R. Gupta's®

National Testing Agency (NTA)

UGC-NET/JRF

Junior Research Fellowship & Assistant Professor Eligibility Exam

COMMERCE

Previous Years' Papers

PAPER II

by

Dr. Sima Kumari

Ph.D (HRM), M.Com., M.B.A., UGC-NET (Management),
Dean & Professor, Echelon Institute of Technology,
Faridabad, Haryana-121101

2027
EDITION

RAMESH PUBLISHING HOUSE, NEW DELHI

Published by

O.P. Gupta *for* Ramesh Publishing House

Admin. Office

12-H, New Daryaganj Road, Opp. Officers' Mess,
New Delhi-110002 ✆ 23275224, 23245124

E-mail: info@rameshpublishinghouse.com

For Online Shopping: www.rameshpublishinghouse.com

Showroom

• Balaji Market, Nai Sarak, Delhi-110006 ✆ 23282525 📱 9354373464
• 4457, Nai Sarak, Delhi-110006

Book Code: R-2659

ISBN: 978-93-5477-732-5

Price: ₹ 730

Printed at: Deepak Offset, Delhi

CONTENTS

UGC-NET/JRF—(PAPER-II) COMMERCE

Previous Years' Paper

National Testing Agency (NTA)

UGC-NET Junior Research Fellowship & Assistant Professor Eligibility Exam

COMMERCE, JANUARY-2026

(Exam held on 03-01-2026)

PAPER-II

1. Which of the following statements are correct for tax Evasion?

A. All methods by which tax liability is illegally avoided is termed as tax evasion

B. Tax evasion takes into account loopholes of Law

C. Tax evasion is tax godging within framework of Law

D. Tax evasion has legal sanction

E. Tax evasion is intentional attempt to avoid payment of tax after the liability to tax has arisen

Choose the ***correct*** answer from the options given below:

1. B and D only
2. B, C and D only
3. A, B and C only
4. A and E only

2. Select the correct option from the followings.

The Balance of Payment (BoP):

1. Includes only exports and imports of goods and services.
2. Is always balanced because every credit entry has a corresponding debit entry.
3. Excludes unilateral transfers like remittance.
4. Shows only the financial account of transactions.

3. What are the GST rates applicable after 22nd September 2025?

A. 5% B. 12%

C. 18% D. 28%

E. 40%

Choose the ***correct*** answer from the options given below:

1. A, B, C and D only
2. B, C, D and E only
3. A, C and E only
4. B, C and E only

4. Arrange the followings on the basis of Sections of Indian Contract Act, 1872 in ascending order:

A. Agreement in restraint of Marriage

B. Agreement made without consideration

C. Agreement with unlawful objects or consideration

D. Agreement in restraint of Trade

E. Agreement by way of wager

Choose the ***correct*** answer from the options given below:

1. C, B, A, D, E
2. C, A, D, B, E
3. A, B, C, E, D
4. D, B, A, C, E

5. Which of the followings are the properties of Indifference Curve?

A. Indifference curve slopes downward to right
B. Indifference curve is concave to origin
C. Indifference curve is convex to origin
D. Indifference curves cannot intersect each other but can be tangent to each other
E. Higher indifference curve represents higher level of satisfaction

Choose the *correct* answer from the options given below:

1. A, B, D and E only
2. A, C, D and E only
3. A, C and E only
4. A, B, C and D only

6. For assessment year 2025-26, 'Health and Education Cess' shall be levied at the rate of:

1. 1% on Income Tax
2. 2% on Income Tax
3. 3% on Income Tax
4. 4% on Income Tax

7. Where a company incurs any expenditure (not being expenditure in the nature of cost of any land or building) on any notified skill development project, then such company can claim as deduction under section 35CCD:

1. Only 25% of such expenditure
2. Only 50% of such expenditure
3. Only 75% of such expenditure
4. 100% of such expenditure

8. Which one of the followings are not the Objectives of HRM?

1. Societal Objectives
2. Organizational Objectives
3. Functional Objectives
4. Group Objectives

9. Charge collected from the investors by a Mutual Fund Scheme when it sells its units to investors is called:

1. Exit Load 2. Entry Load
3. Switch 4. Sale Price

10. Given below are two statements : one is labelled as Assertion (A) and the other is labelled as Reason (R).

Assertion (A): The minimum level of service the customer expects represents the threshold level of expectations.

Reason (R): The gap between the desired and adequate service has been called as the zone of intolerance.

In the light of the above statements, choose the ***most appropriate answer*** from the options given below

1. Both (A) and (R) are correct and (R) is the correct explanation of (A)
2. Both (A) and (R) are correct but (R) is not the correct explanation of (A)
3. (A) is correct but (R) is not correct
4. (A) is not correct but (R) is correct

11. Which of the followings are the techniques of Monetary Control adopted by RBI?

A. Loans and Advances to the Industries
B. Cash Reserve Ratio
C. Open Market Operations
D. Statutory Liquidity Ratio
E. Repo Rates

Choose the *correct* answer from the options given below:

1. A, B, C, D only
2. A, B, D, E only
3. B, C, D, E only
4. A, C, D, E only

12. Arrange the following steps of Personal Selling in sequence:

A. Pre approach
B. Presentation and Demonstration
C. Approach
D. Prospecting and Qualifying
E. Handling Objections

Choose the *correct* answer from the options given below:

1. A, D, C E, B 2. A, C, D, E, B
3. C, A, D, B, E 4. D, A, C, B, E

13. Which one of the followings is not a category under Balance of Payments?

1. Current Account
2. Capital Account
3 Drawings Account
4. Official Reserve Account

14. Arrange the following steps of Capital Budgeting Process in correct order:

A. Preliminary Screening Process
B. Project Generation
C. Detailed Project Evaluation
D. Control of Capital Expenditure
E. Project Selection and its implementation

Choose the ***correct*** answer from the options given below:

1. A, B, C, D, E
2. B, A, C, E, D
3. A, B, C, E, D
4. B, A, C, D, E

15. Given below are two statements : one is labelled as Assertion (A) and the other is labelled as Reason (R).

Assertion (A): Heckscher and Ohlin developed a theory to explain the reasons for differences in relative commodity prices and competitive advantages between two nations. According to this theory, a nation will export the commodity whose production requires intensive use of nation's relatively abundant and cheap factors and import the commodity whose production requires intensive use of the nation's scarce and expensive factors.

Reason (R): Thus, a country with an abundance of cheap labour would import labour intensive products and export capital intensive goods and vice-versa.

In the light of the above statements, choose the ***most appropriate answer*** from the options given below:

1. Both (A) and (R) are correct and (R) is the correct explanation of (A)
2. Both (A) and (R) are correct but (R) is not the correct explanation of (A)
3. (A) is correct but (R) is not correct
4. (A) is not correct but (R) is correct

16. Which one of the followings is not a type of conflict?

1. Task Conflict
2. Relationship Conflict
3. Process Conflict
4. Product Conflict

17. Which statement best captures the difference between FDI and FPI?

1. FDI is investment with lasting interest and managerial control; FPI is passive investment without control.
2. FDI involves only equity investment; FPI involves both equity and debt security.
3. FDI is recorded in current account; FPI is recorded in capital account.
4. Both FDI and FPI give investors voting rights in the host country.

18. An empirical test was carried out in 1951 on Heckscher Ohlin model to find out whether or not the US, which has abundant capital resources, exports capital intensive goods and imports labour intensive goods. But, it was found that the US exported more labour -intensive commodities and imported more capital intensive products, which was contrary to the result of Heckscher - Ohlin model. Who has conducted the test?

1. Staffan B Linder 2. David Ricardo
3. J.B. Say 4. Wassily Leontief

19. Given below are two statements : one is labelled as Assertion (A) and the other is labelled as Reason (R).

Assertion (A): Section 91 provides for grant of unilateral relief in the case of resident taxpayers on income which has been taxed in India as well as in the country with which there is no Double Taxation Avoidance Agreement.

Reason (R): The relief under section 91 is granted by allowing to the tax payer a deduction from tax liability of an amount equal to the tax calculated at the average Indian rate of tax or the amount of tax calculated at the rate of tax of that other country on the doubly taxed income, whichever is higher.

In the light of the above statements, choose the ***most appropriate answer*** from the options given below:

1. Both (A) and (R) are correct and (R) is the correct explanation of (A)
2. Both (A) and (R) are correct but (R) is not the correct explanation of (A)
3. (A) is correct but (R) is not correct
4. (A) is not correct but (R) is correct

20. Given below are two statements : one is labelled as Assertion (A) and the other is labelled as Reason (R).

Assertion (A): The skimming price policy is adopted where close substitute of a new product are not available.

Reason (R): This policy requires fixing a lower initial price designed to penetrate the market as quickly as possible and is intended to maximize the profit in the long run.

In the light of the above statements, choose the ***most appropriate answer*** from the options given below:

1. Both (A) and (R) are correct and (R) is the correct explanation of (A)
2. Both (A) and (R) are correct but (R) is not the correct explanation of (A)
3. (A) is correct but (R) is not correct
4. (A) is not correct but (R) is correct

21. Arrange the following in ascending order of sections of Income Tax Act related to permissible deduction from Gross Total Income:

A. Deduction in respect of Medical Insurance Premia
B. Deduction in respect of Royalty Income of Author
C Deduction in respect of Payment of Interest on Loan taken for Higher Education
D. Deduction in respect of Interest on Deposits in Saving Accounts
E. Deduction in respect of Donations to Certain Funds, charitable Institutions, etc.

Choose the ***correct*** answer from the options given below:

1. A, B, C, D, E 2. E, D, C, B, A
3. A, C, E, D, B 4. A, C, E, B, D

22. Match List-I with List-II.

List-I (*Tax Deducted at Source*)	**List-II** (*Sections of Income Tax Act*)
A. Deduction of Tax at Source on Fees for Professional or Technical Services	I. Section 194A
B. Deduction of Tax at Source from Payment of life Insurance Policy	II. Section 194B
C. Deduction of Tax at Source from Winnings from Lotteries or Crossword Puzzles	III. Section 194DA
D. Deduction of Tax at Source from Interest other than Interest on Securities	IV. Section 194J

Choose the ***correct*** answer from the options given below:

1. A-I, B-II, C-III, D-IV
2. A-IV, B-III, C-II, D-I
3. A-I, B-II, C-IV, D-III
4. A-II, B-I, C-III, D-IV

23. The Break Even point expressed in amount of sales in rupees of X Ltd having selling Price of ₹ 20 per unit, variable cost of ₹ 14 per unit and fixed cost of ₹ 7,92,000 is:

1. ₹ 11,28,571
2. ₹ 1,32,000
3. ₹ 39,600
4. ₹ 26,40,000

24. The right of the insurer to stand in the place of insured after the settlement of a claim and it gives the insurer right to recover from an alternative source, the principle involved in this case is called:

1. Principle of Insurable Interest
2. Principle of Subrogation
3. Principle of Causa Proxima
4. Principle of Contribution

25. Which of the followings are the myths about Rural Market?

A. All Villages are equally populated
B. Rural Consumers are a hetrogeneous lot
C Being illiterate, rural consumer is not able to discriminate between products and brands
D. Only low priced products will sell in rural India
E. Rural markets are the consumer durable markets

Choose the ***correct*** answer from the options given below:

1. A, B, C and D only
2. A, C and D only
3. C, D and E only
4. B, C, D and E only

26. Given below are two statements : one is labelled as Assertion (A) and the other is labelled as Reason (R).

Assertion (A): New Issue of Capital is costlier than Retained Earnings.

Reason (R): The cost of Retained Earnings is the return foregone by the shareholders on the dividend income.

In the light of the above statements, choose the ***most appropriate answer*** from the options given below:

1. Both (A) and (R) are correct and (R) is the correct explanation of (A)
2. Both (A) and (R) are correct but (R) is not the correct explanation of (A)
3. (A) is correct but (R) is not correct
4. (A) is not correct but (R) is correct

27. Match List-I with List-II.

List-I	List-II
A. Operating Leverage	I. Contribution/EBT
B. Combined Leverage	II. Contribution/EBIT
C. Earning Per Share	III. EBIT/EBT
D. Financial Leverage	IV. EAT/No. of Equity Shares

Choose the ***correct*** answer from the options given below:

1. A-I, B-II, C-IV, D-III
2. A-II, B-I, C-IV, D-III
3. A-II, B-I, C-III, D-IV
4. A-I, B-II, C-III, D-IV

28. Which one of the followings is not a type of organizational culture?

1. Non-Entrepreneurial Culture
2. Power Culture
3. Role Culture
4. Task Culture

29. Which one of the followings is not a component of formal (organized) financial system?

1. Financial Markets
2. Financial Instruments
3. Chit-fund Companies
4. Financial Services

30. Match List-I with List-II.

List-I

A. Probable Error of Correlation Coefficient
B. Standard Error of Correlation Coefficient
C Coefficient of Determination
D. Coefficient of Alienation

List-II

I. $\frac{\text{Explained Variation}}{\text{Total Variation}}$

II. $\frac{\text{Unexplained Variation}}{\text{Total Variation}}$

III. $\frac{1-r^2}{\sqrt{n}}$

IV. $0.6745\left[\frac{1-r^2}{\sqrt{n}}\right]$

Choose the ***correct*** answer from the options given below:

1. A-I, B-II, C-III, D-IV
2. A-IV, B-III, C-II, D-I
3. A-III, B-IV, C-I, D-II
4. A-IV, B-III, C-I, D-II

31. Match List-I with List-II.

List-I	List-II
A. Ind AS 7	I. Impairment of Assets
B. Ind AS 24	II. Related Party Disclosures
C. Ind AS 36	III. Consolidated Financial Statement
D. Ind AS 110	IV. Statement of Cash Flows

Choose the ***correct*** answer from the options given below:

1. A-I, B-II, C-III, D-IV
2. A-IV, B-II, C-I, D-III
3. A-III, B-IV, C-I, D-II
4. A-IV, B-III, C-II, D-I

32. Arrange the following in descending order on the basis of number of sellers in the Market.

A. Duopoly
B. Oligopoly
C. Monopolistic Competition
D. Perfect Competition

Choose the ***correct*** answer from the options given below:

1. D, C, B, A   2. B, A, C, D
3. A, B, C, D   4. B, D, A, C

33. Which of the followings is/are the part of external environment (macro) of Business?

A. Customers
B. Economic factors
C. Natural factors
D. Marketing Intermediaries
E. Competitors

Choose the ***correct*** answer from the options given below:

1. B and D only
2. B and C only
3. A, B, C and D only
4. B, C, D and E only

34. Arrange the followings in the correct sequence in which they are computed for determining Net Cash from operating activities as per AS-3 (Revised):

A. Operating profit before Working Capital Changes
B. Cash flow before extra ordinary items
C. Cash generated from operations
D. Net Profit before taxation and extra ordinary items

Choose the ***correct*** answer from the options given below:

1. A, B, C, D   2. D, B, A, C
3. C, D, B, A   4. D, A, C, B

35. Suppose a production function is given as $Q = -L^3 + 5L^2 + 10L$

Which law of production is revealed by this production function:

1. Law of diminishing return
2. Law of increasing return
3. Law of constant return
4. Law of return to scale

36. Arrange the following steps of process of consumer buying in proper sequence:

A. Evaluation of Alternatives
B. Search for Alternatives
C. Need Recognitions
D. Decision
E. Development of Decision Criteria

Choose the ***correct*** answer from the options given below:

1. C, B, A, E, D 2. C, A, B, E, D
3. C, E, B, A, D 4. B, A, C, E, D

37. An infinite series of equal cash flow occurring at regular time interval is known as:

1. An Annuity 2. An Annuity Due
3. Perpetuity 4. Future Value

38. Match List-I with List-II.

List-I	List-II
A. Occurs when a true null hypothesis is rejected	I. Type II Error
B. Occurs when false null hypothesis does not get rejected	II. Type I Error
C. Used for data from interval or ratio scales	III. Nonparametric Tests
D. Used to test hypotheses with nominal and ordinal data	IV. Parametric Tests

Choose the ***correct*** answer from the options given below:

1. A-I, B-II, C-III, D-IV
2. A-I, B-II,, C-IV, D-III
3. A-II, B-I, C-IV, D-III
4. A-II, B-I, C-III, D-IV

39. Which one of the followings is not a method of New Issues?

1. Public Issue through Prospectus
2. Right Issue
3. Bonus Issue
4. Book Building

40. If demand equation is given by
D = 10,000 – P
and the supply equation is given by
S = 1000 + 4P, the equilibrium price would be:

1. 1600 2. 1800
3. 1700 4. 2000

41. Which of the following statements is incorrect for Amalgamation in the nature of merger?

1. All assets and liabilities of the transferor company taken over by the transferee company
2. Shareholders of the transferor company need not become equity shareholders of the transferee company
3. Payment of purchase consideration is made in cash only for fractional shares, if any
4. The business of Transferor Company is intended to be carried on, after amalgamation, by the transferee company

42. Process of ensuring access to appropriate financial products and services needed by all sections of the society in general and vulnerable group such as weaker sections and low-income groups in particular at an affordable cost in a fair and transparent manner by mainstream institutional players is referred to as:

1. Financial Integration
2. Financial Instability
3. Financial Inclusion
4. Monetary Instability

43. Mr. A, a resident in India, aged 60 years, earned agricultural income of ₹ 5,00,000 and non-agricultural income of ₹ 3,80,000 for assessment year 2025-26. The tax liability of Mr. A assuming that he does not opt to be taxed under the old tax regime is:

1. ₹ 38,000 2. ₹ 3,640
3. ₹ 8,000 4. Nil

44. What will be the value of AR, if elasticity of demand is unit elastic and the value of MR is 5?

1. 2.5 2. 5
3. 1 4. 10

45. Arrange the following steps of Sampling Design Process in correct order:

A. Determine the sample size
B. Select a sampling technique
C. Selection of sampling frame
D. Target Population definitions

Choose the ***correct*** answer from the options given below:

1. A, B, C, D 2. D, C, B, A
3. C, D, B, A 4. B, D, C, A

46. Arrange the following steps of Selection Process in correct order:

A. Selection Tests
B. Reference and Background Analysis
C. Preliminary Interview
D. Employment Interview
E. Job Offer

Choose the ***correct*** answer from the options given below:

1. A, B, C, D, E 2. C, A, B, D, E
3. C, A, D, B, E 4. A, C, B, D, E

47. Which of the followings are the types of decentralisation in an organisation?

A. Profit Centres
B. Service Centres
C. Cost Centres
D. Investment Centres

Choose the ***correct*** answer from the options given below:

1. A, B and C only
2. A, C and D only
3. A, B and D only
4. B, C and D only

48. Arrange the following committees as per their year of formation in ascending order:

A. Narsimham Committee-I
B. Pad manathan Committee
C. Verma Committee
D. Saraf Committee
E. Rashid Jilani Committee

Choose the ***correct*** answer from the options given below:

1. A, B, C, D, E 2. A, E, D, B, C
3. A, E, B, D, C 4. A, D, E, B, C

49. Arrange the following institutions as per their year of establishment in ascending order:

A. NAFTA B. EU
C. ASEAN D. UNCTAD

Choose the ***correct*** answer from the options given below:

1. A, B, C, D 2. D, A, C, B
3. B, D, C, A 4. B, C, A, D

50. Match List-I with List-II.

List-I	List-II
A. Standard Deduction under Section 16(*ia*)	I. Income under the head Capital Gains
B. Standard Deduction under Section 24	II. Income under the head Profits and Gains of Business or Profession
C. Depreciation Allowance under Section 32	III. Income Under the Head Income from House Property
D. Exemption Under Section 54 for Profit on transfer of house property used for residence	IV. Income Under the Head Salaries

Choose the ***correct*** answer from the options given below:

1. A-I, B-II, C-III, D-IV
2. A-IV, B-III, C-II, D-I
3. A-III, B-IV, C-II, D-I
4. A-III, B-IV, C-I, D-II

51. India's participation in SAARC and ASEAN trade pacts primarily reflects which level of Regional Economic Integration?

1. Customs Union 2. Free Trade Area
3. Economic Union 4. Common Market

52. Which of the followings is not a core function of WTO?

1. Providing a forum for trade negotiation
2. Administering agreement such as GATS, TRIPS and TRIMS
3. Monitoring trade policies
4. Providing Concessional loans and financial aid to developing countries

53. Non-receipt of dividend by Investors is categorised in which type of complaints received by the SEBI?

1. Type I 2. Type II
3. Type III 4. Type IV

54. Which of the following statements are incorrect?

A. Management audit is not compulsory under any law.
B. Vouching is concerned only with items of balance sheet.
C. Section 148 of the Companies Act, 2013 has made Cost Audit mandatory for some limited companies
D. The object of vouching is to satisfy the auditor as to existence, ownership, possession, completeness, valuation and disclosure of items mentioned in the Balance Sheet.
E. Independent financial audit has been made compulsory for many entities established under respective Acts.

Choose the *correct* answer from the options given below:

1. B, C and E only
2. A, B and C only
3. B and D only
4. A, C and E only

55. Match List-I with List-II.

List-I (*Human Resource Valuation Approaches*)	List-II (*Propounders*)
A. Historical Cost Approach	I. Brummet, Flamholtz and Plye
B. Opportunity Cost Approach	II. Hekimian and Jones
C. Standard Cost Approach	III. David Watson
D. Present Value of Future Earning Model	IV. Lav and Schwartz

Choose the *correct* answer from the options given below:

1. A-I, B-II, C-III, D-IV
2. A-II, B-I, C-IV, D-III
3. A-III, B-IV, C-I, D-II
4. A-IV, B-III, C-I, D-II

56. Match List-I with List-II.

List-I	List-II
A. Greenfield Investment	I. Direct Investment overseas aimed to sell the output of a firm's domestic production process
B. Foreign Portfolio Investment	II. Overseas investment to acquire existing facilities
C. Forward Vertical FDI	III. Overseas investment to create new facilities from the ground up
D. Brownfield Investment	IV. Investment in foreign financial instruments such as foreign stock, government bonds etc.

Choose the *correct* answer from the options given below:

1. A-III, B-IV, C-II, D-I
2. A-I, B-II, C-III, D-IV
3. A-IV, B-III, C-I, D-II
4. A-III, B-IV, C-I, D-II

57. Which of the following sections of research reports contains Executive Summary?

1. Prefatory Information
2. Introductory Information
3. Main Research Body
4. Supplementary Information

58. Which one of the followings is not a type of Organisation charts?

1. Vertical Chart
2. Circular Chart
3. Diagonal Chart
4. Horizontal Chart

59. Match List-I with List-II.

List-I	List-II
A. Making provision for bad and doubtful debts and for discount on debtors	I. Cost-Concept
B. Expenses should be recognised in the period in which associated revenue is recognised	II. Going Concern
C. Assets are not shown at their current realisable value	III. Matching Concept
D. Internally generated goodwill is not recorded in the books of account	IV. Conservatism

Choose the ***correct*** answer from the options given below:

1. A-I, B-II, C-III, D-IV
2. A-IV, B-III, C-II, D-I
3. A-IV, B-II, C-III, D-I
4. A-II, B-I, C-IV, D-III

60. Arrange the following Acts in ascending order as per their year of enactment:

A. RTI (Rights to Information Act)
B. Competitions Act
C. Information Technology Act
D. Negotiable Instrument Act
E. Indian Contract Act

Choose the ***correct*** answer from the options given below:

1. E, D, C, B, A
2. A, B, C, D, E
3. A, B, E, D, C
4. E, D, C, A, B

61. Kail Pearson's Coefficient of Skewness for a distribution having mean of 6.82, median of 6.8 and standard Deviation of 1.4 is:

1. 0.014
2. 0.028
3. 0.043
4. 0.056

62. Match List-I with List-II.

List-I	List-II
A. Doctrine of Caveat Emptor	I. Special Contract
B. Bailment and Pledge	II. Limited Liability Partnership
C. Holder in due Course	III. Sales of Goods Act
D. DPIN	IV. Negotiable Instrument

Choose the ***correct*** answer from the options given below:

1. A-IV, B-I, C-II, D-III
2. A-I, B-II, C-IV, D-III
3. A-II, B-I, C-III, D-IV
4. A-III, B-I, C-IV, D-II

63. Given below are two statements : one is labelled as Assertion (A) and the other is labelled as Reason (R).

Assertion (A): An effective appraisal system can contribute to competitive advantage by improving employee job performance.

Reason (R): One serious challenge facing the performance appraisal relates to assessment of self-managed teams.

In the light of the above statements, choose the ***most appropriate answer*** from the options given below:

1. Both (A) and (R) are correct and (R) is the correct explanation of (A)
2. Both (A) and (R) are correct but (R) is not the correct explanation of (A)
3. (A) is correct but (R) is not correct
4. (A) is not correct but (R) is correct

64. A, B and C were partners in a firm sharing profits and losses in the ratio of 4 : 3 : 2. A died on September 15, 2025. At that time, the capitals of B and C after all the adjustments were ₹ 3,56,000 and ₹ 2,44,000 respectively. B and C decided to adjust their capitals according to their new profit sharing ratio by opening current accounts. The new capital of B is:

1. ₹ 1,33,333
2. ₹ 2,00,000
3. ₹ 2,40,000
4. ₹ 3,60,000

65. If the first quartile is 48 and quartile deviation is 6, the value of median assuming the distribution to be symmetrical is:

1. 50　　2. 52
3. 54　　4. 56

66. Match the List-I with List-II.

List-I	List-II
A. Highest Reach	I. Publicity
B. Most Persuasive	II. Advertising
C. Immediate Effect on Sales	III. Personal Selling
D. No Cost Involved	IV. Sales Promotion

Choose the ***correct*** answer from the options given below:

1. A-I, B-II, C-III, D-IV
2. A-II, B-I, C-III, D-IV
3. A-II, B-III, C-IV, D-I
4. A-IV, B-I, C-II, D-III

67. Arrange the following steps of Control Process in the correct order:

A. Measurement of Actual Performance
B. Establishment of Standards
C. Corrective action where required
D. Comparison of actual performance with the standards

Choose the ***correct*** answer from the options given below:

1. B, A, C, D　　2. B, A, D, C
3. A, B, C, D　　4. A, B, D, C

68. An assessee who declares his business/ professional income in accordance with the provisions of Section 44 AD(1) or Section 44 ADA(l), must pay up to 100 per cent of advance tax payable on or before:

1. December 15 of the previous year
2. January 15 of the previous year
3. February 15 of the previous year
4. March 15 of the previous year

69. Given below are two statements : one is labelled as Assertion (A) and the other is labelled as Reason (R).

Assertion (A): Filter questions in questionnaire measure the familiarity of the respondents with the topic of research.

Reason (R): Questions that try to capture multiple information at once are referred to as leading questions.

In the light of the above statements, choose the ***most appropriate*** answer from the options given below:

1. Both (A) and (R) are correct and (R) is the correct explanation of (A)
2. Both (A) and (R) are correct but (R) is not the correct explanation of (A)
3. (A) is correct but (R) is not correct
4. (A) is not correct but (R) is correct

70. According to Walter's Model of Dividend, market value of the share of a declining firm (having $r < ke$) will be maximum at:

1. 0% Dividend Payout
2. 100% Dividend Payout
3. 50% Dividend Payout
4. 75% Dividend Payout

71. Which one of the followings is not an external technique of Foreign Exchange Risk Management?

1. Forward Contracts
2. Currency Futures
3. Netting
4. Swaps

72. Under which of the following, a firm well publicized changes in price and price changes are generally followed by the rival firms. This kind of price leadership may not necessarily come from the largest firm of the industry.

1. Biometric Price Leadership
2. Barometric Price Leadership
3. Price Leadership by low cost firm
4. Price Leadership by dominant firm

73. Arrange the following types of motivating needs as identified by Maslow in ascending order:

A. Physiological Needs
B. Social Needs
C. Self-actualization Needs
D. Safety Needs
E. Esteem Needs

Choose the ***correct*** answer from the options given below:

1. A, D, B, C, E 2. A, D, B, E, C
3. A, B, D, E, C 4. A, B, C, D, E

74. Arrange the following steps of research process in correct order:

A. Developing an approach to the problem
B. Problem definition
C. Data Collection, Preparation and analysis
D. Research design formulation
E. Report writing and presentation

Choose the ***correct*** answer from the options given below:

1. A, B, C, D, E 2. B, A, D, C, E
3. D, B, A, E, C 4. A, B, D, E, C

75. Given below are two statements : one is labelled as Assertion (A) and the other is labelled as Reason (R).

Assertion (A): RTGS system is a funds transfer mechanism where transfer of money takes place from one bank to another on a real time and on gross basis.

Reason (R): There is no minimum ceiling for the RTGS transactions.

In the light of the above statements, choose the ***most appropriate answer*** from the options given below:

A. Both (A) and (R) are correct and (R) is the correct explanation of (A)
B. Both (A) and (R) are correct but (R) is not the correct explanation of (A)
C. (A) is correct but (R) is not correct
D. (A) is not correct but (R) is correct

76. Which of the following is a measure of relative risk and is calculated by dividing the standard deviation by its expected value?

1. Variance
2. Coefficient of Variance
3. Co-Variance
4. Geometric Mean

77. Which of the followings are properties of Normal Distribution?

A. The normal curve approaches the *x*-axis asymptotically as we proceed in either direction away from the mean.
B. The normal curve has its points of inflection at $\bar{X} \pm 2\sigma$.
C. Irrespective of the shape, the total area under the normal curve and above the horizontal axis is always equal to 1.
D. About 68.27% of the total area under the normal curve is covered from $\mu - 2\sigma$ to $\mu + 2\sigma$.
E. The normal distribution is unimodal.

Choose the ***correct*** answer from the options given below:

1. A, B and E only
2. B, C and D only
3. C, D and E only
4. A, C and E only

78. Match the List-I with List-II.

List-I	List-II
A. Managerial Grid	I. Charles Bird
B. Hawthorne Experiments	II. Alderfer
C. Trait Theory	III. Blake and Mouton
D. ERG Theory	IV. Elton Mayo

Choose the *correct* answer from the options given below:

1. A-I, B-II, C-III, D-IV
2. A-III, B-IV, C-I, D-II
3. A-I, B-III, C-II, D-IV
4. A-III, B-IV, C-II, D-I

79. A possible cost of FDI to the host country is:

A. Employment opportunities may increase in the short run but long run competitiveness will be reduced.

B. Technology transfer always leads to dependency and no local innovation gets encouraged.

C. Repatriation of profits may lead to capital outflows.

D. FDI inflows always worsen the host country's BoP position.

80. The probability that a leap year selected at random contains either 53 Sundays or 53 Mondays is:

1. $\frac{1}{7}$
2. $\frac{2}{7}$
3. $\frac{3}{7}$
4. $\frac{4}{7}$

81. Given below are two statements : one is labelled as Assertion (A) and the other is labelled as Reason (R).

Assertion (A): A gentlemen died leaving a young widow. The relatives of the deceased threatened the widow to adopt a boy otherwise they would not allow her to remove the dead body of her husband for cremation. The widow adopted the boy.

Reason (R): The widow subsequently cancelled the adoption. The court held her consent was not free due to coercion.

In the light of the above statements, choose the ***most appropriate answer*** from the options given below:

1. Both (A) and (R) are correct and (R) is the correct explanation of (A)
2. Both (A) and (R) are correct but (R) is not the correct explanation of (A)
3. (A) is correct but (R) is not correct
4. (A) is not correct but (R) is correct

82. Match the List-I with List-II.

List-I (*Theories of Profit*)	List-II (*Propounders*)
A. Risk theory of Profit	I. Joseph A Schumpeter
B. Dynamic theory of Profit	II. F.A. Waker
C. Innovation theory of Profit	III. F.B. Hawley
D. Profit as rent of ability	IV. J.B. Clark

Choose the *correct* answer from the options given below:

1. A-III, B-II, C-I, D-IV
2. A-III, B-IV, C-I, D-II
3. A-II, B-III, C-I, D-IV
4. A-IV, B-II, C-I, D-III

83. Which of the followings are the approaches of determining the financing mix for working capital:

A. Matching Approach

B. Conservative Approach

C. Operating Cycle Approach

D. Aggressive Approach

Choose the *correct* answer from the options given below:

1. B, C and D only
2. A, B and D only
3. A, C and D only
4. A, B and C only

84. Given below are two statements : one is labelled as Assertion (A) and the other is labelled as Reason (R).

Assertion (A): Minority interest is that part of the net assets of a subsidiary attributable to interest which is held by outsiders.

Reason (R): Minority interest should be presented in the consolidated balance sheet as a part of equity of the parent's shareholders.

In the light of the above statements, choose the ***most appropriate answer*** from the options given below:

1. Both (A) and (R) are correct and (R) is the correct explanation of (A)
2. Both (A) and (R) are correct but (R) is not the correct explanation of (A)
3. (A) is correct but (R) is not correct
4. (A) is not correct but (R) is correct

85. Which of the following types of audit report is issued when the auditor concludes that the financial statements are prepared, in all material respects, in accordance with the applicable financial reporting framework?

1. Audit report with an 'emphasis of matter' paragraph
2. Qualified report
3. Disclaimer of opinion report
4. Unmodified opinion report

86. Match List-I with List-II.

List-I	List-II
A. NPV	I. Which equates the aggregate present value of the net cash Inflows with the aggregate present value of cash outflows.
B. IRR	II. Dividing the average annual profit after tax by average investment over the life of the project.
C. ARR	III. Summation of the present values of cash proceeds in each year minus the summation of the present values of the net cash outflow in each year.
D. PI	IV. Dividing the present value of future cash inflow by the present value of cash outflow.

Choose the ***correct*** answer from the options given below:

1. A-I, B-III, C-II, D-IV
2. A-III, B-II, C-IV, D-I
3. A-III, B-I, C-II, D-IV
4. A-I, B-II, C-III, D-IV

87. Which of the followings is not valid for ordinal school of consumer preferences?

1. Consumer preferences can be plotted on an indifference curve
2. Ranking of Utility is important
3. Magnitude of Utility is important
4. Utility is not additive

88. Arm's length price as per section 92 F of the Income Tax Act is the price applied or proposed to be applied when:

1. two related persons enter into a transaction in uncontrolled conditions.
2. two unrelated persons enter into a transaction in controlled conditions.
3. two related persons enter into a transaction in controlled conditions.
4. two unrelated persons enter into a transaction in uncontrolled conditions.

89. Match List-I with List-II.

List-I	List-II
A. EXIM Bank	I. Advancing Credit for agriculture and other economic activities in rural area
B. NHB	II. Financing Exports and Imports
C. IDBI	III. Promoting Housing Finance Institution
D. NABARD	IV. Financing, Promoting and Developing industries

Choose the ***correct*** answer from the options given below:

1. A-I, B-II, C-III, D-IV
2. A-II, B-I, C-IV, D-III
3. A-II, B-III, C-IV, D-I
4. A-II, B-III, C-I, D-IV

90. Identify the correct equation of Cobb-Douglas production function:

1. $Q = A + L^{\alpha}K^{\beta}$
2. $Q = A \times L^{\alpha}K^{\beta}$
3. $Q = A \div L^{\alpha}K^{\beta}$
4. $Q = A - L^{\alpha}K^{\beta}$

Directions (Qs. No. 91 to 95): *Read the following passage and answer the questions:*

An application was sent to registrar of companies to obtain the certificate of incorporation on 30 June 2024. One of the promotors, Raj, made the allotment of shares of the company on 28 June 2024. He also made a contract to buy a certain machinery from Pooja by representing himself as an agent of the company on 20 June 2024.

Raj also signed the Memorandum of Association (MOA) of the company on behalf of all seven members to obtain the certificate of incorporation.

Inspite of all these, the certificate of incorporation was issued in respect of ABC company but wrongly dated as 25 June 2024.

After sometimes, it is also found that two of the members out of seven members named in MOA were minors.

He also entered into a contract after the incorporation of company to buy a building from Prakash for ₹ 1,00,00,000 but before obtaining the certificate of commencement of business.

91. The certificate of incorporation of ABC is:

1. Void as it is obtained by forged document
2. Void as it is obtained by including minor promotors
3. Valid, even if irregular, cannot be cancelled
4. Valid, but from 30th June 2024 and not from 25th June

92. Which of the followings is correct?

1. Pooja can claim payment of machinery from the company as Raj acted on behalf of the company.
2. Pooja can claim the payment from Raj, who will be personally liable as she is considering that it is a provisional contract.
3. Raj will be personally liable as for all pre-incorporation contracts, promotors are personally liable
4. Raj will not be liable as the machinery was used by the company not by Raj for his personal benefits.

93. The allotment of shares was challenged as it was done before sending the application to the Registrar of Companies. Choose the correct answer:

1. The allotment of shares is void as the certificate of incorporation is not valid
2. The allotment of shares is valid as it is made after obtaining the certificate of incorporation
3. The allotment of shares is void as application to obtain certificate was sent on 30th June
4. The allotment of shares is void as the certificate was obtained by forged document

94. The contract to buy a building from Prakash for ₹ 1,00,00,000 will be called:

1. Pre-incorporation Contract
2. Provisional Contract
3. Preliminary Contract
4. Void Contract

95. The contract made with Pooja on 20 June 2024 will be called:

1. Pre-incorporation Contract
2. Provisional Contract
3. Preliminary Contract
4. Standard Contract

Directions (Qs. No. 96 to 100): *Read the following passage and answer the questions:*

Ecofresh Pvt. Ltd, a startup in India, produces eco-friendly home cleaning products such as liquid detergents, floor cleaners and dishwashing liquids.

The company follows a green marketing approach and highlights its products as biodegradable, safe and affordable.

To reach its customers, Ecofresh sells through online Platforms, retail stores and direct sales agents. The firm has designed its marketing mix carefully. Pricing is slightly above competitors due to its ecofriendly positioning but promotions include digital campaigns, social media advertising and discounts on bulk purchases.

Recently Ecofresh launched a new product; a herbal air freshener. During its product life cycle's introduction stage, the firm invested heavily in promotion and awareness building activities. The company also engages in customer relationship management by offering loyalty points and personalised recommendation to repeat buyers.

96. By selling through online platforms, retail stores and direct sales agents, Ecofresh is focusing on:
1. Pricing Strategies
2. Promotional Mix
3. Service Marketing
4. Multi Channel distribution

97. Ecofresh use of digital campaigns, social media and discounts reflects decisions related to:
1. Distribution Mix
2. Promotion Mix
3. Product Mix
4. Pricing Policy

98. The launch of herbal air freshener during its introduction stage of the product life cycle primarily requires heavy investment in promotion and awareness building activity. It will lead to (in short run):
1. High Profit
2. Low/Negative Profit
3. High Revenue, Low cost
4. High Revenue, High cost

99. The use of loyalty points is an example of:
1. Advertising 2. Sales Promotion
3. Personal Selling 4. Sponsorship

100. Ecofresh's emphasis on biodegradable safe product reflects which marketing approach?
1. Production approach
2. Selling approach
3. Societal marketing approach
4. Product approach

ANSWERS

1	**2**	**3**	**4**	**5**	**6**	**7**	**8**	**9**	**10**
4	2	3	1	3	4	4	4	2	3
11	**12**	**13**	**14**	**15**	**16**	**17**	**18**	**19**	**20**
3	4	3	2	3	4	1	4	3	3
21	**22**	**23**	**24**	**25**	**26**	**27**	**28**	**29**	**30**
4	2	4	2	2	1	2	1	3	4
31	**32**	**33**	**34**	**35**	**36**	**37**	**38**	**39**	**40**
2	1	2	4	1	3	3	3	3	2
41	**42**	**43**	**44**	**45**	**46**	**47**	**48**	**49**	**50**
2	3	4	*	2	3	2	2	3	2
51	**52**	**53**	**54**	**55**	**56**	**57**	**58**	**59**	**60**
2	4	2	3	1	4	1	3	2	1
61	**62**	**63**	**64**	**65**	**66**	**67**	**68**	**69**	**70**
3	4	2	4	3	3	2	4	3	2

71	72	73	74	75	76	77	78	79	80
3	2	2	2	3	2	4	2	3	3
81	**82**	**83**	**84**	**85**	**86**	**87**	**88**	**89**	**90**
1	2	2	3	4	3	3	4	3	2
91	**92**	**93**	**94**	**95**	**96**	**97**	**98**	**99**	**100**
3	3	2	2	1	4	2	2	2	3

EXPLANATORY ANSWERS

1. A. Tax evasion refers to every method where a person illegally reduces or avoids tax liability (for example, hiding income, showing false expenses, or using fake documents).

The defining element here is violation of law, so it is correctly treated as evasion and not a lawful arrangement.

E. Tax evasion is an intentional attempt to avoid paying tax when the taxable event has already happened and liability has arisen under law.

This matches the core idea of evasion: wilful non-compliance after tax becomes payable.

2. The Balance of Payments (BoP) records all economic transactions between residents of a country and the rest of the world over a given period. It is prepared according to the double-entry bookkeeping system, under which every transaction has two equal entries — one credit and one debit. For example, an export is recorded as a credit, while the corresponding payment received (such as increase in foreign assets or reduction in foreign liabilities) is recorded as a debit. Similarly, imports create a debit entry matched by a credit entry in the financial or capital account. Even if the current account shows a deficit or surplus, it is exactly offset by opposite entries in the capital/financial account or changes in official reserves. Therefore, in an accounting sense, the total BoP always balances, because total credits equal total debits.

3. A. (5%): After 22nd September 2025, 5% continues as the lower "merit" slab for a large set of commonly used items and many items shifted down.

So 5% is clearly an applicable GST rate after that date.

C. (18%): 18% continues as the standard slab, covering a wide range of goods and services under the simplified structure.

Hence 18% remains applicable after 22nd September 2025.

E. (40%): A higher rate is applied to specified luxury/sin categories under the revised structure.

Therefore 40% is also applicable after 22nd September 2025 for those specified items.

4. C. (Agreement with unlawful objects or consideration): This is governed by Section 23, which comes earliest among the listed topics.

Since the question asks ascending order of sections, this must be placed first.

B. (Agreement made without consideration): This is covered under Section 25, which comes after Section 23.

Therefore it must follow "unlawful objects/consideration" in the sequence.

A. (Agreement in restraint of Marriage): This falls under Section 26, next in order. Hence it must come after Section 25.

D. (Agreement in restraint of Trade): This is dealt with by Section 27, which is after Section 26.

So it is placed after restraint of marriage.

E. **(Agreement by way of wager):** Wagering agreements are addressed in Section 30, which comes later than all the above. Therefore it is placed at the end in ascending order.

5. A. Indifference curves slope downward to the right because if a consumer has less of one good, they must have more of the other to stay equally satisfied.

With "goods" (not bads), maintaining the same utility requires this trade-off, giving a negative slope.

C. Indifference curves are generally convex to the origin due to diminishing marginal rate of substitution.

As consumption shifts toward more of one good, the consumer is willing to give up less and less of the other good per extra unit, creating convexity.

E. A higher indifference curve represents a higher level of satisfaction because it contains bundles with more of at least one good without reducing the other.

Under the usual assumption of "more is preferred to less," curves farther from the origin indicate greater utility.

6. For Assessment Year 2025–26, Health and Education Cess continues to be levied at the rate of 4% on the amount of income tax plus surcharge, if any. This cess replaced the earlier education cesses and has remained unchanged in recent Finance Acts. It is calculated after computing the total income tax liability and applicable surcharge, and then 4% is added as cess. Therefore, the applicable rate is 4% on Income Tax.

7. Under Section 35CCD of the Income-tax Act, if a company incurs expenditure (other than cost of land or building) on a notified skill development project approved by the prescribed authority, it is eligible to claim 100% of such expenditure as deduction. The provision was amended to allow deduction equal to the full amount of qualifying expenditure. Hence, the allowable deduction is 100%.

8. The objectives of Human Resource Management are generally classified as Societal Objectives, Organizational Objectives, Functional Objectives, and Personal Objectives. "Group Objectives" is not a standard classification under HRM objectives. Therefore, it is not included among the recognized objectives of HRM.

9. The charge collected from investors by a mutual fund scheme at the time of selling units to them is known as Entry Load. It is deducted upfront from the investment amount when units are purchased. Exit load, in contrast, is charged when investors redeem units. Hence, the correct term for charge collected at the time of sale of units is Entry Load.

10. The minimum level of service that a customer is willing to accept is termed "adequate service," and it represents the threshold level of expectations; thus Assertion (A) is correct. However, the gap between desired service and adequate service is called the "zone of tolerance," not the "zone of intolerance." Therefore, Reason (R) is incorrect.

11. B. Cash Reserve Ratio: CRR is a quantitative monetary policy tool used by RBI to control liquidity by mandating banks to keep a percentage of deposits as reserves with RBI.

Increasing CRR reduces money supply, while decreasing it increases liquidity in the economy.

C. Open Market Operations: RBI buys and sells government securities in the open market to regulate money supply.

Sale of securities absorbs liquidity; purchase injects liquidity, making it a direct monetary control instrument.

D. Statutory Liquidity Ratio: SLR requires banks to maintain a fixed percentage of their net demand and time liabilities in specified liquid assets.

It influences banks' capacity to extend credit, thereby controlling money supply.

E. Repo Rates: Repo rate is the rate at which RBI lends to commercial banks against securities.

It directly affects borrowing cost and credit expansion, thus serving as a key monetary policy instrument.

A. Loans and Advances to Industries: These are commercial banking activities, not direct tools of monetary control adopted by RBI.

12. D. Prospecting and Qualifying: The first step is identifying potential customers and determining whether they have the need, authority, and capacity to buy.

Without prospecting, the selling process cannot begin effectively.

A. Pre-approach: After identifying prospects, the salesperson gathers information and plans the sales strategy.

This preparation ensures effective communication in later stages.

C. Approach: The salesperson makes initial contact with the customer.

This stage focuses on creating a positive first impression and establishing rapport.

B. Presentation and Demonstration: The product's features, advantages, and benefits are explained and demonstrated.

The aim is to persuade the customer by linking product value to their needs.

E. Handling Objections: Customer doubts or resistance are addressed after the presentation.

Clearing objections moves the process closer to closing the sale.

13. The Balance of Payments consists of the Current Account, Capital Account, Financial Account, and Official Reserve Account. Drawings Account is a concept related to partnership or sole proprietorship accounting and does not form part of BoP. Hence, it is not a category under Balance of Payments.

14. B. Project Generation: The process begins with identification and generation of investment proposals.

Without project ideas, capital budgeting cannot proceed.

A. Preliminary Screening Process: Feasibility and suitability of proposals are examined at a basic level.

This step filters out non-viable projects early.

C. Detailed Project Evaluation: Financial appraisal using techniques like NPV, IRR, or Payback is conducted.

This ensures objective assessment before selection.

E. Project Selection and its implementation: Based on evaluation results, projects are selected and executed.

Resources are committed at this stage.

D. Control of Capital Expenditure: After implementation, monitoring and control ensure that costs and performance align with plans.

15. The Heckscher–Ohlin theory states that a country exports goods that intensively use its abundant and relatively cheap factors of production and imports goods that use its scarce and expensive factors. Thus, a labour-abundant country exports labour-intensive goods and imports capital-intensive goods. The Reason statement reverses this logic by stating that a labour-abundant country would import labour-intensive products and export capital-intensive goods, which contradicts the theory. Therefore, Assertion is correct but Reason is incorrect.

16. In organizational behavior, the commonly recognized types of conflict are Task Conflict (disagreement about work content or goals), Relationship Conflict (interpersonal incompatibility among individuals), and Process Conflict (disagreement about how work should be done, roles, or responsibilities). "Product Conflict" is not identified as a standard type of organizational conflict in management literature. Therefore, it is not a recognized category of conflict.

17. Foreign Direct Investment (FDI) involves a long-term relationship and significant degree of influence or managerial control in the enterprise located in another country. It usually includes ownership of a substantial stake and participation in management decisions. In contrast, Foreign Portfolio Investment (FPI) refers to investment in financial assets such as shares or bonds without the intention of controlling management. FPI investors typically do not exercise managerial control and remain passive investors. Thus, this statement correctly distinguishes between FDI and FPI.

18. The empirical test conducted in 1951 to examine the validity of the Heckscher–Ohlin model was carried out by Wassily Leontief. He analyzed U.S. trade data and found that the United States, though capital abundant, exported more labor-intensive goods and imported more capital-intensive goods. This unexpected result came to be known as the "Leontief Paradox." Therefore, the test was conducted by Wassily Leontief.

19. Section 91 of the Income-tax Act provides unilateral relief to resident taxpayers where income has been taxed both in India and in a foreign country with which India does not have a Double Taxation Avoidance Agreement. Thus, Assertion (A) is correct. However, the relief under Section 91 is allowed at the lower of the Indian rate of tax or the foreign rate of tax on such doubly taxed income, not the higher. Since the Reason incorrectly states "whichever is higher," it is incorrect.

20. Skimming pricing is adopted when a new product has no close substitutes and the firm initially sets a high price to skim maximum revenue from segments willing to pay more. This is suitable when demand is relatively inelastic and competition is limited, making Assertion (A) correct. The Reason, however, describes penetration pricing, which involves fixing a low initial price to quickly enter the market and gain market share. Since it explains a different pricing policy, Reason (R) is incorrect.

21. **A. Medical Insurance Premia:** Deduction under Section 80D comes first among the listed provisions.

Since Section 80D precedes the other relevant sections numerically, it is placed first in ascending order.

C. Interest on Loan for Higher Education: Covered under Section 80E.

Section 80E comes after Section 80D, so it follows next.

E. Donations to Certain Funds, etc.: Covered under Section 80G.

Section 80G comes after Section 80E, hence it is placed third.

B. Royalty Income of Author: Covered under Section 80QQB.

This section appears later in sequence compared to 80G.

D. Interest on Deposits in Saving Accounts: Covered under Section 80TTA.

Section 80TTA comes after Section 80QQB, so it is placed last in ascending order.

22. **A. Fees for Professional or Technical Services:** Governed by Section 194J.

This section specifically deals with deduction of tax at source on professional and technical services.

B. Payment of Life Insurance Policy: Covered under Section 194DA.

It relates to TDS on certain sums paid under life insurance policies.

C. Winnings from Lotteries or Crossword Puzzles: Covered under Section 194B.

This section mandates TDS on winnings from lotteries, crossword puzzles, and similar games.

D. Interest other than Interest on Securities: Covered under Section 194A.

It governs TDS on interest payments other than interest on securities.

23. Selling price per unit = 20

Variable cost per unit = 14

Contribution per unit = 20 − 14 = 6

Break-even point (in units)

= Fixed Cost ÷ Contribution per unit
= 7,92,000 ÷ 6
= 1,32,000 units

Break-even sales (in rupees)
= 1,32,000 × 20 = 26,40,000

Therefore, break-even point in terms of sales value is ₹ 26,40,000.

24. After indemnifying the insured for a loss, the insurer acquires the legal right to step into the shoes of the insured and recover the loss amount from a third party responsible for the damage. This transfer of rights after settlement of claim is known as subrogation. It prevents the insured from receiving double compensation and ensures equitable recovery.

25. **A.** The belief that all villages are equally populated is incorrect; villages differ widely in population size and purchasing power.

C. The idea that rural consumers cannot discriminate between products due to illiteracy is a misconception; rural consumers are increasingly aware and brand conscious.

D. The notion that only low-priced products sell in rural India is also a myth; rural markets demand quality and even premium products in certain categories.

Statements B and E are not myths because rural consumers are heterogeneous and rural markets also include consumer durable segments.

26. The new issue of capital is generally costlier than retained earnings because issuing new equity involves flotation costs such as underwriting commission, brokerage, advertisement expenses, and administrative charges, which increase the effective cost. Retained earnings, though not involving explicit cash outflow, have an opportunity cost, which is the return shareholders forgo when profits are retained instead of distributed as dividends. Since shareholders could have invested the dividend elsewhere to earn a return, this foregone return represents the cost of retained earnings. New equity includes both this opportunity cost and additional flotation costs, making it costlier. Hence both statements are correct and the reason properly explains the assertion.

27. **A. Operating Leverage:** Degree of Operating Leverage = Contribution/EBIT.

It measures the sensitivity of EBIT to changes in sales.

B. Combined Leverage: Degree of Combined Leverage = Contribution/EBT.

It reflects the combined effect of operating and financial leverage on earnings before tax.

C. Earning Per Share: EPS = EAT/Number of Equity Shares.

It indicates earnings attributable to each equity share.

D. Financial Leverage: Degree of Financial Leverage = EBIT/EBT.

It measures the effect of fixed financial charges on earnings.

28. Common types of organizational culture include Power Culture, Role Culture, Task Culture, and Person Culture. "Non-Entrepreneurial Culture" is not recognized as a standard classification of organizational culture. Therefore, it is not considered a type of organizational culture.

29. The formal or organized financial system consists of financial markets, financial instruments, financial services, banks, and other regulated financial institutions. Chit-fund companies typically operate in the unorganized or semi-formal sector and are not considered a core component of the formal organized financial system. Therefore, chit-fund companies are not part of the formal financial system.

30. **A. (Probable Error of Correlation Coefficient):** The formula for probable error is 0.6745 × Standard Error of r, and

Standard Error of $r = \left[\frac{1-r^2}{\sqrt{n}}\right]$

Therefore,

Probable Error $= 0.6745\left[\frac{1-r^2}{\sqrt{n}}\right]$, which matches IV.

B. Standard Error of Correlation Coefficient:

Standard Error of r is given by $\frac{1-r^2}{\sqrt{n}}$.

This directly corresponds to III.

C. Coefficient of Determination: It represents the proportion of explained variation to total variation.

Hence it matches I, $\frac{\text{Explained Variation}}{\text{Total Variation}}$.

D. Coefficient of Alienation: It represents the proportion of unexplained variation to total variation.

Therefore, it corresponds to II, $\frac{\text{Unexplained Variation}}{\text{Total Variation}}$.

31. A. Ind AS 7 → IV: Ind AS 7 deals with the Statement of Cash Flows and prescribes classification of cash flows into operating, investing, and financing activities.

It focuses on cash and cash equivalents and reporting cash movements during the period.

B. Ind AS 24 → II: Ind AS 24 relates to Related Party Disclosures to ensure transparency of relationships and transactions that may influence financial statements.

It requires disclosure of related parties, key management personnel, and related party transactions/balances.

C. Ind AS 36 → I: Ind AS 36 covers Impairment of Assets, ensuring assets are not carried above their recoverable amount.

It prescribes impairment testing, recognition of impairment loss, and reversal rules (where permitted).

D. Ind AS 110 → III: Ind AS 110 deals with Consolidated Financial Statements based on the concept of control over subsidiaries.

It lays down when to consolidate and how to present group financials as a single economic entity.

32. D. Perfect Competition: It has the maximum number of sellers, typically very large, with each seller being a price taker.

Entry and exit are relatively easy, so the number of sellers remains very high.

C. Monopolistic Competition: It has many sellers, but fewer than perfect competition, because products are differentiated.

Firms have some pricing power due to branding and differentiation, yet sellers are still numerous.

B. Oligopoly: It has a few sellers, often large firms, and each firm's decisions affect rivals.

Entry barriers and strategic interdependence keep the number of sellers limited.

A. Duopoly: It is a special case of oligopoly with exactly two sellers in the market.

Hence, it comes last when arranging by descending number of sellers.

33. B. Economic factors: These are part of the macro (external) environment, affecting overall demand, costs, interest rates, inflation, and growth conditions.

They influence all firms broadly, not just a single industry participant.

C. Natural factors: These are also macro forces, including climate, natural resources, environmental regulations, and ecological constraints.

They shape production possibilities, sustainability costs, and long-term business risk.

(A) Customers, (D) Marketing intermediaries, (E) Competitors: These belong to the micro/immediate environment (task environment), directly linked to the firm's market operations. They affect the firm closely and industry-specifically rather than economy-wide.

34. D. Net Profit before taxation and extra ordinary items: This is the starting point in the indirect method to compute operating cash flow under AS-3 (Revised).

It represents the profit base before making cash-flow adjustments.

A. Operating profit before Working Capital Changes: Next, non-cash/non-operating adjustments (like depreciation, provisions, non-operating gains/losses) convert profit into operating profit before working capital changes.

This step isolates operating performance on an accrual basis before current asset/ current liability movements.

C. Cash generated from operations: Then working capital changes (inventory, receivables, payables, etc.) are adjusted to convert accrual operating profit into cash from operations.

This yields the cash generated from operational activities before considering extraordinary items presentation.

B. Cash flow before extra ordinary items: Finally, the operating cash figure is presented as cash flow before extraordinary items (with extraordinary items shown separately as required).

This aligns the presentation so extraordinary items do not distort the normal operating cash flow figure.

35.

$$Q = -L^3 + 5L^2 + 10L$$

$$MP_L = \frac{dQ}{dL}$$

$$MP_L = -3L^2 + 10L + 10$$

Since the marginal product is a downward-opening quadratic (coefficient of L^2 is negative), after some level of labour, MP_L starts falling and can even become negative for large L. This means additional units of labour add less and less to output after a point, which is exactly the law of diminishing returns.

36. **C. Need Recognition:** The buying process begins when a consumer recognizes a difference between the desired state and the actual state.

This triggers the motivation to satisfy a need.

E. Development of Decision Criteria: After recognizing the need, the consumer identifies criteria (price, quality, features, brand) that will guide the purchase decision.

These criteria serve as standards for evaluating alternatives.

B. Search for Alternatives: The consumer then gathers information about available products or brands that meet the decision criteria.

This may involve internal memory search or external information sources.

A. Evaluation of Alternatives: The identified alternatives are compared against the developed criteria.

The consumer assesses relative advantages and disadvantages before narrowing choices.

D. Decision: Finally, the consumer selects the most suitable alternative and makes the purchase decision.

37. An infinite series of equal cash flows occurring at regular intervals is known as a perpetuity. Unlike an ordinary annuity or annuity due, which run for a fixed number of periods, a perpetuity continues indefinitely. Therefore, the correct term is perpetuity.

38. **A. True null hypothesis is rejected:** This is a Type I Error, where a correct null hypothesis is incorrectly rejected.

B. False null hypothesis does not get rejected: This is a Type II Error, where a false null hypothesis is wrongly accepted.

C. Used for data from interval or ratio scales: These are analyzed using Parametric Tests, which assume specific distributional properties.

D. Used to test hypotheses with nominal and ordinal data: These data types are analyzed using Nonparametric Tests, which do not require strict distributional assumptions.

39. A new issue refers to raising fresh capital from the public or existing shareholders. Public issue through prospectus, rights issue, and book building are methods of issuing new shares to raise funds. A bonus issue, however, involves issuing additional shares to existing shareholders out of accumulated reserves without raising fresh capital. Hence, it is not a method of new issue.

40. Given demand equation,

$$D = 10,000 - PP$$

Given supply equation,

$$S = 1000 + 4P$$

At equilibrium,

$$D = S$$

So,

$$10,000 - P = 1000 + 4P$$

Bringing like terms together,

$$10,000 - 1000 = 4P + P$$

$$9000 = 5P$$

$$P = \frac{9000}{5}$$

$$P = 1800$$

Therefore, the equilibrium price is 1800.

41. In an amalgamation in the nature of merger (as per accounting standards), all assets and liabilities of the transferor company are taken over by the transferee company and the business of the transferor company is intended to be continued by the transferee. One essential condition is that shareholders holding at least 90% of the equity shares of the transferor company (excluding shares already held by transferee or its subsidiaries) must become equity shareholders of the transferee company. Hence, the statement that shareholders need not become equity shareholders is incorrect.

42. Financial inclusion refers to the process of ensuring access to appropriate financial products and services to all sections of society, especially weaker and low-income groups, at affordable cost and in a transparent manner through formal institutional channels. It aims at integrating vulnerable groups into the mainstream financial system to promote inclusive growth.

43. Under the new tax regime (default regime for AY 2025–26), agricultural income is considered only for rate purposes if non-agricultural income exceeds the basic exemption limit. For an individual aged 60 years opting for the new regime, the basic exemption limit is ₹ 3,00,000. Mr. A's non-agricultural income is ₹ 3,80,000. Under the new regime slabs, income up to ₹ 3,00,000 is nil, and the next slab up to ₹ 6,00,000 is taxed at 5%. Tax on ₹ 80,000 = ₹ 4,000. However, since total income does not exceed ₹ 7,00,000, rebate under section 87A makes the tax liability nil. Therefore, the tax payable is Nil.

44. No option fits the correct economic relationship: The correct formula connecting AR, MR and elasticity of demand (e) is

$$MR = AR\left(\frac{e-1}{e}\right)$$

Given unit elasticity,

$$e = 1$$

Substituting,

$$MR = AR\left(\frac{1-1}{1}\right)$$

$$MR = AR \times 0$$

$$MR = 0$$

But the question states MR = 5.

Since Marginal Revenue must be zero when demand is unit elastic, the given value MR = 5 contradicts the condition of unit elasticity. Therefore, no value of AR can satisfy both conditions simultaneously.

Hence, none of the given options (2.5, 5, 1, 10) is correct.

45. **D. Target Population Definition:** First, clearly define the population to which the study results will apply.

C. Selection of Sampling Frame: Next, identify the list or source from which the sample will be drawn.

B. Select a Sampling Technique: Then choose an appropriate sampling method (random, stratified, etc.).

A. **Determine the Sample Size:** Finally, decide how many units will be included in the sample based on accuracy and resource considerations.

46. C. **Preliminary Interview:** The process begins with an initial screening interview to eliminate clearly unsuitable candidates.

It helps verify basic qualifications and assess initial suitability.

A. **Selection Tests:** After screening, candidates undergo aptitude, intelligence, personality, or skill tests.

These tests objectively measure the candidate's capabilities.

D. **Employment Interview:** Candidates who clear tests appear for a formal interview.

This step evaluates communication skills, attitude, and job fit.

B. **Reference and Background Analysis:** Once selected provisionally, references and background details are verified.

This ensures authenticity of qualifications and past experience.

E. **Job Offer:** Finally, an offer of employment is issued to the selected candidate.

47. A. **Profit Centres:** A unit responsible for both revenues and costs, and evaluated on profit performance.

It represents a decentralized structure with autonomy over income and expenditure.

C. **Cost Centres:** A unit responsible only for controlling costs without direct revenue responsibility.

It reflects functional decentralization.

D. **Investment Centres:** A unit responsible for profit and investment decisions.

It represents the highest form of decentralization where managers control assets and returns.

B. **Service Centres:** These are support units and not classified as formal decentralization types in standard management control systems.

48. A. **Narasimham Committee-I:** Constituted in 1991 to recommend reforms in India's banking and financial system.

This is the earliest among the listed committees.

E. **Rashid Jilani Committee:** Formed in the early 1990s after Narasimham-I to examine cheque clearing and payment system reforms.

It predates the later reform-oriented committees of the late 1990s and 2000s.

D. **Saraf Committee:** Set up in the mid-1990s to examine legal and structural aspects of the banking and financial sector.

It followed the earlier 1990s reform committees.

B. **Padmanabhan Committee:** Constituted in the early 2000s to review risk management and supervision in banks.

Its formation was later than the 1990s reform committees.

C. **Verma Committee:** Established in the mid-2000s concerning banking sector restructuring and related reforms.

Hence, it comes last in ascending order of formation.

49. B. **EU:** European Union originated from the European Economic Community established in 1957 (Treaty of Rome).

D. **UNCTAD:** Established in 1964 as a permanent intergovernmental body under the UN.

C. **ASEAN:** Formed in 1967 to promote economic and regional cooperation in Southeast Asia.

A. **NAFTA:** Came into force in 1994 as a trilateral trade agreement between USA, Canada, and Mexico.

50. A. **Standard Deduction under Section 16(ia):** Allowed under the head Income under Salaries.

B. **Standard Deduction under Section 24:** Allowed under Income from House Property.

C. Depreciation Allowance under Section 32: Allowed under Profits and Gains of Business or Profession.

D. Exemption under Section 54 for profit on transfer of residential house: Falls under Income under the head Capital Gains.

51. India's participation in SAARC (SAFTA) and ASEAN trade agreements mainly involves reduction or elimination of tariffs among member countries while allowing each country to maintain its own external trade policy with non-members. There is no common external tariff, free movement of factors, or unified economic policy. These features correspond to a Free Trade Area, not a Customs Union, Common Market, or Economic Union.

52. The WTO's core functions include providing a forum for trade negotiations, administering multilateral trade agreements such as GATS, TRIPS, and TRIMS, and monitoring members' trade policies through review mechanisms. It also settles trade disputes. However, providing concessional loans and financial aid is the function of institutions like the World Bank or IMF, not the WTO. Therefore, this is not a core function of WTO.

53. Complaints regarding non-receipt of dividend by investors are categorized as investor service-related complaints. Under SEBI's complaint classification system, non-receipt of dividend falls under Type II complaints, which relate to issues concerning payment or transfer of securities benefits. Hence, it is classified under Type II.

54. B. Vouching is not concerned only with items of the Balance Sheet; it mainly relates to verification of transactions recorded in the books of accounts, particularly those in the Profit and Loss Account. Hence, this statement is incorrect.

D. The objectives mentioned (existence, ownership, valuation, etc.) relate to verification rather than vouching. Vouching primarily deals with examining documentary evidence supporting transactions. Therefore, this statement is also incorrect.

Statements A, C, and E are correct as management audit is generally not compulsory, Section 148 mandates cost audit for certain companies, and independent financial audit is compulsory for many entities under respective laws.

55. A. Historical Cost Approach: Propounded by Brummet, Flamholtz and Pyle, focusing on capitalizing recruitment and training costs of employees.

B. Opportunity Cost Approach: Propounded by Hekimian and Jones, valuing employees based on their alternative uses within the organization.

C. Standard Cost Approach: Associated with David Watson, emphasizing standard costing techniques for human resource valuation.

D. Present Value of Future Earnings Model: Developed by Lev and Schwartz, which calculates the present value of expected future earnings of employees.

56. A. Greenfield Investment: It refers to overseas investment to create new facilities from the ground up.

Hence, it matches III.

B. Foreign Portfolio Investment: It involves investment in foreign financial instruments like stocks and bonds without managerial control.

Therefore, it matches IV.

C. Forward Vertical FDI: It is a type of direct investment overseas aimed at selling the output of a firm's domestic production process in foreign markets.

Thus, it corresponds to I.

D. Brownfield Investment: It involves acquiring or merging with existing facilities abroad rather than building new ones.

Hence, it matches II.

57. The Executive Summary appears at the beginning of a research report and provides a concise overview of objectives, methodology, findings, and recommendations. It forms part of the prefatory section, which includes title page, table of contents, and acknowledgements. Therefore, it is included under Prefatory Information.

58. Common types of organization charts include vertical (top-down), horizontal (left-to-right), and circular (radial) charts. "Diagonal chart" is not recognized as a standard type of organization chart in management literature. Hence, it is not a valid type.

59. A. **Provision for bad and doubtful debts:** Reflects the Conservatism concept, which anticipates possible losses.

B. **Expenses recognised with revenue:** Represents the Matching Concept, where expenses are matched with related revenues.

C. **Assets not shown at current realisable value:** Reflects the Going Concern concept, assuming business continuity and valuation at historical cost rather than liquidation value.

D. **Internally generated goodwill not recorded:** Reflects the Cost Concept, as only purchased goodwill is recorded at actual cost.

60. E. **Indian Contract Act:** Enacted in 1872.

D. **Negotiable Instruments Act):** Enacted in 1881.

C. **Information Technology Act):** Enacted in 2000.

B. **Competition Act):** Enacted in 2002.

A. **Right to Information Act:** Enacted in 2005.

61. "Karl Pearson's Coefficient of Skewness"

$$= \frac{3(\text{Mean} - \text{Median})}{\text{S.D.}}$$

$$= \frac{3(6.82 - 6.80)}{1.4}$$

$$= \frac{3(0.02)}{1.4} = \frac{0.06}{1.4}$$

$$= 0.042857 \approx 0.043.$$

62. A. **Doctrine of Caveat Emptor → III Sales of Goods Act:** Caveat emptor means "let the buyer beware," and it is a key principle of sale of goods transactions.

Hence it is primarily governed under the Sales of Goods Act.

B. **Bailment and Pledge → I Special Contract:** Bailment and pledge are treated as specific/special contractual relationships under contract law.

Therefore, they fall under the category of Special Contract.

C. **Holder in due Course → IV Negotiable Instrument:** "Holder in due course" is a concept unique to negotiable instruments like cheques, bills, and promissory notes.

So it belongs to the Negotiable Instruments law area.

D. **DPIN → II Limited Liability Partnership:** DPIN refers to Designated Partner Identification Number used for designated partners under LLP framework.

Hence it matches Limited Liability Partnership.

63. Assertion (A) is correct because an effective performance appraisal system improves employee performance through clearer expectations, feedback, development planning, and performance-linked decisions, which strengthens organizational capability and competitive advantage. Reason (R) is also correct because evaluating self-managed teams is a recognized difficulty in appraisal due to shared responsibility, interdependence, and measuring individual contributions. However, this challenge does not explain why appraisal creates competitive advantage; it is a separate issue related to implementation difficulty.

64. After A's death, B and C continue with their remaining old ratio 3 : 2 (since no new ratio is stated).

Total adjusted capital = 3,56,000 + 2,44,000
= 6,00,000

$$\text{B's new capital} = 6,00,000 \times \frac{3}{3+2}$$

$$= 6,00,000 \times \frac{3}{5}$$

$$= 3,60,000.$$

65. Quartile Deviation $= \frac{Q_3 - Q_1}{2} = 6$

So, $Q_3 - Q_1 = 12$

Given $Q_1 = 48$, hence $Q_3 = 48 + 12 = 60$

For a symmetrical distribution, "Median"

$$= \frac{Q_1 + Q_3}{2}$$

$$= \frac{48+60}{2} = \frac{108}{2} = 54.$$

66. A. Highest Reach → Advertising: Advertising can reach the largest audience quickly through mass media like TV, digital platforms, newspapers, and outdoor media.

Its strength is wide coverage and repeated exposure to large, geographically dispersed markets.

B. Most Persuasive → Personal Selling: Personal selling is the most persuasive because it involves face-to-face (or direct) interaction, allowing explanation, customization, and immediate handling of objections.

This two-way communication makes it strongest for convincing and converting buyers.

C. Immediate Effect on Sales → Sales Promotion: Sales promotion (discounts, coupons, limited-period offers, contests) is designed to trigger quick purchase decisions.

It produces short-term spikes in sales by creating urgency and extra value.

D. No Cost Involved → Publicity: Publicity is typically not paid directly like advertising; it is media coverage gained through newsworthiness or public relations efforts.

Although some PR activity has indirect costs, publicity itself is treated as "no direct media cost" in promotional mix comparisons.

67. B. Establishment of Standards: Control begins by setting performance standards as benchmarks (targets, norms, or expected output).

Without standards, performance cannot be judged meaningfully.

A. Measurement of Actual Performance: Actual results are then measured using reports, observations, audits, or performance data.

This step produces the factual basis for evaluating control.

D. Comparison of actual performance with the standards: Measured performance is compared with standards to identify deviations.

The deviation analysis shows whether control is required and where gaps exist.

C. Corrective action where required: Finally, corrective steps are taken to remove causes of deviation and improve performance.

This may include retraining, process changes, tighter supervision, or revising standards if needed.

68. For assessees opting for presumptive taxation under Section 44AD or 44ADA, the advance tax requirement is simplified. They must pay the entire advance tax liability in one installment on or before 15th March of the previous year. This special rule replaces the usual multiple installment schedule applicable to other taxpayers.

69. Assertion (A): Filter questions are used to screen respondents and check whether they are relevant to the study—often by testing awareness, familiarity, eligibility, or experience.

Hence, saying they measure familiarity with the research topic is correct in questionnaire design.

Reason (R): Questions that capture multiple pieces of information at once are called double-barrelled questions, not leading questions.

Leading questions are those that push the respondent toward a particular answer, so the Reason is incorrect.

70. In Walter's Model, if a firm is declining such that $r < k_e$, reinvested earnings earn less than shareholders' required rate of return. In this situation, retaining profits destroys value, so shareholders prefer maximum dividends. Therefore, the market value of shares is maximized when the firm pays out all earnings as dividends, i.e., 100% dividend payout.

71. External techniques of foreign exchange risk management include instruments obtained from outside parties such as forward contracts, currency futures, and currency swaps, which are derivative-based hedging tools. Netting, however, is an internal technique where a multinational adjusts intra-group receivables and payables to reduce foreign exchange exposure without using external financial instruments. Hence, it is not an external technique.

72. In barometric price leadership, one firm (not necessarily the largest or lowest-cost firm) takes the initiative in announcing price changes, and other firms follow. The leading firm acts as a "barometer" reflecting market conditions. This leadership arises due to reputation, forecasting ability, or strategic positioning rather than sheer dominance or cost advantage.

73. According to Maslow's hierarchy of needs, the order from lowest to highest is Physiological Needs (basic survival), followed by Safety Needs (security and protection), then Social Needs (belongingness and love), followed by Esteem Needs (recognition and respect), and finally Self-actualization Needs (self-fulfillment and realization of potential). Thus, the ascending order is A, D, B, E, C.

74. The research process begins with Problem Definition, where the issue is clearly identified. Then Developing an Approach to the Problem is undertaken to frame theoretical and analytical perspectives. Next comes Research Design Formulation, which outlines the structure for data collection. After that, Data Collection, Preparation, and Analysis are performed. Finally, the process concludes with Report Writing and Presentation to communicate findings.

75. RTGS (Real Time Gross Settlement) is a system in which funds are transferred from one bank to another on a real-time basis and on a gross basis, meaning each transaction is settled individually without being netted with other transactions. Therefore, the Assertion is correct. However, the Reason is incorrect because RTGS transactions are subject to a prescribed minimum limit (₹ 2 lakh in India), even though there is no upper ceiling. Since the statement claims there is no minimum ceiling, it is factually wrong.

76. The measure of relative risk is calculated as Coefficient of Variation (CV)

$$= \frac{\text{Standard Deviation}}{\text{Expected Value}}$$

It expresses dispersion relative to the mean and allows comparison of risk across different investments or distributions with different expected returns. Variance measures absolute dispersion, co-variance measures joint variability, and geometric mean measures compounded growth rate. Hence, Coefficient of Variance is the correct measure of relative risk.

77. **A.** The normal curve approaches the *x*-axis asymptotically as we move away from the mean in either direction. The tails never touch the axis but extend infinitely.

C. The total area under the normal curve above the horizontal axis is always equal to 1, representing total probability.

E. The normal distribution is unimodal, having only one peak at the mean.

Statements B and D are incorrect because the points of inflection occur at $\mu \pm \sigma$, not $\pm 2\sigma$, and approximately 68.27% of area lies between $\mu \pm \sigma$, not $\pm 2\sigma$.

78. **A. Managerial Grid → III Blake and Mouton:** The Managerial Grid theory was developed by Blake and Mouton focusing on concern for people and concern for production.

B. Hawthorne Experiments → IV Elton Mayo: The Hawthorne Studies were conducted under the leadership of Elton Mayo.

C. Trait Theory → I Charles Bird: Charles Bird contributed significantly to early trait-based leadership studies.

D. ERG Theory → II Alderfer: ERG theory was proposed by Clayton Alderfer, categorizing needs into Existence, Relatedness, and Growth.

79. A possible cost of FDI to the host country is the repatriation of profits by multinational corporations to their home country. This can lead to capital outflows and may create pressure on the balance of payments in the long run. Statement A is not necessarily correct because long-run competitiveness does not automatically reduce. Statement B is incorrect due to the word "always," since technology transfer can also encourage local innovation. Statement D is incorrect because FDI does not always worsen the BoP; it may initially improve the capital account. Therefore, only statement C correctly represents a possible cost of FDI.

80. A leap year has 366 days.

366 = 52 weeks + 2 days

So every weekday occurs 52 times, and the extra 2 consecutive days determine which days occur 53 times.

There are 7 possible pairs of consecutive extra days:

(Mon, Tue)
(Tue, Wed)
(Wed, Thu)
(Thu, Fri)
(Fri, Sat)
(Sat, Sun)
(Sun, Mon)

Total possible outcomes = 7

For 53 Sundays, Sunday must be one of the extra days.

Favourable cases:

(Sat, Sun)
(Sun, Mon)

For 53 Mondays, Monday must be one of the extra days.

Favourable cases:

(Sun, Mon)
(Mon, Tue)

Now for "53 Sundays or 53 Mondays", we take the union of both events:

(Sat, Sun)
(Sun, Mon)
(Mon, Tue)

Total favourable outcomes = 3

Probability $= \frac{3}{7}$.

Therefore, the correct answer is 3: $\frac{3}{7}$.

81. The situation described involves coercion under contract law, where consent is obtained by committing or threatening to commit an act forbidden by law. Preventing cremation of the deceased unless adoption is made amounts to coercion because it compels the widow to act against her free will. Since her consent was not free, she was legally entitled to cancel the adoption. The court held that the consent was obtained under coercion and therefore invalid. Thus, both the Assertion and the Reason are correct, and the Reason properly explains why the adoption was cancelled.

82. **A. Risk Theory of Profit → III F.B. Hawley:** Hawley propounded that profit is the reward for risk-bearing. The entrepreneur undertakes uncertainty and possible loss, and profit compensates for assuming that risk.

B. Dynamic Theory of Profit → IV J.B. Clark: J.B. Clark explained that profits arise in a dynamic economy due to continuous changes such as technological progress, capital accumulation, and population growth. In a purely static economy, profits would tend to disappear.

C. **Innovation Theory of Profit → I Joseph A. Schumpeter:** Schumpeter emphasized innovation as the central function of the entrepreneur. Profit is the temporary reward earned for introducing new combinations such as new products, new methods, or new markets.

D. **Profit as Rent of Ability → II F.A. Walker:** Walker compared profit to economic rent, stating that entrepreneurs differ in ability just as land differs in fertility. Profit represents the surplus earned by superior entrepreneurs over the marginal entrepreneur.

83. A. **Matching Approach:** Also called hedging approach, it matches the maturity of assets with the maturity of financing sources.

B. **Conservative Approach:** Long-term financing is used even for part of temporary working capital to reduce risk.

D. **Aggressive Approach:** Short-term financing is used for permanent and temporary working capital, increasing risk but potentially increasing profitability.

The Operating Cycle Approach determines working capital requirement, not financing mix.

84. Minority interest (non-controlling interest) represents the portion of equity in a subsidiary not attributable to the parent company. It is shown separately in consolidated financial statements. However, it is not presented as part of equity of the parent's shareholders; instead, it is shown separately within equity but distinct from parent shareholders' equity. Hence, Assertion is correct but Reason is incorrect.

85. When the auditor concludes that the financial statements present a true and fair view and are prepared, in all material respects, in accordance with the applicable financial reporting framework, an unmodified (clean) opinion is issued. It indicates no material misstatements or scope limitations.

86.
- **A (NPV → III):** Net Present Value is calculated as the summation of the present values of cash inflows minus the summation of the present values of cash outflows. It measures the absolute increase in wealth.
- **B (IRR → I):** Internal Rate of Return is the rate of discount at which the aggregate present value of cash inflows equals the aggregate present value of cash outflows, making NPV equal to zero.
- **C (ARR → II):** Accounting Rate of Return is computed by dividing the average annual profit after tax by the average investment over the life of the project.
- **D (PI → IV):** Profitability Index is obtained by dividing the present value of future cash inflows by the present value of cash outflows.

87. The ordinal school of consumer preferences states that utility cannot be measured in absolute terms; only ranking or ordering of preferences is possible. Hence, the magnitude (cardinal measurement) of utility is not important. Indifference curves represent ranked preferences, and utility is not considered additive in ordinal analysis.

88. Arm's length price refers to the price that would be charged in a transaction between unrelated parties dealing at arm's length in uncontrolled conditions. It ensures fairness in transfer pricing between associated enterprises.

89.
- **A (EXIM Bank → II):** EXIM Bank finances exports and imports.
- **B (NHB → III):** National Housing Bank promotes housing finance institutions.
- **C (IDBI → IV):** Industrial Development Bank of India finances and promotes industrial development.
- **D (NABARD → I):** NABARD advances credit for agriculture and rural development activities.

90. The Cobb-Douglas production function is expressed in multiplicative form as

$$Q = AL^{\alpha}K^{\beta},$$

where A is total factor productivity, L is labour, K is capital, and α and β represent output elasticities.

91. Once the Registrar issues the certificate of incorporation, it becomes conclusive evidence that all legal requirements of incorporation have been complied with. Even if there are procedural irregularities, wrong dating, or inclusion of minors as subscribers, the validity of incorporation cannot be questioned. Therefore, the certificate remains valid and cannot be cancelled.

92. A contract entered into before incorporation is called a pre-incorporation contract. Since the company did not exist on 20 June 2024, it could neither authorize Raj nor ratify the contract later. Therefore, Raj, as the promoter who entered into the contract, will be personally liable to Pooja.

93. The certificate of incorporation, once issued by the Registrar, is conclusive evidence of the date of incorporation. Even if it is wrongly dated, the date mentioned on the certificate is legally binding and cannot be challenged. Since the certificate bears the date 25 June 2024, the company is deemed to have come into existence from that date. The allotment of shares was made on 28 June 2024, which is after the legally recognized date of incorporation. Therefore, in the eyes of law, the allotment is valid as it was made after the company had come into existence.

94. A contract entered into after incorporation but before obtaining the certificate of commencement of business (in case required) is known as a provisional contract. Such a contract becomes binding only after the company is entitled to commence business. Hence, the contract with Prakash is a provisional contract.

95. The contract with Pooja was entered into on 20 June 2024, before the certificate of incorporation was issued. Since the company did not legally exist at that time, the contract is termed a pre-incorporation contract.

96. Selling through online platforms, retail stores, and direct sales agents means the company is using multiple channels to reach customers. This reflects a multi-channel distribution strategy, where products are made available through different intermediaries and platforms to increase market coverage and convenience.

97. Digital campaigns, social media advertising, and discounts are elements of promotional activities aimed at creating awareness and stimulating demand. These tools are part of the promotion mix, which includes advertising, sales promotion, public relations, and personal selling.

98. During the introduction stage of the product life cycle, companies typically incur high promotional and awareness-building costs while sales volume is still low. As a result, profits are usually low or even negative in the short run due to heavy marketing expenditure and limited initial revenue.

99. Loyalty points are incentives offered to encourage repeat purchases and build customer retention. Such schemes provide additional value to customers and are categorized under sales promotion rather than advertising or personal selling.

100. Emphasizing biodegradable and safe products shows concern not only for customer satisfaction but also for environmental and societal welfare. This aligns with the societal marketing approach, which balances company profits, consumer needs, and long-term societal well-being.

Previous Years' Paper

National Testing Agency (NTA)

UGC-NET Junior Research Fellowship & Assistant Professor Eligibility Exam

COMMERCE, JUNE-2025

(Exam held on 27-06-2025)

PAPER-II

1. Match the LIST-I with LIST-II.

LIST-I (Concept)	LIST-II (Formula)
A. Present Value	I. Cash flow $x\ (1 + r)^t$
B. Future Value	II. Cash flow$/(1 + r)^t$
C. Future Value of Annuity	III. R $(PVIF_{i,n})$
D. Present Value of Annuity	IV. R $(FVIFA_{i,n})$

Choose the **correct** answer from the options given below:

1. A-II, B-I, C-IV, D-III
2. A-I, B-II, C-IV, D-III
3. A-III, B-IV, C-I, D-II
4. A-I, B-III, C-II, D-IV

2. Match the LIST-I with LIST-II.

LIST-I (Trade Tariff)	LIST-II (Explanation)
A. Specific Tariff	I. Fixed percentage of the value of the commodity
B. Ad valorem Tariff	II. Fixed amount of money per unit
C. Compound Tariff	III. Duty fixed to bring the price of imported commodity to the level of domestic support price
D. Variable Tariff	IV. Combination of Ad valorem and Specific Tariff

Choose the **correct** answer from the options given below:

1. A-I, B-II, C-III, D-IV
2. A-II, B-I, C-IV, D-III
3. A-III, B-IV, C-II, D-I
4. A-IV, B-III, C-II, D-I

3. Which of the following is NOT the feature of business environment?

1. Complex
2. Dynamic
3. Multi faceted
4. Static

4. Identify the correct sequence of Research Design Process:

A. Measurement technique selection
B. Research approach selection
C. Data collection technique selection
D. Sample design selection
E. Data analysis method selection

Choose the **correct** answer from the options given below:

1. A, B, C, D, E
2. B, A, D, C, E
3. D, C, E, A, B
4. C, E, D, B, A

5. A Ltd. makes plastic buckets. Selling price per bucket is ₹ 210 and variable cost per bucket is ₹ 60. Fixed cost of making buckets is ₹ 1,50,000 for the year. The number of buckets to be sold to get a profit of ₹ 90000 is:

1. 714 buckets 2. 428 buckets
3. 1000 buckets 4. 1600 buckets

6. Identify the correct sequence of sampling design process:

A. Determine the Sample size
B. Select a sampling technique
C. Selection of sampling frame
D. Defining target population

Choose the **correct** answer from the options given below:

1. A, B, C, D 2. B, A, D, C
3. A, B, D, C 4. D, C, B, A

7. The ongoing process of systematically identifying, assessing and developing organizational leadership to enhance performance is known as which of the following?

1. Strategy and workforce planning
2. Predictive workforce monitoring
3. Succession planning
4. Managerial decision making

8. Arrange the following examples of business cycles in chronological order. (Old to New)

A. Dot Com Bubble Burst
B. Great Depression
C. Covid Pandemic
D. Global Financial Crisis

Choose the **correct** answer from the options given below:

1. A, B, C, D 2. B, A, D, C
3. D, B, A, C 4. C, D, A, B

9. Arrange the following Development Financial Institution in chronological order of their establishment. (Old to New)

A. IFCI
B. IDBI
C. NABARD
D. SIDBI

Choose the **correct** answer from the options given below:

1. A, B, C, D 2. B, A, C, D
3. C, D, A, B 4. D, C, B, A

10. Which of the following is a horizontal agreement?

1. Tie in arrangement
2. Resale Price maintenance
3. Cartel
4. Exclusive Distribution

11. Match the LIST-I with LIST-II.

LIST-I	LIST-II
A. Deduction of Tax at source on fees for professional and technical services	I. Section 194 B
B. Deduction of Tax at source from income by way of rent	II. Section 193
C. Deduction of Tax at source from winnings from lotteries or crossword puzzles, etc.	III. Section 194-I
D. Deduction of Tax at source from interest on securities	IV. Section 194-J

Choose the **correct** answer from the options given below:

1. A-I, B-II, C-III, D-IV
2. A-IV, B-III, C-II, D-I
3. A-IV, B-III, C-I, D-II
4. A-II, B-I, C-IV, D-III

12. Which of the following statements are correct with regard to mathematical properties of standard deviation?

A. Standard deviation is independent of change of origin and change of scale.
B. Standard deviation is independent of change of origin but not of scale.
C. The standard deviation of first n natural numbers is $\sqrt{\frac{n^2-1}{12}}$
D. The standard deviation of first n natural numbers is $\sqrt{\frac{n^2-1}{6}}$

E. For moderately skewed distributions standard deviation is 0.8 of mean deviation.

Choose the **correct** answer from the options given below:

1. B and C only
2. B, C and E only
3. A and C only
4. B, D and E only

13. Arrange the following steps of incorporation of a new Limited Liability Partnership in proper sequence.

A. Reserve LLP Name
B. Preparation of Documents for Incorporation of LLP
C. Procure Digital Signature Certificate
D. LLP incorporation and DIN Application and apply for PAN and TAN
E. Drafting and filling LLP Agreement

Choose the **correct** answer from the options given below:

1. B, A, C, D, E
2. A, B, C, E, D
3. C, A, B, D, E
4. D, E, B, A, C

14. A company has 10%, 20 lakh debentures. The EBIT of the company is ₹ 5,00,000 and the equity capitalisation rate is 16%. Calculate overall cost of capital.

1. 9.5%
2. 10.8%
3. 12.9%
4. 14.5%

15. Symbols, Icons, Rituals and values are the manifestations of:

1. Social class
2. Culture
3. Sub-culture
4. Social Factors

16. What refer to 'L' in the PESTLE Framework?

1. Labour
2. Legal
3. Land
4. Latest

17. Match the LIST-I with LIST-II.

LIST-I (Relative measures of Skewness)	LIST-II (Formula)
A. Karl Pearson's coefficient of skewness	I. $\frac{(\mu_3)^2}{(\mu_2)^3}$
B. Bowley's coefficient of skewness	II. $(P_{90} + P_{10} - 2 \text{ Median})/(P_{90} - P_{10})$
C. Kelly's coefficient of skewness	III. $(Q_3 + Q_1 - 2 \text{ Median})/(Q_3 - Q_1)$
D. Moment coefficient of skewness	IV. (Mean-Mode)/Standard Deviation

Choose the **correct** answer from the options given below:

1. A-I, B-II, C-III, D-IV
2. A-IV, B-III, C-II D-I
3. A-II, B-III, C-IV, D-I
4. A-III, B-IV, C-I, D-II

18. Match the LIST-I with LIST-II.

LIST-I (Stages of Product Life Cycle)	LIST-II (Types of Customers)
A. Introduction	I. Laggards
B. Growth	II. Early Adopters
C. Maturity	III. Middle Majority
D. Obsoletion	IV. Innovators

Choose the **correct** answer from the options given below:

1. A-I, B-II, C-III, D-IV
2. A-II, B-III, C-I, D-IV
3. A-IV, B-II, C-III, D-I
4. A-III, B-II, C-IV, D-I

19. Geographical Price differentials include which of the following?

A. F.O.B Factory Pricing
B. Zone Pricing
C. Loss Leader Pricing

D. Postage Stamp Pricing
E. Basing Point Pricing

Choose the **correct** answer from the options given below:

1. A, B, C and D only
2. B, C, D and E only
3. A, B, D and E only
4. B, D and E only

20. Match the LIST-I with LIST-II.

LIST-I (Components commonly present in reports)	LIST-II (Contents)
A. Prefatory Information	I. Executive Summary
B. Introductory Information	II. Glossary
C. Main Research Body	III. Problem Definition
D. Supplementary Information	IV. Research Design

Choose the **correct** answer from the options given below:

1. A-I, B-II, C-III, D-IV
2. A-II, B-I, C-IV, D-III
3. A-I, B-III, C-II, D-IV
4. A-I, B-III, C-IV, D-II

21. Any assessee (except an eligible assessee in respect of an eligible business referred to in section 44 AD or 44 ADA) must pay upto 75 per cent of advance tax payable:

1. on or before June 15 of the previous year
2. on or before September 15 of the previous year
3. on or before December 15 of the previous year
4. on or before March 15 of the previous year

22. Arrange the following human needs as per Maslow's Hierarchy of needs.

A. Social Needs
B. Safety Needs
C. Esteem Needs
D. Physiological Needs
E. Self-actualisation Needs

Choose the **correct** answer from the options given below:

1. D, B, A, C, E
2. A, B, C, D, E
3. B, D, C, E, A
4. D, A, B, C, E

23. Match the LIST-I with LIST-II.

LIST-I (Concept)	LIST-II (Formula)
A. Total Utility	I. $MU_1 + MU_2 + \ldots\ldots\ldots MU_n$
B. Marginal Utility	II. $TU_n - TU_n - 1$
C. Average Fixed Cost	III. $\Delta TC/\Delta Q$
D. Marginal Cost	IV. TFC/Q

Choose the **correct** answer from the options given below:

1. A-IV, B-III, C-II, D-I
2. A-II, B-I, C-III, D-IV
3. A-I, B-II, C-IV, D-III
4. A-III, B-II, C-I, D-IV

24. Match the LIST-I with LIST-II.

LIST-I	LIST-II
A. Section 2 (85)	I. Associate Company
B. Section 455	II. Producer Company
C. Section 378A	III. Dormant Company
D. Section 2 (6)	IV. Small Company

Choose the **correct** answer from the options given below:

1. A-I, B-II, C-III, D-IV
2. A-I, B-III, C-II, D-IV
3. A-II, B-III, C-I, D-IV
4. A-IV, B-III, C-II, D-I

25. What rights does an unpaid seller have against the goods?

A. Right of lien
B. Right to sue for specific performance
C. Right of resale
D. Right of stoppage of goods in transit
E. Right to reorganise possession of goods

Choose the **correct** answer from the options given below:

1. A, B and C only
2. B, C and D only
3. C, D and E only
4. A, C, D only

26. What is the amount of net cash from operating activities of A Ltd. if it has net profit before tax ₹ 5,90,000: Depreciation on Property, Plant and Equipment ₹ 4,30,000: Decrease in current Assets ₹ 30,000: Decrease in Current Liabilities ₹ 85,000: and Tax Paid ₹ 80,000.

1. ₹ 9,65,000 2. ₹ 8,85,000
3. ₹ 10,75,000 4. ₹ 9,95,000

27. Match the LIST-I with LIST-II.

LIST-I	LIST-II
A. Ind AS 2	I. Property, Plant and Equipment
B. Ind AS 16	II. Fair Value Measurement
C. Ind AS 103	III. Inventories
D. Ind AS 113	IV. Business Combinations

Choose the **correct** answer from the options given below:

1. A-I, B-II, C-III, D-IV
2. A-IV, B-III, C-II, D-I
3. A-III, B-I, C-IV, D-II
4. A-III, B-I, C-II, D-IV

28. Which of the following statements are incorrect for amalgamation in the nature of merger?

A. All the assets and liabilities of the transferor company are taken over by transferee company.
B. Shareholders holding not less than 95% of the face value of the equity shares of the transferor company become equity shareholders of the transferee company.
C. Payment of purchase consideration may be made in cash per share.
D. Journal entries for recording the merger are passed by pooling of interest method.
E. The business of the transferor company is not intended to be carried on by the transferee company.

Choose the **correct** answer from the options given below:

1. A, B and C only
2. B, C and D only
3. A and D only
4. B, C and E only

29. The term 'marketing myopia' was coined by:

1. Philip Kotler 2. Gary Armstrong
3. Peter Drucker 4. Theodore Levitt

30. In case the income of an individual includes the income of ₹ 25,000 of his minor child in terms of section 64(IA), such individual shall be entitled to an exemption under section 10(32) of:

1. ₹ 25,000 2. ₹ 1,500
3. ₹ 2,500 4. ₹ 15,000

31. The cross price elasticity between two goods 'A' and 'B' is (–) 0.8. If the price of good 'B' rise by 20%, how will the demand for 'A' change?

1. (–) 16% 2. 6%
3. (–) 8% 4. (–) 12%

32. ABC Ltd. issued 2,000, 10% preference shares of ₹ 100 each at ₹ 95. Calculate the cost of preference shares.

1. 8.50% 2. 10.53%
3. 12.35% 4. 15.25%

33. Match the LIST-I with LIST-II.

LIST-I (Item)	LIST-II (Section)
A. Deduction in respect of medical insurance premium	I. Section 80CCH
B. Deduction in case of a person with disability	II. Section 80D

C. Deduction in respect of interest on loan taken for higher education	III. Section 80U
D. Deduction in respect of contribution to Agnipath Scheme	IV. Section 80E

Choose the **correct** answer from the options given below:

1. A-IV, B-I, C-II, D-III
2. A-III, B-IV, C-I, D-II
3. A-II, B-III, C-IV, D-I
4. A-I, B-II, C-III, D-IV

34. Arm's length price as per section 92F is the price applied or proposed to be applied when:

1. two unrelated persons enter into a transaction in uncontrolled conditions
2. two related persons enter into a transaction in uncontrolled conditions
3. two unrelated persons enter into a transaction in controlled conditions
4. two related persons enter into a transaction in controlled conditions

35. Which of the following are the applications of the conservatism principle of accounting?

A. Valuation of stock in trade at the lower of cost or market value
B. Debiting drawings account and crediting purchases account when goods are withdrawn by the proprietor
C. Making provision for bad and doubtful debts
D. Making provision for discount on creditors
E. Creation of investment fluctuation fund

Choose the **correct** answer from the options given below:

1. A and C only
2. A, B and D only
3. B, C and E only
4. A, C and E only

36. Which of the following methods belong to the category of demand/market-based pricing?

A. Surge pricing
B. Premium pricing
C. 'What the traffic can bear' pricing
D. Discount pricing
E. Parity pricing

Choose the **correct** answer from the options given below:

1. A, B, C and D only
2. B, C and D only
3. A, B and C only
4. C, D and E only

37. A term loan becomes Non-Performing Asset (NPA) if its interest and/or instalment of principal remains overdue for a period of more than:

1. 30 days
2. 60 days
3. 75 days
4. 90 days

38. The scheme of partial integration of tax or non-agricultural income with income derived from agricultural is applicable if an individual has:

1. Non-Agricultural income of more than the exemption limit or agricultural income exceeding ₹ 5000
2. Non-Agricultural income of more than the exemption limit or agricultural income exceeding ₹ 2500
3. Non-Agricultural income of more than the exemption limit and agricultural income exceeding ₹ 2500
4. Non-Agricultural income of more than the exemption limit and agricultural income exceeding ₹ 5000

39. Which of the following are the key objectives of WTO?

A. To set rules for international trade
B. To resolve trade disputes
C. To resolve border disputes
D. To provide a forum for negotiating trade liberalisation

Choose the **correct** answer from the options given below:

1. A, B, D only
2. A, C only
3. B, C, D only
4. A, B, C and D

40. In India, the term of every utility patent granted shall be of .... years.

1. 10
2. 20
3. 30
4. 50

41. The working of current Purchasing Power Accounting requires classification of balance sheet items into Monetary Items and Non-Monetary Items. Which of the following is a Non-Monetary Item as per current Purchasing Power Accounting?

1. Cash
2. Debentures
3. Debtors
4. Inventories

42. Arrange the following steps of Multinational Capital Budgeting in correct order:

A. Estimate net cash flow from the project
B. Determine net investment outlay
C. Apply appropriate evaluation technique
D. Identify appropriate discount rate

Choose the **correct** answer from the options given below:

1. A, B, C, D
2. C, A, B, D
3. D, C, B, A
4. B, A, D, C

43. Which of the following Ind AS specifically deals with consolidated financial statements?

1. Ind AS 29
2. Ind AS 101
3. Ind AS 110
4. Ind AS 41

44. Which of the following types of FDI includes creation of new assets and production facilities in the country?

1. Brownfield investment
2. Merger and Acquisition
3. Strategic alliances
4. Greenfield investment

45. What is the Harmonic Mean of two numbers whose Arithmetic Mean and Geometric Mean are 30 and 24 respectively?

1. 4.8
2. 9.6
3. 19.2
4. 76.8

46. What is the primary liability of the drawer of a bill of exchange or cheque?

1. Liability to compensate the holder in case of dishonour.
2. Liability to pay the amount at maturity.
3. Liability to provide sufficient funds to the drawee.
4. Liability to pay the holder without any condition.

47. In case of transmission of shares, which of the following is correct?

A. No instrument of transfer is required.
B. Transmission of securities is generally made without any consideration.
C. Shares continue to be subject to the original liabilities.
D. Transmission takes place on death or insolvency of a holder of securities.
E. Stamp duty is payable on transmission of securities.

Choose the **correct** answer from the options given below:

1. A, B, C and D only
2. B, C and D only
3. C, D and E only
4. A, B, C only

48. Which of the following statements are correct with regard to tax avoidance?

A. Tax avoidance is legitimate arrangement of affairs in such a way so as to minimize tax liability.
B. There is an element of malafide motive involved in tax avoidance.
C. Tax avoidance takes into account the loop-holes of law.
D. Tax avoidance is intentional attempt to avoid payment of tax after the liability to tax has arisen.
E. Tax avoidance is same as tax omission.

Choose the **correct** answer from the options given below:

1. A and C only
2. A, B and C only
3. B, D and E only
4. A, C and E only

49. Arrange the following steps of New Product Development in sequential order:

A. Product Development
B. Feasibility Analysis
C. Concept Development and Testing
D. Identifying Prospective Customers
E. Idea Generation

Choose the **correct** answer from the options given below:

1. A, B, C, E, D
2. D, E, B, C, A
3. E, D, C, B, A
4. E, B, C, A, D

50. Which of the following are properties of regression coefficient?

A. The coefficient of correlation and the two regression coefficients have the same signs.
B. The coefficient of correlation is the harmonic mean between the regression coefficients.
C. If one of the regression coefficient is greater than unity, the other must also be greater than unity.
D. If one of the regression coefficient is greater than unity, the other must be less than unity.
E. The regression coefficient are independent of change of origin but not of scale.

Choose the **correct** answer from the options given below:

1. A and D only
2. B, C and E only
3. A, B and C only
4. A, D and E only

51. Arrange the following stages of Adoption process in correct order:

A. Interest
B. Awareness
C. Trial
D. Evaluation
E. Adoption

Choose the **correct** answer from the options given below:

1. A, D, C, B, E
2. A, B, C, D, E
3. B, C, A, E, D
4. B, A, D, C, E

52. Arrange the following in chronological order of their establishment. (Old to New)

A. NAFTA
B. European Union
C. SAARC
D. ASEAN

Choose the **correct** answer from the options given below:

1. A, B, C, D
2. B, A, D, C
3. D, C, A, B
4. C, D, A, B

53. Match the LIST-I with LIST-II.

LIST-I (Concept)	LIST-II (Formula)
A. Production Function	I. K (K, L)
B. Average Product	II. $TP_n - TP_{n-1}$
C. Marginal Product	III. Total Product/ No. of units of variable factor
D. Constant Return to scale	IV. $Q = f(a, b, c, \ldots\ldots n)$

Choose the **correct** answer from the options given below:

1. A-I, B-II, C-III, D-IV
2. A-II, B-I, C-IV, D-III
3. A-I, B-II, C-IV, D-III
4. A-IV, B-III, C-II, D-I

54. Which of the following are the discounted cash flow techniques of capital budgeting?

A. Payback Period
B. Accounting Rate of Return (ARR)
C. Net Per cent Value (NPV)
D. Internal Rate of Return (IRR)
E. Profitability Index

Choose the **correct** answer from the options given below:

1. A, C, D only
2. B, C, E only
3. C and D only
4. C, D and E only

55. If a random variable X follows a Poisson distribution such that $P(X=1) = 4P(X=2)$ The variance of X is:

1. 1/2
2. 1
3. 2
4. 1/4

56. A type of validity which demonstrates statistically a relationship between scores on a selection procedure and job performance is called:

1. Test validity
2. Criterion validity
3. Content validity
4. Construct validity

57. Which of the following is NOT an element of Micro environment?

1. Customers
2. Suppliers
3. Technology
4. Competitors

58. "Active concealment of fact" is associated with which one of the following?

1. Misrepresentation
2. Undue influence
3. Fraud
4. Mistake

59. A company hold raw material for 60 days. It gets credit from suppliers for 15 days, production process take 15 days, finished goods are held for 30 days and 30 days credit is given to debtors. Calculate the total working capital cycle.

1. 150 days
2. 120 days
3. 100 days
4. 90 days

60. Match the LIST-I with LIST-II.

LIST-I	LIST-II
A. Job enlargement	I. A list of jobs 'human requirements', i.e., the requisite education, skills, personality etc.
B. Job descriptions	II. A list of jobs duties, responsibilities, reporting relationships, working conditions and supervisory responsibilities.
C. Job specifications	III. Assigning workers additional same level activities.
D. Job enrichment	IV. Redesigning jobs in a way that increases the opportunities for the workers to experience feelings of responsibility, achievement, growth and recognition.

Choose the **correct** answer from the options given below:

1. A-III, B-II, C-I, D-IV
2. A-IV, B-II, C-I, D-III
3. A-III, B-I, C-II, D-IV
4. A-IV, B-II, C-III, D-I

61. Which of the following requirements have to be satisfied in order that an assessee is entitled to claim deduction under section 91 for doubly taxed income?

A. The assessee must have been non-resident in India in the relevant previous year.

B. The assessee must have been resident in India in the relevant previous year.

C. Income must have been accrued or arisen to him during that previous year in India.

D. Income must have been accrued or arisen to him during that previous year outside India.

E. In respect of that income which accrued or arouse outside India, he must have paid by deduction or otherwise tax under the law in force in the country in question.

Choose the **correct** answer from the options given below:

1. A and C only
2. B and D only
3. B, D and E only
4. A, C and E only

62. The price of a product decreases from ₹ 100 to ₹ 60 per unit. If the price elasticity of demand in 1.5 and the original quantity demanded in 30 units. What will be the new quantity demanded?

1. 38
2. 48
3. 56
4. 62

63. Which of the following statement is incorrect for Management Audit?

1. Management audit is a statutory requirement.
2. Management audit is a comprehensive and critical review of all aspects of management process.
3. Management audit covers wide area of management activities and may be for more than one financial year.
4. The shareholders or board of directors may appoint the management auditor.

64. The questions that are actually asked from the respondent are known as:

1. Management Questions
2. Research Questions
3. Investigative Questions
4. Measurement Questions

65. State Bank of India came into existence in which of the following year?

1. 1947
2. 1950
3. 1955
4. 1969

66. Identify the areas of macro economics:

A. National Income
B. Balance of Payments
C. Level of savings and investment
D. Location of industry
E. Behaviour of firms

Choose the **correct** answer from the options given below:

1. A, B and C only
2. B, C and E only
3. B, C and D only
4. A, B, C, D and E

67. In which of the following year Investor Protection and Education Fund Regulations was issued by the Securities and Exchange Board of India?

1. 1992
2. 1999
3. 2003
4. 2009

68. According to Levitt and Drucker, the essence of marketing is:

1. Profit Orientation
2. Product Orientation
3. Market Orientation
4. Customer Orientation

69. Arrange the following in chronological order of the Milestone achieved by the National Stock Exchange of India:

A. Commencement of Trading in Index options
B. Launch of securities Lending and Borrowing Scheme
C. Commencement of Derivatives Trading in Index Futures
D. Launch of Mutual Fund Service System
E. Launch of S & P CNX Nifty

Choose the **correct** answer from the options given below:

1. B, D, E, A, C
2. A, C, E, B, D
3. E, A, C, D, B
4. E, C, A, B, D

70. Which of the following types of audit report are termed together as modified reports as per standards on Auditing (SA) 705?

A. Qualified Report
B. Audit Report with an 'Emphasis of Matter' paragraph
C. Disclaimer of Opinion Report
D. Adverse Report

Choose the **correct** answer from the options given below:

1. A and B only
2. A, B and C only
3. B and C only
4. A, C and D only

71. Which of the following formula correctly show the relationship Average Revenue (AR), Marginal Revenue (MR) and Price elasticity of demand?

1. $MR = AR + e - 1$
2. $AR = MR \times e - 1/e$
3. $MR = AR \times (e - 1)/e$
4. $MR = AR + e - 1/e + 1$

72. Arrange the following exchange rate arrangements of international monetary system in chronological order. (Old to New)

A. Gold Standard
B. Commodity Specie Standard
C. Fixed Parity System
D. Floating Exchange Rate

Choose the **correct** answer from the options given below:

1. A, B, C, D
2. B, A, C, D
3. C, B, D, A
4. B, C, A, D

73. Who can file petition to the Tribunal for the Winding up of a Limited Liability Partnership?

A. Secured Creditors
B. LLP or any of its Partners
C. Registrar of Companies
D. Any person authorised by the Central Government
E. Any Voluntary Association

Choose the **correct** answer from the options given below:

1. A, B, C only
2. A and B only
3. A, B, C and D only
4. B, C and E only

74. If the employee pays tax within the parameters of alternative tax regime under section 115 BAC then from assessment year 2025-26, standard deduction from salary income is:

1. NIL
2. ₹ 50,000 or gross salary, whichever is lower
3. ₹ 75,000 or gross salary, whichever is lower
4. ₹ 40,000 or gross salary, whichever is lower

75. Which of the following are part of micro economics?

A. Product pricing
B. Consumer behaviour
C. Interest rate
D. Factor pricing

Choose the **correct** answer from the options given below:

1. A, B and C only
2. A, B and D only
3. A and D only
4. A, B, C and D

76. An unsecured short term promissory note, negotiable and transferable by endorsement and delivery with a fixed maturity period, issued at a discount by creditworthy corporates, primary dealers and all-India financial institutions is known as:

1. Treasury Bill
2. Commercial Paper
3. Certificates of Deposit
4. Repo

77. The type of market where few sellers are selling competing products to many buyers is known as:

1. Monopoly
2. Monopolistic Competition
3. Oligopoly
4. Perfect Competition

78. A company produces and sells 10,000 toys. The selling price per toy is ₹ 500, variable cost is ₹ 200 per unit and fixed operating cost is ₹ 25,00,000. Calculate operating Leverage.

1. 4 times
2. 5 times
3. 6 times
4. 8 times

79. Which of the following statements is correct?

A. If a company is an Indian company, it will automatically be considered as a domestic company.

B. Foreign company means a company which is not a domestic company.

C. The exit status of an Indian company can be non-resident in India.

D. The resident status of a foreign company can never be resident in India.

E. The foreign income of a resident company is taxable in India.

Choose the **correct** answer from the options given below:

1. A, B and C only
2. B, C and D only
3. A, C and E only
4. A, B and E only

80. Identify the correct order in which the assets of the firm shall be applied in case of dissolution of a partnership firm:

A. Paying to each partner rateably what is due to him from the firm for advances as distinguished from capital.

B. Paying the residues if any to partners in the proportion in which they were entitled to share profit.

C. Paying the debts of the firm to third parties.

D. Paying to each partner rateably what is due to him on account of capital.

Choose the **correct** answer from the options given below:

1. A, C, D, B
2. C, A, B, D
3. C, A, D, B
4. A, B, C, D

81. Identify the factors that determine the demand.

A. Price of the Commodity

B. Income of the Consumer

C. Taste and Preferences of Consumer

D. Size of Population

Choose the **correct** answer from the options given below:

1. A and B only
2. A, B and C only
3. B, C and D only
4. A, B, C and D

82. Arrange the following steps involved in the process of Voluntary Liquidation of a Limited Liability Partnership in correct order.

A. Declaration of Solvency

B. Designated Partners' Meeting

C. Partners' Meeting

D. Identification of an Insolvency Professional as liquidator

E. Filling of resolutions with registrar of Companies and Insolvency and Bankruptcy Board of India (IBBI)

Choose the **correct** answer from the options given below:

1. A, B, C, D, E
2. C, B, D, A, E
3. A, D, B, C, E
4. E, D, C, B, A

83. Matrix Structure can be made more effective by following which of the guidelines given below?

A. Collective learning, coordination and integration of skills for obtaining the streams of technology.

B. Define the objectives of the project or task.

C. Clarify the roles, authority and responsibilities of managers and team members.

D. Ensure that influence is based on knowledge, information, rather than on rank.

E. Balance the power of functional and project managers.

Choose the **correct** answer from the options given below:

1. A, B, C, D only
2. A, B, D and E only
3. B, C, D, and E only
4. A, B, C, E only

84. Match the LIST-I with LIST-II.

LIST-I	LIST-II
A. Perception	I. A descriptive thought that a person holds about something.
B. Learning	II. A person's consistently favourable or unfavourable evaluations, feelings and tendencies toward an object or idea.
C. Belief	III. Changes in an individual's behaviour arising from experience.
D. Attitude	IV. The process by which people select, organise and interpret information to form a meaningful picture of the world.

Choose the **correct** answer from the options given below:

1. A-I, B-II, C-III, D-IV
2. A-III, B-IV, C-II, D-I
3. A-IV, B-III, C-I, D-II
4. A-II, B-III, C-I, D-IV

85. Match the LIST-I with LIST-II.

LIST-I (BOP)	LIST-II (Concept)
A. Balance of payment-current A/C	I. Inflow and outflow of capital
B. Balance of payment-capital A/C	II. International Transactions of goods and services
C. Balance of Trade	III. Import and export of goods only
D. Balancing item	IV. Entry for net errors and omissions

Choose the **correct** answer from the options given below:

1. A-I, B-II, C-III, D-IV
2. A-III, B-II, C-IV, D-I
3. A-IV, B-III, C-I, D-II
4. A-II, B-I, C-III, D-IV

86. Which of the following countries were part of NAFTA?

A. United States B. Canada
C. Mexico D. Brazil

Choose the **correct** answer from the options given below:

1. A, B only 2. A, B, C only
3. B, C, D only 4. B, C only

87. Arrange the following theories of international trade in chronological order. (old to new)

A. Mercantilism Theory
B. Comparative Advantage Theory
C. Product Life Cycle Theory
D. Hecksher-Ohlin Theory

Choose the **correct** answer from the options given below:

1. A, B, C, D 2. A, B, D, C
3. C, B, A, D 4. B, A, C, D

88. Keeping a record of uncommonly good or undesirable examples of an employee's work-related behaviour and reviewing it with the employee at pre-determined times is known as:

1. Behaviourally Anchored Rating Scale
2. Critical Incident Method
3. Paired Comparison Method
4. Mixed Standard Scales

89. The parametric test that can be used for hypothesis testing of paired samples is:

1. *t*-test
2. *z*-test
3. Chi-Square test
4. Mann-Whitney test

90. Match the LIST-I with LIST-II.

LIST-I (Term)	LIST-II (Explanation)
A. Nostro Account	I. Account held by a foreign bank with a local bank
B. Vostro Account	II. An Indian Bank's Swiss Franc A/C with a hank in Switzerland.

C. Bid	III.	Price at which the dealer is willing to buy another currency.
D. Offer	IV.	Price at which the dealer is willing to sell another currency.

Choose the **correct** answer from the options given below:

1. A-I, B-II, C-III, D-IV
2. A-II, B-I, C-III, D-IV
3. A-III, B-II, C-IV, D-I
4. A-IV, B-III, C-I, D-II

Directions (Qs. No. 91-95): *Read the following passage and answer the questions:*

A mid-sized IT firm in India is facing multiple HR challenges as it expands. The company recently hired 200 employees but is struggling with high attrition, lack of structured training program and a weak performance appraisal system. Employees often feel over worked and under-appreciated, leading to low engagement and motivation. The HR manager Priya wants to improve HR practices by implementing a structured performance appraisal system launching employee wellness program and using HR technology for recruitment. However she face resistance from senior management, who think those initiative will increase cost without direct financial benefits.

Additionally, employee feedback indicates dissatisfaction with work life balance and unclear career progression. Some employees also feel that promotions are biased and that the company lack a proper succession plan.

Priya is considering introducing flexible work arrangements, setting up leadership development program and adopting AI-driven HR analytics to improve decision making. However, she needs to convince top management of the long term benefits of these changes.

91. Which strategy would be most effective in retaining employees and reducing attrition rate?

1. Making the resignation process more difficult
2. Increasing workload
3. Offering voluntary retirement
4. Offering increments and career growth opportunities

92. Priya needs to address employee dissatisfaction with career progression. What should be her first step?

1. Encouraging employee to find new jobs
2. Reducing training budgets
3. Conducting skill gap analysis and creating career development plan
4. Promoting only senior employee

93. To convince senior management about HR investments, Priya should highlight:

1. The number of training program conducted
2. The positive feed back of customers
3. The financial impact of HR initiatives on business growth
4. The employees performance appraisal methods

94. If Priya wants to use HR analytics to predict labour turn over. Which data should she analyse?

1. Employees social media engagements
2. Attrition trends and exit interview feedback
3. The number of training program
4. The number of leaves taken by employees

95. Which HR strategy will help develop future leaders in the organization?

1. Implementing intensive employee development programs
2. Hiring only external candidates for leadership roles
3. Implementing performance-linked bonuses
4. Promoting employees based on seniority

Directions (Qs. No. 96-100): *Read the following passage and answer the questions:*

A large real estate company in India is facing challenges in raising funds for expansion. Despite solid track record the company is struggling to attract investors due to increasing concern about liquidity in the financial market. The company has earlier relied on bank loans and debt instruments for financing but now looking for other funding option.

The CFO of the company is evaluating different option such as corporate bonds, Private equity, public deposit and securitization to raise capital. He is also looking at the evolving role of financial institution such as investment banks, development banks and insurance companies in providing finance. However, he is concerned about the volatility of the stock market and the risk of inflation affecting company's future cashflow.

To address these challenges, the company plan to consult with financial advisors and explore new avenues of funding, including green bonds and venture capital. The CFO must navigate the complex world of financial markets to ensure that the company secures the right funding at the right cost.

96. In a volatile stock market, how the company can reduce financing risk when raising funds through equity?

1. Issue share only when market is at peak
2. Raise funds through long term bonds only
3. Reduce dividend payout to increase internal funds
4. Diversify source of funds by combining debt and equity financing

97. Which of the following is a primary function of financial markets in the economy?

1. Facilitating buying and selling of financial instruments
2. Offering financial advice to individual investors
3. Providing loan without collateral
4. Increasing revenues for the Government

98. What would be the main concern for the company if it has to issue green bonds for financing?

1. High interest rate
2. Less repayment period
3. Limited investor demand due to niche market
4. Government restriction

99. What is the main advantage of raising capital through venture capital?

1. To avoid giving up ownership or control
2. To access expertise and guidance from investors
3. To get the fund for a very long term
4. To get a low cost funding

100. The company is considering corporate bonds as a funding option. Which factor is most likely to affect the interest rate of bond?

1. The number of projects completed by the company
2. The interest rate on Government securities
3. The credit rating of the bond
4. The level of Foreign Direct Investment

ANSWERS

1	2	3	4	5	6	7	8	9	10
1	2	4	2	4	4	3	2	1	3
11	**12**	**13**	**14**	**15**	**16**	**17**	**18**	**19**	**20**
3	1	3	3	2	2	2	3	3	4
21	**22**	**23**	**24**	**25**	**26**	**27**	**28**	**29**	**30**
3	1	3	4	4	2	3	4	4	2

31	32	33	34	35	36	37	38	39	40
1	2	3	1	4	3	4	4	1	2
41	**42**	**43**	**44**	**45**	**46**	**47**	**48**	**49**	**50**
4	4	3	4	3	1	1	1	3	4
51	**52**	**53**	**54**	**55**	**56**	**57**	**58**	**59**	**60**
4	3	4	4	1	2	3	3	2	1
61	**62**	**63**	**64**	**65**	**66**	**67**	**68**	**69**	**70**
3	2	1	4	3	1	4	4	4	4
71	**72**	**73**	**74**	**75**	**76**	**77**	**78**	**79**	**80**
3	2	3	3	2	2	3	3	4	3
81	**82**	**83**	**84**	**85**	**86**	**87**	**88**	**89**	**90**
4	3	3	3	4	2	2	2	1	2
91	**92**	**93**	**94**	**95**	**96**	**97**	**98**	**99**	**100**
4	3	3	2	1	4	1	3	2	3

EXPLANATORY ANSWERS

1. Present Value (PV) is the current worth of a future cash flow discounted at a specific rate. Its formula is:

$$PV = \frac{\text{Cash Flow}}{(1+r)^t}$$

Thus, A matches with II.

Future Value (FV) represents the value of a current cash flow compounded into the future. Its formula is:

$$FV = \text{Cash Flow} \times (1 + r)^t$$

Thus, B matches with I.

Future Value of an Annuity involves calculating the compounded value of a series of equal payments. The formula is:

$$\text{FV of Annuity} = R \times (FVIFA_{i,n})$$

Thus, C matches with IV.

Present Value of an Annuity refers to discounting a series of equal payments to their present value. The formula is:

$$\text{PV of Annuity} = R \times (PVIFA_{i,n})$$

Thus, D matches with III.

2. Specific Tariff is a duty levied as a fixed amount per physical unit of an imported commodity. This corresponds to II.

Ad valorem Tariff is calculated as a fixed percentage of the commodity's value. This matches with I.

Compound Tariff combines both Ad valorem and Specific tariffs, meaning a combination of a percentage and a fixed amount per unit. This matches with IV.

Variable Tariff is adjusted to align the imported commodity's price with the domestic support price to protect domestic producers. This corresponds to III.

3. The business environment is known for being:

- **Complex:** Due to numerous interacting factors.
- **Dynamic:** Constantly changing with external influences.
- **Multifaceted:** Different interpretations by different observers.

However, the business environment is never Static, as it continuously evolves.

Hence, "Static" is not a feature.

4. The correct sequence of steps in Research Design Process is as follows:

1. **Research Approach Selection (B):** Decide whether the study will be exploratory, descriptive, or causal.
2. **Measurement Technique Selection (A):** Choose how variables and data points will be quantified.
3. **Sample Design Selection (D):** Determine the sampling methods and size.

4. **Data Collection Technique Selection (C):** Decide on surveys, interviews, observations, etc.

5. **Data Analysis Method Selection (E):** Choose analytical tools and techniques to process data.

Thus, the sequence is: B → A → D → C → E.

5. Given: Selling Price per bucket (SP) = ₹ 210

Variable Cost per bucket (VC) = ₹ 60

Fixed Cost (FC) = ₹ 1,50,000

Desired Profit = ₹ 90,000

First, calculate Contribution per bucket (C):

$$C = SP - VC$$
$$= 210 - 60 = ₹\ 150$$

Total Contribution required:

$$\text{Total Contribution} = FC + \text{Profit}$$
$$= 1,50,000 + 90,000$$
$$= ₹\ 2,40,000$$

Number of buckets to be sold:

$$\text{Units} = \frac{\text{Total Contribution}}{C}$$
$$= \frac{2,40,000}{150}$$
$$= 1,600 \text{ buckets.}$$

6. The correct sequence of the Sampling Design Process is as follows:

   D. Defining Target Population – First, identify the overall population relevant to the study.

   C. Selection of Sampling Frame – Next, prepare a list or source from which the sample will be drawn.

   B. Select a Sampling Technique – Choose whether to use random, stratified, cluster sampling, etc.

   A. Determine the Sample Size – Finally, decide the number of units to include in the sample.

   Hence, the sequence is: D → C → B → A.

7. Succession Planning is a continuous process through which organizations systematically identify, assess, and develop future leaders to ensure leadership continuity, improve performance, and reduce risks related to sudden leadership vacancies. It involves grooming internal talent for future leadership roles.

8. Chronological order of the given business cycles:

   B. Great Depression – Started in 1929, the most severe global economic depression.

   A. Dot Com Bubble Burst – Occurred in 2000-2001 when internet company valuations crashed.

   D. Global Financial Crisis – Originated in 2008 due to subprime mortgage collapse.

   C. Covid Pandemic – Began in 2020, causing a global economic slowdown.

   Correct sequence: B → A → D → C.

9. Chronological order of establishment of Development Financial Institutions (DFIs):

   A. IFCI (Industrial Finance Corporation of India) – Established in 1948 as the first DFI in India.

   B. IDBI (Industrial Development Bank of India) – Established in 1964.

   C. NABARD (National Bank for Agriculture and Rural Development) – Established in 1982.

   D. SIDBI (Small Industries Development Bank of India) – Established in 1990.

   Correct sequence: A → B → C → D.

10. A Cartel is an agreement between competing firms at the same level of production or distribution to control prices or limit competition. This is a classic example of a Horizontal Agreement, where firms at the same market level collude.

    Tie-in arrangements, resale price maintenance, and exclusive distribution are examples of Vertical Agreements between firms at different levels of the supply chain.

11. A. **Deduction of Tax at source on fees for professional and technical services** is governed by Section 194J of the Income Tax Act, which mandates TDS on payments made for services such as consultancy, technical, professional, and royalty payments.

    B. **Deduction of Tax at source from income by way of rent** falls under Section 194I, which requires TDS to be deducted on rental payments exceeding the prescribed limit for land, buildings, machinery, etc.

    C. **Deduction of Tax at source from winnings from lotteries, crossword puzzles, etc.** is covered under Section 194B, which specifies

TDS provisions on winnings exceeding ₹ 10,000 from lotteries, card games, betting, etc.

D. Deduction of Tax at source from interest on securities is governed by Section 193, which applies to interest payments on debentures, securities issued by companies, and government securities, with certain exemptions.

Correct matching: A-IV (194J), B-III (194I), C-I (194B), D-II (193).

12. Statement B is correct because Standard Deviation is independent of change of origin. Adding or subtracting a constant to all data points does not affect the dispersion, so standard deviation remains unchanged. However, it is not independent of change of scale; multiplying or dividing data points by a constant will proportionally affect the standard deviation.

Statement C is also correct. The Standard Deviation of the first *n* natural numbers is given by the formula:

$$\sigma = \sqrt{\frac{n^2 - 1}{12}}$$

This is a standard result derived from statistical properties of natural numbers.

Statement A is incorrect because it wrongly claims independence from both origin and scale, while standard deviation is not scale-independent.

Statement D is wrong because it mentions a denominator of 6, which is incorrect; it should be 12.

Statement E is incorrect because for moderately skewed distributions, Mean Deviation ≈ 0.8 × Standard Deviation, not the reverse.

Thus, only statements B and C are correct.

13. Correct sequence of LLP Incorporation Process:

C. Procure Digital Signature Certificate (DSC) — This is required for filing forms electronically.

A. Reserve LLP Name — Name approval through RUN-LLP service.

B. Preparation of Documents for Incorporation of LLP — Including consent, affidavits, etc.

D. LLP Incorporation and DIN Application and apply for PAN and TAN — Filing of Form FiLLiP.

E. Drafting and Filing LLP Agreement — Mandatory within 30 days of incorporation.

Correct sequence: C → A → B → D → E.

14. Given: Debenture amount = ₹ 20,00,000

Interest rate on Debentures = 10%

EBIT = ₹ 5,00,000

Equity Capitalization Rate = 16%

Debenture Interest = 20,00,000 × 10%

= ₹ 2,00,000

Earnings available to Equity Shareholders = EBIT − Debenture Interest

= 5,00,000 − 2,00,000

= ₹ 3,00,000

Market Value of Equity =

$$= \frac{\text{Earnings}}{\text{Equity Capitalization Rate}} = \frac{3,00,000}{0.16}$$

= ₹ 18,75,000

Total Value of Firm =

Market Value of Equity + Debentures

= 18,75,000 + 20,00,000 = ₹ 38,75,000

$$\text{Overall Cost of Capital (Ko)} = \frac{\text{EBIT}}{\text{Total Value}}$$

$$= \frac{5,00,000}{38,75,000}$$

= 0.129

= 12.9%.

15. Symbols, Icons, Rituals, and Values are core elements of Culture. Culture represents the shared patterns of behaviour, beliefs, and values that characterize a society or group.

16. In the PESTLE Framework, the letter 'L' stands for Legal. PESTLE is an analytical tool used to evaluate external macro-environmental factors affecting an organization.

- P – Political
- E – Economic
- S – Social
- T – Technological
- L – Legal
- E – Environmental

Thus, 'L' refers to Legal aspects like laws, regulations, compliance policies, etc.

17. Matching the Relative Measures of Skewness with their correct formulas:

A. Karl Pearson's Coefficient of Skewness

$$= \frac{\text{Mean} - \text{Mode}}{\text{Standard Deviation}} \rightarrow \text{Matches with IV.}$$

B. Bowley's Coefficient of Skewness

$$= \frac{(Q_3 + Q_1 - 2 \times \text{Median})}{(Q_3 - Q_1)}$$

→ Matches with III.

C. Kelly's Coefficient of Skewness

$$= \frac{(P_{90} + P_{10} - 2 \times \text{Median})}{(P_{90} - P_{10})}$$

→ Matches with II.

D. Moment Coefficient of Skewness

$$= \frac{(\mu_3)^2}{(\mu_2)^3} \rightarrow \text{Matches with I.}$$

Thus, the correct matching is:
A-IV, B-III, C-II, D-I.

18. Matching Product Life Cycle stages with types of customers:

A. Introduction Stage — Customers: Innovators

B. Growth Stage — Customers: Early Adopters

C. Maturity Stage — Customers: Middle Majority

D. Obsoletion Stage — Customers: Laggards

Correct matching sequence: A-IV, B-II, C-III, D-I.

19. Geographical Pricing differentials include:

A. F.O.B Factory Pricing — Buyer pays transport from factory.

B. Zone Pricing — Uniform price for buyers within a geographical zone.

D. Postage Stamp Pricing — Uniform delivery price across regions.

E. Basing Point Pricing — Freight is calculated from a fixed location (basing point).

C. Loss Leader Pricing is not a geographical price differential; it's a promotional strategy.

Thus, correct set: A, B, D and E only.

20. Matching report components with their contents:

A. Prefatory Information — Contains Executive Summary → Matches I.

B. Introductory Information — Contains Problem Definition → Matches III.

C. Main Research Body — Contains Research Design → Matches IV.

D. Supplementary Information — Contains Glossary, Appendices, etc. → Matches II.

Thus, correct matching: A-I, B-III, C-IV, D-II.

21. As per the Income Tax Act, any assessee (other than an eligible assessee under Section 44AD or 44ADA) is required to pay advance tax in installments. Up to 75% of the advance tax payable must be paid on or before December 15 of the previous year. The remaining 25% is due by March 15.

Thus, for non-eligible assessees:

- 15% by June 15
- 45% (cumulative) by September 15
- 75% (cumulative) by December 15
- 100% by March 15.

22. Maslow's Hierarchy of Needs (from bottom to top) is arranged as:

1. **Physiological Needs (D)** – Basic survival needs like food, water, shelter.
2. **Safety Needs (B)** – Security, stability, protection from harm.
3. **Social Needs (A)** – Belongingness, love, relationships.
4. **Esteem Needs (C)** – Respect, recognition, self-esteem.
5. **Self-actualization Needs (E)** – Realizing personal potential, self-fulfillment.

Correct sequence: D → B → A → C → E.

23. A. Total Utility (TU) is the sum of Marginal Utilities of each unit consumed:

$$TU = MU_1 + MU_2 + \ldots + MU_n$$

→ Matches with I.

B. Marginal Utility (MU) is the change in Total Utility when an additional unit is consumed:

$$MU = TU_n - TU_n - 1$$

→ Matches with II.

C. Average Fixed Cost (AFC) is given by:

$$AFC = \frac{TFC}{Q}$$

→ Matches with IV.

D. **Marginal Cost (MC)** is the change in Total Cost per unit change in output:

$$MC = \frac{\Delta TC}{\Delta Q} \rightarrow \text{Matches with III.}$$

Correct matching: A-I, B-II, C-IV, D-III.

24. A. **Section 2(85)** defines a Small Company, characterized by paid-up capital and turnover not exceeding prescribed limits. This is intended for small-scale businesses that are not public companies.

B. **Section 455** pertains to a Dormant Company, which is formed for future projects or to hold assets and intellectual properties without significant financial transactions.

C. **Section 378A** deals with the definition and provisions related to a Producer Company, which mainly involves activities linked to primary produce and is governed under Chapter XXIA of the Companies Act.

D. **Section 2(6)** defines an Associate Company, where another company exercises significant influence but it is neither a subsidiary nor a joint venture.

Thus, the correct match is: A-IV (Small Company); B-III (Dormant Company); C-II (Producer Company); D-I (Associate Company).

25. An unpaid seller has the following rights against the goods:

A. **Right of lien** - Retaining possession until payment is made.

C. **Right of resale** - Reselling the goods after notifying the buyer.

D. **Right of stoppage in transit** - Stopping goods in transit if buyer becomes insolvent.

B. **Right to sue for specific performance** is a personal remedy against the buyer, not a right against the goods.

E. **Right to reorganise possession of goods** is not a recognized right.

Thus, correct rights are: A, C, D only.

26. Given: Net Profit before Tax = ₹ 5,90,000

Depreciation = ₹ 4,30,000

Decrease in Current Assets = ₹ 30,000

Decrease in Current Liabilities = ₹ 85,000

Tax Paid = ₹ 80,000

Calculation:

Add Depreciation:

5,90,000 + 4,30,000 = 10,20,000

Add Decrease in Current Assets:

10,20,000 + 30,000 = 10,50,000

Subtract Decrease in Current Liabilities:

10,50,000 - 85,000 = 9,65,000

Subtract Tax Paid:

9,65,000 - 80,000 = 8,85,000

Net Cash from Operating Activities = ₹ 8,85,000.

27. Matching Indian Accounting Standards (Ind AS) with their subjects:

A. **Ind AS 2** — Relates to Inventories → Matches III

B. **Ind AS 16** — Relates to Property, Plant and Equipment (PPE) → Matches I

C. **Ind AS 103** — Relates to Business Combinations (Amalgamations, Mergers) → Matches IV

D. **Ind AS 113** — Relates to Fair Value Measurement → Matches II.

28. In Amalgamation in the Nature of Merger:

A. **Correct** — All assets and liabilities are transferred to the transferee company.

B. **Correct** — Shareholders holding at least 90% (not 95%) of face value must become shareholders of transferee. Statement mentions 95%, so Incorrect.

C. **Incorrect** — Purchase consideration must not be paid in cash, except for fractional shares.

D. **Correct** — Pooling of Interests Method is used for accounting.

E. **Incorrect** — The business of transferor must be intended to be carried on by transferee.

Thus, statements B, C, E are incorrect.

29. The term 'Marketing Myopia' was coined by Theodore Levitt in his 1960 Harvard Business Review article. It describes a shortsighted focus on selling products rather than understanding customer needs and market evolution.

30. As per Section 10(32) of the Income Tax Act, when an individual's income includes the income of a minor child under Section 64(1A), an exemption of ₹ 1,500 per child is allowed. Thus, the exemption is ₹ 1,500.

31. Given: Cross Price Elasticity of Demand (E_p) between goods A and B = –0.8

Price Increase of Good B = +20%

Formula: %Change in Demand of A

= Cross Price Elasticity × %Change in Price of B

Substitute values:

%Change in Demand of A

= (–0.8) × 20 = –16%

A negative cross elasticity indicates that Goods A and B are complementary goods. Hence, an increase in the price of Good B will lead to a decrease in the demand for Good A by 16%.

32. Given Data:

Face Value of Preference Share = ₹ 100

Dividend Rate = 10% → Dividend = ₹ 10

Issue Price = ₹ 95 (Issued at a discount of ₹ 5)

Formula for Cost of Preference Shares (K_p):

$$K_p = \frac{\text{Annual Dividend}}{\text{Net Proceeds}} = \frac{10}{95} = 0.1053$$

Convert to Percentage:

K_p = 10.53%

Thus, the cost of preference shares is 10.53%.

33. Matching deductions under various sections of Income Tax Act:

A. **Medical Insurance Premium Deduction →** Section 80D allows deduction for premium paid towards Mediclaim policies.

B. **Deduction for Person with Disability →** Section 80U provides a flat deduction for individuals with disabilities.

C. **Deduction for Interest on Education Loan** → Section 80E covers deduction of interest on loans taken for higher education.

D. **Contribution to Agnipath Scheme →** Section 80CCH allows deductions for contributions to the Agnipath scheme.

Correct Matching: A-II (80D), B-III (80U), C-IV (80E), D-I (80CCH).

34. The concept of Arm's Length Price under Section 92F of the Income Tax Act is pivotal in Transfer Pricing regulations. It ensures that transactions between associated enterprises (related parties) are priced fairly, as if they were conducted between independent (unrelated) entities under uncontrolled (market-driven) conditions.

The definition explicitly mentions that Arm's Length Price is the price which would have been applied between two unrelated persons in an uncontrolled situation. The purpose is to prevent tax evasion through manipulation of transaction prices between related entities.

Thus, though the context is about transactions between related parties, the Arm's Length Price benchmark is derived from how unrelated persons would transact in an open market.

35. The Conservatism Principle (Prudence Concept) in accounting ensures that liabilities and losses are recognized as soon as they are foreseeable, while revenues and gains are only recorded when realized.

Correct applications of Conservatism:

A. **Stock Valuation at Lower of Cost or Market Value** — Ensures that unrealized losses are accounted for, not unrealized gains.

C. **Provision for Bad and Doubtful Debts** — Anticipating potential non-recovery of debts, even if actual default hasn't occurred.

E. **Creation of Investment Fluctuation Fund** — Setting aside reserves to absorb potential future investment losses.

B. (Drawings adjustment) and D. (Provision for discount on creditors) are not applications of conservatism.

36. Demand/Market-Based Pricing methods focus on consumer demand and market conditions rather than cost structures.

A. **Surge Pricing** — Prices fluctuate based on real-time demand.

B. **Premium Pricing** — Setting a high price to create a perception of superior quality.

C. **'What the Traffic Can Bear' Pricing** — Charging the maximum price that customers are willing to pay.

All three are classic demand-based pricing strategies.

D. **Discount Pricing** — Though influenced by market factors, it's generally seen as a tactical cost-based strategy.

E. **Parity Pricing** — Involves setting prices based on competitors, categorized under competition-based pricing.

Thus, correct methods: A, B, C.

37. As per RBI guidelines, a Term Loan is classified as a Non-Performing Asset (NPA) if the principal or interest remains overdue for more than 90 days. This 90-day norm is applicable for all banks and financial institutions to identify loan defaults.

38. Under the Partial Integration Scheme of Agricultural and Non-Agricultural Income in India:

- Non-Agricultural Income must exceed the exemption limit applicable to the individual.
- Agricultural Income must exceed ₹ 5,000 for the partial integration provisions to apply.

Thus, the correct condition is when Non-Agricultural Income exceeds the exemption limit and Agricultural Income exceeds ₹ 5,000.

39. Key Objectives of World Trade Organization (WTO):

A. To set rules for international trade — WTO formulates trade agreements and rules.

B. To resolve trade disputes — WTO has a formal mechanism for resolving disputes between nations.

C. To resolve border disputes — Incorrect, WTO doesn't handle geopolitical/border disputes.

D. To provide a forum for negotiating trade liberalisation — Core WTO function is trade negotiations to lower trade barriers.

Thus, correct objectives are A, B, D.

40. In India, the term of every utility patent (which is a regular patent for inventions) is 20 years from the date of filing of the patent application, as per The Patents Act, 1970 (as amended in 2005).

41. In Current Purchasing Power (CPP) Accounting, balance sheet items are classified as:

- **Monetary Items:** Fixed in terms of currency (Cash, Debtors, Creditors, Debentures, etc.)
- **Non-Monetary Items:** Not fixed in monetary terms; their values change with inflation (Inventories, Fixed Assets, etc.)

Among the given options:

1. **Cash** — Monetary Item
2. **Debentures** — Monetary Item
3. **Debtors** — Monetary Item
4. **Inventories** — Non-Monetary Item (as their value fluctuates with price level changes)

42. Correct sequence of steps in Multinational Capital Budgeting:

B. Determine Net Investment Outlay — Compute initial project cost.

A. Estimate Net Cash Flow from the Project — Forecast expected inflows/outflows.

D. Identify Appropriate Discount Rate — Consider country risk, cost of capital.

C. Apply Appropriate Evaluation Technique — Use NPV, IRR, etc., to assess viability.

Correct sequence: B → A → D → C.

43. Ind AS dealing with Consolidated Financial Statements is:

- **Ind AS 110:** Consolidated Financial Statements — It lays down principles for presenting consolidated financials where a parent company controls one or more subsidiaries.

Other options:

Ind AS 29 — Financial Reporting in Hyperinflationary Economies

Ind AS 101 — First-time Adoption of Indian Accounting Standards

Ind AS 41 — Agriculture.

44. FDI involving the creation of new assets, infrastructure, and production facilities is known as Greenfield Investment.

- Brownfield involves acquiring existing assets.
- Mergers and Acquisitions involve taking over existing companies.
- Strategic alliances are partnerships without direct ownership.

Thus, Greenfield is new infrastructure creation.

45. Given: Arithmetic Mean (A.M.) = 30

Geometric Mean (G.M.) = 24

Let the two numbers be x and y.

From Arithmetic Mean:

$$\frac{x+y}{2} = 30$$

$$\Rightarrow \quad x + y = 6$$

From Geometric Mean:

$$\sqrt{xy} = 24$$

$$\Rightarrow \quad xy = 576$$

Harmonic Mean (H.M.) formula:

$$\text{H.M.} = \frac{2xy}{x+y} = \frac{2 \times 576}{60} = \frac{1152}{60}$$

$$= 19.2.$$

46. The primary liability of the drawer of a bill of exchange or cheque is to compensate the holder in case of dishonour.

- If the drawee fails to accept or pay, the drawer becomes liable to compensate for the loss.
- The drawee is primarily liable to pay upon acceptance or presentation.

Thus, the drawer's liability is contingent on dishonour.

47. Correct statements about Transmission of Shares:

A. **No instrument of transfer is required** — Transmission occurs by operation of law.

B. **Made without consideration** — It is not a sale or transfer for value.

C. **Original liabilities continue** — Shares retain their obligations post-transmission.

D. **Takes place on death or insolvency of a holder** — It happens due to legal events, not voluntary actions.

E. **Stamp duty is NOT payable on transmission** — Stamp duty applies on transfer, not transmission.

Thus, correct set: A, B, C, D.

48. Statements on Tax Avoidance:

A. **Correct** — Tax avoidance involves legitimate arrangements to reduce tax liability within the law.

B. **Correct** — Though legal, tax avoidance involves exploiting loopholes with an intent that may be malafide.

C. **Correct** — It relies on legal loop-holes to minimize tax.

D. **Incorrect** — Describes tax evasion, not avoidance.

E. **Incorrect** — Tax avoidance is not the same as tax omission (which is accidental).

Correct set: A, B, C.

49. Correct sequence of New Product Development Process:

E. **Idea Generation** — First step, gathering raw ideas.

D. **Identifying Prospective Customers** — Understand target market early.

C. **Concept Development and Testing** — Refine idea and test its feasibility.

B. **Feasibility Analysis** — Analyze financial, technical, and market feasibility.

A. **Product Development** — Build the actual product.

Sequence: E → D → C → B → A.

50. Properties of Regression Coefficient:

A. **Correct** — The regression coefficients and correlation coefficient always have the same sign.

D. **Correct** — If one regression coefficient is greater than unity, the other must be less than unity (because product of regression coefficients = square of correlation coefficient ≤ 1).

E. **Correct** — Regression coefficients are independent of origin, but affected by change of scale.

Thus, correct statements: A, D, E.

51. The correct sequence of the Adoption Process Stages is:

B. **Awareness** — Consumer becomes aware of the product.

A. **Interest** — Consumer seeks information.

D. **Evaluation** — Consumer considers whether to try the product.

C. **Trial** — Consumer tries the product on a small scale.

E. **Adoption** — Consumer decides to make full use of the product.

Correct sequence: B → A → D → C → E.

52. Chronological order of establishment:

D. **ASEAN (Association of Southeast Asian Nations)** — Established in 1967

C. **SAARC (South Asian Association for Regional Cooperation)** — Established in 1985

A. **NAFTA (North American Free Trade Agreement)** — Came into effect in 1994

B. **European Union (EU)** — Formally established in 1993

Thus, correct order: D → C → A → B.

53. **A. Production Function** → Q = $f(a, b, c...n)$ — Represents output as a function of inputs → IV

B. Average Product (AP) → Total Product ÷ No. of units of variable factor → III

C. Marginal Product (MP) → $TP_n - TP_{n-1}$ – Change in total product when an additional unit is used → II

D. Constant Returns to Scale → Function where K(K, L) is multiplied by a constant and output increases by the same proportion → I.

54. Discounted Cash Flow (DCF) techniques are methods that consider the time value of money.

C. Net Present Value (NPV) — DCF method.

D. Internal Rate of Return (IRR) — DCF method.

E. Profitability Index (PI) — DCF method.

A. Payback Period and B. ARR are non-discounted techniques.

Correct set: C, D, E.

55. Given: P(X = 1) = 4 × P(X = 2)

For Poisson distribution:

$$P(X = x) = \frac{e^{-\lambda}\lambda^x}{x!}$$

Compute probabilities:

$$\frac{e^{-\lambda}\lambda^1}{1!} = 4 \times \frac{e^{-\lambda}\lambda^2}{2!}$$

Simplifying: $\lambda = 4 \times \frac{\lambda^2}{2}$

$$\lambda = 2\lambda^2$$

$$2\lambda^2 - \lambda = 0$$

$$\lambda(2\lambda - 1) = 0$$

$$\lambda = 0 \text{ or } \lambda = \frac{1}{2}$$

Reject $\lambda = 0$ (since $\lambda > 0$ in Poisson).

Thus, $\lambda = 1/2$.

Variance of a Poisson distribution = λ.

So, Variance = 1/2.

56. When a selection procedure (like a test or assessment) is statistically correlated with actual job performance, it refers to Criterion Validity. This type of validity shows how well scores predict future job performance, making it a key metric in recruitment tests.

57. Elements of the Micro Environment include Customers, Suppliers, Competitors, Intermediaries, etc., which directly interact with the firm.

Technology is a part of the Macro Environment, affecting entire industries over time rather than direct business interactions.

Thus, Technology is NOT part of Micro Environment.

58. "Active concealment of fact" is a deliberate act to hide material information, which constitutes Fraud under contract law. Fraud involves intentional deceit, while misrepresentation refers to false statements made innocently.

59. Given Data:

- Raw Material Holding = 60 days
- Credit from Suppliers = 15 days
- Production Time = 15 days
- Finished Goods Holding = 30 days
- Credit to Debtors = 30 days

Working Capital Cycle formula:

WCC = Raw Material Holding Period + Production Time + Finished Goods Holding + Debtor Collection Period - Credit from Suppliers

WCC = 60 + 15 + 30 + 30 - 15

= 120 days

60. **A. Job Enlargement** — Assigning additional same-level activities to workers → Matches III.

B. Job Description — Document listing job duties, responsibilities, reporting relationships, etc. → Matches II.

C. Job Specification — Document outlining human requirements like education, skills, personality → Matches I.

D. Job Enrichment — Redesigning jobs to enhance responsibility, achievement, and growth → Matches IV.

Correct matching: A-III, B-II, C-I, D-IV.

61. For claiming deduction under Section 91 (Relief for Double Taxation) of the Income Tax Act, the following conditions must be satisfied:

B. The assessee must be Resident in India during the relevant previous year.

D. The income must have accrued or arisen outside India.

E. Tax must have been paid or deducted in the foreign country in respect of that income.

A is incorrect because Section 91 applies to Residents, not Non-Residents.

C is incorrect because the income must have arisen outside India, not in India.

Correct set: B, D, E.

62. Given: Initial Price (P_1) = ₹ 100

New Price (P_2) = ₹ 60

Price Elasticity of Demand (E_d) = 1.5

Initial Quantity Demanded (Q_1) = 30 units

Percentage Change in Price:

$$\%\Delta P = \frac{P_2 - P_1}{P_1} \times 100 = \frac{60 - 100}{100} \times 100 = -40\%$$

Percentage Change in Quantity Demanded:

$$\%\Delta Q = E_d \times \%\Delta P$$
$$= 1.5 \times (-40\%) = -60\%$$

But since price has decreased, quantity demanded will increase by 60%.

New Quantity Demanded:

$$Q_2 = Q_1 \times \left(1 + \frac{60}{100}\right) = 30 \times 1.6 = 48.$$

63. Statement 1 is Incorrect because Management Audit is not a statutory requirement. It is a voluntary and comprehensive review of the efficiency and effectiveness of management practices. The other statements are correct.

64. The actual questions that are posed to the respondent during a survey or questionnaire are called Measurement Questions.

- Management Questions are broad and strategic.
- Research Questions define the problem.
- Investigative Questions break down the research question into sub-questions.
- Measurement Questions are the direct questions asked from respondents to collect data.

65. The State Bank of India (SBI) was established on 1st July 1955, following the nationalization of the Imperial Bank of India through the State Bank of India Act, 1955.

66. Macroeconomics focuses on aggregate economic variables and overall economic environment.

A. National Income — Macro variable.

B. Balance of Payments (BoP) — Macro area involving external sector balance.

C. Level of Savings and Investment — Macro variable affecting national income and growth.

D. Location of Industry — Microeconomic aspect (concerned with firm/industry decisions).

E. Behaviour of Firms — Microeconomic subject.

Correct Macro areas: A, B, C.

67. The Investor Protection and Education Fund (IPEF) Regulations were issued by SEBI in 2009 to promote investor awareness and education, funded through unclaimed dividends, application money, etc.

68. Both Theodore Levitt and Peter Drucker emphasized that the essence of marketing is Customer Orientation. They stressed that marketing begins with identifying and satisfying customer needs, not just selling a product.

69. Chronological milestones of NSE:

E. Launch of S&P CNX Nifty — 1996

C. Commencement of Derivatives Trading in Index Futures — 2000

A. Commencement of Trading in Index Options — 2001

B. Launch of Securities Lending and Borrowing Scheme (SLBS) — 2008

D. Launch of Mutual Fund Service System (MFSS) — 2009

Correct sequence: E → C → A → B → D.

70. As per SA 705 (Modifications to the Opinion in the Independent Auditor's Report), the following are classified as Modified Reports:

A. Qualified Report — Opinion modified due to material but not pervasive issues.

C. Disclaimer of Opinion — No opinion expressed due to lack of sufficient audit evidence.

D. Adverse Report — Material and pervasive misstatements found.

B. Emphasis of Matter paragraph is not a modified opinion; it is an addition to highlight an important matter without modifying the audit opinion.

Correct set: A, C, D.

71. The correct formula showing the relationship between Marginal Revenue (MR), Average Revenue (AR), and Price Elasticity of Demand (*e*) is:

$$MR = AR \times \frac{(e-1)}{e}$$

This formula reflects how MR depends on AR and elasticity.

72. Chronological order of exchange rate arrangements:

B. Commodity Specie Standard — Earliest, based on actual commodities (e.g., silver).

A. Gold Standard — Fixed gold exchange system established later.

C. Fixed Parity System — Bretton Woods system post-World War II.

D. Floating Exchange Rate System — Adopted after the collapse of Bretton Woods in 1971.

Correct order: B → A → C → D.

73. Petition for winding up of an LLP can be filed by:

A. Secured Creditors — Can file if dues are unpaid.

B. LLP or any of its Partners — Can file voluntarily.

C. Registrar of Companies (ROC) — Can file if statutory requirements are violated.

D. Person authorized by the Central Government — Can file on behalf of the government.

E. Voluntary Associations — Not eligible to file winding-up petitions.

Correct set: A, B, C, D.

74. Under Section 115BAC, the alternative tax regime initially did not allow for standard deduction. However, the Finance Act, 2023 amended this and permitted a standard deduction of ₹ 50,000 for salaried employees and pensioners from Assessment Year (AY) 2024-25 onwards.

Recent updates indicate that for Assessment Year 2025-26 (corresponding to FY 2024-25), the standard deduction has been increased to ₹ 75,000. This increase was specified to align with efforts to provide relief to middle-class taxpayers under the default new tax regime. Multiple credible sources confirm that from AY 2025-26, the standard deduction allowed under Section 115BAC for salaried individuals will be ₹ 75,000 or gross salary, whichever is lower.

Therefore, the correct provision applicable for AY 2025-26 is ₹ 75,000 standard deduction under the new regime.

75. Microeconomics deals with individual economic units:

A. Product Pricing — Microeconomic topic.

B. Consumer Behaviour — Microeconomic study of individual decision-making.

D. Factor Pricing — Micro topic involving pricing of inputs (land, labour, capital).

C. Interest Rate — Though it can be micro when studying specific markets, it is generally a Macroeconomic variable when analyzed in context of monetary policy.

Correct set: A, B, D.

76. An unsecured, short-term promissory note, negotiable and transferable by endorsement and delivery, issued at a discount by corporates and financial institutions with a fixed maturity, is known as a Commercial Paper (CP).

- Treasury Bills are issued by the Government.
- Certificates of Deposit are time deposits issued by banks.
- Repo is a money market instrument involving repurchase agreements.

77. A market where few sellers dominate and sell competing or similar products to many buyers is known as an Oligopoly.

- **Monopoly:** Single seller dominates.
- **Monopolistic Competition:** Many sellers with differentiated products.
- **Perfect Competition:** Many buyers and sellers dealing in identical products.

78. Given: Units Sold = 10,000

Selling Price per unit = ₹ 500

Variable Cost per unit = ₹ 200

Fixed Operating Cost = ₹ 25,00,000

Contribution per unit

= Selling Price – Variable Cost

= ₹ 500 – ₹ 200 = ₹ 300

Total Contribution

= 10,000 × ₹ 300 = ₹ 30,00,000

Operating Leverage = Total Contribution ÷ EBIT

EBIT = Total Contribution – Fixed Costs

= ₹ 30,00,000 – ₹ 25,00,000

= ₹ 5,00,000

Operating Leverage

= ₹ 30,00,000 ÷ ₹ 5,00,000 = 6 times.

79. **A.** **Correct** — An Indian company is automatically treated as a Domestic Company.

B. **Correct** — Foreign company is one which is not a Domestic Company.

C. **Incorrect** — An Indian company can never become a non-resident in India; it is always resident.

D. **Incorrect** — A Foreign Company can be considered Resident in India if its place of effective management (POEM) is in India.

E. **Correct** — The global income of a Resident Company (Indian or foreign) is taxable in India.

Correct set: A, B, E.

80. Correct order of application of assets during Dissolution of Partnership Firm as per the Indian Partnership Act:

1. Paying debts of the firm to third parties (C)
2. Paying to each partner rateably what is due to him from the firm for advances as distinguished from capital (A)
3. Paying to each partner rateably what is due to him on account of capital (D)
4. Paying the residues, if any, to partners in the profit-sharing ratio (B)

Sequence: C → A → D → B.

81. The factors that determine demand are:

A. **Price of the Commodity** — Inverse relationship with demand.

B. **Income of the Consumer** — Direct relationship with demand for normal goods.

C. **Taste and Preferences of Consumer** — Changes can increase or decrease demand.

D. **Size of Population** — Larger population usually leads to higher market demand.

Thus, all four factors influence demand.

82. Correct order of steps for Voluntary Liquidation of LLP:

A. **Declaration of Solvency** — Ensure that the LLP is solvent.

D. **Identification of Insolvency Professional as Liquidator** — Appointment of liquidator.

B. **Designated Partners' Meeting** — Pass resolution for winding up.

C. **Partners' Meeting** — Approve the resolution passed by designated partners.

E. **Filing of Resolutions with ROC and IBBI** — Legal formalities and notifications.

Correct sequence: A → D → B → C → E.

83. For effective Matrix Structure, the following guidelines are essential:

A. **Collective learning, coordination and integration of skills** — To manage technological and functional complexities.

B. **Define the objectives of the project or task** — Clarity in purpose.

C. **Clarify roles, authority, responsibilities** — Avoids conflicts.

D. **Ensure influence is based on knowledge, not rank** — Encourages meritocracy.

E. **Balance power of functional and project managers** — Prevents power struggles.

Correct set: A, B, C, D, E.

Since "all five" is not given, the closest match is:

Answer: 3. B, C, D and E only.

84. Matching psychological concepts correctly:

A. **Perception** — The process of selecting, organizing, interpreting information → IV

B. **Learning** — Change in behaviour due to experience → III

C. **Belief** — Descriptive thought held about something → I

D. **Attitude** — Consistent evaluation/feeling towards object/idea → II

Correct matching: A-IV, B-III, C-I, D-II.

85. Matching Balance of Payment (BOP) components:

A. **Balance of Payment - Current Account** — International trade in goods and services → II

B. **Balance of Payment - Capital Account** — Inflows and outflows of capital → I

C. **Balance of Trade** — Import and export of goods only → III

D. **Balancing Item** — Entry for net errors and omissions → IV

Correct matching: A-II, B-I, C-III, D-IV.

86. The North American Free Trade Agreement (NAFTA) was signed between:

A. United States

B. Canada

C. Mexico

Brazil was not a member of NAFTA; it is part of MERCOSUR.

87. Chronological order of International Trade Theories:

A. Mercantilism Theory — Oldest (16th-18th century)

B. Comparative Advantage Theory (David Ricardo) — Early 19th century (1817)

D. Heckscher-Ohlin Theory — 1930s

C. Product Life Cycle Theory (Raymond Vernon) — 1960s

Correct order: A → B → D → C.

88. Keeping a record of exceptionally good or bad incidents of an employee's work behaviour for evaluation purposes refers to the Critical Incident Method of performance appraisal.

89. For paired samples hypothesis testing, the appropriate parametric test is the *t*-test (specifically the paired sample *t*-test).

- ***z*-test:** Large sample sizes.
- **Chi-Square:** Non-parametric test.
- **Mann-Whitney:** Non-parametric for two independent samples.

90. Correct matching of terms:

A. Nostro Account — An account that an Indian bank holds in a foreign bank → II

B. Vostro Account — An account that a foreign bank holds with an Indian bank → I

C. Bid — Price at which dealer is willing to buy foreign currency → III

D. Offer (Ask Price) — Price at which dealer is willing to sell foreign currency → IV

Correct matching: A-II, B-I, C-III, D-IV.

91. To effectively retain employees and reduce attrition, the firm should focus on offering increments and career growth opportunities. Providing clear career paths, skill enhancement, and financial incentives increases employee motivation and reduces voluntary exits. The other options (making resignation harder, increasing workload, voluntary retirement) would worsen attrition.

92. The first step to address dissatisfaction with career progression is to conduct a skill gap analysis to identify where employees need development and then create career development plans. This structured approach aligns employee aspirations with organizational needs.

93. To persuade senior management, Priya should present the financial impact of HR initiatives on business growth. Demonstrating how HR investments improve productivity, reduce turnover costs, and enhance profitability will align with management's focus on financial returns.

94. For predicting labour turnover using HR analytics, Priya should analyse attrition trends and exit interview feedback. These data points directly reflect the reasons for employee exits and help forecast future turnover risks.

95. To develop future leaders, the best HR strategy is to implement intensive employee development programs. Leadership development initiatives nurture internal talent, preparing them for future leadership roles.

96. In a volatile stock market, the best way to reduce financing risk is to diversify sources of funds by combining debt and equity financing. This approach balances risk and avoids over-dependence on equity markets, providing financial stability.

97. A primary function of financial markets is to facilitate the buying and selling of financial instruments (shares, bonds, derivatives, etc.). This ensures liquidity, capital formation, and efficient allocation of resources.

98. The main concern while issuing green bonds is the limited investor demand due to its niche market. Although green bonds are gaining popularity, the market size is still limited compared to conventional debt instruments, which can pose challenges in raising large sums.

99. The key advantage of venture capital is that, apart from funding, it provides access to expertise, strategic guidance, and networking opportunities. Venture capitalists support businesses with mentoring and market insights, crucial for growth.

100. While issuing corporate bonds, the credit rating of the bond is a critical factor influencing the interest rate. A higher credit rating reflects lower risk and results in lower interest rates, whereas a lower rating demands higher interest to compensate investors for the increased risk.

Previous Years' Paper

National Testing Agency (NTA)

UGC-NET Junior Research Fellowship & Assistant Professor Eligibility Exam

Commerce, January-2025

(Exam held on 07-01-2025)

PAPER-II

1. Which one of the following is not the behavioural factor of the customer profile involved in tactical targeting?

A. Purchase Frequency
B. Income
C. Purchase Quantity
D. Price Sensitivity

2. Match the List-I with List-II.

List-I (Product Life Cycle (PLC) Stage)	List-II (Distribution Strategy)
(*a*) Introduction	I. Phase out unprofitable outlets
(*b*) Growth	II. Build Selective distribution
(*c*) Maturity	III. Build intensive distribution
(*d*) Decline	IV. Build more intensive distribution

Choose the ***correct*** answer from the options given below:

	(*a*)	(*b*)	(*c*)	(*d*)
A.	III	II	IV	I
B.	III	II	I	IV
C.	II	III	IV	I
D.	IV	III	I	II

3. Arrange the following management research questions in the ascending order.

(*a*) Management Question
(*b*) Measurement Question
(*c*) Management Dilemma
(*d*) Research Question
(*e*) Investigative Question

Choose the ***correct*** answer from the options given below:

A. (*c*), (*a*), (*b*), (*d*), (*e*)
B. (*c*), (*a*), (*d*), (*e*), (*b*)
C. (*a*), (*c*), (*d*), (*e*), (*b*)
D. (*b*), (*c*), (*a*), (*d*), (*e*)

4. Determine the P/V ratio from the following particulars.

Total Fixed Cost ₹ 12,000
Actual Sales ₹ 48,000
Margin of Safety ₹ 8,000

A. 20% B. 25%
C. 30% D. 40%

5. The Consumer Protection Act came into force first on:

A. 14 June, 1986
B. 20 January, 1987
C. 24 December, 1986
D. 14 July, 1987

6. Quasi contracts are based on the doctrine of:

A. Unjust enrichment
B. Just enrichment
C. Unjust Richment
D. Misrepresentation

7. Match the List-I with List-II.

List-I (Personality Type)	List-II (Congruent Occupation)
(*a*) Social	I. Mechanic
(*b*) Conventional	II. Mathematician
(*c*) Investigative	III. Corporate Manager
(*d*) Realistic	IV. Teacher

Choose the ***correct*** answer from the options given below:

	(*a*)	(*b*)	(*c*)	(*d*)
A.	IV	III	II	I
B.	III	IV	II	I
C.	IV	II	III	I
D.	II	IV	I	III

8. Match the List-I with List-II.

List-I (Conflict Handling Intentions)	List-II (Description)
(*a*) Competing	I. A situation in which each party in a conflict desires to satisfy fully the concerns of all parties.
(*b*) Collaborating	II. The willingness of one party in a conflict to place the negotiating partners interest above their own.
(*c*) Accommodating	III. A situation in which each party to a conflict is willing to give up something to resolve the conflict.
(*d*) Compromising	IV. A desire to satisfy one's interests regardless of the impact on the other party to the conflict.

Choose the ***correct*** answer from the options given below:

	(*a*)	(*b*)	(*c*)	(*d*)
A.	I	IV	II	III
B.	IV	I	II	III
C.	IV	I	III	II
D.	IV	II	I	III

9. Which of the following are True for a random variable?

(*a*) A random variable is a certain quantity, whose value depends on chance.
(*b*) A continuous random variable can assume at most two countable number of values.
(*c*) A discrete random variable can assume at most a countable number of values.
(*d*) A random variables is a function of the simple space.
(*e*) A random variables is a uncertain quantity, whose value depends on chance.

Choose the ***correct*** answer from the options given below:

A. (*a*), (*b*), (*d*) only
B. (*a*), (*b*), (*c*) only
C. (*b*), (*c*), (*d*) only
D. (*c*), (*d*), (*e*) only

10. Which of the following is a non-probability method of selecting sample from a population?

A. Simple Random Sampling
B. Multi Stage Sampling
C. Cluster Sampling
D. SnowBall Sampling

11. A proposal requires a cash outflow of ₹ 18,500 and is expected to generate cash inflows of ₹ 8,000, ₹ 6,000, ₹ 4,000, ₹ 2,000 and ₹ 2,000 over next 5 years respectively. The payback period is:

A. 4 years B. 3.25 years
C. 3.50 years D. 4.25 years

12. The Securities Exchange Board of India (SEBI) regulates and supervises the securities through:

(*a*) Regulations (*b*) Rules
(*c*) Guidelines (*d*) Scheme
(*e*) Orders

Choose the ***correct*** answer from the options given below:

A. (*a*), (*b*), (*e*) only
B. (*b*), (*c*), (*d*) only
C. (*a*), (*b*), (*c*), (*d*), (*e*)
D. (*a*), (*c*), (*d*), (*e*) only

13. In which one of the following the effectiveness of brainstorming as group decision making technique is high?

A. Social Pressure
B. Task Orientation
C. Potential for interpersonal conflict
D. Money Costs

14. Match the List-I with List-II.

List-I (Accounting Concept & Convention)	List-II (Meaning)
(*a*) Conservatism	I. Use of same accounting policies by a firm from period to period
(*b*) Dual aspect	II. Enterprise is treated as separate from owner and other persons associated with it
(*c*) Separate Business entity	III. Every transaction has a two - fold effect
(*d*) Consistency	IV. Anticipate no profit, but provide for all possible losses

Choose the ***correct*** answer from the options given below:

	(*a*)	(*b*)	(*c*)	(*d*)
A.	IV	III	II	I
B.	I	II	III	IV
C.	II	III	I	IV
D.	III	IV	I	II

15. Match the List-I with List-II.

List-I (Theory)	List-II (Author(s))
(*a*) Theory of Comparative Cost Advantage	I. Heckseher & Ohlin
(*b*) Theory of Opportunity Cost	II. David Ricardo
(*c*) Theory of Factor Endowment	III. Haberler
(*d*) Theory of Absolute Advantage	IV. Adam Smith

Choose the ***correct*** answer from the options given below:

	(*a*)	(*b*)	(*c*)	(*d*)
A.	II	III	I	IV
B.	II	III	IV	I
C.	III	II	I	IV
D.	IV	III	II	I

16. Match the List-I with List-II.

List-I (Concept)	List-II (Meaning)
(*a*) Exchange Rate	I. It refers to the price of one unit of foreign currency in terms of some units of home currency
(*b*) Forward market	II. It is the process of making risk less profits by exploiting price differences of assets in different market.

(*c*) Arbitrage	III. Where transactions are entered into for settlement on a future date
(*d*) Direct Quotation	IV. It is a price of one unit of a currency in terms of some units of another currency

Choose the ***correct*** answer from the options given below:

	(*a*)	(*b*)	(*c*)	(*d*)
A.	IV	III	II	I
B.	III	IV	II	I
C.	I	II	III	IV
D.	I	III	II	IV

17. Which one of the following conditions is not true in case of marketing skimming as the pricing objective?

A. The market is highly price sensitive

B. A sufficient number of buyers signal a high demand

C. The high initial price does not attract more competitors to the market

D. The high price communicates the image of a superior product

18. Which one of the following is the developmental role of RBI?

A. Formulates, implements and monitors the monitary policy

B. Prescribes broad parameters of banking operations

C. Issues, exchanges and destroys currency notes

D. Performs a wide range of promotional functions to support national objectives

19. Which one of the following consists of comparing entries in the books of account with documentary evidence in support thereof.

A. Internal check B. Internal control

C. Vouching D. Verification

20. Bret Lee, an Australian cricket player visits India for 100 days in every financial year. This has been his practice for the past 10 financial Years. Find out his residential status for the assessment Year 2023-24.

A. Resident in India

B. Resident and ordinarily resident in India

C. Resident but not ordinarily resident in India

D. Non-resident in India

21. Which of the following curves cannot be U-shaped?

A. A.V.C Curve B. A.F.C Curve

C. A.C. Curve D. M.C. Curve

22. Arrange the following actions of a manager in the increasing degree of control.

(*a*) Manager defines limits and asks for group decisions

(*b*) Manager offers tentative decisions to change

(*c*) Manager sells decisions

(*d*) Manager lets subordinates function within limits defined by him

(*e*) Manager presents problems, invites suggestions and makes decisions

Choose the ***correct*** answer from the options given below:

A. (*a*), (*d*), (*b*), (*e*), (*c*)

B. (*c*), (*b*), (*e*), (*a*), (*d*)

C. (*d*), (*a*), (*e*), (*b*), (*c*)

D. (*d*), (*a*), (*b*), (*e*), (*c*)

23. Which of the following are taxes (GST) applicable in the case of supply of goods?

I. From West Bengal to Chandigarh

II. From Puducherry to Chennai

Note:

CGST: Central Goods and Services Tax

IGST: Integrated Goods and Services Tax

UTGST: Union territory Goods and Services Tax

SGST: State Goods and Services Tax

A. I. CGST II. IGST	B. I. IGST II. IGST
C. I. UTGST II. UTGST	D. I. SGST II. UTGST

24. Match the List-I with List-II.

List-I (Direct Material Variance)	List-II (Formula)
(*a*) Direct material cost variance	I. Standard price × (Revised Standard Quantity - Actual Quantity)
(*b*) Direct material price variance	II. Standard price × (Standard Quantity for actual output quantity - Actual Quantity)
(*c*) Direct material usage variance	III. Actual Quantity × (standard price - actual price)
(*d*) Direct material mix variance	IV. Standard cost for actual output - actual cost

Choose the ***correct*** answer from the options given below:

	(*a*)	(*b*)	(*c*)	(*d*)
A.	I	II	III	IV
B.	IV	III	I	II
C.	IV	III	II	I
D.	III	IV	II	I

25. Which of the following points are considered as factors determinating the working capital of a firm?

(*a*) Basic nature of Business
(*b*) Business cycle fluctuations
(*c*) Credit Policy of the firm
(*d*) Long term source of finance
(*e*) Employee Skills

Choose the ***correct*** answer from the options given below:

A. (*a*), (*b*) and (*d*) only
B. (*b*), (*c*) and (*d*) only
C. (*a*), (*b*) and (*c*) only
D. (*d*) and (*e*) only

26. Arrange the following levels of economic integration in increasing order.

(*a*) Political Union
(*b*) Free Trade Area
(*c*) Customs Union
(*d*) Common Market
(*e*) Economic Union

Choose the ***correct*** answer from the options given below:

A. (*b*), (*c*), (*d*), (*e*), (*a*)
B. (*b*), (*a*), (*c*), (*d*), (*e*)
C. (*b*), (*a*), (*d*), (*c*), (*e*)
D. (*e*), (*d*), (*b*), (*a*), (*c*)

27. Which section of the Income Tax Act 1961 mentions unilateral relief?

A. 90	B. 89
C. 91	D. 92

28. Which of the following statements are true regarding admission of a new partner?

(*a*) According to section 25 of the Indian Partnership Act, 1932, a person can be admitted as partner.
(*b*) New Profit - sharing ratio is the ratio in which all partners, including new partners, will share future profits and loses of the firm.
(*c*) New Profit Share = Profit Share Sacrificed - Old Profit Share
(*d*) Sacrificing Ratio = Old Profit Share - New Profit Share
(*e*) The Profit or loss which arises from Revaluation Account will be transferred to partner's capital account.

Choose the ***correct*** answer from the options given below:

A. (*b*), (*d*) and (*e*) only
B. (*a*), (*b*) and (*c*) only
C. (*b*), (*c*) and (*d*) only
D. (*c*), (*d*) and (*e*) only

29. Current assets are ₹ 4,00,000
Inventories are ₹ 2,00,000
Working capital is ₹ 2,40,000
Calculate Current Ratio.

A. 2 : 1 B. 2.5 : 1
C. 1.5 : 1 D. 1 : 2

30. Match the List-I with List-II.

List-I (Act)	**List-II (Year)**
(*a*) Indian Contract Act	I. 2013
(*b*) Sales of Goods Act	II. 1872
(*c*) Negotiable Instruments Act	III. 1930
(*d*) Companies Act	IV. 1881

Choose the ***correct*** answer from the options given below:

	(*a*)	(*b*)	(*c*)	(*d*)
A.	II	III	IV	I
B.	I	II	III	IV
C.	IV	III	II	I
D.	III	IV	I	II

31. Which of the following are the assumptions of the oligopoly?

(*a*) One seller and large number of buyers
(*b*) A few sellers and large number of buyers
(*c*) Large number of sellers and large number of buyers
(*d*) Entry of new seller is restricted
(*e*) Firms Interdependence

Choose the ***correct*** answer from the options given below:

A. (*c*), (*d*), (*e*) only
B. (*a*), (*b*), (*c*) only
C. (*b*), (*d*), (*c*) only
D. (*b*), (*d*), (*e*) only

32. Which of the following are the features of Treasury Bills?

(*a*) Negotiable Securities
(*b*) Issued at par and are repaid at premium on maturity
(*c*) High liquidity on account of short tenure
(*d*) Assured Yield
(*e*) High transaction cost

Choose the ***correct*** answer from the options given below:

A. (*a*), (*b*), (*e*) only
B. (*a*), (*c*), (*d*) only
C. (*b*), (*c*), (*d*) only
D. (*a*), (*c*), (*d*), (*e*) only

33. Which one of the following refers to the composition of long term fluids such as debentures, long term borrowing, preference shares, equity shares in the capitalization of a company?

A. Cost of capital
B. Capital budgeting
C. Working capital
D. Capital structure

34. What is the value of Standard Deviation of first seven natural numbers?

A. $\sqrt{48}$ B. 2
C. $\sqrt{8}$ D. 4

35. Arrange the prefatory information of report writing in a logical sequence.

(*a*) Executive Summary
(*b*) Authorization Statement
(*c*) Title Page
(*d*) Letter of transmittal
(*e*) Table of Contents

Choose the ***correct*** answer from the options given below:

A. (*a*), (*b*), (*c*), (*d*), (*e*)
B. (*c*), (*d*), (*e*), (*b*), (*a*)
C. (*d*), (*c*), (*b*), (*a*), (*e*)
D. (*d*), (*b*), (*c*), (*e*), (*a*)

36. Arrange the following points step by step regarding computation of Gross Total Income:

(*a*) Computation of Gross Total Income
(*b*) Set off and carry forward of Losses

(*c*) Clubbing of Income of spouse, minor child etc.
(*d*) Computation of Income under each head of Income
(*e*) Determination of Residential Status

Choose the ***correct*** answer from the options given below:

A. (*e*), (*d*), (*c*), (*b*), (*a*)
B. (*a*), (*b*), (*c*), (*d*), (*e*)
C. (*c*), (*d*), (*e*), (*a*), (*b*)
D. (*b*), (*c*), (*d*), (*e*), (*a*)

37. When price of a good X rises, the demand for substitute good Y will;

A. Rise
B. Fall
C. Remain unchanged
D. Falls initially and then rises

38. Arrange the organizational aspect of employees need hierarchy in the increasing order.

(*a*) Cohesive and supportive co-workers
(*b*) Work place conditions
(*c*) Work safety
(*d*) Responsibilities
(*e*) Job Challenge

Choose the ***correct*** answer from the options given below:

A. (*c*), (*b*), (*d*), (*a*), (*e*)
B. (*b*), (*c*), (*a*), (*d*), (*e*)
C. (*a*), (*c*), (*b*), (*e*), (*d*)
D. (*b*), (*a*), (*c*), (*d*), (*e*)

39. According to Job characteristics model, the psychological state of an experienced meaningfulness of the work is due to the following core job dimensions:

(*a*) Autonomy (*b*) Skill Variety
(*c*) Task Identity (*d*) Feedback
(*e*) Task Significance

Choose the ***correct*** answer from the options given below:

A. (*a*), (*b*), (*d*) only
B. (*b*), (*c*), (*e*) only
C. (*a*), (*c*), (*e*) only
D. (*a*), (*b*), (*d*), (*e*) only

40. Match the List-I with List-II.

List-I (Institution)	**List-II (Year of Establishment)**
(*a*) UNCTAD	I. 1967
(*b*) WTO	II. 1994
(*c*) NAFTA	III. 1964
(*d*) ASEAN	IV. 1995

Choose the ***correct*** answer from the options given below:

	(*a*)	(*b*)	(*c*)	(*d*)
A.	I	II	III	IV
B.	III	IV	II	I
C.	I	III	IV	II
D.	I	II	IV	III

41. Which of the following is not a monetary measure for correcting disequilibrium in Balance of Payment?

A. Monetary Contraction
B. Devaluation
C. Exchange Control
D. Abolution of Export Duties

42. Arrange the following steps in the proper sequence to develop effective marketing communication.

(*a*) Design the communication
(*b*) Select the communication channel
(*c*) Identify the target audience
(*d*) Choose the communication mix
(*e*) Choose the communication objectives

Choose the ***correct*** answer from the options given below:

A. (*e*), (*a*), (*c*), (*b*), (*d*)
B. (*c*), (*a*), (*b*), (*d*), (*e*)
C. (*e*), (*b*), (*c*), (*a*), (*d*)
D. (*c*), (*e*), (*a*), (*b*), (*d*)

43. Identify, which of the following statements are True.

(*a*) Commuted pension received by a government employee is fully exempted from Income Tax

(*b*) Section 30 of the Income Tax Act 1961 discusses deduction in respect of rent, rates, taxes, repairs and insurance of building used by the assessee for the purpose of business

(*c*) Section 33 of the Income Tax Act 1961, defines provision regarding depreciation of tangible assets

(*d*) Capital gain arises from transfer of any assets

(*e*) Short term Capital assets is defined under section 2(42A) of the Income Tax Act 1961

Choose the ***correct*** answer from the options given below:

A. (*a*), (*b*) and (*e*) only
B. (*c*), (*d*) and (*e*) only
C. (*a*) and (*b*) only
D. (*c*) and (*d*) only

44. Which of the following are the disadvantages of Graphics rating scale as an appraisal tool?

(*a*) Standards may be unclear
(*b*) Halo Effect
(*c*) Time consuming
(*d*) Difficult to develop
(*e*) Leniency

Choose the ***correct*** answer from the options given below:

A. (*a*), (*b*), (*e*) only
B. (*a*), (*b*), (*c*) only
C. (*b*), (*c*), (*e*) only
D. (*a*), (*c*), (*d*), (*e*) only

45. Arrange the following channels in the increasing order of value-addition of sales.

(*a*) Retail Store
(*b*) Sales force
(*c*) Internet
(*d*) Value-added partners
(*e*) Distributors

Choose the ***correct*** answer from the options given below:

A. (*a*), (*e*), (*c*), (*d*), (*b*)
B. (*c*), (*a*), (*e*), (*b*), (*d*)
C. (*c*), (*a*), (*e*), (*d*), (*b*)
D. (*b*), (*c*), (*a*), (*e*), (*d*)

46. Which of the following are true for Skewness:

(*a*) It is a measure of symmetry of a frequency distribution.
(*b*) For the right-skewed distribution, the mean is to be to the right of median.
(*c*) For the right-skewed distribution, the mean is to be to the right of mode.
(*d*) For the right-skewed distribution, the mean is to be to the left of median.
(*e*) For the right-skewed distribution, the mean is to be to the left of mode.

Choose the ***correct*** answer from the options given below:

A. (*a*), (*b*), (*c*) only
B. (*a*), (*c*), (*d*) only
C. (*a*), (*d*), (*e*) only
D. (*a*), (*b*), (*d*) only

47. Arrange the following Institutions in ascending order of their year of establishment.

(*a*) SEBI
(*b*) Reserve Bank of India
(*c*) State Bank of India
(*d*) SIDBI
(*e*) NABARD

Choose the ***correct*** answer from the options given below:

A. (*c*), (*b*), (*e*), (*a*), (*d*)
B. (*b*), (*c*), (*e*), (*d*), (*a*)
C. (*b*), (*c*), (*a*), (*e*), (*d*)
D. (*e*), (*b*), (*c*), (*d*), (*a*)

48. "To what degree will there be rules and regulations to direct employees and managers" is defined as:

A. Departmentalization

B. Centralization and decentralization

C. Formalization

D. Boundary Spanning

49. Prepaid Insurance is which type of account?

A. Real Account

B. Personal Account

C. Nominal Account

D. Real and Nominal Both

50. A contract of Indemnity is a:

A. Wagering Agreement

B. Quasi Contract

C. Void Contract

D. Contingent Contract

51. The Capital Adequacy Ratio (CAR) for Indian Public Sector banks set by RBI is:

A. 9% B. 10%

C. 11% D. 12%

52. Identify correct statements from the following regarding Time Value of money.

(*a*) The interest which may be earned/saved on the money held at present underlines the concept of time value of money.

(*b*) The money which is receivable at present has less value than the money receivable in future.

(*c*) The relationship that exists between the value of money receivable at present and the value of money receivable in future is referred as time value of the money.

(*d*) Value of money receivable at present = Value of money receivable in future – Time value of money

(*e*) Future value of money is the value of money held presently at some given future time at a given rate of Interest.

Choose the ***correct*** answer from the options given below:

A. (*b*) and (*d*) only

B. (*a*), (*c*) and (*e*) only

C. (*b*), (*c*) and (*d*) only

D. (*c*), (*d*) and (*e*) only

53. Match the List-I with List-II.

List-I (Section)	List-II (TDS)
(*a*) Section 194 of the Income Tax Act, 1961	I. Payment on account of repurchase of units by mutual fund
(*b*) Section 194C of the Income Tax Act, 1961	II. Payment to the non-resident sportsman
(*c*) Section 194E of the Income Tax Act, 1961	III. Payment to contractor and sub-contractor
(*d*) Section 194F of the Income Tax Act, 1961	IV. Dividend

Choose the ***correct*** answer from the options given below:

	(*a*)	(*b*)	(*c*)	(*d*)
A.	IV	III	II	I
B.	I	II	III	IV
C.	I	III	II	IV
D.	III	IV	I	II

54. Arrange the following Securities Exchange Board of India (SEBI) regulations in the ascending year of their enactment.

(*a*) ICDR regulations

(*b*) Intermediaries regulations

(*c*) Real estate investment Trusts regulations

(*d*) Buy - Back of Securities by listed companies regulations

(*e*) Listing Obligations and Disclosures Requirements Regulations

Choose the ***correct*** answer from the options given below:

A. (*d*), (*b*), (*a*), (*c*), (*e*)
B. (*d*), (*a*), (*e*), (*c*), (*b*)
C. (*a*), (*c*), (*d*), (*e*), (*b*)
D. (*b*), (*a*), (*e*), (*d*), (*c*)

55. When all the factors of production are changed in same proportion, it is called as:

(*a*) Long run production function
(*b*) Law of equal proportion
(*c*) Law of return to scale
(*d*) Law of return to a factor
(*e*) Law of Variable proportion

Choose the ***correct*** answer from the options given below:

A. (*a*), (*b*), (*c*) only
B. (*b*), (*c*), (*d*) only
C. (*c*), (*b*), (*e*) only
D. (*a*), (*c*), (*e*) only

56. Which of the following statements are true regarding the buying dynamics of individual consumers?

(*a*) To successfully compete in the market and create customer value, managers must fully understand the reality rather than theory of consumer behaviour.
(*b*) In marketing, perceptions are more important than reality because they affect consumers actual behaviour.
(*c*) People emerge with same perceptions of the same object.
(*d*) Consumers are constructive decision makers and are subject to many contextual influences.
(*e*) A consumer's buying behaviour is influenced by cultural, social and personal tactics. Of these personal factors exert the broadest and deepest influence on people's perception and desires.

Choose the ***correct*** answer from the options given below:

A. (*b*), (*d*) only
B. (*a*), (*b*), (*d*) only
C. (*a*), (*c*), (*e*) only
D. (*b*), (*c*), (*d*), (*e*) only

57. Which one of the following structure of the marketing department will be most suitable for the companies that produce many products for many markets?

A. Geographic Organization
B. Product or Brand Organization
C. Functional Organization
D. Matrix Organization

58. Which of the following are the characteristics of a high customer centric Organization?

(*a*) Market Driven
(*b*) Process Oriented
(*c*) Value Driven
(*d*) Price Driven
(*e*) Making competitor irrelevant

Choose the ***correct*** answer from the options given below:

A. (*a*), (*b*), (*e*) only
B. (*a*), (*c*), (*e*) only
C. (*b*), (*c*), (*d*) only
D. (*c*), (*d*), (*e*) only

59. Identify which of the following statements are True:

(*a*) Assessment Year means the period of 12 months commencing on the first day of April every year
(*b*) Rounding off of total income is defined under section 288B of the Income Tax Act, 1961
(*c*) Rounding off of tax is defined under section 288 A of the Income Tax Act. 1961
(*d*) Assessee is always a person but a person may or may not be an assessed
(*e*) A person may not have assessable income but may still be an assessed

Choose the ***correct*** answer from the options given below:

A. (*b*) and (*c*) only
B. (*a*), (*d*), (*e*) only
C. (*a*), (*b*), (*c*) only
D. (*b*), (*c*), (*d*) only

60. Match the List-I with List-II.

List-I (Concept)	List-II (Explanation)
(*a*) Higher Indifference Curve	I. Higher Satisfaction
(*b*) Converse Indifference Curve	II. Diminishing Marginal Rate of Substitution
(*c*) Price Line	III. Same satisfaction on the curve
(*d*) Indifference Curve	IV. Constant Price Ratio

Choose the ***correct*** answer from the options given below:

	(*a*)	(*b*)	(*c*)	(*d*)
A.	I	II	III	IV
B.	I	II	IV	III
C.	I	III	IV	II
D.	IV	II	III	I

61. Arrange the following steps in logical sequence regarding how to compute Net Present Value (NPV).

(*a*) Calculate Net Present Value (NPV) i.e. Present Value of all cash inflows - present value of all cash outflows

(*b*) Calculate all the cash outflows associated with the project

(*c*) Calculate all the cash inflows associated with the project

(*d*) Calculate the present value of all cash inflows associated with the project

(*e*) Calculate the present value of all cash outflows associated with the project

Choose the ***correct*** answer from the options given below:

A. (*a*), (*b*), (*c*), (*e*), (*d*)
B. (*b*), (*c*), (*e*), (*d*), (*a*)
C. (*a*), (*c*), (*b*), (*e*), (*d*)
D. (*a*), (*c*), (*b*), (*d*), (*e*)

62. Arrange the following point (Section wise from Section 14 to 18) of the Indian Contract Act.

(*a*) Definition of free consent
(*b*) Misrepresentation
(*c*) Fraud
(*d*) Undue influence
(*e*) Coercion

Choose the ***correct*** answer from the options given below:

A. (*e*), (*d*), (*c*), (*b*), (*a*)
B. (*d*), (*e*), (*c*), (*a*), (*b*)
C. (*b*), (*d*), (*e*), (*a*), (*c*)
D. (*a*), (*e*), (*d*), (*c*), (*b*)

63. Which one of the following refers to the firms investment in the current assets?

A. Gross Working Capital
B. Net Working Capital
C. Gross Current liabilities
D. Operating cycle

64. Arrange the practical steps involved in the preparation of process account where there is work in progress.

(*a*) Prepare process account
(*b*) Prepare statement of Evaluation
(*c*) Prepare statement of cost per equivalent unit
(*d*) Prepare statement of equivalent production
(*e*) Determine and analyze the number of physical units in the form of inputs (transferred from previous process) and output

Choose the ***correct*** answer from the options given below:

A. (*a*), (*b*), (*c*), (*d*), (*e*)
B. (*e*), (*d*), (*c*), (*b*), (*a*)
C. (*c*), (*d*), (*e*), (*a*), (*b*)
D. (*b*), (*c*), (*d*), (*a*), (*e*)

65. Which one of the following is value added service of EXIM Bank?

A. Export Facilitation
B. Export product Development
C. Workshops and Seminars
D. Export Marketing

66. Arrange the following stages of conflict process in the proper sequence.

(*a*) Outcomes
(*b*) Potential opposition or incompatibility
(*c*) Behaviour
(*d*) Cognition and personalization
(*e*) Intentions

Choose the ***correct*** answer from the options given below:

A. (*d*), (*b*), (*e*), (*c*), (*a*)
B. (*b*), (*d*), (*e*), (*c*), (*a*)
C. (*a*), (*b*), (*e*), (*d*), (*c*)
D. (*d*), (*c*), (*b*), (*e*), (*a*)

67. Which of the following statements are correct:

(*a*) Call-in-advance is the amount paid by the shareholders in excess of amount due from them.
(*b*) When the number of shares applied is more than the number of shares offered to the public for subscription, the issue is termed as under subscription.
(*c*) Section 49 of the Companies Act prohibits the issue of shares other than sweat equity shares at discount.
(*d*) Unless or until the fortified shares are re-issued, the balance on the shares fortified account will be deducted from the paid up capital.
(*e*) The securities premium is an amount in excess of nominal value of face value of the securities.

Choose the ***correct*** answer from the options given below:

A. (*a*) and (*e*) only
B. (*b*), (*c*) and (*d*) only
C. (*a*), (*b*) and (*c*) only
D. (*a*), (*d*) and (*e*) only

68. Which of the following research designs is the most precise one?

A. Experimental B. Exploratory
C. Diagnostic D. Descriptive

69. Which one of the following sections of the Income Tax Act, 1961 defines method for computing Arm Length Price?

A. 90C B. 91C
C. 92C D. 93C

70. Which of the following is a situation of adverse balance of trade?

A. Import more than exports
B. Exports more than imports
C. Exports equal to imports
D. Export Surplus

71. Match the List-I with List-II.

List-I (Financial Inclusion Yojana)	List-II (Year)
(*a*) PM Jan Dhan	I. 2016
(*b*) PM Mudra	II. 2014
(*c*) Stand Up India	III. 2017
(*d*) Vaya Vandana	IV. 2015

Choose the ***correct*** answer from the options given below:

	(*a*)	(*b*)	(*c*)	(*d*)
A.	II	IV	I	III
B.	II	I	IV	III
C.	IV	I	III	II
D.	II	III	I	IV

72. Standard Deviation of Sampling Distribution is called:

A. Sampling Error B. Probable Error
C. Standard Error D. Measurable Error

73. Which of the following tool is used for projecting supply of personnel?

A. Trend Analysis
B. Ratio Analysis
C. Markov Analysis
D. Managerial Judgement

74. Total production is maximum when:

A. Average production is maximum
B. Marginal production is maximum
C. Marginal production is zero
D. Average production is zero

75. Which one of the following is not a social network of social media platform?

A. Facebook B. Blogs
C. Twitter D. YouTube

76. Match the List-I with List-II.

List-I (Economists)	List-II (Contribution)
(*a*) Adam Smith	I. Principles of Economics
(*b*) A. Marshall	II. Value and Capital
(*c*) J.R. Hicks	III. The Wealth of Nations
(*d*) Wassily Leontief	IV. Input Output Economics

Choose the ***correct*** answer from the options given below:

	(*a*)	(*b*)	(*c*)	(*d*)
A.	I	III	II	IV
B.	I	II	IV	III
C.	III	I	II	IV
D.	III	II	I	IV

77. Which of the following is not the characteristics of theory of comparative cost advantage?

(*a*) There is full employment of the factors of production.
(*b*) There are two countries, two commodities and two factors of production.
(*c*) There are two countries, two commodities and one factor of production.
(*d*) There is absence of transportation cost.
(*e*) The countries are capital intensive only.

Choose the ***correct*** answer from the options given below:

A. (*a*), (*b*), (*c*) only
B. (*b*), (*c*), (*d*) only
C. (*a*), (*c*), (*d*) only
D. (*a*), (*b*), (*e*) only

78. Beta Company Ltd issued 10% perpetual debt of ₹ 1,00,000. The company's tax rate is 50%. Determine the cost of capital (before tax as well as after tax) assuming the debt is issued at 10 per cent premium.

A. Before tax cost = 9.09% and after tax cost = 4.54%
B. Before tax cost = 4.54% and after tax cost = 9 %
C. Before tax cost = 9.90% and after tax cost = 4.45%
D. Before tax cost = 10.09% and after tax cost = 5.54%

79. Which one of the following conditions is not true as per IRDA Act, 1999, for entry of private players into the insurance market?

A. The company's sole purpose is to carry on life insurance business or general insurance business or reinsurance business.
B. The minimum paid up equity capital for life insurance or general insurance business is ₹ 100 crore.
C. The minimum paid up capital for carrying reinsurance business is ₹ 300 crore.
D. Insurance companies are required to invest not less than 15 per cent of their funds in infrastructure and social sectors.

80. Arrange the following points in their section-wise order (Section 23 to 27) as per the Income Tax Act, 1961.

(*a*) Deemed ownership
(*b*) Provision for arrears of rent and unrealized rent received subsequently
(*c*) Determination of annual value
(*d*) Treatment of income from co-owned property
(*e*) Deduction from (Annual Value) Income from house property

Choose the ***correct*** answer from the options given below:

A. (*a*), (*c*), (*b*), (*d*), (*e*)
B. (*c*), (*e*), (*b*), (*d*), (*a*)
C. (*a*), (*b*), (*c*), (*d*), (*e*)
D. (*b*), (*c*), (*d*), (*e*), (*a*)

81. If new contract is substituted in place of an existing contract, it is called:

A. Waiver B. Remission
C. Novation D. Alteration

82. ______ is the result of the Bretton Wood Conference of nations held in 1944.

A. WTO B. IMF
C. IBRD D. ADB

83. Which one of the following is not a behavioural symptom of stress?

A. Lower Job Satisfaction
B. Lower Job Performance
C. Higher Absenteeism
D. Higher Labour Turnover

84. Which of the following is correct?

A. A firm under perfect competition is in equilibrium where AR = MR
B. A firm under monopoly is in equilibrium where TR = MR
C. A firm under monopolistic competition is in equilibrium where AC = MC
D. A firm under oligopoly is in equilibrium where MR = MC

85. Which of the following are the features of F.E.M.A?

(*a*) Central government can regulate payments to and from a person situated outside country.
(*b*) Holding of immovable property outside India is restricted.
(*c*) R.B.I can restrict the transaction from capital account even if it is done by authorized person.
(*d*) All foreign financial transactions are to be done through F.E.M.A authorized person.
(*e*) F.E.M.A applies to Indian citizens living abroad.

Choose the ***correct*** answer from the options given below:

A. (*a*), (*b*), (*c*) only
B. (*b*), (*d*), (*e*) only
C. (*a*), (*b*), (*e*) only
D. (*a*), (*c*), (*d*) only

86. Match the List-I with List-II.

List-I (Key definition Under IT Act 2000)	**List-II (Sections)**
(*a*) Addressee	I. Section 2(1)(f) of the Information Technology Act 2000
(*b*) Adjudicating Officer	II. Section 2(1)(d) of the Information Technology Act 2000
(*c*) Affixing Electronic Signature	III. Section 2(1)(c) of the Information Technology Act 2000
(*d*) Asymmetric Crypto System	IV. Section 2(1)(b) of the Information Technology Act 2000

Choose the ***correct*** answer from the options given below:

	(*a*)	(*b*)	(*c*)	(*d*)
A.	IV	III	II	I
B.	III	IV	I	II
C.	II	I	III	IV
D.	I	II	III	IV

87. Which of the following points are considered as salient features of Limited Liability Partnership (LLP)?

(*a*) LLP is a body corporate
(*b*) LLP is a legal entity separate from its partners
(*c*) LLP does not enjoy a perpetual succession
(*d*) Partners of LLP have unlimited liability
(*e*) LLP is an artificial legal person

Choose the ***correct*** answer from the options given below:

A. (*a*), (*b*) and (*e*) only
B. (*b*), (*c*) and (*d*) only
C. (*c*), (*d*) and (*e*) only
D. (*c*) and (*d*) only

88. Which of the following refers to an attempt to avoid payment of taxes by using illegal means?

A. Tax Management
B. Tax Planning
C. Tax Avoidance
D. Tax Evasion

89. Match the List-I with List-II.

List-I (Statistical Test)	List-II (Explanation)
(*a*) Z-Test	I. Tests the significance of the association between two attributes
(*b*) Chi-Square	II. Compares the difference in the mean values of two independent sample groups (non-parametric data)
(*c*) ANOVA	III. Tests the significance of the different between average of two large sized sample groups (Parametric data)
(*d*) Mann-Whitney Test (U-test)	IV. Compares the difference in the mean values of more than two sample groups (Parametric data)

Choose the ***correct*** answer from the options given below:

	(*a*)	(*b*)	(*c*)	(*d*)
A.	I	II	III	IV
B.	III	I	IV	II
C.	II	III	I	IV
D.	IV	I	III	II

90. Which of the following points are considered as essential characteristics of a Promissory Note?

(*a*) It must be in writing
(*b*) It must not contain an undertaking or promise to pay
(*c*) The promise to pay must be conditional
(*d*) A promissory note must be signed by the maker.
(*e*) Promise to pay money only

Choose the ***correct*** answer from the options given below:

A. (*a*), (*d*) and (*e*) only
B. (*a*), (*b*) and (*e*) only
C. (*b*), (*c*) and (*d*) only
D. (*b*) and (*d*) only

Directions (Qs. No. 91 to 95): *Read the following passage carefully and answer the questions based on it:*

The first phase of modern banking in India began after independence in 1947, when the government nationalized the major banks and introduced various reforms to promote financial inclusion and social welfare. The second phase started in the 1990s, when the liberalization of the economy and the advent of technology enabled the emergence of new private and foreign banks, offering competitive and innovative products and services to the customers. In the 2000s, the third phase commenced when the Internet and mobile penetration increased, leading to the rise of online and mobile banking, as well as the entry of Non-Banking Financial Companies (NBFCs) and fintech startups, offering digital solutions to cater to the unbanked and underbanked segments of the population. The fourth and current phase of banking in India is characterized by the emergence of neo banks, which are digital-only banks that operate without physical branches and offer a range of banking and financial services through mobile apps and web platforms. Neo banks often function by partnering with licensed banks to provide their services to customer. While the digital banking landscape in India is evolving rapidly, there are still many challenges and gaps that need to be addressed. One of the major challenges is the lack of standardization and interoperability among the various players, platforms, and systems in the ecosystem. For instance, there are multiple payment methods, such as UPI, IMPS, NEFT, RTGS, cards, wallets and QR codes, each with its own features, limitations and charges. This creates confusion and inconvenience for customers, who have to switch between different apps and interfaces to make payments and access their accounts.

Artificial Intelligence (AI) is a potent technology that can help digital banks to overcome the challenges and gaps mentioned above, and add value to their customers and stakeholders. AI can enable digital banks to leverage data and analytics, machine learning, natural language processing, computer vision, and other advance techniques to automate and enhance various banking processes, such as customer identification and verification, customer service and support, product recommendation and cross-selling, fraud detection and risk management, credit scoring and underwriting, and regulatory compliance and reporting.

91. What is the primary focus of neo banks in India?

A. Offering physical branch services
B. Catering to the unbanked and underbanked segments
C. Providing traditional banking services
D. Emphasizing paper-based transaction

92. What is one of the major challenges in the digital banking landscape in India?

A. Lack of internet penetration
B. Overabundance of physical branches
C. Lack of standardization and interoperability
D. Over regulation by the government

93. How can artificial intelligence (AI) help digital banks to overcome challenges?

A. By reducing Internet penetration
B. By increasing physical branches
C. By providing advanced analytics
D. By reducing customer base

94. What marked the beginning of the second phase of modern banking in India?

A. Nationalization of major banks
B. Liberalization of the economy
C. Emergence of fintech startup
D. Introduction of Internet banking

95. What is consequence of the lack of standardization and interoperability in the digital banking ecosystem?

A. Convenience for customers
B. Increased trust in digital banking
C. Confusing and inconvenience for costumers
D. Reduction in transaction costs

Directions (Qs. No. 96 to 100): *Read the following passage carefully and answer the questions based on it:*

The major source for the revenue for the government is indirect tax. The Central Board of Indirect Taxes and Customs (CBIC) (erstwhile Central Board of Excise and Customs) is the apex regulatory body that supervises the levy and administration of Indirect Taxes in India. CBIC is a part of the Department of Revenue under the Ministry of Finance, Government of India. It deals with the tasks of formulation of policy concerning levy and collection of customs, Central Excise duties, Central Goods & Services Tax and IGST, prevention of smuggling and administration of matter relating to customs, Central Excise, Central Goods & Services Tax (CGST), IGST and narcotics to the extent under CBIC's purview. The board is the administrative authority for its subordinate organizations, including Custom Houses, Central Excise and Central GST Commissionerate's and the Central Revenue Control Laboratory In recent years, the Indian government has undertaken significant reforms under the indirect taxation system. This includes the implementation of Goods and Services Tax (GST). Goods and Services Tax (GST) is an indirect tax that has replaced many indirect taxes in India. The Goods and Services Tax Act was passed in the Parliament on March 29, 2017.

This Act came into effect on July 01, 2017. GST is a destination based tax on consumption with credit of taxes paid at previous stages available as set-off. In nutshell, only value addition will be taxed and the burden of tax is to be borne by the final consumer.

Destination based tax on consumption means the tax would accrue to the taxing authority which has jurisdiction over the place of consumption which is also termed as place of supply. GST has removed the cascading effect of taxes. This cascading effect implies charging tax on tax. In other words, at the time of levy of tax, the total value is considered which is inclusive of all taxes paid up to the points. In this manner, if the tax is always charged on the selling price of the products, the burden of tax keeps on increasing at each point of sales. In this process, the effect of taxation magnifies as at each level tax is calculated on value, which includes taxes already levied and paid. The charging of tax on tax is called the 'Cascading Effect of Tax'.

96. Who bears the burden of tax in the GST system?

A. Manufacturers B. Retailers
C. Final Consumer D. Government

97. How does GST eliminate the cascading effect of taxes?

A. By increasing tax rates
B. By reducing the number of tax types
C. By allowing tax credit on previous stages
D. By exempting certain product from tax

98. Which department oversees the administration of matters related to custom, central excise, Central Goods & Services Tax (CGST), (IGST), and narcotics under the Indian government?

A. Ministry of Finance
B. Central Board of Direct Taxes
C. Central Board of Indirect Taxes and Customs (CBIC)
D. Department of Revenue

99. What does the term "cascading effect of taxes" refer to?

A. Tax evasion
B. Tax avoiding
C. Charging tax on tax
D. Tax exemption

100. What is the significance of the term "destination - based tax" in the context of GST?

A. Tax is based on the destination of goods only.
B. Tax is levied based on the origin of goods.
C. Tax is collected at the point of sale.
D. Tax accrues to the taxing authority at the place of consumption.

ANSWERS

1. (B): Income is not a behavioural factor in customer profiling for tactical targeting. Behavioural factors typically include aspects such as purchase frequency, purchase quantity, and price sensitivity, which relate to how customers interact with products and make purchasing decisions. Income, however, is a demographic factor that classifies customers based on financial capability rather than their purchasing behaviour.

2. (C): (*a*) Introduction - II. Build Selective Distribution: In the introduction stage of the Product Life Cycle (PLC), selective distribution is used to carefully control product availability and target specific market segments.

(*b*) Growth - III. Build Intensive Distribution: As the product gains acceptance, businesses expand distribution to maximize reach and increase market penetration.

(*c*) Maturity - IV. Build More Intensive Distribution: In this stage, companies further increase distribution to maintain sales and market share against competitors.

(*d*) Decline - I. Phase Out Unprofitable Outlets: As sales decline, businesses reduce distribution efforts by closing unprofitable outlets and focusing on cost management.

3. (B): (*c*) Management Dilemma: The first step is recognizing a problem or opportunity that needs to be addressed.

(*a*) Management Question: This is a broad question derived from the dilemma that guides managerial decision-making.

(*d*) Research Question: The management question is further refined into a research question, specifying the focus of study.

(*e*) Investigative Question: These are detailed questions that break down the research question into measurable components.

(*b*) Measurement Question: The final step involves formulating precise questions for data collection, ensuring quantifiable analysis.

4. (C): To calculate the P/V (Profit/Volume) ratio, we use the formula:

Margin of Safety = Actual Sales − Break-even Sales

Given:

Actual Sales = ₹ 48,000

Margin of Safety = ₹ 8,000

Break-even Sales = 48,000 − 8,000 = ₹ 40,000

$$\text{P/V Ratio} = \frac{\text{Margin of Safety} \times 100}{\text{Actual Sales}}$$

$$= \frac{8,000 \times 100}{40,000} = 30\%.$$

5. (C): The Consumer Protection Act was enacted on 24th December 1986 to safeguard consumers from unfair trade practices, defective goods, and deficient services. This law established consumer rights, including protection against hazardous products, the right to be informed, and mechanisms for grievance redressal through consumer courts. It was a landmark legislation aimed at ensuring consumer welfare in India.

6. (A): Quasi-contracts are based on the doctrine of unjust enrichment, which states that no person should unfairly benefit at the expense of another. Even in the absence of a formal contract, the law imposes an obligation on a person who has received an unfair benefit to compensate the other party.

7. (A): (*a*) Social - IV. Teacher: Social personality types are people-oriented and enjoy helping others, making teaching a suitable profession.

(*b*) Conventional - III. Corporate Manager: Conventional types prefer structured tasks and organization, aligning with managerial roles.

(*c*) Investigative - II. Mathematician: Investigative personalities are analytical and prefer problem-solving, making them suitable for research-based roles like mathematicians.

(*d*) Realistic - I. Mechanic: Realistic personalities prefer hands-on and practical work, fitting occupations like mechanics.

8. (C): (*a*) Competing - IV. A desire to satisfy one's interests regardless of the impact on the other party to the conflict: In competing, individuals focus on winning without concern for others' interests.

(*b*) Collaborating - I. A situation in which each party in a conflict desires to satisfy fully the concerns of all parties: Collaboration seeks a win-win resolution where both parties' interests are met.

(c) Accommodating - III. A situation in which each party to a conflict is willing to give up something to resolve the conflict: Accommodation involves one party sacrificing their position to maintain harmony.

(d) Compromising - II. The willingness of one party in a conflict to place the negotiating partner's interest above their own: Compromise involves mutual concessions for conflict resolution.

9. (D): (c) A discrete random variable can assume at most a countable number of values: A discrete random variable takes on distinct values, often finite or countably infinite.

(d) A random variable is a function of the sample space: A random variable assigns numerical values to outcomes in the sample space.

(e) A random variable is an uncertain quantity, whose value depends on chance: Since random variables represent outcomes of experiments, their values are uncertain and determined probabilistically.

10. (D): Snowball sampling is a non-probability sampling technique where existing study subjects recruit future subjects from their acquaintances. It is commonly used when the target population is hard to reach, such as in social research on marginalized groups. Unlike probability sampling, this method does not give every individual an equal chance of selection.

11. (B): The payback period is calculated as the time taken to recover the initial investment of ₹ 18,500 from cumulative cash inflows.

Given cash inflows:

Year 1: ₹ 8,000
Year 2: ₹ 6,000
Year 3: ₹ 4,000
Year 4: ₹ 2,000
Year 5: ₹ 2,000

Cumulative cash inflows:

End of Year 1: ₹ 8,000
End of Year 2: ₹ 14,000 (₹ 8,000 + ₹ 6,000)
End of Year 3: ₹ 18,000 (₹ 14,000 + ₹ 4,000)
End of Year 3.25: ₹ 18,500 (₹ 18,000 + ₹ 500 from Year 4's ₹ 2,000)

Since the remaining ₹ 500 is recovered in 0.25 years (500/2000), the payback period is 3.25 years.

12. (C): SEBI regulates and supervises securities markets through:

(a) Regulations: SEBI issues regulations to govern various aspects of securities markets, such as insider trading and mutual funds.

(b) Rules: It sets rules to ensure the proper functioning of securities exchanges.

(c) Guidelines: SEBI provides guidelines to ensure transparency and investor protection.

(d) Schemes: It introduces schemes to develop financial markets, such as mutual fund schemes.

(e) Orders: SEBI issues orders to take enforcement actions against violators.

13. (B): The effectiveness of brainstorming is high in a task-oriented environment because:

- It focuses on generating multiple ideas and solutions without immediate criticism.
- Task-oriented groups prioritize achieving objectives over personal conflicts.
- A structured brainstorming approach enhances creativity and problem-solving capabilities.

14. (A): (a) Conservatism - IV. Anticipate no profit, but provide for all possible losses: This principle ensures financial prudence by recognizing expenses and liabilities early while deferring the recognition of revenues until they are realized.

(*b*) Dual Aspect - III. Every transaction has a two-fold effect: This concept states that every financial transaction affects two accounts, maintaining the balance in the accounting equation.

(*c*) Separate Business Entity - II. Enterprise is treated as separate from the owner and other persons associated with it: The business is considered an independent entity, distinct from its owners.

(*d*) Consistency - I. Use of the same accounting policies by a firm from period to period: Firms should maintain consistency in their accounting methods to ensure comparability of financial statements over time.

15. (A): (*a*) Theory of Comparative Cost Advantage - II. David Ricardo: Ricardo's theory explains how countries benefit from trade by specializing in goods with a comparative cost advantage.

(*b*) Theory of Opportunity Cost - III. Haberler: Haberler refined Ricardo's concept by introducing opportunity cost, showing how nations allocate resources efficiently.

(*c*) Theory of Factor Cost - I. Heckseher & Ohlin: This theory states that countries export goods that intensively use their abundant production factors.

(*d*) Theory of Absolute Advantage - IV. Adam Smith: Smith's theory states that a country should produce and export goods in which it has an absolute production advantage over other nations.

16. (A): (*a*) Exchange Rate - IV. It is a price of one unit of a currency in terms of some units of another currency: Exchange rate refers to the value of one currency in terms of another, such as 1 USD = 83 INR.

(*b*) Forward Market - III. Where transactions are entered into for settlement on a future date: The forward market involves contracts to buy or sell an asset at a predetermined price at a future date, commonly used in forex trading.

(*c*) Arbitrage - II. It is the process of making risk-less profits by exploiting price differences of assets in different markets: Arbitrage involves taking advantage of price differences of the same asset in different markets to earn a profit.

(*d*) Direct Quotation - I. It refers to the price of one unit of foreign currency in terms of some units of home currency: In direct quotation, the exchange rate expresses the foreign currency's value per unit in domestic currency (e.g., 1 USD = 83 INR).

17. (A): Market skimming involves setting a high initial price for a new product to maximize revenue from early adopters. It works best when demand is inelastic, meaning consumers are willing to pay a premium. If the market is highly price-sensitive, skimming is ineffective because consumers will not accept the high price.

18. (D): The Reserve Bank of India (RBI) has a developmental role, including:

- Promoting financial inclusion by encouraging banking in rural areas.
- Supporting economic growth by facilitating credit flow to priority sectors.
- Developing payment and settlement systems.

It also regulates monetary policy and banking operations, but those are regulatory rather than developmental roles.

19. (C): Vouching is the process of verifying accounting records by checking supporting documents like invoices, bills and receipts. It ensures that all transactions are valid, authorized, and supported by proper evidence. Internal check and internal control are broader frameworks, while verification is related to checking assets and liabilities.

20. (C): As per the Income Tax Act, 1961, an individual's residential status depends on their stay in India:

- If a person stays in India for 182 days or more in a financial year, they are a Resident.
- If a person stays for less than 182 days, they are a Non-Resident.
- A person is Resident but Not Ordinarily Resident (RNOR) if they were a Non-Resident in 9 out of the last 10 years or stayed in India for less than 729 days in the last 7 years.

Since Brett Lee visits only for 100 days per year for 10 years, he qualifies as RNOR for the assessment year 2023-24.

21. (B): The Average Fixed Cost (A.F.C) Curve is not U-shaped; instead, it is a downward-sloping curve.

Fixed costs remain constant, but as output increases, AFC decreases continuously because it is calculated as:

AFC = Total Fixed Cost Output

AFC = Output Total Fixed Cost

Other curves (AVC, AC, and MC) are U-shaped due to the law of variable proportions, but AFC never rises again after declining.

22.(C): (*d*) Manager lets subordinates function within limits defined by him → Least control, as subordinates operate independently.

(*a*) Manager defines limits and asks for group decisions → Slightly more control, but still involves group participation.

(*e*) Manager presents problems, invites suggestions, and makes decisions → The manager retains decision-making power but seeks input.

(*b*) Manager offers tentative decisions to change → More control, as decisions are already made but subject to modifications.

(*c*) Manager sells decisions → Highest control, as the manager has already decided and persuades others to accept it.

23. (B): Interstate supply of goods (i.e., between different states or a union territory and a state) is taxed under Integrated Goods and Services Tax (IGST).

I. West Bengal to Chandigarh → IGST applies because it is an interstate transaction.

II. Puducherry to Chennai → Puducherry is a Union Territory, and Chennai (Tamil Nadu) is a state; IGST applies here as well.

24. (C): (*a*) Direct Material Cost Variance - IV. Standard cost for actual output − Actual cost

(*b*) Direct Material Price Variance - III. Actual Quantity × (Standard Price − Actual Price)

(*c*) Direct Material Usage Variance - II. Standard Price × (Standard Quantity for Actual Output − Actual Quantity)

(*d*) Direct Material Mix Variance - I. Standard Price × (Revised Standard Quantity − Actual Quantity)

25. (C): (*a*) Basic Nature of Business → Some businesses require more working capital (e.g., manufacturing) than others (e.g., services).

(*b*) Business Cycle Fluctuations → During boom periods, firms need more working capital to handle increased demand.

(*c*) Credit Policy of the Firm → A firm offering longer credit terms to customers requires more working capital.

(*d*) Long-term Source of Finance and (*e*) Employee Skills do not directly determine working capital needs.

26. (A): (*b*) Free Trade Area → The simplest form of economic integration where member countries eliminate trade barriers but maintain independent external policies.

(*c*) Customs Union → A higher level of integration, where member countries adopt a common external trade policy.

(*d*) Common Market → Allows free movement of goods, services, capital, and labor among member countries.

(*e*) Economic Union → Further integration with harmonized economic policies and regulations.

(*a*) Political Union → The highest level of integration, where member countries unify political and economic policies under a single government structure.

27. (C): Section 91 of the Income Tax Act, 1961, provides unilateral relief to taxpayers to avoid double taxation in cases where no bilateral agreement exists between India and the foreign country. It applies when an Indian resident has paid tax on the same income in another country.

28. (A): (*b*) New Profit - sharing ratio is the ratio in which all partners, including new partners, share future profits and losses.

(*d*) Sacrificing Ratio = Old Profit Share - New Profit Share: This determines the portion of profit sacrificed by existing partners in favour of the new partner.

(*e*) Profit or loss from Revaluation Account is transferred to partners' capital accounts, ensuring that old partners receive the effect of asset and liability revaluation before admitting a new partner.

29. (B): Current Ratio Formula:

$$\text{Current Ratio} = \frac{\text{Current Assets}}{\text{Current Liabilities}}$$

Given:

Current Liabilities = Current Assets - Working Capital

= 4,00,000 - 2,40,000

= ₹ 1,60,000

$$\text{Current Ratio} = \frac{4,00,000}{1,60,000} = 2.5:1.$$

30. (A): (*a*) Indian Contract Act - II. 1872: Governs contract law in India, establishing the legal framework for agreements.

(*b*) Sales of Goods Act - III. 1930: Defines rules regarding the sale of goods, including conditions, warranties, and rights of buyers and sellers.

(*c*) Negotiable Instruments Act - IV. 1881: Governs financial instruments like promissory notes, cheques, and bills of exchange.

(*d*) Companies Act - I. 2013: Regulates the incorporation, operation, and governance of companies in India.

31. (D): (*b*) A few sellers and a large number of buyers → Oligopoly is characterized by a few dominant firms in the market, competing with each other, while consumers are numerous.

(*d*) Entry of new sellers is restricted → Oligopolistic markets often have barriers to entry, such as high costs or regulations, preventing new firms from easily joining.

(*e*) Firms' interdependence → Since there are only a few firms, their pricing and production decisions are interdependent, meaning one firm's actions influence the others.

32. (B): (*a*) Negotiable Securities → Treasury Bills (T-Bills) are short-term negotiable instruments that can be bought and sold in the secondary market.

(*c*) High liquidity on account of short tenure → T-Bills have high liquidity as they mature within 91, 182, or 364 days, making them attractive for short-term investment.

(*d*) Assured yield → Since T-Bills are issued by the government, they provide assured returns with no risk of default.

(*b*) Incorrect → T-Bills are issued at a discount and repaid at face value, not at a premium.

(*e*) Incorrect → T-Bills have low transaction costs, making them efficient investment tools.

33. (D): Capital structure refers to the composition of long-term sources of finance used by a company, such as:

- Debentures (long-term borrowings)
- Preference shares (fixed dividends)
- Equity shares (ownership capital)

It determines the financial stability and risk associated with the firm's operations.

34. (B): Standard Deviation Formula:

$$\sigma = \sqrt{\frac{\Sigma(x-\bar{x})^2}{n}}$$

First seven natural numbers

$$= \{1, 2, 3, 4, 5, 6, 7\}$$

$$\text{Mean } (\bar{x}) = \frac{1+2+3+4+5+6+7}{7} = 4$$

Variance

$$= \frac{(1-4)^2+(2-4)^2+(3-4)^2+(4-4)^2+(5-4)^2+(6-4)^2+(7-4)^2}{7}$$

$$= \frac{9+4+1+0+1+4+9}{7} = \frac{28}{7} = 4$$

Standard Deviation (σ) = $\sqrt{4} = 2$.

35. (C): (*d*) Letter of transmittal → A formal letter that introduces the report to the recipient.

(*c*) Title Page → Contains the title of the report, author, and date.

(*b*) Authorization Statement → Indicates who authorized the report and its purpose.

(*a*) Executive Summary → A brief overview summarizing the key points of the report.

(*e*) Table of Contents → Lists sections and page numbers for easy navigation.

36. (A): (*e*) Determination of Residential Status → The first step is to determine whether an individual is a resident or non-resident for tax purposes, as taxation rules differ accordingly.

(*d*) Computation of Income under each head of Income → Income is classified into different heads: Salary, House Property, Business/Profession, Capital Gains, and Other Sources.

(*c*) Clubbing of Income of spouse, minor child, etc. → Certain incomes earned by close family members must be clubbed with the taxpayer's income.

(*b*) Set off and carry forward of losses → Losses from one head of income may be set off against gains from another head, or carried forward as per tax rules.

(*a*) Computation of Gross Total Income → After considering all heads of income and adjustments, Gross Total Income is determined.

37. (A): When the price of Good X rises, the demand for its substitute Good Y will increase because consumers will switch from the more expensive Good X to the relatively cheaper Good Y.

Example: If the price of tea increases, more people may switch to coffee (assuming they are substitutes).

This follows the law of demand and cross-elasticity of substitutes, where an increase in the price of one good leads to a rise in demand for its substitute.

38. (B): (*b*) Work place conditions → The most basic employee need, ensuring a comfortable and functional work environment.

(*c*) Work safety → Employees prioritize job security and safe working conditions before considering social and psychological needs.

(*a*) Cohesive and supportive co-workers → Social belonging comes after physical and safety needs are met.

(*d*) Responsibilities → Employees seek meaningful roles and responsibilities once basic and social needs are satisfied.

(*e*) Job challenge → The highest-order need, involving motivation through challenging and fulfilling work.

39. (B): (*b*) Skill Variety → Employees find their work more meaningful when they can use diverse skills.

(*c*) Task Identity → The degree to which an employee completes a whole, identifiable task rather than just a portion of it.

(*e*) Task Significance → If employees believe their work has a meaningful impact, they experience higher job satisfaction.

Autonomy and feedback are related to job responsibility and knowledge of results rather than meaningfulness.

40. (B): (*a*) UNCTAD (United Nations Conference on Trade and Develop-ment) - III. 1964 → Established to promote international trade and economic development.

(*b*) WTO (World Trade Organization) - IV. 1995 → Succeeded GATT, regulating international trade among nations.

(*c*) NAFTA (North American Free Trade Agreement) - II. 1994 → A trade agreement between the U.S., Canada, and Mexico.

(*d*) ASEAN (Association of Southeast Asian Nations) - I. 1967 → A regional organization promoting economic and political cooperation among Southeast Asian countries.

41. (D): Monetary measures for correcting balance of payment (BOP) disequilibrium include policies that influence money supply and exchange rates, such as Monetary Contraction, Devaluation, and Exchange Control.

Abolition of Export Duties is a fiscal measure, not a monetary measure. It affects government revenue and trade policy but does not directly control money supply or exchange rates.

42. (D): (*c*) Identify the target audience → The first step is to determine whom the marketing communication is directed at.

(*e*) Choose the communication objectives → Define what the company wants to achieve (e.g., brand awareness, lead generation).

(*a*) Design the communication → Develop the message, format, and appeal to attract the target audience.

(*b*) Select the communication channel → Choose whether to use TV, social media, print, or digital platforms for delivery.

(*d*) Choose the communication mix → Decide the proportion of advertising, sales promotions, personal selling, and public relations.

43. (A): (*a*) Commuted pension received by a government employee is fully exempted from Income Tax → As per Section 10(10A) of the Income Tax Act, 1961, a government employee's commuted pension is fully exempted.

(*b*) Section 30 of the Income Tax Act 1961 discusses deduction in respect of rent, rates, taxes, repairs, and insurance of building used for business → This section allows deductions related to business premises.

(*e*) Short-term capital asset is defined under Section 2(42A) of the Income Tax Act, 1961 → This section defines short-term capital assets based on their holding period (less than 36 months for immovable property and 12 months for listed securities).

(*c*) Incorrect → Section 33 does not deal with depreciation; depreciation is covered under Section 32.

(*d*) Incorrect → Capital gain does not arise from every asset transfer; certain transfers (like gifts or inheritance) are exempt.

44. (A): (*a*) Standards may be unclear → Rating scales may be subjective and lack clear differentiation between performance levels.

(*b*) Halo Effect → A single characteristic (e.g., punctuality) may influence overall ratings, leading to biased appraisals.

(*e*) Leniency → Some raters may consistently give higher ratings, making the evaluation unreliable.

(*c*) and (*d*) Incorrect → Graphics rating scales are not time-consuming or difficult to develop compared to other methods like Behaviourally Anchored Rating Scales (BARS).

45. (C): (*c*) Internet → Provides the least value addition as customers browse and purchase products online without personal interaction.

(*a*) Retail Store → Adds more value by allowing customers to physically examine products before purchasing.

(*e*) Distributors → Act as intermediaries in the supply chain, adding logistical efficiency to sales.

(*d*) Value-added partners → Offer additional services like customization, training, or after-sales support.

(*b*) Sales Force → Provides maximum value addition through personalized service, customized solutions, and relationship-building with clients.

46. (A): (*a*) It is a measure of symmetry of a frequency distribution → Skewness describes the asymmetry of a data distribution. A perfectly symmetrical distribution has zero skewness.

(*b*) For the right-skewed distribution, the mean is to the right of the median → In a positively skewed (right-skewed) distribution, the mean is greater than the median because larger values pull it to the right.

(*c*) For the right-skewed distribution, the mean is to the right of mode → In a right-skewed distribution, the relationship is: Mode < Median < Mean

(*d*) and (*e*) are incorrect because in right-skewed distributions, the mean is to the right (not left) of the median and mode.

47. (B): (*b*) Reserve Bank of India (RBI) - 1935 → India's central bank, established to regulate monetary policy and financial stability.

(*c*) State Bank of India (SBI) - 1955 → India's largest public-sector bank, nationalized in 1955.

(*e*) NABARD (National Bank for Agriculture and Rural Development) - 1982 → Supports rural development and agricultural finance.

(*d*) SIDBI (Small Industries Development Bank of India) - 1990 → Focuses on financing micro, small, and medium enterprises (MSMEs).

(*a*) SEBI (Securities and Exchange Board of India) - 1992 → Regulates and oversees the stock market and securities transactions in India.

48. (C): Formalization refers to the degree to which rules, procedures, and regulations are established to guide employees and managers in an organization.

Highly formalized organizations have strict rules and policies, while low formalization allows flexibility.

Other options are incorrect:

- Departmentalization → Dividing an organization into different units based on functions or geography.
- Centralization and Decentralization → Determines decision-making authority distribution.
- Boundary Spanning → Involves interactions across organizational boundaries to share knowledge.

49. (B): Prepaid Insurance represents an advance payment for insurance coverage and is classified as a Personal Account in accounting.

Rule of Personal Accounts: Debit the receiver, Credit the giver Debit the receiver, Credit the giver

Since an insurance company is the receiver of payment in advance, Prepaid Insurance is an Asset (not a nominal or real account).

50. (D): A contract of indemnity is a contingent contract as per Section 31 of the Indian Contract Act, 1872.

A contingent contract depends on the occurrence or non-occurrence of an uncertain event.

Indemnity contracts ensure compensation to a party in case of a specified loss, making them contingent in nature.

Other options are incorrect:

- Wagering Agreement → Based on chance, not indemnity.
- Quasi Contract → Implied by law, not an agreement.
- Void Contract → Indemnity contracts are legally valid unless otherwise specified.

51. (D): The Capital Adequacy Ratio (CAR) is a measure of a bank's financial stability, ensuring that it has sufficient capital to absorb potential losses.

As per the Reserve Bank of India (RBI) guidelines, Indian Public Sector Banks are required to maintain a CAR of 12% under Basel III norms, which is higher than the minimum 9% set by the Basel Committee.

This ratio is calculated as:

$$\text{CAR} = \frac{\text{Tier 1 Capital} + \text{Tier 2 Capital}}{\text{Risk-Weighted Assets}} \times 100$$

A higher CAR helps banks mitigate risks and ensures financial stability.

52. (B): (*a*) The interest which may be earned/saved on the money held at present underlines the concept of time value of money → True, as money today has more value than money in the future due to its earning potential.

(*c*) The relationship that exists between the value of money receivable at present and the value of money receivable in the future is referred to as time value of money → True, as this concept helps in evaluating investments and financial decisions.

(*e*) Future value of money is the value of money held presently at some given future time at a given rate of interest → True, as future value considers the impact of compounding over time.

(*b*) Incorrect → Money receivable at present has more value than money receivable in the future due to inflation and opportunity cost.

(*d*) Incorrect → The formula should be: Present Value = Future Value (1 + *r*)*n* Present Value = (1 + *r*)*n* Future Value

53. (A): (*a*) Section 194 - IV. Dividend → TDS is deducted on dividends paid to shareholders if the amount exceeds ₹ 5,000 in a financial year.

(*b*) Section 194C - III. Payment to contractor and sub-contractor → TDS is applicable on contract payments exceeding ₹ 30,000 per transaction or ₹ 1,00,000 annually.

(*c*) Section 194E - II. Payment to the non-resident sportsman ₹ TDS applies to payments made to foreign sportsmen, associations, and entertainers for participating in India.

(*d*) Section 194F - I. Payment on account of repurchase of units by mutual fund → TDS is deducted when mutual funds repurchase units from investors.

54. (A): (*d*) Buy-Back of Securities by Listed Companies Regulations - 1998 → Governs share buybacks by listed companies.

(*b*) Intermediaries Regulations - 2008 → Covers SEBI-registered market intermediaries like stockbrokers.

(*a*) ICDR (Issue of Capital and Disclosure Requirements) Regula-tions - 2009 → Regulates the public issue of shares.

(*c*) Real Estate Investment Trusts (REITs) Regulations - 2014 → Establishes a framework for REITs in India.

(*e*) Listing Obligations and Disclosure Requirements (LODR) Regulations - 2015 → Sets compliance requirements for listed companies.

55. (A): (*a*) Long run production function → In the long run, all factors of production (land, labour, capital) are variable.

(*b*) Law of equal proportion → Refers to changes in all inputs in the same ratio, leading to returns to scale.

(*c*) Law of return to scale → If all inputs are increased proportionally, output changes accordingly:

Increasing returns to scale → Output increases more than input increase.

Constant returns to scale → Output increases in the same proportion as inputs.

Decreasing returns to scale → Output increases at a lower rate than inputs.

(*d*) and (*e*) Incorrect → These laws apply when only one factor of production is varied, holding others constant (e.g., Law of Variable Proportion).

56. (A): (*b*) In marketing, perceptions are more important than reality because they affect consumers' actual behaviour → True, because consumer decisions are influenced by their perceptions rather than objective reality. A product perceived as high quality will sell more, even if another product is objectively superior.

(*d*) Consumers are constructive decision-makers and are subject to many contextual influences → True, as consumer behaviour is affected by psychological, cultural, and environmental factors, making their decisions context-dependent.

(*a*) Incorrect → Managers should understand both reality and theory of consumer behaviour, as theory helps predict patterns.

(*c*) Incorrect → People do not always emerge with the same perceptions of the same object due to personal experiences and biases.

(*e*) Incorrect → Cultural factors exert the broadest influence, not personal factors.

57. (D): A Matrix Organization is the most suitable structure for companies producing multiple products for multiple markets, as it allows for dual reporting relationships where employees have both product-based and market-based responsibilities.

This structure is effective for complex organizations with diverse products and geographic reach.

Other options are incorrect:

- Geographic Organization → Best for companies expanding across different locations.
- Product or Brand Organization → Best when managing a few key product lines.
- Functional Organization → Best when focusing on specialized functions like sales, HR, and finance.

58. (B): (*a*) Market Driven → A high customer-centric organization aligns its operations with market demands.

(*c*) Value Driven → Focuses on creating customer value rather than just reducing costs.

(*e*) Making competitors irrelevant → By differentiating through superior value and customer experience, such organizations reduce the impact of competition.

(*b*) Incorrect → Being process-oriented is important but does not define a customer-centric organization.

(*d*) Incorrect → A high customer-centric company focuses on value, not just price.

59. (B): (*a*) Assessment Year means the period of 12 months commencing on the first day of April every year → True; as per Section 2(9) of the Income Tax Act, 1961.

(*d*) An assessee is always a person, but a person may or may not be an assessee → True, as a person is only considered an assessee when they have tax obligations.

(*e*) A person may not have assessable income but may still be an assessee → True, as individuals can file tax returns despite having zero taxable income (e.g., filing for refund purposes).

(*b*) and (*c*) Incorrect → Rounding off of total income is under Section 288A, and rounding off of tax is under Section 288B, not vice versa.

60. (B): (*a*) Higher Indifference Curve - I. Higher Satisfaction → A consumer prefers higher indifference curves as they represent greater utility and higher levels of satisfaction.

(*b*) Converse Indifference Curve - II. Diminishing Marginal Rate of Substitution → As a consumer moves along the curve, they are willing to give up less of one good for an additional unit of another, showing diminishing marginal rate of substitution.

(*c*) Price Line - IV. Constant Price Ratio → The price line represents a fixed budget constraint, showing the trade-off between two goods at constant prices.

(*d*) Indifference Curve - III. Same Satisfaction on the Curve → Every point on an indifference curve represents the same level of satisfaction or utility for the consumer.

61. (B): (*b*) Calculate all the cash outflows associated with the project → Identify the total initial and recurring costs involved.

(*c*) Calculate all the cash inflows associated with the project → Estimate future revenues and savings generated by the project.

(*e*) Calculate the present value of all cash outflows associated with the project → Discount future cash outflows to their present value using an appropriate discount rate.

(*d*) Calculate the present value of all cash inflows associated with the project → Similarly, discount all future cash inflows to their present value.

(*a*) Calculate Net Present Value (NPV) i.e., Present Value of all cash inflows - Present Value of all cash outflows → Subtract total discounted outflows from discounted inflows.

If NPV > 0, the project is financially viable; if NPV < 0, it should be rejected.

62. (D): (*a*) Definition of free consent (Section 14) → A contract is valid only if both parties enter into it voluntarily, without coercion, undue influence, fraud, or misrepresentation.

(*e*) Coercion (Section 15) → The use of force or threats to make someone enter into a contract.

(*d*) Undue Influence (Section 16) → One party unfairly exerts pressure or influence over another, affecting free consent.

(*c*) Fraud (Section 17) → Intentional misrepresentation or concealment of facts to deceive another party.

(*b*) Misrepresentation (Section 18) → False statements made without fraudulent intent, but still leading to an unfair contract.

63. (A): Gross Working Capital (GWC) refers to a firm's total investment in current assets, which include:

- Cash & Cash Equivalents
- Accounts Receivable
- Inventory
- Marketable Securities

Other options are incorrect:

- Net Working Capital (NWC) = Current Assets – Current Liabilities.
- Gross Current Liabilities refers only to short-term liabilities, not assets.
- Operating Cycle measures the time taken to convert inventory into cash.

64. (B): (*e*) Determine and analyze the number of physical units in the form of inputs (transferred from previous process) and output → Identify raw materials, labour, and overhead costs in production.

(*d*) Prepare statement of equivalent production → Calculate the work-in-progress (WIP) units to determine equivalent production.

(*c*) Prepare statement of cost per equivalent unit → Compute the cost per fully completed and WIP unit.

(*b*) Prepare statement of evaluation → Assign total production cost across completed and WIP units.

(*a*) Prepare process account → Summarize all transactions in a process account.

65. (C): EXIM Bank offers Workshops and Seminars as value-added services to:

- Educate exporters on international trade finance.
- Train businesses on export credit risk management.
- Provide insights on global trade policies and documentation.

Other options are part of EXIM Bank's functions but not necessarily "value-added services":

- Export Facilitation → Supports exports through financing and guarantees.
- Export Product Development → Helps firms improve product quality for international markets.
- Export Marketing → Focuses on market expansion strategies for Indian exporters.

66. (B): (*b*) Potential opposition or incompatibility → The first stage where conflict arises due to differences in goals, values, or communication gaps.

(*d*) Cognition and personalization → The parties involved become aware of the conflict and start developing emotional responses toward it.

(*e*) Intentions → At this stage, individuals form strategies for dealing with conflict, whether competitive or cooperative.

(*c*) Behaviour → This is the actual expression of conflict, ranging from verbal disagreements to organizational disruptions.

(*a*) Outcomes → Conflict resolution leads to either a functional (positive) or dysfunctional (negative) outcome.

67. (A): (*a*) Call-in-advance is the amount paid by the shareholders in excess of the amount due from them → True, as shareholders sometimes pay additional amounts voluntarily before they are due.

(*e*) The securities premium is an amount in excess of the nominal value of face value of the securities → True, as per Section 52 of the Companies Act, 2013, securities premium is the extra amount received over and above the face value.

(*b*) Incorrect → If applications exceed the shares offered, it is called oversubscription, not under-subscription.

(*c*) Incorrect → Section 53 of the Companies Act, 2013 prohibits issuing shares at a discount, except in specific cases like sweat equity shares.

(*d*) Incorrect → Forfeited shares are not deducted from paid-up capital until they are reissued. They are recorded as a separate account under reserves.

68. (A): Experimental research design is the most precise because:

- It involves controlled experiments to establish cause-and-effect relationships.
- Uses independent and dependent variables with minimal external influences.
- Randomized trials and controlled settings enhance accuracy.

Other options are less precise:

- Exploratory → Used for initial research, lacks precision.
- Diagnostic → Identifies causes but does not establish precise cause-effect relationships.
- Descriptive → Focuses on data collection without control over variables.

69. (C): Section 92C of the Income Tax Act, 1961 defines methods for computing the Arm's Length Price (ALP) in international transactions.

ALP is used for transfer pricing regulations to ensure that transactions between associated enterprises are fair and comparable to market rates.

Methods under Section 92C include:

- Comparable Uncontrolled Price (CUP) Method
- Resale Price Method (RPM)
- Cost Plus Method (CPM)
- Profit Split Method (PSM)
- Transactional Net Margin Method (TNMM)

70. (A): Adverse Balance of Trade occurs when a country imports more than it exports, leading to a trade deficit.

It indicates higher dependency on foreign goods and can affect the country's foreign exchange reserves and currency value.

Other options are incorrect:

- Exports more than imports → Leads to trade surplus (positive balance of trade).
- Exports equal to imports → Creates a balanced trade situation.
- Export surplus → Means exports exceed imports, which is not an adverse balance.

71. (A): (*a*) PM Jan Dhan Yojana - II. 2014 → Launched in August 2014, this scheme aims to provide universal banking access to all households in India, especially for the unbanked population.

(*b*) PM Mudra Yojana - IV. 2015 → Introduced in April 2015, Mudra loans provide financial support to micro and small enterprises through Shishu, Kishor, and Tarun categories.

(*c*) Stand Up India - I. 2016 → Launched in April 2016, this scheme facilitates loans for SC/ST entrepreneurs and women entrepreneurs to promote business development.

(*d*) Vaya Vandana Yojana - III. 2017 → Launched in 2017, it is a pension scheme designed for senior citizens (aged 60 and above), providing a guaranteed pension with an assured return.

72. (C): The Standard Deviation of a Sampling Distribution is known as the Standard Error (SE), which measures the dispersion of sample means from the true population mean.

Formula: $SE = \frac{\sigma}{\sqrt{n}}$

Where:

- σ = Population Standard Deviation
- n = Sample Size

Other options are incorrect:

- Sampling Error → The difference between a sample statistic and the actual population parameter.
- Probable Error → Used to estimate the reliability of correlation coefficients.
- Measurable Error → A general term for errors in statistical measurements.

73. (C): Markov Analysis is used to project the supply of personnel by analyzing employee movement patterns (promotion, transfers, exits, and retirements) within an organization.

It helps in forecasting future workforce availability based on historical data.

Other options are incorrect:

- Trend Analysis → Examines past employment patterns to predict future needs.
- Ratio Analysis → Uses ratios like employees per department to forecast staffing needs.
- Managerial Judgment → A qualitative approach based on expert opinions.

74. (C): Total production is maximum when Marginal Production (MP) = 0, meaning that adding one more unit of input does not increase total output.

Concepts of Production:

- Marginal Production (MP) → The additional output from one more unit of input.
- Average Production (AP) → Total output divided by input quantity.
- Total Production (TP) → The sum of all output produced.

Other options are incorrect:

- MP is maximum when TP is increasing at an increasing rate, not at the maximum TP.
- AP does not determine maximum TP; it helps in assessing efficiency.

75. (B): Blogs are not a social network but a content-sharing platform where individuals or businesses publish articles, news, and opinions.

Other options are social media networks:

- Facebook → A widely used social networking platform for personal and business interactions.
- Twitter → A microblogging platform used for sharing short messages and trending discussions.
- YouTube → A video-sharing platform where users interact via comments, likes, and subscriptions, making it a social media site.

76. (C): (*a*) Adam Smith - III. The Wealth of Nations → Published in 1776, this book laid the foundation of classical economics, emphasizing free markets and the division of labour.

(*b*) A. Marshall - I. Principles of Economics → Published in 1890, it introduced concepts like consumer surplus, price elasticity of demand, and marginal utility.

(*c*) J.R. Hicks - II. Value and Capital → Published in 1939, this work contributed to general equilibrium theory and the concept of elasticity of substitution.

(*d*) Wassily Leontief - IV. Input-Output Economics → Leontief developed Input-Output Analysis, which studies interdependencies between economic sectors.

77. (*)

78. (A): Before-tax cost of perpetual debt (Kd):

$$Kd = \frac{\text{Interest}}{\text{Net Proceeds}}$$

Given:

Interest rate = 10% on ₹ 1,00,000 → ₹ 10,000 interest

Issued at 10% premium, so proceeds = ₹ 1,10,000.

$$Kd = \frac{10,000}{1,10,000} \times 100$$

$$= 9.09\%$$

After-tax cost of debt:

$$Kd_{\text{after tax}} = Kd \times (1 - \text{Tax Rate})$$
$$= 9.09\% \times (1 - 0.50)$$
$$= 4.54\%.$$

79. (C): As per the IRDA Act, 1999, private insurance companies must follow these conditions:

A. Correct → The company's sole purpose must be life insurance, general insurance, or reinsurance.

B. Correct → Minimum ₹ 100 crore paid-up capital for life or general insurance business.

C. Incorrect → Minimum ₹ 200 crore (not ₹ 300 crore) is required for reinsurance business.

D. Correct → At least 15% of investments must be in infrastructure and social sectors.

80. (B): (*c*) Determination of annual value (Section 23) → Calculation of the gross annual value of a house property.

(*e*) Deduction from (Annual Value) Income from house property (Section 24) → Includes deductions for interest on loans and standard deduction (30%).

(*b*) Provision for arrears of rent and unrealized rent received subsequently (Section 25A) → Tax treatment of rent received after eviction or recovery.

(*d*) Treatment of income from co-owned property (Section 26) → Specifies how rental income is divided among co-owners.

(*a*) Deemed ownership (Section 27) → Defines cases where a person is considered the owner without formal ownership (e.g., leasehold rights, transferred property, etc.).

81. (C): Novation occurs when a new contract replaces an existing contract, with the mutual consent of all parties involved.

This can involve either changing the contractual terms or substituting one party with another.

Other options are incorrect:

- Waiver → Refers to voluntarily giving up a right or claim under a contract.
- Remission → Involves accepting a lesser performance than originally agreed.
- Alteration → Modifies some terms of an existing contract without replacing it entirely.

82. (B, C): The Bretton Woods Conference (1944) led to the creation of:

- IMF (International Monetary Fund) → Established to stabilize exchange rates and facilitate global financial cooperation.
- IBRD (International Bank for Reconstruction and Development, also known as the World Bank) → Aimed at financing post-war reconstruction and economic development.

Other options are incorrect:

- WTO (World Trade Organization) was established in 1995 as a successor to GATT.
- ADB (Asian Development Bank) was established in 1966 to promote economic development in Asia.

83. (A): Lower job satisfaction is a major behavioural symptom of stress, as stressed employees feel demotivated and disengaged.

Other symptoms are more indicative of organizational outcomes rather than individual behaviour:

- Lower Job Performance → A consequence of stress but not strictly a behavioural symptom.
- Higher Absenteeism → A result of physical or psychological stress, not necessarily a direct behaviour.
- Higher Labour Turnover → A long-term effect of dissatisfaction, not an immediate behavioural response.

84. (D): Under oligopoly, firms maximize profit where Marginal Revenue (MR) = Marginal Cost (MC).

Other options are incorrect:

A. Incorrect → In perfect competition, equilibrium occurs where Price (P) = AR = MR = MC, not just AR = MR.

B. Incorrect → In monopoly, equilibrium occurs where MR = MC, not TR = MR.

C. Incorrect → In monopolistic competition, equilibrium occurs where MR = MC, not AC = MC.

85. (D): (*a*) Central government can regulate payments to and from a person situated outside the country → True, as FEMA controls foreign exchange transactions to prevent economic instability.

(*c*) RBI can restrict transactions from capital accounts even if done by an authorized person → True, as FEMA allows RBI to regulate capital account transactions to prevent currency fluctuations.

(*d*) All foreign financial transactions are to be done through a FEMA-authorized person → True, to ensure transactions comply with foreign exchange laws.

(*b*) Incorrect → Holding of immovable property outside India is not completely restricted; certain conditions apply.

(*e*) Incorrect → FEMA does not apply to Indian citizens living abroad unless they have Indian assets or earnings subject to FEMA rules.

86. (A): (*a*) Addressee - IV. Section 2(1)(b) of the Information Technology Act, 2000 → Defines an addressee as a person who is intended by the originator to receive an electronic record but does not include an intermediary.

(*b*) Adjudicating Officer - III. Section 2(1)(c) of the Information Technology Act, 2000 → The Adjudicating Officer has the power to impose penalties for violations of the Act.

(*c*) Affixing Electronic Signature - II. Section 2(1)(d) of the Information Technology Act, 2000 → Describes the process of using digital signatures to authenticate electronic documents.

(*d*) Asymmetric Crypto System - I. Section 2(1)(f) of the Information Technology Act, 2000 → Defines cryptographic techniques using a pair of keys (public and private) to enable secure communication.

87. (A): (*a*) LLP is a body corporate → True, as per the Limited Liability Partnership (LLP) Act, 2008, LLPs are legally recognized entities.

(*b*) LLP is a legal entity separate from its partners → True, as LLPs enjoy separate legal status, meaning they can own property, enter into contracts, and sue or be sued independently of their partners.

(*e*) LLP is an artificial legal person → True, like companies, LLPs exist in the eyes of the law and can perform legal functions.

(*c*) Incorrect → LLPs enjoy perpetual succession, meaning the LLP continues to exist even if partners change.

(*d*) Incorrect → Partners of an LLP have limited liability, meaning they are not personally liable for the debts of the LLP beyond their contribution.

88. (D): Tax Evasion refers to illegally avoiding tax payments by underreporting income, inflating deductions, or hiding assets. It is a criminal offense.

Other options are incorrect:

- Tax Management → Legitimate tax compliance through proper accounting.

- Tax Planning → Legal strategies to minimize tax liability using deductions and exemptions.
- Tax Avoidance → Legally reducing tax liabilities through loopholes but without violating laws.

89. (B): (*a*) Z-Test - III. Tests the significance of the difference between the average of two large-sized sample groups (Parametric data) → Used for large samples ($n > 30$) when population variance is known.

(*b*) Chi-Square - I. Tests the significance of the association between two attributes → Used for categorical data analysis, such as independence and goodness-of-fit tests.

(*c*) ANOVA - IV. Compares the difference in the mean values of more than two sample groups (Parametric data) → Used for analyzing variance among multiple groups.

(*d*) Mann-Whitney Test (U-test) - II. Compares the difference in the mean values of two independent sample groups (Non-parametric data) → Used when data is not normally distributed.

90. (A): (*a*) It must be in writing → True, a promissory note must be documented and signed.

(*d*) A promissory note must be signed by the maker → True, without a signature, it is not legally valid.

(*e*) Promise to pay money only → True, it must involve only monetary transactions.

(*b*) Incorrect → A promissory note must contain a promise to pay, not just an undertaking.

(*c*) Incorrect → The promise to pay must be unconditional, meaning no extra conditions should be attached.

91. (B): Neo banks in India primarily focus on digital-only banking services, targeting unbanked and underbanked populations through mobile apps and web platforms. Unlike traditional banks, they do not operate physical branches and instead partner with licensed banks to provide services such as savings accounts, loans, and digital payments. This helps in increasing financial inclusion and reaching customers who have limited or no access to traditional banking.

92. (C): One of the major challenges in India's digital banking landscape is the lack of uniformity and interconnectivity between different banking systems, platforms, and payment methods such as UPI, NEFT, IMPS, RTGS, wallets, and QR codes. This creates confusion and inconvenience for customers, as they need to switch between multiple apps and payment interfaces. Ensuring interoperability across all digital banking services would improve customer experience and efficiency.

93. (C): Artificial Intelligence (AI) can help digital banks overcome challenges by using data analytics, machine learning, and automation to enhance banking operations. AI-driven solutions can optimize customer identification and verification, fraud detection, credit scoring, risk management, and personalized product recommendations. By analyzing large volumes of data, AI improves efficiency, reduces operational costs, and enhances customer experience in digital banking.

94. (B): The second phase of modern banking in India began in the 1990s with the liberalization of the economy, which led to the entry of new private and foreign banks. This phase introduced competitive and innovative banking products and services, increasing customer choice and improving banking efficiency. The reforms during this period encouraged technology adoption and modernized the financial sector.

95. (C): The lack of standardization and interoperability in India's digital banking ecosystem results in confusion and inconvenience for customers. Different payment methods such as UPI, NEFT, IMPS, RTGS, wallets, and QR codes have their own rules, limitations, and charges, making transactions more complicated. Customers often have to use multiple apps and interfaces to complete transactions, reducing the ease and efficiency of digital banking.

96. (C): In the GST system, the final consumer bears the burden of tax.

GST is a destination-based tax, meaning it is levied at the place of consumption rather than the place of production.

Businesses such as manufacturers, wholesalers, and retailers act as intermediaries who collect GST from buyers and pass it to the government, ensuring that only the value addition at each stage is taxed.

The system eliminates the cascading effect, making tax payment fairer and reducing double taxation.

97. (C): GST eliminates the cascading effect of taxes by allowing businesses to claim Input Tax Credit (ITC) on the tax paid at previous stages.

Input Tax Credit (ITC) allows businesses to deduct the tax they have already paid on purchases from the tax they owe on sales, ensuring that tax is only paid on the value added at each stage.

This avoids "tax on tax", reduces the overall tax burden, and makes the system more efficient and transparent.

98. (D): The Department of Revenue, under the Ministry of Finance, Government of India, oversees the administration of customs, central excise, Central GST (CGST), Integrated GST (IGST), and narcotics.

The Central Board of Indirect Taxes and Customs (CBIC), a part of the Department of Revenue, is responsible for enforcing indirect tax laws and policies.

CBIC handles policy formulation, implementation, and compliance to ensure smooth tax collection and prevent tax evasion.

99. (C): The cascading effect of taxes refers to charging tax on tax, which results in an increase in the total tax burden at each stage of the supply chain.

Before GST, indirect taxes such as excise duty, VAT, and service tax were applied at different levels, leading to a higher cost of goods and services.

GST eliminates this issue by ensuring that tax is only levied on the value addition at each stage.

100. (D): GST is a destination-based tax, meaning the revenue is collected by the state where the goods or services are consumed.

This contrasts with the origin-based tax system, where tax is levied at the place of production.

The place of supply determines which government (state or central) gets the tax revenue, ensuring a fair distribution of tax collection.

YOUR SPACE

Previous Years' Paper

National Testing Agency (NTA)

UGC-NET Junior Research Fellowship & Assistant Professor Eligibility Exam

Commerce, September-2024

(Exam held on 03-09-2024)

PAPER-II

1. Which of the following is the apex decision-making body of WTO?

A. General Council
B. Executive Council
C. Ministerial Conference
D. TRIMS

2. The authentication to be affected by use of asymmetric crypto system and hash function is known as:

A. E-commerce
B. Virtual signature
C. Digital signature
D. E-verification

3. Revenue from sale of products, ordinarily is reported as part of the earning in the period when:

A. The sale is made
B. The cash is collected
C. The products are manufactured
D. The profit is computed

4. Arrange the following new product planning process in proper sequence.

(*a*) Idea screening
(*b*) Idea generation
(*c*) Concept Development and testing
(*d*) Market strategy development
(*e*) Business Analysis

Choose the ***correct*** answer from the options given below:

A. (*a*), (*b*), (*c*), (*d*), (*e*)
B. (*b*), (*a*), (*c*), (*d*), (*e*)
C. (*a*), (*b*), (*c*), (*e*), (*d*)
D. (*e*), (*d*), (*b*), (*a*), (*c*)

5. Which of the following are the participants in T-Bills Market?

(*a*) Reserve Bank of India
(*b*) Commercial Banks
(*c*) Foreign Banks
(*d*) Provident Funds
(*e*) Corporates

Choose the ***correct*** answer from the options given below:

A. (*b*), (*c*), (*d*) & (*e*) only
B. (*a*), (*b*), (*c*) & (*e*) only
C. (*a*), (*b*), (*d*) & (*e*) only
D. (*a*), (*b*), (*c*), (*d*) & (*e*)

6. Compute the tax liability under default tax regime of Mr. X (35 year), having total income of ₹ 51,75,000 for the assessment year 2024-25. Assume that his total income comprises salary, income from house property and interest on fixed deposit:

A. 13,75,000 B. 13,77,750
C. 14,30,000 D. 14,75,000

7. Match the List-I with List-II.

List-I (Section)	List-II (Ceiling limit)
(*a*) 80-C	I. 50,000
(*b*) 80-CCD (1)	II. 10% of salary or 20% of gross total income as per case
(*c*) 80-CCD (1B)	III. 14% of salary
(*d*) 80-CCD (2)	IV. 1,50,000

Choose the ***correct*** answer from the options given below:

	(*a*)	(*b*)	(*c*)	(*d*)
A.	I	II	III	IV
B.	IV	II	I	III
C.	IV	III	II	I
D.	III	IV	I	II

8. What is the time limit within which an information is to be provided regarding the life and liberty of a person under RTI Act, 2005?

A. 30 days B. 60 days
C. 24 hours D. 48 hours

9. Match the List-I with List-II.

List-I	List-II
(*a*) Right to Safety	I. Consumers have a right against the marketing of goods, products or services which are hazardous to life & property.
(*b*) Right to be assured	II. Consumers have a right to know about the quality, quantity, potency, purity, standard and price of goods or services.
(*c*) Right to be informed	III. Consumers have a right to be assured that their interest will receive due consideration at appropriate commission
(*d*) Right to be heard	IV. Consumer has the opportunity to choose from a wide range of products at reasonable rates

Choose the ***correct*** answer from the options given below:

	(*a*)	(*b*)	(*c*)	(*d*)
A.	I	IV	II	III
B.	II	III	I	IV
C.	III	II	I	IV
D.	IV	III	II	I

10. Which of the following are the benefits of globalisation?

(*a*) Increase in competition would make companies more cost & quality conscious and innovative.

(*b*) An open economy spurs innovation with fresh ideas from abroad.

(*c*) Liberalisation & global competition enhances consumer choice and consumer surplus.

(*d*) Developing countries could be very vulnerable to the harmful effects of globalisation.

(*e*) Globalisation opens up enormous domestic and global opportunities for firms in developing countries.

Choose the ***correct*** answer from the options given below:

A. (*a*), (*b*), (*c*) & (*d*) only
B. (*c*), (*d*) & (*e*) only
C. (*b*), (*c*), (*d*) & (*e*) only
D. (*a*), (*b*), (*c*) & (*e*) only

11. Match the List-I with List-II.

List-I (Instruments)	List-II (Market)
(*a*) Forwards	I. Primary Market
(*b*) Certificate of Deposits	II. Money Market
(*c*) FPO	III. Derivative Market
(*d*) IPO	IV. Stock Market

Choose the ***correct*** answer from the options given below:

	(*a*)	(*b*)	(*c*)	(*d*)
A.	I	III	II	IV
B.	II	IV	I	III
C.	IV	II	III	I
D.	III	II	IV	I

12. Arrange the online registration process of a new private limited company in proper sequence.

(*a*) Select and Reserve Company Name
(*b*) Acquire DIN & DSC of promoters
(*c*) Draft Memorandum and Articles of Association
(*d*) Get Company Registration Certificate
(*e*) File SPICE+ Application

Choose the ***correct*** answer from the options given below:

A. (*a*), (*b*), (*c*), (*e*), (*d*)
B. (*a*), (*b*), (*e*), (*d*), (*c*)
C. (*b*), (*a*), (*c*), (*e*), (*d*)
D. (*b*), (*a*), (*c*), (*d*), (*e*)

13. Match the List-I with List-II.

List-I	**List-II**
(*a*) Transfer of ownership	I. Negotiable Instrument
(*b*) Sale of goodwill after dissolution	II. Contract of Sale of Goods
(*c*) Buy back of shares	III. Dissolution of Partnership Firm
(*d*) Promissory Note	IV. Share Capital of Company

Choose the ***correct*** answer from the options given below:

	(*a*)	(*b*)	(*c*)	(*d*)
A.	II	III	IV	I
B.	I	II	III	IV
C.	II	III	I	IV
D.	I	III	II	IV

14. When the number of trials (n) is large but the probability of success (p) is small, Binomial probability distribution can be approximated using:

A. Normal Distribution
B. Hypergeometric Distribution
C. Poisson Distribution
D. Bernoulli Distribution

15. Match the List-I with List-II.

Match the offences and their corresponding penalties as per IT Act-2000.

List-I	**List-II**
(*a*) Tampering with computer source documents (Sec.65)	I. Imprisonment upto 2 years and/or fine upto ₹ 1 lakh
(*b*) Penalty for mis-representation (Sec. 71)	II. Imprisonment upto 3 years, or fine of ₹ 2 lakh or both
(*c*) Penalty for Breach of confidentiality and privacy (Sec.72)	III. Imprisonment upto 2 years or fine which may extend to one lakh rupees or with both
(*d*) Punishment for cyber terrorism (Sec.66F)	IV. Imprisonment extends to imprisonment for life.

Choose the ***correct*** answer from the options given below:

	(*a*)	(*b*)	(*c*)	(*d*)
A.	I	II	III	IV
B.	II	I	IV	III
C.	II	III	I	IV
D.	III	IV	I	II

16. Arrange the following strategic decisions in international business in proper sequence.

(*a*) Market Selection Decision
(*b*) International Business Decision
(*c*) Entry and Operating Decision
(*d*) International organisation & HR Decisions
(*e*) Marketing Mix Decision

Choose the ***correct*** answer from the options given below:

A. (*a*), (*b*), (*c*), (*d*), (*e*)
B. (*a*), (*b*), (*c*), (*e*), (*d*)
C. (*b*), (*a*), (*c*), (*e*), (*d*)
D. (*b*), (*c*), (*a*), (*e*), (*d*)

17. "Fiduciary relationship" is a relationship based on:

A. Legal obligations
B. Absolute trust and reliance
C. Trade relation
D. Monetary benefits

18. Match the List-I with List-II.

List-I	List-II
(*a*) Capital Asset Pricing Model	I. $\frac{E}{V}\gamma_E + \frac{D}{V}\gamma_D(1 - T_C)$
(*b*) Gordon Model	II. $R_E = R_f + \beta_E (R_M - R_f)$
(*c*) Weighted Average Cost of Capital	III. $P = m\left(D + \frac{E}{3}\right)$
(*d*) Traditional Model	IV. $P_0 = \frac{E_1(1-b)}{k - br}$

Choose the ***correct*** answer from the options given below:

	(*a*)	(*b*)	(*c*)	(*d*)
A.	IV	I	II	III
B.	II	III	I	IV
C.	I	II	III	IV
D.	II	IV	I	III

19. From the following identify the measures of dispersion:

(*a*) Mean Deviation
(*b*) Range
(*c*) Standard Deviation
(*d*) Coefficient of Variation
(*e*) Coefficient of Correlation

Choose the ***correct*** answer from the options given below:

A. (*b*), (*c*), (*d*) & (*e*) only
B. (*a*), (*b*), (*d*) & (*e*) only
C. (*a*), (*c*), (*d*) & (*e*) only
D. (*a*), (*b*), (*c*) & (*d*) only

20. Determine the correct sequence of the steps involved in the process of hypothesis testing.

(*a*) Setting the null and alternative hypothesis
(*b*) Setting the level of significance
(*c*) Determining the appropriate statistical test
(*d*) Setting the decision rule
(*e*) Analysing the collected data

Choose the ***correct*** answer from the options given below:

A. (*b*), (*a*), (*c*), (*d*), (*e*)
B. (*b*), (*c*), (*a*), (*d*), (*e*)
C. (*a*), (*c*), (*b*), (*d*), (*e*)
D. (*a*), (*b*), (*c*), (*d*), (*e*)

21. The tax planning strategies used by multinational enterprises that exploit gaps and mismatches in tax rules to avoid paying tax is known as:

A. AEPS B. BEPS
C. EBPS D. CEPS

22. Which environment shapes the attitudes of human beings, though there may be great diversity in its impact?

A. The Political Environment
B. International Environment
C. The Socio-Cultural Environment
D. The Economic Environment

23. The liquidator after realizing the assets of the company should distribute the proceeds among below mentioned claimants in which order?

(*a*) Liquidator's remuneration and cost of expenses of winding up.
(*b*) Legal charges
(*c*) Claims of secured creditors

(*d*) Preferential creditors and creditors secured by floating charges
(*e*) Unsecured creditors

Choose the ***correct*** answer from the options given below:

A. (*a*), (*b*), (*c*), (*d*), (*e*)
B. (*b*), (*a*), (*c*), (*d*), (*e*)
C. (*b*), (*c*), (*a*), (*d*), (*e*)
D. (*a*), (*c*), (*b*), (*e*), (*d*)

24. Match the List-I with List-II.

List-I	List-II
(*a*) Buyer's Mind	I. Members of Social-club
(*b*) Personal Factor	II. Motivation
(*c*) Psychological Factor	III. Life Style
(*d*) Reference Group	IV. Black Box

Choose the ***correct*** answer from the options given below:

	(*a*)	(*b*)	(*c*)	(*d*)
A.	I	II	III	IV
B.	II	III	IV	I
C.	III	IV	I	II
D.	IV	III	II	I

25. The profit volume ratio of a company is 50% and the margin of safety is 40%. Calculate net profit if the sales volume is ₹ 1,00,000.

A. 10,000 B. 18,000
C. 20,000 D. 25,000

26. The supply function is given as $q = -100 + 10p$. Find the elasticity of supply (Es) using point method, when price is ₹ 15.

A. Es = 2 B. Es = 3
C. Es = 3.5 D. Es = 4

27. Arrange the following phases of International Monetary System in chronological order (old to new).

(*a*) Gold Bullion Standard
(*b*) Gold Specie Standard
(*c*) Floating Exchange Rate
(*d*) Gold Exchange Standard
(*e*) Bretton Woods System

Choose the ***correct*** answer from the options given below:

A. (*a*), (*b*), (*e*), (*d*), (*c*)
B. (*a*), (*d*), (*e*), (*c*), (*b*)
C. (*b*), (*a*), (*d*), (*e*), (*c*)
D. (*b*), (*d*), (*a*), (*c*), (*e*)

28. Matrix organisation violates which of the following management principles?

A. Span of Management
B. Scalar Chain
C. Unity of Direction
D. Unity of Command

29. The effect of exchange rate fluctuations on a firm's future cost and revenues is termed as:

A. Transaction Exposure
B. Translation Exposure
C. Accounting Exposure
D. Operating Exposure

30. The Bretton Woods monetary system was based on the fixed rate monetary system. It lasted between the years:

A. 1946 to 1974 B. 1944 to 1974
C. 1940 to 1974 D. 1944 to 1971

31. Which of the following is ***not*** a feature of capitalist economy?

A. Right of private property
B. Freedom of choice to consumers
C. Government Interference
D. High level of competition

32. Which of the following is correct to compute Labour Mix Variance (LMV)?

A. LMV = Actual rate (Revised Std. time-Actual time)
B. LMV = Actual time (Std. Rate-Actual rate)
C. LMV = Std. Rate (Revised Std. time - Actual time)
D. LMV = Std. time (Actual rate - Std. Rate)

33. Which of the following is the most frequently held meeting of a company?

A. Statutory Meeting
B. Annual General Meeting
C. Class Meeting
D. Director's Meeting

34. Arrange the following steps of sampling design process in correct order.

(*a*) Sampling frame must be determined
(*b*) Target population should be defined according to objective
(*c*) Sampling process must be effectively executed
(*d*) Selecting a sampling technique
(*e*) Number of elements to be included in the study must be carefully determined.

Choose the ***correct*** answer from the options given below:

A. (*b*), (*d*), (*e*), (*c*), (*a*)
B. (*a*), (*b*), (*d*), (*e*), (*c*)
C. (*a*), (*c*), (*b*), (*d*), (*e*)
D. (*b*), (*a*), (*d*), (*e*), (*c*)

35. Arrange the steps of research process in the correct logical order.

(*a*) Formulate a research question
(*b*) Literature review
(*c*) Collect data
(*d*) Develop a research plan
(*e*) Interpret the result

Choose the ***correct*** answer from the options given below:

A. (*b*), (*a*), (*d*), (*c*), (*e*)
B. (*a*), (*b*), (*d*), (*c*), (*e*)
C. (*a*), (*c*), (*d*), (*b*), (*e*)
D. (*b*), (*a*), (*c*), (*d*), (*e*)

36. Providing a total package of related goods and services to solve a customer's needs is called:

A. Complete Selling
B. Conglomerate Selling
C. Wholesale Selling
D. Systems Selling

37. The distribution of data which has a long left tail is known as:

A. Positively skewed distribution
B. Negatively skewed distribution
C. Symmetrical distribution
D. Mesokurtic distribution

38. Nicosia Model of consumer behaviour is divided into four major fields, which of the following is the third field under this model?

A. Feedback
B. Act of purchase
C. Firm's and consumer's attributes
D. Search and evaluation

39. Match the List-I with List-II.

List-I	List-II
(*a*) Personal selling	I. Commercially significant news
(*b*) Advertising	II. Advertising within buses, railway compartments
(*c*) Transit advertising	III. Non-personal communication
(*d*) Publicity	IV. Two way communication

Choose the ***correct*** answer from the options given below:

	(*a*)	(*b*)	(*c*)	(*d*)
A.	I	II	III	IV
B.	II	III	IV	I
C.	I	III	II	IV
D.	IV	III	II	I

40. Match the List-I with List-II.

List-I (Act/Institution)	List-II (Year)
(*a*) Consumer Protection Act	I. 1964
(*b*) FEMA	II. 1945
(*c*) IMF	III. 1999
(*d*) UNCTAD	IV. 2019

Choose the ***correct*** answer from the options given below:

	(a)	(b)	(c)	(d)
A.	IV	III	II	I
B.	II	III	I	IV
C.	III	IV	II	I
D.	I	II	III	IV

41. Match the List-I with List-II.

List-I (Technique)	List-II (Description)
(a) Gordon Technique	I. Teaching the importance of resolving matters
(b) Morphological Analysis	II. Insight into a given interaction
(c) Built-in-Tension	III. Listing of alternative solution to problems
(d) Monodrama	IV. Steering a discussion to crystallise solutions

Choose the ***correct*** answer from the options given below:

	(a)	(b)	(c)	(d)
A.	I	II	III	IV
B.	II	III	I	IV
C.	III	IV	II	I
D.	IV	III	I	II

42. Transmission of shares is effected by which of the following?

(a) Sale
(b) Death
(c) Insolvency
(d) Maturity

Choose the ***correct*** answer from the options given below:

A. (a) & (b) only
B. (a) & (c) only
C. (b) & (d) only
D. (b) & (c) only

43. Arrange the following forums in correct sequence of first appeal to final appeal by an assessee under Income Tax Act-1961.

(a) Supreme Court
(b) High Court
(c) Appellate Tribunal
(d) Joint Commissioner

Choose the ***correct*** answer from the options given below:

A. (a), (b), (c), (d)
B. (d), (c), (b), (a)
C. (b), (d), (a), (c)
D. (c), (a), (d), (b)

44. What will be the dividend per share of Rohtas Industries for the year 2024 given the following information about the company?

EPS for 2024 = ₹ 3
DPS for 2023 = ₹ 1.2
Target Payout Ratio = ₹ 0.6
Adjustment Rate = ₹ 0.7

A. ₹ 1.8
B. ₹ 1.62
C. ₹ 1.52
D. ₹ 1.72

45. Arrange the following steps involved in the process of IPO issue in correct order.

(a) Verification by SEBI
(b) Hiring an under writer
(c) Registration for IPO
(d) Pricing of IPO
(e) Allotment of shares

Choose the ***correct*** answer from the options given below:

A. (a), (c), (d), (b), (e)
B. (a), (d), (c), (b), (e)
C. (b), (c), (d), (a), (e)
D. (b), (c), (a), (d), (e)

46. Which of the following is the pre-condition for applying Chi-square test?

A. Data should not be presented in percentage or ratio form.
B. The sample should consists of at least 100 observations.
C. The sample should not be drawn randomly.
D. All the individual observations in a sample should not be independent.

47. Which of the following is/are included in salary as per section-17 of Income Tax Act 1961?

(*a*) Wages
(*b*) Perquisite
(*c*) Profits in lieu of salary
(*d*) Compensation on termination of employment

Choose the ***correct*** answer from the options given below:

A. (*a*) & (*b*) only
B. (*b*) & (*c*) only
C. (*a*), (*b*) & (*c*) only
D. (*a*), (*b*), (*c*) & (*d*)

48. Which of the following are the assumption underlying MM Theory of capital structure?

(*a*) Perfect Capital Market
(*b*) Heterogeneous Expectations
(*c*) Absence of Taxes
(*d*) 100% Dividend Payout
(*e*) Equivalent Risk Class

Choose the ***correct*** answer from the options given below:

A. (*a*), (*c*) & (*e*) only
B. (*b*), (*c*) & (*e*) only
C. (*a*), (*b*), (*c*) & (*d*) only
D. (*b*), (*c*), (*d*) & (*e*) only

49. According to Proposition II of Modigliani-Miller theory of capital structure, which of the following statement is true?

A. Financial Leverage has no effect on the wealth of shareholders.
B. Financial Leverage increases with wealth of shareholders.
C. Rate of return expected by shareholders increases with the increase in equity financing.
D. Rate of return expected by shareholders increases with financial leverage.

50. Which organisational structure promotes control and co-ordination within a department because of similarity in the tasks being performed?

A. Divisional Structure
B. Functional Structure
C. Formal Structure
D. Matrix Structure

51. Which of the following means management should promote a team-spirit of unity and harmony among employees?

A. Unity of Command
B. Unity of Direction
C. Scalar chain
D. Esprit De Corps

52. Which of the following are the rights of the equity shareholders?

(*a*) Right to Income
(*b*) Right to claim Dividend
(*c*) Right to Control
(*d*) Right to Liquidation
(*e*) Pre-emptive Rights

Choose the ***correct*** answer from the options given below:

A. (*a*), (*b*), (*c*), (*d*) & (*e*)
B. (*b*), (*c*) & (*e*) only
C. (*a*), (*b*), (*c*) & (*d*) only
D. (*a*), (*c*), (*d*) & (*e*) only

53. Tax treaties are generally based on which of the following convention?

(*a*) OECD Model Tax Convention
(*b*) UN Model Tax Convention
(*c*) WTO Model Tax Convention
(*d*) IMF Model Tax Convention

Choose the ***correct*** answer from the options given below:

A. (*a*) & (*b*) only
B. (*a*) & (*c*) only
C. (*b*) & (*d*) only
D. (*a*), (*b*) & (*c*) only

54. An appeal that elaborate on a non-product related benefit or image and attempts to induce emotional responses from consumers is called:

A. Physiological Appeals
B. Informational Appeal
C. Sociological Appeal
D. Transformational Appeal

55. Calculate Debt Service coverage ratio from the following data.
Net profit before interest and Tax ₹ 50,000
10% Debenture (payable in 10 years in equal instalments) ₹ 1,00,000
Tax rate is 50%

A. 1.27 B. 1.67
C. 2.27 D. 2.67

56. Which of the following are included in Foreign Direct Investment?

(*a*) Wholly owned subsidiary
(*b*) Joint venture
(*c*) Investment in GDR
(*d*) Acquisition
(*e*) Investment by FIIs

Choose the ***correct*** answer from the options given below:

A. (*a*) & (*b*) only
B. (*b*), (*c*) & (*d*) only
C. (*c*), (*d*) & (*e*) only
D. (*a*), (*b*) & (*d*) only

57. The price of one kg of tea is ₹ 30. At this price ₹ 5 kg of tea is demanded. If the price of coffee rises from ₹ 25 to ₹ 35 per kg, the quantity demanded of tea rises from 5 kg to 8 kg. Find the cross price elasticity of tea.

A. (+) 0.5 B. (+) 1.0
C. (+) 1.5 D. (-) 1.8

58. According to Dividend Growth Model, the cost of Equity is equal to:

A. Retained Earning + Dividend yield
B. Dividend yield + Expected Growth in Dividend
C. Retained Earning + Expected Growth in Dividend
D. Dividend yield + Intrinsic value

59. What is the valuation formula based on the Walter's model if

P : Price per equity share
D : Dividend per share
E : Earnings per share
r : Rate of return on investment
k : Cost of equity

A. $P = \frac{D + (E - k)/r}{r}$

B. $P = \frac{E + (D - E)r/k}{k}$

C. $P = \frac{D + (E - D)r/k}{k}$

D. $P = \frac{E + (E - D)r/k}{k}$

60. In the context of an organisation, the process of making subordinates to act in a desired manner to achieve certain organisational goals is known as:

A. Employee participation
B. Co-partnership
C. Affiliation
D. Motivation

61. Which of the following are true about chi-square test and chi-square distribution?

(*a*) Chi-square test is a non-parametric test.
(*b*) Chi-square test was developed by spearman.
(*c*) Chi-square distribution can never be negative.
(*d*) Chi-square distribution is a discrete distribution.
(*e*) Chi-square distribution is a function of its degree of freedom.

Choose the ***correct*** answer from the options given below:

A. (*b*), (*c*) & (*d*) only
B. (*a*), (*c*) & (*e*) only
C. (*a*), (*b*) & (*d*) only
D. (*b*), (*d*) & (*e*) only

62. The general consideration applicable to tax planning in the field of business deduction revolve around which of the following?

(*a*) Allowability
(*b*) Year of allowability

(*c*) Extent of allowability
(*d*) Carry forward to future years

Choose the ***correct*** answer from the options given below:

A. (*a*) & (*b*) only
B. (*a*) & (*c*) only
C. (*a*), (*b*) & (*c*) only
D. (*a*), (*b*), (*c*) & (*d*)

63. Match the List-I with List-II.

List-I	List-II
(*a*) Unity of Command	I. Maintaining high morale among employees is imperative
(*b*) Unity of Direction	II. Hierarchical, formalised communication channel
(*c*) Scalar Chain	III. Functions have only one plan and one boss
(*d*) Espirit de Corps	IV. Sub-ordinates reports to only one boss

Choose the ***correct*** answer from the options given below:

	(*a*)	(*b*)	(*c*)	(*d*)
A.	I	II	III	IV
B.	I	IV	III	II
C.	IV	III	II	I
D.	II	III	IV	I

64. Arrange the following process of incorporation of a new LLP in proper sequence.

(*a*) Reserve LLP name
(*b*) Procure Digital Signature Certificate
(*c*) Prepare documents for incorporation of LLP
(*d*) LLP incorporation and DIN Application
(*e*) Drafting and Filling LLP Agreement
(*f*) Apply for PAN and TAN

Choose the ***correct*** answer from the options given below:

A. (*a*), (*b*), (*c*), (*d*), (*f*), (*e*)
B. (*b*), (*a*), (*d*), (*c*), (*e*), (*f*)
C. (*b*), (*a*), (*c*), (*d*), (*f*), (*e*)
D. (*a*), (*b*), (*c*), (*d*), (*e*), (*f*)

65. Arrange the steps of Capital Budgeting Process in correct sequence.

(*a*) Preparation of Capital Budget and Appropriation
(*b*) Performance Review
(*c*) Assembling of Investment proposals
(*d*) Identification of Investment opportunities
(*e*) Decision Making

Choose the ***correct*** answer from the options given below:

A. (*d*), (*c*), (*e*), (*a*), (*b*)
B. (*a*), (*c*), (*d*), (*b*), (*e*)
C. (*a*), (*d*), (*c*), (*b*), (*e*)
D. (*b*), (*d*), (*c*), (*e*), (*a*)

66. Match the List-I with List-II.

List-I	List-II
(*a*) Organisational Structure	I. Refers to the delegation of authority throughout the organisation.
(*b*) Span of Management	II. Groups activities on the basis of products.
(*c*) Divisional Structure	III. Refers to the number of subordinates under a supervisor.
(*d*) Decentralisation	IV. The framework within which managerial and operating tasks are operated.

Choose the ***correct*** answer from the options given below:

	(*a*)	(*b*)	(*c*)	(*d*)
A.	I	II	III	IV
B.	III	II	I	IV
C.	II	III	IV	I
D.	IV	III	II	I

67. Which of the following sections of the Income-Tax Act-1961, provide for double taxation relief in India?

(*a*) Section-89 (*b*) Section-90
(*c*) Section-91 (*d*) Section-92
(*e*) Section-93

Choose the ***correct*** answer from the options given below:

A. (*a*) & (*b*) only
B. (*b*) & (*c*) only
C. (*c*) & (*d*) only
D. (*a*), (*b*) & (*e*) only

68. In case of performance appraisal, an assessment should focus on:

(*a*) Technology to intervene between appraiser and appraisee
(*b*) Individual traits
(*c*) Behaviours exhibited by the assesses
(*d*) Knowledge/skills possessed
(*e*) Results achieved

Choose the ***correct*** answer from the options given below:

A. (*a*), (*b*), (*c*) & (*d*) only
B. (*a*), (*b*), & (*c*) only
C. (*b*), (*c*) & (*d*) only
D. (*b*), (*c*), (*d*) & (*e*) only

69. Arrange the following stages of investigation in proper sequence.

(*a*) Plan work to be done and timing.
(*b*) Obtain instructions from the client and prepare terms of reference.
(*c*) Make necessary calculation to eliminate inconsistencies.
(*d*) Collect necessary information and documents.
(*e*) Formulate conclusions/analysis of findings.

Choose the ***correct*** answer from the options given below:

A. (*a*), (*b*), (*c*), (*d*), (*e*)
B. (*a*), (*c*), (*b*), (*d*), (*e*)
C. (*b*), (*a*), (*d*), (*c*), (*e*)
D. (*a*), (*b*), (*d*), (*c*), (*e*)

70. Which of the following are included under EPRG framework of internationalisation?

(*a*) Eco centrism
(*b*) Ethno centrism
(*c*) Poly centrism
(*d*) Regio centrism
(*e*) Geo centrism

Choose the ***correct*** answer from the options given below:

A. (*b*), (*c*), (*d*) & (*e*) only
B. (*a*), (*b*), (*c*) & (*e*) only
C. (*a*), (*c*), (*d*) & (*e*) only
D. (*a*), (*b*), (*d*) & (*e*) only

71. A firm wants to launch a new brand of television and refrigerator. The firm conducted a survey and found that 60% of the households have television, 65% have a refrigerator and 35%, both a television and a refrigerator. If a household is randomly selected, what is the probability that the household has either a television or refrigerator?

A. 0.70
B. 0.90
C. 0.80
D. 0.60

72. Which of the following capital budgeting Techniques follows the discounting criteria?

(*a*) Net Present Value
(*b*) Benefit-cost Ratio
(*c*) Accounting Rate of Return
(*d*) Internal Rate of Return
(*e*) Payback Period

Choose the ***correct*** answer from the options given below:

A. (*a*), (*b*), (*c*), (*d*) only
B. (*b*), (*c*), (*d*) only
C. (*a*), (*b*), (*d*) only
D. (*a*), (*c*), (*d*) only

73. Which of the following is **NOT** a part of micro environment?

A. Suppliers
B. Customers
C. Competitors
D. Technology

74. Which of the following are different types of dumping?

(*a*) Persistent dumping
(*b*) Predatory dumping
(*c*) Sporadic dumping
(*d*) Nomadic dumping

Choose the ***correct*** answer from the options given below:

A. (*a*) & (*b*) only
B. (*a*), (*b*) & (*c*) only
C. (*b*) & (*c*) only
D. (*c*) & (*d*) only

75. What is the privilege of a holder in due course?

A. The right to cancel the instrument at any time.
B. Instrument cleansing of all defects.
C. Exemption from legal obligations.
D. Unrestricted transfer of the instrument.

76. Match the List-I with List-II.

List-I	List-II
(*a*) Joint occurrence of Events	I. Collective Exhaustive Events
(*b*) Outcome of an experiment consisting of all possible events	II. Equally likely Events
(*c*) One of the events can not be expected to occur in preference over the other	III. Compound Event
(*d*) The occurrence of one event implies that the other can not occur	IV. Mutually Exclusive Events

Choose the ***correct*** answer from the options given below:

	(*a*)	(*b*)	(*c*)	(*d*)
A.	III	I	II	IV
B.	IV	II	I	III
C.	III	II	I	IV
D.	I	II	III	IV

77. Which of the following can file a petition for winding up of a company?

(*a*) Shareholders
(*b*) The creditor or prospective creditors
(*c*) The legal heirs
(*d*) The person authorised by the central government

Choose the ***correct*** answer from the options given below:

A. (*a*), (*b*) & (*c*) only
B. (*b*), (*c*) & (*d*) only
C. (*a*), (*c*) & (*d*) only
D. (*a*), (*b*) & (*d*) only

78. Arrange the following anti-dumping process in proper sequence.

(*a*) Initiation
(*b*) Preliminary screening
(*c*) Rejection under de minimis, unsubstantiated information etc.
(*d*) Exporting country allowed to modify practice.
(*e*) Preliminary findings followed by final finding and measures.

Choose the ***correct*** answer from the options given below:

A. (*b*), (*c*), (*a*), (*d*), (*e*)
B. (*a*), (*b*), (*c*), (*d*), (*e*)
C. (*b*), (*a*), (*c*), (*d*), (*e*)
D. (*b*), (*c*), (*a*), (*e*), (*d*)

79. A company has Return on Assets (ROA) of 10% and profit margin of 2%. Compute the total assets turnover.

A. 2.5% B. 5%
C. 7.5% D. 10%

80. Match the List-I with List-II.

List-I	List-II
(*a*) Informal organisation	I. Grouping of jobs of similar nature
(*b*) Formal organisation	II. Interaction among people at work gives rise to a network of social relationship among employees
(*c*) Divisional structure	III. The organisation structure comprises separate business units
(*d*) Functional structure	IV. Specifies clearly the boundaries of authority and responsibility

Choose the ***correct*** answer from the options given below:

	(*a*)	(*b*)	(*c*)	(*d*)
A.	II	III	IV	I
B.	II	III	I	IV
C.	II	IV	III	I
D.	II	IV	I	III

81. A company prices one litre bottle of its mineral water at ₹ 20 but 100 ml of the same water in a moisturizer spray for ₹ 50. This is an example of which one of the following pricing practices?

A. Customer-Segment Pricing
B. Image Pricing
C. Product-form Pricing
D. Mark-up Pricing

82. Which of the following are the schemes promoted by NABARD?

(*a*) Kisan Credit Card (KCC)
(*b*) Capital Investment Subsidy Scheme
(*c*) Special Economic Zone Scheme
(*d*) Rural Innovation Fund
(*e*) Tribal Development Fund

Choose the ***correct*** answer from the options given below:

A. (*a*), (*b*), (*c*) & (*d*) only
B. (*b*), (*c*), (*d*) & (*e*) only
C. (*a*), (*b*), (*d*) & (*e*) only
D. (*a*), (*c*), (*d*) & (*e*) only

83. Which of the following are the principal functions of UNCTAD?

(*a*) To promote International trade with a view to accelerating economic development.
(*b*) To assist economic development of developing countries by promoting private enterprises.
(*c*) To negotiate multinational trade agreements.
(*d*) To make proposals for putting its principles and policies into effect.

Choose the ***correct*** answer from the options given below:

A. (*a*), (*b*) & (*c*) only
B. (*b*), (*c*) & (*d*) only
C. (*a*), (*b*) & (*d*) only
D. (*a*), (*c*) & (*d*) only

84. Arrange the following steps of securitisation in a correct sequence.

(*a*) Forming SPV
(*b*) Transfer to SPV
(*c*) Credit Enhancement
(*d*) Seasoning
(*e*) Issuance of securities

Choose the ***correct*** answer from the options given below:

A. (*a*), (*b*), (*c*), (*d*), (*e*)
B. (*b*), (*c*), (*a*), (*d*), (*e*)
C. (*d*), (*c*), (*a*), (*b*), (*e*)
D. (*d*), (*c*), (*b*), (*a*), (*e*)

85. Assessment made not only from inside the company but from groups outside the organisation is known as:

A. 360-Degree Feedback
B. 720-Degree Feedback
C. Performance Appraisal
D. MBO

86. Match the List-I with List-II.

List-I (Trader)	List-II (Function/Activity)
(*a*) Hedger	I. Buying and selling shares quickly
(*b*) Speculator	II. Reducing investment Risk
(*c*) Arbitrageur	III. Taking increased Risk willingly
(*d*) Scalper	IV. Taking advantage of the mismatch of the prices in two markets

Choose the ***correct*** answer from the options given below:

	(*a*)	(*b*)	(*c*)	(*d*)
A.	I	II	III	IV
B.	II	I	III	IV
C.	II	III	IV	I
D.	III	IV	II	I

87. The management of Vibgyor Fabrics subscribes to the NOI approach and believes that its cost of debt and overall cost of capital will remain at 9% and 12% respectively. If the debt-equity ratio is 0.8, what is the cost of equity?

A. 16.4% B. 12.4%
C. 14.4% D. 8.12%

88. Which of the following section of Companies Act, 2013 deals with amalgamation, absorption and reconstruction?

A. Section 139
B. Section 219
C. Section 319
D. Section 391

89. Who among the following has given this definition of CSR? "Wealth created from society has to be ploughed back into society."

A. Milton
B. Henry Ford
C. Mahatma Gandhi
D. Kay and Silberston

90. Which of the following are the price-adaption strategies?

(*a*) Price discounts and allowances
(*b*) Target return pricing
(*c*) Geographical pricing
(*d*) Differentiated pricing
(*e*) Going rate pricing

Choose the ***correct*** answer from the options given below:

A. (*a*), (*c*) & (*e*) only
B. (*b*), (*c*) & (*d*) only
C. (*a*), (*c*) & (*d*) only
D. (*a*), (*b*) & (*d*) only

Direction (Qs. No. 91 to 95): *Read the following passage carefully and answer the questions:*

Solar Tech Ltd., a global solar panel manufacturer, sought to expand into emerging markets to counteract stagnation in its domestic market. After analyzing global opportunities, the company targeted India due to its favourable renewable energy policies and growing demand for sustainable energy solution.

Solar Tech Ltd. established a joint venture with a local firm to leverage their market knowledge and distribution network. They also customized their products to meet local regulatory standards and climatic conditions. Despite initial challenges, such as navigating regulatory complexities and cultural differences, solar tech achieved a 25% market share within two years.

The success of the company was attributed to strategic partnerships, product customization and effective market entry tactics. However it faced ongoing issues with supply chain-disruption and the need for continuous innovation to stay competitive.

91. What was a key factor in Solar Tech. ability to achieve a 25% market share in India?

A. Price reduction
B. Aggressive advertising campaigns
C. Strategic partnership and product customisation
D. Government subsidies

92. How did Solar Tech Ltd. initially approached the market entry into India?

A. By setting up a wholly owned subsidiary
B. Through a joint venture with a local firm
C. By acquiring a local competition
D. By exporting products directly

93. Despite its success, what ongoing issue did Solar Tech Ltd. encounter?

A. Decreasing customer base
B. Increased competition from local brands
C. Supply chain disruption
D. Difficulties in securing financing

94. What was the primary reason for Solar Tech. to expand its business to Indian market?

A. Declining domestic demand
B. Favourable policies and growing demand in India
C. Lower production cost in India
D. Saturated international market

95. What were some of the challenges Solar Tech. Ltd. faced in Indian Market?

A. Labour shortage and high tariffs
B. High inflation rate
C. Political instability and poor infrastructure
D. Regulatory complexities and cultural differences

Direction (Qs. No. 96 to 100): *Read the following passage carefully and answer the questions:*

The finance manager of ABC Ltd., a company based in Bangalore has gone on vacation to an island with his family. The island has very poor connectivity and hence he is unable to make or receive calls. The CEO of the company send him a SMS to provide certain information related to financial statement as he was unable to connect due to network problems and CEO has a meeting with the chairman next day.

The finance manager has no documents with him and he was also not able to take the help of internet to send the desired information due to lack of internet facility on the island. On the basis of his memory, he was able to send the following information to the CEO through SMS. which was delivered after 2 hours.

(*a*) Current Debt to Total Debt Ratio : 0.40
(*b*) Total Debt to owner's equity : 0.60
(*c*) Fixed Assets to owner's equity: 0.60
(*d*) Total Assets turnover : 2 Times
(*e*) Inventory turnover : 8 Times
(*f*) Owner's equity : ₹ 1,00,000

The CEO is puzzled to get the SMS, as he was unable to find the required information. You are required to help the CEO in finding relevant information from the SMS as indicated in the following questions:

96. What would be the value of sales as per the data given in case?

A. ₹ 1,60,000
B. ₹ 2,20,000
C. ₹ 3,00,000
D. ₹ 3,20,000

97. What would be the value of fixed assets as per the ratio given in the case?

A. ₹ 50,000
B. ₹ 60,000
C. ₹ 70,000
D. ₹ 75,000

98. Compute the value of inventory from the data given in case.

A. ₹ 40,000
B. ₹ 45,000
C. ₹ 50,000
D. ₹ 60,000

99. Find out the value of total assets from the given information.

A. ₹ 80,000 B. ₹ 1,20,000
C. ₹ 1,45,000 D. ₹ 1,60,000

100. Identify the value of long term debt from the given data.

A. ₹ 32,000 B. ₹ 35,000
C. ₹ 36,000 D. ₹ 39,500

ANSWERS

1. **(C):** The Ministerial Conference is the apex decision-making body of the World Trade Organization (WTO). It comprises representatives from all member countries and typically meets at least once every two years. The Ministerial Conference has the authority to make decisions on all matters under any of the multilateral trade agreements. This includes functions such as interpreting the trade rules and agreements to ensure smooth operation and progression of trade across global markets. For example, in past meetings, the Ministerial Conference has been responsible for major decisions that led to the launch of new trade negotiation rounds and the approval of accession for new members, thereby shaping the international trade landscape significantly.

2. **(C):** Digital signatures use asymmetric cryptography and hash functions to authenticate the identity of the sender of a message or the signer of a document, ensuring that the original content of the message or document has been sent without tampering. Asymmetric cryptography involves a pair of keys, a public key, and a private key. The private key, which is kept secret, is used to create a digital signature, and the corresponding public key is used to verify it. The hash function creates a unique digital fingerprint of the data; if the document changes after signing, the digital signature will fail to verify, thereby ensuring data integrity.

3. **(A):** Revenue from the sale of products is typically recognized at the point of sale, which is when the ownership and risks of the goods have transferred to the buyer, and the seller has fulfilled their part of the deal by making the goods available to the purchaser. This principle aligns with the accrual basis of accounting, which recognizes income when earned and expenses when incurred, regardless of when the cash transactions occur. This approach provides a more accurate picture of the company's financial health and performance during a particular accounting period, as it matches revenues with the expenses related to those revenues.

4. **(B):** The correct sequence for a new product planning process typically starts with Idea Generation (*b*), where potential product ideas are developed. This is followed by Idea Screening (*a*), where ideas are evaluated to determine if they are feasible and align with company goals. Next is Concept Development and Testing (*c*), which involves creating product concepts, defining marketing and engineering details, and testing the concepts to refine them further. Market Strategy Development (*d*) comes afterward, focusing on developing marketing strategies and sales approaches. Finally, Business Analysis (*e*) assesses the market attractiveness, competition, potential sales, and profitability of the new product.

5. **(D):** Participants in the T-Bills Market include the Reserve Bank of India (*a*), which plays a crucial role in issuing and managing Treasury Bills as part of government debt management. Commercial Banks (*b*) and Foreign Banks (*c*) participate as investors seeking low-risk short-term investment opportunities. Provident Funds (*d*) and Corporates (*e*) also invest in T-Bills to manage their short-term liquidity needs effectively. T-Bills are considered safe investments with maturities typically ranging from a few days to a year, offering participants a secure place to park funds temporarily.

6. (C): To compute the tax liability of Mr. X, a 35-year-old individual with a total income of ₹ 51,75,000 for the assessment year 2024-25 under the default tax regime, we need to apply the prevailing income tax slabs. Assuming Mr. X falls under the general category (not senior citizen), the tax rates for assessment year 2024-25 for income exceeding ₹ 50,00,000 are typically around 30%, plus applicable surcharge and cess. Therefore, the primary tax calculation on ₹ 50,00,000 would be approximately ₹ 12,50,000 (excluding initial tax-free slabs and considering different slabs leading up to 30%). For the remaining ₹ 1,75,000, a 30% rate yields ₹ 52,500. Adding surcharge (typically around 10% on the tax for incomes exceeding ₹ 50 lakh) and a 4% health and education cess results in an estimated tax liability around ₹ 14,30,000.

7. (B): Matching the sections of the Income Tax Act with their ceiling limits, we find that Section 80-C, which pertains to deductions on investments like PF contributions, life insurance premiums, etc., has a ceiling limit of ₹ 1,50,000, hence matched with IV. Section 80-CCD(1) refers to deductions for contributions to pension accounts, limited by 10% of salary (or 20% if self-employed), thus II is correct. Section 80-CCD(1B) provides an additional deduction of ₹ 50,000 over and above the ceiling limit under Section 80-CCD(1), making I correct. Section 80-CCD(2) pertains to the employer's contribution to an employee's pension account, which can go up to 14% of salary for government employees, corresponding to III.

8. (D): The Right to Information Act, 2005 stipulates a specific provision for cases concerning the life and liberty of a person. Under this provision, the information must be provided within 48 hours from the time of the request. This accelerated timeline ensures urgent access to information that could impact a person's immediate safety or freedom, reflecting the critical nature of such requests.

9. (A): The correct matches for the rights under consumer protection are as follows: The Right to Safety, denoted by (*a*), means that consumers have a right against the marketing of goods and services which are hazardous to life and property, matched with I. The Right to be Assured (*b*), corresponds to the ability to choose from a range of products at reasonable prices, making IV correct. The Right to be Informed (*c*) is about consumers' right to know details like quality, quantity, potency, etc., matching with II. Lastly, the Right to be Heard (*d*) ensures that consumers' interests receive due consideration at appropriate forums, corresponding to III.

10. (D): The benefits of globalization include several economic and social impacts. Increased competition (*a*) often drives companies to focus on cost reduction, quality improvement, and innovation to stand out in a global marketplace. An open economy (*b*) facilitates the influx of fresh ideas and technologies, which can spur domestic innovation. Liberalization and global competition (*c*) expand consumer choices and lead to better pricing, which can increase consumer surplus. Finally, globalization (*e*) opens up new markets and platforms for domestic companies, especially in developing countries, allowing them to scale up and participate more actively in international trade.

Note, however, that while (*d*) highlights a potential downside of globalization, it is not a benefit and is thus excluded from the correct options.

11. (D): Matching the financial instruments with the appropriate markets, Forwards are a type of financial contract used in the

Derivative Market, hence (*a*) matches with III. Certificates of Deposit are short-term debt instruments typically issued by banks and are traded in the Money Market, so (*b*) matches with II. A Follow-on Public Offer (FPO) is a method used by already publicly traded companies to issue additional shares, which relates to the Stock Market, thus (*c*) matches with IV. An Initial Public Offering (IPO) is the first sale of stock by a company to the public and is part of the Primary Market, making (*d*) match with I.

12. (C): The online registration process for a new private limited company involves several steps. First, the promoters need to Acquire the Director Identification Number (DIN) and Digital Signature Certificate (DSC) (*b*), which are essential for legal identification and electronic submission of documents. Next, Select and Reserve Company Name (*a*) is done, which ensures the proposed company name is available and not similar to any existing company names. Drafting the Memorandum and Articles of Association (*c*) follows, which are the key documents outlining the company's structure and rules of operation. Then, File SPICE+Application (*e*) is the next step; this integrated form simplifies the application process by combining multiple services into a single form (e.g., DIN, mandatory issue of PAN, TAN, bank account number). Finally, the company receives the Get Company Registration Certificate (*d*), which is the official incorporation document.

13. (A): Matching the legal terms with their appropriate contexts, Transfer of ownership (*a*) pertains to the Contract of Sale of Goods (II), which legally transfers ownership from seller to buyer. Sale of goodwill after dissolution (*b*) relates to the Dissolution of a Partnership Firm (III), where assets including goodwill are disposed of and proceeds distributed among partners. Buy back of shares (*c*) concerns the Share Capital of a Company (IV), where a company repurchases its own shares from shareholders. A Promissory Note (*d*) is a Negotiable Instrument (I), which is a legal document guaranteeing the payment of a specified amount of money at a set time or on demand.

14. (C): When the number of trials (*n*) is large but the probability of success (*p*) is very small, the Binomial probability distribution can be approximated using the Poisson distribution. This approximation is particularly useful in situations where events occur independently and the total number of occurrences is low relative to the possible number of trials. The Poisson distribution simplifies calculations by focusing on the average rate of success over many trials without tracking the exact number of successes and failures, making it ideal for modeling rare events in large populations.

15. (C): Matching the offences under the IT Act-2000 with their corresponding penalties, Tampering with computer source documents (Sec. 65) is punishable by Imprisonment up to 3 years, or a fine of ₹ 2 lakh or both, matching (*a*) with II. Penalty for misrepresentation (Sec. 71), involving false information, incurs a penalty, which may extend to one lakh rupees or with both imprisonment and fine, thus (*b*) with III. Breach of confidentiality and privacy (Sec. 72) pertains to unauthorized access and release of personal or confidential information, with penalties of up to 2 years or fine up to ₹ 1 lakh, aligning (*c*) with I. Lastly, Punishment for cyber terrorism (Sec. 66F) carries a severe penalty, potentially extending to life imprisonment, correctly associating (*d*) with IV.

16. (C): The proper sequence of strategic decisions in international business begins with the International Business Decision (*b*), which encompasses the initial consideration and decision to engage in or expand international operations. This decision sets the stage for all subsequent strategic considerations. Next is the Market Selection Decision (*a*), where a company identifies and selects specific international markets to enter, based on factors such as market size, potential growth, and competitive landscape. Following this is the Entry and Operating Decision (*c*), which involves choosing the mode of entry (e.g., export, joint venture, wholly owned subsidiary) and operational strategies for the selected markets. The Marketing Mix Decision (*e*) comes afterward, focusing on adapting or standardizing the marketing strategies (product, price, place, promotion) to fit the needs and preferences of the target international market. Finally, International Organization & HR Decisions (*d*) are made to structure the organization and manage human resources effectively across different cultural, legal, and business environments. This sequence ensures a strategic, organized approach to expanding into international markets, optimizing resource allocation, and enhancing global competitiveness.

17. **(B):** A "fiduciary relationship" is fundamentally based on absolute trust and reliance between two parties. This type of relationship is crucial in contexts where one party, the fiduciary, is obligated to act in the best interests of another party, the principal. The defining element of a fiduciary relationship is that one party places trust and confidence in another who has a legal or ethical duty to act primarily for the benefit of the trusting party. Examples of fiduciary relationships include those between a trustee and a beneficiary, a lawyer and a client, or a director and the shareholders of a company. In these relationships, the fiduciary is expected to demonstrate the highest levels of honesty, loyalty, and integrity, often foregoing their own interests in favour of those of the principal. This relationship is not primarily defined by legal obligations, trade relations, or monetary benefits, but by the high level of trust and ethical conduct expected of the fiduciary.

18. **(D)**

19. **(D):** The measures of dispersion are statistical tools used to describe the spread or variability within a set of data. The correct answers include:

    (*a*) **Mean Deviation:** This measure represents the average of the absolute differences between each data point and the mean of the dataset. It provides an overview of dispersion by showing how far, on average, each value lies from the center.

    (*b*) **Range:** The simplest measure of dispersion, the range is the difference between the maximum and minimum values in a dataset. It gives a quick sense of the spread of the data but can be easily affected by outliers.

    (*c*) **Standard Deviation:** Perhaps the most widely used measure of dispersion, standard deviation quantifies the amount of variation or dispersion of a set of data values. A low standard deviation means that the data points tend to be close to the mean (also called the expected value) of the set, while a high standard deviation means that the data points are spread out over a wider range of values.

    (*d*) **Coefficient of Variation:** This measure is the ratio of the standard deviation to the mean. It is particularly useful because it is a dimensionless number that allows for comparisons of the degree of variation between datasets with vastly different means and units.

(*e*) **Coefficient of Correlation**, however, is not a measure of dispersion but rather a measure of the strength and direction of a linear relationship between two variables. Therefore, it does not fit with the other options.

Hence, the correct answer is D, which includes (*a*), (*b*), (*c*), and (*d*) only, as these are the relevant measures of dispersion.

20. (C): The process of hypothesis testing involves a systematic series of steps to determine whether to reject a null hypothesis (H0H_0H0) based on sample data. The correct sequence, as per the instructions, is outlined below in detail:

(*a*) **Setting the null and alternative hypothesis:** This is the foundational step where the researcher specifies the null hypothesis (H0H_0H0), which typically states that there is no effect or no difference between groups or conditions. Alongside, the alternative hypothesis (H1H_1H1) is set, which states that there is an effect, a difference, or a relationship. These hypotheses frame the scope and direction of the statistical analysis.

(*c*) **Determining the appropriate statistical test:** Once the hypotheses are defined, the next step involves selecting the correct statistical test that aligns with the data type, distribution, and the hypothesis itself. This choice is crucial as it impacts the analysis' validity. Possible tests include *t*-tests, chi-square tests, ANOVA, regression analysis, among others, depending on the data's nature and the hypothesis specifics.

(*b*) **Setting the level of significance:** After choosing the test, the level of significance (α) is decided. This value defines the threshold for rejecting the null hypothesis. Common levels are 0.05, 0.01, or 0.10, translating into a 5%, 1%, or 10% risk of wrongly rejecting the null hypothesis, respectively. This step sets the critical values for the subsequent statistical test.

(*d*) **Setting the decision rule:** Based on the selected level of significance and the chosen statistical test, the decision rule is established. This rule outlines the conditions under which the null hypothesis will be rejected or not rejected, incorporating the test statistic's critical values derived from the statistical test's distribution.

(*e*) **Analyzing the collected data:** Finally, with the decision rule in place, the actual data collected through research is analyzed. This analysis involves calculating the test statistic from the data and applying the decision rule. Based on whether the test statistic falls within the critical region, the null hypothesis is either rejected or not rejected, concluding the hypothesis testing process.

Thus, the sequence (C): (*a*), (*c*), (*b*), (*d*), (*e*) provides a logical and systematic approach to hypothesis testing, ensuring that the test is properly aligned with the research questions, correctly executed, and that conclusions are based on predetermined criteria, reducing the risk of error in hypothesis testing.

21. (B): The tax planning strategy used by multinational enterprises that exploit gaps and mismatches in tax rules to avoid paying tax is known as Base Erosion and Profit Shifting (BEPS). BEPS refers to tax planning strategies that exploit gaps and mismatches in tax rules to artificially shift profits to low or no-tax locations where there is little or no economic activity, resulting in little or no overall corporate tax being paid. Strategies such as abusing tax treaties, transferring intangibles for less than market value, and using artificial arrangements to avoid establishing a tax residence are commonly used in BEPS. This strategy has significant implications for the global economy, leading to billions of dollars in tax revenue losses for governments worldwide. Efforts by the OECD and G20 have led to the development of the BEPS Action Plan aimed at providing governments with domestic and international instruments to address tax avoidance.

22. (C): The environment that shapes the attitudes of human beings, though there may be great diversity in its impact, is the Socio-Cultural Environment. This environment encompasses the beliefs, values, norms, customs, and practices of people within a given geographic area. These cultural aspects deeply influence human behaviour, including consumer preferences, work attitudes, management styles, and interpersonal relations. Cultural diversity can result in significant differences in how these elements manifest in different regions or among different groups within the same society. Understanding the socio-cultural environment is crucial for businesses to tailor their products and marketing strategies to meet the unique cultural needs and expectations of their target markets.

23. (B): The liquidator, after realizing the assets of a company, should distribute the proceeds among the below-mentioned claimants in the following order: first, legal charges (*b*) must be addressed as these are fundamental to ensuring that the proceedings follow legal mandates and secure the assets involved. Next, the liquidator's remuneration and cost of expenses of winding up (*a*) are covered, recognizing the costs associated with administering the liquidation process itself. The claims of secured creditors (*c*) are prioritized following these, as secured creditors have claims that are backed by specific assets as collateral. Following this, preferential creditors and creditors secured by floating charges (*d*) are handled, with these creditors generally including employees and certain other preferential claims. Finally, unsecured creditors (*e*) receive any remaining funds, as their claims are not secured against the company's assets. This order ensures that the distribution is fair, respects legal priorities, and meets statutory obligations.

24. (D): Matching List-I with List-II based on the context of marketing and consumer behaviour:

(*a*) Buyer's Mind is matched with IV, "Black Box," which refers to the internal thought processes and decision-making mechanisms that are not visible but influence the buyer's decisions.

(*b*) Personal Factor is matched with III, "Life Style," as personal factors include individual characteristics that impact consumer behaviour, such as lifestyle, personality, economic status, and occupation.

(*c*) Psychological Factor is matched with II, "Motivation," since psychological factors driving consumer behaviour include motivation, perception, learning, beliefs, and attitudes.

(*d*) Reference Group is matched with I, "Members of Social-club," which fits as reference groups are groups that a person identifies with or aspires to join, influencing their purchasing behaviour and attitudes.

25. (C): The calculation for net profit when the profit volume ratio is 50% and the margin of safety is 40% with sales volume being ₹ 1,00,000 proceeds as follows:

The profit volume ratio indicates that for each unit of sale, 50% contributes to the profit. The margin of safety indicates that actual sales are 40% higher than what is needed to break even, which means actual sales cover all fixed costs and provide additional revenue that contributes entirely to profit.

1. **Calculate Break-Even Sales:** The margin of safety tells us that the actual sales are 40% above the break-even point. Thus, the break-even sales can be calculated as:

Break-Even Sales = Total Sales − (Margin of Safety × Total Sales)

Break-Even Sales = 1,00,000 − (0.40 × 1,00,000)
= 60,000

2. **Calculate Profit:** The net profit can then be derived from the difference between total sales and break-even sales, factoring in the profit volume ratio:

Net Profit = Profit Volume Ratio × (Total Sales − Break-Even Sales)

Net Profit = 0.50 × (1,00,000 − 60,000)
= 20,000

Hence, the net profit when the sales volume is ₹ 1,00,000, given a profit volume ratio of 50% and a margin of safety of 40%, is ₹ 20,000. This calculation shows how the margin of safety impacts profit by accounting for the additional sales over and above the break-even point.

26. (B): The elasticity of supply (Es) can be calculated using the point elasticity method from the given supply function

$$q = -100 + 10p.$$

When the price p is 15, we first calculate the quantity supplied q by substituting p into the supply function:

$$q = -100 + 10 \times 15$$
$$= -100 + 150 = 50$$

The elasticity of supply is then calculated using the formula:

$$\text{Es} = \frac{dq}{dp} \times \frac{p}{q}$$

Here, $\frac{dq}{dp}$ (the derivative of the supply function with respect to price) is 10, as given by the coefficient of p in the supply function. Thus, substituting the values, we have:

$$\text{Es} = 10 \times \frac{15}{50}$$
$$= 10 \times 0.3 = 3.0$$

Therefore, the elasticity of supply at a price of ₹ 15 is 3, indicating that a 1% increase in price leads to a 3% increase in the quantity supplied. This result aligns with option (B).

27. (C): The chronological order of the phases of the International Monetary System from old to new is:

(*b*) **Gold Specie Standard:** This was the earliest system where currencies were directly convertible into gold.

(*a*) **Gold Bullion Standard:** Under this system, currency was convertible into gold bullion, primarily for international trade payments, rather than domestic use.

(*d*) **Gold Exchange Standard:** Established during the interwar period, under this system, currencies were pegged to other currencies that were convertible into gold, rather than directly to gold itself.

(*e*) **Bretton Woods System:** Initiated post-World War II in 1944, this system involved fixed exchange rates where currencies were pegged to the U.S. dollar, which was convertible into gold.

(*c*) **Floating Exchange Rate:** Adopted after the collapse of the Bretton Woods System, currencies' values are determined by market forces without a peg to gold.

28. (D): A matrix organization violates the management principle of Unity of Command. In a traditional hierarchy, each employee reports to one manager, ensuring clear authority and responsibility lines. However, in a matrix structure, an employee typically reports to multiple managers – often a functional manager and a project or product manager. This dual-reporting structure can lead to conflicts in authority and confusion in responsibility, thus conflicting with the principle of Unity of Command, which states that an employee should receive orders from only one superior.

29. (D): The effect of exchange rate fluctuations on a firm's future costs and revenues is termed Operating Exposure. This type of exposure, also known as economic exposure, encompasses the impact of exchange rate changes on a company's future cash flows and overall financial health. It is broader than transaction or translation exposure, as it considers the long-term effect of changes in exchange rates on market demand, prices, sales, and costs. Operating exposure is strategic and can influence fundamental business decisions and competitive positioning globally.

30. (D): The Bretton Woods monetary system, established in 1944 at a conference in Bretton Woods, New Hampshire, was based on a fixed exchange rate system. Under this system, currencies were pegged to the U.S. dollar, which was, in turn, convertible into gold at a fixed rate of $35 per ounce. This system aimed to provide stability in international economic transactions and prevent competitive devaluations of currencies. The system lasted until 1971 when the United States unilaterally terminated convertibility of the dollar to gold, effectively leading to the system's collapse and the transition to floating exchange rates. This period from 1944 to 1971 marks the duration of the Bretton Woods system.

31. (C): A capitalist economy is characterized primarily by the lack of government interference in economic activities. The hallmark of capitalism is the operation of the free market where supply and demand determine prices and production levels without direct intervention by the state. Features that are common in a capitalist economy include the right of private property, where individuals and businesses have the right to own and use property as they see fit. Freedom of choice allows consumers to decide what to purchase based on their preferences and budgets, and a high level of competition exists because businesses are free to enter the market and compete for profit. In contrast, government interference is generally minimal except for regulations necessary to protect property rights and ensure a competitive market environment. Therefore, government interference is not a feature of a capitalist economy but rather a feature associated with mixed or command economies where the government has significant control over economic resources and decisions.

32. (C): Labour Mix Variance (LMV) measures the impact of a deviation in the labour mix used from the standard labour mix planned. The correct computation of Labour Mix Variance involves using the standard rate to quantify the financial impact of the difference between the revised standard time—time expected if the actual mix had been used at standard efficiency—and the actual time recorded. This formula highlights how much more or less cost has been incurred due to the variance in the labour mix, assuming that workers were paid at the standard rate. It helps in analyzing how the change in labour composition affects the production costs relative to the standard setup.

33. (D): Among the types of meetings listed, the Director's Meeting is typically the most frequently held. Director's meetings (or board meetings) are essential for the ongoing management of a company, where directors convene to make decisions about the strategic direction, management practices, and organizational policies of the company. These meetings occur regularly, often monthly or quarterly, to address immediate and strategic issues of the company. In contrast, Annual General Meetings (AGMs) are held once a year, Statutory Meetings are held once in the lifetime of a company shortly after incorporation, and Class Meetings are occasional, depending on specific needs related to shareholders of a particular class.

34. (D): The correct order for the steps in the sampling design process in a research setting involves:

(*b*) **Defining the target population:** The first step is to clearly define who or what will be studied, specifying the population that is relevant to the research objectives.

(*a*) **Determining the sampling frame:** This step involves identifying a list or database from which the sample will be drawn, which should ideally include all elements of the defined target population.

(*d*) **Selecting a sampling technique:** Based on the nature of the research and the characteristics of the population, an appropriate sampling method (random, stratified, cluster, etc.) is chosen to ensure representativeness and manageability.

(*e*) **Determining the number of elements to be included in the study:** Deciding how large the sample should be to achieve reliable results without being unnecessarily large, which could complicate or increase the cost of the research.

(*c*) **Executing the sampling process:** The final step is the actual process of selecting elements according to the defined plan and procedure, ensuring that the sample accurately represents the population.

35. (B): The correct sequence of steps in the research process involves:

(*a*) **Formulating a research question:** This is the initial step where a clear, focused question is developed, which guides the entire research.

(*b*) **Literature review:** Following the formulation of the research question, a thorough review of existing literature is conducted to gather information on what has previously been discovered about the topic, helping to refine the research question or hypothesis.

(*d*) **Developing a research plan:** This involves designing the methodology for the study, including how data will be collected, what instruments will be used, and how the data will be analyzed.

(*c*) **Collecting data:** After the plan is in place, the next step is to collect the data according to the methods specified in the research plan.

(*e*) **Interpreting the results:** Finally, the data collected is analyzed and interpreted to draw conclusions that address the research question, completing the process of research.

Each step builds upon the previous to ensure that the research is well-grounded, methodologically sound, and effectively addresses the initial research question.

36. (D): Systems selling refers to the practice of providing a total package of related goods and services designed to address a customer's needs comprehensively. This approach is particularly prevalent in industries where products and services are interrelated and where a solution-based approach enhances value for the customer. Systems selling enables businesses to solve complex customer problems through a seamless, integrated offering rather than requiring the customer to integrate products and services from multiple vendors. It's a strategic approach in sales that aligns closely with customers' broad needs, often leading to enhanced customer satisfaction and loyalty due to the convenience and tailored nature of the solutions provided.

37. (B): A distribution of data that has a long left tail is known as a negatively skewed distribution. In such a distribution, the bulk of the data is concentrated toward the right side of the scale, with the tail extending to the left. This implies that the mean and median of the dataset are less than the mode, and there are a number of outliers or lower values stretching out on the left side. Negatively skewed distributions are indicative of data scenarios where most occurrences are high but a few low values pull the mean down, often seen in scenarios where floor effects or lower bounds limit the data range.

38. (B): In the Nicosia Model of consumer behaviour, which is divided into four major fields, the third field is the "Act of purchase." This model outlines the decision-making process of consumers from the initial contact with a marketing message to the final purchase decision. The third field specifically deals with the actions taken by consumers towards purchasing, influenced by their attitudes and the evaluation of the product. This stage is critical as it translates consumer attitudes and intentions into actual purchasing behaviour, reflecting the culmination of the process begun with awareness and moving through interest and desire.

39. (D): Matching List-I with List-II based on marketing communication types: (*a*) Personal selling is matched with IV, "Two-way communication." Personal selling involves direct interactions between a salesperson and a customer, with immediate feedback and adaptability in communication, characteristic of a two-way communication process. (*b*) Advertising is matched with III, "Non-personal communication." Advertising typically involves mass media messages directed at a broad audience, not tailored to individuals, representing non-personal communication. (*c*) Transit advertising is matched with II, "Advertising within buses, railway compartments." This specific description matches the context of transit advertising, which occurs in and around public transportation. (*d*) Publicity is matched with I, "Commercially significant news." Publicity involves disseminating information to the public through media which can be seen as news items, not paid for directly by the beneficiary.

40. (A): Matching the Act/Institution with the correct Year of enactment or establishment: (*a*) Consumer Protection Act is correctly matched with IV, "2019." The latest iteration of the Consumer Protection Act in India, which overhauled previous legislation, was enacted in 2019. (*b*) FEMA (Foreign Exchange Management Act) is correctly matched with III, "1999." FEMA was enacted in 1999 to replace the Foreign Exchange Regulation Act (FERA), liberalizing restrictions on foreign exchange. (*c*) IMF (International Monetary Fund) is matched with II, "1945." The IMF was established in 1945 as part of the Bretton Woods Agreement to oversee the international monetary and financial system. (*d*) UNCTAD (United Nations Conference on Trade and Development) is matched with I, "1964." UNCTAD was founded in 1964 to support developing countries to participate more effectively in the global economy.

These answers provide a detailed explanation of each choice, emphasizing how they align with the respective options provided in the questionnaire.

41. (D): This question involves matching various techniques with their correct descriptions:

(*a*) Gordon Technique is matched with IV, "Steering a discussion to crystallise solutions." The Gordon Technique is often utilized to guide discussions toward clear and specific solutions in group settings, helping participants focus on problem-solving.

(*b*) Morphological Analysis is matched with III, "Listing of alternative solution to problems." This technique involves systematically exploring all possible solutions to a problem by examining multiple dimensions and combinations, often used in innovation and design.

(*c*) Built-in Tension is matched with I, "Teaching the importance of resolving matters." This technique is used to build awareness and emphasize the need for resolving issues, ensuring that conflicts or tensions are addressed constructively.

(*d*) Manodrama is matched with II, "Insight into a given interaction." Manodrama involves role-playing scenarios that provide deep insights into interpersonal dynamics and individual behaviours within those interactions.

42. (D): Transmission of shares occurs when the legal title to shares passes from one person to another without the action of the owner, usually due to statutory or automatic reasons. This can happen in scenarios such as:

(*b*) **Death:** Upon the death of a shareholder, the shares are transmitted to the heirs or legal representatives of the deceased.

(*c*) **Insolvency:** In the event of insolvency, the shares owned by the insolvent are transmitted to a trustee or similar entity managing the insolvent's assets. Transmission is distinct from the sale of shares, which is a voluntary action taken by the shareholder, and maturity is not applicable as shares do not have a maturity date like bonds or other fixed-income securities.

43. (B): The correct sequence of forums for appeal by an assessee under the Income Tax Act-1961 from the first appeal to the final appeal is:

(*d*) **Joint Commissioner:** The first level of appeal is usually before the Joint Commissioner or Commissioner (Appeals), where initial grievances regarding assessments are addressed.

(*c*) **Appellate Tribunal:** If the assessee is not satisfied with the decision of the Joint Commissioner, they may appeal to the Income Tax Appellate Tribunal, which is the second level of appeal.

(*b*) **High Court:** Further appeals can be made to the High Court if the matter involves a substantial question of law.

(*a*) **Supreme Court:** The final appeal can be made to the Supreme Court, which is the highest judicial authority, if the High Court certifies that the case is fit for appeal to the Supreme Court.

44. (B): To calculate the dividend per share for Rohtas Industries for the year 2024, we use the following data and a formula that integrates both the target payout ratio and the adjustment rate:

Earnings Per Share (EPS) for 2024: ₹ 3

Dividend Per Share (DPS) for 2023: ₹ 1.2

Target Payout Ratio: 0.6 (60% of EPS)

Adjustment Rate: 0.7

The dividend adjustment model applied is typically used to gradually shift the dividend payment towards a target payout ratio, reflecting a policy of stabilizing dividend payments. The formula to calculate the adjusted dividend per share for the next year is:

$$\text{Adjusted DPS}_{2024} = \text{DPS}_{2023} + \text{Adjustment Rate} \times (\text{Target Payout Ratio} \times \text{EPS}_{2024} - \text{DPS}_{2023})$$

Substituting the given values into the formula:

$$\begin{aligned}\text{Adjusted DPS}_{2024} &= 1.2 + 0.7 \times (0.6 \times 3 - 1.2)\\ &= 1.2 + 0.7 \times (1.8 - 1.2)\\ &= 1.2 + 0.7 \times 0.6\\ &= 1.2 + 0.42 = 1.62\end{aligned}$$

Therefore, the calculated dividend per share for Rohtas Industries for the year 2024, using the provided EPS for 2024, the previous year's DPS, the target payout ratio, and the adjustment rate, is ₹ 1.62. This calculation shows a controlled approach to increasing the dividend, aligning it closer to the target payout ratio while considering the previous year's dividend level.

45. (D): The correct sequence for the steps involved in the process of an Initial Public Offering (IPO) issue is:

(*b*) **Hiring an underwriter:** The first step involves selecting an underwriting firm that will help in preparing the IPO, including drafting the prospectus and performing due diligence.

(*c*) **Registration for IPO:** Once the underwriter is hired, the company files a registration statement with the Securities and Exchange Board of India (SEBI), which includes all pertinent financial and business information.

(*a*) **Verification by SEBI:** After registration, SEBI reviews the submitted documents to ensure compliance with regulations and to protect investor interests.

(*d*) **Pricing of IPO:** The price band of the IPO is determined based on the valuation of the company, market conditions, and investor interest.

(*e*) **Allotment of shares:** Finally, shares are allotted to investors, and the company receives the funds raised from the IPO. This step marks the completion of the IPO process and the beginning of the company's life as a publicly-traded entity.

46. (A): A key precondition for applying the Chi-square test is that the data must be presented in frequency counts rather than in percentages, ratios, or other transformed values. The Chi-square test is a statistical test commonly used to compare observed data with data we would expect to obtain according to a specific hypothesis. The test's validity depends on the fact that the data are frequencies of occurrences in different categories, allowing it to measure how the observed frequencies deviate from the expected frequencies. Using percentages or ratios instead of actual counts can lead to inaccuracies in the calculation of the Chi-square statistic because the original data scale is altered, potentially affecting the sum of squared differences crucial for the test's computation.

47. (D): According to section-17 of the Income Tax Act 1961, 'salary' includes several components that constitute the total remuneration received by an employee. These components include:

(*a*) **Wages:** Basic day-to-day earnings paid to an employee.

(*b*) **Perquisite:** Benefits or perks provided by the employer that are above and beyond the wages or salaries. These could be in various forms like rent-free accommodation, cars, etc.

(*c*) **Profits in lieu of salary:** This includes any compensation due to or received by an employer from an employer or former employer, if not in pursuance of his employment.

(*d*) **Compensation on termination of employment:** This includes any payments due to termination, such as severance pay or compensation for loss of office. These elements collectively make up what is legally recognized as salary for tax purposes under the Income Tax Act, covering not only the direct payments but also additional benefits and compensations.

48. (A): The assumptions underlying the Modigliani-Miller (MM) Theory of capital structure are critical to understanding their conclusions about the irrelevance of capital structure in a perfect market. The assumptions include:

(*a*) **Perfect capital market:** This implies that there are no transaction costs, all information is freely available to all market participants, and there are no restrictions on the buying or selling of securities.

(*c*) **Absence of taxes:** The MM theory assumes that there are no tax advantages to debt over equity financing.

(*e*) **Equivalent risk class:** Companies are compared only if they are in equivalent risk classes or have business risks that are similar. These assumptions ensure that the theory's core idea, that the value of a firm is independent of its capital structure, holds under ideal conditions. Assumptions about heterogeneous expectations, 100% dividend payout do not directly support the foundational ideas of MM theory.

49. (D): According to Proposition II of the Modigliani-Miller theory of capital structure, the expected rate of return on equity (cost of equity) increases linearly as financial leverage (debt/equity ratio) increases. This relationship reflects the higher risk perceived by shareholders as more debt is used to finance the firm's operations, requiring a higher return to compensate for the increased risk. This theory essentially holds that while leverage does not change the total value of the firm (Proposition I), it does affect the cost of equity.

50. (B): The functional structure is an organizational design that groups together employees who perform similar tasks or processes. This structure is known for promoting control and coordination within departments due to the similarity in tasks being performed. Each department specializes in a particular function, such as marketing, finance, or production, which allows for efficiencies and expertise development specific to each function. This organizational structure enhances the ability to monitor and direct efforts within a department effectively, leading to improved performance in specific functional areas.

51. (D): The term "Espirit De Corps" refers to the management principle that emphasizes promoting a team spirit of unity and harmony among employees. This principle is based on fostering a positive work environment where teamwork and mutual respect are highly valued. Encouraging espirit de corps helps in building strong relationships among employees, which is crucial for maintaining morale, enhancing cooperation, and achieving organizational goals effectively. By promoting a sense of solidarity, management can ensure that employees feel part of a cohesive group, leading to better communication, reduced conflicts, and increased productivity.

52. (D): Equity shareholders typically enjoy several fundamental rights associated with their investment in a company. These rights include:

(*a*) **Right to Income:** Equity shareholders have the right to share in the profits of the company, typically in the form of dividends.

(*c*) **Right to Control:** Equity shareholders often have voting rights that allow them to influence the management and major decisions of the company, such as electing directors.

(*d*) **Right to Liquidation:** In the event of the company's liquidation, after settling all debts, equity shareholders have a claim over the remaining assets of the company.

(*e*) **Pre-emptive Rights:** Shareholders may have pre-emptive rights to purchase new shares issued by the company, which helps them maintain their proportional ownership. This combination of rights ensures that equity shareholders can benefit financially from the company's success, participate in its governance, and protect their investment interests.

53. (A): Tax treaties are international agreements designed to avoid double taxation and prevent tax evasion, enhancing economic cooperation between countries. The most commonly referenced models for these treaties are:

(*a*) **OECD Model Tax Convention:** Developed by the Organisation for Economic Co-operation and Development, this model serves as a framework for bilateral tax treaties between developed nations, aiming to promote consistent and fair tax practices.

(*b*) **UN Model Tax Convention:** This model, provided by the United Nations, is similar to the OECD's but includes provisions that are particularly relevant to developing countries, recognizing their specific needs and economic circumstances. Both these models are influential in shaping tax treaties worldwide, providing a basis for negotiations and helping countries to draft agreements that reflect their economic and fiscal environments.

54. (D): Transformational appeal in advertising refers to a technique that focuses on the non-product related benefits or images associated with a product or service, which attempts to evoke emotional responses from consumers. This type of appeal seeks to transform the consumer's perception by associating the product with desirable qualities or lifestyles, suggesting that using the product will enhance their life in some way. Transformational appeals are often used in branding and marketing strategies to create a strong, memorable image that resonates on an emotional level, influencing consumer behaviour more deeply than just the functional attributes of the product.

55. (B)

56. (D): Foreign Direct Investment (FDI) involves investment made by a company or individual in one country in business interests located in another country, typically in the form of either establishing business operations or acquiring business assets in the foreign country. The types of investments that are commonly included in FDI are:

(*a*) **Wholly owned subsidiary:** This involves a parent company owning 100% of the company's stock, thereby fully controlling the subsidiary in another country.

(*b*) **Joint venture:** Here, the foreign investor partners with local companies or other foreign entities to create a new company together, sharing resources, risks, and profits.

(*d*) **Acquisition:** This includes acquiring a controlling interest in a foreign company, where the foreign investor buys enough shares in a foreign company to manage and control it.

Investments such as Global Depository Receipts (GDR) (*c*) and investments by Foreign Institutional Investors (FIIs) (*e*) are generally classified under portfolio investments rather than direct investments because they do not confer management control.

57. (C): To calculate the cross-price elasticity of tea with respect to the price of coffee, we use the formula for cross-price elasticity of demand, which is the percentage change in quantity demanded of one good divided by the percentage change in price of another good. The formula and values are:

Initial price of coffee = ₹ 25 per kg

Final price of coffee = ₹ 35 per kg

Initial quantity demanded of tea = 5 kg

Final quantity demanded of tea = 8 kg

Cross Price Elasticity

$$= \frac{\text{Change in Quantity of Tea/Initial Quantity of Tea}}{\text{Change in Price of Cofee/Initial Price of Coffee}}$$

Change in Quantity of Tea = 8 – 5 = 3

Percentage Change in Quantity of Tea

$$= \frac{3}{5} = 0.6$$

Change in Price of Coffee

= 35 – 25 = 10

Percentage Change in Price of Coffee

$$= \frac{10}{25} = 0.4$$

$$\text{Cross Price Elasticity} = \frac{0.6}{0.4} = 1.5$$

Thus, the cross-price elasticity of tea with respect to coffee is 1.5, indicating that a 1% increase in the price of coffee results in a 1.5% increase in the quantity demanded of tea.

58. (B): According to the Dividend Growth Model (also known as the Gordon Growth Model), the cost of equity can be estimated using the dividend yield plus the expected growth rate in dividends. This model posits that the current price of a stock is equal to the present value of all future dividends it will pay, which are assumed to grow at a constant rate indefinitely. The formula to estimate the cost of equity is:

$$r = \frac{D_1}{P_0} + g$$

Where r is the cost of equity, D_1 is the expected dividend per share one year from now, P_0 is the current price per share, and g is the growth rate in dividends. This formula captures both the immediate income from dividends relative to the price of the stock (dividend yield) and the value of future growth in these dividends.

59. (C)

60. (D): In the context of an organization, the process of making subordinates act in a desired manner to achieve certain organizational goals is known as motivation. Motivation involves the set of processes that arouse, direct, and maintain human behaviour towards attaining some goal. It's essential for managers to understand what drives their employees to perform effectively and to use this knowledge to encourage them to work towards the organization's objectives. Motivation can stem from internal factors like personal satisfaction and achievement or from external factors such as incentives, recognition, and rewards. Effective motivation strategies can enhance productivity, improve workplace morale, and reduce turnover, thereby contributing significantly to the success of the organization.

61. (B): Regarding the chi-square test and chi-square distribution:

(*a*) **Chi-square test is a non-parametric test:** True, as it does not assume a normal distribution of the data. It is used for categorical data to determine if there are significant associations between variables.

(*c*) **Chi-square distribution can never be negative:** True, as the chi-square distribution is based on squared values, it cannot result in negative numbers.

(*e*) **Chi-square distribution is a function of its degree of freedom:** True, the shape of the chi-square distribution is determined by the degrees of freedom associated with the data.

These points reflect the characteristics and applications of the chi-square test and its distribution in statistical analysis. Misconceptions about the developer of the test (not Spearman) and the nature of the distribution (not discrete but continuous on the positive side) are common and should be clarified.

62. (D): The general considerations applicable to tax planning in the field of business deductions revolve around:

(*a*) **Allowability:** Determining which expenses are legally deductible according to tax regulations.

(*b*) **Year of allowability:** Identifying the correct tax year in which a deduction should be claimed to optimize tax benefits.

(*c*) **Extent of allowability:** Calculating how much of an expense can be deducted, as some expenses may be only partially deductible.

(*d*) **Carry forward to future years:** Understanding whether unused deductions can be carried forward to future tax years, which is important for strategic tax planning.

These considerations are crucial for ensuring that deductions are maximized legally and effectively, thus reducing the overall tax liability for a business while complying with tax laws.

63. (C): Matching the organizational principles with their descriptions:

(*a*) Unity of Command (IV): Subordinates report to only one boss, ensuring clear directives and responsibility.

(*b*) Unity of Direction (III): Functions have only one plan and one boss, aligning all activities under a single plan and leadership to achieve organizational goals.

(*c*) Scalar Chain (II): Hierarchical, formalized communication channel, signifying a clear and formal line of authority within the organization.

(*d*) Espirit de Corps (I): Maintaining high morale among employees is imperative, as it fosters teamwork and unity, enhancing overall productivity and satisfaction.

This correct matching underscores the fundamental principles of organizational structure that facilitate effective management and communication within companies.

64. (C): The correct sequence for the incorporation of a new Limited Liability Partnership (LLP) is as follows:

(*b*) **Procure Digital Signature Certificate:** The first step is to procure Digital Signature Certificates (DSCs) for all the designated partners of the LLP. DSCs are required for digitally signing the incorporation forms and other submissions to the Registrar of Companies (ROC).

(*a*) **Reserve LLP Name:** After obtaining DSCs, the next step is to reserve a unique name for the LLP. An application is submitted to the ROC through the LLP portal, ensuring that the name complies with naming guidelines and is not similar to any existing company or LLP.

(*c*) **Prepare Documents for Incorporation of LLP:** Once the name is approved, necessary documents for incorporation are prepared. These include forms like Form 2 (Incorporation application), details of the registered office, and the consent of designated partners.

(*d*) **LLP Incorporation and DIN Application:** The incorporation application is filed with the ROC along with a request for the allotment of Director Identification Numbers (DINs) for the designated partners if they do not already have one.

(*f*) **Apply for PAN and TAN:** After incorporation, the next step is to apply for a Permanent Account Number (PAN) and Tax Deduction and Collection Account Number (TAN) for the LLP, as these are mandatory for financial and taxation purposes.

(*e*) **Drafting and Filing LLP Agreement:** The final step involves drafting the LLP Agreement, which outlines the mutual rights, duties, and obligations of the partners. This agreement is required to be filed with the ROC within 30 days of incorporation.

By following this sequence, the LLP can be incorporated efficiently while meeting all legal and procedural requirements in the correct order.

65. (A): The correct sequence of the capital budgeting process is:

(*d*) **Identification of Investment opportunities:** Recognizing and evaluating potential investment opportunities that could benefit the business.

(*c*) **Assembling of Investment proposals:** Gathering detailed proposals for identified investment opportunities.

(*e*) **Decision Making:** Making decisions based on the analysis of various investment proposals.

(*a*) **Preparation of Capital Budget and Appropriation:** Formulating a budget that allocates resources for the approved investments.

(*b*) **Performance Review:** Monitoring and evaluating the performance of the investments against the expected outcomes.

This sequence ensures a comprehensive approach to capital budgeting, from opportunity identification to post-implementation review, aiming to maximize returns and align investments with strategic objectives.

66. (D): The correct matching of List-I with List-II is as follows:

(*a*) Organisational Structure (IV): This refers to the framework within which managerial and operating tasks are operated. It defines the hierarchy, roles, and responsibilities within an organization and provides a clear structure for operational efficiency.

(*b*) Span of Management (III): This relates to the number of subordinates under a supervisor. It helps determine the extent of managerial control and influences the efficiency of communication and decision-making.

(*c*) Divisional Structure (II): This structure groups activities on the basis of products, services, or markets. It ensures better management of diverse product lines or markets by assigning separate divisions for each.

(*d*) Decentralisation (I): Refers to the delegation of authority throughout the organization. It involves distributing decision-making authority to lower levels, empowering subordinates to make decisions independently.

This matching emphasizes the organizational principles that govern efficient management and operations.

67. (B): The provisions for double taxation relief in India are contained in the following sections of the Income-Tax Act, 1961:

(*b*) **Section 90:** This section deals with agreements with foreign countries or specified territories to grant relief from double taxation. It applies to Indian residents who have earned income in a country with which India has a Double Taxation Avoidance Agreement (DTAA).

(*c*) **Section 91:** This section provides unilateral relief from double taxation for residents of India who have earned income in a country that does not have a DTAA with India.

These sections ensure that Indian residents are not taxed twice on the same income earned in foreign countries.

68. (D): In performance appraisal, an assessment should focus on:

(*b*) **Individual traits:** Evaluating inherent characteristics like attitude, integrity, and reliability.

(*c*) **Behaviours exhibited by the assessee:** Observing and measuring job-related behaviours, which reflect how well the employee performs assigned tasks.

(*d*) **Knowledge/skills possessed:** Assessing the employee's expertise and proficiency required for the job.

(*e*) **Results achieved:** Evaluating tangible outcomes and goals accomplished by the employee.

These factors ensure a holistic and fair appraisal process, considering both qualitative and quantitative aspects of employee performance.

69. (C): The correct sequence of stages in an investigation is:

(*b*) **Obtain instructions from the client and prepare terms of reference:** Establishing the scope, objectives, and framework of the investigation with the client.

(*a*) **Plan work to be done and timing:** Designing a detailed plan for the investigation, including a timeline and resource allocation.

(*d*) **Collect necessary information and documents:** Gathering all relevant data and evidence needed for the analysis.

(*c*) **Make necessary calculations to eliminate inconsistencies:** Analyzing the data and resolving discrepancies for accurate findings.

(*e*) **Formulate conclusions/analysis of findings:** Drawing conclusions and presenting recommendations based on the analysis.

This logical order ensures an organized and systematic approach to investigations.

70. (A): The EPRG (Ethnocentric, Polycentric, Regiocentric, and Geocentric) framework of internationalization includes:

(*b*) **Ethnocentrism:** Focuses on home-country management and practices being applied to international operations.

(*c*) **Polycentrism:** Emphasizes tailoring operations to meet the specific needs of host countries.

(*d*) **Regiocentrism:** Involves viewing markets and operations from a regional perspective, grouping countries into regions.

(*e*) **Geocentrism:** Adopts a global perspective, integrating home and host country practices for worldwide efficiency.

These orientations guide firms in their approach to international business strategy and market entry.

71. (B): The probability that a household has either a television or a refrigerator is calculated using the formula for the union of two events in probability:

$$P(T \cup R) = P(T) + P(R) - P(T \cap R)$$

Where:

$P(T)$ = Probability of having a television $= 0.60$

$P(R)$ = Probability of having a refrigerator $= 0.65$

$P(T \cap R)$ = Probability of having both $= 0.35$

Substituting the values:

$$P(T \cup R) = 0.60 + 0.65 - 0.35 = 0.90$$

Thus, the probability that a randomly selected household has either a television or a refrigerator is 0.90, or 90%.

72. **(C):** Capital budgeting techniques that follow the discounting criteria consider the time value of money. These techniques are:

(*a*) **Net Present Value (NPV):** It calculates the difference between the present value of cash inflows and outflows, taking the time value of money into account.

(*b*) **Benefit-Cost Ratio (BCR):** Also called profitability index, it calculates the ratio of the present value of benefits to the present value of costs, using discounting.

(*d*) **Internal Rate of Return (IRR):** This method calculates the discount rate at which the net present value of cash flows equals zero, considering time value.

Techniques such as Accounting Rate of Return (*c*) and Payback Period (*e*) do not use discounting and are therefore excluded.

73. **(D):** Technology is **not** considered as a part of the micro-environment. The micro-environment comprises factors that are close to the company and directly affect its ability to serve customers, including:

Suppliers: Provide inputs for production.

Customers: Form the target market for the company's goods or services.

Competitors: Entities competing for the same market. Technology, on the other hand, is part of the macro-environment, influencing industries broadly and affecting operations, innovation, and productivity across multiple sectors.

74. **(B):** The different types of dumping in international trade are:

(*a*) **Persistent Dumping:** Continuous selling of goods in a foreign market at lower prices than in the home market to establish or maintain market dominance.

(*b*) **Predatory Dumping:** Selling goods at very low prices to eliminate competition and gain monopoly power in the foreign market.

(*c*) **Sporadic Dumping:** Selling surplus goods at reduced prices in a foreign market to avoid losses or stockpiling.

"Nomadic dumping" is not a recognized type of dumping and is therefore excluded.

75. **(B):** A holder in due course enjoys significant privileges under the Negotiable Instruments Act. The most important privilege is that the instrument in their possession is cleansed of all prior defects in title or irregularities, ensuring its validity and enforceability. This means:

The holder in due course can claim the amount due under the instrument without being affected by any disputes, fraud, or irregularities that may have existed in prior transactions.

This privilege protects the holder and ensures smooth transferability of negotiable instruments in financial transactions.

Thus, the holder in due course has a legally protected right to enforce the instrument without concerns about prior defects.

76. (A): The correct matching of List-I with List-II is as follows:

(*a*) Joint occurrence of Events (III): Compound Event refers to the occurrence of multiple events together, such as the probability of one or more events occurring simultaneously.

(*b*) Outcome of an experiment consisting of all possible events (I): Collective Exhaustive Events include all possible outcomes of an experiment, ensuring that no possibility is excluded.

(*c*) One of the events cannot be expected to occur in preference over the other (II): Equally Likely Events imply that all events have the same probability of occurring.

(*d*) The occurrence of one event implies that the other cannot occur (IV): Mutually Exclusive Events occur when the occurrence of one event precludes the occurrence of the other.

77. (D): A petition for winding up of a company can be filed by:

(*a*) **Shareholders:** Members of the company have the right to petition for winding up under specific circumstances, such as the company being unable to carry out its objectives.

(*b*) **Creditors or prospective creditors:** They can file a petition if the company is unable to pay its debts or fulfill obligations, thereby jeopardizing creditors' interests.

(*d*) **The person authorized by the central government:** Under certain regulatory or compliance violations, an authorized representative of the government may petition for winding up to safeguard public interest.

Legal heirs (*c*) cannot independently file for winding up unless they represent a shareholder or creditor.

78. (A): The correct sequence for the anti-dumping process is:

(*b*) **Preliminary Screening:** Initial evaluation to assess the legitimacy of the complaint and whether the information provided meets the necessary criteria for further investigation.

(*c*) **Rejection under deminimis, unsubstantiated information, etc.:** If the evidence does not meet the required threshold, the case may be rejected at this stage.

(*a*) **Initiation:** If the preliminary screening supports the case, formal anti-dumping proceedings are initiated.

(*d*) **Exporting country allowed to modify practice:** Before concluding, the exporting country is given an opportunity to adjust its trade practices.

(*e*) **Preliminary findings followed by final findings and measures:** A detailed investigation leads to preliminary findings, and based on further review, final measures are implemented to counteract dumping.

79. (B): To calculate the Total Asset Turnover:

$$\text{ROA} = \text{Profit Margin} \times \text{Total Asset Turnover}$$

Given

$$\text{ROA} = 10\% = 0.10$$

$$\text{Profit Margin} = 2\% = 0.02$$

Rearranging the formula:

Total Asset Turnover

$$= \frac{\text{ROA}}{\text{Profit Margin}}$$

$$= \frac{0.10}{0.02} = 5$$

Thus, the Total Asset Turnover is 5 (or 500%), indicating that for every unit of assets, the company generates five times the revenue.

80. (C): The correct matching of List-I with List-II is:

(*a*) Informal Organisation (II): Refers to the network of social relationships that arise spontaneously among employees at the workplace, outside the formal structure.

(*b*) Formal Organisation (IV): Specifies clearly the boundaries of authority and responsibility within the organization, based on hierarchical structures.

(*c*) Divisional Structure (III): This organizational structure comprises separate business units or divisions that focus on distinct product lines, markets, or geographies.

(*d*) Functional Structure (I): Groups jobs of similar nature together, focusing on specialized functions like marketing, finance, or production.

This matching emphasizes how organizational types and structures cater to different management needs and operational efficiencies.

81. (C): Product-form pricing is a pricing strategy where a company prices different versions or forms of the same product differently, not based on cost differences but on the perceived value of the product form.

In this case, the company sells 1 litre of mineral water for ₹ 20 and 100 ml of the same water in a moisturizer spray for ₹ 50. The significant price difference arises not from the cost of production but from the perception of the product's utility, convenience, and additional packaging in the moisturizer spray form.

This practice highlights how companies leverage the perceived value of different product forms to set varied price points, catering to different customer needs or use cases.

82. (C): The following are schemes promoted by NABARD (National Bank for Agriculture and Rural Development):

(*a*) **Kisan Credit Card (KCC):** A scheme that provides timely and adequate credit to farmers for their agricultural and other needs.

(*b*) **Capital Investment Subsidy Scheme:** Encourages agricultural and rural development by supporting capital investments in infrastructure and technology.

(*d*) **Rural Innovation Fund:** Focuses on fostering innovation in rural areas to address unique challenges in agriculture, rural development, and livelihoods.

(*e*) **Tribal Development Fund:** Provides financial assistance to tribal communities for sustainable development and empowerment.

The Special Economic Zone (SEZ) Scheme (*c*) is not promoted by NABARD; it is primarily overseen by the Ministry of Commerce and Industry.

83. (D): The principal functions of UNCTAD (United Nations Conference on Trade and Development) include:

(*a*) **To promote international trade with a view to accelerating economic development:** UNCTAD facilitates trade, especially for developing countries, to boost their economic growth.

(*c*) **To negotiate multinational trade agreements:** UNCTAD provides a platform for negotiating trade agreements that align with global trade principles while addressing developing countries' needs.

(*d*) **To make proposals for putting its principles and policies into effect:** It develops actionable recommendations to implement its policies and principles for trade and development.

Promoting private enterprises (*b*) is not a core function of UNCTAD, as its focus is on facilitating trade and development through international cooperation.

84. (C): The correct sequence of the securitization process is:

(*d*) **Seasoning:** Initial assessment of the assets to ensure that they are seasoned, meaning they have performed consistently over a period of time.

(*c*) **Credit Enhancement:** Measures taken to improve the creditworthiness of the securitized assets, such as guarantees or reserve funds.

(*a*) **Forming SPV:** Creating a Special Purpose Vehicle (SPV) to handle the securitized assets, isolating them from the originating entity's risks.

(*b*) **Transfer to SPV:** The underlying assets are transferred to the SPV to facilitate securitization.

(*e*) **Issuance of Securities:** The SPV issues securities backed by the underlying assets to investors, generating liquidity for the originating entity.

This process ensures the efficient conversion of assets into tradable securities.

85. (B): 720-degree feedback is an advanced form of performance evaluation where the assessment is conducted not only internally (within the organization) but also externally (from groups outside the organization). This approach includes feedback from:

Internal Sources: Supervisors, peers, subordinates, and the employee themselves.

External Sources: Customers, suppliers, and other stakeholders who interact with the employee.

This comprehensive method provides a holistic view of the employee's performance, considering multiple perspectives. It is particularly useful for leadership roles or roles requiring significant external interaction, enabling organizations to develop employees effectively while addressing all stakeholder expectations.

86. (C): The correct matching of List-I with List-II is:

(*a*) Hedger (II): Hedgers aim to reduce investment risk by using financial instruments like derivatives to offset potential losses in the market. For example, farmers hedge the prices of their crops to protect against fluctuations.

(*b*) Speculator (III): Speculators willingly take increased risk by betting on price changes in financial markets to earn profits. They play a significant role in providing liquidity to the market.

(*c*) Arbitrageur (IV): Arbitrageurs exploit price mismatches in two or more markets by buying in one market and selling in another for a profit, helping in price correction across markets.

(*d*) Scalper (I): Scalpers engage in high-frequency trading, buying and selling shares quickly to earn small profits on each trade. They rely on market volatility for their gains.

87. (C): To calculate the cost of equity under the Net Operating Income (NOI) approach, the formula used is:

$$k_e = k_o + (k_o - k_d) \times \frac{D}{E}$$

Where:

k_e : Cost of equity (to be calculated)

k_o : Overall cost of capital = 12% = 0.12

k_d : Cost of debt = 9% = 0.09

$\frac{D}{E}$: Debt-Equity Ratio = 0.8

Substitute the values:

$$k_e = 0.12 + (0.12 - 0.09) \times 0.8$$
$$k_e = 0.12 + 0.03 \times 0.8$$
$$k_e = 0.12 + 0.024$$
$$= 0.144 = 14.4\%$$

Thus, the cost of equity is 14.4%.

88. (*)

89. (C): Mahatma Gandhi defined Corporate Social Responsibility (CSR) as: "Wealth created from society has to be ploughed back into society." This definition emphasizes the ethical responsibility of businesses to give back to society. Gandhi advocated for trusteeship, where businesses act as trustees of societal wealth, promoting equitable distribution and welfare. This aligns CSR with the concept of serving society's needs and enhancing overall development, particularly for the disadvantaged sections.

90. (C): Price adaptation strategies are techniques that adjust prices based on market conditions, customer segments, or geographical locations. The strategies include:

(*a*) **Price discounts and allowances:** These offer price reductions to incentivize purchases or clear inventory.

(*c*) **Geographical pricing:** Adjusting prices based on geographical factors like transportation costs or regional market conditions.

(*d*) **Differentiated pricing:** Charging different prices to different customer groups or markets based on perceived value or demand elasticity.

"Target return pricing (*b*)" and "Going rate pricing (*e*)" are not price adaptation strategies but belong to pricing objectives and competition-based pricing, respectively.

91. (C): Solar Tech Ltd. achieved a 25% market share in India primarily due to its strategic partnerships with a local firm and product customization tailored to meet Indian regulatory standards and climatic conditions. The partnership allowed Solar Tech Ltd. to leverage the local firm's market knowledge and distribution network, ensuring effective penetration into the Indian market. Additionally, customizing products to meet specific Indian requirements helped the company gain a competitive edge. These strategies ensured that Solar Tech Ltd. addressed the unique needs of the Indian market while overcoming initial entry challenges. This combination of approaches enabled the company to rapidly capture a significant share of the market within just two years.

92. (B): Solar Tech Ltd. initially entered the Indian market by establishing a joint venture with a local firm. This approach was strategic as it allowed the company to benefit from the local partner's market knowledge and established distribution network. By collaborating with a local firm, Solar Tech Ltd. was able to navigate the complexities of the Indian market, including regulatory requirements and cultural differences, more effectively than if it had chosen to enter the market independently. This partnership was instrumental in ensuring a smooth market entry and laid the foundation for the company's success in India.

93. (C): Despite its success in achieving a 25% market share, Solar Tech Ltd. faced ongoing issues with supply chain disruptions. These disruptions likely impacted the company's ability to maintain a consistent flow of raw materials and deliver products on time. In the renewable energy sector, efficient supply chain management is critical due to the high demand for timely installation and operational readiness. Additionally, supply chain challenges can arise from global uncertainties, such as fluctuating raw material prices or geopolitical factors, further affecting the company's operations and competitiveness.

94. (B): Solar Tech Ltd. chose to expand its business to the Indian market due to favourable renewable energy policies and growing demand for sustainable energy solutions in India. The Indian government has actively promoted renewable energy through initiatives and incentives, creating a conducive environment for companies like Solar Tech Ltd. Additionally, the rising awareness of sustainable energy among Indian consumers and the need for alternative energy sources due to environmental concerns made India an attractive market for Solar Tech Ltd. to counteract stagnation in its domestic market.

95. (D): Solar Tech Ltd. faced significant challenges in the Indian market, including regulatory complexities and cultural differences. Navigating India's regulatory environment required understanding and complying with local laws, policies, and standards, which can be complex and time-consuming for foreign companies. Additionally, cultural differences posed challenges in understanding consumer behaviour, business practices, and communication styles. By addressing these issues effectively, Solar Tech Ltd. was able to establish itself successfully, but these challenges required continuous effort and adaptation to sustain its operations in the Indian market.

96. (D): The value of sales is calculated using the Total Assets Turnover ratio:

- Sales = Total Assets Turnover × Total Assets

Where:

Total Assets Turnover = 2

Total Assets = ₹ 1,60,000

(calculated as Owner's Equity + Total Debt)

Sales = 2 × 1,60,000

= ₹ 3,20,000

Thus, the value of sales is ₹ 3,20,000.

97. (B): The value of Fixed Assets is calculated using the Fixed Assets to Owner's Equity Ratio:

Fixed Assets = Fixed Assets to Owner's Equity Ratio × Owner's Equity

Where:

Fixed Assets to Owner's Equity Ratio = 0.60

Owner's Equity = ₹ 1,00,000

Fixed Assets = 0.60 × 1,00,000

= ₹ 60,000

Thus, the value of fixed assets is ₹ 60,000.

98. (A): The value of inventory is calculated using the Inventory Turnover Ratio:

$$\text{Inventory} = \frac{\text{Sales}}{\text{Inventory Turnover}}$$

Where:

Sales = ₹ 3,20,000

Inventory Turnover = 8

$$\text{Inventory} = \frac{3,20,000}{8}$$

= ₹ 40,000

Thus, the value of inventory is ₹ 40,000.

99. (D): The value of Total Assets is calculated as:

Total Assets = Owner's Equity + Total Debt

Where:

Owner's Equity = ₹ 1,00,000

Total Debt = ₹ 60,000

(Calculated as Total Debt of Owner's Equity Ratio × Owner's Equity)

Total Assets = 1,00,000 + 60,000

= ₹ 1,60,000

Thus, the value of total assets is ₹ 1,60,000.

100. (C): The value of Long-Term Debt is calculated as:

Long-Term Debt = Total Debt - Current Debt

Where:

Total Debt = ₹ 60,000

Current Debt = Current Debt to Total Debt Ratio × Total Debt

= 0.40 × ₹ 60,000

= ₹ 24,000

Long-Term Debt = 60,000 - 24,000

= ₹ 36000

Thus, the value of long-term debt is ₹ 36,000.

YOUR SPACE

Previous Years' Paper

National Testing Agency (NTA)

UGC-NET Junior Research Fellowship & Assistant Professor Eligibility Exam

COMMERCE, December-2023

(Exam held on 07-12-2023)

PAPER-II

1. Match List-I with List-II.

List-I (Bond rates and risk)	List-II (Description)
(*a*) Coupon rate	I. The interest rate required in the market on a bond
(*b*) Yield to maturity	II. It is obtained by dividing annual coupon (stated interest payment) by the bond price
(*c*) Interest rate risk	III. It germinates and originates from fluctuating interest rates
(*d*) Current (bond) yield	IV. The annual coupon (stated interest payment) divided by the face value of a bond

Choose the correct answer from the option given below:

	(*a*)	(*b*)	(*c*)	(*d*)
A.	IV	I	III	II
B.	II	III	I	IV
C.	III	II	IV	I
D.	I	III	II	IV

2. In a certain population, 22% of people are smokers, 57% of people are males and 12% males are smokers. If a person is chosen at random from the population, what is that probability that selected person is either a male or a smoker?

A. 0.79 B. 0.22
C. 0.45 D. 0.67

3. Which of the following are deemed to be dividend for the purpose of computing income chargeable under the head, Income from other sources, as per the Income Tax Act, 1961?

(*a*) Payment on buy-back of shares
(*b*) Payment to shareholders on reduction of capital
(*c*) Distribution of debentures to shareholders
(*d*) Loan granted to shareholders in the ordinary course of business
(*e*) Loan granted to shareholders by a closely held company

Choose the correct answer from the options given below:

A. (*b*) and (*c*) only
B. (*b*), (*c*) and (*e*) only
C. (*a*), (*b*) and (*c*) only
D. (*a*) and (*c*) only

4. Which of the following managerial actions are followed to reduce resistance to change?

(*a*) Education and communication are strong tools for resistance to change
(*b*) Allows participation to those who oppose a change to participate in decision making
(*c*) Negotiation may become vital when resistance comes from a powerful source
(*d*) Employee counseling does not serve the purpose
(*e*) Coercion can be used to get support easily

Choose the correct answer from the options given below:

A. (*a*), (*b*) and (*c*) only
B. (*b*), (*c*) and (*d*) only
C. (*b*), (*c*) and (*e*) only
D. (*a*), (*c*) and (*d*) only

5. As per the sub-section (8A) of Section 139 of the Income Tax Act, a person may furnish an updated return of his income for the previous year relevant to such assessment year, within ________ from the end of assessment year?

A. 6 months B. 12 months
C. 24 months D. 36 months

6. Which of the following frameworks is considered as the Open International Standard for Digital Business Reporting?

A. CSR reporting B. TBL reporting
C. XBRL reporting D. PPP reporting

7. The exporting firm is termed 'rider' where the other firm with an established distribution channel in the target country is termed as 'Carrier'.

This phenomenon is known as:

A. Counter Trade B. Barter
C. Piggy Backing D. Switch Trading

8. Which one of the following concepts measures the amount of capital that the firm can give up by using one additional unit of labour and still remain on the same isoquant?

A. Diminishing Marginal Rate of Substitution
B. Economic Trade-off Region
C. Diminishing Marginal Rate of Technical Substitution
D. Diminishing Marginal Utility

9. Match List-I with List-II.

List-I (Types of Effect)	**List-II (Description)**
(*a*) Veblen effect	I. Conspicuous consumption
(*b*) Snob effect	II. Reduction in relative price of commodity
(*c*) Bandwagon effect	III. Negative network externality
(*d*) Substitution effect	IV. Positive network externality

Choose the correct answer from the option given below:

	(*a*)	(*b*)	(*c*)	(*d*)
A.	I	II	III	IV
B.	IV	III	II	I
C.	II	III	IV	I
D.	I	III	IV	II

10. Arrange the following in a sequence with regard to price leadership sustainability:

(*a*) Small firms in the industry are allowed to sell all they want at that price
(*b*) Dominant firm acts as the residual supplier of the commodity
(*c*) The dominant firm sets the price for the commodity that maximizes its profits
(*d*) Small firms in the industry behave as price takers
(*e*) Dominant firm then comes into fill the market

Choose the correct answer from the option given below:

A. (*a*), (*b*), (*c*), (*d*), (*e*)
B. (*e*), (*d*), (*c*), (*b*), (*a*)
C. (*a*), (*c*), (*b*), (*d*), (*e*)
D. (*c*), (*a*), (*e*), (*b*), (*d*)

11. A charitable trust (registered under section 12 AB of the Income Tax Act) is registered under GST in New Delhi. It provided yoga training to middle-aged people, coaching for Basket-ball to teenagers and skill development services to persons over the age of 65 years residing in New Delhi in the month of July. This trust is liable to pay GST on

A. Yoga training
B. Skill-development services
C. Coaching for basket-ball
D. Coaching for basket-ball and Yoga training

12. Sequentially arrange the following impacts of the evolving global monetary system on the economies.
(*a*) Protectionism and nationalism
(*b*) Capital flows driving economic development
(*c*) Increased world trade with limited capital flows
(*d*) Expanded open economies
(*e*) Industrial economies increasingly open and emerging nations open slowly

Choose the correct answer from the option given below:
A. (*b*), (*d*), (*a*), (*c*), (*e*)
B. (*c*), (*a*), (*d*), (*e*), (*b*)
C. (*c*), (*e*), (*d*), (*a*), (*b*)
D. (*e*), (*b*), (*d*), (*a*), (*c*)

13. Given below are two statements:

Statement I: The ordinary treasury bills that are marketable and have a secondary market are issued to the public and financial institutions.

Statement II: Ad hoc treasury bills are issued only in favour of the Reserve Bank of India which is authorized to issue currency notes against them.

In the light of the above statements, choose the most appropriate answer from the options given below:
A. Both Statement I and Statement II are true
B. Both Statement I and Statement II are false
C. Statement I is true, but Statement II is false
D. Statement I is false, but Statement II is true

14. Which one of the following committees has suggested the establishment of NBFCs' regulatory framework?
A. Raj Study Group (1975)
B. Chakkravarty Committee (1985)
C. Vaghul Committee (1987)
D. Shah Committee (1992)

15. Which of the following ratios are critically significant for an investor:
(*a*) Debt-Equity ratio
(*b*) Price-Earning ratio
(*c*) Dividend yield
(*d*) Asset turnover ratio
(*e*) Debtor turnover ratio

Choose the correct answer from the options given below:
A. (*a*), (*b*) and (*c*) only
B. (*d*) and (*e*) only
C. (*b*), (*c*) and (*d*) only
D. (*a*). (*d*) and (*e*) only

16. Which one of the following are disposed to promote financial inclusion?
A. Poor quality of services rendered
B. High transaction costs
C. Universal access to financial services
D. Lack of trust in the system

17. Which one of the following is the allowable deduction as per the Income Tax Act, 1961 in respect of entertainment allowance paid to a government employee?
A. Lower of one-fourth of basic salary or ₹ 5000 or entertainment allowance received
B. Lower of one-fifth of basic salary or ₹ 5000 or entertainment allowance received
C. Lower of one-fifth of salary or ₹ 5000 or entertainment allowance received.
D. Lower of one-fourth of salary or ₹ 5000 or entertainment allowance received

18. Arrange the following steps of a well planned experiment in the sequential order.
(*a*) Specify the treatment levels
(*b*) Assign subject to groups and conduct pilot test
(*c*) Choose an experimental design suited to the hypotheses

(*d*) Control the environmental and extraneous factors

(*e*) Select relevant variables for testing

Choose the correct answer from the option given below:

A. (*c*), (*d*), (*e*), (*a*), (*b*)
B. (*a*), (*c*), (*d*), (*e*), (*b*)
C. (*e*), (*a*), (*d*), (*c*), (*b*)
D. (*d*), (*c*), (*b*), (*a*), (*e*)

19. Which are the states where every supplier of goods and/or services is required to obtain registration if his aggregate turnover exceeds the threshold limit of ₹ 20 lakh for supply of goods and/or services?

(*a*) Arunachal Pradesh
(*b*) Meghalaya
(*c*) Manipur
(*d*) Mizoram
(*e*) Sikkim

Choose the most appropriate answer from the option given below:

A. (*b*), (*c*) and (*a*) only
B. (*c*), (*d*) and (*e*) only
C. (*e*), (*b*) and (*a*) only
D. (*a*), (*b*) and (*d*) only

20. Given below are two statements: one is labelled as Assertion (A) and the other is labelled as Reason (R).

Assertion (A): Persons with high self-esteem are less susceptible to influence, more confident of achieving goals and more effective in social networking

Reason (R): Self-esteem manifests in several behaviours. Persons with high self-esteem tend to report fewer negative emotions than persons with low self-esteem.

In the light of the above statements, choose the most appropriate answer from the options given below:

A. Both (A) and (R) are true and (R) is the correct explanation of (A)
B. Both (A) and (R) are true, but (R) is NOT the correct explanation of (A)
C. (A) is true, but (R) is false
D. (A) is false, but (R) is true

21. Honeywell Inc's move from a hierarchical management structure to a much flatter and team-based structure is a good description of which one of the following?

A. Centralisation
B. Decentralisation
C. Span of control
D. Work specialization

22. In order to conduct exploratory data analysis, which of following are used by a researcher in the five number summary?

(*a*) Median
(*b*) First quartile
(*c*) Mean
(*d*) Third quartile
(*e*) Smallest and largest values

Choose the correct answer from the options given below:

A. (*a*), (*c*), (*d*) and (*e*) only
B. (*a*), (*b*), (*d*), and (*e*) only
C. (*b*), (*c*), (*d*) and (*e*) only
D. (*a*), (*b*), (*c*) and (*e*) only

23. In International Commercial Terms (INCOTERMES), identify the one, under which the delivery of goods to the named place of destination (discharge) takes place at the seller's expense. Buyers assumes the cargo insurance, import custom clearance, payment of custom duties, taxes and other costs and risk:

A. Carriage and Insurance Paid To (CIP)
B. Cost, Insurance and Freight (CIF)
C. Carriage Paid To (CPT)
D. Cost and Freight (CFR)

24. Given below are two statements:

Statement I: For a given sample size and level of significance (α), the critical value of Student's t always exceeds that of z.

Statement II: For a given level of significance (α), the critical value of Student's t increases as n increases.

In the light of the above statements, choose the correct answer from the options given below:

A. Both Statement I and Statement II are true

B. Both Statement I and Statement II are false

C. Statement I is true but Statement II is false

D. Statement I is false but Statement II is true

25. Which one of the following accounting concepts and conventions consider it reasonable to use the historical cost to record long-lived assets?

A. The entity concept

B. Going concern convention

C. Materiality convention

D. The periodicity convention

26. Every seller who receives an amount exceeding ________ as consideration for sale of a motor vehicle, shall collect tax @ 1% of the sale consideration from the buyer at the time of receipt of such an amount.

A. ₹ 25 lakhs B. ₹ 15 lakhs

C. ₹ 10 lakhs D. ₹ 50 lakhs

27. The concept of product life cycle is based on which of the following key assumptions?

(*a*) Profits remain stable at different stages of product life cycle

(*b*) Products have an unlimited life

(*c*) Product sales pass through distinct stages, each posing different challenges, opportunities and problems to the seller

(*d*) Products require different marketing, financial, manufacturing, purchasing and human resource strategies in each of the life cycle stages

(*e*) Products have a limited life

Choose the most appropriate answer from the option given below:

A. (*b*), (*c*) and (*d*) only

B. (*a*), (*b*) and (*c*) only

C. (*a*), (*c*) and (*d*) only

D. (*c*), (*d*) and (*e*) only

28. Arrange the following group member's behaviour outcomes in a sequence as per the successive stages of group building process

(*a*) Eager, Anxious, Gather data about similarities and differences among members and keep things simple

(*b*) Upset and Depressed

(*c*) Less dissatisfied and a feeling of belongings to the group

(*d*) Confront the differences, feel angry or frustrated, lot of competition and hostilities

(*e*) Inter dependence in personal relations, tendency to get involved in and problem solving

Choose the correct answer from the option given below:

A. (*a*), (*d*), (*c*), (*e*), (*b*)

B. (*a*), (*b*), (*c*), (*d*), (*e*)

C. (*e*), (*c*), (*d*), (*b*), (*a*)

D. (*b*), (*c*), (*e*), (*a*), (*d*)

29. Which of the following are constituents of the trilemma of international finance?

(*a*) Fixed exchange rate

(*b*) Independent monetary policy

(*c*) Free mobility of capital

(*d*) Global recessionary tendency

(*e*) Rising inflationary conditions

Choose the correct answer from the options given below:

A. (*a*), (*b*) and (*c*) only

B. (*c*), (*d*) and (*e*) only

C. (*b*), (*c*) and (*e*) only

D. (*a*), (*c*) and (*d*) only

30. Which one of the following instruments is often used to protect the value of a foreign currency denominated transaction?

A. Forward contract B. Forward swap
C. Forward hedge D. Forward premium

31. Which of the following are objectives of Immediate Payment Service (IMPS)?

(*a*) To enable bank clients to use mobile instruments as a channel for accessing their bank accounts and remit funds

(*b*) To build the foundation for a full range of mobile based banking services

(*c*) To sub-serve the goal of Reserve Bank of India (RBI) in digital payments.

(*d*) To make payments simpler with the mobile number of the baneficiary

(*e*) To restrain a nation-wide payment system facilitating one-to-one funds transfer

Choose the most appropriate answer from the option given below:

A. (*a*), (*c*), (*d*) and (*e*) only
B. (*a*), (*b*), (*c*) and (*d*) only
C. (*b*), (*c*), (*d*) and (*e*) only
D. (*b*), (*a*), (*e*) and (*d*) only

32. Which amongst the following methods is not a method of generating sales leads in personal selling?

A. Referrals
B. Networking
C. Coupons
D. Cold calls

33. Match List-I with List-II.

List-I (Asset classes)	List-II (Type of Investments)
(*a*) Asset Class A	I. Equity shares of companies traded in futures and options segmenets
(*b*) Asset Class C	II. Government securities and state development loans
(*c*) Asset Class E	III. Alternate Assests
(*d*) Asset Class G	IV. Corporate bonds/ debentures which are listed and rated not below A

Choose the correct answer from the option given below:

	(*a*)	(*b*)	(*c*)	(*d*)
A.	I	IV	II	III
B.	III	II	IV	I
C.	III	IV	I	II
D.	I	III	II	IV

34. Companies use _______ when they lack financial resources to carry out direct marketing and when they can earn more by doing so.

A. Intermediaries
B. Internationalisation
C. Influences
D. Innovation

35. Match List-I with List-II.

List-I (Management Thinkers)	List-II (Approach Dimensions)
(*a*) Kurt Lewin	I. Position power, Task structure, Leader member relations
(*b*) Fred E Fiedler	II. Authority and Responsibility, Unity of command, Scalar chain
(*c*) Henri Fayol	III. Power, Affiliation, Achievement
(*d*) David C. McClelland	IV. Unfreezing, Moving, Refreezing

Choose the correct answer from the option given below:

	(*a*)	(*b*)	(*c*)	(*d*)
A.	I	II	III	IV
B.	IV	I	II	III
C.	IV	III	I	II
D.	II	IV	III	I

36. Which of the following are relevant in deciding among different courses of action, the manager needs to consider the differential revenue and costs of alternatives?

(*a*) Opportunity costs and economic profits

(*b*) Fixed and Sunk Costs

(*c*) Marginal Revenue and Marginal Cost
(*d*) Incremental and marginal costs
(*e*) Economies and dis-economies of scale

Choose the correct answer from the options given below:

A. (*a*) and (*d*) only B. (*b*) and (*c*) only
C. (*d*) and (*e*) only D. (*a*) and (*b*) only

37. For Foreign Direct Investment, it is argued that a location in question attracts FDI because it combines the unique advantage of which of the following conditions?

(*a*) Internalisation Advantage
(*b*) First Mover Advantage
(*c*) Knowledge Advantage
(*d*) Ownership Advantage
(*e*) Location Advantage

Choose the correct answer from the options given below:

A. (*e*), (*a*) and (*c*) only
B. (*e*), (*a*) and (*d*) only
C. (*c*), (*b*) and (*d*) only
D. (*c*), (*e*) and (*d*) only

38. The price earnings ratio for firms in a certain industry follows the normal distribution. A firm's price-earnings ratio has a standardized value (Z) = 1.0 and it is included in the highest ________ of firms in the industry.

A. 99.73% B. 68.27%
C. 15.87% D. 34.13%

39. Which one of the following beliefs and behaviours does not characterise 'collectivism'?

A. Relations are moral not contractual
B. Relations take precedence over tasks
C. Individual opinions are independent of collective opinions
D. Maintaining harmony is highly valued

40. The earning per share for Avanti corporation is ₹ 4.0. The rate of return on investments is 16 per cent and the return required by its shareholders is 12 per cent. What will be the price per share as per the Walter model, if the payout ratio is 40 per cent?

A. ₹ 24 B. ₹ 36
C. ₹ 40 D. ₹ 72

41. SAFTA (South Asian Free Trade Agreement) categorises member nations as Non-Least Developed Contracting States (NLDCS) and Least Developed Contracting States (LDCS). Identify the NLDSC states from the following

(*a*) Bangladesh (*b*) Pakistan
(*c*) Bhutan (*d*) India
(*e*) Sri Lanka

Choose the correct answer from the options given below:

A. (*a*), (*b*) and (*d*) only
B. (*a*), (*c*) and (*e*) only
C. (*e*), (*a*) and (*b*) only
D. (*e*), (*d*) and (*b*) only

42. Which of the following are considered as the limitations of Cost-Volume-Profit analysis?

(*a*) Constant selling price regardless of sales volume
(*b*) Firm efficiency and productivity are constant and the costs are linear
(*c*) Margin of safety is constant at varied levels of sales
(*d*) Sales mix and the inventory levels are constant
(*e*) Profit is constant at varied levels of sales price

Choose the correct answer from the options given below:

A. (*a*), (*b*) and (*c*) only
B. (*b*), (*c*) and (*d*) only
C. (*c*), (*d*) and (*e*) only
D. (*a*), (*b*) and (*d*) only

43. Match List-I with List-II.

List-I (Description Identifiers)	**List-II (Research design)**
(*a*) The time dimension	I. Exploratory study
(*b*) The purpose of the study	II. Statistical study

(*c*) The topical scope of the study	III.	Descriptive study
(*d*) The degree to which the research question has been crystallized	IV.	Cross-sectional study

Choose the correct answer from the option given below:

	(*a*)	(*b*)	(*c*)	(*d*)
A.	I	II	III	IV
B.	III	I	IV	II
C.	IV	III	II	I
D.	II	IV	I	III

44. Which of the following theories of capital structure articulates that a firm borrows up to the point where the tax benefit from extra debt is exactly equal to the cost that comes from the increased probability of financial distress?

A. The static theory
B. Net income approach
C. Modigliani-Miller theory
D. Net operating income approach

45. Mr. X is holding equity shares of ABC Ltd with voting power of 26 per cent. Mrs. X is working in ABC Ltd at a salary of ₹ 20,000 p.m. The other income of Mr. X and Mrs. X are ₹ 6,00,000 and ₹ 3,00,000 respectively. The gross total income of Mr X and Mrs. X are ________, ________ respectively for the Assesment Year 2023-24.

A. ₹ 6,00,000 and ₹ 5,40,000
B. ₹ 7,90,000 and ₹ 3,00,000
C. ₹ 6,00,000 and ₹ 4,90,000
D. ₹ 8,40,000 and ₹ 3,00,000

46. Identify the source of oligopoly which is also applicable to monopoly firms:

A. Economies of scale may operate over a small range of outputs
B. Huge capital investments and specialized inputs are required to enter the market
C. Large firms may own a patent for the exclusive right to produce a commodity
D. New firms have chances to win customer loyalty

47. Which of the following are relavant in technological innovations?

(*a*) Most innovations are incremental
(*b*) Most innovations involve the commercial utilization of ideas
(*c*) Innovations cannot be explained with isoquants
(*d*) Introduction of innovations is not stimulated by strong domestic rivalry and geographic concentrations
(*e*) The risk in introducing innovations is usually high

Choose the correct answer from the options given below:

A. (*b*), (*d*) and (*e*) only
B. (*a*), (*c*) and (*e*) only
C. (*a*), (*b*) and (*e*) only
D. (*a*), (*b*) and (*c*) only

48. Which one of the following consists of physical working conditions, work schedule, incentives and the number of people with whom the employee would normally intract?

A. Job profile
B. Job content
C. Job context
D. Job specification

49. Which one of the following is an exception to the doctrine of Constructive Notice?

A. Doctrine of Subrogation
B. Doctrine of Ultra Vires
C. Corporate Veil
D. Turquand Rule

50. Match List-I with List-II

List-I (Concepts (Targeting))		List-II (Definition)
(*a*) Target Compatibility	I.	Reflects the ability of a market segment to create superior value for the company
(*b*) Tactical Targeting	II.	A reflection of the company's ability, to create superior customer value

(*c*) Target Attractiveness	III.	Focuses on customising company's offerings according to the customers' needs
(*d*) Strategic Targeting	IV.	Ways in which the company can reach strategically important customers

Choose the correct answer from the option given below:

	(*a*)	(*b*)	(*c*)	(*d*)
A.	I	II	III	IV
B.	II	IV	I	III
C.	II	III	I	IV
D.	IV	III	II	I

51. A discrete probability distribution ______.

A. is a listing of all possible values of the random variable
B. assigns a probability to each possible value of the random variable
C. can assume the value between –1 and +1
D. is independent of the parameters of the distribution

52. When a country's currency is accepted as a reserve currency, the potential conflict may arise between which of following policy objectives?

(*a*) Domestic monetary policy
(*b*) Domestic fiscal policy
(*c*) External currency policy
(*d*) Foreign trade policy
(*e*) Inland trade policy

Choose the correct answer from the options given below:

A. (*a*), (*b*) and (*c*) only
B. (*a*), (*c*) and (*d*) only
C. (*b*), (*d*) and (*e*) only
D. (*c*), (*d*) and (*e*) only

53. Given below are two statements : one is labelled as Assertion (A) and the other is labelled as Reason (R).

Assertion (A): Consumers may prefer to choose the channels based on their own shopping goals as well as price, product assortment and convenience.

Reason (R): Some consumers are unwilling to "trade-up" to retailers offering higher-end goods, and "trade down" to discount retailers for private-label.

In the light of the above statements, choose the most appropriate answer from the options given below:

A. Both (A) and (R) are correct and (R) is the correct explanation of (A)
B. Both (A) and (R) are correct, but (R) is NOT the correct explanation of (A).
C. (A) is correct, but (R) is not correct
D. (A) is not correct, but (R) is correct

54. Arrange the following rounds for multilateral trade negotiations under GATT/WTO in a chronological order.

(*a*) Kennedy (*b*) Doha
(*c*) Annecy (*d*) Torquay
(*e*) Tokyo

Choose the correct answer from the option given below:

A. (*c*), (*d*), (*a*), (*e*), (*b*)
B. (*d*), (*c*), (*e*), (*a*), (*b*)
C. (*b*), (*a*), (*e*), (*c*), (*d*)
D. (*b*), (*e*), (*a*), (*d*), (*c*)

55. When a target company makes a counter bid for the stock of the bidder, the defensive strategy in reference is called?

A. Greenmail B. Poison pill
C. Pacman defense D. Golden parachute

56. In which ratio, will the remaining partners compensate the retiring partner for a share of goodwill?

A. Profit-sharing ratio
B. Sacrificing ratio
C. Gaining ratio
D. Capital ratio

57. Match List-I with List-II.

List-I (Features)	List-II (Remedies for breach of contract)
(*a*) Breach of promise to marry	I. Suit for injuction
(*b*) Part performance (as much as earned)	II. Rescission of contract
(*c*) Absolvation from all obligations	III. Sue for quantum meruit
(*d*) Mode of securing the specific performance of negative terms of contract	IV. Vindictive damage

Choose the correct answer from the option given below:

	(*a*)	(*b*)	(*c*)	(*d*)
A.	IV	III	II	I
B.	I	II	III	IV
C.	III	IV	I	II
D.	II	I	IV	III

58. In one-factor ANOVA, the computed F-value will be negative:

A. when there is no difference in the treatment of means.

B. when there is no difference within treatments.

C. when SST (total variance) is larger than SSE (error variance)

D. under no circumstances

59. Which of the following are functions of the Reserve Bank of India?

(*a*) Bank of issue

(*b*) Banker's bank and lender of the last resort

(*c*) Regulator of fiscal policy

(*d*) Controller of credit

(*e*) Custodian of foreign exchange reserves

Choose the most appropriate answer from the option given below:

A. (*a*), (*b*), (*c*) and (*d*) only

B. (*a*), (*b*), (*d*) and (*e*) only

C. (*b*), (*c*), (*d*) and (*e*) only

D. (*a*), (*b*) and (*d*) only

60. Which one of the following is invalid for the relationship among the agent, the sub-agent and the principal?

A. Sub-agent works under the control and on the directions of the agent

B. Sub-agent is responsible to the agent only

C. Privity of contract exists between the principal and the sub-agent

D. Agent is responsible to the principal for the acts of the sub-agent

61. Luxmi industries issued shares of ₹ 1000 at a premium of ₹ 10 per share, payable ₹ 20 on application, ₹ 35 on allotment (including premium) and the balance on the first and final call, Mr, X who held 200 shares has paid only the application money and these shares were subsequently forfeited by the company. In this regard, by which amount share forfeiture account will be credited?

A. ₹ 4000 B. ₹ 2000

C. ₹ 3000 D. ₹ 200

62. Which of the following are pre-experimental designs?

(*a*) One-group pre test-post test

(*b*) Pre-test post-test control group

(*c*) Quasi-experiments

(*d*) Static group comparison

(*e*) After-only study

Choose the correct answer from the options given below:

A. (*d*), (*b*), (*c*) only B. (*a*), (*d*), (*e*) only

C. (*a*), (*c*), (*e*) only D. (*e*), (*b*), (*d*) only

63. Arrange the following steps in the investigation process of combinations by the Competition Commission of India in the correct order.

(*a*) Call for a report from the Director General

(*b*) Invite any person, affected parties to file written objections

(*c*) Direct the parties of combination to publish details of the combination
(*d*) Call for additional information from the parties of the combination
(*e*) Issue a notice for show-cause to the parties of the combination

Choose the correct answer from the option given below:

A. (*a*), (*b*), (*c*), (*d*), (*e*)
B. (*e*), (*a*), (*c*), (*b*), (*d*)
C. (*b*), (*a*), (*c*), (*d*), (*e*)
D. (*c*), (*a*), (*d*), (*e*), (*b*)

64. Channel power is the ability to alter channel members' behaviour so that they take actions they would not have taken otherwise. From the following channel powers, list the ones which are subjective in nature:

(*a*) Legal Power
(*b*) Coercive Power
(*c*) Expert Power
(*d*) Referent Power
(*e*) Reward Power

Choose the correct answer from the options given below:

A. (*d*), (*a*) and (*c*) only
B. (*d*), (*a*) and (*b*) only
C. (*a*), (*b*) and (*e*) only
D. (*a*), (*c*) and (*e*) only

65. Arrange the following SBI-sponsored RRBs in an increasing order of their existence since formation.

(*a*) Rajasthan Marudhara Gramin Bank
(*b*) Telangana Gramin Bank
(*c*) Saurashtra Gramin Bank
(*d*) Madhyanchal Gramin Bank
(*e*) Arunachal Pradesh Rural Bank

Choose the correct answer from the option given below:

A. (*a*), (*d*), (*b*), (*e*), (*c*)
B. (*c*), (*e*), (*d*), (*a*), (*b*)
C. (*b*), (*a*), (*c*), (*e*), (*d*)
D. (*d*), (*e*), (*a*), (*b*), (*c*)

66. Match List-I with List-II.

List-I (Assets Transferred)	**List-II (Exemptions of capital gains Sections 54-54 EC Income Tax Act)**
(*a*) Agricultural Land	I. Section 54 B
(*b*) Residential House	II. Section 54 EC
(*c*) Land or Building or Both	III. Section 54 D
(*d*) Land and Building forming part of an industrial undertaking	IV. Section 54

Choose the correct answer from the option given below:

	(*a*)	(*b*)	(*c*)	(*d*)
A.	III	II	I	IV
B.	I	IV	II	III
C.	IV	III	I	II
D.	III	I	IV	II

67. In case of anti-competitive activities by a firm, the Competition Commission of India can impose a penalty which shall be not more than:

A. Five per cent of the average turnover/ income of the firm of the three preceding financial years.
B. Ten per cent of the average turnover/ income of firm of the three preceding financial years
C. Fifteen per cent of the average turnover/ income of firm of the three preceding financial years
D. Five per cent of the average turnover/ income of firm of the five preceding financial years

68. The sequential stages of moral development in business organisations are characterised by:

A. Conceptualised disposition, consistency and harmony, principled oriented
B. Consistency and harmony, conceptualised disposition, principled oriented

C. Principled oriented, conventional and preconventional
D. Preconventional, conventional, principled oriented

69. _______ takes into account a host of inputs, such as buyer's image of the product performance, the channel deliverables, the warranty quality, customer support and softer attributes such as the suppliers reputation, trust worthiness and esteem.

A. Target rate-of-return pricing
B. Auction-type pricing
C. Economic-value-to-customer pricing
D. Competitive pricing

70. Which of the following factors are attributed to the weakening of Indian rupee?

(*a*) Rupee payment for international trade
(*b*) Rising cost of imports
(*c*) Widening trade deficit
(*d*) Opening of Rupee vostro accounts
(*e*) Rupee UPI payments for overseas transactions

Choose the most appropriate answer from the options given below

A. (*a*), (*b*) and (*c*) only
B. (*c*), (*d*) and (*e*) only
C. (*a*), (*d*) and (*e*) only
D. (*b*), (*c*) and (*d*) only

71. Which of the following can become the member of an LLP?

(*a*) Resident Indians
(*b*) Limited Liability Partnership
(*c*) Corporation Sole
(*d*) Co-operative society
(*e*) Companies (including foreign companies)

Choose the most appropriate answer from the option given below:

A. (*a*), (*b*) and (*c*) only
B. (*a*), (*c*) and (*d*) only
C. (*a*), (*b*) and (*d*) only
D. (*a*), (*e*) and (*b*) only

72. Arrange the following in the ascending order of applicable TDS (Tax deducted at source) rates for the Financial Year, 2023-24.

(*a*) Payment of ₹ 6,55,000 rent by an individual in a year
(*b*) Payment of ₹ 20,000 on winnings from horse races
(*c*) Payment of ₹ 8,000 as dividend by cheque
(*d*) Payment of ₹ 35,000 to an individual contractor for repair by a university
(*e*) Payment of ₹ 38,000 as fees for professional and technical services by a call center

Choose the correct answer from the option given below:

A. (*a*), (*b*), (*c*), (*d*), (*e*)
B. (*d*), (*e*), (*a*), (*c*), (*b*)
C. (*e*), (*d*), (*c*), (*b*), (*a*)
D. (*a*), (*e*), (*c*), (*d*), (*b*)

73. Match List-I with List-II.

List-I (Activity Based Cost Centers)	List-II (Costs incurred and accounted for)
(*a*) Unit-level activity center	I. Patent, trademark and copyright fees
(*b*) Batch level activity center	II. Direct material and labour costs
(*c*) Product level activity center	III. Plant depreciation and maintenance expenses
(*d*) Facility level activity center	IV. Material handling costs

Choose the correct answer from the option given below:

	(*a*)	(*b*)	(*c*)	(*d*)
A.	II	IV	I	III
B.	II	IV	III	I
C.	I	III	II	IV
D.	III	I	IV	II

74. Given below are two statements: one is labelled as Assertion (A) and the other is labelled as Reason (R).

Assertion (A): A promoter, invariably is the one who has been associated with formation of the company.

Reason (R): A promoter is the one who undertakes to form a company with reference to a given object and who takes the necessary steps to accomplish that purpose.

In the light of the above statements, choose the most appropriate answer from the options given below:

A. Both (A) and (R) are correct and (R) is the correct explanation of (A).
B. Both (A) and (R) are correct, but (R) is NOT the correct explanation of (A).
C. (A) is correct, but (R) is not correct
D. (A) is not correct, but (R) is correct

75. Effective mentoring requires trust and the level of trust reflects the mentor's:

A. Competence, consistency, communication abilities and control sharing readiness
B. Concerned, cooperativeness, communication abilities and coordination skills
C. Competence, consistency, complexity and communication abilities
D. Communication abilities, competence, concerned behaviour, control sharing readiness

76. By reducing the sales price from ₹ 80 per unit to ₹ 78 per unit, the sales manager has succeeded in selling 1000 units more of a product. Which of the following decisive conclusions can be drawn from this?

(*a*) Sales price variance is unfavourable
(*b*) Sales volume variance is favourable
(*c*) Total sales variance is unfavourable
(*d*) Sales activity variance is ₹ 80000 (favourable)
(*e*) Sales price variance is ₹ 2000 (unfavourable)

Choose the correct answer from the options given below:

A. (*a*), (*b*) and (*c*) only
B. (*c*), (*d*) and (*e*) only
C. (*a*), (*b*) and (*d*) only
D. (*b*), (*d*) and (*e*) only

77. Which of the following are the reasons for substitution between domestic and MNC goods?

(*a*) Increased knowledge of foreign products due to international information revolution
(*b*) No need to conduct advertising campaigns
(*c*) Transportation costs having fallen to very low levels for most products
(*d*) Restricted international travel
(*e*) Tastes are consistent at the global level

Choose the correct answer from the options given below:

A. (*a*) and (*c*) only B. (*d*) and (*e*) only
C. (*c*) and (*d*) only D. (*a*) and (*b*) only

78. The trademarks can be broadly classified into which of the following categories?

(*a*) Descriptive (*b*) Normative
(*c*) Generic (*d*) Explanatory
(*e*) Invented

Choose the most appropriate answer from the option given below:

A. (*a*), (*b*) and (*d*) only
B. (*d*), (*e*) and (*c*) only
C. (*b*), (*c*) and (*e*) only
D. (*c*), (*a*) and (*e*) only

79. Which of the following will be clubbed into the income of Mr. Q whose income from Profession is ₹ 85,000?

(*a*) Income from Mrs Q's profession, ₹ 45,000
(*b*) Mrs. Q's salary as a clerk, ₹ 66,000
(*c*) Minor son's earned interest on deposits of money gifted to him by his uncle, ₹ 15,000
(*d*) Minor daughter's earnings from sports, ₹ 85,000
(*e*) Minor son's winnings from lottery, ₹ 1,05,000

Choose the correct answer from the options given below:

A. (*a*), (*c*), (*d*) and (*e*) only
B. (*c*), (*d*) and (*e*) only
C. (*c*) and (*d*) only
D. (*c*) and (*e*) only

80. Which one of the following statements is the most relevant to the substitution effect?

A. In the real world, substitution effect is much larger than the income effect
B. Most of the goods are not reasonable substitutes
C. In reality, the income effect represents its predominance over the substitution effect
D. Substitution and income effects cannot be separated easily

81. _________ as defined under the Foreign Trade Policy (FTP), implemented by Director General of Foreign Trade has the main aim to "mentor new and potential exporters on the intricacies of foreign trade through counselling, training and outreach programmes" so that they can get into international trade:

A. Niryat Bharat Scheme
B. Niryat Bandhu Scheme
C. Niryat Benefit Scheme
D. Niryat Border Scheme

82. Which one of the following statements does not support the concept of third degree price discrimination?

A. The firm must have monopoly power
B. This type of price discrimination is most likely to occur in the manufacturing industries
C. The firm must be able to keep the two markets separate
D. The price elasticity and demand for the commodity must be different in the two markets

83. _______ is a marketing term for any design to prompt an immediate response or encourage an immediate sale.

A. Call for Promotion
B. Call for Activity
C. Call to Action
D. Call to Aspiration

84. Match List-I with List-II.

List-I (Nature of Business Activity)	**List-II (FDI Permitted under Automatic Route)**
(*a*) Trading in Transferable Development Rights (TDR)	I. 49%
(*b*) Multi-Brand Retail Trading	II. Prohibited
(*c*) Satellite (Establishment and Operations)	III. 51%
(*d*) Petroleum Refining (by PSUs)	IV. 100%

Choose the correct answer from the option given below:

	(*a*)	(*b*)	(*c*)	(*d*)
A.	IV	II	III	I
B.	II	III	IV	I
C.	I	III	II	IV
D.	IV	II	I	III

85. Which of the following are considered while avoiding conflict?

(*a*) Conflict based on interpersonal relationships
(*b*) All conflicts are not bad and can be taken positively
(*c*) Conflict over content and goals of the work
(*d*) Conflicts do not support a group's goal and improve its performance
(*e*) Conflict over how work gets done

Choose the correct answer from the options given below:

A. (*a*), (*b*) and (*c*) only
B. (*a*), (*b*) and (*e*) only
C. (*a*), (*c*) and (*e*) only
D. (*b*), (*c*) and (*d*) only

86. The present value of future profits, the individual or segment will generate over a lifetime relationship with a brand or firm, is known as:

A. Lifelong Value
B. Lifetime Value
C. Longlife Value
D. Longterm Value

87. Emotional appeal is one of the types of advertising appeals, based on three ideas, namely:

(*a*) Rational appeals generally go unnoticed
(*b*) Consumers watch all ads
(*c*) It can capture attention and foster an attachment
(*d*) Consumers ignore most ads
(*e*) Rational appeal generally gets noticed

Choose the correct answer from the options given below:

A. (*c*), (*e*), and (*d*) only
B. (*c*), (*e*) and (*b*) only
C. (*c*), (*a*) and (*d*) only
D. (*c*), (*a*) and (*b*) only

88. Place the following service differentiators in a logical sequence:

(*a*) Speed and timing of delivery
(*b*) Maintenance and repair
(*c*) Returns
(*d*) Installation, training and consulting
(*e*) Ease of ordering

Choose the correct answer from the option given below:

A. (*e*), (*d*), (*b*), (*c*), (*a*)
B. (*e*), (*a*), (*d*), (*b*), (*c*)
C. (*e*), (*d*), (*a*), (*c*), (*b*)
D. (*e*), (*c*), (*a*), (*b*), (*d*)

89. Arrange the steps in the book building process for public issue of shares in India:

(*a*) Determine issue price, market clearing price and price discovery
(*b*) Book runner and syndicate members generate awareness, create demand and run the order book
(*c*) Appointment of the merchant banker and syndicate members (SEBI registerd intermediaries) as underwriters
(*d*) Preparation and filing of red herring prospectus with the SEBI for approval
(*e*) Allotment and listing of shares on stock exchange(s)

Choose the correct answer from the option given below:

A. (*c*), (*d*), (*b*), (*a*), (*e*)
B. (*d*), (*c*), (*a*), (*b*), (*e*)
C. (*a*), (*b*), (*c*), (*d*), (*e*)
D. (*b*), (*c*), (*d*), (*e*), (*a*)

90. Which one of the following digital payment systems is developed and managed by the National Payments Corporation of India?

A. Paytm
B. BharatPe
C. Mastercard
D. RuPay

Directions (Qs. No. 91-95): *Read the given passage and answer the questions that follow:*

For most of its existence as a modern field of study since the 18th century, economics has fared reasonably well at explaining consumer and producer behaviour. It explained why buyers choose the products they do, how firms produce them to maximize profit, and how markets discover the most efficient prices. This changed with the Great Depression, when aggregate variables came into play that needed a better understanding than an assumption that markets return to equilibrium after shocks. Thus came into existence macro-economics, the most dismal aspect of the dismal science. Economics has since diversified into quite a few other branches, such as those employing statistics and psychology, but most of its disrepute originates from its failure to predict financial crises

'Macro' by its very nature - dealing with GDP, employment, inflation and other important but soporific matters and parameters - is headline-grabbing stuff. Governments come into play here, as do international relations. Yet, macro eludes the scientific method of testing hypotheses with repeated experiments one can't conceivably wreck an economy to establish the effects of a shock. Instead, macroeconomists can only back-test their models against data that may be of questionable provenance. This makes prediction of the next stock market crash forever embarrassingly less exact than the return of Halley's Comet.

Microeconomics, the reputable part of the endeavour, suffers from fewer limitations to controlled parameter experiments and delivers less equivocal insights. The explosion of commerce in the modern world owes itself in no small measure to predicting actions by the smallest economic agents: humans. Here, too, heroic assumptions are made, the foremost being that human beings are rational and information is free. The crisis in economic modelling arises from aggregating billions of micro truths into one macro truth. Models are improving, so are quantitative capabilities, and the qualitative judgements that drive macro policy will become more refined.

91. Which of the following is the reason, as per the passage, for driving more effective macro policies?

A. Assumption that markets return to equilibrium after shocks

B. Improved economic models are capable to understand qualitative and quantitative factors

C. Economics has fared reasonably well during financial crises

D. Every small measure is not capable to predict economic outcomes

92. Which of the following, as per the passage, are the major contribution of economics?

(*a*) Buyers behaviour towards the products

(*b*) Firm's behaviours for maximizing profit

(*c*) Retailers behaviour to maximize sale

(*d*) Market behaviour to the most efficient prices

(*e*) Stakeholder's behaviours to maximize wealth

Choose the correct answer from the options given below:

A. (*a*), (*b*) and (*d*) only

B. (*a*), (*b*) and (*c*) only

C. (*b*), (*d*) and (*e*) only

D. (*a*), (*b*) and (*e*) only

93. Match List-I with List-II.

List-I (Phenomenon)	List-II (Reasons)
(*a*) Economics defines	I. Better understanding of aggregate variables
(*b*) Learning of Great Depression	II. GDP, Employment, and Inflation
(*c*) Macro-economic variables	III. Human beings are rational and information is free
(*d*) Pitfalls of Micro economics	IV. How markets discover the most efficient prices

Choose the correct answer from the options given below:

	(*a*)	(*b*)	(*c*)	(*d*)
A.	I	II	III	IV
B.	II	III	I	IV
C.	III	IV	II	I
D.	IV	I	II	III

94. Which one of the following is the reason, as per the given passage, for crises in economic modelling?

A. Aggregating billions of micro truths into one macro truth

B. Only equalization factors are considered in economic models

C. Economic activities are not sufficient to study the macro environment

D. Human beings behave irrationally

95. Given below are two statements.

Statement I: Macroeconomists can only back-test their models against data that may be of questionable provenance.

Statement II: Macroeconomic variables elude the scientific method of testing hypotheses with repeated experiments.

In the light of the above statements, choose the most appropriate answer from the options given below:

A. Both Statement I and Statement II are true
B. Both Statement I and Statement II are false
C. Statement I is true, but Statement II is false
D. Statement I is false, but Statement II is true

Directions (Qs. No. 96-100): *Read the given passage and answer the questions that follow:*

Over $350 billion of private capital has been deployed over the last decade, which has propelled more than 5,000 enterprises. These new businesses are anchored in innovative business models combining the full potential of technology, facilitating every Indian to fulfil their aspirations.

The big shift in the last decade is the reimagination of India as an addressable market of 300 million households, a massive shift from only 20 million households in tier-1 cities earlier. This has been propelled by the strong partnership between entrepreneurs and the PE/VC ecosystem. The share of FDI funnelled into PE/VC has surged to 50-60%, up from 20-30% two decades back.

Besides the tremendous focus on value creation, the PE/VC industry has brought about multidimensional progress in the economy. The principles of responsible investing that this industry is committed to have enabled the building of a more equitable, inclusive economy, and one that has earned the trust of large global investors as an attractive investment destination.

The PE/VC ecosystem sparked a renaissance, empowering young minds to take a bold leap. This led to a change in mindset where entrepreneurship is now an accepted livelihood and, indeed, a proud way of life. Today, startups and new businesses are celebrated, and many are giving up established careers to follow their heart, with families standing as stalwart supporters of entrepreneurship.

The proportionality of risk and reward has been embraced, forging a harmonious relationship between uncertainty and achievement.

Stories at home and those that went global are a testament to the power of partnerships between the capital provider and entrepreneurs, transforming a large democracy to be self-reliant, and elevating over a billion people to a new world of greater aspirations and confidence.

This revolution has been largely possible because of GoI's thrust towards attracting capital. The frameworks of alternative investment funds (AIFs), GIFT City IFSC, Startup India programme and budget allocations, coupled with progressive amendments such as GST and India Stack, have made India an attractive destination for investment.

96. Given below are two statements: one is labelled as Assertion (A) and the other is labelled as Reason (R).

Assertion (A): The private equity and venture capital ecosystem has sparked a renaissance, empowering young minds to take a bold leap.

Reason (R): Today, startups and new business are celebrated and many are given up their established careers to follow their heart, with families standing as stalwart supporters.

In the light of the above statements, choose the correct answer from the options given below:

A. Both (A) and (R) are true and (R) is the correct explanation of (A)
B. Both (A) and (R) are true, but (R) is NOT the correct explanation of (A)
C. (A) is true, but (R) is false
D. (A) is false, but (R) is true

97. According to the passage, which of the following is now being accepted as a way of life and livelihood?

A. PE/VC ecosystem
B. Risk and uncertainty
C. Innovation and achievement
D. Entrepreneurship

98. The principles of responsible investing to which private equity and venture capital industry is committed have resulted in which of the following outcomes for the Indian economy?

(*a*) Democratic decentralization

(*b*) Balanced regional growth

(*c*) Inclusive and equitable economy

(*d*) Larger export orientation

(*e*) Earned the trust of global investors

Choose the correct answer from the options given below:

A. (*b*) and (*c*) only

B. (*a*) and (*d*) only

C. (*c*) and (*e*) only

D. (*b*), (*c*) and (*d*) only

99. In the recent years, the focus of private equity and venture capital in India, has been on:

A. Self-reliance B. Job creation

C. Inclusive growth D. Value creation

100. Which of the following, according to the passage, have made India an attractive destination for investments?

(*a*) Startup India program

(*b*) Make in India program

(*c*) Goods and Services Tax facilitation

(*d*) Alternative Investment funds

(*e*) Standup India program

Choose the most appropriate answer from the options given below:

A. (*a*), (*b*) and (*c*) only

B. (*a*), (*c*) and (*d*) only

C. (*a*), (*d*) and (*e*) only

D. (*c*), (*d*) and (*e*) only

ANSWERS

1. (A): The correct match for each term from List-I to the descriptions in List-II is as follows:

(*a*) Coupon rate is matched with IV, which describes it as the annual coupon (stated interest payment) divided by the face value of a bond. This definition matches the concept of a coupon rate, which is the rate of interest the bond issuer agrees to pay the bondholder on the bond's face value, typically expressed as an annual percentage.

(*b*) Yield to maturity (YTM) is matched with I, indicating it as the interest rate required in the market on a bond. YTM is a comprehensive measure of a bond's return that accounts for all potential income streams from the bond until its maturity, including coupon payments and any gain or loss if the bond is held to maturity.

(*c*) Interest rate risk is correctly paired with III, highlighting that it originates from fluctuating interest rates. Interest rate risk is the risk that arises for bond owners from fluctuating interest rates, which inversely affect bond prices, meaning that as interest rates rise, bond prices fall, and vice versa.

(*d*) Current (bond) yield is matched with II, which is defined as the annual coupon divided by the bond price. This measure gives the investor an idea of the income they can expect to receive from the bond as a percentage of its current price, not its face value.

2. (D): To find the probability that a randomly selected person is either a male or a smoker, we use the formula for the union of two events: $P(A \cup B) = P(A) + P(B) - P(A \cap B)$. In this context, P(A) is the probability of being a male (0.57), P(B) is the probability of being a smoker (0.22), and $P(A \cap B)$ is the probability of being a male smoker (0.12). By substituting these values into the formula, we calculate the probability of selecting a person who is either a male or a smoker,

i.e., $P(A \cup B) = 0.57 + 0.22 - 0.12$
$= 0.79 - 0.12 = 0.67$.

This calculation is intended to capture the overall chance of selecting from the population someone who falls into at least one of the categories, considering the overlap between male smokers in the calculation to avoid double-counting those individuals.

3. **(B):** The correct options are (*b*), (*c*), and (*e*), which are deemed to be dividends for the purpose of computing income chargeable under the head, "Income from other sources," according to the Income Tax Act, 1961.

   (*b*) Payment to shareholders on reduction of capital is considered a return of capital to shareholders and is treated as a dividend because it distributes the company's assets to shareholders.

   (*c*) Distribution of debentures to shareholders is similarly treated as a dividend because it involves distributing corporate assets to shareholders, though in the form of debt rather than cash or stock.

   (*e*) Lastly, a loan granted to shareholders by a closely held company can be considered a dividend, especially under certain conditions outlined by the Income Tax Act, as it may be seen as a distribution of profits to shareholders under the guise of a loan, particularly when the loan is granted by a company with substantial accumulated profits.

   These provisions aim to tax under "Income from other sources" certain distributions or payments by companies that, while not traditional dividends, are akin to distributions of profit.

4. **(C):** The actions that are typically followed to reduce resistance to change include:

   (*b*) Allowing those who oppose the change to participate in the decision-making process can lead to a greater acceptance of the change, as it gives them a sense of ownership and control over the situation.

   (*c*) Negotiation is essential when resistance emanates from a powerful source, as it helps to reach a compromise that can facilitate the implementation of change.

   (*e*) While coercion might sometimes be used in practice, it is generally not recommended as a strategy to reduce resistance to change because it can lead to further resistance and damage trust.

5. **(C):** According to the sub-section (8A) of Section 139 of the Income Tax Act, a person is allowed to furnish an updated return of income for the previous year relevant to such assessment year within 24 months from the end of the assessment year. This provision enables taxpayers to rectify any mistake or to include any income that was not previously reported in their original tax return. It offers a significant period for taxpayers to ensure that their tax affairs are in order, acknowledging that errors or omissions can occur. This extended timeframe is designed to facilitate compliance and accuracy in tax reporting, allowing individuals and businesses to make corrections that reflect their income more accurately without immediate penal consequences, thus promoting a fair and efficient tax administration.

6. **(C):** XBRL (eXtensible Business Reporting Language) is recognized as the open international standard for digital business reporting. This framework is designed to communicate business and financial information electronically, providing an efficient and accurate method for preparing, sharing, and analyzing financial data. XBRL allows for the tagging of financial information, which enables automated processing of business information by computers, thereby enhancing the reliability, speed, and cost-effectiveness of business reporting. It is widely adopted by regulatory bodies around the world for the submission of financial and regulatory data, facilitating

greater transparency, comparability, and accessibility of financial information. This standard is crucial for investors, regulators, and other stakeholders who rely on accurate and timely business information for decision-making processes.

7. (C): Piggybacking is a global market entry strategy where an exporting firm (referred to as the 'rider') utilizes the distribution system of another firm (called the 'carrier') that already has an established distribution channel in the target country. This strategy is beneficial for the rider because it allows access to the market with reduced distribution costs and takes advantage of the carrier's existing knowledge, relationships, and infrastructure in the target market. For the carrier, it can mean additional revenue without significant extra costs. Piggybacking is a cost-effective way for companies to enter foreign markets, leveraging the strengths of partners to mutual advantage.

8. (C): The concept referred to is the Diminishing Marginal Rate of Technical Substitution (MRTS). MRTS measures how many units of capital (or any other input) can be replaced by one additional unit of labor (or another input), while keeping output constant, i.e., remaining on the same isoquant. It reflects the rate at which a firm can substitute between inputs without affecting the level of output. As more of one input is used, the firm must give up increasingly smaller amounts of the other input to maintain the same level of production, due to the law of diminishing returns. This concept is crucial in understanding how firms optimize their production processes and input combinations.

9. (D): The correct matches between the types of effects and their descriptions are as follows:

(*a*) Veblen effect is correctly matched with I, Conspicuous consumption, which refers to the phenomenon where people buy expensive goods to display wealth rather than for the utility of the product.

(*b*) Snob effect is matched with III, Negative network externality, indicating a preference for exclusivity or goods that become less desirable as they become more widely owned.

(*c*) Bandwagon effect is paired with IV, Positive network externality, where the value of a product increases as more people use it, leading individuals to follow the trend.

(*d*) Substitution effect is accurately linked with II, Reduction in relative price of a commodity, which occurs when consumers react to a change in the price of a good relative to other goods, altering their consumption preferences in favor of the cheaper options.

10. (D): The sequence with regard to price leadership sustainability starts with the dominant firm setting the price for the commodity that maximizes its profits (*c*). Once the price is set, small firms in the industry are allowed to sell all they want at that price (*a*), effectively behaving as price takers. The dominant firm then comes in to fill the market (*e*), acting as the residual supplier of the commodity (*b*), to meet the remaining demand at the set price. Finally, small firms in the industry behave as price takers (*d*), adhering to the price set by the dominant firm without attempting to alter it. This sequence illustrates the process of price leadership where a dominant firm sets the price, and other firms in the market follow suit, reflecting the dynamics of price leadership in markets where one firm has a significant influence over the industry's pricing structure.

11. (B): A charitable trust registered under section 12 AB of the Income Tax Act and registered under GST in New Delhi is liable to pay GST on the services it provides depending on the nature of the services and the exemptions available under GST law. Among the options given, skill-development services provided to persons over the age of 65 years are taxable under GST unless specifically exempted. However, services like yoga training and coaching for basketball might be considered exempt under certain conditions if they are deemed charitable activities promoting health, sports, or education. The specific mention of skill-development services to persons over the age of 65 years without specifying its charitable nature or alignment with exempt categories makes it the most likely subject to GST, assuming no specific exemptions apply to this service.

12. (B): The sequential arrangement of the impacts of the evolving global monetary system on economies begins with increased world trade with limited capital flows (*c*), indicating an early stage of global economic integration. This is followed by protectionism and nationalism (*a*), as countries might respond to the challenges of globalization by protecting domestic industries. Expanded open economies (*d*) come next, illustrating a move towards more liberalized trade and investment regimes. Industrial economies becoming increasingly open and emerging nations opening slowly (*e*) reflect the gradual integration of developing countries into the global economy. Finally, capital flows driving economic development (*b*) signifies a stage where global financial markets significantly impact economic growth, indicating a mature phase of globalization where capital mobility supports development across borders.

This sequence captures the evolution from initial stages of trade integration to a complex global system characterized by significant capital flows and economic interdependence.

13. (A): Both Statement I and Statement II are true. Ordinary treasury bills are indeed marketable securities with a secondary market, allowing them to be bought and sold among investors after their initial issuance. This makes them attractive to a wide range of investors, including the general public and financial institutions, as they provide a relatively risk-free investment option with short-term maturities. Ad hoc treasury bills, on the other hand, are specifically issued in favour of the Reserve Bank of India (RBI). They are not intended for market circulation but are a tool for managing the finances between the central bank and the government. The RBI can issue currency notes against these ad hoc treasury bills, which are essentially an accounting mechanism to finance the government's short-term liquidity needs.

14. (D): The Shah Committee, established in 1992, is credited with suggesting the establishment of a regulatory framework for Non-Banking Financial Companies (NBFCs). This committee's recommendations laid the foundation for the regulatory structure under which NBFCs operate today, aiming to ensure their sound functioning and to protect the interests of depositors. The recommendations made by the Shah Committee have been instrumental in shaping the policies and regulations governing NBFCs in India, emphasizing the need for a structured approach to oversight and regulation to ensure financial stability and integrity within this sector.

15. (A): The ratios critically significant for an investor are the Debt-Equity ratio, Price-Earning ratio, and Dividend yield. The Debt-Equity ratio provides insights into the financial leverage of a company and its reliance on debt financing compared to equity financing, which can influence investment risk. The Price-Earning (P/E) ratio offers a valuation measure that helps investors evaluate if a stock is overvalued, undervalued, or fairly valued based on its current market price relative to its earnings per share. The dividend yield, which is the dividend per share divided by the stock price, gives investors an idea of the income they can expect from an investment in a stock, independent of its price movements.

These ratios are essential for investors as they assess the financial health, performance, and attractiveness of an investment opportunity, allowing for informed decision-making.

16. (C): Universal access to financial services is a key strategy to promote financial inclusion. Financial inclusion aims to make financial services accessible and affordable to all individuals and businesses, regardless of their net worth or company size. It involves ensuring that everyone has access to useful and affordable financial products and services that meet their needs—transactions, payments, savings, credit, and insurance—delivered in a responsible and sustainable way.

Universal access addresses barriers such as high transaction costs, poor quality of services, and lack of trust in the system, thereby enabling more people, especially those in underserved and low-income groups, to participate in the financial system.

17. (B): Entertainment Allowance [Section 16(ii)]

- Deduction in respect of entertainment allowance is allowed only for Government Employees.
- The deduction is irrespective of the actual amount spent by the employee, out of the entertainment allowance received by him.
- Quantum of deduction–Least of the following is allowed as deduction:
    - Actual amount received
    - Statutory limit– ₹ 5000
    - 1/5th of Basic Salary.

18. (C): The correct sequence for the steps of a well-planned experiment is to:

(*e*) First select relevant variables for testing, which involves identifying the independent and dependent variables that will be the focus of the experiment.

(*a*) Next, specify the treatment levels, determining the different conditions or interventions that the experimental subjects will undergo.

(*d*) Controlling the environmental and extraneous factors is crucial to ensure that the results are as accurate as possible and not influenced by outside variables.

(*c*) Choosing an experimental design suited to the hypotheses follows, selecting the framework that will best test the hypotheses under investigation.

(*b*) Finally, assigning subjects to groups and conducting a pilot test is performed to ensure the experiment's design is feasible and to identify any potential issues before the full-scale study begins. This sequence ensures a thorough and systematic approach to experimental design, enhancing the validity and reliability of the findings.

19. (*)

20. (A)

21. (B): Honeywell Inc's move from a hierarchical management structure to a much flatter and team-based structure is a description of decentralization. Decentralization refers to the process of distributing or dispersing decision-making authority closer to the point of action or operational level within an organization. It involves a shift from a centralized structure, where decisions are made at the top of the organization, to a flatter structure, where decision-making powers are spread out among various levels and departments. This approach aims to improve responsiveness, enhance creativity and innovation, and empower employees by giving them more autonomy in their roles. Decentralization can lead to more flexible and agile organizations that are better able to adapt to changes and meet the needs of their stakeholders.

22. **(B):** In exploratory data analysis, the five number summary is used to describe the distribution of the data. This summary includes the following:

(*a*) Median, which divides the dataset into two equal parts;

(*b*) First quartile (Q1), which is the median of the data points to the left of the median in an ordered dataset;

(*d*) Third quartile (Q3), which is the median of the data points to the right of the median; and

(*e*) Smallest and largest values in the dataset.

The mean is not part of the five number summary because the summary focuses on median and quartiles to provide a quick overview of the data distribution, including its center, spread, and tail length without being affected by outliers and skewness in the data.

23. **(C):** In International Commercial Terms (INCOTERMS), "Carriage Paid To (CPT)" is the term under which the seller pays for the carriage of goods to the named place of destination. Under CPT, the seller delivers the goods to the carrier nominated by them but the buyer assumes the risk once the goods have been handed over to the first carrier. This means that while the seller covers the transport costs to the destination, the buyer is responsible for additional costs including cargo insurance, import customs clearance, payment of customs duties, taxes, and any other costs from the moment the goods are delivered to the first carrier. Therefore, under CPT, the risk and insurance responsibility shifts to the buyer once the seller has fulfilled their obligation of delivering the goods to the carrier.

24. **(C):** Statement I is true but Statement II is false. For a given sample size and level of significance (α), the critical value of Student's *t*-distribution indeed exceeds that of the *z*-distribution (or normal distribution). This is because the *t*-distribution accounts for the added uncertainty in the estimation of the population standard deviation from a sample, especially relevant in smaller sample sizes, making its tails heavier than those of the *z*-distribution. As the sample size increases, the *t*-distribution approaches the *z*-distribution, and their critical values converge.

Statement II is false because as the sample size (n) increases, the critical value of Student's t decreases and approaches that of the z value, not increases. This convergence reflects the decreasing uncertainty in the estimate of the standard deviation with larger sample sizes.

25. **(B):** The Going Concern Convention assumes that an entity will continue to operate indefinitely. This assumption allows for the use of historical cost to record long-lived assets rather than continually adjusting them to reflect current market values. The rationale is that if the business is expected to continue operating, it is reasonable to record the cost of assets at their purchase price, adjusting for depreciation over time, rather than speculating on future values that may fluctuate due to market conditions. This convention supports the stability and consistency of financial reporting, making it easier for users of financial statements to compare performance over time.

26. **(C):** Every seller who receives an amount exceeding ₹ 10 lakhs as consideration for the sale of a motor vehicle is required to collect tax at the rate of 1% of the sale consideration from the buyer at the time of receipt of such an amount. This provision is part of the tax collected at source (TCS) regulations under the Income Tax Act, which aims to curb tax evasion by collecting tax at the point of transaction for certain high-value transactions, including the sale of motor vehicles exceeding the specified threshold.

27. (D): The concept of the product life cycle is based on several key assumptions, notably that (*c*) product sales pass through distinct stages, each posing different challenges, opportunities, and problems to the seller; (*d*) products require different marketing, financial, manufacturing, purchasing, and human resource strategies in each of the life cycle stages; and (*e*) products have a limited life. This framework suggests that a product will typically start with a development phase, followed by growth, maturity, and eventually decline. Each stage demands different business strategies and operations adjustments to navigate the changing market dynamics, consumer preferences, and competitive pressures effectively. Contrary to options (*a*) and (*b*), profits and product life are not stable or unlimited but vary significantly throughout the product life cycle.

28. (A): The correct sequence of group member's behaviour outcomes according to the successive stages of group building process is as follows:

(*a*) In the initial stage, members are eager and anxious as they gather data about similarities and differences among each other and try to keep things simple. This stage is typically characterized by orientation and testing.

(*d*) As the group progresses, confrontations over differences may occur, leading to feelings of anger or frustration, with a lot of competition and hostilities manifesting. This represents the storming stage, where conflicts arise.

(*c*) Moving past the conflicts, members feel less dissatisfied and develop a sense of belonging to the group, indicating the norming stage where consensus develops.

(*e*) Interdependence in personal relations and a tendency to get involved in problem-solving indicate the performing stage, where the group effectively works towards its goals.

(*b*) Feeling upset and depressed may occur during any stage as individuals process conflicts and challenges but is not typically a stage in group development models like Tuckman's stages of group development, which include forming, storming, norming, and performing.

29. (A): The trilemma of international finance, also known as the impossible trinity, states that it is impossible to have all three of the following at the same time:

(*a*) a fixed exchange rate,

(*b*) an independent monetary policy, and

(*c*) free mobility of capital.

This concept suggests that a country can only choose two of these three policy objectives simultaneously. For example, if a country wants to maintain a fixed exchange rate and allow for free capital movement, it cannot have an independent monetary policy because it would need to adjust its interest rates to maintain the fixed rate, which could conflict with domestic economic goals. Similarly, if a country wants an independent monetary policy and free mobility of capital, it cannot maintain a fixed exchange rate as changes in interest rates would affect exchange rates.

30. (C)

31. (B): The objectives of Immediate Payment Service (IMPS) include:

(*a*) enabling bank clients to use mobile instruments as a channel for accessing their bank accounts and remitting funds,

(*b*) building the foundation for a full range of mobile-based banking services, (*c*) subserving the goal of the Reserve Bank of India (RBI) in digital payments, and

(*d*) making payments simpler with the mobile number of the beneficiary.

These objectives highlight IMPS's role in enhancing the convenience, efficiency, and reach of digital payments in India, supporting the RBI's broader goals of promoting digital transactions and financial inclusion. IMPS is designed to facilitate instant, 24 × 7, interbank electronic fund transfers, making it an important component of the country's digital payment ecosystem.

32. (C): Among the options provided, Coupons are not a method of generating sales leads in personal selling. Coupons are typically used in marketing to offer discounts or deals to encourage purchases, rather than directly generating sales leads. Sales leads in personal selling are generated through methods that involve personal interaction or the potential for direct follow-up, such as Referrals (where existing customers or contacts recommend potential clients), Networking (building relationships within specific groups or industries to identify potential leads), and Cold calls (contacting potential customers directly without prior interaction).

33. (C)

34. (A): Companies use Intermediaries when they lack the financial resources to carry out direct marketing and when they can earn more by doing so. Intermediaries, such as distributors, wholesalers, and retailers, play a crucial role in the distribution chain by bridging the gap between producers and consumers. They help companies reach a wider market with lower upfront costs compared to establishing and managing their own distribution channels. By leveraging the expertise, infrastructure, and customer base of intermediaries, companies can enhance their market penetration and focus on their core competencies while still maximizing their profits.

35. (B): Matching the management thinkers with their approach dimensions:

- Kurt Lewin is known for the change management process of Unfreezing, Moving, Refreezing, which describes the stages of preparing for change, making the change, and solidifying the change into the organization.
- Fred E. Fiedler developed the contingency theory, which includes dimensions such as Position power, Task structure, and Leader-member relations, suggesting that the effectiveness of a leader's style is contingent on the situation.
- Henri Fayol is associated with the principles of management, including Authority and Responsibility, Unity of Command, and Scalar Chain, focusing on the structural framework of organizing and managing companies.
- David C. McClelland is known for his theory on the need for Power, Affiliation, and Achievement, which are motivational dimensions influencing leadership style and effectiveness.

36. (A): When deciding among different courses of action, managers need to consider the differential revenue and costs of alternatives, including:

(*a*) Opportunity costs and economic profits, which involve evaluating the benefits forgone by not choosing the next best alternative and the surplus after covering all costs, respectively, and

(*d*) Incremental and marginal costs, which are the additional costs incurred by producing one more unit of a product or service.

These concepts are crucial for making informed decisions that maximize economic benefits while minimizing costs. Fixed and sunk costs are typically not relevant for marginal decision-making because they do not change with the level of output in the short term. Marginal Revenue and Marginal Cost are indeed critical in decision-making but the correct options according to the question's phrasing are Opportunity costs and Incremental and marginal costs.

37. (B): A location attracts Foreign Direct Investment (FDI) because it combines the unique advantage of Location Advantage, Internalization Advantage, and Ownership Advantage. Location Advantage refers to the specific benefits offered by a host country, such as natural resources, strategic location, labour cost advantages, market size, and regulatory environment that make it attractive for foreign investments. Internalization Advantage explains why a company finds it more profitable to exploit its advantages itself rather than to license them to others. Ownership Advantage refers to the firm's specific assets, technology, brand, or product differentiations that can be leveraged internationally. These three advantages together explain why certain locations are more attractive for FDI, as they allow firms to capitalize on their unique strengths in a favourable external environment.

38. (C): A firm's price-earnings ratio with a standardized value (Z) of 1.0 falls within the top 15.87% of firms in the industry. The Z-score indicates how many standard deviations an element is from the mean. A Z-score of 1.0 typically corresponds to the 84.13th percentile, meaning that the firm's price-earnings ratio is higher than approximately 84.13% of the firms.

Therefore, it is included in the highest 15.87% (100% – 84.13%) of firms in the industry in terms of its price-earnings ratio.

39. (C): Collectivism is characterized by the belief that group goals precede individual goals, relations are moral and often placed above tasks, and maintaining harmony within the group is highly valued. The statement that "Individual opinions are independent of collective opinions" does not characterize collectivism. In collectivist cultures, individual opinions are often aligned with and subordinate to the collective or group opinions, reflecting a priority for group consensus and harmony over individual dissent.

40. (C)

41. (D): The Non-Least Developed Contracting States (NLDCS) among the provided options are:

(*b*) Pakistan

(*d*) India

(*e*) Sri Lanka

Therefore, the correct answer is (D).

42. (D): The correct considerations that are limitations of CVP analysis include:

(*a*) Constant selling price regardless of sales volume

(*b*) Firm efficiency and productivity are constant and the costs are linear

(*d*) Sales mix and the inventory levels are constant

CVP analysis assumes certain conditions for its applicability, such as constant selling prices, linear costs, and unchanged sales mix and inventory levels, which may not hold true in real-world scenarios, making these its limitations.

Therefore, the correct answer is (D).

43. (C): The correct matches between the description identifiers and the types of research design are as follows:

(*a*) The time dimension is matched with IV, Cross-sectional study, which involves collecting data at a single point in time. This design is used to capture a snapshot of the current state of the subjects being studied.

(*b*) The purpose of the study, when it aims to depict the characteristics of a group or the nature of a situation, is III, Descriptive study. Descriptive research is concerned with describing the characteristics of a particular individual, or of a group.

(*c*) The topical scope of the study, when it focuses on the extent and relationships of variables, aligns with II, Statistical study. This type of study involves analyzing data to find relationships between variables.

(*d*) The degree to which the research question has been crystallized, if it's in the preliminary stages of investigation, is linked with I, Exploratory study. Exploratory research is conducted for a problem that has not been clearly defined. It allows the researcher to gather information that provides insights and understanding of the issue at hand.

44. (A): The Static Theory of Capital Structure, also known as the Trade-Off Theory, articulates that a firm borrows up to the point where the tax benefit from extra debt is exactly equal to the cost that comes from the increased probability of financial distress. This theory suggests an optimal capital structure at which the value of the firm is maximized through the balance of these costs and benefits. The tax shield on debt interest payments can increase the value of the firm because these payments are deductible expenses that reduce the firm's taxable income. However, as a firm increases its leverage, the risk of financial distress and bankruptcy costs also increase, which can deter value. The static theory thus proposes a balance between these factors to determine the optimal level of debt a firm should maintain.

45. (B)

46. (B)

47. (C): Relevant factors in technological innovations include:

(*a*) most innovations are incremental, which means they build upon existing technologies or products, making gradual improvements rather than revolutionary changes;

(*b*) most innovations involve the commercial utilization of ideas, indicating that innovation is not just about inventing new technologies but also about finding commercial applications for those technologies; and

(*e*) the risk in introducing innovations is usually high, reflecting the uncertainty associated with developing and marketing new technologies or products. These aspects underscore the gradual, applied, and risky nature of most technological innovations.

48. (C): Job context consists of physical working conditions, work schedule, incentives, and the number of people with whom the employee would normally interact. It encompasses the environment and external conditions under which the job is performed, including the non-task-related aspects that can affect an employee's performance and satisfaction. Job context differs from job content, which refers to the duties and responsibilities of the job itself, and job specification, which outlines the qualifications and skills required for the job. Job profile may provide an overview of the position, including both job content and context, but does not specifically refer to the external factors influencing the job environment as described.

49. (D): The Turquand Rule, also known as the "Indoor Management Rule," is an exception to the doctrine of Constructive Notice. The doctrine of Constructive Notice suggests that persons dealing with a company are assumed to have knowledge of the company's public documents, such as its memorandum and articles of association. However, the Turquand Rule provides that outsiders dealing with a company have the right to assume that the internal requirements and procedures specified in the company's public documents have been properly observed. This rule protects third parties who enter into contracts with the company in good faith, without having to inquire into the compliance of internal company procedures.

50. **(B)**

51. **(B):** A discrete probability distribution assigns a probability to each possible value of the random variable. It characterizes the distribution of discrete outcomes, such as counts or categories, as opposed to continuous outcomes. This means that for each specific outcome that the random variable can take, there is an associated probability that precisely that outcome will occur. This property is fundamental to the understanding and application of discrete probability distributions in statistical analysis, helping to predict the likelihood of various outcomes.

52. **(B):** When a country's currency is accepted as a reserve currency, the potential conflict may arise between (*a*) Domestic monetary policy, (*c*) External currency policy, and (*d*) Foreign trade policy. The use of a country's currency as a global reserve currency can complicate its ability to conduct independent monetary policy because the demand for the currency can affect its value independently of domestic economic conditions. Additionally, maintaining the currency as attractive for international reserves may require the country to prioritize external currency stability over domestic objectives. This can also influence its foreign trade policy, as the country may need to balance the benefits of a strong currency (such as cheaper imports and attractiveness as a reserve currency) against the potential drawbacks (like more expensive exports).

53. **(A):** Both Assertion (A) and Reason (R) are correct, and (R) is the correct explanation of (A). Consumers do indeed choose retail channels based on various factors including shopping goals, price, product assortment, and convenience, as stated in Assertion (A). Reason (R) provides a specific example of this behaviour, explaining that consumers' willingness or unwillingness to "trade-up" to higher-end goods or "trade down" to discount retailers for private-label products is a reflection of their preference based on perceived value, assortment, and convenience. This behaviour underlines the broader assertion that consumer choice of retail channels is influenced by a variety of factors beyond just price or product availability.

54. **(A):** The chronological order for the rounds of multilateral trade negotiations under GATT/WTO is as follows:

(*c*) Annecy was held in 1949 as one of the early rounds of negotiations.

(*d*) Torquay followed in 1951, continuing the work of reducing tariffs and expanding global trade.

(*a*) Kennedy came later, in the mid-1960s (1964-1967), and focused on further tariff reductions and also introduced anti-dumping measures.

(*e*) Tokyo was held in the 1970s (1973-1979), significantly expanding the scope of the negotiations to include non-tariff barriers and framework agreements.

(*b*) Doha, the most recent round, began in 2001 and has been focused on further liberalizing trade, with particular attention to the needs of developing countries.

Thus, the correct chronological order is (*c*), (*d*), (*a*), (*e*), (*b*).

55. (C): The defensive strategy where a target company makes a counter bid for the stock of the bidder is called the Pacman Defense. This strategy turns the tables on the original bidder by attempting to acquire them instead. Named after the Pac-Man video game, where the character eats ghosts that chase it, this defense tactic is used by a company to fend off a hostile takeover attempt by making a counteroffer to purchase the shares of the company attempting the takeover.

56. (C): The remaining partners compensate the retiring partner for their share of goodwill in the Gaining Ratio. The Gaining Ratio is determined by comparing the old profit-sharing ratio to the new profit-sharing ratio of the remaining partners. It reflects the proportion in which the remaining partners gain from the outgoing partner's share of profits and, consequently, the goodwill. The compensation for the retiring partner's goodwill share is thus based on how much more of the profits the remaining partners will receive after the retirement, relative to their previous shares.

57. (A): Matching the features with the remedies for breach of contract:

(*a*) Breach of promise to marry is typically addressed with IV, Vindictive damages, which are awarded in cases where the breach of contract causes personal suffering or distress, as in the case of a breached promise to marry.

(*b*) Part performance (as much as earned) can be remedied by III, Sue for quantum meruit, where the party who has performed part of the contract can claim payment for the work actually done or services rendered.

(*c*) Absolvation from all obligations corresponds to II, Rescission of contract, which allows the aggrieved party to cancel the contract and be relieved from all its obligations.

(*d*) Mode of securing the specific performance of negative terms of contract is addressed by I, Suit for injunction, which can prevent a party from doing something that would breach the contract's terms, thereby enforcing the contract's negative terms.

58. (D): In one-factor ANOVA (Analysis of Variance), the computed F-value will be negative under no circumstances. The F-value is a ratio of the variance between the groups (mean squares between) to the variance within the groups (mean squares within), and since variance cannot be negative, the F-value also cannot be negative. It's a statistical method used to compare the means of three or more samples to see if at least one of the means is different from the others. A negative F-value is not possible because variances (which are squared differences) are always non-negative.

59. (B): The functions of the Reserve Bank of India (RBI) include:

(*a*) Bank of issue, where it has the sole right to issue currency notes in India except for one rupee notes and coins which are issued by the Ministry of Finance,

(*b*) Banker's bank and lender of the last resort, where it acts as a banker to the government and banks and provides funds to them in times of need,

(*d*) Controller of credit through its monetary policy measures to control inflation and stabilize the currency, and

(*e*) Custodian of foreign exchange reserves, managing the Foreign Exchange Management Act, 1999.

(*c*) The RBI does not regulate fiscal policy as fiscal policy is managed by the government through its spending and taxation decisions.

60. (C): The relationship among the agent, the sub-agent, and the principal usually does not involve direct privity of contract between the principal and the sub-agent. Privity of contract exists between the agent and the principal, and separately between the agent and the sub-agent. The principal's relationship with the sub-agent is indirect, mediated through the agent. The agent is responsible to the principal for the acts of the sub-agent, and the sub-agent works under the control and on the directions of the agent. The sub-agent is responsible to the agent only for his actions unless there's an express or implied agreement to the contrary that directly involves the principal.

61. (A): To determine the amount by which the Share Forfeiture Account will be credited when Mr. X's shares are forfeited, we calculate the total amount paid by him and then apply it to the forfeiture process. Mr. X held 200 shares and paid only the application money of ₹ 20 per share.

The total amount paid by Mr. X for the 200 shares = 200 shares × ₹ 20/share = ₹ 4000.

The Share Forfeiture Account will be credited by ₹ 4000, which is the total amount paid by Mr. X for the application money on 200 shares.

62. (B): Pre-experimental designs include simple structures that do not control for all variables, which might influence the outcome of an experiment. Among the options given:

(*a*) One-group pre-test-post-test involves testing a single group before and after a treatment to observe changes.

(*d*) Static group comparison involves comparing two groups, one that receives the treatment and one that does not, without random assignment.

(*e*) After-only study involves measuring the outcome after the treatment has been applied, without a pre-test.

These designs are characterized by a lack of random assignment and control, making them less rigorous than true experimental designs but useful in preliminary or exploratory research contexts.

63. (B): The investigation process of combinations by the Competition Commission of India involves several steps, typically starting with the initial assessment and moving towards more detailed inquiries if needed. The correct order reflecting the procedural steps is:

(*e*) Issue a notice for show-cause to the parties of the combination, asking them to explain why their combination should not be investigated.

(*a*) Call for a report from the Director General, which involves a detailed investigation into the combination.

(*c*) Direct the parties of the combination to publish details of the combination, ensuring transparency and allowing for public comments.

(*b*) Invite any person, affected parties to file written objections, which allows stakeholders to present their concerns.

(*d*) Call for additional information from the parties of the combination, which is often necessary for a thorough analysis of the combination's impact.

This sequence ensures that the Competition Commission gathers all necessary information to assess the combination's compliance with competition laws and its potential impact on the market.

64. (A)

65. (B)

66. (B): Matching the assets transferred with the exemptions of capital gains under Sections 54 to 54EC of the Income Tax Act:

(*a*) Agricultural Land is covered under Section 54B, which provides an exemption on capital gains arising from the transfer of agricultural land, subject to certain conditions.

(*b*) Residential House is associated with Section 54, which offers an exemption on capital gains from the sale of a residential house, provided another residential house is purchased or constructed under specified conditions.

(*c*) Land or Building or Both can be eligible for exemption under Section 54EC, provided the capital gains are invested in specified bonds issued by the government or a public sector company within a specified timeframe.

(*d*) Land and Building forming part of an industrial undertaking falls under Section 54D, which provides an exemption for capital gains arising from the compulsory acquisition of land and buildings of an industrial undertaking.

Therefore, the correct match is B (I, IV, II, III), aligning each asset type with the appropriate Section of the Income Tax Act that provides an exemption for capital gains.

67. (B): The Competition Commission of India (CCI) can impose a penalty for anti-competitive activities by a firm which shall be not more than ten per cent of the average turnover/income of the firm of the three preceding financial years.

This penalty is meant to deter anti-competitive practices and ensure fair competition within the market. The CCI plays a crucial role in monitoring and managing competition in the Indian market, and this power to impose penalties is a key tool in enforcing compliance with competition laws.

68. (D): The sequential stages of moral development in business organizations, as proposed by Lawrence Kohlberg, are characterized by: Preconventional, Conventional, and Principled Oriented stages. This model suggests that individuals' moral reasoning develops through these stages:

- In the Preconventional stage, individuals make decisions based on self-interest and the consequences of actions (punishment or reward).
- In the Conventional stage, individuals adhere to societal norms and laws.
- In the Principled Oriented stage, individuals follow universal ethical principles and internalized moral standards, even if they conflict with laws and social agreements. This framework is applied to understand ethical behaviour and decision-making in business contexts.

69. (C): Economic-value-to-customer pricing (EVC) takes into account a host of inputs, such as buyer's image of the product performance, the channel deliverables, the warranty quality, customer support, and softer attributes such as the supplier's reputation, trustworthiness, and esteem. This pricing strategy is based on the perceived value of the product or service to the customer, rather than solely on the seller's costs or the prices set by competitors. EVC pricing aims to capture the total value that a product or service provides to a customer, including both tangible and intangible benefits, to set a price that reflects its overall worth to the customer.

70. (D): The factors attributed to the weakening of the Indian rupee typically include:

(*b*) Rising cost of imports,

(*c*) Widening trade deficit, and

(*d*) Opening of Rupee vostro accounts.

Rising costs of imports make the country spend more foreign currency, putting pressure on the domestic currency. A widening trade deficit, where the value of imports significantly exceeds the value of exports, also contributes to the weakening of the currency due to higher demand for foreign currency. Opening of Rupee vostro accounts, aimed at facilitating trade settlements in rupees, could have varied impacts on the currency's strength, depending on the balance of trade and other economic factors. Rupee payment for international trade (*a*) and Rupee UPI payments for overseas transactions (*e*) are initiatives that could potentially strengthen the rupee by increasing its usability in international transactions but are not direct causes of weakening.

71. (D): Members of a Limited Liability Partnership (LLP) can include:

(*a*) Resident Indians,

(*b*) Limited Liability Partnership itself (another LLP can be a member of an LLP), and

(*e*) Companies (including foreign companies).

These entities can be partners in an LLP, contributing to its capital and participating in its management depending on the LLP agreement. Corporations Sole and Co-operative societies are typically not eligible to become members of an LLP under the LLP Act.

72. (B)

73. (A): Matching Activity Based Cost Centers with the Costs Incurred and Accounted for:

(*a*) **Unit-level activity center:** Costs incurred are directly related to the production volume, such as II. Direct material and labour costs. These costs vary with the number of units produced.

(*b*) **Batch level activity center:** Costs associated with specific batches of production, like IV. Material handling costs, which are incurred each time a batch is handled or processed.

(*c*) **Product level activity center:** Costs related to specific products, including I. Patent, trademark, and copyright fees. These are costs that can be directly attributed to the development and maintenance of a product.

(*d*) **Facility level activity center:** Costs that are not directly tied to a specific product but are necessary for the overall operation of the facility, such as III. Plant depreciation and maintenance expenses, which are incurred regardless of the production volume or the number of batches run.

74. (D)

75. (A): Effective mentoring requires trust, and the level of trust reflects the mentor's:

- **Competence:** The mentor's ability and expertise in their field.
- **Consistency:** The mentor's reliability in behaviour and actions.
- **Communication abilities:** The mentor's skill in conveying information, listening, and providing feedback.
- **Control sharing readiness:** The mentor's willingness to share control and empower the mentee.

These factors contribute to building a strong, trustful mentoring relationship where the mentee feels supported and valued, and the mentor can effectively guide and facilitate the mentee's growth and development.

76. (C)

77. (A): The reasons for substitution between domestic and MNC (Multinational Corporation) goods include:

(*a*) Increased knowledge of foreign products due to the international information revolution, which has made consumers more aware of the availability and attributes of foreign products, influencing their purchasing decisions.

(*c*) Transportation costs having fallen to very low levels for most products, making it economically feasible to import and export goods, thereby increasing the competition between domestic and MNC goods on price, quality, and availability.

These factors contribute to the dynamic interchangeability between domestic and international products in the consumer market.

78. (D): Trademarks can be broadly classified into the following categories:

(*a*) **Descriptive:** Marks that describe the goods or services on which the mark is used.

(*c*) **Generic:** Terms that refer to the general category or class of products and cannot function as trademarks because they do not distinguish the products of one provider from those of others.

(*e*) **Invented:** Marks that are made-up words or coined terms that have no dictionary or known meaning.

These categories reflect the spectrum of trademark types, from those that directly describe or relate to the product, to generic terms that are ineligible for trademark protection, to completely invented words created for the purpose of branding.

79. (D): In the context of the Income Tax Act, certain types of income are clubbed together under the income of an individual for tax purposes. For Mr. Q, the incomes that would be clubbed into his income include:

(*c*) Minor son's earned interest on deposits of money gifted to him by his uncle, ₹ 15,000. The income earned by minors is usually clubbed with the income of the parent unless the minor earns income due to his or her own skill, talent, or specialized knowledge.

(*e*) Minor son's winnings from lottery, ₹ 1,05,000. Winnings from lotteries, game shows, etc., earned by minors are also typically clubbed with the income of the parent for tax purposes.

Incomes from Mrs. Q's profession or salary (options *a* and *b*) are not clubbed with Mr. Q's income as they are considered separate entities for income tax purposes. Similarly, a minor daughter's earnings from sports (option *d*) would not be clubbed with Mr. Q's income if the earnings are attributable to her skills, talent, or specialized knowledge.

80. (A): The most relevant statement regarding the substitution effect is that, in the real world, the substitution effect is often much larger than the income effect. This assertion is based on the economic theory that when the price of a good decreases, consumers are likely to substitute the cheaper good for more expensive ones, holding the utility constant. This substitution effect, which reflects changes in consumption patterns due to changes in relative prices, tends to dominate because consumers adjust their consumption to maintain or increase their utility by taking advantage of lower-priced goods. The income effect, which describes how a consumer's purchasing power is affected by changes in prices, can either reinforce or counteract the substitution effect but is generally considered to be smaller in magnitude in many cases.

81. (B): The "Niryat Bandhu Scheme" as defined under the Foreign Trade Policy (FTP), implemented by the Director General of Foreign Trade, has the main aim to "mentor new and potential exporters on the intricacies of foreign trade through counselling, training, and outreach programmes". The scheme is designed to help new and inexperienced exporters understand the nuances of international trade and become successful in the global market.

It provides guidance and support to ensure that new exporters can navigate the complexities of exporting goods and services from India, making it an important initiative for promoting exports and enhancing India's trade relations globally.

82. (B): The statement that does not support the concept of third-degree price discrimination is "This type of price discrimination is most likely to occur in the manufacturing industries". Third-degree price discrimination involves charging different prices to different segments of the market, based on varying demand elasticities or willingness to pay among those segments. It does not inherently relate to the industry type (manufacturing, service, etc.) but rather to the ability of a firm to segment the market, maintain separation between segments, and recognize differences in price sensitivity. The other options correctly describe necessary conditions for third-degree price discrimination.

83. (C): "Call to Action" (CTA) is a marketing term for any design intended to prompt an immediate response or encourage an immediate sale. CTAs are used in various forms of media, including online marketing, advertisements, and promotional emails, to direct the audience towards taking a specific action, such as making a purchase, registering for a webinar, subscribing to a newsletter, or visiting a website. Effective CTAs are crucial for converting prospects into customers by guiding them on what steps to take next.

84. (B)

85. (C)

86. (B): The present value of future profits that an individual or segment will generate over a lifetime relationship with a brand or firm is known as Lifetime Value. This concept is used in marketing to estimate the total value a customer brings to a business over the entire period of their relationship. It helps businesses in allocating marketing resources efficiently by focusing on customers who offer the highest return over time.

87. (C): Emotional appeal in advertising is based on the idea that:

(*c*) It can capture attention and foster an attachment to the brand or product,

(*a*) Rational appeals generally go unnoticed because many purchase decisions are made with emotional rather than rational considerations at the forefront, and

(*d*) Consumers ignore most ads, which implies that emotional appeals are more likely to break through the clutter and resonate with the audience.

Emotional appeals aim to evoke feelings that influence consumers' perceptions and buying behaviour, making them more effective in certain contexts than rational appeals, which focus on the practical or functional aspects of a product.

88. (B): The logical sequence for service differentiators, starting from the initial interaction with the customer to the post-sale support, would be:

(*e*) **Ease of ordering:** This is the first step where the customer engages with the service, making it critical for a positive initial impression.

(*a*) **Speed and timing of delivery:** Once an order is placed, the promptness and timing of delivery become the next crucial differentiator.

(*d*) **Installation, training, and consulting:** For services requiring setup or knowledge transfer, the quality and effectiveness of these activities significantly impact customer satisfaction.

(*b*) **Maintenance and repair:** Ongoing support and the ability to maintain and repair any issues ensure long-term customer satisfaction and loyalty.

(*c*) **Returns:** The process for handling returns smoothly and efficiently is a key part of post-purchase customer service.

Therefore, the correct sequence is (B) *i.e.*, (*e*), (*a*), (*d*), (*b*), (*c*).

89. (A): The steps in the book building process for the public issue of shares in India typically follow this sequence:

(*c*) Appointment of the merchant banker and syndicate members (SEBI registered intermediaries) as underwriters: This is the initial step where the company appoints financial experts to manage the issue.

(*d*) Preparation and filing of red herring prospectus with the SEBI for approval: The next step involves preparing and submitting the necessary documentation to the regulatory authority for approval.

(*b*) Book runner and syndicate members generate awareness, create demand and run the order book: Once the regulatory approvals are in place, the focus shifts to market outreach and demand generation.

(*a*) Determine issue price, market clearing price, and price discovery: Based on the demand and bids received, the issue price is determined through a process of price discovery.

(*e*) Allotment and listing of shares on stock exchange(s): The final step involves allocating shares to investors and listing the shares on stock exchanges for trading.

The correct order is (*c*), (*d*), (*b*), (*a*), (*e*).

90. (D): RuPay is the digital payment system developed and managed by the National Payments Corporation of India (NPCI). RuPay is India's own card payment network, similar to international payment networks like Visa and Mastercard, but focused on providing a domestic, cost-effective alternative to these global systems. RuPay cards are accepted at ATMs, POS devices, and e-commerce websites across India, making it a significant component of India's push for financial inclusion and enhanced digital payment infrastructure.

91. (B): Improved economic models are capable of understanding qualitative and quantitative factors, which is the reason, as per the passage, for driving more effective macro policies. The passage suggests that as models improve and quantitative capabilities enhance, alongside the refinement of qualitative judgments, macroeconomic policy-making will become more precise and effective.

This is in contrast to earlier times when the predictive power of macroeconomic models was less reliable due to the inability to test hypotheses with repeated experiments and reliance on data of questionable provenance.

92. (A): The major contributions of economics, as per the passage, include explaining (*a*) buyers' behaviour towards the products, (*b*) firms' behaviours for maximizing profit, and (*d*) market behaviour to discover the most efficient prices.

These aspects are foundational to the study of economics, which has excelled at understanding and explaining how individuals and firms make decisions within markets to maximize utility and profit, respectively, and how these interactions determine price levels in the market.

93. (D): Matching the phenomenon with the reasons given in the passage:

(*a*) Economics defines how markets discover the most efficient prices (IV).

(*b*) Learning of the Great Depression led to a better understanding of aggregate variables like GDP, Employment, and Inflation (I) because it highlighted the need for a branch of economics that could explain phenomena not accounted for by microeconomics alone.

(*c*) Macro-economic variables include GDP, Employment, and Inflation (II), which are central to the study of macroeconomics.

(*d*) The pitfalls of Microeconomics include assumptions that human beings are rational and information is free (III), which can lead to over simplifications in economic models.

94. **(A):** The reason for crises in economic modelling, as per the given passage, is aggregating billions of micro truths into one macro truth. This process is inherently complex and challenging because it involves synthesizing a vast array of individual decisions, behaviours, and interactions into a coherent macroeconomic model. The difficulty lies in the fact that these micro-level behaviours may not aggregate in a straightforward or predictable manner, leading to potential inaccuracies or over simplifications in macroeconomic models.

95. **(A):** Both Statement I and Statement II are true. Statement I highlights the limitation faced by macroeconomists in testing their models, as they can only back-test against historical data, which may not be entirely reliable or indicative of future conditions. Statement II points out a fundamental challenge in macroeconomics: the inability to apply the scientific method of hypothesis testing through repeated experiments due to the impracticality of experimenting with real economies. Together, these statements underscore the difficulties in macroeconomic prediction and model validation.

96. **(A)**

97. **(D):** According to the passage, entrepreneurship is now being accepted as a way of life and livelihood. The narrative emphasizes the changing mindset towards entrepreneurship, celebrating startups and new businesses, and recognizing entrepreneurship as a respectable and viable career path, supported by families and society at large.

98. **(C):** The principles of responsible investing to which the private equity and venture capital industry is committed have resulted in (*c*) an inclusive and equitable economy, and (*e*) earned the trust of global investors. The passage underlines how these principles have contributed to building an economy that is more equitable and inclusive, attracting significant trust and investment from global investors due to its commitment to responsible and sustainable growth.

99. **(D):** In the recent years, the focus of private equity and venture capital in India has been on value creation. The passage highlights the emphasis on creating value through innovative business models and the deployment of private capital to support enterprises that contribute to the economy's multi-dimensional progress.

100. **(B):** According to the passage, factors that have made India an attractive destination for investments include (*a*) the Startup India program, (*c*) Goods and Services Tax (GST) facilitation, and (*d*) Alternative Investment Funds (AIFs). The passage specifically mentions these frameworks and progressive amendments as key contributors to attracting capital and enhancing India's appeal as an investment destination.

Previous Years' Paper

National Testing Agency (NTA)

UGC-NET Junior Research Fellowship & Assistant Professor Eligibility Exam

COMMERCE, June-2023

(Exam held on 13-06-2023)

PAPER-II

1. Which of the following cause demand of a product to increase?

(*a*) An increase in consumer's income
(*b*) An increase in the prices of substitutes
(*c*) An increase in the price of complements
(*d*) An increase in the number of substitutes
(*e*) An increased taste for the commodity.

Choose the correct answer from the options given below:

A. (*a*), (*b*) and (*c*) only
B. (*c*), (*d*) and (*e*) only
C. (*b*), (*d*) and (*e*) only
D. (*a*), (*b*) and (*e*) only

2. Which one of the following values is not a part of OCTAPACE framework?

A. Openness
B. Extension
C. Proactivity
D. Autonomy

3. Under which of the following market structures, products are differentiated and close substitutes?

(*a*) Perfect competition
(*b*) Monopolistic competition
(*c*) Oligopoly
(*d*) Duopoly
(*e*) Monopoly

Choose the correct answer from the options given below:

A. (*a*), (*b*) and (*c*) only
B. (*b*), (*c*) and (*d*) only
C. (*c*), (*d*) and (*e*) only
D. (*a*), (*c*) and (*d*) only

4. The problem-definition process involves following steps. Arrange them in a logical sequence.

(*a*) Determine the unit of analysis
(*b*) Determine the relevant variables
(*c*) Write managerial decision statement and research objectives
(*d*) Write research question and/or research hypothesis
(*e*) Identify key problems

Choose the correct answer from the options given below:

A. (*a*), (*b*), (*e*), (*d*), (*c*)
B. (*c*), (*d*), (*a*), (*b*), (*e*)
C. (*b*), (*e*), (*a*), (*c*), (*d*)
D. (*e*), (*c*), (*a*), (*b*), (*d*)

5. Empirical studies indicate that long run average cost (LAC) curve is _____

A. L-shaped
B. U-shaped
C. S-shaped
D. V-shaped

6. Which of the following are the reasons for manufacturers and retailers to brand their offerings?

(*a*) Helps to gauge the level of product quality
(*b*) Enables premium pricing
(*c*) Contributes to corporate identity programmes
(*d*) Informs about the source of a product
(*e*) Develops customer loyalty.

Choose the most appropriate answer from the options given below:

A. (*a*), (*b*), (*c*) and (*e*) only
B. (*b*), (*c*) and (*e*) only
C. (*a*), (*b*), (*c*) and (*d*) only
D. (*a*), (*d*) and (*e*) only

7. A population has a mean of 200 and a standard deviation of 50. Suppose a simple random sample of size 100 is selected then the probability that the sample mean will be ± 5 of the population mean is ____

A. 0.7523
B. 0.6928
C. 0.9544
D. 0.6826

8. On attaining the age of majority, a minor's agreement

A. Can be ratified by him
B. Cannot be ratified by him
C. Becomes void
D. Becomes valid

9. Which one group of the following countries are members of ASEAN?

A. Laos, Cambodia, Brunei
B. Malaysia, Thailand, Taiwan
C. Myanmar, Singapore, Hong Kong
D. Fiji, Laos, Cambodia

10. Who was of the opinion that labour was "the father of wealth" and it must be included in any estimate of national wealth?

A. William Far
B. William Petty
C. William C. Pyle
D. Flamholtz

11. The Competition (Amendment) Act, 2023 revamped the competition Act in which of the following perspectives:

(*a*) The CCI needs to be intimated if the value of merger and acquisition deal exceeds ₹ 2000 crores

(*b*) The overall timeline for assessment of combination has been reduced to 150 days from 210 days

(*c*) "Exclusive selling agreements" has been replaced with "exclusive dealing agreement"

(*d*) Entities who are not engaged in identical or similar trade shall also be part of an Anti-competitive Agreement under Section 3(3) of the Act

(*e*) Anti-competitive conduct like "tie-up arrangements", "re-sale price maintenance" and "exclusive distribution agreement" have been redefined.

Choose the correct answer from the options given below:

A. (*a*), (*b*) and (*c*) only
B. (*c*) and (*e*) only
C. (*a*), (*b*), (*c*) and (*d*) only
D. (*a*), (*b*), (*c*), (*d*) and (*e*)

12. In totalitarianism, called authoritarianism, individual freedom is subordinated to the power of the authority of a group or state. Which of the following is not a type of totalitarianism?

A. Theocratic
B. Right Wing
C. Tribal
D. Conservative

13. 'A' sells a mobile phone to 'B', a minor who pays for it by his cheque. 'A' endorses the cheque to 'C' who takes it in good faith and for value. The cheque is dishonoured on presentation. Can 'C' enforce payment of the cheque?

A. 'C' can enforce the payment of cheque only against 'A'
B. 'C' can enforce the payment of cheque either against 'A' or 'B'
C. 'C' can enforce payment of cheque both against 'A' and 'B'
D. 'C' can enforce the payment of cheque only against 'B'

14. Match List-I with List-II.

List-I (A.T. Kearney Globalization Index)	**List-II (Variables)**
(*a*) Economic Integration	I. International Tourism and Travel
(*b*) Personal Integration	II. Internet users

(*c*) Technological Integration	III. Foreign Direct Investment		
(*d*) Political Integration	IV. Ratification and multilateral treaties		

Choose the correct answer from the options given below:

	(*a*)	(*b*)	(*c*)	(*d*)
A.	IV	III	II	I
B.	III	I	II	IV
C.	III	II	I	IV
D.	IV	I	II	III

15. According to the theory of contestable markets, vigorous competition can take place even among few sellers if ___ and ____ .

(*a*) Product is differentiated
(*b*) Demand is infinitely elastic
(*c*) Entry into the market is absolutely free
(*d*) There are strong entry-exit barriers
(*e*) Exit from the market is entirely costless.

Choose the correct answer from the options given below:

A. (*a*) and (*d*) only B. (*b*) and (*e*) only
C. (*a*) and (*c*) only D. (*c*) and (*e*) only

16. Experimental treatment in research design signifies which of the following?

A. Selection of dependent variable
B. Manipulating independent variable
C. Selection of independent variable
D. Manipulating dependent variable

17. The steps to be followed by a firm while strategizing to go international are as follows:

(*a*) Deciding when to enter
(*b*) Deciding which markets to enter
(*c*) Deciding whether to go global
(*d*) Choosing a mode of entry
(*e*) Deciding how to enter the chosen market.

Choose the correct answer from the options given below:

A. (*e*), (*d*), (*c*), (*b*), (*a*)
B. (*c*), (*a*), (*e*), (*d*), (*b*)
C. (*c*), (*b*), (*a*), (*e*), (*d*)
D. (*a*), (*b*), (*c*), (*e*), (*d*)

18. In the context of banking sector, spread is defined as a function of the following:

(*a*) Forex
(*b*) Net Interest income
(*c*) Rate Sensitive Assets
(*d*) Asset Ratio
(*e*) Leverage Ratio

Choose the correct answer from the options given below:

A. (*c*) and (*e*) only B. (*a*) and (*c*) only
C. (*b*) and (*d*) only D. (*b*) and (*e*) only

19. If the application for information is rejected under the Right to Information Act 2005, the CPIO/SPIO is obligated which of the following to furnish the person seeking the information?

(*a*) Power and functions of information commission
(*b*) Reasons for such rejection
(*c*) Obligation of public authorities
(*d*) The particulars of the appellant authority
(*e*) The period within which an appeal against such rejection may be preferred

Choose the correct answer from the options given below:

A. (*a*), (*b*) and (*c*) only
B. (*b*), (*c*) and (*d*) only
C. (*a*), (*c*) and (*e*) only
D. (*b*), (*d*) and (*e*) only

20. A multinational company can use which prices to create profits in low tax regimes and loss in high tax regimes?

A. Divisional prices
B. Inter-Divisional Prices
C. Holding company prices
D. Transfer prices

21. Which are the RBI notified domestic accredited credit rating agencies?

(*a*) Brickwork ratings
(*b*) Acuite ratings
(*c*) CRISIL ratings
(*d*) Standard and Poor's
(*e*) Moody's

Choose the correct answer from the options given below:

A. (*b*) and (*c*) only B. (*c*) and (*d*) only
C. (*a*) and (*c*) only D. (*c*) and (*e*) only

22. When the income of a minor child is clubbed with the income of mother or father, how much the deduction will be allowed to mother or father?

A. ₹ 1500
B. ₹ 2000
C. Actual income clubbed with the income of mother or father, whichever is less
D. No deduction

23. Arrange the following service gaps as per SERVQUAL approach in the logical sequence.

(*a*) The gap between service quality specifications and service delivery
(*b*) The gap between the customer's expectations end management perception
(*c*) The gap between perceived service and expected service
(*d*) The gap between management perception and service quality specification
(*e*) The gap between service delivery and external communications.

Choose the correct answer from the options given below:

A. (*d*), (*a*), (*b*), (*e*), (*c*)
B. (*b*), (*d*), (*a*), (*e*), (*c*)
C. (*a*), (*c*), (*b*), (*d*), (*e*)
D. (*c*), (*a*), (*b*), (*e*), (*d*)

24. As suggested by Collins, arrange the following leadership levels in the sequentially higher order.

(*a*) The leader is a competent manager
(*b*) The leader is an executive
(*c*) The leader is a highly capable individual
(*d*) The leader is an effective leader
(*e*) The leader is a contributing team member

Choose the correct answer from the options given below:

A. (*b*), (*c*), (*d*), (*a*), (*e*)
B. (*c*), (*e*), (*a*), (*d*), (*b*)
C. (*c*), (*a*), (*e*), (*d*), (*b*)
D. (*c*), (*e*), (*a*), (*b*), (*d*)

25. The sales step in which a salesperson learns as much as possible about a prospective customer before making a sales call is known as ______.

A. Approach
B. Prospecting
C. Pre-approach
D. Presentation

26. Match List-I with List-II.

List-I (Accounting Concepts)	**List-II (Purpose/ Applicability)**
(*a*) Going Concern Concept	I. The same accounting method used by a firm from one period to another
(*b*) Consistency	II. Relate to the relative size or importance of an item or event
(*c*) Cost concept	III. An inappropriate assumption for firm undergoing bankruptcy
(*d*) Materiality	IV. The normal basis used to account for assets

Choose the correct answer from the options given below:

	(*a*)	(*b*)	(*c*)	(*d*)
A.	II	III	IV	I
B.	I	II	III	IV
C.	I	II	IV	III
D.	III	I	IV	II

27. Which of the following are skills and capabilities related competencies?

(*a*) Analysis
(*b*) Intellectual curiosity
(*c*) Organization
(*d*) Problem solving
(*e*) Ownership of assignments

Choose the most appropriate answer from the options given below:

A. (*a*), (*c*) and (*d*) only
B. (*a*), (*b*) and (*c*) only
C. (*b*), (*c*) and (*d*) only
D. (*a*), (*d*) and (*e*) only

28. The Directorate General of Foreign Trade (DGFT) facilitates and promotes foreign trade in India and also implements the foreign trade policy of India. Which of the following union ministry governs the DGFT?

A. Ministry of Commerce and Industry
B. Ministry of Science and Technology
C. Ministry of Finance
D. Ministry of External Affairs

29. Match List-I with List-II.

List-I (Schedules under the companies Act, 2013)	**List-II (Underlying themes)**
(*a*) Schedule I	I. Computation of Depreciation
(*b*) Schedule II	II. Code for Independent directors
(*c*) Schedule III	III. Memorandum of Association
(*d*) Schedule IV	IV. Preparation of Balance sheet and statement of profit and loss

Choose the correct answer from the options given below:

	(*a*)	(*b*)	(*c*)	(*d*)
A.	II	I	IV	III
B.	III	I	IV	II
C.	III	IV	I	II
D.	I	III	II	IV

30. An attacking strategy which involves introducing new products or technologies that rewrite the rules of competition in the market and avoid direct conflict with a rival is known as _______.

A. Flanking B. Bypass
C. Encirclement D. Guerrilla

31. Which of the following describe an intervention currency:

A. The currency in which exporter choose to invoice their exports
B. The currency in which cross-border transactions are paid for and closed
C. The currency in terms of which a domestic currency is quoted
D. The vehicle currency

32. From the following information you are required to compute Return on Total Capital employed.

Net Profit .... ₹ 1,00,000

Provision for tax.................. ₹ 1,00,000

Income from Investment .... ₹ 10,000

Fixed Assets.......................... ₹ 4,50,000

Current assets .... ₹ 1,50,000

Interest on debenture .... ₹ 10,000

Reserves .... ₹ 1,00,000

A. 30% B. 50%
C. 60% D. 40%

33. In which of the following segmentation criteria, the predictability of consumer choice behaviour is the highest?

A. Psychological
B. Demographic
C. Behavioural
D. Geodemographic

34. Which one of the following is a fully owned subsidiary of the R.B.I?

A. Indian Institute of Bank Management (IIBM)
B. National Institute of Bank Management (NIBM)
C. Indian Institute of Banking and Finance (IIBF)
D. Indian Financial Technology and Allied Services (IFTAS)

35. Arrange the following steps in a logical sequence in recourse to dishonouring a negotiable instrument:

(*a*) Noting (*b*) Compensation
(*c*) Protesting (*d*) Notice of dishonour
(*e*) Penalties

Choose the correct answer from the options given below:

A. (*d*), (*a*), (*c*), (*b*), (*e*)
B. (*c*), (*d*), (*a*), (*b*), (*e*)
C. (*c*), (*d*), (*e*), (*b*), (*a*)
D. (*a*), (*c*), (*d*), (*b*), (*e*)

36. Sequence the following steps in the operational functioning of the Asset reconstruction companies (as per SARFAESI Act 2002)

(*a*) Charge a 2 per cent management fee
(*b*) Issue security receipts to bank
(*c*) Make payment to bank
(*d*) Buys loans of bank at a discount
(*e*) Carry out the recovery

Choose the correct answer from the options given below:

A. (*d*), (*c*), (*a*), (*e*), (*b*)
B. (*d*), (*b*), (*e*), (*a*), (*c*)
C. (*d*), (*b*), (*c*), (*e*), (*a*)
D. (*d*), (*a*), (*b*), (*e*), (*c*)

37. Section 61 to 64 of the Company Act, 2013 states 'Alteration proper' which includes:

(*a*) Cancellation of the unissued shares
(*b*) Cancellation of issued shares
(*c*) Increase in share capital by issue of new share
(*d*) Decrease of share capital by redemption of shares
(*e*) Conversion of fully paid shares into stock and vice versa.

Choose the most appropriate answer from the options given below:

A. (*b*), (*c*) and (*d*) only
B. (*a*), (*c*) and (*e*) only
C. (*c*), (*d*) and (*e*) only
D. (*a*), (*b*) and (*c*) only

38. Mutual Funds in India are regulated by:

A. Unit Trust of India
B. Department for Promotion of Industries and Internal trade
C. The Securities and Exchange Board of India
D. Department of Financial Services

39. Given below are two statements: One is labelled as Assertion (A) and the other is labelled as Reason (R)

Assertion (A): Usually manufacturing companies use sale and lease back arrangement to unlock investment in fixed assets.

Reason (R): In a sale of lease back arrangement, the companies sell the asset to a leasing company, and lease it back to enjoy the uninterrupted use of asset in their business.

In the light of the above statements, choose the most appropriate answer from the options given below:

A. Both (A) and (R) are true and (R) is the correct explanation of (A)
B. Both (A) and (R) are true, but (R) is not the correct explanation of (A)
C. (A) is true, but (R) is not false
D. (A) is false, but (R) is true

40. Which of the following are correct for Agricultural Income?

(*a*) Income from self grown grass, trees, bamboo
(*b*) Rent and Rates derived from land
(*c*) Income from making the produce fit for marketing
(*d*) Income from land used for storing agriculture produce
(*e*) Income from farmhouse

Choose the correct answer from the options given below:

A. (*b*), (*c*) and (*e*) only
B. (*b*), (*d*) and (*e*) only
C. (*a*), (*c*) and (*d*) only
D. (*c*), (*d*) and (*e*) only

41. Match List-I with List-II.

List-I (Herfindahe Index Value)	**List-II (Market Type)**
(*a*) Zero	I. Oligopoly with high risk of cartels
(*b*) 0 -1,000	II. Oligopoly
(*c*) 1,000-1,800	III. Monopolistic competition
(*d*) 1,800-10,000	IV. Extremely competitive market

Choose the correct answer from the options given below:

	(*a*)	(*b*)	(*c*)	(*d*)
A.	I	II	III	IV
B.	IV	III	II	I
C.	II	I	III	IV
D.	I	III	II	IV

42. A box-plot is a graphical summary measures of data that displays

(*a*) Mean

(*b*) Q_1

(*c*) Median

(*d*) Q_3

(*e*) Mode

Choose the correct answer from the options given below:

A. (*c*) and (*e*) only

B. (*a*), (*c*) and (*e*) only

C. (*c*), (*d*) and (*b*) only

D. (*d*), (*b*) and (*a*) only

43. An agent is personally liable to third parties in which of the following situations?

(*a*) If an agent acts for an undisclosed Principal

(*b*) Trade usage and customs makes agent personally liable

(*c*) If an agent signs a contract in Principal's name

(*d*) If an agent acts for the named Principal

(*e*) If an agent works for a foreign Principal.

Choose the correct answer from the options given below:

A. (*a*), (*b*) and (*c*) only

B. (*a*), (*b*) and (*e*) only

C. (*c*), (*d*) and (*e*) only

D. (*b*), (*c*) and (*d*) only

44. Given below are two statements:

Statement I: Certificate of incorporation is conclusive evidence that all the requirements of the Companies Act have been complied with in respect of registration.

Statement II: After incorporation, if the company makes a fresh contract in terms of the pre-incorporation contract, the liability of the promoters shall come to an end.

In the light of the above statements, choose the correct answer from the options given below:

A. Both Statement I and Statement II are true

B. Both Statement I and Statement are false

C. Statement I is true, but Statement II is false

D. Statement I is false, but Statement II is true

45. Which of the interventions can be used to manage the anxiety created by mergers and acquisitions

(*a*) Speed-up of the integration process

(*b*) Articulate a new vision, common goals and organizational symbols

(*c*) Employee counselling and stress management training

(*d*) Disengage efforts such as termination ceremonies

(*e*) Social support from spouse, friends, supervisors and co-workers

Choose the most appropriate answer from the options given below:

A. (*a*), (*b*) and (*c*) only

B. (*b*), (*c*) and (*d*) only

C. (*a*), (*c*) and (*e*) only

D. (*a*), (*b*) and (*e*) only

46. Which of the following one considered as supply factors affecting the flow of Foreign Direct Investment (FDI):

(*a*) Customer Access
(*b*) Economic Priorities
(*c*) Resource Availability
(*d*) Avoidance of Trade Barrier
(*e*) Logistics

Choose the most appropriate answer from the options given below:

A. (*a*) and (*b*) only B. (*b*) and (*d*) only
C. (*c*) and (*e*) only D. (*a*) and (*e*) only

47. Arrange the following advance payment of tax in ascending order (Section 207 to section 211) of the Income Tax Act, 1961.

(*a*) Instalment of advance tax and due date
(*b*) Liability for payment of Advance Tax
(*c*) Payment of advance tax by the assessee on own record
(*d*) Condition of liability to pay advance tax
(*e*) Computation of advance tax

Choose the correct answer from the options given below:

A. (*a*), (*b*), (*c*), (*d*), (*e*)
B. (*b*), (*d*), (*e*), (*c*), (*a*)
C. (*b*), (*d*), (*e*), (*a*), (*c*)
D. (*c*), (*d*), (*e*), (*a*), (*b*)

48. A letter of acceptance sufficiently stamped and duly addressed is put into course of transmission. There is a ______

A. Contract voidable at the option of acceptor
B. Contract voidable at the option of offeror
C. No contract at all
D. Valid contract

49. The doctrine of "Caveat emptor" applies in which of the following situations?

A. When goods are sold by description
B. When goods are sold by sample
C. When goods are sold under implied conditions and warranties
D. When the buyer does not intimate the purpose to the seller and depends upon his own skill and judgement.

50. X was appointed on 1st July 2022 as a lecturer in an University. He was continued on 30th April 2023. What would be the duration of the previous year for the assessment year 2023-24 for computation of income under the head Salary?

A. 1 July 2022 to 30 April 2023
B. 1 April 2022 to 31 March 2023
C. 1 April 2022 to 30 April 2023
D. 1 July 2022 to 31 March 2023

51. Match List-I with List-II.

List-I (Non-parametric test (Counterpart of parameter test))	**List-II (Parametric test)**
(*a*) Friedman Test	I. One-way ANOVA
(*b*) Mann-Whitney U Test	II. t-test
(*c*) Kriskal Wallis Test	III. Paired t-test
(*d*) Wilcoxon signed Rank Test	IV. two-way ANOVA

Choose the correct answer from the options given below:

	(*a*)	(*b*)	(*c*)	(*d*)
A.	I	III	IV	II
B.	IV	II	I	III
C.	III	I	II	IV
D.	II	IV	III	I

52. Match List-I with List-II.

List-I (Purpose)	**List-II (Committee)**
(*a*) Study all aspects of Electronic Fund Transfer (EFT)	I. Rashid Jilani Committee (1992)
(*b*) Working group on NBFCs	II. Soduani Committee (1994)
(*c*) Suggest alternate methods of Lending	III. Malegam Committee (1995)
(*d*) Expert group on Foreign exchange markets	IV. Shere Committee (1995)

Choose the correct answer from the options given below:

	(a)	(b)	(c)	(d)
A.	III	I	II	IV
B.	II	I	III	IV
C.	I	III	II	IV
D.	IV	III	I	II

53. Match List-I with List-II.

List-I (Technique)	List-II (Feature)
(a) Pooling	I. Setting up production facilities in a number of countries
(b) Financial hedge	II. Reduction of Foreign exchange risk through leading and lagging
(c) Natural hedge	III. Simultaneous borrowing and lending in two different currencies
(d) Netting	IV. Holding and managing of cash by the affiliates

Choose the correct answer from the options given below:

	(a)	(b)	(c)	(d)
A.	I	IV	II	III
B.	IV	III	I	II
C.	IV	II	III	I
D.	I	II	III	IV

54. The assumptions of Purchasing Power Parity Theory includes:

(a) No costs for converting one currency to another

(b) No restrictions on the movement of capital between countries

(c) No restrictions on the movement of commodities between countries

(d) No transaction costs for buying and selling financial security

(e) No transportation costs for transporting a commodity from one country to another.

Choose the most appropriate answer from the options given below:

A. (a), (b) and (c) only

B. (b), (d) and (c) only

C. (e), (a) and (c) only

D. (d), (a) and (e) only

55. A and B are equal partners, when partnership is dissolved, their capital are ₹ 40,000 and ₹ 50,000 respectively. After all assets are sold and liabilities paid, there is a cash balance of ₹ 80,000. What is the amount of profit or loss on realization?

A. 10,000 (Profit)

B. 20,000 (Profit)

C. 30,000 (Profit)

D. 10,000 (Loss)

56. From the followings which is an uncommon feature of Private Equity and Venture Capital.

A. Both invest in companies that are not able to or ready to gain capital from the public

B. Their investment is used for financial or operating restructuring of the invester companies

C. They are set up an independent pools of capital contributed by institutions or the high net worth individuals

D. Their activities are subject to few regulations

57. Starting from the earliest, sequence the steps taken to develop the money market in India

(a) Introduction of Interest Rate Swaps (IRSs)

(b) Introduction of Commercial Paper

(c) Introduction of Ways and Means Advances (WMA) linked to bank rate

(d) Introduction of Liquidity Adjustment Facility (LAF)

(e) Implementation of Real Time Gross Settlement (RTGS)

Choose the correct answer from the options given below:

A. (c), (b), (d), (a), (e)

B. (d), (c), (b), (e), (a)

C. (b), (d), (c), (a), (e)

D. (b), (c), (d), (a), (e)

58. Match List-I with List-II.

List-I (Motive of human behaviour in organizations)	List-II (Characteristic)
(*a*) Achievement	I. Concern for others
(*b*) Control	II. Concern for self-development
(*c*) Extension	III. Concern for excellence
(*d*) Dependency	IV. Concern for orderliness

Choose the correct answer from the options given below:

	(*a*)	(*b*)	(*c*)	(*d*)
A.	III	IV	II	I
B.	IV	III	II	I
C.	II	IV	I	III
D.	III	IV	I	II

59. "It is an art of dodging tax without actually breaking the law". This is related with:

A. Tax Management B. Tax Avoidance
C. Tax Planning D. Tax Evasion

60. Which of the following are the disadvantages of straight salary sales compensation plan?

(*a*) Sales volume is emphasized over profits
(*b*) Sales representative may overstock the customer
(*c*) Low motivational impact
(*d*) Difficult to attract or retain top sales performers
(*e*) Sales representatives may focus on products that require least effort to sell

Choose the most appropriate answer from the options given below:

A. (*c*), (*d*) and (*e*) only
B. (*a*), (*b*) and (*c*) only
C. (*b*), (*d*) and (*e*) only
D. (*a*), (*c*) and (*d*) only

61. A point estimator is said to be consistent when:

A. It has smaller standard error
B. Its expected value is equal to the population parameter
C. It tend to become closer to the population parameter as the sample size become larger
D. It is based on all available information

62. In case of two variables, the estimated regression equation is $y = 60 + 5x$. The total sum of squares is 15730 and sum of square due to error is 1530. The estimated regression line based on this information is a:

A. Poorest fit B. Moderate fit
C. Good fit D. Best fit

63. Which is the legal framework governing the Regional Rural Banks (RRBs)?

(*a*) Regional Rural Banks Act, 1976
(*b*) Regional Rural Banks Act, 1966
(*c*) Small Industries Development Bank of India, 1989
(*d*) Banking Regulations Act, 1949
(*e*) Indian Partnership Act, 1932

Choose the correct answer from the options given below:

A. (*a*) and (*d*) only B. (*b*) and (*d*) only
C. (*a*) and (*c*) only D. (*b*) and (*e*) only

64. The practice of setting a price target by the firm and then developing a product that would allow the firm to maximize total profits at that price is called

A. Prestige pricing B. Price lining
C. Price matching D. Value pricing

65. Which of the following are the tools for consumer promotions?

(*a*) Price off (*b*) Refunds
(*c*) Coupons (*d*) Event sponsorship
(*e*) Off-invoice

Choose the correct answer from the options given below:

A. (*a*), (*b*) and (*c*) only
B. (*b*), (*c*), (*d*) and (*e*) only
C. (*a*), (*d*) and (*e*) only
D. (*b*), (*c*) and (*d*) only

66. From the operational point of view, which are the part of Environmental Audit

(*a*) Environment Management System Audit
(*b*) Social Audit
(*c*) Compliance Audit
(*d*) Site Property Audit
(*e*) Energy Audit

Choose the correct answer from the options given below:

A. (*c*), (*d*) and (*e*) only
B. (*a*), (*c*) and (*d*) only
C. (*b*), (*c*) and (*d*) only
D. (*a*), (*d*) and (*e*) only

67. Which of the following is not the limitation of activity based costing?

A. It involves various support activities in the process of making products.
B. It does not provide relevant information for decision making.
C. All costs cannot be identified easily with a particular activity
D. Set up cost as well as costs of running and updating the ABC system are very high.

68. Which committee had recommended a comprehensive framework of reform in the insurance sector?

A. Ghosh Committee (1993)
B. Sodhani Committee (1994)
C. Malhotra Committee (1993)
D. Kalia Committee (1994)

69. Which one of the following normative ethical theories has "Net benefit from the decision" as consideration in ethical decision making?

A. Ethics of duty
B. Theory of justice
C. Stock holder ethics
D. Utilitarianism

70. In the process of perception, which one of the following is not an external factor influencing selection of stimuli?

A. Experience B. Familiarity
C. Repetition D. Novelty

71. Arrange the following goods and services in the increasing order of the underlying income elasticity of demand.

(*a*) Normal consumption goods
(*b*) Necessities
(*c*) Luxuries
(*d*) Inferior goods
(*e*) Services

Choose the correct answer from the options given below:

A. (*d*), (*b*), (*a*), (*e*), (*c*)
B. (*d*), (*c*), (*b*), (*a*), (*e*)
C. (*c*), (*e*), (*b*), (*a*), (*d*)
D. (*b*), (*a*), (*d*), (*c*), (*e*)

72. In case of presence of outliers in a data set, which of the following can better measure the central tendency?

(*a*) Mode (*b*) Trimmed Mean
(*c*) Arithmetic Mean (*d*) Median
(*e*) Harmonic Mean

Choose the correct answer from the options given below:

A. (*a*) and (*b*) only B. (*b*) and (*c*) only
C. (*c*) and (*e*) only D. (*b*) and (*d*) only

73. Which one of the following is the hiring related turnover cost when an employee quits an organization?

A. Advertising B. Interviewing
C. Training D. Recruiter fees

74. In which of the following balance of payment accounts changes in holdings of gold and foreign currencies by official monetary institutions are accounted for:

A. Current Account
B. Capital Account
C. Official Reserves Account
D. Foreign Exchange Account

75. The optimal capital budget of a firm is reflected by intersection point of:

A. Security market line and capital market line
B. Weighted average cost of capital curve and marginal cost of capital curve

C. Investment opportunity curve and marginal cost of capital curve
D. Weighted average cost of capital curve and investment opportunity curve.

76. Substitution effect is usually larger than the income effect in real world because:
A. Consumer usually spends only a small proportion of income on any one commodity
B. Consumer often consumes a small number of commodities
C. Consumer only spends small portion of income on consumption
D. Consumers income is relatively smaller in relation to the consumption.

77. For customers, which are the areas of ethical and social responsibility concerns?
(*a*) Product safety (*b*) Fair Price
(*c*) Fan Wages (*d*) TQM
(*e*) Proper disclosures and information

Choose the correct answer from the options given below:
A. (*c*) and (*d*) only
B. (*c*), (*d*) and (*e*) only
C. (*a*) and (*e*) only
D. (*a*), (*b*) and (*e*) only

78. Regional Economic Integration is an attempt to achieve economic gains from the free flow of trade and investment between countries. One such association is NAFTA. NAFTA comprises of the following countries:
A. USA, Canada, Mexico
B. USA, Canada, Brazil
C. USA, Mexico, Brazil
D. Canada, Mexico, Panama

79. Given below are two statements: One is labelled as Assertion (A) and the other is labelled as Reason (R).

Assertion (A): When a partner retires, all the assets and liabilities are revalued according to current value.

Reason (R): The balance sheet should show the correct values of assets and liabilities.

In the light of the above statements, choose the most appropriate answer from the options given below:
A. Both (A) and (R) are correct and (R) is the correct explanation of (A)
B. Both (A) and (R) are correct, but (R) is not the correct explanation of (A)
C. (A) is correct, but (R) is not correct
D. (A) is not correct, but (R) is correct

80. The total return for an equity stock during a year was 12.5 per cent. The rate of inflation during that year was 3.5 per cent. The real (inflation-adjusted) return was:
A. 9.26 per cent B. 16.00 per cent
C. 7.65 per cent D. 8.70 per cent

81. Which of the following form of market organization is the most prevalent in the manufacturing sector?
A. Perfect competition
B. Monopolistic competition
C. Oligopoly
D. Duopoly

82. Which of the following are the characteristics of the Euro Currency market?
(*a*) The euro currency market does not have geographical limits
(*b*) The euro currency market is unregulated
(*c*) The euro currency market does not have deposit insurance
(*d*) There are no restriction on the maximum interest payable or chargeable.
(*e*) The euro currency market does not attract CRR and SLR restrictions.

Choose the most appropriate answer from the options given below:
A. (*a*), (*b*) and (*c*) only
B. (*b*), (*e*) and (*d*) only
C. (*e*), (*c*) and (*a*) only
D. (*d*), (*a*) and (*e*) only

83. To remove 'order bias' in a questionnaire, usually researcher use which of the following:
(*a*) Pivot questions
(*b*) Multiple grid questions

(*c*) Funnel technique
(*d*) Filter questions
(*e*) Leading questions

Choose the most appropriate answer from the options given below':

A. (*b*), (*e*) and (*a*) only
B. (*d*), (*e*) and (*b*) only
C. (*e*), (*b*) and (*c*) only
D. (*c*), (*d*) and (*a*) only

84. Given below are two statements: One is labelled as Assertion (A) and the other is labelled as Reason (R)

Assertion (A): By removing barriers between national markets, trading blocks create competition due to bigger trading area.

Reason (R): Increased competition can lead to the closure of local industry and harm domestic consumption.

In the light of the above statements, choose the most appropriate answer from the options given below:

A. Both (A) and (R) are correct and (R) is the correct explanation of (A)
B. Both (A) and (R) are correct, but (R) is not the correct explanation of (A)
C. (A) is correct, but (R) is not correct
D. (A) is not correct, but (R) is correct

85. Match List-I with List-II.

List-I (Consequent outcome)	List-II (Taxation Perspective)
(*a*) The person is liable to penalty and prosecution	I. Tax Management
(*b*) Tax is reduced by taking advantage of loopholes of the law	II. Tax Avoidance
(*c*) Main aim is compliance with legal formalities	III. Tax Evasion
(*d*) It is a guide in decision making	IV. Tax planning

Choose the correct answer from the options given below:

	(*a*)	(*b*)	(*c*)	(*d*)
A.	II	III	IV	I
B.	II	IV	III	I
C.	III	II	I	IV
D.	III	I	IV	II

86. Which one of the advertising planning strategies is suitable for cars and appliances?

A. Informative strategy
B. Affective strategy
C. Habitual strategy
D. Satisfaction strategy

87. Arrange the steps of process costing from beginning and ending with the work in process inventory

(*a*) Summarize total costs to account for work-in-process inventory
(*b*) Compute output in terms of equivalent unit
(*c*) Compute cost per equivalent unit
(*d*) Summarize the flow of physical units (of output)
(*e*) Assign total cost to units completed and to units in ending work in process.

Choose the correct answer from the options given below:

A. (*d*), (*b*), (*a*), (*c*), (*e*)
B. (*b*), (*c*), (*d*), (*a*), (*e*)
C. (*c*), (*b*), (*a*), (*d*), (*e*)
D. (*e*), (*d*), (*a*), (*b*), (*c*)

88. Given below are two statements :

Statement I: The only purpose of logistics management is to coordinate activities of moving products from the factory to customers.

Statement II: Logistics management is only the responsibility of marketing function.

In the light of the above statements choose the most appropriate answer from the options given below:

A. Both Statement I and Statement II are correct
B. Both Statement I and Statement II are incorrect

C. Statement I is correct, but Statement II is incorrect

D. Statement I is incorrect, but Statement II is correct.

89. Which are the appropriate tax planning perspectives in case of shut down or continue decision under Income Tax Act, 1961?

(*a*) Business loss and unabsorbed depreciation can be carry forward and set off against profit and gain.

(*b*) The loss making company and profit making company may merge to avail the tax benefit

(*c*) Tax benefit of deduction u/s 33 AB and 115 VT may be withdrawn and liable to tax for the year in which business is discontinued.

(*d*) The condition of section 80 IB / 80 IC of the Act, a deduction is allowed to such undertaking

(*e*) If a person has more than one business, the loss making business may not be discontinued.

Choose the most appropriate answer from the options given below:

A. (*a*), (*c*) and (*d*) only

B. (*b*), (*d*) and (*e*) only

C. (*c*), (*d*) and (*e*) only

D. (*a*), (*c*) and (*e*) only

90. Match List-I with List-II.

List-I (Retail Store Format)	**List-II (Product assortment)**
(*a*) Discount	I. Very narrow and deep
(*b*) Specialty	II. Broad and shallow
(*c*) Category Killer	III. Broad and deep
(*d*) Supermarket	IV. Narrow and very deep

Choose the correct answer from the options given below:

	(*a*)	(*b*)	(*c*)	(*d*)
A.	II	I	III	IV
B.	I	II	III	IV
C.	IV	II	III	I
D.	II	I	IV	III

Directions (Qs. No. 91-95): *Read the following passage carefully* and *answer these questions.*

Interoperability guidelines for prepaid payment instruments with United Payments Interface (UPI) bolster the business case for digital wallets. For a loading fee on transactions through UPI, payments banks, for instance, can widen the adoption of wallets among customers and merchants. This increase use cases for UPI, which largely works on a model of free peer-to-peer merchant transactions. The opportunity provided by the scorching growth of UPI transactions must, however, cross the hurdle of consumer behaviour that is shaped by zero fees for payments made from their bank accounts. For survival, payments banks - which can accept deposits but are prohibited from lending - need to be part of the UPI ecosystem. They also need to carve out a distinct business segment where they have an advantage over full-service banks.

Those use cases are expected to grow as UPI diversifies into cross- border remittances, introduces consumer lending through RuPay credit cards and offers currency exchange to foreign travelers, and bill payments using standing instructions gain traction. UPI will also have to integrate with the digital rupee that is undergoing tests for retail and wholesale transactions. The digital payments platform will continue to play a key role in the infrastructure that is being developed around contactless payments.

This involves building additional UPI context around digital transactions such as billing and credit-profiling. Initial adoption has surpassed the most optimistic expectations. But that is principally on account of the waiver of the merchant discount rate. In the next leg, UPI will grow by providing solutions for the conduct of business. It will have to incorporate lending at some point to become a comprehensive medium of commerce. The infrastructure must encourage fintechs to push innovation in finance. Payments banks have a strong correlation with the growth of digital transactions. They are vital piece of the machinery being built. The interoperability with UPI guidelines plugs them deeper.

91. Given below are two statements:

Statement I: Initial UPI adoption has surpassed the most optimistic expectations on account of the waiver of the merchant discount rate.

Statement II: The future growth of the UPI will be facilitated by providing solution for the conduct of business and to becoming a medium of commerce.

In the light of the above statements, choose the most appropriate answer from the options given below:

A. Both Statement I and Statement II are correct

B. Both Statement I and Statement II are incorrect

C. Statement I is correct, but Statement II is incorrect

D. Statement I is incorrect, but Statement II is correct.

92. Given below are two statements: One is labelled as Assertion (A) and the other is labelled as Reason (R).

Assertion (A): Payment banks - which can accept deposits but are prohibited from lending - need to be part of the UPI ecosystem.

Reason (R): Loading fee on transactions through UPI, payment banks can widen the adoption of wallets among customers and merchants.

In the light of the above statements, choose the correct answer from the options given below:

A. Both (A) and (R) are true and (R) is the correct explanation of (A)

B. Both (A) and (R) are true, but (R) is not the correct explanation of (A)

C. (A) is true, but (R) is not false

D. (A) is false, but (R) is true

93. Contactless payments infrastructure, as per the passage, will empower fintechs for:

A. Interoperability with the UPI

B. Innovation in finance

C. Integration with the UPI ecosystem

D. Integration with the full service banks

94. As per the passage, why do the payment banks need to carve out a distinct business segment for themselves?

A. To be a part of the UPI ecosystem

B. Because payment banks are in competition with full service banks

C. Because payment banks are mandated to push innovation in finance

D. In order to entitle themselves for lending

95. Which of the following use cases are expected to promotes the growth of payment basses?

(*a*) UPI integration with the digital rupee

(*b*) Dislocation of payment banks from digital transactions

(*c*) UPI facilitation of cross-border remittances

(*d*) Keeping a safe distance from the contactless payment infrastructure

(*e*) Consumer lending through Rupay Credit Cards.

Choose the most appropriate answer from the operations given below:

A. (*a*), (*b*) and (*c*) only

B. (*c*), (*d*) and (*e*) only

C. (*a*), (*c*) and (*e*) only

D. (*b*), (*d*) and (*e*) only

Directions (Qs. No. 96-100): *Read the following passage carefully* and *answer these questions.*

The proposed facility similar to the Applications Supported by Blocked Amount (ASBA) for secondary markets has elements to protect investors while increasing their potential earnings. The way it works now in the primary market is that money remains blocked in investor accounts, earning interest till issues of Initial Public Offerings (IPO) accept subscriptions. Replicating this for the secondary market is more complicated because of the number of parties, as well as the kinds of transactions, involved. Investors place a variety of orders over differing time horizons with or without leverage for multiple securities in the secondary market. Incorporating all these variables for a mechanism like ABSA involves escrow arrangements with counter parties in a dynamic environment.

The technical challenge may be considerable but not insurmountable. In this, the Securities and Exchange Board of India (SEBI) is on the right course in its effort to provide such a structure for investors. The Unified Payments Interface (UPI) allows money used for trading to be transferred directly to clearing corporations, which can then settle with brokers. This flushes out money idling with brokers, lowering risk of abuse and containing the fallout in case of broker default. This also offers a pathway for direct settlement, bypassing the pool accounts of intermediaries. SEBI has thus, acted on its regulatory remit of protecting investors' cash as well as their securities.

SEBI has offered relief to brokerages that stand to lose float income on account of upstreaming client money to clearing corporations. Brokerages have been allowed to upstream clients' funds in the form of fixed deposit lien or mutual funds units. This should keep intermediation fees low while the market regulator nudges the system to clear excess funds from the broker channel. Higher upfront brokerage fees are an improvement over those subsidised by float income, bettering systemic oversight. This could lead to concentration among brokerages discount players lose their advantage.

96. The Application Supported by Blocked Amount (ASBA) used in the passage refers to which market.
A. Primary Market
B. Secondary Market
C. Money Market
D. Forex Market

97. The money used for trading is allowed to be transferred directly to clearing corporation, through:
A. Escrow arrangement
B. Unified Payments Interface
C. E-banking
D. Credit cards

98. Given below are two statements: One is labelled as Assertion (A) and the other is labelled as Reason (R).

Assertion (A): SEBI has offered relief to brokerages that stand to lose float income on account of upstreaming client money to clearing corporations.

Reason (R): Brokerage have been allowed to upstream clients' fund in the form of fixed deposit lien or mutual fund units.

In the light of the above statements, choose the correct answer from the options given below:
A. Both (A) and (R) are true and (R) is the correct explanation of (A)
B. Both (A) and (R) are true, but (R) is not the correct explanation of (A)
C. (A) is true, but (R) is false
D. (A) is false, but (R) is true

99. The SEBI has acted on its regulatory remit of protecting investors cash and ______.
A. Securities
B. Dividend Income
C. Grievances of payment
D. Public Deposits

100. Which are reasons that make replication of ASBA for the secondary market complicated:
(*a*) Kinds of transactions
(*b*) Presence of large number of brokers
(*c*) Applicability of SEBI guideline
(*d*) Number of Parties
(*e*) Differing time horizon

Choose the most appropriate answer from the options given below:
A. (*c*), (*d*) and (*e*) only
B. (*a*), (*b*) and (*c*) only
C. (*a*) and (*d*) only
D. (*b*) and (*c*) only

ANSWERS

1. **(D):** The demand for a product can increase due to:
   - **An increase in consumer income:** As income rises, consumers have more purchasing power and can afford to buy more goods and services.
   - **An increase in the prices of substitutes:** When the prices of substitute goods rise, consumers may switch to buying the product instead, leading to an increase in demand.
   - **An increased taste for the commodity:** Changes in consumer preferences can lead to an increase in demand. If a product becomes more popular or fashionable, more people will want to buy it.

2. **(B):** The OCTAPACE framework comprises eight key organizational values designed to cultivate a positive and effective workplace culture. Openness underscores transparent communication, promoting a free exchange of ideas. Confrontation encourages addressing conflicts openly and constructively., fostering a culture of healthy debate. Trust focuses on building interpersonal reliability among team members. Authenticity emphasizes the importance of genuine expression and being true to oneself. Proactivity encourages employees to take initiative and be proactive in driving positive change. Autonomy advocates for individual decision-making and empowerment, allowing employees the freedom to make decisions within their roles. Collaboration underscores the significance of teamwork and collective efforts. Experimentation promotes a culture of innovation and the willingness to explore new ideas. However, among the options provided, "Extension" is not a part of the OCTAPACE framework, which highlights the value of each component in shaping a robust organizational culture.

3. **(B):** In an oligopoly, duopoly, and monopolistic competition, products can indeed be differentiated and serve as close substitutes for each other:
   - **Monopolistic competition:** Each firm sells a differentiated product that can serve as a close substitute for a product from another firm.
   - **Oligopoly:** This market structure is characterized by a small number of firms where products can be either differentiated or homogeneous. When differentiated, they serve as close substitutes.
   - **Duopoly:** A duopoly is a type of oligopoly with only two producers. The products they provide can be differentiated and can serve as a close substitute.

4. **(D):** The logical sequence in the problem-definition process typically follows these steps:
   1. **Identify key problems:** This is the starting point where you identify what problems need to be addressed.
   2. **Write managerial decision statement and research objectives:** Next, define the goal of the research based on the identified problems and what decision management needs to make.
   3. **Determine the unit of analysis:** This is where you determine what or who is to be analyzed to address the research question.
   4. **Determine the relevant variables:** Identify what measurable factors you believe influence the problem and decision at hand.
   5. **Write the research question and/or research hypothesis:** Finally, based on the identified problems, goals, units, and variables, develop a research question or hypothesis that the research should answer or test.

5. (A): Empirical evidence indicates that initially the long-run average cost rapidly falls but after a point it remains flat throughout or at its right-hand end it may even slope gently downward. For example, Joel Dean in his cost function studies funds that long run average cost curve is L-shaped. In an L-shaped curve, the average cost remains relatively constant over a wide range of production levels. This could be attributed to factors like learning by doing, technical progress, and efficient managerial practices that allow firms to achieve cost stability over a large scale of production.

6. (B): Branding transcends mere product identification. It's a potent tool forged in the fires of customer perception, forging emotional connections that drive loyalty and profitability for both manufacturers and retailers.

(*b*) **Premium Pricing:** A strong brand acts as a halo, casting its glow upon its offerings. Consumers, captivated by the brand's story and reputation, readily accept a higher price tag. Think Apple - sleek design, cutting-edge technology, and a distinct ecosystem command a premium, willingly paid by brand loyalists. For manufacturers, this translates to increased profit margins, while retailers bask in the prestige of stocking sought-after products.

(*c*) **Corporate Identity:** Branding isn't just about individual products; it's about weaving a tapestry of values that resonates with customers. Think Patagonia- its commitment to environmentalism and activism is woven into its branding, attracting like-minded consumers who identify with its ethos. This builds a loyal community, not just for Patagonia's products, but for its overall message. By aligning their corporate identity with a well-defined brand, both manufacturers and retailers attract customers who share their values, fostering long-term relationships.

(*e*) **Customer Loyalty:** Branding builds bridges of trust and familiarity. Consistent messaging, quality products, and positive customer experiences solidify these bonds, transforming transient buyers into loyal advocates. Think Amazon - its focus on convenience and reliability has cultivated a legion of loyal customers who turn to it first for a plethora of needs. This translates to sustained sales and market share for manufacturers and retailers, a testament to the power of a brand that resonates with its audience.

7. (D)

8. (B): Upon attaining the age of majority, a minor's agreement cannot be ratified by the individual. This is because, in legal terms, agreements made by minors are typically considered void or voidable due to the presumption that minors lack the legal capacity to fully comprehend the implications of their contracts. When a minor reaches the age of majority, they are capable of entering into new agreements that are inherently valid. However, they cannot retroactively validate or ratify agreements made during their minority, as these agreements remain legally void regardless of the individual's current understanding or intentions. While there may be exceptions depending on specific jurisdictions and the nature of the agreements, the general principle holds that agreements made by minors cannot be ratified after reaching the age of majority.

9. (A): The group of countries that are members of ASEAN (Association of Southeast Asian Nations) consists of Laos, Cambodia, and Brunei. ASEAN is a regional intergovernmental organization aimed at promoting economic and political cooperation among its member states in Southeast Asia.

These nations collaborate on various issues such as economic integration, regional security, and cultural exchange. The inclusion of Laos and Cambodia, landlocked countries in the region, and Brunei, a small but wealthy nation on the island of Borneo, underscores the diverse membership within ASEAN, reflecting a commitment to fostering regional stability and development through collaboration.

10. **(B):** William Petty, a 17th-century English economist and philosopher, is famously known for his assertion that labor is "the father of wealth." In his work, Petty emphasized the essential role of labor in the creation of national wealth and argued that it should be a fundamental component of any assessment of a nation's economic prosperity. Petty's ideas were influential in the early development of economic thought, highlighting the significance of productive human effort in the generation of wealth for a nation. His contributions laid the groundwork for later economic theories and discussions on the factors influencing a country's economic well-being.

11. **(D):** It indicates that the Competition (Amendment) Act, 2023 in India might have brought several changes to the original Act from these perspectives:

    1. **Greater CCI oversight:** With the amendment requiring companies to inform the Competition Commission of India (CCI) about mergers and acquisitions exceeding ₹ 2000 crores, it appears there would be greater regulatory scrutiny for higher-value business transactions.
    2. **Increased Efficiency:** The reduction in the overall timeline for the assessment of the combination from 210 days to 150 days may improve efficiency in the decision-making process.
    3. **Broadened Interpretation:** By replacing "exclusive selling agreements" with "exclusive dealing agreements", it seems the Act has expanded the scope to potentially cover a broader range of exclusive agreements that may affect competition.
    4. **Expanded Scope of Anti-Competitive Agreements:** If entities not engaged in identical or similar trade can now form part of an anti-competitive Agreement under Section 3(3) of the Act, this could potentially widen the net of businesses affected by this legislation and require increased vigilance to ensure compliance.
    5. **More precise definitions:** The redefinition of anti-competitive conduct like "tie-up arrangements", "resale price maintenance", and "exclusive distribution agreement" could provide more clarity and specificity, helping businesses better understand and comply with the rules.

12. **(D):** Conservatism is a political ideology rather than a type of totalitarianism. Totalitarianism, a political system where an overarching authority wields comprehensive control over public and private spheres, exhibits diverse forms such as theocratic, right-wing, and tribal totalitarianism. Theocratic totalitarianism involves religious institutions dictating government and societal norms.

    Right-wing totalitarianism emphasizes authoritarian governance, nationalism, and conservative social values. Tribal totalitarianism manifests when a dominant tribe or ethnic group holds absolute control. In contrast, conservatism is not a type of totalitarianism but a political ideology emphasizing the preservation of traditional values. While conservatism may resist societal changes, it typically operates within democratic frameworks and does not inherently imply totalitarian control, distinguishing it from the explicitly authoritarian characteristics of theocratic, right-wing, and tribal forms of totalitarianism.

13. (A): In the given scenario, where 'A' sells a mobile phone to 'B,' a minor, and 'A' endorses the cheque to 'C,' the legal principles regarding contracts with minors come into play. Generally, contracts with minors are considered voidable at the option of the minor, meaning the minor can choose to affirm or disaffirm the contract upon reaching the age of majority.

Given that 'B' is a minor, the contract for the mobile phone sale is voidable. If 'B' chooses to disaffirm the contract upon reaching the age of majority, the contract becomes void. Consequently, any negotiable instrument (like a cheque) related to that voidable contract is also affected.

Therefore, 'C' can enforce the payment of the cheque only against 'A'

14. (B)

15. (D):

(*c*) **Entry into the market is absolutely free:** In contestable markets, potential competitors face minimal legal, financial, and technological hurdles to enter and offer their products or services. This translates to readily available licenses, streamlined regulatory processes, and accessible resources. The lack of entry barriers fosters a dynamic environment where incumbents constantly face the pressure of potential entrants. This motivates them to maintain operational efficiency, offer competitive prices, and continuously innovate to retain market share. Imagine a telecommunications market characterized by low licensing fees and readily available infrastructure. New operators can easily enter, offering innovative services and competitive pricing, leading to improved services and lower costs for consumers.

(*e*) **Exit from the market is entirely costless:** Contestable markets facilitate low sunk costs and minimal exit barriers for struggling firms. This allows them to readily divest resources, sell equipment, and terminate contracts upon encountering competitive pressure. Low exit barriers promote resource allocation efficiency. Unprofitable firms can exit the market, freeing up resources for more efficient entrants who can utilize them optimally. This ensures a dynamic market where only the most competitive firms survive and thrive. Visualize a garment manufacturing industry with flexible leases and readily transferable production licenses. Companies struggling against cheaper competitors can easily exit, allowing more efficient producers to enter and cater to evolving consumer preferences.

In conjunction, these characteristics create a potent environment where the threat of competition acts as an invisible hand, driving efficiency, innovation, and ultimately, consumer welfare. Understanding the dynamics of contestable markets can inform policy decisions aimed at fostering competitive landscapes and maximizing economic benefits for all stakeholders.

16. (B): Experimental treatment in research design refers to the deliberate manipulation of the independent variable by researchers to observe and assess its impact on the dependent variable. The independent variable is the factor or condition that researchers intentionally vary or manipulate during an experiment, while the dependent variable is the outcome or response that is measured. By systematically altering the independent variable, researchers aim to establish a causal relationship and understand how changes in this variable influence the dependent variable. This experimental approach enables researchers to control and isolate specific factors, providing a rigorous framework for drawing conclusions about cause-and-effect relationships within the study.

17. (C): The process of international expansion for a firm involves several strategic decisions, and the order of these decisions is crucial for effective implementation. The steps to be followed while strategizing to go international are:

(*c*) **Deciding whether to go global:** This initial step involves a comprehensive assessment of whether international expansion aligns with the firm's overall business strategy, considering factors such as market potential, risk, and resource requirements.

(*b*) **Deciding which markets to enter:** Once the decision to go global is made, the firm must identify and evaluate potential markets. This involves analyzing market size, growth prospects, competition, and cultural factors to determine the most suitable markets for expansion.

(*a*) **Deciding when to enter:** Timing is critical in international expansion. Firms need to consider economic conditions, market readiness, and other external factors to determine the opportune moment for entering a specific market.

(*e*) **Deciding how to enter the chosen market:** After selecting the target market, the firm needs to decide on the entry strategy. This involves choosing the mode of entry, such as exporting, licensing, joint ventures, or wholly-owned subsidiaries, based on factors like control, risk, and resource requirements.

(*d*) **Choosing a mode of entry:** This step involves selecting the specific method or approach for entering the chosen market. Firms must weigh the advantages and disadvantages of various entry modes to determine the most appropriate strategy for their international expansion.

The strategic sequence involves assessing the decision to go global, selecting target markets, determining the timing of entry, choosing the entry strategy, and finally, selecting the specific mode of entry. Each step builds upon the previous one, contributing to a comprehensive and well-thought-out international expansion strategy.

18. (C): In the context of the banking sector, the spread refers to the difference between the interest earned on assets, such as loans and investments, and the interest paid on liabilities, such as deposits and borrowings. The spread is a critical indicator of a bank's profitability and is influenced by various factors. The two relevant factors mentioned in the options are:

(*b*) **Net Interest Income:** Net Interest Income (NII) is a key component of a bank's profitability, representing the difference between interest earned on loans and investments and interest paid on deposits and borrowings. The larger the positive spread, the more profitable the bank is likely to be.

(*d*) **Asset Ratio:** The asset ratio, or loan-to-deposit ratio, is a measure of the proportion of a bank's assets that are funded by deposits. It is calculated by dividing total loans by total deposits. This ratio influences the spread, as a higher ratio suggests that a larger portion of the bank's assets is earning interest, potentially contributing to a wider spread.

19. (D): If the CPIO/SPIO decides that the information is requested is covered by an exemption, then the application will be rejected. In such case the CPIO/SPIO is obligated to sent a rejection notice.

The rejection notice should contain:

- Reason for such rejection.
- The particulars of the appellant authority.
- The period with in which an appeal against such rejection may he preferred.

20. (D): Transfer prices refer to the prices at which goods, services, or intangible property are transferred between different divisions or entities within a multinational company. By manipulating these transfer prices, a company can strategically allocate profits and losses among its various divisions or subsidiaries, taking advantage of tax disparities between countries. This practice can be employed to shift income to jurisdictions with lower tax rates, allowing the company to minimize its overall tax liability. It is essential to note that while transfer pricing is a legitimate business practice, it must comply with international tax laws and regulations to avoid legal issues and penalties.

21. (A):

(*b*) **Acuite Ratings:** Acuite Ratings & Research Limited (Acuite) is a credit rating agency established in 2008. It received its accreditation from the RBI in 2012. Acuite primarily focuses on providing credit ratings for corporate debt instruments, structured finance products, and municipal bonds. They also offer services like research, due diligence, and portfolio analysis. Acuite's presence in the market provides an alternative to CRISIL, potentially leading to increased competition and potentially more diverse perspectives on creditworthiness.

(*c*) **CRISIL Ratings:** CRISIL Ratings Limited (CRISIL) is the oldest and largest credit rating agency in India, established in 1987. It received its accreditation from the RBI in 1993. CRISIL has a broader range of offerings compared to Acuite, including ratings for sovereign debt, bank loans, infrastructure projects, and small and medium-sized enterprises (SMEs). Their extensive experience and market share make them a significant player in the Indian financial landscape. CRISIL's accreditation by the RBI underscores its adherence to stringent regulations and quality standards, making it a trusted source of credit information for investors and lenders.

22. (A): The ₹ 1500 deduction for clubbed income from a minor child, as per Section 64(1A) of the Income Tax Act, 1961, serves to acknowledge the financial responsibility parents bear for their children's upbringing and education. This fixed deduction simplifies tax filing procedures by providing a standardized allowance, irrespective of actual expenses. While it may not fully cover all costs, it establishes a baseline financial acknowledgment for parents, ensuring fairness and uniformity in deduction allowances across different income levels. Importantly, this deduction does not alter the taxable income but reduces the portion of clubbed income considered for tax calculation, offering significant tax benefits to parents. Therefore, option A is the correct answer, emphasizing the established ₹ 1500 deduction as a practical and standardized measure to recognize parental responsibilities in the tax framework.

23. (B): The logical sequence of the service gaps according to the SERVQUAL model, a popular service quality measurement framework, goes as follows:

- **The gap between the customer's expectations and management's perception:** This is the first gap where management doesn't accurately perceive what customers want.
- **The gap between management perception and service quality specification:** After understanding the customer's expectations, the next gap could occur when specifying those perceptions in delivering service quality.
- **The gap between service quality specifications and service delivery:** The next stage is the actual delivery of service, where there might be a gap between the planned service quality and what is actually delivered.

- **The gap between service delivery and external communications:** This gap arises if promotional efforts do not match what is actually delivered to the customer.
- **The gap between perceived service and expected service:** This is the gap between what customers expect of the service and their perceptions of the service they actually receive.

24. (B):

(*c*) **The leader is a highly capable individual:** This comes at the beginning because it emphasizes the importance of individual capability. Before someone can effectively lead a team or manage tasks, they need to possess the necessary skills, knowledge, and competence in their domain.

(*e*) **The leader is a contributing team member:** Once an individual has proven themselves to be highly capable, they often start by contributing effectively within a team environment. This stage emphasizes collaboration, teamwork, and the ability to work alongside others towards common goals.

(*a*) **The leader is a competent manager:** As the individual gains experience and demonstrates their ability to contribute within a team, they may be entrusted with managerial responsibilities. This stage involves overseeing tasks, resources, and potentially other team members, ensuring that objectives are met efficiently and effectively.

(*d*) **The leader is an effective leader:** With continued development and experience, the individual may progress to becoming an effective leader. This involves not only managing tasks and resources but also guiding, motivating, and inspiring others towards achieving shared goals. Effective leadership goes beyond mere management; it involves influencing and empowering others to perform at their best.

(*b*) **The leader is an executive:** Finally, in certain organizational contexts, individuals may reach executive positions where they hold significant decision-making authority and strategic responsibility. This is often the highest level of leadership within an organization, where leaders shape the overall direction and vision of the company.

This sequence highlights a progression from individual capability to higher levels of responsibility and leadership within an organization. It illustrates the journey that individuals often undertake as they develop their leadership skills and advance in their careers.

25. (C): Pre-approach: The pre-approach in the sales process is a critical step where a salesperson engages in thorough research and learning about a prospective customer before making the actual sales call. During this phase, the salesperson gathers information about the customer's needs, preferences, industry challenges, and any relevant background details.

This preparation allows the salesperson to tailor their approach, aligning their product or service with the specific needs and characteristics of the customer.

The goal of the pre-approach is to enhance the effectiveness of the sales interaction by demonstrating a deep understanding of the customer's context and positioning the product or service as a tailored solution to address their unique requirements.

This strategic preparation contributes to building rapport, credibility, and increases the likelihood of a successful sales outcome.

26. (D)

27. (A):

(*a*) **Analysis:** This competency involves the ability to critically examine information, break down complex data, and derive meaningful insights. Individuals with strong analytical skills can assess situations, identify patterns, and make informed decisions based on evidence and logic. Analytical skills are valuable in various domains, including problem-solving, strategic planning, and decision-making.

(*c*) **Organization:** The competency of organization pertains to an individual's ability to structure tasks, information, or resources in a systematic and efficient manner. Organized individuals can prioritize, plan, and manage their workload effectively. This skill is crucial for maintaining order, meeting deadlines, and optimizing productivity in both personal and professional settings.

(*d*) **Problem-solving:** Problem-solving is a competency that reflects an individual's capacity to identify, analyze, and resolve challenges or issues. Those with strong problem-solving skills can approach difficulties methodically, evaluate potential solutions, and implement effective resolutions. This competency is fundamental in various roles and industries where addressing complex issues is a routine part of the job.

These competencies collectively represent a set of skills and capabilities that are highly valued in professional settings. Individuals possessing strong analytical, organizational, and problem-solving skills are well-equipped to navigate complex tasks, contribute to effective decision-making, and enhance overall productivity within an organization.

28. (A): The Directorate General of Foreign Trade (DGFT) plays a pivotal role in facilitating and promoting foreign trade activities in India. It operates under the purview of the Ministry of Commerce and Industry. As the implementing authority for India's foreign trade policy, DGFT is tasked with creating an environment conducive to international commerce. Its responsibilities encompass the formulation and execution of trade-related policies, regulation of imports and exports, and the administration of various incentive schemes to boost India's trade and economic engagements globally. The Ministry of Commerce and Industry oversees DGFT's activities, ensuring alignment with broader economic objectives and contributing to India's integration into the global marketplace.

29. (B)

30. (B): Bypass: This strategy perfectly aligns with the scenario. By introducing innovative products or technologies, an ailing company can create an entirely new market space, making the existing competition irrelevant. They effectively "bypass" the current competitive landscape and carve out a new niche for themselves.

31. (C): "The currency in terms of which a domestic currency is quoted," refers to the base currency when considering exchange rates. In the context of foreign exchange markets, currencies are often quoted in terms of another currency. The currency being quoted is the "quote currency," and the currency against which its value is measured is the "base currency."

For example, if you see an exchange rate quote like USD/EUR = 1.20, it means 1 US Dollar (USD) is equivalent to 1.20 Euros (EUR). Here, the USD is the base currency, and the exchange rate tells you how much of the quote currency (EUR) you need to exchange for one unit of the base currency (USD).

Now, the term "intervention currency" can be relevant in cases where a country pegs its domestic currency to another currency, effectively determining the exchange rate between the two. In such a scenario, the foreign currency to which the domestic currency is pegged can be considered an "intervention currency." This is because the authorities may actively intervene in the foreign exchange market to maintain the peg, influencing the value of their domestic currency in terms of the intervention currency.

32. (D)

33. (C): The highest predictability of consumer choice behaviour is typically associated with Behavioural Segmentation. This segmentation strategy focuses on analyzing consumers' actual behaviours, including their purchasing patterns, product usage, brand loyalty, and responses to marketing stimuli. By categorizing consumers based on their observable actions and interactions with products or services, marketers can gain valuable insights into preferences and decision-making processes. This practical approach to understanding consumer behavior enhances the ability to predict future choices and tailor marketing strategies more effectively. Unlike demographic or psychological factors, which may not always correlate with actual purchasing actions, behavioural segmentation directly taps into observable actions, providing a robust foundation for predicting and influencing consumer choices.

34. (D): Indian Financial Technology and Allied Services (IFTAS) is a fully owned subsidiary of the Reserve Bank of India (RBI), established to cater to the technological needs and advancements in the financial sector. IFTAS plays a crucial role in developing, implementing, and managing various financial technologies to enhance the efficiency and effectiveness of banking and financial services in India. As an entity directly under the RBI, IFTAS is at the forefront of driving innovation and technological solutions that align with the evolving demands of the financial industry. Its mandate includes fostering the adoption of secure and efficient technological platforms, contributing to the modernization of banking operations, and ensuring that India's financial landscape remains resilient and technologically advanced.

35. (A):

(*d*) **Notice of Dishonour:** This essential step kicks off the recourse process. You must formally inform all parties on the instrument (drawer, endorsers, etc.) about the dishonour within a specific timeframe as mandated by law. This serves as a crucial notification of their potential liability and triggers their obligation to address the situation.

(*a*) **Noting:** This step strengthens case by preserving evidence. A notary public officially records the details of the dishonour in a public register. This documentation adds credibility and facilitates a smoother legal challenge if negotiations with the liable parties fail.

(*c*) **Protesting:** This step applies only to bills of exchange and involves a formal declaration of dishonour by a notary public. It can be particularly valuable in international transactions and serves as additional evidence for recourse procedures abroad.

(*b*) **Compensation :** The core objective of recourse is to recover the instrument's value. Once all parties are informed, you can demand the due amount, along with interest, charges, and potential damages incurred due to the dishonour. This negotiation or legal enforcement remains the primary focus of recourse.

(*e*) **Penalties:** Should the liable parties fail to fulfill their obligations, including compensation, legal measures may involve imposing additional financial penalties. These serve as consequences for non-compliance and can significantly increase the pressure on them to rectify the situation.

This sequence prioritizes official notification, evidence gathering, and then transitions to seeking compensation or, if necessary, escalating through legal channels with potential penalties.

36. (B): Operational functioning of Asset Reconstruction Companies (ARCs) in accordance with the SARFAESI Act 2002:

(*d*) **Buys loans of bank at a discount:** ARCs acquire non-performing assets (NPAs) from banks at a discounted value. This allows banks to offload distressed assets from their balance sheets and recover some value from these troubled loans.

(*b*) **Issue security receipts to the bank:** In exchange for acquiring the NPAs, ARCs issue security receipts to the selling bank. These receipts represent the value of the assets acquired and serve as a promise to share the proceeds from the eventual recovery.

(*e*) **Carry out the recovery:** ARCs focus on the recovery of the acquired assets. This involves employing various strategies such as restructuring, rehabilitation, or liquidation of the assets to maximize the returns.

(*a*) **Charge a 2 per cent management fee:** ARCs charge a management fee for their services in managing and overseeing the recovery process. This fee is typically around 2 per cent of the realized value of the assets.

(*c*) **Make payment to the bank:** Once the recovery process is successful, ARCs make payments to the selling bank. The payments are made based on the proceeds generated from the recovery efforts, and they are distributed in proportion to the security receipts held by the bank.

This sequence outlines the key steps in the functioning of ARCs under the SARFAESI Act, providing a systematic approach to handling distressed assets and facilitating the cleanup of banks' balance sheets.

37. (B):

(*a*) **Cancellation of the unissued shares:** Unissued shares refer to shares that have been authorized but not yet issued to shareholders. The company might decide to cancel these unissued shares, perhaps to simplify its capital structure or eliminate the possibility of future dilution.

(*c*) **Increase in share capital by issue of new shares:** This alteration involves the company issuing new shares, thereby increasing its share capital. Companies often opt for this when they need to raise additional funds or when there's a strategic decision to expand the capital base.

(*e*) **Conversion of fully paid shares into stock and vice versa:** Fully paid shares are those for which the shareholders have already paid the entire nominal or face value. Conversion of fully paid shares into stock (and vice versa) provides flexibility. Stock represents a collective ownership interest without a nominal value per share, making it a versatile financial instrument.

38. (C): Mutual Funds in India are regulated by the Securities and Exchange Board of India (SEBI), which is the primary regulatory authority overseeing the securities market in the country. SEBI plays a crucial role in formulating and implementing regulations to ensure the fair and transparent functioning of mutual funds. It regulates various aspects, including fund management, disclosure norms, investor protection, and market conduct. SEBI's regulatory framework aims to safeguard the interests of investors, promote market integrity, and maintain the overall stability and development of the mutual fund industry in India.

39. (B): Assertion (A): Usually manufacturing companies use sale and leaseback arrangements to unlock investment in fixed assets. This assertion is true. Sale and leaseback is a financial strategy where a company, in this case, a manufacturing company, sells its fixed assets (such as machinery or equipment) to a leasing company and then leases the same assets back for regular use. This allows the manufacturing company to convert the ownership of the asset into capital, providing liquidity and unlocking funds that were tied up in the fixed assets. This capital can then be utilized for other business needs, such as expansion, debt reduction, or working capital requirements.

Reason (R): In a sale of lease back arrangement, the companies sell the asset to a leasing company, and lease it back to enjoy the uninterrupted use of the asset in their business. This reason is true and describes the basic process of a sale and leaseback arrangement. The company sells the asset to a leasing company, receives funds, and then leases the same asset back to continue using it for its operations. This allows the company to maintain the operational use of the asset while converting the asset's ownership into capital. While both the assertion and the reason are true, the reason doesn't directly explain why manufacturing companies, in particular, use sale and leaseback arrangements. The primary motivation, as mentioned in the assertion, is to unlock investment in fixed assets, providing financial flexibility for other business needs.

40. (A):

(*b*) **Rent and Rates derived from land:** Income earned as rent and rates from land is considered agricultural income. This includes the money received by the landowner for leasing or renting out agricultural land. Rates refer to the payments made for the use of the land, and both rent and rates are integral parts of agricultural income.

(*c*) **Income from making the produce fit for marketing:** Income derived from activities that make agricultural produce suitable for the market is considered agricultural income. This may include processing, cleaning, sorting, or any other activities that enhance the marketability of the agricultural produce. The income generated from such activities is considered part of agricultural income.

(*e*) **Income from a farmhouse:** Income from a farmhouse is considered agricultural income when the farmhouse is used in conjunction with agricultural operations. If the farmhouse is used for residential purposes only, the income may not be treated as agricultural income. However, if the farmhouse is used for activities related to agriculture, such as storage of agricultural produce or accommodation for agricultural workers, the income from the farmhouse is considered part of agricultural income.

41. (B)

42. (C): A boxplot, also known as a box-and-whisker plot, is a graphical representation that provides a visual summary of the distribution of a dataset.

(*c*) **Median (Second Quartile):** The median is represented by a line inside the box. It is the middle value of the dataset when it is ordered. In a boxplot, the box is divided into two parts by this line. Half of the data points lie below the median, and half lie above it. The median is a measure of central tendency that provides insight into the typical or central value of the data.

(*d*) **Q_3 (Third Quartile):** Q_3, or the third quartile, is the point below which 75% of the data falls. In a boxplot, the upper end of the box represents Q_3. The length of the box, therefore, spans from Q_1 to Q_3, covering the interquartile range (IQR). Q_3 is a valuable measure to understand the spread of the upper half of the dataset.

(*b*) **Q_1 (First Quartile):** Q_1, or the first quartile, is the point below which 25% of the data falls. In a boxplot, the lower end of the box represents Q_1. Together with Q_3, it defines the interquartile range (IQR). The IQR is a measure of statistical dispersion, giving an idea of how spread out the middle 50% of the data is.

43. (B): An agent is personally liable to third parties in following situations:

- Where the agents acts for an undisclosed principal.
- An agent who is not having any authority to act as an agent or who has exceed the authority and the same has not been ratified by the principal is personally liable for any loss beard by a third party (Section 235).
- Trade, usage and customs makes agent personally liable.
- If an agent works for a foreign principal.
- When the agent sign a negotiable instrument in his own name without making it clear that he is signing as an agent.

44. (A): Statement I: Certificate of incorporation is conclusive evidence that all the requirements of the Companies Act have been complied with in respect of registration. - This statement is true. The issuance of a certificate of incorporation is a formal acknowledgment by the government or regulatory authority that a company has completed all the necessary legal requirements for registration under the Companies Act. It serves as conclusive evidence that the company is officially incorporated, and its legal existence has begun.

Statement II: After incorporation, if the company makes a fresh contract in terms of the pre-incorporation contract, the liability of the promoters shall come to an end. - This statement is also true. Yes, if a company enters into a new contract with the same terms as a pre-incorporation contract, the liability of the promoters, the company, and any other person involved ends. Promoters are usually personally liable for pre-incorporation contracts. If a company doesn't ratify or adopt a pre-incorporation contract, the common law principle applies and the promoter is liable for breach of contract. A company can ratify preliminary contracts after incorporation. However, the company can't be forced to honor these contracts. A company can ratify a pre-incorporation contract by expressly or impliedly confirming it. For example, the company can make a payment for the contracted amount. Promoters are responsible for raising capital and entering into the first agreements for a business and the pre-incorporation of a company. A promoter's status usually ends when the Board of Directors is formed and begins governing the company.

45. (C): The uncertainty resulting from merger or acquisition can increase stress levels and signal risk to target company employees.

Following intervention can be used to manage the anxiety created by mergers and acquisitions:

- Speed-up of the integration process.
- Employee counselling and stress management training.
- Social support from spouse, friend, supervisors and co-workers.

46. (C):

(*c*) **Resource Availability:** Resource availability is a critical factor influencing the flow of Foreign Direct Investment (FDI). Companies often seek locations where they can access essential resources such as raw materials, skilled labor, and advanced technologies. The availability of these resources can impact the efficiency, cost-effectiveness, and competitiveness of the business operations. For example, a manufacturing company might be attracted to a country with abundant natural resources or a well-educated workforce.

(*e*) **Logistics:** Logistics plays a vital role in the decision-making process for Foreign Direct Investment. It encompasses the entire supply chain process, including transportation, warehousing, distribution, and information flow. Efficient logistics infrastructure in a host country can significantly reduce operational costs and enhance the overall competitiveness of the investment destination. This involves considerations such as the quality of transportation networks, the reliability of supply chains, and the ease of moving goods and services within and outside the country.

Resource availability and logistics are key supply-side factors influencing the flow of Foreign Direct Investment. Companies are often attracted to locations where they can efficiently access essential resources and benefit from a well-developed logistics infrastructure to support their operations. These factors contribute to the overall competitiveness of a destination for FDI.

47. (B):

(*b*) **Liability for payment of Advance Tax:** This section outlines the circumstances under which an individual or entity becomes liable to pay advance tax. It typically pertains to cases where the total tax liability for the financial year exceeds a specified threshold. It sets the groundwork for determining who must pay taxes in advance.

(*d*) **Condition of liability to pay advance tax:** Section D establishes the specific conditions or criteria that trigger the liability to pay advance tax. It may include factors such as the nature and amount of income, tax liability in the previous year, and other relevant considerations. This section clarifies the prerequisites that lead to the obligation of paying taxes in advance.

(*e*) **Computation of advance tax:** Once the liability and conditions are determined, Section E comes into play. This section provides guidelines for calculating the amount of advance tax that an individual or entity is required to pay. It may involve estimating income, considering deductions, and applying the applicable tax rates to arrive at the advance tax amount.

(*c*) **Payment of advance tax by the assessee on own record:** This section focuses on the practical aspect of making advance tax payments. It explains how the assessee is expected to make these payments based on their own calculations and assessments. This involves periodic payments throughout the financial year rather than waiting until the end of the year.

(*a*) **Instalment of advance tax and due date:** The final section, A, provides details on the installment schedule and due dates for paying advance tax. It specifies the deadlines by which the taxpayer needs to make these periodic payments. This ensures a structured and timely fulfillment of the advance tax obligation throughout the financial year.

These sections collectively create a comprehensive framework for the determination, computation, and payment of advance tax, providing a systematic approach for individuals and entities to fulfill their tax obligations in advance of the regular assessment cycle.

48. **(D):** When a letter of acceptance is sufficiently stamped, duly addressed, and set in the course of transmission, it forms the basis for a valid contract. The acceptance is considered effective as soon as it is posted, and the contract becomes legally binding from that moment. This principle is based on the "postal rule," which deems acceptance to occur when the acceptance is posted, not when it is received. As long as the acceptance complies with the specified requirements and is properly transmitted, it establishes a valid and enforceable contract between the parties involved, and neither party can unilaterally revoke their commitment.

49. **(D):** The doctrine of 'Caveat emptor' emphasizes the buyer's responsibility for due diligence and careful consideration in a purchase, particularly when the buyer does not communicate the intended purpose to the seller and relies on their own expertise. In such situations, the buyer is expected to exercise caution and thoroughly assess the goods, as the seller may not be held responsible for any defects or shortcomings in the product. Essentially, it places the burden on the buyer to inspect and verify the quality, suitability, and condition of the goods, and the principle is often invoked when the buyer relies on their own skill and judgment in the transaction, without explicitly communicating specific requirements to the seller.

50. **(D):** The duration of the previous year for the assessment year 2023-24, concerning the computation of income under the head Salary for X, who was appointed as a lecturer in a university on 1st July 2022 and continued in the role until 31st March 2023, spans from 1st July 2022 to 31st March 2023. In this context, the period considered for assessing income tax is based on the financial year in which the individual earned the salary income, encompassing the duration of employment from the date of appointment until the end of the financial year, i.e., from the 1st of July 2022 to the 31st of March 2023.

51. **(B)** **52.** **(D)** **53.** **(B)**

54. **(C):**

(*e*) **No transportation costs for transporting a commodity from one country to another:** This assumption is grounded in the idea that transportation costs should not impact the prices of goods and commodities in different countries. By assuming no transportation costs, the PPP theory simplifies the analysis, focusing on the relative price levels of identical goods in different locations without factoring in the costs associated with moving those goods.

(*a*) **No costs for converting one currency to another:** This assumption is essential for the PPP theory to hold, as it asserts that there are no transaction costs or barriers associated with converting one currency into another. In a world with no currency conversion costs, exchange rates would reflect the relative prices of goods and services in different currencies accurately, allowing for a direct comparison of purchasing power across countries.

(*c*) **No restrictions on the movement of commodities between countries:** This assumption posits that there are no restrictions or barriers to the free movement of goods and commodities between countries. In a scenario where commodities can move seamlessly across borders, the PPP theory can better analyze and compare the relative price levels of identical goods in different countries without being influenced by trade restrictions or limitations.

These assumptions collectively form the foundation of the Purchasing Power Parity Theory, simplifying the analysis by assuming no transportation costs, no currency conversion costs, and no restrictions on the movement of commodities. These assumptions facilitate the theory's goal of comparing the relative price levels and purchasing power across different countries based on a basket of identical goods and services.

55. (D): The amount of profit or loss on realization can be calculated using the following steps:

Combine the partners' capital: Total capital = A's capital + B's capital

= ₹ 40,000 + ₹ 50,000 = ₹ 90,000.

Compare total capital with cash balance: = ₹ 90,000 (total capital) – ₹ 80,000 (cash balance) = ₹ 10,000.

Therefore, based on the comparison, they experienced a loss of ₹ 10,000 during the realization process.

So, the correct answer is ₹ 10,000 (Loss).

56. (B): Private Equity and Venture Capital are both types of investment strategies that involve providing capital to companies in exchange for ownership stakes. While they share similarities in terms of their structure and goals, they also have distinct characteristics that differentiate them. One of the key differences lies in their investment focus, particularly regarding the use of funds for financial or operating restructuring of the investee companies. Private Equity firms typically target mature companies that are already established in their respective industries. When Private Equity firms invest in these companies, they often do so with the intention of implementing significant changes to improve their performance and increase their value. This may involve undertaking financial restructuring measures, such as refinancing debt, optimizing capital structure, or improving cash flow management practices. Additionally, operational restructuring initiatives may be pursued, including streamlining processes, implementing cost-saving measures, or restructuring management teams. These efforts are aimed at enhancing the company's profitability and overall value, ultimately leading to a successful exit for the investors.

On the other hand, Venture Capital firms typically focus on investing in early-stage companies that have high growth potential but may lack the resources or experience to scale their operations rapidly. Unlike Private Equity, Venture Capital investments are often directed towards funding the growth and expansion of these startups rather than implementing significant restructuring measures. Venture Capitalists provide capital to fuel the development of innovative products or services, expand market reach, and build strong management teams. While some operational improvements may occur as part of the growth process, the emphasis is primarily on supporting the company's expansion and achieving market success.

57. (D):

(*b*) **Introduction of Commercial Paper:** Commercial Paper (CP) was introduced in 1989 as a short-term money market instrument. It provides corporations with a means of raising funds for a short duration, typically to meet working capital needs. Investors purchase commercial paper at a discount, and it matures at face value.

(*c*) **Introduction of Ways and Means Advances (WMA) linked to bank rate:** Ways and Means Advances (WMA) are temporary advances provided by the

Reserve Bank of India (RBI) and was launched in the year 1997 to the central and state governments to help them meet short-term mismatches in their receipts and payments. Linking WMA to the bank rate ensures that the government has access to funds at an interest rate reflecting prevailing market conditions.

(*d*) **Introduction of Liquidity Adjustment Facility (LAF):** The Liquidity Adjustment Facility (LAF) was introduced by the RBI in 1999 to manage liquidity and interest rates in the banking system. It consists of repo (repurchase agreement) and reverse repo operations. Banks use LAF to borrow or lend money from/to the RBI, helping to stabilize short-term interest rates.

(*a*) **Introduction of Interest Rate Swaps (IRSs):** Interest Rate Swaps (IRSs) were introduced to the Indian financial markets as a derivative instrument in the year 2000. IRSs allow market participants to exchange interest rate cash flows, helping them manage and hedge against interest rate risks.

(*e*) **Implementation of Real Time Gross Settlement (RTGS):** Real Time Gross Settlement (RTGS) is a funds transfer system implemented for high-value and time-sensitive transactions launched in the year 2004. It facilitates real-time settlement on a gross basis, where each transaction is settled individually and immediately, enhancing the efficiency and safety of money market transactions.

This sequence of steps represents the key developments in the Indian money market, ranging from the introduction of financial instruments like Commercial Paper to the establishment of advanced systems like Real Time Gross Settlement (RTGS), contributing to the overall growth and efficiency of the money market in the country.

58. (D)

59. (B): Tax Avoidance: Tax avoidance is a legal and strategic approach to managing one's financial affairs in a way that minimizes tax liability within the boundaries of the law. The statement "It is an art of dodging tax without actually breaking the law" suggests a deliberate and lawful effort to minimize tax payments. Individuals or businesses engaging in tax avoidance often leverage legal provisions, exemptions, and deductions provided by the tax laws to optimize their tax position.

In this context, the term "dodging tax" implies a proactive effort to reduce tax liability through legitimate means, such as taking advantage of tax credits, deductions, and other incentives provided by tax regulations. The emphasis on "without actually breaking the law" underscores that the practice is within legal boundaries, distinguishing it from tax evasion, which involves illegal activities to evade taxes. Therefore, the statement aligns with the concept of tax avoidance, where individuals or entities employ legal strategies to optimize their tax position without violating tax laws.

60. (A):

(*c*) **Low motivational impact:** In a straight salary plan, sales representatives receive a fixed salary regardless of their sales performance. This lack of a direct link between effort and financial reward can result in lower motivation among sales teams. Without the incentive of additional earnings tied to higher sales achievements, individuals may not be as motivated to go above and beyond their minimum job requirements.

(*d*) **Difficult to attract or retain top sales performers:** Top-performing sales professionals are often motivated by the potential for higher earnings. In a straight salary plan, where earnings are fixed, it may be challenging for companies to attract or retain high-performing salespeople who are seeking greater financial rewards for their exceptional efforts. Commission-based or performance-based plans are often more appealing to top performers.

(*e*) **Sales representatives may focus on products that require the least effort to sell:** Without specific incentives tied to product performance or sales achievements, sales representatives under a straight salary plan might opt to focus on selling products that are perceived as easier to sell or require less effort. This could lead to a skewed focus on certain products, potentially neglecting other products in the company's portfolio that may be strategically important.

These disadvantages highlight the limitations of a straight salary sales compensation plan, including potential challenges in motivating the sales team, attracting and retaining top performers, and ensuring a balanced focus on the entire product or service offering. Alternative compensation structures, such as commission-based or performance-based plans, are often implemented to address these drawbacks and provide stronger incentives for sales success.

61. (C): A point estimator is considered consistent when it tends to become closer to the population parameter as the sample size becomes larger. In statistical estimation, consistency is a desirable property indicating that as more data points are included in the sample, the estimator converges in probability to the true population parameter. In practical terms, this means that as we collect more observations, the estimate produced by the estimator becomes more accurate and approaches the actual value of the parameter we are trying to estimate. Consistency provides confidence that, with larger sample sizes, the point estimator becomes increasingly reliable in capturing the true characteristics of the population, enhancing the precision and accuracy of statistical inferences.

62. (C)

63. (A):

(*a*) **Regional Rural Banks Act, 1976:** The Regional Rural Banks Act, 1976, is the primary legal framework governing the establishment, operation, and regulation of Regional Rural Banks (RRBs) in India. This Act was enacted to create a special category of banks, known as Regional Rural Banks, to cater to the banking needs of rural and semi-urban areas. RRBs are a crucial component of rural credit structure, and this Act provides the legal basis for their formation, governance, and functions.

(*d*) **Banking Regulation Act, 1949:** The Banking Regulation Act, 1949, is a broader piece of legislation that regulates various aspects of banking in India. It applies to all types of banks, including commercial banks, cooperative banks, and development banks. While the Banking Regulation Act sets the framework for the functioning of banks, it also works as specific legislation that governs the establishment and operation of Regional Rural Banks. Each category of banks, including RRBs, has its own specific legislation.

64. (B): Price lining is a strategic pricing approach employed by businesses, where a range of products within a specific category is offered at predetermined price points. In this strategy, a company sets clear price targets based on various factors such as market conditions, competitive landscape, and internal profit goals. These price points represent different tiers or levels within the product line, each associated with specific features, qualities, or specifications.

The unique aspect of price lining is that the firm establishes these prices before developing the products, essentially setting a pricing structure first and then creating products to align with each targeted price point. This approach enables the company to cater to diverse consumer segments with varying preferences and budgets. The ultimate objective is to maximize total profits by strategically positioning products across different price levels, providing options for a broader customer base while ensuring that each product contributes to the overall profitability of the business.

65. (D):

(*b*) **Refunds:** Offering money back, whether as a temporary incentive, a loyalty reward, or a goodwill gesture after purchase, can be a powerful promotional tool. It directly addresses price sensitivity and potential concerns about product satisfaction, encouraging trial and repeat purchases. While not always a direct discount, it acts as a tangible benefit for consumers.

(*c*) **Coupons:** These versatile promotional tools come in various forms, offering discounts, free trials, or bundled deals. They directly incentivize specific purchases, attracting new customers and encouraging existing ones to try new products or services. Coupons can be targeted to specific demographics or distributed through diverse channels, making them a flexible and effective way to reach desired audiences.

(*d*) **Event sponsorship:** While not a direct one-on-one interaction with consumers, sponsoring events relevant to your target market can be a strategic promotional move. It creates brand awareness and association with positive experiences, potentially leading to increased purchase consideration and brand loyalty. Partnering with events that align with your brand values and target demographics allows you to connect with potential customers in a more engaging and immersive setting.

66. (B):

(*a*) **Environment Management System (EMS) Audit:** An Environment Management System (EMS) Audit assesses the effectiveness and compliance of an organization's environmental management system. This involves reviewing the policies, procedures, and processes in place to manage environmental aspects and impacts. The audit aims to ensure that the organization is following established environmental management practices and standards.

(*c*) **Compliance Audit:** A Compliance Audit evaluates whether an organization is adhering to applicable laws, regulations, and standards related to environmental matters. It ensures that the organization is in compliance with environmental legislation, permits, and any other requirements governing its operations. This type of audit helps identify any areas of non-compliance and ensures that the organization is meeting its legal obligations.

(*d*) **Site Property Audit:** A Site Property Audit focuses on the physical aspects of a site or facility, including land, buildings, and infrastructure, with an emphasis on environmental considerations. This audit assesses the environmental impact of the site, identifies potential risks or hazards, and evaluates the organization's management of site-related environmental aspects. It helps ensure that the organization is effectively managing its physical assets in an environmentally responsible manner.

These three components (EMS Audit, Compliance Audit, and Site Property Audit) contribute to the broader Environmental Audit framework by examining the organization's environmental management practices, ensuring legal compliance, and evaluating the environmental aspects of its physical facilities.

67. **(A):** The statement "It involves various support activities in the process of making products" highlights a key characteristic of activity-based costing (ABC). ABC is a costing methodology that goes beyond traditional methods by not only considering direct production costs but also incorporating various support activities or overhead costs into the product cost calculation. Support activities, such as setup, inspection, and maintenance, contribute to the overall production process, and ABC recognizes their significance in determining the true cost of products. By identifying and allocating these support activity costs more accurately, ABC provides a more detailed and nuanced understanding of the cost structure, enabling businesses to make informed decisions about pricing, product mix, and resource allocation.

68. **(C):** The Malhotra Committee, formed in 1993, played a crucial role in recommending comprehensive reforms in the Indian insurance sector. Led by former Finance Secretary R.N. Malhotra, the committee was appointed to assess the structure and functioning of the insurance industry and propose measures for its modernization. The committee's recommendations aimed at liberalizing and opening up the insurance market to private players, encouraging competition, and introducing innovative products. The reforms suggested by the Malhotra Committee, such as increasing the Foreign Direct Investment (FDI) limit, paved the way for the Insurance Regulatory and Development Authority Act (IRDA Act) of 1999, which established the Insurance Regulatory and Development Authority (IRDA) to regulate and supervise the insurance business in India. The committee's recommendations marked a significant turning point in the evolution of the insurance sector, ushering in a new era of growth and development.

69. **(D):** Utilitarianism is a normative ethical theory that emphasizes the principle of maximizing overall well-being or happiness as the primary criterion for ethical decision-making. In the context of utilitarianism, the key consideration is to assess the consequences of an action and determine whether it leads to a net increase in overall happiness or pleasure.

The ethical value of an action is measured by the extent to which it produces the greatest overall benefit for the greatest number of individuals. Utilitarianism encourages decision-makers to evaluate the outcomes of different options and choose the one that result in the greatest net positive impact on well-being.

This approach prioritizes the collective welfare and aims to create the greatest overall happiness, making it a consequentiality ethical theory focused on the consequences or outcomes of actions.

70. **(A):** In the process of perception, external factors play a crucial role in influencing the selection of stimuli. However, experience is considered an internal factor rather than an external one. Experience refers to an individual's personal history, knowledge, and past encounters, shaping how they interpret and perceive stimuli. External factors typically involve elements in the immediate environment, and in this context, familiarity, repetition, and novelty are examples of external factors influencing the selection of stimuli. Familiarity relates to recognition and previous exposure, repetition emphasizes the frequency of encountering stimuli, and novelty refers to the degree of newness or uniqueness in the stimuli. These external factors collectively contribute to the way individuals perceive and respond to the information presented in their surroundings.

71. (A):

(*d*) **Inferior goods:** Inferior goods typically have negative income elasticity of demand. As consumers' income increases, the demand for inferior goods tends to decrease because consumers often shift to higher-quality substitutes.

(*b*) **Necessities:** Necessities are goods for which demand is relatively insensitive to changes in income. They have low income elasticity, meaning that the percentage change in demand is less than the percentage change in income. These goods are considered essential for daily living, and as income increases, the demand for necessities does not increase significantly.

(*a*) **Normal consumption goods:** Normal goods usually have positive but less than unity income elasticity. As consumers' income rises, the demand for normal goods increases, but not at the same proportion as the increase in income. The demand for these goods grows, but not as rapidly as income.

(*e*) **Services:** The income elasticity of services can vary. Some services may be considered necessities, while others, particularly those perceived as luxuries, may have higher income elasticity. The demand for certain services may increase more than proportionately with an increase in income.

(*c*) **Luxuries:** Luxuries are goods and services for which demand is highly sensitive to changes in income. They typically have income elasticity greater than one, indicating that as income rises, the demand for luxury items increases at a greater proportion than the increase in income.

72. (D):

(*b*) **Trimmed Mean:** A Trimmed Mean is a measure of central tendency that involves excluding a certain percentage of extreme values or outliers from both ends of a dataset and then calculating the average of the remaining values. This approach is less sensitive to outliers, making it a robust alternative to the traditional mean. The trimming process offers flexibility, allowing analysts to adjust the percentage based on the characteristics of the data, and it enhances transparency by clearly identifying which data points are excluded and why. This method is particularly useful in situations where outliers may significantly skew the results of the arithmetic mean.

(*d*) **Median:** The Median is a measure of central tendency calculated as the middle value of a dataset when arranged in ascending or descending order. If there is an even number of observations, the median is the average of the two middle values. Unlike the mean, the Median is not influenced by extreme values, making it a robust measure that provides an accurate representation of the center of a distribution. Its intuitive interpretation, dividing the dataset into two equal halves, makes the Median a straightforward choice, especially when dealing with skewed data or datasets containing outliers. The simplicity of calculation further adds to its appeal in various analytical contexts.

73. (C): The hiring-related turnover cost associated with an employee quitting an organization is primarily related to training. When an employee leaves, the organization may incur costs related to training the replacement or ensuring that the new hire is familiar with the role and responsibilities. This includes the time and resources invested in on boarding, orientation programs, and any specialized training required for the position. Training costs are a significant component of turnover expenses, as organizations strive to equip new hires with the necessary skills and knowledge to perform effectively in their roles.

74. (C): In the balance of payments framework, changes in holdings of gold and foreign currencies by official monetary institutions are recorded in the Official Reserves Account. This account is a subcomponent of the capital account, which tracks transactions involving financial assets. Official reserves represent a country's holdings of valuable assets, such as gold and foreign currencies, often managed by central banks. Fluctuations in these reserves can impact a nation's ability to manage its currency's value and ensure stability in international trade. The Official Reserves Account provides a detailed record of these transactions, reflecting changes in a country's official reserves due to factors like purchases, sales, or changes in the market value of these assets.

75. (C): The optimal capital budget of a firm is determined by the intersection point of the investment opportunity curve and the marginal cost of capital curve. The investment opportunity curve represents various potential projects ranked by their expected returns, while the marginal cost of capital curve illustrates the cost of raising additional capital for investment. The point where these two curves intersect signifies the optimal capital budget, indicating that the firm should allocate funds to projects up to this intersection point. Beyond this point, the marginal cost of capital exceeds the return on investment opportunities, leading to a suboptimal allocation of resources. This approach ensures that the firm maximizes shareholder wealth by investing in projects that yield returns higher than the cost of capital.

76. (A): "Consumers usually spend only a small proportion of income on any one commodity." This statement suggests that consumers allocate a relatively small portion of their total income to the purchase of any specific commodity.

In the context of consumer behaviour and the substitution effect, this could imply that consumers have a diverse range of goods and services that they purchase, and any one particular item represents only a fraction of their overall budget. When the price of a specific commodity changes consumers may find it relatively easier to substitute that commodity with alternatives because it constitutes only a small share of their total spending.

For example, if the price of a particular brand of coffee increases, and coffee is just a small portion of a consumer's overall food and beverage budget, they may be more inclined to switch to a different brand or type of coffee without significantly altering their overall consumption pattern. This behaviour emphasizes the substitution effect, where consumers adjust their preferences based on relative price changes, especially when the impact on their overall budget is limited due to the small share of income allocated to a specific commodity.

77. (D):

(*a*) **Product safety:** This refers to the ethical responsibility of companies to ensure that the products they offer are safe for consumers to use. This involves rigorous testing, compliance with safety standards, and transparent communication about potential risks. Customers are concerned about the safety of the products they purchase, and ethical companies prioritize the well-being of their customers.

(*b*) **Fair Price:** Customers are concerned about the fairness of pricing strategies employed by companies. Ethical considerations involve setting prices that are reasonable and fair, avoiding price gouging or deceptive pricing practices. Fair pricing ensures that customers are not exploited and can make informed purchasing decisions based on transparent and ethical pricing practices.

(*e*) **Proper disclosures and information:** Ethical companies are expected to provide accurate and complete information about their products and services. This includes clear and transparent disclosure of relevant details such as ingredients, potential risks, pricing, and terms of service. Customers rely on truthful information to make informed decisions, and ethical responsibility entails openness and honesty in communication.

These areas collectively contribute to building trust between businesses and consumers, emphasizing the importance of ethical and socially responsible practices in meeting customer expectations and fostering a positive relationship between companies and their clientele.

78. **(A):** The North American Free Trade Agreement (NAFTA) was a regional economic integration agreement that aimed to promote economic gains through the free flow of trade and investment between participating countries. It was established in 1994 to create a trilateral trade bloc between the United States, Canada, and Mexico. It eliminates tariffs and other trade barriers between the three countries, encouraging the free flow of goods, services, and investment. NAFTA included three member countries.

USA as one of the largest economies in the world, the United States played a central role in NAFTA. The agreement facilitated trade between the U.S. and its North American neighbours, Canada and Mexico. Canada, being geographically close to the United States, also benefited from NAFTA by fostering increased trade and economic cooperation with its North American partners. Mexico, as the southernmost member of NAFTA, experienced significant economic benefits from increased access to the U.S. and Canadian markets, leading to the expansion of trade and investment.

These three countries formed the core of NAFTA, and the agreement aimed to eliminate trade barriers, reduce tariffs, and create a more integrated and efficient economic space within North America. It was an important milestone in regional economic integration efforts, promoting cooperation and collaboration among the participating nations.

79. **(B): Assertion (A):** When a partner retires, all the assets and liabilities are revalued according to current value : When a partner retires from a partnership, it often leads to a significant change in the ownership structure and financial dynamics of the firm. To ensure that the financial statements provide an accurate representation of the partnership's financial position, it is common practice to revalue the assets and liabilities. This revaluation involves updating the values of assets and liabilities to their current market or fair values.

Reason (R): The balance sheet should show the correct values of assets and liabilities: The reason is correct, emphasizing the fundamental principle of financial reporting. The balance sheet is a snapshot of a company's financial position at a specific point in time. To provide a true and fair view, it is crucial that the values assigned to assets and liabilities reflect their current market values. This ensures that stakeholders, including partners or shareholders, have an accurate understanding of the financial health of the partnership.

However, while the reason highlights the importance of showing correct values on the balance sheet, it doesn't specifically explain why the revaluation is done when a partner retires. The revaluation process is more directly tied to changes in ownership structure and ensuring an accurate representation of the partnership's financial position after a significant event like a partner's retirement.

80. (D)

81. (C): Oligopoly is a market structure characterized by a small number of large firms that dominate the industry. In the manufacturing sector, oligopolies are prevalent due to factors such as high barriers to entry, significant economies of scale, and the need for substantial capital investment. The presence of a few major players in an oligopoly allows these firms to have a considerable impact on market conditions, including pricing strategies, product development, and overall industry dynamics. Oligopolistic markets often exhibit inter-dependence among firms, where the actions of one major player can influence and shape the strategies of others. This concentration of market power makes oligopoly a common and influential form of market organization in the manufacturing sector.

In the Indian manufacturing sector, an example of an oligopoly can be observed in the cement industry. The cement industry in India is characterized by a small number of major players who dominate the market. Companies such as UltraTech Cement, ACC Limited, Ambuja Cements, and Shree Cement are among the key players in the Indian cement industry. These companies control a significant portion of the market share, have large production capacities, and play a crucial role in determining pricing strategies and market conditions. The barriers to entry, capital requirements, and the scale of operations in cement manufacturing contribute to the oligopolistic nature of the industry in India. The actions and decisions of these major players have a substantial impact on the overall dynamics of the cement market in the country.

82. (C):

(*a*) **The euro currency market does not have geographical limits:** The Euro Currency market operates globally, allowing transactions to take place without specific geographical constraints. It is not confined to a particular region or country, providing participants with the flexibility to engage in transactions worldwide.

(*c*) **The euro currency market does not have deposit insurance:** Unlike domestic markets that may have deposit insurance schemes to protect depositors in case of a bank failure, the Euro Currency market generally lacks such deposit insurance. Participants in this market should be aware of the absence of this protective measure.

(*e*) **The euro currency market does not attract CRR and SLR restrictions:** Cash Reserve Ratio (CRR) and Statutory Liquidity Ratio (SLR) are regulatory requirements imposed by central banks in some countries to ensure financial stability. In the Euro Currency market, participants are not subjected to these restrictions, providing more flexibility in managing their reserves.

These characteristics collectively contribute to the unique nature of the Euro Currency market, making it an attractive and versatile platform for international financial transactions. Participants, however, should be mindful of the differences and considerations associated with operating in this market compared to domestic financial markets.

83. (D):

(*c*) **Funnel Technique:** The Funnel Technique involves structuring the questionnaire in a way that starts with broad, general questions and progressively narrows down to more specific inquiries. The benefits include minimizing the influence of early responses on later ones and allowing for a gradual exploration of the topic.

(*d*) **Filter Questions:** Filter Questions act as a screening mechanism to identify and exclude respondents who don't meet specific criteria before they reach the main part of the questionnaire. The advantages include reducing irrelevant data and bias, ensuring that responses come from qualified participants who fit the target population.

(*a*) **Pivot Questions:** Pivot Questions are dynamic and adapt based on the respondent's prior answers. They are designed to reduce redundancy, avoid asking irrelevant follow-up questions, and provide personalized insights by tailoring questions to the respondent's individual experiences.

84. (C): Assertion (A): By removing barriers between national markets, trading blocks create competition due to a bigger trading area. This assertion is generally correct in the context of economics. When barriers, such as tariffs or restrictions on the movement of goods and services between countries, are removed within trading blocks, businesses operating within those blocks have access to a larger market. The increased market size often leads to heightened competition among businesses as they vie for consumer attention and market share.

Reason (R): Increased competition can lead to the closure of local industry and harm domestic consumption. While it is not correct that increased competition can pose challenges to local industries, the statement in Reason (R) oversimplifies the potential outcomes. Increased competition can have both positive and negative effects. While some local industries may struggle or face closure due to the intensified competition, others may thrive by innovating, improving efficiency, and adapting to the changing market conditions. Additionally, consumers may not benefit from increased choices and potentially lower prices.

85. (C)

86. (A): The Informative strategy is suitable for advertising cars and appliances due to the high involvement nature of these purchases. Consumers extensively research features, specifications, and benefits before making decisions. Informative advertising provides detailed information about safety features, performance, energy efficiency, and technological advancements, aiding consumers in making informed choices. Transparency in advertising builds trust, and the strategy allows for comparative information, helping consumers weigh options. While emotional appeals or satisfaction elements may complement the campaign, the core focus for cars and appliances involves conveying detailed and accurate information to meet the informational needs of potential buyers, contributing to a well-informed decision-making process.

87. (A):

(*d*) **Summarize the flow of physical units:** This step involves tracking the movement of units through different stages of the production process. It summarizes how many units were started and completed during the period and how many are still in process.

(*b*) **Compute output in terms of equivalent units:** Calculate the equivalent units of production. This involves considering both fully completed units and partially completed units at various stages of the production process. It provides a more accurate measure of the work done.

(*a*) **Summarize total costs to account for work-in-process inventory:** Summarize all costs incurred during the period, including costs added to the beginning work-in-process inventory and costs incurred in the current period. This step helps in determining the total cost to be accounted for.

(*c*) **Compute cost per equivalent unit:** Determine the cost per equivalent unit for each cost component (e.g., materials, labor, overhead). This involves dividing the total cost by the equivalent units, providing the cost allocated to each unit of production.

(*e*) **Assign total cost to units completed and to units in ending work in process:** Allocate the total costs to both completed units, which have been transferred out of the process, and units still in the ending work-in-process inventory. This step finalizes the cost allocation and provides a clear understanding of the costs associated with completed and partially completed units.

So, the sequence reflects the logical flow of process costing steps, starting with summarizing the physical flow of units and concluding with the assignment of costs to completed and in-process units.

88. (B): Statement I: The only purpose of logistics management is to coordinate activities of moving products from the factory to customers: This statement is incorrect. While coordinating the movement of products is a significant aspect of logistics management, it is not the sole purpose. Logistics management involves a broader set of functions, including inventory management, transportation, warehousing, and distribution. The ultimate goal is to optimize the entire supply chain, ensuring efficiency and cost-effectiveness beyond just the coordination of physical movement.

Statement II: Logistics management is only the responsibility of the marketing function: This statement is also incorrect. Logistics management is a cross-functional activity that involves coordination among various departments, including marketing, operations, procurement, and distribution. While marketing plays a role in determining customer requirements and communicating them to the logistics function, logistics is not exclusively the responsibility of the marketing department. It requires collaboration across multiple functions to ensure a seamless flow of goods and information.

89. (D):

(*a*) **Business loss and unabsorbed depreciation can be carried forward and set off against profit and gain:** This tax planning strategy involves carrying forward business losses and unabsorbed depreciation to future years. These losses can be set off against future profits and gains, reducing the overall taxable income in subsequent years.

(*c*) **Tax benefit of deduction under section 33AB and 115VT may be withdrawn and liable to tax for the year in which business is discontinued:** Section 33AB provides a deduction for specified reserves created by a specified entity. When a business is discontinued, the tax benefit associated with this deduction may be withdrawn, and the reserves may become liable to tax in the year of discontinuation.

(*e*) **If a person has more than one business, the loss-making business may not be discontinued:** This perspective acknowledges the overall business portfolio and considers the possibility of continuing a loss-making business if the overall tax implications, synergy with other businesses, or strategic reasons makes it favorable. It emphasizes a holistic approach to tax planning and business strategy.

90. (D)

91. (A): Statement I: Initial UPI adoption has surpassed the most optimistic expectations on account of the waiver of the merchant discount rate: This statement is correct. The initial adoption of the United Payments Interface (UPI) indeed exceeded optimistic expectations. One of the contributing factors mentioned is the waiver of the merchant discount rate, which likely encouraged more users and merchants to adopt UPI for transactions.

Statement II: The future growth of UPI will be facilitated by providing solutions for the conduct of business and becoming a medium of commerce: This statement is also correct. The passage suggests that the future growth of UPI is expected to be facilitated by not only providing solutions for the conduct of business but also by incorporating lending at some point to become a more comprehensive medium of commerce. This aligns with the evolving role of UPI beyond peer-to-peer transactions to support a wider range of commercial and financial activities.

92. (A): Assertion (A): Payment banks - which can accept deposits but are prohibited from lending - need to be part of the UPI ecosystem: Payment banks have limitations on lending activities but can accept deposits. Being part of the UPI ecosystem allows them to participate in digital transactions, broaden their service offerings, and potentially attract more customers. The ability to engage in digital transactions aligns with the core function of UPI, making it beneficial for payment banks to be involved.

Reason (R): Loading fee on transactions through UPI, payment banks can widen the adoption of wallets among customers and merchants: This reason supports the idea that payment banks, by charging a loading fee on transactions through UPI, can encourage the adoption of digital wallets among both customers and merchants. The loading fee acts as an incentive, and by participating in UPI transactions, payment banks can play a role in expanding the usage of digital wallets.

93. (B): According to the passage, the contactless payments infrastructure is expected to empower fintechs primarily by fostering innovation in finance. The infrastructure is seen as a catalyst for encouraging financial technology companies (fintechs) to push boundaries and introduce novel solutions within the finance sector. The passage highlights the importance of creating an environment that stimulates creativity and originality in financial services, indicating that the contactless payments infrastructure plays a pivotal role in providing opportunities for fintechs to innovate and contribute to the evolving landscape of financial technology.

94. (B): The passage indicates that payment banks, which are restricted from lending but can accept deposits, need to strategically carve out a distinct business segment for themselves. The rationale behind this move is the competition with full-service banks. By creating a unique business segment, payment banks aim to position themselves in a way that leverages their strengths and advantages, despite the limitations on lending. This strategic differentiation allows payment banks to effectively compete with full-service banks in areas where they have a comparative advantage, contributing to their viability and success within the broader financial services landscape.

95. (C):

(*a*) **UPI integration with the digital rupee:** The integration of UPI with the digital rupee signifies the advancement of digital transactions and payment systems. Payment banks, being part of the UPI ecosystem, would likely benefit from this integration as it expands the scope and usage of digital payments, contributing to the growth of payment banks.

(*c*) **UPI facilitation of cross-border remittances:** UPI's facilitation of cross-border remittances opens up new opportunities for payment banks to engage in international transactions. This use case not only broadens their service offerings but also attracts a more diverse user base, fostering growth for payment banks.

(*e*) **Consumer lending through RuPay Credit Cards:** The introduction of consumer lending through RuPay Credit Cards represents a significant expansion of services for payment banks. Offering credit services enhances their role in the financial ecosystem, potentially attracting more customers and contributing to revenue growth.

These selected options align with the passage's suggestion that specific use cases, such as UPI integration, cross-border remittances, and consumer lending, can promote the growth of payment banks.

96. **(B):** The Application Supported by Blocked Amount (ASBA) facility, as discussed in the passage, is proposed to be extended to the secondary market, emphasizing investor protection and increased earnings potential. The passage underscores the complexity of implementing such a mechanism in the secondary market due to the multitude of transactions involving various securities and investor orders with differing time horizons. The Securities and Exchange Board of India (SEBI) is acknowledged for its efforts to introduce a structure that mirrors the ASBA model, providing a safeguard for investors' cash and securities in the dynamic environment of the secondary market. The proposal envisions a technical challenge but deems it surmountable, suggesting that the Unified Payments Interface (UPI) could play a pivotal role in facilitating direct money transfers for trading, thereby minimizing risks and streamlining settlement processes. Overall, the proposed ASBA-like facility for the secondary market aligns with SEBI's regulatory objective of safeguarding investors and enhancing the efficiency of financial transactions.

97. **(B):** The passage discusses the role of the Unified Payments Interface (UPI) in facilitating the direct transfer of money used for trading to clearing corporations. UPI is highlighted as a key enabler, allowing funds utilized in trading activities to be seamlessly transferred directly to the clearing corporations. This process is described as flushing out money that may otherwise be idling with brokers, reducing the risk of misuse and containing potential fallout in case of broker default. The passage commends UPI for providing a pathway for direct settlement, bypassing traditional intermediary pool accounts and ensuring more efficient and secure transactions in the financial market. In summary, the use of UPI emerges as a significant advancement in financial infrastructure, contributing to enhanced transparency and risk management in the trading process.

98. **(B): Assertion (A):** SEBI has offered relief to brokerages that stand to lose float income on account of up-streaming client money to clearing corporations: This assertion is true. The passage mentions that SEBI has provided relief to brokerages facing potential loss of float income by allowing them to upstream clients' funds in the form of fixed deposit lien or mutual fund units.

Reason (R): Brokerages have been allowed to upstream clients' fluid in the form of fixed deposit lien or mutual fund units: This reason is also true, as it corresponds to the relief measures mentioned in Assertion (A).

However, it does not serve as a complete or correct explanation of Assertion (A). The reason provides details about how relief is granted (allowing up-streaming of clients' funds), but it doesn't explain why SEBI offered this relief.

99. (A): The Securities and Exchange Board of India (SEBI) has diligently fulfilled its regulatory mandate by prioritizing the safeguarding of investors' interests, specifically their cash and securities. The passage underscores SEBI's commitment to ensuring the protection of both financial assets, emphasizing its role in creating a secure investment environment.

By actively addressing challenges and proposing structures such as the Application Supported by Blocked Amount (ASBA) for the secondary market, SEBI demonstrates its dedication to maintaining the integrity of investors' financial holdings. This commitment extends to efforts in reducing risks associated with trading practices, such as allowing the direct transfer of trading funds to clearing corporations through the Unified Payments Interface (UPI). In summary, SEBI's regulatory initiatives are geared towards preserving the financial well-being of investors by safeguarding both their cash and securities.

100. (C):

(*a*) **Kinds of transactions:** In the secondary market, investors engage in a variety of transactions involving different securities and trading strategies. Unlike the more straightforward process in the primary market, the secondary markets involves a diverse range of buy and sell orders, including options like leverage and multiple securities. Adapting ASBA to accommodate this complexity becomes a challenge.

(*d*) **Number of Parties:** The secondary market involves a larger number of parties compared to the primary market. Multiple investors, brokers, and other intermediaries participate in various transactions. Coordinating and implementing a mechanism like ASBA, which involves blocking funds until the transaction is settled, becomes more intricate in a system with numerous participants. Escrow arrangements and coordination with multiple parties add to the complexity of implementing such a mechanism.

Previous Years' Paper (Solved)

National Testing Agency (NTA)

UGC-NET Junior Research Fellowship & Assistant Professor Eligibility Exam

COMMERCE, March 2023

(Online exam held on 04-03-2023)

PAPER-II

Note: *This paper contains* ***hundred (100)*** *objective type questions of* ***two (2)*** *marks each.* ***All*** *questions are* ***compulsory.***

1. Which of the following is the right description of the "Duty Free Import Authorization (DFIA)" Scheme?
   A. Duty free imports of inputs required for export production subject to certain export obligations, as stipulated in the foreign trade policy.
   B. Exemption in respect of custom duty, additional duty, education cess and anti-dumping or safeguard duties for inputs used in exports.
   C. Import of capital goods at concessional rate of duty subject to an appropriate export obligation accepted by the importer.
   D. Grant of credit on post-export basis as specified percentage of F.o.B value of exports made in a freely convertible currency.

2. An Indian company receiving investment from outside India for issuing shares/ convertible debentures/preference shares under the FDI Scheme should report the details of the inflow to the RBI. What is the time limit for reporting these details to RBI?
   A. Within 10 days from the date of receipt
   B. Within 15 days from the date of receipt
   C. Within 30 days from the date of receipt
   D. Within 45 days from the date of receipt

3. Which one of the following theories of attitude change states that changes in opinions can result in to an attitude change?
   A. Balance Theory
   B. Cognitive Consistency Theory
   C. Reinforcement Theory
   D. Cognitive Dissonance Theory

4. According to Porter's diamond, which of the following is NOT a factor of national competitive advantage?
   A. Relating and supporting industry
   B. Firm strategy, structure and rivalry
   C. Bargaining power of buyers
   D. Demand conditions

5. X and Y are partners sharing profits and losses in the ratio of 3 : 2. They admit Z as a new partner with 1/5 share in the profits. Calculate the new profit sharing ratio of the partners.
   A. 12 : 8 : 5 B. 12 : 8 : 6
   C. 12 : 7 : 6 D. 12 : 3 : 7

6. At the break-even point, contribution is equal to:
   A. Variable cost
   B. Profit
   C. Fixed cost
   D. Sales

7. Which one of the following is NOT true?
   A. Capital expenditure results in extra capacity
   B. Capital expenditure results in a benefit which will last for a long time
   C. Capital expenditure results in the acquisition of a permanent asset
   D. Heavy expenditure on advertisement campaigns in order to introduce a new product in the market

8. As per the information given below, what is the correct material yield variance?
Standard input = 100 kg
Standard yield = 90 kg
Standard cost per kg of output = ₹ 20
Actual input = 200 kg
Actual yield = 182 kg
Actual cost per kg of output = ₹ 19
A. ₹ 40 (Favourable)
B. ₹ 400 (Favourable)
C. ₹ 400 (Unfavourable)
D. ₹ 38 (Favourable)

9. When the negative income effect overwhelms the positive substitution effect so much that the demand curve is positively sloped, the commodity in consumption is described as;
A. Normal good B. Inferior good
C. Giffen good D. Luxury good

10. In the extreme case of perfect price discrimination, the entire consumer surplus in the market goes:
A. to consumers
B. to monopoly producer
C. as deadweight loss
D. to capital

11. A situation, in which economic actors interacting with one another, each choose their best strategy, given the strategies that all the other actors have chosen, is called:
A. Nash equilibrium
B. Prisoners' dilemma
C. Dominant strategy
D. Predatory strategy

12. In the Cobb- Douglas production function, $Q = AK^aL^b$, where 'a' and 'b' are output elasticities of capital and labour, respectively. If $a + b > 1$, the underlying return to scale will be:
A. increasing B. decreasing
C. constant D. linear

13. Which one of the following institutions is not a part of the World Bank Group?
A. International Bank for Reconstruction and Development (IBRD)
B. International Development Association (IDA)
C. Multilateral Investment Guarantee Agency (MIGA)
D. The Bank for International Settlements (BIS)

14. According to the traditional approach, what is the effect of increase in degree of leverage on the valuation of a firm?
A. Increases
B. Decreases
C. Remains unaffected
D. Increases first and then decreases

15. An economic enterprise requires 90,000 units of certain item annually. The cost per unit is ₹ 3. The cost per purchase order is ₹ 300 and the inventory carrying cost is ₹ 6 per unit per year. What is EOQ?
A. 3000 units B. 1500 units
C. 6000 units D. 4500 units

16. Dell Ltd. has ₹ 100 preference shares redeemable at a premium of 10% with 15 years maturity. The coupon rate is 12%; the flotation cost is 5% and the sale price is ₹ 95. Calculate the cost of preference shares and select the correct option.
A. 12% B. 12.67%
C. 13% D. 13.33%

17. Which of the following is not a characteristic of normal distribution?
A. The mean of the normal distribution may be negative or positive
B. For any normal random variable x, $P(x \le \mu) = P(x \ge \mu) = 0.50$
C. For every pair of values μ and σ, the curve of the distribution is bell-shaped and symmetric
D. The kurtosis of the distribution is always less than 3

18. For a Poisson distribution $P(x) = \frac{e^{-5}(5)^2}{2!}$ the mean value is:
A. 2 B. 5
C. 10 D. 25

19. Which of the following is used to assess the relationship between two ordinal variables?
A. Spearman's rho B. Phi
C. Cramer's V D. Chi-square

20. A "Spurious" relationship between two variables is expressed as:

A. An apparent relationship that is so curious that it demands further attention.

B. A relationship that appears to be true because each variable is related to a third one.

C. One that is so ridiculously illogical that it cannot be possibly true.

D. One that produces a perfect negative correlation on a scatter diagram.

21. Which one of the following motives characterizes dominant organizational climate of clubs?

A. Extension B. Affiliation

C. Dependency D. Achievement

22. Which one of the following is the description of Ego Regression Mechanism?

A. Returning to a previous stage of psyche development

B. Avoiding unacceptable emotions by focusing on the intellectual aspects

C. Taking out impulses on a less threatening target

D. Pulling into the unconscious situation

23. Which one of the following is not an advantage of organization structure by product in a manufacturing company?

A. Places attention and effort on product line

B. Requires less persons with general managerial abilities

C. Improves coordination of functional activities

D. Permits growth and diversity of products

24. Which one of the following is not an assumption under the McGregor's Theory Y?

A. The degree of commitment to objectives is in proportion to the size of the rewards associated with their achievement.

B. Under the conditions of modern industrial life, the intellectual potentialities of the average human being are only partially utilized.

C. External control and the threat of punishment are the only means for producing effort towards organizational objectives.

D. Average human beings learn, under proper conditions, not only to accept responsibility but also to seek it.

25. The minimum capital requirement for a life insurance company in India is:

A. ₹ 300 crores B. ₹ 200 crores

C. ₹ 500 crores D. ₹ 100 crores

26. Universal banks that function as investment banks in India are regulated by:

A. SEBI

B. RBI

C. Ministry of Finance

D. IRDA

27. When the RBI desires to restrict expansion of credit, it:

A. increases the bank rate

B. decreases the bank rate

C. decreases the CRR for banks

D. decreases the SLR for banks

28. Which of the following refers to default-risk intermediation?

A. Borrowing short-term funds from savers and making long-term loans to borrowers

B. Making loans to risky borrowers by attracting savings from the savers who are risk-averse

C. Using information gathering skills of the intermediary

D. Pooling small amounts of savings from individuals to give loans to others

29. The knowledge and courtesy of employees and their ability to convey trust and confidence indicates which of the following?

A. Responsiveness B. Assurance

C. Empathy D. Reliability

30. Which of the following is not true about rural markets?

A. Growth opportunities in rural markets are driving companies to them.

B. Information and communication technology are the drivers of change in rural markets.

C. Socioeconomic changes are yet to happen to rural markets.

D. Rural consumers shop for grocery, apparels, consumer durables of agri-inputs in nearby urban shops.

31. "Manufacturers of razors and cameras often price these products low and set high mark ups on razor blades and films."

As per the above statement, manufacturers of razors and cameras are using which one of the following?

A. Captive-product pricing
B. Two-part pricing
C. Product-bundling pricing
D. By-product pricing

32. A vertical marketing system (VMS) combining successive stages of production and distribution under single ownership, is known as:

A. Corporate VMS
B. Administered VMS
C. Contractual VMS
D. Conventional VMS

33. The act of throwing on board cargo and other things from the ship to safeguard it from total loss in times of peril is called:

A. Jettisoning
B. Moral hazards
C. Consequential peril
D. Reverse indemnity

34. The right to 'stoppage in transit' exercised by an unpaid seller is to:

A. recover price B. retain possession
C. regain possession D. recover damages

35. Which one among the following is the duty of the Central Assistant Public Information Officer or a State Assistant Public Information Officer?

A. To receive the applications for information or appeals under the RTI Act for forwarding the same forthwith to the CPIO/SPIO
B. To receive the fee for the RTI applications
C. To assist the CPIO/SPIO in furnishing the reply to the applicant
D. To ensure that RTI applications are replied within the prescribed period

36. The relationship between a bank and its customers is basically that of:

A. Debtor and Creditor
B. Trustee and Beneficiary
C. Principal and Agent
D. Drawer and Payee

37. Provisions of the Vivad se Vishwas Act, 2020 does not apply in respect of tax arrears relating to which one of the following?

A. an assessment year in respect of which prosecution has been instituted on or before the date of filing of declaration
B. any income from agricultural land in India
C. Section 10(3) dealing with tax deductions
D. assessments under Section 80Gl of the Act

38. Under Section 80TTB of the Income Tax Act, which amount of benefits is available to senior citizens on account of interest income from deposits with banks or post-office or cooperative banks?

A. ₹ 50,000 B. ₹ 1,00,000
C. ₹ 75,000 D. ₹ 1,50,000

39. Provisional Input Tax Credit can be utilised against:

A. Any tax liability
B. Self-assessed tax liability
C. Differential income tax gains
D. Fine

40. Penalty for late filing of the Income Tax Return for individuals under the Income Tax Act, 1961 is up to a maximum of amount of:

A. ₹ 10,000
B. ₹ 25,00,000
C. 10% of Gross Total Income
D. 2% of Tax liability

41. Revenue expenditure of the Central government includes:

(*a*) Debt relief to farmers
(*b*) Subsidy for fertilizers
(*c*) Grants to states
(*d*) Central plan allocations for rural development
(*e*) Central plan allocation for irrigation and flood control

Choose the ***correct*** answer from the options given below:

A. (*a*), (*b*) and (*e*) only
B. (*a*), (*c*) and (*d*) only
C. (*c*), (*d*) and (*e*) only
D. (*a*), (*b*) and (*c*) only

42. Exchange depreciation rate of one currency in relation to another currency is, approximately, equal to their:

(*a*) Inflation rate differential
(*b*) Interest rate differential
(*c*) Growth rate differential
(*d*) Fiscal deficit differential
(*e*) Forex reserve differential

Choose the ***correct*** answer from the options given below:

A. (*a*), (*b*) and (*c*) only
B. (*c*), (*d*) and (*e*) only
C. (*a*) and (*b*) only
D. (*d*) and (*e*) only

43. Which of the following activities are included under investing activities in the Cash Flow Statement?

(*a*) Cash receipts from disposal of fixed assets (including intangible)
(*b*) Cash advances and loans made to third parties (other than advances and loans made by a financial enterprise)
(*c*) Cash receipts from repayment of advances and loans made to third parties (other than advances and loans of a financial enterprise)
(*d*) Cash repayments of amount borrowed
(*e*) Cash payments to suppliers for goods and services

Choose the ***correct*** answer from the options given below:

A. (*a*), (*b*) and (*c*) only
B. (*c*), (*d*) and (*e*) only
C. (*c*) and (*d*) only
D. (*a*), (*c*) and (*d*) only

44. Identify cost drivers used in Activity Based Costing from the following:

(*a*) Volume
(*b*) Transaction
(*c*) Intensity
(*d*) Currency
(*e*) Duration

Choose the ***correct*** answer from the options given below:

A. (*a*), (*b*) and (*c*) only
B. (*c*), (*d*) and (*e*) only
C. (*a*), (*c*) and (*d*) only
D. (*b*), (*c*) and (*e*) only

45. Increasing returns to scale arise because as the scale of operation increases it causes:

(*a*) more division of labour and specialisation
(*b*) productive utilisation of machinery
(*c*) lower procurement and logistic costs
(*d*) more difficulties in managing firm effectively
(*e*) more economies in advertising

Choose the ***correct*** answer from the options given below:

A. (*a*), (*b*) and (*c*) only
B. (*c*), (*d*) and (*e*) only
C. (*a*), (*b*), (*c*) and (*d*) only
D. (*a*), (*b*), (*c*) and (*e*) only

46. Consumer rationality implies which of the following assumptions?

(*a*) Non-satiety of needs
(*b*) Transitivity of preferences
(*c*) Cardinal measurement
(*d*) Selfish economic motive
(*e*) Ordinal measurement

Choose the ***correct*** answer from the options given below:

A. (*a*) and (*b*) only
B. (*c*) and (*d*) only
C. (*a*), (*c*) and (*e*) only
D. (*a*), (*b*) and (*d*) only

47. Which of the following relationships raise presumptions of undue influence?

(*a*) Parent and child
(*b*) Doctor and patient
(*c*) Husband and wife
(*d*) Fiance and fiancee
(*e*) Creditor and debtor

Choose the ***correct*** answer from the options given below:

A. (*a*), (*b*) and (*c*) only
B. (*a*), (*b*) and (*d*) only
C. (*a*), (*b*) and (*e*) only
D. (*b*), (*c*) and (*d*) only

48. The Internal Rate of Return (IRR) method offer which of the following advantages?

(*a*) It recognises the time value of money
(*b*) It is consistent with the shareholders' profit-maximization objective also

(*c*) It considers all cash flows occurring over the entire life of the project
(*d*) It generally gives the same acceptance rule as the NPV method
(*e*) It considers all positive NPV over the entire life of the project

Choose the ***correct*** answer from the options given below:
A. (*a*), (*b*) and (*c*) only
B. (*b*), (*c*) and (*e*) only
C. (*a*), (*b*), (*c*) and (*d*) only
D. (*a*), (*d*) and (*e*) only

49. Which of the following are the off-balance sheet source(s) of finance?
(*a*) Securitisation (*b*) Factoring
(*c*) Forfaiting (*d*) Operational lease
(*e*) Credit rating

Choose the ***correct*** answer from the options given below:
A. (*a*) and (*e*) only
B. (*b*), (*c*) and (*e*) only
C. (*a*), (*b*) and (*c*) only
D. (*a*), (*b*), (*c*) and (*d*) only

50. Which of the following factors influence portfolio beta?
(*a*) Portfolio size
(*b*) Investment longevity
(*c*) Trading volume
(*d*) Return interval (weekly vs. monthly)
(*e*) Portfolio leverage

Choose the ***correct*** answer from the options given below:
A. (*a*), (*b*) and (*c*) only
B. (*b*), (*c*) and (*d*) only
C. (*d*) and (*e*) only
D. (*a*), (*b*), (*c*) and (*d*) only

51. A contract of life insurance is a/an:
(*a*) Indemnity
(*b*) Wagering agreement
(*c*) Contingent agreement
(*d*) Assurance
(*e*) Guarantee

Choose the ***correct*** answer from the options given below:
A. (*a*), (*c*) and (*e*) only
B. (*a*) and (*d*) only
C. (*b*), (*c*) and (*e*) only
D. (*c*) and (*d*) only

52. Which of the following statements are rightly expressed in relation to statistical testing?
(*a*) When the expected frequencies are too small, the value of χ^2 will be over-estimated and will result in too many rejections of the null-hypothesis
(*b*) Mann-Whitney test assumes that population is normal
(*c*) Kruskal-Wallis test is similar to one-way analysis of variance
(*d*) The homogeneity of variance means that the test is concerned with the hypothesis that the identical means came from the same population
(*e*) Student's t-Distribution is by definition normal

Choose the ***correct*** answer from the options given below:
A. (*a*), (*b*) and (*d*) only
B. (*b*), (*c*) and (*d*) only
C. (*a*), (*c*) and (*e*) only
D. (*c*) and (*d*) only

53. Which of the following are distinctive characteristics of the Performing stage of the Group Building Process?
(*a*) The Group gains its identity
(*b*) Leadership is shared
(*c*) Disengagement from relationships
(*d*) Group morale is high
(*e*) Group loyalty is intense

Choose the ***correct*** answer from the options given below:
A. (*a*) and (*b*) only
B. (*b*) and (*c*) only
C. (*a*), (*d*) and (*e*) only
D. (*c*), (*d*) and (*e*) only

54. Which of the following are characteristic quadrants of the BCG matrix?
(*a*) Cash cows (*b*) Question mark
(*c*) White Elephant (*d*) Crown Jewel
(*e*) Dogs

Choose the ***correct*** answer from the options given below:
A. (*a*), (*b*) and (*e*) only
B. (*a*), (*c*) and (*d*) only

C. (*b*), (*c*) and (*e*) only
D. (*c*), (*d*) and (*e*) only

55. The following tools are used for forecasting the supply of inside candidates for human resource planning:
(*a*) Scatter Plot
(*b*) Personnel replacement charts
(*c*) Managerial judgement
(*d*) Markov Analysis
(*e*) Trend Analysis

Choose the ***correct*** answer from the options given below:
A. (*a*) and (*c*) only
B. (*c*), (*d*) and (*e*) only
C. (*b*), (*c*) and (*e*) only
D. (*b*) and (*d*) only

56. Which of the following statements are correct?
(*a*) NEFT allows the customer to transfer funds with a maximum limit of ₹ 3,00,000 per day
(*b*) IMPS allows to transfer funds in an Insta Payment Mode
(*c*) The minimum limit to transfer funds via RTGS is ₹ 2,50,000
(*d*) Instant Real Time Payment System developed by National Payment Corporation of India is UPI
(*e*) For clearing of cheques under Positive Pay System (PPS), the minimum limit is ₹ 50,000

Choose the ***correct*** answer from the options given below:
A. (*b*) and (*d*) only B. (*c*) and (*e*) only
C. (*a*) and (*b*) only D. (*c*) and (*d*) only

57. Which of the following statements are correctly expressed in relation to capital and credit flows?
(*a*) Theoretically, regulators of financial markets believe that increasing capital requirements on banks could reduce the likelihood of their failure
(*b*) Open financial markets are solely influenced by the currency rate movements
(*c*) Financial inflow reflects the net flow of capital into one country in the form of increased purchases of domestic assets by foreigners
(*d*) Tier II Capital for banks include Perpetual Debt Instruments
(*e*) Only private banks in India have implemented Basel III guidelines

Choose the ***correct*** answer from the options given below:
A. (*c*), (*d*) and (*e*) only
B. (*b*), (*c*) and (*e*) only
C. (*a*), (*c*) and (*d*) only
D. (*a*) and (*b*) only

58. Holistic marketing recognizes that a broad integrated perspective is necessary. Which of the following are the components of Holistic marketing?
(*a*) Direct marketing
(*b*) Relationship marketing
(*c*) Internal marketing
(*d*) Socially responsible marketing
(*e*) Green marketing

Choose the ***correct*** answer from the options given below:
A. (*b*) and (*c*) only
B. (*b*), (*c*) and (*d*) only
C. (*a*), (*b*) and (*c*) only
D. (*c*), (*d*) and (*e*) only

59. Which of the following statements are true for Direct Marketing?
(*a*) Direct marketing is an interactive mode of marketing
(*b*) Direct marketing model is based on Network marketing and multi-cultural marketing
(*c*) Globalisation of markets and the internet have facilitated the growth of direct marketing
(*d*) Future of direct marketing in India is independent of use of debit and credit cards
(*e*) Direct marketing activities are not location specific

Choose the ***correct*** answer from the options given below:
A. (*a*) and (*b*) only
B. (*b*), (*c*) and (*d*) only
C. (*a*), (*c*) and (*e*) only
D. (*a*), (*c*), (*d*) and (*e*) only

60. An ideal advertisement (ad) campaign would ensure that:

(*a*) The ad motivates consumers to consider purchases of the brand

(*b*) The ad gives maximum possible product knowledge to the customer

(*c*) The ad causes the consumer to pay attention but does not distract from the intended message

(*d*) The ad properly reflects the consumer's level of understanding and behaviours with the product and the brand

(*e*) The right consumer is exposed to the right message at the right place and at the right time

Choose the ***correct*** answer from the options given below:

A. (*a*), (*b*) and (*e*) only
B. (*c*), (*d*) and (*e*) only
C. (*a*), (*b*), (*c*) and (*d*) only
D. (*a*), (*c*), (*d*) and (*e*) only

61. The Information Technology Act, 2000 in India provides legal recognition to which of the following?

(*a*) Electronic books of accounts in banks

(*b*) Electronic commerce

(*c*) Electronic negotiable instrument

(*d*) Electronic signature

(*e*) Electronic sale and conveyance of immovable property

Choose the ***correct*** answer from the options given below:

A. (*a*), (*b*) and (*c*) only
B. (*c*), (*d*) and (*e*) only
C. (*b*), (*d*) and (*e*) only
D. (*a*), (*b*) and (*d*) only

62. To make the resolution process faster and maximize the realisable value of assets under Insolvency and Bankruptcy Code (IBC), the Parliamentary Standing Committee has recommended strengthening India's insolvency resolution ecosystem by:

(*a*) A professional code of conduct for the committee of creditors

(*b*) Constitution of specialized National Company Law Tribunals (NCLT) benches to hear IBC matters

(*c*) Strengthening the role of resolution professionals

(*d*) Digitising IBC platforms

(*e*) Strengthening and promotion of Asset Reconstruction Companies

Choose the ***correct*** answer from the options given below:

A. (*a*), (*b*) and (*c*) only
B. (*b*), (*c*) and (*d*) only
C. (*c*), (*d*) and (*e*) only
D. (*a*), (*b*), (*c*) and (*d*) only

63. In which of the following methods, a contract is said to be discharged by mutual consent?

(*a*) Novation

(*b*) Recission

(*c*) Remission

(*d*) Alteration

(*e*) Accord and Satisfaction

Choose the ***correct*** answer from the options given below:

A. (*a*), (*b*) and (*e*) only
B. (*b*), (*c*) and (*d*) only
C. (*a*), (*b*), (*c*) and (*d*) only
D. (*a*), (*b*), (*c*), (*d*) and (*e*)

64. Duties of bailor include:

(*a*) Take care of goods

(*b*) Bear extraordinary expenses

(*c*) Return accretion to the goods

(*d*) Indemnify the bailee

(*e*) Disclose known faults

Choose the ***correct*** answer from the options given below:

A. (*a*), (*b*) and (*e*) only
B. (*a*), (*c*) and (*d*) only
C. (*b*), (*c*) and (*d*) only
D. (*b*), (*d*) and (*e*) only

65. Expenses that are not deductible under Section 58 of the Indian Income Tax Act for computing the income chargeable under the head "Income From Other Sources":

(*a*) Personal expenses

(*b*) Interest payable outside India on which tax has not been paid or deducted at source

(*c*) Wealth tax

(*d*) Commission for realizing dividend income or interest on securities

(*e*) Expenses which are not of capital nature like repairs, depreciation on plant and insurance premium

Choose the ***correct*** answer from the options given below:

A. (*a*), (*b*) and (*d*) only

B. (*a*), (*b*) and (*c*) only

C. (*a*), (*b*), (*d*) and (*e*) only

D. (*a*), (*b*), (*c*), (*d*) and (*e*)

66. Match List-I with List-II:

List-I (Name of Theory of International Trade)	***List-II (Description)***
(*a*) Heckscher-Ohlin Theory	(*i*) The ability of a nation to produce the goods more efficiently and effectively than any other country
(*b*) Country Similarity Theory	(*ii*) Theory stating that trade occurs between nations that have similar characteristics such as economic, geography and cultural characteristics
(*c*) Theory of Mercantilism	(*iii*) The theory that a nation will export the goods whose production requires intensive use of the nation's relatively abundant and cheap factors and import goods when production requires intensive use of its scarce and expensive factors
(*d*) Absolute Advantage Theory	(*iv*) Theory that aims at accumulating financial wealth in terms of gold by encouraging exports and discouraging imports

Choose the ***correct*** answer from the options given below:

	(*a*)	(*b*)	(*c*)	(*d*)
A.	(*iv*)	(*iii*)	(*ii*)	(*i*)
B.	(*iv*)	(*ii*)	(*i*)	(*iii*)
C.	(*iii*)	(*ii*)	(*iv*)	(*i*)
D.	(*iii*)	(*ii*)	(*i*)	(*iv*)

67. Match List-I with List-II:

List-I (Ind AS)	***List-II (Topic (Subjects))***
(*a*) Ind AS 37	(*i*) Insurance contracts
(*b*) Ind AS 104	(*ii*) Inventories
(*c*) Ind AS 2	(*iii*) Provisions, Contingent Liabilities and Contingent Assets
(*d*) Ind AS 19	(*iv*) Employee Benefits

Choose the ***correct*** answer from the options given below:

	(*a*)	(*b*)	(*c*)	(*d*)
A.	(*iii*)	(*i*)	(*ii*)	(*iv*)
B.	(*i*)	(*ii*)	(*iii*)	(*iv*)
C.	(*iv*)	(*iii*)	(*ii*)	(*i*)
D.	(*ii*)	(*iii*)	(*i*)	(*iv*)

68. Match List-I with List-II:

List-I (Cost Concepts)	***List-II (Description)***
(*a*) Explicit cost	(*i*) Costs that do not require any outlay of money by the firm
(*b*) Implicit cost	(*ii*) A cost that has already been committed and cannot be recovered
(*c*) Total cost	(*iii*) Costs that require an outlay of money by the firm
(*d*) Sunk cost	(*iv*) Market value of all inputs that a firm uses in production

Choose the ***correct*** answer from the options given below:

	(*a*)	(*b*)	(*c*)	(*d*)
A.	(*iii*)	(*iv*)	(*i*)	(*ii*)
B.	(*ii*)	(*iv*)	(*iii*)	(*i*)
C.	(*iii*)	(*i*)	(*iv*)	(*ii*)
D.	(*iii*)	(*iv*)	(*ii*)	(*i*)

69. Match List-I with List-II

List-I *(Type of Bonds)*	*List-II* *(Description)*
(*a*) Euro bonds	(*i*) Bonds denominated in US dollar and issued in the USA
(*b*) Global bonds	(*ii*) Bonds denominated in a foreign currency and are offered for simultaneous placement in different countries
(*c*) Yankee bonds	(*iii*) When the bonds issued in a foreign country and are denominated in a currency other than the currency of the country where the bonds are issued
(*d*) Samurai bonds	(*iv*) Bonds denominated in Japanese Yen and issued in Japan

Choose the ***correct*** answer from the options given below:

	(*a*)	(*b*)	(*c*)	(*d*)
A.	(*iii*)	(*ii*)	(*i*)	(*iv*)
B.	(*iv*)	(*iii*)	(*ii*)	(*i*)
C.	(*iii*)	(*iv*)	(*i*)	(*ii*)
D.	(*iii*)	(*ii*)	(*iv*)	(*i*)

70. Match List-I with List-II:

List-I *(Sampling methods)*	*List-II* *(Descriptions of situation)*
(*a*) Multi-stage Sampling	(*i*) Specified number of respondents in best position to provide the desired information
(*b*) Systematic Sampling	(*ii*) Heterogenous sub-populations
(*c*) Judgement Sampling	(*iii*) Widely spread population and random sampling not possible
(*d*) Stratified Sampling	(*iv*) Elements of population arranged in some order

Choose the ***correct*** answer from the options given below:

	(*a*)	(*b*)	(*c*)	(*d*)
A.	(*ii*)	(*iv*)	(*i*)	(*iii*)
B.	(*iii*)	(*iv*)	(*i*)	(*ii*)
C.	(*i*)	(*ii*)	(*iii*)	(*iv*)
D.	(*ii*)	(*iii*)	(*i*)	(*iv*)

71. Match List-I with List-II

List-I *(Leadership Style)*	*List-II* *(Description)*
(*a*) Proactive management	(*i*) People with trust and respect and interdependence through common partnership with the organizational objective to get work done
(*b*) Team management	(*ii*) Requires minimal effort to function and to maintain organizational morale
(*c*) Country club management	(*iii*) To achieve efficiency organize work in such a way that the influence of human element is minimized
(*d*) Voluntary work manager	(*iv*) Pre-contemplation for the needs of the people, and leads to a harmonious and smooth organizational environment and working style

Choose the ***correct*** answer from the options given below:

	(*a*)	(*b*)	(*c*)	(*d*)
A.	(*i*)	(*ii*)	(*iv*)	(*iii*)
B.	(*ii*)	(*i*)	(*iii*)	(*iv*)
C.	(*ii*)	(*i*)	(*iv*)	(*iii*)
D.	(*iv*)	(*i*)	(*iii*)	(*ii*)

72. Match List-I with List-II:

List-I *(Interest rates)*	*List-II* *(Description)*
(*a*) Policy Rate	(*i*) RBI lending rate to commercial banks without security

(*b*) Repo Rate	(*ii*)	RBI lending rate when commercial banks borrow money by purchasing securities issued by RBI
(*c*) MCLR	(*iii*)	Internal benchmark rate for financial institutions and banks
(*d*) Bank Rate	(*iv*)	Rate established by RBI to influence the main monetary variables in the economy

Choose the ***correct*** answer from the options given below:

	(*a*)	(*b*)	(*c*)	(*d*)
A.	(*i*)	(*iv*)	(*iii*)	(*ii*)
B.	(*iv*)	(*i*)	(*iii*)	(*ii*)
C.	(*iv*)	(*ii*)	(*iii*)	(*i*)
D.	(*ii*)	(*iv*)	(*i*)	(*iii*)

73. Match List-I with List-II

List-I (Market Expansion Strategies)		***List-II (Description)***
(*a*) Market Penetration	(*i*)	New products, New markets
(*b*) Market Development	(*ii*)	Existing markets, Existing products
(*c*) Product Development	(*iii*)	Existing products, New markets
(*d*) Diversification	(*iv*)	Existing markets, New products

Choose the ***correct*** answer from the options given below:

	(*a*)	(*b*)	(*c*)	(*d*)
A.	(*i*)	(*ii*)	(*iii*)	(*iv*)
B.	(*i*)	(*iii*)	(*ii*)	(*iv*)
C.	(*ii*)	(*iv*)	(*i*)	(*iii*)
D.	(*ii*)	(*iii*)	(*iv*)	(*i*)

74. Match List-I with List-II:

List-I (Insurance contracts)		***List-II (Presence (time) of insurable interest)***
(*a*) Marine insurance	(*i*)	Both at the time of contract as well at the loss of subject matter
(*b*) Life insurance	(*ii*)	Throughout the contract of insurance
(*c*) Fire insurance	(*iii*)	At the time of loss of the subject matter
(*d*) General insurance	(*iv*)	At the time of insurance contract effected

Choose the ***correct*** answer from the options given below:

	(*a*)	(*b*)	(*c*)	(*d*)
A.	(*iv*)	(*ii*)	(*iii*)	(*i*)
B.	(*iii*)	(*iv*)	(*i*)	(*ii*)
C.	(*i*)	(*iv*)	(*ii*)	(*iii*)
D.	(*iii*)	(*i*)	(*iv*)	(*ii*)

75. Match List-I with List-II:

List-I (Tax deductions)	***List-II (Relevant Sections)***
(*a*) Deduction in respect of rent paid	(*i*) 80 GGC
(*b*) Deduction in respect of contribution given by company to political parties	(*ii*) 80 GG
(*c*) Deduction in respect of contribution given by any person to political parties	(*iii*) 80 GGA
(*d*) Deduction in respect of certain donations for scientific research	(*iv*) 80 GGB

Choose the ***correct*** answer from the options given below:

	(*a*)	(*b*)	(*c*)	(*d*)
A.	(*iii*)	(*i*)	(*iv*)	(*ii*)
B.	(*iv*)	(*ii*)	(*iii*)	(*i*)
C.	(*ii*)	(*iii*)	(*i*)	(*iv*)
D.	(*i*)	(*iv*)	(*ii*)	(*iii*)

76. In relation to the export from India, arrange the following steps of port procedure and customs cleareance sequentially:

(*a*) C&F agent present mate's receipt to shipping company

(*b*) Shipping company issues bill of lading. C&F agent dispatches bill of lading and other documents to the importer

(*c*) C&F agent receives documents from the exporter, takes delivery of cargo and stores cargo in warehouse till shipment

(*d*) Master of vessel issues mate's receipt to shed superintendent of port

(*e*) Cargo brought to the port shed for loading

Choose the ***correct*** answer from the options given below:

A. (*c*), (*e*), (*d*), (*b*), (*a*)
B. (*c*), (*e*), (*d*), (*a*), (*b*)
C. (*e*), (*c*), (*d*), (*a*), (*b*)
D. (*c*), (*d*), (*e*), (*a*), (*b*)

77. The following are contextual auditing with wider intensities:

(*a*) Special Audit (*b*) Internal Audit
(*c*) Internal Check (*d*) Annual Audit
(*e*) Interim Audit

Choose the ***correct*** answer from the options given below in increasing order of underlying intensity.

A. (*c*), (*b*), (*e*), (*d*), (*a*)
B. (*b*), (*c*), (*d*), (*a*), (*e*)
C. (*a*), (*b*), (*c*), (*d*), (*e*)
D. (*b*), (*c*), (*a*), (*e*), (*d*)

78. Sequence the following steps in the process of estimating demand equation using regression analysis.

(*a*) Obtaining data on each variable or its proxy
(*b*) Estimating slope coefficients
(*c*) Model specifications
(*d*) Deciding on the functional form of the demand equation
(*e*) Evaluation of regression results

Choose the ***correct*** answer from the options given below:

A. (*c*), (*a*), (*d*), (*b*), (*e*)
B. (*d*), (*c*), (*b*), (*a*), (*e*)
C. (*a*), (*b*), (*c*), (*d*), (*e*)
D. (*d*), (*a*), (*c*), (*b*), (*e*)

79. Arrange the following in the logical sequence of the international arbitrage operation.

(*a*) Identify an opportunity
(*b*) Purchase the asset
(*c*) Review the transaction cost
(*d*) Pocket the profit
(*e*) Sell the asset

Choose the ***correct*** answer from the options given below:

A. (*a*), (*c*), (*b*), (*e*), (*d*)
B. (*c*), (*a*), (*d*), (*b*), (*e*)
C. (*b*) (*a*), (*d*), (*e*), (*c*)
D. (*b*), (*d*), (*a*), (*c*), (*e*)

80. Arrange the following steps in sequence for testing a statistical hypothesis:

(*a*) Test statistics
(*b*) Framing the hypothesis
(*c*) Collecting the sample data
(*d*) Level of significance
(*e*) Obtaining results and taking decisions

Choose the ***correct*** answer from the options given below:

A. (*b*), (*d*), (*c*), (*a*), (*e*)
B. (*c*), (*b*), (*a*), (*d*), (*e*)
C. (*b*), (*c*), (*a*), (*d*), (*e*)
D. (*a*), (*c*), (*b*), (*e*), (*d*)

81. Arrange the following steps of employee training in the proper sequence:

(*a*) Familiarize the employee with equipment, materials, tools, and trade terms
(*b*) Create interest and find out what the employee already knows about the job
(*c*) Explain why the employee is being trained
(*d*) Place the trainee/employee as close to the normal working position as possible
(*e*) Explain the whole job and relate it to some other job which the employee already knows

Choose the ***correct*** answer from the options given below:

A. (*c*), (*e*), (*b*), (*a*), (*d*)
B. (*c*), (*b*), (*e*), (*d*), (*a*)
C. (*b*), (*e*), (*c*), (*d*), (*a*)
D. (*e*), (*a*), (*c*), (*d*), (*b*)

82. Risk management process follows the following steps in which logical sequence?

(*a*) Selection of appropriate risk model for analysis
(*b*) Identification of risk variable
(*c*) Determination of frequency and severity of risk
(*d*) Feedback on the risk management process
(*e*) Application of a suitable risk instrument

Choose the ***correct*** answer from the options given below:

A. (*e*), (*a*), (*b*), (*c*), (*d*)
B. (*c*), (*b*), (*a*), (*d*), (*e*)
C. (*b*), (*c*), (*a*), (*e*), (*d*)
D. (*a*), (*c*), (*b*), (*d*), (*e*)

83. Arrange the following purchases made by a customer as per Maslow's hierarchy of needs theory starting with the lower order needs.

(*a*) Purchase of House
(*b*) Purchase of an expensive car
(*c*) Taking a club membership
(*d*) Enrolling in a learn-by-yourself course
(*e*) Purchase of bathing soap

Choose the ***correct*** answer from the options given below:

A. (*e*), (*a*), (*b*), (*c*), (*d*)
B. (*a*), (*e*), (*c*), (*b*), (*d*)
C. (*e*), (*a*), (*c*), (*b*), (*d*)
D. (*a*), (*e*), (*b*), (*c*), (*d*)

84. Arrange the following decision outcomes under the Indian Consumer Protection Act, 1986 in a rising sequence of severity of offences.

(*a*) Removal of defects
(*b*) Impose cost on parties
(*c*) Return of price paid
(*d*) Discontinuation of unfair practices
(*e*) Compensation to consumer

Choose the ***correct*** answer from the options given below:

A. (*a*), (*b*), (*c*), (*e*), (*d*)
B. (*a*), (*c*), (*e*), (*d*), (*b*)
C. (*c*), (*d*), (*a*), (*b*), (*e*)
D. (*d*), (*e*), (*b*), (*c*), (*a*)

85. Steps involved in computation of tax on agricultural income in India are followed in which sequence?

(*a*) Add basic exemption limit to Net agriculture income and calculate tax
(*b*) Deduct rebate u/s 87A from the total income
(*c*) Add Health Cess
(*d*) Add Agricultural and Non-agriculture income and calculate tax on total income
(*e*) Calculate difference of tax in both computations

Choose the ***correct*** answer from the options given below:

A. (*a*), (*d*), (*b*), (*c*), (*e*)
B. (*a*), (*c*), (*d*), (*b*), (*e*)
C. (*a*), (*d*), (*c*), (*e*), (*b*)
D. (*d*), (*a*), (*e*), (*b*), (*c*)

86. Given below are two statements:

Statement I: Thousands of small firms in developing countries have closed their shutters because of the competition from large MNCs.

Statement II: MNCs have played a significant role in the development of poor countries by transfer of technology, introducing best management practices and help in improving productivity.

In light of the above statements, choose the ***correct*** answer from the options given below:

A. Both Statement I and Statement II are true
B. Both Statement I and Statement II are false
C. Statement I is true, but Statement II is false
D. Statement I is false, but Statement II is true

87. Given below are two statements, one is labelled as Assertion (A) and the other is labelled as Reason (R).

Assertion (A): Economic profit is smaller than accounting profit.

Reason (R): Accounting profit = Revenue – Explicit costs

Economic Profit = Revenue – Explicit costs – Implicit costs

In light of the above statements, choose the ***correct*** answer from the options given below:

A. Both (A) and (R) are true and (R) is the correct explanation of (A)
B. Both (A) and (R) are true, but (R) is NOT the correct explanation of (A)
C. (A) is true, but (R) is false
D. (A) is false, but (R) is true

88. Given below are two statements:

Statement I: The stage in the manufacturing process where joint products are separately identifiable is called split-off point.

Statement II: The production costs incurred after the split-off point are called separable costs.

In light of the above statements, choose the ***correct*** answer from the options given below:

A. Both Statement I and Statement II are true
B. Both Statement I and Statement II are false

C. Statement I is true, but Statement II is false.
D. Statement I is false, but Statement II is true

89. Given below are two statements

Statement I: Long term capital loss can only be set off against the long term capital gains.

Statement II: Long-term capital gains exceeding ₹ one lakh are subject to tax at the rate of 10% with indexation and at 20% without indexation.

In light of the above statements, choose the ***most appropriate*** answer from the options given below:

A. Both Statement I and Statement II are correct
B. Both Statement I and Statement II are incorrect
C. Statement I is correct, but Statement II is incorrect
D. Statement I is incorrect, but Statement II is correct

90. Given below are two statements, one is labelled as Assertion (A) and the other is labelled as Reason (R).

Assertion (A): One of the most difficult product to sell is 'life insurance' such that one who sells life insurance can sell anything under the Sun.

Reason (R): What is sought to be marketed in life insurance is an assurance whereby payment of money is assured upon death or the happening of any contingency depended upon human life.

In light of the above statements, choose the ***correct*** answer from the options given below:

A. Both (A) and (R) are true and (R) is the correct explanation of (A)
B. Both (A) and (R) are true, but (R) is NOT the correct explanation of A
C. (A) is true, but (R) is false
D. (A) is false, but (R) is true

Directions (Qs. No. 91 to 95): *Read the passage below carefully and answer the five questions that follow.*

The invention of the office – from the Latin opus (work) + facere (do) = officium (performance of work) – was necessitated by the inability of work to be done remotely. Until very recently, the prevalent technology was simply not available or very limited to allow work away from office. If you had to conduct stocktaking, copy documents or engage in a brainstorming session, one had to be physically close to the tools of work and co-workers. Even as the technology was becoming increasingly available, it was the forced disruption of pandemic that finally showed that office, like the stock exchange trading floor, as a shared physical-only space was no longer essential to carry out work. Today, as Covid restrictions thankfully recede, the push that had become the shove of working from home (WFH) is becoming a nudge for working from anywhere (WFA).

Neither can all work be conducted WFA nor to all workers prefer remote working. Several reasons for the primacy of the 'face-to-face' work model are trotted out - 'water-cooler' engagements; ideas flying 'better' at corporeally attended meeting; company values welded only under 'one roof, one team' norms. But studies, including pre-pandemic ones conducted by the likes of Harvard Business School's Prithwiraj Choudhury, have shown that WFA is a win-win for 'Workers, Companies and for Society'. WFA slashes time and energy expanded in commutes; allows workers the choice of their work surroundings that may actually improve their quantitative and qualitative output; provides less crowded space for those who choose offices as their comfort work zone. Most importantly, for companies, it allows HFA - hiring from anywhere, thereby breaking the talent pool distance barrier.

The new hybrid work culture is still a work-in progress. Floor managers will have to be trained to manage a different kind of floor. Company values will need to flourish in a digital-deeper environment. The idea of work-life balance itself has to be rejigged. But the bottomline is work optimisation. For which WFA, without the stress of a pandemic around, makes damn good pitch.

91. Given below are two statements, one is labelled as Assertion (A) and the other is labelled as Reason (R).

Assertion (A): Work from Anywhere is only possible in case of employees working independently.

Reason (R): Brainstorming sessions are possible in the case of Work from Anywhere.

In light of the above statements, choose the ***most appropriate*** answer from the options given below:

A. Both (A) and (R) are correct and (R) is the correct explanation of (A)
B. Both (A) and (R) are correct, but (R) is NOT the correct explanation of (A)
C. (A) is correct, but (R) is not correct
D. (A) is not correct, but (R) is correct

92. Work from Office was preferred because of:
(*a*) 'Water cooler' engagements
(*b*) Ideas fly better at corporeally attended meetings
(*c*) Promotes one team norm
(*d*) Improves work-life balance
(*e*) Inability of work to be done remotely

Choose the ***most appropriate*** answer from the options given below:

A. (*a*), (*b*) and (*c*) only
B. (*c*), (*d*) and (*e*) only
C. (*a*), (*b*), (*c*) and (*e*) only
D. (*a*), (*b*) and (*e*) only

93. Given below are two statements:

Statement I: Work from home concept was not initiated in the past because no one had conceptualised it.

Statement II: It was not possible to Work from home in the past.

In light of the above statements, choose the ***most appropriate*** answer from the options given below:

A. Both Statement I and Statement II are correct
B. Both Statement I and Statement II are incorrect
C. Statement I is correct, but Statement II is incorrect
D. Statement I is incorrect, but Statement II is correct

94. Which one of the following is NOT true for Work from Anywhere?

A. It reduces time and energy expended in commuting
B. It increases talent pool distance barrier
C. It allows an employee to choose his work surroundings
D. It improves quality and quantity of work output

95. Given below are two statements in relation to the passage:

Statement I: With ease in the stress of the pandemic around, the relevance of Work from Anywhere will reduce

Statement II: For the new hybrid work culture to prevail, companies will have to invest more in technology

In light of the above statements, choose the ***most appropriate*** answer from the options given below:

A. Both Statement I and Statement II are correct
B. Both Statement I and Statement II are incorrect
C. Statement I is correct, but Statement II is incorrect
D. Statement I is incorrect, but Statement II is correct

Directions (Qs. No. 96 to 100): *Read the passage below carefully and answer the five questions that follow:*

Capital flows, exchange rates and the interest rates are causes of immediate concern to the national economies. Central banks of various countries have been using a variety of methods with the excessive capital inflows. Foreign portfolio investment have a direct and indirect impact on exchange rates, valuation of traded assets and yields of various government and corporate securities.

RBI, in the post-pandemic scenario and the recent Russia-Ukraine war situation is working on multiple options to stabilize the exchange rates by protecting both the exporters and importers. One way which RBI adopts to maintain a desirable level of exchanges rates is to mop up nets foreign exchange assets from scheduled commercial banks in exchanges of domestic currency (₹) assets. The liquidity flows are, in essence, inflationary. RBI has projected a comfortable GDP rate for the current fiscal and believes a reasonable level of CPI inflation as 5.3%.

The retail inflation, according to the RBI governor, recently is likely to be 4.5% in 2023 fiscal. With this perspective, the repo rate and reverse repo rate remain at 4% and 3.35%, respectively, since May 22, 2020. A balancing act between economic growth and inflation is visible. Though the RBI rates are consistent, the burden on borrowers for the short-term and longterm, is still unpredictable.

96. The primary purpose of the monetary policy of RBI is to maintain:
A. Wealth
B. Exchange Rate Volatility
C. Income Equality
D. Stability of prices

97. The stance of a monetary policy wherein the interest rates may move either way, upwards or downwards, is called:
A. Accommodative stance
B. Neutral stance
C. Calibrated stance
D. Hawkish stance

98. An increase in investment is most likely to be caused by:
A. Decrease in marginal propensity to consume
B. Expectations of lower GDP
C. Lowering of interest rates
D. Writing-off of Non-performing Assets

99. Quantitative easing by the Central bank implies:
A. Selling of assets by the Central bank
B. Lowering of interest rates for commercial bank leading
C. Purchase of assets by the Central bank
D. Central bank reducing the policy rate

100. Changes in foreign portfolio investments is directly related to:
A. Money demanded
B. Exchange rates
C. Prices
D. Circulation of money

ANSWERS

1. (B): Duty Free Import Authorisation (DFIA) Scheme: Under the scheme, the inputs required for export production are exempt from basic customs duty, additional customs duty, education cess, anti-dumping duty and safeguard duty. The scheme is similar to Advance Licence Scheme with certain differences. One significant difference is that unlike the Advance Licence Scheme where the value addition requirement is only positive value addition, under the new scheme minimum value addition requirement is 20% (except for items in gem & jewellery sector). Another vital difference is that under the new scheme once the export obligation is fulfilled, the licence or the inputs imported (other than fuel) against it can be transferred/sold.

2. (C): According to India's Foreign Exchange Management Act (FEMA), an Indian company that receives investment from outside India for issuing shares, convertible debentures, or preference shares under the FDI Scheme, is required to report the details of the inflow to the Reserve Bank of India (RBI). This reporting must be done within 30 days of the date of receipt of the funds.

3. (C)

4. (C): Porter's diamond model, a framework that illustrates the competitive advantage of nations, includes four elements: factor conditions, demand conditions, related and supporting industries, and firm strategy, structure, and rivalry. The bargaining power of buyers is not a factor included in Porter's diamond model. This factor is actually from Porter's Five Forces Framework which is used to analyze the competitive environment of an industry, not the competitive advantage of nations.

5. (A): In a partnership, when a new partner is admitted, the profit-sharing ratio among partners changes. Originally, X and Y shared profits in a 3 : 2 ratio, meaning there were 5 parts in total. When Z is admitted with a 1/5 share in the profits, Z's share will be 1/5 of 5 parts which is 1 part. Therefore, the new profit-sharing ratio will be 3 : 2 : 1 or, when expressed with a common denominator, 12 : 8 : 5.

6. **(C):** In cost-volume-profit analysis, the break-even point is the point at which total revenue equals total costs. At this point, there's no net income or loss. The contribution margin, which is the selling price per unit minus the variable cost per unit, covers the fixed costs at the break-even point. So, at the break-even point, contribution is equal to the fixed cost.

7. **(D):** While capital expenditure does typically result in extra capacity, a long-term benefit, and the acquisition of a permanent asset, heavy expenditure on advertising campaigns to introduce a new product in the market does not fit this description. Advertising costs are typically treated as revenue expenditure and not capital expenditure because the benefits from advertising are usually short-term and consumed within the accounting period in which they occur.

8. **(A):** Material yield variance measures the difference between the standard cost of the expected yield and the standard cost of the actual yield.

   Standard cost per kg of output is 20, so the total standard cost is 20 * 90 kg = 1800. The actual cost is 19 * 182 kg = 3458. Therefore, the variance is 1800 – 3458 = –658, which indicates an unfavorable variance. The value in the question seems to be incorrect.

9. **(C):** Giffen goods are an exception to the law of demand, which states that as the price of a good increases, the quantity demanded decreases. In the case of a Giffen good, when the price increases, the quantity demanded also increases due to the overwhelming negative income effect, causing the demand curve to be positively sloped.

10. **(B):** Perfect price discrimination refers to the scenario in which a monopoly producer is able to charge each consumer the maximum amount they are willing to pay for each unit of a good or service. In this situation, the entire consumer surplus, which is the difference between the maximum price a consumer is willing to pay and the actual price they pay, is transferred to the producer. There is no consumer surplus left for consumers in the market.

11. **(A):** A Nash equilibrium refers to a situation in which, in a game involving two or more players, each player is assumed to know the equilibrium strategies of the other players and no player has anything to gain by changing their own strategy unilaterally. If a player has chosen a strategy and no player can benefit by changing strategies while the other players keep theirs unchanged, then the current set of strategy choices constitutes a Nash equilibrium.

12. **(A):** The Cobb-Douglas production function, $Q = AK^aL^b$, describes the relationship of output to inputs (capital and labor). The sum of '*a*' and '*b*' reflects the returns to scale. If $a + b > 1$, it implies increasing returns to scale. That is, a proportionate increase in all inputs will result in a more than proportionate increase in output.

13. **(D):** The Bank for International Settlements (BIS) is not part of the World Bank Group. The World Bank Group consists of five institutions: the International Bank for Reconstruction and Development (IBRD), the International Development Association (IDA), the International Finance Corporation (IFC), the Multilateral Investment Guarantee Agency (MIGA), and the International Centre for Settlement of Investment Disputes (ICSID).

14. **(D):** According to the traditional approach to capital structure, a firm's value first increases, then remains stable, and finally decreases with an increase in leverage. This approach suggests

that there is an optimal level of debt that maximizes the value of a firm, beyond which additional debt will decrease the firm's value due to the increasing costs of financial distress and bankruptcy risk.

15. (A): The Economic Order Quantity (EOQ) is the number of units that a company should add to its inventory with each order to minimize the total cost of inventory-such as holding costs, order costs, and shortage costs. Using the EOQ formula √((2DS)/H), where D is the demand, S is the order cost, and H is the holding cost per unit, the EOQ is √((290000300)/6) = 3000 units.

16. (D): The cost of preference shares is the dividend on the shares divided by the net proceeds from the sale of shares. In this case, the dividend is 12% of 100 = 12. The net proceeds are the sale price minus the flotation cost, which is 95 – 5% of 100 = 90. Therefore, the cost of preference shares is 12/90 = 13.33%.

17. (D): Normal distribution has several key characteristics, but it doesn't have a kurtosis of less than 3. In fact, the kurtosis of a normal distribution is 3. A normal distribution is symmetric about its mean, with its shape described as bell-shaped. The distribution is fully defined by its mean and standard deviation. The probability of a random variable being less than the mean is equal to it being greater than the mean (0.50).

18. (B)

19. (A): Spearman's rho, also known as Spearman's rank correlation coefficient, is a non-parametric measure of rank correlation. It assesses how well an arbitrary monotonic function could describe the relationship between two variables without making any assumptions about the frequency distribution of the variables. This makes it suitable for studying the relationship between two ordinal variables.

20. (B): A spurious relationship refers to a situation where two variables appear to be related to each other but are actually both related to a third variable. The apparent relationship between the two original variables is, therefore, misleading or spurious because it's the third variable that's driving the changes in both of the original variables.

21. (B): The organizational climate of clubs tends to be characterized by a strong sense of affiliation. Clubs are essentially social organizations where members join to share common interests and activities. As such, affiliation, or a sense of belonging and shared identity, is a key driver for such organizations. This fosters social connections, mutual support, cooperation, and collective action among members.

22. (A): Ego regression, in psychological terms, is when an individual returns to a previous stage of psychological development. This usually occurs during times of extreme stress or trauma, where the individual regresses to a time where they felt safer or more at ease. This regression can manifest as a temporary or long-term response to stress or emotional trauma.

23. (B): In an organizational structure based on products, the focus tends to be more on the individual product lines rather than a general managerial approach. While this can help improve focus and coordination for each product, it may require more specialized managerial abilities, as each product may have unique needs and challenges. Thus, it might require more personnel with specialized, rather than general, managerial skills.

24. (C)

25. (D): As per the Insurance Regulatory and Development Authority (IRDA) regulations in India, the minimum capital requirement for a life insurance company is ₹ 100 crores. This minimum capital requirement is to ensure that the insurance company has sufficient financial resources to honor the insurance claims of policyholders.

26. (A)

27. (A): The RBI can restrict the expansion of credit by increasing the bank rate. By increasing this rate, the cost of borrowing for commercial banks from the RBI increases. As a result, the commercial banks would also increase their lending rates to maintain their profit margins. This increase in lending rates discourages borrowing and hence, restricts the expansion of credit.

28. (B): Default-risk intermediation refers to the process where financial intermediaries make loans to risky borrowers while attracting savings from risk-averse savers. In this process, the financial intermediaries assume the risk of default by the borrowers, thus allowing the risk-averse savers to lend their money without bearing this risk.

29. (B): Assurance in service quality refers to the knowledge and courtesy of employees, and their ability to convey trust and confidence to customers. Employees' skills, competence, and behavior can significantly impact customers' trust and confidence in the service provider. This dimension of service quality emphasizes the importance of staff being knowledgeable, polite, and trustworthy in their interactions with customers.

30. (C)

31. (A): The strategy described in the question is known as Captive-product pricing. This pricing strategy is used by companies that make products that must be used along with a main product. The main products (such as razors and cameras) are sold at a relatively low price and the captive products (like blades and film) that are indispensable to the function of the main product, are marked up significantly. This strategy is often effective because once consumers have purchased the main product, they are "captive," and must continue to buy the associated products.

32. (A): A Corporate Vertical Marketing System (VMS) is one in which successive stages of production and distribution, are combined under a single ownership. This implies that one company owns multiple levels of the distribution chain, enabling it to control the entire process from manufacturing to retail. This leads to better coordination and control over the entire value chain, reduces costs, and can improve efficiency.

33. (A): The term for throwing cargo overboard to lighten a vessel in distress is Jettisoning. In marine insurance, jettisoning is considered a voluntary sacrifice made to prevent the total loss of a ship or its cargo. The cost of such losses is shared among all of the cargo's owners based on the maritime law principle of General Average.

34. (C): The 'right to stoppage in transit' is the right of an unpaid seller to regain possession of goods while they are in transit to the buyer, in order to secure payment. If the buyer becomes insolvent after the goods have been dispatched but before they've been delivered, the seller can stop the goods in transit and resume possession to mitigate potential losses.

35. (A): The primary duty of the Central Assistant Public Information Officer (CAPIO) or a State Assistant Public Information Officer (SAPIO) under the Right to Information Act is to receive applications for information or appeals and forward them to the Central Public Information Officer or the State Public Information Officer. They act as a point of contact for citizens who wish to request information.

36. (B)

37. (A): The Vivad se Vishwas Act, 2020, does not apply in respect of tax arrears relating to an assessment year for which prosecution has been instituted on or before the date of filing of the declaration. This means if the taxpayer has already been prosecuted for an offense related to tax arrears for a particular year, he/

she cannot utilize the provisions of this Act for that year.

38. (A): Under Section 80TTB of the Income Tax Act, senior citizens are eligible for benefits of up to ₹ 50,000 on account of interest income from deposits with banks or post-office or cooperative banks. This provision was introduced to provide tax relief to senior citizens who often rely on interest income for their financial needs.

39. (B): The Provisional Input Tax Credit under the Goods and Services Tax (GST) regime in India can be utilized against Self-assessed tax liability. This means that the taxpayers can claim a provisional credit of the amount of input tax which they have paid on their purchases, and utilize this credit to offset their GST liability as computed in their own tax returns.

40. (A): As per the Income Tax Act, 1961, the penalty for late filing of the Income Tax Return for individuals is up to a maximum of 10,000. However, if the income doesn't exceed 5 lakhs, the maximum penalty is restricted to ₹ 1,000. The objective behind imposing a penalty is to ensure compliance with the due dates as specified by the tax authorities.

41. (D): Revenue expenditure of the Central government includes debt relief to farmers, subsidy for fertilizers, and grants to states. Revenue expenditure is the government's spending on the day-to-day running of the country, including salaries, subsidies, and interest payments on debt. Here, debt relief to farmers, subsidies for fertilizers, and grants to states are all forms of revenue expenditure as they do not create assets but rather are expenses incurred for operational purposes.

42. (C): Exchange depreciation rate of one currency in relation to another is approximately equal to their inflation rate differential and interest rate differential. In international finance, exchange rate movements are heavily influenced by differences in inflation rates and interest rates between countries. If one country has higher inflation or lower interest rates than another, its currency is likely to depreciate relative to the other country's currency.

43. (A): Investing activities in the Cash Flow Statement include cash receipts from disposal of fixed assets, cash advances and loans made to third parties, and cash receipts from repayment of advances and loans made to third parties. Investing activities refer to the purchase and sale of long-term assets and other investments, not included in cash equivalents. These mentioned actions all relate to such long-term assets and investments.

44. (D): Cost drivers used in Activity Based Costing include transaction, intensity, and duration. Activity-Based Costing (ABC) is a method of assigning overhead costs to products based on the idea of cost pools. Cost drivers are the actual activities that cause the total cost in a cost pool to increase. In this case, the number of transactions, the intensity of the activity, and the duration of the activity all influence the total cost and therefore serve as cost drivers.

45. (D): Increasing returns to scale arise because as the scale of operation increases, it causes more division of labor and specialization, productive utilization of machinery, lower procurement and logistic costs, and more economies in advertising. As firms increase the scale of production, they are able to achieve higher efficiencies due to these reasons, leading to increasing returns to scale.

46. (D): Consumer rationality implies non-satiety of needs, transitivity of preferences, and selfish economic motive. These are assumptions underpinning the concept of rational behavior in economics, where it's assumed that consumers aim to maximize utility, have consistent preferences (transitivity), and act in self-interest (selfish economic motive).

47. (B)

48. (C): The Internal Rate of Return (IRR) method offers advantages such as recognizing the time value of money, being consistent with shareholders' profit-maximization objective, considering all cash flows occurring over the entire life of the project, and generally providing the same acceptance rule as the NPV method. IRR is a method used in capital budgeting that calculates the profitability of potential investments and is a discount rate that makes the net present value (NPV) of all cash flows equal to zero.

49. (D): Off-balance sheet sources of finance include securitization, factoring, forfaiting, and operational lease. These sources do not appear on a company's balance sheet as liabilities, hence the term "off-balance sheet." These forms of financing help companies raise capital without increasing their debt or equity.

50. (D)

51. (D): A contract of life insurance is a Contingent agreement and an Assurance. A contract of life insurance isn't an indemnity contract because the value of a life cannot be measured monetarily, unlike objects like cars or houses. Instead, it's a contract of assurance wherein the event (death or survival) is certain to happen, only the time of occurrence is uncertain. It's a contingent agreement because the obligation to pay by the insurer depends on an uncertain future event (the death or survival of the policyholder).

52. (C)

53. (C): The Performing stage of the Group Building Process is characterized by the group gaining its identity, high group morale, and intense group loyalty. In this stage, the group members are well-aware of their roles and responsibilities and are highly productive. The leadership isn't necessarily shared, and disengagement from relationships generally signifies the adjourning or termination stage, not the performing stage.

54. (A): The characteristic quadrants of the BCG matrix are Cash cows, Question mark, and Dogs. The BCG matrix, developed by the Boston Consulting Group, is a strategic tool used for portfolio management. It categorizes business units into four quadrants based on market growth and market share - Stars, Question Marks, Cash Cows, and Dogs. The terms 'White Elephant' and 'Crown Jewel' are not part of this matrix.

55. (D): Personnel replacement charts and Markov Analysis are the tools used for forecasting the supply of inside candidates for human resource planning. The personnel replacement chart shows the present performance and promotability of inside candidates for the most important positions. Markov analysis is a method of analyzing the current movement of employees within an organization and predicting the future availability of employees.

56. (A): IMPS allows to transfer funds in an Insta Payment Mode, and the Instant Real Time Payment System developed by National Payment Corporation of India is UPI. NEFT doesn't have a maximum limit per day, it depends on individual bank's policies. The minimum limit for RTGS is ₹ 2,00,000, not ₹ 2,50,000. The Positive Pay System (PPS) is for cheque clearing, but the minimum limit is not ₹ 50,000, it's ₹ 50,00,000.

57. (C): The correct statements are: Regulators of financial markets believe that increasing capital requirements on banks could reduce the likelihood of their failure; Financial inflow reflects the net flow of capital into one country in the form of increased purchases of domestic assets by foreigners; and Tier II Capital for banks include Perpetual Debt Instruments. The statement about open financial markets being solely influenced by the currency rate movements is incorrect as they are influenced by several other factors as well. Not only private banks, but all commercial banks in India have implemented Basel III guidelines.

58. (B): The components of Holistic marketing are Relationship marketing, Internal marketing, and Socially responsible marketing. Holistic marketing recognizes that "everything matters" with marketing and that a broad, integrated perspective is often necessary. Relationship marketing focuses on building long-lasting relationships with customers. Internal marketing ensures that everyone in the organization embraces appropriate marketing principles. Socially responsible marketing involves recognizing and acting upon the societal responsibilities of the organization. Direct marketing and green marketing can be elements of a holistic marketing approach, but they aren't considered core components.

59. (C): The correct statements for Direct Marketing are: it's an interactive mode of marketing; Globalisation of markets and the internet have facilitated the growth of direct marketing; and Direct marketing activities are not location specific. Direct marketing isn't necessarily based on network marketing and multi-cultural marketing, it can use a wide variety of channels, including mail, email, and telemarketing. The future of direct marketing in India isn't independent of the use of debit and credit cards, as they facilitate transactions for direct marketing.

60. (D): An ideal advertisement campaign would ensure that the ad motivates consumers to consider purchases of the brand, the ad causes the consumer to pay attention but doesn't distract from the intended message, the ad properly reflects the consumer's level of understanding and behaviours with the product and the brand, and the right consumer is exposed to the right message at the right place and at the right time. While providing maximum possible product knowledge can be useful, it might overwhelm or bore the consumer, so it's not necessarily a component of an ideal ad campaign.

61. (D): The Information Technology Act, 2000 in India provides legal recognition to electronic books of accounts in banks, electronic commerce, and electronic signatures. The Act allows these electronic records to have the same legal effect, validity, and enforcement as physical documents. The aim was to facilitate and give legal recognition to the carrying out of commercial and business transactions electronically, reducing the need for physical paperwork, and thus reducing time and costs. Electronic commerce and electronic signatures are recognised, facilitating secure electronic commerce and electronic communications. Electronic books of accounts in banks are also recognised, helping in maintaining transparency and ease of conducting audits. However, it's noteworthy that electronic negotiable instruments and sale/conveyance of immovable property are not recognized by this Act.

62. (D): Strengthening India's insolvency resolution ecosystem has been recommended by the Parliamentary Standing Committee with various measures including a professional code of conduct for the committee of creditors, the establishment of specialized National Company Law Tribunals (NCLT) benches to hear IBC matters, strengthening the role of resolution professionals, and digitizing IBC platforms. Each of these measures aims to improve the efficiency of the IBC process. A professional code of conduct for the committee of creditors ensures ethics and accountability in the process. Specialized NCLT benches would speed up the resolution process. Strengthening the role of resolution professionals and digitizing IBC platforms would increase the effectiveness of the process, ensuring a smooth resolution.

63. (D)

64. (D): The duties of a bailor include bearing extraordinary expenses, indemnifying the bailee, and disclosing known faults. Extraordinary expenses are those expenses which are unusual or not inherent to the particular type of bailment. The bailor is responsible for indemnifying the bailee against any loss arising from the bailor's negligence or failure to disclose known faults. This might include faults or defects in the goods which could harm or cause damage to the bailee.

65. (B): Under Section 58 of the Indian Income Tax Act, personal expenses, interest payable outside India on which tax has not been paid or deducted at source, and wealth tax are not deductible when computing the income chargeable under the head "Income From Other Sources". These expenses are considered to be unrelated to the earning of income, or in the case of wealth tax, it's a personal obligation and therefore not deductible. Commission for realizing dividend income or interest on securities, however, is deductible as they are necessary expenses incurred for earning that income.

66. (C): The correct matchings are as follows: Heckscher-Ohlin theory aligns with description (iii) stating that a nation will export the goods whose production requires intensive use of the nation's relatively abundant and cheap factors and import goods when production requires intensive use of its scarce and expensive factors.

The Country Similarity theory corresponds to description (ii), stating that trade occurs between nations that have similar characteristics.

The Theory of Mercantilism corresponds to description (iv), stating that this theory aims at accumulating financial wealth in terms of gold by encouraging exports and discouraging imports.

The Absolute Advantage theory matches with description (i), the ability of a nation to produce the goods more efficiently and effectively than any other country.

67. (A): Indian Accounting Standard (Ind AS) are developed in accordance with the International Financial Reporting Standards (IFRS). The correct matching is as follows: Ind AS 37 is related to (iii) Provisions, Contingent Liabilities and Contingent Assets; Ind AS 104 is associated with (i) Insurance contracts; Ind AS 2 is about (ii) Inventories; Ind AS 19 is on (iv) Employee Benefits. These standards provide guidelines on how these specific financial topics should be reported in financial statements.

68. (C): The correct associations for the cost concepts are:

Explicit cost corresponds to description (iii), stating that these are costs that require an outlay of money by the firm.

Implicit cost aligns with description (i), costs that do not require any outlay of money by the firm.

Total cost aligns with description (iv), the market value of all inputs that a firm uses in production.

Sunk cost matches with description (ii), a cost that has already been committed and cannot be recovered. Understanding these cost concepts is important in both managerial and financial accounting.

69. (A): The correct matches for the bond types are:

Euro bonds correspond to description (iii), bonds issued in a foreign country and are denominated in a currency other than the currency of the country where the bonds are issued.

Global bonds align with description (ii), bonds denominated in a foreign currency and are offered for simultaneous placement in different countries.

Yankee bonds align with description (i), bonds denominated in US dollar and issued in the USA.

Samurai bonds align with description (iv), bonds denominated in Japanese Yen and issued in Japan. Understanding these bond types is crucial for international finance.

70. (B): The matching for the sampling methods are:

Multi-stage Sampling corresponds to description (iii), used for widely spread populations where random sampling is not possible.

Systematic Sampling matches with description (iv), used when elements of the population are arranged in some order.

Judgement Sampling matches with description (i), used when a specified number of respondents are in the best position to provide the desired information.

Stratified Sampling aligns with description (ii), used for heterogenous sub-populations. These sampling methods are crucial for conducting research and gathering representative data.

71. (C): The Proactive management (a) style matches with (iv) where managers anticipate future needs and make strategic moves to address them. They don't wait for issues to arise but take steps to prevent them, which is akin to pre-contemplation of the needs of the people.

Team management (b) corresponds to (i) as it's all about creating an environment where people can work collaboratively, driven by mutual respect, trust, and shared objectives. The Country club management (c) matches with (ii), which involves a work environment that requires minimal efforts to maintain morale as it emphasizes the comfort and happiness of team members.

The Voluntary work manager (d) style aligns with (iii) where the structure of work is organized to minimize the influence of the human element, often seen in voluntary work where tasks are divided equitably among participants.

72. (C): The Policy Rate (a) refers to (iv), the rate established by RBI to influence key monetary variables in the economy, impacting the overall lending rates in the country.

Repo Rate (b) corresponds to (ii), where commercial banks borrow money from RBI by purchasing securities, using them as collateral.

MCLR (c) or Marginal Cost of funds-based Lending Rate is indeed (iii), an internal benchmark rate set by individual banks.

The Bank Rate (d) corresponds to (i), which is the rate at which RBI lends money to commercial banks without any security.

73. (D): Market Penetration (a) aligns with (ii), it involves selling existing products in existing markets, often through aggressive marketing and competitive pricing.

Market Development (b) aligns with (iii), it entails expanding into new markets with existing products.

Product Development (c) matches with (iv), it means introducing new products into existing markets to meet changing customer needs. Diversification (d) is associated with (i), where companies venture into new markets with new products, often as a risk management strategy.

74. (B): In Marine insurance (a), insurable interest needs to be present at the time of the loss of the subject matter (iii).

Life insurance (b) requires insurable interest to be present throughout the contract of insurance (ii).

In Fire insurance (c), the insurable interest must be present at the time of loss of the subject matter (iii).

In General insurance (d), insurable interest needs to be present at the time of the insurance contract (iv).

75. (*)

76. (B): The correct sequence of port procedure and customs clearance for export from India begins with the C&F agent receiving documents from the exporter, taking delivery of the cargo and storing the cargo in a warehouse till shipment (c). After this, the cargo is brought to the port shed for loading (e). Once the cargo has been loaded onto the vessel, the master of the vessel issues a mate's receipt to the shed superintendent of the port (d). This mate's receipt is then presented to the shipping company by the C&F agent (a). Upon receipt of the mate's receipt, the shipping company issues a bill of lading. The C&F agent then dispatches the bill of lading and other documents to the importer (b).

77. (A): The process of auditing often involves different levels of intensity depending on the nature and the scope of the audit. Starting with the lowest intensity, we have the Internal Check (c), where internal controls and procedures are evaluated. This is followed by the Internal Audit (b), a more comprehensive audit conducted by a company's internal auditors. The Interim Audit (e) is conducted during a financial year with a focus on particular periods or specific areas. The Annual Audit (d) involves a complete examination of financial statements and records at the end of a financial year, while the Special Audit (a) is conducted for specific reasons or areas and is the most intense due to its specific and detailed nature.

78. (A): The correct sequence in the process of estimating a demand equation using regression analysis starts with Model Specifications (c) where the dependent and independent variables are identified. Next, obtaining data on each variable or its proxy (a) is carried out. The third step is deciding on the functional form of the demand equation (d), followed by estimating the slope coefficients (b). The final step involves the evaluation of regression results (e) to validate the model.

79. (A): In the logical sequence of international arbitrage operation, the first step is to Identify an Opportunity (a), where a price difference in different markets is identified. This is followed by reviewing the Transaction Cost (c) to ensure the opportunity is profitable. Next, the arbitrageur would Purchase the Asset (b) in the lower-priced market. The asset is then Sold (e) in the higher-priced market, and finally, the Profit is pocketed (d).

80. (A)

81. (B): The process of training an employee should first start with Explaining why the Employee is being Trained (c). This would involve describing the objectives of the training program and outlining the skills that the employee will gain. The next step is to Create Interest and Find Out What the Employee Already Knows About the Job (b), this step will help to customize the training to the employee's existing knowledge base. Then, it's important to Explain the Whole Job and Relate it to Some Other Job Which the Employee Already Knows (e) to enhance understanding. This should be followed by Placing the Trainee/Employee as Close to the Normal Working Position as Possible (d) to provide practical, hands-on experience. Finally, the training should Familiarize the Employee with Equipment, Materials, Tools, and Trade Terms (a) related to their specific job responsibilities.

82. (C): The risk management process should ideally follow these steps: The first step should be the Identification of Risk Variables (b), where possible risks that could affect the project or business are recognized. The next step should be the Determination of Frequency and Severity of Risk (c), which entails assessing the potential impact and the likelihood of each risk occurring. This is followed by the Selection of an Appropriate Risk Model for Analysis (a), where a model is selected to analyze and rank the risks. After this, the Application of a Suitable Risk Instrument (e) is done, which could be any number of risk mitigation strategies. The final step in this process is Feedback on the Risk

Management Process (d), where the effectiveness of the risk management process is evaluated and necessary adjustments are made.

83. (C): As per Maslow's hierarchy of needs theory, the first purchase a customer makes is usually based on physiological needs which is Purchase of Bathing Soap (e). Next, comes the need for safety and security - Purchase of a House (a). The need to belong and be accepted usually prompts the Taking of a Club Membership (c). The Esteem needs lead to the Purchase of an Expensive Car (b). Lastly, the need for self-actualization and personal development results in Enrolling in a Learn-by-Yourself Course (d).

84. (B): According to the Indian Consumer Protection Act, 1986, the least severe outcome of an offense is Removal of Defects (a), followed by the Return of Price Paid (c) by the consumer. The next is Compensation to Consumer (e) for the harm or loss they have suffered. After this comes the Discontinuation of Unfair Practices (d), which might be enforced by the consumer court if the defendant has been found to practice unfair trade. The most severe outcome is to Impose Cost on Parties (b) as a penalty or as a means of discouraging future occurrences of such behavior.

85. (D): In computation of tax on agricultural income in India, first, the agricultural and non-agricultural income is added together and the tax is calculated on the total income (d). The next step is to add the basic exemption limit to the net agricultural income and calculate the tax (a). The difference in both computations is then calculated (e). This is followed by deducting rebate under section 87A from the total income (b). Finally, the health cess is added (c) to arrive at the total tax payable.

86. (A): Both statements are accurate and reflect the complex realities of global economic dynamics. Large multinational corporations (MNCs) often have significant economic advantages, such as advanced technology, economies of scale, and vast marketing networks, enabling them to compete effectively on a global scale (Statement I). This sometimes leads to the closure of smaller firms in developing countries that cannot compete. On the other hand, MNCs also contribute to the development of these countries (Statement II) by transferring technology, introducing modern management practices, and enhancing productivity. Thus, MNCs can have both positive and negative impacts on developing economies.

87. (A): Both Assertion (A) and Reason (R) are correct, and (R) is the correct explanation of (A). Accounting profit is indeed calculated by deducting explicit costs (actual out-of-pocket expenses) from revenue. Economic profit, on the other hand, takes into account both explicit and implicit costs (opportunity costs of all resources involved in production). Since implicit costs are an additional deduction in the calculation of economic profit, it is often smaller than accounting profit unless the implicit costs are zero or negative.

88. (A): Both statements are true. The Split-Off Point (Statement I) is the stage in the manufacturing process where joint products can be identified separately. For instance, in oil refining, the crude oil enters the refinery as a single product but is split into multiple distinct products like gasoline, diesel, and jet fuel. The costs associated with this separation process are known as Separable Costs (Statement II) and are allocated to the different products based on certain allocation bases, such as the physical units or the sales value at the split-off point.

89. (C): Statement I is correct. As per Indian Income Tax laws, a Long-Term Capital Loss can only be set off against a Long-Term Capital Gain. This means that if you suffer a loss on the sale of a long-term capital asset, this loss can only be offset against any gain you may have from the sale of other long-term capital assets. However, Statement II is incorrect. As per the current laws, Long-term capital gains exceeding INR one lakh are taxed at the rate of 20% with indexation. The rate of 10% is applicable only when certain conditions are met, such as the asset being listed shares or units of equity-oriented mutual funds, and these are sold on a recognized stock exchange in India.

90. (A): Both Assertion (A) and Reason (R) are true, and (R) is indeed the correct explanation of (A). Life insurance is a complex product to sell because it involves selling a promise of future financial security, usually upon the death of the policyholder or the happening of a contingency based on human life. It involves discussing unpleasant but possible future events. This requires a high degree of trust and excellent communication skills, leading to the assertion that a successful life insurance salesperson can potentially sell anything.

91. (D): Assertion (A) is not correct. Work from Anywhere (WFA) is not limited to employees working independently. It can be applicable to employees in various roles and positions, depending on the nature of their work and the organization's flexibility. Reason (R) is incorrect because brainstorming sessions can still take place in a Work from Anywhere setup. While physical proximity may have certain advantages, virtual collaboration tools and video conferencing platforms enable remote brainstorming and idea sharing.

92. (C) **93. (D)** **94. (B)**

95. (D): Statement I is incorrect. The passage does not suggest that the relevance of Work from Anywhere (WFA) will reduce with the ease of the pandemic. On the contrary, it emphasizes that the push towards remote work during the pandemic has led to a shift from working from home (WFH) to working from anywhere (WFA). Statement II is correct. For the new hybrid work culture to prevail, companies will indeed need to invest more in technology to support flexible work arrangements, virtual collaboration, and efficient communication across physical and remote workspaces.

96. (D): Stability of prices. The primary purpose of the monetary policy of RBI (Reserve Bank of India) is to maintain stability of prices. This refers to controlling inflation and ensuring that prices of goods and services do not experience excessive volatility. The RBI uses various tools, such as interest rates and liquidity management, to achieve this objective. By implementing appropriate monetary measures, the RBI aims to keep inflation within a desired range to promote economic stability and sustainable growth.

97. (B): Neutral stance. The stance of a monetary policy wherein the interest rates may move either way, upwards or downwards, is called a neutral stance. In this approach, the central bank neither emphasizes a tightening (increasing interest rates) nor an easing (decreasing interest rates) bias. It indicates that the central bank is maintaining a balanced view and is ready to adjust the policy rates based on the prevailing economic conditions and objectives.

98. (C): Lowering of interest rates. An increase in investment is most likely to be caused by the lowering of interest rates. When the interest rates are reduced, borrowing costs decrease, making it more attractive for individuals and businesses to borrow money for investment purposes. Lower interest rates incentivize spending and borrowing, leading to increased investment activity, which can stimulate economic growth.

99. (C): Purchase of assets by the Central bank. Quantitative easing by the central bank implies the purchase of assets by the central bank. It is a monetary policy tool used by central banks to inject liquidity into the economy.

The central bank purchases assets, such as government bonds or other securities, from the market, which increases the money supply and aims to stimulate economic activity. Quantitative easing is typically employed during periods of economic downturn or when there is a need to provide additional liquidity to the financial system.

100. (B): Exchange rates. Changes in foreign portfolio investments are directly related to exchange rates. Foreign portfolio investments involve the purchase and sale of financial assets, such as stocks and bonds, in a country by foreign investors. The decision to invest in a particular country's financial assets is influenced by various factors, including the exchange rate. Fluctuations in exchange rates can impact the returns and attractiveness of foreign investments. A strengthening currency may make investments more expensive, while a weakening currency may make investments more attractive, affecting the flow of foreign portfolio investments.

Previous Years' Paper (Solved)

National Testing Agency (NTA)

UGC-NET Junior Research Fellowship & Assistant Professor Eligibility Exam

COMMERCE, SEPTEMBER–2022*

(Online exam held on 29-09-2022)

PAPER-II

Note: *This paper contains* ***hundred (100)*** *objective type questions of* ***two (2)*** *marks each.* ***All*** *questions are* ***compulsory.***

1. Pricing of housing loan by a commercial bank may follow the following steps in a logical sequence:

(*a*) Competitive price determination
(*b*) Specification of spread
(*c*) Application of MCLR
(*d*) Conduct of Credit Assessment
(*e*) Quoting to prospective borrower

Choose the correct answer from the options given below:

A. (*c*), (*b*), (*a*), (*d*), (*e*)
B. (*a*), (*b*), (*d*), (*c*), (*e*)
C. (*b*), (*a*), (*d*), (*e*), (*c*)
D. (*d*), (*c*), (*b*), (*a*), (*e*)

2. Presumptive taxation involves which one of the following?

A. The use of indirect methods to calculate tax liability, which differ from the usual sales based on the tax payers accounts.
B. Transfer of tax liability from State to the Centre.
C. Calculation of short term capital gain
D. Calculation of rebate U/S 89

3. Sequentially arrange the following themes related to globalization of Indian businesses since independence:

(*a*) FDI in various sectors opened along with slashing of custom duties.
(*b*) Partial opening of economy to external trade and de-licensing of some key sectors.
(*c*) Govt. led investments in large public sector units in steel, chemicals and power.
(*d*) Indian businesses became competitive and started to reap rewards of various phases cf development learning.
(*e*) Increased government involvement in industry with sustained focus on import substitution.

Choose the correct answer from the options given below:

A. (*c*), (*e*), (*b*), (*d*), (*a*)
B. (*e*), (*c*), (*b*), (*a*), (*d*)
C. (*c*), (*e*), (*b*), (*a*), (*d*)
D. (*a*), (*c*), (*e*) (*b*), (*d*)

4. Which one of the following is a myth about rural markets?

A. All villages are not equally populated.
B. Rural buyers are a heterogenous lot.
C. Rural buyers are able to discriminate between products and brands.
D. Only low priced products sell in rural markets.

5. The pricing practice to extract all of the consumer surplus from consumers to maximize the total revenue and profits from the sale of a particular quantity of product is called:

A. First-degree price discrimination
B. Second-degree price discrimination
C. Third-degree price discrimination
D. Penetration pricing

* Exam of December 2021 & June 2022.

6. As per the Agency Theory of Corporate Governance, which of the following statements are relevant?

(*a*) Governance approach is materialistic.
(*b*) Managers are motivated by the principals objectives.
(*c*) Interests of the managers and principals converge.
(*d*) Behaviour pattern is opportunistic.
(*e*) Owner's attitude is to avoid risks.

Choose the most appropriate answer from the options given below:

A. (*a*), (*c*), (*e*) only B. (*b*), (*c*), (*d*) only
C. (*b*), (*d*), (*e*) only D. (*a*), (*d*), (*e*) only

7. A company should undergo a step-wise process before selecting a final price. Accordingly, arrange the following steps of pricing-policy process to help 'XYZ' company to decide the final price of its product.

(*a*) Selecting the pricing method.
(*b*) Examining competitor's costs, prices and offers.
(*c*) Estimating the demand curve and the probable quantities company will sell at each possible price.
(*d*) Selecting the pricing objective of the company.
(*e*) Estimating costs for different levels of output, for different levels of accumulated production experience, and for differentiated marketing offers.

Choose the correct answer from the options given below:

A. (*d*), (*b*), (*e*), (*c*), (*a*)
B. (*d*), (*c*), (*e*), (*b*), (*a*)
C. (*a*), (*b*), (*c*), (*e*), (*d*)
D. (*a*), (*d*), (*e*), (*c*), (*b*)

8. Match List-I with List-II:

List-I (Legal Latin Phrase)	List-II (Description)
(*a*) *Consensus ad idem*	(*i*) Something in return
(*b*) *Quid pro quo*	(*ii*) As much as earned
(*c*) *Quantum meruit*	(*iii*) Buyer beware
(*d*) *Caveate emptor*	(*iv*) Meeting of minds

Choose the correct answer from the options given below:

	(*a*)	(*b*)	(*c*)	(*d*)
A.	(*i*)	(*iii*)	(*iv*)	(*ii*)
B.	(*iv*)	(*i*)	(*ii*)	(*iii*)
C.	(*ii*)	(*i*)	(*iii*)	(*iv*)
D.	(*i*)	(*iv*)	(*ii*)	(*iii*)

9. Arrange the following stages of delegation in correct sequence:

(*a*) Establish proper controls.
(*b*) Select the person in light of the job to be done.
(*c*) Reward effective delegation and successful assumption of authority.
(*d*) Define assignments and delegate authority in light of results expected.
(*e*) Maintain open lines of communication.

Choose the correct answer from the options given below:

A. (*a*), (*b*), (*c*), (*e*), (*d*)
B. (*b*), (*d*), (*e*), (*a*), (*c*)
C. (*d*), (*b*), (*e*), (*a*), (*c*)
D. (*c*), (*d*), (*b*), (*e*), (*a*)

10. Rates of Income Tax under new regime applicable for financial year 2021-22 in India are:

(*a*) 5% (*b*) 10%
(*c*) 12% (*d*) 15%
(*e*) 20%

Choose the correct answer from the options given below:

A. (*a*), (*b*), (*c*) only
B. (*a*), (*b*), (*d*) only
C. (*a*), (*b*), (*d*), (*e*) only
D. (*b*), (*c*), (*d*), (*e*) only

11. If the subject matter of insurance is the ship, the marine insurance is called:

A. Cargo insurance B. Hull insurance
C. Freight insurance D. Voyage insurance

12. As per Section 68 of the Indian Companies Act, a company may purchase its own shares out of which of the following?

(*a*) Free reserves
(*b*) Securities premium account
(*c*) General reserve

(*d*) Proceeds of any other shares
(*e*) Proceeds of same kind of shares

Choose the correct answer from the options given below:

A. (*a*), (*b*), (*c*) and (*e*) only
B. (*a*), (*b*), (*c*) and (*d*) only
C. (*b*), (*c*), (*d*) and (*e*) only
D. (*a*), (*c*), (*d*) and (*e*) only

13. Match List-I with List-II:

List-I (Type of Exposure)	**List-II (Description)**
(*a*) Economic Exposure	(*i*) Potential changes in all future cash flows of a firm that result from unanticipated changes in exchange rates.
(*b*) Translation Exposure	(*ii*) It arises when items of financial statements that are stated in foreign currencies are restated in the home currency of an MNC.
(*c*) Transaction Exposure	(*iii*) It arises when a firm's contract obligations are exposed to unanticipated changes in exchange rate.
(*d*) Operating Exposure	(*iv*) When a firm's real assets are exposed to unanticipated changes in exchange rates.

Choose the correct answer from the options given below:

	(*a*)	(*b*)	(*c*)	(*d*)
A.	(*iii*)	(*iv*)	(*ii*)	(*i*)
B.	(*i*)	(*ii*)	(*iii*)	(*iv*)
C.	(*iv*)	(*iii*)	(*ii*)	(*i*)
D.	(*i*)	(*iv*)	(*iii*)	(*ii*)

14. Match List-I with List-II:

List-I (Statistical Distribution)	**List-II (Characteristical Expression)**
(*a*) Negatively Skewed Distribution	(*i*) Mean = Mode, $P(x \leq \mu) = 0.50$
(*b*) Positively Skewed Distribution	(*ii*) $\bar{x}$ > Median > Mode: P > 0.5
(*c*) Binomial Distribution	(*iii*) $\bar{x}$ < Median < Mode
(*d*) Normal Distribution	(*iv*) $\bar{x}$ > Median > Mode

Choose the correct answer from the options given below:

	(*a*)	(*b*)	(*c*)	(*d*)
A.	(*iii*)	(*i*)	(*ii*)	(*iv*)
B.	(*i*)	(*ii*)	(*iii*)	(*iv*)
C.	(*ii*)	(*iii*)	(*iv*)	(*i*)
D.	(*iii*)	(*iv*)	(*ii*)	(*i*)

15. Which of the following are key assumptions of Gordon's Dividend Model?

(*a*) Ke > br
(*b*) *r* and Ke are changing
(*c*) The firm is not all-equity firm
(*d*) The firm has perpetual life
(*e*) The retention ratio, once decided, is constant

Choose the correct answer from the options given below:

A. (*a*), (*d*), (*e*) only B. (*b*), (*c*), (*e*) only
C. (*a*), (*b*), (*d*) only D. (*c*), (*d*), (*e*) only

16. Given below are two statements:

Statement I: Display of goods by a shopkeeper with prices marked on them, is not an offer but an invitation to the public to make an offer to buy the goods.

Statement II: Price quotations, catalogues and advertisements in newspaper for sale of an article do constitute a valid offer.

In the light of the above statements, choose the most appropriate answer from the options given below:

A. Both Statement I and Statement II are correct
B. Both Statement I and Statement II are incorrect
C. Statement I is correct, but Statement II is incorrect
D. Statement I is incorrect, but Statement II is correct

17. Which of the following are key features of prudent accounting concepts and conventions?

(*a*) It includes revenues and profits in the accounts when they are realised.

(*b*) It prevents profits from being overstated.

(*c*) It prevents a trader from more withdrawing from the business than is wise.

(*d*) Managerial efficiency and expertise.

(*e*) Good customer relations.

Choose the most appropriate answer from the options given below:

A. (*c*), (*d*) and (*e*) only

B. (*a*), (*d*) and (*e*) only

C. (*b*), (*c*) and (*d*) only

D. (*a*), (*b*) and (*c*) only

18. Match List-I with List-II:

List-I (Description)	**List-II (Conceptualisation)**
(*a*) Net Stable Funding Ratio	(*i*) Asset Liability Management
(*b*) Innovative Perpetual Debt Instrument	(*ii*) Tier-I capital
(*c*) Time Maturity Gap	(*iii*) Tier-II capital
(*d*) Risk Weighted Assets	(*iv*) Basel-III norms

Choose the correct answer from the options given below:

	(*a*)	(*b*)	(*c*)	(*d*)
A.	(*iv*)	(*ii*)	(*i*)	(*iii*)
B.	(*i*)	(*iv*)	(*iii*)	(*ii*)
C.	(*ii*)	(*iii*)	(*iv*)	(*i*)
D.	(*iv*)	(*iii*)	(*ii*)	(*i*)

19. Economists' adjustment to reality limited by individual consumers' preferences, intelligence and environmental factors is called:

A. Rationality

B. Homo economicus

C. Bounded rationality

D. Consumer sovereignity

20. A contract is discharged by supervening impossibility under which of the following situations?

(*a*) Destruction of subject matter

(*b*) Death or disablement of parties

(*c*) Rescission

(*d*) Remission

(*e*) Accord and satisfaction

Choose the most appropriate answer from the options given below:

A. (*a*), (*c*) and (*d*) only

B. (*a*) and (*b*) only

C. (*a*), (*b*) and (*e*) only

D. (*c*) and (*d*) only

21. Which of the following statements are correct?

(*a*) Internal reliability is described as the consistency of a measure taken at two different points of time.

(*b*) A distribution is random walk if it has a mean of 0 and variance of 1.

(*c*) Increase and decrease in scores measured overtime that produce a variance of less than 50% is reliable.

(*d*) Normal distribution cannot be applied to real life situations.

(*e*) Factor Analysis supersedes multiple discriminant analysis.

Choose the most appropriate answer from the options given below:

A. (*a*), (*b*), (*e*) only B. (*c*), (*d*), (*e*) only

C. (*b*), (*c*), (*d*) only D. (*b*), (*d*), (*e*) only

22. Total revenue of a business firm increases as long as:

A. | Ep | > 1 B. | Ep | = 1

C. | Ep | < 1 D. | Ep | < 0

23. Which of the following are thinly veiled disguises that essentially restrict imports?

(*a*) Voluntary import restrictions

(*b*) Labelling requirements showing origin and contents

(*c*) Import tarrifs and quotas

(*d*) Safety regulations for automobile and electrical equipments

(*e*) Health regulations for hygiene production and packaging of imported food production

Choose the most appropriate answer from the options given below:

A. (*a*), (*b*) and (*c*) only

B. (*b*), (*c*) and (*d*) only
C. (*c*), (*d*) and (*e*) only
D. (*b*), (*d*) and (*e*) only

24. According to Herzberg's Two Factor Theory, which one of the following is not a maintenance factor?
A. Affiliation or Acceptance
B. Esteem or Status
C. Security or Safety
D. Physiological Needs

25. Steps involved in computation of Book Profit under MAT regime are as follows:
(*a*) Arrive NP as per statement of P/L A/C of the company.
(*b*) Specific adjustments in case of merger.
(*c*) Make adjustments pertaining to OCI items.
(*d*) Adjust the book profit with stipulated exclusion and inclusion.
(*e*) Net amount of Book Profit for application of MAT rate

Choose the correct sequence from the options given below:
A. (*a*), (*d*), (*b*), (*c*), (*e*)
B. (*a*), (*b*), (*d*), (*c*), (*e*)
C. (*a*), (*c*), (*b*), (*d*), (*e*)
D. (*a*), (*b*), (*c*), (*d*), (*e*)

26. Given below are two statements:
Statement I: Policies are guides to action, rather than to thinking.
Statement II: Policies define an area within which a decision is to be made.

In the light of the above statements, choose the most appropriate answer from the options given below:
A. Both Statement I and Statement II are correct
B. Both Statement I and Statement II are incorrect
C. Statement I is correct, but Statement II is incorrect
D. Statement I is incorrect, but Statement II is correct

27. Given below are two statements: One is labelled as Assertion (A) and the other is labelled as Reason (R):
Assertion (A): Capital structure is determined within debt capacity of a company and it should not be exceeded.
Reason (R): Debt capacity of a company depends on its ability to generate cash flows. It should generate cash enough to pay lenders' fixed charges and principal sum.

In the light of the above Statements, choose the most appropriate answer from the options given below:
A. Both (A) and (R) are correct and (R) is the correct explanation of (A)
B. Both (A) and (R) are correct, but (R) is NOT the correct explanation of (A)
C. (A) is correct, but (R) is not correct
D. (A) is not correct, but (R) is correct

28. Michael Porter has identified five forces that determine the intrinsic long-term attractiveness of a market. According to the model, which of the following are true?
(*a*) A segment is unattractive if it already contains numerous aggressive competitors.
(*b*) A segment is unattractive if it is stable or declining.
(*c*) A segment is unattractive if it has high entry barriers and low exit barriers.
(*d*) A segment is unattractive if the company's suppliers are able to raise prices.
(*e*) A segment is unattractive when there are actual or potent substitutes for the product.

Choose the most appropriate answer from the options given below:
A. (*a*) and (*b*) only
B. (*b*) and (*c*) only
C. (*a*), (*c*) and (*d*) only
D. (*a*), (*b*), (*d*) and (*e*) only

29. Dimensions of VALS™ framework to include which one of the following?
A. Consumer motivation and consumer resources
B. Consumer personality and consumer resources
C. Consumer motivation and consumer preferences
D. Consumer needs and consumer resources

30. Under Indian Income Tax Act, allowances which are non-taxable for the individual assessee are:

(*a*) Sumptuary allowances.
(*b*) Compensatory allowance paid to judges.
(*c*) Overtime allowance.
(*d*) Allowances paid to Govt, employees posted abroad
(*e*) Non-practicing allowance.

Choose the most appropriate answer from the options given below:

A. (*a*), (*b*), (*d*), (*e*) only
B. (*a*), (*c*), (*d*), (*e*) only
C. (*a*), (*b*), (*d*) only
D. (*a*), (*b*), (*c*), (*d*), (*e*)

31. A prudent financial policy suggested by Marris Hypothesis to maximize balanced growth of the firm is based on which of following financial ratios?

(*a*) Return on investment ratio
(*b*) Debt equity ratio
(*c*) Return on capital employed ratio
(*d*) Liquidity ratio
(*e*) Retention ratio

Choose the most appropriate answer from the options given below:

A. (*a*), (*b*) and (*c*) only
B. (*b*), (*c*) and (*d*) only
C. (*a*), (*c*) and (*d*) only
D. (*b*), (*d*) and (*e*) only

32. Preference share in India is issued by a company for a maximum period of:

A. 10 years
B. 15 years
C. 20 years
D. Unlimited period

33. Which one of the following theories describes FDI flows in ecosystems?

A. Product Life Cycle Theory
B. Factor Endowment Theory
C. Waterfall Theory
D. New Trade Theory

34. Break-even point is not affected with the changes in which one of the following?

A. Sale price per unit
B. Variable cost per unit
C. Number of units sold
D. Total fixed costs

35. Match List-I with List-II:

List-I (International Trade Theories)	**List-II (Expounders)**
(*a*) Absolute Advantage	(*i*) David Ricardo
(*b*) Factor Endowments	(*ii*) Minhas, Leontief *et al.*
(*c*) Factor-Intensity Reversal	(*iii*) Adam Smith
(*d*) Comparative Advantage	(*iv*) Heckscher-Ohlin

Choose the correct answer from the options given below:

	(*a*)	(*b*)	(*c*)	(*d*)
A.	(*iii*)	(*ii*)	(*iv*)	(*i*)
B.	(*iii*)	(*iv*)	(*ii*)	(*i*)
C.	(*i*)	(*iv*)	(*ii*)	(*iii*)
D.	(*iii*)	(*i*)	(*ii*)	(*iv*)

36. The qualified characteristics determining (constituting) consumer 'rationality' includes which of the following?

(*a*) Economic selfish motives
(*b*) Risk-return optimiser
(*c*) Clarity of preferences
(*d*) Possession of information
(*e*) Non-satiation of needs

Choose the most appropriate answer from the options given below:

A. (*a*), (*b*) and (*c*) only
B. (*c*), (*d*) and (*e*) only
C. (*a*), (*b*), (*c*) and (*d*) only
D. (*a*), (*c*), (*d*) and (*e*) only

37. The current market price per share of New Age Limited is ₹ 80. The dividend expected a year from now is ₹ 4 and it is expected to grow at a constant rate of 10 per cent. The floatation (issue) cost for the new issue will be 8 per cent. What is the cost of new equity?

A. 15.43 per cent
B. 15.00 per cent
C. 5.00 per cent
D. 5.43 per cent

38. From the following, select the right option with reference to the working capital:

A. Higher net working capital leads to higher liquidity and higher profitability

B. According to hedging approach, current assets should be financed from long-term sources.
C. There is an inverse relationship between the length of operating cycle of a firm and its working capital requirements.
D. Trade-off plan, in general, is considered an appropriate financing strategy for working capital.

39. Arrange the following steps in the process of GDR Issues:
(*a*) Registration with prescribed authority
(*b*) Appointment and vesting of shares with the custodian
(*c*) Approval of the regulatory authorities
(*d*) Listing of GDR
(*e*) GDR allotment

Choose the correct answer from the options given below:
A. (*c*), (*a*), (*b*), (*e*), (*d*)
B. (*a*), (*b*), (*c*), (*d*), (*e*)
C. (*a*), (*c*), (*b*), (*e*), (*d*)
D. (*b*), (*a*), (*c*), (*d*), (*e*)

40. Arrange the following negotiation rounds of WTO (World Trade Organisation) in reverse chronological order:
(*a*) Uruguay Round (*b*) Geneva Round
(*c*) Kennedy Round (*d*) Doha Round
(*e*) Tokyo Round

Choose the correct answer from the options given below:
A. (*a*), (*c*), (*d*), (*b*), (*e*)
B. (*d*), (*a*), (*e*), (*c*), (*b*)
C. (*b*), (*a*), (*c*), (*e*), (*d*)
D. (*d*), (*e*), (*a*), (*c*), (*b*)

41. In case of a warranty, the buyer can:
A. Repudiate the contract
B. Claim damages only
C. Return the goods
D. Refuse to pay the price

42. Written plan containing the details regarding the conduct of a particular audit is called:
A. Audit Memorandum
B. Audit Planning Procedure
C. Audit Notebook
D. Audit Programme

43. A price ceiling below the equilibrium price possibly leads to which of the following?
(*a*) Black marketing
(*b*) Commodity glut
(*c*) Shortage of commodity
(*d*) Commodity export
(*e*) Price decline

Choose the correct answer from the options given below:
A. (*a*) and (*b*) only
B. (*d*) and (*e*) only
C. (*a*) and (*c*) only
D. (*a*), (*b*) and (*c*) only

44. Which one of the following is an example of Secondary Reserves?
A. Cash in hand and balances with other banks in current account
B. Balances with RBI for CRR
C. Investment in Commercial Paper
D. Investment in Government Securities for SLR

45. When a monopolist switches from charging a single price to perfect price discrimination, it reduces:
A. The quantity produced
B. The firm's profit
C. Consumer surplus
D. Total surplus

46. Choose the correct options regarding banking:
(*a*) Chain banking indicates the form of bank cartel that occurs when a small group of people control at least three banks that are independently chartered.
(*b*) PAN number is required for deposits in a commercial bank for ₹ 50,000 and above.
(*c*) Upon detection of counterfeit notes at the counter, the bank can impound the note and issue receipt.
(*d*) The interest rates on bank's contribution to Rural Infrastructure Development Fund is fixed by NABARD.
(*e*) RBI Act, 1934 prohibits the making or issuing of a promissory note expressed to be payable to the bearers thereof.

Choose the most appropriate answer from the options given below:

A. (*b*), (*d*), (*e*) only B. (*b*), (*c*) only
C. (*a*), (*d*), (*e*) only D. (*a*), (*b*), (*c*) only

47. Under the Vivad se Vishwas Act, 2020 the amount payable by the declarant U/S 3 on or after January 1, 2021 is:

A. Amount of disputed tax
B. The aggregate of the amount of disputed tax and 10% of disputed tax
C. Amount of penalty and amount computed by CBDT.
D. Average of tax arrears for last three assessment years.

48. In a statistical experiment, an effect size is described as:

A. Effective testing of hypothesis
B. Probable success of an experimental manipulation
C. Quantitative measurement of the magnitude of the experimental effect
D. Standardised measure of the magnitude of the effect observed in an experiment

49. Sequence the following in copyright ecosystem for literary creation under the Indian Copyright Act, 1957:

(*a*) Public communication
(*b*) Copyright assignment
(*c*) Content development
(*d*) Relinquish copyright
(*e*) Copyright transmission

Choose the correct answer from the options given below:

A. $(a) \rightarrow (e) \rightarrow (b) \rightarrow (d) \rightarrow (c)$
B. $(c) \rightarrow (a) \rightarrow (b) \rightarrow (e) \rightarrow (d)$
C. $(e) \rightarrow (c) \rightarrow (b) \rightarrow (d) \rightarrow (a)$
D. $(b) \rightarrow (c) \rightarrow (e) \rightarrow (a) \rightarrow (d)$

50. The standard error is a statistical measure of:

A. The normal distribution of scores around the sample mean.
B. The extent to which a sample mean is likely to differ from the population mean.
C. The clustering of scores at each end of a survey scale.
D. The degree to which the sample has been accurately stratified.

51. Logically sequence the following economic entities/identities in understanding the theory of consumer choice:

(*a*) Budget line
(*b*) Utility analysis
(*c*) Demand curve analysis
(*d*) Indifference curve analysis
(*e*) Consumer equilibrium

Choose the correct answer from the options given below:

A. $(d) \rightarrow (e) \rightarrow (a) \rightarrow (b) \rightarrow (c)$
B. $(b) \rightarrow (d) \rightarrow (a) \rightarrow (e) \rightarrow (c)$
C. $(b) \rightarrow (c) \rightarrow (d) \rightarrow (a) \rightarrow (e)$
D. $(b) \rightarrow (d) \rightarrow (a) \rightarrow (c) \rightarrow (e)$

52. "If you know the enemy and know yourself, you need not fear the result of a hundred battles."

Above statement of Sun Tzu corresponds to which one of the following components of Porter's Five Forces Model?

A. Threat of substitutes
B. Threat of Competitor
C. Bargain Power of Supplier
D. Threat of New Entrants

53. Which one of the following is false with respect to interest rate structure in the Indian money market?

A. A very tight liquidity position will increase the call rates while excess liquidity will give fairly low and stable rates.
B. If the liquidity crunch of the banks is passed on to the system, it may lead to high volatility in the call rates.
C. Call rates under normal liquidity conditions are the cap rate for the term money market.
D. In a volatile call market situation, lending will yield high return and by selling Inter-bank participation, the bank will have more money to play in the call market.

54. A co-efficient of correlation having a value of +0.87 implies that:

A. Co-efficient of correlation is strong and positive.

B. Co-efficient of determination is extremely weak.
C. The relationship between two variables is weak, but positive.
D. The relationship between two variables is strong.

55. In Fund Flow Statement, which one of the following is not a valid statement?
A. It is prepared to know the total sources and their uses in a year.
B. Dividend received is a source of funds.
C. Its preparation is at the discretion of the management.
D. It is useful for external financial management.

56. Which of the following statements are correct?
(*a*) The difference between sample variance and population variance computation is μ replaced by $\overline{x}$.
(*b*) Cronbach alpha value less than 0.30 indicates reliability of research instrument.
(*c*) The value of $R^2 = 1$ may imply that regression is spurious.
(*d*) The identical observation of sample and population parameters shows that every sample can be substituted as population.
(*e*) Randomise control trial is a qualitative approach to research.

Choose the correct answer from the options given below:
A. (*c*), (*d*), (*e*) only
B. (*a*), (*b*), (*c*), (*d*) only
C. (*a*), (*c*), (*d*), (*e*) only
D. (*b*), (*c*), (*d*) only

57. The banks wherein a majority of depositors are non-residents are called:
A. Cross Payment Banks
B. Currency Banks
C. Foreign Banks
D. Offshore Banks

58. Given below are two statements:
Statement I: Marketing managers must calculate customer lifetime values of their customer base to understand their profit implications.
Statement II: Activity-based costing, an accounting technique, is very useful for conducting customer profitability analysis.

In the light of the above Statements, choose the most appropriate answer from the options given below:
A. Both Statement I and Statement II are correct
B. Both Statement I and Statement II are incorrect
C. Statement I is correct, but Statement II is incorrect
D. Statement I is incorrect, but Statement II is correct

59. Which one of the following motives characterizes dominant organizational climate of university teaching departments/scientific organizations?
A. Affiliation B. Extension
C. Expert power D. Achievement

60. Which of the following decision choices are valid in relation to marginal costing?
(*a*) Costing 'special' or one off opportunities.
(*b*) Deciding whether to make or buy a product.
(*c*) Most appropriate technique because of application of more automation in the industry.
(*d*) Choosing between competing alternative actions.
(*e*) Employing a penetration or destroyer pricing strategy.

Choose the correct answer from the options given below:
A. (*a*), (*b*), (*d*) and (*e*) only
B. (*a*), (*b*), (*c*) and (*d*) only
C. (*b*), (*c*), (*d*) and (*e*) only
D. (*a*), (*d*) and (*e*) only

61. "Hospital administration may think that patients want better food, but patients may be more concerned with nurse responsiveness".
Above statement pertains to which one of the following service gaps?
A. Gap between consumer expectation and management perception.

B. Gap between management perception and service-quality specification.
C. Gap between service delivery and external communication.
D. Gap between service-quality specifications and service delivery.

62. Which of the following constructs hold true for research analysis and design?
(*a*) Research design is a framework for every stage of the collection and analysis of data.
(*b*) The choice between qualitative and quantitative methods in a research experiment depends upon Cronbach alpha.
(*c*) Experiments as source of data is not appropriate for a qualitative study.
(*d*) Plagarism is the failure of researcher to acknowledge the borrowed material in his/her publication.
(*e*) Content Analysis is a method commonly used in qualitative research to aid data collection.

Choose the most appropriate answer from the options given below:
A. (*a*), (*b*), (*e*) only
B. (*b*), (*c*), (*d*) only
C. (*a*), (*c*), (*d*), (*e*) only
D. (*b*), (*e*) only

63. Answer the correct material usage variance from the information given below:

Standard material cost for manufacturing 1000 units of an output is 400 kgs of material at ₹ 2.50 per kg. When 2000 units are produced, it is found that actual consumption was of 825 kgs material at a price of ₹ 2.70 per kg.?
A. ₹ 67.50 Favourable
B. ₹ 67.50 Adverse
C. ₹ 62.50 Favourable
D. ₹ 62.50 Adverse

64. A spot sale of a currency combined with a forward repurchase of the same currency is called which one of the following?
A. Forex swap
B. Swap rate
C. Forward rate
D. Spot rate

65. Under which one of the following the Basel framework places restrictions on participation by banks in system-wide credit booms with the aim of reducing their losses in credit bust?
A. Catastrophic Reserve Capital
B. Countercyclical Capital Buffer
C. Deferred Capital
D. Conservative Preference Capital

66. Which one of the following is not an advantage of organization structure by territory?
A. Makes control easy for top management
B. Places responsibility at a lower level
C. Improves coordination in a region
D. Takes advantage of economies of local operations

67. From which of the following, employees derive authority?
(*a*) Position
(*b*) Experience
(*c*) Moral worth
(*d*) Past service
(*e*) Intelligence

Choose the most appropriate answer from the options given below:
A. (*a*), (*b*) only
B. (*a*), (*e*) only
C. (*b*), (*c*), (*e*) only
D. (*a*), (*b*), (*c*), (*d*), (*e*)

68. Arm's length price computation method under 92(C) of the Income Tax Act, 1961 does not include which one of the following?
A. Comparable uncontrolled price
B. Transaction net margin
C. Resale price
D. Slum sale price method

69. Match List-I with List-II:

List-I (Ind AS)	List-II (Topic)
(*a*) Ind AS 1	I. Income Taxes
(*b*) Ind AS 12	II. Related Party Disclosures
(*c*) Ind AS 24	III. Intangible Assets
(*d*) Ind AS 38	IV. Presentation of Financial Statements

Choose the correct answer from the options given below:

	(a)	(b)	(c)	(d)
A.	I	II	III	IV
B.	IV	I	II	III
C.	IV	III	II	I
D.	II	IV	I	III

70. Match List-I with List-II:

List-I (Promotional Campaign)	**List-II (Company)**
(a) # StayStrongMoms	I. Pepsico India
(b) # JeetKiOre	II. Hindustan Uniliver (HUL)
(c) # Lets unstereotypeIndia	III. Indian Tobacco Company (ITC)
(d) # Freedomtolove	IV. Brooke Bond India

Choose the correct answer from the options given below:

	(a)	(b)	(c)	(d)
A.	III	I	IV	II
B.	II	IV	I	III
C.	II	I	III	IV
D.	I	III	IV	II

71. Which one of the following is a Trade related entry mode in international markets?

A. Management Contract
B. International Licensing
C. International Leasing
D. Portfolio Investments

72. Which of the following are essentially anti-competetive agreements as per the Competition Act, 2002 in India?

(a) Exclusive distribution agreement
(b) Resale price maintenance
(c) Exclusive supply agreement
(d) Non-compete agreement
(e) Tie-in agreement

Choose the correct answer from the options given below:

A. (a), (b) and (c) only
B. (c), (d) and (e) only
C. (a), (b), (c) and (d) only
D. (a), (b), (c) and (e) only

73. Match List-I with List-II:

List-I (Personality Factor)	**List-II (Bipolar Dimension)**
(a) Warmth	I. Imaginative vs practical
(b) Abstractedness	II. Controlled vs casual
(c) Openness to change	III. Outgoing vs reserved
(d) Perfectionism	IV. Experimental vs conservative

Choose the correct answer from the options given below:

	(a)	(b)	(c)	(d)
A.	II	I	IV	III
B.	III	I	IV	II
C.	I	IV	III	II
D.	III	II	IV	I

74. Which one of the following is not valid as per the Limited Liability Partnership Act, 2008?

A. LLP shall maintain its books of accounts on double entry system and on cash or accrual basis.
B. LLP shall prepare a Statement of Account and Solvency for each financial year.
C. Every LLP shall file an annual return with the Registrar of Companies.
D. Every LLP is a separate legal entity independent of its partners.

75. Which are the major factors that lead to capital rationing?

(a) Imperfection of capital market.
(b) Reluctance to broaden the equity share-base for the fear of losing control.
(c) Inability to manage.
(d) Deficiencies in market information which might affect the availability of capital.
(e) Efficiency of Capital Market.

Choose the correct answer from the options given below:

A. (a), (b), (d) only
B. (c), (d), (e) only
C. (a), (b), (c), (e) only
D. (a), (b), (c), (d) only

76. Match List-I with List-II:

List-I (Income Tax Disposition)	List-II (Particular Section)
(*a*) Donation to National Defence Fund	I. Section 140 (A)
(*b*) Hedging of Tax	II. Tax Management
(*c*) Compliance with Legal Formalities	III. Tax Avoidance
(*d*) Permanent Account Number (PAN)	IV. 100% Deduction

Choose the correct answer from the options given below:

	(*a*)	(*b*)	(*c*)	(*d*)
A.	III	II	I	IV
B.	IV	III	II	I
C.	II	I	III	IV
D.	I	IV	II	III

77. Why do Central banks intervene to affect exchange rates?

(*a*) To influence domestic production
(*b*) To influence trade flows
(*c*) To influence domestic interest rates
(*d*) To inject liquidity in domestic markets
(*e*) To smoothen fluctuations in exchange rates.

Choose the most appropriate answer from the options given below:

A. (*a*), (*b*) and (*c*) only
B. (*c*), (*d*) and (*e*) only
C. (*b*), (*c*) and (*d*) only
D. (*a*), (*b*) and (*e*) only

78. If the information sought has been supplied by third party or is treated as confidential by that third party, the third party must give a representation before the PIO in reply to the notice issued to it within how many days from the date of receipt of such notice?

A. 5 days B. 15 days
C. 10 days D. 7 days

79. Which of the following factors favour product standardization in the international markets?

(*a*) High cost of adaptation.
(*b*) Variations in conditions of use.
(*c*) Country of origin effect.
(*d*) Economies in R&D.
(*e*) Differences in technical standards.

Choose the most appropriate answer from the options given below:

A. (*a*) and (*e*) only
B. (*a*), (*c*) and (*d*) only
C. (*a*), (*b*), (*c*) and (*d*) only
D. (*c*) and (*d*) only

80. Banker sale of a mortgage portfolio by setting up a mortgage pass-through securities is an example of:

A. Credit enhancement
B. Unbundling
C. Derivatives
D. Securitisation

81. Match List-I with List-II:

List-I (Nature of goods)	List-II (Income Elasticity (E_i) of demand)
(*a*) Normal goods	I. E_i is greater than one
(*b*) Inferior goods	II. E_i is greater than zero
(*c*) Luxury goods	III. E_i is between zero and one
(*d*) Necessities	IV. E_i is less than zero

Choose the correct answer from the options given below:

	(*a*)	(*b*)	(*c*)	(*d*)
A.	II	IV	I	III
B.	III	I	IV	II
C.	II	I	III	IV
D.	I	III	II	IV

82. Which one of the following is not an assumption of simple linear regression model?

A. The set of expected values of the dependent variable *y* for given values of independent variable *x*, are normally distributed.
B. The standard deviation and variance of expected values of the dependent variable about the regression line are constant for all values of the independent variable *x* for the set of observations in a sample.
C. The dependent variable *y* is a continuous random variable.
D. The errors in the value of *y* are identical in successive observations.

83. Tax holiday under the Income Tax Act 1961 has been used in the context of which one of the following?
A. Section 80 IA B. Section 80 D
C. Section 80 CCC D. Section 10(5)

84. Given below are two statements: One is labelled as Assertion (A) and the other is labelled as Reason (R):
Assertion (A): Substitution effect is usually much larger than the income effect.
Reason (R): Consumer usually spends only a small portion of her/his income on any one commodity.

In the light of the above Statements, choose the correct answer from the options given below:
A. Both (A) and (R) are true and (R) is the correct explanation of (A)
B. Both (A) and (R) are true, but (R) is NOT the correct explanation of (A)
C. (A) is true, but (R) is false
D. (A) is false, but (R) is true

85. Which one of the following tools is not used for forecasting personnel needs (Labour Demand) by an organization?
A. Trend Analysis B. Markov Analysis
C. Ratio Analysis D. Scatter Plot

86. Who among the following are indentified as the Key managerial personnel in the Indian Companies Act, 2013?
(*a*) Chief Executive Officer
(*b*) Whole Time Director
(*c*) Company Secretary
(*d*) Chief Risk Officer
(*e*) Manager

Choose the most appropriate answer from the options given below:
A. (*a*), (*b*) and (*d*) only
B. (*a*) and (*b*) only
C. (*a*), (*b*), (*c*) and (*d*) only
D. (*a*), (*b*), (*c*) and (*e*) only

87. In order to maintain its market share, a market follower can employ:
A. Counter feiting strategy
B. Specialization strategy
C. Counter offensive strategy
D. Preemptive strategy

88. Under Indian Income Tax Act, in order to claim deduction of interest on home loan for house property, which of the following things need to be taken care of?
(*a*) The home loan must be used for the purchase/construction of the house property.
(*b*) The loan must be taken on or after 1st April, 2019.
(*c*) The amount of loan must be used within 10 days from the date of loan taken.
(*d*) The purchase or construction must be completed within 5 years from the end of Financial Year in which the loan was taken.
(*e*) The rate of interest on loan cannot exceed 22%.

Choose the most appropriate answer from the options given below:
A. (*a*), (*b*), (*d*) only
B. (*a*), (*c*), (*d*), (*e*) only
C. (*b*), (*c*), (*d*), (*e*) only
D. (*a*) and (*d*) only

89. What will be the sequence of steps involved in 'Net Benefit Model' of Human Resource Accounting?
(*a*) The gross value of services to be rendered in future by the employee in their individual as well as their collective capacity is determined.
(*b*) The excess of the value of future human resources over the value of future payments is ascertained.
(*c*) The present value of the net benefit is determined by applying a pre-determined discount rate.
(*d*) The value of future payments to the employees is determined.
(*e*) The amount calculated under 'C' will be the value of human resources to the organisation.

Choose the correct sequence from the options given below:
A. (*a*), (*d*), (*b*), (*c*), (*e*)

B. (*a*), (*b*), (*c*), (*d*), (*e*)
C. (*a*), (*c*), (*d*), (*b*), (*e*)
D. (*b*), (*a*), (*c*), (*d*), (*e*)

90. Which of the following are the main platforms for social media?
(*a*) Search Engines
(*b*) Online communities and forums
(*c*) Blogs
(*d*) Social Networks
(*e*) Web 1.0

Choose the correct answer from the options given below:
A. (*b*), (*c*) and (*d*) only
B. (*b*) and (*d*) only
C. (*b*), (*c*), (*d*) and (*e*)
D. (*a*), (*b*), (*c*) and (*d*) only

Directions (Qs. No. 91-95): *Read the following passage and answer the question.*

GOI has reaffirmed its intent in amendments to the Finance Bill to use tax as a deterrent to speculation in virtual digital assets. The amendments disallow losses on the sale of one crypto asset to be set off against gains on another. No deduction is permitted for any expenditure other than the cost of acquisition for computation of income from sale of cryptos and non-fungible tokens (NFTs). Every transfer of crypto assets will be taxed at the proposed 30% rate, irrespective of whether they are a capital asset or not. Only the proposed 1% rate of tax deducted at source will apply to transactions in digital assets. Penalties have been imposed for taxpayers who have claimed a deduction of surcharge and cess from their taxable income, but have not, on their own accord, paid the tax and interest on the deduction they have claimed.

The inability to set off losses will skew the risk-reward profile of digital assets, and crypto exchanges fear it could push trading activity beyond Indian jurisdiction to decentralized exchanges and foreign platforms accessed through virtual private networks. The industry feels not allowing tax deduction on the costs of mining cryptos will eventually force blockchain companies and the talent they hire to operate outside the country. To the extent that the proposed tax regime drives users from exchanges compliant with know-your-customer (KYC) rules towards underground peer-to-peer platforms, deterrence would be diluted.

Nirmala Sitharaman, in her statement while moving the amendments, has clarified the tax on private digital assets does not indicate GoI's stance on their legitimacy. The regulatory position could become clearer once the Reserve Bank of India (RBI) is ready with its digital currency. Fiat digital currencies, which make transactions and monetary transmission more efficient, are inevitable as the use of cash plateaus in several countries. Speculation, and a reflex to curb it, must not draw attention away from the inherent superiority of digital currencies. This is the future of money.

91. Which one of the following is done by the Digital Currency Regulatory Framework?
A. Eventually force blockchain companies to operate from outside.
B. Attract users towards exchanges which are compliant with know-your-customer rules.
C. Motivate the operators to operate outside the country.
D. Promote underground peer to peer crypto platforms.

92. Digital currency regulations will result into which one of the following?
A. Scare digital currencies away.
B. Permit deduction of any expenditure other than the cost of acquisition for computation of income.
C. Impose penalties for tax payers who have claimed a deduction of surcharge and cess from their taxable income.
D. Attract 30% tax on every transfer of crypto asset.

93. Given below are two statements:
Statement I: Non-fungible tokens cannot be splitted.
Statement II: Non-fungible tokens can be replicated at convenience.

In the light of the above Statements, choose the most appropriate answer from the options given below:

A. Both Statement I and Statement II are correct
B. Both Statement I and Statement II are incorrect
C. Statement I is correct, but Statement II is incorrect
D. Statement I is incorrect, but Statement II is correct

94. Government of India's intent towards virtual digital assets is which one of the following?

A. To promote speculation
B. To be silent on speculation
C. To discourage speculation
D. To stop speculation

95. Given below are two statements: One is labelled as Assertion (A) and the other is labelled as Reason (R):

Assertion (A): Crypto exchanges fear that the new amendments could push trading activity beyond Indian jurisdiction to decentralized exchanges.

Reason (R): The new amendments disallow losses on the sale of new crypto asset to be set off against gains on another.

In the light of the above Statements, choose the most appropriate answer from the options given below:

A. Both (A) and (R) are correct and (R) is the correct explanation of (A)
B. Both (A) and (R) are correct, but (R) is NOT the correct explanation of (A)
C. (A) is correct, but (R) is not correct
D. (A) is not correct, but (R) is correct

Directions (Qs. No. 96-100): *Read the given passage and answer the question.*

Naik, AGM Materials, is fuming and fretting. He bumped into Kamath, GM (Materials), threw the resignation letter on his table, shouted and walked out of the room swiftly.

Naik has reason for his sudden outburst. He has been driven to the wall. Perhaps, details of the story will tell the reasons for Naik's bile and why he put in his papers, barely four months after he took up his present assignment.

The year was 2021 when Naik quit the prestigious SAIL plant at Vishakapatnam. As a manager materials, Naik enjoyed powers—he could even place an order for materials worth ₹ 25 lakh. He needed nobody's prior approval.

Naik joined a pulp-making plant located at Harihar in Karnataka, as AGM Materials. The plant is a part of the multi-product and multiplant-conglomerate owned by a prestigious business house in India.

Obviously, perks, designation and reputation of the conglomerate lured Naik away from the public sector steel monolith.

When he joined the eucalyptus pulp making company, little did Naik realise that he needed prior approval to place an order for materials worth ₹ 12 lakh. He had presumed that he had the authority to place an order by himself worth half the amount of what he used to do at the mega steel maker. He placed the order, materials arrived, were received, accepted and used up in the plant.

Trouble started when the bill for ₹ 12 lakh came from the vendor. The accounts department withheld payment for the reason that the bill was not endorsed by Kamath. Kamath refused to sign on the bill as his approval was not taken by Naik before placing the order.

Naik felt fumigated and cheated. A brief encounter with Kamath only aggravated the problem. Naik was curtly told that he should have known company rules before venturing. Naik decided to quit.

96. What is the most ineffective in the organisation?

A. Recruitment policy
B. Selection policy
C. Induction programme
D. Promotion policy

97. The job of AGM materials is to:

A. Place order B. Receive material
C. Inspect material D. Issue material

98. Given below are two statements:

Statement I: Mr. Naik's presumption that he could place an order for materials worth ₹ 25 lakh was right.

Statement II: Perks and reputation of the conglomerate were the reasons for Mr. Naik joining the eucalyptus pulp making company.

In the light of the above Statements, choose the most appropriate answer from the options given below:

A. Both Statement I and Statement II are correct

B. Both Statement I and Statement II are incorrect

C. Statement I is correct, but Statement II is incorrect

D. Statement I is incorrect, but Statement II is correct

99. As per the passage, who is at fault?

A. Mr. Naik

B. Mr. Kamath

C. Both Mr. Naik and Mr. Kamath

D. Human Resource Department

100. Given below are two statements: One is labelled as Assertion (A) and the other is labelled as Reason (R):

Assertion (A): It was right on the part of accounts department to withheld payment.

Reason (R): Mr. Naik had the authority to place the order for materials worth ₹ 25 lakh.

In the light of the above Statements, choose the correct answer from the options given below:

A. Both (A) and (R) are true and (R) is the correct explanation of (A)

B. Both (A) and (R) are true, but (R) is NOT the correct explanation of (A)

C. (A) is true, but (R) is false

D. (A) is false, but (R) is true

ANSWERS

1. (D)

2. (A): Presumptive taxation allows you to pay your tax based on presumptive income. Meaning, you don't really need to estimate your income by deducting your expenses from revenue. You can simply take a percentage of your total revenue and pay tax on that. Presumptive taxation for businesses is covered under section 44AD of the income tax act. Any business which has a turnover of less than ₹ 2 crore can opt to be taxed presumptively. They must declare profits of 8% for non-digital transactions or 6% for digital transactions, whichever one is applicable. The following businesses are excluded from presumptive taxation:

(*a*) Life insurance agents.

(*b*) Commission of any kind.

(*c*) Running the business of plying, hiring or leasing goods carriages.

3. (C)

4. (D): "Only low priced products sell in rural markets." This statement is incorrect because the statement assumes that the all people residing in rural India have low per capita income and cannot afford high priced products. This is an unrealistic assumption.

5. (A): Under first-degree price discrimination, the monopolist tries to know the maximum amount of money that each consumer will pay and he/she will set the price equal to their willingness to pay and take the entire consumer surplus away from each consumer. It is also known as perfect price discrimination and involves charging consumers the maximum price that they are willing to pay for a good or service. Here, consumer surplus is entirely captured by the firm. In practice, a consumer's maximum willingness to pay is difficult to determine. Therefore, such a pricing strategy is rarely employed.

6. (D): Agency theory posits that corporations act as agents of its shareholders. That is, shareholders invest in corporate ownership and thereby entrust their resources to the management of the directors and officers of the corporation. In larger corporations, there is often a sharp divergence between the short and long-term interest of officers and shareholders. This is primarily brought on by short-term demand for profits and the asymmetry of information that officers and directors possess compared with that of shareholders. Agency theory may be used to design these incentives appropriately by considering what interests motivate the agent to act. Incentives encouraging the wrong behaviour must be removed, and rules discouraging moral hazard must be in place. Understanding the mechanisms that create problems helps businesses develop better corporate policy.

7. (B)

8. (B): *Consensus ad idem* in contract law means there has been a meeting of the minds of all parties involved and everyone involved has accepted the offered contractual obligations of each party.

Quid pro quo is a Latin term for "something for something" that originated in the middle ages in Europe. It describes a situation when two parties engage in a mutual agreement to exchange goods or services reciprocally. In a quid pro quo agreement, one transfer is thus contingent upon some transfer from the other party.

Quantum meruit means "the amount one deserves" or "as much as one has earned". In most cases it denotes a claim for a reasonable sum in respect of services or goods supplied to the defendant.

Caveat emptor is a common law doctrine that places the burden on buyers to reasonably examine property before making a purchase. A buyer who fails to meet this burden is unable to recover for defects in the product that would have been discovered had this burden been met. The phrase "caveat emptor" is Latin for "let the buyer beware."

9. (C)

10. (C):

Income Tax Slab	New Regime Income Tax Slab Rates FY 2021-22 (Applicable for All Individuals & HUF)
₹ 0.0 – ₹ 2.5 lakh	NIL
₹ 2.5 lakh – ₹ 5.00 lakh	5% (tax rebate u/s 87a is available)
₹ 5.00 lakh – ₹ 7.5 lakh	10%
₹ 7.5 lakh – ₹ 10.00 lakh	15%
₹ 10.00 lakhs – ₹ 12.50 lakh	20%
₹ 12.5 lakhs – ₹ 15.00 lakh	25%
> ₹ 15 lakh	30%

11. (B): Hull and machinery insurance is an insurance policy specially designed for covering ship damage expenses. Where the 'Hull' refers to the main body of the ship, Hull insurance includes fixtures attached to the ship hull as a functional part, into the definition of the hull. Since the policy mostly applies to water-going vessels, it is more popularly called Marine Hull Insurance and is a part of marine insurance. It covers all types of vessels operating in the oceans, lakes, and rivers like bulk carriers, fishing boats, ships, tankers, cruises, yachts, jetties, and wharves.

12. (B): Sections 68 to 70 of the Companies Act, 2013 and Rule 17 of the Companies (Share Capital and Debentures) Rules, 2014 deal with buy-back of shares.

- **Sources of Buy-Back:** A company may purchase its shares out of: its free reserves; the securities premium account; or the proceeds of the issue of any shares or other specified securities. However, no buy-back of any kind of shares can be made out of the proceeds of an earlier issue of the same kind of shares.

- **Prohibitions on Buy-Back:** No company shall directly or indirectly purchase its own shares.

13. (B): Economic exposure, also sometimes called operating exposure, is a measure of the change in the future cash flows of a company as a result of unexpected changes in foreign exchange rates (FX).

Translation exposure (also known as translation risk) is the risk that a company's equities, assets, liabilities, or income will change in value as a result of exchange rate changes. This occurs when a firm denominates a portion of its equities, assets, liabilities, or income in a foreign currency. It is also known as "accounting exposure."

Transaction exposure is the level of uncertainty businesses involved in international trade face. Specifically, it is the risk that currency exchange rates will fluctuate after a firm has already undertaken a financial obligation. A high level of vulnerability to shifting exchange rates can lead to major capital losses for these international businesses.

Operating exposure, is a measure of the change in the future cash flows of a company as a result of unexpected changes in foreign exchange rates (FX).

14. (D)

15. (A): Gordon Growth Dividend Model Assumptions:

(*a*) **No external financing:** There is no external financing available. Companies' retained earnings are used to finance the projects.

(*b*) **All-equity firm:** The firm is financed through equity capital and there in no debt financing.

(*c*) **Returns are constant:** The internal rate of return that is *r* of the firm is constant. This implies that it ignores the diminishing marginal efficiency.

(*d*) **Cost of capital is also constant:** The discount rate (k) remains constant. This implies it completely ignores the effect due to change in firms risk class.

(*e*) **Retention ratio is constant:** The retention ratio (br) and the growth rate(g) is constant.

(*f*) The cost of capital is greater than growth rate: The discount rate is greater than the growth rate, that is, k > br = g.

16. (C): An offer is a proposal while an invitation to offer is inviting someone to make a proposal. An Invitation to Offer is an act prior to an offer, in which one person induces another person to make an offer to him, it is known as invitation to offer, display of goods in a shop window with prices marked upon them is an invitation to offer. Thus, statement I is correct.

Generally speaking, advertisements, catalogs, brochures, and announcements to the public associated with the sale of merchandise at a specified price are not considered to be offers to enter into a binding contract. Rather, they are considered to be invitations to make a deal. As such, it is not generally a breach of contract when the advertiser refuses to sell an item at a price that they advertised.Thus, statement II is incorrect.

An advertisement may be considered a valid offer if it meets the following three elements:

- It is sufficiently definite in its terms, meaning descriptions, quality, quantity, & price;
- It is communicated to a specific person or people, generally a limited group of people; and
- The circumstances surrounding the publication show that the advertiser intends to enter into a contract.

17. (D): Prudence Concept or Conservatism principle is a key accounting principle that makes sure that assets and income are not overstated, and provision is made for all known expenses and losses whether the amount is known for certain or just an estimation, *i.e.*, expenses and liabilities are not understated in the books of accounting.

18. (A): Net stable funding ratio (NSFR): The net stable funding ratio is a liquidity standard requiring banks to hold enough stable funding to cover the duration of their long-term assets. For both funding and assets, long-term is mainly defined as more than one year, with lower requirements applying to anything between six months and a year to avoid a cliff-edge effect. Banks must maintain a ratio of 100% to satisfy the requirement. Introduced as part of the post-crisis banking reforms known as Basel III, the ratio ensures banks do not undertake excessive maturity transformation, which is the practice of using short-term funding to meet long-term liabilities. It was finalised by the Basel Committee in October 2014.

The total amount raised by a bank through Innovative Perpetual Debt Instruments (IPDI) shall not be reckoned as liability for calculation of net demand and time liabilities for the purpose of reserve requirements and, as such, will not attract CRR/SLR requirements. An innovative perpetual debt instrument definition is an asset rather than an establishment. There are numerous debt instruments such as bonds, debentures, national saving certificates (NSC), and fixed deposits. The total amount raised by a bank through IPDIs shall not exceed 15 per cent of total Tier 1 capital. The eligible amount will be computed with reference to the amount of Tier 1 capital as on March 31 of the previous financial year, after deduction of goodwill and other intangible assets but before the deduction of investments.

The maturity gap analysis compares the value of assets that either mature or are repriced within a given time interval to the value of liabilities that either mature or are repriced during the same time period. Reprice means there's the potential to receive a new interest rate.

Risk-weighted assets are used to determine the minimum amount of capital a bank must hold in relation to the risk profile of its lending activities and other assets. This is done in order to reduce the risk of insolvency and protect depositors. The more risk a bank has, the more capital it needs on hand. The capital requirement is based on a risk assessment for each type of bank asset.

19. (C): According to Bounded Rationality theory, a rational individuals will make satisfactory decisions instead of optimal ones. Even the economists' adjustment to reality limited by individual consumers' preferences, intelligence and environmental factors. This is due to the limitations that the theory deconstructs the idea of "perfect" rationality. Perfect rational decisions are often impossible in practice due to the natural decision problems and constrained computational resources available.

20. (B): Doctrine of Supervening Impossibility:

- The Indian Contract Act, 1872 states in Section 56, paragraph 2, that if the doctrine of supervening impossibility applies and a contract becomes impossible or illegal to perform after it is formed, it will be void.
- It's interesting to note that, generally speaking, the inability to perform a contract is not a reason for failing to do so.
- It only applies where this impossibility results from causes outside the parties' control. They can only be released from any additional contract obligations in that scenario.
- Here, Impossibilities are known to the parties at the time of making of the contract that's why it will be applied.

Doctrine of Supervening Impossibility will be applied in following cases:

- **Destruction of Subject Matter of Contract:** A contract is dismissed if, after it is formed, its subject matter is destroyed without any of the parties' fault.
- **Non-existence or non-occurrence of a particular state of things:** There are occasions when a contract is made based on the occurrence or existence of a specific condition. However, if the circumstances that formed the contract's very foundation change or cease to exist, the agreement is null and void.
- **Death or Incapacity of Services:** If the performance of a contract depends on a party's qualifications or personal skills and that party's demise, illness, or incapacity renders the contract void, the contract may also be discharged by supervening impossibility. This is true because the contract's implied terms include a man's life.
- **Change of law or stepping in of a new law:** After the creation of a contract, it is possible that the law changes or that an amendment is made to an ordinance, a special act, or a set of government regulations. The contract is discharged since the change makes it impossible to carry out the terms of the agreement.
- **Outbreak of war:** When two parties from separate nations sign in to a contract with one another and a war is subsequently declared between the countries, the contract typically becomes void since it cannot be carried out.

The doctrine of Supervening impossibility will not apply in following cases:

- **Difficulty in performance:** The mere fact that it is now more difficult to carry out a contract due to unforeseen circumstances or delays does not deem it to be fulfilled.
- **Commercial Impossibility:** A contract is not discharged for these reasons if an anticipation of larger profits is not met, the required raw material becomes available at a very expensive price due to the start of a war, or if a sudden depreciation of currency happens.
- **Impossibility due to failure of third party:** A contract is also not discharged if it was unable to be carried out because a third party the promisor had depended on defaulted.
- **Strikes, lock-outs, and civil disturbances:** Events like strikes, lockouts, or public unrest do not discharge a contract unless the parties explicitly consented to such terms at the time the contract was signed.
- **Failure of one of the objects:** In addition to the aforementioned situations, if a contract is made for a number of purposes, the simple failure of one of those purposes does not cancel the agreement.

21. (A): "Increase and decrease in scores measured overtime that produce a variance of less than 50% is reliable" is an incorrect statement as reliability concerns how accurately a test represents variation between subjects.

The normal distribution, also known as the Gaussian distribution, is the most important probability distribution in statistics for independent, random variables. Most people recognize its familiar bell-shaped curve in statistical reports. The normal distribution is a continuous probability distribution that is symmetrical around its mean, most of the observations cluster around the central peak, and the probabilities for values further away from the mean taper off equally in both directions. The normal distribution approximates many natural phenomena, such as, height, rolling a dice, tossing a coin, IQ level.

IQ GRAPH

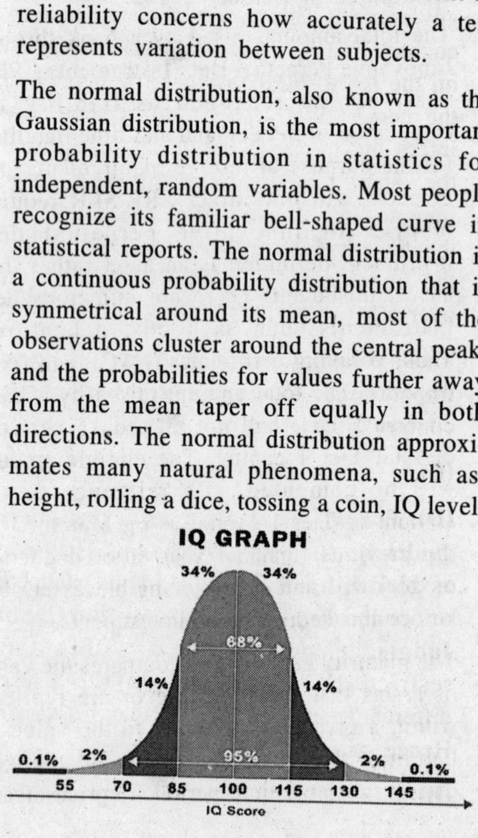

In this scenario of increasing competition, most parents, as well as children, want to analyze the Intelligent Quotient level. Well, the IQ of a particular population is a normal distribution curve; where IQ of a majority of the people in the population lies in the normal range whereas the IQ of the rest of the population lies in the deviated range. Thus, statement "(*d*)" is also incorrect.

22. (A)

23. (D): Thinly veiled disguises can be defined as factors which are able to be seen or understood but not openly shown or stated, or expressed in a way that is not clear and direct. A voluntary export restraint (VER) is a self-imposed limit on the quantity of a good that an exporting country is allowed to export.

Tariffs are described as levies that a government imposes on imports entering a country. The government does this by passing on the tax to the consumers by heightening the commodities' prices. An import quota infers the numerical limit set to determine the quantity of a commodity that can be imported into a country. It is a trade restriction that the government puts in place to minimize the importation of a particular commodity over a given period.

Thus, voluntary export restraint (VER), and Import tariffs and quota restricts imports in a country.

24. (B) **25. (A)**

26. (D): Policies are standing plans that provide guidelines for decision making. They serve as thinking frameworks that set the parameters or constraints for making judgments. Judgment must be used within these restrictions. Depending on the policy, different levels of discretion may be allowed. Hence statement I is the incorrect.

27. (B)

28. (D): According to Michael Porter's Five Forces, an attractive industry has the following characteristics:

1. **Threat of intense segment rivalry:** A segment is unattractive if it already contains numerous, strong, or aggressive competitors. It's even more unattractive if fixed costs or exit barriers are high.
2. **Threat of new entrants:** The most attractive segment has high entry barriers, and low exit barriers, so few new firms can enter, while poor-performing firms can exit easily.
3. **Threat of substitute products.** A segment is unattractive when there are actual or potential substitutes for the product. If technology advances or competition increases in these substitute industries, prices and profits in the segment are likely to fall.
4. **Threat of buyer's growing bargaining power:** A segment is unattractive if the buyers possess strong or growing bargaining power. Buyer's bargaining power grows when the product or service is undifferentiated or when switching costs and effort is low.
5. **Threat of suppliers' growing bargaining power:** A segment is unattractive if the company's suppliers can raise prices or reduce quantity supplied. Suppliers tend to be powerful when the costs of switching suppliers are high, and when suppliers can go direct-to-consumer.

29. (A): VALS (Values, Attitudes, and Lifestyles) is a framework developed by Arnold Mitchell and his colleagues in the year 1978 at SRI International.

- The VALS is a system used for grouping consumers with the help of psychographic segmentation.
- It was developed in the 1970s and was inaugurated in 1978 by Mitchell at SRI International.

- The VALS places adult customers into one of the eight segments based on their responses to the questionnaire.
- The main scope of the VALS framework is the resources in the vertical dimension and primary motivation at the horizontal dimension.
- The people in the vertical dimension are based on the degree to which they are innovative and have enough resources like education, income, intelligence, self-control, energy, and leadership skills.
- At the top of the VALS framework are innovators, who have high resources that can have any of the 3 primary motivations.
- At the bottommost are the survivors who live within their means without primary motivation.

Below are the 8 types of consumer clusters defined in the VALS framework, which divides consumers according to their buying motivation behaviour.

1. **Innovators:** These consumers have the *highest incomes,* abundant resources as well as *high self-esteem.* These consumers indulge in *self-orientation.* In the VALS framework, innovators are located above the rectangle. Innovators have the confidence to experiment and *take new information.*
2. **Thinkers:** These consumers have a tendency towards analysis. Consumers have *high resources* and are generally motivated by new ideas. They have enough knowledge about *social change and new ideas.* Thinkers choose traditional knowledgeable pursuits. They *plan and research before taking any decision.*
3. **Believers:** Believers are the consumers who have low resources and are motivated by ideals. They believe in faith and spirituality. Thinkers are *conservative* who *purchase established brands and local products.*
4. **Achievers:** These consumers have high resources and are motivated by their achievements. Such people are work-oriented and get *satisfaction from their work and families.* Achievers respect the authority and are politically conservative. They *prefer services* and products that *show off their growth to their peers.*
5. **Striver:** Strivers are low-resource group consumers, they get highly motivated by their achievements. Their values are just like achievers but *strivers have less resources as compared to achievers.*
6. **Experiencers:** Experiencers have high resources who get *motivated by self-expression.* Experiencers are the *youngest* in all the segments with an *age of 25.* They have the *highest energy* and take part in social activities. They spend heavily on fast foods, clothing, and new products and services.
7. **Makers:** Makers have low resources and are motivated by self-expression. These consumers have self-sufficiency. Makers focus on work, family and have little interest in the world. They *appreciated* functional and practical products.
8. **Survivors:** They are the consumers with the lowest income. They have so few resources that they cannot be included in any group thus they lie below the rectangle. Survivors are the oldest segment of age 61. They have limited means and are brand-loyal.

30. (C): As per Indian Income Tax Act,

Taxable Allowances are:

- Dearness allowance
- Entertainment allowance
- Overtime allowance
- City compensatory allowance
- Interim allowance
- Project allowance
- Tiffin/meals allowance

- Cash allowance
- Non-practicing allowance
- Warden allowance
- Servant allowance

Partly-Taxable Allowances are:

- HRA
- Fixed medical allowance
- Special allowance

Tax-exempt allowances

- Govt. employees posted abroad
- Sumptuary allowance
- Allowance for UNO employees
- City compensatory allowance

31. (D): Marris proposed that a sound financial policy will be based on at least three financial ratios, which set the limit for the firm's growth. These are debt-equity ratio, liquidity ratio, and retained profit ratio.

- **Debt equity ratio:** This is the ratio between borrowed capital and owners' capital. This ratio indicates the financial strength of a firm.
- **Liquidity ratio:** This is the ratio between current assets and current liabilities. Liquidity ratio indicates the coverage of current assets by current liabilities.
- **Retention ratio:** It is the ratio between retained profits and total profits. The retained profits are that portion of the net profit, that is not distributed as dividend among shareholders. A high retention implies that more funds are available to the firm.

32. (C) **33. (A)**

34. (C): A company's breakeven point is the point at which its sales exactly cover its expenses.

Fixed Costs ÷ (Price – Variable Costs) = Breakeven Point in Units.

35. (B) **36. (D)**

37. (A): The following details about a company are available with us:

Current Stock price = ₹ 80

Current dividend (D_0) = ₹ 4

Growth rate = 10%

Floatation cost = 8%

The cost of equity will be calculated as follows:

$$r_e = \frac{D_1}{P_0(1-f)} + g$$

$$r_e = \frac{4}{80(1-8\%)} + 10\%$$

$$r_e = \frac{1}{20(0.92)} + 0.10$$

$$r_e = \frac{1}{18.4} + 0.10$$

$$r_e = 0.0543 + 0.10$$

$$r_e = 15.43\%$$

38. (D): The concept of risk-return tradeoff represents a balance between low-risk and high potential return. It is a tradeoff that an investor must carefully consider between risk and return while weighing investment decisions. For example, in the case of a business dealing with working capital management, the fewer inventories kept, the higher the expected return (since fewer current assets are tied up); however, there is increased risk of running out of stock and thus losing potential customers and revenues. Taking on some risk is the price of achieving returns. The greater the risk, the greater the expected return, although an investor can never truly predict with absolute certainty the outcome of any financial or investment decision.

39. (C)

40. (B):

Negotiation rounds of WTO	**Started in**	**Lasted until**
Uruguay Round	1986	1994
Geneva Round	1955	1956
Kennedy Round	1964	**1967**
Doha Round	2001	
Tokyo Round	1973	

There have been nine rounds of trade negotiations since the Second World War. The list of WTO rounds (initially as GATT) is mentioned below:

- **Geneva Round (April 1947):** GATT was signed.
- **Doha Round (November 2001):** development of the developing and lesser developed countries at the heart of the trade negotiations
- **Uruguay Round (September 1986):** WTO was created, tariffs and agricultural subsidies were reduced.
- **Tokyo Round (September 1973):** Tariff, Non-Tariff measures discussed.
- **Kennedy Round (May 1964):** Tariff Concessions and Anti-Dumping covered.
- **Dillion round (September 1960):** Tariff Concessions.
- **Geneva II Round (January 1956):** Japan was admitted and tariff reductions.
- **Torquay Round (September 1950):** Cut in tariff levels.
- **Annecy Round (April 1949):** Tariff Concessions discussed.

41. (B): According to Section 12(3) of the Sale of Goods Act, 1930, a warranty, is a stipulation collateral to the main purpose of the contract, the breach of which gives rise to a claim for damages but not to a right to reject the goods and treat the contract as repudiated. In other words, warranty is a stipulation which is not essential to the main purpose of the contract i.e., it is of a subsidiary or collateral nature.

If there is a breach of warranty, the buyer cannot repudiate the contract, but he can only claim damages from the seller.

In the case discussed above if the buyer had asked for a good car and while selling the car the dealer said that it could run for 15 km per liter of petrol. But it was discovered that it could run only 12 km per liter of petrol. Here, the statement made by the seller would amount to a warranty and the buyer could not terminate the contract and he was entitled to claim damages only.

42. (D): An audit program, also called an audit plan, is an action plan that documents what procedures an auditor will follow to validate that an organization is in conformance with compliance regulations. The goal of an audit program is to create a framework that is detailed enough for any outside auditor to understand what official examinations have been completed, what conclusions have been reached and what the reasoning is behind each conclusion.

43. (C): When a price ceiling is set below the equilibrium price, **quantity demanded will exceed quantity supplied**, and excess demand or shortages will result. When a price floor is set above the equilibrium price, the quantity supplied will exceed the quantity demanded, and excess supply or surpluses will result. The **Shortage of the commodity and black-marketing** economy drives out legitimate industries that can't compete with the lower costs of illegal operations. Some **black market** players deliberately create **shortages in legal goods** to force people to purchase from them. The tax-free nature of the black market means the **government loses revenue**.

44. (C): Banks can't lend out all the deposits they collect, or they wouldn't have funds to pay out to depositors. Therefore, they keep primary and secondary reserves.

Primary reserves consist of cash on hand in the bank and deposits owed to it by other banks. These are also called the legal reserves. From this cash on hand tellers are able to meet customer demands for withdrawals, exchanges, and loans. Any excess reserves may be invested in larger banks in the form of the loans; in the United States these are called federal funds. Primary Reserve also called "First line of Defense".

Assets invested in short-term marketable securities, usually Treasury bills and short-term government securities. Legal reserve kept in a Central Reserve Bank don't earn interest, but secondary reserves are a source of supplemental liquidity. These earn interest and can be used to adjust a bank's reserve position. If loan demand is slow, deposit funds often are invested in short-term securities that are easily converted to cash. Secondary reserves are not listed as a separate balance sheet item. Secondary Reserve is also called "Second line of Defense".

45. (C): When a monopoly practices, perfect price discrimination (PPD) the firm knows what each customer is willing to pay and charges them exactly that amount. When this happens, the monopoly gains the entirety of the surplus for every transaction.

Consumer surplus is the difference between the price that customers pay and the price they're willing to pay. When the monopoly practices PPD they are taking that surplus away from every customer. So, option (C) is correct.

46. (B)

47. (B): Amount Payable Under Direct Tax Vivad Se Vishwas Scheme

Nature of Tax Arrear	Amount payable on / before 31.12.2020	Amount payable on / after 01.01.2021 but before last date [yet to be notified]
Quantum appeals, writ, SLP, DRP objections, revision and specified proceedings Where the 'tax arrears' is the aggregate amount of 'disputed tax', interest chargeable or charged on such disputed tax or penalty leviable or levied on such disputed tax	Disputed tax (100%)	Disputed tax + Further 10% of Disputed tax [if 10% of disputed tax exceeds aggregate amount of interest and penalty on such disputed tax, the excess shall be ignored for the purpose of computation of amount payable under this Act]

48. (C): Effect size is a statistical concept that measures the strength of the relationship between two variables on a numeric scale. For instance, if we have data on the height of men and women and we notice that, on average, men are taller than women, the difference between the height of men and the height of women is known as the effect size. The greater the effect size, the greater the height difference between men and women will be. Statistic effect size helps us in determining if the difference is real or if it is due to a change of factors. In hypothesis testing, effect size, power, sample size, and critical significance level are related to each other.

49. (B)

50. (B): The mean, median, mode, percentiles, range, variance, and standard deviation are the most commonly used numerical measures for quantitative data

The standard error is a statistical term that measures the accuracy with which a sample distribution represents a population by using standard deviation.

In statistics, a sample mean deviates from the actual mean of a population; this deviation is the standard error of the mean.

The standard error tells you how accurate the **mean** of any given sample from that population is likely to be compared to the true population mean.

When the standard error increases, *i.e.*, the means are more spread out, it becomes more likely that any given mean is an inaccurate representation of the true population means.

In cluster sampling, researchers divide a population into smaller groups known as clusters. They then randomly select among these clusters to form a sample. Cluster sampling is a method of probability sampling that is often used to study large populations, particularly those that are widely geographically dispersed.

The normal distribution is symmetrical, bell-shaped distribution in which the mean, median, and mode are all equal. It is a central component of inferential statistics.

Therefore, the standard error is a statistical measure of the extent to which a sample mean is likely to differ from the population mean.

51. (B): Budget line: The budget line is a graphical delineation of all possible combinations of the two commodities that can be bought with provided income and cost so that the price of each of these combinations is equivalent to the monetary earnings of the customer.

Utility analysis: It investigates consumer behaviour, especially market purchases, based on the satisfaction of wants and needs (that is, utility) generated from the consumption of a good.

Demand curve analysis: The demand curve is a graphical representation of the relationship between the price of a good or service and the quantity demanded for a given period of time.

Indifference curve analysis: An indifference curve is a graphical representation of a combined products that gives similar kind of satisfaction to a consumer thereby making them indifferent. Every point on the indifference curve shows that an individual or a consumer is indifferent between the two products as it gives him the same kind of utility.

Consumer equilibrium: Consumer's Equilibrium means a state of maximum satisfaction. A situation where a consumer spends his given income purchasing one or more commodities so that he gets maximum satisfaction and has no urge to change this level of consumption, given the prices of commodities, is known as the consumer's equilibrium.

52. (B): Porter's Five Forces is a framework for analyzing a company's competitive environment. It is frequently used guideline for evaluating the competitive forces that influence a variety of business sectors. It was created by Harvard Business School professor Michael E. Porter in 1979 and has since become an important tool for managers. These forces include:

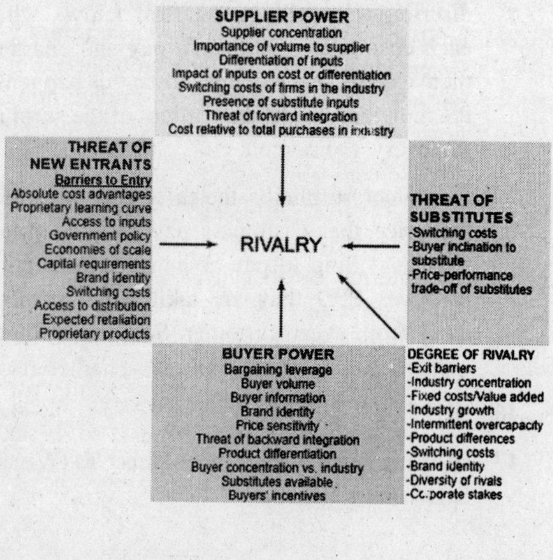

53. (C): Call money rate is the rate at which short term funds are borrowed and lent in the money market. The duration of the call money loan is 1 day. Banks resort to these types of loans to fill the asset liability mismatch, comply with the statutory CRR and SLR requirements and to meet the sudden demand of funds. RBI, banks, primary dealers etc are the participants of the call money market. Demand and supply of liquidity affect the call money rate. A tight liquidity condition leads to a rise in call money rate and vice versa.

54. (A): Correlation Coefficient is a statistical concept, which helps in establishing a relation between predicted and actual values obtained in a statistical experiment. The calculated value of the correlation coefficient explains the exactness between the predicted and actual values.

Correlation Coefficient value always lies between –1 to +1. If correlation coefficient value is positive, then there is a similar and identical relation between the two variables. Else it indicates the dissimilarity between the two variables.

55. (D): A funds flow statement explains the changes in a company's working capital. It considers the inflows and outflow of funds (source of funds and application of funds) for a particular period. The statement helps in analysing the changes in a company's financial position between two balance sheet periods. The statement helps in determining how the funds are being used. As a result, analysts can assess the company's fund flow in the future. Thus, statement D is incorrect.

56. (C): Cronbach's alpha coefficient measures the internal consistency, or reliability, of a set of survey items. Use this statistic to help determine whether a collection of items consistently measures the same characteristic. Cronbach's alpha quantifies the level of agreement on a standardized 0 to 1 scale. Higher values indicate higher agreement between items.

Cronbach alpha value less than 0.30 indicates non-reliability of research instrument. The values above 0.70 is considered as reliable.

57. (D): An offshore banking unit (OBU) is a bank shell branch, located in another international financial center. For instance,.a London-based bank with a branch located in Delhi. Offshore banking units make loans in the Eurocurrency market when they accept deposits from foreign banks and other OBUs. Eurocurrency simply refers to money held in banks located outside of the country which issues the currency.

58. (A) **59. (C)**

60. (A): Marginal cost is an important concept in managerial accounting, as it can help an organization optimize its production through economies of scale. A company can maximize its profits by producing to where marginal cost (MC) equals marginal revenue (MR). Fixed costs are constant regardless of production levels, so higher production leads to a lower fixed cost per unit as the total is allocated over more units. Variable costs change based on production levels, so producing more units will add more variable costs. Companies must be mindful of when increasing production necessitates results in step costs due to changes in relevant ranges (*i.e.*, automation, additional machinery or storage space needed). Thus, the statement C is incorrect.

61. (A)

62. (C): Quantitative research is expressed in numbers and graphs. It is used to test or confirm theories and assumptions. This type of research can be used to establish generalizable facts about a topic. Qualitative research is expressed in words. It is used to understand concepts, thoughts or experiences. This type of research enables you to gather in-depth insights on topics that are not well understood. The choice between quantitative and qualitative research depends on following differences:

Quantitative Research	Qualitative Research
Focuses on testing hypotheses and theories	Focuses on exploring ideas and formulating a theory or hypothesis
Analyzed through math and statistical analysis	Analyzed by summarizing, categorizing and interpreting
Mainly expressed in numbers, graphs and tables	Mainly expressed in words
Requires many respondents	Requires few respondents
Closed (multiple choice) questions	Open-ended questions
Key terms: testing, measurement, objectivity, replicability	Key terms: understanding, context, complexity, subjectivity

Further, Cronbach's alpha is a measure of internal consistency, that is, how closely related a set of items are as a group. It is considered to be a measure of scale reliability. Thus, statement (*b*) is incorrect.

63. (D): Actual Output = 2000

Standard			Actual		
Qty. of Material	Rate	Amt.	Qty. of Material	Rate	Amt.
800* kg	2.5	2000	825 kg	2.70	2227.5

*1000 units ——— 400kg

Std. qty. required for 1 unit = 400/1000 kg

Std. qty. for actual output

= 400/1000 × 2000 = 800 kg

Material Cost Variance (MCV)

= Std. Cost – Actual Cost

= 2000 – 2227.5 = 227.5 (Adverse)

Material Price Variance (MPV)

= (Std. Price – Actual price) × Actual Qty.

= (2.5 – 2.7) × 825 = 165 (Adverse)

Material Usage Variance (MUV)

= (Std. Qty. – Actual Qty.) × Std. Price

= (800 – 825) × 2.5 = 62.50 (Adverse)

To check,

MCV = MPV + MUV

= 165 (Adverse) + 62.5 (Adverse)

= 227.5 (Adverse)

64. (A): In finance, a foreign exchange swap (forex swap, or FX swap in short) is a simultaneous purchase and sale of identical amounts of one currency for another with two different value dates and may use foreign exchange derivatives. A forex swap allows sums of a certain currency to be used to fund charges designated in another currency without acquiring foreign exchange risk. It permits companies that have funds in different currencies to manage them efficiently.

65. (B): The Countercyclical Capital Buffer (CCyB) is designed to counter procyclicality in the financial system. When cyclical systemic risk is judged to be increasing, institutions should accumulate capital to create buffers that strengthen the resilience of the banking sector during periods of stress when losses materialise. This will help maintain the supply of credit to the economy and dampen the downswing of the financial cycle. The CCyB can also help dampen excessive credit growth during the upswing of the financial cycle.

66. (A) **67. (D)**

68. (D): The arm's length price in relation to an international transaction (or specified domestic transaction) shall be determined by any of the following methods, being the most appropriate method, having regard to the nature of transaction or class of transaction or class of associated persons or functions performed by such persons or such other relevant factors as the Board may prescribe, namely:

- comparable uncontrolled price method;
- resale price method;
- cost plus method;
- profit split method;
- transactional net margin method;
- such other method as may be prescribed by the Board.

In a slump sale, the company's assets and liabilities are sold as is without any valuations being placed on them. Companies may choose to sell their assets in this manner by entering into a Business Transfer Agreement by Section 230-232 of the Companies Act, 2013.

69. (B) **70. (A)**

71. (A): Types of Entry Modes in International Business:

(*a*) **Exporting** is the act of selling goods and services produced domestically in other countries is known as exporting. Exports are classified into two types:

- Direct exports are transactions in which a company sells its products directly to a buyer in another country.
- Indirect exports include hiring a third party's skills to facilitate the transaction.

(*b*) **Licensing:** In this mode of entry, a manufacturer from the home country rents the right to their intellectual properties, such as technology, copyrights, brand names, and so on, to a manufacturer from a foreign country. To obtain the license, you must pay a set fee. Lessees are manufacturers who lease, and licensees are manufacturers from the country that receives the license.

(*c*) **Franchising:** A separate company known as the franchisee operates under the brand of a different organisation known as the franchisor in this model.

(*d*) **Management Contracts:** A company essentially rents out its knowledge or know-how to a government or business in the form of individuals who enter the foreign setting and manage the business under management contracts and do contract manufacturing. This strategy of entering international markets is frequently used with a new facility after a company has been seized by the national government or when a business is experiencing difficulties.

(*e*) **Foreign Direct Investment:** A corporation can enter a foreign market through foreign direct investment by investing significantly there. Foreign direct investment can be used to enter the global market through mergers and acquisitions, joint ventures, and greenfield investments. This strategy is appropriate when there is sufficient demand, market size, or market growth potential to justify the investment.

(*f*) **Joint Endeavors:** A joint venture is one of the preferred ways to enter the global market for companies that don't mind sharing their brand, knowledge, and expertise.

72. (D): Anti-Competitive Agreement Prohibition: Section 3 (1) of the Act states that:

"No enterprise shall enter into any agreement with respect of production, supply, distribution, storage, acquisition or control of goods/provision of services, which causes or is likely to cause appreciable adverse effect on competition within India"

There are two kinds of anti-competitive agreements viz.

I. Horizontal Anti-Competitive Agreements [Section 3(3)]: They are agreements between parties in the same line of production. Types of Horizontal Anti-Competitive Agreements are:

- Price-Fixing Agreements [Section 3(3)(a)]
- Limiting Or Controlling Production And Investment [Section 3(3)(b)]
- Market Allocation And Sharing [Section 3(3)(c)]
- Bid Rigging Or Collusive Bidding [Section 3(3)(d)]

II. Vertical Anti-Competitive Agreements [Section 3(4)]: Vertical anti-competitive agreements are entered between two or more companies each of which operates, at a different level of production or distribution chain, and relating to conditions under which the parties may purchase, sale or resell certain goods or services. Types of Vertical anti-competitive agreements are:

- Tie-In Arrangement
- Exclusive Supply Arrangement
- Exclusive Distribution Arrangement
- Refusal To Deal
- Resale Price Maintenance

73. **(B)**

74. **(D):** The LLP is a separate legal entity, is liable to the full extent of its assets but liability of the partners is limited to their agreed contribution in the LLP. Hence, D statement is incorrect.

75. **(D)** **76.** **(B)** **77.** **(D)**

78. **(C)** **79.** **(B)** **80.** **(D)**

81. **(A):** Elasticities of Demand — Income elasticity of demand is the degree of responsiveness of changes in quantity demanded of goods to the changes in consumer's income.

Income Elasticity of Demand = % Change in Demand Quantity / % Change in Income of Consumer

- **Normal goods:** Normal goods are commodities with positive income elasticity of demand. It describes a situation where a commodity's demand increases with an increase in consumer income and decreases with a decrease in consumer income. Thus, Income elasticity of Normal Goods is Greater than zero or Positively Elastic.
- **Inferior goods:** Inferior goods are those goods whose demand decreases with increase in income of consumer. That' why income elasticity of inferior goods is negative and less than one which describes a situation in which demand for a commodity increases as consumer income increases and drops when consumer income decreases.
- **Luxurious commodities:** Luxury goods are directly correlated with consumer income. Consumers buy more of these things when their income rises and vice versa. Income elasticity of these goods is more than one.
- **Necessities:** It reflects the condition in which increased household income has little effect on the production of commodities. We call these products "necessary goods." Income Elasticity of Necessities goods will be between zero and one which is unitary.

82. **(D):** Assumptions for Simple Linear Regression

- **Linearity:** The relationship between \(X\) and \(Y\) must be linear. Check this assumption by examining a scatterplot of *x* and *y*.
- **Independence of errors:** There is not a relationship between the residuals and the \(Y\) variable; in other words, \(Y\) is independent of errors. Check this

assumption by examining a scatterplot of "residuals versus fits"; the correlation should be approximately 0. In other words, there should not look like there is a relationship.

- **Normality of errors:** The residuals must be approximately normally distributed. Check this assumption by examining a normal probability plot; the observations should be near the line. You can also examine a histogram of the residuals; it should be approximately normally distributed.
- **Equal variances:** The variance of the residuals is the same for all values of \(X\).Check this assumption by examining the scatterplot of "residuals versus fits"; the variance of the residuals should be the same across all values of the *x*-axis. If the plot shows a pattern (*e.g.*, bowtie or megaphone shape), then variances are not consistent, and this assumption has not been met.

83. **(A):** Tax holiday is a period when people or companies do not have to pay any tax or not as much tax as usual on goods, services, or profits. It is covered under Section 80 IA of Income Tax Act 1961.

Section 80 IA deduction of the Income Tax Act provides a tax deduction for certain Industrial Undertakings involved in Infrastructure Development. Section 80IA provides income deduction for enterprises in the business of developing, operating or maintaining the following:

- Infrastructure Facilities
- Telecommunication Services
- Industrial Parks
- Reconstruction of Power Plant
- Distribution of Natural Gas

84. **(A):** The substitution effect is the decrease in sales for a product that can be attributed to consumers switching to cheaper alternatives when its price rises. When the price of a product or service increases but the buyer's income stays the same, the substitution effect generally kicks in. The substitution effect is strongest for products that are close substitutes. An increase in consumer spending power can offset the substitution effect.

85. **(B):** Markov analysis is a method used to forecast the value of a variable whose predicted value is influenced only by its current state. The primary advantages of Markov analysis are simplicity and out-of-sample forecasting accuracy. Markov analysis is not very useful for explaining events, and it cannot be the true model of the underlying situation in most cases. Markov analysis is useful for financial speculators, especially momentum investors.

86. **(D):** Section 2(51) of the Act defines Key Managerial Personnel (KMP). It states that the KMP of a company means:

- Chief executive officer, manager or managing director
- Company Secretary
- Whole-time director
- Chief financial officer
- Such other officers, designated by the Board as KMP but are not more than one level below the directors in whole-time employment
- Such other officer as may be prescribed

87. **(A):** Defensive marketing refers to the actions of a brand, especially a market leader, to protect its brand and maintain its position as a market leader. If a brand fails to maintain its position, then it might lose some of its customers to the competitors.

Types of Defensive marketing:

- **Flank defense:** It is a competitive marketing strategy used by a market leader to identify and strengthen its own weak points, market segments where it is under-performing before a smaller rival can mount an attack against it.
- **Preemptive defense:** This strategy works well when the market is segmented and one of the segments is not catered well by the competitor. Market leaders use this strategy to gain an advantage over competitors and upset industry balance.
- **Mobile defense:** The market leader shifts domain to new territories that will serve as a future center for defense and offense. It can be done through Market broadening *i.e.*, shift focus from current product to generic product, and Market diversification *i.e.*, shift into unrelated industries.
- **Contractor defense:** It is a competitive strategy in which a market leader withdraws from a market segment in which it is not strong in order to concentrate on other market segments where it is strong. It is also known as strategic withdrawal.
- **Counteroffensive defense:** This strategy is used when the market leader is attacked by the other company. This involves that the market leader will attack the attacker in its main territories so that the attacker will have to put back some resources for the attacked territories and will have to divert its attention from launching an attack on the market leader.

Therefore, Counter feiting strategy is used by marketer to maintain its market share.

88. (D) **89. (A)**

90. (A): A search engine is a software program that helps people find the information they are looking for online using keywords or phrases.

Web 1.0 was all about fetching, and reading information. Web 2.0 is all about reading, writing, creating, and interacting with the end user. It was famously called the participative social web. Web 3.0 is the third generation of the World Wide Web, and is a vision of a decentralized web which is currently a work in progress. It is all about reading, writing, and owning.

Thus, option (*a*) and (*e*) are not the main platforms for social media?

91. (B) **92. (D)** **93. (C)**
94. (C) **95. (A)** **96. (C)**
97. (A) **98. (D)** **99. (D)**
100. (C)

Previous Years' Paper (Solved)

National Testing Agency (NTA)

UGC-NET Junior Research Fellowship & Assistant Professor Eligibility Exam

COMMERCE, June–2021

(Online exam held on 25-11-2021)

PAPER-II

Note: *This paper contains* ***hundred (100)*** *objective type questions of* ***two (2)*** *marks each.* ***All questions*** *are* ***compulsory****.*

1. Which is the most potent driver of business transformation during Covid-19 pandemic?
A. Ethical consciousness
B. Scale economies and pricing power
C. Technology adoption and innovation
D. Supply chain logistics and government interventions

2. Counter Vailing Duties (CVD) are often imposed on imports to offset the impact of:
A. Predatory pricing
B. Export subsidies
C. Dumping
D. Low cost financing

3. To prevent opportunistic takeover of domestic firms amid Covid-19 pandemic. Foreign Direct Investment (FDI) from countries that share borders with India is allowed through:
A. Automatic route
B. Government route
C. FIPB route
D. DPIIT route

4. Factor conditions in Michael Porter's competitive advantage of Nations include:
A. Market size
B. Demand conditions
C. Internationally competitive suppliers
D. Skilled labour and scientific knowledge

5. In case the purchasing company agrees to act as the agent of the vendor for collection of the book debts, in the books of the purchasing company, the amount of debtors should be credited to:
A. Vendor's debtors account
B. Vendor's suspense account
C. Debtors account
D. Creditors account

6. When the value of "Investment in subsidiary" in the holding company's balance sheet is more than the book value of the net assets acquired, the difference represents:
A. Capital reserve on consolidation
B. Goodwill on consolidation
C. Minority interest
D. Post acquisition profit

7. The basic method of valuing human assets is:
A. Adjustment B. Amortization
C. Capitalization D. Quasi equity

8. X and Y are partners, sharing profits and losses in the ratio of 4 : 3. They admit Z into the partnership for 1/5th share. X and Y decide to share future profits in the ratio of 2 : 1. What is the sacrificing ratio of X and Y?
A. 4 : 3 B. 13 : 8
C. 8 : 13 D. 4 : 17

9. The value of the firm in wealth maximisation objective is measured by:
A. Present value of all expected future cash flows

B. All expected future cash flows
C. Present value of all expected future profits
D. All expected future profits

10. For a decline in price, total revenue declines if the demand of the product is:

A. Inelastic B. Elastic
C. Unitary elastic D. Zero elastic

11. In Cobb-Douglas production function, $Q = AK^{\alpha}L^{\beta}$ increasing returns to scale occurs when:

A. $\alpha + \beta > 1$ B. $K + L > 1$
C. $\alpha + \beta < 1$ D. $K + L < 1$

12. The extreme case of non-price competition in an Oligopoly is:

A. Formation of cartels
B. Interdependent decision-making
C. Attaining economies of scale
D. Formation of duopoly

13. Pecking order theory in finance is based on the assertion of:

A. Asymmetric information between managers and investors
B. Symmetric information between managers and investors
C. Outside information
D. Asymmetric information among investors only

14. If a project cost is ₹ 40,000. Its stream of earning before depreciation and tax during first year through five years is expected to be ₹ 10,000, ₹ 12,000, ₹ 14,000, ₹ 16,000 and ₹ 20,000. Assume a 50% tax rate and depreciation on straight line basis; project's ARR is:

A. 14.40% B. 72%
C. 16% D. 55.56%

15. According to the theory of dividend, the firm should follow its investment policy of accepting all positive NPV projects and paying out dividends if and only if, funds are available:

A. Bird in hand theory
B. Investor rationality theory
C. 100 per cent retention theory
D. Residual theory

16. In Securitisation when no assets are acquired and the collateral is fixed for the life of the asset, the type of a structure is called as:

A. Revolving structure
B. Amortized structure
C. Collateralized structure
D. Self-liquidating strucutre

17. For a very large sample size the ratio between $SE_{\bar{X}}$ and σ is 8 : 40. Determine the sample size *n*:

A. 25 B. 5
C. 4 D. 16

18. For a given set of paired data, the correlation and regression coefficients have been calculated as being equal to *r*, *bxy* and *byx* respectively. Now, each of the values of the *x* series is divided by 5. What effect does it have on each of these co-efficients?

A. The three co-efficients remain unchanged
B. There is no change in *r* but by *x* changes to *byx*/5 and *bxy* changes to 5*bxy*
C. Each of the co-efficients will be reduced to one fourth of its value.
D. There is no change in *r* but *byx* changes to 5*byx* and *bxy* changes to *bxy*/5

19. Which of the following statement is correct?

A. Co-efficient of variance = $\frac{\sigma}{\bar{X}} \times 100$
B. If value in a series are negative, the standard deviation is also negative
C. If value in a series multiplied by σ, the variance would be multiplied by 36
D. Standard deviation is equal to square of variance.

20. For a poisson distribution variable X, $P(X = 0) = 2P(X = 1)$, its standard deviation would be:

A. $\sqrt{2}$ B. 0.5
C. $\sqrt{0.5}$ D. 2

21. A test that contains a fair sample of the tasks and skills actually needed for the job in question is:
A. Construct validity
B. Content validity
C. Test validity
D. Criterion validity

22. Which among the following is not a primary determinant of organizational structure?
A. Chain and span
B. Capacity and lower needs
C. Power and control
D. Differentiation and integration

23. An act in a way that results in the greatest good for the greatest number is:
A. The golden rule
B. The utilitarian principle
C. The four way test
D. Kant's categorical imperative

24. People repeat behaviours that bring them satisfaction and pleasure and stop those that bring them dissatisfaction or pain is known as:
A. Law of exercise B. Law of redo
C. Law of effect D. Law of readiness

25. Which one of the following statements is true about under the Basel I Accord, BCBS, fixed the minimum requirement of capital fund for banks at?
A. 8 per cent of the total risk weighted assets
B. 9 per cent of the total risk weighted assets
C. 10 per cent of the total risk weighted assets
D. 1000 crore

26. Which of the following statements is correct relating to Indian Financial System?
A. RBI has direct supervision over depositories and mutual funds.
B. Monetary control is exercised through cash reserve ratio and statutory liquidity ratio.
C. Primary dealers mainly deal in shares, mutual fund units.
D. The decrease in statutory liquidity ratio contracts the credit creation.

27. Which one of the following is not one of the advantages of Derivatives market?
A. Leveraging increases risk
B. They enhance liquidity in the market for underlying assets
C. They represent a form of insurance against risks
D. They reduce price volatility

28. Which one of the following statements is not true about Indian Money Market?
A. Non-Banking Finance Companies (NBFCs) are financial institutions that constitute organised component of money market.
B. Money market mutual funds are allowed to sell units to corporates and individuals.
C. A Well-developed money market is essential for a modern economy.
D. In the Indian Money Market, the predominant place is enjoyed by government and semi-government securities.

29. Which of the following is not true while determining length of distribution channel?
A. The larger the market size, the longer the channel.
B. If the average lot size is large, it is better to have a longer channel.
C. If the product and the market require a high level of service, it is advisable to keep a shorter channel.
D. If customers shop for an assortment of products, it demands for a water channel of distribution.

30. Which of the following can be categorized as people processing services?
A. Health care B. Legal services
C. Education D. Transportation

31. SBUs or products that have lost their position of leadership and are in the low growth markets, are known as:
A. Star B. Problem child
C. Dog D. Cash cow

32. Which of the following is not a valid basis for market segmentation?
A. Customer Based Segmentation
B. Technology Oriented Segmentation
C. Competition Related Segmentation
D. Product Related Segmentation

33. Which one of the following statements is a promissory note?
A. I promise to pay Q ₹ 7,000, 7 days after my marriage.
B. On demand, I promise to pay B or bearer ₹ 5,000
C. I promise to pay ₹ 5,000 on C's death provided C leaves with me enough money to pay that sum.
D. I acknowledge to be indebted to you for ₹ 10,000 to be paid on demand for value received.

34. A claim for 'quantum meruit' cannot succeed:
A. When a divisible contract is partly performed.
B. When an indivisible contract for a lumpsum is partly performed.
C. When a contract is discovered to be un-enforceable due to some technical defect.
D. In the case of breach of contract, the aggrieved party can claim reasonable compensation for what he has done under the contract.

35. The first offence for infringement of copyright can be for a maximum of imprisonment for a term of:
A. 6 months and a fine of ₹ 20,000
B. 3 years and a fine of ₹ 50,000
C. 3 years and a fine of ₹ 2,00,000
D. 1 year and a fine of ₹ 3,00,000

36. Which one of the following conditions does not constitute a valid agency by necessity?
A. There should have been actual and definite commercial necessity for the agent to act promptly.
B. The agent should have acted bonafide and for the benefit of the principal.
C. The agent should have adopted the most reasonable and practicable course under the circumstances.
D. Destruction of the subject matter of the contract of agency.

37. If assessee is engaged in the business of growing and manufacturing tea in India, the non-agricultural income in that case be:
A. 40% the income from such business
B. 25% the income from such business
C. 60% the income from such business
D. 75% the income from such business

38. AMT provisions are applicable on:
A. Corporate assessee
B. Non Corporate assessee
C. HUF
D. An Individual

39. X, an employee of the private company, gets ₹ 30,000 p.m. basic salary and entitled to ₹ 1,500 p.m. as entertainment allowance. What are the deductions u/s 16(ii) from gross salary in respect of entertainment allowance?
A. ₹ 5,000 B. ₹ 18,000
C. ₹ 72,000 D. Nil

40. Which of the following provident fund is approved by the provident fund commissioner?
A. Statutory provident fund
B. Recognised provident fund
C. Unrecognised provident fund
D. Public provident fund

41. Which of the following institutions are included in the 'World Bank Group'?
(*a*) International Finance Corporation
(*b*) International Monetary Fund
(*c*) World Trade Organization
(*d*) Multilateral Investment Guarantee Agency
(*e*) International Development Association

Choose the correct answer from the options given below:
A. (*a*), (*b*) and (*c*) only
B. (*a*), (*b*) and (*d*) only
C. (*a*), (*b*), (*d*) and (*e*) only
D. (*a*), (*d*) and (*e*) only

42. Corporate social responsibility is the continuing commitment by business to behave ethically and contribute to:

(*a*) Political awareness, social security and inclusion.

(*b*) Public health, education and literacy.

(*c*) Maintaining ecological balances and protecting environment.

(*d*) Gender diversity, profiteering and market controlling.

(*e*) Rendering, Sponsoring and donating to social and charitable activities.

Choose the correct answer from the options given below:

A. (*a*), (*b*) and (*d*) only

B. (*b*), (*c*) and (*e*) only

C. (*c*), (*d*) and (*e*) only

D. (*a*), (*b*) and (*c*) only

43. Firm characteristics that help managers identify core compentencies include:

(*a*) Potential access to wide variety of markets

(*b*) Significantly contribute to the perceived customer benefits

(*c*) Value accretive and non competitive

(*d*) Distinctive and difficult for competitors to imitate

Choose the most appropriate answer from the options given below:

A. (*a*), (*b*) and (*c*) only

B. (*b*), (*c*) and (*d*) only

C. (*a*), (*b*) and (*d*) only

D. (*a*), (*c*) and (*d*) only

44. Which of the following distinction(s) is/are not correct between public issue and rights issue?

(*a*) In public issue, applications for shares are invited from the general public and in rights issue, the shares are offered to existing shareholders.

(*b*) In public issue there is no question of any over-subscription and in rights issue the shares may be under subscribed or over subscribed leading to prorata allotment.

(*c*) The price of public issue is generally less than the market price and in rights issue, the price is deliberately made less than the market price.

(*d*) In a public issue, the communication of the issue is through prospects or advertisements and in rights issue the communication is between the company and the existing members of the company.

Choose the most appropriate answer from the options given below:

A. (*b*) only

B. (*d*) only

C. (*a*) and (*c*) only

D. (*c*) and (*d*) only

45. According to AS-2, which of the following costs should be included in valuing the inventories of a manufacturing company?

(*a*) Freight and insurance

(*b*) Carriage outwards

(*c*) Depreciation of factory plant

(*d*) General administrative overheads

Choose the most appropriate answer from the options given below:

A. (*a*) and (*d*) only

B. (*a*), (*b*) and (*d*) only

C. (*b*) and (*c*) only

D. (*a*) and (*c*) only

46. Which of the following rules stands true while preparing schedule of changes in working capital?

(*a*) An increase in current assets increases working capital.

(*b*) An increase in current assets decreases working capital.

(*c*) An increase in current liabilities decreases working capital.

(*d*) An increase in current liabilities increases working capital.

Choose the most appropriate answer from the options given below:

A. (*a*) and (*c*) only

B. (*a*) and (*d*) only

C. (*b*) and (*d*) only

D. (*a*), (*b*) and (*c*) only

47. Characteristics constituting the core of consumers rationality includes:

(*a*) Homogeneous expectations

(*b*) Non-satiation

(*c*) Selfish motive

(*d*) Clarity of preferences

(*e*) Possession of information

Choose the correct answer from the options given below:

A. (*a*), (*b*) and (*c*) only

B. (*b*), (*c*) and (*d*) only

C. (*a*), (*b*), (*c*) and (*d*) only

D. (*b*), (*c*), (*d*) and (*e*) only

48. Why is an indifference curve convex to the origin?

(*a*) Indifference curve slope downward to the right.

(*b*) Two commodities are imprefect substitutes.

(*c*) Declining marginal rate of substitution between commodities.

(*d*) Diminishing marginal utilities.

Choose the most appropriate answer from the options given below.

A. (*a*) and (*b*) only B. (*b*) and (*c*) only

C. (*c*) and (*d*) only D. (*a*) and (*d*) only

49. Financial crises takes the form of:

(*a*) Currency crisis

(*b*) Banking crisis

(*c*) Systematic financial crisis

(*d*) Foreign debt crisis

Choose the correct answer from the options given below:

A. (*a*), (*b*), (*c*) only

B. (*a*), (*b*), (*d*) only

C. (*b*), (*c*), (*d*) only

D. (*a*), (*b*), (*c*), (*d*) only

50. Following are the problems that mar an optimal international diversification:

(*a*) Unfavourable exchange rate movements

(*b*) Frictions in international markets

(*c*) Manipulation of security prices

(*d*) Unequal access to information

Choose the most appropriate answer from the options given below:

A. (*a*), (*b*), (*c*) only

B. (*b*), (*c*), (*d*) only

C. (*a*), (*c*), (*d*) only

D. (*a*), (*b*), (*c*), (*d*) only

51. Which of the following statement is correct about Mann-Whitney U-test?

(*a*) It is non parametric test.

(*b*) It requires that samples are independent.

(*c*) It can be used when populations involved are normally distributed.

(*d*) It is used to test the null hypothesis that the two populations are involved are identical.

(*e*) It is always a two tailed test.

Choose the correct answer from the options given below:

A. (*a*), (*b*), (*d*) only B. (*a*), (*c*), (*d*) only

C. (*a*), (*d*), (*e*) only D. (*a*), (*b*), (*e*) only

52. Which of the following are correct about complementary events?

(*a*) Mutually exclusive

(*b*) Independent

(*c*) Such that their probabilities add up to 1

(*d*) Collective exhaustive

Choose the most appropriate answer from the options given below:

A. (*a*), (*b*), (*c*) only

B. (*a*), (*b*), (*d*) only

C. (*b*), (*c*), (*d*) only

D. (*a*), (*c*), (*d*) only

53. Which of the following statements are correct about Chi-Square test?

(*a*) The only parameter of a Chi-Square distribution is its number of degrees of freedom.

(*b*) The null hypothesis in given Chi-Square test is rejected when calculated value of variable exceed its critical value.

(*c*) The rejection region in a goodness of fit test lies only in the right tail of the distribution.

(*d*) The Chi-Square test is a parametric test.
(*e*) At $\alpha = .05$ and V = 1 the critical value of χ^2 is equal to Z-value at the same level of significance.

Choose the most appropriate answer from the options given below:

A. (*b*), (*d*), (*e*) only
B. (*a*), (*c*), (*e*) only
C. (*a*), (*b*), (*c*) only
D. (*b*), (*c*), (*d*) only

54. The principles of management have the following distinct features:

(*a*) Flexibility
(*b*) Universal application
(*c*) Principles are relative, not absolute
(*d*) Based on situation

Choose the most appropriate answer from the options given below:

A. (*a*), (*b*) only B. (*b*), (*c*) only
C. (*a*), (*c*), (*d*) only D. (*a*), (*b*), (*c*), (*d*)

55. Use of interviews as a training needs assessment technique has the following advantages:

(*a*) Questions can be modified
(*b*) Easy to analyze
(*c*) Can explore unanticipated issues that come up
(*d*) Less time consuming

Choose the most appropriate answer from the options given below:

A. (*a*), (*b*) only
B. (*b*), (*c*) only
C. (*a*), (*c*) only
D. (*b*), (*c*), (*d*) only

56. The advantages of incentive payments are:

(*a*) Ease in the introduction of new machines
(*b*) Better utilization of equipment
(*c*) Reduced absenteeism and turnover
(*d*) Increased scrap

Choose the most appropriate answer from the options given below:

A. (*a*), (*b*) only B. (*b*), (*c*) only
C. (*b*), (*c*), (*d*) only D. (*a*), (*b*), (*c*) only

57. Which of the following forms may not result in credit risk?

(*a*) Principle and/or interest amount may not be repaid in the case of direct lending.
(*b*) In case of guarantees or letter of credit, fund may not be forth coming from the constituents upon crystallisation of the liability.
(*c*) Funds/Securities settlement may not be effected, in case of securities trading business.
(*d*) Provide information for determining adequacy of loan loss provision.

Choose the correct answer from the options given below:

A. (*a*), (*b*) and (*c*) only
B. (*a*), (*c*) and (*d*) only
C. (*b*) and (*c*) only
D. (*d*) only

58. Which of the following statements are false regarding electronic purse? Indicate the correct code.

(*a*) Retinal pattern verification
(*b*) Visual recognition
(*c*) No risk of bad payment
(*d*) Method of accepting payments with no cash float to manage and no risk of theft.

Choose the correct answer from the options given below:

A. (*a*), (*b*) and (*c*) only
B. (*b*), (*c*) and (*d*) only
C. (*a*) and (*b*) only
D. (*c*) and (*d*) only

59. Which of the following statements are the defects of Indian Money Market?

(*a*) Profitable Investment
(*b*) Dichotomy in Indian Money Market
(*c*) Financing Industry
(*d*) Diversity in interest rates

Choose the correct answer from the options given below:

A. (*a*), (*b*) and (*c*) only
B. (*b*) and (*c*) only

C. (*a*), (*b*) and (*d*) only
D. (*b*) and (*d*) only

60. Penetration pricing strategy delivers results:
(*a*) Where price quality association is weak
(*b*) When the product is perceived as a 'high technology' product
(*c*) When the market is characterised by intensive competition
(*d*) When the firm uses it as an entry strategy

Choose the most appropriate answer from the options given below:
A. (*b*), (*c*) only
B. (*a*), (*d*) only
C. (*a*), (*c*), (*d*) only
D. (*a*), (*b*), (*c*) only

61. Which of the following represents traditional logistics management approach?
(*a*) Independent inventory management efforts.
(*b*) Minimise firm costs.
(*c*) Amount of information sharing and monitoring limited to current processes.
(*d*) Small breadth of supplier base to increase coordination.

Choose the correct answer from the options given below:
A. (*a*), (*b*) only B. (*b*), (*c*) only
C. (*a*), (*c*), (*d*) only D. (*b*), (*c*), (*d*) only

62. Which of the following statements are false? Indicate the correct code.
(*a*) No company has to file any prescribed declaration before commencement of business.
(*b*) A company can ratify the contract entered into by the promoters with third parties on behalf of the company before its formation.
(*c*) The date mentioned in the certificate for commencement of business is taken as the date of birth of a public company.
(*d*) A private company has to file a "Settlement in lieu of prospectus" with the registrar.

Choose the correct answer from the options given below:
A. (*a*), (*b*) and (*d*) only
B. (*a*) and (*b*) only
C. (*b*), (*c*) and (*d*) only
D. (*c*) and (*d*) only

63. Which of the following are not the objectives of competition act, 2002?
(*a*) Ensure freedom of trade for other participants in incidental and connected markets.
(*b*) Provide a reasonable level of reliability and connect operation.
(*c*) Adhere to generally accepted security procedures.
(*d*) Protect the interests of consumers.

Choose the correct answer from the options given below:
A. (*a*), (*c*), (*d*) only
B. (*b*), (*c*), (*d*) only
C. (*a*), (*c*) only
D. (*b*), (*c*) only

64. Which of the following persons cannot use ITR-4?
(*a*) Who is director of a company
(*b*) Who has held any unlisted equity shares
(*c*) Who has any asset located outside India
(*d*) A firm (other than LLP) if assessee is a Resident
(*e*) Who has income from other sources

Choose the most appropriate answer from the options given below:
A. (*a*), (*b*), (*c*) only
B. (*a*), (*b*), (*d*) only
C. (*b*), (*d*), (*e*) only
D. (*c*), (*d*), (*e*) only

65. Which of the following losses are not deductible from business income?
(*a*) Loss sustained before the business is commenced.
(*b*) Lossess incurred in the closing down of the business.

(*c*) Loss incurred due to damage, destruction, etc., of capital assets.

(*d*) Loss of raw material and finished goods in transit.

(*e*) Loss of stock-in-trade due to enemy action.

Choose the correct answer from the options given below:

A. (*a*), (*b*), (*c*) only

B. (*b*), (*c*), (*d*) only

C. (*a*), (*d*), (*e*) only

D. (*a*), (*b*), (*d*) only

66. Match List-I with List-II:

List-I	List-II (International Trade Theories)
(*a*) David Ricardo (1817)	I. Theory of absolute advantage
(*b*) Michael Porter (1990)	II. Factor endowment theory
(*c*) Adam Smith (1776)	III. Theory of comparative advantage
(*d*) Heckscher (1919)-Ohlin (1933)	IV. Theory of competitive advantage

Choose the correct answer from the options given below:

	(*a*)	(*b*)	(*c*)	(*d*)
A.	I	II	III	IV
B.	III	IV	I	II
C.	IV	III	II	I
D.	III	IV	II	I

67. Match List-I with List-II:

List-I (Method)	List-II (Purchase consideration)
(*a*) Lump-sum payment method	I. Calculated by adding up the total amount (money value) of existing shares, preference shares and cash received from the purchasing company for the shareholders of the vendor company.
(*b*) Net Assets Method	II. On the basis of ratio in which the shares of the transferee company are to be exchanged for the shares of the transferor company.
(*c*) Net Payment Method	III. The amount to be paid by the transferee company to transferor company for amalgamation of its business.
(*d*) Swap Ratio Method	IV. Arrived at by adding the agreed value of assets taken over and deducting there from the agreed values of liabilities.

Choose the correct answer from the options given below:

	(*a*)	(*b*)	(*c*)	(*d*)
A.	III	II	I	IV
B.	III	IV	I	II
C.	IV	I	II	III
D.	IV	III	II	I

68. Match List-I with List-II:

List-I (Pricing Strategies)	List-II (Description)
(*a*) Ramsay pricing	I. Setting a high price when a product is first introduced and gradually lowering price as it gains scale
(*b*) Price skimming	II. Firm charges lower price (than the ongoing price) to gain market entry
(*c*) Cost plus pricing	III. Price deviations from marginal cost should be inversely proportional to price elasticity of the product
(*d*) Penetration pricing	IV. It is full cost pricing strategy that also includes mark up for target return, degree of competition, price elasticity and availability of substitutes.

Choose the correct answer from the options given below:

	(a)	(b)	(c)	(d)
A.	III	IV	I	II
B.	II	I	III	IV
C.	III	I	IV	II
D.	I	IV	II	III

69. Match List-I with List-II:

List-I	List-II
(a) Market risk	I. Associated with the efficiency with which a firm conducts its operations within the broader environment imposed upon it.
(b) Financial risk	II. Arises due to change in operating conditions caused by conditions thrust upon the firm which are beyond its control.
(c) External business risk	III. Variations in price sparked off due to real, social, political and economic events.
(d) Internal business risk	IV. Associated with the capital structure of a firm.

Choose the correct answer from the options given below:

	(a)	(b)	(c)	(d)
A.	I	II	III	IV
B.	III	IV	II	I
C.	III	I	II	IV
D.	IV	III	I	II

70. Logically sequence the following in the process of entering international markets outlined in the uppsala model.

(a) Sporadic (Ad hoc) exports
(b) Foreign production and manufacturing
(c) Establishing a foreign sales subsidiary
(d) Domestic operations and production
(e) Exporting via independent representative

Choose the correct answer from the options given below:

A. (a), (b), (c), (d) and (e)
B. (c), (b), (d), (a) and (e)
C. (d), (a), (e), (c) and (b)
D. (e), (b), (d), (c) and (a)

71. Match List-I with List-II:

List-I (Personality dimensions)	List-II (Individual Traits)
(a) Extroversion	I. Calm, happy and secure
(b) Conscien-tiousness	II. Talkative, assertive, sociable and outgoing
(c) Emotional stability	III. Creative, curious, intellectual, imaginative and artistically sensitive
(d) Openess to experience	IV. Self-disciplined, hard-working, organised, dependable and persistent.

Choose the correct answer from the options given below:

	(a)	(b)	(c)	(d)
A.	II	IV	III	I
B.	II	IV	I	III
C.	III	II	I	IV
D.	IV	I	II	III

72. Match List-I with List-II:

List-I	List-II
(a) Insurance Act	I. 1988
(b) Life Insurance Corporation Act	II. 1963
(c) Motor Vehicles Act	III. 1938
(d) Marine Insurance Act	IV. 1956

Choose the correct answer from the options given below:

	(a)	(b)	(c)	(d)
A.	IV	III	I	II
B.	I	II	III	IV
C.	III	IV	I	II
D.	IV	III	II	I

73. Match List-I with List-II:

List-I (Books)	List-II (Author(s))
(*a*) Wealth of Nations, 1776	I. Thomas Malthus
(*b*) Principles of Political Economy and Taxation, 1817	II. Karl Marx
(*c*) Principle of Population, 1798	III. Adam Smith
(*d*) Das Capital, 1867	IV. David Ricardo

Choose the correct answer from the options given below:

	(*a*)	(*b*)	(*c*)	(*d*)
A.	I	III	IV	II
B.	III	IV	I	II
C.	II	III	I	IV
D.	III	I	IV	II

74. Match List-I with List-II:

List-I	List-II
(*a*) Ordinary damages	I. Never granted by way of compensation for the loss
(*b*) Special damages	II. They are quite heavy in amount and are awarded by way of punishment only
(*c*) Exemplary damages	III. Arise in the ordinary course of events from the breach of contract
(*d*) Nominal damages	IV. The constitute indirect loss suffered by the aggrieved party on account of breach of contract

Choose the correct answer from the options given below:

	(*a*)	(*b*)	(*c*)	(*d*)
A.	III	IV	II	I
B.	IV	III	II	I
C.	I	II	IV	III
D.	II	I	III	IV

75. Match List-I with List-II:

List-I	List-II
(*a*) Section 35 (2AA)	I. Payment made to certain institutions for scientific
(*b*) Section 35(1) (ii a)	II. Payment made to certain institutions for research in social sciences.
(*c*) Section 35(1) (iii)	III. Payment made to a company to be used for scientific research.
(*d*) Section 35(1) (ii)	IV. Payment made to Indian Institute of Technology for Scientific Research.

Choose the correct answer from the options given below:

	(*a*)	(*b*)	(*c*)	(*d*)
A.	IV	II	III	I
B.	IV	III	II	I
C.	I	II	III	IV
D.	I	II	IV	III

76. Sequence the following in increasing order of integration of member economies.

(*a*) Free Trade Area
(*b*) Economic Union
(*c*) Custom Union
(*d*) Preferential Trade Agreements
(*e*) Common Market

Choose the correct answer from the options given below:

A. (*a*), (*c*), (*e*), (*b*), (*d*)
B. (*b*), (*e*), (*c*), (*a*), (*d*)
C. (*d*), (*a*), (*c*), (*e*), (*b*)
D. (*c*), (*e*), (*b*), (*d*), (*a*)

77. The liquidator after realizing the assets of the company should distribute the proceeds among below mentioned claimants in the following order:

(*a*) Legal charges
(*b*) Liquidators remuneration and cost of expenses of winding up
(*c*) Workman's dues and claims of the secured creditors
(*d*) Preferential creditors and creditors secured by floating charge
(*e*) Unsecured creditors

Choose the correct answer from the options given below:

A. (*b*), (*c*), (*a*), (*d*), (*e*)
B. (*d*), (*c*), (*b*), (*a*), (*e*)
C. (*a*), (*b*), (*c*), (*d*), (*e*)
D. (*b*), (*c*), (*e*), (*a*), (*d*)

78. Arrange the following market structures in the increasing order of pricing power to firms.

(*a*) Monopolistic competition
(*b*) Perfect competition
(*c*) Duopoly
(*d*) Monopoly
(*e*) Oligopoly

Choose the correct answer from the options given below:

A. (*b*), (*d*), (*a*), (*e*), (*c*)
B. (*b*), (*a*), (*e*), (*c*), (*d*)
C. (*a*), (*c*), (*b*), (*d*), (*e*)
D. (*d*), (*c*), (*e*), (*a*), (*b*)

79. Arrange the following items, *i.e.*, stages of capital budgeting in correct sequence:

(*a*) Identification of potential investment opportunities.
(*b*) Assembling of proposed investments.
(*c*) Decision making.
(*d*) Implementation and performance review.
(*e*) Preparation of capital budget and appropriations.

Choose the correct answer from the options given below:

A. (*b*), (*a*), (*e*), (*c*), (*d*)
B. (*e*), (*c*), (*a*), (*b*), (*d*)
C. (*c*), (*e*), (*d*), (*b*), (*a*)
D. (*a*), (*b*), (*c*), (*e*), (*d*)

80. Arrange the following stages of processing of data in a correct sequence:

(*a*) Coding (*b*) Editing
(*c*) Tabulation (*d*) Classification
(*e*) Using Percentages

Choose the correct answer from the options given below:

A. (*a*), (*b*), (*c*), (*d*), (*e*)
B. (*d*), (*a*), (*b*), (*c*), (*e*)
C. (*c*), (*d*), (*a*), (*b*), (*e*)
D. (*b*), (*a*), (*d*), (*c*), (*e*)

81. Arrange the following characteristics of stages of group development in the increasing order:

(*a*) Members begin to resolve differences and clarify the purpose of the group and the roles of group members.
(*b*) It includes recognition for participation and achievement.
(*c*) Members are highly task-oriented and there is unity in the group.
(*d*) Conflicts start arising due to the differences of opinion among members.
(*e*) Members are moderately eager, have positive expectations, anxious about why they are there, and who other members are.

Choose the correct answer from the options given below:

A. (*e*), (*d*), (*a*), (*b*), (*c*)
B. (*d*), (*e*), (*c*), (*a*), (*b*)
C. (*e*), (*d*), (*a*), (*c*), (*b*)
D. (*d*), (*b*), (*a*), (*e*), (*c*)

82. Arrange the following steps in logical sequence of operation of the registration of portfolio managers:

(*a*) Prior approval of the SEBI.
(*b*) Adequate steps for redressal of investors grievances.
(*c*) Maintenance of the specified capital adequacy requirements.
(*d*) Payment of fee.
(*e*) Abide by the regulations under the SEBI Act.

Choose the correct answer from the options given below:

A. (*c*), (*e*), (*a*), (*b*), (*d*)
B. (*d*), (*a*), (*b*), (*e*), (*c*)
C. (*a*), (*d*), (*b*), (*c*), (*e*)
D. (*d*), (*e*), (*a*), (*c*), (*b*)

83. Arrange the following stages of consumer decision making process in a sequential order with regard to a young person Divya:

(*a*) looks for a specific colour and showroom delivery as she does not want to wait.

(*b*) narrows down to a dark grey car of a specific brand.
(*c*) belongs to an executive group and all her colleagues have their own vehicles.
(*d*) uses media and other social channels to collect information about different models.
(*e*) feels that fuel efficiency should be the most critical factor while making a choice.

Choose the correct answer from the options given below:
A. (*a*), (*c*), (*b*), (*d*), (*e*)
B. (*c*), (*e*), (*d*), (*a*), (*b*)
C. (*c*), (*a*), (*d*), (*e*), (*b*)
D. (*e*), (*c*), (*a*), (*d*), (*b*)

84. Arrange the following stages of formation of companies in a proper sequence:
(*a*) Promotion stage
(*b*) Raising of share capital stage
(*c*) Incorporation stage
(*d*) Commencement stage
(*e*) Selection of name

Choose the correct answer from the options given below:
A. (*c*), (*a*), (*e*), (*d*), (*b*)
B. (*b*), (*e*), (*a*), (*c*), (*d*)
C. (*a*), (*e*), (*c*), (*b*), (*d*)
D. (*d*), (*a*), (*b*), (*c*), (*e*)

85. Sequence the steps for computing gross annual value of income from house property:
(*a*) Find out the rent actually received or receivable after excluding unrealised rent before deducting loss due to vacancy.
(*b*) Find out the loss because of vacancy.
(*c*) Find out the reasonable expected rent of the property.
(*d*) Find out which one is the higher amount computed in (*c*) or (*a*).
(*e*) (*d*)—(*b*) is gross annual value

Choose the correct answer from the options given below:
A. (*c*), (*a*), (*d*), (*b*), (*e*)
B. (*a*), (*d*), (*c*), (*b*), (*e*)
C. (*d*), (*a*), (*c*), (*b*), (*e*)
D. (*a*), (*b*), (*c*), (*d*), (*e*)

86. Given below are two statements:
Statement I : Deferred Tax Liabilities (Net) is the amount of tax on the temporary difference between the accounting income and taxable income. It arises when the accounting income is more than the taxable income.
Statement II : Deferred Tax Liabilities (Net) and Deferred Tax Assets (Net) are only book entires *i.e.,* they are neither actual liability nor actual asset.

In the light of the above statements, choose the correct answer from the options given below:
A. Both Statement I and Statement II are true.
B. Both Statement I and Statement II are false.
C. Statement I is true, but Statement II is false
D. Statement I is false, but Statement II is true

87. Given below are two statements:
Statement I : Modified Internal rate of return is based on reinvestment assumption.
Statement II : Value-additivity principle is not applicable in NPV.

In the light of the above statements, choose the most appropriate answer from the options given below:
A. Both Statement I and Statement II are correct.
B. Both Statement I and Statement II are incorrect.
C. Statement I is correct, but Statement II is incorrect.
D. Statement I is incorrect, but Statement II is correct.

88. Given below are two statements:

Statement I : Delegation is an interpersonal transactions based on behaviour analysis.

Statement II : Delegation is an evolutionary and developmental process which needs encouragement and reinforcement.

In the light of the above statements, choose the most appropriate answer from the options given below:

A. Both Statement I and Statement II are correct.

B. Both Statement I and Statement II are incorrect.

C. Statement I is correct, but Statement II is incorrect.

D. Statement I is incorrect, but Statement II is correct

89. Given below are two statements:

Statement I : Only low priced products will sell in rural India.

Statement II : Rural consumers are a homogenous lot.

In the light of the above statements, choose the most appropriate answer from the options given below:

A. Both Statement I and Statement II are correct.

B. Both Statement I and Statement II are incorrect.

C. Statement I is correct, but Statement II is incorrect.

D. Statement I is incorrect, but Statement II is correct.

90. Given below are two statements: One is labelled as Assertion (A) and the other is labelled as Reason (R).

Assertion (A) : ITR-1 can be used by an individual whose total income does not exceed ₹ 1 Crore.

Reason (R) : ITR -1 cannot be used by an individual who is director in a company.

In the light of the above statements, choose the most appropriate answer from the options given below:

A. Both (A) and (R) are correct and (R) is the correct explanation of (A)

B. Both (A) and (R) are correct, but (R) is ***not*** the correct explanation of (A)

C. (A) is correct, but (R) is not correct

D. (A) is not correct, but (R) is correct

Directions (Qs. No. 91-95): *Read the following passage and answer these questions.*

In 2019, India's ten largest trading partners were USA, China, UAE, Saudi Arabia, Hong Kong, Iraq, Singapore. Germany, South Korea and Switzerland. In 2018-19, the Foreign Direct Investment (FDI) in India was $64.4 billion with service sector, computer and telecom industry remains leading sectors for FDI inflows. India has free trade agreements with several nations, including ASEAN, SAFTA, Mercosur, South Korea, Japan and few others which are in effect or under negotiating stage.

The service sector makes up 55.6% of GDP and remains the fastest growing sector, while the industrial sector and the agricultural sector employs a majority of the labour force. The Bombay Stock Exchange and National Stock Exchange are one of the World's largest stock exchanges by market capitalisation. India is the world's sixth-largest manufacturer, representing 3% of global manufacturing output and employs over 57 million people. Nearly 66% of India's population is rural whose primary source of livelihood is agriculture and contributes less than 50% of India's GDP. It has the world's fifth-largest foreign-exchange reserves worth ₹ 38,832.21 billion (US $540 billion). India has a high national debt with 68% of GDP, while its fiscal deficit remained at 3.4% of GDP. However, as per 2019 CAG report, the actual fiscal deficit is 5.85% of GDP.

India's government—owned banks faced mounting bad debt, resulting in low credit growth; simultaneously the NBFC sector has been engulfed in a liquidity crisis. India faces high unemployment, rising income inequality and major slump in aggregate demand.

91. India has significant trading partners from which of the following regions:
(*a*) Europe
(*b*) America
(*c*) Asia
(*d*) Africa

Choose the correct answer from the options given below:
A. (*a*), (*b*), (*c*) only
B. (*b*), (*c*), (*d*) only
C. (*a*), (*b*), (*d*) only
D. (*a*) and (*d*) only

92. Which of the following sectors have significant Foreign Direct Investment (FDI) in India?
(*a*) Service Sector
(*b*) Secondary Sector
(*c*) Primary Sector
(*d*) Fisheries and Animal Husbandry

Choose the correct answer from the options given below:
A. (*a*) and (*b*) only B. (*b*) and (*c*) only
C. (*c*) and (*d*) only D. (*a*) and (*d*) only

93. Which among the following statements is the correct one? (Choose the most appropriate one)?
A. India has a better trade relations with European countries.
B. MSE is the largest stock exchange in the world.
C. Indian primary sector is contributing less as compared to other sectors.
D. India attracts highest FDI from USA.

94. The Comptroller and Auditor General has reported a different estimate than of governments, in terms of:
A. GDP
B. Fiscal Deficit
C. FDI
D. Liquidity of private banks

95. Which of the following has not been articulated in the passage?
(*a*) GDP Growth
(*b*) Currency flows
(*c*) Liquidity
(*d*) Demographics

Choose the correct answer from the options given below:
A. (*a*) and (*b*) only B. (*b*) and (*c*) only
C. (*b*) only D. (*c*) and (*d*) only

Directions (Qs. No. 96-100): *Read the following passage carefully and answer the question.*

XYZ Ltd. funrnished you with the following information:

	Budget	**Actual (in a particular month)**
No. of working days	25	27
Production (in units)	20,000	22,000
Fixed overhead (in Rupees)	30,000	31,000

Budgeted overhead rate is ₹ 1 per unit. In a particular month the actual hours worked were 31,500.

96. What is the total overhead variance in the given month experienced by the XYZ Ltd?
A. ₹ 4,000 (Favourable)
B. ₹ 2,000 (Adverse)
C. ₹ 1,000 (Adverse)
D. ₹ 2,000 (Favourable)

97. What is the expenditure variance of XYZ Ltd as on given month?
A. ₹ 1,000 (Adverse)
B. ₹ 1,500 (Adverse)
C. ₹ 2,000 (Favourable)
D. ₹ 1,500 (Favourable)

98. From given information in the passage, what is the volume variance of XYZ Ltd in given month?
A. ₹ 3,000 (Favourable)
B. ₹ 2,000 (Adverse)
C. ₹ 1,500 (Favourable)
D. ₹ 1,500 (Adverse)

99. Find the capacity variance for the month from the information given in the passage.

A. ₹ 1,000 (Favourable)
B. ₹ 900 (Adverse)
C. ₹ 1,500 (Favourable)
D. ₹ 1,000 (Adverse)

100. Given the information in the passage, what is the calendar variance for the month?

A. ₹ 2,000 (Favourable)
B. ₹ 3,000 (Adverse)
C. ₹ 2,400 (Favourable)
D. ₹ 1,000 (Adverse)

ANSWERS

1	**2**	**3**	**4**	**5**	**6**	**7**	**8**	**9**	**10**
C	B	B	D	B	B	B	D	C	A
11	**12**	**13**	**14**	**15**	**16**	**17**	**18**	**19**	**20**
A	A	A	C	D	D	A	D	A	C
21	**22**	**23**	**24**	**25**	**26**	**27**	**28**	**29**	**30**
B	B	B	C	A	B	A	A	B	A
31	**32**	**33**	**34**	**35**	**36**	**37**	**38**	**39**	**40**
C	B	D	B	C	D	A	B	D	B
41	**42**	**43**	**44**	**45**	**46**	**47**	**48**	**49**	**50**
D	B	C	A	D	A	D	B	B	D
51	**52**	**53**	**54**	**55**	**56**	**57**	**58**	**59**	**60**
A	D	C	D	C	B	D	C	D	C
61	**62**	**63**	**64**	**65**	**66**	**67**	**68**	**69**	**70**
A	C	D	A	A	B	B	C	B	C
71	**72**	**73**	**74**	**75**	**76**	**77**	**78**	**79**	**80**
B	C	B	A	B	C	C	B	D	D
81	**82**	**83**	**84**	**85**	**86**	**87**	**88**	**89**	**90**
C	C	B	C	A	A	C	D	B	D
91	**92**	**93**	**94**	**95**	**96**	**97**	**98**	**99**	**100**
A	A	C	B	C	D	A	A	B	C

EXPLANATORY ANSWERS

2. Countervailing duty (CVD) is a specific form of duty that the government imposes in order to protect domestic producers by countering the negative impact of import subsidies. CVD is thus an import tax by the importing country on imported products.

To make their products cheaper and boost their demand in other countries, foreign governments sometimes provide subsidy to their producers. To avoid flooding of the market in the importing country with these goods, the government of the importing country imposes countervailing duty, charging a specific amount on import of such goods.

The duty nullifies and eliminates the price advantage (low price) enjoyed by an imported product when it is given subsidies or exempted from domestic taxes in the country where they are manufactured.

4. **Porter's Theory of Competitive Advantage**

In his book, *The Competitive Advantage of Nations,* published originally in 1990, Michael Porter developed a theory of national **competitive advantage**. His considerable reasearch, which is set out in the book, attempts to find out why some countries are more successful than others. Each nation, he says, has four broad attributes that shape its national competitive environment.

- ***Factor conditions***: The nation's position in factors of production, such as skilled labour or infrastructure and natural resources necessary to compete in a given industry.
- ***Demand conditions***: The nature and depth of home demand for the industry's product or service.
- ***Related and supporting industries***: The presence or absence in the nation of supplier industries and related industries that are internationally competitive.
- ***Firm strategy, structure and rivalry***: The conditions in the nation governing how companies are created, organized and managed; and the nature of domestic rivalry.

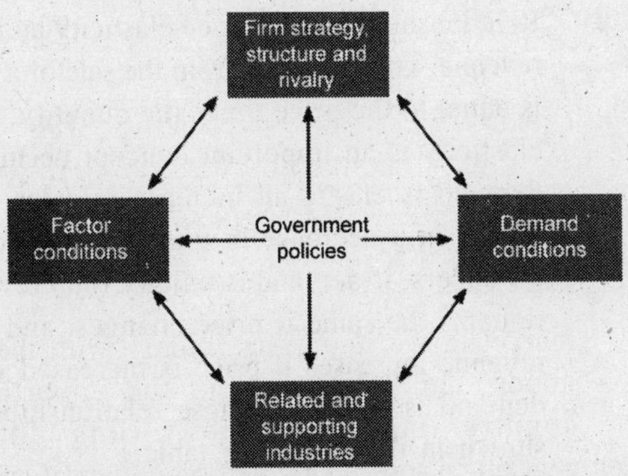

5. **Debtors and Creditors Suspense Accounts:**

- A company taking over a running business may also agree to collect its debts as an agent for the vendor and may further undertake to pay the creditors on behalf of the vendors in such a case, the debtors and creditors of a vendors will include in the accounts for the company by debit or credit separate total accounts in the general ledger to distinguish them from the debtors and creditors of the business and contra entries will make in corresponding suspense account. Also details of debtors and creditors balance will thus kept in separate ledger.
- The vendor hence treated as a creditor for the cash received by the purchasing company in respect of the debts due to the vendor, just as if he has himself collected cash from his debtors and remitted the proceeds to the purchasing company.
- The vendor thus considers a debtor in respect of cash paid to his creditors by the purchasing company. The balance of cash collected, less paid, will represent the amount due to or by the vendor, arising from debtors and creditors balances which have taken over, subject to any collection expenses.
- Balance in suspense account will be equal to the amount of debtor and creditors taken over remaining unadjusted at any time.

7. Amortization of intangible asset is a process under which the cost of an intangible asset is reduced over a specified period of time, also called as expected useful life. The general meaning of intangible is 'without physical substance'. Intangibles are assets that may not have a physical substance but are still valuable resources for an entity.

Like depreciation for tangible assets, amortization transfers part of the value of the intangible asset from the balance sheet to the income statement as a cost. Depreciation is done for tangible assets, and amortization is done for intangible assets.

8. The remaining share $= 1 - \frac{1}{5} = \frac{4}{5}$ is shared by X & Y in the ratio of 2 : 1

Future ratio of X = $\frac{4}{5}\times\frac{2}{3}=\frac{8}{15}$

Furture ratio of Y = $\frac{4}{5}\times\frac{1}{3}=\frac{4}{15}$

∴ Sacrifice ratio = Old ratio – New ratio

Sacrifice ratio of X = $\frac{4}{7}-\frac{8}{15}=\frac{4}{105}$

Sacrifice ratio of Y = $\frac{3}{7}-\frac{4}{15}=\frac{17}{105}$

∴ Sacrifice ratio of X & Y = 4 : 17.

9. The original theory of the firm was based on the assumption that the goal or objective of the firm was to maximize current or short-term profits. Firms, however, are often observed to sacrifice short-term profits for the sake of increasing future or long-term profits. The modern theory of the firm postulates that the primary goal of the firm is to maximize the wealth or value of the firm. The shareholder value maximization or the shareholder wealth maximization model assumes that the objective of the firm is to maximize the value of the firm as measured in the market place, *i.e.*, maximize the market value of firm's share. Various alternative definitions of the term *value of the firm* have been suggested by economists and management theorists like book value, market value, liquidating value, going-concern value, and so on *Prima facie*, the value can be defined as the present value of the expected future cash flows of the firm. Cash flows are often equated with profits. Therefore the value of the firm today, known as present value in the literature of financial management, is the value of its expected future profits, discounted back to the present by an appropriate rate of inerest. Since in a coporate form of business it is the shareholders who are the owners of the firm, the value of a firm represents the shareholders' wealth. Thus, the value maximization of a firm implies the maximization of shareholder's wealth. In other words, we can say:

Value of the firm = Net persent value (NPV) of expected future profits

$$PV = \frac{\pi_1}{(1+r)}+\frac{\pi_2}{(1+r)^2}+\ldots+\frac{\pi_n}{(1+r)^n}$$

$$= \sum_{i=1}^{n}\frac{\pi_i}{(1+r)^i}$$

Here, PV is is the present value of all expected future profits of the firm, $\pi_1, \pi_2, \ldots, \pi_n$ represent the expected profits in each year i; r is the appropriate rate of interest, which acts as the discount factor.

In a market-oriented economy, it is impossible to earn a profit unless the firm is economically viable, *i.e.*, creating economic value. The firm undertakes actions designed to maximize its wealth by maximizing the net present value (NPV) of its future income stream.

10. Relationship between price elasticity and total revenue. Total revenue from the sale of a good is equal to the price times the quantity. Price elasticity is an important concept because if demand is elastic an increase in sales price results in a decrease in total revenue for all producers. If demand is unitary total revenue remains the same if price changes, and total revenue increases if price is increased when demand is inelastic. These relationships are shown in the following table:

Effect of Price Changes on Various Types of Goods

Price change	Elastic Demand E > 1	Inelastic Demand E < 1	Unitary Demand E = 1
Price increase	Total revenue decreases	Total revenue increases	Total revenue does not change
Price decrease	Total revenue increases	Total revenue decreases	Total revenue does not change

11 • If $\alpha + \beta > 1$, the Cobb-Douglas production function displays increasing returns to scale.

• If $\alpha + \beta = 1$, the Cobb-Douglas production function displays constant returns to scale.

• If $\alpha + \beta < 1$, the Cobb-Douglas production function displays decreasing returns to scale.

12. The extreme case of non price competition is the formation of *cartels* or *collusive oligopoly*, where all the firms openly or tacitly agree to sell their products at the same price. Oil and Petroleum Exporting Countries (OPEC) is an international cartel, in which all the suppliers of crude oil have openly declared to charge a single price for the product all over the world. Firms may also *tacitly* agree to sell their products in separate markets and/or at the same price, like in the case of soft drinks and cellular phone services.

13. The pecking-order theory starts with *asymmetric information*—a fancy term indicating that managers know more about their companies' prospects, risks, and values than do outside investors.

Managers obviously know more than investors. We can prove that by observing stock price changes caused by announcements by managers. When a company announces an increased regular dividend, stock price typically rises, because investors interpret the increase as a sign of management's confidence in future earnings. In other words, the dividend increase transfers information from managers to investors. This can happen only if managers know more in the first place.

Asymetric information affects the choice between internal and external financing and between new issues of debt and equity securities. This leads to a *pecking order*, in which investment is financed first with internal funds, reinvested earning primarily; then by new issues of debt; and finally with new issues of equity. New equity issues are a last resort when the company runs out of debt capacity, that is, when the threat of costs of financial distress brings regular insomnia to existing creditors and to the financial manager.

14. $$\text{ARR} = \frac{\text{Average Net Income (after tax ad dep.)}}{\text{Average Investment}} \times 100$$

$$\text{Average Investment} = \frac{\text{Initial Investment}}{2}$$

$$= \frac{40,000}{2} = 20,000$$

$$\therefore \quad \text{ARR} = \frac{3200}{20000} \times 100$$

$$= \frac{3200 \times 100}{20000} = 16\%.$$

15. According to residual dividend theory, a company should use all its funds not needed for operations investing in positive net present value (NPV) projects, until no further positive NPV project opportunities remain. Following this line of thinking, once a company has invested in all available positive NPV projects, any remaining excess long-term capital (*i.e.*, residual funds) should be distributed as a dividend to its shareholders. This theory is built on the view that a shareholder should be happy to forgo receiving dividends, so long as the company that they own shares in is investing in projects that, over the long term, will generate profits that will enable shareholders to be provided with returns that exceed their required rate of return. If a company can provide returns to shareholders that exceed their required rate of return, all things being equal, demand for the company's shares will rise, causing an increase in the share price.

17. $SE_{\overline{X}} = \sigma/\sqrt{n}$

Therefore, $\sqrt{n} = \sigma/SE_{\overline{X}}$

$\sqrt{n} = 40/8$

$$\sqrt{n} = 5 \Rightarrow n = 25$$

Therefore, for a very large population the ratio between $SE_{\bar{X}}$ and σ is 8 : 40. The sample size n will be 25.

18. The regression coefficient is independent of change of origin, but not scale. That is, 'change of scale' means, by dividing or multiplying every value of X and/or Y by some constant, the value of '$\hat{b}$' (regression coefficient) changes.

The correlation coefficient is not affected by change of origin or scale or both. When a constant term is added or subtracted from the original values of a variable, we say that the origin is changed. When the original values of a variable is multiplied or divided by a constant term we say that the scale is changed.

20. The probability function for the Poisson distribution is defined as

$$P(X = x) = \frac{e^{-\lambda}\lambda^{x}}{x!} \text{ where } \lambda \text{ is a parameter}$$

Standard deviation of X is $\sqrt{x}$

Here, we have

$$P(X = 0) = 2P(X = 1) \quad ...(i)$$

$$P(X = 0) = \frac{e^{-\lambda}\lambda^{0}}{0!} = e^{-\lambda}$$

$$P(X = 1) = \frac{e^{-\lambda}\lambda^{1}}{1!} = e^{-\lambda}\lambda$$

From equation (*i*)

$$e^{-\lambda} = 2e^{-\lambda}\lambda$$

$$\lambda = \frac{1}{2} = 0.5$$

So, the standard deviation = $\sqrt{\lambda} = \sqrt{0.5}$.

21. Content validity is a demonstration that the content of a selection procedure is representative of important aspects of performance on the job. For example, employers may demonstrate the *content validity* of a test by showing that the test constitutes a fair sample of the job's content. The basic procedure here is to identify job tasks that are critical to performance, and then randomly select a sample of those tasks to test. In selecting students for dental school, one might give applicants chunks of chalk, and ask them to carve something like a tooth. If the content you choose for the test is a representative sample of the job, then the test is probably content valid. Clumsy dental students need not apply. Subject matter experts (SMEs, such as practicing dentists) help choose the tasks.

23. ***Principle of Utilitarianism*:** Many ethicists have held that the correctness or fairness of an action can be determined best by looking at its overall results or consequences. If the consequences are good, the action or decision is considered good. If the consequences are bad, the action or decision is considered wrong. An example of utilitarianism might be in the case of a pharmaceutical firm that has released a new drug that has been approved by the government but it does have side effects. But, the drug is able to help more people than are bothered by the side effects so it is considered a good drug though it has problems for some.

The **principle of utilitarianism** is therefore a *consequential* principle, or as stated earlier, a *teleological* principle. In its simplest form, **utilitarianism** asserts: "we should always act so as to produce the greatest ratio of good to evil for everyone." Another way of stating utilitarianism is to say that one should take the course of action that represents the "greatest good for the greatest number." Two of the most influential philosophers who advocated this consequential view were Jeremy Bentham (1748-1832) and John Stuart Mill (1806-1873).

24. In learning, 'law of effect' principle developed by 'Edward Thorndike' which suggested that responses closely followed by satisfaction will become firmly attached to the situation and therefore more likely to reoccur when the situation is repeated. In other word any behaviour that is followed by pleasant consequences is likely to be repeated, and any behaviour followed by unpleasant consequences is likely to be stopped.

25. Basel is a city in Switzerland. It is the headquarters of Bureau of International Settlement (BIS), which fosters co-operation among central banks with a common goal of financial stability and common standards of banking regulations. Basel guidelines refer to broad supervisory standards formulated by this group of central banks - called the Basel Committee on Banking Supervision (BCBS). The set of agreement by the BCBS, which mainly focuses on risks to banks and the financial system are called Basel accord. The purpose of the accord is to ensure that financial institutions have enough capital on account to meet obligations and absorb unexpected losses.

Basel I: BCBS introduced capital measurement system called Basel capital accord, also called as Basel I in 1988. It focused almost entirely on credit risk. It defined capital and structure of risk weights for banks. The minimum capital requirement was fixed at 8% of risk weighted assets (RWA).

Basel II: Basel II guidelines were published by BSBS in June 2004, it is considered to be the refined and reformed versions of Basel I accord. The guidelines were based on three parameters:

- ***Capital Adequacy Requirements***: Banks should maintain a minimum capital adequacy requirement of 8% of risk assets.
- ***Supervisory Review***: According to this, banks were needed to develop and use better risk management techniques in monitoring and managing all the three types of risks that a bank faces.
- ***Market Discipline***: This need increased disclosure requirements.

Basel III: Basel III guidelines were released in 2010. These guidelines were introduced in response to the financial crisis of 2008. A need was felt to further strengthen the system as banks in the developed economies were under-capitalised, over-leveraged and had a greater reliance on short-term funding. Also the quantity and quality of capital under Basel II were deemed insufficient to contain any further risk. Basel III norms aim at making most banking activities such as their trading book activities more capital-intensive. The guidelines aim to promote a more resilient banking system by focusing on four vital banking parameters viz. capital, leverage, funding and liquidity.

27. A derivative is a contract that derives its value from the performance of an underlying entity. This underlying entity can be an asset, index, cryptocurrency and so on. Derivatives can be used for many purposes, including insuring against price movements (hedging), increasing exposure to price movements for speculation, or getting access to otherwise hard-to-trade assets or markets. Some of the more common derivatives include forwards, futures, options swaps, contracts for difference, and variations of these such as synthetic collateralised debt obligations and credit default swaps.

28. A Non-Banking Financial Company (NBFC) is a company registered under the Companies Act, 1956 engaged in the business of loans and advances, acquisition of shares/stocks/ bonds/debentures/securities issued by Government or local authority or other marketable securities of a like nature, leasing, hire-purchase, insurance business, chit business but does not include any institution whose principal business is that of agriculture activity, industrial activity, purchase or sale of any goods (other than securities) or providing any services and sale/purchase/ construction of immovable property. A non-banking institution which is a company and has principal business of receiving deposits under any scheme or arrangement in one lump sum or in installments by way of contributions or in any other manner, is also a non-banking financial company (Residuary non-banking company).

29. The design of a distribution channel is an important strategic decision because customers must be able to purchase goods and services when and where they find it most satisfying and convenient. Marketing intelligence data can be used to determine customers' buying habits and channel preferences as input for channel design decisions. Channel structure also depends on the firm's resources and objectives. For instance, the opportunity to distribute computer software directly over the Internet may provide a shorter lead time and a better return on assets than distributing through wholesalers or storefronts.

Bucklin explains channel structures in terms of four service level outputs: spatial convenience, lot size, waiting or delivery time, and product variety. *Spatial convenience* refers to the degree of market decentralizaion or a distribution strategy that is designed to reduce customers' travel time and search costs through convenient locations of intermediaries. As customers place greater value on travel time and search costs, the channel becomes more decentralized and requires more channel intermediaries.

Lot size refers to the number of units that a customer will purchase at any one time. Products that are consumed quickly and replenished frequently require higher levels of service outputs to maintain inventories. When customers can rely on their suppliers to maintain an inventory of wanted items, they can purchase in smaller quantities and hold smaller inventories. The smaller the lot size that is available in a channel, the higher is the service output of that channel, and the higher is the price that can be charged to customers for convenience.

Waiting time or *delivery time* is the time a customer must wait between ordering and receiving goods. Longer waiting times generally mean that the customer will experience greater inconvenience and will need to plan purchases in advance. However, when the customer is willing to wait longer to receive purchases, prices usually are lower.

Product variety refers to the width and depth of assortments. When customers demand a broad assortment of goods, channel members must carry a higher level of inventory. This results in higher channel output and higher distribution costs.

As customers require a higher level of service outputs, the channel expands to include more intermediaries to provide the necessary marketing functions and flows. When channel outputs are higher, customers will pay higher prices for additional service and convenience. Conversely, channel outputs and prices are lower when customers provide more of the marketing functions themselves.

30. ***People processing*** **(services directed at people's bodies):**

- Passenger transportation
- Health care
- Lodging
- Beauty salons
- Physical therapy
- Fitness center
- Restaurant/bars
- Barbers
- Funeral services

Possession processing **(services directed at physical possessions):**

- Freight transportation
- Repair and maintenance
- Warehousing/storage
- Office cleaning services
- Retail distribution
- Laundy and dry cleaning
- Refueling
- Landscaping/gardening
- Disposal/recycling

***Mental stimulus processing* (services directed at people's minds):**

- Advertising/PR
- Arts and entertainment
- Broadcasting/cable
- Management consulting
- Education
- Information services
- Music concerts
- Psychotherapy
- Religion
- Voice telephone

***Information processing* (services directed at intangible assets):**

- Accounting
- Banking
- Data processing
- Data transmission
- Insurance
- Legal services
- Programming
- Research
- Securities investment
- Software consulting

31. The BCG matrix categorised SBUs into four groups:

- **Question marks:** These are SBUs struggling to make their presence felt in a high market growth area. Generally, most SBUs in this segment are in the initial period after their launch.
- **Stars:** These are the SBUs in which a firm has acquired market leadership. This situation occurs only when the firm has been able to successfully evolve strategies to convert question marks into stars.
- **Cash cows:** These are the SBUs that generate the much desired cash for a company. This is because, the market has stopped growing and the firm already occupies a market leader position. Its brands are a household name and the firm has to do very little to market them. Consumer demand for these brands exists. Generally, the brand is the front runner in the consumer's mind and also claims reasonable brand loyalty. Cash generated through these SBUs is used for R&D, converting question marks into stars, and maintaining stars in their positions. Strategically, the more cash cows in a firm's product portfolio, the stronger its financial position. It should milk these cows before they go dry.
- **Dogs:** These are the SBUs that have lost their glamour. The firm has lost leadership in a market which is not growing at a high rate. Often this stage is characterised by losses, as the firm has to plough in resources to maintain the SBU. The strategy recommended here is to 'kill the dog' or drop the product from the product line. However, most marketers, for emotional reasons, are hesitant to take this decision and one does find that a loss-making SBU is allowed to continue.

32. Base for segmenting a market: There is no single way to segment a market. A marketer has to try different segmentation variables, alone and in combination, hoping to find the best way to view the market structure.

- Geographic segmentation calls for dividing the market into different geographic units, such as nations, states, regions, counties, cities, or neighbourhoods.
- Demographic segmentation consists of dividing the market into groups based on demographic variables such as age, gender, family life cycle, income, occupation, education, religion, race, and nationality.
- Psychographic segmentation divides buyers into different groups based on social class, lifestyle and personality characteristics.
- Behaviour segmentation divides buyers into groups based on their knowledge, attitude, use or response to a product.

33. According to section 4 of the Negotiable Instruments Act of 1881, "Promissory note is an instrument in writing containing an unconditional undertaking by the maker to pay a certain sum of money only to or to the order of a certain person, or to the bearer of the instrument."

Essential features of a promissory note: The above definition reveals the following essential features:

- The instrument must be in writing.
- Mere acknowledgement of debt is not sufficient and must be an undertaking of a promise to pay. That is, an I.O.U. (I owe you) is not a promise to pay.
- The promise to pay must be unconditional, because, a conditional promise destroys the character negotiability of an otherwise negotiable instrument, but a promise to pay at a particular place or after a specified time or on the happening of an event certain to happen is not conditional For e.g. "I promise to pay ₹ 10,000, fifteen days after Ram's retirement" is not conditional.
- The instrument needs to be signed by the maker. In the case of an illiterate person, he should fix his thumb impression or any other mark. The signature could be indicated by a facsimile or by stamping the name.
- The promise to pay should be a certain sum of money in legal tender. The payee should be certain.

Normally promissory notes bear date and place but these are not required under the law. But a stamp is necessary as is required under the Indian Stamp Act.

34. The phrase *quantum meruit* literally means "as much as earned". When a person has done some work under a contract and the other party repudiates the contract or some event happens which makes the further performance of the contract impossible, then the party who has performed the work can claim remuneration for the work he has already performed. Similarly, where a party has expressly or impliedly requested another to render him a service without specifying the remuneration, but the circumstances of the request imply that the service is to be paid since there is an implied promise to pay as much as the party rendering the service deserves.

The conditions of *quantum meruit* are:

- The claim for *quantum meruit* arises only when the original contract is discharged.
- The claim for *quantum meruit* can be brought only by the party who is not in default.

The right to claim *quantum meruit* does not arise out of a contract as the right to damages does. It is a claim on the quasi contractual obligation which the law implies in the circumstances.

A party in default may sue on *quantum meruit* for what he has done if the contract is divisible and the other party has had the benefit of the part which he has performed.

Claim of *quantum meruit* arises in the following cases:

- When agreement is discovered to be void (Section 65).
- When something is done without any intention to do so gratuitously (Section 70).
- When there is express or implied contract to render services but there is no agreement as to remuneration.
- When the completion of the contract has been prevented by the act of the other party to the contract.
- When a contract is divisible.
- When an indivisible contract is completely performed but badly.

35. The copyright Act, 1957 has provided for enforcement of copyright through a series of penal provisions under Chapter 13 of the Act. The following are the principal penal provisions under the Act.

- Under section 63, where any person knowingly infringes or abets infringement of the copyright in a work and any other right as covered by the Copyright Act, 1957 (broadcast reproduction rights, performers' rights, moral rights, etc), such person may be punished with imprisonment of a minimum term of six months and a maximum term of three years, and a fine of between 50,000 and 200,000 rupees.

- Section 65A penalises circumvention of effective technological measures that may be applied to copies of a work with the purposes of protecting any of the rights conferred under the Act (*i.e.,* copyright, performance rights). The punishment under this provision is imprisonment that may extend to two years and payment of a fine. Section 65A was inserted by the Copyright (Amendment) Act, 2012.
- Section 65B makes unauthorised removal or alteration of 'rights management information' punishable with imprisonment of up to two years and payment of a fine. The provision makes the unauthorised distribution, broadcast or communication to the public of copies of the work punishable in the same manner if the person is aware that electronic rights management information in the copy has been removed or altered. Section 65B was inserted by the Copyright (Amendment) Act, 2012.
- Section 63A provides for enhanced penalty on second or subsequent convictions under section 63 (see point (i)).
- Other provisions in the chapter provide penalities for offences such as using infringing copies of a computer program, making or possessing plates for the purpose of making infringing copies of works, and making false entries in the Register of Copyrights.

36. Agency by necessity: In certain circumstances the law confers an authority on one person to act as agent for another without any regard to the consent of the principal. Such an agency is called an agency of necessity. Bowstead has rightly observed: "An agency by necessity is conferred by law in certain cases, where a person is faced with an emergency in which the property or interests of another are in imminent danger, and it becomes necessary in order to preserve the property or interest, to act before the instructions of the owner can be obtained. The law assumes the consent of the owner to the creation of the relationship of principal and agent." Thus, the conditions which enable a person to act as an agent of necessitiy of another are as follows:

- There should be a real necessity for acting on behalf of the principal.
- It should be impossible to communicate with the principal within the time available.
- The alleged agent should act *bona fide* in the interests of the principal.

Generally the 'agency by necessity' arises in the following cases:

- *Where the agent exceeds his authority, bona fide, in an emergency*. For example, where A consigns fruits to B at Allahabad with directions to send them immediately to C at Varanasi, and B, finding that the fruits are perishing rapidly, sells them at Allahabad itself for the best price obtainable, the sale will bind the principal and the agent cannot be held liable for exceeding his authority as under the circumstances of the case there arises agency of necessity.
- *Where the carriers of goods acting as a bailee, does any thing to protect or preserve the goods, in an emergency,* although there is no express authority in that regard. Thus a master of a ship is entitled, in cases of accident and emergency, to sell or pledge the goods in order to save their value and the sale or pledge will bind the cargo owners. Similarly, a land carrier of goods, in case of accident or emergency, becomes an agent of necessity, for example, if a public carrier develops an engine trouble, the driver can pledge a part of the goods loaded thereon in order to raise the money necessary for repairs and the pledge will be binding on the owner of goods.

Notice that in these cases it is not practicable to communicate with the principal.

- *Where a husband improperly leaves his wife without providing proper means for her sustenance*. In a special circumstance the case of husband and wife also provides an instance of agency by necessity. When the wife has been deserted by the husband and thus forced to live separate from him, the wife is regarded as the agent of necessity of the husband and she has the authority of pledging her husband's credit for necessaries even against her husband's wishes. However, this rule does not apply where the wife improperly leaves the husband.

It is relevant to state that in the ordinary course of things there is an implied agency between the husband and wife and the wife is presumed to have implied authority to pledge her husband's credit for necessaries suiting to the couple's joint style of living. But a husband enjoys no corresponding right to pledge his wife's credit for necessaries.

38. As per section 115JC of Income Tax Act, 1961, AMT is Alternate Minimum Tax computed on the adjusted total income of a non-corporate assessee.

39. The deduction against entertainment allowance is not available to non government employees. Only the Central or State Government employees are eligible for the deduction. Moreover, the employees of local authorities and statutory corporations are not eligible for the deduction.

40. Provident fund is a kind of security fund in which the employees contribute a part of their salary and the employer also contributes on behalf of their employees. Section 10(11) and 10(12) of the Income Tax Act defines the exemption on the amount added to the provident fund. Additionally, the amount allowed as a deduction on contributing to the provident fund is dealt in section 80C of the Income Tax Act. The types of provident funds are:

- Recognised Provided Fund (RPF) as recognised by Commissioner of Income Tax under EPF and Miscellaneous Provision Act, 1952. It applies to enterprises employing at least 20 employees.
- Unrecognised Provident Fund (UPF) is not recognised by the Commissioner of Income Tax. The employers and employees start these schemes.
- Public Provident Fund (PPF) under Public Provident Fund Act, 1968 is another system of contributing to the provident fund. Self-employed people can also take part in this scheme. A minimum contributing limit of ₹ 500 per annum and a maximum of ₹ 150000 per annum are set.
- Statutory Provided Fund (SPF) is meant for employees of Government or Universities or Educational Institutes affiliated to University.

41. The World Bank Group (WBG) is a family of five international organizations that are the International Bank for Reconstruction and Development (IBRD), the International Development Association (IDA), The International Finance Corporation (IFC), The Multilateral Investment Guarantee Agency (MIGA) and the International Centre for Settlement of Investment Disputes (ICSID). IFC was established in July, 1956 that provides loans to private industries for developing nations without any government guarantee and also promotes the additional capital investment in these countries. MIGA came into existence in April, 1988.

43. C.K. Prahalad and Gary Hamel are mainly credited for the dynamic capabilities approach that considers strategic managements as a collective learning process aimed at developing and then exploiting distinctive competencies by an organisation that are difficult to replicate by their rivals. Through a series of publications such as 'The Core Competence of the Corporation' (1990) and 'Strategy as Stretch and Leverage' (1993) in the *Harvard*

Business Review, and a book *Competing for the Future* (1994), they have sought to propagate the idea of dynamic capabilities. This idea rests on the thinking that strategy depends on learning, and learning depends on the capabilities of an organisation.

According to Prahalad and Hamel, the competitive (or strategic, as we call it here) advantage can be traced to the core competencies of an organisation. They take the analogy of a tree in describing core competence. 'The diversified corporation is a large tree. The trunk and major limbs are core products, the smaller branches are business units; the leaves, flowers, and fruit are end products. The root system that provides nourishment, sustenance, and stability is the core competence.'

Further they explain core competence as: '... the collective learning in the organisation, especially how to coordinate diverse production skills and integrated multiple streams of technologies... . It is also about the organisation of work and the delivery of value... . (It) is communication, involvement and a deep commitment to working across organisational boundaries. It involves many levels of people and all functions... (and it) does not diminish with use.'

To identify a core competence, Prahalad and Hamel prescribe three tests:

- it should be able to provide potential access to a wide variety of markets;
- it should make a significant contribution to the perceived customer benefits of the end product; and
- it should be difficult for the competitors to imitate.

From the several examples of corporations that Prahalad and Hamel use to exemplify their concept of core competence, we quote here a few. Canon's core competence lies in optics, imaging and microprocessor controls, Sony's in miniaturisation, Philip's in optical-media, 3M's in stick tape and Honda's in engines and power trains. The core competencies of these corporations have enabled them to operate in diverse markets offering different products. For instance, Canon has entered, and even dominated, diverse markets such as copiers, laser printers, cameras and image scanners.

44. Distinction Between Rights Issue and Public Issue

S.No.	Rights Issue	Public Issue
1.	In rights issue; the shares are offered to *the existing shareholders* or members of the company.	In public issue, *applications for shares are invited from the general public.*
2.	The price of rights issue is made much less than the current market price.	The price of public issue is generally lower than the expected market price.
3.	There is *no chance of over-subscription.*	In a public issue, the shares may be *under-subsribed or over-subscribed.*
4.	In case of rights issue, the *cost of issue* is comparatively *low*.	In a public issue, the *cost of issue* is obviously high.

46. The working capital flow arises when net effect of a transaction is to increase or decrease the amount of working capital. Normally, a firm have some transactions that will change net working capital and some transactions that will cause no change in net working capital. The transactions which change net working capital include most of the items of the income statement (profit and loss account) and thopse business events which affect both current and non-current balance sheet items. On the other hand, the transactions which do not increase or decrease net working capital include those which affect only current accounts or only non-current accounts. From above the following can be deduced:

Transactions Affecting Working Capital

- An increase in current assets increases working capital.
- A decrease in current assets decreases working capital.
- An increase in current liabilities decreases working capital.
- A decrease in current liabilities increases working capital.

Transactions not affecting Working Capital

- An increase in current assets with corresponding increase in current liabilities does not affect working capital.
- A decrease in current assets with corresponding decrease in current liabilities does not affect working capital.

48. An indifference curve may be defined as the *locus of points each representing a different combination of two substitute goods, which yield the same utility or level of satisfaction to the consumer. Therefore, he is indifferent between any two combinations of two goods when it comes to making a choice between them.* Such a situation arises because he consumes a large number of goods and services and often finds that one commodity can be substituted for another. The consumer can, therefore, substitute one commodity for another, and can make various combinations of two substitute goods which give him the same level of satisfaction. Since each combination yields the same level of satisfaction, he would be indifferent between the combinations when he has to make a choice. When such combinations are plotted graphically, it produces a curve. This curve is called the *indifference curve*. An indifference curve is also called *iso-utility curve* or *equal utility curve.*

Indifference curves are not only negatively sloped, but are also *convex to the origin*. The *convexity of the indifference curves* is caused by two factors:

- the two commodities are *imperfect substitutes* for one onother, and
- the marginal rate of substitution (MRS) between the two goods decreases as a consumer moves along an indifference curve.

49. In a financial crisis, asset prices notice a sharp decline in value, consumers and business are unable to pay their debts, and financial entities face a shortage of liquidity. Often, a financial crisis is related to a bank run or panic during which investors sell their assets or withdraw money from their savings accounts because they believe that if they stay in a financial institution, the value of those assets will decrease.

Certain circumstances that could be described as a financial crisis include a global financial bubble bursting, a sovereign default, a stock market crash, or a currency crisis. Financial crises can be confined to banks or spread across a single economy, a region's economy, or worldwide economies.

50. An investor opts for international portfolio investment because international diversification of portfolio of assets helps achieve a higher risk-adjusted return. This means that an investor is able to reduce risk and raise return through international investment.

Problems of International Investment: It is an established fact that the international diversification of portfolio is gainful. But there are also some problems that mar an optimal international diversification of portfolio. These problems are broadly:

- Unfavourable exchange rate movement
- Frictions in international financial market
- Manipulation of security prices
- Unequal access to information

51. The Mann-Whitney U-test is a nonparametric alternative to the t-test for two independent samples and can be used to test whether two independent samples have been taken from the same population. Therefore, when the assumptions of the parametric t-test are violated or are difficult to evaluate, such as with small samples, the Mann-Whitney U-test should be applied. This test is equivalent to the Wilcoxon-Mann-Whitney rank-sum test described in many textbooks as a t-test on the rank-transformed data.

52. Complementary events are two mutually exclusive events whose probabilities that add up to 1. $P(\overline{A})$ is the complement event of P(A). Tossing a coin, and complement of probability of head is $P(\overline{H}) = 0.5 = P(T)$. Similarly, tossing two coins, and $P(\overline{HH}) = 1 - P(HH) = P(HT) + P(TH) + P(TT)$, i.e., 0.75.

53. The chi-square random variable, denoted by χ^2, assumes only non-negative real numbers. The distribution has one parameter, the number of degrees of freedom. The family of chi-square distributions, like the "Student's" t distributions, has an infinite number of members, one for each number of degrees of freedom. The expectation of a chi-square distribution is equal to the number of degrees of freedom, and the variance of the distribution is equal to two times the number of degrees of freedom. The distribution is skewed to the right, the mean is greater than the median and the median is greater than the mode. The skewness decreases as the number of degrees of freedom increases. The chi-square distribution tends to the normal distribution as the number of degrees of freedom approaches infinity.

54. Management is a social science as well as an art. Thus the principles are not expected to be thoroughly exact as is the case with physical and natural sciences, The following basic nature of management principles should be kept in mind:

- ***Universality of Principles***: Henri Fayol has emphasized that management principles are universal. These can be applied in different organizations—business, government, hospital, military, etc. The basic task before every human organization is to get the desired results through integrated human efforts. Thus, the principles may be used with equal utility by the managers of different managerial levels. This shows the flexibility of a manager to handle different departments of an organization or the functions of different organizations. Some management thinkers, however, are against this universality.
- ***Dynamic Nature of Principles***: Management principles are flexible in nature and change with the changes in the environment in which an organization exists. Many of the golden principles of management which were thought to be very useful at one time are being replaced by others because of changes in the society. Continuous researches are being carried on the establish principles in the changing society and no principles can be regarded as a final truth. Nothing is permanent in the landslide of management.
- ***Relative, Not Absolute Principles***: Management principles are relative, not absolute and they should be applied according to the need of the organization. Organizations differ in respect of place, time, social, culture, etc. Moreover, individuals working in the same organization also differ. Thus a particular management principle has different strength in different conditions and the principle should be modified or placed by another. As Fayol has indicated 'principles of management are flexible, not absolute but must be utilized in the light of changing and twice conditions.' Seldom does one have to apply the same principles twice in identical conditions; allowance must be made for different changing circumstances.

- ***Limitations Due to Human Nature***: Management involves the reaction of human behaviour in the organization. It is also related with other human factors—suppliers, customers, owners, government, etc. The complex nature of human behaviour has considerably affected the progress of management principles. The principles of other disciplines dealing with human nature such as pyschology also are taken into account.

56. One important advantage of incentive plans is that they motivate employees to show superior performance. Employees are induced to produce more and earn more. Increased earnings would help employees to improve their standard of living. The other benefits of incentive plans are better utilisation of equipment, reduced supervision, reduced scrap, reduced lost time, reduced absenteeism and turnover. All these would, in the end, result in the reduction of total as well as unit cost of production.

57. Credit risk is the possibility of losses associated with a diminution in the credit quality of borrowers/counterparties. In a bank's credit portfolio, losses stem from outright default due to inability of unwillingness of a customer/ counterparty to meet his commitments in relation to lending, trading, settlement, and other financial transactions. Alternatively, losses result from a reduction in the portfolio value arising from actual or perceived deterioration in credit quality.

Credit risk emanates from the bank's dealings with an individuals, corporate, bank, financial institution or a sovereign and may take any of the following forms:

- In the case of direct lending: the principal and/or interest amount may not be repaid;
- In the case of guarantees or letter of credits; funds may not be coming from the constituents upon crystallisation of the liability;
- In the case of treasury operations: payment(s) due from the counterparties under the respective contacts may not be forthcoming or ceases;
- In the case of security trading business: funds/securities settlement may not be effected; and
- In the case of cross-border exposure: availability and free transfer of foreign currency funds may either be frozen or restrictions imposed by the action of, or because of political/economic conditions in the country where the borrower is located.

58. The advantages of the Electronic Purse:

- ***For the Bank***: Electronic purse provides a new method of payment which allows the bank to enter into a transatction market which is complementary to the credit or debit card transaction market. Electronic purse presents no risk of bay payment. Revenue is guaranteed from existence of the float account.
- ***For the Purse Holder***: The cash in an electronic purse cannot be spent if the purse is reported stolen or lost. A new electronic purse can be issued after loss, theft or destruction with the original balance restored. A single card can conveniently pay all small to medium purchases.
- ***For the Merchants***: Electronic purse represents a single method of accepting payments with no cash float to manage and no risk of theft.

60. A market-penetration pricing strategy involves setting a relatively low initial price for a new product to tap a substantial segment of large and growing market. The low price established for the new product helps a firm to penetrate deep into the market easily, capture a large share of a substantial market and earn profits quickly. Besides, low prices discourage competitors from entering the market because the profit margin is relatively small. The penetration pricing strategy has been successfully used by well-known companies. For example, Micromax entered the washing powder market by using penetration pricing; McDonald's success is primarily because it offers a wide range of food at low prices; and Dell is typically associated with penetration pricing.

61. Comparison of Traditional Logistics and Supply Chain Management Approaches

Element	Approach	
	Traditional	**Supply Chain**
Inventory management approach	Independent efforts	Joint reduction in channel inventories
Total cost approach	Minimise firm costs	Channel wide cost efficiencies
Time horizon	Short term	Long term
Amount of information sharing and monitoring	As required for planning and transaction	Limited to needs of current monitoring processes
Amount of coordination of levels in multiple levels in the channel and levels of channel	Single contact for the channel	Multiple contacts between transaction between firms
Joint Planning	Transaction-based	Ongoing
Compatibility of corporate philosophies	Not relevant	Compatible at least for keys relationships
Breadth of supplier base	Large ot increase competition and spread risk	Small to increase coordination
Channel leadership	Not needed	Needed for coordination focus
Amount of sharing of risks and the rewards	Each on its own	Risks and rewards shared over long term
Speed of operations, , information and inventory interconnecting flows	"Warehouse" orientation (storage, safety stock) interrupted by barriers to flow: localised to channel pairs	"Distribution Centre' orientation (inventory velocity) flows; JIT, Quick response across the channel

63. The Competition Act is an Act to provide, keeping in view of the economic development of the country, for the establishment of a commission to prevent practices having adverse effect on competition in the market. The Act provides for the protection of the interest of consumers and ensures the freedom of trade carried on by other participants in the markets, in India, and for matters connected therewith or incidental thereto.

Objectives: The preamble of this Act states that this is an Act to establish a commission, protect the interest of the consumers and ensure freedom of trade in markets in India. Following are some elements or the objectives for the act.

- to prohibit the agreements or practices th^t restrict free trading and also the competition between two business entities;
- to ban the abusive situation of the market monopoly;
- to provide the opportunity to the entrepreneur for the competition in the market;
- to have the international support and enforcement network across the world; and
- to prevent from anti-competition practices and to promote fair and healthy competition in the market.

64. Who is required to file ITR 4?

ITR 4 is to be filled by the individuals/HUF/ Partnership firm whose total income of AY 2020-21 includes as below:

- Business income under section 44AD or 44AE.
- Income from profession calculated under section 44ADA.

- Salary/pension having income up to ₹ 50 lakh.
- Income from One House Property having income up to ₹ 50 lakh (excluding the brought forward loss or loss to be carried forward cases under this head).
- Income from Other Sources having income up to ₹ 50 lakh (Excluding winning from lottery and income from horse races).

Who is not required to file ITR 4?

- An individual having income from salary, house property or other sources above ₹ 50 lakh cannot use this form.
- An individual who is either a director in a company and has invested in unlisted equity shares cannot use this form.
- An individual, HUF or partnership firm whose books of accounts should be audited under the Income Tax Act, 1961.

65. Business losses incurred by taxpayers in previous financial years can be adjusted against the taxable income of the current financial year. In keepint with the principles of natural justice, the Income Tax Act allows such adjustments to be made. Hence, the Income Tax Act has provisions for business loss setoff.

The following types of business loss are not deductible from business income:

- Losses sustained before the business is commenced.
- Losses incurred in the closing down of a business.
- Losses incurred due to damage, destructions, etc., of capital assets.
- A loss which is not incidental to the carrying on of the business of the assessee.
- Loss due to the sale of securities held as investments as it will be a capital loss and not the business loss.
- Loss caused by forfeiture of advance given for the purchase of capital assets.
- Violation of the law is not a normal incident of trade and an expense incurred by way of penalty for infraction of laws is not allowed for deduction as a business loss.
- Trading loss due to loss of goods in transit in the normal course of business.

76. Regional trade agreements in general exist in five types which are:

- Custome Union
- Free Trade Agreement
- Common Market
- Economic Union
- Preferential Trade Agreement

In custom union, two or more nations who form a union eliminate tariffs and non-tariff barriers among themselves but maintain and implement separate tariffs for outside nation and simultaneously the member countries agree to maintain common external tariffs. Few examples of custom union are East African community (EAC), European Union Custom Union (EUCU), Southern African Custom Union (SACU). Free trade agreement is almost similar to custom union but member countries do not maintain common external tariffs. Some of free trade agreement includes North Area Free Trade Area (NAFTA), AFTA, SAFTA, COMESA and GAFTA. Common market is the platform where there is a free movement of capital and services but major trade barrier remains. In general all tariff and quotas are eliminated for imported goods traded within the members but non-tariff barrier remains.

Major focus of common market is economic convergence and the formation of integrated single market. ASEAN and MERCOSUR are the example of common market. Economic union is another form of regional trade bloc which is an amalgamation of custom union and common market where the members of the trading bloc practice common policies on free movement of goods and services, factor of production and on product regulation and also follow common external trade policies.

Caribbean single market economy (CSME), European Union (EU) is the RTAs which comes under economic union. Pre-ferential trade agreement is another form of union where all the members of that union lowers the trade barriers. Regional trade Agreements though signed amongst nations to realize mutual gains but it does not guarantee the same because of regional bias.

77. Realisation of amount by a Liquidator: At the time of winding up, the Liquidator of the company realises the amount due from the debtors, the sale of the assets of the company, surplus from fully secured creditors, and makes calls on the contributories and realise the amount from them.

Disbursement of the amount realised among various claimants: The Liquidator has to disburse the amount in a prescribed order of payment. This is as follows:

- Payment to fully secured creditors.
- Payment of legal expenses, cost of winding up.
- Remuneration of the Liquidator.
- Epenses of Liquidator.
- Payment to debenture-holders or creditors secured by the floating charge as the assets of the company.
- Payment to unsecured creditors including the preferential creditors.
- Payment of preferential shareholders including arrears of dividend.
- Paym nt of equity shareholders (the remaining amount).

79. The capital budgeting process includes identifying and then evaluating capital projects for the company. Capital budgeting is a complex process, which may be divided into the following phases.

- ***Identification of project*:** The capital budgeting process begins with the identification of potential investment opportunities. A project is an investment proposal. At a given point of time, while the investible funds are limited, a firm may come across with mutually competing projects and mutually exclusive projects as well. Usually, the planning body (it can be an individual or a committee, formal or informal) develops estimates for future sales which serve as the basis of setting production targets. The expected level of sales and the required production capacity will help in arriving at the amount of investment.

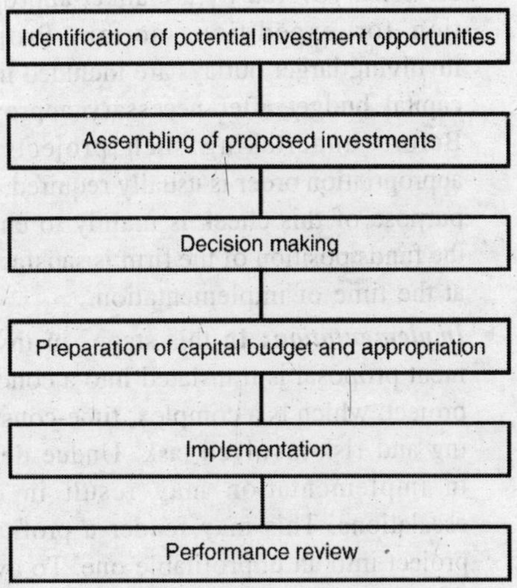

Capital budgeting process

- ***Assembling of proposed investments*:** Investment proposals identified by the production department and other departments are submitted in a standardized capital investment proposal form. Generally, most of the proposals are routed through several persons before they reach the planning body to ensure that the proposal is viewed from different angles. This not only enables the groups to have a sense of involvement in the decision-making process, but also brings abut coordination. Investment proposals are classified into various categories for facilitating decision making, budgeting, and control.

- ***Decision-making***: Executives are vested with the power to approve investment proposals keeping in mind of the constraints. Depending on the financial power, the executive decision-maker may range from a plant engineer to the *Managing Director* or a *Capital Budgeting Committee*.
- ***Preparation of capital budget and appropriations***: The decisions to invest is followed by financing alternatives. Projects involving smaller outlays and which can be decided by executives at lower levels are often covered by a blanket appropriation for expeditious action. Projects involving larger outlays are included in the capital budget after necessary approvals. Before undertaking such projects, an appropriation order is usually required. The purpose of this check is mainly to ensure the funds position of the firm is satisfactory at the time of implementation.
- ***Implementation***: In this stage, an investment proposal is translated into a concrete project, which is a complex, time-consuming and risk-involved task. Undue delays in implementation may result in cost escalations. This may render a profitable project into an unprofitable one. To avoid this, those in charge of implementation are assigned specific responsibilities for completion within the time-frame.

82. Conditions of Registration: The registration/renewal of portfolio managers is subject to the following conditions:

- Prior approval of the SEBI would be required for change of its status/constitution including amalgamation/demerger/consolidation/any other kinds of corporate restructuring, change in its managing/whole-time director(s), and any change in control over the body corporate, that is:
  - ❑ in case of listed shares, change in control in terms of the SEBI Substantial Acquisition of Shares and Takeover Regulations.
  - ❑ in any other case, change in controlling interest in the body corporate to the extent of at least 51 per cent of its voting rights;
- Payment of fee;
- Adequate steps for redressal of investors grievances within one month of the receipt of the complaint and keep the SEBI informed about the number/nature/other particulars of these complaints;
- Maintenance of the specified capital adequacy requirements; and
- Abide by the regulations under the SEBI Act in respect of its activities.

83. Stages in formation of a company: Steps involved in the formation of a company are:

- **Promotion:** It involves conceiving a business opportunity and taking an initiative to form a company after exploiting the available business opportunity. The person who performs all the tasks during the promotion stage is known as promoter.

  Steps in Promotion

  (Function of a Promoter)

  - ❑ Identification of business opportunity
  - ❑ Feasibility studies (include technical, financial and economic feasibility)
  - ❑ Name approval
  - ❑ Fixing up signatories to the memorandum of association
  - ❑ Appointment of professionals
  - ❑ Preparation of necessary documents
- **Incorporation:** Incorporation means registration of the company as a body corporate under the Indian Companies Act, 2013 and receiving 'Certificate of Incorporation'. A private company can start its business immediately after obtaining the 'Certificate of Incorporation'.

  Steps in Incorporation

  - ❑ Filing of necessary documents
  - ❑ Payment of fees
  - ❑ Registration
  - ❑ Certificate of incorporation

- **Capital Subsription:** A public company can raise funds from the public by issuing shares and debentures. For this, it has to issue a prospectus and undergo various other formalities.

Steps for Raising Funds from Public

- SEBI approval
- Filling of prospectus
- Appointment of bankers, brokers, underwriters
- Minimum subscription
- Application of stock exchange
- Allotment of shares

- **Commencement of Business:** A public company has to apply to the Registrar of Companies for the certificate of commencement of business along with the declaration that
  - Shares payable in cash have been subscribed and minimum subscription has been received.
  - Every director has paid in cash the money due on his/her shares.
  - No money is payable to applicants.
  - The above requirements have been complied with.

The Registrar, upon satisfaction, issues Certificate of Commencement of Business.

This certificate is also a conclusive evidence of completion of formation requirements.

85.

Provisions in Brief		
Basis of charge	Income is taxable under the head "Income from house property" only when the following three conditions are satisfied: 1. The property should consist of any buildings or lands appurtenant thereto. 2. The assessee should be owner of the property. 3. The property should not be used by the owner for the purpose of any business or profession carried on by him, the profits of which are chargeable to income tax.	
Computation of income of let out house property	Income from let out house property is computed as under.	₹
	Gross annual value	xxxx
	Less: Municipal taxes	xxxx
	Net annual value	xxxx
	Less: Deduction under section 24	
	-Standard deduction	xxxx
	-Interest on borrowed capital	xxxx
	Income from house property	xxxx

- Gross annual value will be calculated as follows:

Step I : Find out reasonable expected rent of the property

Step II : Find out rent actually received or receivable after excluding unrealized rent but before deducting loss due to vacancy

Step III : Find out which one is higher-amount computed in *Step I* or *Step II*.

Step IV : Find out loss because of vacancy.

Step V : *Step II* minus *Step IV* is gross annual value.

- *Reasonable expected rent*: The higher of municipal valuation (MV) and fair rent (FR), subject to maximum of standard rent (SR) (*i.e.*, rent as per the Rent Control Act), is reasonable expected rent.
- *Rent actually received or receivable*: It shall be calculated as follows:

Rent of the previous year (or that part of the previous year) for which the property is available for letting out	xxxx
Less: Unrealized rent if a rew conditions are satisfied	xxxx
Rent received/receivable before deducting loss due to vacancy	xxxx

- *Loss due to vacancy*: It is separately dedycted under *Step IV*. Not to be dudycted under *Step III* from actually received or receivable

Deductiable only if (*a*) these taxes are borne by the owner, and (*b*) are actually paid by him during the previous year.

For Q.No. (96 to 100)

It is given that budgeted overhead rate is ₹ 1 per hour. It is also given that budgeted fixed overheads is ₹ 30,000.

Therefore budgeted hours
= 30,000 hours.

Hours allowed per unit of output
= 30,000 hours/20,000 units
= 1.5 hours.

96. Total Overhead Variance
= (SR × SH) – AFC

Where,
SR = Standard fixed overhead, rate per hour
= ₹ 1
SH = Standard hours allowed for actual output
= 1.5 hours × 22,000 units
= 33,000 hours
AFC = Actual fixed cost = ₹ 31,000

Total Overhead Variance
= (₹ 1 × 33,000) – ₹ 31,000
= ₹ 2,000 (Favourable)

97. Expenditure Variance
= (Budgeted Fixed Overhead Cost)
– (Actual Fixed Overhead Cost)
= ₹ 30,000 – ₹ 31,000
= ₹ 1,000 (Adverse)

98. Volume Variance
= (Budgeted Fixed Overhead Cost)
– (Fixed Overhead Absorbed)
= ₹ 30,000 – ₹ 33,000
= ₹ 3,000 (Favourable)

99. Capacity Variance = SR(BH – AH)

Where,
SR = Standard fixed overhead rate per hour
= ₹ 1
BH = Budgeted hours
= 30,000 hours/25 days × 27 days
= 32,400 hours
AH = Actual hours worked = 31,500 hours

Capacity Variance
= ₹ 1(32,400 hours – 31,500 hours)
= ₹ 900 (adverse)

100. Calendar Variance = SRD (BD – AD)

Where,
SRD = Standard fixed overhead per day
= ₹ 30,000/25 = ₹ 1,200
BD = Budgeted number of days per month
= 25 days
AD = Actual number of days per month
= 27 days

Calendar Variance
= ₹ 1,200 (25 days – 27 days)
= ₹ 2,400 (Favourable)

Previous Years' Paper (Solved)

National Testing Agency (NTA)

UGC-NET Junior Research Fellowship & Assistant Professor Eligibility Exam

COMMERCE, June–2020

(Online exam held on 17-10-2020)

PAPER-II

Note: *This paper contains* ***hundred (100)*** *objective type questions of* ***two (2)*** *marks each.* ***All questions are compulsory.***

1. As per Section 80G maximum deduction allowed for any cash donation is upto:

A. ₹ 1,000 B. ₹ 2,000
C. ₹ 5,000 D. ₹ 10,000

2. In Leontief production function, L is considered as:

A. Structural constraint in the production process
B. Degree of Homogeneity
C. Binding constraint in the production process
D. Optimisation constraint in the production process

3. EPRG framework in International Business refers to:

A. Ethno, Poly, Regio, Geo Transformations
B. Ethnocentric, Polycentric, Regiocentric and Geocentric Orientations
C. Ethics, Policies, Regulations, Guidelines Orientations
D. Every Person Refers Global Framework

4. Which one of the following is not a major direct selling company in India?

A. Eureka Forbes
B. Amway India Enterprises
C. Modicare
D. Hindustan Unilever Ltd.

5. Which one of the following statements is 'True' in partnership?

A. In the absence of any provision in the partnership deed, only a working partner is entitled to remuneration.
B. Any firm which earns normal profit has no goodwill.
C. The business of the firm must be carried on by all the partners.
D. Interest on loan given by a partner to the firm shall be paid if there are profits.

6. Which of the following relationships is true in a model distribution?

A. Mean – Mode = 3 (Mean – Median)
B. Mode = 3 Median – 2 Mean
C. 3 Median = 2 Mean + Mode
D. 2 Median – 3 Quartile Deviation = 2 Mean

7. In continuous compounding, the time it takes to double the sum grossly follow 'Rule of 69'. If it is changed to discrete compounding, the relevant rule of thumb is _____.

A. Rule of 69.3 B. Rule of 72
C. Rule of 84 D. Rule of 64

8. The 'going concern concept' is the underlying basis for:

A. Disclosing the market value of securities
B. Consolidating the accounts of subsidiary companies with those of parent company
C. Depreciating fixed assets over their useful lives
D. Disclosing the sales and other operating information in the income statement

9. 'Constraint Optimisation' is closer to which of the following objectives of business firm?
A. Sales maximisation
B. Profit maximisation
C. Satisfying behaviour
D. Rent seeking behaviour

10. In a rising consumer income scenario, the preferred decision choice of business firms for low income elastic products will be ______.
A. Product promotion
B. Cost control
C. Product repositioning
D. Product improvement

11. If an estimated Cobb-Douglas production function is $Q = 10K^{0.6}L^{0.8}$, what type of returns to scale does this production function indicate?
A. Increasing returns
B. Decreasing returns
C. Constant returns
D. Negative returns

12. Pricing strategy of setting a high price when a product is introduced and gradually lowering its price is known as:
A. Skimming
B. Penetration pricing
C. Peak load pricing
D. Dumping

13. Which one of the following is not true for Mass Marketing?
A. Provides very little scope for customisation
B. Deals with customers directly
C. Normally followed in case of FMCG and SMCG Goods
D. Relies heavily on advertising

14. A manufacturing enterprise monthly consumes 1,350 units of raw material at the cost of ₹ 20 per unit. Determine its economic order quantity given the ordering cost of ₹ 2,400 and carrying cost of inventory being 30 per cent of the price paid.
A. 3,600 units B. 2,400 units
C. 4,800 units D. 2,700 units

15. The portfolio theory articulates diversification to reduce which of the following risks?
A. Market risk B. Financial risk
C. Unsystematic risk D. Business risk

16. When foreign currency assets and liabilities match in terms of amount of exposure and timing of maturities, it is described as:
A. Financial hedge B. Natural hedge
C. Perfect hedge D. Netting

17. What is the probability that a randomly choosen card from a deck of cards will either be a King or a Spade?
A. 0.3077 B. 0.3269
C. 0.0384 D. 0.3169

18. The standard deviation of the binomial distribution is:
A. np B. $\sqrt{np}$
C. npq D. $\sqrt{npq}$

19. When sampling is done without replacement then standard error of mean is:
A. $SE_{\bar{X}} = \frac{\sigma}{\sqrt{n}}$
B. $SE_{\bar{X}} = \frac{\sigma}{\sqrt{n}}\sqrt{\frac{N-n}{N-1}}$
C. $SE_{\bar{X}} = \frac{\sigma}{\sqrt{n}}\sqrt{\frac{N-1}{N-n}}$
D. $SE_{\bar{X}} = \frac{\sigma}{\sqrt{n}}\sqrt{1-\frac{n}{N}}$

20. Which of the following is not an example of compressed data?
A. Data array
B. Frequency distribution
C. Histogram
D. Ogive

21. The Human Relations Approach rejected the 'rabble hypothesis' by giving which of the following argument?

A. The worker does not work for money only.
B. A worker operates in a techno-economic system with no room for emotions.
C. Authoritarian style of leadership is more productive.
D. Individual pays attention to self-achievement irrespective of informal group norms.

22. Which of the following is not correct with respect to matrix organisation?
A. It is a combination of functional and product organisation
B. Functional departments are not permanent fixtures of a matrix organisation
C. Product departments are created as the need for them arises
D. Team members have functional home when they are not needed on a project

23. As per Carroll Model, the four levels of Corporate Social Responsibility are:
A. Physical, economic, social and legal
B. Physical, economic, legal and ethical
C. Philanthropic, economic, legal and ethical
D. Philanthropic, economic, social and ethical

24. Who coined the term 'Collective Bargaining'?
A. Reed Richardson
B. Kurt Lewin
C. W.E. Deming
D. Sydney Webb and Beatrice Webb

25. The headquarters of the ASEAN is located in which of the following country?
A. Indonesia B. Vietnam
C. Thailand D. Singapore

26. What is the rate of tax deduction at source from insurance commission in case of 'Person'?
A. 2 per cent B. 5 per cent
C. 10 per cent D. 4 per cent

27. Which of the following is a long term source of finance?
A. Commercial Paper (CP)
B. External Commercial Borrowings (ECB)
C. Factoring
D. Line of Credit (LOC)

28. What is a 'Repo Rate'?
A. Is the rate at which RBI lends to State Government
B. Is the rate at which International aid agencies lends to RBI
C. Is the rate at which the RBI lends to Banks in case of short maturity
D. Is the rate at which RBI borrows funds from the Commercial Banks in the country

29. In Marketing, DSA stands for _____.
A. Delivery Staff Agency
B. Direct Supplier Agent
C. Direct Selling Agent
D. Distribution and Supply Agency

30. In which of the following stages of product life cycle a company reduces sales promotion to take advantage of heavy consumer demand?
A. Introduction B. Growth
C. Maturity D. Decline

31. In which of the following price adjustment strategies, a company reduces prices to reward customer responses such as volume purchases, paying early or promoting the product?
A. Discount and allowance pricing
B. Psychological pricing
C. Promotional pricing
D. Dynamic pricing

32. Some doctors charge patients for missed appointments because the service value existed only at that point and disappeared when the patient did not show up, is an example of which one of the following four service characteristics?
A. Inseparability B. Intangibility
C. Variability D. Perishability

33. Which one is False as per the relevant provisions of the Indian Contract Act, 1872?
A. A void agreement is one that is not enforceable by law

B. Assignment is the obvious mode of discharge of a contract

C. Where a party waives its rights under the contract, the other party is released of its obligations under the contract

D. Where the subject matter of a contract is destroyed for no fault of the promisor, the contract does not become void by impossibility of performance

34. Which of the following is not an implied condition in a contract of sale?

A. Condition as to quality or fitness

B. Condition as to merchantable quality

C. Condition as to wholesomeness

D. Condition as to free from encumbrances

35. Which of the following does not come under the definition of "Information" under RTI Act, 2005?

A. Log Books

B. Circulars

C. File Notings in the process

D. Data material held in any electronic form

36. Under which section of Information Technology Act of 2000, updated in 2008, stealing any digital asset or information is considered as cyber crime?

A. 65 B. 65D

C. 67 D. 70

37. Which one of the following statements is true for the set off and carry forward of loss under the head 'house property' in India?

A. Can be carried forward for 8 years

B. Can not be carried forward

C. Can be carried forward for 4 years

D. Can be carried forward infinitely

38. Surcharge of 10% (per cent) is payable by an individual where the total income exceeds:

A. ₹ 7,50,000 B. ₹ 8,50,000

C. ₹ 50,00,000 D. ₹ 20,00,000

39. Mohan, has rendered his services in India and retired in 2015. He then shifted and settled in Singapore. The pension received by him for such services would be ______?

A. Deemed to accure or arise outside India

B. Deemed to accure or arise in India only when it is received in India

C. Deemed to accure or arise in India only when it is received outside India

D. Deemed to accure or arise in India

40. Sugam is also known as:

A. ITR-1 B. ITR-2

C. ITR-4 D. ITR-6

41. Mercosur, a South American Trade block is a:

A. Free Trade Area

B. Common Market

C. Custom Union

D. Economic Cooperation

42. Which of the following are possible negative impacts of FDI on domestic firms in host countries?

(*a*) Market monopoly

(*b*) Technology dependence

(*c*) Increased competition

(*d*) Profit outflow

Choose the correct answer from the options given below:

A. (*a*), (*b*) only

B. (*b*), (*c*) only

C. (*a*), (*b*), (*d*) only

D. (*b*), (*c*), (*d*) only

43. Charging different prices for the same product in different markets until the MR of last unit sold equals the MC of the product sold in each market is described by ____.

(*a*) Price discrimination of first degree

(*b*) Price discrimination of second degree

(*c*) Price discrimination of third degree

(*d*) Equilibrium price

(*e*) Price discrimination

Choose the correct answer from the options given below:

A. (*a*) and (*b*) only

B. (*a*) and (*c*) only

C. (*c*) and (*e*) only

D. (*a*) and (*d*) only

44. Arrange the following steps in logical sequence of operation of the Arbitrage Pricing Theory (APT).

(*a*) Estimate the Factor Sensitivities
(*b*) Estimate the Risk Premium for Factor(s)
(*c*) Identify the Macroeconomic Factors

Choose the correct answer from the options given below:

A. (*a*), (*b*), (*c*) B. (*b*), (*a*), (*c*)
C. (*c*), (*b*), (*a*) D. (*c*), (*a*), (*b*)

45. Cost audit for Materials covers:

(*a*) Goods inward procedure.
(*b*) Methods of calculating standard cost variance
(*c*) Classification of overhead.
(*d*) Accounting for scrap, wastage, materials transfers
(*e*) Accounting treatment of under or over absorption

Choose the most appropriate answer from the options given below:

A. (*a*), (*d*) only B. (*a*), (*e*) only
C. (*a*), (*b*) only D. (*e*), (*c*) only

46. Which of the following explains the declining slope of indifference curves?

(*a*) Diminishing marginal utility
(*b*) Diminishing Marginal Rate of substitutions between the commodities
(*c*) Diminishing Marginal Rate of technical substitution
(*d*) Ordinal measurement of utilities
(*e*) Diminishing Marginal utility of money

Choose the most appropriate answer from the options given below:

A. (*a*) and (*d*) only B. (*b*) and (*d*) only
C. (*c*) and (*d*) only D. (*a*) and (*e*) only

47. Which of the following is/are condition(s) for price discrimination of product?

(*a*) Firm must have some monopoly power.
(*b*) Price elasticities of demand for the product in different market must differ
(*c*) Market must be separable or able to be segmented
(*d*) Free entry and exit of firms

Choose the correct answer from the options given below:

A. (*a*) and (*d*) only
B. (*b*), (*c*) and (*d*) only
C. (*a*), (*c*) and (*d*) only
D. (*a*), (*b*) and (*c*) only

48. Consumer rationality in business economics is collective manifestation of which of the following assumptions?

(*a*) Non-Satiation
(*b*) Clarity of preferences
(*c*) Divisibility of goods and services
(*d*) Economic selfish motive
(*e*) Possession of information

Choose the most appropriate answer from the options given below:

A. (*a*), (*b*) and (*d*) only
B. (*a*), (*c*) and (*e*) only
C. (*a*), (*b*), (*c*) and (*d*) only
D. (*a*), (*b*), (*d*) and (*e*) only

49. Net Present Value (NPV) and Internal Rate of Return (IRR) methods yield conflicting outcomes due to ______.

(*a*) Unconventional cash flows
(*b*) Investment size disparity
(*c*) Investment life disparity
(*d*) Cash flow pattern disparity

Choose the most appropriate answer from the options given below:

A. (*a*) and (*b*) only
B. (*a*) and (*c*) only
C. (*a*), (*b*) and (*c*) only
D. (*b*), (*c*) and (*d*) only

50. In which of the following situations, the payback period method is advised for evaluation of investment opportunities?

(*a*) Overleveraged businesses
(*b*) Cash rich businesses
(*c*) Uncertain market conditions
(*d*) Stable market conditions

Choose the most appropriate answer from the options given below:

A. (*a*) and (*b*) only B. (*a*) and (*c*) only
C. (*b*) and (*c*) only D. (*c*) and (*d*) only

51. The Regression Coefficient is independent of the change of:
(*a*) Scale only
(*b*) Origin only
(*c*) Both Scale and Origin
(*d*) Neither Scale nor Origin
Choose the most appropriate answer from the options given below:
A. (*a*) only B. (*b*) only
C. (*c*) only D. (*d*) only

52. Which of the following are positional averages?
(*a*) Arithmetic Mean
(*b*) Median
(*c*) Mode
(*d*) Geometric Mean
(*e*) Harmonic Mean
Choose the most appropriate answer from the options given below:
A. (*b*), (*c*) only
B. (*b*), (*c*), (*d*) only
C. (*b*), (*c*), (*a*) only
D. (*a*), (*b*), (*c*), (*d*) only

53. Which of following is not correct about properties of correlation coefficient?
(*a*) Depends on the origin.
(*b*) Depends on the scale.
(*c*) Depends on both origin and scale.
(*d*) Is independent with respect to origin.
(*e*) Is independent with respect to unit of scale.
Choose the correct answer from the options given below:
A. (*a*), (*d*), (*e*) only B. (*a*), (*b*), (*d*) only
C. (*a*), (*b*), (*c*) only D. (*d*), (*e*), (*b*) only

54. What type of defense mechanism is used by a person when he gets angry at his child or spouse because he had a bad day at work?
(*a*) Denial (*b*) Repression
(*c*) Projection (*d*) Displacement
(*e*) Regression
Choose the most appropriate answer from the options given below:
A. (*a*) and (*b*) only B. (*b*) only
C. (*d*) only D. (*e*) only

55. Out of the following statements which of them explains the difference between enculturation and acculturation as a part of Cross-Cultural Training?
(*a*) Enculturation refer to the process of learning and adopting host cultural norms, and acculturation is the process of learning our own native culture.
(*b*) Enculturation is a anthropological term used for socialisation like acculturation.
(*c*) Both terms refer to the process of Learning through social interaction.
(*d*) Enculturation refers to the process of learning our own culture, and acculturation refers to the process of learning host cultural norms.
Choose the most appropriate answer from the options given below:
A. (*a*), (*b*), (*c*) only
B. (*b*), (*d*) only
C. (*b*), (*c*), (*d*) only
D. (*a*), (*b*), (*c*) and (*d*) only

56. Which of the following financial institution(s) got merged with their subsidiary?
(*a*) UTI
(*b*) IFCI
(*c*) ICICI
(*d*) IDBI
(*e*) Global Trust Bank
Choose the correct answer from the options given below:
A. (*a*), (*b*) only B. (*b*), (*c*) only
C. (*c*), (*d*) only D. (*c*), (*e*) only

57. Objectives of IMPS (Immediate Payment Service) are:
(*a*) To enable bank customers to use mobile instruments as a channel for accessing their banks accounts and remit funds 24 × 7.
(*b*) Making payments simpler just with the mobile number of the beneficiary.
(*c*) To build the foundation for a full range of mobile based banking services
(*d*) To create competition with NEFT and RTGS

Choose the most appropriate answer from the options given below:

A. (*a*), (*b*), (*c*) only
B. (*b*), (*c*), (*d*) only
C. (*a*), (*b*), (*d*) only
D. (*b*), (*d*) only

58. Which among the followings are correct statements with regard to NBFC in India?

(*a*) All NBFCs should be registered with RBI.
(*b*) NBFCs cannot accept demand deposits.
(*c*) NBFCs do not form part of the payment and settlement system and cannot issue cheques drawn on itself.
(*d*) Deposit insurance facility of Deposit Insurance and Credit Guarantee Corporation is not available to depositors of NBFCs.

Choose the correct answer from the options given below:

A. (*a*), (*b*), (*c*) only
B. (*a*), (*b*), (*c*), (*d*) only
C. (*a*), (*b*), (*d*) only
D. (*a*), (*d*) only

59. Which of the following are true about delivering customer value?

(*a*) A company can go alone in creating customer value
(*b*) Company must work within a broader network of partners to accomplish customer value.
(*c*) Individual companies and brands compete; their entire value delivery networks don't.
(*d*) Individual companies and brands don't compete; their entire value delivery networks do.
(*e*) Value = Contribution/cost (offer higher contribution through product or service to clients and lowers the cost)

Choose the most appropriate answer from the options given below:

A. (*a*) and (*e*) only
B. (*a*), (*b*) and (*e*) only
C. (*b*), (*c*) and (*e*) only
D. (*b*), (*d*) and (*e*) only

60. Market for automobiles needs to be segmented on the basis of:

(*a*) Buying behaviour
(*b*) Psychographies
(*c*) Geographies
(*d*) Demographics

Choose the most appropriate answer from the options given below:

A. (*a*), (*d*) only
B. (*c*), (*d*) only
C. (*a*), (*b*), (*d*) only
D. (*a*), (*b*), (*c*), (*d*)

61. The strategies of flanking defense, preemptive defense, mobile defense, contractor defense and counter offensive defense is used by which market player?

(*a*) Market challenger
(*b*) Market leader
(*c*) Market follower
(*d*) Market Nicher
(*e*) Start up Marketer

Choose the most appropriate answer from the options given below:

A. (*a*) only
B. (*b*) only
C. (*c*) only
D. (*b*), (*e*) only

62. Out of the following statements, which is not correct about the RTI Act, 2005?

(*a*) The RTI Act come into force from October 13, 2005.
(*b*) Any citizen may request information from a Public Authority (Both Govt. and Private)
(*c*) Reply for information asked can be given within 30 days.
(*d*) There is a nominal application fee that are needs to pay to get information under the RTI application.
(*e*) For getting information, applicant has to pay ₹ 10 per page of information for Central Govt. Departments.

Choose the correct answer from the options given below:

A. (*a*), (*b*), (*e*) only
B. (*b*), (*e*) only
C. (*c*), (*e*) only
D. (*b*), (*c*), (*d*), (*e*) only

63. Out of the following, which are not the features of GST 2017 in India.

(*a*) GST is applicable on 'supply' of Goods and Services.

(*b*) GST is based on the principle of origin based taxation rather than principle of destination based consumption.

(*c*) Import of Goods is treated as Inter-State supplies and would be subject to IGST in addition to applicable Custom Duties.

(*d*) It is a dual taxation with Centre and State simultaneously levying it on a common base.

(*e*) GST is applicable to all Goods and Services without any exemptions.

Choose the correct answer from the options given below:

A. (*a*), (*b*), (*e*) only B. (*b*), (*c*), (*e*) only
C. (*b*), (*e*) only D. (*c*), (*d*), (*e*) only

64. Which of the followings is correct about deduction available in respect of contribution to various provident funds in case of salaried employees?

(*a*) Employer's contribution to recognised provident fund is exempted upto 12% of salary.

(*b*) Employer's contribution to unrecognised provident fund is exempted from tax.

(*c*) Employer does not contribute to Public Provident Fund.

(*d*) Deduction under Section 80 C is available for employer's contribution in unrecognized provident fund.

Choose the correct answer from the options given below:

A. (*a*), (*b*), (*c*) only
B. (*a*), (*b*), (*d*) only
C. (*b*), (*c*), (*d*) only
D. (*a*), (*c*), (*d*) only

65. Which of the following expenses debited to Profit and Loss A/c but disallowed while computing income from Business?

(*a*) General Expenses

(*b*) Personal Expenses

(*c*) Expenses of Income which is taxable under the other heads of income

(*d*) Charities and donations

Choose the correct answer from the options given below:

A. (*a*), (*b*), (*c*) only
B. (*b*), (*c*), (*d*) only
C. (*c*), (*d*) only
D. (*a*), (*b*), (*c*), (*d*) only

66. Match List-I with List-II:

List-I (Authors of Trade Theory)	List-II (Name of Theory)
(*a*) Steffan Linder	(*i*) Product Life Cycle Theory
(*b*) Raymond Vernon	(*ii*) Country Similarity Theory
(*c*) Hecksher-Ohlin	(*iii*) Absolute Advantage Theory
(*d*) Adam Smith	(*iv*) Factor Proportion Theory

Choose the correct answer from the options given below:

	(*a*)	(*b*)	(*c*)	(*d*)
A.	(*iv*)	(*iii*)	(*ii*)	(*i*)
B.	(*ii*)	(*i*)	(*iv*)	(*iii*)
C.	(*i*)	(*iii*)	(*iv*)	(*ii*)
D.	(*iii*)	(*ii*)	(*i*)	(*iv*)

67. Match List-I with List-II:

List-I	List-II
(*a*) Standard Costing	(*i*) Financial forecasting and planning
(*b*) Margin of Safety	(*ii*) Sales minus break-even sales
(*c*) Ratio Analysis	(*iii*) Control of inventory
(*d*) JIT System	(*iv*) Management by exception

Choose the correct answer from the options given below:

	(*a*)	(*b*)	(*c*)	(*d*)
A.	(*iv*)	(*ii*)	(*i*)	(*iii*)
B.	(*iii*)	(*i*)	(*ii*)	(*iv*)
C.	(*ii*)	(*iii*)	(*i*)	(*iv*)
D.	(*i*)	(*ii*)	(*iv*)	(*iii*)

68. Match the market forms in the List-I and the role of the selling costs in the List-II:

List-I (Market Forms)	List-II (Role of selling costs)
(*a*) Perfect Competition	(*i*) Sustained survival of firm
(*b*) Monopoly	(*ii*) Influencing buying behaviour
(*c*) Monopolistic	(*iii*) Increasing market size
(*d*) Oligopoly Competition	(*iv*) Intimation of product or service

Choose the correct answer from the options given below:

	(*a*)	(*b*)	(*c*)	(*d*)
A.	(*i*)	(*iii*)	(*iv*)	(*ii*)
B.	(*iv*)	(*ii*)	(*i*)	(*iii*)
C.	(*iii*)	(*iv*)	(*ii*)	(*i*)
D.	(*ii*)	(*i*)	(*iii*)	(*iv*)

69. Match List-I with List-II:

List-I	List-II
(*a*) Mezzanine Capital	(*i*) It is the speedy source of finance less regulated by the regulatory environment of debt and capital markets.
(*b*) Private Equity	(*ii*) It is long term capital embraced by the high networth and high risk appetite investors.
(*c*) Global Depository Receipts	(*iii*) It is an equity instrument issued in overseas markets and is listed and traded on bourses on an OTC basis.
(*d*) Venture Capital	(*iv*) It refers to subordinated debt or preferred equity that allows firms to borrow additional capital beyond the levels lenders are willing to finance through the bank loans.

Choose the correct answer from the options given below:

	(*a*)	(*b*)	(*c*)	(*d*)
A.	(*ii*)	(*iv*)	(*i*)	(*iii*)
B.	(*i*)	(*iii*)	(*iv*)	(*ii*)
C.	(*iv*)	(*i*)	(*iii*)	(*ii*)
D.	(*iii*)	(*ii*)	(*i*)	(*iv*)

70. Match List-I with List-II:

List-I	List-II
(*a*) Bayes' Theorem	(*i*) $P(\bar{E}) = 1 - P(E)$
(*b*) Conditional Probability	(*ii*) $P(E_1 \cup E_2) = P(E_1) + P(E_2)$
(*c*) Theorem of complementary events	(*iii*) $P\left(\frac{E_2}{E_1}\right) = \frac{P(E_1 \cap E_2)}{P(E_1)}$
(*d*) Theorem of addition	(*iv*) $P\left(\frac{H_i}{E}\right) = \frac{P(H_i \cap E)}{P(E)}$

Choose the correct answer from the options given below:

	(*a*)	(*b*)	(*c*)	(*d*)
A.	(*i*)	(*iv*)	(*iii*)	(*ii*)
B.	(*iii*)	(*iv*)	(*ii*)	(*i*)
C.	(*iii*)	(*iv*)	(*i*)	(*ii*)
D.	(*iv*)	(*iii*)	(*i*)	(*ii*)

71. Match List-I with List-II:

List-I	List-II
(*a*) I am Not OK, you are Not OK	(*i*) Dependent
(*b*) I am OK, you are Not OK	(*ii*) Confronting
(*c*) I am OK, you are OK	(*iii*) Withdrawn
(*d*) I am Not OK, you are OK	(*iv*) Task obsessive

Choose the correct answer from the options given below:

	(*a*)	(*b*)	(*c*)	(*d*)
A.	(*iii*)	(*iv*)	(*ii*)	(*i*)
B.	(*iii*)	(*ii*)	(*iv*)	(*i*)
C.	(*i*)	(*ii*)	(*iii*)	(*iv*)
D.	(*ii*)	(*i*)	(*iii*)	(*iv*)

72. Match List-I with List-II:

List-I (Capital Structure Preposition(s))	List-II (Description(s))
(*a*) Target Capital Structure	(*i*) Expected yield on the equity capital is equal to the pure equity return plus a premium for financial risk.
(*b*) Optimum Capital Structure	(*ii*) It refers to the perceived costs due to increased ratio of debt in the firm.
(*c*) Cost of financial distress	(*iii*) It is the debt ratio the firm strives to achieve.
(*d*) MM preposition-II	(*iv*) It is the debt-equity ratio that maximises the value of the firm.

Choose the correct answer from the options given below:

	(*a*)	(*b*)	(*c*)	(*d*)
A.	(*ii*)	(*iii*)	(*i*)	(*iv*)
B.	(*iii*)	(*iv*)	(*ii*)	(*i*)
C.	(*iv*)	(*ii*)	(*iii*)	(*i*)
D.	(*i*)	(*iii*)	(*ii*)	(*iv*)

73. Match List-I with List-II:

List-I (Authors)	List-II (Ideas)
(*a*) Bill Bishop	(*i*) Managing in the Market Space
(*b*) D. Bird	(*ii*) Commonsense Direct Marketing
(*c*) Daniel S. Jonal	(*iii*) Strategic Marketing for the Digital Age
(*d*) Jeffery F. Rayport	(*iv*) On-line Marketing

Choose the correct answer from the options given below:

	(*a*)	(*b*)	(*c*)	(*d*)
A.	(*iii*)	(*ii*)	(*iv*)	(*i*)
B.	(*i*)	(*ii*)	(*iii*)	(*iv*)
C.	(*ii*)	(*i*)	(*iv*)	(*iii*)
D.	(*iv*)	(*iii*)	(*ii*)	(*i*)

74. Match List-I with List-II:

List-I	List-II
(*a*) Limited Liability Partnership	(*i*) It can be formed with a minimum of two individuals or body corporate through their nominees.
(*b*) Particular Partnership	(*ii*) It is formed for a specific venture or for a particular period.
(*c*) Partnership	(*iii*) It is an association of two or more individuals.
(*d*) Mutual Agency	(*iv*) A partner is both an agent and a principal in a partnership firm.

Choose the correct answer from the options given below:

	(*a*)	(*b*)	(*c*)	(*d*)
A.	(*i*)	(*ii*)	(*iii*)	(*iv*)
B.	(*ii*)	(*iii*)	(*i*)	(*iv*)
C.	(*ii*)	(*i*)	(*iii*)	(*iv*)
D.	(*iv*)	(*ii*)	(*i*)	(*iii*)

75. Match List-I with List-II

List-I	List-II
(*a*) 80 GG	(*i*) Deduction in respect of contribution given by companies to political parties.
(*b*) 80 GGA	(*ii*) Deduction in respect of contribution given by any person to political parties.
(*c*) 80 GGB	(*iii*) Deduction in respect of scientific research.
(*d*) 80 GGC	(*iv*) Deduction in respect of rent paid.

Choose the correct answer from the options given below:

	(*a*)	(*b*)	(*c*)	(*d*)
A.	(*iv*)	(*iii*)	(*i*)	(*ii*)
B.	(*iii*)	(*iv*)	(*ii*)	(*i*)
C.	(*iv*)	(*iii*)	(*ii*)	(*i*)
D.	(*iv*)	(*ii*)	(*i*)	(*iii*)

76. Arrange the following legal enactments in India in the chronological sequence from the first to the last.

(*a*) The Mines Act
(*b*) The Minimum Wages Act
(*c*) The Payment of Gratuity Act
(*d*) The Child Labour (Prohibition and Regulation) Act
(*e*) The Apprentices Act

Choose the correct answer from the options given below:

A. (*b*), (*d*), (*c*), (*a*), (*e*)
B. (*b*), (*a*), (*e*), (*c*), (*d*)
C. (*a*), (*e*). (*b*), (*c*), (*d*)
D. (*e*), (*b*), (*a*), (*c*), (*d*)

77. Arrange in the sequence of decisions in manufacturing enterprises:

(*a*) Making of forecasts
(*b*) Determination of key factors
(*c*) Consideration of alternative combination of forecasts
(*d*) Preparation of budgets
(*e*) Combination of factors

Choose the correct answer from the options given below:

A. (*a*), (*b*), (*c*), (*e*), (*d*)
B. (*c*), (*a*), (*e*), (*b*), (*d*)
C. (*b*), (*a*), (*c*), (*e*), (*d*)
D. (*a*), (*c*), (*b*), (*e*), (*d*)

78. Arrange the following products in the increasing order of price elasticities:

(*a*) Homogeneous products
(*b*) Differentiated products
(*c*) Necessities
(*d*) Durable goods

Choose the correct answer from the options given below:

A. (*c*), (*b*), (*d*) and (*a*)
B. (*a*), (*b*), (*c*) and (*d*)
C. (*a*), (*c*), (*b*) and (*d*)
D. (*c*), (*a*), (*b*) and (*d*)

79. Arrange the following financing choices in order of preference suggested by the pecking order theory:

(*a*) Reinvestment of earnings
(*b*) New issue of equity
(*c*) Issue of debt

Choose the correct answer from the options given below:

A. (*a*), (*b*), (*c*)
B. (*a*), (*c*), (*b*)
C. (*b*), (*c*), (*a*)
D. (*b*), (*a*), (*c*)

80. Arrange the following stages of research in a proper sequence:

(*a*) Report Writing
(*b*) Budgeting
(*c*) Data Collection
(*d*) Field Work
(*e*) Research outcomes

Choose the correct answer from the options given below:

A. (*b*), (*d*), (*c*), (*e*), (*a*)
B. (*d*), (*a*), (*b*), (*c*), (*e*)
C. (*d*), (*c*), (*b*), (*e*), (*a*)
D. (*b*), (*e*), (*d*), (*c*), (*a*)

81. Arrange the following steps of creating a market-competitive pay plan in a sequence from the first to the last:

(*a*) Choose benchmark jobs and select compensable factors
(*b*) Define each compensable factor and determine its degree in each job
(*c*) Establish rate changes
(*d*) Develop pay grades
(*e*) Compare and adjust current and market wage rates for jobs

Choose the correct answer from the options given below:

A. (*b*), (*a*), (*e*), (*d*), (*c*)
B. (*a*), (*c*), (*b*), (*d*), (*e*)
C. (*a*), (*b*), (*e*), (*d*), (*c*)
D. (*a*), (*b*), (*c*), (*e*), (*d*)

82. Arrange the following initiatives taken by the Government of India to tackle the Non performing assets in their ascending order of chronology:

(*a*) Corporate Debt Restructuring
(*b*) Compromise Settlement

(*c*) The Debt Recovery Tribunals (DRTs)
(*d*) Credit Information Bureau
(*e*) SARFAESI Act

Choose the correct answer from the options given below:

A. (*c*), (*d*), (*a*), (*b*), (*e*)
B. (*a*), (*b*), (*e*), (*c*), (*d*)
C. (*c*), (*d*), (*b*), (*e*), (*a*)
D. (*d*), (*c*), (*b*), (*e*), (*a*)

83. Arrange the following steps of marketing process in proper sequence:

(*a*) Construct an integrated marketing programme that delivers superior value
(*b*) Capture value from customers to create profits and customer equity
(*c*) Understand the market place and customer needs and wants
(*d*) Engage customers, build profitable relationships, and create customer delight
(*e*) Design a customer value-driven marketing strategy

Choose the correct answer from the options given below:

A. (*c*), (*a*), (*e*), (*d*), (*b*)
B. (*b*), (*e*), (*a*), (*c*), (*d*)
C. (*d*), (*a*), (*b*), (*c*), (*e*)
D. (*c*), (*e*), (*a*), (*d*), (*b*)

84. Which one is the correct sequence implied in the Indian Contract Act 1872?

(*a*) Offer of proposal
(*b*) Contract
(*c*) Promise
(*d*) Agreement
(*e*) Acceptance

Choose the correct answer from the options given below:

A. (*c*), (*e*), (*a*), (*d*), (*b*)
B. (*d*), (*b*), (*c*), (*a*), (*e*)
C. (*b*), (*d*), (*c*), (*e*), (*a*)
D. (*a*), (*e*), (*c*), (*d*), (*b*)

85. Arrange the following procedure of Income Tax return e-Filling in India:

(*a*) Login
(*b*) Register
(*c*) Verification
(*d*) Downloading utility and preparing return
(*e*) e-filing Income Tax Return

Choose the correct answer from the options given below:

A. (*a*), (*b*), (*c*), (*d*), (*e*)
B. (*a*), (*c*), (*b*), (*e*), (*d*)
C. (*b*), (*a*), (*e*), (*d*), (*c*)
D. (*b*), (*a*), (*d*), (*e*), (*c*)

86. Given below are two statements.

Statement (I) : Monetary policy causes a deliberate change in government revenue and expenditure with a view to influencing the price level and the quantum of national output.

Statement (II) : Fiscal Policy regulates the money supply and the cost and availability of credit.

In the light of the above statements, choose the most appropriate answer from the options given below:

A. Both Statement (I) and Statement (II) are correct
B. Both Statement (I) and Statement (II) are incorrect
C. Statement (I) is correct but Statement (II) is incorrect
D. Statement (I) is incorrect but Statement (II) is correct

87. Given below are two statements: One is labelled as Assertion (A) and the other is labelled as Reason (R).

Assertion (A) : Firms opt for buying an asset if the equivalent annual cost of ownership and operation is less than the best lease rate it can get.

Reason (R) : Operating leases are attractive to equipment users if the lease payment is less than the user's equivalent annual cost of buying the equipment.

In the light of the above statements, choose the most appropriate answer from the options given below:

A. Both (A) and (R) are correct and (R) is the correct explanation of (A)

B. Both (A) and (R) are correct, but (R) is NOT the correct explanation of (A)

C. (A) is correct, but (R) is not correct

D. (A) is not correct, but (R) is correct

88. Given below are two statements: One is labelled as Assertion (A) and the other is labelled as Reason (R).

Assertion (A): According to Herzberg, preventing or reducing dissatisfaction at work is not the same as providing satisfaction.

Reason (R) : Under the 'two factor theory', job satisfaction and dissatisfaction are the two different aspects of work motivation.

In the light of the above statements, choose the correct answer from the options given below:

A. Both (A) and (R) are true and (R) is the correct explanation of (A)

B. Both (A) and (R) are true, but (R) is NOT the correct explanation of (A)

C. (A) is true, but (R) is false

D. (A) is false, but (R) is true

89. Given below are two statements: One is labelled as Assertion (A) and the other is labelled as Reason (R).

Assertion (A): Trade mark registration gives exclusive proprietary rights to the trademark owner.

Reason (R) : A trademark is a recognizable sign, design or expression which identifies products or services of a particular source from those of others, and are used to claim exclusive proprietary rights of products or services.

In the light of the above statements, choose the correct answer from the options given below:

A. Both (A) and (R) are true and (R) is the conect explanation of (A)

B. Both (A) and (R) are true, but (R) is NOT the correct explanation of (A)

C. (A) is true, but (R) is false

D. (A) is false, but (R) is true

90. Given below are two statements.

Statement (I) : Gratuity received by Government employee is exempted from tax under Section 10(10)(*i*) of the Indian Income Tax Act, 1961.

Statement (II) : Gratuity received by local authority employee is exempted from tax.

In the light of the above statements, choose the correct answer from the options given below:

A. Both Statement (I) and Statement (II) are true

B. Both Statement (I) and Statement (II) are false

C. Statement (I) is correct but Statement (II) is false

D. Statement (I) is incorrect but Statement (II) is true

Directions (Qs. No. 91-95): *Answer the question on the basis of the following passage:*

Burnout is a psychological syndrome emerging as a prolonged response to chronic interpersonal stressors on the job. The three key dimensions of this response are an overwhelming exhaustion, feelings of cynicism and detachment from the job, and a sense of ineffectiveness and lack of accomplishment. The significance of this three-dimensional model is that it clearly places the individual stress experience within a social context and involves the person's conception of both self and others.

The exhaustion dimension was also described as wearing out, loss of energy, depletion, debilitation, and fatigue. The cynicism dimension was originally called depersonalization (given the nature of human services occupations), but was also described as negative or inappropriate attitudes towards clients, irritability, loss of idealism, and withdrawal. The inefficacy dimension was originally called reduced personal accomplishment, and was also described as reduced productivity or capability, low morale, and an inability to cope.

There have been various conceptual models about the development of burnout and its subsequent impact. At first, the focus was on the relationship between the three dimensions of burnout, which was often described in sequential stages. Exhaustion was assumed to develop first, in response to high demands and overload, and then this would precipitate detachment and negative reactions to people and the job (depersonalization or cynicism). If this continued, then the next stage would be feelings of inadequacy and failure (reduced personal accomplishment or professional inefficacy).

More recently, burnout models have been based on theories about job stress, and the notion of imbalances leading to strain. Its three stages are: (*a*) Job stressors, (*b*) individual strain, and (*c*) defensive coping. Subsequently, two developmental models of the demands-resources imbalance have emerged: the Job Demands-Resources (JD-R) model and the conservation of Resources (COR) model. The JD-R model focuses on the notion that burnout arises when individuals experience incessant job demands and have inadequate resources available to address and to reduce those demands. The COR model follows a basic motivational theory assuming that burnout arises as a result of persistent threats to available resources. A different variation of an imbalance model of burnout is the Areas of Worklife (AW) model, which frames job stressors in terms of person-job imbalances, or mismatches, but identifies six key areas in which these imbalances take place: workload, control, reward, community, fairness and values. Mismatches in these areas affect an individual's level of experienced burnout, which in turn determines various outcomes, such as job performance, social behaviours, and personal wellbeing.

91. Which of the following has the correct sequence of the stages of burnout?

A. Fatigue due to excessive work, dislike for work. failure to achieve targets
B. Negative feelings about work, dislike for work, effort to quit work
C. Initial good interpersonal relations, depersonalization, loss of idealism
D. Cynicism, inadequacy, inefficiency

92. Given below are two statements.

Statement (I) : Cynicism stage of Burnout is often experienced by employees, engaged in production activity, due to excessive work pressure.

Statement (II) : In Cynicism stage of burnout, person withdraws from others and shows lack of interest towards them.

In the light of the above statements, choose the correct answer from the options given below:

A. Both Statement (I) and Statement (II) are true
B. Both Statement (I) and Statement (II) are false
C. Statement (I) is correct but Statement (II) is false
D. Statement (I) is incorrect but Statement (II) is true

93. Match List-I with List-II:

List-I	List-II
(*a*) Exhaustion	(*i*) Not able to complete work
(*b*) Cynicism	(*ii*) No energy for work
(*c*) Inefficiency	(*iii*) No interest in customer

Choose the correct answer from the options given below:

	(*a*)	(*b*)	(*c*)
A.	(*i*)	(*ii*)	(*ii*)
B.	(*iii*)	(*ii*)	(*i*)
C.	(*ii*)	(*iii*)	(*i*)
D.	(*ii*)	(*i*)	(*iii*)

94. Which of the following is not a resource-imbalance model of Burnout?
A. Job Demands-Resources Model
B. Conservation of Resources Model
C. Three Dimensional Model
D. Areas of Worklife Model

95. Which of the following are caused by Burnout?
(*a*) Concern for clients
(*b*) Negative Social Behaviour
(*c*) Physical and Mental Strain
Choose the most appropriate answer from the options given below:
A. (*a*) only   B. (*a*) and (*b*) only
C. (*b*) and (*c*) only   D. (*a*) and (*c*) only

Directions (Qs. No. 96-100): *Answer the question on the basis of the following passage:*

It is desirable for consumers to be aware of their rights, and to exercise those rights responsibly and intelligently. In these days of audio-video publicity on the public and private media, it is indeed very difficult, if not impossible, to verify the exaggerated or false claims made by producers, manufacturers, distributors and dealers of various goods and services. The all-pervasive, exaggerated and often false claims, made for services and goods, emphasize the imperative need for Consumer Protection Legislation and creation of awareness about it among the general public.

In this connection, there are a number of enactments, in India such as the prevention of Food Adulteration Act, 1954, the Essential Commodities Act, 1955, the Hire Purchases Act, 1972, the Standards Weight and Measure Act, 1976 etc. However, the remedies prescribed there under are time-consuming, inadequate and expensive. As in other areas of Judicial Processes, the offenders are hardly caught, proceeded against and rarely, if ever, got convicted. When violators go scot-free, the victims have no remedy and gets frustated.

96. Which among the following is a correct statement based on the passage?
A. Consumers' laws are not explained well in India
B. Indian Judiciary System needs a drastic reform to facilitate consumers' welfare
C. Indian manufacturers are clever
D. The Indian Consumers have no remedy and get frustated

97. Which among the following is a correct statement based on the passage?
A. Consumers in India are aware of their rights
B. Consumers in India exercise their rights responsibly
C. Consumers in India are unaware of their rights and hence, they do not exercise them
D. None of the above could be ascertained on the basis of paragraph given here above

98. Which among the following is a correct statement based on the passage?
A. The Government of India has enacted sufficient number of laws for protection of consumer interests
B. The paragraph does not give comprehensive list of laws in favour of consumers
C. Legal environment for consumers in India is not conducive
D. Legal environment for consumers in India is conducive

99. Who among the followings could be considered at the center point in the passage?
A. Consumers
B. Judicial Process
C. Manufacturers
D. Government

100. Which among the following is a correct statement based on the passage?
A. Producers and manufacturers are sensitive about consumers' rights.
B. Producers and manufacturers are insensitive about consumers rights.
C. Producers and manufacturers are neutral about consumers' rights.
D. Producers and manufacturers are basically governed by ethics and values.

ANSWERS

1	2	3	4	5	6	7	8	9	10
B	C	B	D	B	A, B, C	B	C	C	D
11	**12**	**13**	**14**	**15**	**16**	**17**	**18**	**19**	**20**
A	A	B	A	C	B	A	D	B	A
21	**22**	**23**	**24**	**25**	**26**	**27**	**28**	**29**	**30**
A	B	C	D	A	B	B	C	C	B
31	**32**	**33**	**34**	**35**	**36**	**37**	**38**	**39**	**40**
A	D	B	D	C	A	A	C	D	C
41	**42**	**43**	**44**	**45**	**46**	**47**	**48**	**49**	**50**
B	*	C	C	A	B	D	D	D	B
51	**52**	**53**	**54**	**55**	**56**	**57**	**58**	**59**	**60**
B	A	C	C	C	C	A	B	D	D
61	**62**	**63**	**64**	**65**	**66**	**67**	**68**	**69**	**70**
B	A	C	A	D	B	A	C	C	D
71	**72**	**73**	**74**	**75**	**76**	**77**	**78**	**79**	**80**
A	B	A	A	A	B	C	A	B	A
81	**82**	**83**	**84**	**85**	**86**	**87**	**88**	**89**	**90**
C	A	D	D	D	B	B	A	A	A
91	**92**	**93**	**94**	**95**	**96**	**97**	**98**	**99**	**100**
A	D	C	C	C	B	D	B	A	B

* *No option is correct or the question is wrong.*

EXPLANATORY ANSWERS

1. A deduction can be claimed under section 80G only when the contribution is made to specified funds and institutions either via cheque or cash.

Effective from the assessment year 2018-19, a person can avail a maximum deduction of ₹ 2,000 if the donation is made in cash. However, there is no maximum limit on the deduction amount if the payment is made via cheque or digital payment methods.

2. *Leontief* production technology represents the extreme case of *perfect complements* or the case in which capital is a perfect complement for labour. As explained earlier, such production functions have 'L' shaped or right angled isoquants. In this case the firm cannot give up one input in exchange for the other input and still maintain the same level of output. This production function is also known as fixed *coefficient* production function.

In Leontief production functions the production technology always involves inputs labour (L) and capital (K) in fixed proportions to produce a unit of output and α and β are the fixed coefficients. In case of fixed coefficient production function, a certain amount of each input is required technologically to produce one unit of output. In this case the demand for the inputs is uniquely determined, because inputs are required in exact quantities per unit of output.

Leontief Production function:

$$Q = \min\left(\frac{L}{\alpha}, \frac{K}{\beta}\right)$$

If $\frac{L}{\alpha} < \frac{K}{\beta}$, then $Q = \frac{L}{\alpha}$, and L is considered as the binding constraint in the production process. This is because an increase in the labour input is necessary to increase output, but an increase in K in such a situation will not increase output. Conversely, If $\frac{L}{\alpha} > \frac{K}{\beta}$, then $Q = \frac{K}{\beta}$ and K becomes the limitative factor or binding constraint on output. So any additional increase in labour will not lead to an increase in output.

3. A marketer organizes marketing activities in international marketplace according to his degree of involvement in foreign marketing. Thus, the marketing activities at/in different levels of involvement are influenced by different orientations, which have been advocated by Wind, Douglas and Perlmutter (1973) in an acronym, EPRG that stands for ethnocentric, polycentric, regiocentric, and geocentric. According to the KPRG framework, a marketer applies the following four orientations in a foreign market depending on his level of involvement in the international marketplace:
   1. Ethnocentric orientation
   2. Polycentric orientation
   3. Regiocentric orientation
   4. Geocentric orientation.

4. Over a period of time, a well-established business develops an advantage of good name, reputation and wide business connections. This helps the business to earn more profits as compared to newly set-up business. In accounting, the monetary value of such advantage is known as goodwill. Goodwill is regarded as an intangible asset. In other words, goodwill is the value of the reputation of a firm respect of the profits expected in future over and above the normal profits earned by other units. It is generally observed that when a person pays for goodwill, he/she pays for something, which places him in the position of being able to earn super-profit. Goodwill exists only when the firms earns more profits than normal. Any firm that earns normal profits or is incurring losses has no goodwill.

6. **Relationship between Mean, Mode and Median:** In order to study the relationship between Mean, Mode and Median, we will have to ascertain whether the distribution is symmetrical or asymmetrical:

   In Case of Symmetrical Distribution: In such distribution Mean, Mode and Median are identical. The frequency curve in this situation is bell shaped.

   In Case of Asymmetrical Distribution: In an asymmetrical series Mean, Mode and Median have different values. Frequency curve in this case is not bell shaped. The height of the curve is not in the middle just like bell. It may be either leftward or rightward. Ordinarily the relationship between Mean, Mode and Median is as under:

   According to Karl Pearson the following relationship exists between Mean, Mode and Median in an asymmetrical distribution.

   Mode = 3 Median − 2 Mean

   $Z = 3 \text{ Median} - 2\bar{X}$

   $\text{Median} = \text{Mode} + \frac{2}{3} (\text{Mean} - \text{Mode})$.

7. There are two useful rules of thumb. The "Rule of 72" says that with discrete compounding the time it takes for an investment to double in value is roughly 72/interest rate (in per cent). The "Rule of 69" says that with continuous compounding the time that it takes to double is exactly 69.3/interest rate (in per cent).

8. **Going Concern Concept:** This concept states that a business firm will continue to carry on its activities for an indefinite period of time. Simply stated, it means that every business entity has continuity of life. Thus, it will not be dissolved in the near future. This is an important assumption of accounting, as it provides a basis for showing the value of

assets in the balance sheet; For example, a company purchases a plant and machinery of ₹ 100000 and its life span is 10 years. According to this concept every year some amount will be shown as expenses and the balance amount as an asset. Thus, if an amount is spent on an item which will be used in business for many years, it will not be proper to charge the amount from the revenues of the year in which the item is acquired. Only a part of the value is shown as expense in the year of purchase and the remaining balance is shown as an asset.

Significance: The following points highlight the significance of going concern concept;

- This concept facilitates preparation of financial statements.
- On the basis of this concept, depreciation is charged on the fixed asset.
- It is of great help to the investors, because, it assures them that they will continue to get income on their investments.
- In the absence of this concept, the cost of a fixed asset will be treated as an expense in the year of its purchase.
- A business is judged for its capacity to earn profits in future.

9. Some economists argue that the real business world is full of uncertainty; acurate and adequate data are not readily available; where data are available managers have little time and ability to process them; and managers work under a number of constraints. Under such conditions, it is not possible for the firms to act in terms of postulated profit maximisation hypothesis. Nor do the firms seek to maximise sales, growth or anything else. Instead they seek to achieve a *'satisfactory profit'*, or *'satisfactory growth'* and so on. This behaviour of firms, he terms, as 'satisficing behaviour'. The underlying assumption of satisficing behaviour of firms is that a firm is a coalition of different groups connected with various activities of the firm, *e.g.*, shareholders, managers, workers, input suppliers, customers, bankers, tax-authorities and so on. All of these groups have some kind of expectations—often conflicting—from the firm, and the firm seeks to satisfy all of them in one way or another.

11. If $\alpha + \beta > 1 \Rightarrow$ Increasing Return

Here, $0.6 + 0.8 = 1.4 > 1$

Hence, there is increasing return to scale.

12. Skimming pricing refers to the setting of a high price when a product is first introduced and gradually lowering its price subsequently to capture the other segments of the market. When a product is first introduced it is often difficult to determine exactly the strength of demand, therefore, the best way is to set a high price which allows the firm to recover its cost of production by selling the products to those selected rich consumers (the cream of the market) who are willing to pay the high price to possess the product as an exclusive item.

13. Conventional marketing is mass marketing; the marketer approaches the customers on a mass basis and sells to them indirectly. He goes for mass production, mass communication and mass distribution. Conventional marketing has several limits; for example, it affords little scope for customisation, which is the key in most businesses today. In contrast, direct marketing is demassified marketing; here the marketer deals with the customers direct and on a one-to-one basis and markets the products directly to them. He approaches the customers individually, communicates with them on a one-to-one basis and offers products that are modified to suit the requirements of the chosen customers. In other words, DM relies on customised production, individualised distribution and individualised communication/promotion. And, this is precisely why direct marketing is referred to as demassified marketing. Building relationship with customers, one at a time, is essential in today's marketing. While mass marketing targets the average customer of the chosen segment and develops its offer for the average customer, DM targets an individual customer and develops its offer specifically for him.

Differences between Conventional Marketing and Direct Marketing

Conventional Marketing	Direct Marketing
Conventional marketing is mass marketing	Direct marketing is demassified marketing; it deals with customers one-to-one
Conventional marketing deals with the customers indirectly	Direct marketing deals with them directly
Conventional marketing is a one-way activity	Direct marketing is interactive marketing, with two-way communication between the firm and each one of the customers
Conventional marketing relies heavily on marketing channels/stores	Direct marketing is channel-less
Conventional marketing relies heavily on advertising/mass promotion	Direct marketing does not involve them

14. $\text{EOQ} = \sqrt{\dfrac{2\times16200\times2400}{30\%\text{ of }20}}$

$= \sqrt{\dfrac{2\times16200\times2400}{6}} = 3600$ unit.

15. The economist and Nobel Prize Laureate Harry M. Markowitz proved by means of his modern portfolio theory (MPT) that a portfolio's risk can be reduced by adequate diversification. The risk of a diversified portfolio of assets is therefore considerably lower than that of a portfolio with a small number of assets (see Figure). Diversification lowers or mitigates the unsystematic risk so that the overall portfolio will only contain the market risk, *i.e.* the systematic, non-diversifiable risk. The diversification effect is based on the correlation (statistical interdependence) of the different assets in the portfolio. While positive correlations point to a parallel movement of return of both assets, negative correlation as a rule leads to counter movements, *i.e.* diversification.

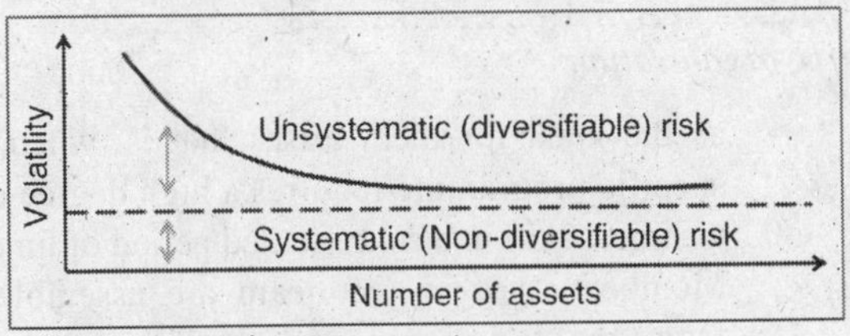

Figure: *Diversification*

16. Natural Hedging: The most popular method to mitigate currency exchange risk is the simple natural hedge when exporter and importer complete a transaction in the same currency. A natural hedge is the reduction in risk that can arise from institutions normal operating procedures. Banks involved in international trade. Often attempt to match the currency denomination of their receipts and payments in order to limit foreign exchange exposure.

Matching and Netting: Netting and matching is a feature of foreign exchange risk management. They are carried out to reduce the scale of external hedging required, and netting refers to netting off group receipts and payments. Matching extends this concept to include third parties to banks, banks can reduce the size of their counter party exposures by entering into legally binding agreements to net settlements bilaterally, and netting arrangements permit banks to offset trade against each other. So only net amount in each currency is paid or received by each institution.

17. P (a spade card) $= \dfrac{13}{52}$

P (a king [(P(B)]) $= \dfrac{4}{52}$

Hence, Required Probability,

$$P(A \text{ or } B) = P(A) + P(B) - (P\ A\ \&\ B)$$

$$= \frac{13}{52} + \frac{4}{52} = \frac{1}{52}$$

$$P\ (A \text{ or } B) = \frac{17}{52} - \frac{1}{52} = \frac{16}{52} = \frac{4}{13}$$

Note: One king of spade is included in a kings of all cards. Hence, the probability of a king of spade will be deducted, because its probability $\frac{1}{13}$ is included in both probability.

20. Compressed data are defined as the data that are converted from the larger dataset into a smaller dataset. In this case, the frequency distribution, histogram and ogive are all used to represent the large data in a smaller graphical form. Hence, these are the examples of compressed data.

21. Rabble Hypothesis: The word 'rabble' means crowd or mob or horde. Rabble is a segment of the human population that is poor, uneducated, mostly unemployed, discontent and likely to form an angry mob. Rabble hypothesis presumes that man is an isolated human, motivated by only monetary incentives. In other words, rabble hypothesis assumes mankind as a horde of unorganised individuals actuated by self interest. Scientific management subscribes to this view.

Rabble hypothesis is made by famous British classical economist David Ricardo. It asserts that each individual in a group setting is interested in pursuing only a narrow, rational self-interest. The argument is made that workers behave like a rabble of isolated individuals, and that they are motivated primarily by financial rewards. Human relations theory rejected proved rabble hypothesis. Against the assumptions of Rabble hypothesis of mankind as horde, human relations theory, popularised by Elton Mayo, assumes mankind as herd— a group of people sharing a common bond. The rabble hypothesis (or *horde hypothesis*) thus, gave way to *herd hypothesis* having a sharing culture.

22. In Matrix organisation (also called grid or lattice pattern), two types of departmentali-sation—functional and product—exist simultaneously as shown in Fig.

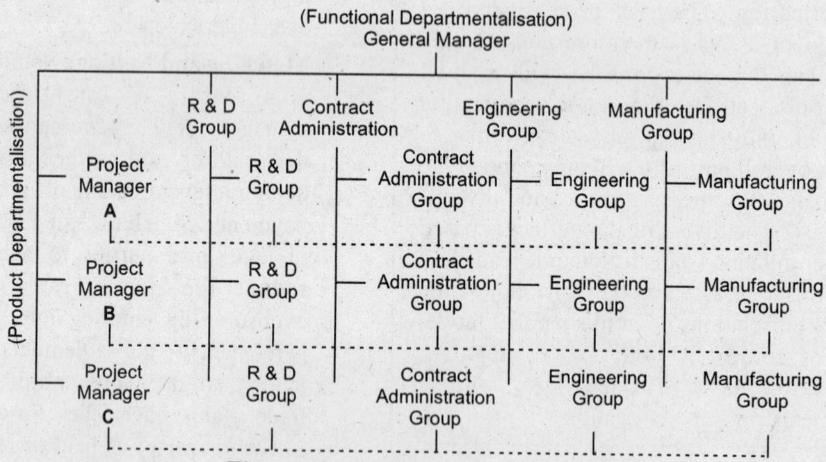

Fig. *A typical matrix organisation*

Functional departments are a permanent fixture of the matrix organisation; they retain authority for the overall operation of their respective units. Product departments or project teams, on the other hand, are created as the need for them arises that is, when a specific programme requires a high degree of technical skill in a concentrated period of time. Members of a project team are assembled from the functional departments and are placed under the direction of a project manager. The manager for each project is responsible and accountable for its success; thus he has authority over the other team members for the duration of the project. (This temporary authority is shown in Fig. by broken lines) On the completion of the project, the members of the team, including the project manager revert back to their respective departments until the next assignment to a project.

Benefits: The benefits of such an organisation are as follows:

1. Combination of all necessary inputs of manpower, facilities and information at one place reduces problems of communication and coordination. There is also economy in cost because there is no unnecessary surplus.
2. Stress on optimization of the total project eliminates chances of suboptimisation of goals.
3. Assignment of specific jobs to employees makes passing of buck difficult.
4. Change of projects promotes the intellectual growth and development of employees.

23. The four-part model of CSR, as formulated in 1979 and later refined by Carroll, is often applied to distinguish among the different responsibilities of a company. Carroll's four-part model characterizes CSR as a multi-layered concept consisting of four interrelated responsibilities: economic, legal, ethical, and philanthropic responsibilities. The economic responsibility of a company is to provide goods and services to society and to be profitable. The legal responsibility expects business operations to comply with applicable laws as codified ethics established by lawmakers. The ethical responsibility lies in opting for activities that meet the ethical and moral expectations of society which are not codified in law. The philanthropic responsibility is to contribute to the improvement of society through activities that are appreciated or desired by society but not expected in an ethical or moral sense.

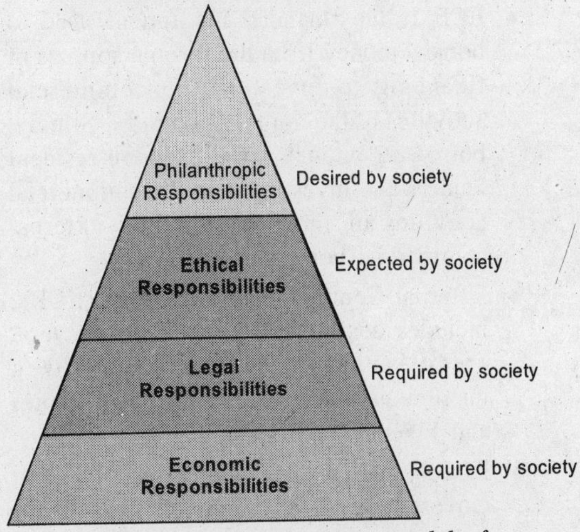

Fig. *Carroll's four-part model of corporate social responsibility*

24. Collective bargaining is a technique adopted by the organizations of workers and employers collectively to resolve their differences with or without the assistance of a third party. Its ultimate aim is to reach some settlements acceptable to both the parties involved in labour-management relations. The phrase 'Collective Bargaining' was coined and at first used by Sydney and Beatrice Webb in 1891 and Great Britain is said to be the 'Home of Collective Bargaining'. Subsequently, Samuel Gompers, the president of American Federation of Labour in USA considered 'Collective Bargaining' as the most important for determining the terms and conditions of employment. Gradually, the term came to be extensively used not only by trade unionist and employers, but also by the governmental agencies, academicians and even social organizations and others. It becomes a very important institution in the realm of industrial relations.

25. The Association of Southeast Asian Nations, or ASEAN, was established on 8 August, 1967 in Bangkok, Thailand. Currently there are 10 permanent members of this association. Its headquarter is in Jakarta (Indonesia).

27. External Commercial Borrowings or ECBs

- ECB is the financial instrument used to borrow money from the foreign sources of financing to invest in the commercial activities of the domestic country. Simply, borrowing money from the non-resident lenders and investing it in the commercial activities of India is called as external commercial borrowings.
- External Commercial Borrowings (ECBs) includes commercial bank loans, buyers' credit, suppliers' credit, securitized instruments such as Floating Rate Notes and Fixed Rate Bonds etc.
- ECBs are being permitted by the Government as a source of finance for Indian Corporate for expansion of existing capacity as well as for fresh investment.
- ECBs provide opportunity to borrow large volume of funds. The funds are available for relatively long term. Interest rate are also lower compared to domestic funds.
- ECBs are in the form of foreign currencies. Hence, they enable the corporate to have foreign currency to meet the import of machineries etc.
- Corporate can raise ECBs from internationally recognised sources such as banks, export credit agencies, international capital markets etc.
- The ECBs have emerged as a major form of foreign capital called as FDI. PSUs and corporate use this ECB as a major platform for the source of investment.

28. Repo (Repurchase) rate is the rate at which the RBI lends short-term money to the banks. When the repo rate increases borrowing from RBI becomes more expensive. Therefore, we can say that in case, RBI wants to make it more expensive for the banks to borrow money, it increases the repo rate; similarly, if it wants to make it cheaper for banks to borrow money, it reduces the repo rate.

29. Direct Selling Agent (DSA) are people or business entities interested in functioning as sales agents on their behalf by multiple banks, financial institutions or a company. A direct selling agent is different from an in-house dealer, because the DSA would not be on the company's payroll, would have a defined contract period and would have a performance-based payment. On the other hand, a sales person would be hired by the company, have a fixed monthly salary, and can only be fired according to India's terms of employment and labour laws.

30. Every product passes through four stages in its life cycle—Introduction, Growth, Maturity and Decline. The marketing objectives of each stage are different. During the Introduction stage, the objective is to create product awareness and trial and therefore intensive advertising and personal selling is required. Moreover, to entice trial companies depend heavily on sales promotion. During the Growth stage the marketing objective is to maximise the market share and then advertising can build awareness and interest in the mass market. During the growth stage sales promotion is reduced to take advantage of the heavy consumer demand. During the Maturity stage the company aims at maximising profits while defending its market share and advertising then stresses on brand differences and benefits. Sales promotion efforts are to be increased during maturity stage to encourage brand switching. Finally, during the Decline stage the marketing objective is to reduce expenditures and milk the brand. Advertising is then reduced to a minimum level to retain hardcore loyals and sales promotion too is reduced to the minimum of the level.

31. Companies will often adjust their basic prices to allow for differences in customers, products and locations. In segmented pricing, the company sells a product or service at two or more prices, even though the difference in prices is not based on differences in costs.

Strategy	Description
Discount and Allowance pricing	Reducing prices to reward customer responses such as paying early or promoting theproduct
Segmented pricing	Adjusting prices to allow for differences in customers, products, or locations
Psychological pricing	Adjusting prices for psychological effect
Promotional pricing	Temporarily reducing prices to increase short-run sales
Geographical pricing	Adjusting prices to account for the geographic location of customers
Dynamic pricing	Adjusting prices continually to meet the characteristics and needs of individual customers and situations
International pricing	Adjusting prices for international markets

33. Discharge of a Contract: Discharge of a contract means termination of contractual relation between the parties to a contract, in other words a contract is discharged when the rights and obligations created by it are extinguished (*i.e.* comes to an end).

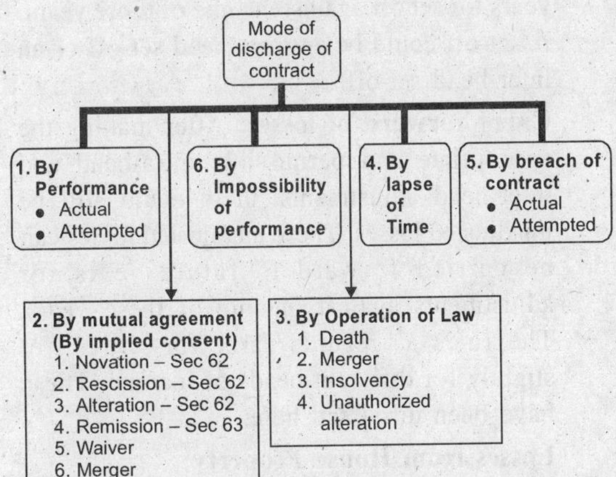

34. Implied conditions are the stipulations which have not been included in the Contract of sale in express words. But the law presumes that the parties have incorporated them into their contract.

Following are the implied conditions which are contained in the Sale of Goods Act, 1930.

1. **Conditions as to title**—According to this implied condition, it is presumed that the seller has a valid title to the geods, in other words, he has the right to sell the goods. [Sec, 14(a)]
2. **Condition as to description**—Where there is a contract for sale of goods by description, there is an implied condition that the goods shall correspond with the description. [Sec. 15]
3. **Condition as to sample**—A contract of sale is a contract for sale by sample where there is a term in the contract, express or implied to that effect. [Sec. 17]
4. **Condition as to sample as well as description**—Sometimes the seller shows sample of the goods to the buyer and also gives him their description. In such cases, the implied condition is that the goods shall correspond with both, the sample as well as description.
5. **Condition as to quality or fitness for buyer's purpose**—If the buyer makes his purpose clear to the seller and buys the goods 'relying upon his skills and judgement', than there is an implied condition that the goods shall be fit for the buyer's specific purpose. [Sec. 16(1)]
6. **Condition as to merchantable quality**—Where goods are bought by description from a seller who deals in goods of that description, there is an implied condition that the goods shall be of merchantable quality. [Sec. 16 (2)]
7. **Condition as to wholesomeness**—In case of contract of sale of eatables or foodstuffs, there is in implied condition as to whole someness of the product. It implies that the eatables or provision sold are wholesome.

8. **Condition implied by custom—**An implied condition as to quality or fitness for a particular purpose may be annexed by the usage and custom of trade. [Sec, 16 (3)].

35. **Definition of the term 'Information' under the RTI Act-2005—**Section 2(F) of the Right to Information Act states that *"Information means any material in any form, press releases, circulars, orders, logbooks, contracts, reports, papers, samples, models, data material held in any electronic form and information relating to any Private body which can be accessed by a Public authority under any other law for the time being in force."*

Chapter 1 section 2 para (f) of the Right to Information Act defines 'information' as "any material in any form, including records, documents, memos, e-mails, opinions, advices, press releases, circulars, orders, logbooks, contracts, reports, papers, samples, models, data material held in any electronic form and information relating to any private body which can be accessed by a public authority under any other law for the time being in force".

Though the Act makes no express provision on 'file notings', the RTI regulator, the Central Information Commission, ruled in January, 2006 that, "a citizen has the right to seek information contained in file notings and no file (or information) would be complete without note-sheets having file notings". In short, 'file notings' are considered integral part of 'information' and, as the CTC stated, "file notings are not, as a matter of law, exempted from disclosure."

For a better understanding, we must first consider the definition of the term. 'Infromation' under the Right to Information Act, Section 2(f) of the RTI Act states that information, means any material in any form, including records, documents, memos, emails, opinions, advices, press releases, circulars, orders, logbooks, contracts, reports, papers, samples, models, data material held in any electronic form and information relating to any private body which can be accessed by a public authority under any other law for the time being in force.

This definition of the term "information" is very wide. In order to deter-mine whether 'file notings' fall within the ambit of information, an understanding of the legal connotation of certain terms like—record, document, file, and opinion is essential. The nature of a file noting comes within the ambit of opinion, advice, reports, and papers.

37. **Set off of losses:** Set off of losses means adjusting the losses against the profit or income of that particular year. Losses that are not set off against income in the same year can be carried forward to the subsequent years for set off against income of those years. A set-off could be an intra-head set-off or an inter-head set-off.

Carry forward of losses: After making the appropriate and permissible intra-head and inter-head adjustments, there could still be unadjusted losses. These unadjusted losses can be carried forward to future years for adjustments against income of these years. The rules as regards carry forward differ slightly for different heads of income. These have been discussed here:

Losses from House Property:

- Can be carry forward up to next 8 assessment years from the assessment year in which the loss was incurred.
- Can be adjusted only against Income from house property.
- Can be carried forward even if the return of income for the loss year is belatedly filed.

40. The Sugam ITR-4S Form is the Income Tax Return form for those taxpayers who have opted for the presumptive income scheme as per Section 44AD and Section 44AE of the Income Tax Act.

41. Mercosur, also known as the Common Market of the South, is a trade bloc agreement that exists between the following South American countries: Argentina, Brazil, Paraguay, Uruguay, and Venezuela. The trade bloc was established under the Treaty of Asuncion in March 1991; it was then expanded under the 1994 Treaty of Ouro Preto, which set up a formal customs union. The main objective of Mercosur is to bring about the free movement of goods, capital, services, and people among its member states. The official languages of the trade bloc are Portuguese and Spanish. In addition to the four founding members of Mercosur and Venezuela, there are five countries with associate member status. These countries are Bolivia, Chile, Colombia, Ecuador, and Peru. As associate members, they are able to join free-trade agreements but do not receive the benefits of the customs union.

43. Price discrimination is the practice of charging a different price for the same good or service. There are three types of price discrimination—first-degree, second-degree, and third-degree price discrimination.

Third-degree price discrimination is the strategic behaviour of a monopolistic firm which charges different prices for the same product in different sub-markets until the marginal revenue of the last unit of the product sold in each submarket equals the marginal cost of producing it. Therefore, third-degree price discrimination is based on the neoclassical profit-maximising rule of MR = MC.

44. Arbitrage Pricing Model Theory: The arbitrage pricing model can be thought of as a multivariate extension of the CAPM, incorporating several systematic risk factors, one of which may be sensitivity to market returns as defined in the CAPM.

Arbitrage Pricing Model Formula: The econometric estimation of the cost of capital by the arbitrage pricing model takes the following form:

$$E(R_i) = R_f + (B_{i1}K_1) + (B_{i2}K_2) + \ldots (B_{in}K_n)$$

where:

$E(R_i)$ = expected rate of return on the subject security

R_f = rate of return on a risk-free security

$K_i \ldots K_n$ = risk premium associated with factor K for the average asset in the market (general macro-economic factors such as changes in investor confidence, inflation, and so on)

$B_{i1} \ldots B_{in}$ = sensitivity of the security to each risk factor relative to the market average condition to that factor.

The variables used are generally based on measures of macroeconomic risk factors expected to have different impacts on different companies. The arbitrage pricing model is not widely used today; to the extent that the arbitrage pricing model is used, it is usually applied to the valuation of very large companies.

45. The Institute of Cost and Management Accountants (UK) defines cost audit "as the verification of cost accounts and a check on the adherence to the cost accounting plan." Cost audit is verifying the correctness of cost accounts, cost reports, cost data and costing methods.

Cost audit covers the following important areas:

1. **Materials:** The cost auditor generally varifies the following items relating to materials:
   (*i*) Goods inward procedure.
   (*ii*) Store-keeping arrangement.
   (*iii*) Accounting for scrap, wastage, materials transfers.
   (*iv*) Perpetual inventory system.
   (*v*) Materials pricing methods used.
   (*vi*) Adequacy of stock checking methods.
2. **Wages:**
   (*i*) Documents used in preparation of payroll.

(*ii*) Wage rate changes authorisation for wage payments and overtime payments.

(*iii*) Time recording.

(*iv*) Internal check system.

3. Overhead

(*i*) Classification of overhead.

(*ii*) Overhead budgets.

(*iii*) Apportionment and allocation of overhead.

(*iv*) Methods of absorption.

(*v*) Policy regarding inclusion of overhead in work-in-progress.

(*vi*) Accounting treatment of under- or over-absorption.

4. General

(*i*) Methods of establishing standards, revision of standards.

(*ii*) Methods of calculating standards cost variances.

(*iii*) Accounting codes and instructions.

46. Indifference curve analysis has the following main assumptions:

1. **Rational Consumer:** It is assumed that the consumer will behave rationally. It means the consumer would like to get maximum satisfaction out of his total income.
2. **Ordinal Utility:** A consumer can determine his preferences on the basis of satisfaction derived from different goods or their combinations. Utility can be expressed in terms of ordinal numbers, *i.e.*, first, second, etc.
3. **Diminishing Marginal Rate of Substitution:** In the words of *Prof. Boumol, "Indifference curve analysis assumes that marginal rate of substitution diminishes."* It means, as the stock of a commodity increases with the consumer, he substitutes it for the other commodity at a diminishing rate.
4. **Non-satiety:** A consumer does not possess any good in more than the required quantity. He does not reach the level of satiety. Consumer prefers more quantity of a good to less quantity, *i.e.*, five *rasgullas* instead of two *rasgullas*.
5. **Consistency in Selection:** There is consistency in consumer's behaviour. It means that if at any given time a consumer prefers A combination of goods to B combination, then at another time he will not prefer B combination to A combination.

   If $A > B$

   Then, $B \not> A$.

The basic assumption of indifference theory is that the marginal rate of substitution is negative.

This means that to gain an increase in consumption of one commodity, the consumer is prepared to reduce her consumption of a second. Graphically, the negative marginal rate of substitution is shown by the downward slope of indifference curves.

47. Conditions For Successful Price Discrimination: A monopolist practices prices discrimination because, by doing so, it earns higher profits. However, for price discrimination to be successful the following four condibons have to be satisfied:

1. **Multiple Demand Elasticities:** Firstly, it must be possible to categorize different markets in terms of price elasticity of demand in each. As K.K. Seo has put it: "There must be differences in demand elasticity among buyers due to differences in income, location, available alternatives, tastes, or other factors. If the underlying conditions that normally determine demand elasticity are the same for all purchasers, the separate demand elasticities for each buyer or group of buyers will be approximately equal and a single rather than multiple price structure may be warranted."
2. **Market Power:** Secondly, the firm must have some control over price. This means that the firm must face a downward-sloping demand curve for its product. A monopolist

meets this condition but a pure competitor does not. Obviously a price-taker in a perfectly competitive market is not in a position to engage in price discrimination.

3. **Market Segmentation:** Thirdly, it is essential for the monopolist to be able to identify the separate markets.
4. **Market Selling:** Fourthly, the seller must be able to prevent the customers who are charged a low price from reselling the product to customers who are charged higher prices.

49. Where there is a conflict among alternatives (*i.e.*, where two or more alternatives are equally favoured by different techniques), decision can be based on NPV and IRR techniques.

However, in the following situations, there might be a conflict between the alternative favoured by NPV and IRR Techniques:

(*a*) In case of Size Disparity (*i.e.*, cash outflows of different alternatives are different, for example, low in one case and high in another case);

(*b*) In case of disparity in Cash Inflows (*i.e.*, different behaviour of cash inflows in different alternatives). For example, increasing cash inflows in one case and decreasing cash inflows in another case.

(*c*) In case of disparity in useful life (*i.e.*, different useful lives for different alternatives). For example, 3 years of life for one alternative and 5 years for another alternative.

Whenever there is a conflict in the decision between NPV Technique and IRR Technique, it is most advisable to make decision based on NPV technique.

50. There are four main methods of appraisal. They have in common a concern with cash flows. They all therefore require an evaluation of the initial cost, the running expenses, the estimated life of the project, and the income over the life of the project. Only cash items are included in the calculation of these factors. This means that depreciation is ignored, but the expected residual value of the item in the market place is included. Taxation, which may be a cash inflow or outflow, can have a significant effect on an investment decision and should always be included.

The four methods are payback, average rate of return, net present value, and yield or internal rate of return.

(*a*) **Payback:** This method calculates the time for cash inflows to recoup the initial investment on the project. The payback period indicates to management the time that the investment is at risk: the shorter the length of the period to payback the better. This method is widely used because it is simple to understand. It provides a clear indication of the time required to convert a "risky" investment into a safe one. It does not, however, pay any heed to several factors: the timing of cash flows, the situation after the payback period, and the return on capital invested.

(*b*) **Average rate of return:** This method calculates the average annual net cash inflow as a percentage of the initial cash outflow.

51. The regression coefficients are independent of the change of the origin. But, they are not independent of the change of the scale. It means there will be no effect on the regression coefficients if any constant is subtracted from the value of x and y. If x and y are multiplied by any constant, then the regression coefficient will change.

52. Positional averages determine the position of variables in given sets of data. Median and mode are the most important positional averages as these are computed on the basis of their position in the statistical series. There are mainly three positional averages—median, partition values and mode.

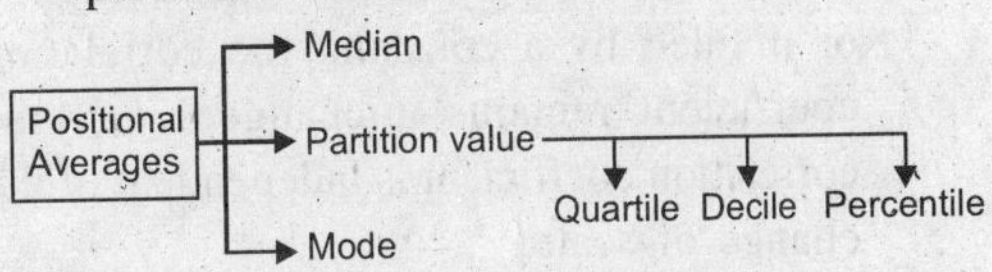

53. Properties of Correlation Coefficient: The following are the important properties of the coefficient of correlation:

1. The coefficient of correlation r lies between -1 and $+1$, *i.e.*, $-1 \le r \le 1$, *i.e.*, a number between -1 and 1 both inclusive that describes the linear relationship between pairs of quantitative variables.
2. The correlation coefficient is independent of the change of origin and scale.
3. The correlation coefficient is the ratio of two quantities having same units, thus it is a pure number having no units.
4. The value of r does not change if all the values of either variable are converted to a different scale. For example, if the units of X are changed from feet to meters, the value of r does not change.
5. The value of r is not affected by the choice of X and Y. Interchange of all X and Y values will not change the value of r, *i.e.*, the correlation coefficient between X and Y is equal to the correlation coefficient between Y and X.
6. r measures the strength of linear relationship. It is not designated to measure the strength of a relationship that is not linear.
7. If the sign of all the values of one of the variables is changed, the sign of the correlation coefficient changes, *i.e.*, the correlation between X and Y is opposite in sign to the correlation between –X and Y or X and –Y.
8. If each value of X and (or) Y a constant amount is added or subtracted, the correlation coefficient remains unchanged, *i.e.*, the correlation coefficient is independent of the change of origin.
9. If each value of X and (or) Y is multiplied or divided by a constant, the correlation coefficient remains unchanged, *i.e.*, the correlation coefficient is independent of the change of scale.

54. Defense mechanisms: Described by Sigmund Freud; unconscious thinking patterns of the ego to either decrease pain or increase pleasure.

Denial: One of the primary defense mechanisms noted by Freud in which one disbelieves what occurred when personally threatened.

Repression: The involuntary removal of thoughts, memories, and feelings from the conscious mind so they are less threatening to the ego.

Projection: The act of attributing one's thoughts and feelings to other people so that they are less threatening to the ego.

Rationalization: The reinterpretation of the current reality to match one's liking: a reinterpretation of the truth.

Displacement: When something that causes pain to the ego is inaccessible or otherwise cannot be responded to directly, the painful feelings can be transferred to an unrelated person or object. This is what Freud called displacement. Displacement involves transferring emotional plain and its related behaviour from an unacceptable object (*e.g.*, an authority figure) to a non-threatening object (usually children and pets). For example, your boss is a jerk and you would love to choke him, but instead you go home and shoo away the cat who begs for attention. Even though feelings and anger and aggression are most commonly cited as those that are displaced, it is also possible to displace feelings and behaviours associated with joy and love to those you perceive to be most receptive to them, rather than those you believe would not respond favourably.

55. Intercultural encounters between people of different races, ethnic backgrounds and lifestyles are multiplying. As well as understanding the technical nature of their business transactions, those engaged in international business must also understand differences in the way people think, feel and act.

Hoebel and Frost define enculturation as 'conscious or unconscious conditioning occurring within that process whereby the individual, as child and adult, achieves competence in a particular culture.' Learning about culture can be:

- unconscious (as we absorb and imitate the daily habits, speech patterns and roles of our parents from infancy) or
- deliberate (as we are taught specific manners for greeting people, religious rites and rituals, and reading the Bible, Koran, Torah or other literature).

A member of a culture or subculture learns how to use, formally and informally, the patterns of cultural behaviour prescribed by that culture.

Acculturation is the process by which people adjust to the host culture by adopting its values, symbols and behaviour. Acculturation is a multi-dimensional process involving the adaptation of language, cultural beliefs and values of one group (usually the minority group) to the norms and structures of another (usually the majority group). Reasons for difficulties in adjusting to a new culture include:

- conflicting social norms and attempts to retain previous culture
- focusing on differences between own and the new culture
- perceiving differences as weaknesses, rather than adopting a balanced view of the new culture.

Acculturation is an active ongoing process of cultural involvement. People develop new norms of behaviour as they adapt and adjust to the cultural worldviews, customs and traditions of another group. The process may involve direct social interaction or exposure to other cultures through mass media. Rather than abandoning their past for the new culture, people are more likely to accommodate new ideas into their own culture and try to achieve 'synergy' between the two cultures.

57. IMPS: *Immediate Payment Service,* this is one of instant and real-time inter-bank electronic funds transfer system through mobile phones in India. Unlike NEFT and RTGS, the service is available 24/7 throughout the year including bank holidays.

It is managed by the National Payments Corporation of India (NPCI) and is built upon the existing National Financial Switch network (NFSN). NFSN was designed, developed and deployed by the Institute for Development and Research in Banking Technology (IDRBT) in 2004, with the goal of inter-connecting all ATMs in the county. IMPS was publicly launched on November 22, 2010. The versatility of this service that it can be accessed through various platforms like banking internet site, apps, and USSD on basic phones. This is only system can run on basic mobile to access the banking.

58. NBFCs are doing functions akin to that of banks, however there are a few differences: (*i*) an NBFC cannot accept demand deposits; (*ii*) an NBFC is not a part of the payment and settlement system and as such an NBFC cannot issue cheques drawn on itself; and (*iii*) deposit insurance facility of Deposit Insurance and Credit Guarantee Corporation is not available for NBFC depositors unlike in case of banks.

Every NBFC Should Be Registered with RBI: In terms of Section 45-1A of the RBI Act, 1934. It is mandatory that every NBFC should be registered with RBI to commence or carry on any business of non-banking financial institution as defined in clause (*a*) of Section 45 I of the RBI Act, 1934. However, to obviate dual regulation, certain categories of NBFCs which are regulated by other regulators are exempted from the requirement of registration with RBI viz. Venture Capital Fund/Merchant Banking companies/Stock broking companies registered with SEBI, Insurance Company holding a valid certificate of Registration issued by IRDA. Nidhi companies as notified under Section 620A of the Companies Act, 1956, Chit companies as defined in clause (*b*) of Section 2 of the Chit Funds Act, 1982 or Housing Finance Companies regulated by National Housing Bank.

61. Kotler and Singh (1981) have identified the following six strategies that can help a leader attain the objective of market share protection:

- Position Defence
- Flanking Defence
- Pre-emptive Defence
- Counter-offensive Defence
- Mobile Defence
- Contraction Defence.

63. Salient Features of GST

- The GST has two components—Central Goods and Service Tax (CGST) and State Goods and Service Tax (SGST)/ Union Territory Goods and Service Tax (UTGST).
- CGST is to be administered by the Central Government and SGST is to be administered by State Governments. UTGST is to be administered by Administrator appointed by the Central Government for the Union Territory.
- CGST has replaced existing Central Excise, Service Tax, Additional Excise Duty, Special Additional Duty of Customs, etc. whereas SGST has replaced State VAT, CST, Luxury Tax, Octroi and Entry Tax, Purchase Tax, etc.
- Taxable Event under GST shall be supply of goods or services or both. It is an event the occurrence of which attracts the liability to tax. Under earlier system of indirect taxes there were different taxable event in each of the indirect taxes. "Manufacture" was a taxable event under Central Excise, "Transfer of property in goods" under VAT/CST, and services "Provided or agreed to be provided" in Service Tax.
- GST is based on destination based consumption tax principle. On the contrary, erstwhile Central Sales Tax was origin based tax.

  Destination Based Taxation as the name suggests is the taxation based on destination or consumption of the goods or services. This principle seeks to tax the goods and services on simple theory that the goods or services should be taxed at the place where their consumption takes place rather than the point where their origin takes place. The entire revenue relating to the goods or services should accrue in the jurisdiction where they are being ultimately consumed.

  Example: If A in Delhi produces the goods and sells the goods to B in Haryana, then in such case the tax should accrue to the State of Haryana and not to the State of Delhi. On the other hand, Origin Based Taxation as the name suggests was the taxation system where the tax accrued to the State from where the transaction originated.

  Example: If A in Delhi produces the goods and sells the goods to B in Haryana, then in such case the central sales tax was levied and collected in the State of Delhi and not in the State of Haryana. The revenue in the case of origin based taxation should accrue to the place, where the transaction originates and not to the State where such goods or services or both are consumed.
- Under former indirect taxes, two separate legal entities were required to complete the transaction. Whereas in GST in specified situations even self-supply is also subject to tax. Transfer of goods from one branch of a person in a State to a branch in other State is also subject to tax under GST.

  Example: If A transfer the goods from its head office in Delhi to its branch in Ludhiana (Punjab), it will be subject to GST.

64. Tax Treatment of Provident Fund (EPF): Contribution is made in the Provident Fund for the employee's welfare by the employee and the employer. The deduction is available under section 80C.

Provident fund is a kind of security fund in which the employees contribute a part of their salary and the employer also contributes on behalf of their employees. Section 10(11) and 10(12) of the Income Tax Act defines the exemption on the amount added to the provident fund. Additionally, the amount allowed as a deduction on contributing to the provident fund is dealt in section 80C of the Income Tax Act. The types of provident funds are:

1. Recognised Provident Fund (RPF) as recognised by Commissioner of Income Tax under EPF and Miscellaneous Provision Act, 1952. It applies to enterprises employing at least 20 employees.
2. Unrecognised Provident Fund (UPF) is not recognised by the Commissioner of Income Tax. The employers and employees start these schemes.
3. Public Provident Fund (PPF) under Public Provident Fund Act, 1968 is another system of contributing to the provident fund. Self-employed people can also take part in this scheme. A minimum contributing limit of ₹ 500 per annum and a maximum of ₹ 150000 per annum are set.
4. Statutory Provident Fund (SPF) is meant for employees of Government or Universities or Educational Institutes affiliated to University.

Tax Treatment of Provident Fund

Particulars	Recognised PF	Unrecognised PF	Statutory PF	Public PF
Employer's Contribution	Contribution to 12% of salary is exempt, above that is added to salary income of the employee.	Not taxable	Not taxable	Not taxable
Employee's Contribution	Section 80C Deduction	No Section 80C deduction	Section 80C Deduction	Section 80C Deduction
Interest on PF	Any interest over and above 9.5% is added to Income from Salaries Until 9.5% interest is exempt.	Not taxable	Exempt	Exempt
Amount withdrew at retirement time	Exempt subject to certain conditions*.	Contribution from employer and interest on that is taxable under the head Income from Salaries; Contribution by an employee is not taxable, and employee's contribution interest is taxable under the head Income from Other Sources.	Exempt	Exempt

Conditions:

1. Employee leaves the job after five years of employment; or
2. Where the service period is less than five years, the reason for termination is discontinuance of employer's business or ill health; or
3. The balance in RPF is reassigned to RPF with the new employer on re-employment.

66. Adam smith's theory of absolute advantage

- In 1776, Adam smith propounded a different theory, in his book titled 'The wealth of nations'.
- Smith offered a new trade theory called absolute advantage, which focused on the ability of a country to produce a good more efficiently than any other nation.
- The theory stated that trade between countries shouldn't be regulated or restricted by government policy or intervention. He stated that trade should flow naturally according to market forces.
- He introduced the idea of 'mutual benefit' through trade.

Hecksher-Ohlin theory

- It is also known as fac. .r proportions/ endowment theory.
- They determined that the cost of any factor or resource was a function of supply and demand. Factors that were in great supply relative to demand would be cheaper.
- Their theory stated that countries would produce and export goods that required resources or factors that were in great supply and, therefore, cheaper production factors. In contrast, countries would import goods that required resources that were in short supply, but higher demand.
- E.g. India and China.

Country similarity theory

- Swedish economist Steffan Linder developed the country similarity theory in 1961, he tried to explain the concept of intra-industry trade.
- This theory proposed that consumers in countries that are in the same or similar stage of development would have similar preferences.
- Firms seek the comfort of familiarity, the companies can trade in products that are inherently different of different versions of the same basic product.
- E.g.: USA and Germany trade in automobiles as the design and engineering is different.

Product life cycle theory

- Raymond Vernon, a Harvard Business School professor, developed the product life cycle theory in the 1966.
- The theory, originating in the field of marketing, stated that a product life cycle has three distinct stages: (1) new product, (2) growth, (3) maturity and (4) standardized product.
- In the 1960s this was a useful theory to explain the manufacturing success of the United States.
- The product life cycle theory has been less able to explain current trade patterns where innovation and manufacturing occur around the world. Global companies even conduct research and development in developing markets where highly skilled labour and facilities are usually cheaper.

69. Private equity can be broadly defined to include the following four different forms of investment:

1. **Leveraged buyout** (LBO) refers to the purchase of all or most of a company or a business unit by using equity from a small group of investors in combination with a significant amount of debt. The targets of LBOs are typically mature companies that generate strong operating cash flow.
2. **Growth capital** typically refers to minority equity investments in mature companies that need capital to expand or restructure operations, finance an acquisition, or enter a new market, without a change of control of the company.
3. **Mezzanine capital** refers to an investment in subordinated debt or preferred stock of a company, without taking voting control of the company. Often these securities have attached warrants or conversion rights into common stock.
4. **Venture capital** refers to equity investments in less mature non-public companies to fund the launch, early development, or expansion of a business.

76. (*a*) The Mines Act – 1952
(*b*) The Minimum Wages Act – 1948
(*c*) The Payment of Gratuity Act – 1972
(*d*) The Child Labour (Prohibition and Regulation) Act – 1986
(*e*) The Apprentices Act – 1961

78. Branded Product: The branded products get an identity through a name. It belongs to a specific company and the marketer separates this product from the rest.

The differentiated product: All the branded products are supposed to be differentiated products, but in certain cases where the brand name alone has not earned enough distinction the case may be different. Here the marketer tries to differentiated his product from the clutter created by competitor products by highlighting some of the special attributes/ features /qualities his brand is endowed with. The difference could be tangible or psychological. For example Knorr's Soups are tasty and healthy soups and can be prepared easily.

Homogeneous Products: They are products which are alike, with the sellers engaging on price war. Manufacturers end up distinguishing based on design, services offered or other freebies.

Non durable goods: Non durable goods are tangible goods normally consumed in either one or a couple of uses. These are purchased regularly and also consumed frequently. Smooth distribution and easy availability at all possible locations makes these products succeed in the market. The marketer has to advertise heavily to increase the purchase and build brand preference. Most of the fast moving consumer goods category products belong to this class. Examples include food items and toiletries.

Durable goods: Durable goods are tangible goods that can normally be used for many years. These products need more personal selling, after sales service, are often supported by guarantee and warranty programs. Examples include LCD TVs, mobile phones, washing machines and microwaves.

79. The pecking-order theory starts with *asymmetric information*—a fancy term indicating that managers know more about their companies' prospects, risks, and values than do outside investors.

Asymmetric information affects the choice between internal and external financing and between new issues of debt and equity securities. This leads to a *pecking order,* in which investment is financed first with internal funds, reinvested earnings primarily; then by new issues of debt; and finally with new issues of equity. New equity issues are a last resort when the company runs out of debt capacity, that is, when the threat of costs of financial distress brings regular insomnia to existing creditors and to the financial manager.

81. In a ***Market Competitive Pay Plan*** a job's compensation reflects the job's value in the company, as well as what other employers are paying for similar jobs in the marketplace.

Steps to create A Market-competitive Pay Plan:

1. Choose benchmark jobs
2. Select compensable factors
3. Assign weights to compensable factor
4. Convert percentages to points for each factor
5.. Define each factor's degree
6. Determine for each factor its factor degrees' points
7. Review job descriptions and job specifications
8. Evaluate the jobs
9. Draw the current (internal) wage curve
10. Conduct a Market Analysis: Salary Surveys
11. Draw the Market (external) Wage Curve
12. Compare and adjust Current and Market Wage Rates for jobs
13. Develop Pay Grades
14. Establish Rate Ranges
15. Address remaining jobs
16. Correct out-of-line rates.

82. **Technical definition by RBI on NPA on different cases:** NPA is a loan or an advance where:

- Interest and/or instalment of principal remain overdue for a period of more than 90 days in respect of a term loan.
- The account remains 'out of order' in respect of an Overdraft/Cash Credit (OD/CC).
- The bill remains overdue for a period of more than 90 days in the case of bills purchased and discounted.
- The instalment of principal or interest thereon remains overdue for two crop seasons for short duration crops.
- The instalment of principal or interest thereon remains overdue for one crop season for long duration crops.
- The amount of liquidity facility remains outstanding for more than 90 days, in respect of a securitisation transaction undertaken in terms of guidelines on securitisation dated February 1, 2006.
- In respect of derivative transactions, the overdue receivables representing positive mark-to-market value of a derivative contract, if these remain unpaid for a period of 90 days from the specified due date for payment.

Various steps taken to tackle NPAs: NPAs story is not new in India and there have been several steps taken by the GOI on legal, financial, policy level reforms. In the year 1991, **Narsimham Committee** recommended many reforms to tackle NPAs. Some of them were implemented.

The Debt Recovery Tribunals (DRTs)–1993: To decrease the time required for settling cases. They are governed by the provisions of the Recovery of Debt Due to Banks and Financial Institutions Act, 1993. However, their number is not sufficient therefore they also suffer from time lag and cases are pending for more than 2-3 years in many areas.

Credit Information Bureau–2000: A good information system is required to prevent loan falling into bad hands and therefore prevention of NPAs. It helps banks by maintaining and sharing data of individual defaulters and willful defaulters.

Lok Adalats–2001: They are helpful in tackling and recovery of small loans however they are limited up to 5 lakh rupees loans only by the RBI guidelines issued in 2001. They are positive in the sense that they avoid more cases into the legal system.

Compromise Settlement–2001: It provides a simple mechanism for recovery of NPA for the advances below ₹ 10 Crores. It covers lawsuits with courts and DRTs (Debt Recovery Tribunals) however willful default and fraud cases are excluded.

SARFAESI Act–2002: The Securitization and Reconstruction of Financial Assets and Enforcement of Security Interest (SARFAESI) Act, 2002 - The Act permits Banks / Financial Institutions to recover their NPAs without the involvement of the Court, through acquiring and disposing of the secured assets in NPA accounts with an outstanding amount of ₹ 1 lakh and above. The banks have to first issue a notice. Then, on the borrower's failure to repay, they can:

1. Take ownership of security and/or
2. Control over the management of the borrowing concern;
3. Appoint a person to manage the concern.

ARC (Asset Reconstruction Companies): The RBI gave license to 14 new ARCs recently after the amendment of the SARFAESI Act of 2002. These companies are created to unlock value from stressed loans. Before this law came, lenders could enforce their security interests only through courts, which was a time-consuming process.

Corporate Debt Restructuring–2005: It is for reducing the burden of the debts on the company by decreasing the rates paid and increasing the time the company has to pay the obligation back.

5:25 rule–2014: Also known as, **Flexible Structuring of Long Term Project Loans to Infrastructure and Core Industries.** It was proposed to maintain the cash flow of such companies since the project timeline is long and they do not get the money back into their books for a long time, therefore, the requirement of loans at every 5-7 years and thus refinancing for long term projects.

Joint Lenders Forum–2014: It was created by the inclusion of all PSBs whose loans have become stressed. It is present so as to avoid loan to the same individual or company from different banks. It is formulated to prevent the instances where one person takes a loan from one bank to give a loan of the other bank.

Mission Indradhanush–2015: The Indradhanush framework for transforming the PSBs represents the most comprehensive reform effort undertaken since banking nationalization in the year 1970 to revamp the Public Sector Banks (PSBs) and improve their overall performance by **ABCDEFG.**

83. Marketing is the process by which companies create value for customers and build strong customer relationships in order to capture value from customers in return.

The marketing process involves five steps. The first four steps create value for customers. First, marketers need to understand the marketplace and customer needs and wants. Next, marketers design a customer-driven marketing strategy with the goal of getting, keeping, and growing target customers. In the third step, marketers construct a marketing program that actually delivers superior value. All of these steps form the basis for the fourth step, building profitable customer relationships and creating customer delight. In the final step, the company reaps the rewards of strong customer relationships by capturing value from customers.

84. Meaning of Contract—Contract is defined under section 2h of The Indian Contract Act, 1872. According to this, an agreement enforceable by law is a contract.

Agreement—Agreement is defined under section 2e of The Indian Contract Act, 1872. According to this, every promise and every set of promises, forming the consideration for each other, is an agreement.

Promise—According to section 2b of the Indian Contract Act, 1872, when a person to whom the proposal is made signifies his assent thereto, the proposal is said to be accepted. A proposal when accepted, becomes a promise. It can be said that for promise, the proposal is said to be accepted, or there should be proposal and acceptance.

Proposal + Acceptance = Promise

Types of Agreement—Agreement has many types. On ground of enforceability agreement has two types:

(*a*) **Void Agreement—**According to section 2g, an agreement not enforceable by law is said to be void. Examples of these agreements are:

(*i*) If considerations and objects unlawful in part (Section 24)

(*ii*) Agreement without consideration (Section 25)

(*iii*) Agreement in restraint of marriage (Section 26)

(*iv*) Agreement in restraint of trade (Section 27)

(*v*) Agreement in restraint of legal proceedings (Section 28)

(*vi*) Agreement for uncertainty (Section 29)

(*vii*) Agreement by way of wager (Section 30)

(*viii*) Agreement contingent on impossible event (Section 31)

(*ix*) Agreement to impossible act [Section 56(1)]

(*x*) Where both parties are under mistake of law (Section 20)

(*xi*) Agreement to minor.

(*b*) **Valid Agreement—**An agreement enforceable by law is a contract.

Proposal or Offer—Definition of proposal is given in section 2a of The Indian Contract Act, 1872, according to this when one person signifies to another his willingness to do or to abstain from doing anything, with a view to obtaining the assent of that other to such act or abstinence, he is said to make a proposal.

According to section 2c, The person making the proposal is called the promisor and the person accepting the proposal is called the promisee.

86. The following are the differences between these two policies:

(*i*) The objective of monetary policy is to maintain price stability, full employment and economic growth. On the other hand, the objective of fiscal policy is to change aggregate demand, to control inflation and overcome recession.

(*ii*) The monetary policy regulates money supply and the cost and availability of credit. It also influences lending and borrowing rates of commercial banks. The fiscal policy, on the other hand, causes a deliberate change in government revenue and expenditure with a view to influencing the price level and the quantum of national output.

(*iii*) The monetary policy is the policy statement announced twice a year by the RBI along with an economic overview and future forecasts. The fiscal policy is showcased by the union budget announced on the last day of February even year, preceded by an economic survey.

87. A lease is just an extended rental agreement. The owner of the equipment (the *lessor*) allows the user (the *lessee*) to operate the equipment in exchange for regular lease payments.

There is a wide variety of possible arrangements. Short-term, cancelable leases are known as *operating leases.* In these leases the lessor bears the risks of ownership. Long-term, non-cancelable leases are called *full-payout, financial,* or *capital leases.* In these leases the lessee bears the risks. Financial leases are *sources of financing* for assets the firm wishes to acquire and use for an extended period.

The key to understanding operating leases is equivalent annual cost. In a competitive leasing market, the annual operating lease payment will be forced down to the lessor's equivalent annual cost. Operating leases are attractive to equipment users if the lease payment is less than the *user's* equivalent annual cost of buying the equipment. Operating leases make sense when the user needs the equipment only for a short time, when the lessor is better able to bear the risks of obsolescence, or when the lessor can offer a good deal on maintenance. Remember too that operating leases often have valuable options attached.

89 The "trademark" is a sign or symbol that distinguishes the goods or services of one enterprise from another in commerce. Trademarks may consist of virtually any form of sign, including letters and words, designs, colours, shapes, sounds, and scents. A trademark allows its holder to prevent others from using an identical or confusingly similar sign to identify its goods or services in commerce. Trademark rights may last as long as the right holder continues to use the mark in commerce. In civil law jurisdictions, trademark rights are most typically based on registration, although use in commerce may also establish trademark rights. In common law jurisdictions, trademark rights may be based either on registration or on use in commerce (the latter referred to as "common law" trademarks). In some jurisdictions, trademark rights may extend beyond the prevention of consumer confusion to encompass the prevention of "dilution" of the trademark holder's interests, that is, third parties may be prevented from "tarnishing" or "blurring" the trademark.

Previous Years' Paper (Solved)

National Testing Agency (NTA)

UGC-NET Junior Research Fellowship & Assistant Professor Eligibility Exam

Commerce, December-2019*

PAPER-II

Note; *This paper contains* ***hundred (100)*** *objective type questions of* ***two (2)*** *marks each.* ***All*** *questions are* ***compulsory***.

1. Match the following methods of capital budgeting with their respective formula:

Method	Formula
(*a*) ARIR method	(*i*) Present Value of Cash Inflows – Present Value of Cash Outflows
(*b*) Pay back Period Method	(*ii*) Present Value of Cash Inflows ÷ Present Value of Cash Outflows
(*c*) NPV Method	(*iii*) Average Income ÷ Average Investment
(*d*) Probability Index	(*iv*) Investment ÷ Annual Cash Inflows

Choose the correct option from those given below:

	(*a*)	(*b*)	(*c*)	(*d*)
A.	(*iii*)	(*i*)	(*iv*)	(*ii*)
B.	(*iii*)	(*iv*)	(*i*)	(*ii*)
C.	(*i*)	(*ii*)	(*iii*)	(*iv*)
D.	(*i*)	(*iv*)	(*ii*)	(*iii*)

2. Non-Banking Financial Companies can be classified as:

(*a*) Asset Finance Company (AFC)
(*b*) Investment Company (IC)
(*c*) loan Company (LC)
(*d*) Foreign Trade Company (FTC)

Choose the correct answer from the options given below:

A. (*a*), (*b*) and (*c*) only
B. (*b*), (*c*) and (*d*) only
C. (*a*), (*c*) and (*d*) only
D. (*a*), (*b*) and (*d*) only

3. Which two of the following are correct about the due date of issue of the TDS certificate?

(*a*) Form No 16 – Annual
(*b*) Form No 16 A – Quarterly
(*c*) Form No 16 B – Half Yearly
(*d*) Form No 16 C – Monthly

Choose the correct option from those below:

A. (*a*) and (*d*) B. (*a*) and (*c*)
C. (*a*) and (*b*) D. (*c*) and (*d*)

4. The theories that explain the formation of 'Informal Groups' are to include which of the following?

(*a*) Propinquity Theory
(*b*) Similarity (or) Balance Theory
(*c*) Displacement Theory
(*d*) Need for achievement Theory

Choose the correct option from those given below:

A. (*a*) and (*d*) only
B. (*a*) and (*b*) only
C. (*a*), (*b*) and (*c*) only
D. (*a*), (*b*), (*c*) and (*d*)

5. Under which of the following categories, a partner of partnership firm will be assessed?

A. An individual
B. HUF
C. Firm
D. Body of an Individual

*Held on 06/12/2019

6. What are the drivers of globalization?
(*a*) Population mobility especially of labour
(*b*) financial flows
(*c*) Exporting
(*d*) Assembly operations

Choose the correct answer from the following
A. (*a*) and (*d*) B. (*b*) and (*d*)
C. (*a*) and (*b*) D. (*c*) and (*d*)

7. Which of the following sections of Companies Act, 2013 facilitates amalgamation, absorption and reconstruction of companies?
A. 319 B. 320
C. 410 D. 502

8. What percentage of income from compensation on disaster is exempted from tax liability?
A. 100% B. 75%
C. 50% D. 25%

9. Which two of the following statements are true?
(*a*) The sum of the deviations from mean (ignoring algebraic signs) is greater than the sum of the deviations from median (ignoring algebraic signs)
(*b*) Standard deviation is independent of change of origin and change of scale
(*c*) In a symmetrical distribution, mean deviation equals 4/5 of standard deviation
(*d*) In a symmetrical and bell shaped distribution, quartile deviation is 1/3 of standard deviation

Choose the correct answer from the options given below:
A. (*b*) and (*d*) B. (*a*) and (*c*)
C. (*c*) and (*d*) D. (*a*) and (*b*)

10. Under which of the following approaches, the cost of equity is assumed to increase linearly with leverage, *i.e.*, the average cost of capital remains constant with increased use of leverage?
A. Net Operating Income Approach
B. Net Income Approach
C. Traditional Approach
D. Walter Approach

11. For calculating posterior probabilities (conditional probabilities under statistical dependence), the following information is available
(*a*) conditional probabilities
(*b*) original probability estimates (prior - probabilities) of mutually exclusive and collectively exhaustive events
(*c*) Arbitrary event with probability # 0 and for which conditional probabilities are also known
(*d*) joint probabilities of prior probability and conditional probability

Given the information that the arbitrary event has occurred, arrange the above information in a sequence of their requirement as per Baye's Theorem

Choose the correct option:
A. (*a*) → (*b*) → (*d*) → (*c*)
B. (*c*) → (*b*) → (*a*) → (*d*)
C. (*b*) → (*c*) → (*d*) → (*a*)
D. (*b*) → (*a*) → (*d*) → (*c*)

12. Which two of the following are the function of WTO?
(*a*) To facilitate the implementation, administration and operation of trade agreement
(*b*) To carry out periodic reviews of the trade policies of its member countries
(*c*) To assist in the establishment of a multilateral system of payments
(*d*) To promote international monetary cooperation

Choose the correct option from the following:
A. (*a*) and (*d*) B. (*b*) and (*c*)
C. (*c*) and (*d*) D. (*a*) and (*b*)

13. Which of the following statements is false?
A. When value of correlation coefficient is one, the two regression lines coincide
B. The regression coefficients are independent of the change of origin and of scale

C. The sign of the regression coefficients are always the same
D. The square of the coefficient of correlation is called coefficient of determination

14. Which of the following laws affect business organizations?
A. Incorporation and Bankruptcy laws
B. Environmental Protection Laws
C. Occupational Health and Safety Laws
D. Competition Laws

15. Who are the parties to a cheque?
(*a*) Drawer
(*b*) Payee
(*c*) Acceptor
(*d*) Holder
Choose the correct answer from the following options:
A. (*a*) and (*b*) only
B. (*a*), (*b*) and (*d*) only
C. (*a*) and (*c*) only
D. All of these – (*a*), (*b*), (*c*) and (*d*)

16. Companies that are becoming skilled in Customer Relationship Management (CRM) focus on:
A. Understanding the perceived performance and buyer's expectations
B. Giving benefits to the customers by reducing cost
C. Developing programs to attract and retain the right customers and meeting the individual needs of valued customers
D. Giving the quality in features and characteristics of a product or service that bear on its ability to satisfy stated or implied needs

17. Which of the following are the methods of determining cost behaviour?
(*a*) High and low point method
(*b*) Least square regression method
(*c*) Accounting or analytical approach
(*d*) Non-parametric method
Choose the correct answer from the options given below:
A. (*a*), (*b*) and (*d*)
B. (*a*), (*c*) and (*d*)
C. (*b*), (*c*) and (*d*)
D. (*a*), (*b*) and (*c*)

18. Arrange the steps to e-filing of Income Tax Return in correct sequence:
(*a*) Register yourself
(*b*) Verify ITR V
(*c*) Select the requisite form
(*d*) Fill form and upload
Choose the correct option from those below:
A. (*a*) → (*c*) → (*d*) → (*b*)
B. (*a*) → (*b*) → (*c*) → (*d*)
C. (*a*) → (*b*) → (*d*) → (*c*)
D. (*c*) → (*a*) → (*d*) → (*b*)

19. Michael Porter proposed generic strategies that provide good starting points for strategic thinking. Identify them from the below mentioned strategies
(*a*) Overall cost leadership
(*b*) Innovation
(*c*) Focus
(*d*) Differentiation
Choose the correct answer from the options given below
A. (*a*) and (*b*) only
B. (*a*), (*c*) and (*d*) only
C. (*a*), (*b*) and (*d*) only
D. All of these – (*a*), (*b*), (*c*) and (*d*)

20. Given below are two statements. One is labelled as Assertion (A) and the other is labelled as Reason (R).

Assertion (A): If the firm is prepared to incur increased cost on transportation, it may be in a position to reduce its inventory cost.

Reason (R): As in such a case, the firm can use the fastest mode of transport and rush the goods/stocks to the desired warehouse, unmindful of the cost of transportation.

In the context of the above two statements related to logistics management, which of the following options is correct.

A. Both (A) and (R) are true and (R) is the correct explanation of (A)
B. Both (A) and (R) are true, but (R) is NOT the correct explanation of (A)
C. (A) is true, but (R) is false
D. (A) is false, but (R) is true

21. Which of the following statements are true?
(*a*) Transaction exposure is inherent in all foreign currencies denominated contractual transactions
(*b*) Translation exposure relates to the change in accounting income and balance sheet statements caused by change in exchange rate
(*c*) Economic exposure has an impact on the valuation of a firm
(*d*) Operating exposure does not have any impact on the firm's future operating revenues or future operating costs

Choose the correct option from those below:
A. (*a*) and (*b*) only
B. (*b*) and (*c*) only
C. (*b*) and (*d*) only
D. (*a*), (*b*) and (*c*) only

22. Which of the following is NOT a method for calculating or ascertaining the amount of purchase consideration?
A. Net Payment Method
B. Net Assets Method
C. Gross Receipts Method
D. Share Exchange Method

23. Which of the following is NOT a presumption about a negotiable instrument?
A. Date
B. Consideration
C. Stamp
D. Absolute and good title to the transferee

24. Which of the following statements is NOT correct regarding the duties of an auditor?
A. Physical verification of fixed assets is primarily the responsibility of the auditor
B. Ownership of fixed assets should be verified by examining the title deed by the auditor
C. Auditor should ascertain that the assets are in the possession of the client
D. The auditor should satisfy himself that the assets have been valued in the financial statements according to the accounting principles

25. Which two of the following are correct in terms of rate of tax deduction at source (TDS)?
(*a*) Income by way of winning from horse race: @ 30%
(*b*) Insurance Commission: @ 10%
(*c*) Rent of Plant & Machinery: @ 5%
(*d*) Rent of furniture: @ 5%

Choose the correct option from the following:
A. (*a*) and (*b*)
B. (*a*) and (*c*)
C. (*a*) and (*d*)
D. (*b*) and (*c*)

26. Which one of the following is NOT correct according to the Consumer Protection Act?
A. District Forum shall consist of a lady social worker
B. State Commission shall consist of person who is or has been a Judge of a High Court
C. District Forum shall consist of four members
D. National Consumer Disputes Redressal Commission shall consist of a person who is or has been a Judge of the Supreme Court

27. What is the typical sequence in which the following selection devices are used by the company?
(*a*) Reference checks
(*b*) Physical examination
(*c*) Application Blank
(*d*) Hire
(*e*) Conditional Offers
(*f*) More interviews
(*g*) Screening interviews
(*h*) Tests

Choose the correct answer from the options given below:
A. (*c*) → (*g*) → (*h*) → (*f*) → (*a*) → (*e*) → (*b*) → (*d*)

B. $(d) \rightarrow (g) \rightarrow (f) \rightarrow (h) \rightarrow (a) \rightarrow (e) \rightarrow (b) \rightarrow (c)$
C. $(c) \rightarrow (h) \rightarrow (g) \rightarrow (a) \rightarrow (f) \rightarrow (e) \rightarrow (b) \rightarrow (d)$
D. $(d) \rightarrow (g) \rightarrow (h) \rightarrow (f) \rightarrow (a) \rightarrow (e) \rightarrow (b) \rightarrow (d)$

28. According to Sale of Goods Act which two of the following are defined as 'goods'?

(*a*) Moveable property
(*b*) Growing crops
(*c*) Actionable claims
(*d*) Book debt

Choose the correct answer from the following options:

A. (*a*) and (*d*) B. (*b*) and (*c*)
C. (*a*) and (*b*) D. (*d*) and (*b*)

29. Which among the following are NOT qualified to be appointed as auditor of a company?

(*a*) An individual who is a Chartered Accountant and holds a Certificate of Practice as per CA Act, 1949
(*b*) A limited liability partnership firm, which has all partners as Chartered Accountants
(*c*) Officer or employee of a company who is qualified Chartered Accountant degree holder too
(*d*) Any Chartered Accountant whose appointment will result in the person being the auditor of more than 10 companies

Choose the most appropriate option:

A. (*a*) and (*b*)
B. (*b*), (*c*) and (*d*)
C. (*c*) and (*d*)
D. (*a*), (*b*) and (*d*)

30. Which one of the following is a void contract?

A. Unilateral contract
B. A contract which ceases to be enforceable by law
C. Implied contract
D. Express contract

31. Match List-I with List-II:

List-I	List-II
(*a*) Transfer of ownership	(*i*) Negotiable Instrument
(*b*) Sale of goodwill after dissolution	(*ii*) Contract of sale of goods
(*c*) Buy-back of securities	(*iii*) Dissolution of partnership firm
(*d*) Promissory Note	(*iv*) Share capital of company

Choose the correct option from those given below:

	(*a*)	(*b*)	(*c*)	(*d*)
A.	(*ii*)	(*iii*)	(*iv*)	(*i*)
B.	(*iii*)	(*iv*)	(*ii*)	(*i*)
C.	(*iv*)	(*ii*)	(*i*)	(*iii*)
D.	(*i*)	(*ii*)	(*iii*)	(*iv*)

32. Given below are two statements. One is labelled as Assertion (A) and the other is labelled as Reason (R).

Assertion (A): In the case of short run cost behaviour, MC curve intersects AC curve at its minimum.

Reason (R): While AC continues to decrease, MC begins to rise. Also, when AC is at its minimum, it is neither increasing nor decreasing. It is constant when AC is constant, it is equal to MC at the point of intersection.

Choose the correct option from those below

A. Both (A) and (R) are true and (R) is the correct explanation of (A)
B. Both (A) and (R) are true, but (R) is NOT the correct explanation of (A)
C. (A) is true, but (R) is false
D. (A) is false, but (R) is true

33. ADEN Rules, 1953 is related to which of the following?

A. Tax exemption
B. Residential status
C. Double taxation relief
D. Assessment of corporate entity

34. Which of the following types of authorities are found in most organizations?

(*a*) Division Authority

(*b*) line Authority

(*c*) Staff Authority

(*d*) functional Authority

Choose the correct option from those given below:

A. (*a*) and (*b*) only

B. (*b*) and (*c*) only

C. (*a*), (*b*) and (*c*) only

D. (*b*), (*c*) and (*d*) only

35. Which of the following is NOT true about web marketers?

A. Web marketers usually try to attract prospects to their site through email, advertisements in newspapers

B. Use attractions like discounts, gifts and contests

C. Ask customers to give their personal data mandatorily

D. Give a lot of publicity to the discount schemes

36. Which among the following is a correct statement about residential status of a company?

A. A company can be classified as "not ordinarily resident"

B. A company can never be classified as "not ordinarily resident"

C. A company can be classified as "not ordinarily resident" with the permission from Ministry of finance

D. A company can be classified as "not ordinarily resident" with the permission from Ministry of Commerce

37. In which of the following years, the Bretton Woods Agreement was signed by the delegates from 44 nations which led to the establishment of the IMF?

A. 1940 B. 1952

C. 1944 D. 1957

38. Which of the following statements are true?

(*a*) Pay-back period method considers all cash flows of a project

(*b*) Pay-back period method concerns more with the recovery of cost than profitability

(*c*) Net Present Value represents net addition to the wealth of shareholders

(*d*) Accounting Rate of Return method incorporates risk as well as time value of money

Choose the correct option from those below:

A. (*a*) and (*b*) B. (*a*) and (*d*)

C. (*b*) and (*c*) D. (*b*) and (*d*)

39. Match List-I with list-II

List-I	List-II
(*a*) Qualified Report	(*i*) Auditor Duty
(*b*) Examine Valuation and Disclosure	(*ii*) Auditor Liabilities
(*c*) Access to records of Company and its subsidiaries	(*iii*) Auditor Report
(*d*) Mis-statement in prospectus in company issue of capital	(*iv*) Auditor Right

Choose the correct option from those given below:

	(*a*)	(*b*)	(*c*)	(*d*)
A.	(*ii*)	(*i*)	(*iv*)	(*iii*)
B.	(*iii*)	(*i*)	(*iv*)	(*ii*)
C.	(*iii*)	(*i*)	(*ii*)	(*iv*)
D.	(*iv*)	(*ii*)	(*iii*)	(*i*)

40. The sum total of the values of two variables 'X' and 'Y' is equal for all the observations, The value of the coefficient of correlation between 'X' and 'Y' is:

A. +1 (perfectly positive)

B. –1 (perfectly negative)

C. Zero (No correlation)

D. $> 0 < 1$ (Imperfect correlation)

41. Which of the following is the non-random method of selecting samples from a given population?

A. Stratified Sampling

B. Systematic Sampling

C. Quota Sampling
D. Multi-stage Sampling

42. Which of the following are true about conditions according to the Sale of Goods Act?
(*a*) Title
(*b*) Description
(*c*) Quite possession
(*d*) Encumbrances

Choose the correct answer from the following options:
A. (*a*) and (*d*) only
B. (*b*) and (*c*) only
C. (*a*), (*c*) and (*d*) only
D. (*a*) and (*b*) only

43. Which of the following is an incomplete experimental research design?
A. Before and after with control group design
B. Factorial design
C. One group before-after design
D. Latin Square design

44. Which of the following statements are correct?
(*a*) Dividend payout ratio refers to that portion of total earnings which is distributed among equity shareholders of the company
(*b*) 'Bird in hand' argument is given by Gordon's model
(*c*) MM model suggest that dividend payment is very relevant for value of the firm
(*d*) Walter's Model suggests that dividend payment does not affect the market price of the share

A. (*a*) and (*b*) B. (*a*) and (*c*)
C. (*b*) and (*c*) D. (*c*) and (*d*)

45. Choose incorrect statement from the following:
A. 28 Days T-bills were introduced in 1998
B. 364 Days T-bills were introduced in 1992
C. 182 Days T-bills were introduced in 1986
D. 273 Days T-bills were introduced in 2006

46. Arrange the following financial institutions in ascending order of their year of establishment:
(*a*) National Housing Bank
(*b*) Export-Import Bank of India
(*c*) NABARD
(*d*) Unit Trust of India

Choose the correct option from those below:
A. $(b) \rightarrow (d) \rightarrow (c) \rightarrow (a)$
B. $(d) \rightarrow (b) \rightarrow (a) \rightarrow (c)$
C. $(d) \rightarrow (b) \rightarrow (c) \rightarrow (a)$
D. $(d) \rightarrow (c) \rightarrow (b) \rightarrow (a)$

47. Match List-I with List-II

List-I	List-II
(*a*) Size of the market	(*i*) Globalization of business
(*b*) Demographic environment	(*ii*) Foreign trade policy
(*c*) Export-oriented units	(*iii*) Macro-environment
(*d*) Multinational corporations	(*iv*) Non-economic environment

Choose the correct option from those given below:

	(*a*)	(*b*)	(*c*)	(*d*)
A.	(*iv*)	(*ii*)	(*iii*)	(*i*)
B.	(*ii*)	(*iii*)	(*i*)	(*iv*)
C.	(*iii*)	(*ii*)	(*i*)	(*iv*)
D.	(*iii*)	(*iv*)	(*ii*)	(*i*)

48. Which of the following are part of Corporate Social Responsibility (CSR) to consumers?
(*a*) Reasonable chances and proper system for accomplishment and promotion
(*b*) To supply goods at reasonable prices even when there is seller's market
(*c*) Improving the efficiency of the business operation
(*d*) To provide an opportunity for being heard and redress genuine grievances

Choose the correct answer from the options given below:
A. (*a*) and (*b*) B. (*b*) and (*d*)
C. (*b*) and (*c*) D. (*a*) and (*c*)

49. In e-commerce, one of the key design elements of an effective website-community refers to:

A. Its layout and design
B. The way site enables user to user communication
C. Site's ability to tailor itself to different users or to allow users to personalize the site
D. Degree that the site is linked to the other sites

50. Given below are two statements, one labelled as Assertion (A) and the other labelled as Reason (R).

Assertion (A): Auto companies and other consumer goods companies offer cash rebates to encourage purchase of the manufacturer's products within a specified period.

Reason (R): The same product is priced differently at different times.

In the context of the two statements above related to pricing strategy, which one of the following options is correct?

A. Both (A) and (R) are correct
B. Both (A) and (R) are not correct
C. (A) is correct, but (R) is not correct
D. (A) is not correct, but (R) is correct

51. Which one is odd?

A. Economic Policies
B. Economic Planning
C. Socio-cultural factors
D. Macro-economic scenario

52. Which one of the following is the correct sequence of various stages of operating cycle of a manufacturing company?

A. Raw material conversion period, work-in-progress conversion period, Finished goods conversion period, Receivables conversion period
B. Raw material conversion period, work-in-progress conversion period, Creditors payment period, Receivables conversion period
C. Creditor payment period, Raw material conversion period, Receivables conversion period, work-in-progress conversion period
D. Raw material conversion period, Finished goods conversion period, work-in-progress conversion period, Receivables conversion period

53. Which of the following is NOT part of the process of management audit?

A. Identification of responsibility center
B. Review of performance of each responsibility center
C. Review of organizational structure
D. Investigating the depreciation method and its application on fixed assets in the company

54. A production function expressed as

$$Q = A\left[\alpha K^{-\beta} + (1-\alpha)L^{-\beta}\right]^{\frac{-1}{\beta}}$$

or

$$Q = A\left[\alpha L^{-\beta} + (1-\alpha)K^{-\beta}\right]^{\frac{-1}{\beta}}$$

When $A > 0$, $0 < \alpha < 1$ and $\beta > -1$

Where L = Labour, K = Capital and A, α and β are three parameters is called

A. Constant elasticity substitution function
B. Variable elasticity substitution function
C. Leontief-type function
D. Cobb-Douglas function

55. Match the following theories of profit with their propounders

Theory	Propounder
(*a*) Profit as Rent of Ability	(*i*) F.B. Hawley
(*b*) Dynamic Theory of Profit	(*ii*) Joseph A Schumpeter
(*c*) Risk Theory of Profit	(*iii*) J.B. Clark
(*d*) Innovation Theory of Profit	(*iv*) F.A Walker

Choose the correct option from those given below:

	(a)	(b)	(c)	(d)
A.	(iv)	(ii)	(iii)	(i)
B.	(i)	(ii)	(iii)	(iv)
C.	(iv)	(iii)	(i)	(ii)
D.	(iii)	(i)	(ii)	(iv)

56. Which three of the following types of cyber attacks may occur in the process of mobile banking?

(*a*) Backdoor attack
(*b*) Front door attack
(*c*) Denial of service attack
(*d*) Direct access attack

Choose the correct option from those given below:

A. (*a*), (*b*) and (*c*) B. (*b*), (*c*) and (*d*)
C. (*a*), (*b*) and (*d*) D. (*a*), (*c*) and (*d*)

57. In the recent years—the major gain in logistical efficiency have come from which one of the following?

A. Advances in Information Technology
B. Reduction in petroleum prices
C. Fast order processing
D. Increase in production of commercial vehicles

58. On which of the following assumptions, the theory of consumer behaviour on cardinal utility approach is NOT based?

A. Consumer is rational
B. Limited money income of the consumer
C. Maximization of total satisfaction
D. Diminishing marginal utility of money

59. Functions of a first-level or front line supervisors are to include which of the following?

(*a*) To determine individual job assignment
(*b*) To attend to grievances and resolve conflicts
(*c*) To provide technical knowledge and guidance to workers
(*d*) To supply strategic information relating to production to management

Choose the correct answer from the options given below:

A. (*a*) and (*b*) only
B. (*a*) and (*c*) only
C. (*a*), (*b*) and (*c*) only
D. All of them - (*a*), (*b*), (*c*), and (*d*)

60. According to FEMA, foreign exchange does NOT include:

A. Deposits payable in any foreign currency
B. Bills of exchange drawn in Indian currency but payable in any foreign currency
C. Travellers cheques drawn by institutions outside India but payable in Indian currency
D. Drafts drawn by banks outside India and payable in foreign currency

61. Market logistic planning has the following four steps. Arrange the steps in correct sequence.

(*a*) Develop operational excellence in sales forecasting, warehouse management, transportation and material management
(*b*) Select the best channel design and network strategy for reaching the customers
(*c*) Implement the solution with the best information systems, equipment, policies and procedures
(*d*) Decide on company's value proposition to its customers Select the correct option from those below

Select the correct option from those below:

A. (*a*) → (*b*) → (*c*) → (*d*)
B. (*d*) → (*b*) → (*a*) → (*c*)
C. (*d*) → (*b*) → (*c*) → (*a*)
D. (*d*) → (*c*) → (*b*) → (*a*)

62. A company raises ₹ 1,00,000 by issue of 11000, 10% debentures of ₹ 100 each at a discount of 2% redeemable after 10 years. If the corporate tax rate is 40%, what would be the cost of capital]?

A. 6.82% B. 5.98%
C. 6.18% D. 5.5%

63. Match the following Banking Sector reform committees with their respective purposes:

Committee	**Purpose**
(*a*) Y.V. Reddy Committee	(*i*) Revised method of lending in place of cash credit system
(*b*) Rashid Jilani Committee	(*ii*) Rationalization of interest rate on small savings
(*c*) S.M. Kelkar Committee	(*iii*) Working capital lending norms
(*d*) I.T. Vaz Committee	(*iv*) Regional Rural Banks

Choose the correct option from those given below:

	(*a*)	(*b*)	(*c*)	(*d*)
A.	(*i*)	(*ii*)	(*iii*)	(*iv*)
B.	(*ii*)	(*i*)	(*iv*)	(*iii*)
C.	(*iv*)	(*iii*)	(*ii*)	(*i*)
D.	(*ii*)	(*iii*)	(*iv*)	(*i*)

64. Given below are two statements. One is labelled as Assertion (A) and the other is labelled as Reason (R).

Assertion (A): Tax should not be charged on dividend income from the shareholders.

Reason (R): Some economists are of the opinion that when tax has already been paid on the profit of the company and balance is distributed as dividend to the owners, tax need not be levied on them.

In the light of the above two statements, choose the correct answer from the options given below

A. Both (A) and (R) are true and (R) is the correct explanation of (A)

B. Both (A) and (R) are true, but (R) is NOT the correct explanation of (A)

C. (A) is true, but (R) is false

D. (A) is false, but (R) is true

65. Match the 'Category of Compensation' with 'Compensation Plan':

(Category of Compensation)	**(Compensation Plan)**
(*a*) Pay for time not worked	(*i*) Savings Plan
(*b*) Services and Perquisites	(*ii*) Stock Option
(*c*) Protection Programme	(*iii*) Pension
(*d*) Incentive Pay	(*iv*) Sick Leave
(*e*) Deferred Pay	(*v*) Low Cost Meals

Choose the correct option from those given below:

	(*a*)	(*b*)	(*c*)	(*d*)	(*e*)
A.	(*iii*)	(*iv*)	(*ii*)	(*i*)	(*v*)
B.	(*iv*)	(*v*)	(*iii*)	(*ii*)	(*i*)
C.	(*iv*)	(*v*)	(*i*)	(*ii*)	(*iii*)
D.	(*iii*)	(*v*)	(*i*)	(*iv*)	(*ii*)

66. Which one of the following relates to warranty?

A. It is of vital importance for completion of contract

B. If there is breach, the aggrieved party can repudiate the contract

C. It is essential to the main purpose of the contract

D. In case of breach, the aggrieved party can claim only damages

67. The indemnity holder is NOT entitled to:

A. All damages which he may be compelled to pay in any suit in respect of any matter to which the promise applies

B. All costs that he may be compelled to bear in defending any such suit

C. All sums that he may have paid under the terms of any compromise of such suit

D. Damages for liability incurred which is not absolute

68. Which two of the following measures of central tendency are NOT capable of algebraic treatment?

(*a*) Geometric Mean

(*b*) Median

(*c*) Arithmetic Mean

(*d*) Mode

(*e*) Harmonic Mean

Choose the correct answer from the options given below:

A. *(a)* and *(b)* B. *(d)* and *(e)*
C. *(b)* and *(d)* D. *(c)* and *(e)*

69. 'Maximization of firm's growth rate subject to managerial and financial constraints' as one of the important alternative objectives of especially large business corporation was pleaded by:

A. Milton Friedman
B. Robin Marris
C. Cyert and March
D. H.A. Simon

70. Which two of the following statements are correct?

(a) In the short-run, Δ TFC = 0, therefore Δ TC = Δ TVC
(b) If decrease in AFC < increase in AVC, then AC decreases
(c) If decrease in AFC = increase in AVC, AC remains constant
(d) If decrease in AFC > increase in AVC, then AC increases

Choose the correct answer from the options given below

A. *(a)* and *(c)* B. *(b)* and *(c)*
C. *(b)* and *(d)* D. *(a)* and *(d)*

71. Match the tests with suitable situations of their application for hypothesis-testing:

Test	Situation
(a) z-test	*(i)* Comparing the differences in the mean values of more than two sample groups (Parametric data)
(b) ANOVA	*(ii)* Testing the significance of the difference between averages of two large sized sample groups (Parametric data)
(c) Chi-Square Test	*(iii)* Comparing the differences in the mean values of more than two sample groups (Non-parametric data)
(d) Kruskal - Wallis Test	*(iv)* Testing the significance of the association between two attributes

Choose the correct option from those given below:

	(a)	*(b)*	*(c)*	*(d)*
A.	*(i)*	*(ii)*	*(iii)*	*(iv)*
B.	*(ii)*	*(i)*	*(iv)*	*(iii)*
C.	*(ii)*	*(iii)*	*(i)*	*(iv)*
D.	*(i)*	*(iv)*	*(ii)*	*(iii)*

72. Quality circle is a type of:

A. Problem-solving team
B. Cross-functional team
C. Self-directed team
D. Project team

73. Given below are two statements. One is labelled as Assertion (A) and the other is labelled as Reason (R).

Assertion (A): Indian Accounting Standards contain some 'carve outs' and for convergence with IFRS with some changes applied in India.

Reason (R): Financial statements prepared in India with Indian Accounting Standards will not be IFRS compliant.

In the light of the above two statements, choose the correct option

A. Both (A) and (R) are true and (R) is the correct explanation of (A)
B. Both (A) and (R) are true, but (R) is NOT the correct explanation of (A)
C. (A) is true, but (R) is false
D. (A) is false, but (R) is true

74. 14 Days intermediate T-bills were brought into effect from 1996-97 after the abolition of which of the following?

A. 91 Days T-bills
B. 182 Days T-bills
C. 273 Days T-bills
D. 364 Days T-bills

75. National Housing Bank was established in 1987 as wholly owned subsidiary of which of the following?

A. State Bank of India
B. Life Insurance Corporation of India
C. Reserve Bank of India
D. Industrial Finance Corporation of India

76. Which two of the following statements are true?

(*a*) Skewness studies the flatness or peakedness of the distribution
(*b*) A positively skewed distribution curve is stretched more to the right than to the left
(*c*) On the basis of empirical relationship between mean, mode and median for moderately asymmetrical distribution, Karl Pearson's coefficient of skewness can be measured by 3 (Mean- Median) divided by Standard Deviation
(*d*) If mean < mode, the distribution is positively skewed

Choose the correct option from those below:

A. (*a*) and (*b*) B. (*b*) and (*c*)
C. (*c*) and (*d*) D. (*b*) and (*d*)

77. Match the modes of communication in marketing and their communication platforms

(Mode of Communication)	**(Communication Platform)**
(*a*) Advertising	(*i*) Blogs
(*b*) Sales Promotion	(*ii*) Brochures & Booklets
(*c*) Word of mouth marketing	(*iii*) Sales meetings
(*d*) Personal selling	(*iv*) Contests

Choose the correct option:

	(*a*)	(*b*)	(*c*)	(*d*)
A.	(*ii*)	(*iii*)	(*iv*)	(*i*)
B.	(*ii*)	(*iv*)	(*i*)	(*iii*)
C.	(*iv*)	(*iii*)	(*ii*)	(*i*)
D.	(*iv*)	(*iii*)	(*i*)	(*ii*)

78. Which of the following terms means the tendency of a supervisor to rate a subordinate lower than his performance?

A. Horns Effect
B. Halo Effect
C. Central Tendency
D. Pointing Tendency

79. Given below are two statements. One is labelled as Assertion (A) and the other is labelled as Reason (R).

Assertion (A): Globalization refers to the free cross-border movement of goods, services, capital, information and people.

Reason (R): Countries are consistently evolving innovative marketing barriers that are WTD compatible.

In the light of the above statements, choose the correct answer from the options given below

A. Both (A) and (R) are true and (R) is the correct explanation of (A)
B. Both (A) and (R) are true, but (R) is NOT the correct explanation of (A)
C. (A) is true, but (R) is false
D. (A) is false, but (R) is true

80. The following are the two statements regarding elasticity of demand and its measurement

Statement I: On every point on the straight line demand curve, the point elasticities are all equal.

Statement II: On every point on the rectangular hyperbola shaped demand curve, the point elasticities are not equal.

Select the correct option for those below:

A. Both the statements are correct
B. Both the statements are not correct
C. Statement I is correct while Statement II is incorrect
D. Statement I is incorrect while Statement II is correct

81. Which two of the following statements are true?

(*a*) A simple monopoly firm always earns super normal profit
(*b*) Sweezy's kinked demand curve model is the best known model explaining relatively more satisfactory behaviour of oligopoly firm for price rigidity
(*c*) A perfectly competitive firm is price-taker

(*d*) Firms under monopolistic competition earn only normal profits

Choose the correct option from those below:

A. (*a*) and (*d*) B. (*b*) and (*d*)
C. (*b*) and (*c*) D. (*a*) and (*c*)

82. Match the following countries with the types of Double Taxation Avoidance Agreement signed by India with them:

Country	Type of Agreement
(*a*) Austria	(*i*) Limited Agreement
(*b*) Bahamas	(*ii*) Comprehensive Agreements
(*c*) Lebanon	(*iii*) Comprehensive Agreements/Limited Multilateral Agreement
(*d*) Sri Lanka	(*iv*) Tax Information Exchange Agreement

Choose the correct option from those given below:

	(*a*)	(*b*)	(*c*)	(*d*)
A.	(*iv*)	(*ii*)	(*i*)	(*iii*)
B.	(*ii*)	(*iv*)	(*i*)	(*iii*)
C.	(*ii*)	(*iv*)	(*iii*)	(*i*)
D.	(*i*)	(*ii*)	(*iii*)	(*iv*)

83. Which of the following is the odd one out?

A. Specific goods
B. Un-ascertained goods
C. Future goods
D. Ascertained goods

84. Which two of the following are correct about TDS Certificates?

(*a*) TDS on non-salary payment - Form 16
(*b*) TDS on salary payment - Form 16 A
(*c*) TDS on sale of property - Form 16 B
(*d*) TDS on rent - Form 16 C

Choose the correct option from those given below:

A. (*a*) and (*b*) B. (*c*) and (*d*)
C. (*a*) and (*d*) D. (*b*) and (*c*)

85. In the case consumers' equilibrium to be explained through an ordinal approach, when there are two commodities with their prices given and with limited income of the consumer, the following information is required:

(*a*) Price line/budget line
(*b*) Indifference map
(*c*) Point of tangency between IC and budget line
(*d*) Equality of the slopes of IC and budget line

Arrange the information required in the correct sequence and choose the right option from those below

A. (*b*) → (*d*) → (*a*) → (*c*)
B. (*b*) → (*a*) → (*d*) → (*c*)
C. (*a*) → (*d*) → (*b*) → (*c*)
D. (*a*) → (*b*) → (*c*) → (*d*)

86. If the risk-free return (Rf) is 6%, Beta value (β) is 1.5 and market rate of return (Km) is 10%, the expected rate of return would be:

A. 15% B. 12%
C. 17.5% D. 16%

87. The informal group's communication system is called

A. Group Dynamics
B. Grapevine
C. Exchange
D. Interaction

88. Which of the following is NOT a factor contributing to MBO program failure?

A. Altering goals to meet changes in circumstances
B. Easy goals
C. Lack of management support
D. Setting of unrealistically difficult goals

89. Which among the following is NOT a correct statement?

A. The Reserve Bank of India worked as Central Bank of Burma till April 1947
B. The Reserve Bank of India worked as Central Bank of Pakistan till June 1948
C. The Reserve Bank of India worked as Central Bank of Bangladesh from January 1972 to December 1975
D. The Reserve Bank of India commenced its operations on April 1, 1935

90. Following are the events which generally happen in the life of a public limited company

(*a*) Public issue of shares (IPO)

(*b*) Firm incorporation

(*c*) Preliminary expenditures

(*d*) Issue of equity shares to promoters of the company

Choose the correct sequence (chronological order) of the events from the options given below:

A. (*a*) → (*b*) → (*c*) → (*d*)
B. (*b*) → (*c*) → (*d*) → (*a*)
C. (*c*) → (*b*) → (*a*) → (*d*)
D. (*c*) → (*b*) → (*d*) → (*a*)

Directions (Qs. No. 91 to 95): *Read the passage carefully and answer the questions that follow:*

Life Insurance in its modern form came to India from England in the year 1818. The Oriental We Insurance Company started by Europeans in Calcutta was the first life insurance company on Indian soil. All the insurance companies established during that period were brought up with the purpose of looking after the needs of the European community and Indian natives were not being insured by these companies. However, later with the efforts of eminent people like Babu Muttylal Seal, foreign insurance companies started insuring Indian lives too. But Indian lives were being treated as sub standard lives and heavy extra premium were being charged upon them. The Bombay Mutual Life Assurance Society heralded the birth of the first Indian life insurance company in the year 1870 and covered Indian lives at normal rates. Starting as an Indian enterprise with highly patriotic motives, insurance companies came into existence to carry the message of insurance and social security through insurance to various sectors of society. In 1907, the Hindustan Co-operative Insurance Company took birth in one of the rooms of 'The Jorsanko', house of the great poet Rabindranath Tagore in Calcutta. The Indian Mercantile, General Assurance and Swadeshi Life (later Bombay Life) were some of the companies established during the same period. Prior to 1912, India had no legislation to regulate the insurance business. In the year 1912, Life Insurance Companies Act and Provident Fund Act were passed. The Life Insurance Companies Act, 1912 made it necessary that the pıemium rate tables and periodical valuations of companies should be certified by an actuary. But the Act discriminated between foreign and Indian Companies on many accounts, putting Indian Companies at a disadvantage.

91. The insurance business in India was started first by which one of the following?

A. Americans
B. Indian merchants
C. Europeans
D. Afro-Indians

92. Identify the correct statement from the following:

A. Initially, insurance companies used to discriminate Indian and European clients
B. There was no discrimination in Indian and European clients by the insurance companies initially
C. Indian clients were charged lower premium by the insurance companies ,in the beginning
D. Indian insurance companies charged higher premium to Europeans at a later stage

93. The paragraph is about which of the following?

A. Genesis of insurance in India
B. Struggle of insurance business
C. Conflict of insurance business
D. Complications of insurance business

94. Which one among the following grew along with insurance business in India?

A. Pension Fund B. Provident Fund
C. Gratuity D. Arbitrage

95. Which among the following was later renamed as Bombay Life?

A. The Indian Mercantile General Assurance
B. The Oriental Life Insurance Company
C. National Insurance
D. Swadeshi Life

Directions (Qs. No. 96 to 100): *Read the given, passage carefully and answer the questions that follow:*

Companies often define themselves in terms of products: They are in the "auto business" or the "clothing business". 'Market definitions of a business, however, describe the business as a customer-satisfying process. Products are transient, basic needs and customer groups endure forever. Transportation is a need: the horse and carriage, automobile, railroad, airline, ship and truck are products that meet the need. Viewing business in terms of customers can suggest additional growth opportunities, There exists a difference between a target market definition and a strategic market definition. To define its mission, a company should address Peter Drucker's classic question: What is our business?

96. Which of the following is NOT a major characteristic of a good mission statement?
- A. They have very limited words
- B. They focus on a limited number of goals
- C. They stress the company's major competitive spheres in which company will operate
- D. They have a long term view

97. Which of the following is the correct product definition of 'Blue Star'?
- A. We provide climate control in homes and offices
- B. We supply air conditioners
- C. We make air cooling systems
- D. We make air conditioners

98. Which of the following is the correct market definition of 'BPCL'?
- A. We distribute oil products
- B. We are the largest oil supply company in India
- C. We supply energy
- D. Bharat's own oil distribution company

99. Pepsi could define its 'target market' as:
- A. Everyone who drinks carbonated soft drinks and are competitors
- B. Anyone who drinks liquid
- C. Everyone who drinks non-milk drinks
- D. Anyone who drinks competitor's drinks

100. Which of the following is the correct combination Product Definition and Market Definition of Xerox Company?
- A. Product Definition - We sell photocopies
  Market Definition - We help improve office efficiency
- B. Product Definition - We make photo machines
  Market Definition - We improve copy speeds
- C. Product Definition - We sell copying equipment
  Market Definition - We make office more efficient
- D. Product Definition - We make copying equipment
  Market Definition - We help improve office productivity

ANSWERS

1	2	3	4	5	6	7	8	9	10
B	A	C	B	C	C	A	A	B	A
11	**12**	**13**	**14**	**15**	**16**	**17**	**18**	**19**	**20**
D	D	B	A	B	C	D	A	B	A
21	**22**	**23**	**24**	**25**	**26**	**27**	**28**	**29**	**30**
D	C	D	A	C	C	A	C	B	B
31	**32**	**33**	**34**	**35**	**36**	**37**	**38**	**39**	**40**
A	A	C	D	C	B	C	C	B	B

41	42	43	44	45	46	47	48	49	50
C	D	C	A	D	C	D	B	B	C
51	52	53	54	55	56	57	58	59	60
C	A	D	A	C	D	A	D	D	D
61	62	63	64	65	66	67	68	69	70
B	C	B	A	B	D	D	C	B	A
71	72	73	74	75	76	77	78	79	80
B	A	B	A	C	B	B	A	B	B
81	82	83	84	85	86	87	88	89	90
C	B	C	B	B	B	B	A	C	D
91	92	93	94	95	96	97	98	99	100
C	A	A	B	D	A	D	C	A	D

EXPLANATORY ANSWERS

2. Reserve Bank of India has classified NBFCs as:

(*i*) Asset financing company (AFC) — it is a company (a financial institution) whose principal business is the financing of physical assets supporting productive/economic study, such as automobiles, tractors, lathe machines, generator sets, earth moving and material handling equipments, moving on own power and general purpose industrial machines.

(*ii*) Investment company (IC).

(*iii*) Loan company (LC).

3. Section of IT Act that mandates TDS

The Income Tax (IT) Act, 1961 and IT Rules (1962) govern the payment of Income Tax by all income earning individuals, companies, organizations, associations and trusts as the case may be. Section 203 mandates that the employer shall deduct tax at source and issue certificates in the Forms 16 and 16A to the deductees as a proof of the same.

Form 16A

Like Form 16 is for salaries, Form 16A is a certificate of tax deduction at source (TDS) by an employer which shows the amount of tax deducted at source, nature of payment, and the tax deposited with IT department on income other than salaries. The IT Act stipulates that TDS to be deducted at source on all payments than ₹ 30,000 unless otherwise exempted.

Also TDS is deducted on salaries as per existing Income Tax rate slabs. TDS on all other income such as interest and house rent as applicable. Form 16A shows TDS deductions made and deposited on all other income except salary.

The basic difference between Form 16 and Form 16A is that the former reflects deductions made from salary and the later shows deductions on income other than salary. Form 16 is usually issued annually while the latter is issued quarterly.

4. A number of theories have been advanced by social and organisational psychologists to explain the formation of informal groups. These are as under:

- **Propinquity Theory:** The most basic theory explaining the formation of groups is propinquity. This means that individuals affiliate with one another because of spatial or geographical proximity. In an organisation, employees who work in the same area of the plant or office or managers with offices close to one another would more probably form into groups than those who are not physically located together.

- **Similarity Theory:** According to Theodore Newcomb "birds of a feather flock together". People with similar attitudes, interests and work-related needs are attracted to one another. Thus, employees may form a union for fighting indiscrimination or unilateral treatment of the employer.
- **Complementarity Theory:** According to Winch, "opposites attract each other", i.e., people with complementary needs and/or abilities are attracted to one another.
- **Social Comparison Theory:** According to Festinger, an individual joins a group because be suffers from the need for self-evaluation, *i.e.*, he wants to "test" himself against other members to determine whether or not his opinions, ideas, and judgements correspond to those of others in the group.
- **Interaction Theory:** According to George Homans, group formation is the result of activities, interactions and sentiments. The more activities persons share, the more numerous will be their interactions and the stronger will be their sentiments; the more interactions between persons, the more will be their shared activities and sentiments; and the more positive sentiments persons have for one another, the more will be their shared activities and interactions.
- **Exchange Theory:** The approach to group formation, receiving the most recent emphasis is the exchange theory. It is based upon reward-cost outcomes of interaction. A minimum positive level (rewards greater than costs) of an outcome must exist in order for attraction or affiliation to take place. Rewards from interactions gratify needs while costs incur anxiety frustration, fatigue or boredom.

5. In entire income tax act, 1961 partnership is not defined any where, therefore we can refer section 4 of Indian partnership act, 1932.

"*Parternship is the relationship between persons who have agreed to share the profits of a business carried on by all or any of them.*"

Firms are assessed as a separate entity, as per section 2(31) definition of the person includes ***firm***. Therefore assessment of the same is done separately.

Secondly, There are certain conditions which are required to be satisfied by partnership firm to be assessed as a firm and for claiming deductions of interest, salary to the partners. Conditions are mentioned in **section 184** of the act.

6. In general, globalisation represents the increasing integration of the world economy base on five inter-related drivers of change:

- International trade (Lower trade barriers and more competition).
- Financial flows (Foreign direct investment, technology transfer, investments).
- Communication (Traditional media and Interest).
- Technology advancement in transportation, electronics, bio-engineering and related fields.
- Population mobility, especially labour.

7. Section 319 of the Companies Act, 2013 facilitates amalgamation, absorption and reconstruction of companies. It provides that the liquidator of a company can accept shares, policies or like interest in consideration of the sale of the company's undertaking to another company with the object of distributing them amongst the members of the transferor company provided the following two conditions are satisfied:

(*i*) A special resolution is passed by the company to that effect.

(*ii*) The liquidator purchases the interest of any dissenting member at a price to be determined by agreement or the registered valuer.

The money to the dissenting member should be paid before the company is dissolved and should be raised in such manner as determined by a special resolution.

10. Net Operating Income Approach (NOI Approach)

This approach was put forth by Durand and totally differs from the Net Income Approach. Also famous as traditional approach, Net Operating Income Approach suggests that change in debt of the firm/company or the change in leverage fails to affect the total value of the firm/company. As per this approach, the WACC and total value of a company are independent of the capital structure decision or financial leverage of a company.

As per this approach, the market value is dependent on the operating income and the associated business risk of the firm. Both these factors cannot be impacted by the financial leverage. Financial leverage can only impact the share of income earned by debt holders and equity holders but cannot impact the operating incomes of the firm. Therefore, change in debt to equity ratio cannot make any change in the value of the firm.

It further says that with the increase in the debt component of a company, the company is faced with higher risk. To compensate that, the equity shareholders expect more returns. Thus, with increase in financial leverage, the cost of equity increases.

Assumptions/Features of Net Operating Income Approach:

1. The overall capitalisation rate remains constant irrespective of the degree of leverage. At a given level of EBIT, value of the firm would be "EBIT/Overall capitalisation rate".
2. Value of equity is the difference between total firm value less value of debt *i.e.*, Value of Equity = Total Value of the Firm – Value of Debt
3. WACC (Weightage Average Cost of Capital) remains constant; and with the increase in debt, the cost of equity increases. Increase in debt in the capital structure results in increased risk for shareholders. As a compensation of investing in highly leveraged company, the shareholders expect higher return resulting in higher cost of equity capital.

11. Bayes' theorem is applicable when the events for which we want to compute posterior probabilities are mutually exclusive and their union is the entire sample space. For the case of n mutually exclusive events $A_1, A_2, ..., A_n$, whose union is the entire sample space, Bayes' theorem can be used to compute any posterior probability $P(A_i \mid B)$ as shown here.

Bayes' theorem

$$P(A_i \mid B) = \frac{P(A_i)P(B \mid A_i)}{P(A_1)P(B \mid A_1) + P(A_2)P(B \mid A_2) + ... + P(A_n)P(B \mid A_n)}$$

With prior probabilities $P(A_1)$, $P(A_2)$ .... $P(A_n)$ and the appropriate conditional probabilities $P(B|A_1)$, $P(B|A_2)$, ..., $P(B|A_n)$, above equation can be used to compute the posterior probability of the events $A_1, A_2, ..., A_n$.

The Tabular Approach

The tabular approach is helpful in conducting the Bayes' theorem calculations simultaneously for all events A_i. The computations shown there involve the following steps.

Step 1. Prepare three columns:

Column 1 — The mutually exclusive events for which posterior probabilities are desired

Column 2 — The prior probabilities for the events

Column 3 — The conditional probabilities of the new information given each event

Step 2. In column 4, compute the joint probabilities for each event and the new information *B* by using the multiplication law. To get these joint probabilities, multiply the prior probabilities in column 2 by the corresponding conditional probabilities in column 3—that is, $P(A_i \cap B) = P(A_i)P(B|A_i)$.

Step 3. Sum the joint probabilities in column 4 to obtain the probability of the new information, P(B). In the example there is a 0.0130 probability that a part is from supplier 1 and is bad and a 0.0175 probability that a part is from supplier 2 and is bad. These are the only two ways by which a bad part can be obtained, so the sum 0.0130 + 0.0175 shows an overall probability of 0.0305 of finding a bad part from the combined shipments of both suppliers.

Step 4. In column 5, compute the posterior probabilities by using the basic relationship of conditional probability:

$$P(A_i|B) = \frac{P(A_i \cap B)}{P(B)}$$

Note that the joint probabilities $P(A_i \cap B)$ appear in column 4, whereas P(B) is the sum of the column 4 values.

12. Functions of WTO

The Agreement establishing WTO provides that it should perform the following four functions:

WTO Agreement, Article III, 1: First, it shall facilitate the implementation, administration and operation of the Uruguay Round legal instruments and of any new agreements that may be negotiated in the future.

WTO Agreement, Article III, 2: Second, it shall provide a forum for further negotiations among member countries on matters covered by the agreements as well as on new issues falling within its mandate.

WTO Agreement, Article III, 3: Third, it shall be responsible for the settlement of differences and disputes among its member countries.

WTO Agreement, Article III, 4: Fourth, it shall be responsible for carrying out periodic reviews of the trade policies of its member countries.

13. The regression coefficients are independent of the change of origin, but not of the scale. By origin, we mean that there will be no effect on the regression coefficients if any constant is subtracted from the value of *x* and *y*. By scale, we mean that if the value of *x* and *y* is either multiplied or divided by some constant, then the regression coefficients will also change.

14. Laws Affecting Business Incorporation and Constitution

Although companies are free to organize their employees as they see suitable, to enhance the survival of business organizations, many countries have enacted laws concerning their incorporations and bankruptcy.

Incorporation and Bankruptcy Laws

Most legal jurisdictions specify the forms of ownership that a business can take. Though the forms of business organization vary across jurisdictions, there are some common forms, such as sole proprietorship, partnership, privately and publicly held corporations, and co-operative. Incorporation laws vary as per the type of organization. These laws dictate the type of information and the format in which the relevant information need to be made public by a particular type of organization. For example, companies raising capital from the stock markets need to provide detailed information about their financial conditions periodically.

Bankruptcy laws also vary as per the type of organization. For example, in the USA there are three types of bankruptcy — Liquidation, Restructuring and Personal bankruptcy applicable for sole proprietorship form of organization. In India also bankruptcy laws vary as per the type of organization. For example, if a private limited company becomes insolvent then only the assets of the company are used to clear the debts. The managers of the company have no personal liabilities in such forms of organizations and their assets remain untouched. Managers of such companies can incorporate another company if they wish to do so. On the contrary, if a sole proprietorship or a partnership firm becomes insolvent then the creditors can claim not only the assets of the company but also the property of the person who is the sole proprietor or partners in the company.

15. Every Negotiable instrument has many parties, depending on nature of instruments. In addition to original parties like the maker, the payee and the drawee, there are many other parties associated with an instrument, such as indorser, indorsee and holder etc. As the instrument goes on negotiating the number of parties does also increase.

Following are the parties involved in various types of negotiable instruments.

- Parties to promissory note Maker, Payee, Holder, Indorser and Indorsee.
- Parties to a bill of exchange Drawer, Drawee, Payee, Holder, Drawee in case of need and Acceptor for honour.
- Parties to a cheque Drawer, Drawee (Bank) Payee, Holder, Indorser and Indorsee.

16. Customer relationship management helps in profiling prospective customers, understanding their needs, and in building relationships with them by providing the most suitable products and enhanced customer service.

Therefore, Customer Relationship Management is a comprehensive strategy and process of acquiring, retaining, and partnering with selective customers to create superior value for the company and the customer.

17. Cost behaviour can be defined as the manner in which costs changes due to changes in volume or activity. In relation to cost behaviour analysis, fixed and variable cost classifications are generally found. A proper analysis of cost behaviour patterns is the basis of all profit planning and cost control. The separation of costs into fixed, variable and semi-variable is necessary in order to determine, analyse, control, measure or evaluate the following:

1. Departmental expenses allowed at various levels of production.
2. Operating efficiency of a department.
3. Use of variable costing method.
4. Utilisation of facilities.
5. Break-even point.
6. Relative profitability of territories, departments and customers.
7. Company profit position.
8. Cost-volume-profit analysis.
9. Marginal or differential cost for various decision making purposes.
10. Effect of proposed, capital, expenditures.
11. Effect of alternative courses of action.

Methods of Determining Cost Behaviour

Several methods are used for segregating semi-variable costs into fixed and variable. There are four major techniques that are found in practice and they may be listed as follows:

1. High and low points method
2. Scattergraph method
3. Least squares regression method
4. Accounting or analytical approach.

18. Six steps to e-filing the income tax return

Step 1. Register yourself.

Step 2. Choose how you want to e-file.

Step 3. Select the requisite form.

Step 4. Keep the documents ready.

Step 5. Fill form and upload.

Step 6. Verify ITR V.

19. Michael Porter in 1985 in his book *Competitive Advantage: Creating and Sustaining Superior Performance* has set out three approaches as examples of "generic strategies", because they can be applied to products or services in all industries, and to organizations of all sizes. Porter called the generic strategies "Cost Leadership" (no frills), "Differentiation" (creating uniquely desirable products and services) and "Focus" (offering a specialized service in a niche market). He then subdivided the Focus strategy into two parts: "Cost Focus" and "Differentiation Focus". These are shown in Figure below.

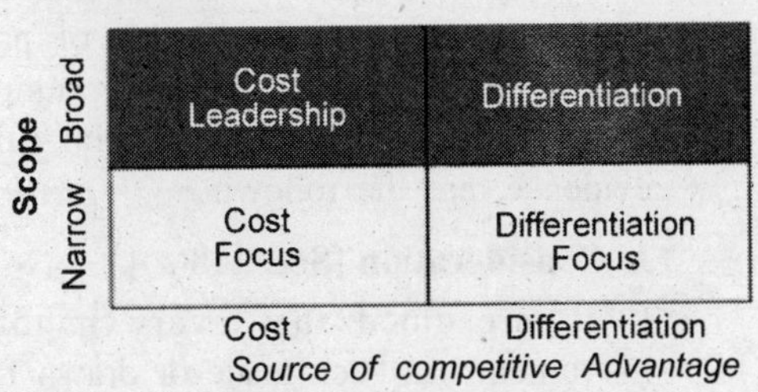

Fig.: *Porter's Generic Strategies*

The terms "Cost Focus" and "Differentiation Focus" can be a little confusing, as they could be interpreted as meaning "A focus on cost" or "A focus on differentiation". Remember that Cost Focus means emphasizing cost-minimization within a focused market, and Differentiation Focus means pursuing strategic differentiation within a focused market.

21. Business firms, having international business operations, primarily encounter three types of exposure: (*i*) transaction exposure, (*ii*) translation exposure and (*iii*) economic exposure.

Transaction Exposure

Transaction exposure is inherent in all foreign currency denominated contractual obligations/transactions. This involves gain or loss arising out of the various types of transactions that require settlement in a foreign currency. The transactions may relate to cross-border trade in terms of import or export of goods, the borrowing or lending in foreign currencies, domestic purchases and sales of goods and services of the foreign subsidiaries and the purchase of assets or take over of the liability involving foreign currency. The actual profit the firm earns or loss it suffers, of course, is known only at the time of settlement of these transactions.

Translation Exposure

Translation exposure relates to the change in accounting income and balance sheet statements caused by the changes in exchange rates. These changes may take place by/at the time of finalisation of accounts compared to the time when the asset was purchased or liability was assumed. In other words, translation exposure results from the need to translate foreign currency assets or liabilities into the local currency at the time of finalising accounts.

Economic Exposure

Of all the three exposures, economic exposure is considered the most important as it has an impact on the valuation of a firm. It is defined as the change in the value of a company that accompanies an unanticipated change in exchange rates. It is important to note that anticipated changes in exchange rates are already reflected in the market value of the company. For instance, when an Indian firm transacts business with an American firm, it has the expectation that the Indian rupee is likely to weaken *vis-à-vis* the US dollar. This weakening of the Indian rupee will not affect the market value (as it was anticipated, and hence already considered in valuation). However, in case the extent/margin of weakening is different from expected, it will have a bearing on the market value. The marker value may enhance if the Indian rupee depreciates less than expected. In case, the Indian rupee value weakens more than expected, it may entail erosion in the firm's market value. In brief, the unanticipated changes in exchange rates (favourable or unfavourable) are not accounted for in valuation and, hence, cause economic exposure.

22. Purchase consideration can be calculated by different methods. The method to be adopted by students in an examination problem will depend upon the information given.

The following are the different methods for calculating or ascertaining the amount of purchase consideration:

- **Direct ascertainment method:** The question may directly state the amount of purchase consideration. For example, it may be provided that the purchasing company agrees to take over the business of the vendor company for a sum of ₹ 1 lakh. In such a case the purchase consideration will be taken as ₹ 1 lakh. No calculations are required in such a case.

- **Net payment method:** In this case, the purchase consideration is to be calculated by adding the different amounts which the purchasing company has agreed to pay to the vendor company. The payments by the purchasing company are for different parties interested in the vendor company. For example, if the purchasing company agrees to pay ₹ 1 lakh in shares for shareholders, ₹ 1 lakh in debentures for debenture-holders and ₹ 50,000 in cash for the creditors of the vendor company, the amount of consideration would be a sum of ₹ 2,50,000.

- **Net assets method:** In case of this method, the purchase consideration is calculated by finding out the net assets of the company. The term net assets refers to vendor company's assets, less liabilities taken over by the purchasing company. For this purpose assets and liabilities are to be taken at the values mutually agreed.

- **Shares exchange method:** In case of this method, the purchase consideration is ascertained on the basis of the ratio in which the shares of the purchasing company are to be exchanged for the shares of the vendor company. This exchange ratio is generally determined on the basis of the value of each company's shares.

23. Sections 118 and 119 of the Negotiable Instruments Act, 1881, lay down certain presumptions to all negotiable instruments, unless the contrary is proved. In case of any disputes about these presumptions, these need not be proved by the person who holds the negotiable instrument, until contrary is proved. These are rebuttable presumptions. The party liable, proves the non-existence of presumptions, then the burden of proving them shifts to plaintiff. These presumptions, which are also known as special rules of evidence, are the following:

1. Consideration [Sec. 118(*a*)]

It is presumed that every negotiable instrument has been made or drawn for the consideration. Moreover, when a negotiable instrument is accepted, indorsed, negotiated or transferred, it is also presumed that it was so accepted, indorsed etc. for a consideration.

2. Date [Sec. 118(*b*)]

It is also a presumption under the Act, that every negotiable instrument bearing a date, was made or drawn on such date.

3. Time of Acceptance [Sec. 118(*c*)]

It shall be presumed that every accepted bill of exchange was accepted within a reasonable time after its date and before its maturity.

4. Time of Transfer [Sec. 118(*d*)]

Until the contrary is proved, it shall be

presumed that every transfer of a negotiable instrument was made before its maturity.

5. Order of Endorsement [Sec. 118(*e*)]

Until the contrary is proved, it shall be presumed that the indorsement appearing upon a negotiable instrument were made in the order in which they appear thereon.

6. Stamp [Sec.118(*f*)]

Sometimes, a negotiable instrument is lost or destroyed. In such cases it is presumed that it was duly stamped.

7. Holder in due Course (Sec. 118(*g*)]

The holder of a negotiable instrument is a holder in due course. But when a negotiable instrument is obtained by a person from its lawful holder by means of an offence or fraud or for unlawful consideration, the holder will have to prove that he is a holder in due course.

For this purpose, he will have to prove:

(*a*) that there was consideration for it;

(*b*) that the defect, if any, in the instrument was not known to him; and

(*c*) that he became its holder before its due date.

8. Proof of Protest (Sec. 119)

In a suit upon an instrument, which has been dishonoured, the court on proof of the protest, presumes the fact of dishonour, unless and until such fact is disproved.

26. The Consumer Protection Act provides for the establishment of the following consumer dispute redressed agencies—

- **A District Forum:** A complaint where the value of goods or services and the compensation, if any, is less than ₹ 20 lakh is to be dealt with the District Forum. It shall consist of—

  (*i*) A person who is, or has been qualified to be a District Judge and is nominated by the State Govt.

  (*ii*) A person of eminence in the field of education trade or commerce.

  (*iii*) A lady social worker.

- **State Commission:** Where the value of goods and services exceeds rupees 20 lakh but is under rupees one crore, it is to be dealt with the State Commission. It shall consist of (a) a person who is or has been a judge of High Court, appointed by a State Government who shall be its President and two others who shall be persons of ability, integrity and standing and have adequate knowledge of; or has shown capacity in dealing with the problems related to law, economics etc.

- **National Commission:** Cases involving more than ₹ one crore fall within the jurisdiction of the National Commission.

It shall consist of a person who is or has been a judge of Supreme Court; appointed by the Central Government (who shall be its President) and two other members, who shall be persons of ability, integrity and standing and have adequate knowledge or experience of or have shown capacity to deal with the problems related to economics, law etc.

28. Meaning of Some of the Important Terms Defined Under the Sale of Goods Act, 1930

'Goods' means every kind of moveable property (other than actionable claims and money) and includes

- stock and shares
- growing crops, grass
- things attached to or forming part of the land which are agreed to be severed before sale or under the contract of sale.

'Buyer' means a person who buys or agrees to buy goods.

'Seller' means a person who sells or agrees to sell goods.

'Price' means the money consideration for a sale of goods.

'Delivery' means voluntary transfer of possession from one person to another.

'Document of title to goods' includes bill of lading, dock-warrant, warehouse-keeper's certificate, wharfingers' certificate, railway receipt, multimodal transport document, warrant or order for the delivery of goods and any other document used in the ordinary course of business as proof of the possession or control of goods authorised by endorsement or delivery to transfer or receive goods as possessor of document.

'Future goods' means goods to be manufactured or produced or acquired by the seller after making of the contract of sale.

'Specific goods' means goods identified and agreed upon at the time a contract of sale is made.

'Mercantile agent' means an agent having authority either to sell goods, or to consign goods for the purposes of sale, or to buy goods, or to raise money on the security of goods.

29. A person shall be qualified for appointment as an auditor of a company, only if one is a Chartered Accountant within the meaning of the Chartered Accountants Act, 1949. Under the Chartered Accountants Act, 1949, only a chartered accountant holding the certificate of practice can engage in public practice.

30. **Void contract:** According to Section 2(j) of the Contract Act, 1872 "a contract which ceases to be enforceable by law becomes void when it ceases to be enforceable." A void contract entails a useless contract which has no legal effect at all. Such a contract is a nullity, as there has been no contract at all. It follows from the definition that a void contract is not void ab initio and that it is valid and binding on the parties when originally entered but subsequent to its formation, it becomes invalid and lack legal effects because of certain reasons. The reasons are:

- Supervening impossibility (Section 56)
- Subsequent illegality (Section 56)
- Repudiation of voidable contract.
- In case of a contract contingent on happening of an uncertain future event, if that event becomes impossible (Section 32).

33. 1. In exercise of the powers available under section 49A of the 1922 Act, the Government of India had issued a Notification dated 24-3-1953 called the Income-tax (Double Taxation Relief) (Aden) Rules, 1953 providing for grant of relief in respect of income on which tax has been paid both in India and in Aden. These Rules being consistent with the corresponding provisions of the 1961 Act, continued to be operative by virtue of the provisions contained in section 297(2)(*k*).

2. The Government of the Peoples' Democratic Republic of Yemen (formerly Aden) has, however, stated that the Agreement on the basis of which the above Rules were applicable is no longer binding on it after November 30, 1967, the date of attainment of independence by it. Thus, *there is no subsisting agreement between India and Aden for the avoidance of double taxation of income after November 30, 1967.*

3. The cases of Indian residents will, therefore, be covered by the provisions for grant of unilateral relief under section 91 of the 1961 Act. This will be applicable in respect of the assessment years commencing from the assessment year immediately following the financial year in which Aden attained independence. Thus, the provision for unilateral relief will become applicable in the case of income in the Peoples' Democratic Republic of Yemen for and from the assessment year 1968-69.

34. Line and staff relationships are important in all organisational ways of life, and these relationships must necessarily affect the operation of the enterprise. *Line functions are those that have direct impact on the accomplishment of the objectives of the enterprise.* On the other hand, *staff functions are those that help the line persons work most effectively in accomplishing the objectives.* Based on this view, people classify production and sales (and sometimes finance) as line functions, and purchasing, accounting, personnel, plant maintenance, quality control etc., as staff functions.

In other words, line and staff are characterised by relationships and not by people or departments. Line authority (some people call it as line organisation) is that relation in which a superior exercises direct supervision over subordinates. The staff relationship, on the other hand, consists of giving advice and counsel.

Another type of authority that exists beside line and staff authorities is *functional authority. It is the right which is delegated to an individual or a department to control specified processes, practices, policies, or other matters, relating to activities undertaken by persons in other departments.*

Functional authority is not restricted to managers of a particular types of department. It may be exercised by line, service, or staff department heads, although more often by the latter two because service and staff departments are usually composed of specialists whose knowledge becomes the basis for financial controls.

36. How to find out the residential status of a company [Sec 6(3)]

A company is said to be a resident in India in any previous year, if

(*i*) it is an Indian company; or

(*ii*) its place of effective management, in that year, is in India

Place of effective management means a place where key management and commercial decisions that are necessary for the conduct of business of an entity as a whole are in substance made.

An Indian company is always resident in India. A foreign company is resident in India only if during the previous year, place of effective management is situated wholly in India. Conversely, a foreign company is treated as non-resident if during the previous year, place of effective management is either is wholly or partly situated out of India. A company can never be ordinarily or not ordinarily resident in India. In case of a foreign company even the slightest place of effective management is exercised from outside India, it would be treated as a non-resident. Income Tax Benefits to Residents & Indian Companies.

37. In 1944, 730 delegates from 44 nations gathered for a conference at Bretton Woods, United States. They aimed to create a new international monetary system which would allow cooperation among countries as the classic gold standard was abandoned after World War I and competitive devaluations along with imposed heavy trade restrictions by countries was deepened the Great Depression.

With the Bretton Woods agreement signed on July 1944, the delegates agreed to establish two new institutions. The first institution, "International Monetary Fund" (IMF) aimed to ensure worldwide financial stability by monitoring exchange rates and lending currencies to countries with balance of payment deficits. The second institution "The International Bank for Reconstruction and Development", today known as the "World Bank", aimed to provide financial assistance to reconstruction after World War II and help the economic development of less developed countries.

38. The basic methods of making investment decisions include the payback period, the accounting rate of return and the average rate of return. While these simple methods ignore the time value of money they are quick and simple to use.

Payback method

This method attempts to forecast how long it will take for the expected net cash inflows to pay back the net investment outflows. The payback period is calculated as follows:

Payback period (years)

$$= \frac{\text{Net Investment Outflows}}{\text{Average Net Cash Inflows}}$$

The net present value method computes the present worth of a project's benefits over its costs, evaluated using the firm's cost of capital. If a project has a positive net present value, it means that investors are receiving the minimum required rate of return, as measured by the cost of capital, plus they are receiving something extra. This positive net present value is an additional increment to shareholder wealth.

41. **Quota Sampling:** A method of non-random sampling which is popular in market research. It uses street interviewers, armed with quotas of people to interview in a range of groups, to collect information from passers-by. For example, obtaining peoples' attitudes regarding the worth of secondary double glazing.

42. Implied conditions are the stipulations which have not been included in the contract of sale in express words. But the law presumes that the parties have incorporated them into their contract.

Following are the implied conditions which are contained in the Sale of Goods Act, 1930.

- **Conditions as to title:** According to this implied condition, it is presumed that the seller has a valid title to the goods, in other words, he has the right to sell the goods. [Sec. 14(a)]
- **Condition as to description:** Where there is a contract for sale of goods by description, there is an implied condition that the goods shall correspond with the description. [Sec. 15]
- **Condition as to sample:** A contract of sale is a contract for sale by sample where there is a term in the contract, express or implied to that effect. [Sec. 17]
- **Condition as to sample as well as description:** Sometimes the seller shows sample of the goods to the buyer and also gives him their description. In such cases, the implied condition is that the goods shall correspond with both, the sample as well as description.
- **Condition as to quality or fitness for buyer's purpose:** If the buyer makes his purpose clear to the seller and buys the goods 'relying upon his skills and judgement', then there is an implied condition that the goods shall be fit for the buyer's specific purpose. [Sec. 16 (1)]
- **Condition as to merchantable quality:** Where goods are bought by description from a seller who deals in goods of that description, there is an implied condition that the goods shall be of merchantable quality. [Sec. 16 (2)]
- **Condition as to wholesomeness:** In case of contract of sale of eatables or foodstuffs, there is in implied condition as to wholesomeness of the product. It Implies that the eatables or provision sold are wholesome.
- **Condition implied by custom:** An implied condition as to quality or fitness for a particular purpose may be annexed by the usage and custom of trade. [Sec. 16 (3)]

43. An experimental design is a sketch to execute an experiment where a researcher is able to control or manipulate at least one independent variable. The experimental designs can be broadly segregated into two groups: **classical experimental designs** and **statistical experimental designs**. Classical experimental designs consider the impact of only one treatment level of independent variable taken for the study at a time, whereas statistical experimental design considers the impact of different treatment levels of independent (explanatory) variable as well as the impact of two or more independent variables. On the basis of these two factors, the experimental designs can be broadly classified as pre-experimental designs, **post-experimental designs, quasi-experimental designs**, and **statistical experimental designs**. The first three designs can be placed under the classical experimental design category and the last one can be placed under the statistical experimental design. Figure presents a classification of the experimental designs.

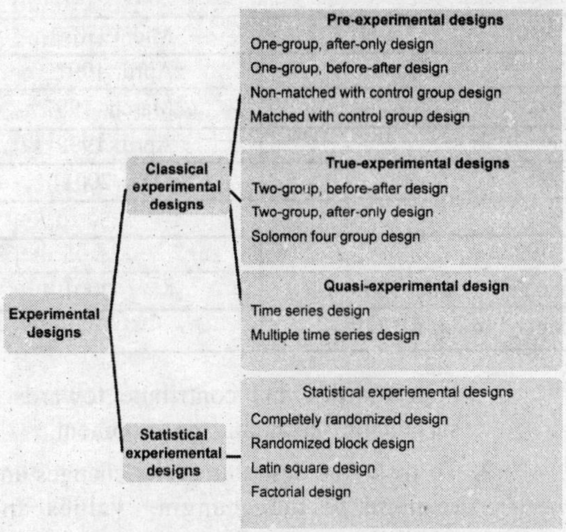

Fig.: *A classification of experimental designs*

Pre-Experimental Design

Pre-experimental design is an exploratory type of research design and has no control over extraneous factors. These designs cannot be easily put under the category of the experimental designs, because these are not able to establish the cause and effect relationship. These designs are exploratory in nature and are mainly used to frame the hypotheses about the casual relationship and that is why a detailed description of these designs is of paramount importance. Hence, these designs are mainly applied for developing causal relationship hypotheses and not for testing the hypotheses. In addition to this design, further research should be executed to make the researcher firm about the casual relationship between variables. There are four commonly used pre-experimental designs. These are one-group, after only design; one-group, before-after design; non-matched with control group design, and matched with control group design.

True-Experimental Design

Most of the problems of the pre-experimental design can be tackled with the help of randomization procedure. "Randomization" is the key of difference between pre-experimental design and true experimental design. The randomized experiments are more likely to yield unbiased estimates of causal effects than typical observational studies, because the randomization of treatment makes the treatment and control groups equal on average in terms of all (observed and unobserved) characteristics (Horiuchi et al., 2007). True experimental design involves the random assignment of test units to the experimental group and various treatments to the experimental groups. This random assignment provides an opportunity to neutralize the impact of extraneous variables in the experiment. True experimental designs are commonly classified as two-group, before-after design; two-group, after-only design, and Solomon four-group design.

45. Treasury bills (T-bills market): Treasury bills are short-term financial instruments issued by the central government. Unlike commercial bills, they do not represent genuine trade transactions. They are promissory notes issued by the Reserve Bank on behalf of the Government of India for financing temporary deficits arising out of the mismatch between revenue and capital receipts and payments. The main features of treasury bills are:

(*a*) Treasury bills are negotiable securities.

(*b*) They are issued at a discount and the face value would be paid on maturity.

(*c*) The difference between the price at which they are sold and the face value is the return on these bills.

(*d*) The duration of these bills vary from 91 days to 364 days and enjoys high liquidity.

(*e*) They are supported by government guarantee and therefore do not have default risk.

(*f*) T-Bills offer an assured yield.

(*g*) The transaction cost in respect of Treasury-bills are comparatively low.

(*h*) Banks can include these bills for the purpose of calculating SLR requirements.

(*i*) The purchase and sale of these bills are done through auctions and are settled through SGL (Security General Ledger) account with RBI.

Treasury bills with a maturity period of 182 days were introduced by the RBI in 1986 to promote short-term liquidity requirements.

Treasury Bills – Chronology of Developments

Type of T-Bill	Introduced	Discontinued
28 days T-Bills	1998	2001
91 days T-Bill on weekly auction	Before 1950s	Mid-1950s
91 days Ad-hoc T-Bill	Mid 1950s	April, 1997
91 days T-Bill on Tap	Mid 1950s	March, 1997
182 days T-Bill on weekly auction	November, 1986	April, 1992
14 days T-Bill on weekly auction	April, 1997	May, 2001
364 days T-Bill on fortnightly auction	April, 1992	
91 days T-Bill on weekly auction	January, 1993	
182 days T-Bill on weekly auction	Re-introduced in June, 1999	May, 2001
182 days T-Bill on weekly auction	Re-introduced in April, 2005	

46. (*a*) National Housing Bank 1988

(*b*) Export-Import Bank of India 1982 (1 January)

(*c*) NABARD 1982 (12 July)

(*d*) Unit Trust of India 1964

48. CSR can be understood in both micro and macro perspectives. In the micro perspective, it is the responsibility of one business unit or company; in the macro perspective, CSR encompasses the whole gamut of corporate social activities where the entire corporate sector is engaged, and also in some cases, the involvement of government is ensured.

There are the following three basic constituents of CSR:

1. One part of CSR is to supply socially necessary products, create employment opportunities and contribute towards a sustainable economic development.
2. To make the desirable social changes and respond to the changing values and priority patterns of the society.
3. Actively contribute towards the improvement of social environment and discontinue or internalise all the negative externalities (harmful impact).

There are basically the following five types of social responsibilities:

1. Responsibilities towards the Society
2. Responsibilities towards the Government
3. Responsibilities towards Employees
4. Responsibilities towards Shareholders
5. Responsibilities towards Consumers

Types of Social Responsibilities

Responsibilities towards Government:	• Obey rules and regulations • Regular payment of taxes • Cooperating with the Govt. to promote social values • Resisting bribery and corrupt practices • Cooperating with the Govt. for economic growth and development • Cooperating with the Govt. for promoting R and D • Not to take advantage of loopholes in business laws
Responsibilities towards Society as a whole:	• Carrying on business with moral values and ethical standards • Prevention of environmental pollution • Minimizing ecological imbalance • Implementing the strategy of sustainable development • Making the use of appropriate technology • Contributing towards the development of social health, education and cultural milleu
Responsibilities towards Consumer:	• Supplying socially harmless products • Supplying the quality, standard, as promised • Providing good and services at reasonable prices • Providing efficient timely after-sales services • Resisting black-marketing and profiteering • Maintaining consumers' grievance cell • Trying to improve the quality of products and reduce prices over time through competition
Responsibilities towards Shareholders:	• To work for the survival and the growth of the concern • To build reputation and goodwill of the company • To ensure a reasonable rate of return over time • To remain transparent and accountable
Responsibilities towards Employees:	• To provide a healthy working environment • To grant regular and fair wages • To provide regular welfare services • To provide training and promotion facilities • To provide reasonable working standard and norms • To provide efficient mechanism to redress workers' grievances • Proper recognition of efficiency and hard work

49. Designing an effective Web site: The seven Cs provide a framework for designing a Web site: context, the site's layout and design; content, the text, pictures, sound, and video that the Web site contains; community, the ways that the site enables user-to-user communication; customization, the site's ability to tailor itself to different users or to allow users to personalize the site; communication, the ways the site enables site-to-user, user-to-site, or two-way communication; connection, the degree that the site is linked to other sites; and commerce, the site's capabilities to enable commercial transactions.

52. The optimization of investment in working capital of an industrial undertaking depends to a great extent on its operating cycle. It measures the time gap between investment of cash and its realization out of sales revenue.

The operating cycle represents the period during which investments of one unit of money remain blocked in the normal course of operation till recovery out of revenue. The length of the operating cycle differs from one undertaking to another. Fig. below shows the operating cycle of a typical small-scale industry.

In a typical small-scale industry, the operating cycle for the element of cost starts with the purchasing of materials. The materials are not consumed immediately. The next stage in the cycle involves 'Raw Materials Conversion Period'. Once the materials are issued to production, it again involves a time gap between the issue of materials and the production of the finished product. This time gap is called the 'Work-in-Progress Conversion Period'. The finished goods are made by the company on the basis of expectation of demand. Till the demand for the finished product materializes, the product would remain in the store. This period is termed 'Finished Goods Conversion Period'.

The company extends credit facilities to its customers due to competition and other reasons. This time gap between sale and realization of cash is known as 'Book Debts Conversion Period'.

The company receives credit on the purchase of raw materials from suppliers. This period is known as 'Payment Deferral Period' which reduces the length of the operating cycle.

Thus the length of the operating cycle of the industry (in the case of direct raw materials) is the sum of:

1. Raw Materials Conversion Period (RMCP)
2. Work-in-Progress Conversion Period (WIPCP)
3. Finished Goods Conversion Period (FGCP)
4. Book Debts Conversion Period (BDCP)

53. Management audit is a complex task closely linked with the process of management. It usually involves the following steps.

1. Identification of the objectives of the organisation. Sometimes, the objectives are stated in specific terms but, in most cases, they remain undefined. It is important that the objectives are clearly perceived and identified.
2. The overall objectives of the organisation are broken down into detailed targets and plans for various segments.
3. The organisational structure is reviewed to assess whether or not it can effectively achieve the overall objectives and the detailed targets. If possible, specific responsibility centres may be identified in the organisation.
4. The performance of each functional area or responsibility centre is examined. In many cases, the performance can be expressed in quantitative terms. Also, it should be compared with the objectives and targets.
5. On the basis of the above examination, a realistic course of action may be suggested. A motivation system can be operated whereby incentives are given to various personnel on the basis of the results of management audit.

54. The Constant Elasticity of Substitution Production Function or CES implies, that any change in the input factors, results in the constant change in the output. In CES, the elasticity of substitution is constant and may not necessarily be equal to one or unity.

The constant elasticity of substitution production function can be shown algebraically as:

$$Q = A\left[\alpha K^{-\beta} + (1-\alpha)L^{-\beta}\right]^{\frac{-1}{\beta}}$$

or

$$Q = A\left[\alpha L^{-\beta} + (1-\alpha)K^{-\beta}\right]^{\frac{-1}{\beta}}$$

When $A > 0$, $0 < \alpha < 1$ and $\beta > -1$

Where L = Labour, K = Capital and A, α and β are three parameters.

The Constant elasticity of substitution production function shows, that any change in the technology or organizational aspects, the production function changes with a shift in the efficiency parameter.

The homogeneity of the production function can be determined by the value of the substitution parameter (β), if it is equal to one, then it is said to be linearly homogenous *i.e.*, the proportionate change in the input factors results in the increase in the output in the same proportion.

In constant elasticity of substitution production function, all the input factors are taken into the consideration such as raw material, technology, labour, capital, etc. The marginal product of one factor increases with the increase in the value of the other factors of production. Also, the marginal product of labour and capital will be positive in case of constant returns to scale.

56. A cyber attack, in simple terms, is an attack on your digital systems originating from malicious acts of an anonymous source. Cyber attack allows for an illegal access to your digital device, while gaining access or control of your digital device. A different types of cyber attacks can be defined as an offensive tactic to gain an illegal control or access to your digital device, called the target system, initiated by a person or computer against a website, computer system or a single digital device as well as a whole, which poses a serious threat to computer systems, information stored, financial structures and the entire network itself. Cyber attacks work towards compromising the integrity of the digital device and the information stored in it.

Types of Cyber Attack or Threats

- Backdoors
- Denial-of-Service Attack
- Direct-Access Attack
- Eavesdropping
- Spoofing
- Tampering
- Repudiation Attack
- Information Disclosure
- Privilege Escalation Attack
- Exploits
- Social Engineering
- Indirect Attack
- Computer Crime
- Malware
- Adware
- Bots
- Ransomware
- Rootkits
- Spyware
- Scareware
- Trojan Horses
- Virus
- Worm
- Phishing
- Identity Theft
- Intellectual Property Theft
- Password Attacks
- Bluesnarfing
- Bluejacking
- DDoS
- Key Logger

58. The cardinal utility approach or what is called also as the Marshallian approach to consumer's equilibrium is based on the following assumptions:

- **Rationality:** It is assumed that the consumer is a rational being in the sense that he satisfies his wants in order of their merit. It means that he buys first a commodity which yields the highest utility and he buys last a commodity which gives the least utility.
- **Limited money income:** The consumer has a limited money income to spend on the goods and services he chooses to consume.
- **Maximisation of satisfaction:** Every rational consumer intends to maximise his satisfaction from his given money income.
- **Utility is cardinally measurable:** The cardinalists assume that utility is cardinally measurable, *i.e.*, it can be measured in absolute terms and in cardinal numbers.
- **Diminishing marginal utility:** The cardinalist assumed that the utility gained from successive units of a commodity consumed decreases as a consumer consumes more and more units of it.
- **Constant utility of money:** The marginal utility of money remains constant whatever the level of consumer's income and each unit of money has utility equal to 1.
- **Utility is additive:** Cardinalists maintain that utility is not only cardinally measurable but also it is additive. The additivity of the utility can be expressed through a utility function. Suppose that the basket of goods and services consumed by a consumer contains n items, and their

quantities may be expressed as x_1, x_2, x_3, ..., x_n. The utility function of the consumer may be expressed as

$$U = f(x_1, x_2, x_3, ..., x_n).$$

Given the utility function, the total utility obtained from n items may be expressed as:

$$U_n = U_1(x_1) + U_2(x_2) + U_3(x_3) ... + U_n(x_n).$$

60. Foreign exchange is defined in terms of Section 2 of FEMA, 1999 as a foreign currency including:

- All deposits, credits, balance payable in any foreign currency.
- Any drafts, traveller's cheques, letters of credit and bills of exchange expressed or drawn in Indian currency and payable in foreign currency.
- Any instrument giving anyone the option of making it payable either partly or fully in a foreign currency.

Here the term currency in "foreign currency" includes coins, bank notes, postal notes, postal orders and money orders.

In other words, foreign exchange includes all kinds of claims of the residents of a country to foreign currency payable abroad.

61. Market logistics includes planning the infrastructure to meet demand, then implementing and controlling the physical flows of materials and final goods from points of origin to points of use, to meet customer requirements at a profit. Market logistics planning has four steps:

- Deciding on the company's value proposition to its customers. (What on-time delivery standard should we offer? What levels should we attain in ordering and billing accuracy?)
- Selecting the best channel design and network strategy for reaching the customers. (Should the company serve customers directly or through intermediaries? What products should we source from which manufacturing facilities? How many warehouses should we maintain and where should we locate them?)
- Developing operational excellence in sales forecasting, warehouse management, transportation management, and materials management.
- Implementing the solution with the best information systems, equipment, policies, and procedures.

Studying market logistics leads managers to find the most efficient way to deliver value. For example, a software company might traditionally produce and package software disks and manuals, ship them to wholesalers, which ship them to retailers, which sell them to customers, who bring them home to download onto their PCs. Market logistics offers two superior delivery systems. The first lets the customer download the software directly onto his or her computer. The second allows the computer manufacturer to download the software onto its products. Both solutions eliminate the need for printing, packaging, shipping, and stocking millions of disks and manuals.

62.

$$\text{Cost of Capital} = \frac{10000}{98000}(1-0.4)$$
$$= \frac{10000}{98000}(0.6)$$
$$= 0.102 \times 0.6$$
$$= 0.061$$
$$= 6.1\%.$$

66. The sales of goods act, 1930:

Meaning of Warranty [Section 12(3) of the Sales of Goods Act, 1930]

A warranty is a stipulation—

- which is collateral to the main purpose of the contract, and
- the breach of which gives the aggrieved party a right to claim damages but not a right to reject goods and to terminate the contract.

Example:

X asked a car dealer to suggest him a good car and while suggesting the car, the dealer said that it could run for 20 km per litre of petrol. But the car could run only 15 kms per litre of petrol. In this case, the statement made by the seller was a warranty. *X* was, therefore not entitled to reject the car but he was entitled to claim the damages.

67. Rights of Indemnity Holder [Section 125]: An indemnity holder is entitled to recover the following amounts from the indemnifier provided he acts within the scope of his authority.

- *All damages* which he is compelled to pay in any suit in respect of any matter to which the promise to indemnify applies;
- *All costs* which he is compelled to pay, in bringing or defending such suit.

  Condition: (*a*) he did not contravene the orders of the promisor, and acted as it would have been prudent for him to act in the absence of any contract of indemnity, or (*b*) the promisor authorized him to bring or defend the suit.
- *All sums* which he has paid under the terms of any compromise of any such suit

  Condition: (*a*) the compromise was not contrary to the orders of the promisor, and was one which it would have been prudent for the promisee to make in the absence of any contract of indemnity, or (*b*) the promisor authorized him to compromise the suit.

Whether Contract of indemnity Covers the Cases of Loss Caused by the Events or Accidents which do not Depend upon the Conduct of the Promisor or any other Person

If the definition of contract of indemnity as per Section 124 is strictly interpreted, it would not cover the cases of loss caused by the events or accidents which do not depend upon the conduct of the promisor or any other person.

When does the Liability of Indemnifier Commence? Although the Indian Contract Act, 1872 is silent on the time of commencement of liability of indemnifier but on the basis of judicial pronouncement of courts, it can be said that the liability of an indemnifier commences as soon as the liability of the indemnity-holder becomes absolute and certain. In other words, if the indemnity-holder has incurred an absolute liability even though he has himself paid nothing, he is entitled to ask the indemnifier to indemnify him.

Example:

X promises to compensate *Y* for any loss that he may suffer by filling a suit against *Z*. The court orders *Y* to pay *Z* damages of ₹ 5,000. As the loss has become certain, *Y* may claim the amount of loss from *X* and pass it on to *Z*.

68. The median, a positional average, is that value of the variable which divides the group of observations into two equal parts. One part comprising all values greater, and the other values less than median. It is a simple, rigidly defined average and is not affected by extreme observations. It can be graphically located and recommended for open-end classes. However, it is not capable of algebraic treatment and has less sampling stability as compared to mean. The use of median is recommended when very large or small values occur in the observations or we wish to average a qualitative phenomena, *e.g.*, intelligence honestly etc. Like median, we can define other partition values also. Partition values divide a series into a number of parts. For instance, quartiles are those values which divide the distribution into four equal parts, deciles divide it into ten parts and percentiles divide it into hundred equal parts.

Mode is another measure of location. The Mode of a distribution is the value around which the observations tend to be most heavily concentrated. Mode is a simple descriptive measure of an average which is not affected by extreme observations and can be determined even for open end distributions. But, neither it is rigidly defined nor is capable of further algebraic treatment, and thus one has to be very careful in its determination. Still, the use of mode is recommended in many practical situations relating to market studies. For example, the terms like modal output per machine, average size of ready-made garments, most common income etc. refer to mode.

69. According to Robin Marris, managers maximize firm's balanced growth rate subject to managerial and financial constraints. He defines firm's balanced growth rate (G) as follows:

$$G = G_D = G_C$$

where G_D = growth rate of demand for firms product, and G_C = growth rate of capital supply to the firm.

In simple words, a firm's growth rate is balanced when demand for its product and supply of capital to the firm increase at the same rate. The two growth rates are according to Marris, translated into two utility functions: (*i*) manager's utility function, and (*ii*) owner's utility function.

The manager's utility function (U_m) and owner's utility function (U_o) may be specified as follows.

$U_m = f$(salary, power, job security, prestige, status),

and $U_o = f$(output, capital, market-share, profit, public esteem).

Owners' utility function (U_o) implies growth of demand for firms product and supply of capital. Therefore, maximization of U_o means maximization of 'demand for firm's product' or growth of capital supply'. According to Marris, by maximizing these variables, managers maximise both their own utility function and that of the owners. The managers can do so because most of the variables (*e.g.*, salaries, status, job security, power, etc.) appearing in their own utility function and those appearing in the utility function of the owners (*e.g.*, profit, capital market, share, etc.) are positively and strongly correlated with a single variables, *i.e.*, size of the firm. Maximization of these variables depends on the maximization of the growth rate of the firms. The managers, therefore, seek to maximize a steady growth rate.

70. Total cost is the sum of each input (fixed and variable) used in the production. Therefore to obtain the firm's total cost (TC) at a given output, we have to add total fixed cost (TFC) and its total variable cost (TVC). Thus,

$$TC = TFC + TVC$$

TFC is constant with respect to output changes. Therefore, in short run, the change in total cost resulting from a change in the level of output is equal to the change in total variable cost.

At zero level of output, TVC is zero.

$$TC = TFC + TVC$$

$$TC = TFC + \text{zero}$$

$$\therefore \quad TC = TFC$$

Hence, TC and TFC are equal at zero level of output. Therefore, TC curve starts from starting point of TFC.

Also $\quad TC - TVC = TFC$

that is, total cost and total variable cost differ by the amount of total fixed costs, which remains constant at every output. Tnus, TC and TVC curves are parallel to each other. In other words, TC curve have the same shape as TVC curve but will lie above the TVC curve.

Therefore TC curve behaves just like TVC curve. Initially it increases at decreasing rate and then at increasing rate according to increasing and diminishing returns. This is illustrated in Figure.

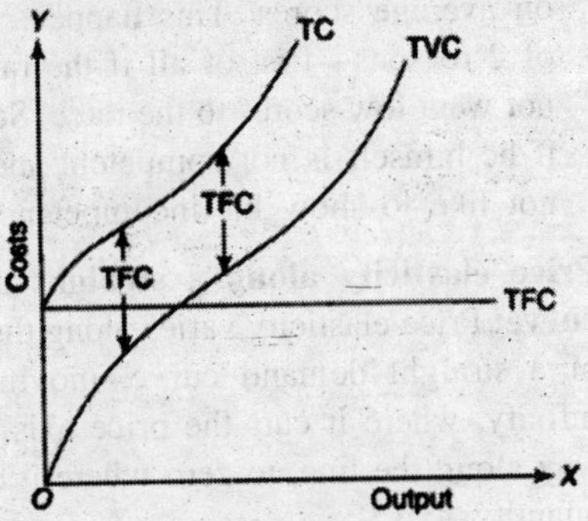

Fig.: Total Cost, Total Fixed Cost and Total Variable Cost

72. Problem-Solving Work Groups

The use of teams or work groups to solve problems is an integral part of quality programs. There are different ways of implementing this aspect of the program, however. The method of choice is best made at the organization or department level. Two specific variations of problem-solving teams are explored here: quality circles and task forces.

Quality Circles: A quality circle, for our purposes, is defined as an ongoing group of employees who systematically work together to identify and solve problems that affect their work. The problems that are addressed by these groups can include such issues as safety, morale, productivity, and costs. Quality circles are used extensively in the American manufacturing setting.

Task Forces: A task force is described as a structured group of employees who join together to solve a specific problem systematically. The issues that are addressed by task forces are comparable to those solved by quality circles. Moore and Miller-Kovach (1988) have described the use of this method as it applies to the provision of nutrition services.

75. National Housing Bank (NHB), a wholly owned subsidiary of Reserve Bank of India (RBI), was set up on 9 July, 1988 under the National Housing Bank Act, 1987. NHB is an apex financial institution for housing. NHB has been established with an objective to operate as a principal agency to promote housing finance institutions both at local and regional levels and to provide financial and other support incidental to such institutions and for matters connected therewith.

NHB registers, regulates and supervises Housing Finance Company (HFCs), keeps surveillance through on-site and off-site mechanisms and coordinates with other regulators.

77. Common Communication Platforms

Advertising	Sales Promotion	Events & Experiences	Public Relations & Publicity	Direct & Interactive Marketing	Word-of-Mouth Marketing	Personal Selling
Print and broadcast ads Packaging-outer Packaging inserts Motion pictures Brochures and booklets Posters and leaflets Directories Reprints of ads Billboards Display signs Point-of-purchase displays Audiovisual material Symbols and logos Videotapes	Contests, games, sweepstakes, lotteries Premiums and gifts Sampling Fairs and trade shows Exhibits Demonstrations Coupons Rebates Low-interest financing Entertainment Trade-in allowances Continuity programs Tie-ins	Sports Entertainment Festivals Arts Causes Factory tours Company Museums Street activities	Press kits Speeches Seminars Annual reports Charitable donations Publications Community relations Lobbying Identity media Company magazine	Catalogs Mailings Telemarketing Electronic shopping TV shopping Fax mail E-mail Voice mail Blogs Web sites	Person-to-person Chat rooms Blogs	Sales presentations Sales Meetings Incentive programms Samples Fairs and trade shows

78. Limitations of Performance Appraisal:

- **Personal Bias:** The biggest limitation of performance Appraisal is subjectivity. Due to human element in Appraisal, there is always a fear of one's own opinion coming in the way of Appraisal.
- **Halo Effect:** The tendency of an individual to rate an employee consistently high due to some earlier good performance rather than his existing performance is called as carrying a halo around oneself.
- **Horn Effect:** The tendency of a superior to rate a subordinate lower than his performance justifies due to some recent/earlier failures.
- **Lack of Uniform Standards:** The standards used by different departments in the organization may not be the same, hence, rating becomes unscientific and employees suffer. Some rates are too liberal while others are too strict causing lack of uniformity.
- **Appropriate Appraisal Technique:** Selection of appropriate appraisal technique is important to give the correct result. Some of the techniques are time-consuming and costly and so avoided. If wrong techniques are applied performance appraisal results may prove defective.
- **Wrong Appraisal by Superior:** Superiors have continuous and daily relations with the subordinates, giving accurate ratings may lead to spoiling relations with them which the superiors may want to avoid, hence higher rating to the subordinates.
- **Stress on Individual and not on Performance:** Performance Appraisal must lay stress on the performance of the individual and not on his individual and not on his personal characteristics. Many a times this is overlooked and the personnel characteristics comes in the way of his performance appraisal.
- **Central Tendency:** Many a times to be on the safer side the rater would put the rate on average scores. This happens because of 2 reasons—first of all if the rater does not want low scores to the ratee. Secondly, if he himself is not competent and would not like to show his incompetency.

80. Price elasticity along a straight demand curve: Price elasticity varies along the length of a straight demand curve, moving from infinity, where it cuts the price axis, to half way along the line, to zero where it cuts the quantity axis.

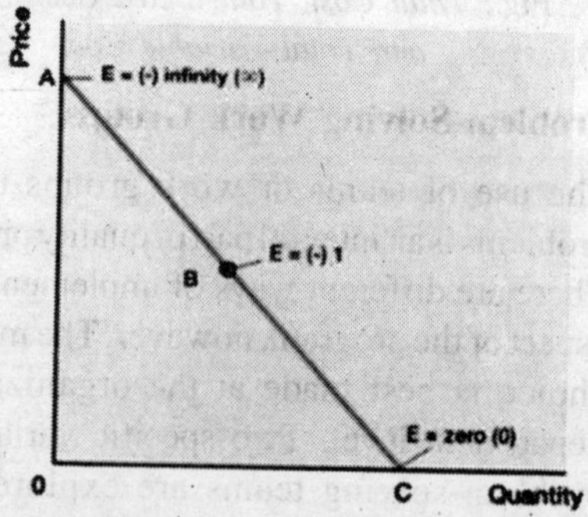

Unitary Elastic Demand: Demand for a commodity will be said to be unitary elastic, if the percentage change in the quantity demanded equals to the percentage change in the price. Cloth is its example. The numerical measurement of the elasticity will be equal to one (=1). In other words, when the demand changes in the same proportion as in the price of the commodity, the elasticity of demand is equal to one. Demand curve takes the shape of rectangular hyperbola. Here, area under the demand curve will always be equal. It is shown in Fig.

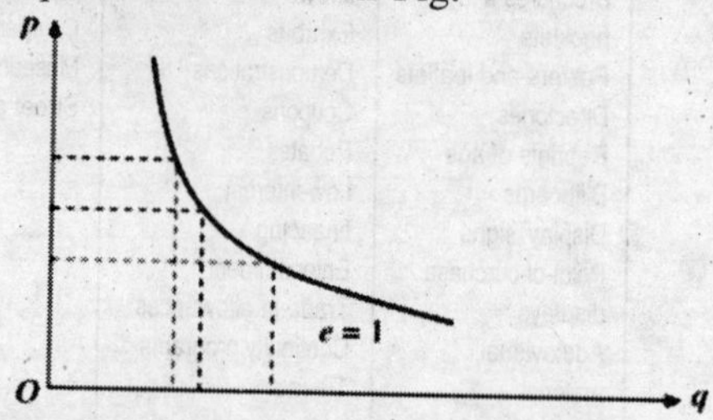

Fig.: *Unitary Elastic Demand*

[Demand curve with unitary elasticity of demand at all points is rectangular hyperbola. For such demand curve, expenditure is constant at all prices.]

81. The concept and form of the kinked-demand curve was first developed and used by Chamberlin in his theory of monopolistic competition. Later, Hall and Hitch used kinked-demand curve to explain rigidity of prices in oligopolistic market. But, neither Chamberlin nor Hall and Hitch used kinked-demand curve as a tool of analysis in their respective theories. It was Paul M. Sweezy who used the kinked-demand curve in his model of price stability in oligopolistic market.

The kinked-demand curve model developed by Paul M. Sweezy has features common to most oligopoly pricing models. This is the best-known model to explain, relatively more satisfactorily, the behaviour of the oligopolistic firms. It must, however, be noted at the outset that kinked-demand curve analysis does not deal with price and output determination. Rather, it seeks to establish that once a price-quantity combination is determined, an oligopoly firm does not find it profitable to change its price even when there is a considerable change in the cost of production and change in demand for the product.

The logic behind this proposition is as follows. An oligopoly firm believes that if it reduces the price of its product, the rival firms would follow and neutralize the expected gain from price reduction. But, if it raises the price, the firms would either maintain their prices or even go for price cutting, so that the price-raising firm loses a part of its market to the rival firms. This behaviour is true of all the firms. The oligopoly firms would, therefore, find it more desirable to maintain the prevailing price and output.

83. Types of Goods [Section 6 of the Sale of Goods Act, 1930]

The goods which form the subject of a contract of sale may be classified into following categories as shown below in Fig.

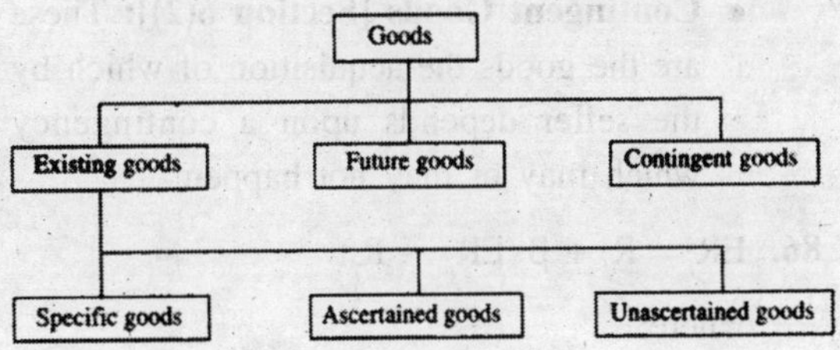

Fig.: Types of Goods

Let us discuss these types of goods one by one:

- **Existing Goods:** Existing goods mean the goods which are either owned or possessed by the seller at the time of contract of sale. The existing goods may be specific or ascertained or unascertained as follows:
  (a) ***Specific Goods [Section 2(14)]:*** These are the goods which are identified and agreed upon at the time when a contract of sale is made—For example, a specified TV, VCR, Car, Ring.
  (b) ***Ascertained Goods:*** Goods are said to be ascertained when out of a mass of unascertained goods, the quantity extracted for is identified and set aside for a given contract. Thus, when part of the goods lying in bulk are identified and earmarked for sale, such goods are termed as ascertained goods.
  (c) ***Unascertained Goods:*** These are the goods which are not identified and agreed upon at the time when a contract of sale is made. *e.g.*, goods in stock or lying in lots.
- **Future Goods [Section 2(6)]:** Future goods mean goods to be manufactured or produced or acquired by the seller after

the making of the contract of sale. There can be an agreement to sell only. There can be no sale in respect of future goods because one cannot sell what he does not possess.

- **Contingent Goods [Section 6(2)]:** These are the goods the acquisition of which by the seller depends upon a contingency which may or may not happen.

86. $ER_i = R_f + \beta_i(ER_m - R_f)$

where:

ER_i = expected return of investment

R_f = risk-free rate

β_i = beta of the investment

$(ER_m - R_f)$ = market risk premium

Expected Rate of Return

= 6 + 1.5(10 – 6)

= 6 + 1.5 × 4

= 12%.

87. The Grapevine: A grapevine is the unofficial and informal communication system. It sometimes conflicts with the formal system and complements and reinforces it at other times. The grapevine will remain in organizations as long as people are working in a group environment. It has both positive and negative sides. From a positive side, the grapevine communication can help management learn how employees truly feel about policies, procedures, and programs—a type of feedback mechanism. However, a negative consequence to the grapevine is rumors.

88. Inspite of many advantages, MBO may not be considered as a panacea for all the evils of the organisation. The success of the program depends on several factors. If the program fails, it is largely due to the following reasons:

- Lack of top management involvement and support. For an MBO program to succeed, it must have the complete support of top management.
- Lack of understanding of the philosophy behind MBO. MBO program in some organisations meet the resistance of employees because it is imposed on them as 'control device' to curb their freedom.
- Difficultly in setting realistic and meaningful objectives. Some jobs and areas of performance cannot be quantified and hence are not amenable for objective evaluation.
- Increased time pressure. To use MBO program, managers must learn to establish priorities and use the time effectively.
- Lack of relevant skills. Managers may not have the requisite skills for identifying objectives, communication and interpersonal interaction such as counselling and receiving feedback.
- Lack of individual motivation. The rewards and incentives for superior performance have to be specified clearly. Ambiguity or uncertainty regarding the outcome of the efforts is one of the reasons for the non-performance.
- Poor integration with other systems. Objective setting and review phases must be performed in conjunction with other activities such as budgeting, forecasting and the like. Often managers are neither taught how to set the objectives nor familiarized with the various plans and policies of the organisation. In such cases, each department ends up going its own way and the results are counter-productive to the overall organisation.

89. Reserve Bank of India—Brief History

1926	:	Royal Commission on Indian Currency and Finance popularly known as the Hilton-Young Commission submitted its report and made recommendations to the British Government of India for creation of a Central Bank. ***Objectives:*** • To separate the control of currency and credit from the government. • To augment banking facilities throughout the country.
1933	:	White Paper on Indian Constitutional Reforms recommended the creation of a Reserve Bank. A fresh bill was introduced in the Legislative Assembly.
1934	:	The bill was passed and received the Governor General's assent
April 1, 1935		• Reserve Bank of India was established via the RBI Act of 1934 as the banker to the central government. • RBI launched its operations from April 1, 1935. • Its headquarters were in Kolkata in the beginning, but it was shifted to Shaheed Bhagat Singh Marg, Mumbai in 1937. • RBI started as a privately owned bank. It started with a Share Capital of ₹ 5 Crore, divided into shares of ₹ 100 each fully paid up. • In the beginning, this entire capital was owned by private shareholders. Out of this ₹ 5 Crore, the amount of ₹ 4,97,8000 was subscribed by the private shareholders while ₹ 2,20,000 was subscribed by central government.
1942	:	Reserve Bank ceased to be the currency issuing authority of Burma (now Myanmar).
1947	:	Reserve Bank stopped acting as banker to the Government of Burma.
1948	:	Reserve Bank stopped rendering central banking services to Pakistan.
1949		• Government of India nationalized the Reserve Bank under the Reserve Bank (Transfer of Public Ownership) Act, 1948. • Thus, the government passed Reserve Bank (Transfer to Public Ownership) Act, 1948 and took over RBI from private shareholders after paying appropriate compensation. Thus, nationalisation of RBI took place in 1949 and from January 1, 1949, RBI started working as a government owned Central Bank of India. • Banking Regulation Act was enacted.

Previous Years' Paper (Solved)

National Testing Agency (NTA)

UGC-NET Junior Research Fellowship & Assistant Professor Eligibility Exam

Commerce, June-2019*

PAPER-II

Note: *This paper contains **hundred (100)** objective type questions of **two (2)** marks each. **All** questions are **compulsory**.*

1. A statement of change in financial position typically would NOT disclose the effect of:
   A. share capital issued to acquire productive facilities
   B. dividends on share declared
   C. cash dividend declared but not yet paid
   D. purchase and retirement of treasury stock

2. **Assertion (A) :** At times, a business may face the situation where it has to shut down its operations.
   Reason (R) : If the revenue is less than its variables cost, the operation should be closed down.

   In the context of the above two statements, which one of the following codes is correct?
   A. (A) is correct, but (R) is not correct
   B. (A) and (R) both are correct and (R) is the right explanation of (A)
   C. (A) and (R) both are correct and (R) is not the right explanation of (A)
   D. Both (A) and (R) are incorrect

3. A 'sale and lease back' arrangement is more suitable for a lessee having:
   A. liquidity crisis B. surplus fund
   C. high profit D. no-profit no-loss

4. Which one is NOT true regarding the Market Stabilization Scheme (MSS)?
   A. It absorbs surplus liquidity of enduring nature arising out of large capital flows
   B. It absorbs surplus liquidity through sale of short-dated government securities and treasury bills
   C. Mobilised surplus liquidity is held in the MSS account with the Reserve Bank of India
   D. MSS account liquidity can be used for normal government expenditure of capital nature

5. Arrange the following in order of their manifestations:
   (*a*) Offer (*b*) Acceptance
   (*c*) Breach of contract (*d*) Contract
   Choose the correct option from the following:
   A. (*a*), (*b*), (*c*) and (*d*)
   B. (*a*), (*b*), (*d*) and (*c*)
   C. (*b*), (*c*), (*a*) and (*d*)
   D. (*a*), (*d*), (*c*) and (*b*)

6. Which among the following institutions is NOT a part of World Bank group?
   A. International Development Association (IDA)
   B. International Monetary Fund (IMF)
   C. International Finance Corporation (IFC)
   D. Multilateral Investment Guarantee Agency (MIGA)

7. In which of the following pricing policies, a firm charges higher initial price for the product and reduces it over time as the demand at higher price is satisfied?
   A. Peak load pricing
   B. Incremental pricing
   C. Skimming
   D. Penetration pricing

*Held on 26-06-2019.

8. If two regression coefficients are –0.8 and –0.2, then the value of coefficient of correlation is:
A. –0.16
B. –0.50
C. +0.40
D. –0.40

9. Which one of the following is used for international money transfer?
A. RTGS
B. NEFT
C. SWIFT
D. DD

10. Which among the following is NOT true about BASEL?
A. Initially it was named as Committee of Banking Regulations and Supervisory Practices (CBRS)
B. BASEL was established by the Central Bank Governors of fifteen countries
C. It was established by the end of 1974
D. Disturbances in international currency and banking markets were responsible for its establishment

11. A company issues 10% irredeemable preference shares. The face value per share is ₹ 100, but the issue price is ₹ 95. What is the cost of preference share?
A. 10.63%
B. 10.73%
C. 10.83%
D. 10.53%

12. As per Section 52 of the companies Act, 2013, the balance in the Security Premium Account cannot be utilized for:
A. payment of dividend
B. writing off discount on issue of shares
C. issue of fully paid-up bonus share
D. capital losses

13. Under which of the following situations, the decision outcome on evaluation of investment opportunities vary under NPV and IRR methods *per se*?
(*a*) Time disparity (*b*) Cost disparity
(*c*) Life disparity (*d*) Volume disparity
Choose the correct combination of situations:
A. (*a*) and (*d*) only
B. (*b*) and (*d*) only
C. (*a*), (*b*) and (*c*) only
D. (*b*), (*c*) and (*d*) only

14. Find the marginal revenue of a firm that sells a product at a price of ₹ 10 and the price elasticity of demand for the product is (–)2.
A. ₹ 5
B. ₹ 10
C. ₹ 30
D. ₹ 15

15. Which of the following is an instance of non-conventional dumping?
A. Sporadic dumping
B. Predatory dumping
C. Reverse dumping
D. Persistent dumping

16. In which of the following commodities, when a consumer spends so much that negative income effect overwhelms the positive substitution effect so as the underlying demand curve is positively sloped?
A. Inferior goods
B. Superior goods
C. Giffen goods
D. Normal goods

17. Match List-I with List-II:

List-I	List-II
(*a*) $j = \frac{\overline{X} - M_o}{\sigma}$	(*i*) Kelly's coefficient of skewness
(*b*) $j = \frac{Q_3 - Q_1 - 2M_e}{Q_3 - Q_1}$	(*ii*) Bowley's measure of skewness
(*c*) $j = \frac{P_{90} + P_{10} - 2P_{50}}{P_{90} - P_{10}}$	(*iii*) Karl Pearson's coefficient of skewness

Choose the correct option from those given below:

	(*a*)	(*b*)	(*c*)
A.	(*iii*)	(*ii*)	(*i*)
B.	(*iii*)	(*i*)	(*ii*)
C.	(*i*)	(*ii*)	(*iii*)
D.	(*ii*)	(*i*)	(*iii*)

18. Excess capacity is NOT noticed in which of the following market conditions?
A. Monopoly
B. Monopolistic competition
C. Oligopoly
D. Perfect competition

19. Assertion (A) : Reserve Bank of India is an important regulatory and administrative authority to execute FEMA provisions.

Reason (R) : Being monetary authority and custodian of foreign exchange, Reserve Bank of India enjoys requisite expertise of FEMA administration.

In the context of the above two statements, which one of the following option is correct?

A. Both (A) and (R) are correct and (R) is the right explanation of (A)

B. Both (A) and (R) are correct, but (R) is not the right explanation of (A)

C. Both (A) and (R) are incorrect

D. (A) is correct and (R) is not correct

20. Amount unutilised in capital gain account scheme for which exemption claimed u/s 54 shall be treated as long-term capital gain, if:

A. 2 years have expired from the date of transfer

B. 2 years have expired from the date of deposit

C. 3 years have expired from the date of transfer

D. 3 years have expired from the date of deposit

21. Which of the following is true about India Trade Policy (Export-Import), 2015-2019?

(*a*) Doubling the exports (both merchandise and services)

(*b*) Achieve 3.5% share in global exports

(*c*) Introduced two new schemes (MEIS and SEIS)

(*d*) Introduced simplified Aayat-Niryat Form

Choose the correct answer from the following:

A. (*a*) and (*b*) only

B. (*a*) and (*c*) only

C. (*a*), (*b*) and (*c*) only

D. All are correct

22. Promoting team spirit, harmony and unity within the organization is the principle of:

A. order B. scalar chain

C. spirit de corps D. equity

23. Match List-I with List-II:

List-I	List-II
(*a*) Interbank call market	(*i*) Money Market
(*b*) Commercial bills	(*ii*) Promissory note
(*c*) Commercial papers	(*iii*) Short-term maturity
(*d*) Treasury bills	(*iv*) Government papers

Choose the correct option from those given below:

	(*a*)	(*b*)	(*c*)	(*d*)
A.	(*i*)	(*ii*)	(*iv*)	(*iii*)
B.	(*iii*)	(*i*)	(*ii*)	(*iv*)
C.	(*i*)	(*iii*)	(*iv*)	(*ii*)
D.	(*iv*)	(*iii*)	(*ii*)	(*i*)

24. Assertion (A) : Brainstorming technique demands generation of a number of alternatives to a problem.

Reason (R) : Participants generate as many alternatives as possible without evaluating them in brainstorming sessions.

In the context of the above two statements, which one of the following option is correct?

A. Statement (A) is correct and (R) is the correct explanation of (A)

B. Both (A) and (R) are correct, but (R) is not the right explanation of (A)

C. Statement (A) is correct, but (R) is incorrect

D. Both (A) and (R) are correct

25. Redeemable preference shares of ₹ 2,00,000 are to be redeemed at par for which fresh equity shares of ₹ 80,000 are issued at a discount of 10%. What amount should be transferred to Capital Redemption Reserve Account?

A. ₹ 2,00,000 B. ₹ 1,20,000

C. ₹ 1,28,000 D. ₹ 72,000

26. Which of the following does NOT come under the definition of 'information' as per the Right to Information Act (RTI Act), 2005?

A. Logbooks

B. Data material held in electronic from

C. File noting

D. Circular

27. X is an individual of 55 years of age having gross total income ₹ 3,50,000. What is the tax liability for assessment year 2018-19?

A. ₹ 5,000 B. ₹ 2,500
C. ₹ 2,580 D. ₹ 3,000

28. Which of the following does NOT fall in the ambit of the objectives of Competition Act, 2002?

A. Encourage Competition
B. Prevent abuse of dominant position
C. Prevent monopolistic rights are arising out of intellectual property
D. Regulate mergers and acquisitions

29. **Statement (I) :** If the tax liability has been reduced within the legal framework, it is tax planning.

Statement (II) : If tax liability has been reduced to get benefit of deduction available under the income tax, it is called tax evasion.

In the context of the above two statements, which one of the following codes is correct?

A. Both the Statements (I) and (II) are correct
B. Statement (I) is correct, but (II) is incorrect
C. Both Statements (I) and (II) are incorrect
D. Statement (II) is correct, but (I) is incorrect

30. The retail supply chain does NOT include:

A. manufactures B. retailers
C. wholesalers D. regulators

31. Which of the following characteristics are related to relationship marketing?

(*a*) Product feature orientation
(*b*) Product benefit orientation
(*c*) Frequent consumer contact
(*d*) High concern for quality

Choose the correct answer from the following:

A. (*b*), (*c*) and (*d*) B. (*a*), (*b*) and (*c*)
C. (*a*), (*c*) and (*d*) D. (*a*), (*b*) and (*d*)

32. Miller-Orr model is used in the management of:

A. inventory B. leverage
C. receivables D. cash

33. Match List-I with List-II:

List-I	List-II
(*a*) 80 TTA	(*i*) Deduction in respect of payment of interest on loan taken for higher education
(*b*) 80 CCD	(*ii*) Deduction in respect of interest on loan taken for residential house property
(*c*) 80 E	(*iii*) Deduction in respect of interest on deposits in savings account
(*d*) 80 EE	(*iv*) Deduction in respect of contribution to national pension system

Choose the correct option from those given below:

	(*a*)	(*b*)	(*c*)	(*d*)
A.	(*iii*)	(*iv*)	(*i*)	(*ii*)
B.	(*iii*)	(*iv*)	(*ii*)	(*i*)
C.	(*iii*)	(*i*)	(*ii*)	(*iv*)
D.	(*i*)	(*ii*)	(*iii*)	(*iv*)

34. Product A requires 10 kg of material at the rate of ₹ 5 per kg. The actual consumption of material for the manufacturing of product A comes to 12 kg of material at the rate of ₹ 6 per kg. Direct material cost variance is:

A. ₹ 22 (favourable)
B. ₹ 22 (unfavourable)
C. ₹ 12 (favourable)
D. ₹ 12 (unfavourable)

35. 'Doctrine of Caveat Emptor' means:

A. buyer should make payment well in time
B. buyer should be beware of all aspects of buying
C. buyer will be responsible for the whole payment
D. buyer will not be responsible at any cost

36. The attitude based on beliefs, opinion, knowledge or information about the particular event which the employees possesses is:

A. behavioural attitude
B. positive attitude
C. cognitive attitude
D. affective attitude

37. Which among the following is NOT included in negotiable instrument?

A. Cheque B. Demand Draft
C. Promissiory Note D. Mutual Fund

38. Redressal mechanism for consumer disputes under Section 9 of the Consumer Protection Act envisages a:

A. single-tier system
B. two-tier system
C. three-tier system
D. open system independent of hierarchy

39. Match List-I with List-II:

List-I (Theories of Profit)	List-II (Economists)
(*a*) Risk theory of profit	(*i*) Schumpeter
(*b*) Innovation theory of profit	(*ii*) Walker
(*c*) Rent theory of profit	(*iii*) Hawley
(*d*) Dynamic theory of profit	(*iv*) Clark

Choose the correct option from those given below:

	(*a*)	(*b*)	(*c*)	(*d*)
A.	(*iii*)	(*iv*)	(*ii*)	(*i*)
B.	(*iv*)	(*ii*)	(*iii*)	(*i*)
C.	(*iii*)	(*i*)	(*ii*)	(*iv*)
D.	(*iv*)	(*i*)	(*ii*)	(*iii*)

40. Statement (I) : Though closely related, job evaluation and performance appraisal are not the same.

Statement (II) : The purpose of job evaluation is to fix the remuneration and other relevant benefits.

In the context of the above two statements, which one of the following codes is correct?

A. Both the Statements (I) and (II) are correct
B. Both the Statements (I) and (II) are incorrect
C. Statement (I) is correct, while Statement (II) is incorrect
D. Statement (I) is incorrect, while Statement (II) is correct

41. Building long-term mutually satisfying relations with key customers, suppliers, distributors in order to earn and retain their long-term preference and business is known as:

A. relationship marketing
B. social marketing
C. niche marketing
D. service marketing

42. Which of the following are the rights of a Statutory Auditor?

(*a*) To receive remuneration
(*b*) To attend Board of Directors Meeting
(*c*) To attend the General Meeting
(*d*) To visit the branch office

Choose the correct answer from the following:

A. (*a*) and (*b*) B. (*a*), (*b*) and (*d*)
C. (*a*), (*c*) and (*d*) D. (*a*), (*b*), (*c*) and (*d*)

43. Following are the steps in the activity-based cost allocation:

(*a*) Identification of the main activities
(*b*) Collection of cost pool
(*c*) Determination of the activity cost drivers
(*d*) Calculation of activity driver rate
(*e*) Charging the cost of activities to products

Select the correct sequence of the above steps:

A. (*a*), (*b*), (*c*), (*e*), (*d*) B. (*a*), (*b*), (*e*), (*d*), (*c*)
C. (*a*), (*b*), (*c*), (*d*), (*e*) D. (*a*), (*d*), (*c*), (*b*), (*e*)

44. Which among the following is NOT a correct statement?

A. Hedge funds are not mutual funds.
B. Hedge funds can be sold to public.
C. Investors in mutual funds must pay various fees and expenses.
D. Mutual funds provide economies of scale to investment decisions.

45. SIDBI was set up as a subsidiary of IDBI to:

A. takeover the functions of small business financing of IDBI
B. takeover the venture capital operation of IDBI
C. reconstruct and rehabilitate the sick and closed industrial units financed by IDBI
D. facilitate, finance and promote India's foreign trade

46. For a very large population the ratio between SE_X and σ is 8 : 40. The Sample size *n* will be:

A. 5 B. 25
C. 32 D. 48

47. Which of the following are NOT sources of secondary data?

(*a*) Interview (*b*) Questionnaire
(*c*) Observation (*d*) Unpublished thesis
(*e*) Annual report

Choose the correct option from the following:

A. (*a*), (*d*) and (*e*) B. (*b*), (*c*) and (*d*)
C. (*c*), (*d*) and (*e*) D. (*a*), (*b*) and (*c*)

48. Which of the following committees is related to the investor protection?

A. Bhagwati Committee
B. N.K. Mitra Committee
C. J.R. Verma Committee
D. L.C. Gupta Committee

49. The social environment of the job affects people and is also affected by them and not by management alone, is the main proposition of:

A. contingency theory of organization
B. system theory of organization
C. classical theory of organization
D. Neo-classical theory of organization

50. Assertion (A) : U-shaped long-run average cost curve is based on the assumption that economies of scale prevails at small levels of production and dis-economies of scale prevails at larger level of production.

Reason (R) : Decreasing returns to scale arises primarily because as the scale of operation increases, it becomes even more difficult to manage the firm effectively.

In the context of the above two statements, which one of the following codes is correct?

A. Both (A) and (R) are correct and (R) is the right explanation of (A)
B. Both (A) and (R) are correct and (R) is not the right explanation of (A)
C. (A) is correct and (R) is not incorrect
D. Both (A) and (R) are incorrect

51. Statement (I) : The arithmetic mean is an all purpose average.

Statement (II) : Median and mode are called positional averages.

In the context of the above two statements, which one of the following codes is correct?

A. Both the Statements (I) and (II) are correct
B. Both the Statements (I) and (II) are incorrect
C. Statement (I) is correct, but (II) is incorrect
D. Statement (II) is correct, but (I) is incorrect

52. Consumer behaviour does NOT consist which of the following activities?

A. Obtaining B. Consuming
C. Disposition D. Producing

53. A firm consumes 90,000 units of a certain item of raw material in its production process annually. It costs ₹ 3 per unit, the cost per purchase order is ₹ 300 and the inventory carrying cost is 20% per year. What is the EOQ?

A. 9470 units B. 9487 units
C. 9480 units D. 9840 units

54. Which of the following types of goodwill is considered to be the best?

A. Dog goodwill B. Cat goodwill
C. Rat goodwill D. Cow goodwill

55. Match List-I with List-II:

List-I	List-II
(*a*) Net income approach	(*i*) Inventory management
(*b*) Gordan model	(*ii*) Capital budgeting
(*c*) Internal rate of return	(*iii*) Capital structure theory
(*d*) Reorder level	(*iv*) Dividend theory

Choose the correct option from those given below:

	(*a*)	(*b*)	(*c*)	(*d*)
A.	(*ii*)	(*iii*)	(*iv*)	(*i*)
B.	(*iii*)	(*iv*)	(*ii*)	(*i*)
C.	(*iii*)	(*iv*)	(*i*)	(*ii*)
D.	(*ii*)	(*i*)	(*iv*)	(*iii*)

56. Statement (I) : Agreement without consideration is always valid.

Statement (II) : All contracts are agreements but all agreements are not contracts.

In the context of the above two statements, which one of the following codes is correct?

A. Statements (I) and (II) both are correct
B. Both Statements (I) and (II) are incorrect
C. Statement (I) is incorrect and Statement (II) is correct
D. Statement (I) is correct but Statement (II) is incorrect

57. Match List-I with List-II:

List-I (Objectives of business firms)	List-II (Hypothesis)
(*a*) Maximization of firms' growth rate	(*i*) Baumol's hypothesis
(*b*) Managerial utility function	(*ii*) Marris hypothesis
(*c*) Satisfying behaviour	(*iii*) Williamson hypothesis
(*d*) Sales Maximization	(*iv*) Cyert March hypothesis

Choose the correct option from those given below:

	(*a*)	(*b*)	(*c*)	(*d*)
A.	(*ii*)	(*iii*)	(*iv*)	(*i*)
B.	(*iii*)	(*iv*)	(*i*)	(*ii*)
C.	(*iv*)	(*i*)	(*ii*)	(*iii*)
D.	(*i*)	(*ii*)	(*iii*)	(*iv*)

58. In tax laws, donation to approved and notified association for scientific research is allowed as:

A. 125% of the donation
B. 100% of the donation
C. 175% of the donation
D. 150% of the donation

59. Match List-I with List-II:

List-I	List-II
(*a*) Ind AS-16	(*i*) Income tax
(*b*) Ind AS-38	(*ii*) Leasing
(*c*) Ind AS-17	(*iii*) Intangible assets
(*d*) Ind AS-12	(*iv*) Property, plant and equipment

Choose the correct option from those given below:

	(*a*)	(*b*)	(*c*)	(*d*)
A.	(*iv*)	(*iii*)	(*i*)	(*ii*)
B.	(*iv*)	(*iii*)	(*ii*)	(*i*)
C.	(*iii*)	(*ii*)	(*iv*)	(*i*)
D.	(*iv*)	(*ii*)	(*i*)	(*iii*)

60. Which of the following are considered non-parametric tests?

(*a*) Mann-Whitney U test
(*b*) Kruskal-Wallis test
(*c*) F-test
(*d*) T-test
(*e*) Chi-square test

Choose the correct option from the following:

A. (*a*), (*b*) and (*e*)
B. (*a*), (*b*) and (*c*)
C. (*a*), (*b*), (*c*) and (*d*)
D. (*a*), (*b*), (*c*), (*d*) and (*e*)

61. Assertion (A) : According to Net Income (NI) approach, capital structure decision is relevant in the valuation of firm.

Reason (R) : A firm can change its total value and its overall cost of capital by change in the degree of leverage in its capital structure.

In the context of the above two statements, which one of the following codes is correct?

A. Both (A) and (R) are correct and (R) is the right explanation of (A)
B. Both (A) and (R) are correct and (R) is not the right explanation of (A)
C. Both (A) and (R) are incorrect
D. (A) is correct and (R) is not correct

62. The arithmetic mean of 10 items is 50. If each item is increased by 5, then new arithmetic mean would be:

A. 50 B. 55
C. 60 D. 45

63. After US dollar, which of the following currencies has largest weightage in determining the value of SDR?

A. Japanese Yen
B. Chinese Yuan (Renminbi)
C. Euro
D. British Pound

64. Credit worthiness score in India ranges between:
A. 300 to 600 B. 300 to 900
C. 500 to 1000 D. 900 to 1600

65. SUGAM is also known as:
A. ITR-1 B. ITR-2
C. ITR-3 D. ITR-4

66. **Statement (I)** : *t*-test and F-test are based on the identical assumptions.
Statement (II) : *t*-test is used for comparison between two groups whereas F-test is used for comparison between more than two groups.

In the context of the above two statements, which one of the following codes is correct?
A. Both the Statements (I) and (II) are correct
B. Both the Statements (I) and (II) are incorrect
C. Statement (I) is correct, but (II) is incorrect
D. Statement (II) is correct, but (I) is incorrect

67. Which of the following is the predecessor of the IRDA Act, 1999?
A. The Insurance Act, 1938
B. The Life Insurance Corporation Act, 1956
C. The Marine Insurance Act, 1963
D. The Public Liability Insurance Act, 1991

68. 'Motivation-force or level of efforts is not equal to satisfaction and performance' is propounded by:
A. Porter-Lawler model
B. Vroom's expectancy theory
C. X and Y theory
D. Adam's equity theory

69. Which is the most appropriate mode of entry in international business to an enterprise with little experience of international markets?
A. Acquisition B. Strategic Alliance
C. Joint Venture D. Exporting

70. Match List-I with List-II:

List-I (Trade and Finance Institution)	List-II (Headquarters)
(*a*) WTO	(*i*) Brussels
(*b*) IMF	(*ii*) Geneva
(*c*) FAO	(*iii*) Washington
(*d*) EU	(*iv*) Rome

Choose the correct option from those given below:

	(*a*)	(*b*)	(*c*)	(*d*)
A.	(*ii*)	(*iii*)	(*iv*)	(*i*)
B.	(*i*)	(*ii*)	(*iii*)	(*iv*)
C.	(*iii*)	(*ii*)	(*i*)	(*iv*)
D.	(*i*)	(*iii*)	(*ii*)	(*iv*)

71. When a company distributes its products through a channel structure that includes one of more resellers, it is known as:
A. direct marketing
B. indirect marketing
C. integrated marketing
D. multi-level marketing

72. Organization structure that shows a unique combination of strategy, structure and management process is known as:
A. free-form organization
B. virtual organization
C. network organization
D. horizontal organization

73. Shopping goods have which of the following features?
(*a*) These products are generally durable in nature
(*b*) Consumers generally compare the goods of various sellers and then buy such goods
(*c*) Per unit price of these goods is generally high
(*d*) These goods are regularly and continuously in demand
(*e*) These goods are sold as a result of aggressive promotional efforts

Choose the correct option from the following:
A. (*c*), (*d*) and (*e*) B. (*a*), (*b*) and (*c*)
C. (*b*), (*c*) and (*d*) D. (*a*), (*c*) and (*e*)

74. Which one of the following analyses is suitable for risk-return analysis in financial decisions?

A. CAPM analysis B. SWOT analysis
C. Capital gearing D. EVA analysis

75. Which of the following is NOT a main stage in a customer relationship life cycle?

A. Customer acquisition
B. Customer development
C. Customer satisfaction
D. Customer annoyance

76. One belt, one road initiative (BRI) is NOT intended to:

A. trade protectionism
B. strengthening logistic and supply chain
C. improve cost competitiveness
D. rebalance trade dominance

77. Following are the events of an organizational culture:

(*a*) Customer orientation and employee policies
(*b*) Quality orientation, directing and motivating styles
(*c*) Decision-making, products and services and responsibilities to society
(*d*) Reaction to competitors and gratitude towards nation
(*e*) Role ambiguities, trade union and policies

Select the correct sequence for the above events:

A. (*a*), (*b*), (*d*) and (*e*) B. (*a*), (*c*), (*d*) and (*e*)
C. (*b*), (*c*), (*d*) and (*e*) D. (*a*), (*b*), (*c*) and (*d*)

78. What is the probability that sum of outcomes on pair of dice is equal to 8?

A. $\frac{6}{36}$ B. $\frac{5}{36}$
C. $\frac{4}{36}$ D. $\frac{3}{36}$

79. The essence of the law of diminishing returns is:

A. inelastic production
B. negative marginal production
C. declining total production
D. declining average production

80. Under which of the following situations, economies of scale exists to the potential and persists?

A. When firm is too small and too specialized
B. When firms' decision to hire inputs do not result in an increase in the input costs
C. When firm is too large and over-diversified
D. When long-run cost of producing a unit falls as the output increases

81. Following are the information for a house property:

Municipal value	:	₹ 4,50,000
Fair rental value	:	₹ 5,00,000
Standard rent	:	₹ 4,80,000
Actual rent	:	₹ 4,20,000

What is the gross annual value of the house property?

A. ₹ 4,80,000 B. ₹ 5,00,000
C. ₹ 4,20,000 D. ₹ 4,50,000

82. Study the following information:

Covariance between X and Y series = –17.8
Standard deviation of X series = 6.6
Standard deviation of Y series = 4.2
Number of pairs of observation = 20

The coefficient of correlation is:

A. –0.642 B. 0.642
C. 0.253 D. –0.253

83. Match List-I with List-II:

List-I	List-II
(*a*) Fiscal, monetary and industrial policies	(*i*) Social responsibilities
(*b*) Social obligation towards several stakeholders	(*ii*) Stakeholders/ interest group
(*c*) Consumers, shareholders, suppliers, creditors etc.	(*iii*) Business ethics
(*d*) Moral principles that defines the right or wrong	(*iv*) Economic policies

Choose the correct option from those given below:

	(a)	(b)	(c)	(d)
A.	(iii)	(i)	(iv)	(ii)
B.	(i)	(ii)	(iv)	(iii)
C.	(ii)	(iv)	(iii)	(i)
D.	(iv)	(i)	(ii)	(iii)

84. Capital structure and leverage decisions come in the ambit of:
A. investment decisions
B. distribution decisions
C. financing decisions
D. dividend decisions

85. Match List-I with List-II:

List-I	List-II
(a) Sec 6(i)	(i) Agriculture Income
(b) Sec 10AA	(ii) Leave Travel Concession
(c) Sec 10(i)	(iii) Resident
(d) Sec 10(5)	(iv) Leave Salary

Choose the correct option from those given below:

	(a)	(b)	(c)	(d)
A.	(i)	(iv)	(iii)	(ii)
B.	(iii)	(iv)	(ii)	(i)
C.	(iii)	(ii)	(iv)	(i)
D.	(iii)	(iv)	(i)	(ii)

86. The channel alternative is NOT to be assessed on the basis of:
A. economic criteria
B. control criteria
C. adaptive criteria
D. accumulation criteria

87. Return of income is submitted under which Section of Income Tax Act?
A. Section 138(1) B. Section 142(1)
C. Section 139(1) D. Section 129(1)

88. Which one of the following is NOT the pre-requisite of price discrimination?
A. Firm must have monopoly power
B. Product have multiple close substitutes and different uses
C. Markets are separated and segmented
D. Price elasticity of product must differ in different markets

89. Match List-I with List-II:

List-I	List-II
(a) Cyber Crime	(i) Intellectual Property Right Act
(b) Doctrine of Caveat Emptor	(ii) Negotiable Instrument Act
(c) Dishonour of Bill	(iii) Sale of Goods Act
(d) Patent and Copyrights	(iv) The Information Technology Act

Choose the correct option from those given below:

	(a)	(b)	(c)	(d)
A.	(iii)	(iv)	(i)	(ii)
B.	(iii)	(ii)	(iv)	(i)
C.	(iv)	(iii)	(ii)	(i)
D.	(ii)	(iv)	(iii)	(i)

90. Which of the following commodities is kept outside the purview of GST?
A. Tobacco products
B. Petroleum products
C. Edible oils
D. Insurance products

91. List out from the given statements the important ethical principles that a business should follow:
(a) To take the necessary action for the development of the concerned industry or business
(b) Pay taxes and discharge other obligations promptly
(c) To ensure the best utilisation of the human resources
(d) Refrain from secret kickbacks or pay-offs to customers, suppliers, administrators, etc.
(e) Ensure payment of fair wages and fair treatment of employees

Choose the correct answer from the options given below.
A. (c), (d) and (e) B. (b), (d) and (e)
C. (a), (b) and (c) D. (a), (c) and (e)

92. Deduction u/s 37(1) is allowed under tax laws for those expenditures which are:
A. revenue
B. capital

C. both revenue and capital
D. deferred revenue expenses

93. Which of the following reflects the sum of perceived tangible and intangible benefits and costs to a customer?
A. Customer satisfaction
B. Customer delight
C. Customer value
D. Customer expectation

94. Which of the following are included in digital payment system?
(*a*) RTGS (*b*) Demand draft
(*c*) NEFT (*d*) Cheque

Choose the correct option from the following:
A. (*a*), (*c*) and (*d*) B. (*b*) and (*d*) only
C. (*a*) and (*c*) only D. (*b*), (*c*) and (*d*)

95. The current market price of a company's share is ₹ 90 and the expected dividend per share next year is ₹ 4.5. If the dividend is expected to grow at a constant rate of 8%, the shareholder's required rate of return will be:
A. 8% B. 5%
C. 20% D. 13%

96. New reform in Indian banking system include:
(*a*) Digitisation of bank operations
(*b*) Banking consolidation
(*c*) Borrowing from Government
(*d*) Agency work

Choose the correct option from the following:
A. (*a*) and (*b*) B. (*c*) and (*d*)
C. (*b*), (*d*) and (*c*) D. (*a*), (*c*) and (*d*)

97. Currency swap is a method of:
A. hedging against foreign exchange risk
B. speculating in foreign exchange
C. leverage instrument used by cooperative banks
D. mode of payment in international trade

98. Peter F. Drucker noted the relationship between selling and marketing in which of the following terms?
A. Marketing is a subsidiary component of selling
B. The aim of marketing is to make selling superfluous
C. The aim of selling is to make marketing superfluous
D. Selling and marketing are essentially the same thing

99. Quantitative import restrictions that limit the quantity of a product being imported is called:
A. embargo B. quota
C. trade restraint D. import tariff

100. Chalapathi Rao Committee was constituted for restructuring of:
A. State Financial Corporation in India
B. Commercial Banks in India
C. Co-operative Banks in India
D. Regional Rural Banks in India

ANSWERS

1	2	3	4	5	6	7	8	9	10
B	B	A	D	B	B	C	D	C	B
11	**12**	**13**	**14**	**15**	**16**	**17**	**18**	**19**	**20**
D	A	C	A	C	C	A	D	A	C
21	**22**	**23**	**24**	**25**	**26**	**27**	**28**	**29**	**30**
D	C	B	A	C	C	C	C	B	D
31	**32**	**33**	**34**	**35**	**36**	**37**	**38**	**39**	**40**
A	D	A	B	B	C	D	C	C	A
41	**42**	**43**	**44**	**45**	**46**	**47**	**48**	**49**	**50**
A	C	C	B	A	B	D	B	D	B
51	**52**	**53**	**54**	**55**	**56**	**57**	**58**	**59**	**60**
A	D	B	B	B	C	A	D	B	A

61	62	63	64	65	66	67	68	69	70
A	B	C	B	D	A	A	A	D	A
71	72	73	74	75	76	77	78	79	80
*	C	B	A	C	A	D	B	B	D
81	82	83	84	85	86	87	88	89	90
A	A	D	C	D	D	C	B	C	B
91	92	93	94	95	96	97	98	99	100
B	A	C	C	D	A	A	B	B	D

EXPLANATORY ANSWERS

1. Accounting Standard 3 (Revised) issued by Institute of Chartered Accounts of India has made it mandatory for listed companies and other enterprises whose turnover exceeds ₹ 50 crore to prepare and present the Statement of Changes in Financial Position along with the Financial Statement Realising the importance of such a statement, a number of companies in India have started providing an analysis of their funds and cash flow position in their annual reports. Companies who are required to comply with Accounting Standard (Revised), the presentation of cash flow statement has become a part of the financial statements. The Statement of changes in Financial Position presents condensed and summarised information (prepared from data collected from Income Statement and Balance Sheet) which is not readily available in these statements. In fact the statement of changes in Financial Position in a refined form or an extension of the funds flow or cash flow statement. It is more informative and comprehensive in indicating the financial position of an enterprise.

2. A firm generating an economic loss faces a tough choice: Should it continue to produce or should it shut down its operation? To make this decision, we need to add another variable to our discussion of economic profits and losses: average variable cost, Variable costs are costs that vary with output—for example, wages, raw material, transportation, and electricity. If a firm cannot generate enough revenues to cover its variable costs, it will have larger losses if it operates than if it shuts down (when losses are equal to fixed costs). That is, the firm will shut down if its total revenue ($p \times q$) is less than its variable costs (VC). If we divide $p \times q$ by q, we get p, and if we divide VC by q we get AVC, so if $p <$ AVC, a profit-maximizing firm will shut down. Thus, a firm will not produce at all unless the price is greater than its average variable cost.

3. 'Sale and Lease-back' arrangements provide the advantage of better liquidity, since it enables the lessee to make a sale of the asset owned to the prospective lessor, and then take the asset back on lease. This helps a lessee-firm to overcome a liquidity crunch by being in a position to sell and realize cash. This helps overcome working capital crises.

4. **Market Stabilization Scheme (MSS):** This instrument for monetary management was introduced in 2004. Surplus liquidity of a more enduring nature arising from large capital inflows is absorbed through sale of short-dated government securities and treasury bills. The cash so mobilized is held in a separate government account with the Reserve Bank.

5. Offer and acceptance are two very important elements, among other things, which constitute a contract. In fact, the making of a contract consists the proposal or offer by the proposer and the acceptance of the proposal or offer by the person to whom the said proposal is made. The contract becomes complete as soon as the acceptance is made and communicated to the proposer. An offer and its acceptance by the person to whom such offer is made becomes an agreement under the Law of Contract.

Offer and acceptance which are essential elements of a contract must be absolutely clear and unambiguous. In order to see the sustainability of offer and acceptance from legal angle, one has to see whether the offer and acceptance are founded on three components, namely, certainty, commitment and communication. If any of these components is missing, either in the offer or in the acceptance, the validity of a contract may be open to question.

6. **World Bank Group:** The World Bank Group consists of five institutions: The International Bank for Reconstruction and Development (IBRD), the International Development Association (IDA), the International Finance Corporation (IFC), the International Centre for Settlement of Investment Disputes (ICSID), and the Multilateral Investment Guarantee Agency (MIGA). IBRD and IDA together are known as the World Bank. The term World Bank Group refers collectively to all five of the institutions. Although each institution has a distinct purpose, history and set of founding documents, they have a common commitment to reducing poverty, increasing shared prosperity, and promoting sustainable development.

IBRD: The International Bank for Reconstruction and Development aims to reduce poverty in middle-income countries and creditworthy poorer countries by promoting sustainable development through loans, guarantees, risk management products, and analytical and advisory services. Established in 1944 as the original institution of the World Bank Group, IBRD is structured like a cooperative that is owned and operated for the benefit of its 188 member countries. IBRD raises most of its funds on the world's financial markets and has become one of the most established borrowers since issuing its first bond in 1947. The income that IBRD has generated over the years has allowed it to fund development activities and to ensure its financial strength, which enables it to borrow at low cost and offer clients good borrowing terms.

ICSID: The International Centre for Settlement of Investment Disputes provides international facilities for conciliation and arbitration of investment disputes.

IDA: The International Development Association is the part of the World Bank that helps the world's poorest countries. Established in 1960, IDA aims to reduce poverty by providing loans (called 'credits'), grants and guarantees for programs that boost economic growth, reduce inequalities, and improve people's living conditions. IBRD and IDA share the same staff and headquarters and evaluate projects with the same rigorous standards.

IFC: The International Finance Corporation is the largest global development institution focused exclusively on the private sector. It helps developing countries achieve sustainable growth by financing investment, mobilizing capital in international financial markets, and providing advisory services to businesses and governments.

MIGA: The Multilateral Investment Guarantee Agency was created in 1988 to promote foreign direct investment into developing countries to support economic growth, reduce poverty and improve people's lives. MIGA fulfills this mandate by offering political risk insurance and credit enhancement to investors and lenders.

7. Skimming price is one of the strategies used by a firm when it introduces a new product in the market. In this strategy, the firm charges a very high price for the product and, later, gradually reduces the price. The reason for using this strategy is that the firm has incurred

a substantial cost on development of the new product, and, before the competitors enter the market, the firm wants to take back the development cost. Once competition picks up in the market, the firm gradually reduces price. Though the sale volume would be low when skimming price is charged, the profit margin being high, the firm would be able to recoup its development cost.

8. Since the coefficient of correlation is the G.M. between the regression coefficients, therefore,

$$r^2 = 0.8 \times 0.2 = 0.16$$

$$\therefore \quad r = \pm\, 0.4$$

Since r has the same sign as the two regression coefficients, so r must be –ve.

Hence, r = –0.4.

9. SWIFT stands for: Society for Worldwide Interbank Financial Telecommunications. SWIFT is a Cooperative Society registered in May 1973 in Brussels, Belgium. In an era of information technology SWIFT offers unique message processing services and provides a very fast, accurate and authenticated transfer of financial messages on global basis. It is a cooperative society of international banks and operates a computerized telecommunication system, which allows rapid, economical, secure and accurate transmission system for essential financial data. SWIFT services enable the retail as well as corporate customers to transfer funds around the world.

11. Issue price ₹ 95

$$K_P = \frac{DIV}{P_0} = \frac{10}{95} = 0.1053 \text{ or } 10.53\%.$$

12. Securities premium, similar to share capital, can't be returned to the shareholders. However, Section 52 of the Companies Act, 2013 provides that the balance in the securities premium account can be utilized for the following purposes:

1. Issuing fully paid bonus shares.
2. Writing off the preliminary expenses of the company.
3. Writing off the expenses of, or commission paid or discount allowed on, an issue of shares or debenture of the company.
4. Providing for the premium payable on the redemption of redeembale preference shares or debentures of the company.

14. The relationship between price, elasticity and marginal revenue is given as follows:

$$MR = P\left(1 - \frac{1}{e_d}\right)$$

$$= 10\left(1 - \frac{1}{2}\right) = 10\left(\frac{2-1}{2}\right) = 5.$$

15. Dumping is a form of price discrimination. Under dumping the international company charges different prices for the same product in different markets. Dumping means selling the products at below the cost of production or at below the on going price in the market. Consequently, the imported goods are sold at prices so low as to be detrimental to local producers of the same kind of merchandise.

Types of Dumping

- *Sporadic dumping:* Sporadic dumping occurs when an international company sells its unsold inventories in a foreign country to get rid of them.
- *Predatory dumping:* Predatory dumping is selling the product in a foreign market at a loss as a strategy of entering the market. Zenith uses this strategy for selling televisions and computers.
- *Persistent dumping:* Persistent dumping involves consistently selling the product at lower prices in one market than in other markets. Japan sells its electronic products at high prices in Japan and sells the same products consistently at lower prices in the USA and India.
- *Reverse dumping:* Under reverse dumping the product is sold at a high price in international markets and at a low price in the domestic market.

16. Giffen Paradox: The Positively Slopped Demand Curve: If the commodity in question is an inferior good, the increase in real income resulting from the reduction in its price will lead the consumer to purchase less, not more, of the commodity.

Thus, the income effect will be negative while the substitution effect continues to be positive to lead the consumer to purchase more of the commodity when its price falls. For most of the inferior goods, the positive substitution effect will be more than offset the negative income effect so that the demand curve is negatively sloped.

However, in the very rare case when the consumer spends so much on the inferior commodity that the strong negative income effect overwhelms the positive substitution effect the quantity demanded of the commodity will fall when its price falls and rise when its price rises.

In other words, the demand curve in this case will be positively sloped. The commodity in question is then called a Giffen goods, after the 19th century English economist Robert Giffen, who first discussed it. This is what is called Giffen Paradox that makes the demand curve to have a positive slope.

18. Excess capacity is a long-run concept. Excess capacity, broadly speaking, *measures the difference between least cost output and the profit-maximizing output;* least cost output corresponds to the minimum point on the LAC curve and the profit maximising output corresponds to that point where MR = MC.

Excess Capacity in Perfect Competition: In perfect competition, due to free entry and exit of firms, normal profit are earned in the long-run. There is no excess capacity as the firm earns normal profit and stays at the minimum point of LAC curve (Fig.) That is, the least cost output coincides with the profit maximising output *i.e.*, $X_c = X_e$. It is shown in fig.

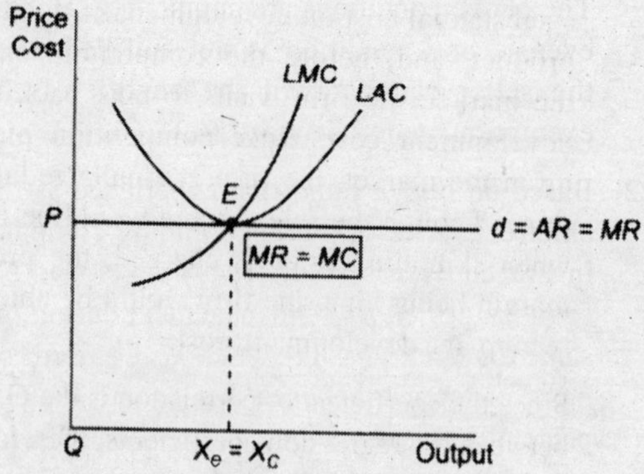

Fig. *Long-run Equilibrium Under Perfect Competition: Case of Zero Excess Capacity*

20. Exemption under Section 54: When an individual sells a residential property and buys another residential property, he will be eligible for exemption under Section 54. Conditions to avail the benefit of exemption under Section 54 includes:

- The tax payer (i.e., seller) needs to be an individual or HUF. Thus, firms, LLP's and companies cannot utilize the benefits of this section.
- Asset needs to be classified as a long-term capital asset.
- The asset sold is a Residential House. Income from such a house should be chargeable as Income from House Property.
- The seller should purchase a residential house either 1 year before the date of sale/ transfer or 2 years after the date of sale/ transfer. In case the seller is constructing a house, the seller has an extended time, i.e., the seller will have to construct the residential house within 3 years from the date of sale/transfer. In case of compulsory acquisition, the period of acquisition or construction will be determined from the date of receipt of compensation (whether original or additional compensation).
- The new residential house should be in India. The seller cannot buy or purchase a residential house abroad and claim the exemption.

The above conditions are cumulative. Hence, even if one condition is not fulfilled, then the seller cannot avail the benefit of the exemption under Section 54.

22. Based on his vast and rich experience as the chief executive of a French mining company in France, Henri Fayol (1949) developed his fourteen principles of management during the same time period as Frederick W. Taylor. The basic difference between Taylor and Fayol's principles of management was that Taylor was concerned with management at the shop level and used the scientific method, Fayol who was a practitioner, was concerned with the activities of all managers. His management thought is known as *'administrative management'* and he is considered as the *'father of the administrative management.'* Following are the widely talked and discussed fourteen principles of management developed by Henri Fayol:

1. **Division of Work:** Sepecialization of labour increases output by making employees more efficient.
2. **Authority:** Managers must be given authority which, in turn, gives them right to give orders. However, along with authority must go responsibility too.
3. **Discipline:** Employees must obey and respect the rules that govern the organization. This helps an organization run smoothly.
4. **Unity of Command:** Every employee should receive orders from only one superior.
5. **Unity of Direction:** The efforts of each employee in the organization having the same objective should be directed by one manager in the same direction.
6. **Subordination of Individual Interests to General Interests:** The interests of the organization as a whole should be above the interests of the individual employees.
7. **Remuneration:** Employees should be paid fair remuneration for the services rendered by them.
8. **Centralization:** A proper proportion should be evolved between involving the employees in decision-making activity (decentralization) and decision made by the management (centralization).
9. **Scalar Chain:** Communication should follow from the top management to the lowest ranks of the employees.
10. **Order:** Both people and materials should be in the right place at the right time.
11. **Equity:** Managers should be fair and kind to their subordinates.
12. **Stability of Tenure of Personnel:** Management should make proper personnel planning to ensure that replacements are available to fill vacancies.
13. **Initiative:** Employees should be allowed and encouraged to initiate the preparation of plans.
14. ***Esprit de corps:*** Promoting team spirit will build harmony and unity within the organization. The team spirit is the key to organizational success.

Based on his above *'Fourteen Principles of Managemnet,'* Henri Fayol regarded the basic elements of management as the functions of—planning, organizing, commanding, coordinating, and controlling.

24. Brainstorming was developed by A.F. Osborn, an advertising executive, to increase creativity. Brainstorming is used to help groups generate multiple ideas and alternatives for solving problems. This technique is effective because it helps reduce interference caused by critical and judgmental reactions to one's ideas from other group members.

When brainstorming, a group is convened, and the problem at hand is reviewed. Individual members then are asked to silently generate ideas/alternatives for solving the problem. Silent idea generation is recommended over the practice of having group members randomly shout out their ideas because it leads to a greater number of unique ideas. Next, these ideas/alternatives are solicited and written on a board or flip chart. A recent study suggests that managers or team leaders may want to collect the brainstormed ideas anonymously. Results demonstrated that more controversial ideas and more nonredundant ideas were generated by anonymous than nonanoymous brainstorming groups. Finally, a second session is used to critique and evaluate the alternatives.

25. Transfer of Capital Redemption Reserve
= Nominal value of preference shares to be redeemed – proceeds from issue of shares
= 2,00,000 – (80,000 – 80,000 × 10%)
= 2,00,000 – (80,000 – 8,000)
= 2,00,000 – 72,000 = 1,28,000.

26. The Right to Information Bill was introduced in the Lok Sabha in December 2004. It was passed by both houses of Parliament in May 2005. The assent of the President was received on 15th June and the Act was notified in The Gazette of India on 21st June. The Right to Information Act has become operational by the 12th October, 2005 after the completion of 120 days from the date of Presidential assent. The Freedom of Information Act passed by Parliament in 2002 has been repealed.

The Right to Information Act (RTI Act) will cover all levels of government-Centre, State, district and local-self governing bodies like Panchayats and Municipal bodies. It will also cover non-governmental organisations, i.e., NGOs and other private bodies—that are financed substantially with the public funds provided by the government. This means every citizen has the right to put in an application requesting information or copies of records held by these bodies and such information should be given by the concerned body.

The citizens' right to information is not explicitly mentioned in the Fundamental Rights chapter of the Constitution. But in many cases, the Supreme Court of India has declared that the fundamental right to life and liberty [Art. 21] and the fundamental right to freedom of speech and expression [Art. 19(1)] include every citizen's fundamental right to access information. Parliament passed the RTI Act to enable all citizens to use their fundamental right to access information from public bodies.

The main objectives of the RTI Act are:

- to promote transparency and accountability in the working of every public authority; and
- to set-up a practical regime for giving citizens access to information that is under the control of public authorities.

Definition of Information

- Information means material in any form including records, documents, memos, e-mails, opinions, advices, press releases, circulars, orders, logbooks, contracts, reports, papers, samples, models, data material held in any electronic form; and
- Information relating to any private body which can be accessed by a public authority under any other law for the time being in force.

Definition of Record

- Any document, manuscript or file;
- Any microfilm, microfiche and facsimile copy of a document;
- Any reproduction of image or images embodied in such micro-film (whether enlarged or not); and
- Any other material produced by a computer or any other device.

Definition of Right to Information: Right to information accessible under this Act which is held by or under the control of any public authority and includes the right to:

- Inspection of work, documents, records;
- Taking notes, extracts or certified copies of documents or records;
- Taking certified samples of material; and

- Obtaining information in the form of diskettes, floppies, tapes, video cassettes or in any other electronic mode or through printouts where such information is stored in a computer or in any other device.

One of the guiding principles of the RTI Act is—"information" which cannot be denied to Parliament or a State Legislature shall not be denied to any person".

28. Objectives of the Competition Act 2002 are:

1. To protect the interests of the consumers by providing them good products and services at reasonable prices.
2. To promote healthy competition in the Indian market.
3. To prevent the interests of the smaller companies or prevent the abuse of dominant position in the market.
4. To prevent those practices which have adverse impact on competition in the Indian markets.
5. To ensure freedom of trade in Indian markets.
6. To regulate the operation and activities of combinations (acquisitions, mergers and amalgamation).

30. While the complexities of supply chains have increased in recent years, the basic structures of supply chains are fairly straightforward, as shown in Figure. The figure shows three basic supply chain structures, divided into two types: indirect and direct supply chains. Indirect supply chains utilize one or more marketing intermediaries to get products from the producer to the consumer. The number of intermediaries can vary widely depending on the product type and place strategy. The trend in recent years has been to use fewer intermediaries as power and control has shifted to retailers who have begun taking on their own wholesaling operations. Traditional indirect supply chains include wholesalers, while others only include a retailer. The tendency for retailers to bring wholesaling in-house has led to a decline in the number of independent wholesalers.

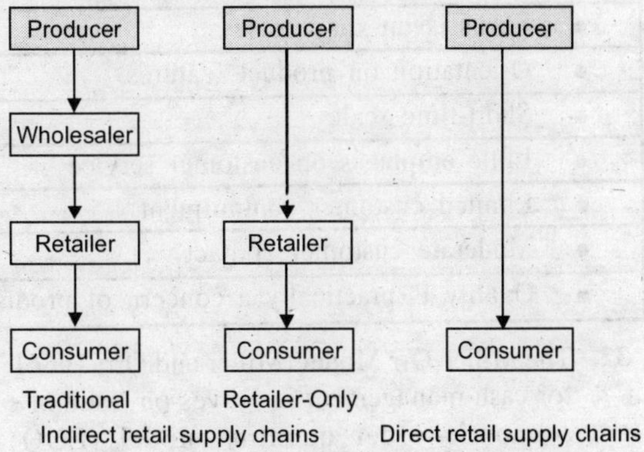

Fig. *Comparison between Indirect and Direct Retail Supply Chains*

Producers use direct retail supply chains when selling directly to consumers. Online retailing had driven growth in direct supply chains that bypass physical stores and sell directly to consumers through their websites.

31. Relationship marketing (RM) refers to all marketing activities directed toward establishing, developing and maintaining successful relational exchanges. It is widely held that the majority of marketers are in the transactional, and not in the relationship, mode. Transactional marketing (TM) fundamentally aims at viewing sales as a discrete terminating activity. Relationship marketing on the other hand, treats sales as a continuous relationship that goes beyond the sale. Experts share that TM's orientation is on product features over a short-term period, while RM's orientation is on product benefits over a long-term period. The transactional mode pays little attention to customer service and offers limited commitment to the customers. On the other hand, the relationship mode pays greater attention to customer service and commitment. Quality is primarily a concern for production in the former, whereas, quality is the concern of all in the latter. Table below provides the differences between Transactional and Relationship Marketing.

Table : *Difference between Transactional and Relationship Marketing*

Transactional Marketing	Relationship Marketing
• Focus is on single sales	• Focus is on customer retention
• Orientation on product features	• Orientation on product benefits
• Short-time scale	• Long-time scale
• Little emphasis on customer service	• High customer service emphasis
• Limited customer commitment	• High customer commitment
• Moderate customer contact	• High customer contact
• Quality is practically a concern of production	• Quality is the concern of all

32. The Miller-Orr Model (Miller and Orr, 1966), for cash management improves on Baumol's economic order quantity model (EOQ) methodology in significant ways. Miller and Orr start with the assumption that the firm has only two forms of assets: cash and marketable securities. The model allows for cash balance movement in both positive and negative directions and it can state the optimal cash balance as a range of values, rather than a single-point estimate. This makes the model especially useful for firms with unpredictable day-to-day cash inflows and outflows.

While the Miller-Orr model is an improvement over the EOQ model, it too makes some assumptions. The most important is the assumption that cash flows are random, which in many cases is not completely valid. Under certain circumstances and at particular times of the year, consecutive periods' cash flows may be dependent upon one another, the volatility of net cash flow may sharply increase, or cash balances may demonstrate a definite trend. The frequency and extent of these events will affect the Miller-Orr model's effectiveness. Actual tests using daily cash flow for various firms indicate that the model minimizes cash holding costs as well as or better than the intuitive decisions of these firms' financial managers. However, others studies have shown that simple rules of thumb have performed just as well. Still, the Miller-Orr model is valuable because of the insight it offers concerning the forces that influence a firm's optimal cash balance.

34. Material Cost Variance = Standard Cost for Actual Output – Actual Cost
= (SP × SQ) – (AP × AQ)
= (5 × 10) – (6 × 12)
= 50 – 72 = ₹ 22 (Unfavourable or Adverse).

35. In case of sale of goods, the doctrine 'caveat emptor' means 'let the buyer beware'. When sellers display their goods in the open market, it is for the buyers to make a proper selection of the goods. If the goods turn out to be defective, the buyer cannot hold the seller liable. The seller is in no way responsible for the bad selection of the buyer. The seller is not bound to disclose the defects in the goods which he is selling. It is the duty of the buyer to satisfy himself before buying the goods that the goods will serve the purpose for which they are being bought. If the goods turn out to be defective or do not serve his (buyer) purpose or if he depends on his own skill or judgement, the buyer cannot hold the seller responsible. It is contained in Section 16 of the Sale of Goods Acts, 1930 which reads as under: "Subject to the provisions of this Act and any other law for the time being in force, there is no implied warranty on condition as to the quality or fitness for any particular purpose of goods supplied under a contract of sale."

Birds's Eye View: Doctrine of caveat emptor [Section 16(1)]

- Caveat emptor is a Latin word which means 'let the buyer beware'.
- The buyer must take care of his own purpose while purchasing the goods.

- If the buyer makes a wrong choice of goods, he cannot make the seller responsible and ask compensation.
- Exceptions to the rule 'caveat emptor' are:
  - Fitness for buyer's purpose.
  - Sale under patent or trade name.
  - Merchantable quality.
  - Usage of trade.
  - Misrepresentation or fraud.
  - Goods by sample.
  - Goods by sample as well as description.
  - Goods by quality or fitness.

37. According to Section 13 of Negotiable Instrument Act, 1881, "Negotiable instrument means a promissory note, a bill of exchange or a cheque payable either to order or to bearer, whether the word 'orderf' or 'bearer' appear on the instrument or not."

According to Justice Willis, "A negotiable instrument is one, the property in which is acquired by anyone who takes it bonafide and for value notwithstanding any defects of the title in the person from whom he took it."

Thus, the term, negotiable instrument means a written document which creates a right in favour of some person and which is freely transferable. The Act mentions only these three instruments such as a promissory note, a bill of exchange and cheque. However other similar instruments satisfying the conditions of the act can also be included in the ambit of negotiable instruments.

Negotiable instrument is such instrument–a written document for the transfer of money value or for the settlement of payment by the exchange of such written document called instrument of payment. Cheque, demand draft, bills of exchange, promissory notes, hundi and similar such instruments (written documents) are the most frequently used negotiable instruments. Negotiability of these instruments means that these can be transferred or endorsed from one party to another party for the settlement of monetary claims.

38. Section 9 of the Consumer Protection Act advocates three-tier redressal of consumer disputes at the national, state and the district levels.

District Consumer Disputes Redressal Forum (DCDRF): These are also known as district forums. These forums are established by the state government in every district to deal with cases of complaints valuing up to ₹ 5 lakh. It has the power of a civil court.

State Consumer Disputes Redressal Commission (SCDRC): It is the apex body for consumer redressal in states. It has been established in each state and union territory. State commissions could entertain complaints up to INR 10 million. In rare cases, it has the power to take the cases pending at a District Forum in its own hands.

National Consumer Disputes Redressal Commission (NCDRC): The national commission has been established by the central government. It is the highest forum for consumer disputes Redressal in the country. It can entertain cases where the value of claims exceeds ₹ 20 lakh. It has both appellate and revisional jurisdiction.

41. With reference to the definition of Shani and Chalasani, relationship marketing is "an integrated effort to identify, maintain, and build up a network with individual consumers and to continuously strengthen the network for the mutual benefit of both sides, through interactive, individualized, and value-added contacts over a long period of time". Thus the relationship marketing is performed to benefit both the company and its customers. Through it, an increasing fraction of each customer's business is received. It aims at building long term, mutually satisfying relations with customers, suppliers and distributors with the objective to earn and retain their long-term preference and businesses (Armstrong and Kotler).

42. **Statutory Audit:** An audit which is undertaken under any specific statute or Act is called 'statutory audit'. The term 'statutory' signifies anything regulated by laws of the state. Accordingly, a statutory audit is the official inspection of an organisation's books accounts by an independent body as per the requirements of a statute. The objective of this audit is to ensure fair and accurate representations of the financial statements of an entity. The forms of organisations for which audit is mandatory in India under any statute are as follows:

Statutory Audit is Applicable for	Relevant Statute
Joint Stock Companies	Companies Act, 2013
Banking Companies	Banking Regulations Act, 1949
Electricity Companies	Electric Supply Act, 1948
Co-operative Societies	Co-operative Societies Act, 1912
Trusts	Respective State Acts

Non-statutory Audit: A non-statutory audit is such an audit which is neither required by the law nor by any regulatory authority. They are usually carried out at the will of an organisation or in some cases to adhere to the internal policies of the organisation. This audit is often used by sole proprietors, limited and unlimited liability partnerships, associations, clubs, charitable trusts etc. in order to enhance their reliability.

43. Activity Based Costing refers to an approach to the costing and monitoring of activities, which involves tracing resource consumption and costing final outputs. Resources are assigned to activities, and activities to cost objects, based on consumption estimates. The latter utilise Cost Drivers to attach activity costs to outputs.

Activity Based Costing is a technique which involves identification of costs with each cost driving activity and making it as the basis of apportionment of costs over different cost objects/jobs/products/customers or services.

Absorbing Overheads into the cost of product or service under Activity Based Costing involves the following steps:

- Identification of various activities within the organisation.
- Estimation of the cost of each activity.
- Apportionment of cost of support activities across primary activities on suitable basis.
- Determination of Activity Cost Drivers for each activity or Cost Pool.
- Calculation of Activity Cost Driver Rate.
- Assigning of Overheads to cost objects on the basis of Activity Cost Driver Rate.

44. Definition: Hedge fund is a private investment partnership and funds pool that uses varied and complex proprietary strategies and invests or trades in complex products, including listed and unlisted derivatives.

Put simply, a hedge fund is a pool of money that takes both short and long positions, buys and sells equities, initiates arbitrage, and trades bonds, currencies, convertible securities, commodities and derivative products to generate returns at reduced risk. As the name suggests, the fund tries to hedge risks to investor's capital against market volatility by employing alternative investment approaches.

Description: Hedge fund investors typically include high net worth individuals (HNIs) and families, endowments and pension funds, insurance companies, and banks. These funds work either as private investment partnerships or offshore investment corporations. They are not required to be registered with the securities markets regulator and are not subject to the reporting requirements, including periodic disclosure of NAVs.

There are many strategies a hedge fund may use to generate returns. One such strategy is global macros, where the fund takes long and short positions in large financial markets based on the views influenced by economic trends. Then there are funds that work on market-neutral strategies. Here, the goal of the fund manager is to minimise market risks by investing in long/short equity funds, convertible bonds, arbitrage funds, and fixed income products.

Another type includes event-driven funds that invest in stocks to take advantage of price movements generated by corporate events. Merger arbitrage funds and distressed asset funds fall into this category.

46. Since the population is large sized, we have

$$SE_{\overline{X}} = \frac{\sigma}{\sqrt{n}}$$

$$\therefore \quad n = \left(\frac{\sigma}{SE_{\overline{X}}}\right)^2 = \left(\frac{40}{8}\right)^2 = 25.$$

47. Secondary data is a published data by some other agency. If the investigator uses already collected and published data (or unpublished) it is secondary data for him.

Meaning: As the name 'Secondary Data' indicates, it is used for a second time but not first time. It implies a collected, used and published data. It is defined by W.A. Neiswanger as "A secondary source is a publication reporting data which has been gathered by other authorities and for which others are responsible". Usually data once collected is made available through internal records, reports, personal records etc.

Sources of secondary data can be broadly classified into two: Published sources and Unpublished sources.

1. **Government Publications:** Various Ministries and Departments of the Government publish data regularly on number of subjects such as national income, exports, foreign exchange reserves, industrial production etc. Some of these are annual others are monthly statistics and some are weekly. Ex. Important publications of the Government of India are Statistical Abstract of India (Annual) Agricultural Statistics etc.
2. **Publications by International Organisations:** International organisations such as United Nations Organization, World Bank, IMF, WTO, WHO etc. collect and publish reliable data on various topics regularly, which is a greatest source of secondary data.
3. **Reports of Committees and Commissions:** Special committees are appointed internationally and nationally by the governments or organizations to conduct special studies. Such committees submit detailed reports which contain valuable data and rich information. Ex. Basele's Committee Report on financial sector reforms, Finance Commission Report etc.
4. **Trading, Banking and Non-Trade Organisations:** In India LIC, ECGC, RBI, SEBI etc., publish monthly and annual reports along with relevant data, which are reliable and useful for any purpose of statistical studies.
5. **Data Published by Chambers of Commerce and Associations:** Chambers of Commerce, Trade Associations, Bankers Associations, Export Promotion Councils etc. collect data and publish regularly.
6. **Journals and News Papers:** News agencies, newspapers, journals etc. also publish annual and monthly reports with supportive data. The Hindu paper publishes annual reports on various topics. Prominent among them are survey of industries, agriculture etc. Economic and Political Weekly publishes monthly and annual reports regularly.
7. **Universities, Research Organizations and other Institutions:** Universities such as Oxford, Andhra, Osmania, Central University, JNU etc. are great source of data collected by research scholars on various topics. Research and training institutions such as Indian Institute of Foreign Trade, Indian Institute of Packaging also publish research data regularly.
8. **Others:** Market surveys, project reports, research papers published by authors, surveys conducted by individuals and institutions are great source of secondary data.
9. **Internet:** Internet became the largest single supplier of the latest information and data on different subjects through web sites.

10. **Books:** Ancient works stored in libraries are great source of information. Even today there are researchers who refer to ancient scriptures for some information.

11. **Institutions:** Every institution big or small, trade or non-trade, maintains internal records where data is recorded regularly. This is a good source of secondary data.

48. The N.K. Mitra Committee on Investor Protection: This Committee chaired by N.K. Mitra submitted its report on investor protection, in April, 2001, with the following recommendations:

(*i*) There is a need for a specific Act to protect investor interest. The Act should codify, amend and consolidate laws and practices for the purpose of protecting investors interest in corporate investment.

(*ii*) Establishment of a judicial forum and award of compensation for aggrieved investors.

(*iii*) Investor Education and Protection Fund which is under the Companies Act should be shifted to the SEBI Act and be administered by SEBI.

(*iv*) SEBI should be the only capital market regulator, clothed with the powers of investigation.

(*v*) The regulator, SEBI should require all IPOs to be insured under third party insurance with differential premium based on the risk study by the insurance company.

49. Neo-Classical Theory: It has introduced the human relations approach in the classical theory of organisation. The main propositions of this theory are:

(*i*) The organisation in general is a social system composed of several interacting parts.

(*ii*) The social environments on the job affect people and are also affected by them.

(*iii*) Besides formal organisation, informal organisation also exists and it affects and is affected by formal organisation.

52. Consumer behaviour consists of all the activities people undertake when obtaining, consuming and disposing of products and services. Studying consumer behaviour involves looking at what influences people to behave in particular ways when obtaining products, using them and disposing of them. Understanding the way people think when they go about their purchasing behaviour is a key factor in successful marketing. The motivations, decision-making processes and post-purchase behaviour of consumers are useful when seeking to persuade people to choose one product rather than another, and to encourage people to recommend products to their friends.

53. $\text{EOQ} = \sqrt{\dfrac{2AB}{CS}}$

Where, A = annual consumption

B = ordinary cost per order

CS = carrying cost per unit per annum

$\therefore \text{EOQ} = \sqrt{\dfrac{2 \times 90000 \times 300}{0.6}} = 9487$ units.

54. According to Wilson, "Goodwill has been very ably divided into three types—cat, dog and rat—in view of the peculiar habits of these three animals. The cat tends to stick to the abode, cat goodwill is therefore that which will adhere to the business which is being transferred and is the most valuable. The dog follows his master, dog goodwill is difficult to transfer and is correspondingly less valuable. The rat is a migrant, rat goodwill is practically valuless, as it represents those customers who have no specialities either to the business or its properties and who may be here today and gone tomorrow. Summed up, cat goodwill is adherent; dog personal and rat fugitive. Adherent goodwill is only valuable as attaching to the business; personal goodwill is unsaleable, fugitive goodwill is only valuable in that as one fugitive goes another may arrive."

60. Non-parametric tests vs. Parametric tests: Tests appropriate for analyzing ordinal and nominal data are called non-parametric tests. In contrast, tests for analyzing interval or ratio scale are called parametric tests. Parametric tests (z, t or F) require that certain assumptions be valid concerning the population from where the samples were drawn while non-parametric require few assumptions.Tests involving ranks of data are non-parametric. Non-parametric tests are not as powerful as parametric statistics and tend to err on the conservative side.

Examples of Non-parametric tests:

- **Chi-square test:** Test of hypothesis to determine if categorical data shows dependency or if two classifications are independent.
- **One sample sign test:** Test of hypothesis related single value for given data.
- **Two sample sign test, Fisher-Irwin test, Rank sum test (Wilcoxon-Mann-Whitney test i.e., U test, Kruskal-Wallis test i.e., H test), Wilcoxon Matched pairs test/Signed Rank test:** Test of hypothesis related no difference among two or more sets of data.
- **Charles Spearman's rank correlation, Kendall's Coefficient of concordance:** Test of hypotheses related to relationship between variables.
- **Kruskal-Wallis test:** Test of hypothesis between more than two sets of data are analogous to ANOVA in parametric test.

62. If all the items increase by 5, average (arithmetic mean) will also increase by 5.

63. The value of the SDR is the sum of the values of specified amounts of the four currencies that satisfy the following criteria:

(*i*) they are issued by IMF members, or by monetary unions that include IMF members, that have the largest value of exports of goods and services; and

(*ii*) they have been deemed by the IMF to be freely usable currencies.

These four currencies currently are the U.S. dolalr, the Euro, the Japanese Yen, and the Pound sterling. The SDR value is calculated daily in terms of the U.S. dollar, using the mid-point of the buying and selling spot exchange rates for each currency against the US dollar at noon on the London exchange market as determined by the Bank of England.

Table: *Calculation of the SDR Value*

Currency	Initial weight (in per cent)
Euro	34
Japanese yen	11
Pound sterling	11
US dollar	44
SDR	

64. The Reserve Bank of India has licensed four major credit information organization to accumulate data and provide credit scores for the people of the country. These four organizations are Credit Information Bureau of India Limited (CIBIL), CRIF High Mark, Equifax and Experian. CIBIL is oldest organization and its scores are deemed to be the most acceptable by lenders. It started its operation in 2000 the rest of the three companies received licenses to operate in 2010.

A CIBIL score ranges between 300 and 900 where 900 is considered to be the best score. The credit score of an individual is built over a period of 18 to 36 months. A credit history which is less than 6 months old will have a CIBIL score of 0 while people with no credit history at all will show a CIBIL score of –1.

65. Forms of Return of Income

Forms–These forms are given below:

New ITR Forms	Subject
ITR 1 (*i.e.,* SAHAJ)	For individuals having income from salary, one house property (excluding loss brought forward from previous years) and income from other sources (not being loss and not being winnings from lottery and income from race horses).

New ITR Forms	Subject
ITR 2	For individuals and HUF's not having business/professional income.
ITR 3	For individuals/HUF's being partners in firms and not carrying out business or profession under any proprietorship.
ITR 4	For individuals and HUF's having income from a proprietary business or profession.
ITR 4S (*i.e.*, Sugam)	For individual/HUFs deriving business income and such income is computed in accordance with special provisions referred to in sections 44AD and 44AE
ITR 5	For firms, AOPs and BOIs or any other person (not being individual or HUF or company or to whom ITR-7 is applicable).
ITR 6	For companies other than companies claiming exemption under section 11.
ITR 7	For persons including companies required to furnish return under section 139(4A)/(4B)/(4C)/(4D).
ITR V	Where the data of the return of income/ fringe benefits in Forms ITR-1, ITR-2, ITR-3, ITR-4, ITR-5 and ITR-6 transmitted electronically without digital signature.

67. The Indian insurance industry is governed by Insurance Act, 1938, General Insurance Business Act, 1972, Life Insurance Corporation Act, 1956 and Insurance Regulatory Development Authority Act, 1999. General Insurance Industry is guided by all the above acts except the Life Insurance Corporation Act, 1956, which is specifically meant for Life business. Indian insurance industry has recently been opened up for private companies, both domestic and foreign. The opening of the insurance sector has been facilitated through IRDA.

The Government of India realized the necessities of setting-up Insurance Regulatory and Development Authority (IRDA) in 1999. The IRDA was set-up to provide for the establishment of an Authority, for protecting the interests of holders of insurance policies, to regulate, promote and insurer orderly growth of the insurance industry and for matters connected therewith or incidental thereto. With the birth of IRDA, the Government amended the Insurance Act, 1938, the Life Insurance Corporation Act, 1956 and the General Insurance Business (Nationalization) Act, 1972 for the sake of proper control at apex level.

Insurance Development and Regulatory Authority (IRDA) exercise the supervisory control or insurance companies and these powers flow from Insurance Act, 1983 as well as from IRDA Act, 1999. IRDA Act, 1999 states: "Subject to the provisions of this Act and any other law for the time being in force, the Authority shall have the duty to regulate, promote and ensure orderly growth of insurance business and reinsurance business." Regulatory and supervisory powers of the authority are wide and pervasive.

68. The content theories implicitly assume that satisfaction leads to improved performance and that dissatisfaction detracts from performance. The Herzberg model is really a theory of job satisfaction, but still it does not deal with the relationship between satisfaction and performance. The Vroom model also largely avoids the relationship between satisfaction and performance. Although satisfaction make an input into Vroom's concept of valence and although the outcomes have performance implications, it was not until Porter and Lawler refined and extended Vroom's model that the relationship between satisfaction and performance was dealt with directly by a motivation model.

Porter and Lawler start with the premise that motivation (effort or force) does not equal satisfaction or performance. Motivation, satisfaction, and performance are all separate variables and relate in ways different from what was traditionally assumed. Figure depicts the multivariable model used to explain the complex relationship that exists between motivation, performance, and satisfaction. It is important, however, that Porter and Lawler point out that effort (force or motivation) does not lead directly to performance. It is dedicated by abilities and traits and by role perceptions. More important in the Porter-Lawler is a significant turn of events from traditional thinking that performance leads to satisfaction.

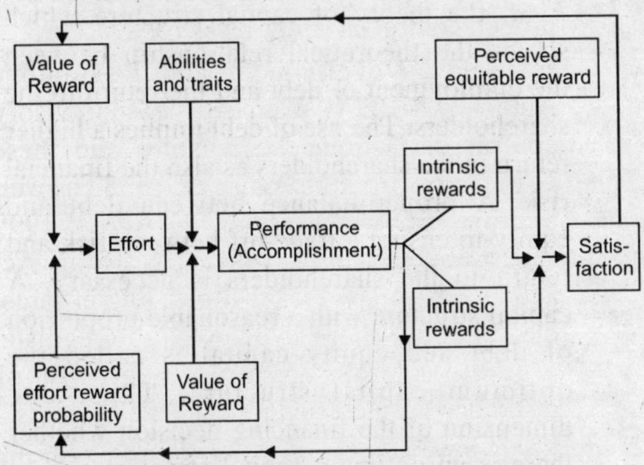

Fig. *Porter-Lawler Motivation Model*

The model has had a fair degree of research support over the years. For example, a recent field study found that effort level and direction of effort are important in explaining individual performance or reward in the relationship between performance and satisfaction. Specially, it was concluded that performance and satisfaction will be more strongly related when rewards are made contingent upon performance than when they are not.

73. Shopping Products: They are purchased after due shopping efforts. The shopping efforts include search and comparison of goods on the basis of price, quality, suitability etc. **Examples:** Furniture, Television, Washing Machine, Music systems.

Characteristics:

(*i*) The shopping products are generally of durable nature;

(*ii*) The unit price as well as profit margin of shopping products is generally high;

(*iii*) Customers compare the prices of products of different companies before making selection.

(*iv*) Purchases of shopping products are generally pre-planned;

(*v*) Lot of persuasive effort is needed to convince the buyers to purchase such products, for this services of retailers are availed.

74. William F. Sharpe and John Linter developed the Capital Asset Pricing Model (CAPM). The model is based on the portfolio theory developed by Harry Markowitz. The model emphasises the risk factor in portfolio theory is a combination of two risks, systematic risk and unsystematic risk. The model suggests that a security's return is directly related to its systematic risk, which cannot be neutralised through diversification. The combination of both types of risks stated above provides the total risk. The total variance of returns is equal to market related variance plus company's specific variance. CAPM explains the behaviour of security prices and provides a mechanism whereby investors could assess the impact of a proposed security investment on the overall portfolio risk and return. CAPM suggests that the prices of securities are determined in such a way that the risk premium or excess returns are proportional to systematic risk, which is indicated by the beta coefficient. The model is used for analysing the risk-return implications of holding securities. CAPM refers to the manner in which securities are valued in line with their anticipated risks and returns. A risk-averse investor prefers to invest in risk-free securities. For a small investor having few securities in his portfolio, the risk is greater. To reduce the unsystematic risk, he must build up well-diversified securities in his portfolio.

75. Customer Life Cycle is typically has 3 phases—Acquisition, Growth and Retention.

Customer Acquisition: Focus is targeting & reaching out to prospects, explaining them about the products and services and on-boarding the customers.

Customer Development/Build/Growth: In this phase organizations leverage the existing relationship for growing the engagement with newly acquired customers or existing customers. So, the focus is both on increasing level of engagement on the existing product or relationship (*i.e.,* spend/balance build on credit card) and identifying customers' needs & soliciting for a right product (*i.e.,* cross sell a credit card to mortgage customers).

Customer Retention: The most valuable customers are the most sought after customers by the competitors. The organizations have to develop strategies to manage and retain the most valuable customers. Acquiring a new customer is 3-5 times more costly, but still organizations are finding difficult to retain their customers.

78. The outcomes of favourable to the event 'sum of two numbers is 8' are (6, 2), (5, 3), (4, 4), (3, 5) and (2, 6). There are 5 in number:

$\therefore$ P (sum of 8) = $\frac{5}{36}$.

79. The law of diminishing marginal returns states that as more of a variable resource is combined with a given amount of another resource, marginal product eventually declines. *The law of diminishing marginal returns is the most important feature of production in the short run.*

81. Step-1 : Higher of Municipal value and Fair Rent in this case it will be higher of 450,000 and 5,00,000, So it will be 5,00,000 (let us call it as A).

Step 2 : Lower of A and Standard Rent so it will be lower of 5,00,000 and 4,80,000, So will be 4,80,000. (let us call it B)

Step 3 : Higher of 'B' and Actual Rent, So it will be Higher of 4,80,000 and 4,20,000. So the GAV will be 4,80,000.

82. Coefficient of Correlation

$$= \frac{\text{Covariance between X and Y}}{\text{SD of X} \times \text{SD of Y}}$$

$$= -\frac{17.8}{6.6 \times 4.2} = -\frac{17.8}{27.72} = -0.642.$$

84. The concern of the financing decision is with the financing-mix or capital structure or leverage. The term capital structure refers to the proportion of debt (fixed-interest sources of financing) and equity capital (variable-dividend securities/source of funds). The financing decision of a firm relates to the choice of the proportion of these sources to finance the investment requirements. There are two aspects of the financing decision. *First,* the theory of capital structure which shows the theoretical relationship between the employment of debt and the return to the shareholders. The use of debt implies a higher return to the shareholders as also the financial risk. A proper balance between debt and equity to ensure a trade-off between risk and return to the shareholders is necessary. A capital structure with a reasonable proportion of debt and equity capital is called the optimum capital structure. Thus, one dimension of the financing decision whether there is an optimum capital structure and in what proportion should funds be raised to maximise the return to the shareholders? The second aspect of the financing decision is the determination of an appropriate capital structure, given the facts of a particular case. Thus, the financing decision covers two interrelated aspects: (1) the capital structure theory, and (2) the capital structure decision.

86. Major Channel Alternatives: Companies can choose from a wide variety of channels for reaching customers - from sales forces to agents, distributors, dealers, direct mail, etc. Most companies now use a mix of channels where each channel reaches a different segment of buyers and delivers the right products to each at the least cost.

Evaluation of the Channel Alternatives:

Each channel alternative can be evaluated against the following criteria:

(*i*) **Economic Criteria:** Each alternative channel design will result in different levels of sales and cost as shown in Figure.

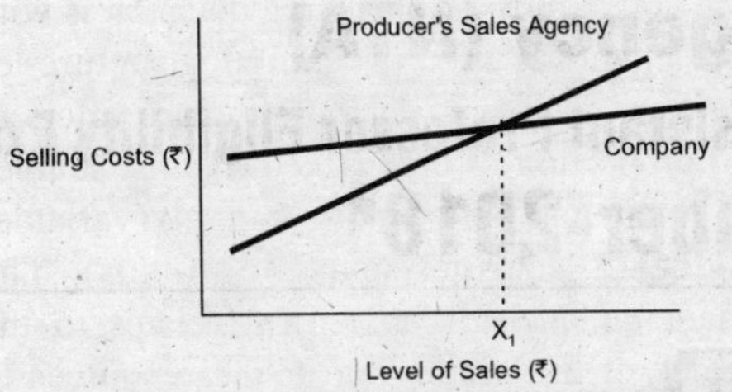

Fig. *Economic Criteria for Channel Alternatives*

For level of sales below X_1 (as shown in the figure above) provider's sales agency will have economic advantage over their own sales force. But when the level of sales increases above the level X_1, the company's sales force will be more economical.

(*ii*) **Control and Adaptive Criteria:** The channel alternatives are evaluated in terms of companies having better control and more adaptable channels.

93. *Value* reflects the sum of the perceived tangible and intangible benefits and costs to customers. It's primarily a combination of quality, service, and price, called the "customer value triad." Value increases with quality and service and decreases with price, although other factors can also play an important role in perceptions of value.

Value is a central marketing concept. Marketing can be seen as the identification, creation, communication, delivery, and monitoring of customer value. *Satisfaction* reflects a person's comparative judgement of a product's perceived performance (or outcome) in relation to expectations. If product performance falls short of expectations, the customer is dissatisfied and disappointed. If it matches expectations, the customer is satisfied–and if it exceeds expectations, the customer is delighted.

95. The required rate of return is

$$= \frac{4.5}{90} + 0.08 = 0.05 + 0.08 = 0.13 = 13\%.$$

97. A currency swap is the simultaneous purchase and sale of a given amount of foreign exchange for two different value dates. Swaps are transacted between international businesses and their banks, between banks, and between governments when it is desirable to move out of one currency into another for a limited period without incurring foreign exchange risk.

Currency swaps between multinationals are frequently used both as a hedge and as a means of securing overseas financing. The swaps may be bilateral or multilateral. They may be simple or highly complex. As a relatively simple example, a French company may have a Brazilian subsidiary that needs more local currency for expansion. Through an investment bank or a broker, the French company locates a British firm whose Brazilian subsidiary has surplus domestic currency. The French company makes the swap by buying the Brazilian cruzados from the British company and simultaneously entering into an agreement to reserve the sale at some future date. Nominal interest rates are agreed upon at the outset.

The swap is a hedge in the sense that foreign currency liability is matched by a similar foreign currency asset. Furthermore, neither loan requires the approval of any government agency, and the cost of funds can be cheaper than funds from alternative sources. Besides, the swap may be one of the few sources open to non-resident companies for securing the use of foreign exchange over a period of time at a fixed rate.

99. A quota is a quantitative restriction on imports. Quotas limit the amount of a product that can be imported into a country over a specified period of time, such as a calendar year. Quotas are a form of non-tariff barrier (NTB), *i.e.,* they are not tariffs but have the same impact in terms of restricting free trade and protecting domestic industries. Quotas restrict the availability of the foreign product in the domestic market and, therefore, provide an advantage to local producers. There are various forms of quotas.

Previous Years' Paper (Solved)

National Testing Agency (NTA)

UGC-NET Junior Research Fellowship & Assistant Professor Eligibility Exam

Commerce, December-2018*

PAPER-II

Note: *This paper contains* ***hundred (100)*** *objective type questions of* ***two (2)*** *marks each.* ***All*** *questions are* ***compulsory.***

1. Which one of the following statements is correct?
   A. The purpose of issuing different types of rules and regulations by SEBI is to bring monetary gains to investors.
   B. SEBI has been constituted under the Securities (Contract and Regulation) Act, 1956.
   C. One of the objectives of setting up SEBI is to protect the interests of investors.
   D. SEBI is constituted from amongst the directors of various stock exchanges.

2. Match the items of List-I with the items of List-II and choose the correct answer from the code given below.

LIST-I	LIST-II
(*a*) Rival Firms	(*i*) External Environments
(*b*) Technology	(*ii*) Social and Cultural Environment
(*c*) Improving Quality	(*iii*) Internal Environment
(*d*) Ethics in Business	(*iv*) Global Environment

Code:

	(*a*)	(*b*)	(*c*)	(*d*)
A.	(*ii*)	(*iii*)	(*iv*)	(*i*)
B.	(*iv*)	(*i*)	(*ii*)	(*iii*)
C.	(*i*)	(*ii*)	(*iii*)	(*iv*)
D.	(*iii*)	(*i*)	(*iv*)	(*ii*)

3. Combined leverage can be used to measure the relationship between:
   A. Sales and EPS B. PAT and EPS
   C. EBIT and EPS C. Sales and EBIT

4. Which among the following is not an internal factor of pricing decision?
   A. Price elasticity as per sales of product
   B. Consumers expectation from company by past pricing
   C. Consumer behaviour for given product
   D. Position of product in product cycle

5. Match the items of List-I with the items of List-II and choose the correct answer from the code given below.

LIST-I	LIST-II
(*a*) Compensation received by an employee from his employer on termination of job	(*i*) Exemption up to specified limit
(*b*) Pension received by the widow of an employee	(*ii*) Profits in lieu of salary
(*c*) Foreign allowance for rendering services abroad	(*iii*) Income from other sources
(*d*) Children hostel allowance	(*iv*) Fully exempt from tax

Code:

	(*a*)	(*b*)	(*c*)	(*d*)
A.	(*ii*)	(*iv*)	(*iii*)	(*i*)
B.	(*ii*)	(*iii*)	(*iv*)	(*i*)
C.	(*iv*)	(*iii*)	(*i*)	(*ii*)
D.	(*iii*)	(*iv*)	(*ii*)	(*i*)

*Held on 22 Dec. 2018.

6. The companies having business in a large number of countries around the world at present are called:

A. Multinational Enterprises (MNEs)
B. Global Corporations (GCs)
C. Transnational Corporations (TNCs)
D. Multinational Corporations (MNCs)

7. Banking Ombudsman Scheme was introduced by RBI with effect from:

A. 2005 B. 1998
C. 2001 D. 1995

8. If a perpendicular on X-axis from the point of intersection of both 'less than' and 'more than' frequency curves is drawn, it gives the value of:

A. Median
B. Mode
C. Third quartile
D. Arithmetic mean

9. Choose the correct code for the following statements being correct or incorrect.

Statement I : An identifiable group of people contributing their efforts towards attainment of goals is called organization.

Statement II: In its broadest sense, organization refers to the relationship between the various factors present in a given endeavour.

Code:

A. Both the statements I and II are incorrect.
B. Both the statements I and II are correct.
C. Statement II is correct, but I is incorrect.
D. Statement I is correct, but II is incorrect.

10. Match the items of List-I with the items of List-II and choose the correct answers from the code given below.

LIST-I	LIST-II
(*a*) Job context	(*i*) Procedures used
(*b*) Job-related tangibles and intangibles	(*ii*) Work schedule
(*c*) Work activities	(*iii*) Work standards
(*d*) Work performance	(*iv*) Services rendered

Code:

	(*a*)	(*b*)	(*c*)	(*d*)
A.	(*ii*)	(*iv*)	(*i*)	(*iii*)
B.	(*iv*)	(*iii*)	(*i*)	(*ii*)
C.	(*iii*)	(*iv*)	(*ii*)	(*i*)
D.	(*i*)	(*iv*)	(*ii*)	(*iii*)

11. Given below are two statements, one labelled as Assertion (A) and the other labelled as Reason (R). Read the statements and choose the correct answer using the code given below.

Assertion (A): There exists excess capacity of the production for the firms if these incur losses.

Reason (R): Their production level has to remain below their economic capacity level.

Code:

A. (A) is incorrect, but (R) is correct.
B. Both (A) and (R) are correct, but (R) is not the right explanation of (A).
C. (A) is correct, but (R) is incorrect.
D. Both (A) and (R) are correct and (R) is the right explanation of (A).

12. Second generation reforms in our country do not comprise of which one of the following?

A. Exploiting the knowledge based global economy
B. Population control measures
C. Growing Indian transnational corporations
D. Clean environment

13. Match the items of List-I with the items of List-II and choose the correct answer from the code given below.

LIST-I	LIST-II
(*a*) Claims	(*i*) Company car, club membership, paid holidays, furnished house
(*b*) Fringe benefits	(*ii*) Telephone/mobile allowance, internet allowance, medical allowance
(*c*) Perquisites	(*iii*) Canteen, uniform, accident relief

Code:

	(a)	(b)	(c)
A.	(iii)	(ii)	(i)
B.	(ii)	(iii)	(i)
C.	(ii)	(i)	(iii)
D.	(i)	(ii)	(iii)

14. The monopoly involves a social cost mainly due to its emphasis on which one of the following?

A. Earning net profit in all possible situations.

B. Charging different prices from different categories of buyers of the same product.

C. Attempting to stall entry of other firms in the market.

D. Lower output at a higher cost in a normal profit situation.

15. Arrange the following stages of staffing in correct sequence and indicate the code of correct sequence.

(i) Performance appraisal
(ii) Recruitment
(iii) Transfers
(iv) Selection
(v) Induction and orientation

Choose the correct answer from the code given below.

Code:

A. (iv), (ii), (v), (iii), (i)
B. (i), (ii), (iv), (v), (iii)
C. (ii), (iv), (v), (i), (iii)
D. (ii), (i), (iv), (v), (iii)

16. Which one of the following demands states consumers are adequately buying all the products put into the marketplace?

A. Latent demand B. Irregular demand
C. Full demand D. Overfull demand

17. Choose the correct code for the following statements being correct or incorrect.

Statement I: Thousands of employees die every day in factories due to accidents.

Statement II: To make an accident-free plant adds to cost and decreases productivity.

Code:

A. Both the statements I and II are correct.
B. Both the statements I and II are incorrect.
C. Statement I is correct, but II is incorrect.
D. Statement II is correct, but I is incorrect.

18. Who among the following is not an observer country of the SAARC?

A. Iran B. China
C. Canada D. USA

19. Which one of the following is not true for introducing multiple brands in a category?

A. Increasing shelf presence and retailer dependence in the store

B. Yielding economies of scale in advertising, sales, merchandising and physical distribution

C. Decreasing internal competition within the firm

D. Attracting consumers seeking variety who may otherwise have switched to another brand

20. Given below are two statements, one labelled as Assertion (A) and the other labelled as Reason (R). Read the statements and choose the correct answer using the code given below.

Assertion (A): Databases assist in market segmentation, especially behavioural segmentation such as developing loyalty segments.

Reason (R): Customer Relationship Management (CRM) databases have become an asset for the analysis of customer behaviour.

Code:

A. Both (A) and (R) are correct and (R) is the right explanation of (A).
B. (A) is correct, but (R) is not correct.
C. Both (A) and (R) are correct, but (R) is not the right explanation of (A).
D. Both (A) and (R) are incorrect.

21. "Skimming" in e-banking is a method of:

A. stealing credit card information.

B. transferring cash from one account to another account.
C. converting Debit Card into Credit Card.
D. intimating the customer about his heavy withdrawals

22. Everyone benefits when the focus is on common interest and promotion of harmony is the underlying assumption of which one of the approaches to industrial relations:
A. Pluralistic approach
B. Human relation approach
C. Unitary approach
D. Marxist approach

23. Sales of firm are ₹ 40 Lakh; variable costs ₹ 10 lakh; fixed costs ₹ 15 lakh; Interest ₹ 5 lakh combined leverage of the firm will be:
A. 2 B. 2-5
C. 3 D. 8

24. Under Sec. 194 1B of the Income Tax Act, 1961 an individual or HUF (who is not required to get his accounts audited u/s 44 AB) who is responsible for paying to a resident any rent, shall deduct income tax, for the use of any land and building or both, if the rent exceeds:
A. 50,000 per month
B. 15,000 per month
C. 25,000 per month
D. 40,000 per month

25. Which one of the following is not an advantage of external recruitment?
A. Scope for resentment, jealousies and heartburn are avoided
B. Benefits of new skills, new talents and new experiences to organisations are available
C. Compliance with reservation policy becomes easy
D. Good performance is rewarded

26. When RBI reduces CRR, it results into:
A. Increase in deposits
B. Increase in lendable resources
C. Decrease in lendable resources
D. Decrease in deposits

27. The Industrial Policy, 1956 has been prompted by which combination of the following developments?
(*i*) Adoption of the Constitution of India.
(*ii*) Implementation of Economic Planning.
(*iii*) Acceleration of Economic Growth and Industrialisation.
(*iv*) Availability of Sufficient Funds for Investment in Public Sector.

Choose the correct answer from the code given below:

Code:
A. Only (*i*) and (*ii*)
B. Only (*ii*), (*iii*) and (*iv*)
C. Only (*ii*) and (*iv*)
D. Only (*i*), (*ii*) and (*iv*)

28. Match the items of List-I with the items of List-II and choose the correct answer from the code given below.

LIST-I	LIST-II
(*a*) Balance of trade	(*i*) Imports and exports of goods and services and unilateral transfer of goods and services
(*b*) Current account	(*ii*) Transactions leading to changes in the financial assets and liabilities of a country
(*c*) Balance of payments	(*iii*) All economic transactions between a countries residents and residents of other countries
(*d*) Capital account	(*iv*) Value of exports and imports of a country

Code:

	(*a*)	(*b*)	(*c*)	(*d*)
A.	(*iii*)	(*ii*)	(*iv*)	(*i*)
B.	(*i*)	(*ii*)	(*iii*)	(*iv*)
C.	(*iv*)	(*iii*)	(*ii*)	(*i*)
D.	(*iv*)	(*i*)	(*iii*)	(*ii*)

29. Choose the correct code for the following statements being correct or incorrect.

Statement I: Punctuality and team spirit among employees of an organisation has great contribution in enhancing profits of the business but they do not appear as an asset in the balance sheet.

Statement II: Financial statements do not reflect the correct financial position of a business.

Code:

A. Both the statements I and II are incorrect.
B. Both the statements I and II are correct.
C. Statement I is correct, but II is incorrect.
D. Statement I is incorrect, but II is correct.

30. Choose the correct code for the following statements being correct or incorrect.

Statement I: Intellectual Property (IP) is a category of property that includes intangible creations of the human intellect.

Statement II: IPR does not include trade secrets and moral rights.

A. Both the statements I and II are incorrect.
B. Statement II is correct, but I is incorrect.
C. Both the statements I and II are correct.
D. Statement I is correct, but II is incorrect.

31. Choose the correct code for the following statements being correct or incorrect.

Statement I: If the value of $\beta 2$, i.e., $\mu 4/\sigma 4$, of a distribution gives the value more than 3, its Curve is platykurtic.

Statement II: In a moderately asymmetrical distribution, the standard deviation is 1.25 times of mean deviation.

Code:

A. Both the statements I and II are incorrect.
B. Both the statements I and II are correct.
C. Statement I is correct, but II is incorrect.
D. Statement II is correct, but I is incorrect.

32. Which one of the following statements is not true?

A. Cost of sales is a better numerator than sales while calculating stock turnover.
B. Conversion of debentures into preference shares will decrease debt-equity ratio.
C. Higher operating ratio indicates higher profits.
D. Long-term liabilities due for payment within a year should be treated as current liabilities.

33. Which of the following sources of finance has an implicit cost of capital?

A. Equity share capital
B. Preference share capital
C. Debentures
D. Retained earnings

34. Given below are two statements, one labelled as Assertion (A) and the other labelled as Reason (R). Read the statements and choose the correct answer using the code given below.

Assertion (A): Technological change and skill requirements have been made a subject of investigation in an organization.

Reason (R): The neo-classical economic theory stated that technological changes require a broader variety of skills and higher average skills from the workers.

Code:

A. Both (A) and (R) are correct, but (R) is not the right explanation of (A).
B. (A) is correct, but (R) is incorrect.
C. Both (A) and (R) are correct and (R) is the right explanation of (A).
D. Both (A) and (R) are incorrect.

35. Choose the correct code for the following statements being correct or incorrect.

Statement I: An option which gives its holder the privilege of selling to other party a fixed amount of some stock at a stated price on or before a predetermined date is known as call option.

Statement II: In an option, the holder has the privilege of purchasing from other party a fixed amount of some stock at a stated price on or before a predetermined date is known as put option.

Code:

A. Both the statements I and II are correct.
B. Statement II is correct, but I is incorrect.

C. Statement I is correct, but II is incorrect.
D. Both the statements I and II are incorrect.

36. Which one of the following is agricultural income under Income Tax Act?
A. Income from the sale of replanted trees where denuded parts of the forest are replanted and subsequent operations in forestry are carried out.
B. Income from dairy farm, poultry farm, etc.
C. Dividend from a company engaged in agriculture.
D. Income from the land used for storing agricultural produce.

37. The inverse relationship between the variation in the price and the variation in the quantity demanded is not due to:
A. Price effect
B. Gossen's laws of consumption
C. Entry and exit of buyers
D. Law of substitution

38. Which one of the following is not the fund based business of commercial banks?
A. RTGS/NEFT transactions
B. Issuance of Letters of Credit
C. Overdraft facility
D. Acceptance of deposits

39. For performance assessment of employees, "helping to meet legal requirements" is the application of which one of the following?
A. Administrative purpose
B. Organisational maintenance purpose
C. Documentation purpose
D. Developmental purpose

40. Which one of the following items is not a part of job specification?
A. Judgement
B. Initiative
C. Location
D. Emotional characteristics

41. In which one of the following modes of entry into foreign market are risk and profit potential the highest?
A. Indirect exporting
B. Direct investment
C. Direct exporting
D. Joint ventures

42. Cost plus pricing is considered appropriate for which combination of the following?
(*i*) Product Tailoring
(*ii*) Public Utility Pricing
(*iii*) Refusal Pricing
(*iv*) Monopoly Pricing

Choose the correct answer from the code given below:

Code:
A. Only (*i*) and (*ii*)
B. Only (*ii*), (*iii*) and (*iv*)
C. Only (*iii*) and (*iv*)
D. Only (*i*), (*ii*) and (*iii*)

43. Which one of the following is not the function of the Reserve Bank of India?
A. Custodian of Cash Reserves of Commercial Banks
B. Controller of credit
C. Accepting deposits and advancing loans to public
D. Issue of Bank notes

44. Choose the correct code for the following statements being correct or incorrect.

Statement I: The geometric mean of the two regression coefficients of X and Y variables gives the value of the coefficient of correlation.

Statement II: If the population distribution is not normal and a sampling distribution of mean is prepared by taking small sized samples, the sampling distribution of mean is not normal.

Code:
A. Statement I is correct, but II is incorrect.
B. Statement II is correct, but I is incorrect.
C. Both the statements I and II are correct.
D. Both the statements I and II are incorrect.

45. Given below are two statements, one labelled as Assertion (A) and the other labelled as Reason (R). Read the statements and choose the correct answer using the code given below.

Assertion (A): The multilateral trading system is an attempt by governments to make the business environment stable and predictable.

Reason (R): Promising not to raise trade barriers can be as important as lowering one, because the promise gives businesses a clearer view of their future market opportunities.

Code:

A. (A) is correct, but (R) is incorrect.
B. Both (A) and (R) are correct and (R) is the right explanation of (A).
C. Both (A) and (R) are correct, but (R) is not the right explanation of (A).
D. Both (A) and (R) are incorrect.

46. Which among the following is not included in seven Ps of marketing and Bitner?

A. Politics
B. Process
C. People
D. Physical Evidence mix given by Booms

47. Match the items of List-I with the items of List-II and choose the correct code given below.

LIST-I	LIST-II
(*a*) The economy was characterised by marketing small regional suppliers who sold goods on a local basis	(*i*) Mass marketing
(*b*) Standardised, branded goods were sold at national level	(*ii*) Hyper-segmentation
(*c*) Era of market differentiation based on demographic, socio-economic and life style factors	(*iii*) Segmentation
(*d*) Technological advancements, especially in the area of digital communication, allow marketers to communicate with individual consumers or very small groups	(*iv*) Fragmentation

Code:

	(*a*)	(*b*)	(*c*)	(*d*)
A.	(*iv*)	(*i*)	(*iii*)	(*ii*)
B.	(*iv*)	(*i*)	(*ii*)	(*iii*)
C.	(*i*)	(*ii*)	(*iii*)	(*iv*)
D.	(*i*)	(*iv*)	(*ii*)	(*iii*)

48. Which one among the following is the oldest form of organization?

A. Project Organization
B. Functional Organization
C. Committee Organization
D. Line Organization

49. Merger of two companies under the Board for Industrial and Financial Reconstruction (BIFR) supervision is known as:

A. Offer for sale
B. Negotiated merger
C. Reverse merger
D. Arranged merger

50. According to Donald Kirkpatrick, training programmes can be evaluated at four levels. Indicate the code of correct sequence from the following:

(*i*) Result
(*ii*) Reaction
(*iii*) Learning
(*iv*) Behaviour

Choose the correct answer from the code given below:

Code:

A. (*iv*), (*iii*), (*ii*), (*i*)
B. (*i*), (*ii*), (*iii*), (*iv*)
C. (*ii*), (*iii*), (*iv*), (*i*)
D. (*iii*), (*iv*), (*i*), (*ii*)

51. Which of the following statements relating to the sampling theory are correct?

(*i*) The values of the statistical measures based on the sampled units are called values of statistic.
(*ii*) In the simple random sampling technique, the element of the population and the unit of the sample are different.
(*iii*) Snow-ball sampling technique is a probability-based sampling technique.

(*iv*) The 'law of statistical regularity' and the 'law of inertia of large' are the main bases of the sample to become representative of the population.

Choose the correct answer from the code given below.

Code:

A. (*i*) and (*iv*) B. (*ii*) and (*iii*)
C. (*ii*), (*iii*) and (*iv*) D. (*i*), (*ii*) and (*iii*)

52. Which one of the following statements is not true?

A. Profits earned from non-operating activities is added to net profit while calculating profits from operations.
B. Major source of working capital in the long run, is profits from operations.
C. Depreciation is a source of funds.
D. Any transaction that increases working capital is a source of funds.

53. Which one of the following is not the advantage of database management system?

A. Improved data integrity
B. Centralized control
C. High acquisition costs
D. Shared data

54. The probable error of the coefficient of correlation (*r*) is calculated by which one of the following formulae?

A. 1 B. 2
C. 3 D. 4

55. To examine whether the company is pursuing its best opportunities with respect to markets, products, and channels is the purpose of which one of the following types of marketing control?

A. Strategic control
B. Annual-plan control
C. Efficiency control
D. Profitability control

56. Choose the correct code for the following statements being correct or incorrect.

Statement I: A well-chosen marketing channel must be aligned to company's marketing strategy with respect to segmentation, targeting and positioning.

Statement II: Marketing channels are set of interdependent organizations participating in the process of making the product available for the use of consumption.

Code:

A. Statement II is correct, but I is incorrect.
B. Both the statements I and II are incorrect.
C. Both the statements I and II are correct.
D. Statement I is correct, but II is incorrect.

57. Foreign investment can be made through which of the following routes?

(*i*) Foreign Direct Investment (FDI)
(*ii*) Foreign Portfolio Investment (FPI)
(*iii*) Private Equity Investment (PEI)
(*iv*) Foreign Venture Capital Investors (FVCI)

Choose the correct answer from the code given below:

Code:

A. (*i*), (*iii*) and (*iv*)
B. (*i*), (*ii*), (*iii*) and (*iv*)
C. (*i*), (*ii*) and (*iv*)
D. (*i*) and (*iv*)

58. Given below are two statements, one labelled as Assertion (A) and the other labelled as Reason (R). Read the statements and choose the correct answer using the code given below.

Assertion (A): Training aids in encouraging and achieving self-development and self-confidence.

Reason (R): It helps a person handle stress, tension, frustration and conflict.

Code:

A. Both (A) and (R) are correct, but (R) is not the right explanation of (A).
B. Both (A) and (R) are incorrect.
C. (A) is correct, but (R) is not correct.
D. Both (A) and (R) are correct and (R) is the right explanation of (A).

59. Match the items of List-I with the items of List-II and choose the correct answer from the code given below.

LIST-I	LIST-II
(a) AS-I	(i) Accounting for fixed assets
(b) AS-3	(ii) Disclosure of accounting policies
(c) AS-10	(iii) Leases and its accounting
(d) AS-19	(iv) Cash flow statements

Code:

	(a)	(b)	(c)	(d)
A.	(iii)	(i)	(iv)	(ii)
B.	(iii)	(iv)	(ii)	(i)
C.	(i)	(ii)	(iii)	(iv)
D.	(ii)	(iv)	(i)	(iii)

60. Which of the following are included in the international liquidity? Indicate the correct code.

(i) Foreign exchange reserve

(ii) Borrowing capacity of the various countries

(iii) Gold reserves

Choose the correct answer from the code given below:

Code:

A. (ii) and (iii) B. (i) and (ii)

C. (i) and (iii) D. (i), (ii) and (iii)

61. X Ltd. forfeited 40 shares of 10 each and on which 4 per share were paid. If the forfeited shares are reissued as 8 per share paid up, what is the minimum price the company must charge?

A. 2 per share B. 4 per share

C. 10 per share D. 8 per share

62. Which one of the following initiatives is not the strategy for managing shortage of employees in an organisation?

A. Attempt to reduce turnover

B. Employee training

C. Hire temporary employees

D. Offer incentives to postpone retirement

63. A firm has inventory turnover of 3 and cost of goods sold is ₹ 2,70,000 with better inventory management, the inventory turnover is increased to 5. This would result in:

A. Decrease in inventory by 90,000

B. Increase in cost of goods sold by 20,000

C. Decrease in inventory by 36,000

D. Increase in inventory by 54,000

64. Which of the following variables is not known in Internal Rate of Return method of capital budgeting?

A. Life of the project

B. Discount rate

C. Amount of cash outflows

D. Amount of cash inflows

65. Match the items of List-I with the items of List-II and choose the correct answer from the code given below.

LIST-I (Propounder of Theory)	LIST-II (Theory of Motivation)
(a) Dr. William Ouchi	(i) X Theory
(b) Douglas McGregor	(ii) Need Hierarchy Theory
(c) Frederick Herzberg	(iii) Z Theory
(d) A.H. Maslow	(iv) Hygiene Theory

	(a)	(b)	(c)	(d)
A.	(iii)	(i)	(iv)	(ii)
B.	(iv)	(i)	(iii)	(ii)
C.	(ii)	(iii)	(iv)	(i)
D.	(ii)	(i)	(iii)	(iv)

66. Which one of the following is not the correct property of normal distribution?

A. Equality of central values (Mean, Mode and Median)

B. Uni-modal distribution

C. Standard deviation is the sole parameter of the distribution

D. Continuous distribution

67. Production function is based on which combination of the main characteristics of the inputs from the following:

(i) Substitutability

(ii) Complementarity

(iii) Flexibility

(iv) Specificity

Choose the correct answer from the code given below:

Code:

A. Only (*iii*) and (*iv*)
B. Only (*i*), (*ii*) and (*iv*)
C. Only (*i*) and (*ii*)
D. Only (*ii*), (*iii*) and (*iv*)

68. Indicate the most popular route of privatisation adopted by the Government of India in recent decades.

A. Spontaneous Privatisation
B. Cross Holdings
C. Management-Employee Buyout
D. Strategic sale

69. Which of the following is not a method of preparation of cash budget?

A. Adjusted Net Income method
B. Proforma Balance Sheet method
C. Cash Cycle method
D. Receipts and Payments method

70. Corporations are controlled and directed by which one of the following?

A. Corporate codes
B. Corporate governance
C. Corporate ethics
D. Corporate mechanism

71. Choose the correct code for the following statements being correct or incorrect.

Statement I: FX Spot is an agreement between two parties to buy one currency against selling another currency at an agreed price for settlement on the spot date.

Statement II: The date of maturity of a forward contract is more than two business days in future.

Code:

A. Both the statements I and II are correct.
B. Statement II is correct, but I is incorrect.
C. Statement I is correct, but II is incorrect.
D. Both the statements I and II are incorrect.

72. Which of the following statements is/are true?

1. Tax-shield on depreciation and interest is an important variable both for the lessor and the lessee.
2. Lease transactions in India are governed by the Lease Act.
3. A lessee should evaluate the lease options against the buying option.
4. As per AS-19, financial lease is shown in the balance sheet of the lessee as an asset.

Choose the correct answer from the code given below:

Code:

A. (*i*), (*iii*) and (*iv*)
B. Only (*ii*)
C. (*ii*), (*iii*) and (*iv*)
D. (*i*) and (*iv*)

73. A company proposes to introduce a new product in the market. The company wants to maintain P/V ratio at 25%. If variable cost of the product is 300, what will be the selling price?

A. ₹ 400 B. ₹ 100
C. ₹ 200 D. ₹ 300

74. Choose the correct code for the following statements being correct or incorrect.

Statement I: When the two securities returns are perfectly positively correlated, the risk of their portfolio is just a weighted average of the individual risks of the securities. In such case, diversification does not provide risk reduction but only risk averaging.

Statement II: Total risk of a portfolio of two risk securities can be completely eliminated when their returns are perfectly negatively correlated and their proportionate holdings in the portfolio are inversely related to the relative individual risks of the securities.

Code:

A. Both the statements I and II are incorrect.
B. Both the statements I and II are correct.
C. Statement I is correct, but II is incorrect.
D. Statement II is correct, but I is incorrect.

75. Match the items of List-I with the items of List-II and choose the correct answer from the code given below.

LIST-I (Type of Interview)	LIST-II (Usual Application)
(*a*) Structured	(*i*) A realistic approach that yields comparable answers plus in-depth insights
(*b*) Unstructured	(*ii*) Useful to understand applicants reasoning and analytical abilities under modest stress
(*c*) Mixed	(*iii*) Useful for valid results, especially when dealing with large number of applicants
(*d*) Behavioural	(*iv*) Useful when the interviewer tries to probe personal details of the candidate to analyse why they are not fit for the job

Code:

	(*a*)	(*b*)	(*c*)	(*d*)
A.	(*iii*)	(*i*)	(*ii*)	(*iv*)
B.	(*i*)	(*iv*)	(*ii*)	(*iii*)
C.	(*iii*)	(*iv*)	(*i*)	(*ii*)
D.	(*iv*)	(*ii*)	(*i*)	(*iii*)

76. Given below are two statements, one labelled as Assertion (A) and the other labelled as Reason (R). Read the statements and choose the correct answer using the code given below.

Assertion (A): Consumers need to be given legal protection against certain trade practices and business methods.

Reason (R): Protection as per market forces and 'Caveat Emptor' is not enough as perfectly competitive market is an economics dream and consumer sovereignty is a myth.

Code:

A. Both (A) and (R) are correct, but (R) is not the right explanation of (A).
B. (A) is correct, but (R) is incorrect.
C. (A) is incorrect, but (R) is correct.
D. Both (A) and (R) are correct and (R) is the right explanation of (A).

77. Banks are required to classify Non-Performing Assets into

A. Doubtful assets, bad debts and loss assets
B. Standard assets and sub-standard assets
C. Sub-standard assets, doubtful assets and loss assets
D. Doubtful assets, and bad debts

78. Cardinal utility analysis of consume/s behaviour is based on which combination of the following assumptions:

(*i*) Utility is measurable in terms of cardinal numbers.
(*ii*) Constancy of the marginal utility of money.
(*iii*) Utilities of different goods are interdependent.
(*iv*) Gossen's first law of consumption.

Choose the correct answer from the code given below:

Code:

A. Only (*iii*) and (*iv*)
B. Only (*i*), (*ii*) and (*iv*)
C. Only (*ii*), (*iii*) and (*iv*)
D. Only (*i*) and (*ii*)

79. Which one of the following is the main government agency responsible for development and monitoring international trade in India?

A. Export Promotion Council
B. Department of Commerce
C. Indian Institute of Foreign Trade
D. Federation of Indian Export Organisations

80. Which of the following statements are false?

(*i*) Capital profits can never be distributed as dividends to the shareholders.
(*ii*) Dividends are paid out of profits and, therefore, do not affect the liquidity position of the firm.
(*iii*) Every company should follow the policy of low dividend payment.
(*iv*) Walter's model suggests that dividend payment does not affect the market price of the shares.

Choose the correct answer from the code given below:

Code:

A. (*iii*) and (*iv*)
B. (*ii*), (*iii*) and (*iv*)
C. (*i*), (*ii*), (*iii*) and (*iv*)
D. (*i*), (*ii*) and (*iii*)

81. A and B are partners in a firm sharing profits in the ratio of 3 : 2. They admit X as a partner for 1/3 share in profits of the firm. The new profit sharing ratio of A, B and X is:

A. 3 : 2 : 2 B. 3 : 2 : 1
C. 6 : 4 : 5 D. 3 : 2 : 3

82. Advertising method in which a commercial is broadcast simultaneously on several radio stations and/or television channels is known as:

A. Road block
B. Road side
C. Exclusive drive
D. Intensified campaign

83. Which one of the following is not the basic function of WTO?

A. To facilitate the expansion and balanced growth of international trade
B. To facilitate the implementation, administration and operation of trade agreements
C. To settle differences and disputes among its member countries
D. To carry out periodic reviews of the trade policies of its member countries

84. Bretton Woods Conference resulted into the establishment of which of the following?

A. IBRD and IFC B. IMF and IDA
C. IDA and ADB D. IMF and IBRD

85. Which one of the following modes is not an example of Direct and Database marketing communication?

A. Mailings
B. Social media marketing
C. Catalogues
D. Telemarketing

86. Given below are two statements, one labelled as Assertion (A) and the other labelled as Reason (R). Read the statements and choose the correct answer using the code given below.

Assertion (A): A low debt-equity ratio is generally recommended for a newly started business.

Reason (R): During the initial years of the business, debt servicing will prove to be less burdensome.

Code:

A. (A) is not correct, but (R) is correct.
B. Both (A) and (R) are correct and (R) is the correct explanation of (A).
C. (A) is correct, but (R) is not correct.
D. Both (A) and (R) are correct, but (R) is not the correct explanation of (A).

87. Match the items of List-I with the items of List-II and choose the correct answer from the code given below.

LIST-I	LIST-II
(*a*) Direct investment overseas aimed at manufacturing products not manufactured by the firm in the home country	(*i*) Inward FDI
(*b*) Direct investment in a foreign country aimed to sell the output of the firm's domestic production.	(*ii*) Backward Vertical FDI
(*c*) Direct investment overseas aimed at providing inputs for the firms production process in the home country	(*iii*) Conglomerate FDI
(*d*) Foreign firms investing overseas and taking control over foreign assets	(*iv*) Forward Vertical FDI

Code:

	(*a*)	(*b*)	(*c*)	(*d*)
A.	(*iv*)	(*iii*)	(*ii*)	(*i*)
B.	(*iii*)	(*iv*)	(*ii*)	(*i*)
C.	(*i*)	(*iv*)	(*ii*)	(*iii*)
D.	(*iii*)	(*ii*)	(*i*)	(*iv*)

88. Given below are two statements, one labelled as Assertion (A) and the other labelled as Reason (R). Read the statements and choose the correct answer using the code given below.

Assertion (A): Among all methods of charging depreciation on fixed assets, diminishing balance method is the best method.

Reason (R): Diminishing balance method of charging depreciation has been permitted under the Income Tax Act, 1961 for claiming deduction for depreciation.

Code:

A. (A) is correct, but (R) is not correct.
B. Both (A) and (R) are correct, but (R) is not the correct explanation of (A).
C. Both (A) and (R) are correct and (R) is the correct explanation of (A).
D. (A) is incorrect, but (R) is correct.

89. The theory suggesting that the patterns of international trade are determined by factor endowment rather than productivity was propounded by which one of the following?

A. Adam Smith
B. Michael Porter
C. David Ricardo
D. Heckscher and Bertil Ohlin

90. Match the items of List-I with the items of List-II and choose the correct answer from the code given below.

LIST-I	LIST-II
(*a*) Behaviour referent	(*i*) Wide ranging cultural, structural and personnel strategies
(*b*) Focus of attention for interventions	(*ii*) Manage climate and culture
(*c*) Conflict handling	(*iii*) Few
(*d*) Job categories and grades	(*iv*) Values/mission

Code:

	(*a*)	(*b*)	(*c*)	(*d*)
A.	(*i*)	(*ii*)	(*iv*)	(*iii*)
B.	(*iii*)	(*i*)	(*ii*)	(*iv*)
C.	(*iv*)	(*i*)	(*ii*)	(*iii*)
D.	(*iv*)	(*ii*)	(*i*)	(*iii*)

91. Critical path indicates which one of the following?

A. Average time of completing a task
B. Shortest route of completing a task
C. Longest route of completing a task
D. Recorded time of completing a task

92. Given is the information related to a house

Municipal Value (M.V.)	₹ 1,50,000
Fair Rent	₹ 1,80,000
Standard Rent	₹ 1,60,000
Actual Rent	₹ 20000

Municipal tax paid by owner is 20% of M.V. Unrealised rent 40,000 (conditions of rule 4 satisfied). What is the annual value of the house?

A. ₹ 1,60,000
B. ₹ 1,50,000
C. ₹ 2,10,000
D. ₹ 1,70,000

93. Match the items of List-I with the items of List-II and choose the correct answer from the code given below.

LIST-I	LIST-II
(*a*) Income elasticity less than unity	(*i*) Competitive goods
(*b*) Cross elasticity less than unity	(*ii*) Inferior goods
(*c*) Cross elasticity less than zero	(*iii*) Superior goods
(*d*) Income elasticity less than zero	(*iv*) Complementary goods

Code:

	(*a*)	(*b*)	(*c*)	(*d*)
A.	(*i*)	(*ii*)	(*iii*)	(*iv*)
B.	(*iv*)	(*i*)	(*ii*)	(*iii*)
C.	(*iii*)	(*i*)	(*iv*)	(*ii*)
D.	(*iv*)	(*iii*)	(*i*)	(*ii*)

94. Match the items of List-I with the items of List-II and choose the correct answer from the code given below.

List-I	List-II
(*a*) Mobile Defense	(*i*) Occupying the most desirable position in consumers' minds, making the brand almost impregnable.
(*b*) Contraction Defense	(*ii*) The leader stretches its domain over new territories through market broadening and market diversification.
(*c*) Position Defense	(*iii*) Large companies give up weaker markets and reassign resources to stronger ones.

Code:

	(*a*)	(*b*)	(*c*)
A.	(*ii*)	(*iii*)	(*i*)
B.	(*i*)	(*ii*)	(*iii*)
C.	(*i*)	(*iii*)	(*ii*)
D.	(*ii*)	(*i*)	(*iii*)

95. Options for the following two statements regarding infrastructural services in the country, choose the correct code for the statements being correct or incorrect.

Statement I: Most infrastructure services are provided by public monopolies which generally suffer with severe problems like lack of accountability, low productivity, poor financial performance and over-employment.

Statement II: There is a need now to induce more private sector investment and participation in provision of social overheads as it may encourage better risk sharing, accountability, monitoring and management of infrastructure sector.

A. Both I and II are correct.
B. I is incorrect, but II is correct.
C. Both I and II are incorrect.
D. I is correct, but II is incorrect.

96. Options in which one of the following forms of workers participation in management is the role of the workers council not just advisory but the management is under a moral obligation to acknowledge, accept and implement the unanimous decision of the council?

A. Associative Participation
B. Administrative Participation
C. Consultative Participation
D. Decisive Participation

97. Match the items of List-I with the items of List-II and choose the correct answer from the code given below.

LIST-I	LIST-II
(*a*) NPA	(*i*) The percentage of deposits to be kept with RBI in the form of cash.
(*b*) SLR	(*ii*) The rate at which RBI lends money to commercial banks.
(*c*) Repo Rate	(*iii*) Loans and advances not paid for more than 90 days.
(*d*) CRR	(*iv*) The percentage of net demand and time liabilities to be kept in the form of liquid assets.

Code:

	(*a*)	(*b*)	(*c*)	(*d*)
A.	(*iii*)	(*ii*)	(*iv*)	(*i*)
B.	(*iii*)	(*iv*)	(*ii*)	(*i*)
C.	(*iii*)	(*iv*)	(*i*)	(*ii*)
D.	(*ii*)	(*iii*)	(*iv*)	(*i*)

98. Given below are two statements, one labelled as Assertion (A) and the other labelled as Reason (R). Read the statements and choose the correct answer using the code given below.

Assertion (A): Purchase decisions are not based on how customers perceive prices but, on the marketers, stated price.

Reason (R): Customers may have a lower price threshold, below which prices signal inferior or unacceptable quality, and an upper price threshold where the product appears not worth the money.

Code:

A. Both (A) and (R) are correct, but (R) is not the right explanation of (A).
B. Both (A) and (R) are incorrect.
C. Both (A) and (R) are correct and (R) is the right explanation of (A).
D. (A) is incorrect, but (R) is correct.

99. 'Finance for exporting companies' as part of major programmes of the Exim Bank of India does not include?

A. Post-shipment credit
B. Overseas investment finance
C. Term loans
D. Working capital

100. On fulfilling certain conditions, for an undertaking set up in special economic zones, deduction under section 10 AA of the Income Tax Act is allowed for?

A. 10 years
B. Unlimited period
C. 5 years
D. 15 YEARS

ANSWERS

1	**2**	**3**	**4**	**5**	**6**	**7**	**8**	**9**	**10**
C	A	A	C	B	B	D	A	B	A
11	**12**	**13**	**14**	**15**	**16**	**17**	**18**	**19**	**20**
D	B	B	D	C	C	C	C	C	A
21	**22**	**23**	**24**	**25**	**26**	**27**	**28**	**29**	**30**
A	C	C	A	D	B	D	D	B	D
31	**32**	**33**	**34**	**35**	**36**	**37**	**38**	**39**	**40**
D	C	D	C	D	A	D	B	C	C
41	**42**	**43**	**44**	**45**	**46**	**47**	**48**	**49**	**50**
B	D	C	C	B	A	A	D	D	C
51	**52**	**53**	**54**	**55**	**56**	**57**	**58**	**59**	**60**
A	C	C	D	A	C	B	A	D	D
61	**62**	**63**	**64**	**65**	**66**	**67**	**68**	**69**	**70**
B	B	C	B	A	C	B	D	B	B
71	**72**	**73**	**74**	**75**	**76**	**77**	**78**	**79**	**80**
A	A	A	B	C	A	C	B	B	C
81	**82**	**83**	**84**	**85**	**86**	**87**	**88**	**89**	**90**
C	A	A	D	B	B	B	D	D	C
91	**92**	**93**	**94**	**95**	**96**	**97**	**98**	**99**	**100**
C	D	C	A	B	A	B	D	A	D

EXPLANATORY ANSWERS

1. Government of India set up the Securities and Exchange Board of India (SEBI) on April 12, 1988 on the basis of the recommendations of the high powered Committee on Stock Exchange Reforms headed by G.S. Patel. SEBI was given a legal status by the Securities and Exchange Board of India Ordinance, 1992. The members of the Board of Management of the SEBI comprised those drawn from professional brokers, financial consultants, merchant bankers, investors, stock exchange authorities, finance ministry, etc.

FEATURES OF THE SEBI BILL

The SEBI has been entrusted with a wide range of responsibilities in regulating the activities of almost all the players in the capital market. After the abolition of the controller of capital issues, the issuer of capital, which is the promoter, has come under SEBI's jurisdiction. The SEBI laid down certain guidelines for the issuers to ensure investor protection. The SEBI was expected to regulate mutual funds, merchant bankers, registrars to issue, share transfer agents, portfolio managers, underwriters, investment advisors, brokers and sub-brokers. SEBI has also been given certain powers to regulate the functioning of stock exchanges in India.

OBJECTIVES

SEBI was set up with the following objectives of assisting and facilitating the mobilization of adequate resources through the securities market and its efficient allocation, keeping in mind the interests of issuers, investors and the intermediaries:

1. **Conducive environment:** SEBI aims at creating a proper and conducive environment required for raising money from the capital market through the rules, regulations, trade practices, customs and relations among institutions, brokers, investors and companies. It also aims at endeavouring to restore and safeguard the trust of investors, especially the interest of the small investors. This is to be achieved by meeting the needs of the players connected with the securities market such as the investors, the corporate sector and the intermediaries. SEBI works for creating proper investment climate to enable corporate sector to float industrial securities easily, efficiently and at affordable minimum cost.
2. **Investor education:** SEBI aims at educating investors so as to make them aware of their rights in clear and specific terms by providing them with information. This way, SEBI aims at maintaining liquidity, them with information. This way, SEBI aims at maintaining liquidity, safety and profitability of the securities in the market that are crucial for any investment. A high degree of protection of investor rights and interests is made possible by providing adequate, accurate and authentic information on a continuous basis. This way, the market efficiency is also ensured.
3. **Infrastructure:** SEBI aims at developing a proper infrastructure for facilitating automatic expansion and growth of business of middlemen like brokers, jobbers, commercial banks, merchant bankers, mutual funds, etc. This is aimed at providing efficient service to their constituents, viz. investors and corporate sector at competitive prices.
4. **Others:** In addition to the above mentioned objectives, SEBI would also make efforts to bring about necessary enactments for regulating business of intermediaries such as mutual funds, NBFCs and chit funds, etc. SEBI would also work towards creating a framework for more open, orderly and unprejudiced conduct in relation to takeover and mergers in the corporate sector so as to ensure fair and equal treatment to all the security holders.

3. COMBINED LEVERAGE

Meaning of Combined Leverage

Combined Leverage is a measure of Total Risk. The percentage change in EPS occurring due to a given percentage change in Sales is known as the degree of combined leverage. It is the product of degree of operating leverage and degree of financial leverage.

Decision with which Combined Leverage is Associated

It is associated with Capital Budgeting Decision (or Assets Mix Decision) and Capital Structure Decision (or Capital Mix Decision). Its degree differs with the use of different forms of financing.

When Does Combined Leverage Exist?

Combined Leverage exists if there are *either* fixed costs or funds bearing fixed financial payments *or* both.

How to Calculate Combined Leverage?

Combined Leverage can be calculated with the help of following formulae:

1. $$\text{D.C.L} = \frac{\text{Percentage Change in EPS}}{\text{Percentage Change in Sales}}$$

$$= \frac{\Delta\text{EPS/EPS}}{\Delta\text{Sales/Sales}}$$

2. D.C.L. (if there is no preference dividend)

$$= \frac{\text{Contribution}}{\text{EBIT}} \times \frac{\text{EBIT}}{\text{EBT}} \times \frac{\text{Contribution}}{\text{EBT}}$$

4. FACTORS INFLUENCING THE PRICING DECISIONS OF SERVICES

Internal and External Factors

The factors that influence price determination can be classified as internal and external factors (Adrein Palmer).

1. Internal Factors

The internal factors are controllable in nature, which are discussed below:

(*a*) **Organisational Policies:** As price decision is an outcome of production and marketing, the pricing (takes at the top level and the lower level of an organisation.)

(*b*) **Service Differentiation:** In order to differentiate own services from that of the competitor, the service provider has to price the services differently.

(*c*) **Service Cost:** It is necessary to assure that the price charged for a service covers the fixed, variable and semi-variable costs incurred in providing that service.

(*d*) **Marketing Mix:** The price of a product or service varies depending upon whether the product or service idea is new or an established one, whether the service provider is an agent or a sub-agent, or the main provider (distribution channels) and also the various pricing objectives.

2. External Factors

On the other hand external factors are uncontrollable in nature, such as:

(*a*) **Demand:** Markets have to be segmented effectively according to:

Different Groups of Users: In order to obtain maximum value from each segment of users, different prices can be charged for offering the same service. Depending on the user's demand for the product or service like heavy user, medium user, on low user the pricing variations are made.

Different Points of Consumption: On the basis of the point of production and consumption, service organisations charge different prices at different service locations. Depending on the place where the consumption takes place, the prices are to be varied. For example, Taj group of hotels will not charge the same price for its deluxe rooms in Delhi, Mumbai, Chennai and Bangalore.

Different Time of Production: Owing to the perishability characteristic of the services, they are priced discriminatorily, depending upon the time at which they are offered. For example, hotels in Goa follow a different price package during the monsoon season as compared to the peak season of the year *i.e.*, October-May.

(*b*) **Competition:** Competition plays a significant role in pricing, due to similarity in the services offered and the satisfaction enjoyed by a customer. Unless the products and services provided by the hotelier are unique in nature, the marketer cannot price the products and services higher than the competitor.

(*c*) **Governmental Control:** Government policy regulations affect the pricing decisions of various services. For example, changes in the luxury tax, sales tax, etc. imposed by the government, from time to time, affect the pricing decisions of a hotel or restaurant business.

7. Banking Ombudsman is a quasi judicial authority functioning under the Banking Ombudsman Scheme, 2006. The authority was created to enable resolution of complaints of customers of banks relating to services rendered by the lenders.

   Banking Ombudsman Scheme is a mechanism created by the RBI to address the complaints raised by bank customers. It is run by the RBI directly to ensure customer protection in the banking industry. According to the RBI, "The Scheme enables an expeditious and inexpensive forum to bank customers for resolution of complaints relating to certain services rendered by banks."

   The Banking Ombudsman Scheme was introduced under Section 35 A of the Banking Regulation Act, 1949 by RBI with effect from 1995. The present Ombudsman scheme was introduced in 2006.

   The Banking Ombudsman is a senior official appointed by the Reserve Bank of India. He has the responsibility to redress customer complaints against deficiency in certain banking services. At present fifteen Ombudsmen were appointed by the RBI to settle complaints and they are appointed in state capitals.

   All Scheduled Commercial Banks, Regional Rural Banks and Scheduled Primary Co-operative Banks are covered under the Scheme.

   The Banking Ombudsman can receive and consider any complaint relating to a number of deficiencies related to banking operations including internet banking. RBI has mentioned a large number of service deficiencies by banks to customers where the customers can approach the Ombudsman through a complaint.

8. **Graphical method of locating the median**

   Median can be located with the help of a cumulative frequency curve or by an 'ogive' curves. From the point of intersection of 'less than' and 'more than' ogives, if a perpendicular is drawn on the X axis, the point so obtained on the horizontal axis gives the value of the median.

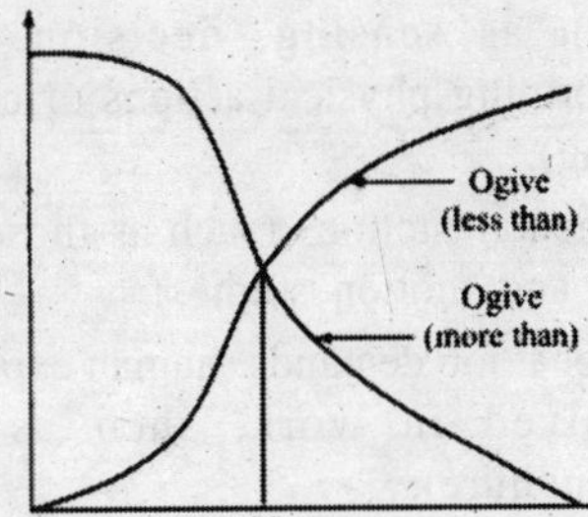

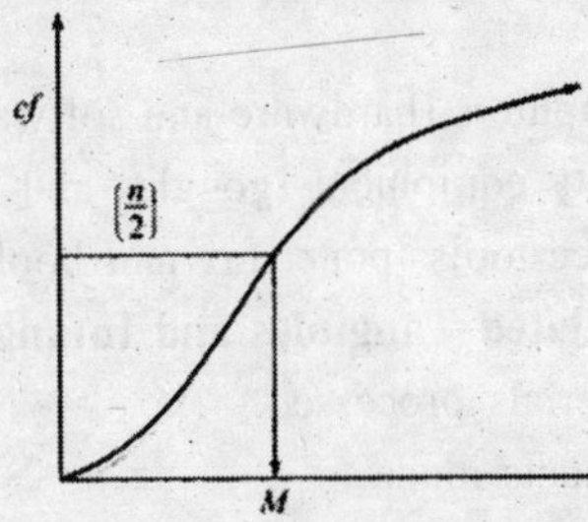

   If ogive is drawn using cumulated percentage frequencies, then we draw a straight line from the point representing 50 percent cumulated frequency on the Y-axis parallel to the X-axis to intersect the ogive. A perpendicular drawn from this point of intersection on the horizontal axis gives the value of the median.

10. **Types of Information to be Collected by Job Analysis**

    Work Activities

    - Job-oriented activities (description of the work activities performed, expressed in "job" terms, usually indicating what is accomplished, such as .galvanising, weaving, cleaning, and so on; sometimes such activity descriptions also indicate how, why and when a worker performs an activity; usually the activities are those involving active human participation, but In certain instances they may characterise machine or system functions).

- Work activities/processes.
- Procedures used.
- Activity records (such as films).
- Personal accountability/responsibility.

Worker-Oriented Activities

- Human behaviours performed in work (such as sensing, decision making, performing physical actions or communicating).
- Elemental motions (such as those used in time and motion studies).
- Personal job demands (human expenditures involved in work, such as energy expenditure).

Machines, Tools, Equipment and Work Aids Used

- Computers (hardware and software).
- Safety equipment (goggles and groves).
- Office tools (pone, fax and books).

Job-Related Tangibles and Intangibles

- Materials processed.
- Products made.
- Knowledge dealt with or applied (such as law or chemistry).
- Services rendered (such as laundering or repairing).

Work Performance

- Work measurements (*i.e.*, time taken).
- Work standards.
- Error analysis.
- Other aspects.

Job Context

- Physical working conditions.
- Work schedule.
- Organised context.
- Social context.
- Incentives (financial and non-financial).

Personal Requirements

- Job-related knowledge and/or skills (such as education, training, or work experience required).
- Personal attributes (such as aptitudes, physical characteristics, personality, interests required).

16. Marketers are skilled at stimulating demand for their products, but that's a limited view of what they do. Just as production and logistics professionals are responsible for supply management, marketers are responsible for demand management. They seek to influence the level, timing, and composition of demand to meet the organization's objectives. Eight demand states are possible:

1. Negative demand—Consumers dislike the product and may even pay to avoid it.
2. Nonexistent demand—Consumers may be unaware of or uninterested in the product.
3. Latent demand—Consumers may share a strong need that cannot be satisfied by an existing product.
4. Declining demand—Consumers begin to buy the product less frequently or not at all.
5. Irregular demand—Consumer purchases vary on a seasonal, monthly, weekly, daily, or even hourly basis.
6. Full demand—Consumers are adequately buying all products put into the marketplace.
7. Overfull demand—More consumers would like to buy the product than can be satisfied.
8. Unwholesome demand—Consumers may be attracted to products that have undesirable social consequences.

17. Thousands of employees die everyday in factories due to accidents. Accidents are partial or total, temporary or permanent. An accident-free plant can save on cost, increase productivity, discharge moral commitment towards workers and comply with legal provision.

The safety programme of a typical organisation comprises six steps—making strategic choice, development of a safety policy; organisation for safety; analysis of the causes, extent and consequences of accidents; implementation of the programme; and evaluation of the safety performance.

18. The South Asian Association for Regional Cooperation (SAARC) was established with the signing of the SAARC Charter in Dhaka on 8 December, 1985. SAARC comprises of eight Member States: **Afghanistan, Bangladesh, Bhutan, India, Maldives, Nepal, Pakistan and Sri Lanka.** The Secretariat of the Association was set up in Kathmandu on 17 January, 1987.

The objectives of the Association as outlined in the SAARC Charter are: to promote the welfare of the peoples of South Asia and to improve their quality of life; to accelerate economic growth, social progress and cultural development in the region and to provide all individuals the opportunity to live in dignity and to realize their full potentials; to promote and strengthen collective self-reliance among the countries of South Asia; to contribute to mutual trust, understanding and appreciation of one another's problems; to promote active collaboration and mutual assistance in the economic, social, cultural, technical and scientific fields; to strengthen cooperation with other developing countries; to strengthen cooperation among themselves in international forums on matters of common interests; and to cooperate with international and regional organizations with similar aims and purposes.

There are currently nine Observers to SAARC, namely: (*i*) Australia; (*ii*) China; (*iii*) the European Union; (*iv*) Iran; (*v*) Japan; (*vi*) the Republic of Korea; (*vii*) Mauritius; (*viii*) Myanmar; and (*ix*) the United States of America.

There is a moratorium on the admission of new Observers to SAARC at present. Observers are invited to participate in the inaugural and closing Sessions of SAARC Summits.

Member States have decided to engage the SAARC Observers into productive, demand-driven and objective project based cooperation in priority areas as identified by the Member States, *i.e.* (*i*) Communication (*ii*) Connectivity (*iii*) Agriculture (*iv*) Public Health (*v*) Energy (*vi*) Environment and (*vii*) Economic Cooperation.

Joint Meeting of Observers and National Focal Points (Ministries of Foreign Affairs) will finalize the projects based on proposals from Member States and Observers.

19. Many firms have to introduce multiple brands because no one brand is viewed equally favourably by all the different market segments the firm would like to target. Some reasons for introducing multiple brands in a category include the following:

- To increase shelf presence and retailer dependence in the store.
- To attract consumers seeking variety who may otherwise switch to another brand.
- To increase internal competition within the firm.
- To yield economies of scale in advertising, sales, merchandising and physical distribution.

21. Skimming: Skimming is a method by which a device is used to steal credit card information. The legitimate credit card is swiped on the device, which steals the data on the magnetic strip of the credit card and they creates a clone of the credit card. This credit card information obtained is either directly used by the skimmer or is also sold online. This information is mostly bought by terrorist organisations.

22. Unitary Approach

Under unitary approach, IR is grounded in mutual co-operation, individual treatment, team-work and shared goals. Work place conflict is seen as temporary aberration, resulting from poor management, from employees who do not mix well with the organisation's culture. Unions co-operate with the management and the management's right to manage is accepted because there is no 'we-they' feeling. The underlying assumption is that everyone benefits when the focus is on common interest and promotion of harmony. Conflict in the form of strikes is not only regarded as unnecessary but destructive.

Pluralistic Approach

The pluralistic approach totally departs from the unitary approach. This approach perceives:

1. Organisations as coalitions of competing interests, where the management's role is to mediate amongst the different interest groups.
2. Trade unions as legitimate representatives of employee interests.
3. Stability in IR as the product of concessions and compromises between management and unions.

Legitimacy of the management's authority is not automatically accepted. Conflict between the management and workers is understood as inevitable and, in fact, is viewed as conducive for innovation and growth. Employees join unions to protect their interests and influence decision-making by the management. Unions thus balance the power between the management and employees. In the pluralistic approach, therefore, a strong union is not only desirable but necessary. Similarly, society's interests are protected by state intervention through legislation and industrial tribunals which provide orderly process for regulation and resolution of conflict.

The theories on pluralism were evolved in the mid-sixties and early seventies when England witnessed a resurgence of industrial conflicts. However, the recent theories of pluralism emanated from British scholars, and in particular from Flanders and Fox. According to pluralists, industrial conflict is inevitable and it needs to be contained within the social mechanism of collective bargaining, conciliation and arbitration.

Marxist Approach

Marxists, like the pluralists, regard conflict between employers and employees as inevitable. However, pluralists believe that the conflict is inevitable in all organisations. Marxists see it as a product of the capitalist society. As Marx himself put it, "the mode of production in material life determines the general character of social, political and spiritual process of life."

Adversarial relations in the workplace are simply one aspect of class conflict. The Marxist approach thus focuses on the type of society in which an organisation functions. Conflict arises not just because or competing interests within the organisation, but because of the division within society between those who own or manage the means of production and those who have only their labour to offer. Industrial conflict is thus seen as being synonymous with political and social unrest. The application of Marxian theory as it relates to industrial relations derives indirectly from later Marxist scholars rather than directly from Marx himself.

Trade unions are seen both as labour reaction to exploitation by capital, as well as a weapon to bring about a revolutionary social change. Concerns with wage-related disputes are secondary. Trade unions focus on improving the position of workers within the capitalist system and not to overthrow. For the Marxists, all strikes are political.

Besides, Marxists regard state intervention via legislation and the creation of industrial tribunals as supporting management's interest rather than ensuring a balance between the competing groups. This view is in contrast to the belief of the pluralists who argue that state intervention is necessary to protect the overall interests of society. To Marxists, the pluralist approach is supportive of capitalism, the unitary approach is anathema. Consequently, enterprise bargaining, employee participation, co-operative work culture, and the like which help usher in cordial IR are not acceptable to Marxists. Such initiatives are regarded as nothing more than sophisticated management techniques designed to reinforce management control and the continuation of the capitalist system.

The Human Relations Approach

The human relations theory was propounded by the human relations school founded by Elton Mayo. The approach offers a coherent view of industrial conflict and harmony. The human relations approach highlights certain policies and techniques to improve harmony, morale, job satisfaction and productivity. The theory stresses the role of small groups to remove irritants in labour management relations. Elton Mayo and his team were humanists and believed in the positive nature of employees. They believed that given human initiatives from managements, workers would respond positively and conflicts would have no place. But excessive stress on positive nature of workers was not appreciated by Marxists and Pluralists.

23. Combined Leverage

$$= \frac{\text{Contribution (Sales} - \text{Variable Cost)}}{\text{PBT}}$$

$$= \frac{(40-10)}{40-(10+15)-5} = \frac{30}{10} = 3.$$

24. Individuals and HUFs paying rent of ₹ 50,000 or more per month will now have to deduct 5% tax at source *i.e.* TDS at the rate of 5%, as per Budget 2017 proposals. This move is aimed at ensuring that recipients of large rental incomes come into the tax net as they would be forced to report the full rental income in their tax returns in order to claim benefit of the TDS amount. This change is proposed to be made effective from 1.6.2017.

The existing provisions of section 194-I of the Act provide for TDS at the time of credit or payment of rent to the payee beyond a threshold limit. Currently, this provision is applicable to Individuals or Hindu undivided family (HUF) which is liable for tax audit under section 44AB.

However, Individuals and HUF other than those liable for tax audit were not liable to deduct tax at source under this section *i.e.*, section 194-I of the Act. In order to widen the scope of tax deduction at source, it is proposed to insert a new section 194-I B in the Act to provide that Individuals or an HUF (other than those covered under 44AB of the Act), paying to a resident, rent of over ₹ 50,000 per month, shall deduct tax at source of 5%.

25. Evaluation of External Recruitment: External sources of recruitment have both merits and demerits. On the plus side, the following may be cited:

1. The organisation will have the benefit of new skills, new talents and new experiences, if people are hired from external sources.
2. The management will be able to fulfil reservation requirements in favour of the disadvantaged sections of the society.
3. Scope for resentment, heartburn and jealousy can be avoided by recruiting from outside.

The demerits are:

1. Better motivation and increased morale associated with promoting own employees are lost to the organisation.
2. External recruitment is costly.
3. If recruitment and selection processes are not properly carried out, chances of right candidates being rejected (false positive error) and wrong applicants being selected (false negative error) occur.

26. Effect of Decrease in Cash Reserve Ratio

Effect on interest rates: When the cash reserve ratio is decreased by the RBI, banks will have more money to invest in other businesses since the amount of funds that needs to be kept with the RBI is low. This shows that banks will have an excess of funds and hence, there will be a decline in the interest rates that are charged on loans.

Effect on inflation: When the cash reserve ratio is minimised, commercial banks will have more funds and hence, the money supply of the banking system will increase. When there is a rise in the money supply, excessive funds will result in high inflation.

When the CRR is minimised, funds are drawn out from the economic system excessively and then the money supply is affected negatively wherein there is a shortage of funds. Since the money supply has declined in this situation, the inflation also reduces.

Effect of Increase in Cash Reserve Ratio

When the cash reserve ratio is raised, banks will have very limited amount of funds because they are asked to retain huge amounts of cash in hand with the Reserve Bank of India. Hence, banks will not have any money to use for other purposes. You also need to remember that the RBI does not pay any interest on balances of the CRR.

Now, since banks are not able to receive any interest, they decide to raise the interest rates. They will be forced to raise the interest rates for their loan products such as personal loans, car loans, home loans, two-wheeler loans, etc. When interest rates are increased, even the equated monthly installments (EMIs) of the borrowers will increase. Your loan costs will rise pretty intensely.

30. "Intellectual Property shall include the rights relating to; literary, artistic and scientific works, performances of performing artists, inventions in all fields of human endeavour, scientific discoveries, industrial designs, trademarks, service marks and commercial names and designations, protection against unfair competition, and all other rights resulting from intellectual activity in the industrial, scientific, literary or artistic fields" (WIPO Convention).

IP is usually divided into two categories: copyright and industrial property. Industrial property rights include patents for inventions, trademarks, industrial designs, plant variety rights, and of course, GIs. The holder of IPR has a legally recognized capacity to authorize and/or prevent others from acting in certain ways with respect to his/her intellectual property.

Nature and Kinds of Intellectual Property

- Creation of human mind (Intellect)
- Intangible property
- Exclusive rights given by statutes
- Attended with limitations and exceptions
- Time-bound
- Territorial (Patent terms vary considerably from country to country)
- Different kinds of properties are-
- Movable Property: Car, Pen, Furniture, Dress
- Immovable Property: Land, Building
- Intellectual Property: Literary works, inventions

Important IP laws that prevail in most of the countries are patents, copyright and related rights, trademarks, trade secrets, industrial designs, industrial property, GIs, layout designs/topographies and protection of new plant varieties.

Rights in the Content

A. The Content Provider is the exclusive owner of the Content and shall retain all rights therein and any Content derived therefrom as well as in the Content Provider Marks and any and all intellectual property rights relating thereto. This shall include all inventions, discoveries, trademarks, patents, trade names, copyrights, moral rights, know-how, intellectual property, software, shop rights, licenses, developments, research data, designs, technology, trade secrets, test procedures, processes, route lists, computer programs, computer discs, computer tapes, literature, reports, and other confidential information, intellectual and similar intangible property rights, whether or not patentable or copyrightable (the "Content Provider Property").

B. The Content Distributor is the exclusive owner of any content created by the Content Distributor (the "Content Distributor Content") and shall retain all right, title and interest to the Content Distributor Content or any content derived therefrom, the Content Distributor's Service, the Content Distributor's trademarks, and all Intellectual Property Rights therein, excluding the Content Provider Property.

C. During the Term of this Agreement, the Content Provider shall not license nor authorize another to license any person other than the Content Distributor the right to use the Content or the Content Provider Marks in connection with promoting in the United States any wireless service that makes the Content available via the Platform.

31. To begin with, we consider the mean deviation and standard deviation. To calculate mean deviation, absolute deviations are used whereas the calculation of standard deviation calls for squaring the deviations before averaging them and taking the square root. The squaring of deviations places relatively larger weights to the bigger deviation values. The result is that the standard deviation is always higher than the mean deviation. Further, quartile deviation is always smaller than the standard deviation and the mean deviation. The relationship between the three measures is defined precisely in respect of a normal distribution.

That mean deviation is about 80 per cent of the standard deviation. Conversely, the standard deviation is about 1.25 times the mean deviation. Further, quartile deviation is approximately two-thirds of the standard deviation and five-sixths of the mean deviation. Thus, the relationships given here may be summarized as follows:

$$4\ SD = 5\ MD = 6\ QD$$

Here, SD is standard deviation, MD is mean deviation and QD is quartile deviation.

34. **Managerial Skills and Competencies:** Skills of managers have now become an important factor to address global competitiveness both at organizational and national level. However, because of the problem of quantification of benefits, imparting skills through training and development is yet not recognized as an important initiative at organizational level for problem of quantification of benefits. Skill is defined as a coordinated series of actions that serves to attain some goal or accomplish a particular task. Operationally, skills are defined widely as overt responses and controlled stimulation. Overt responses may be verbal, motor or perceptual. Verbal response typically stresses on speaking (which requires memorization of words); motor response stresses on movements of limbs and body, whereas, perceptual responses stress on understanding of sensory response. Controlled stimulation, on the other hand, are energy inputs to the workers, which we express in units of frequency, length, time and weight. Technological change and skill requirements have been made a subject of investigation in enormous studies across the world. There is a general consensus that a technological change alters the job but the observations differ in its nature and form. The Neo-c1assical Economic Theory advocated technological changes that require broader variety of skills and higher than average skills from the workers. New forms of skill and responsibility along with technological changes have been studied in Continuous Process Industry and Chemical Manufacturing Units, Petroleum Refining, Metal Working Industries, Banking Operations and in many other industries. Another school of thought advocates that technology is instrumental in fractionating and de-skilling of jobs. Redesigning of jobs subsequent to technological change separates the planning and the concept of job in its totality from the execution aspect of work. De-skilling and skill downgrading also occur due to differential growth of higher-versus low-skill occupations and industries. The focal point of this hypothesis is that the technology induces differential point of growth for different sectors of the economy and produces skill polarization by eventual occupational shift to skilled jobs in some industries and unskilled jobs in many others. These phenomena are especially evident in India. From the 1981 Census Reports onwards, we find a major occupational shift of workers from primary sector to secondary sector and from secondary sector to tertiary sector. Simultaneous structural change in occupational pattern is also evident, as the number of blue-collar workers has been drastically reduced while the number of white-collar workers has significantly increased.

35. TYPES OF OPTIONS

There are two basic types of stock options which can be used separately or combined to derive two additional types of options. Fundamentally, the holder of an option merely possesses the right to buy or sell a specific asset. The option contract specifies between the period of time allowed to exercise this right and the price. The main types of stock options are listed below:

1. Put Option

A put is an option to sell. A put gives its holder the privilege of selling or putting — to a second party a fixed amount of some stock at a stated price on or before a predetermined date.

2. Call Option

Analogously, a call is an option to purchase, its holders has the privilege of purchasing-or-calling from a second party a fixed amount of some stock at a stated price on or before a predetermined day.

36. Examples of Agricultural Income

The following are some of the examples of agricultural income:

- Income derived from sale of replanted trees.
- Income from sale of seeds.
- Rent received for agricultural land.
- Income from growing flowers and creepers.
- Profits received from a partner from a firm engaged in agricultural produce or activities.
- Interest on capital that a partner from a firm, engaged in agricultural operations, receives.

Examples of Non-Agricultural Income

The following are some of the examples of non-agricultural income:

- Income from poultry farming.
- Income from bee hiving.
- Any dividend that an organization pays from its agriculture income.
- Income from the sale of spontaneously grown trees.
- Income from dairy farming.
- Income from salt produced after the land has flooded with sea water.
- Purchase of standing crop.
- Royalty income from mines.
- Income from butter and cheese making.
- Receipts from TV serial shooting in farm house.

39. Multiple Purposes of Performance Assessment

General Applications	*Specific Purpose*
Developmental Uses	Identification of individual needs
	Performance feedback
	Determining transfers and job assignments
	Identification of individual strengths and developmental needs
Administrative Uses/Decisions	Salary
	Promotion
	Retention or termination
	Recognition of individual performance
	Lay-offs
	Identification of poor performers
Organisational Maintenance/ Objectives	HR planning
	Determining organisation training needs
	Evaluation of organisational goal achievement
	Information for goal identification
	Evaluation of HR systems
	Reinforcement of organisational development needs
Documentation	Criteria for validation research
	Documentation for HR decisions
	Helping to meet legal requirements

40. Job Specification: Job specification or employee specification is a statement which answers the question, "What human qualities and traits are necessary to do the job well?" It is a written record of the physical, mental, social, psychological, and behavioural characteristics which a person should possess in order to perform the job effectively. In contrast to the job description it is a standard of personnel and designates the qualities required for acceptable performance. A job description is a profile of the job. A job specification, on the other hand, describes what the job demands of the employee and the human skills that are required. It is a profile of the human characteristics needed by the person performing the job. It is a statement of essential and desirable attributes, which a person must possess. It contains information in terms of education, experience, training, judgement, initiative, physical effort, physical skills, communication skills and emotional characteristics.

The job specification is a major tool in the staffing process. It is also helpful in training and appraisal of employees. It is also useful in testing, interviewing and checking of reference.

41. Three of the strategies for entry into foreign markets — contracts, joint ventures and direct foreign investments — present greater challenges when faced with different goals: social welfare for the developing country and profits for the firm. These market entry strategies may affect multiple market participants and provide the opportunity for a differing risk/reward ratio. The profit potential of each entry mode depends on characteristics of the market to which the strategy is applied.

42. Cost-Plus Pricing: With cost-plus pricing, the seller's costs are determined (usually during a project or after a project is completed), and then a specified dollar, amount or percentage of the cost is added to the seller's cost to establish the price. Cost-plus pricing and competition-based pricing are in fact the most common bases for pricing services. When production cost are difficult to predict, cost-plus pricing is appropriate. Projects involving custom-made equipment and commercial construction are often priced using this technique. The government frequently uses such cost-based pricing in granting defense contracts. One pitfall for the buyer is that the seller may increase costs to establish a larger profit base. Furthermore, some costs, such as over-head, may be difficult to determine. In periods of rapid inflation, cost-plus pricing is popular, especially when the producer must use raw materials that are fluctuating in price. In industries in which cost-plus pricing is common and sellers have similar costs, price competition may not be especially intense.

43. The main functions of the RBI are:

(*i*) To maintain monetary stability so that the business and economic life can deliver welfare gains of a properly functioning mixed economy;

(*ii*) To maintain financial stability and ensure sound financial institutions so that monetary stability can be safely pursued and economic units can conduct their business with confidence;

(*iii*) To maintain stable payments systems so that financial transactions can be safely and efficiently executed;

(*iv*) To promote the development of the financial infrastructure in terms of markets and systems, and to enable it to operate efficiently, that is, to play a leading role in developing a sound financial system so that it can discharge its regulatory function efficiently;

(*v*) To ensure that credit allocation by the financial system broadly reflects the national economic priorities and societal concerns; and

(*vi*) To regulate the overall volume of money and credit in the economy, with a view to ensuring a reasonable degree of price stability.

Roles of RBI

The roles that the RBI plays in the Indian banking and financial system relate to (*i*) Note issuing authority, (*ii*) Government banker. (*iii*) Bankers' bank. (*iv*) Supervising authority, (*v*) Exchange control authority. (*vi*) Promoter of the financial system and (*vii*) Regulator of money and credit.

44. The regression coefficients b_{yx} and b_{xy} may be expressed in terms of the correlation coefficient (r) and the standard deviations of x and y (viz. σ_x and σ_y) by the relations

$$b_{yx} = r\frac{\sigma_y}{\sigma_x}, \quad b_{xy} = r\frac{\sigma_x}{\sigma_y}$$

$$\therefore \quad b_{yx} \times b_{xy} = \left(r\frac{\sigma_y}{\sigma_x}\right)\left(r\frac{\sigma_x}{\sigma_y}\right) = r^2$$

$$\text{or,} \quad r^2 = b_{yx} \times b_{xy}$$

$$\therefore \quad r = \sqrt{b_{yx} \times b_{xy}}$$

Thus, the correlation coefficient r is the geometric mean of the two regression coefficients b_{yx} and b_{xy}.

45. ***Predictability and Stability:*** Predictability and stability are important objectives of the multilateral regulation of trade. The multilateral trading system is an attempt by governments to make the business environment stable and predictable as sometimes, promissing not to raise a trade barrier can be as important as lowering one, because the promise gives businesses a clearer view of their future opportunities. With stability and predictablility, investment is encouraged, employment opportunities are generated and consumers can fully enjoy the benefits of competition.

46. Booms and Bitner suggested in 1981, a seven P's marketing mix model to service firms. The seven P's were later supported by McGrath and other marketing specialists.

The marketing mix for service organisations are product, physical evidence, price, place, people, promotion and process. Fig. exhibits the marketing mix of services. Thus, there are three additional components—physical evidence, people and process in the services marketing mix.

Components of the Services Marketing Mix

Product Service is an intangible product. It consists of a bundle of features and benefits that have relevance to a specific target market. As such, there is a high level of flexibility and opportunity to be innovative in designing a product offer.

Physical evidence: Most services cannot be offered without the support of tangibles. Though customers cannot see the service, they can definitely see the tangibles associated, examine them and try to form an opinion on the service provider, Thus, a passenger transport organisation's promise of a safe, comfortable and timely journey from one place to another will be examined by the transport vehicle's condition, seating facilities and other physical facilities, the personality of the driver and other personnel, the office furniture and equipment being used and also the way in which the employees are responding to customers. All these physical objects are used as evidence by the customer to assess and expect performance from the service provider. Hence, physical evidence plays a critical role in shaping consumer perceptions and also expectations.

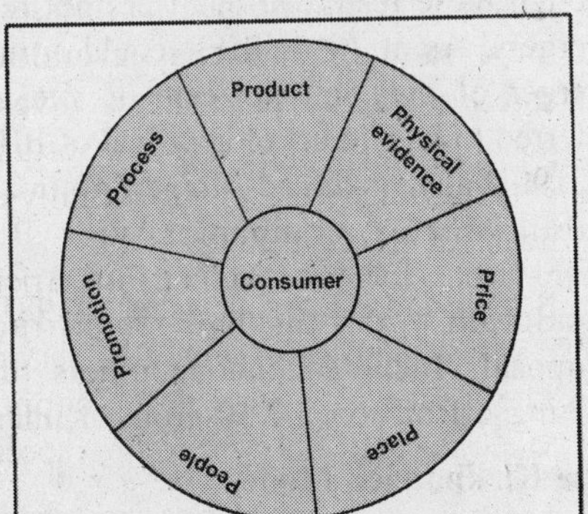

Fig. *Services marketing mix*

Price: The pricing decision is a critical one in services too, as this component of the marketing mix alone determines the revenue of the firm. Consumer sensitivity to price would be higher in services than in goods. Though the basic methods of pricing are the same as in goods, the pricing strategies for services basically depends upon value perceptions of various groups of people that are targeted by the organisation.

Place (distribution): Services are intangible as well as inseparable. These two characteristics do not allow a service firm to follow the same channel options available for goods marketing. Due to the intangible character of service, traditional wholesalers and retailers cannot be used. As services cannot be stored and cannot be separated from producers, retailing cannot be an independent activity in services marketing. Production, distribution and consumption are simultaneous activities in services. However, services have an advantage of using a direct selling approach, through which services can be offered to the customer at a lower cost. This does not mean direct selling is the only way of selling the services. There are certainly other channels of distribution such as agents and brokers, franchisers and electronic channels, that are used for distribution of services.

People: Service organisations are people-oriented and people-based organisations. Employees of a service firm constitute the major competency in undertaking business operations. Every employee of the service organisation is a marketing person, who undertakes either full-time or part-time marketing activity. Whether an employee is involved in direct contact with the customer or not, if he was placed on the line of visibility, his behaviour, activities and performance will have a direct influence on consumers. Service employees are to be trained and motivated, for better performance in marketing activities.

Promotion: Consumers are co-producers in the service business. The quality of services will not only depend upon the performance of the service provider but also on the performance of the service consumer. Very few service organisations or service concepts can have readily available mature performers as consumers. It is the responsibility of service organisations to educate and, if necessary, train customers so as to make them prepared to use the services efficiently. A well designed promotional programme is of immense help to organisations to inform, persuade and train customers to better their experiences.

Process: Process is a functional activity that assures service availability and quality. The way the physical setting is designed technically and how the functions are scheduled and routed to provide promised services to the customers speaks of the efficiency of the process. In simple terms, the management of process is to manage service encounters (the interaction between service employees and customers, customers and service environment, systems and other facilities) effectively. Gronroos has described process as interactive marketing wherein moments of truth occur. The challenges of process management is to improve the moment of truth.

The seven P's of services marketing become the marketing offer of the organisation to the target market. The marketing mix aims to achieve seven distinctive goals. They are matching the offer to the consumer needs and wants, consumer quality expectations, consumer perceptions, consumer satisfaction, customer relationships, customer welfare and protection and societal well-being. The dynamic nature of the target market in all the seven distinctive areas offers challenges to marketing organisations. Service firms can be successful only when they make all the marketing mix elements dynamic and adaptable to the changes in the market environment.

48. Line Organization: Line organization is the oldest form of an organization. In this, the line of authority flows vertically from top to bottom throughout the entire organizational structure. The person at the highest enjoys the highest authority while the person at the last level has the lowest authority. It is also possible that a business is divided into several departments and the authority flows downward from the general manger through the departmental managers to the lower subordinates. In such a type of structure, the head of the departments enjoy equal status while being independent of each other.

49. A number of corporate restructuring ventures were initiated by the Board of Industrial Finance and Reconstruction (BIFR). Most of these restructurings were institutionally driven and the terms and conditions were designed to suit the creditors and lending institutions. Some well-known BIFR cases during the early 1990s, in which a healthy company took over a sick company were: VAM Organic Chemical taking over Ramganga Fertilizer, Straw Products taking over Orissa Synthetic, and Voltas Ltd. taking over Miami Pharma Ltd. In all these cases, BIFR sanction helped the transferee companies enjoy the benefits of carry forward losses of the transferor companies, even though these restructurings were not reverse mergers. As at 1994, BIFR could arrange a merger of only 4.3 per cent of total cases referred to it. The list of approval of BIFR as at 1991 also included merger of two sick public sector companies viz. Bharat Refractories Ltd. and Indian Fire Bricks & Insulation Co. Ltd. The reconstruction proposals Included, among others things, writing off of about ₹ 50 crore of interest.

50. The Kirkpatrick Model

Level 1: Reaction: The degree to which participants find the training favourable, engaging and relevant to their jobs.

Level 2: Learning: The degree to which participants acquire the intended knowledge, skills, attitude, confidence and commitment based on their participation in the training.

Level 3: Behaviour: The degree to which participants apply what they learned during training when they are back on the job.

Level 4: Results: The degree to which targeted outcomes occur as a result of the training and the support and accountability package

54. Probable Error and Standard Error of Coefficient of Correlation

The probable error (PE) of coefficient of correlation indicates extent to which its value depends on the condition of random sampling. If r is the calculated value of correlation coefficient in a sample of n pairs of observations, then the standard error SE_r of the correlation coefficient r is given by

$$SE_r = \frac{1-r^2}{\sqrt{n}}$$

The probable error of the coefficient of correlation is calculated by the expression:

$$PE_r = 0.6745\ SE_r = 0.6745\frac{1-r^2}{\sqrt{n}}$$

Thus with the help of PE_r we can determine the range within which population coefficient of correlation is expected to fall using following formula:

$$\rho = r \pm PE_r$$

where ρ (rho) represents population coefficient of correlation.

Remarks

1. If $r < PE_r$ then the value of r is not significant, that is, there is no relationship between two variables of interest.
2. If $r > 6PE_r$ then value of r is significant, that is, there exists a relationship between two variables.

Illustration: If $r = 0.8$ and $n = 25$, then PE_r is

$$PE_r = 0.6745\ \frac{1-(0.8)^2}{\sqrt{25}}$$

$$= 0.6745 = \frac{0.36}{5} = 0.048$$

Thus the limits within which population correlation coefficient (ρ_r) should fall are

$$r \pm PE_r = 0.8 \pm 0.048$$

or $$0.752 \le \rho_r \le 0.848$$

55.	Type of Control	Responsibility	Purpose of Control	Tools
Levels of Marketing Control	Strategic control	Top management	To examine whether the company is pursuing its best opportunities with respect to markets, products, and channels	Marketing audit
	Annual plan control	Top management, middle management	To examine whether the planned results are being achieved	sales analysis; market-share analysis; expense-to-sales ratios; other ratios; attitude tracking
	Efficiency and effectiveness control	Middle management	To examine how well resources have been utilized in each element of the marketing strategy to accomplish a specific goal	Expense ratios; advertising effectiveness measures; market potential; contribution margin analysis
	Profitability control	Marketing controller	To examine where the company is making and losing money	Profitability by product Territory, market Segment, trade Channel, order size

56. A marketing channel can be defined as follows:

A marketing channel is a set of interdependent organizations involved in the process of making a product or service available for use or consumption.

The definition bears some explication. It first points out that a marketing channel is a *set of interdependent organizations.* That is, a marketing channel is not just one firm doing its best in the market—whether that firm is a manufacturer, wholesaler, or retailer. Rather, many entities are typically involved in the business of channel marketing. Each channel member depends on the others to do their jobs.

57. Types of Investments

Foreign investment into India may take place through foreign direct investment, foreign portfolio investment, foreign venture capital investment, and other investments.

- **Foreign direct investment:** Foreign direct investment may be made in a new company or an existing company. It is now freely permitted up to 100 per cent in almost all sectors. Such investment can be made in shares, convertible debentures, and preference shares of Indian companies in accordance with the FDI Policy.
- **Foreign portfolio investment:** Under the portfolio investment scheme, foreign institutional investors (FIIs) can invest in shares and convertible debentures issued by Indian companies. FIIs are allowed to invest in securities traded on both primary and secondary capital markets as well as through private placement or arrangement. These securities include shares, debentures, warrants, units of mutual funds, government securities, and derivative instruments. FIIs are, however, not permitted to invest in equity issued by an asset reconstruction company.
- **Foreign venture capital investment:** A foreign venture capital investor (FVCI) is permitted to invest in an Indian venture capital undertaking, an Indian venture capital fund, or in a scheme floated by a venture capital fund. FVCIs are permitted to purchase equity, equity linked instruments, debt, debt instruments, and debentures of a venture capital undertaking or a venture capital fund through initial public offer or private placement in units of schemes or funds set up by a ventures capital funds.
- **Other investments:** FIIs can also buy dated government securities or treasury bills, listed nonconvertible debentures, bonds issued by Indian companies, and units of domestic mutual funds, either directly from the issuer of such securities or through a registered stockbroker on a recognized stock exchange in India.

58. Training: *Benefits to the Individual Which in Turn Ultimately Should Benefit the Organisation*

- Helps the individual in making better decisions and effective problem solving.
- Through training and development, motivational variables of recognistion, achievement, growth, responsibility and advancement are internalised and operationalised.
- Aids in encouraging and achieving self-development and self-confidence.
- Helps a person handle stress, tension, frustration and conflict.
- Provides information for improving leadership, knowledge, communication skills and attitudes.
- Increases job satisfaction and recognition.
- Moves a person towards personal goals while improving interactive skills.
- Satisfies personal needs of the trainer (and trainee).
- Provides the trainee an avenue for growth and a say in his/her own future.
- Develops a sense of growth in learning.
- Helps a person develop speaking and listening skills; also writing skills when exercises are required.
- Helps eliminate fear in attempting new tasks.

59. Indian Accounting Standards

Till date (December, 2004), the Institute of Chartered Accountants of India has issued twenty nine accounting standards. The majority of accounting standards are mandatory in the sense that the management of the business enterprise should ensure their compliance in preparation and presentation of financial statements. The list of accounting standard is given below:

- Accounting Standard (AS) 1 – *Disclosure of Accounting Policies*
- Accounting Standard (AS) 2 – *Valuation of Inventories*
- Accounting Standard (AS) 3 – *Cash Flow Statement*
- Accounting Standard (AS) 4 – *Contingencies and Events occurring after the Balance Sheet Date*
- Accounting Standard (AS) 5 – *Net Profit or Loss for the Periods, Prior Period Items and Changes in Accounting Policies*
- Accounting Standard (AS) 6 – *Depreciation Accounting*
- Accounting Standard (AS) 7 – [Revised] *Construction Contracts*
- Accounting Standard (AS) 8 – *Accounting for Research and Development*
- Accounting Standard (AS) 9 – *Revenue Recognition*
- Accounting Standard (AS) 10 – *Accounting for Fixed Assets*
- Accounting Standard(AS) 11 – [Revised] *The Effects of Changes in Foreign Exchange Rates*
- Accounting Standard (AS) 12 – *Accounting for Government Grants*
- Accounting Standard (AS) 13 – *Accounting for Investments*
- Accounting Standard (AS) 14 – *Accounting for Amalgamations*
- Accounting Standard (AS) 15 – *Accounting for Retirement Benefits in the Financial Statements of Employers*
- Accounting Standard (AS) 16 – *Borrowing Costs*
- Accounting Standard (AS) 17 – *Segment Reporting*
- Accounting Standard (AS) 18 – *Related Party Disclosures*
- Accounting Standard (AS) 19 – *Leases*
- Accounting Standard (AS) 20 – *Earning per Share*
- Accounting Standard (AS) 21 – *Consolidated Financial Statements*
- Accounting Standard (AS) 22 – *Accounting for Taxes on Income*
- Accounting Standard (AS) 23 – *Accounting for Investments in Associates in Consolidated Financial Statements*
- Accounting Standard (AS) 24 – *Discontinuing Operations*
- Accounting Standard (AS) 25 – *Interim Financial Reporting*
- Accounting Standard (AS) 26 – *Intangible Assets*
- Accounting Standard (AS) 27 – *Financial Reporting of Interests in Joint Ventures*
- Accounting Standard (AS) 28 – *Impairment of Assets*
- Accounting Standard (AS) 29 – *Provisions, Contingent Liabilities and Contingent Assets*

60. International Liquidity and International Reserves

International liquidity refers to those financial resources and facilities that are available to a country for financing the deficit in its balance of payments. The various components of international liquidity are gold and foreign currencies held by the monetary authority of a country, borrowing facilities available from the IMF, special drawing rights (SDRs), the borrowing capacity of the country in the international market, and so on. Thus, the term "international liquidity" refers to the country's international reserves as well as its capacity to borrow in the international market. Where gold is held as a reserve asset, its market value is listed, but gold cannot be directly used to settle payments between central banks. In other words, gold is no longer used as a means to settle international payments.

Official reserve holdings may include some foreign currency that is universally acceptable and convertible. Throughout the latter part of the nineteenth century, the British pound served as a universally acceptable currency alongside gold, into which it was convertible. Subsequently, the U.S. dollar has rivalled the GBP as a world currency. Any currency which is to serve satisfactorily as a reserve currency for other countries should satisfy certain conditions. It must be the currency of a great trading nation. The currency should be easily acquired via normal trade. It must have a stable value, or at least, in a world where currencies are losing value, it must lose value no faster than other currencies. It must be a currency that is supported in its home country by a strong banking system. Such a currency must also be free from recurrent scarcity. Any currency which is a candidate for the international reserve must be close to meeting these criteria, and the extent to which it conforms to them is likely to determine its success.

The main purposes of holding foreign exchange reserves are: (*i*) to maintain public confidence in the capacity of the country to honour its international obligations; and (*ii*) to increase the capacity of the monetary authority to intervene in the foreign exchange market. In other words, foreign exchange reserves are mainly held for precautionary and transaction motives, and also for achieving a balance between demand and supply of foreign currencies.

62.

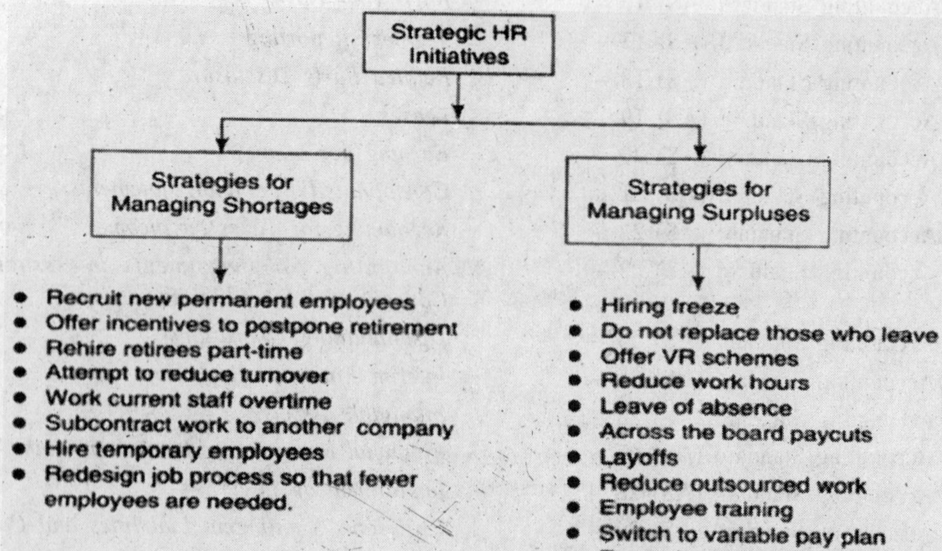

66. Properties of a Normal Distribution

A **normal Distribution** is a continuous probability distribution for a random variable *x*. The graph of a normal distribution is called the **normal curve,** which has all of the following properties:

1. The mean, median and mode are equal.
2. The normal curve is bell-shaped and is symmetric about the mean.
3. The total area under the curve is equal to one.
4. The normal curve approaches, but never touches the *x*-axis.
5. Between $\mu - \sigma$ and $\mu + \sigma$ the graph is concave down and elsewhere the graph is concave up. The points at which the graph changes concavity are called *inflection points.*

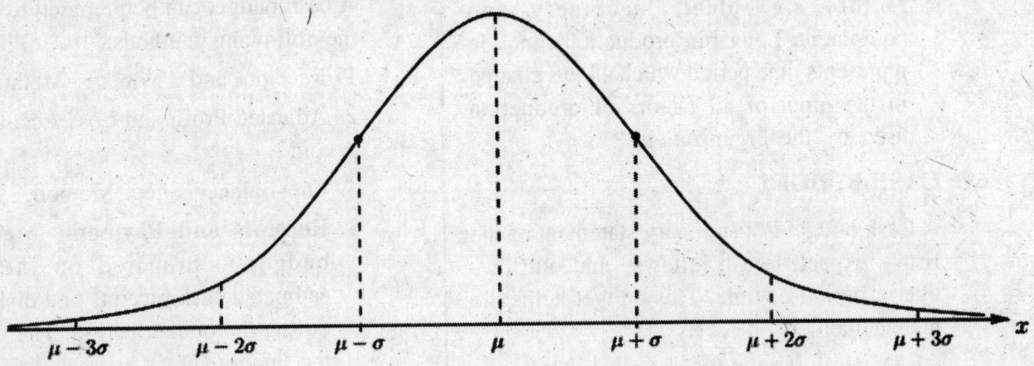

Remarks

- A normal distribution can have any mean and any positive standard deviation
- The two parameters, μ and σ completely determine the shape of the normal curve.
- The equation of the normal curve is $y = \dfrac{1}{\sigma\sqrt{2\pi}} e^{\frac{-(x-\mu)^2}{2\sigma^2}}$.

67. Characteristics of production function

Important characteristics of production function are given below.

1. **Flow concept:** Production function exhibits flow concept. It represents flow of inputs and the resulting output flow for a specified time period.
2. **Physical concept:** It exhibit technical relationship between physical input and physical output only and not in any other firm.
3. **Complementary:** Input show complementary characteristics. For example if man and machine combination produces 5 units of a commodity per day. By employing 2 man and 2 machines, 10 units of that commodity can be produced.
4. **Substitutability:** Some factors may be substitutable. For example, X and Y are substitutable factor, X may be increased instead of Y. X is fixed while Y is variable, one can use less capital and more labour and vice versa for obtaining same output. For example, if agricultural university wants more agricultural produce, it can use more land or can adopt new improved varieties of seeds, fertilizers and other inputs to get more produce from the same land.
5. **Specificity and versatility:** If a factor of production can be used for only one purpose, it is considered as specific on the other hand if it can be used for more than one purpose it is referred to as versatile. In

production some factors are specific and some are versatile. A thrasher and tractor are versatile farm equipment whereas chemical spraying pump is specific.

Short run and long run production function: Short run production function represents a time period in which the inputs of some factors of production cannot be changed. They are referred to as fixed factors *e.g.* plant, machinery and equipment. Long run production function represents time period which allows change in the input of all factors of production used by the organization.

69. CASH BUDGET

A Cash budget is a summary statement of the firm's expected cash inflows and outflows over a period of time. This budget helps the management in

(*i*) Determining the future cash needs of the firm;

(*ii*) Planning for financing of those needs; and

(*iii*) Exercising control over cash and liquidity of the firm.

Objectives and Uses of Cash budget: The preparation of cash budget serves the following purposes:

- It provides a sound basis for cash control.
- It gives estimated cash position due to operating activities.
- Cash generation due to capital receipts can be known promptly.
- It facilitates the planning of cash disbursements on account of capital expenditures, debt redemption, capital redemption and dividend payments.
- Just by having a glance, we can know the opening and closing budgeted balance of cash for a particular period.
- Estimated surplus and deficiency of cash during each period is predetermined; this facilitates proper planning for managing cash deficits and profitable investment of surplus cash.
- It provides perfect synchronization of cash requirements in relation to working capital, sales, raising of debts and capital expenditures.

Methods of Preparing Cash Budgets

A cash budget can be prepared by any one of the following methods:

1. Receipts and Payments Method
2. Adjusted Profit and Loss Account Method and
3. The Balance Sheet Method.

1. **Receipts and Payments Method:** The budget is prepared on the basis of estimated cash receipts and disbursements during the budget period. The first part of the budget shows estimated cash receipts on account of cash sales, collection from debtors, receipt of interest and dividend on investments made outside the business, sale of old assets, issue of capital and debt, etc. The second part shows estimated disbursements of cash on account of cash purchases, payment to creditors, payment of bills on maturity, operating expenses, payment of interest and dividends to the holders of equity/preference capital and interest to debenture holders, payment of direct/indirect taxes, etc. The accumulation of cash receipts and payments is on periodic basis which may be monthly or quarterly. The Closing balance of cash for the current period is net result of the opening balance of cash for the current period plus estimated receipts and minus the estimated disbursements. Symbolically,

$$C = O + R - D$$

Some times closing balance for a particular period may be negative *i.e.*, there is cash deficit. The closing balance of a period becomes the opening balance for the next period. *The budgeted cash balance may be positive or negative but actual cash balance can never be negative.*

Minimum cash balance is predetermined on the basis of working capital requirements. In case the budgeted cash is less than the requisite minimum, arrangements are to be made to meet cash deficits. If the cash balance is in surplus, plans should be made for its profitable deployment.

2. **Adjusted Profit and Loss Account Method:** It is prepared on the basis of opening CASH including Bank balance, Projected Profit and Loss account, and Balance sheet exclusive of cash balance. This method is usually applied for long term cash forecasting. Cash budget prepared using this method is known as Cash Flow Statement. This method of preparing cash budget requires the following information:

   1. Cash and Bank balances at the start of the budget period.
   2. All the operating and non-operating expenses.
   3. Estimated sales revenues.
   4. Estimated non-operating incomes.
   5. Changes in Working capital Assets and liabilities.
   6. Planned capital receipts on account of issue of capital and/ or debentures and sale of assets.
   7. Planned capital outlays, and payments on account of redemption of preference capital, and debentures.
   8. Payment of interest and dividends.

   Net profit in most of the cases is not equal to net inflow of cash from operations and this requires adjustments. This is why this method is known as Adjusted Profit and Loss account. All the non-cash expenses such as depreciation, goodwill written off, and Preliminary expenses written off are added back to the given Net Profit figure. Increases in current liabilities and decreases in current assets are added to the net profit; increases in current assets and decreases in current liabilities are deducted from the net profit so as to arrive at cash from operating activities. Raising of cash through issue of capital and debt, sale of assets, etc. are added and utilisations of cash in the form of redemption of capital and debt, purchase of assets, payments of dividends and interest etc., are deducted to arrive at the budgeted cash balance at the end of the period.

3. **Balance Sheet method:** In this method, closing balances of all (budgeted) Balance Sheet items, except cash and bank balances, are found and put in a budgeted Balance Sheet. If the total of liabilities-side items is more than the total of asset-side items, the balancing figure will be cash/bank balance. On the contrary, if the total of assets-side items is more than the total of liabilities-side items, the balancing figure will be bank overdraft or shortage in cash. The budgeted figures of closing Balance Sheet items can be found after adjusting the opening Balance Sheet items with the transactions anticipated for the year.

   The main defect of this method is that it does not take into account the items of income and expenditure. Another defect is that cash position is ascertained only at the end of the year when the Balance Sheet is prepared.

70. Corporate governance is a set of processes, customs, policies, laws, and institutions that affect the way a corporation is directed, administered or controlled. Corporate governance mechanisms consist of internal and external systems and procedures used to ensure that the agent (the management of the corporation) runs the firm for the benefit of one or more principals (shareholders and other stakeholders). An important theme of corporate governance is to ensure the accountability of a corporation's management through mechanisms designed to reduce the agency problem between managers and shareholders. In the Anglo-American model of corporate governance, shareholder wealth maximization generally holds primacy as the firm's goal. Thus, governance devices attempt to align or ensure that managerial behaviour and actions pursue this goal. Governance control mechanisms work through a broad array of layered and overlapping actions such as monitoring by the boards of directors, compensation systems, ownership structure, takeovers, and government regulations.

71. A foreign exchange spot transaction, also known as FX spot, is an agreement between two parties to buy one currency against selling another currency at an agreed price for settlement on the spot date. The exchange rate at which the transaction is done is called the spot exchange rate.

Forward transactions are classified by forward value date into:

- **Short dates:** maturity of one month or less.
- **Round dates (fixed dates or straight dates):** original terms to maturity of a whole number of months.
- **Broken dates (odd dates):** original maturities of less than round dates.

Forward transactions are of two types: Outright forward contracts and foreign exchange swaps (or spot-forward swaps). An outright forward contract involves the sale or purchase of a currency for delivery more than two business days into the future. Hence, the only difference between an outright forward transaction and a spot transaction is the value date. The word 'out-right' indicates that no spot transaction is involved. On the other hand, a foreign exchange swap (which is different from a currency swap) involves a spot purchase against a matching outright forward sale (or vice versa). For example, a foreign exchange swap transaction is concluded when a trader agrees to sell a currency and simultaneously to repurchase it (thus reversing the operation) some time in the future at an exchange rate determined now. When the reversal is on adjacent days, the term rollover is used.

75.

Types of Interview

Type	*Type of Questions*	*Usual Applications*
Structured	A predetermined checklist of questions, usually asked of all applicants.	Useful for valid results, especially when dealing with large number of applicants.
Unstructured	Few, if any, planned questions. Questions are made up during the interview.	Useful when the interviewer tries to probe personal details of the candidate to analyse why they are not right for the job.
Mixed	A combination of structured and unstructured questions, which resembles what is usually done in practice.	A realistic approach that yields comparable answers plus indepth insights.
Behavioural	Questions limited to hypothetical situations. Evaluation is based on the solution and approach of the applicant.	Useful to understand applicant's reasoning and analytical abilities under modest stress.
Stressful	A series of harsh, rapid fire questions Intended to upset the applicant.	Useful for stressful jobs, such as handling complaints.

77. Bank's loans and advances are to be classified into two broad categories — Standard and Non-Performing. Non-performing assets (NPA) are sub-divided into — Sub-standard; Doubtful and Loss assets.

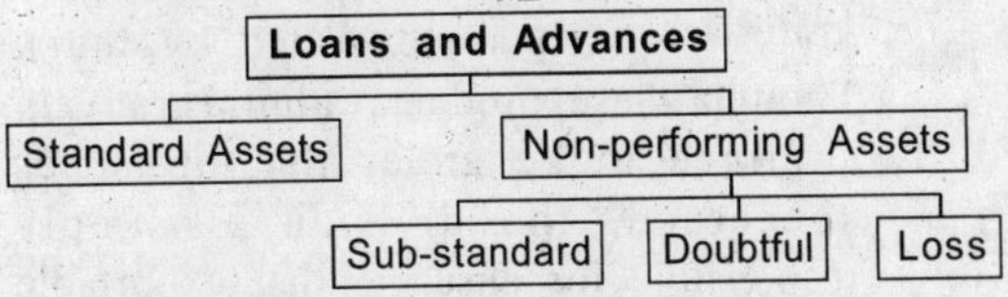

Definitions

Standard Assets: Standard Asset is one which does not disclose any problems and which does not carry more than normal risk attached to the business. Such an asset should not be an NPA.

Sub-Standard Assets

(*i*) With effect from March, 2005 an asset would be classified as sub-standard if it *remained NPA for a period less than or equal to 12 months.* In such cases, the current net worth of the borrowers/guarantors or the current market value of the security charged is not enough to ensure recovery of the dues to the banks in full. In other words, such assets will have well defined credit weaknesses that jeopard the liquidation of the debt and are characterised by the distinct possibility that the banks will sustain some loss, if deficiencies are not corrected.

(*ii*) An asset where the terms of the loan agreement regarding interest and principal have been re-negotiated or rescheduled after commencement of production, should be classified as sub-standard and should remain in such category *for at least 12 months of satisfactory performance* under the re-negotiated or rescheduled terms. In other words, the classification of an asset should not be upgraded merely as a result of rescheduling, unless there is satisfactory compliance of this condition.

Doubtful Assets: With effect from March 31, 2005, an asset is required to be classified as doubtful, if it has *remained NPA for more than 12 months.* For Tier I banks the 12-months period of classification of a sub-standard asset in doubtful category will be effective from April 1, 2008. As in the case of sub-standard assets, rescheduling does not entitle the bank to upgrade the quality of an advance automatically. A loan classified as doubtful has all the weaknesses inherent as that classified as sub-standard, with the added characteristic that the weaknesses make collection or liquidation in full, on the basis of currently known facts, conditions and values, highly questionable and improbable.

Loss Assets: A loss asset is one where loss has been identified by the NBFCs, or internal or external auditors, or the RBI inspection to the extent the amount has not been written off. Alternatively, it may be an asset that is adversely affected by a potential threat of non-recoverability due to either erosion in the value of the security/non-availability of security, or any fraudulent act/omission on the part of the borrower.

79. Role of Department of Commerce in the Ministry of Commerce in Promoting Exports

The Department of Commerce in the Ministry of Commerce is the apex body in the sixtier arrangement of the institutional infrastructure created for the promotion of exports in India. This is the primary Government agency and the brain of entire export promotion system in the India and is responsible for evolving and directing India's foreign trade policy and programmes including developing trade relations with other countries. It also supervises the state trading in India and is also responsible for devising and implementing various trade promotional measures and the development and regulation of certain export-oriented industries. It formulates and regulates country's foreign trade policy and is responsible for external trade including commercial relations with other countries, state trading, various trade promotional measures, and development and regulation of certain export-oriented industries and commodities such as tea and tobacco. The department functions through the following six divisions.

1. **The Economic Division:** This division is headed by the economic adviser to the Government of India. The division is responsible for the development of export planning and export strategies and also for the periodic review and appraisal of foreign trade policy, it co-ordinates the functions of and maintains contacts with the other division as well as with other organizations set up under the Department of Commerce to assist the export drive. It also monitors work relating to technical assistance, management services for exports and overseas investments by Indian entrepreneurs.
2. **The Trade Policy Division:** This division is mainly concerned with the development in the international field like UNCTAD, GATT and ESCAP. It has regular contact with regional groupings like EEC, EFTA, LAFTA etc. and Commonwealth to maintain trade relations. It is also responsible for the tariff and non-tariff barriers imposed by the importing countries on India's exports.
3. **The Foreign Trade Territorial Division:** This division is entrusted with the relating to the development of trade with different regions and countries of the world. It looks after matters relating to state trading, trade fairs and exhibitions, organisation of trade; commercial publicity abroad etc. Besides, it also maintains a liaison with India, commercial missions and representatives abroad and attends to the connective administrative work as also the protocol functions.
4. **The Export Products Division:** The division is concerned with the problems of production, generation of surplus and market development of different products except with the products under the jurisdiction of the export industries division which are exported by India. Though these products administratively continue to be under the ministries concerned, the division is simply responsible for ensuring that exportable surplus is generated on continuous basis and export commitments are met to their full extent besides meeting the home consumption. It also keeps continuous watch over the functioning of export promotion councils, commodity boards and other export organizations dealing with the commodities under its jurisdiction.
5. **The Export Industries Division:** This division is responsible for the problems connected with the production development and regulation of some select commodities, including tobacco, rubber, and cardamom for export purposes. It also looks after the export promotion activities of certain specified products, including textiles, woollens, readymade garments, coir, silk and handicrafts.
6. **The Export Services Division:** This divisions deals with problems of export assistance, facilities and grants to Indian industries and exporters to produce more to general export surplus. The functions of this division include replenishment licenses, cash assistance, marketing development assistance, export credit, export houses, guidance to Indian entrepreneurs to set up joint ventures abroad, capacity creation in export-oriented units etc.

81. X' share $= \frac{1}{3}$

Remaining profit $= \frac{1}{3} = \frac{2}{3}$

$$\text{A's share} = \frac{2}{3} \times \frac{3}{5} = \frac{2}{5}$$

$$\text{D's share} = \frac{2}{3} \times \frac{2}{5} = \frac{4}{15}$$

$$\text{New Ratio} = \frac{6}{15} : \frac{4}{15} : \frac{5}{15}$$

$$= 6 : 4 : 5.$$

82. Road Block: A method of scheduling broadcast commercials to obtain maximum reach by simultaneously showing the identical advertisement on several different stations.

83. Functions of WTO

The Agreement establishing WTO provides that it should perform the following four functions:

- First, it shall facilitate the implementation, administration and operation of the Uruguay Round legal instruments and of any new agreements that may be negotiated in the future.
- Second, it shall provide a forum for further negotiations among member countries on matters covered by the agreements as well as on new issues falling within its mandate.
- Third, it shall be responsible for the settlement of differences and disputes among its member countries.
- Fourth, it shall be responsible for carrying out periodic reviews of the trade policies of its member countries.

84. Bretton Woods Conference, formally **United Nations Monetary and Financial Conference,** meeting at Bretton Woods, New Hampshire (July 1-22, 1944), during World War II to make financial arrangements for the postwar world after the expected defeat of Germany and Japan.

The conference was attended by experts non-committally representing 44 states or governments, including the Soviet Union. It drew up a project for the International Bank for Reconstruction and Development (IBRD) to make long-term capital available to states urgently needing such foreign aid, and a project for the International Monetary Fund (IMF) to finance short-term imbalances in international payments in order to stabilize exchange rates. Although the conference recognized that exchange control and discriminatory tariffs would probably be necessary for some time after the war, it prescribed that such measures should be ended as soon as possible. After governmental ratifications the IBRD was constituted late in 1945 and the IMF in 1946, to become operative, respectively, in the two following years.

85. Forms of Direct Marketing

- Mail Order Marketing/Catalogue Marketing
- Direct Mail Marketing
- Direct Response Marketing
- Database Marketing
- Telemarketing
- Teleshopping (Home Shopping)
- The New Age DM Methods

  Marketing through Mobile Phone

  Marketing through ATMs

  Viral marketing
- Online Marketing/Marketing on the Web

87. Types of FDI

We distinguish between horizontal and vertical FDI. Horizontal FDI occurs when the MNE enters a foreign country to produce the same product(s) produced at home (or offer the same service that it sells at home). It represents, therefore, a geographical diversification of the MNE's domestic product line. Most Japanese MNEs, for instance, begin their international expansion with horizontal investment because they believe that this approach enables them to share experience, resources, and knowledge already developed at home, thus reducing risk. If FDI abroad is to manufacture products not manufactured by the parent company at home, it is called conglomerate FDI. For example, Hong Kong MNEs often set up foreign subsidiaries or acquire local firms in Mainland China to manufacture goods that are unrelated to the parent company's portfolio of products. The main purpose is to seize emerging-market opportunities and capitalize on their established business and personal networks with the mainland that Western MNEs do not have. Vertical FDI occurs when the MNE enters a foreign country to produce intermediate goods that are intended for use as inputs in its home country (or in other subsidiaries') production process (this is called "backward vertical FDI"), to market its homemade products overseas, or to produce final outputs in a host country using its home-supplied intermediate goods or materials (this is called "forward vertical FDI"). An example of backward vertical FDI is offshore extractive investments in petroleum and minerals. An example of forward vertical integration is the establishment of an assembly plant or a sales outlet overseas.

89. Factor Proportions Theory

Almost after a century and a quarter of the classical version of the theory of international trade, two Swedish economists, Eli Heckscher and Bertil Ohlin, propounded a theory that is known as the factor endowment theory or the factor proportions theory. In fact, it was Eli Heckscher who mooted the notion of a country's comparative advantage (disadvantage) based on relative abundance (scarcity) of factors of production. Later on, his student, Bertil Ohlin developed this notion of relative factor abundance into a theory of the pattern of international trade.

The theory explains that in a two-country, two-factor, and two-commodity framework different countries are endowed with varying proportions of different factors of production. Some countries have large populations and large labour resources. Others have abundance of capital but are short of labour resources. Thus, a country with a large labour force will be able to produce the goods at a lower cost using a labour intensive mode of production. Similarly, countries with a large supply of capital will specialise in goods that involve a capital intensive mode of production. The former will export its labour intensive goods to the latter and import capital intensive goods from the latter. After the trade, both the countries will have two types of goods at the least cost.

Factor endowment theory explains that a country should produce and export a commodity that primarily involves a factor of production abundantly available within the country.

90. Differences between HRM and PM

Dimension	*Personnel Management*	*Human Resource Management*
1. Employment contract	Careful delineation of written contracts	Aim to go beyond contract
2. Rules	Importance of devising clear rules	Can do outlook, impatience with rules
3. Guide to management action	Procedures	Business need
4. Behaviour referent	Norms/customs and practices	Values/mission
5. Managerial task vis-à-vis labour	Monitoring	Nurturing
6. Key relations	Labour management	Customer
7. Initiatives	Piecemeal	Integrated
8. Speed of decision	Slow	Fast
9. Management role	Transactional	Transformational

10. Communication	Indirect	Direct
11. Prized management skills	Negotiation	Facilitation
12. Selection	Separate, marginal task	Integrated, key task
13. Pay	Job evaluation (fixed grades)	Performance related
14. Conditions	Separately negotiated	Harmonisation
15. Labour management	Collective-bargaining contracts	Individual contracts
16. Job categories and grades	Many	Few
17. Job design	Division of labour	Team work
18. Conflict handling	Reach temporary truce	Manage climate and culture
19. Training and development	Controlled access to courses	Learning companies
20. Focus of attention for interventions	Personnel procedures	Wide-ranging cultural, structural and personnel strategies
21. Respect for employees	Labour is treated as a tool which is expendable and replaceable	People are treated as assets to be used for the benefit of an organisation, its employees and the society as a whole
22. Shared interests	Interests of the organisation are uppermost	Mutuality of interests
23. Evolution	Precedes HRM	Latest in the evolution of the subject
24. Locus of control	External	Internal
25. Organising principles	Mechanistic Top-down Centralised	Organic Bottom-up Oecentralised

91. The **Critical Path Method** or **CPM** is a network analysis technique concerned with planning and controlling of complex, but routine projects. Simply, Critical path method is generally used for the projects whose time duration is known with certainty and also the amount of resources required for the completion of the project is assumed to be known.

The Critical Path method is deterministic in nature, since the required amount of resources and the time needed for the completion of the whole project is known, and is mainly used in the construction projects. This method was developed by Du Pont Company and the Univac Division of Remington Rand Corporation as a technique for controlling the maintenance of chemical plants.

93. As with own-price elasticity and cross-price elasticity, the good or service can also be classified according to its income elasticity:

$E_Y > 1$ Superior good

$E_Y > 0$ Normal good

$E_Y < 0$ Inferior good

If the product's income elasticity is greater than zero, then the good is categorized as a normal good—that is, the quantity demanded of a normal good increases with any increase in the consumer's income. As we might expect, the vast majority of goods and services can be classified as normal goods, as in the above example. A subcategory of normal goods are superior goods, whose income elasticity is greater than one. Superior goods have a proportional increase in the quantity demanded that is greater than the increase in consumer income. Superior goods usually encompass high-end luxury products such as fancy sport cars and business jet travel.

The other goods categorized according to income elasticity are inferior goods. Inferior goods have income elasticity values less than zero, indicating that, for any increase in income, the quantity demanded decreases.

This peculiar situation occurs when products have a price advantage over competitors but are generally not perceived as quality goods. Therefore, when consumers' income increases, they are more willing to purchase the perceived better product. Examples of inferior goods might include generic products versus brand names or, in some markets, coach travel versus first-class seats.

The concept of elasticity is critical to understanding pricing policies of any industry, especially the air transportation industry, and, as the earlier discussion has shown, elasticity can be used to determine the optimum price level where total revenue is maximized. Ultimately, revenue management has its foundation in this concept since elasticity can be used to help manage both pricing and capacity.

94. Kotler and Singh: have defined the following defensive strategies:

- A *position defense* is designed to defend a position by strengthening the firm's brand power.
- A *pre-emptive defense* is an attempt to anticipate a competitive attack. This may involve covering every segment and niche within a market and flooding the market with products, targeting specific competitors before they can attack or indicating to the market the ways in which the leader intends to defend itself.
- A *flank defense* creates interventions in order to protect the leader's position. For example, a competitor's price attack on a firm's brand may be responded to by introducing two new brands, one designed to be sold at the same price as the competitor's brand, and the second at a lower price in order to outflank the competitor.
- A *mobile defense* involves *market broadening*. This usually involves an attempt to shift the emphasis from a specific product to the underlying need. An example is the repositioning of television companies as multimedia companies. An alternative to market broadening is *market diversification,* which involves the mergers of firms in wholly different industries into conglomerates.
- An *alternative defense* involves concentrating corporate resources in the areas of its greatest strength rather than defending all of the firm's positions.
- A *contraction defense* involves a strategic withdrawal from specific areas of lesser strength.
- A *counteroffensive defense* may lead the organization to respond to a competitor's price cuts in one market sector by slashing prices in another market sector considered to be more important to the competitor.

95. Infrastructure Bottlenecks

Quantitatively, India is rich in transport and communication network but qualitatively it is poor. The industries face shortage of raw materials. To meet this problem, they are located near the source of raw material which may not be richly endowed in terms of other factors of production. In our country, the position of power supply is poor and uncertain. Hence, both agriculture and industries fail to utilise their full capacity. Our economy also suffers from bureaucratic bottlenecks. The time lag in completion of projects, due to procedural hold ups inflates the total cost of the project and makes them financially unviable.

Its Remedy

Most infrastructure services in India have until recently been provided by public monopolies and quasi-monopolies and have been faced by several problems like lack of accountability, low productivity, poor financial performance and over-employment. In older to meet the challenges of rapid economic growth and international competitiveness, there is an urgent need to achieve greater efficiency and accountability in these sectors, much greater prevalence of commercial principles and much more competition in the provision and operation of infrastructure services. As the Government's ability to undertake investment in infrastructure is severely constrained, it is necessary to induce much more private sector investment and participation in the provision of infrastructural services. The entry of private suppliers can also encourage better risk sharing, accountability, monitoring and management in infrastructure sectors. The Government has, however, already introduced several structural reforms in the infrastructural sectors.

Government Steps

The Union Government has recently taken steps to upgrade infrastructure and bring Foreign Direct Investment (FDI) in infrastructure. This is a step in right direction. In this era of globalisation and liberalism, to maintain the competitive edge, we need to modernise and upgrade our infrastructure.

97. Cash Reserve Ratio (CRR)

CRR is the most powerful tool to influence and control the monetary aggregates of the country. Under section 42(1) of RBI act, 1934, every scheduled commercial bank was required to maintain with the RBI every fortnight a minimum average daily cash reserve equivalent to 3% of its Net Demand and Time Liabilities (NDTL) outstanding as on the Friday of the previous week. The RBI is empowered to vary the CRR between 3% and 15%. RBI is using the CRR either to impound the excess liquidity or to release funds needed for the economy from time to time.

Statutory Liquidity Ratio (SLR)

Under section 24(b) of the Banking Regulation Act: 1949, every bank is required to maintain at the close of business every day, a minimum proportion of their Net Demand and Time Liabilities as liquid assets in the form of cash, gold and un-encumbered approved securities. The ratio of liquid assets to demand and time liabilities is known as Statutory Liquidity Ratio (SLR). The RBI is empowered to increase the SLR upto 40%.

Non-Performing (NPA)

RBI has defined NPA as follows (credit facility wise)

NPA - Term Loan: If interest and/instalment of principal remains overdue for a period of more than 180 days.

NPA - Cash credit & overdraft: A CC/OD account will have to be treated as NPA if account remains out of order for more than 180 days.

NPA - Bills purchased & Discounted: If the bill remains overdue for a period of more than 180 days.

Reverse Repo Rate

A Reverse Repo Rate is a rate that RBI offers to banks when they deposit their surplus cash with RBI for shorter periods. In other words, it is the rate at which the RBI borrows from the commercial banks. When banks have excess funds, but don't have any other lending or investment options, they deposit/ lend the surplus funds with the RBI. This way banks can raise additional interest from their funds.

The reverse repo rate has an inverse relationship with the money supply in the economy. During high levels of inflation in the economy, the RBI increases the reverse repo. It encourages the banks to park more funds with the RBI to earn higher returns on idle cash. As a result, every excess rupee is put to use in banking system. Banks are left with lesser cash to extend loans, curbing the purchasing power of individuals.

Repo Rate

Repo rate refers to the rate at which commercial banks borrow money from the Reserve Bank of India (RBI) in case of shortage of funds. It is one of the main tools of RBI to keep inflation under control.

Previous Paper (Solved)

UGC-NET-Junior Research Fellowship & Assistant Professor Eligibility Exam

COMMERCE, July-2018*

PAPER-II

Note: *This paper contains* ***hundred (100)*** *objective type questions of* ***two (2)*** *marks each.* ***All*** *questions are* ***compulsory***.

1. The central bank can significantly influence the savings, investments and consumer spending in the economy through which of the following policy?

A. Fiscal Policy
B. Monetary Policy
C. Industrial Policy
D. Foreign Exchange Policy

2. Which one of the following is **not** the characteristic of capitalism?

A. Individuals and associations behave with economic motive of maximising their profit with least sacrifice or cost.
B. The country's major means of production are either owned by the Government or their use is controlled by the Government.
C. Producers, consumers and employees compete among themselves, as the resources and opportunities are limited.
D. Price, the invisible hand, plays a predominant role in the flow of the factors of production and consumption.

3. Which of the following is **not** the salient feature of the industrial policy developments since 1991?

A. The scope of the private sector has been enormously expanded.
B. Public sector has been withdrawing partially or fully from several of the enterprises by divestment.
C. The Indian industry is increasingly exposed to foreign competition.
D. Monopoly or dominant position for the public sector in most of the industries and control of the commanding heights of the economy by the public sector.

4. Which of the following does **not** form the part of the important information to be incorporated in the Memorandum of Association as specified in the Companies Act, 2013?

A. The name of the company and the state in which it is situated.
B. The objects for which the company is proposed to be incorporated.
C. The rules, regulations and bye-laws for the internal management of the company.
D. The liability of the members of the company, whether limited or unlimited.

5. **Assertion (A):** The volume of imports tends to be very high when there is a conjecture of high rate of economic growth and a sharp fall in the relative price of imports and vice versa.

Reason (R): High rate of growth, ceteris paribus, is associated with rise in imports and increase in the imports, ceteris paribus, is associated with a fall in the relative price of imports.

Code:

A. Both (A) and (R) are correct and (R) is the right explanation of (A).
B. Both (A) and (R) are correct but (R) is not the right explanation of (A).
C. (A) is correct but (R) is not correct
D. (R) is correct but (A) is not correct.

* *Held on 8 July, 2018.*

6. Which of the following statements is **not** correct relating to consumerism?

A. Consumerism is a manifestation of the failure of the business to guarantee and ensure consumer legitimate rights.
B. The government does not have any role in consumer protection as it is the part of business organisations alone.
C. The consumers should accept consumerism as a means of asserting and enjoying their rights.
D. Consumerism evolution is not a set-back for marketing but rather points to the next stage in the evolution of enlightened marketing.

7. Which one of the following is **not** covered in the approach adopted by "Niti Aayog"?

A. Five year planning approach
B. Three year action agenda
C. Seven year strategy
D. Fifteen year vision

8. **Assertion (A):** Personal transactions of the owners of the business are not recorded in the books.

Reasoning (R): According to the business entity concept, each business enterprise is considered as an accounting unit separate from owners.

Code:

A. Both (A) and (R) are correct and (R) is the correct explanation of (A).
B. Both (A) and (R) are correct but (R) is not the correct explanation of (A).
C. (A) is correct but (R) is not correct.
D. (A) is wrong but (R) is correct.

9. Which one of the following is not an example of 'financing activities' with reference to cash flow statement?

A. Repayment of bank loan
B. Interest on debentures/Dividend paid
C. Cash proceeds from public deposits
D. Sale of fixed assets

10. Which one of the following statements is **true** about estimated costs and standard costs?

A. Standard costs are based on scientific analysis and engineering studies while estimated costs are based on historical basis.
B. Standard cost emphasis is on "what cost will be" while estimated cost emphasis is on "what cost should be".
C. Standard costs are more frequently revised compared to estimated cost.
D. Estimated costs are more stable than standard costs.

11. Which one of the following statements is **not** true?

A. An expenditure intended to benefit current year is revenue expenditure.
B. Amount paid for acquiring goodwill is capital expenditure.
C. Wages paid for installation of a new machine is usually debited to wages account.
D. Revenue expenditure is not intended to benefit future period.

12. X Ltd. forfeited 20 shares of ₹ 10 each, ₹ 8 called up, on which John had paid application and allotment money of ₹ 5 per share, of these, 15 shares were reissued to Parker as fully paid up for ₹ 6 per share. What is the balance in the share Forfeiture Account after the relevant amount has been transferred to Capital Reserve Account?

A. NIL B. ₹ 5
C. ₹ 25 D. ₹ 100

13. X and Y sharing profits in the ratio of 7 : 3, admit Z for 3/7 share in the new firm in which he takes 2/7 from X and 1/7 from Y. The new ratio of X, Y and Z will be:

A. 7 : 3 : 3 B. 4 : 2 : 3
C. 14 : 6 : 15 D. 29 : 11 : 30

14. **Assertion (A):** A high operating ratio indicates a favourable position.

Reasoning (R): A high operating ratio leaves a high margin to meet non-operating expenses.

Code:

A. (A) and (R) both are correct and (R) correctly explains (A).

B. Both (A) and (R) are correct but (R) does not explain (A).
C. Both (A) and (R) are incorrect.
D. (A) is correct but (R) is incorrect.

15. The following are the two statements regarding concept of profit. Indicate the correct code of the statements being correct or incorrect.

Statement (I): Accounting profit is a surplus of total revenue over and above all paid-out costs, including both manufacturing and overhead expenses.

Statement (II): Economic or pure profit is a residual left after all contractual costs have been met, including the transfer costs of management, insurable risks, depreciation and payments to shareholders sufficient to maintain investment at its current level.

Code:
A. Both the statements are correct.
B. Both the statements are incorrect.
C. Statement (I) is correct while Statement (II) is incorrect.
D. Statement (I) is incorrect while Statement (II) is correct.

16. Which one of the following sets is incorrect to show the inter-relationships among price elasticity coefficient, change in price and change in total revenue?

Price elasticity coefficient	Change in price	Change in Total Revenue
A. Zero	Increase	Increase
	Decrease	Decrease
B. Less than 1	Increase	Decrease
	Decrease	Increase
C. Equal to 1	Increase	No change
	Decrease	No change
D. More than 1	Increase	Decrease
	Decrease	Increase

17. Which one of the following is not the basic property of indifference curves?
A. Indifference curves have a negative slope.
B. Indifference curves of imperfect substitutes are concave to the origin.
C. Indifference curves do not intersect nor are they tangent to one another.
D. Upper indifference curves indicate higher level of satisfaction.

18. When labour is plotted on X-axis and capital is plotted on Y-axis and an iso-quant is prepared, then which of the following statements is/are **false**?
(*a*) Marginal rate of technical substitution of labour for capital is equal to the slope of the iso-quant.
(*b*) Marginal rate of technical substitution of labour for capital is equal to change in the units of capital divided by the change in the units of labour.
(*c*) Marginal rate of technical substitution of labour for capital is the ratio of marginal productivity of capital to marginal productivity of labour.

Code:
A. (*a*) and (*b*) statements
B. Only (*c*) statement
C. Only (*a*) statement
D. Only (*b*) statement

19. Match the items of List-II with the items of List-I and indicate the code of correct matching. The items relate to economies of scale/scope.

List-I	List-II
(*a*) Economies of scale	(*i*) arise with lower average costs of manufacturing a product when two complementary products are produced by a single firm
(*b*) Internal economies	(*ii*) Mean lowering of costs of production by producing in bulk
(*c*) External economies	(*iii*) Arise when cost per unit depends on size of the firm
(*d*) Economies of scope	(*iv*) Arise when cost per unit depends on the size of the industry, not the firm

Code:

	(a)	(b)	(c)	(d)
A.	(ii)	(iv)	(i)	(iii)
B.	(i)	(ii)	(iii)	(iv)
C.	(ii)	(iii)	(iv)	(i)
D.	(iv)	(iii)	(ii)	(i)

20. A firm that produces highly substitute goods can adopt which one of the following pricing strategies?
A. Transfer pricing
B. Going Rate pricing
C. Product bundling
D. Full cost pricing

21. In a perfectly competitive market, a firm in the long run operates at the level of output where:
A. AC = MC when MC is lowest
B. MC = AR = MR when MC is lowest
C. MR = MC
D. AR = MR = AC = MC

22. Assignment of numerals to the objects to represent their attributes is known as:
A. Nominal data B. Ordinal data
C. Interval data D. Ratio data

23. A graph of a cumulative frequency distribution is called:
A. Frequency polygon
B. Frequency curve
C. Ogive
D. Pie diagram

24. In the case of classification of data, the class having its upper limit is treated as the lower limit of its next class is called:
A. Open ended class
B. Close ended class
C. Exclusive class
D. Inclusive class

25. For a standard normal probability distribution, the mean (μ) and the standard deviation (σ) are:
A. $\mu = 0, \sigma = 1$ B. $\mu = 16, \sigma = 4$
C. $\mu = 25, \sigma = 5$ D. $\mu = 100, \sigma = 10$

26. Match the items of List-II with the items of List-I and select the code of correct matching.

List-I	List-II
(a) Standard error of mean	(i) Ha : $\mu_1 \neq \mu_2$
(b) Base of point estimate of the mean of the population	(ii) Values based on all the observations of the population
(c) Non-specific hypothesis	(iii) Mean of the sampling distribution of mean
(d) Parameter value of descriptive statistics	(iv) Standard deviation of the sampling distribution of mean

Code:

	(a)	(b)	(c)	(d)
A.	(iv)	(iii)	(i)	(ii)
B.	(i)	(ii)	(iii)	(iv)
C.	(iv)	(iii)	(ii)	(i)
D.	(iii)	(iv)	(i)	(ii)

27. There is a very high inverse relationship between measures of 'Overweight' and 'life expectancy'. Which one of the following value of the coefficient of correlation is consistent with the statement?
A. 0.80 B. 0.20
C. –0.20 D. –0.80

28. Match the items of List-II with the items of List-I and select the code of correct matching.

List-I	List-II
(a) Chi-square Test	(i) Testing the significance of the differences of the mean values among more than two sample groups.
(b) ANOVA (F-test)	(ii) Testing the goodness of fit of a distribution
(c) Z-test	(iii) Testing the significance of the difference of the mean values between two large sized samples
(d) *t*-test	(iv) Testing the significance of the difference of the mean values between two small sized samples when population standard deviation is not available

Code:

	(a)	(b)	(c)	(d)
A.	(i)	(ii)	(iii)	(iv)
B.	(iv)	(iii)	(ii)	(i)
C.	(i)	(ii)	(iv)	(iii)
D.	(ii)	(i)	(iii)	(iv)

29. Match the items of List-II with List-I and choose the correct code:

List-I	List-II
(a) Sales Executive	(i) Top-middle Management
(b) Branch Manager	(ii) Middle Management
(c) Foreman	(iii) Lower Management
(d) Production Manager	(iv) Operating Force

Code:

	(a)	(b)	(c)	(d)
A.	(iv)	(ii)	(iii)	(i)
B.	(ii)	(iii)	(iv)	(i)
C.	(iii)	(iv)	(ii)	(i)
D.	(i)	(ii)	(iii)	(iv)

30. Select the **correct** code of the statements being **correct** or **incorrect**.

Statement (I): It is a significant feature of human that he plans.

Statement (II): A plan is a trap to capture the future.

Code:

A. Statement (I) is correct but (II) is incorrect.
B. Statement (II) is correct but (I) is incorrect.
C. Both the statements (I) and (II) are correct.
D. Both the statements (I) and (II) are incorrect.

31. **Assertion (A):** Management is a set of principles relating to its functions.

Reasoning (R): Management is essential to run all types of organizations.

Code:

A. (A) and (R) both are correct ; and (R) is the right explanation of (A).
B. (A) and (R) both are correct ; but (R) is not the right explanation of (A).
C. Both (A) and (R) are incorrect.
D. (A) is correct; but (R) is incorrect.

32. Match the items of List-II with List-I; and choose the correct code:

List-I (Critical Control Standards)	List-II (Critical Points)
(a) Physical standards	(i) Material cost per unit
(b) Cost standards	(ii) Labour hours per unit of output
(c) Revenue standards	(iii) Timing of production
(d) Program standards	(iv) Average sales per customer

Code:

	(a)	(b)	(c)	(d)
A.	(ii)	(i)	(iv)	(iii)
B.	(ii)	(i)	(iii)	(iv)
C.	(i)	(ii)	(iv)	(iii)
D.	(iv)	(i)	(iii)	(ii)

33. Which among the following is **not** a correct statement with regard to Corporate Governance in India?

A. Every company must appoint an individual or firm as auditor.
B. The independent directors must attend at least three meetings a year.
C. One or more women directors are recommended for certain classes of companies.
D. The maximum number of permissible directors cannot exceed 15 in a public limited company.

34. The popular statement, – "if all you have is a hammer, everything looks like a nail", is given by:

A. A.H. Maslow (Hierarchy of Needs)
B. Henry Fayol (Industrial and General Administration)
C. F.W. Taylor (Scientific Management)
D. Fredrick Herzberg (Hygiene Theory)

35. Functional Leadership Theory is associated with:

A. Hackman and Walton and McGrath
B. Bernard and Ordway Tead
C. Koontz and O'Donnell
D. Alford and Beatty

36. When two separate companies or two divisions within the same company agree to place both of their respective brands on a particular product or enterprise, this arrangement is termed as:

A. Differential Branding
B. Cobranding
C. Dual Branding
D. Both Cobranding and Dual Branding

37. The tangible goods for which a consumer wants to compare quality, price and perhaps style in several stores before making a purchase are called:

A. Convenience Goods
B. Shopping Goods
C. Speciality Goods
D. Unsought Goods

38. When a company treats each single customer as a separate segment, this is called:

A. Niche Marketing B. Nano Marketing
C. Single Marketing D. Micro Marketing

39. Under which of the following conditions, the level of consumer's involvement will not be high?

A. The consumer considers the amount of money involved to be large.
B. The product is seen as having low potential for providing significant benefits.
C. The consumer lacks information about alternatives for satisfying the need.
D. The product has considerable social importance.

40. Statement (I): The mindset which is commonly associated with a long - ago era when the demand for goods generally exceeded the supply, and the primary focus in business was to effectively produce medium quantities of products; finding the customers was viewed as a relatively major function.

Statement (II): The firms with product orientation typically focus on the quality and quantity of offerings while assuming that customers will seek out and buy reasonably priced, well made products.

From the above statements indicate the **correct** code of being statements **correct** or **incorrect** The statements relate to concepts of marketing.

A. Both the statements (I) and (II) are not correct.
B. Both the statements (I) and (II) are correct.
C. Statement (I) is correct but statement (II) is not correct.
D. Statement (I) is not correct but statement (II) is correct.

41. Match the items of List-II with List-I to identify the correct code which are related to legal forces affecting international marketers.

List-I	List-II
(*a*) Tariff	(*i*) A regulation specifying the proportion of a finished product's components and labour that must be provided by importing country.
(*b*) Import Quota	(*ii*) Tax imposed on product entering a country and used to protect domestic producers and/or raise revenue.
(*c*) Local-content Law	(*iii*) A requirement that a product contain or exclude certain ingredients or that it be tested and certified as meeting certain restrictive standards.
(*d*) Local-operating Law	(*iv*) Limiting amount of a particular product that can be brought into a country, to protect domestic industry or broadening access to its markets.
(*e*) Standards and Certification	(*v*) A refusal to buy products from a particular company or country.
(*f*) Boycott	(*vi*) A constraint on how, when or where retailing can be conducted.

Code:

	(a)	(b)	(c)	(d)	(e)	(f)
A.	(iii)	(iv)	(ii)	(i)	(vi)	(v)
B.	(vi)	(ii)	(i)	(iv)	(iii)	(v)
C.	(ii)	(iv)	(i)	(vi)	(iii)	(v)
D.	(iv)	(vi)	(i)	(ii)	(iii)	(v)

42. Match the items of List-II with List-I which are related to personal selling process and identify the correct code:

List-I	List-II
(a) Prospecting	(i) Attention, Interest, Desire, Action
(b) Preapproach	(ii) Identifying Profiles, leads, Records and Qualifying capability and willingness
(c) Presentation	(iii) Reduce Dissonance, Build goodwill
(d) Post sales services	(iv) Information, habits, preferences

Code:

	(a)	(b)	(c)	(d)
A.	(i)	(iii)	(iv)	(ii)
B.	(iii)	(iv)	(ii)	(i)
C.	(ii)	(iv)	(i)	(iii)
D.	(iv)	(iii)	(ii)	(i)

43. Which of the following is not an approach to the Capital Structure?

A. Gross Profit Approach
B. Net Operating Income Approach
C. Net Income Approach
D. Modigliani and Miller Approach

44. Which one of the following methods of Capital Budgeting assumes that cash-inflows are reinvested at the project's rate of return?

A. Net Present Value
B. Accounting Rate of Return
C. Internal Rate of Return
D. Discounted Pay Back Period

45. Cost of Equity Share Capital is more than cost of Debt because:

A. Equity shares are not easily saleable.
B. Equity shares do not provide the fixed dividend rate.
C. Generally the face value of equity shares is less than the face value of debentures.
D. Equity shares have high risk than debts.

46. Negative Net Working Capital implies that:

A. Long-term funds have been used for fixed assets.
B. Short-term funds have been used for fixed assets.
C. Long-term funds have been used for current assets.
D. Short-term funds have been used for current assets.

47. Which of the following is an implicit cost of increasing proportion of debt of a company?

A. P.E. Ratio of the company would increase.
B. Rate of return of the company would decrease.
C. Tax-shield would not be available on new debts.
D. Equity shareholders would demand higher return.

48. Profitability Index of a Project is the ratio of present value of cash inflows to:

A. Total cash inflows
B. Total cash outflows
C. Present value of cash outflows
D. Initial cost minus depreciation

49. Which one of the following statements is false?

A. Effective dividend policy is an important tool to achieve the goal of wealth maximisation.
B. According to Walter, the optimal payout ratio for a growth firm is 100%.
C. MM model asserts that the value of the firm is not affected whether the firm pays dividend or not.
D. 'Bird-in-the-hand theory' in reference to dividend decision has been developed by Myron Gordon.

50. Which one of the following statements defines the correct meaning of the term "boundary spanning"?

A. It refers to an obligation of an individual, firm or institution to account for its activities and accept responsibility for them.

B. It refers to the process that helps the organization and its employees to link with their external environment through specific activities/functions.

C. It refers to the science of morals, principles and rules of conduct.

D. It refers to multiculturism management.

51. The VRIO framework, used in HR function in today's era, refers to four criteria. Identify the correct code which stands as correct explanation to VRIO as proposed by Barney.

A. Valence - Recruiting - Industrial relations - Opportunities

B. Vision - Rewards - Improvements - Options

C. Value - Rarity - Imitability - Organization

D. Versatile - Resource - Information - Outsourcing

52. Assertion (A): Induction is an informal information sharing session on miscellaneous issues in an organization.

Reasoning (R): The rationale of induction is to ensure effective integration of staff into or across the organization for their mutual benefit.

Code:

A. Assertion (A) and Reasoning (R) both are correct and (R) is correct explanation of (A).

B. Assertion (A) and Reasoning (R) both are correct but (R) is not the correct explanation of (A).

C. Assertion (A) is correct statement but Reasoning (R) is an incorrect statement.

D. Assertion (A) is an incorrect statement but Reasoning (R) is a correct statement.

53. Match the items of List-II with the items of List-I pertaining to the ranking methods used in performance management systems; and select the code of correct matching.

List-I (Ranking methods)	List-II (Methodology)
(*a*) Simple ranking	(*i*) Based on overall performance.
(*b*) Alternation ranking	(*ii*) Ends up with predetermined number of people in each group.
(*c*) Paired comparison	(*iii*) Based on particular trait only for quantity/quality of work.
(*d*) Forced distribution	(*iv*) Based on a trait or a set of trait and avoids central tendency.

Code:

	(*a*)	(*b*)	(*c*)	(*d*)
A.	(*ii*)	(*iii*)	(*iv*)	(*i*)
B.	(*i*)	(*iv*)	(*iii*)	(*ii*)
C.	(*iv*)	(*ii*)	(*i*)	(*iii*)
D.	(*iii*)	(*i*)	(*ii*)	(*iv*)

54. Assertion (A): Compensation has two vital domains economic concept and psychological concept.

Reasoning (R): Compensation basically represents an employment contract.

Code:

A. (A) is correct and (R) is right explanation of (A).

B. (A) is correct but (R) is not the right explanation of (A).

C. (A) is correct but (R) is incorrect.

D. (A) is incorrect but (R) is correct.

55. Which of the following is not the primary objective of industrial relations and labour laws?

A. Maintaining social equity

B. Providing credit facilities to industries

C. International uniformity

D. Promoting economic growth

56. Assertion (A): In real terms, workers' participation in management has failed in India.

Reasoning (R): There is lack of attitudinal change, multiplicity of unions and absence of a procedure to determine a sole bargaining agent in an organization.

Code:

A. (A) is correct and (R) is correct explanation of (A).

B. (A) is correct but (R) is not the correct explanation of (A).

C. (A) is correct but (R) is incorrect.

D. (A) is incorrect but (R) is correct.

57. Which one of the following is not the function of NABARD?

A. To provide refinance assistance by way of short-term credit to state cooperative banks and sectoral rural banks, etc., approved by the RBI for some specific purposes.

B. To undertake inspection of cooperative societies other than primary cooperative societies and RRBs.

C. To promote research in various aspects of the problems of urban development.

D. To subscribe to share capital or invest in securities of any institution concerned with agricultural and rural development.

58. Which one of the following financial institutions co-ordinates the functions and operations of all the financial institutions into a single integrated financial structure so that each may contribute to the growth of the economy?

A. IFCI B. UTI

C. IDBI D. SIDBI

59. Assertion (A): The Reserve Bank of India is entrusted with the management of the public debt and issue of new loans and treasury bills on behalf of the central and state Governments.

Reasoning (R): The Governor and the Deputy Governors of Reserve Bank of India are appointed by the Central Government.

Code:

A. (A) is correct but (R) is not correct.

B. (A) and (R) both are correct but (R) is not the right explanation of (A).

C. (A) and (R) both are correct and (R) is the right explanation of (A).

D. (A) and (R) both are not correct.

60. ________ refers to the process of removing or stripping the legal status of a currency.

A. Digitisation

B. Financial Inclusion

C. Demonetisation

D. Micro finance

61. Which one of the following is not the objective of UTI?

A. To mobilise savings of the community by offering savers the triple benefits of safety, liquidity and profitability of Investments.

B. To channelise the pooled savings into productive outlets.

C. To provide finance under hire purchase finance and housing finance to its members.

D. To give every one a chance to indirectly own shares and securities in a large number of select companies.

62. Which one of the following is the main objective of IFCI?

A. To offer both small and large investors the means of acquiring shares in the widening prosperity resulting from the steady industrial growth of the country.

B. To upgrade technology, modernization and to promote marketing of products of small scale sector.

C. To serve as the apex institution for term finance for industry with coordination, regulation and supervision of the working of other financial institution.

D. To provide medium and long-term financial assistance to industrial undertakings, particularly in those circumstances in which banking accommodation is in appropriate or resource to capital market is impracticable.

63. Match the items of List-II with the items of List-I and indicate the correct code:

List-I	List-II
(*a*) Term finance	(*i*) Providing finance to new or existing industrial units for encouraging commercial application of technology/expansion.

(*b*) Refinance	(*ii*)	Delivering of banking services at affordable cost to the vast sections of disadvantaged and low income groups.
(*c*) Financial inclusion	(*iii*)	Providing replenishment finance to eligible institutions for their loans to industrial concerns.
(*d*) Venture capital	(*iv*)	Providing finance to the borrowers for expansion and modernization of plant and equipment.

Code:

	(*a*)	(*b*)	(*c*)	(*d*)
A.	(*i*)	(*ii*)	(*iii*)	(*iv*)
B.	(*i*)	(*ii*)	(*iv*)	(*iii*)
C.	(*iv*)	(*iii*)	(*ii*)	(*i*)
D.	(*iv*)	(*iii*)	(*i*)	(*ii*)

64. **Assertion (A):** An export processing zone is different from free trade zone as it promotes units primarily devoted to exports.

Reasoning (R): Goods imported to a free trade zone may be re-exported without any processing, in the same form. But, goods exported by units in an EPZ are expected to have undergone some value addition by manufacturing/processing.

Code:

A. (A) is correct and (R) is correct explanation of (A).

B. (A) is correct but (R) is not the correct explanation of (A).

C. (A) is correct but (R) is incorrect.

D. (A) is incorrect but (R) is correct.

65. Match the items of List-II with the items of List-I relating to liberalisation of agricultural trade.

List-I		**List-II**
(*a*) Tariffication	(*i*)	They have demonstrably adverse effects on other member countries.
(*b*) Prohibited subsidies	(*ii*)	They act on goods which are contingent upon export performance.
(*c*) Actionable subsidies	(*iii*)	Replacement of existing non-tariff restrictions.
(*d*) Non-actionable subsidies	(*iv*)	For industrial research in disadvantaged regions.

Code:

	(*a*)	(*b*)	(*c*)	(*d*)
A.	(*ii*)	(*iii*)	(*i*)	(*iv*)
B.	(*iv*)	(*i*)	(*ii*)	(*iii*)
C.	(*iii*)	(*ii*)	(*i*)	(*iv*)
D.	(*ii*)	(*iv*)	(*iii*)	(*i*)

66. Match the items of List-II and with the items of List-I relating to WTO impact:

List-I		**List-II**
(*a*) NAMA	(*i*)	Liberalisation of international investments.
(*b*) GATTS	(*ii*)	Includes industrial goods, textile, jewellery, fish and fisheries product manufacturing industries.
(*c*) TRIMs	(*iii*)	Liberalisation of trade in goods and services.
(*d*) TRIPs	(*iv*)	Provides monopoly power to owners of intellectual property.

Code:

	(*a*)	(*b*)	(*c*)	(*d*)
A.	(*ii*)	(*i*)	(*iv*)	(*iii*)
B.	(*iv*)	(*ii*)	(*iii*)	(*i*)
C.	(*ii*)	(*iii*)	(*i*)	(*iv*)
D.	(*iii*)	(*ii*)	(*iv*)	(*i*)

67. Indicate the correct code of the following statements being correct or incorrect. The statements relate to the type of transactions recorded in the current/capital accounts of the Balance of Payments.

Statement (I): The capital account consists of long-term capital transactions only.

Statement (II): The current account includes all transactions which give rise to or use up national income.

Code:

A. Both the statements are correct.
B. Both the statements are incorrect.
C. Statement (I) is correct while Statement (II) is incorrect.
D. Statement (I) is incorrect while Statement (II) is correct.

68. Select the **correct** code of the following statements being correct or incorrect.

Statement (I): International liquidity encompasses the international reserves only.

Statement (II): International liquidity covers only official holdings of gold, foreign exchange, SDRs and reserve position in the IMF available for the settlement of the international transactions.

Code:

A. Both the statements are correct.
B. Both the statements are incorrect.
C. Statement (I) is correct while Statement (II) is incorrect.
D. Statement (I) is incorrect while Statement (II) is correct.

69. Match the items of List-II with the items of List-I and select the code of correct matching. The items relate to International Trade Theories.

List-I	List-II
(*a*) Comparative Cost Theory	(*i*) Adam Smith
(*b*) Opportunity Cost Theory	(*ii*) Gottfried Haberler
(*c*) Factor Endowment Theory	(*iii*) David Ricardo
(*d*) Absolute Cost Theory	(*iv*) Eli Heckscher and Bertil Ohlin

Code:

	(*a*)	(*b*)	(*c*)	(*d*)
A.	(*i*)	(*ii*)	(*iii*)	(*iv*)
B.	(*iii*)	(*ii*)	(*iv*)	(*i*)
C.	(*iv*)	(*iii*)	(*ii*)	(*i*)
D.	(*i*)	(*iv*)	(*iii*)	(*ii*)

70. Which one of the following is **not** the guiding principle of the World Bank regarding it's lending operations?

A. Proper assessment of the repayment prospects of loans.
B. Lending should be only for specific projects which are economically and technically sound and of a high priority nature.
C. The lending should be to enable a country to meet foreign exchange content of the project cost.
D. The bank does expect the borrowing country to spend the loan in a particular country.

71. Total return on a security is equal to the following:

A. $\dfrac{\text{Periodic cash receipts + Capital gains}}{\text{Purchase Price of the security}}$

B. $\dfrac{\text{Periodic cash receipts + Capital gains}}{\text{Current Market Price of the security}}$

C. $\dfrac{\text{Periodic cash receipts}}{\text{Current Market price of the security}}$

D. $\dfrac{\text{Periodic cash receipts − Capital gains}}{\text{Purchase Price of the security}}$

72. Risk of a portfolio can be minimised by which one of the following?

A. Combining two securities having perfect positive correlation in their expected returns.
B. Combining two securities having perfect negative correlation in their expected returns.
C. Combining two securities having partially positive correlation in their expected returns.
D. Combining two securities having partially negative correlation in their expected returns.

73. The certificate which evidences an unsecured corporate debt of short-term maturity, is known as:

A. Certificate of Deposit
B. Short-term loan certificate
C. Treasury Bill
D. Commercial paper

74. Which of the following statements are false? Indicate the correct code.

(*a*) Grey market is a market for dealing in listed securities.
(*b*) OTCEI is mainly intended for big investors.
(*c*) Insider Trading is legally permitted in the capital market.
(*d*) The device adopted to make profit out of the differences in prices of a security in two different markets is called 'arbitrage'.

Code:

A. (*a*), (*b*), (*c*) B. (*a*), (*b*), (*d*)
C. (*a*), (*b*), (*c*), (*d*) D. (*b*), (*c*), (*d*)

75. Which of the following statements are false ? Indicate the correct code.

(*a*) Share capital issued by a company for the first time is known as venture capital.
(*b*) All Venture Capital Funds in India are promoted by the Government.
(*c*) In addition to capital, venture capitalists provide managerial and technical support also to the assisted firms.
(*d*) Benefits from venture capital financing can be realised in long run only.

Code:

A. (*a*), (*b*) and (*d*) B. (*a*) and (*b*)
C. (*b*), (*c*) and (*d*) D. (*c*) and (*d*)

76. Match the items of List-II with the items of List-I and select the correct code:

List-I	List-II
(*a*) Liquidity Risk	(*i*) Risk related to purchasing power of Income.
(*b*) Business Risk	(*ii*) Risk related to Firm's capital structure.
(*c*) Financial Risk	(*iii*) Risk related to inability to pay its dues on time.
(*d*) Inflation Risk	(*iv*) Risk related to fluctuation in profits.

Code:

	(*a*)	(*b*)	(*c*)	(*d*)
A.	(*ii*)	(*iii*)	(*iv*)	(*i*)
B.	(*i*)	(*iv*)	(*iii*)	(*ii*)
C.	(*iii*)	(*ii*)	(*iv*)	(*i*)
D.	(*iii*)	(*iv*)	(*ii*)	(*i*)

77. Statement (I): Designing a distribution system for a service (for-profit or non-business context) involves to select the parties only through which ownership will pass.

Statement (II): The ownership channel for most of the services is long and quite complex because of inseparability characteristic.

Statement (III) : Short channels usually mean more control on the part of the seller.

Identify the **correct** code of being the statements correct or incorrect. These statements relate to channel strategies of products/services.

A. Statements (I) and (II) are correct but (III) is not correct.
B. Statements (I) and (III) are correct but (II) is not correct.
C. Statements (I) and (II) are not correct but (III) is correct.
D. Statements (I), (II) and (III) all are not correct.

78. An enormous collection of data on various topics from a variety of internal and external sources, compiled by a firm for its own use or for use by its clients, is called:

A. Data-base B. Data warehouse
C. Data mining D. M.I.S.

79. Statement (I): A form of non-store retailing that uses advertising to contact consumers who, in turn, purchase products without visiting a retail store is called Direct selling.

Statement (II): A form of non-store retailing in which personal contact between a sales person and a consumer occurs away from a retail store is called Direct Marketing.

In the light of above statements, identify the **correct** code of statements being correct or incorrect.

A. Statement (I) is correct but Statement (II) is not correct.
B. Statement (I) is not correct but Statement (II) is correct.
C. Both the statements are correct.
D. Both the statements are not correct.

80. 34% of the customers who fall in one of the categories of diffusion process who are deliberate customers to accept an innovation just before the average adopter in a social system. Such customers who are above average in social and economic measures, rely quite a bit on advertisements and salesmen are known as:

A. Early Adopters B. Early Majority
C. Late Majority D. Late Adopters

81. The G.E. Business Model is explained on which one of the following parameters?

A. Market Attractiveness and Business Position.
B. Business Attractiveness and Market Position.
C. Industry Growth rate and Company's Market share.
D. Company's Growth rate and Industry's Position.

82. A reduction from the list price that is offered by a seller to buyers in payment for marketing functions the buyers will perform is known as:

A. Trade Discount
B. Functional Discount
C. Cash Discount
D. Both Trade and Functional Discount

83. Match the items of List-II with the items of List-I relating to Personnel Management (PM) and Human Resource Management (HRM); and select the code of correct matching.

List-I	List-II
(*a*) Focus of PM	(*i*) Development attitude by making people contribute their best.
(*b*) Focus of HRM	(*ii*) Exercising it as a functional area of management.
(*c*) Philosophy of PM	(*iii*) Exercising it as humane management.
(*d*) Philosophy of HRM	(*iv*) Profit maximization by controlling people.

Code:

	(*a*)	(*b*)	(*c*)	(*d*)
A.	(*ii*)	(*iii*)	(*iv*)	(*i*)
B.	(*iii*)	(*ii*)	(*i*)	(*iv*)
C.	(*iv*)	(*i*)	(*ii*)	(*iii*)
D.	(*i*)	(*iii*)	(*iv*)	(*ii*)

84. Select the **correct** code of the following statements being correct or incorrect.

I. Strategic HRM focuses on specific organizational intentions about what needs to be done while HR strategies focus on long-term issues only.
II. Strategic HRM focuses on macro concerns such as structure and culture while HR strategy focuses on specific issues assigned.
III. Human Resource strategy decisions are derived from strategic HRM.

Code:

A. Statements I and II are correct while III is incorrect.
B. Statements II and III are correct while I is incorrect.
C. Statements I and III are correct while II is incorrect.
D. All the statements are correct.

85. Which of the following code represents the full form of the term "BARS" in performance management systems?

A. Business Appraisal and Rating Systems.
B. Balanced Assessment Reviewing Scorecard.
C. Behaviourally Anchored Rating Scale.
D. Benchmarking Appraisal Reviewing Strategy.

86. Match the items of List-II with the items of List-I relating to training, and select the code of correct matching.

List-I	List-II
(*a*) Andragogy	(*i*) Strategies or styles of instructions
(*b*) Pedagogy	(*ii*) Ultimate knowledge level with which trainee leaves the training sessions
(*c*) Terminal behaviour	(*iii*) Lack of commitment of management and scarcity of resources in training
(*d*) Training impediments	(*iv*) Art and Science of training the adults

Code:

	(*a*)	(*b*)	(*c*)	(*d*)
A.	(*i*)	(*iv*)	(*iii*)	(*ii*)
B.	(*ii*)	(*iii*)	(*i*)	(*iv*)
C.	(*iv*)	(*i*)	(*ii*)	(*iii*)
D.	(*iii*)	(*ii*)	(*iv*)	(*i*)

87. Which of the following statements does not stand as a principle of compensation administration?

A. An enterprise should have a clear-cut plan to determine differential pay level in terms of divergent job requirements.

B. People and jobs should never be mingled.

C. The compensation system should be designed with subjectivity with respect to individual skill sets exercised from time to time.

D. There should be established wage grievance handling procedures.

88. Match the items of List-II with the items of List-I relating to industrial relations and select the code of correct matching.

List-I	List-II
(*a*) Healthy labour–management relations	(*i*) Industrial Disputes Act
(*b*) Industrial Peace Law	(*ii*) Guiding principles for a grievance procedure
(*c*) Industrial Democracy	(*iii*) Workers' participation in management
(*d*) National Commission on Labour, 1969	(*iv*) Voluntary arbitration and responsible trade union

Code:

	(*a*)	(*b*)	(*c*)	(*d*)
A.	(*iv*)	(*i*)	(*iii*)	(*ii*)
B.	(*ii*)	(*iii*)	(*iv*)	(*i*)
C.	(*iii*)	(*i*)	(*iv*)	(*ii*)
D.	(*ii*)	(*iv*)	(*i*)	(*iii*)

89. In recent years which among the following countries has been the largest source of foreign investment in India?

A. Australia
B. Japan
C. China
D. Mauritius

90. **Assertion (A):** The Government of India has been opening up domestic market to foreign players in baby steps.

Reasoning (R): Allowing foreign firms free play in India's retail sector has always been a political hot potato.

Code:

A. (A) and (R) both are correct; and (R) is the right explanation of (A).

B. (A) and (R) both are correct; but (R) is not the right explanation of (A).

C. (A) and (R) both are incorrect.

D. (A) is correct; but (R) is incorrect.

91. Select the correct code of the following statements being correct or incorrect.

Statement (I): A Global Depositary Receipt (GDR) is a bank certificate issued in more than one country for shares in a foreign company.

Statement (II): A GDR is very similar to American Depositary Receipt (ADR)

Statement (III): GDRs are called EDRs when private markets are attempting to obtain Euros.

Code:

A. Statements (I), (II) and (III) are correct.

B. Statements (I) and (II) are correct but (III) is incorrect.

C. Statements (I) and (III) are correct but (II) is incorrect.

D. Statements (II) and (III) are correct but (I) is incorrect.

92. In December 1999, European commission members signed a treaty that committed them to adopting a common currency known as Euro. This is better known as:

A. Treaty of Rome
B. Treaty of Maastricht
C. Treaty of Lisbon
D. Treaty of London

93. Select the correct code of the following statements being correct or incorrect.

Statement (I): The 'law of one price' states that in competitive markets free of transportation costs and barriers to trade, identical products sold in different countries must sell for the same price when their price is expressed in terms of the same currency.

Statement (II): An 'Efficient market' has no impediments to the free flow of goods and services, such as trade barriers.

Code:

A. Statement (I) is correct but (II) is incorrect.
B. Statement (II) is correct but (I) is incorrect.
C. Both statements (I) and (II) are correct.
D. Both statements (I) and (II) are incorrect.

94. Which among the following is not a correct statement regarding patent?

A. A patent is a legal protection granted for an invention that is new, non-obvious and useful.
B. The patent grants the patent holder the exclusive right to make use or sell the patented products or process.
C. The exclusive purpose of the patent system is to benefit the patent holder.
D. The Indian Patent Act, 1970, was amended and made effective from January 1, 2005.

95. Which one of the following is agricultural income under the Income Tax Act, 1961?

A. Interest on arrears of rent in respect of agricultural land.
B. Interest received by a money-lender in the form of agricultural produce.
C. Income from sale of trees of forest which are of spontaneous growth and in relation to which forestry operations alone are performed.
D. Interest on capital received by a partner from the firm engaged in agricultural operations.

96. Under the Income Tax Act, 1961 "block of assets" for the purpose of charging depreciation means:

A. Value of all the assets after depreciation
B. Value of all tangible assets after charging depreciation
C. Value of all those assets to which one rate of depreciation is applicable
D. Gross value of machinery and plant less accumulated depreciation

97. The maximum amount of exemption of compensation received at the time of voluntary retirement U/S 10(10C) of the Income Tax Act, 1961, is:

A. ₹ 1,00,000 B. ₹ 2,50,000
C. ₹ 5,00,000 D. ₹ 10,00,000

98. Which one of the following statements is not correct with reference to the assessment of firms?

A. All partnership firms formed under the Indian Partnership Act, 1932, are assessed as firms under the Income Tax Act, 1961.
B. Income of a firm is taxable at a flat rate of 30% without any exemption.
C. Partners' share in the income of a firm is not chargeable to tax in the hands of partners.
D. Remuneration paid to partners of a firm (assessed as such) is allowed as deduction subject to statutory limit.

99. The due date of first instalment of advance tax by assessees other than companies is:

A. 15th April B. 15th June
C. 15th September D. 15th December

100. Which one of the following items is **not** allowed as deduction while computing income from business and profession?

A. Fees paid to the lawyer for drafting partnership deed
B. Loss due to embezzlement by an employee
C. Legal expenses paid to protect the building of the business
D. Cost of installing a new telephone

ANSWERS

1	2	3	4	5	6	7	8	9	10
B	B	D	C	A	B	A	A	D	A
11	**12**	**13**	**14**	**15**	**16**	**17**	**18**	**19**	**20**
C	C	D	C	A	B	B	B	C	B
21	**22**	**23**	**24**	**25**	**26**	**27**	**28**	**29**	**30**
D	A	C	C	A	A	D	D	A	C
31	**32**	**33**	**34**	**35**	**36**	**37**	**38**	**39**	**40**
B	A	B	A	A	D	B	D	B	D
41	**42**	**43**	**44**	**45**	**46**	**47**	**48**	**49**	**50**
C	C	A	C	D	B	D	C	B	B
51	**52**	**53**	**54**	**55**	**56**	**57**	**58**	**59**	**60**
C	D	B	B	B	A	C	C	B	C
61	**62**	**63**	**64**	**65**	**66**	**67**	**68**	**69**	**70**
C	D	C	A	C	C	D	D	B	D
71	**72**	**73**	**74**	**75**	**76**	**77**	**78**	**79**	**80**
A	B	D	A	B	D	C	B	D	B
81	**82**	**83**	**84**	**85**	**86**	**87**	**88**	**89**	**90**
A	D	C	B	C	C	C	A	D	B
91	**92**	**93**	**94**	**95**	**96**	**97**	**98**	**99**	**100**
A	*	C	C	D	C	C	A	B	A

* Denotes either question or option is worng.

EXPLANATORY ANSWERS

1. **Monetary policy:** The central bank, by its policy towards the cost and availability of credit, can significantly influence the savings, investments and consumer spending in the economy. Depending on the conditions of the economy and the general economic policy of the government, the central bank (called the Reserve Bank in India) may adopt an expansionary or contractionary or neutral monetary policy. For example, a one percentage point reduction in the Cash Reserve Ratio (CRR) or Statutory Liquidity Reserve Ratio (SLR) will significantly increase the loanable funds with the commercial banking system. An increase in these ratios will have the opposite effect. Monetary policy may also be pressed into action to influence the exchange rate of the currency.

2. The main characteristics of capitalism are as follows:

- **Two-class system:** Historically a capitalist society was characterized by the split between two classes of individuals—the capitalist class, which owns the means for producing and distributing goods (the owners) and the working class, who sell their labour to the capitalist class in exchange for wages. The economy is run by the individuals (or corporations) who own and operate companies and make decisions as to the use of resources. But there exists a "division of labour" which allows for specialization, typically occurring through education and training, further breaking down the two class system into sub-classes (*e.g.*, the middle class).

- **Profit Motive:** Companies exist to make a profit. The motive for all companies is to make and sell goods and services only for profits. Companies do not exist solely to satisfy people's needs. Even though some goods or services may satisfy needs, they will only be available if the people have the resources to pay for them.
- **Minimal Government Intervention:** Capitalist societies believe markets should be left alone to operate without government intervention. However, a completely government-free capitalist society exists in theory, only. Even in the United States—the poster child for capitalism, the government regulates certain industries, such as the Dodd-Frank Act for financial institutions. By contrast, a purely capitalist society would allow the markets to set prices based on demand and supply for the purpose of making profits.
- **Competition:** True capitalism needs a competitive market. Without competition, monopolies exist, and instead of the market setting the prices, the seller is the price setter, which is against the conditions of capitalism.
- **Willingness to Change:** The last characteristic of capitalism is the ability to adapt and change. Technology has been a game changer in every society, and the willingness to allow change and adaptability of societies to improve inefficiencies within economic structures is a true characteristic.

3. The government announced a **New Industrial Policy** on July 24, 1991. This new policy deregulates the industrial economy in a substantial manner. The major objectives of the new policy are to build on the gains already made, correct the distortions or weaknesses that might have crept in, maintain a sustained growth in productivity and gainful employment, and attain international competitiveness. In pursuit of these objectives, the government announced a series of initiatives in the new industrial policy as outlined below:

- **Abolition of Industrial Licensing:** In a major move to liberalise the economy, the new industrial policy abolished all industrial licensing irrespective of the level of investment except for certain industries related to security and strategic concerns, and social reasons.

  Now there are only 6 industries for which licensing is compulsory as amended in February 1999. These are alcohol, cigarettes, hazardous chemicals, drugs and pharmaceuticals, electronics, aerospace and defense equipments, and industrial explosives.
- **Public Sector's Role Diluted:** The number of industries reserved for the public sector since 1956 was seventeen. This number has now been reduced to three. They are arms and ammunition and allied items of defense equipment, atomic energy and rail transport.

  The main elements of Government Policy towards Public Sector Undertakings (PSUs) are:

  - ❑ Bring down government equity in all non-strategic PSUs to 26 per cent or lower, if necessary;
  - ❑ Restructure and revive potentially viable PSUs;
  - ❑ Close down PSUs which cannot be revived; and
  - ❑ Fully protect the interests of workers.
- **Abolition of Phased Manufacturing Programmes:** Devaluation of currency and increasing FDI led government to liberalise local content requirement for indigenous firms.
- **MRTP Act:** MRTP Act has been amended to remove the threshold limits of assets in respect of MRTP companies and dominant undertakings.

The new industrial policy also states that the government will undertake review of the existing public enterprises in low technology, small-scale and non-strategic areas. Sick units will be referred to the Board for Industrial and Financial Reconstruction for advice about rehabilitation and reconstruction.

For enterprises remaining in the public sector it is stated that they will be provided a much greater degree of management autonomy through the system of Memorandum of Understanding (MOU).

- **Free Entry to Foreign Investment and Technology:** The Government is committed to promote increased flow of Foreign Direct Investment (FDI) for better technology, modernisation, exports and for providing products and services of international standards.

Therefore, the policy of the Government has been aimed at encouraging foreign investment particularly in core infrastructure sectors so as to supplement national efforts. The salient features of the FDI policy are:

- There are two modalities for FDI approval: (*a*) automatic approval by the Reserve Bank, and (*b*) approval by Foreign Investment Promotion Board (FIPB)/Government.
- 34 categories/groups of high priority industries identified on the basis of National Industrial Classification qualify for automatic approval up to 50/51/74/100 per cent FDI depending on the nature of activity.
- Projects for electricity generation, transmission and distribution, and construction and maintenance of roads, highways, vehicular tunnels, vehicular bridges, ports and harbours have permitted foreign equity participation up to 100 per cent under the automatic route.
- FIPB is required to dispose of applications for FDI within a time frame of six weeks.
- FDI is not permissible in agriculture, real estate and insurance activities.
- Full repatriation of original investment and returns except for dividend balancing and foreign exchange neutrality conditions in certain sectors.
- Liberal access to foreign technology. Automatic approval to lump sum payment of up to US $2 million and royalty at the rate of 5 per cent for domestic sales and 8 per cent for exports subject to a total payment of 8 per cent on sales for a period not exceeding 7 years from the date of commercial production.
- Easy access to domestic debt. Foreign companies that invest in India can leverage in India by way of domestic debt from domestic financial institutions.
- Liberal external commercial borrowings and debt servicing norms.
- No ceiling on raising Global Depository Receipts (GDRs), American Depository Receipts (ADRs), and Foreign Currency Convertible Bonds (FCCBs).

- **Industrial Location Policy Liberalised:** The new industrial policy provides that in locations other than cities of more than 1 million populations, there will be no requirement of obtaining industrial approvals from the centre, except for industries subject to compulsory licensing.

In cities with a population of more than 1 million, industries other than those of a non-polluting nature will be located outside 25 kms of the periphery. Since there is 23 cities in India with a population of more than 1 million each, the new industrial policy has dispensed with government clearance for the location of projects except in the case of these 23 cities.

- **Removal of Mandatory Convertibility Clause:** A large part of industrial investment in India is financed by loans from banks and financial institutions. These institutions have followed a mandatory practice of including a convertibility clause in their lending operations for new projects.

This has provided them an option of converting part of their loans into equity if felt necessary by their management. The new industrial policy has provided that henceforth financial institutions will not impose this mandatory convertibility clause.

4. Important information to be incorporated in the Memorandum of Association as specified in the Companies Act, 2013 mentioned below:

The memorandum of a company shall state—

- the name of the company with the last word "Limited" in the case of a public limited company, or the last words "Private Limited" in the case of a private limited company:
  Provided that nothing in this clause shall apply to a company registered under section 8;
- the State in which the registered office of the company is to be situated;
- the objects for which the company is proposed to be incorporated and any matter considered necessary in furtherance thereof;
- the liability of members of the company, whether limited or unlimited, and also state—
  - ❑ in the case of a company limited by shares, that liability of its members is limited to the amount unpaid, if any, on the shares held by them; and
  - ❑ in the case of a company limited by guarantee, the amount up to which each member undertakes to contribute—
    (*a*) to the assets of the company in the event of its being wound-up while he is a member or within one year after he ceases to be a member, for payment of the debts and liabilities of the company or of such debts and liabilities as may have been contracted before he ceases to be a member, as the case may be; and
    (*b*) to the costs, charges and expenses of winding-up and for adjustment of the rights of the contributories among themselves;
- in the case of a company having a share capital—
  - ❑ the amount of share capital with which the company is to be registered and the division thereof into shares of a fixed amount and the number of shares which the subscribers to the memorandum agree to subscribe which shall not be less than one share; and
  - ❑ the number of shares each subscriber to the memorandum intends to take, indicated opposite his name;
- in the case of One Person Company, the name of the person who, in the event of death of the subscriber, shall become the member of the company.

The name stated in the memorandum shall not—

- be identical with or resemble too nearly to the name of an existing company registered under this Act or any previous company law; or
- be such that its use by the company—
  - ❑ will constitute an offence under any law for the time being in force; or
  - ❑ is undesirable in the opinion of the Central Government.

5. The relative price of imports (*i.e.*, the relative change in the prices of imports and domestic goods). An increase in the imports, *ceteris paribus*, is associated with a fall in the relative price of imports.

From the above factors, it can be inferred that the volume of imports tends to be very high when there is a conjuncture of high rate of economic growth and a sharp fall in the relative price of imports and vice versa.

7. **Vision, Strategy and Three Year Action Agenda of NITI Aayog:**

The 12th and last five year plan of India was completed on March 31, 2017. With this, the five year plans have become a thing of past. It was already announced that there will be no more five year plans. In August, 2017, NITI Aayog has come up with a new idea of planning for future development of India. The core idea is that *India has still not abandoned the process of planning* and the *county still has planned development in action.* However, the only difference is that the process of planning is entirely different. The first major difference is that instead of a single five year plan, the country will have *three plans spread over three different time periods.*

- First is a 15 year *"Vision"* that encompasses overall goals and objectives of the country for next 15 years.
- Second is a 7 year *"Strategy"* which lays the roadmap of development for next seven years dividing those goals and objectives into two parts.
- Third and Final is a *"Three Year Action Agenda"* which states the tasks and targets to be accomplished in next three years time frame, further dividing the strategy into two parts.

NITI Aayog was in process of working out the above plan since May, 2016. A draft was placed in third Governing Council meeting of NITI Aayog on April 23, 2017. Governing Council of NITI Aayog comprises of all States Chief Minister, so the central government including prime minister accord it much priority.

9. **Financing Activities:** The separate disclosure of cash flows arising from financing activities is important because it is useful in predicting claims on future cash flows by providers of funds (both capital and borrowings) to the enterprise. Examples of cash flows arising from financing activities are:

- Cash proceeds from issuing shares or other similar instruments;
- Cash proceeds from issuing debentures, loans, notes, bonds, and other short or long-term borrowings; and
- Cash repayments of amounts borrowed.

Reporting Cash Flows from Operating Activities: An enterprise should report cash flows from operating activities using either:

- The direct method, whereby major classes of gross cash receipts and gross cash payments are disclosed; or
- The indirect method, whereby net profit or loss is adjusted for the effects of transactions of a non-cash nature, any deferrals or accruals of past or future operating cash receipts or payments, and items of income or expense associated with investing or financing cash flows.

10. Differences between standard cost and estimated cost:

Basis of Difference	Standard Cost	Estimated Cost
1. Applicability	Standard cost can be applied in a business operating under standard costing system.	Estimated cost is used in any business even in historical costing system.
2. Objective	Standards are established for the purpose of controlling future performances.	Estimates are prepared mainly for price-fixing purpose
3. Basis of preparation	They are determined on a scientific basis.	They are prepared on the basis of past performance or personal opinion.
4. Usage	They are used as a regular system of accounts from which variances are ascertained	The use of estimated costs is a statistical data only.
5. Coverage	They are to be set with respect to each element of cost. It covers the entire activities of business	They can be determined for a particular activity or a purpose, individually.

11. Capital Expenditures Vs. Revenue Expenditures:

The terms, capital expenditure and revenue expenditure, are used in the context of accounting for property, plant, and equipment. A capital expenditure is one which is expected to benefit two or more accounting periods. A revenue expenditure is one whose benefits are not expected to extend beyond the current period. Thus a revenue expenditure benefits only the current period or no period at all.

Capital expenditures are recorded by increasing an asset account (or by decreasing the balance of the Accumulated Depreciation account). If an asset is of limited life, its cost is depreciated (expensed) over the periods which will be benefited (to comply with the matching principle). Because a revenue expenditure does not yield benefits beyond the current period, it is recorded as an expense in the period it is made.

The distinction between capital and revenue expenditures is of significance because it involves the timing of the recognition of expense and, consequently, the determination of periodic net income. This distinction also affects the costs reflected in asset accounts which will be recovered from future periods revenues.

Examples of capital expenditures include the acquisition of land, building and/or equipment. Examples of revenue expenditures include outlays for maintenance and repair services.

13. X's new share $= \frac{7}{10} - \frac{2}{7}$

$= \frac{49-20}{70}$

$= \frac{29}{70}$

Y's new share $= \frac{3}{10} - \frac{1}{7}$

$= \frac{11}{70}$

Z's new share $= \frac{2}{7} + \frac{1}{7}$

$= \frac{3}{7}$

$= \frac{30}{70}$

Hence, New Ratio of X, Y, & Z will be

$\Rightarrow \frac{29}{70} : \frac{11}{70} : \frac{30}{70}$

$\Rightarrow 29 : 11 : 30.$

14. Operating ratios indicate the percentage of sales that is absorbed to the cost of goods sold and other operating expenses. It is the test of operational efficiency with which the business activities are being carried out. If the ratio is lower, the position is favourable since there is higher operating profit and the management has succeeded in minimising the operating costs. The higher operating ratio is less favourable because it would leave only a smaller margin of operating profit to meet the obligation towards interest, income tax, and dividend. There is no rule of thumb for this ratio, because it varies from firm to firm depending upon the nature of business. While analysing this ratio, it is suggested that the changes in operating ratios over a period of time should be well analysed. The changes in operating expenses can be either within the control of management or beyond the control of management. If the change in operating expense is within the control of management, appropriate steps can be taken to control the same in forthcoming period, based on the results and further probe.

15. The Meaning of Profit and Pure Profit

The meaning and source of 'profit' have always been a centre of controversy. "The word 'profit' has different meanings to businessmen, accountants, tax collectors, workers and economists...". For example, 'profit to a layman means all incomes that go to the capitalist class'. To an accountant, profit means the excess of revenue over all paid-out costs including both manufacturing and overhead expenses. For all accounting purposes, businessmen use accountants' definition of profit.

For all practical purposes, profit or business income means profit in accountancy sense plus non-allowable expenses. Economist's concept of profit is of 'Pure Profit' called 'economic profit' or 'just profit'. Pure profit is a return over and above the opportunity cost, *i.e.*, the income which a businessman might expect from the second best alternative use of his resources. These two concepts of profit are discussed below in detail.

Accounting Profit vs. Economic Profit

The two important concepts of profit that figure in business decisions are 'economic profit' and 'accounting profit'. It will be useful to understand the difference between the two concepts of profit. As already mentioned, in accounting sense, profit is surplus of revenue over and above all paid-out costs, including both manufacturing and overhead expenses. Accounting profit may be calculated as follows:

Accounting profit

$$= TR - (W + R + I + M + OC)$$

where, W = Wages and salaries
R = Rent
I = Interest
M = Cost of materials
OC = Other paid out costs like electricity, transportation, etc.

Obviously, while calculating accounting profit, only explicit or book costs, *i.e.*, the cost recorded in the books of accounts, are considered.

The concept of 'economic profit' differs from that of 'accounting profit'. Economic profit takes into account also the implicit or imputed costs. The implicit cost is opportunity cost. Opportunity cost is defined as the payment that would be 'necessary to draw forth the factors of production from their most remunerative alternative employment'. Alternatively, opportunity cost is the income foregone which a businessman could expect from the second best alternative use of his resources. For example, if an entrepreneur uses his capital in his own business, he foregoes interest which he might earn by purchasing debentures of other companies or by depositing his money with joint stock companies for a period. Furthermore, if an entrepreneur uses his labour in his own business, he foregoes his income (salary) which he might earn by working as a manager in another firm. Similarly, by using productive assets (land and building) in his own business, he sacrifices his market rent. These foregone incomes—interest, salary and rent—are called opportunity costs or transfer costs. Accounting profit does not take into account the opportunity cost whereas all these costs are taken into account while working out the economic profit.

In addition, it should also be noted that in working out economic or pure profit a provision is also made for (*a*) insurable risks, (*b*) depreciation, and (*c*) necessary minimum payment to shareholders to prevent them from withdrawing their capital. Pure profit may thus be defined as 'a residual left after all contractual costs have been met, including the transfer costs of management, insurable risks, depreciation and payments to shareholders sufficient to maintain investment at its current level'.

Thus,

Economic profit = Total Revenue – (Explicit Cost + Implicit Cost)

In real life situation, if economic profit is greater than zero, one thing is certain that people will their money in business. However, in case economic profit is zero or insignificantly different from zero, people prefer to invest their money in business because it has a better future prospect in spite of risk involved.

16. **Relationship between Price Elasticity and Total Revenue:** Total revenue from the sale of a good is equal to the price times the quantity. Price elasticity is an important concept because if demand is elastic and increase in sales price results in a decrease in total revenue for all producers. If demand is unitary total revenue remains the same if price changes, and total revenue increases if price is increased when demand is inelastic. These relationships are shown in the following table:

Effect of Price Changes on Various Types of Goods

Price Change	Elastic Demand E > 1	Inelastic Demand E < 1	Unitary Demand E = 1
Price increase	Total revenue decreases	Total revenue increases	Total revenue does not change
Price decrease	Total revenue increases	Total revenue decreases	Total revenue does not change

17. **Properties of Indifference Curves:**

Indifference curves drawn for two normal substitute goods have the following four basic properties:

- Indifference curves have a negative slope;
- Indifference curves are convex to the origin;
- Indifference curves do not intersect nor are they tangent to one another;
- Upper indifference curves indicate a higher level of satisfaction.

These properties of indifference curves, in fact, reveal the consumer's behaviour, his choices and preferences. They are, therefore, very important in the modern theory of consumer behaviour.

21. In the case of perfect competition, average revenue, AR being equal to the selling price, must be identical to MR curve for the same reason that the firm cannot influence price level. Now the unit profit level for the firm is given by AR = Min. AC.

The long-run equilibrium of the firm is now complete. Optimal output level is determined by equating MR = MC, in which case, the individual entrepreneur has no incentive to alter the optimal level of output.

Long-run 'normal profits' are now earned at, p = Min. AC, in which case there is no incentive for a firm to enter or leave the industry to which the firm belongs.

The concept of competition influencing price and output determination needs to be pointed out. If $p > MC$, then $\pi > 0$. This would induce other firms to enter the industry. Consequently, the total supply of output to the industry by all such firms will increase. Consequently, supply p will be driven down. On the other hand, if $p < MC$, then $\pi < 0$. Now firms will start to leave the industry. The supply of total output will decline. This will drive up price. Finally, with movements from both below and above MC values, the final value of price will be where, $p = MC$.

Because supply prices of output of a perfectly competitive firm are set in this way along the rising portion of the MC curve, this turns out to be the supply curve of the firm's output.

Finally, with all the above results in the situation where the firm is a price-taker in perfect competition, we obtain the compressed result for pricing of output of a firm in perfectly competitive market:

p = MC = Min. AC = AR = MR

Such a firm is the most efficient one in terms of its minimum average cost of production, maximal output that earns the firm the full range of economies of scale, and maximal profits at this level that shows that the entire output is fully distributed among factors of production.

22. **Nominal Scale:** When data are labels or names used to identify the attribute of an element, then the nominal scale is used. For example, assume that a marketing research company wants to conduct a survey in three towns of India—Bhopal, Nagpur and Baroda. While compiling the data, the company assigns the numeric code "1" to Bhopal, "2" to Nagpur, and "3" to Baroda. In this case, "1", "2", and "3" are the labels used to identify the three different towns. Data shows the numeric value but the scale of measurement is nominal. In other words, we cannot say that "1" indicates any ranking or any rating, this is only for the sake of convenience in identification. Employee identification numbers, contributory provident fund numbers, personal identification number (PAN), and the like are some other examples of nominal data. Nominal level measurement is the lowest level of data measurement.

Ordinal Scale: In addition to nominal level data capacities, the ordinal scale can be used to rank or order objects. For example, a manufacturing company administers a questionnaire to 150 consumers for obtaining the consumer perception for one of its products. Each consumer is asked to judge between three given options, excellent, good, or poor. Clearly, excellent is ranked the best and poor the worst with good ranked between the two. If we want to assign numeric values to these three attributes, "1" can be used for excellent, "2" for good, and "3" for poor. In most cases, when we apply statistical tools and techniques, for the sake of interpretation convenience, rankings are set in reverse. In this case, "1" will be used for poor, "2" for good, and "3" for excellent. Therefore, the lowest number has the lowest ranking, and the highest number has the highest ranking. While using this kind of ordinal measurement, the company cannot say that the interval between ranking points 1 and 2 is equal to the interval between ranking points 2 and 3. Here, it can be stated that 1 is superior followed by 2 and 3, or as in the second case 1, the lowest number, has got the lowest ranking followed by the next two numbers, 2 and 3, as the ranking reference for good and excellent. The exact difference between these numeric values cannot be measured in any of these cases. Nominal and ordinal level data measurement are often used for imprecise measurements such as demographic questions, ranking of items under the study, and the like. This is why these data are termed as non-metric data and are referred to as qualitative data.

Interval Scale: In the interval level measurement, the difference between two consecutive numbers is meaningful. Interval data is always numeric. For example, three students of MSc Statistics have scored 65, 75, and 85 in the subject reliability theory. These three students can be rated in terms of their performances. However, the difference in the numbers is also meaningful. The student who secured 85 marks is the highest ranking performer whereas the student who secured 65 is the lowest with the student who secured 75 marks in the middle. In interval level measurement, meaningful difference between two ranking points can be obtained. In the above example, we can also compute that between the highest and the lowest ranking points, the difference is 20 marks.

Ratio Scale: Ratio level measurements possess all the properties of interval data with meaningful ratio of two values. The ratio scale must contain a zero value that indicates that nothing exists for the variable at zero point. For example, a company markets two toothbrushes priced ₹ 30 and ₹ 15, respectively. In the ratio scale, the difference between the two prices, that is, ₹ 30 – ₹ 15 = ₹ 15, can be calculated and is meaningful. With it, we can also say that the price of the first product ₹ 30 is two times that of the second product priced at ₹ 15. Interval and ratio level data are collected using some precise instruments. These data are called metric data and are sometimes referred to as quantitative data.

23. A graph is a geometrical image of frequency distribution. It is a mathematical picture. Frequency distributions are converted into visual models to facilitate understanding. It is easier, more convenient and quicker to draw inferences from graphs than from frequency distribution. Comparison of data also becomes easier. Graphical representation in the form of histogram, frequency polygons, cumulative frequency curves (ogive), Pie graphs etc., appear almost daily in the newspapers, magazines, trade publications, business reports and scientific periodicals.

24. If the upper limit of a class is excluded from the interval, it is exclusive method of classification, otherwise it is inclusive method of classification.

Exclusive Class Limits	Inclusive Class Limits
(i) Class groups will be like 0-10, 10-20, 20-30, etc.	Class group will be like 0-9, 10-19, 20-29, etc.
(ii) An item exactly 10 is put in the group 10-20 not in 0-10	There is no ambiguity to which an item belongs
(iii) Class limits are continuous	Idea of continuity is lost
(iv) Advantages for many further mathematical computations	Stated class limits are also real class limits
(v) Suitable for continuous variable data	Suitable for discrete variable data

Distinguish between Open End Classes and Close End Classes

When lower limit of first class interval and upper limit of last intervals are not given, these are called open end classes and when these limits are given, these are called close end classes.

25. Standard Normal Probability Distribution: To deal with problems where the normal probability distribution is applicable, the value of random variable x is standardized by expressing it as the number of standard deviations (σ) lying on both sides of its mean (μ). Such *standardized normal random variable, z* (also called *z-statistic, z-score* or *normal variable*) is defined as:

$$z = \frac{x - \mu}{\sigma}$$

or equivalently $x = \mu + z\sigma$

The *z-statistic* measures the number of standard deviations that any value of the random variable x falls from the mean. From formula, we may conclude that

(*i*) When x is less than the mean (μ), the value of z is negative.

(*ii*) When x is more than the mean (μ), the value of z is positive.

(*iii*) When $x = \mu$, the value of $z = 0$.

Standard Normal Probability Distribution: A normal probability distribution with mean equal to zero and standard deviation equal to one.

30. Planning Process: Planning, like organising is a fundamental managerial function. In simple words, planning is deciding in advance what is to be done, when, where, how and by whom it is to be done. Thus, a plan is a determined course of action. It is an attempt on the part of a manager to anticipate the future in order to achieve better performance. In the management literature, the word "planning" has been defined like this:

"Generally speaking, planning is deciding in advance, what is to be done."

—*M.H. Newman*

"A plan is a trap laid to capture the future."

—*Allen*

"Planning is an intellectual process, conscious determination of courses of action, the basing of decisions on purpose, facts and considered estimates." —*Koontz & O'Donnell*

32. Types of Critical Point Standards: Every objective, every goal of the many planning programs, every activity of these programs, every policy, every procedure, and every budget can become a standard against which actual or expected performance might be measured. In practice, however, standards tend to be of the following types:

- **Physical Standards:** Physical standards are non-monetary measurements and are common at the operating level, where materials are used, labour is employed, services are rendered, and goods are produced. They may reflect quantities, such as labour-hours per unit of output, pounds of fuel per horsepower per hour, ton-miles of freight traffic carried, units of production per machine-hour, or feet of wire per ton of copper. Physical standards may also reflect quality, such as hardness of bearings, closeness of tolerances, rate of climb of an airplane, durability of a fabric, or fastness of a colour.
- **Cost Standards:** Cost standards are monetary measurements and, like physical standards, are common at the operating level. They attach monetary values to specific aspects of operations. Illustrative of cost standards are such widely used measures as direct and indirect costs per unit produced, labour cost per unit or per hour, material cost per unit, machine-hour costs, cost per seat-mile, selling cost per dollar or unit of sales, and cost per foot of oil well drilled.
- **Capital Standards:** There are a variety of capital standards, all arising from the application of monetary measurements to physical items. They have to do with the capital invested in the firm rather than with operating costs and are therefore primarily related to the balance sheet rather than to the income statement. Perhaps the most widely used standard for new investment, as well as for overall control, is return on investment. The typical balance sheet will disclose other capital standards, such as the ratios of current assets to current liabilities, debt to net worth, fixed investment to total investment, cash and receivables to payables, and bonds to stocks, as well as the size and turnover of inventories.
- **Revenue Standards:** These arise from attaching monetary values to sales. They may vary from such standards as revenue per bus passenger mile and dollars per ton of steel shapes sold to cover sale per customer, rules per capital in a given market area.
- **Programme Standards:** A manager may be assigned to install a variable budget programme, a programme for formally following the development of new products, or a programme for improving the quality of a sales force, while, some subjective judgement may have to be applied in appraising programme performance, timing and other factors can be used as objective standards.
- **Intangible Standards:** More difficult to set are standards not expressed in either physical or monetary measurement. What standard can a manager use for determining the competence of the divisional purchasing agent or Personnel Director, what can be

used for determining whether the public relations program is successful? Are foremen loyal to the company's objectives? Is the office boy alert? Such questions show how difficult it is to establish standards for a goal that cannot be given clear quantitative or qualitative measurement. Many intangible standards exist in business because research into what constitutes desired performance has not been done above the level of the shop, the district sales office, the shopping room, or the accounting department. Perhaps a more important reason is that human relationships, count in performance, as they do above the basic operating levels, it is very hard to measure what is good.

'Effective' or 'Efficient' Tests, surveys and sampling techniques developed by psychologists and sociometrists have made it possible to probe human attitudes and drives, but many managerial controls over interpersonal relationships must continue to be based upon intangible standards considered judgment, trial and error, and even on occasion sheer hunch.

- **Goals for Standards:** However, with the present tendency for better-managed enterprise to establish an entire network of verifiable qualitative or quantitative goals at every level of management, the use of intangible standards, while still important, is diminishing in complex programme operations as well as in the performance of managers themselves, modern managers are finding that through research and thinking it is possible to define goals it is likely to take the form of standards. For example, if the program of district sales office is spelled out to include such elements as training salesmen in accordance with a plan with specific characteristics, the very fact of the plan and its characteristics, furnish standards which tend to become objective and, therefore, 'Tangible'.

35. Functional Theory: Functional leadership theory (Hackman & Walton, 1986; McGrath, 1962) is a particularly useful theory for addressing specific leader behaviours expected to contribute to organizational or unit effectiveness. This theory argues that the leader's main job is to see that whatever is necessary to group needs is taken care of; thus, a leader can be said to have done their job well when they have contributed to group effectiveness and cohesion.

37. Classification of Consumer Goods

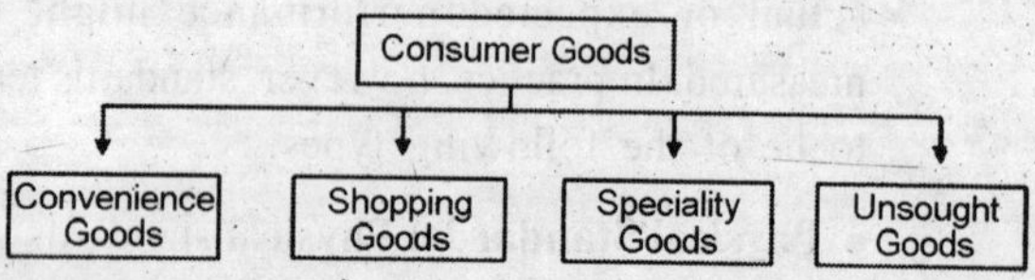

Consumer goods can be classified into four categories:

- **Convenience Goods:** These goods are demanded by customers frequently in small quantities, but they must be immediately available at easily accessible retail shops. These are low cost, highly advertised items that are designed for mass markets and are sold to all income classes. All sales promotions devices are liberally used to stimulate consumer demand. These goods have to be distributed through numerous retailers. Examples of convenience goods are daily use items like soaps, detergents, biscuits, cosmetics and so on.

  Because most retail stores sell only a small volume of the total output of a convenience good, it is not economical for the manufacturer to sell directly to all retail outlets. Instead, the manufacturer depends on distributors or retailers to sell the product to the consumers. Intensive distribution is required for convenience goods.

- **Shopping Goods:** A tangible product for which consumers want to compare quality, price, and perhaps style in several stores before making a purchase is considered a shopping goods. These products need search efforts and special visits to central markets, there are not urgent purchases and buyers can postpone buying according to their convenience. They need not have numerous retail outlets. Buyers want to shop around and select goods after comparing quality, terms, style, price, services and so on. Examples of shopping goods are furniture, jewellery, fashion goods, appliances, automobiles.

  As fewer retailers are required, and retail stores typically buy shopping goods in large quantities, it is common for manufacturers to use short channels of distribution. Usually they sell directly to retailers.

- **Speciality Goods:** A tangible product, for which consumers have a strong brand preference, and are willing to spend substantial time and effort in locating the desired brand is called a speciality good. They are goods with unique features. They demand special shopping efforts. They are sold in speciality shops. Buyers develop brand preferences and make special efforts to buy it. It should be noted that in the modern marketing environment, there is a thin line of difference between shopping and speciality goods.

  Examples of speciality goods can be desired brands of expensive designer clothes (clothes designed by leading designers like J.J. Vallaya or Ritu Beri), expensive sound systems and so on. The most important feature of speciality goods is that consumers insist on a particular brand and are willing to spend considerable effort to find it. Like shopping goods, few retail stores are required to sell speciality goods. Manufacturers may follow exclusive distribution policy for selling speciality goods *i.e.*, opening their own exclusive stores or selling franchise of exclusive stores.

- **Unsought Goods:** An unsought good is a new product that the consumer is not yet aware of or he is aware of that product but does not want it at this moment. An example of unsought goods can be a new product to be launched in the market which does not have a ready demand. Another example is personal insurance. Personal selling combined with advertising is the best strategy to sell unsought goods.

38. Each segment should be *large enough* to be profitable. Procter & Gamble found a segment of candy consumers that wants a low-calorie product. However, it is too small to justify the investment a line of confections would require. In concept, management could treat each single customer as a separate segment. Actually, this situation, called micromarketing.

39. A significant factor influencing how consumer decisions are made is the consumer's level of involvement, reflected in the amount of effort that is expended in satisfying a need. Some situations are *high* involvement. That is, when a need arises a consumer decides to actively collect and evaluate information about the purchase situation. These purchases entail all five stages of the buying-decision process.

Although it is risky to generalize because consumers are so different, involvement tends to be *greater* under any of the following conditions:

- The consumer lacks information about alternatives for satisfying the need.
- The consumer considers the amount of money involved to be large.
- The product has considerable social importance.
- The product is seen as having a potential for providing significant benefits.

40. Product-Orientation Stage: Firms with a product orientation typically focus on the quality and quantity of offerings while assuming that customers will seek out and buy reasonably priced, well-made products.

This mindset is commonly associated with a long-ago era when the demand for goods generally exceeded the supply, and the primary focus in business was to efficiently produce large quantities of products. Finding the customers was viewed as a relatively minor function.

41. Trade Barriers: The most common legal forces affecting international marketers are barriers created by governments to restrict trade and protect domestic industries. Examples include the following:

- **Tariff:** A tax imposed on a product entering a country. Tariffs are used to protect domestic producers and/or raise revenue. To illustrate, for over 40 years the US has imposed a 25% tariff on imported pickup trucks, keeping brands such as Volkswagen and Hyundai out of the market and causing other foreign manufacturers such as Toyota and Nissan to build factories in the US.
- **Import quota:** A limit on the amount of a particular product that can be brought into a country. Like tariffs, quotas can protect a country's domestic industry or can broaden access to its markets. For example, US textile manufacturers want stiff quotas placed on imports from China, while large retailers such as JC Penney, seeking low cost goods, are strongly opposed to such quotas.
- **Local-content Law:** A regulation specifying the proportion of a finished product's components and labour that must be provided by the importing country. For example, to be sold in Taiwan, Japanese cars must be at least partially assembled there. To comply with a local-content law, a firm may import most of a product's parts, buy some locally, and have the final product assembled locally. These laws are used to provide jobs and protect domestic businesses.
- **Local Operating Laws:** A constraint on how, when, or where retailing can be conducted. These regulations, many intended to protect small businesses, are having an impact on Internet shopping. For example, in some countries the retail price of a product has to be the same for everyone. As a result, a system like Priceline.com, where consumers propose a price for an airline seat, rental car, or hotel room and the seller decides if it is acceptable, is illegal.
- **Standards and Certification:** A requirement that a product contain or exclude certain ingredients or that it be tested and certified as meeting certain restrictive standards. European countries, for example, have restricted genetically altered corn and also beef that has been fed growth hormones.
- **Boycott:** A refusal to buy products from a particular company or country. Boycotts, also called embargoes, are used by a government to punish another country for what are perceived to be unfair importation rules.

42. Prospecting: Prospecting refers to locating prospective buyers. Good salesmen do not entirely rely on existing customers, but seek out new ones. They constantly search for 'prospects' or potential customers and rope in as many of them as possible. Prospecting is the first step in the selling process, whenever new customers are sought.

Identifying Prospects and Gathering Leads: Although the company may supply some leads, the salesmen must have the skill to develop their own leads. They can develop leads from many sources, such as current customers, dealers, suppliers, non-competing salesmen, banks, credit agencies, clubs/similar organisations and published data sources like directories, telephone yellow pages, etc. The 'prospecting' will be more effective if the salesmen systematically gather market intelligence and make use of it.

Qualifying the Prospects and Analysing their Purchases: The salesmen have to screen the leads, reject the poor ones and pick the better looking ones for further probing/making sales call. He might phone up or write to prospects before deciding whether to make a sales call. Prospects should be qualified by evaluating their financial ability, likely volume of purchase, specifications adopted, likelihood of continuous business, etc. The leads can also be categorised into *hot leads, warm leads* and *cool leads*, depending on their potential to become customers.

Websites can be Used for Acquiring and Qualifying Leads: Salesmen can use websites of companies/social network sites/blogs for acquiring leads and qualifying the prospects. A lot of details about the prospects can be collected by perusing the sites, and this can help in fine tuning the leads. In some cases, the site can take care of even the actual processing of the business.

Pre-Approach: Pre-approach consists of planning and preparation. The salesmen have to meticulously plan the sales presentation. They must size up the customer characteristics and the sales context. *Need* exploration is an especially important part of Pre-approach. The sales presentation has to be dovetailed with the exact needs of the customer. Securing appointments from the customer is also a part of the preparation.

Approach: Approach refers to the preliminaries and the initial part of the interaction before the substantive sales presentation commences. In particular, it includes the opening remarks in the presentation and the opening style adopted by the salesman. In general, a consultative style of selling is superior to a totally controlled one. The approach should facilitate this requirement.

Sales Presentation: Now, the salesman gets to the actual delivery of the sales story/ message/demonstration. Listening, probing, use of questions, persuasive interceptions are integral elements in the process. Handling and overcoming objections is also a part of it. The salesman must involve the customer in the presentation.

Post Sales Service: The final step in the personal selling process is referred to as the 'follow up'. The follow up involves the salesperson contacting the customer after the sale to ensure that the customer is satisfied. If the customer has any existing issues with the product, the salesperson will address them. A successful follow up stage of personal selling can be very effective in ensuring repeat sales, evaluating the effectiveness of the salesperson, and obtaining additional referrals from the satisfied customer.

43. Theories of Capital Structure: As per as the concept of capital structure is concerned a number of eminent scholars have made their valuable contribution with regard to relationship between capital structure, cost of capital and value of the firm. The main contributors of the theories are David Durand, Ezra Solomon, Modigliani and Miller etc., some important theories is discussed below:

- **Net Income Approach:** The net income approach has been suggested by Durand. Under this approach capital structure decision is relevant to the valuation of the firm. A firm can minimize the weighted average cost of capital and increase the market price of the equity shares by using the debt content in its capital structure. This theory presumes the following assumptions:
  - (*i*) The cost of debt is less than the cost of equity
  - (*ii*) There are no corporate taxes
  - (*iii*) The use of debt content does not change the risk perception of the investors as a result the equity capitalization rate of the company and the debt capitalization rate of the company remains constant with changes in leverage.
- **Net Operating Income Approach:** This approach is also suggested by Durand. It is dramatically opposite to the net income approach. According to this approach any changes in the capital structure of a company

does not affect the market value of the firm and the overall cost of capital remain constant irrespective of the mode of financing. The implication of the above statement is that the overall cost of capital remains the same whether the debt equity mix is 50:50 or 20:80 or 40:60 under this theory all the structures are optimum capital structures. This theory presumes the following assumptions:

(*i*) The debt capitalization rate is a constant.

(*ii*) The market capitalizes the value of the firm as a whole and therefore the split between debt and equity is not important.

(*iii*) Corporate taxes do not exist.

(*iv*) The use of the debt fund having low cost increases the risk of equity shareholders, but it could result in increase the equity capitalization rate.

- **Traditional Approach:** The traditional approach to capital structure advocates that there is a right combination of equity and debt in the capital structure, at which the market value of a firm is maximum. As per this approach, debt should exist in the capital structure only up to a specific point, beyond which, any increase in leverage would result in the reduction in value of the firm.

It means that there exists an optimum value of debt to equity ratio at which the WACC is the lowest and the market value of the firm is the highest. Once the firm crosses that optimum value of debt to equity ratio, the cost of equity rises to give a detrimental effect to the WACC. Above the threshold, the WACC increases and market value of the firm starts a downward movement. This theory presumes the following assumptions:

(*i*) The rate of interest on debt remains constant for a certain period and thereafter with an increase in leverage, it increases.

(*ii*) The expected rate by equity shareholders remains constant or increase gradually. After that, the equity shareholders start perceiving a financial risk and then from the optimal point and the expected rate increases speedily.

(*iii*) As a result of the activity of rate of interest and expected rate of return, the WACC first decreases and then increases. The lowest point on the curve is optimal capital structure.

- **Modigliani-Miller Approach:** The basic premise of the Modigliani and Miller thesis was that there is no optimal capital structure, and moreover, that capital structure would not be able to affect the firm's value. The reason is summarized by the compensatory effect of the market value of the firm's stock that would decrease any time the firm incurs more debt and gets into a higher level of risk. It is because the firm's market value is actually the sum of the market value of debt and market value of stock.

Modigliani and Miller separate between the firm's value and its cost of capital, on one hand, and the form of capital structure on the other. They attribute the firm value to its ability to obtain the highest expected return on investment, utilizing the best capitalization rate, given that:

(*i*) The capitalization is for the firm's pure equity stream for a certain class with a proper consideration of the potential financial risk.

(*ii*) The capitalization rate would not be related to the type of securities that would be utilized for investment.

(*iii*) Finally, their argument gave a lot of weight to the personal arbitrage and its ability to change the dynamics of the financial leverage.

44. Assumptions Underlying Discounted-Cash-Flow Analysis: As is true of any decision model, discounted-cash-flow methods are based on assumptions. Four assumptions underlie the NPV and IRR methods of investment analysis.

- In the present-value calculations used in the NPV and IRR methods, all cash flows are treated as though they occur at year-end. If the city of Mountainview were to acquire the new street cleaner, the $14,000 in annual operating-cost savings actually would occur uniformly throughout each year. The additional computational complexity that would be required to reflect the exact timing of all cash flows would complicate an investment analysis considerably. The error introduced by the year-end cash-flow assumption generally is not large enough to cause any concern.
- Discounted-cash-flow analyses treat the cash flows associated with an investment project as though they were known with certainty. Although methods of capital budgeting under uncertainty have been developed, they are not used widely in practice. Most decision makers do not feel that the additional benefits in improved decisions are worth the additional complexity involved. As mentioned above, however, risk adjustments can be made in an NPV analysis to partially account for uncertainty about the cash flows.
- Both the NPV and IRR methods assume that each cash inflow is immediately reinvested in another project that earns a return for the organization. In the NPV method, each cash inflow is assumed to be reinvested at the same rate used to compute the project's NPV, the organization's hurdle rate. In the IRR method, each cash inflow is assumed to be reinvested at the same rate as the project's internal rate of return.

  What does this reinvestment assumption mean in practice? In the case of Mountainview's proposed new street cleaner, the city must instantly reinvest the money saved each year either in some interest-bearing investment or in some other capital project.
- A discounted-cash-flow analysis assumes a perfect capital market. This implies that money can be borrowed or lent at an interest rate equal to the hurdle rate used in the analysis.

In practice, these four assumptions rarely are satisfied. Neverthless, discounted-cash-flow models provide an effective and widely used method of investment analysis. The improved decision making that would result from using more complicated models seldom is worth the additional cost of information and analysis.

48. Profitability Index (PI) or Benefit-Cost Ratio (B/C Ratio): Yet another time-adjusted capital budgeting technique is profitability index (PI) or benefit-cost ratio (B/C). It is similar to the NPV approach. The profitability index approach measures the present value of returns per rupee invested, while the NPV is based on the difference between the present value of future cash inflows and the present value of cash outlays. A major shortcoming of the NPV method is that, being an absolute measure, it is not a reliable method to evaluate projects requiring different initial investments. The PI method provides a solution to this kind of problem. It is, in other words, a relative measure. It may be defined as the ratio which is obtained dividing the present value of future cash inflows by the present value of cash outlays. Symbolically,

$$PI = \frac{\text{Present value cash inflows}}{\text{Present value of cash outflows}}$$

This method is also known as the B/C ratio because the numerator measures benefits and the denominator costs. A more appropriate description would be *present value index.*

Accept-Reject Rule: Using the B/C ratio or the PI, a project will qualify for acceptance if its PI exceeds one. When PI equals 1, the firm is indifferent to the project.

When PI is greater than, equal to or less than 1, the net present value is greater than, equal to or less than zero respectively. In other words, the NPV will be positive when the PI is greater than 1; will be negative when the PI is less than one. Thus, the NPV and PI approaches give the same results regarding the investment proposals.

The selection of projects with the PI method can also be done on the basis of ranking. The highest rank will be given to the project with the highest PI, followed by others in the same order.

49. **Bird-in-the-Hand Theory: Dividends are Preferred:** The principal conclusion of MM's dividend irrelevance theory is that dividend policy does not affect the required rate of return on equity, r_s. This conclusion has been hotly debated in academic circles. In particular, Myron Gordon and John Lintner argued that r_s *decreases* as the dividend payout is increased because investors are less certain of receiving the capital gains that are supposed to result from retaining earnings than they are of receiving dividend payments. Gordon and Lintner said, in effect, that investors value a dollar of expected dividends more highly than a dollar of expected capital gains because the dividend yield component is less risky than the expected capital gain.

MM disagreed. They argued that r_s is independent of dividend policy, which implies that investors are indifferent between dividends and capital gains. MM called the Gordon-Lintner argument the bird-in-the-hand fallacy because, in MM's view, most investors plan to reinvest their dividends in the stock of the same or similar firms, and, in any event, the risk of the firm's cash flows to investors in the long run is determined by the risk of operating cash flows, not by dividend payout policy.

50. **Boundary-Spanning Roles:** Katz and Kahn (1966, 172-173, italics original) emphasise that organisations consist of *"acts or events... a set of activities"* which "constitute the *role* to be performed". Aldrich and Herker (1977) identified two types of boundary-spanning functions: information processing and external representation. They consider organisational boundaries as well defined with clear organisational structure, while arguing that it is the boundary-spanning activities that need attention given the amount of information the organisation receives from the external environment. This function of information processing serves the organisational decision-making process and therefore the role of boundary spanning is intra-organisational. Another function Aldrich and Herker (1977) investigate is representing the organisation externally in the business environment and the role of boundary spanners is inter-organisational.

51. **HR's Tryst with Competitive Advantage:** In 1950s, Peter Drucker wrote, "Some wit once said maliciously that [personnel management comprises] all those things that do not deal with the work of people and that are not management." (Drucker, 1954). And since then HR has been struggling to be accepted as part of management (or seat at the table). An article published by J. Barney, in *Journal of Management* (1991), for the first time articulated clearly on the resources an organization has and their link to competitive advantage. The article built on resource-based view (RBV) theory by E.T. Penrose (1959). RBV theory has been seen as key in bridging the link between human resource management (HRM) and business strategy. As per RBV theory, any organization has tangible and intangible resources. Tangible resources are land, machinery, or money and intangible are goodwill, patents, or human capital pool.

Barney elaborated that resources can be sources of competitive advantage only if they satisfy four criteria, namely the VRIO framework:

- Valuable,
- Rare,
- Inimitable, and
- Organized.

Any resource—tangible or intangible—satisfying all the four criteria can be a source of competitive advantage. A simple analysis reveals that human capital pool is one resource which cannot be easily imitated or may be unique (rare) to the organization and, hence, has a huge potential to be the source of sustained competitive advantage.

58. The activities of IDBI is to "Co-ordinate the functions and operations of all the financial institutions, including the IFCI, the ICICI, the LIC, and the UTI into a single integrated financial structure so that each may contribute to the total effect—the growth of the economy". For the lessening of Bihar's backwardness and growth of the economy the IDBI again conceived the idea to set up third TCO after North Eastern Industrial and Technical Consultancy Organisation Ltd. (NEITCO) in Bihar.

61. The Unit Trust of India, which was established on February 1, 1964 under the Unit Trust of India Act, 1963 in the public sector, is another organised investment institution in this country.

Objectives of UTI: The primary objective of the UTI is to encourage and mobilise savings of the community and channelise them into productive corporate investments so as to promote the growth and diversification of country's economy. To the achievement of this objective, it is selling 'units' of small denomination of ₹ 10 to the general public. The savings so mobilised are then invested by it in the shares and debentures of industrial companies, and in bonds of Public Corporation and Government Securities. The temporary surplus funds are placed by it with banks in call loans.

65. **Tariffication and Tariff Cuts:** Tariffication means the replacement of existing non-tariff restrictions on trade such as import quotas by such tariffs as would provide substantially the same level of protection.

From the first year of the Agreement's implementation, nearly all border protection was to be bound by tariffs, which (in principle) were to be no higher than the tariff equivalent of the protection levels prevailing in the base periods. Tariff binding means fixing the maximum rate of import duty, above which the country shall not raise the duty unilaterally.

On agricultural tariffs, developing countries have had the flexibility of indicating maximum ceiling binding. India had indicated ceiling bindings of 100 per cent on primary products and 300 per cent on edible oils.

Subsidies and Domestic Support Policies: The UR Agreement deals with three categories of subsidies.

Prohibited Subsidies: Prohibited subsidies are those contingent upon export performance or the use of domestic instead of imported goods.

Actionable Subsidies: Actionable subsidies are those that have demonstrably adverse effects on other member countries.

Non-actionable Subsidies: Non-actionable subsidies include those provided (with stipulated limitations) to industrial research and procompetitive development activity to disadvantaged regions, or to existing facilities to adapt themselves to new environmental requirements.

73. A *Treasury bill* is a short-term debt of the US Government. The bills are sold on an auction basis at a discount from face value. Since the US Government is continually borrowing to pay off debts, Treasury bills are issued on a very frequent basis. Biddings are closed by the US Treasury weekly for 91- and 182-day debt issues and monthly for 9- and 12-month bills. Short maturities and the backing of the US Government make them desirable investments.

Although the market is quite short-term, an active secondary market has developed. Therefore, bills can be traded before the maturity date, adding to their liquidity. Treasury bills are a desirable short-term investment tool for corporate investors because of the high level of liquidity and low level of risk they carry.

Commercial paper is a short-term debt issued by finance companies and some other corporations. Interest rates for commercial paper are generally higher than for Treasury bills because of the risk factors involved in private firms. Many companies use commercial paper to supplement bank loans. In general, it is a less expensive method of financing for prime quality obligatory than loans (because banks are not used as intermediaries) and may fill a need at a time when the issuance of long-term debt is not appropriate. The issuance of commercial paper lacks the supportive, interactive nature of a relationship between a corporation and a commercial bank.

Commercial paper may be sold directly by the issuing corporation or through a dealer. Since dealers screen the instruments to a certain extent, commercial paper placed by a dealer may be less risky for an investor, although commercial paper directly placed by some major corporations is of very high quality. The investor holds an unsecured short-term promissory note as evidence of the debt, and the instrument is tradable in money markets.

76. Interest Rate Risk: The variability in a security's return resulting from changes in the level of interest rates is referred to as interest rate risk. Such changes generally affect securities inversely; that is, other things being equal, security prices move inversely to interest rates. Interest rate risk affects bonds more directly than common stocks, but it affects both and is a very important consideration for most investors.

Market Risk: The variability in returns resulting from fluctuations in the overall market—that is, the aggregate stock market—is referred to as market risk. All securities are exposed to market risk, although it affects primarily common stocks.

Market risk includes a wide range of factors exogenous to securities themselves, including recessions, wars, structural changes in the economy, and changes in consumer preferences.

Inflation Risk: A factor affecting all securities is purchasing power risk, or the chance that the purchasing power of invested dollars will decline. With uncertain inflation, the real (inflation-adjusted) return involves risk even if the nominal return is safe (*e.g.*, a Treasury bond). This risk is related to interest rate risk, since interest rates generally rise as inflation increases, because lenders demand additional inflation premiums to compensate for the loss of purchasing power.

Business Risk: The risk of doing business in a particular industry or environment is called business risk. For example, AT&T, the traditional telephone powerhouse, faces major changes today in the rapidly changing telecommunications industry.

Financial Risk: Financial risk is associated with the use of debt financing by companies. The larger the proportion of assets financed by debt (as opposed to equity), the larger the variability in the returns, other things being equal. Financial risk involves the concept of financial leverage, explained in managerial finance courses.

Liquidity Risk: Liquidity risk is the risk associated with the particular secondary market in which a security trades. An investment that can be bought or sold quickly and without significant price concession is considered liquid. The more uncertainty about the time element and the price concession, the greater the liquidity risk. A Treasury bill has little or no liquidity risk, whereas a small OTC stock may have substantial liquidity risk.

Currency Risk (Exchange Rate Risk): All investors who invest internationally in today's increasingly global investment arena face the prospect of uncertainty in the returns after they convert the foreign gains back to their own currency. Unlike the past when most US investors ignored international investing alternatives, investors today are part of a global economy.

To take another example, a US investor who buys a German stock denominated in marks must ultimately convert the returns from this stock back to dollars. If the exchange rate has moved against the investor, losses from these exchange rate movements can partially or totally negate the original return earned.

Obviously, US investors who invest only in US stocks on US markets do not face this risk, but in today's global environment where investors increasingly consider alternatives from other countries, currency fluctuations have become important US investors who invest in such financial assets as international mutual funds, global mutual funds, closed-end single-country funds, foreign stocks, and foreign bonds are affected by currency risk.

Country Risk: Country risk, also referred to as political risk, is an important risk for investors today—probably more important now than in the past. With more investors investing internationally, both directly and indirectly, the political, and therefore economic, stability and viability of a country's economy need to be considered. The United States has one of the lowest country risks, and other countries can be judged on a relative basis using the United States as a benchmark. Examples of countries that needed careful monitoring in the 1990s because of country risk included the former Soviet Union and Yugoslavia, China, Hong Kong, and South Africa. In the early part of the twenty-first century, Russia, Pakistan, and several countries in South America, among others, require careful attention.

81. GE Variant: the General Electric Business Screen: The General Electric Corporation with the management consulting company McKinsey & Co has developed another portfolio type planning model, Davidson (1997), for example, suggests that the GE matrices overcome some of the disadvantages of the BCG model by incorporating a broader range of measures. The GE business screens can be used to classify SBUs or major products based upon two key factors: market attractiveness and business position.

Market Attractiveness: This includes market share (as with the BCG model), market size, the degree of difficulty in entering the market, the competitors (number, type, size, current and potential future ones), technological requirements (and speed of technological change), external environmental factors, and profit margins.

Business Position: This includes market share (as with the BCG model), the size of the SBU, the strength of differential advantage, research and development capabilities, production and operational capacity, quality of financial management (cost control), core competencies and expertise within the organization.

82. Kinds of discounts given on prices are as follows:

- **Quantity Discount:** It is offered to those customers who buy bulk quantity or larger quantities.
- **Cumulative Quantity Discount:** When the seller offers a discount which increases as the cumulative quantity increases.
- **Cash Discount:** It is a discount given to those customers who are regular and always prompt in paying their bills.
- **Seasonal Discount:** The discount given to customers who purchase during the off-season is called as seasonal discount. This kind of discount is promoted to eliminate the seasonal fluctuations and motivate customers to make purchases even in the off-season.
- **Functional Discount:** It is also called as Trade Discount. This discount is offered by

the manufacturer to trade channel members if they will perform certain functions determined by the manufacturer.

85. Behaviourally Anchored Rating Scales: Behaviourally Anchored Rating Scales (BARS) are 'descriptions provided on appraisal forms and surveys which describe a precise level of performance'. These are designed to reduce the rating errors of conventional scales. The scale includes number of performance dimensions like leadership, teamwork, communication, initiative, adaptability, etc. BARS were developed with the hope of improving rater accuracy by providing job-related behavioural anchors and altering the format of rating scales.

89. According to Census on Foreign Liabilities and Assets of Indian Direct Investment Companies 2016-17 released by Reserve Bank of India (RBI), Mauritius was largest source of foreign investment (FDI) in India.

The census yields carry comprehensive information on market value of foreign liabilities and assets of Indian companies arising on account of FDI, ODI and other investments.

Mauritius was largest source of FDI in India (21.8% share at market value) followed by USA, UK, Singapore and Japan. Singapore (19.7%) was major ODI destination, followed by Netherlands, Mauritius, and US.

18,667 companies had participated in census, of them 17,020 had FDI/overseas direct investment (ODI) in their balance sheets in March 2017. 96% of responding companies were unlisted in March 2017 and most of them had received only inward FDI.

Unlisted companies had higher share of FDI equity capital vis-a-vis listed companies. Further, over 80% of 15,169 companies that reported inward FDI were subsidiaries of foreign companies (single foreign investor holding over 50% of total equity).

The manufacturing sector accounted for nearly half of total FDI at market prices, information and communication services (ICTS) and financial and insurance activities were other major sectors that attracted FDI. Total sales, including exports, of foreign subsidiaries in India increased by 18.7% during 2016-17 whereas their purchases, including imports, increased by 20.1%.

96. Meaning: As per Sec. 2(11) of the Income Tax Act, 1961, unless the context otherwise requires, the term "block of assets" means a group of assets falling within a class of assets comprising:

- Tangible assets, being buildings, machinery, plant or furniture;
- Intangible assets, being know-how, patents, copyrights, trademarks, licences, franchises or any other business or commercial rights of similar nature, in respect of which the same percentage of depreciation is prescribed.

Concept of 'Block of Assets': Income Tax Act has prescribed different rates of depreciation for different types of block of assets. Depreciation on block of assets is mainly charged for the purpose of computing Capital Gains or Business Profit or Loss as per the Income Tax Act, 1961. The concept of block of assets, as explained above, requires working out depreciation in a manner that individual assets are sorted and assigned to the relevant/respective block of assets in the year of purchase itself, based on the terminology prescribed under the Income Tax Act. The written down value needs to be worked out accordingly throughout the existence of that asset or the block, like Land and Buildings, Plant & Machinery, Motor Vehicles, Furniture and Fixtures, etc.

It means the assets which are having similar characteristics are collected together and one block is created. There are twelve block of assets as per The Income Tax Act, 1961, which are as follows:

Block of Assets (Sec. 2(11))

Number	Name of Assets	Rate of Depreciation
Block 1	Buildings—Residential buildings other than hotels and boarding houses	5%
Block 2	Buildings—Office, factory, godown or building which are not mainly used for residential purpose (it covers hotels and boarding houses but does not cover those which are covered under Block 1 & 3	10%
Block 3	Buildings—The following buildings:	
	(a) Buildings acquired on or after September 1, 2002 for installing machinery and plant forming part of water supply project or water treatment system and which is put to use for the purpose of business of providing infrastructure facilities under clause (i) of Section 80-IA	100%
	(b) Temporary erections such as wooden structures	
Block 4	Furniture—Any furniture/fittings including electrical fittings	10%
Block 5	Plant and machinery—Any plant or machinery (not covered by Block 6, 7, 8, 9, 10, 11 or 12) and motor cars (other than those used in a business of running them on hire) acquired or put to use on or after April 1, 1990	15%
Block 6	Ocean-going ships, vessels ordinarily operating on inland waters including speed boats	20%
Block 7	Plant and machinery—Buses, lorries and taxies used in the business of running them on hire, machinery used in semiconductor industry, moulds used in rubber and plastic goods factories.	30%
Block 8	Plant and machinery—Aero planes-Besides, it includes commercial vehicle which is acquired after September 30, 1998 but before April 1, 1999 and it is put to use for any period prior to April 1, 1999, life saving medical equipment	40%
Block 9	Plant and machinery—Containers made of glass or plastic used as refills and plant and machinery which satisfy conditions of rule 5(2)—see the following:	
	(a) New commercial vehicle acquired during 2001-02 and put to use before March 31, 2002 for the purpose of business or profession;	
	(b) Machinery/plant used in weaving processing and garment sector of textile industry which is purchased under Technology Upgradation Fund Scheme during April 1, 2001 and March 31, 2004 and put to use up to March 31, 2004; and	50%
	(c) New commercial vehicle which is acquired during January 1, 2009 and September 30, 2009 and is put to use before October 1, 2009 for the purposes of business or profession.	
Block 10	Plant and machinery—Computers including computer software. Besides, it includes new commercial vehicles acquired in replacement of condemned vehicle of 15 years of age and put to use before April, 1999 (if acquired after September 30, 1998 but before April 1, 1999) or put use before April 1, 2000 (if acquired during the financial year 1999-2000). It also include books (other than annual publication) owned by a professional. It also includes gas cylinders; plant used in field operations by mineral oil concerns; direct fire glass melting furnaces	60%

Number	Name of Assets	Rate of Depreciation
Block 11	Plant and machinery—Energy saving devices; renewal energy devices; rollers in flour mills, sugar works and steel industry.	80%
Block 12	Plant and machinery—Air pollution control equipments; water pollution control equipments; solid waste control equipments, recycling and resource recovery systems; machinery acquired and installed on or after September 1, 2002 in a water supply project or water treatment system or for the purpose of providing infrastructure facility, wooden parts used in artificial silk manufacturing machinery; cinematograph films, bulbs of studio lights; wooden math frames; some plants used in mines, quarries and salt works; and books (being annual publications) owned by assesses carrying on a profession or books (may or may not be annual publications) carrying on business in running lending libraries.	100%
Block 13	Intangible assets (acquired after March 31, 1998)—Know-how, patents, copyrights, trademarks, licenses, franchises and any other business or commercial rights of similar nature.	20%

97. If an employee receives compensation (whether in one go or in installments) on voluntary retirement or separation, Section 10(10C) provides for exemption for such amount, subject to a maximum of ₹ 5,00,000.

This exemption is available to employee of any of the following:

- A public sector company
- Any other company
- An authority established under a Central, State or Provincial Act
- A local authority
- A co-operative society
- A University established or incorporated by or under a Central, State or Provincial Act and an Institution declared to be a University under section 3 of the University Grants Commission Act, 1956
- An Indian Institute of Technology within the meaning of clause (g) of section 378 of the Institutes of Technology Act, 1961 (59 of 1961)
- Any State Government
- The Central Government
- An institution, having importance throughout India or in any State or States, a the Central Government may, by notification in the Official Gazette 82, specify in this behalf
- Such institute of management as the Central Government may, by notification 83 in the Official Gazette, specify in this behalf.

98. Tax on Income of a Partnership Firm and LLP:

- Income Tax at a flat rate of 30% is levied on Partnership Firms and LLP's. Computation of taxes as per Income Tax Slab Rates is not allowed as the benefit of Slab Rates is only available to Individuals and HUF's. Education Cess @2% and SHEC @1% would also be required to be paid. Moreover, in case the income of the partnership firm is more than ₹ 1 crore in any financial year, Surcharge @10% would also be payable.
- Capital Gains arising from the sale of any asset by the partnership firm are taxable under Section 112. Moreover, in case of sale of shares and mutual funds, in case the period of holding is less than 1 year—the

income would be taxable under Section 111A at a flat rate of 15% and in case the period of holding of shares is more than 1 year—the income would be exempted from the levy of tax under Section 10(38).

- Remuneration and Interest is allowed to be paid to the partners. However, the tax deduction for remuneration and interest paid to the partners is allowed subject to the limits and conditions specified in Section 40(b).
- Remuneration and Interest received by the partners shall be taxed in their hands as income under head PGBP. However, the salary and interest which have not been allowed under Section 40(b) or any other section shall not be added to the income of the partners.
- The share of the partners in the total income of the firm is exempt in the hands of the partners as the same has already been taxed in the hands of the partnership firm.
- Losses of the firm should be carried forward and not allowed to be allocated to the partners.
- Deductions under Chapter VI-A would be allowed from the Gross Total Income only for Donations or in case the business falls under the specified category of business.
- In case the partnership firm is unable to pay the tax dues, the partners can be held liable for recovery of the tax dues.
- It is pertinent to note that although LLP's are treated in the same manner as Partnerships, there is only one section which does not apply to LLP's and applies to Partnership Firms which is Section 44AD. LLP's cannot claim benefits of Section 44AD by using Presumptive Taxation.

99. Section 211(1): Advance tax on the current income shall be payable by—all the companies, who are liable to pay the same, in four instalments during each financial year and the due date of each instalment and the amount of such instalment shall be as specified below:

Due Date of Instalment	Amount Payable
On or before the 15th June	Not less than fifteen per cent of such advance tax
On or before the 15th Sept.	Not less than forty-five per cent of such advance tax, as by the amount, if any, paid in the earlier instalment reduced
On or before the 15th Dec.	Not less than seventy-five per cent of such advance tax, as reduced by the amount or amounts, if any, paid in the earlier instalment or instalments.

Previous Paper (Solved)

UGC-NET-Junior Research Fellowship & Assistant Professor Eligibility Exam

COMMERCE, November-2017*

PAPER-II

Note: *This paper contains fifty (50) objective type questions of two (2) marks each. All questions are compulsory.*

1. From the following statements of Assertion (A) and Reasoning (R), indicate the correct code:

Assertion (A) : Industrial liberalisation became an imperative condition for the growth of forces of competition leading to high efficiency and productivity in Indian industries.

Reasoning (R): Industrial development and curbing of poverty is only possible through government intervention.

Code:

A. Both (A) and (R) are not correct.

B. (A) is correct, but (R) is not the correct explanation of (A).

C. (A) is correct and (R) is correct explanation of (A).

D. (A) is not correct, but (R) is correct.

2. Which of the following statements are not correct?

Statement (I) : Sustainable development means an attempt to achieve the balance between economic growth and conservation/protection of environment.

Statement (II) : Sustainable development means meeting the needs of industries without compromising the needs of import - export balancing.

Statement (III) : Sustainable development means creation of sufficient surplus budgets through stock of capital assets including land.

Code;

A. Statements (I) and (III)

B. Statements (II) and (III)

C. Statements (I) and (II)

D. Statements (I), (II) and (III)

3. Match items of List-I with List-II relating to macro environment of business and indicate the code of correct matching:

List-I	***List-II***
(*a*) Economic environment	(*i*) Ethical issues
(*b*) Political and government environment	(*ii*) Trade and transport policies
(*c*) Socio - cultural environment	(*iii*) Economic stratification of population
(*d*) Demographic environment	(*iv*) Judiciary powers

Code:

	(*a*)	(*b*)	(*c*)	(*d*)
A.	(*ii*)	(*iv*)	(*i*)	(*iii*)
B.	(*i*)	(*iii*)	(*ii*)	(*iv*)
C.	(*iv*)	(*ii*)	(*iii*)	(*i*)
D.	(*iii*)	(*i*)	(*iv*)	(*ii*)

4. For which one of the basic reasons, the "Structural Adjustment Programme" was undertaken in India in 1991?

A. Curbing competition among private sectors

B. Establishing predominant role of public sector

* *Held on 5 November, 2017.*

C. Establishing a free market economy
D. Regional balancing through planning and licensing

5. Match the items of List-I with List-II and indicate the correct code of matching:

List-I	***List-II***
(*a*) Micro external environment	(*i*) Economic and political factors
(*b*) Macro external environment	(*ii*) Competition among diverse products targetting disposable income of consumers
(*c*) Non-price competition	(*iii*) Input suppliers
(*d*) Desire competition	(*iv*) Sponsoring of events like sports

Code:

	(*a*)	(*b*)	(*c*)	(*d*)
A.	(*iii*)	(*i*)	(*iv*)	(*ii*)
B.	(*ii*)	(*iii*)	(*iv*)	(*i*)
C.	(*iv*)	(*ii*)	(*iii*)	(*i*)
D.	(*iv*)	(*i*)	(*ii*)	(*iii*)

6. Assertion (A) : Debt-equity ratio indicates the long term solvency of a company.

Reasoning (R) : It measures the ability of the company to pay off its long term liabilities.

Select the correct answer from the code given below:

A. Both (A) and (R) are correct and (R) is the correct reason for (A).
B. Both (A) and (R) are correct, but (R) does not explain (A) correctly.
C. (A) is correct, but (R) is wrong.
D. (A) is wrong, but (R) is correct.

7. The balance of property at cost has been ₹ 20,000 and ₹ 17,000 in 2015 and 2016, respectively. The profit on the sale of property of ₹ 2,000 is credited to Capital Reserve Account. New property costing ₹ 5,000 was bought in 2016. Determine the sale proceeds from property.

A. ₹ 3,000 B. ₹ 7,000
C. ₹ 10,000 D. ₹ 15,000

8. Goodwill of a firm of X and Y is valued at ₹ 30,000. It is appearing in the books at ₹ 12,000. Z is admitted for 1/4 share. What amount he is supposed to bring for goodwill?

A. ₹ 3,000 B. ₹ 4,500
C. ₹ 7,500 D. ₹ 10,500

9. A Ltd. issued a prospectus inviting applications for 2,000 shares. Applications were received for 3,000 shares and pro-rata allotment was made on the applications of 2,400 shares. If A has been allotted 40 shares, how many shares he must have applied for?

A. 40 B. 44
C. 48 D. 52

10. Which one of the following receipts is of revenue nature?

A. Amount realised from the sale of investments
B. Dividend received on investment
C. Amount borrowed from a bank
D. Compensation received from municipal corporation for the acquisition of land for the construction of road.

11. Statement (I) : Business decision makers deal with the complex, rather chaotic, business conditions of the real world and have to find the way to their destination, *i.e*, achieving the goal that they set for themselves.

Statement (II) : Even without application of economic logic and tools of analysis, business decisions are always rational and real and are not counter productive.

Code:

A. Both the statements are correct.
B. Both the statements are incorrect.
C. Statement (I) is correct, while statement (II) is incorrect.
D. Statement (I) is incorrect, while statement (II) is correct.

12. Which one of the following statements is true?

A. Pure profit is the return in excess of the opportunity cost

B. Accounting profit is the excess of total revenue over and above the explicit and implicit costs

C. Profit maximization is the sole objective of the modern firms

D. Profit is maximum when the difference between marginal revenue and marginal cost is maximum

13. Which one of the following is not the assumption on which the theory of consumer behaviour is based on the cardinal utility approach?

A. Rationality

B. Constant marginal utility from successive units

C. Constant marginal utility of money

D. Utility is measurable

14. Statement (I) : Point price elasticity of demand in terms of marginal and average revenues can be measured with the following formula:

$$\frac{AR}{AR - MR}$$

Statement (II) : The point price elasticity of demand is the product of the slope of the demand function and the ratio between corresponding price and quantity.

Code:

A. Both the statements are correct.

B. Both the statements are incorrect.

C. Statement (I) is correct, while statement (II) is incorrect.

D. Statement (I) is incorrect, while statement (II) is correct.

15. Which one of the following is not the basic property of indifference curves?

A. Negative slope

B. Indifference curves of two imperfect substitutes are concave to the point of origin

C. The indifference curves do not intersect nor are they tangent to one another

D. Upper indifference curves indicate a higher level of satisfaction

16. The scale of measurement which has no order, distance and unique origin is known as which one of the following?

A. Nominal scale B. Ordinal scale
C. Interval scale D. Ratio scale

17. The formula to determine the number of classes given by Sturge's Rule is which one of the following?

A. K = 1 + 3.322 (log N)

B. K = (log N) 1.322

C. $K = \frac{1+3.322}{(\log N)}$

D. $K = \frac{3.322}{(\log N)+1}$

Where: K = Number of classes
N = Total number of observations
(log N) = Logarithm of the total number of observations

18. Which one of the following is not the characteristics of normal distribution?

A. Bell - shaped and symmetric

B. Mean, Median and Mode of the distribution are equal

C. The total area under the curve for the normal probability distribution is one

D. The two tails of the distribution in both the directions touch the horizontal axis

19. Assertion (A) : A reasonably sized sample drawn randomly from large sized population contains almost all the characteristics which exist in the population.

Reasoning (R) : The theory of sampling is based on the two important laws of statistics, viz., Law of statistical regularity and law of inertia of large numbers.

Code:

A. Both (A) and (R) are correct and (R) is the complete explanation of (A).
B. Both (A) and (R) are correct, but (R) is not the complete explanation of (A).
C. (A) is not correct, while (R) is correct.
D. Both (A) and (R) are not correct.

20. Statement (I) : If the alternative hypothesis is as Ha: $\mu \neq \mu_0$; a researcher requires two-tailed test in hypothesis-testing.

Statement (II) : The mean of the sampling distribution of mean is not equal to the parametric value of mean.

Code:

A. Both the statements are true.
B. Both the statements are false.
C. Statement (I) is true, while statement (II) is false.
D. Statement (I) is false, while statement (II) is true.

21. Match the items of List-I with List-II; and choose the correct code of combination:

List-I	***List-II***
(*a*) The Fundamentals of Top Management	(*i*) Peter F. Drucker
(*b*) Middle Management	(*ii*) R.C. Davis
(*c*) The Essence of Management	(*iii*) E.L.F. Brech
(*d*) Principles and Practice of Management	(*iv*) Mary Caushing Nile

Code:

	(*a*)	(*b*)	(*c*)	(*d*)
A.	(*ii*)	(*iv*)	(*iii*)	(*i*)
B.	(*ii*)	(*iv*)	(*i*)	(*iii*)
C.	(*ii*)	(*iii*)	(*i*)	(*iv*)
D.	(*iii*)	(*iv*)	(*i*)	(*ii*)

22. Statement (I) : Management is not just a creature of the economy; it is a creator as well.

Statement (II) : He who can manage, can manage anything.

Code:

A. Statement (I) is correct, but (II) is incorrect.
B. Statement (II) is correct, but (I) is incorrect.
C. Both the statements (I) and (II) are incorrect.
D. Both the statements (I) and (II) are correct.

23. Assertion (A) : Due to these experiments (Time, Motion and Fatigue Studies) a factory does not remain a factory, it is converted into a laboratory.

Reasoning (R): Management succeeds or fails as human relations in business are intelligently or unintelligently handled.

Code:

A. Both (A) and (R) are correct and (R) is the right explanation of (A).
B. Both (A) and (R) are correct, but (R) is not the right explanation of (A).
C. (A) is correct, but (R) is not correct.
D. (R) is correct, but (A) is not correct.

24. Who among the following is not associated with theories of motivation?

A. A.H. Maslow B. Cris Argyris
C. Frederick Herzberg D. Peter F. Drucker

25. As per the Herzberg's Hygiene Theory of motivation, which among the following is not a motivational factor?

A. Recognition
B. Working Conditions
C. Responsibility
D. Achievements

26. When Walt Disney World's Magic kingdom lets customers visit a fairy kingdom, a pirate ship, or a haunted house, then what is marketed in this example?

A. Services B. Events
C. Experiences D. Ideas

27. Which one of the following statements is true according to VALS framework of psychographic segmentation?

A. The consumers who are primarily motivated by ideals are guided by knowledge and principles.

B. The consumers who are motivated by achievement look for knowledge and principles.
C. The consumers who are motivated by self expression don't desire social or physical activity, variety, and risk.
D. The consumers who are motivated by achievement desire social or physical activity, variety, and risk.

28. From the following two statements of Assertion (A) and Reason (R), indicate the correct code:

Assertion (A) : A transformational appeal of communication elaborates on a non-product related benefit or image.

Reasoning (R) : Transformational appeals often do not attempt to stir up emotions that will motivate purchase.

Code:

A. Both (A) and (R) are correct.
B. (A) is correct, (R) is not correct.
C. (A) is not correct, (R) is correct.
D. Both (A) and (R) are incorrect.

29. Select the correct sequence for Hierarchy-of-effects model related to marketing communication:

A. Awareness → Knowledge → Liking → Preference → Conviction → Purchase
B. Knowledge → Awareness → Liking → Conviction → Preference → Purchase
C. Awareness → Liking → Knowledge → Conviction → Preference → Purchase
D. Liking → Awareness → Knowledge → Preference → Conviction → Purchase

30. Match the items of List-I with the items of List-II and denote the code of correct matching:

List-I	***List-II***
(*a*) Basic Product	(*i*) Set of attributes and conditions buyers normally expect
(*b*) Expected Product	(*ii*) Possible augmentation and transformation the product might undergo in future
(*c*) Augmented Product	(*iii*) Exceed customer expectations
(*d*) Potential Product	(*iv*) Converting core benefits into product

Code:

	(*a*)	(*b*)	(*c*)	(*d*)
A.	(*iii*)	(*iv*)	(*i*)	(*ii*)
B.	(*i*)	(*iii*)	(*iv*)	(*ii*)
C.	(*i*)	(*iv*)	(*iii*)	(*ii*)
D.	(*iv*)	(*i*)	(*iii*)	(*ii*)

31. Which of the following statements is false?

A. The opportunity cost of an input is considered in capital budgeting
B. Capital budgeting decisions are reversible in nature
C. Cash flows and accounting profits are different
D. An expansion decision is a capital budgeting decision

32. Match the items of List-I with those of List-II and indicate the correct code:

List-I	***List-II***
(*a*) ABC Analysis	(*i*) Dividend Decision
(*b*) Walter Model	(*ii*) Capital Budgeting Decision
(*c*) Capital Rationing	(*iii*) Capital Structure Decision
(*d*) Net Operating Income Approach	(*iv*) Working Capital Management Decision

Code:

	(*a*)	(*b*)	(*c*)	(*d*)
A.	(*i*)	(*iii*)	(*ii*)	(*iv*)
B.	(*ii*)	(*i*)	(*iii*)	(*iv*)
C.	(*iv*)	(*i*)	(*ii*)	(*iii*)
D.	(*iii*)	(*i*)	(*ii*)	(*iv*)

33. Main objective of employing Financial Leverage is to:

A. Reduce the risk associated with profits
B. Maintain the stability in profits
C. Decrease the cost of debt capital
D. Magnify the return on equity share capital

34. Which one of the following is not a method of calculating cost of equity capital?

A. Dividend yield method
B. Dividend yield plus growth method
C. Yield to maturity method
D. Earnings yield method

35. Which one of the following equates the present value of cash out flows and the present value of expected cash inflows from a project?

A. Net Present Value
B. Internal Rate of Return
C. Pay back Period
D. Accounting Rate of Return

36. Which one of the following is not true?

A. Material resources are subject to laws of mechanics and they cannot have an output greater than the input.
B. Human resources are capable of exponential growth and development.
C. Human resources cannot yield an output that may be far greater than what the value of their input warrants.
D. In current scenario, gradually, the emphasis has shifted from muscle power to use of mind power.

37. The pluralistic approach of industrial conflict is based on which one of the following basic assumption/premise?

A. That conflict occurs when the tendency of industrial society is to treat worker as an isolated individual and deprive him of all control over his environment.
B. That an enterprise contains people with coalition of different interests.
C. That industrial conflict is a part of the broader social conflict between classes.
D. That no consensus is possible, in case of conflicts, because people are with different socio-cultural backgrounds.

38. The Job Description Index (JDI) Technique is used for measuring which one of the following?

A. Job attitudes
B. Job descriptions/definitions
C. Job analysis records
D. Job skill requirements

39. From the following two statements of Assertion (A) and Reasoning (R) indicate the correct code:

Assertion (A) : Development in HRM is a short-term educational process with temporary intervention.

Reasoning (R): It is an educational process utilizing a systematic and organized procedure for development of operative employees performance in current jobs.

Code:

A. (A) is correct and (R) is correct explanation of (A).
B. (A) is correct, but (R) is not correct explanation of (A).
C. (A) is not correct, but (R) is correct.
D. Both (A) and (R) are not correct.

40. Match items of List-I with List-II relating to methods of performance appraisal and indicate the correct code of matching.

List-I	***List-II***
(*a*) Paired comparison method	(*i*) Reviewing employee records and holding interview on definite test questions.
(*b*) Forced choice description method	(*ii*) Set of pair phrases or descriptive statements
(*c*) Critical Incidents method	(*iii*) Differentiating between effective and non-effective performance on basis of achievements
(*d*) Field review method	(*iv*) Relative ranking method

Code:

	(*a*)	(*b*)	(*c*)	(*d*)
A.	(*iv*)	(*ii*)	(*iii*)	(*i*)
B.	(*ii*)	(*iii*)	(*iv*)	(*i*)
C.	(*iii*)	(*i*)	(*iv*)	(*ii*)
D.	(*ii*)	(*iv*)	(*i*)	(*iii*)

41. Match the following items of List-I with the items of List-II and indicate the code of correct matching:

List-I (Name of organisation)	*List-II (Year of establishment)*
(*a*) IDBI	(*i*) 1956
(*b*) ICICI	(*ii*) 1955
(*c*) LIC of India	(*iii*) 1990
(*d*) SIDBI	(*iv*) 1964

Code:

	(*a*)	(*b*)	(*c*)	(*d*)
A.	(*iii*)	(*i*)	(*ii*)	(*iv*)
B.	(*iii*)	(*i*)	(*iv*)	(*ii*)
C.	(*iv*)	(*ii*)	(*i*)	(*iii*)
D.	(*i*)	(*ii*)	(*iii*)	(*iv*)

42. Statement (I) : Capital adequacy norms help banks in strengthening their capital base.

Statement (II) : Capital adequacy norms help banks in sanctioning more loans.

Code:

A. Both the Statements (I) and (II) are correct.
B. Both the Statements (I) and (II) are incorrect.
C. Statement (I) is correct, but (II) is incorrect.
D. Statement (I) is incorrect, but (II) is correct.

43. What is Hawala?

A. Tax evasion
B. Illegal trading in stock exchanges
C. Bank robbery
D. Illegal transactions of foreign exchange

44. Read the following events:

(*i*) Capital adequacy norms for commercial banks
(*ii*) Establishment of IDBI
(*iii*) Allowing convertibility of rupee at the market rate in the current account.
(*iv*) Nationalisation of general insurance business

Arrange the events in the ascending order of their occurrance:

A. (*i*), (*ii*), (*iii*), (*iv*) B. (*iv*), (*iii*), (*ii*), (*i*)
C. (*iv*), (*ii*), (*i*), (*iii*) D. (*i*), (*ii*), (*iv*), (*iii*)

45. Assertion (A) : The future will see mostly the electronic money clearance through satellite networking.

Reasoning (R) : RBI is encouraging e-banking.

Code:

A. (A) is true, but (R) is false.
B. (A) is false, but (R) is true.
C. Both (A) and (R) are true and (R) is the correct explanation of (A).
D. Both (A) and (R) are true, but (R) does not support (A).

46. Statement (I) : Developing countries can borrow more than their quota under Extended Fund Facility (EFF) of IMF.

Statement (II) : The Extended Fund Facility (EFF) was created in 1984 to help the developing countries over longer period upto 3 years.

Code:

A. Statement (I) is correct, but (II) is not correct.
B. Statement (II) is correct, but (I) is not correct.
C. Both the statements (I) and (II) are correct.
D. Both the statements (I) and (II) are not correct.

47. Match the items of List-I with those of List-II; and choose the correct code of combination:

List-I	*List-II*
(*a*) Poverty Reduction and Growth Facility (PRGF)	(*i*) 1997
(*b*) Supplemental Reserve Facility (SRF)	(*ii*) 1974
(*c*) Extended Fund Facility (EFF)	(*iii*) 1999

Code:

	(*a*)	(*b*)	(*c*)
A.	(*iii*)	(*i*)	(*ii*)
B.	(*iii*)	(*ii*)	(*i*)
C.	(*ii*)	(*i*)	(*iii*)
D.	(*i*)	(*iii*)	(*ii*)

48. Who among the following has given Absolute Advantage Model of international trade?
A. Adam Smith B. David Recardo
C. Hackscher Ohlin D. William Petty

49. Which among the following is not an international economic institution?
A. IMF B. IBRD
C. ADB D. IFRS

50. Assertion (A) : The fall in aggregate expenditure or aggregate demand in the economy works to reduce imports and help in solving the balance of payment problems.

Reasoning (R) : The important way to reduce imports and thereby reduce deficit in balance of payments is to adopt monetary and fiscal policies that aim at reducing aggregate expenditure in the economy.

Code:
A. Both (A) and (R) are correct and (R) supports (A).
B. Both (A) and (R) are correct, but (R) does not support (A).
C. (A) is correct, but (R) is incorrect.
D. (R) is correct, but (A) is incorrect.

ANSWERS

1	2	3	4	5	6	7	8	9	10
B	B	A	C	A	A	C	B	C	B
11	**12**	**13**	**14**	**15**	**16**	**17**	**18**	**19**	**20**
C	A	B	A	B	A	A	D	A	C
21	**22**	**23**	**24**	**25**	**26**	**27**	**28**	**29**	**30**
*	D	B	D	B	C	A	B	A	D
31	**32**	**33**	**34**	**35**	**36**	**37**	**38**	**39**	**40**
B	C	D	C	B	C	B	A	D	A
41	**42**	**43**	**44**	**45**	**46**	**47**	**48**	**49**	**50**
C	C	D	*	C	A	A	A	D	A

* Discrepancy is found in Question/options.

EXPLANATORY ANSWERS

2. The concept of sustainability is commonly believed to come from the World Conservation Strategy (IUCN, 1980) but was later more fully developed and publicised in the Brundtland Report, *Our Common Future* by the World Commission on Environment and Development (WCED) wherein it is stated that the present generation should develop in such a way that meets their needs 'without jeopardising the ability of future generations to fulfil their needs'. There is a dual emphasis on fulfilling the 'needs' of the present generation and the 'ability' of future generations to do so. Both concepts are subject to different interpretations depending on society norms over time. In particular, 'ability' is difficult to measure and quantify for informing government policies and inducing changes in the behaviour of the present generation.

Therefore, comprehensive sustainability is a broad concept or vision with shared principles and meanings across the globe, but the specific objectives and plans are often place-based and diverse. Comprehensive sustainability aims to balance different needs of the human race in the three major domains of the environment, society and economy. The balance between achieving economic growth and environmental preservation is best described as *sustainable development.* The balance between environmental preservation and social equity is best illustrated by *community liveability.*

The balance between economic growth and social equity is crystallised in social and economic *equity.* However, comprehensive sustainability only exists in the small but important overlapping areas of the three domains of environment, economy and society.

4. Government of India, initiated "Structural Adjustment Programme" since July 1991. It is also known as new economic policy of 1991. The objective is to make the Indian Economy more outward oriented and to provide "free play of market forces". Globalization can not be successful without liberalization. By the term "Liberalization" we means the removal of unnecessary control in laws and procedures, and "Globalization," on the other hand means the opening of the economy to the world by removing barriers against free flow of trade, technology and investment.

5. Classification of External Environment: The external environment can be further classified into two categories: micro environment and macro environment.

Micro Environment: The micro environment consists of different types of stakeholders outside the organisation. The constitutions or stakeholders of the micro environment include customers, suppliers, creditors, distributors, dealers, etc. Although these constituents are not under the direct control of the organisation, still they can be influenced by the organisation through its policies and strategies. Any change in the micro environment affects and impinges on the organisations activities directly. That is why it is also termed as Specific (Task) Environment.

Macro Environment: The macro environment consists of constituents that are beyond the control of a business organisation. These constituents are socio-cultural, technological, economical and political (STEP) factors which constitute their own individual environments. The effect of changes in the macro environment on the business is indirect. Therefore, it is also termed as General (Societal) Environment. An example of a change in the macro environment is the passing of a legislation, which bans smoking in public places. This legislation indirectly affects the business of pubs and restaurants.

Constituents of Macro Environment

The main constituents of the macro environment are: global business environment, socio-cultural environment, technological environment, economic environment, political environment, demographic environment, legal environment and environmental concerns.

6. Long Term Solvency Ratio: The long term solvency ratio indicates the ability of the firm to meet its long term obligations. It includes the loan taken from the financial institutions, banks and issues of debentures and bonds. It is very much essential to study the long term liabilities, consists of the following ratios:

(*i*) Debt-Equity Ratio

(*ii*) Proprietary Ratio/Equity Ratio

(*iii*) Solvency Ratio

Debt Equity Ratio: It indicates the relationship between the outsider funds and shareholder's funds in the business. Outsiders funds includes both the long-term as well as short-term liabilities. The shareholder's fund includes the equity share capital, preference share capital, capital reserves, accumulated profits and surpluses, etc. The formula use to calculate the Debt-Equity Ratio is as follows:

$$\text{Debt-Equity Ratio} = \frac{\text{Outsider's Funds}}{\text{Shareholder's Fund}}$$

There is no rules of thumb to measure the ratio. Usually 1 : 1 ratio may be considered as satisfactory ratio.

Higher debt equity ratio shows lesser margin for long term lenders. This ratio indicates to what extent the firm depends on outsiders' funds for existence.

Purpose of Debt to Equity Ratio: The purpose of debt equity ratio is to measure the long term solvency of the business. A higher debt to equity ratio is not considered good for the business.

7. Sale proceeds from property

$= 20,000 + 2,000 + 5,000 - 17,000$

$= ₹\ 10,000.$

8. The value of goodwill is ₹ 30,000

Book value of goodwill = ₹ 12,000

The share of Z will be 30,000 – 12,000

$$= 18,000 \times \frac{1}{4} = ₹\ 4,500.$$

9. Number of shares applied by A

$$= \frac{\text{Total shares allotted to pro-rata allottees}}{\text{Total shares applied of pro-rata allottees}} \times \text{Number of shares alloted to A}$$

$$= \frac{2,400}{2,000} \times 40 = 48.$$

10. Capital and Revenue Receipts: Contributions to a business enterprise made by a proprietor in the case of sole trader, partners in case of partnership firms, shareholders in case of joint stock company as the capital of the concerns are capital receipts. Loan from third parties, sale of any fixed assets of a business, funds raised by way of debentures are also capital receipts.

Incomes that arise due to the desired results of intense activities in a business enterprise are revenue receipts, such as sales revenue, commission and discount received, interest and dividend received, interest on investments and the like.

11. Managerial Economics Fills the Gap between Theory and Practice: There is undeniably a gap between economic theory and the real economic world. But, at the same time, it is also a mistaken view that economic theories can be directly applied to business decision-making. Economic theories do not offer a custom-made or readymade solution to business problems.

Let us now see how business economics bridges the gap between economic theories and business practices. On one side, there is the complex business world and, on the other, there are abstract economic theories, "The big gap between the problems of logic that intrigue economic theorists and the problems of policy that plague practical management needs to be bridged in order to give executive access to the practical contributions that economic thinking can make to top management policies". Managerial decision-makers deal with the complex, rather chaotic, business conditions of the real world and they have to find their way to their destination, *i.e.,* achieving the goal that they set for themselves. Business economics applies economic models and analytical tools to eliminate unimportant and inconsequential details and identify the major area of analysis to find a solution to the problem. The economic logic and tools of analysis guide the management in the following managerial functions.

(*i*) identifying their problems in achieving their goal.

(*ii*) collecting the relevant data and other relevant information.

(*iii*) processing and analyzing the collected data.

(*iv*) drawing the relevant conclusions,

(*v*) determining and evaluating the alternative means to achieve the goal, and

(*vi*) taking a decision.

12. Economists' concept of profit is of *pure profit.* It is also called 'economic profit' or 'just profit'. 'Pure profit' is a return over and above the opportunity cost, *i.e.,* the payment that would be 'necessary to draw forth the factors of production from their most remunerative alternative employment'. Pure profit may thus be defined as 'a residual left over after all contractual costs have been met, including the transfer costs of management, insurable risks, depreciation, and payments to shareholders sufficient to maintain investment at its current level'. In other words, *pure profit* equals *net profit* less opportunity costs of management, insurable risk, depreciation of capital, necessary minimum payments to shareholders that can prevent them from withdrawing their capital from its current use.

13. Assumptions: The theory of consumer behaviour based on the cardinal utility approach seeks to answer the above questions on the basis of the following assumptions.

(*a*) **Rationality:** It is assumed that the consumer is a rational being in the sense that he satisfies his wants in the order of their preference. That is, he or she buys that commodity first which yields the highest utility and the last which gives the least utility.

(*b*) **Limited money income:** The consumer has a limited money income to spend on the goods and services he chooses to consume. Limitedness of income, along with utility maximization objective makes the choice between goods inevitable.

(*c*) **Maximization of satisfaction:** Every rational consumer intends to maximize his satisfaction from his/her given money income.

(*d*) **Utility is cardinally measurable:** The cardinalists have assumed that utility is cardinally measurable and that utility of one unit of a commodity equals the units of money which a consumer is prepared to pay for it and that 1 util = 1 unit of money.

(*e*) **Diminishing marginal utility:** Following the law of diminishing marginal utility, it is assumed that the utility gained from the successive units of a commodity consumed decreases as a person consumes them. This is an axiom of the theory of consumer behaviour.

(*f*) **Constant marginal utility of money:** The cardinal utility approach assumes that marginal utility of money remains constant whatever the level of a consumer's income. This assumption is necessary to keep the scale of measuring rod of utility fixed. It is important to recall in this regard that cardinalists used 'money' as a measure of utility.

(*g*) **Utility is additive:** Cardinalists assumed not only that utility is cardinally measurable but also that utility derived from various goods and services consumed by a consumer can be added together to obtain the total utility. Suppose a consumer consumes $X_1, X_2, X_3, \ldots X_n$ units of a commodity X and that he derives $U_1, U_2, U_3, \ldots, U_n$, utils respectively, from the various units of commodity X consumed. Given the assumption, the total utility that the consumer derives form *n* units of commodity X can be expressed as

$$U_n = U_1(X_1) + U_2(X_2) + U_3(X_3) + \ldots + U_n(X_n).$$

15. Indifference curves for normal goods have not only a negative slope, but are also convex with reference to the origin. The convexity of the indifference curves implies that:

- The two goods are *imperfect substitutes* for one another.

- The *MRS* between the two goods decreases as a consumer moves along an indifference curve. Convexity in the indifference curve is caused by the diminishing *MRS*.

Properties of Indifference Curve

Indifference curves have the following four basic properties:

1. Indifference curves have a negative slope;
2. Indifference curves of imperfect substitutes are convex to the origin;
3. Indifference curves do not intersect nor are they tangent to one another;
4. Upper indifference curves indicate a higher level of satisfaction.

16. In general, the principles of measurement (scaling) has three characteristics:

1. Numbers are ordered. One number is less than, equal to or greater than another number.
2. Difference between numbers are ordered. The difference between any pair of numbers is greater than, less than or equal to the difference between any other pair of numbers.
3. The number series has a unique origin indicated by the number zero.

The combinations of these characteristics of *order, distance* and *origin* provide the following widely used classification of measurement scales:

Scale of Measurement	*Characteristics of Measurement*	*Basic Empirical Operation*
• Nominal	No order, distance or unique origin	Determination of categorical information. Numbers only identify groups which cannot be ordered.
• Ordinal	Order but no distance or unique origin	Determination of greater or lesser values. Numbers allow ranking but no arithmetic.
• Interval	Both order and distance but not unique	Determination of equality of intervals or differences. Intervals between numbers are meaningful.
• Ratio	Order, distance and unique origin	Determination of equality of ratios. Intervals between numbers are meaningful and also their ratio as the lowest value is a meaningful zero.

17. According to Sturge's rule, the number of classes can be determined by the formula

$$k = 1 + 3.222 \log_e N$$

where k is the number of classes and $\log_e N$ is the logarithm of the total number of observations.

18. Characteristics of the Normal Probability Distribution: There is a family of normal distributions. Each normal distribution may have a different mean μ or standard deviation σ. A unique normal distribution may be defined by assigning specific values to the mean μ and standard deviation σ in the normal probability density function. Large value of σ reduce the height of the curve and increase the spread; small values of σ increase the height of the curve and reduce the spread. Figure 1 shows three normal distributions with different values of the mean μ and a fixed standard deviation σ, while in Figure 2 normal distributions are shown with different values of the standard deviation σ and a fixed mean μ.

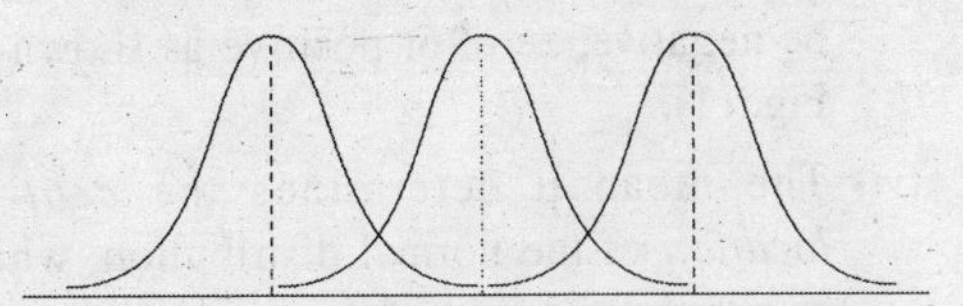

Figure 1: *Normal Distributions with Different Mean Values but Fixed Standard Deviation*

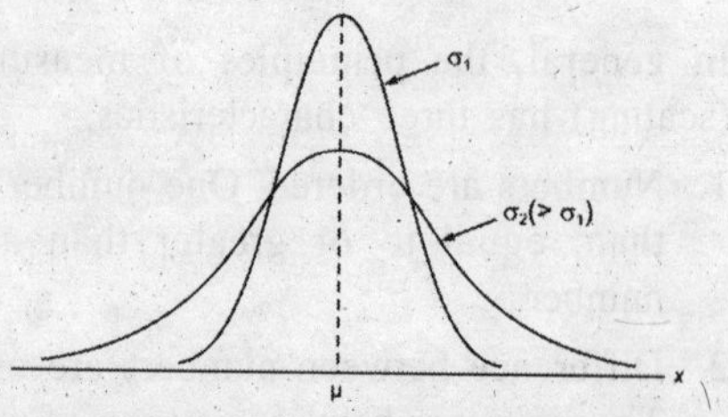

Figure 2: *Normal Distributions with Fixed Mean and Variable Standard Deviation*

From Figs. 1 and 2 the following characteristics of a normal distribution and its density function may be derived:

(*i*) For every pair of values of μ and σ, the curve of normal probability density function is bell shaped and symmetric.

(*ii*) The normal curve is symmetrical around a vertical line erected at the mean μ with respect to the area under it, that is, fifty per cent of the area of the curve lies on both sides of the mean and reflect the mirror image of the shape of the curve on both sides of the mean μ. This implies that the probability of any individual outcome above or below the mean will be same. Thus, for any normal random variable x,

$$P(x \leq \mu) = P(x \geq \mu) = 0.50$$

(*iii*) Since the normal curve is symmetric, the mean, median and mode for the normal distribution are equal because the highest value of the probability density function occurs when value of a random variable, $x = \mu$.

(*iv*) The two tails of the normal curve extend to infinity in both directions and theoretically never touch the horizontal axis.

(*v*) The mean of the normal distribution may be negative, zero, or positive as shown in Fig. (1).

(*vi*) The mean μ determines the *central location* of the normal distribution, while standard deviation σ determines its *spread.* The larger the value of the standard deviation σ, the wider and flatter is the normal curve, thus showing more variability in the data, as shown in Fig. (2). Thus standard deviation σ determines the range of values that any random variable is likely to assume.

(*vii*) The area under the normal curve represents probabilities for the normal random variable, and therefore, the total area under the curve for the normal probability distribution is 1.

20. The parameters of the sampling distribution are related to the parameters of the distribution of data. The means of the two distributions are equal to the same value. This will always be the case for any unbiased estimate. An unbiased estimate is equal to the population's parameter, on the average. This is reflected in the sampling distribution by having the mean equal to the parameter that is being estimated (*i.e.,* mean of the distribution of data).

The variances and standard deviations of the sampling distribution and distribution of data are related, but not equal to the same value. The sampling distribution is less dispersed than is the distribution of data. The reason for this is that the impact of extreme data values in a sample is offset by less extreme data values. Thus, estimates of the mean have less variation than do the data. How much less, depends on the number of observations in the sample. The greater the number of observations, the less variable the estimates. To emphasize the difference in dispersion between the sampling distribution and the distribution of data, the standard deviation of the sampling distribution is usually called the standard error.

22. Professor Drucker regards management as an economic organ which determines how well or ill an enterprise fulfils its essential function: economic performance. His basic assumption is that in determining the economic performance of an enterprise, the manager can improve his performance through the systematic study of principles, the acquisition of organized knowledge, and the systematic analysis of his own performance. This impact of the manager on modern society is so great "as to require of him the self-discipline and the high standards of public service of a true professional."

Within the economic realm, Drucker's view of management requires than mere passive adaptation to changing conditions. "It is management's specific job," he says, "to make what is desirable first possible and then actual. Management is not just a creature of the economy; it is a creator as well."

Since management's job is to make a productive enterprise out of men and materials, it accomplishes its mission by managing managers, who will be effective in fulfilling the two major functions of any business enterprise: to create customers and to innovate. These, according to Drucker are the two entrepreneurial functions.

24. Peter F. Drucker, a management consultant and professor of management has written a number of books on managerial topics like, *The Practice of Management* (1954), *The End of Economic Man* (1939), *The Future of Industrial Man, The Concept of Corporation, Economic Tasks and Risk Taking Decisions etc.* He is also called as *Father of Modern Management.*

Peter Drucker is against bureaucratic management instead he has emphasized creative and innovative management. He has treated management both as discipline and profession. He sees management through its tasks. Drucker stresses the setting up of objectives for each member of organisation, the distribution of all necessary information to each member so that he can make his own change with a view to meet his objectives, and the self control of each unit in the organisation. According to him, control, as domination of a superior over a subordinate is inappropriate in management. He is regarded as a father of *'management by objectives (MBO) Technique'* which has revolutionalised the management process. Drucker's MBO philosophy includes method of planning, setting standards, appraisal of performance and motivation. It applies to every manager, whatever his level of function and to any business enterprise whether large or small. It ensures performance by converting objective needs into personal goals.

25. Herzberg's Motivation-Hygiene Theory

Motivators

- Achievement
- Recognition
- Work itself
- Responsibility
- Advancement
- Growth

Hygiene Factors

- Supervision
- Company Policy
- Relationship with Supervisor
- Working Conditions
- Salary
- Relationship with Peers
- Personal Life
- Relationship with Subordinates
- Status
- Security.

26. Marketing people are involved in 10 types of entities: goods, services, experiences, events, persons, places, properties, organizations, information, and ideas.

Experiences: By orchestrating several services and goods, a firm can create, stage and market experiences. Walt Disney World's Magic Kingdom represents experiential marketing. Customers visit a fairy kingdom, a pirate ship, or a haunted house. So does the Hard Rock Café. There is also a market for customized experiences such as spending a week at a baseball camp playing with some retired baseball greats, paying to conduct the Chicago symphony orchestra for five minutes or climbing mount everest.

Events: Marketers promote time-based events such as the Olympics, company anniversaries, major trade shows, sports events and artistic performances. There is a whole profession of meeting planners who out the details of an event and make sure it comes off perfectly.

Persons: Celebrity Marketing is a major business. Years ago, someone seeking fame would hire a press agent to plant stories in newspapers and magazines. Today every major film star has an agent, a personal manager, and ties to a public relations agency. Various professionals such as lawyers, artists etc are also getting help from celebrity marketers.

Places: Cities, states, regions and whole nations compete actively to attract tourists, factories, company headquarters and new residents. E.g, easter at the mountains. Place marketers include economic development specialists, real estate agents, commercial banks, local business associations, and advertising and public relations agencies.

Properties: Properties are intangible rights of ownership of either real property (real estate) or financial property (stocks and bonds). Properties are bought and sold and this requires marketing. Real estate agents work for property owners or sellers or buy residential or commercial real estate. Investment companies and banks are involved in marketing securities to both institutional and individual investors.

Organizations: organizations actively work to build a strong, favourable image in the minds of their target publics. Companies spend money on corporate identity ads. Philips, the dutch electronic's company puts out ads with the tag "Let's make Things Better". Universities, museums, and performing arts organizations all use marketing to boost their public images and to compete for audiences and funds.

Information: Information can be produced and marketed as a product. This is essentially what schools and universities produce and distribute at a price to parents, students and communities. Encyclopaedias and most nonfiction books market information. The production, packaging, and distribution of information is one of our society's major industries.

Ideas: Every market offering includes a basic idea. Charles Revson of Revlon observed: "In the factory, we make cosmetics; in the store we sell hope". Products and services are platforms for delivering some idea or benefit. Social marketers are busy promoting such as ideas as Say no to drugs, Save the rain forest, exercise daily or avoid fatty foods.

The Decisions Marketers Make: Marketing managers face a host of decisions from major ones such as what product features to design into a new product, how many sales people to hire, or how much to spend on advertising etc.

27. In the United States, lifestyle research has been dominated since 1978 by the VALS system, originally developed by SRI International and now owned and operated by SRI Consulting Business Intelligence (SRI-BI). In 1989 VALS was revised to maximize its ability to predict consumer behaviour. The original system grouped consumers based on their attitudes toward social values such as military spending and abortion rights. Research conducted by SRI, Stanford University, and the University of California, Berkeley, found that psychological characteristics with several key demographics were better predictors of consumer behaviour than social values were. The new VALS system, called VALS 2 for a short time but now known again as VALS, has psychology at its core and is therefore known as a psychographic segmentation system.

VALS systems for Japan and the United Kingdom have also been developed using the same methodology. The U.S. VALS system places U.S. adult consumers into one of eight segments. The two main dimensions of the framework are *primary motivation* (the horizontal dimension) and *resources* (the vertical dimension).

The SRI premise is that consumers are inspired by one of three primary motivations: ideals, achievements, and self-expression. Consumers who are primarily motivated by ideals are guided by knowledge and principles. Consumers who are primarily motivated by achievement look for products and services that demonstrate success to their peers. Consumers who are primarily motivated by self-expression desire social or physical activity, variety and risk.

28. *Creative strategies,* how marketers translate their messages into a specific communication, can be classified as either informational appeal or transformational appeal. An *informational appeal* elaborates on attributes or benefits. Examples in advertising are problem-solution ads (Excedrin stops headache pain quickly), product demonstration ads (Thompson Water Seal can withstand intense rain, snow, and heat), product comparison ads (Verizon offers better Internet access than Comcast), and testimonials from unknown or celebrity endorsers (basketball star LeBron James pitching Coca-Cola and Nike). Such appeals assume the consumer is processing the communication very rationally.

A *transformational appeal* elaborates on a non-product-related benefit or image. It might depict what kind of person uses a brand (as when VW advertised to active, youthful people with its "Drivers Wanted" campaign) or what kind of experience results from using the brand (Coast soap has been advertised as "The Eye Opener!"). Transformational appeals often attempt to stir up emotions that will motivate purchase. Many communicators use negative appeals such as fear, guilt, and shame to prompt action (get people to brush their teeth or stop smoking). Also, communicators can use positive emotional appeals such as humour, love, pride, and joy, sometimes employing "borrowed interest" devices such as frisky puppies or sex appeal to attract interest and raise involvement in the ad. The challenge here is to avoid detracting from comprehension and overshadowing the product.

29. Hierarchy-of-effects models assume mediating processes between the advertisement and the desired outcome on the part of the consumer. These processes are cognitive, affective and conative (behavioural) – in other words, consumers are assumed first to think about the ad, then to form some emotional response and then to act (*e.g.,* purchase the product in the ad). One of the earliest models in this domain was the AIDA model, named as the acronym of its four components: attention, interest, desire, action. According to Fennis and Stroebe, this model dates back at least to the end of the nineteenth century. Later variations of this idea include the model by Lavidge and Steiner, who suggested a sequence of awareness, knowledge, liking, preference, conviction and purchase. In this model, awareness and knowledge refer to the cognitive aspect, focusing on information. Liking and preference, the second two stages, refer to the affective aspects, focusing on favourable attitudes or feelings about the product. Conviction and purchase refer to the conative aspect, focusing on action.

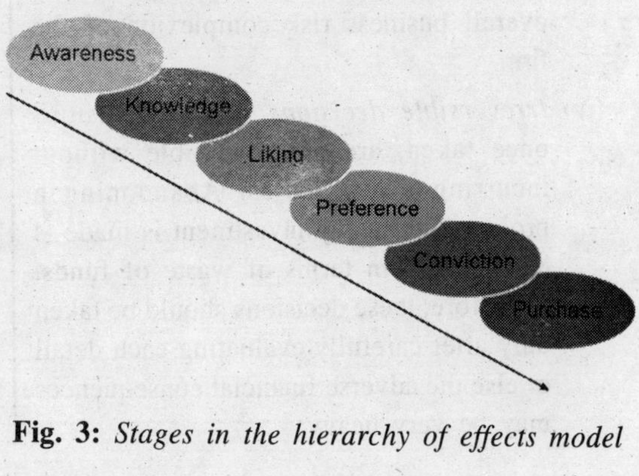

Fig. 3: *Stages in the hierarchy of effects model*

31. Fixed capital refers to investment in long-term assets. Management of fixed capital involves around allocation of firm's capital to different projects or assets with long-term implications for the business.

These decisions are called investment decisions or capital budgeting decisions and affect the growth, profitability and risk of the business in the long run.

The management of fixed capital or investment or capital budgeting decisions are important for the following reasons:

(i) *Long-term growth and effects:* These decisions have bearing on the long-term growth. The funds invested in long-term assets are likely to yield returns in the future. These affect future possibilities and prospects of the business.

(ii) *Large amount of funds involved:* These decisions result in a substantial portion of capital funds being blocked in long-term projects.

Therefore, these investment programmes are planned after a detailed analysis is undertaken. This may involve decisions like where to procure funds from and at what rate of interest.

(iii) *Risk involved:* Fixed capital involves investment of huge amounts. It affects the returns of the firm as a whole in the long-term. Therefore, investment decisions involving fixed capital influence the overall business risk complexion of the firm.

(iv) *Irreversible decisions:* These decisions once taken, are not reversible without incurring heavy losses. Abandoning a project after heavy investment is made is quite costly in terms of waste of funds. Therefore, these decisions should be taken only after carefully evaluating each detail or else the adverse financial consequences may be very heavy.

33. Financial leverage: Financial leverage is associated with financing activities of a firm. It represents the relationship between the firm's earnings before interest and taxes (EBIT) (or operating profit) and earnings available to ordinary shareholders. Financial leverage is sometimes, known as trading on equity.

Definition: Financial leverage may be defined as the payment of fixed rate of interest for the use of fixed interest-bearing securities, to magnify the rate of return as equity shares. Financial leverages arise from the existence of fixed interest expenses. When a firm has fixed interest expenses, one per cent change in EBIT leads to more than one per cent change in PBT or PAT or EPS.

Financial leverage

$$= \frac{\text{Earnings before interest and taxes (EBIT)}}{\text{Earnings before tax (EBT)}}$$

$$= \frac{\text{Operating profit}}{\text{Taxable income}}$$

Degree of financial leverage (DFL)

$$= \frac{\text{Percentage change in EPS}}{\text{Percentage change in EBIT}}.$$

34. Cost of equity capital: Cost of equity is the projected rate of return by the equity shareholders. Cost of equity share capital can be defined as the minimum rate of return which a firm must earn on the equity part of total investment in a project to facilitate no change in the market price of such shares. In order to determine the cost of equity capital, it may be divided into two categories:

- External equity or latest issue of equity shares.
- Retained earnings.

It can be calculated as per the following approaches:

1. Dividend yield/dividend price approach: According to this approach, the cost of equity will be that rate of expected dividends which will sustain the present market price of equity shares. It is computed with the following formula:

$$K_e = D/NP \text{ (for new equity shares)}$$

or

$$K_e = D/MP \text{ (for existing shares)}$$

Where K_e is the cost of equity, D is the expected dividend per share. NP is net proceeds per share and MP is market price per share.

2. **Dividend yield plus growth in dividend methods:** According to this method, the cost of equity is computed on the basis of the expected dividend rate plus the rate of growth in dividend. This technique is used when dividends are projected to grow up at a constant rate. Cost of equity is calculated as:

$$K_e = D_1/NP + g \text{ (for new quity issue)}$$

where D_1 is expected dividend per share at the end of the year. $[D_1 = D_0 (1 + g)]$, NP is net proceeds per share and g is the growth in dividend for existing share calculated as:

$$D_1/MP + g$$

where MP is the market price per share.

3. **Earnings yield method:** According to this approach, the cost of equity is the discount rate that capitalizes a flow of future earnings to calculate the shareholdings. It is called by taking earnings per share (EPS) into consideration. It is calculated as:

1. K_e = Earnings per share/Net proceeds = EPS/NP (for new share)
2. K_e = EPS/MP (for existing equity).

35. Internal Rate of Return (IRR): The discount rate on an investment that equates the present value of the investment's cash outflows with the present value of the investment's cash inflows. For instance, if you spend $50,000 on a given investment, the IRR per cent would be the annualized rate of return of the profit. It's not just the annual rate of return per year multiplied by the number of years. If you loan $50,000 and get no interest the first year, but you get $20,000 in interest or return in the second year, you actually got about $10,000 each year, so the IRR is approximately 20 per cent.

36. Management acts as a creative and invigorating force in the organization. It creates a result that is bigger whole than the sum total of efforts put in by the group. Management adds a real plus value to the operation of any industrial unit by enlisting a little extra value of each person. It provides new ideas, imaginations and visions to the group working and integrates its efforts in such a manner as to account for better results. Productive resources fall into two categories: material and human. Productivity of material resources becomes stagnant after the attainment of their rated capacity. But human resources are capable of tremendous growth and development, and they can yield an output that may be far greater than what the value of their input warrants. And this work of improving human capabilities is done by management. Urwick and Brech have rightly observed, "No ideology, no 'ism', no political theory can win a greater output with less effort from a given complex of human and material resources, only sound management."

37. Experts views on pluralist theory:

1. According to Alan Fox, the pluralistic ideology accepts that an enterprise contains people with different interests, aims and aspirations. It is, therefore, a coalition of different interests rather than the embodiment of one common goal.
2. Sir David Ross has viewed an organization as a plural. Society contains many related but separate interests and objectives which must be maintained in some kind of equilibrium.

3. N.L. Kerr is one of the important exponents of pluralism. He states that social environment is an important factor in industrial conflicts. The isolated groups of workers are more strike-prone as compared to integrated groups. When industrial jobs become more satisfying and when employees get integrated with the wider society, strikes become less frequent.
4. According to H.A. Clegg, pluralism does not imply the inevitability of a compromise in all situations. He accepts that the aim of pluralism is to combine social stability with adaptability and freedom. He states that on most of the occasions, conflicts are resolved by compromises. He further states that associations of governments would prefer to make a further concession rather than take the chance of destroying the social order.
5. **The Donovan Commission (Royal Commission on Trade Unions and Employer's Association 1965-68)** has expressed thus:

   The running of large business is in the hands of professional managers. While in the long term, shareholders, employees and customers all stand to benefit if a concern flourishes, the immediate interests of these groups often conflict. Directors and managers have to balance these conflicting interests and in practice, they generally seek to strike whatever balance will best promote the welfare of the enterprises as such. This is one of the good examples on pluralist approach on industrial relations.

38. To measure job attitudes, the Job Description Index (JDI) technique has been developed. The scale provides the worker with a set of adjectives as possible descriptions of five dimensions of the job, including working conditions, pay, promotion, supervision and co-workers. The worker is required to give 'yes', 'no' or 'don't know' responses, for each adjective. The scale provides a satisfaction score for the five job areas as well as an overall score. This assists the researcher in using the technique as a diagnostic tool. It is possible to ascertain areas in which workers are more satisfied and those in which they are less satisfied. It is, thus, easy to administer.

40. Methods of Performance Appraisal: There are various methods of performance appraisal depending on the size and nature of the organization. Broadly speaking, the methods of performance appraisal may be divided into two–Traditional Methods and Modern Methods.

Methods of Performance Appraisal

Traditional Methods	Modern Methods
• Ranking	• Management by Objectives or Results
• Paired Comparison	• Behaviourally Anchored Rating Scales
• Grading	• Human Resource Accounting
• Forced Distribution	• Assessment Centres
• Forced Choice	• 360-degree
• Checklist	• Balanced Scorecard
• Critical Incidents	
• Graphic Scale	
• Essay	
• Field Review	
• Group	
• Confidential Reports	

Traditional Methods

1. **Ranking Method:** Under this method an employee is ranked against others on the basis of certain traits and characteristics from best to worst. This method is very simple and inexpensive. But its reliability and validity may be open to doubt.
2. **Paired Comparison Method:** Under this method, each employee is compared with

other employees taking only one at a time, usually on one trait. Where the number of employees are less, the number of comparisons required can be deducted by the formulae N(N –1)/2.

3. **Grading Method:** Under this method, different grades of performance are determined in advance such as excellent, very good, good, satisfactory and poor. Employees are placed in any of these grades according to their performance.
4. **Forced Distribution Method:** Under this method, the employees are appraised according to the pattern of a normal curve (bell shaped) in order to check tendency of appraisers to rate most of the employees around high points. This method forces the appraisers to spread their employee evaluations in a prescribed distribution. The distribution in general is as under:

   20% of employees = excellent performers

   60% of employees = average performers

   20% of employees = poor performers

   This method is based on questionable assumption that all groups of employees will have the same distribution of excellent, average and poor performance.
5. **Forced Choice Method:** Under this method, a series of group of statements are given and the appraiser checks how well the statement describes each individual employee being evaluated. Such statements may be both positive and negative. This method does not reveal as to which statement will be considered for final rating and therefore checks rater subjectivity. This method poses lot of problem in framing statements.
6. **Checklist Method:** Under this method, a list of statements or words are given and the appraiser is asked to check statements representing the characteristics and performance of each employee. The statements may carry yes/no alternative or + and – sign representing possession or non-possession of required characteristics and performance.

   This method poses a lot of difficulty in assembling, analyzing and weighing a number of statements about employee characteristics and contributions.
7. **Critical Incidents Method:** Under this method, the appraiser continuously records the critical incidents of the employee performance or behaviour relating to all characteristics both positive and negative in a specially designed notebook. A group of experts then assigns values to them depending on the degree of desirability for the job. This method requires rater to continuously record critical incidents which the rate may resent.
8. **Graphic Scale Method:** Under this method, employee characteristics and performance are evaluated through a graph. Following characteristics are included such as: quantity of work, quality of work, attentiveness, initiative, leadership, health and hygiene, safety habits, planning and organizing skills, analytical skills, innovation and creativity, etc. The rate estimates the degree to which each quality is possessed by the employee on a pre-defined scale, which normally varies from 3 to 7 points.
9. **Essay Method:** Under this method, rater assesses the employee performance on certain parameters in his own words by giving specific examples of employee behaviour.

   This time and effort involved in writing separate essays for all the employees can be a formidable and daunting task.

42. **Capital Adequacy Norms:** Bank's capital is vital as it is the lifeblood that keeps the bank alive; it also gives the bank the ability to absorb shocks and thereby, avoid the likelihood of bankruptcy. Capital adequacy

ratio is a measure of the amount of a bank's capital expressed as a percentage of its risk-weighted credit exposures.

The concept of capital adequacy ratio relates to risk weight assigned to an asset raised by the banks in the process of conducting business and to the proportion of capital to be maintained on such aggregate risk-weighted assets. Capital adequacy ratio is calculated on the basis of risk weightages on assets in the books of banks. Each business transaction carries a specific risk and a portion of capital has to be earmarked for this risk. This portion acts as a 'secret reserve' to cushion any possible future loss. Higher capital adequacy will drive banks towards greater efficiency and this could force banks to bring down operating costs. Capital adequacy enables banks to expand their balance sheet and strengthen their fundamentals, which, in turn, help the banks to mobilise capital at reasonable cost. Hence, quality and risk weightage of assets are the new important parameters which are crucial for the growth of banks.

46. The Extended Fund Facility (EFF) was established in 1974 to allow developing countries to borrow beyond their quotas over longer periods than are allowed under ordinary drawing rights. The EFF arrangement gives members assistance for up to 3 years, with repayment provisions extending over a range of 4–10 years. Drawings under the EFF may be more than 100 per cent of a country's quota over a 3-year period, but the conditions are stringent. The country must provide a detailed statement of policies and measures every 12 months. The resources are provided in instalments, with performance criteria attached. Nonetheless the facility represented an important and significant shift in emphasis from viewing the balance of payments as a stabilization problem, to recognizing the balance of payments as a fundamental long-term constraint on growth that cannot be rectified in a short period of time, if ever.

48. One of the most important theories in international business is comparative advantage model. The theory foundation goes up to Adam Smith, a Scottish economist. In his book, *Wealth of Nations*, he argued that trade is not a zero-sum game. He illustrated how both parties can benefit from trading. His argument is labelled as the *absolute advantage theory*. The logic of absolute advantage is simple and intuitive. If country X can produce a set of goods with lower costs or higher productivity than country Y, and meanwhile, country Y can produce another set of goods with lower costs or higher productivity than country X, the trade of these goods benefit both country X and country Y. But what if a country has all or none absolute advantages in all sets of goods?

Thus, Adam Smith's absolute advantage theory was superseded by the comparative advantage theory in the 1800s.

49. International Financial Reporting Standards (IFRS) are a set of accounting standards developed by the International Accounting Standards Board (IASB) that is becoming the global standard for the preparation of public company financial statements.

PAPER-III

Note: *This paper contains* ***seventy five (75)*** *objective type questions of* ***two (2)*** *marks each. All questions are compulsory.*

1. **Assertion (A) :** Buyers, for several industries, are potential competitors—they may integrate backwards.

   Reasoning (R) : They have different degrees of bargaining power.

   Code:

   A. (A) and (R) are correct and (R) is the correct reasoning of (A).
   B. (A) and (R) are correct, but (R) is not the correct reasoning of (A).
   C. (A) is incorrect, while (R) is a correct statement.
   D. Both (A) and (R) are incorrect.

2. Which one of the following is the governing factor in deciding the type of redressal agency which will deal with the dispute of a consumer?
   A. Area of sale of goods and services
   B. Type of goods and services sold
   C. The choice of the consumer
   D. The value of goods and services sold

3. Match List-I with List-II relating to the roles played by government in an economy and indicate the correct code of their matching.

List-I (Roles)	***List-II (Examples)***
(*a*) Regulatory role	(*i*) Deciding timing and usage of resources
(*b*) Promotional role	(*ii*) Capital intensive projects of public sector
(*c*) Entrepreneurial role	(*iii*) Imposing of high import duty
(*d*) Planning role	(*iv*) Measures to control and cover risk in priority sectors

Code:

	(*a*)	(*b*)	(*c*)	(*d*)
A.	(*iv*)	(*ii*)	(*i*)	(*iii*)
B.	(*iii*)	(*i*)	(*iv*)	(*ii*)
C.	(*iii*)	(*iv*)	(*ii*)	(*i*)
D.	(*i*)	(*iii*)	(*iv*)	(*ii*)

4. Which one of the following statements is not correct relating to Competition Policy and Law?
   A. Collusion and dominance have potential for unfair competition.
   B. The appeal against decisions of Competition Commission of India can be made to the Competition Appellate Tribunal.
   C. State monopolies, government's business policies and functioning of Regulatory Authorities cannot be scrutinized under this law.
   D. Abuse of dominance rather than dominance should be the key to Competition Policy/Law.

5. Which one of the following is not correct with reference to standard costing?
   A. Standard costing is a system where pre determined costs are used for control of entire organisation
   B. Standard may be expressed in quantitative and monetary measures
   C. Only adverse variances are investigated intensively
   D. Standard is determined for each element of cost

6. Which one of the following is not correct?
   A. Margin of Safety $= \dfrac{\text{Profit}}{\text{P/V ratio}}$
   B. P/V Ratio $= \dfrac{\text{Change in Contribution}}{\text{Change in sales}} \times 100$
   C. Break-even point in units $= \dfrac{\text{Fixed cost}}{\text{Contribution per unit}}$
   D. Required sales to earn desired profits $= \dfrac{\text{Desired profit}}{\text{P/V ratio}}$

7. Schedule III Part II of the Companies Act, 2013 deals with which one of the following?

A. Format of Balance Sheet
B. Format of Profit and Loss Account
C. Format of Trading Account
D. Format of Cash Flow

8. Which one of the following statements is not true?

A. When there is one liquidation and one formation it is known as external construction
B. Goodwill or Capital reserve arises only when the amalgamation is in the nature of merger
C. Under the pooling of interest method, the transferee company incorporates the assets and liabilities of the transferor company at book value
D. The vendor company transfers preliminary expenses (at the time of absorption) to equity shareholders' account

9. **Statement-I** : The least-cost or optimal input combination of labour and capital requires that the marginal revenue productivity ratio of the two inputs should be equal to their price ratio.

Statement-II : In a hypothetical production function of the following form $Q = -L^3 + 15\ L^2 + 10\ L$

Where, Q = Quantity of the product and L = No. of variable input (labour), the marginal physical productivity of labour is $-L^2 + 15\ L + 10$.

Code:

A. Both the statements are true.
B. Both the statements are false.
C. Statement-I is true, while statement-II is false.
D. Statement-I is false, while statement-II is true.

10. Match the items of List-I with the items of List-II and indicate the code of correct matching.

List-I	***List-II***
(*a*) Technological advantages	(*i*) Managerial economies
(*b*) Large scale purchase of material inputs	(*ii*) Economies in transport and storage
(*c*) Specialized departments under Specialized personnel	(*iii*) Economies in marketing
(*d*) Oil companies having their own fleet of tankers	(*iv*) Economies in production

Code:

	(*a*)	(*b*)	(*c*)	(*d*)
A.	(*iv*)	(*iii*)	(*i*)	(*ii*)
B.	(*iii*)	(*iv*)	(*ii*)	(*i*)
C.	(*iii*)	(*i*)	(*ii*)	(*iv*)
D.	(*iv*)	(*ii*)	(*iii*)	(*i*)

11. Manufacturing of T.V. sets and refrigerators and their pricing in India belong to which one of the following market structures?

A. Monopolistic competition
B. Perfect competition
C. Monopoly
D. Oligopoly

12. **Statement-I** : Pricing at par with the market price of the existing brands is considered to be the most reasonable pricing strategy for a product which is being sold in a strongly competitive market.

Statement-II : Pricing below the market price has been found to be more successful when a seller intends to achieve a prestigious position among the sellers in the locality for selling prestigious goods of much superior quality.

Code:

A. Both the statements are correct
B. Both the statements are incorrect
C. Statement-I is correct, while Statement-II is incorrect
D. Statement-I is incorrect, while Statement-II is correct

A307

13. Which of the following statements are true? Select the correct code.

(*a*) The coefficient of rank correlation has the same limits as the Karl Pearson's coefficient of correlation.

(*b*) The coefficient of correlation is independent of the change of origin but not of scale.

(*c*) The covariance between X and Y is defined as $\frac{\Sigma xy}{n}$ where $x = (X - \bar{X})$, $y = (Y - \bar{Y})$ and n = no. of paired observations.

(*d*) *bxy* is called regression coefficient of X variable on Y variable.

(*e*) If *bxy* is 0.4 and *byx* is 1.6, coefficient of determination would be 0.8.

Code:

A. (*a*), (*b*) and (*c*)
B. (*a*), (*c*) and (*d*)
C. (*c*), (*d*) and (*e*)
D. (*b*), (*c*) and (*e*)

14. The application of x^2-test as parametric test will be in which one of the following situations?

A. Test of independence of attributes
B. Test of goodness of fit of a specific type of distribution
C. Test for population variance on the basis of small sized sample variance
D. Test of homogeneity of several populations with respect to some characteristic of interest

15. In which one of the following situations is the application of t-test most appropriate?

A. Testing the significance of coefficient of correlation between paired observations of small sized sample
B. Testing the significance of coefficient of correlation between paired observations of large sized sample
C. Comparing variances of two small sized samples
D. Testing the significance of the difference among mean values of more than two samples groups

16. Which of the following is not a logical data structure?

A. Chain B. Stack
C. List D. Tree

17. Match the items of List-I with those of List-II; and choose the correct code of combination:

List-I	***List-II***
(*a*) A committee consists of a group of people specifically designated to perform some administrative work	(*i*) C.I. Barnard
(*b*) Staff service in organisation means the service or advice or counsel, as distinguished from the function of authority or command	(*ii*) W.H. Newman
(*c*) Organisation is informal when the aggregate interpersonal relationships are without conscious joint purpose	(*iii*) McFarland
(*d*) An identifiable group of people contributing their efforts towards the attainment of goals is called organisation	(*iv*) James D. Mooney

Code:

	(*a*)	(*b*)	(*c*)	(*d*)
A.	(*ii*)	(*iv*)	(*i*)	(*iii*)
B.	(*iv*)	(*ii*)	(*iii*)	(*i*)
C.	(*iv*)	(*iii*)	(*i*)	(*ii*)
D.	(*i*)	(*ii*)	(*iv*)	(*iii*)

18. Which among the following is not a physical barrier of communication?

A. Poor vocabulary
B. Noise
C. Improper time
D. Overload information

19. Statement-I : Management control seeks to compel events to conform to plans.

Statement-II : Controlling is determining what is motivational to the employees of the organization.

Code:

A. Statement-I is correct, but II is incorrect
B. Statement-II is correct, but I is incorrect
C. Both the statements I and II are correct
D. Both the statements I and II are incorrect

20. Assertion (A) : Sound planning is one of the essential elements for the success of corporate entities.

Reasoning (R) : Planning is deciding in advance what is to be done. It involves the selection of objectives, policies, procedures and programmes from among alternatives.

Code:

A. Both (A) and (R) are correct and (R) is the right explanation of (A).
B. Both (A) and (R) are correct, but (R) is not the right explanation of (A).
C. Both the statements (A) and (R) are incorrect.
D. (A) is correct, but (R) is incorrect.

21. Match the items of List-I with List-II and denote the code of correct matching:

List-I	*List-II*
(*a*) Acceptability	(*i*) Convenience Aspect
(*b*) Affordability	(*ii*) Functional and Psychological Aspects
(*c*) Accessibility	(*iii*) Information and knowledge Aspects
(*d*) Awareness	(*iv*) Economic and Psychological Aspects

Code:

	(*a*)	(*b*)	(*c*)	(*d*)
A.	(*i*)	(*iii*)	(*ii*)	(*iv*)
B.	(*iii*)	(*ii*)	(*i*)	(*iv*)
C.	(*ii*)	(*iv*)	(*i*)	(*iii*)
D.	(*iv*)	(*ii*)	(*i*)	(*iii*)

22. Match the items of List-I with the items of List-II which are related to dimensions of brand personality. Denote the code of correct matching.

List-I	*List-II*
(*a*) Sincerity	(*i*) Upper class, Charming
(*b*) Excitement	(*ii*) Reliable, Intelligent, Successful
(*c*) Competence	(*iii*) Down to earth, Cheerful, Wholesome
(*d*) Sophistication	(*iv*) Outdoors, Tough
(*e*) Ruggedness	(*v*) Spirited, Imaginative, Up-to-date

Code:

	(*a*)	(*b*)	(*c*)	(*d*)	(*e*)
A.	(*v*)	(*ii*)	(*i*)	(*iii*)	(*iv*)
B.	(*i*)	(*iv*)	(*iii*)	(*ii*)	(*v*)
C.	(*iii*)	(*v*)	(*ii*)	(*i*)	(*iv*)
D.	(*ii*)	(*i*)	(*iii*)	(*v*)	(*iv*)

23. One of the techniques of stimulating creativity for developing new product where you start with an idea then thinking of the next idea and link, then think of the next association and do this with all associations that come up with each new idea, is known as:

A. Attribute Listing
B. Forced Relationship
C. New Contexts
D. Mind Mapping

24. Statement-I : We are motivated to re-evaluate our beliefs, attitudes, opinions or values occurred at two different time.

Statement-II : The difference due to some intervention occurred at either point of time motivates us to search a newer option and thus satisfies our mind/anxiety.

Code:

A. Statement-I is correct, Statement-II is not correct.
B. Statement-II is correct, Statement-I is not correct.
C. Both statements are correct.
D. Both statements are incorrect.

25. Operating Leverage and Financial Leverage of a firm are 3 and 2, respectively. If sales increase by 6%, then earnings before tax will rise by:

A. 18% B. 12%
C. 36% D. 30%

26. Match the items of List-I with those of List-II and indicate the correct code:

List-I	*List-II*
(*a*) Net Income Approach	(*i*) Working Capital Management
(*b*) Profitability Index	(*ii*) Over-capitalisation
(*c*) Concentration Banking	(*iii*) Capital Structure Planning
(*d*) Lower Rate of Return	(*iv*) Capital Budgeting Decision

Code:

	(*a*)	(*b*)	(*c*)	(*d*)
A.	(*iii*)	(*iv*)	(*i*)	(*ii*)
B.	(*iii*)	(*iv*)	(*ii*)	(*i*)
C.	(*iv*)	(*ii*)	(*iii*)	(*i*)
D.	(*ii*)	(*iii*)	(*i*)	(*iv*)

27. Statement-I : In payback period method, the risk of the project is adjusted by lessening the target pay-back period.

Statement-II : Sensitivity Analysis helps in calculation of net present value of the proposal.

Code:

A. Statement-I is correct, but statement-II is wrong
B. Statement-I is wrong, but statement-II is correct
C. Statement-I and statement-II, both are correct
D. Statement-I and statement-II, both are wrong

28. Dividend irrelevance argument of MM Model is based on:

A. Hedging
B. Issue of Debentures
C. Liquidity
D. Arbitrage

29. Match the items of List-I with List-II and indicate the correct code of their matching relating to human resource management philosophy:

List-I	*List-II*
(*a*) Rational System Approach	(*i*) F.W. Taylor
(*b*) The Ahmedabad Experiments to improve productivity	(*ii*) Max Weber's theory of bureaucracy
(*c*) Social System Approach	(*iii*) A.K. Rice
(*d*) Functional organisation concept	(*iv*) Hawthorne studies

Code:

	(*a*)	(*b*)	(*c*)	(*d*)
A.	(*ii*)	(*iv*)	(*iii*)	(*i*)
B.	(*iii*)	(*ii*)	(*iv*)	(*i*)
C.	(*iv*)	(*iii*)	(*i*)	(*ii*)
D.	(*iii*)	(*i*)	(*ii*)	(*iv*)

30. Which one of the following is not a method of deciding acceptable level of reliability or consistency of measurement in selection methods?

A. Regiocentric approach
B. Split half method
C. Test related method
D. Expectancy diagrams

31. Put the following steps of discrete selection process in correct sequence and select the correct code:

(*a*) Preliminary interview
(*b*) Completion of application blank
(*c*) Background investigation
(*d*) Physical examination
(*e*) Employment tests
(*f*) Comprehensive interview
(*g*) Final employment decision

Code:

A. (*b*), (*a*), (*c*), (*d*), (*e*), (*f*), (*g*)
B. (*b*), (*a*), (*e*), (*f*), (*c*), (*d*), (*g*)
C. (*a*), (*b*), (*e*), (*f*), (*c*), (*d*), (*g*)
D. (*a*), (*b*), (*d*), (*c*), (*e*), (*f*), (*g*)

32. Match List-I with List-II relating to wage theories and its propounders and indicate the code representing correct matching:

List-I (Theory)	*List-II (Propounder)*
(*a*) Subsistence Theory	(*i*) Karl Marx
(*b*) Surplus Value Theory	(*ii*) Francis Walker

(*c*) Wage Fund Theory (*iii*) David Ricardo
(*d*) Residual Claimant Theory (*iv*) Adam Smith

Code:

	(*a*)	(*b*)	(*c*)	(*d*)
A.	(*ii*)	(*iv*)	(*i*)	(*iii*)
B.	(*iv*)	(*i*)	(*ii*)	(*iii*)
C.	(*iii*)	(*i*)	(*iv*)	(*ii*)
D.	(*iv*)	(*ii*)	(*iii*)	(*i*)

33. When was paper currency first started in India?
A. 1542 B. 1611
C. 1705 D. 1801

34. 'RWA' with regard to capital adequacy stands for which one of the following?
A. Risk Withdrawal Adjustments
B. Risk Withdrawal Arrangements
C. Risk Weighted Assets
D. Risk-free Weighted Assets

35. Match the items of List-I with List-II and denote the code of correct matching:

List-I	***List-II***
(*a*) Future	(*i*) Consists of purchase or sale of commodities in two different markets with the expectations that a future change in price in one market will be off set by an opposite change in the other market
(*b*) Swap	(*ii*) A contract in which a seller agrees to deliver an asset to a buyer at a predetermined price at some future date as privately negotiated
(*c*) Hedging	(*iii*) A contractual agreement for exchanging a steam of payments with opposite and matching needs, to reap the benefit arising due to market discrepancies
(*d*) Forward	(*iv*) A contract covering the purchase and sale of physical commodities or financial instruments for future delivery on a future exchange floor

Code:

	(*a*)	(*b*)	(*c*)	(*d*)
A.	(*iv*)	(*iii*)	(*ii*)	(*i*)
B.	(*i*)	(*ii*)	(*iii*)	(*iv*)
C.	(*ii*)	(*i*)	(*iii*)	(*iv*)
D.	(*iv*)	(*iii*)	(*i*)	(*ii*)

36. Which of the following are the forms of e-banking? Select the correct code.
(*a*) Internet Banking
(*b*) Telephone Banking
(*c*) Electronic Cheque Conversion
(*d*) Electronic Bill Payment
(*e*) Direct Fund Transfer Through RTGS

Code:
A. (*a*), (*c*) and (*d*)
B. (*a*), (*b*), (*c*) and (*d*)
C. (*b*), (*c*) and (*d*)
D. (*a*), (*b*), (*c*), (*d*) and (*e*)

37. Which one among the following has the largest share of exports from India?
A. Agriculture and Allied Commodity
B. Gems and Jewellery
C. Handicrafts
D. Electronic Goods

38. Which one among the following is not a part of TRIPS agreement?
A. Industrial Design
B. Geographical Indications
C. Interior Design
D. Layout Designs of Integrated Circuits

39. Which one among the following is not correct?
A. IMF's headquarters is in Washington, D.C.
B. IMF has 198 countries as its members.
C. IMF is an outcome of the Bretton Woods Conference.
D. IMF was found on July 7, 1944.

40. Statement-I : Served From India Scheme (SFIS) has been replaced with Service Exports from India Scheme (SEIS).

Statement-II : The rate of reward under SEIS would be based on net foreign exchange earned.

Code:

A. Statement-I is correct, but statement-II is incorrect.
B. Statement-II is correct, but statement-I is incorrect.
C. Both the statements-I and II are incorrect.
D. Both the statements-I and II are correct.

41. Match the items of List-I with those of List-II and indicate the correct code:

List-I (Accounting standard)	*List-II (Relationship)*
(*a*) AS-6	(*i*) Accounting for Consolidated Financial Statements
(*b*) AS-3	(*ii*) Accounting For Fixed Assets
(*c*) AS-10	(*iii*) Depreciation Accounting
(*d*) AS-21	(*iv*) Accounting For Cash Flow Statement

Code:

	(*a*)	(*b*)	(*c*)	(*d*)
A.	(*ii*)	(*iv*)	(*iii*)	(*i*)
B.	(*iii*)	(*iv*)	(*ii*)	(*i*)
C.	(*iv*)	(*iii*)	(*i*)	(*ii*)
D.	(*i*)	(*ii*)	(*iii*)	(*iv*)

42. Which of the following statements are False? Indicate the correct code.

(*a*) RBI has prescribed guidelines for the operations of credit rating agencies in India.
(*b*) All venture capital funds in India have been promoted by Government.
(*c*) A mutual fund can operate as venture capital fund.
(*d*) Credit rating is an authoritative guarantee regarding the credit position of a person.

Code:

A. (*a*), (*b*), (*c*) and (*d*) B. (*a*), (*b*) and (*d*)
C. (*a*), (*b*) and (*c*) D. (*a*) and (*c*)

43. Which of the following are the examples of systematic risk? Indicate the correct code.

(*a*) Elimination of Government Subsidy
(*b*) Increase in Bank Rate
(*c*) Labour Problem
(*d*) High Levered Fund

Code:

A. (*a*), (*b*) and (*c*)
B. (*a*), (*b*) and (*d*)
C. (*a*) and (*b*)
D. (*a*) and (*d*)

44. Which of the following are the benefits of responsibility accounting?

(*a*) It facilitates the centralisation of decision taking.
(*b*) It provides a system of closer control.
(*c*) It measures the performance of individuals in an objective manner.
(*d*) It develops a sense of cost consciousness among managers and their subordinates.

Code:

A. (*a*), (*b*) and (*c*) B. (*b*), (*c*) and (*d*)
C. (*a*), (*b*) and (*d*) D. (*a*), (*c*) and (*d*)

45. Which of the following statements are True? Indicate the correct code.

(*a*) Tax-shield on depreciation and interest is an important variable both for lessor and lessee.
(*b*) A lessee may evaluate the lease options as against the buying option.
(*c*) Sale and Lease-back, and leveraged lease are types of financial lease.
(*d*) Lease financing is a type of capital budgeting decision from the point of view of the lessee.

Code:

A. (*a*), (*b*) and (*d*) B. (*b*), (*c*) and (*d*)
C. (*a*), (*c*) and (*d*) D. (*a*), (*b*) and (*c*)

46. Which one of the following methods of Inflation Accounting has been proposed by Sandilands Committee of U.K?

A. General Price Level Method
B. Specific Price Level Method
C. Current Cost Accounting Method
D. Generally Accepted Accounting Principles

47. Which of the following are the motives of mergers? Indicate the correct code.

(*a*) To gain the economies of scale.
(*b*) To utilise under-utilised resources.
(*c*) To break the monopoly.
(*d*) To reduce the tax liability.

Code:

A. (*a*), (*c*) and (*d*) B. (*a*), (*b*) and (*d*)
C. (*b*), (*c*) and (*d*) D. (*a*), (*b*) and (*c*)

48. A research technique used particularly in retailing (online and offline), in which consumers are recruited by researchers to act as anonymous buyers in order to evaluate customer satisfaction, service quality and customer's own evaluation of their experiences, is known as:

A. Consumer Jury
B. Projective Technique
C. Mystery Shopping
D. Semiotic Research

49. Match the items of List-I with items of List-II and select the correct code of matching:

List-I		*List-II*
(*a*) Market Leader	(*i*)	Avoid hostile attacks on rivals
(*b*) Market Challenger	(*ii*)	Attack the market leader
(*c*) Market Follower	(*iii*)	Provide high level of specialisation
(*d*) Market Nicher	(*iv*)	Attack the market

Code:

	(*a*)	(*b*)	(*c*)	(*d*)
A.	(*iv*)	(*ii*)	(*i*)	(*iii*)
B.	(*ii*)	(*iv*)	(*iii*)	(*i*)
C.	(*iii*)	(*i*)	(*iv*)	(*ii*)
D.	(*i*)	(*iii*)	(*iv*)	(*ii*)

50. Which of the statements are correct? Select correct code.

Statement (I) : Opinions can be described as the slow responses we might give to opinion poll questions about any issue.

Statement (II) : Attitudes are held with a greater degree of conviction, over longer duration and more likely to influence behaviour.

Statement (III) : Values are held more strongly than attitudes and underpin our attitudinal behaviour.

Code:

A. (I) and (II) B. (II) and (III)
C. (I) and (III) D. (I), (II) and (III)

51. Which of the following is not a major aspect of digital marketing?

A. Jurisdiction B. Ownership
C. Security D. Entertainment

52. Which of the following statements are correct? Select the correct code.

Statement (I) : Horizontal conflict between channel members is caused due to channel members impinge on the market territory of other intermediaries at different level.

Statement (II) : Vertical conflict is caused due to intense price competition, disagreement about promotional activities, attempts to bypass intermediary and distribute direct, differing expectations as to channel or intermediary performance.

Statement (III) : Hybrid channel conflict arises due to grey marketing.

Code:

A. (I) and (III) B. (I) and (II)
C. (II) and (III) D. (I), (II) and (III)

53. Which of the following statements are incorrect? Indicate the correct code.

Statement (I) : As consumer's income increases, the percentage of income spent for food items decreases, for rent, fuel and light remains the same, for clothing remains the same and for sundries increases.

Statement (II) : Societal marketing period was from 1960 onwards.

Statement (III) : Our debt to social anthropology decreases more and more as we use qualitative market research approaches.

Statement (IV) : The economic concepts of perfect competition and matching of supply and demand underlie the marketing concept, particularly in relation to the concepts of the price at which goods are sold and quantity distributed.

Code:

A. (I) and (II) B. (II) and (III)
C. (II) and (IV) D. (I) and (IV)

54. Which of the following statements are correct? Indicate the correct code.

Statement (I) : Virtue ethics is a form of ethical approach associated with Aristotle which stresses the importance of developing virtuous principles, 'right' character and the pursuit of a virtuous life.

Statement (II) : Utilitarianism is an ethical approach where an action is right if, and only if, it conforms to the principle of utility, whereby utility is minimised and pain and unhappiness minimised more than any alternative.

Statement (III) : 'Deontological Ethics' is an ethical approach where rightness or wrongness of an action or decision is not judged to be based exclusively on the consequences of that action or decision.

Code:

A. (I), (II) and (III) B. (I) and (II)
C. (I) and (III) D. (II) and (III)

55. Assertion (A) : The matter of succession planning is often deferred.

Reasoning (R) : The succession charts need utmost confidentiality.

Code:

A. (A) is correct and (R) is right reasoning of it.
B. (A) is correct, but (R) is not the correct reasoning of it.
C. (A) is correct, but (R) is not correct statement.
D. (A) is not correct, while (R) is a correct statement.

56. Bethel Maine of USA was the pioneer of which one of the following Laboratory training methods of employee training?

A. Transactional Analysis
B. Business Games
C. Critical Incident Technique
D. T-group

57. Which of the following statements relating to appraisal methods are not correct? Indicate the correct code.

Statement (I) : The MBO program is built on the assumption that individuals always need not be responsible and self-directed and thus need to be motivated to work towards objectives.

Statement (II) : Forced distribution method was developed by Karl Marx.

Statement (III) : Peer evaluation and self - appraisal need to be done on well-defined parameters in check-list method.

Statement (IV) : Forced choice method consists of seven main factors on three point rating scale.

Code:

A. Statements (I) and (II)
B. Statements (III) and (IV)
C. Statements (I), (II) and (III)
D. Statements (I), (II), (III) and (IV)

58. Match the main concerns of HRD sub-systems given in List-I with List-II and choose the correct code of matching:

List-I (HRD sub-systems)	***List-II (Main concerns)***
(*a*) Individual's career	(*i*) Competence
(*b*) Development of teams	(*ii*) Power

(*c*) Socialisation of organisation	(*iii*) Commitment and integration
(*d*) Management of organization	(*iv*) Values

Code:

	(*a*)	(*b*)	(*c*)	(*d*)
A.	(*ii*)	(*iv*)	(*i*)	(*iii*)
B.	(*iv*)	(*ii*)	(*iii*)	(*i*)
C.	(*iii*)	(*i*)	(*iv*)	(*ii*)
D.	(*ii*)	(*iii*)	(*i*)	(*iv*)

59. Match the items of List-I with List-II and indicate the correct code of matching:

List-I (Wage Theory)	***List-II (Basis of determining wage)***
(*a*) Subsistence theory	(*i*) Capitalists first set aside predetermined surplus income and then decide the wages
(*b*) Surplus value theory of wages	(*ii*) Growth of the population brings down to level of subsistence
(*c*) Wage Fund theory	(*iii*) Balance claimed upon the output of industry
(*d*) Residual Claimant theory	(*iv*) Natural price for labour

Code:

	(*a*)	(*b*)	(*c*)	(*d*)
A.	(*iv*)	(*ii*)	(*i*)	(*iii*)
B.	(*ii*)	(*iv*)	(*i*)	(*iii*)
C.	(*iii*)	(*i*)	(*ii*)	(*iv*)
D.	(*i*)	(*iii*)	(*iv*)	(*ii*)

60. Statement (I) : Selection of wrong criteria during performance appraisal can result in serious dysfunctional consequences.

Statement (II) : Generally the evaluator becomes more critical about performance evaluation technique rather than which criteria need to be evaluated.

Code:

A. Both the statements are correct.
B. Both the statements are incorrect.
C. Statement-I is correct, while statement-II is incorrect.
D. Statement-I is incorrect, while statement-II is correct.

61. Which of the statements are not correct? Indicate the correct code.

Statement (I) : Social assistance is financed by tripartite or bipartite contributions.

Statement (II) : Social insurance ignores the income and means of liable relation.

Statement (III) : Social assistance makes the beneficiary a first charge on the liable relations.

Statement (IV) : Social assistance aims at to provide maximum subsistence to those who can not make it on their own.

Code:

A. (I) and (II)
B. (II) and (III)
C. (I) and (IV)
D. (III) and (IV)

62. According to which one of the following theories, differences in nominal interest rates will be eliminated in the exchange rate?

A. Leontief Paradox Trade Theory
B. Fisher Effect Economic Theory
C. Purchasing Power Parity Theory
D. Combined Equilibrium Theory

63. According to the Purchasing Power Parity Theory, the level of foreign exchange rate is determined by which of the following?

A. Domestic Price level (P) divided by foreign price level (P*)
B. P*–P
C. P–P*
D. P*/P

64. Match the items of List-I with List-II and choose the correct code of combination:

List-I	***List-II***
(*a*) It abolishes all restrictions on trade among the members	(*i*) Common Market

(*b*) It not only eliminates all restrictions on trade among members but also adopts a uniform commercial policy against the non-members — (*ii*) Economic Union

(*c*) It allows free movement of labour and capital within the common market — (*iii*) Free Trade Area

(*d*) It achieves some degree of harmonization of national economic policies, through a common central bank, unified monetary and fiscal policy, etc. — (*iv*) Customs Union

Code:

	(*a*)	(*b*)	(*c*)	(*d*)
A.	(*iv*)	(*ii*)	(*i*)	(*iii*)
B.	(*iv*)	(*iii*)	(*i*)	(*ii*)
C.	(*iii*)	(*iv*)	(*i*)	(*ii*)
D.	(*ii*)	(*i*)	(*iv*)	(*iii*)

65. Assertion (A) : Indian companies have established subsidiaries and joint ventures in a number of countries in different manufacturing industries and service sectors.

Reasoning (R) : By restricting the areas of operations and growth, the government policy seriously constrained the potential of Indian companies to make a foray into the foreign countries.

Code:

A. Both (A) and (R) are correct and (R) is the right explanation of (A).
B. Both (A) and (R) are correct, but (R) is not the right explanation of (A).
C. Both (A) and (R) are incorrect.
D. (A) is correct, but (R) is incorrect.

66. Statement (I) : Automatic variations in the exchange rates, in accordance with the variations in the balance of payments position, tend to automatically restore the balance of payments equilibrium.

Statement (II) : A deficiency in the balance of payments increases the exchange rate.

Code:

A. Statement (I) is correct, but (II) is incorrect.
B. Statement (II) is correct, but (I) is incorrect.
C. Both the statements (I) and (II) are incorrect.
D. Both the statements (I) and (II) are correct.

67. Which among the following is not a correct statement?

A. Designated bank refers to any bank in India, which has been authorised by the RBI to act as banker to FII.
B. Domestic custodian includes any person carrying on the activities of providing custodial services in respect of securities.
C. Sub-account includes those institutions, established or incorporated in India, whether incorporated or not, on whose behalf investments are proposed to be made in India by FIIs.
D. A domestic portfolio manager or domestic asset management company shall also be eligible to be registered as FII to manage the funds of sub-accounts.

68. Identify the incorrect statement from the following:

A. Broken-date contract is a full-month forward contract.
B. Currency arbitrage refers to making profit by buying a currency cheap in one market and selling it dear in the other market at a particular point of time.
C. Currency Futures Market refers to organised foreign exchange market where a fixed amount of a currency is exchanged on a fixed maturity date in the pit.
D. Currency Options Market refers to market for the exchange of currency where the option buyer enjoys the privilege of not exercising the option if the rate is not favourable.

69. Dividends declared by Unit Trust of India or by mutual fund is:

A. Fully exempt in the hands of unit holders
B. Fully taxable in the hands of unit holders
C. Fully exempt in the hands of individual unit holders and fully taxable in the hands of institutional unit holders
D. Included in the gross total income but a deduction is allowed under section 80 L

70. Match the items of List-I with the items of List-II and choose the correct answer from the code given below:

List-I (Types of Income)	***List-II (Heads of Income)***
(*a*) Salary, bonus, commission, etc., received by a working partner from the firm	(*i*) Income from other Sources
(*b*) Pension received by the widow of a government employee	(*ii*) Income from (short term) Capital Gains
(*c*) profits on the sale of machinery used in business	(*iii*) Income from Capital Gains
(*d*) Compensation received from the government on compulsory acquisition of land and profit earned	(*iv*) Income from Business and Profession
	(*v*) Income from Salaries

Code:

	(*a*)	(*b*)	(*c*)	(*d*)
A.	(*v*)	(*ii*)	(*i*)	(*iii*)
B.	(*iv*)	(*ii*)	(*iii*)	(*v*)
C.	(*v*)	(*iv*)	(*iii*)	(*ii*)
D.	(*iv*)	(*i*)	(*ii*)	(*iii*)

71. Which of the following will be considered as tax planning effort?

(*a*) Mr. A purchased a house for self residence of ₹ 80 lacs by taking a loan of ₹ 60 lacs from SBI at 10% interest, instead of using his own funds.
(*b*) Mr. A made investment in purchasing 12% redeemable debentures of TISCO worth ₹ 1.50 lac
(*c*) Mr. A purchased 100 gram gold biscuits of ₹ 2.5 lac from SBI on the occasion of Diwali.
(*d*) Mr. A invested ₹ 1 crore in purchasing 5 acres of agricultural land in his native village in Gaya.

Code;

A. (*a*) and (*b*) B. (*b*) and (*c*)
C. (*a*) and (*d*) D. (*c*) and (*d*)

72. Assertion (A) : If the interest is payable outside India, tax must be deducted at source.

Reason (R) : If tax has not been deducted at source, the amount paid as interest will not be allowed as a deduction in computing business income.

Select the correct answer from the code given below:

A. Both (A) and (R) are correct and (R) is the correct explanation of (A).
B. Both (A) and (R) are correct, but (R) is not the correct explanation of (A).
C. (A) is correct, but (R) is wrong.
D. (A) is wrong, but (R) is correct.

73. Under the Income Tax Act, 1961 the education cess of (2% + 1%) is calculated on the amount of:

A. Income Tax
B. Income Tax Plus surcharge (if any)
C. Gross Total Income
D. Taxable Income

74. Exemption, under Sec.54 F of the Income Tax Act, 1961, shall not be allowed if the assessee, on the date of transfer owns:

A. Any residential house
B. A residential house which is let out
C. A house which is self occupied
D. More than one residential house

75. The income from the sale of a machinery used in business is treated as:

A. Income from business and profession
B. Short-term capital gain
C. Long-term capital gain
D. Income from other sources

ANSWERS

1	**2**	**3**	**4**	**5**	**6**	**7**	**8**	**9**	**10**
A	D	C	C	C	D	B	B	C	A
11	**12**	**13**	**14**	**15**	**16**	**17**	**18**	**19**	**20**
A	C	B	C	A	A	A	A	A	A
21	**22**	**23**	**24**	**25**	**26**	**27**	**28**	**29**	**30**
C	C	D	A	C	A	A	D	A	A
31	**32**	**33**	**34**	**35**	**36**	**37**	**38**	**39**	**40**
C	C	*	C	D	D	B	C	B	D
41	**42**	**43**	**44**	**45**	**46**	**47**	**48**	**49**	**50**
B	B	C	B	D	C	B	C	A	B
51	**52**	**53**	**54**	**55**	**56**	**57**	**58**	**59**	**60**
D	C	B	C	B	D	D	C	A	A
61	**62**	**63**	**64**	**65**	**66**	**67**	**68**	**69**	**70**
C	B	A	C	B	A	C	A	A	D
71	**72**	**73**	**74**	**75**					
C	A	B	D	B					

* Discrepancy is found in Question/options.

EXPLANATORY ANSWERS

1. **Structural Analysis of Industries:** Michael E. Porter, the renowned author of *Competitive Strategy, Competitive Advantage and Competitive Advantage of Nations,* has provided a structural analysis of industries. According to this analysis, which has gained great popularity, the state of competition in an industry depends on five basic competitive forces, viz.,

   Rivalry among existing firms

   Threat of new entrants

   Threat of substitutes

   Bargaining power of suppliers

   Bargaining power of buyers.

   Bargaining Power of Buyers: For several industries, buyers are potential competitors–they may integrate backward. Besides, they have different degrees of bargaining power. "Buyers compete with the industry by forcing down prices, bargaining for higher quality or more services, and playing competitors against each other–all at the expense of industry profitability."

   Important determinants of the buyer power, explained by Porter, are the following:

   1. The volume of purchase relative to the total sale of the seller.
   2. The importance of the product to the buyer in terms of the total cost.
   3. The extent of standardization or differentiation of the product.
   4. Switching costs.
   5. Profitability of the buyer (low profitability tends to pressure costs down).
   6. Potential for backward integration by buyer.
   7. Importance of the industry's product with respect to the quality of the buyer's product or services.
   8. Extent of buyer's information.

Bargaining Power of Suppliers: The important determinants of supplier power are the following:

1. Extent of concentration and domination in the supplier industry.
2. Importance of the product to the buyer.
3. Importance of the buyer to the supplier.
4. Extent of substitutability of the product.
5. Switching costs.
6. Extent of differentiation or standardization of the product.
7. Potential for forward integration by suppliers.

2. The law relating to consumer protection is contained in the Consumer Protection Act, 1986. Its objects are:

(*a*) better protection of interests of consumers,

(*b*) protection of rights of consumers,

(*c*) to provide for consumer protection councils, and

(*d*) to provide quasi-judicial machinery for speedy redressal of consumer disputes.

The Act also defines terms like:

(*a*) consumer who buys goods and services for a price,

(*b*) goods means every kind of moveable property,

(*c*) services,

(*d*) complainant,

(*e*) complaint,

(*f*) restrictive trade practices,

(*g*) unfair trade practices,

(*h*) defect,

(*i*) deficiency,

(*j*) persons, and

(*k*) consumer dispute.

Consumer Disputes Redressal Agencies

There are three such agencies: (*a*) District Forum, (*b*) State Commission, and (*c*) National Commission. District Forum is for one or more district and a consumer can file his claim if the limit of the claim is upto ₹ 20 lakhs. Appeal from the decision of the District Forum is to be filed within 30 days of its order to the State Commission. A State Commission is for one or more states. A consumer can file his claim if the claim is above ₹ 20 lakhs but below one crore. Appeal from the decision of the State Commission can be filed within 30 days of its order to the National Commission. National Commission is one for the whole of India. A consumer can file his claim if it is more than ₹ 1 crore. Appeal from the decisions of the National Commission can be made in the Supreme Court of India.

How a complaint is made and dealt with: A complainant can make a complaint before the appropriate consumer dispute redressal agency in relation to any defect in goods or deficiency in service. The complaint relating to any goods or services is given to the opposite party within 21 days to allow him to give his version in 30 days. If the defect in goods needs analysis or testing by a laboratory, a sample of the goods is sent to the laboratory for a report within 45 days. The report is given to the opposite party. Complaint shall be decided within 3 months if no laboratory test is required and within 5 months if the laboratory test is required.

Findings: The consumer dispute redressal agencies can arrive at any of these findings:

(*a*) to remove defects,

(*b*) to replace goods,

(*c*) to return the price,

(*d*) to pay compensation,

(*e*) to remove deficiencies in services,

(*f*) to discontinue the unfair trade practice or the restrictive trade practice,

(*g*) not to offer hazardous goods for sale,

(*h*) to withdraw hazardous goods,

(*i*) to cease manufacture of hazardous goods,

(*j*) to pay such sum as may be determined by such agency,

(*k*) to issue corrective advertisement, and

(*l*) to provide for adequate costs to parties.

4. Competition law is a subset of competition policy which aims at maintaining competition in the market and it has three main prohibitions such as anti-competitive agreements, abuse of dominance, and anti-competitive mergers. In India, the Monopolies and Restrictive Trade Practices (MRTP) Act, 1969 and the Consumer Protection Act, 1986 dealt with anti-competitive practices till the 1990s. It was focussed more on preventing the concentration of economic wealth rather than market power and mergers were allowed or denied by the government without reference to the Monopolies and Restrictive Trade Practices Commission (MRTPC). The MRTP Act, which came into existence after the amendment of 1991, has no provision for merger review. As it was recognised that the provision existed in the MRTP Act was not sufficient enough to address the anti-competitive issues in the new economic environment, the Government of India appointed a high-level Committee on Competition, Policy and Law.

This resulted in a new Competition Policy Act (2002) aimed to counter anti-competitive practices such as cartelisation, collusive bidding, and bid rigging, to check the abuse of market dominance (2005).

5. What is Standard Cost?

The meaning of the term 'Standard Cost' is predetermined cost scientifically computed for measuring the efficiency of the actual performance of an entity. According to CIMA, London, Standard Cost is *'a predetermined calculation of how much costs should be under specified working conditions'. Therefore, Standard Cost is the predetermined cost which should have been under specified operating conditions. It is the yardstick of measuring the efficiency of the actual cost incurred.* Before incurring the actual cost of production, an enterprise determines the Standard Cost of each function production on the basis of its working conditions. After the production, the concern judges the efficiency of its actual costs of production with the predetermined Standard Cost and takes appropriate remedial measures after identifying the deviation from the Standard Cost, if any. Standard Cost is ideal in nature and related to future.

What is Standard Costing?

According to CIMA, London, Standard Costing is *'the preparation and the use of standard costs, their comparison with actual costs and analysis of variances to their causes and points of incidence'. Therefore, Standard Costing is the method of setting up of standard costs and applying them to measure the deviations from the actual costs and analysing the causes of such deviation with a view to maximize the efficiency of the production functions.* It is a technique of costing which uses standards for costs and revenues for the purpose of control through Variance Analysis. Standard Costing is not a distinct system of accounting, but is only a technique which can be applied to all types of costing like job costing or process costing.

Features of Standard Costing

(*i*) Predetermination of appropriate standards for each element of cost and sales.

(*ii*) Comparison of actual performance with the standards and any deviation of actual performance from the standard is being identified as a variance.

(*iii*) Analysis of variances in order to assess the reasons of variances.

(*iv*) Reporting to the management for taking corrective action for any off-standard variance.

6. Calculation of Sales for Desired Profit: To calculate sales for earning a given amount of desired profit, following formula is adopted by modifying the formula of break even point. You are aware that in case of break even sales, the revenues are just equal to the cost incurred; so we have zero profits and total contribution earned is equal to fixed cost. So when we want to earn desired profit, the latter are added in fixed cost and the resultant gives us the formula to earn desired profits.

Break Even Sales (in units)

$$= \frac{\text{Fixed Cost}}{\text{Contribution per unit}}$$

Therefore,

Sales to earn desired profits

$$= \frac{\text{Fixed Cost + Desired Profit}}{\text{Contribution per unit}}$$

or

Sale to earn desired profit (in amount)

$$= \frac{\text{Fixed Cost + Desired Profit}}{\text{P/V ratio}}$$

7. The Schedule III provides the format for the profit and loss account.

The Schedule III continues with the natural classification of expenses. It has retained the concept of exceptional items and extraordinary items. Exceptional items arise from ordinary business but are non-recurring in nature and material enough to require separate disclosure. Examples are: reversal of provisions, sale of real estate, sale of long-term investments and increase in the provision for post-retirement benefits due to change in actuarial assumptions. Extraordinary items do not arise from ordinary business. An example is compensation received from the government to partly cover damage caused by a natural calamity. The profit and loss account structure generally follows the IFRS requirements.

Ind AS does not recognise the concept of 'extraordinary items'. Therefore, Schedule III (Division II), which provides balance sheet and profit and loss account formats consistent with Ind AS, does not require presentation of extraordinary items in the profit and loss account.

8.
- Amalgamation includes mergers and acquisitions. The Companies Act, 1956 has not explicitly defined the term 'amalgamation', whereas the Income Tax Act, 1961 defines clearly the term 'amalgamation'.
- Accounting Standard 14 (AS-14) issued by ICAI states that there are two types of amalgamations—in the nature of merger and in the nature of purchase.
- Amalgamation in the nature of merger should be accounted for by following *'The Pooling of Interests'* method.
- Amalgamation in the nature of purchase should be accounted for by following *'The Purchase'* method.
- Goodwill or capital reserves may arise only in case of amalgamation in the nature of purchase.
- AS-14 is applicable only in those cases of amalgamation where the transferor or company (or Companies) ceases to exist after such amalgamation.

9. Here, $Q = -L^3 + 15L^2 + 10L$ ...(*i*)

Marginal Productivity of Labour (MP_L) can be obtained by differentiating the production function (1). Thus,

$$MP_L \frac{\partial Q}{\partial L} = -3L^2 + 30L + 10 \quad ...(ii)$$

11. Monopolistic competition refers to a market structure in which a large number of sellers sell differentiated products, which are close substitutes for one another. Incidentally, a close substitute is one whose cross-elasticity is close to unity or greater. Monopolistic competition combines the basic elements of both perfect competition and monopoly.

The *element of monopoly* in monopolistic competition arises from the fact that each firm has an absolute right to produce and sell a *branded* or *patented* product. Other firms are prevented by laws from producing and selling a branded product of other firms. This gives a firm *monopoly power* over production, pricing and sale of its own-banded product. For example, consider toilet soap industry. There are a number of brand names available in the market, *e.g.*, Lux, Liril, Palmolive, Fairglow, Pears, Fa, Rexona.

13. Correlation coefficient is independent of change of scale and origin but regression analysis is independent of change of origin but not of scale.

The coefficient of determination thus equals r^2. If the value of $r = 0.9$, r^2 will be 0.81 and this would mean that 81 per cent of the variation in the dependent variable has been explained by the independent variable. The maximum value of r^2 is unity because it is possible to explain all of the variation in Y, but it is not possible to explain more than all of it. The coefficient of determination (r^2) is defined as the ratio of the explained variance to the total variance.

Coefficient of determination

$$= \frac{\text{Explained Variation}}{\text{Total Variance}}$$

The ratio of explained variance to total variance is frequently called coefficient of non-determination. The coefficient of non-determination is denoted by K^2 and its square root is called the coefficient of alienation, or K. The K and K^2 value may also be used as the measure of the degree or relationship between two variables. For example, the higher the unexplained variance with respect to total variance, the higher will be the value of K^2 and the value of K. However, r^2 and r are more convenient in interpreting the result of Correlation.

14. Parametric versus non-parametric: Hypothesis tests based on normally distributed data are known as parametric tests. The t-test is a parametric test. If the data are not normally distributed or the sample is too small a non-parametric test should be used. In non-parametric tests the observations are ordered from low to high and a rank is assigned for each. Statistical tests are performed on the rank not the data values. Non-parametric tests include the Wilcoxon signed rank test (equivalent to a paired t-test) and the Mann-Whitney U-test (equivalent to an unpaired t-test).

15. For ease of understanding, the various tests of significance have been broadly classified as below:

- **Large samples tests**
  - Test of significance of attributes (Sampling of attributes)
    - Test for number of success or presence of an attribute
    - Test for single proportion or proportion of success
    - Test of significance of difference in proportion
  - Test of significance of variables (sampling of variables)
    - Z-test for population mean (known variance)
    - Z-test of significance for difference of means
    - Z-test for difference of standard deviation.
- **Small sample tests**
  - t-test for population mean
  - t-test for difference of means (two population means)
  - Paired t-test for difference of means.
  - t-test for testing significance of sample correlation coefficient
  - t-test for testing significance of the regression coefficient
  - Fisher's z-transformation for tests of correlation coefficient,

16. Classification of Data Structures

Primitive data structures	*Simple data structures*	*Compound data structures*			*File organizations*
		Linear	*Non-linear*		
Integer Boolean Character	String Array Record	Stack Queue Linked List	Binary Tree Binary Search Tree	Graph Binary-Tree	Sequential Relative Index Sequential Multi-key

18. The typical physical barriers that may come to mind are such things as distracting noises that drown out a vocal message. Other examples of physical barriers to communication are distances between the people communicating, walls, static interference with radio messages, and physical impairments of the individuals (*e.g.*, speech impediments or hearing loss). Physical barriers distort the received message.

Another physical barrier that is often disregarded is communication overload. Communication overload occurs when people "receive more communication inputs than they can process or than they need". Communication overload can result from receiving too much information at one time for it to be processed effectively. It can also result from the generation of too much information over a period of time, or having to handle too many types of information in a short period of time. For example, managers often face communication overload due to the necessity for them to deal with many subordinates, peers, and the memos, letters, reports, telephone conversations, e-mail, and face-to-face interactions that are associated with management.

19. Definition of Managerial Control

1. *S.S. Chatterjee:* "Control, is an executive process involving three elements—standards, evaluation and corrective action."
2. *Mary Cussing Niles:* "Control is an aspect and projection of planning, whereas planning sets the course. Control observes deviation from the course and initiates action to return to the chosen course or to an appropriately changed one."
3. *Billy E. Goetz:* "Managerial planning seeks consistent, integrated and articulated programmes while management control seeks to compel events to conform to plans."
4. *Henry Fayol:* "Control consists in verifying whether everything occurs in conformity with the plan adopted, the instructions issued and principles established. It has for object to point out weaknesses and errors in order to rectify them and prevent recurrence."
5. *E.F.L. Brech:* "Control is checking event performance against predetermined standards contained in the plans, with a view to ensuring adequate progress and satisfactory performance."
6. *Koontz and O'Donnell:* "Control like planning is ideally forwad looking, and the best kind of managerial control corrects deviations from plans before they occur."
7. *Peter F. Drucker:* "Control maintains the equilibrium between ends and means, output and efforts."
8. *Mary Parker Follett:* "Control may be defined as power exercised as means towards specific end; authority, as vested control."
9. *George R. Terry:* "Controlling is determining what is being accomplished, that is, evaluating the performance and, if necessary, applying corrective measures so that the performance takes place according to plans."
10. The controlling function consists of actions and decisions managers undertake to ensure that actual results are consistent with desired results."

21. Following the critics of the classic 4 Ps approach, Sheth and Sisodia suggested that modern market realities require a re-evaluation of the marketing tools inventory to enable a better fit to customer specifics. In emerging market economies, for example, one of the most serious challenges is represented by the high level of market heterogeneity. Thus, Sheth and Sisodia advocated an alternative notion to provide marketing with better opportunities for customer value creation. Thus the 4 As concept appeared, including the dimensions of acceptability, affordability, accessibility and awareness. The acceptability dimension is fulfilled if a firm's offerings meet or exceed customer requirements. Affordability relates to customer willingness to pay the price of the offerings. Accessibility is linked to convenience and availability of offerings at the target marketplace. The awareness dimension measures the level of information in the target market on products and brands. The dimensions include further sub-dimensions; for example, affordability is divided into psychological and economic. The value proposition of a firm in a market is formed by the 4 As dimenstions. This approach is very appropriate for emerging market contexts, as they have higher levels of market dynamics, consumer heterogeneity and first-time users. These strategic differences have a strong impact on the tactical decisions firms make, as well as on the adjustment of marketing and customer-related capabilities and processes.

22. Aaker defines brand personality as 'the set of human characteristics associated with a brand". Brand personality is defined as a multi-dimensional and multi-faceted construct that enables consumers to express themselves along several dimensions. Similar to the 'big five' model of human personality, brand personality is measured along five dimensions, that is, *sincerity, excitement, competence, sophistication* and *ruggedness.*

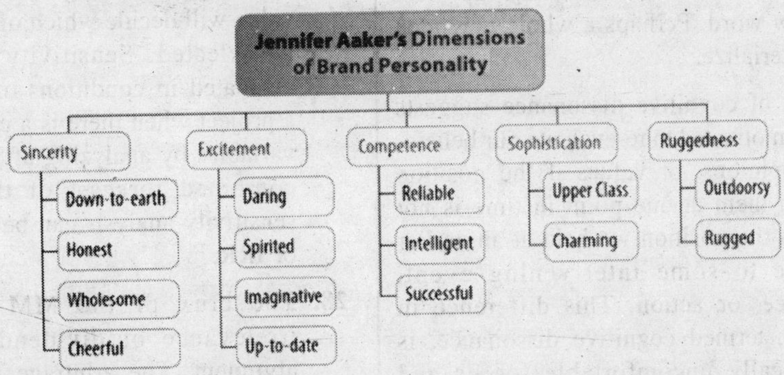

23. Creativity Techniques: The following list is a sampling of techniques for stimulating creativity in individuals and groups:

- **Attribute listing:** List the attributes of an object, such as a screwdriver. Then modify each attribute, such as replacing the wooden handle with plastic, providing torque power, adding different screw heads and so on.
- **Forced relationships:** List several ideas and consider each in relation to each other idea. In designing new office furniture, for example, consider a desk, bookcase, and filing cabinet as separate ideas. Then imagine a desk with a built-in bookcase or a desk with built-in files or a bookcase with built-in files.
- **Morphological analysis:** Start with a problem, such as "getting something from one place to another via a powered vehicle." Now think of dimensions, such as the type of platform (cart, chair, sling, bed), the medium (air, water, oil, rails), and the power source (compressed air, electric motor, magnetic fields). By listing every possible combination, you can generate many new solutions.
- **Reverse assumption analysis:** List all the normal assumptions about an entity and then reverse them. Instead of assuming that a restaurant has menus, charges for food, and serves food, reverse each assumption. The new restaurant may decide to serve only what the chef bought that morning and cooked; may provide some food and charge only for how long the person sits at the table; and may design an exotic atmosphere and rent out the space to people who bring their own food and beverages.

- **New contexts:** Take familiar processes, such as people-helping services, and put them into a new context. Imagine helping dogs and cats instead of people with day care service, stress reduction, psychotherapy, animal funerals, and so on. As another example, instead of sending hotel guests to the front desk to check in, greet them at curbside and use a wireless device to register them.
- **Mind mapping:** Start with a thought, such as a car, write it on a piece of paper, then think of the next thought that comes up (say Mercedes), link it to car, then think of the next association (Germany), and do this with all associations that come up with each new word. Perhaps a whole new idea will materialize.

24. The theory of cognitive dissonance suggests that we are motivated to re-evaluate our beliefs, attitudes, opinions, or values if the position we hold on them at one point in time is not the same as the position we held at an earlier period due to some inter-vening event, circumstance, or action. This difference in evaluations, termed cognitive dissonance, is psychologically uncomfortable for us and causes anxiety. For example, we may feel foolish or regretful about a purchasing decision we have made. So, we are motivated to reduce our anxiety by redefining our beliefs, attitudes, opinions, or values to make them consistent with our circumstances. We will also actively avoid situations that might increase our feeling of dissonance. To reduce dissonance we might.

- selectively forget information;
- minimize the importance of an issue, decision, or act;
- selectively expose ourselves only to new information that agrees with our existing view (rather than information which doesn't); or
- reverse a purchase decision, for instance, by taking a product back or selling it for what it was worth.

25. Operating Leverage = 3. This means that 1% increase in sales would resulting a 3% increase in operating profit and 6% increase in sales would result in 18% increase in operating profit.

Here, Financial leverage is 2, this means that if operating profit goes up by 100%, the earning before tax would go up by 200%.

∴ Here increase in operating profit is 18%. Therefore EBT would rise by 36%.

27. Sensitivity Analysis: This approach helps to take decisions of accepting or rejecting a project through the estimation of net present value. If three situations are given when cash flow estimates are given then the net present value will decide which of the projects should be selected. Sensitivity analysis are also evaluated in conditions of finding out about a project when there is a change in one of the variables by analyzing after tax cash flows of combined forecast of the variables. The sensitivity analysis can be used through NPV or IRR.

28. The crux of the MM position on the irrelevance of dividend is the arbitrage argument. The arbitrage process involves a switching and balancing operation. In other words, arbitrage refers to entering simultaneously into two transactions which exactly balance or completely offset each other. The two transactions here are the acts of paying out dividends and raising external funds–either through the sale of new shares or raising additional loans–to finance investment programmes.

30. Regiocentric approach: This approach advocates the division of operations of the multinational company on the basis of some geographical regions and allows the transfer of employees within a particular region. Many companies have the regional divisions like Europe, America and Asia-Pacific and encourage the transfer of their senior managers within a particular region from one subsidiary to other. Its main advantages are:

(*a*) A major motive for using such an approach is that it allows interaction between executives transferred to regional headquarters from subsidiaries and parent country nationals posted to the regional headquarters.

(*b*) It also reflects some sensitivity to local conditions.

(*c*) Another advantage is that such an approach can prove highly effective for a multinational to move from a purely ethnocentric to geocentric approach.

Some of the disadvantages are:

(*a*) It can produce 'federalism' at a regional rather than a country basis.

(*b*) While this approach does improve career prospects at the national level, it only moves the barrier to the regional level.

34. Risk Weighted Assets: RWA means assets with different risk profiles; it means that we all know that is much larger risk in personal loans in comparison to the housing loan, so with different types of loans the risk percentage on these loans also varies.

38. The 1995 WTO TRIPS Agreement covers eight areas: copyright and related rights, trademarks, geographical indications, industrial designs, patents (and plant variety protection–PVP), layout designs (topographies) of integrated circuits, protection of undisclosed information, and control of anticompetitive practices in contractual licenses.

39. The International Monetary Fund (IMF) is an organization of 189 countries, working to foster global monetary cooperation, secure financial stability, facilitate international trade, promote high employment and sustainable economic growth, and reduce poverty around the world.

40. Service Exports from India Scheme (SEIS)

1. Served From India Scheme (SFIS) has been replaced with Service Exports from India Scheme (SEIS). SEIS shall apply to 'Service Providers located in India' instead of 'Indian Service Providers'. Thus SEIS provides for rewards to all Service providers of notified services, who are providing services from India, regardless of the constitution or profile of the service provider.
2. The rate of reward under SEIS would be based on net foreign exchange earned.

43. Risk in Investment: Risk means the probability of having adverse or low returns as compared to the expected returns. All investment activities are subject to risk; even 'safe investment' like treasury bills, government securities and post office deposits are not free from risk. Risk can broadly be classified into two types:

- Systematic Risk
- Non-systematic Risk

Systematic Risk: It is also termed as non-diversifiable risk because it can not be avoided—it is inherent in almost all the investment avenues. As long as one does the investment, he gets influenced with these risk factors—these are the universal factors and these influence the performance of all the investment avenues. Because some get affected hardly and others softly, it is non-diversifiable. These are as follows:

- Inflation Risk
- Interest Rate Risk
- Political Risk
- Market Risk
- Risk due to government policies
- Natural calamities
- Scams/Malpractices
- Monsoon
- Industrial growth or output
- International events
- War-like situation/Internal Peace

Non-systematic Risk: This kind of risk is created due to industry or company-specific factors—performance of a company, merger or acquisition, industry-specific announcement by the government—which might affect a particular industry. This type of risk can either be reduced or eliminated through diversification. Since it can be minimised or eliminated, it is called diversifiable risk. The following are non-systematic risks:

- Business Risk
- Financial Risk
- Risk due to industry-specific policies
- Disputes.

44. Eric Kohler defines responsibility accounting as "a method of accounting in which costs are identified with persons assumed to be capable of controlling them rather than with products or functions. It differs from activity accounting in that it does not in itself requires an organisational grouping by activities and sub activities or provide a systematic criterion of system design."

Robert Anthony defines responsibility accounting as "the type of management accounting that collects and reports both planned and actual accounting information in terms of responsibility centres."

Advantages of Responsibility Accounting

The ultimate aim of the responsibility accounting is to help and guide the management to achieving organisational goals. The following are some important advantages of responsibility accounting.

(*i*) It provides a system of closer control.

(*ii*) It defines and communicates the corporate objectives and individual goals in an efficient manner.

(*iii*) It helps to improve the quality of decision making.

(*iv*) Each and every employee knows what is expected of him. And at the same time no one can escape from anything that goes wrong.

(*v*) It measures the performance of individual employee in an objective manner.

(*vi*) It fosters a sense of cost-consciousness among managers and their subordinates.

(*vii*) It acts as a suitable tool of cost control.

(*viii*) It is helpful in planning for future costs and revenues.

(*ix*) It guides the management to make an effective delegation of authority and responsibility.

(*x*) If necessary, corrective action can be taken and efficient control over the cost can be obtained.

46. Current Cost Accounting (CCA) Method: This method differs from General Purchasing Power Accounting and has now emerged as an important variant of the replacement cost. This method was first suggested in 1975 by the Sandilands Committee—an independent committee of inquiry into inflation accounting appointed by the Government of U.K. under the Chairmanship F.E.P. Sandilands, the then Chancellor of the Exchequer in the United Kingdom.

So the current cost accounting method gains popularity and this evident in the report of inflation accounting committee in the United Kingdom (Sandilands 1975): "CCA will indicates, more clearly than existing accounting conventions, the effect of inflation on a company's affairs and that it is urgent that it should be introduced as soon as possible. However, it should not be assumed that accounting for inflation is in itself a panacea for the difficulties during a time of inflation.

47. Motives Behind M&As

In general, mergers and acquisitions are performed in the hopes of realising economic gains. Some of the potential advantages of M&As include achieving economics of scale, pooling complimentary resources, obtaining tax benefits and eliminating inefficiencies. Obtaining proprietary rights to products or services, expanding market share, penetrating into new geographic regions and providing managers with newcomer advancement opportunities are other reasons motivating mergers and acquisitions.

Some other motives are:

- To provide improved capacity utilisation.

- To make better use of the existing sales force.
- To reduce managerial staff.
- To gain economies of scale.
- To smooth out seasonal trends in sales.
- To gain access to new suppliers, distributors, customers, products and creditors.
- To gain new technology.
- To reduce tax obligations.

48. Quantitative research methods, *e.g.*, the survey questionnaire, are designed to elicit responses to pre-determined, standardized questions from a large number of respondents. This involves collecting information from many people, quantifying the responses as frequencies or percentages, and descriptive statistics, and statistically analysing them. Other quantitative research methods include mass observation techniques and experiments. Experiments are designed to determine cause and effect relationships, particularly in psychological studies. More recently, structural equation modelling has become a common technique to identify how variables interact and relate to each other. Mystery shopping is a common research technique, used particularly in retailing (on- and offline), where consumers are recruited by researchers to act as anonymous buyers in order to evaluate customer satisfaction, service quality, and the customer's own evaluation of their experiences. In contrast, qualitative research techniques are typically used at the preliminary stages of a research project to identify the basic factors affecting the management problem. The most common forms of qualitative research are discussion groups and in-depth interviews. Projective techniques can also be used in both forms. Qualitative research techniques attempt to uncover the underlying motivations behind consumers' opinions, attitudes, perceptions, and behaviour. Consequently, they adopt unstructured methods to elicit information from respondents. We would use a number of basic issues to guide the research but we would not use a structured set of questions for each respondent, as done with surveys.

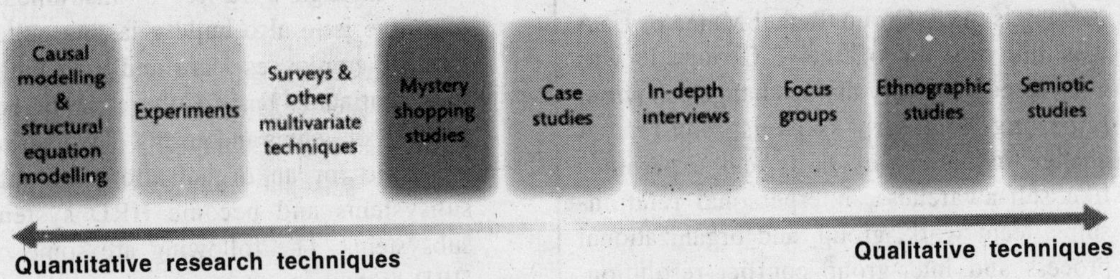

Fig. *A continuum of research techniques.*

49. **Table :** ***Types of market position***

	Characteristics	**Prime Strategies**
Market leader	The market leader has the single largest share of the market. Market leadership is important as it is these offerings and brands that can shape the nature of competition in the market, set out standards relating to price, quality, speed of innovation, and communications, as well as influencing the key distribution channels.	Attack the market: create new uses, users or increase frequency of use. Defend the position; regular innovation, larger ranges, price cutting and discounts, increased promotion.

	Characteristics	Prime Strategies
Market challengers	Products that aspire to the leadership position are referred to as market challengers. These may be positioned as number two, three or even four in the market. They actively seek market share and use aggressive strategies to take share from all of their rivals.	Attack the market leader; use pricing, new product attributes, sharp increase in advertising spend. Attack rivals; special offers and limited editions, offer superior competitive advantages. Maintain status quo.
Market followers	These firms have low market shares and do not have the resources to be serious competitors. They pose no threat to the market leader or challengers and often adopt me-too strategies when the market leader takes an initiative.	Avoid hostile attacks on rivals. Copy the market leader and provide good quality products that are well differentiated. Focus on differentiation and profits, not market share.
Market nichers	Nichers are specialists. They select small segments within target markets that larger companies fail to exploit. They develop specialized marketing mixes designed to meet the needs of their customers.	Provide high level of specialization: geographic, proposition, service, customer group. Provide tight fit between market needs and the organization's resources.

56. T-Groups: One of the methods of sensitivity training is the T-Group. Bethel Maine of USA was the pioneer of the T-Group. It was considered necessary that to change behaviour imparting necessary skills is required. A change in variety of skills and experience like self-awareness, interpersonal relationships, team work, group, and organizational process and inter-group conflict resolution. Sensitivity training has developed to the status of an intervention in organizational development. T-Group training is process oriented and not content oriented where people operate a feeling level of communication, observing, revealing, listening and unravelling messages.

58. A system has its own objectives, components or elements and a process. It has inputs, an output and a throughput. The purpose of any HRD system is broadly to build the competencies and/or commitment of individuals, dyads, teams and the entire organisation as a whole through a variety of instruments. Its objective is to also build a lasting culture so that the employees learn and give their best on a continuous basis. Culture can be defined in terms of values and norms. The instruments available for an organisation are put into subsystems and become HRD systems or subsystems. The following are some of the HRD systems most commonly used.

1. Competency mapping
2. Recruitment and placement
3. Induction and integration.

59. Theory of Wages: How much and on which basis wages should be paid to the workers for services rendered by them has been a subject matter of great concern and debate among economic thinkers for a long time. This has given birth to several wage theories, *i.e.,* how wages are determined. Out of them, some important theories of wages are discussed here.

Wages Fund Theory: This theory was developed by Adam Smith. His theory was based on the basic assumption that workers are paid wages out of a pre-determined fund of wealth. This fund, he called, wages fund created as a result of savings. Accordingly to Adam Smith, the demand for labour and rate of wages depend on the size of the wages fund. According, if the wages fund is large, wages would be high and vice versa.

Subsistence Theory: This theory was propounded by David Recardo. According to this theory, "The labourers are paid to enable them to subsist and perpetuate the race without increase or diminution". This payment is also called as 'subsistence wages'. The basic assumption of this theory is that if workers are paid wages more than subsistence level, workers' number will increase and, as a result, wages will come down to the subsistence level. On the contrary, if workers are paid less than subsistence wages, the number of workers will decrease as a result of starvation death, malnutrition, disease, etc. and many would not marry. Then, wage rates would again go up to subsistence level. Since wage rate tends to be at subsistence level at all cases, that is why this theory is also known as *'Iron Law of Wages'*. The subsistence wages refers to minimum wages.

The Surplus Value Theory of Wages: This theory was developed by Karl Marx. This theory is based on the basic assumption that like other article, labour is also an article which could be purchased on payment of its price *i.e.,* wages. This payment, according to Karl Marx, is at subsistence level which is less than in proportion to time labour takes to produce items. The surplus, according to him goes to the owner. Karl Marx is wߙll known for his advocation in the favour of labour.

Residual Claimant Theory: This theory owes its development to Francis A. Walker. According to Walker, there are four factors of production or business activity, viz., land, labour, capital, and entrepreneurship. He views that once all other three factors are rewarded what remains left is paid as wages to workers. Thus, according to this theory, worker is the residual claimant.

Marginal Productivity Theory: This theory was propounded by Phillips Henry Wicksteed (England) and John Bates Clark of U.S.A. According to this theory, wages is determined based on the production contributed by the last worker, *i.e.,* marginal worker. His/her production is called 'marginal production'.

The Bargaining Theory of Wages: John Davidson was the propounder of this theory. According to this theory, the fixation of wages depends on the bargaining power of workers/ trade unions and of employers. If workers are stronger in bargaining process, then wages tends to be high. In case, employer plays a stronger role, then wages tends to be low.

Behavioural Theories of Wages: Based on research studied and action programmes conducted, some behavioural scientists have also developed theories of wages. Their theories are based on elements like employee's acceptance to a wage level, the prevalent internal wage structure employee's consi-deration on money or wages and salaries as motivators.

62. Important theory used to explain currency exchange rates is the international Fisher effect, named for economist Irving Fisher. The *domestic Fisher effect* says simply that the nominal rate of interest equals the real rate plus the expected inflation rate. When this concept is used in an international setting, however, the international Fisher effect states that changes in the nominal interest rates for two countries will be offset by equal changes, in the opposite direction, in the exchange rate. The difference in nominal interest rates across countries reflects the difference in expected rates of inflation in those countries. According to Irving Fisher, the exchange rate would change by the same amount, but in the opposite direction, as the difference between the nominal interest rates of the two countries. Changes in nominal interest rates are determined by changes in expected inflation, and exchange rates change for the same reason. The rationale is that investors must be compensated, or will offer compensation, to accommodate the expected change in the exchange rate.

63. Purchasing power parity says that the nominal exchange rate should equal the foreign price level divided by the domestic price level, so that,

$$e_{\text{nom}} = \frac{P_{\text{For}}}{P}$$

66. Under a floating exchange rate system, monetary authorities do not assume the responsibility to fix the exchange rate, so the exchange rate will fluctuate with market demand and supply, and central banks cannot alter foreign exchange reserves to deal with a balance of payments deficit or surplus. However, if a country's balance of payments exhibits a deficit, the domestic demand for foreign currency will be greater than the supply of foreign currency, thereby appreciating the value of foreign currency and devaluing domestic currency. Conversely, if a country's balance of payments exhibits a surplus, the demand for foreign currency will be less than supply of foreign currency, thereby appreciating the domestic currency and devaluing foreign currencies. Fluctuations in the exchange rate will automatically change the relative prices of exports and imports, and thus, the deficit in the balance of payments will be automatically eliminated due to exchange rate fluctuations.

68. A broken-date contract is a forward contract for a maturity which is not a whole month or for which a quote is not readily available. For example, if the quotes are available for a 6-month forward and a 9-month forward, but a customer wants a quote for a 7-month forward, it will be a broken-date contract. The rate for a broken-date contract is calculated by interpolating between the available quotes for the preceding and the succeeding maturities.

69. Where an individual is a shareholder of the domestic company, any dividend paid, distributed or declared on or after 1 April, 2003 is exempt in the hands of the shareholder under Sec. 10(34) as the domestic company is liable to dividend tax on such distribution under Sec. 115-O. However, any loan advanced by a closely held company to a shareholder holding 10% equity shares is taxable as deemed dividend to the extent it is covered by the accumulated profits.

From 1 April 2003, the Unit Trust of India and mutual fund, specified under Sec. 10 (23D) are also required to pay dividend tax under Sec. 115-R. Accordingly, dividend from the UTI and mutual fund are exempt from tax in the hands of unit holders under Sec. 10(35).

74. Exemption u/s 54-F shall be allowed if following conditions are fulfilled.

(*i*) The assessee is only an individual or a H.U.F.

(*ii*) The assessee does not own more than one residential house on the date of transfer of the above mentioned assets.

(*iii*) The assessee transfers above mentioned asset or assets (other than a residential building) and there is a long term capital gain.

(*iv*) The assessee invests the net sale consideration of above mentioned assets to construct a residential house within 3 years of the sale of the asset or purchases an already built house within one year before or two years after the sale of the above mentioned asset.

(*v*) The assessee is required not to purchase another residential house within a period of one year after or constructs within a period of 3 year after the date of transfer of the above mentioned asset/assets.

75. Meaning of short-term capital gain and long-term capital gain

Capital gain arising on sale of short-term capital asset is termed as short-term capital gain and capital gain arising on transfer of long-term capital asset is termed as long-term capital gain. However, there are a few exceptions to this rule, like gain on depreciable asset is always taxed as short-term capital gain.

Illustration

In January, 2017 Mr. Raja sold his residential house property which was purchased in May, 2000. Capital gain on such sale amounted to ₹ 8,40,000. In this case the house is sold after holding it for a period of more than 24 months and, hence, capital gain of ₹ 8,40,000 will be charged to tax as Long Term Capital Gain.

Illustration

In April, 2017 Mr. Rahul sold his residential house property which was purchased in May, 2015. Capital gain on such sale amounted to ₹ 8,40,000. In this case the house property is sold after holding for a period of less than 24 months and, hence, gain of ₹ 8,40,000 will be charged to tax as Short Term Capital Gain.

Reason for bifurcation of capital gains into long-term and short-term

The taxability of capital gains depends on the nature of gain, *i.e.,* whether short-term or long-term. Hence, to determine the taxability, capital gains are to be classified into short-term and long-term. In other words, the tax rates for long-term capital gain and short-term capital gain are different.

Tax on short-term capital gain

For the purpose of determination of tax rate, short-term capital gains are classified as follows:

- Short-term capital gains covered under section 111A.
- Short-term capital gains other than covered under section 111A.

Illustration : STCG covered under section 111A

Examples of STCG covered under section 111A:

- STCG arising on sale of equity shares listed in a recognised stock exchange, which is chargeable to STT.
- STCG arising on sale of units of equity oriented mutual fund sold through a recognised stock exchange which is chargeable to STT.
- STCG arising on sale of units of a business trust.
- STCG arising on sale of equity shares, units of equity oriented mutual fund or units of a business trust through are cognised stock exchange located in any International Financial Services Centre and consideration is paid or payable in foreign currency even if transaction of sale is not chargeable to securities transaction tax (STT).

Illustration : STCG other than covered under section 111A

Examples of STCG not covered under section 111A:

- STCG arising on sale of equity shares other than through a recognised stock exchange.
- STCG arising on sale of shares other than equity shares.
- STCG arising on sale of units of non-equity oriented mutual fund (debt oriented mutual funds).
- STCG on debentures, bonds and Government securities.
- STCG on sale of assets other than shares/ units like STCG on sale of immovable property, gold, silver, etc.

Previous Paper (Solved)

UGC-NET-Junior Research Fellowship & Assistant Professor Exam

COMMERCE, January-2017*

PAPER-II

Note: *This paper contains **fifty (50)** objective type questions of **two (2)** marks each. **All** questions are compulsory.*

1. Assertion (A) : Corporate culture is generally considered as either closed and threatening or as open and participatory.

Reason (R) : Corporate culture and style of functioning of top managers is an important factor for determining the internal environment of a company.

Codes:

A. (A) is correct, but (R) is incorrect.
B. Both (A) and (R) are correct and (R) is the correct explanation of (A).
C. Both (A) and (R) are correct, but (R) is not the correct explanation of (A).
D. (R) is correct, but (A) is incorrect.

2. Statement-I : If the workers develop an attitude of non-cooperation with Management, a repressive economic system may be needed to set right this industrial disorder.

Statement-II : By fulfilling social responsibility towards shareholders, employees, consumers, government and community, a business achieves economic growth and increases public image.

Codes:

A. Statement I is correct, but II is incorrect.
B. Both the statements I and II are correct.
C. Statement II is correct but I is incorrect.
D. Both the statements are incorrect.

3. Match the items of List-I with List-II.

List–I	*List–II*
(*a*) Planning Commission	1. 1993
(*b*) Competition Act	2. 2002
(*c*) Adrian Cadbury Committee	3. 1951
(*d*) Rangrajan Committee on Disinvestment in PSEs	4. 1991

Codes:

	(*a*)	(*b*)	(*c*)	(*d*)
A.	1	2	3	4
B.	3	1	4	2
C.	3	2	4	1
D.	3	2	1	4

4. From which Five Year Plan "Growth with Social Justice" has received emphasis?

A. 5th
B. 6th
C. 7th
D. 10th

5. Which of the following is not the objective of the Competition Act, 2002?

A. Prohibition of Restrictive Trade Practices.
B. Prohibition of Dominant Position
C. Prohibition of Anti-competitive Agreements
D. Regulation of Combinations

6. Consolidated financial statements are prepared on the principle

A. In form the companies are one entity, in substance they are separate.
B. In form companies are separate, in substance they are one.
C. In form and substance the companies are one entity.
D. In form and substance the companies are separate.

* *Held on 22 January, 2017.*

7. Match the items of List-I with those of List-II and indicate the correct code:

List–I	*List–II*
(*a*) Acid Test Ratio	1. Profitability analysis
(*b*) Debt Service Coverage Ratio	2. Activity analysis
(*c*) Debt Equity Ratio	3. Liquidity analysis
(*d*) Stock Turnover Ratio	4. Long-term solvency analysis

Codes:

	(*a*)	(*b*)	(*c*)	(*d*)
A.	2	1	3	4
B.	2	3	4	1
C.	3	4	1	2
D.	3	1	4	2

8. From the following two statements of Assertion (A) and Reason (R), indicate the correct code:

Assertion (A) : From the marginal costing approach point of view, the marginal cost is compared with the purchase price.

Reason (R) : If the marginal cost is less than the purchase price it should be purchased rather than manufactured.

Codes:

A. Both (A) and (R) are correct.
B. (A) is correct, but (R) is not correct.
C. (A) is not correct, but (R) is correct.
D. Both (A) and (R) are incorrect.

9. Which one of the following statements is true about standard labour time?

A. Standard labour time indicates the time in hours needed for a specific process.
B. It is standardized on the basis of past experience.
C. In fixing standard time due allowance should not be given to fatigue and tool setting.
D. The Production Manager does not provide any input in setting the labour time standards.

10. Under the yield method of valuation of equity share capital, if for an equity share of ₹ 50, the normal rate of return is 10% and expected rate of return is 5%, then the value of an equity share will be

A. ₹ 25 B. ₹ 40
C. ₹ 50 D. ₹ 100

11. Match the items of List-I with the items of List-II and denote the code of correct matching.

List–I	*List–II*
(*a*) Hypothesis of Sales Revenue Maximization	1. W.J. Baumol
(*b*) Hypothesis of Maximization of Firm's Growth Rate	2. Robin Marris
(*c*) Hypothesis of Maximization of Managerial Utility Function	3. O.E. Williamson
(*d*) Hypothesis of Satisfying Behaviour	4. Cyert and March

Codes:

	(*a*)	(*b*)	(*c*)	(*d*)
A.	2	1	3	4
B.	2	3	1	4
C.	1	2	3	4
D.	1	4	2	3

12. Which of the following is not a correct matching with regard to price elasticity, change in price and change in total revenue?

Price elasticity coefficient	***Change in price***	***Change in total revenue***
A. Zero	Increase	Increase
	Decrease	Decrease
B. Less than one	Increase	Decrease
	Decrease	Increase
C. Equal to one	Increase	No change
	Decrease	No change
D. More than one	Increase	Decrease
	Decrease	Increase

13. The short-run production function for a firm is as follows:

$$Q = -L^3 + 15L^2 + 10L$$

Where Q denotes total output in physical units and L denotes units of labour which are homogeneous, but are not perfectly divisible and change in labour does not tend to become zero.

Statement I : In this production function, the marginal product of 5th unit of labour is 85.

Statement II : Similarly, in this production function, the average product of the 5th unit of labour is 60.

Codes:

A. Both the Statements are true.
B. Both the Statements are false.
C. Statement I is true, while Statement II is false.
D. Statement I is false, but Statement II is true.

14. The Kinked demand curve model of oligopoly was developed by

A. Augustin Cournot B. Stackelberg
C. Edgeworth D. Sweezy

15. For the success of the penetration price policy, which one of the following is not desirable?

A. Short-run demand for the product to have elasticity greater than unity.
B. Availability of economies of large scale production.
C. Product to have very low cross-elasticity of demand.
D. Easy acceptance and adoption of the product by the consumers.

16. Statement I : The absolute value of the difference between an unbiased estimate and the corresponding population parameter is called sampling error.

Statement II : Multi-stage sampling is a restricted non-probability based sampling technique.

Indicate the correct code:

A. Both the Statements are correct.
B. Both the Statements are incorrect.
C. Statement I is correct, while Statement II is incorrect.
D. Statement I is incorrect, while Statement II is correct.

17. Match the following items of List-I and List-II with regard to hypothesis-testing and indicate the code of correct matching.

List–I	***List–II***
(*a*) The ability of test to reject the null hypothesis when it is false.	1. Level of significance
(*b*) The probability of accepting a false null hypothesis.	2. Type I error
(*c*) The probability of rejecting a true null hypothesis due to sampling error.	3. Type II error
(*d*) The probability of rejecting a true null hypothesis.	4. Power of a test

Codes:

	(*a*)	(*b*)	(*c*)	(*d*)
A.	4	2	1	3
B.	4	3	1	2
C.	1	2	3	4
D.	2	3	1	4

18. Which one of the following is a false statement?

A. The signs of the regression coefficients are always the same.
B. Correlation coefficient is the geometric mean of the two regression coefficients.
C. The co-variance between two variables divided by the product of their standard deviations produces the value of coefficient of correlation.
D. Coefficient of correlation is independent of origin but not of scale.

19. If the two regression coefficients are 0.8 and 0.2, then the value of coefficient of correlation is

A. – 0.16 B. + 0.50
C. + 0.40 D. – 0.40

20. Process of arranging data into a new order is called

A. Manipulation of data
B. Standardization of data
C. Sequencing of data
D. Standardized input

21. Developed by the Special Projects Office of the U.S. Navy; this technique was first formally applied to the planning and control of the Polaris Weapon System in 1958 and worked well in expediting the completion of that programme. The technique is known as

A. Gantt Chart
B. PERT
C. CRM
D. Milestone budgeting

22. Consider the following statements relating to planning and find out which of the following is/are correct :

Statement I : The operating personnel should not be associated with the preparation of the budget.

Statement II : A programme indicates the principal operations to be carried out to accomplish a work.

Statement III: Under MBO technique, the Managers should be provided with a freehand to laydown the objectives.

Codes:

A. Only Statement I is correct.
B. Only Statement II is correct.
C. Only Statement III is correct.
D. Both Statements I and III are correct.

23. Assertion (A) : Sympathetic listening in upward communications often leads to resentment in communicator.

Reason (R) : Sympathetic listening and encouraging remarks often lead the communicator to believe that his proposal will receive action not contemplated by superior (communicatee).

Codes:

A. (A) is correct and (R) is the right explanation to it.
B. (A) is correct, but (R) is not the right explanation to it.
C. (A) is not correct while (R) is a correct statement.
D. Both (A) and (R) are incorrect.

24. Assertion (A) : Herzberg believes that today's motivators are tomorrow's hygiene factors.

Reason (R) : Some job conditions operate primarily to dissatisfy employees when they are absent, but their presence does not motivate them in strong way.

Codes:

A. Both (A) and (R) are correct and (R) is the right explanation of (A).
B. Both (A) and (R) are correct, but (R) is not the right explanation of (A).
C. (A) is not correct while (R) is correct.
D. Both (A) and (R) are incorrect.

25. Which of the following statements relating to Henry Fayol are correct?

Statement I : Authority and responsibility are related and former arises from latter.

Statement II : Espirit de Corps is an extension of the principle of unity of command.

Statement III : Unity of command means only one command at a time.

Statement IV : There are fourteen basic principles identified by Henry Fayol.

Codes:

A. Statements I, II and IV
B. Statements II and III
C. Statements I and IV
D. Statements II and IV

26. Match the following items of List-I (sources of competition) with List-II (examples for these sources of competition) and indicate the code of correct matching.

List–I	***List–II***
(*a*) Directly similar products	1. OLA Taxi and Metro Rail
(*b*) Available substitutes	2. Mercedes and BMW
(*c*) Unrelated products	3. PVR and Amusement park

Codes:

	(a)	(b)	(c)
A.	3	2	1
B.	1	3	2
C.	1	2	3
D.	2	1	3

27. The marketing task which finds ways to alter the time pattern of demand through flexible pricing, promotion and other incentives is called

A. Demarketing B. Synchromarketing
C. Fleximarketing D. Gorilla Marketing

28. Which of the following is *not* a reason for a firm to lose its market share to competitors?

A. A product/model is perceived by the target customer group as satisfying needs.
B. Customers not being covered by the company's sales force and distribution outlets.
C. Customers may have been lost to competitors due to poor service by the firm or its sales personnel or product becoming obsolete or more expensive.
D. All the above are correct reasons for given condition.

29. Match the items of List-I with List-II and denote the code of correct matching.

List–I	*List–II*
(*a*) Invest Strategy	1. No receiving of new resources.
(*b*) Protect Strategy	2. Well financed marketing efforts.
(*c*) Harvest Strategy	3. Selective resource allocation
(*d*) Divest Strategy	4. Not warranting substantial new resources.

Codes:

	(a)	(b)	(c)	(d)
A.	2	3	4	1
B.	1	3	2	4
C.	2	1	4	3
D.	4	3	2	1

30. An elaborated version of the idea expressed in meaningful consumer term is called

A. Product image B. Product idea
C. Product concept D. Prototype

31. Which one of the following combinations of rules stands true while preparing schedule of changes in working capital?

A. An increase in current assets increases working capital.
B. An increase in current assets decreases working capital.
C. An increase in current liabilities decreases working capital.
D. An increase in current liabilities increases working capital.

Codes:

A. A and D B. A and C
C. B and C D. C and D

32. Assertion (A) : The primary motive of a company in using financial leverage is to magnify shareholders' return under favourable economic conditions.

Reason (R) : To magnify shareholders' return fixed charges funds can be obtained at a cost higher than the firm's rate of return on net assets.

Codes:

A. (A) is correct and (R) is the correct explanation of (A).
B. (A) is correct, but (R) is wrong.
C. (R) is correct, but (A) is wrong.
D. Both (A) and (R) are wrong.

33. Debt financing is a cheaper source of finance because of

A. Time value of money
B. Rate of interest
C. Tax deductibility of interest
D. Dividends are not payable to lenders

34. Which of the following is not true with reference to capital budgeting?

A. Capital budgeting is related to asset replacement decisions.
B. Cost of capital is equal to minimum required rate of return.
C. Timing of cash flows is relevant.
D. Existing investment in a project is not treated as sunk cost.

35. Which of the following statements is not correct?

A. The cost of capital is required rate of return to ascertain the value of the firm.

B. Different sources of funds have a specific cost of capital related to that source only.

C. Cost of capital does not comprise any risk premium.

D. Cost of capital is basic data for NPV technique.

36. Which of the following is not the quality of human resources in any organization?

A. Their behaviour to stimuli is often inconsistent and unpredictable.

B. They depreciate with passage of time in terms of skills.

C. They are heterogeneous.

D. Retaining qualified human resources is a challenge for managers.

37. Human Resource Planning benefits to an organization are reflected in which of the following combinations?

(*a*) Balance between demand and supply of human resources.

(*b*) Non-compulsion on management to assess critically and continuously the employees and personnel policies.

(*c*) Duplication of efforts and conflicts are avoided.

(*d*) Minimizing the future returns on investment in human resources.

Codes:

A. (*a*) and (*b*) B. (*a*) and (*c*)

C. (*a*), (*b*) and (*c*) D. (*a*), (*c*) and (*d*)

38. A statement containing items such as job title, location, summary, duties, materials used, working conditions, etc., is called

A. Job specification B. Job evaluation

C. Job description D. Job analysis

39. Match List-I with List-II relating to theory of wages.

List–I (Wage Theory)	***List–II (Propounder)***
(*a*) Wage Fund Theory	1. John Davidson
(*b*) Subsistence Theory	2. David Recardo
(*c*) Residual Claimant Theory	3. Adam Smith
(*d*) Bargaining Theory of Wages	4. Francis Walker

Codes:

	(*a*)	(*b*)	(*c*)	(*d*)
A.	2	4	1	3
B.	3	2	4	1
C.	4	1	3	2
D.	2	3	4	1

40. Which organizational analysis method is used, among the following, to develop various efficiency indices relating to contribution of human capital in meeting the organizational goals?

A. Objectives analysis

B. Resource utilization analysis

C. Task analysis

D. Organizational climate analysis

41. Match the items of List-I with the items of List-II regarding evaluation of project application and suggest the correct code.

List–I	***List–II***
(*a*) Managerial Appraisal	1. Analysis of working results.
(*b*) Economic Appraisal	2. Disposal of factory effluents.
(*c*) Financial Appraisal	3. Analysis about traits of an entrepreneur
(*d*) Technical Appraisal	4. Analysis on employment potential

Codes:

	(*a*)	(*b*)	(*c*)	(*d*)
A.	1	2	4	3
B.	2	1	3	4
C.	3	4	1	2
D.	4	3	2	1

42. Match the items of Column-I with the items of Column-II and suggest the correct code.

Column–I	***Column–II***
(*a*) Relationship Banking	1. Dealing in hundis and acceptance of deposits.

(b) Merchant Banking	2. Widening the entrepreneurial base and assist in a rapid rate of industrial growth.
(c) Indigenous Banking	3. Engaged in the business of Issue Management.
(d) Development Banking	4. Creating, maintaining and enhancing strong relationship with customers.

Codes:

	(a)	(b)	(c)	(d)
A.	4	2	1	3
B.	2	4	3	1
C.	4	3	1	2
D.	2	1	4	3

43. In which year, IFCI Act was amended in order to make it possible to provide assistance, inter alia, for medical, health or other allied services?

A. 1960 B. 1970

C. 1973 D. 1986

44. SIDBI was set up as a subsidiary of IDBI to

A. Take over the functions of small business financing of IDBI.

B. Take over the venture capital operations of ICICI.

C. Reconstruct and rehabilitate the sick and closed industrial units financed by IDBI.

D. Facilitate, finance and promote India's Foreign trade.

45. Letters of credit, Guarantees, Forward Contracts, etc., come under which one of the following?

A. Liabilities of a bank

B. Assets of a bank

C. Foreign exchange items of a bank

D. Off-balance sheet items of a bank

46. Consider the following statements with regard for the "Theory of Absolute Cost Advantage":

(i) Productive efficiency differed among different countries because of diversity in natural and acquired resources possessed by them.

(ii) The difference in natural advantage manifests in varying climate, quality of land, availability of minerals, water and other resources.

(iii) The difference in acquired resources manifests in different levels of technology and skills available.

Identify the correct code from the following:

A. Statement (i) is correct, but (ii) and (iii) are incorrect.

B. Statements (i) and (ii) are correct, but (iii) is incorrect.

C. All the statements (i), (ii) and (iii) are correct.

D. None of the statements is correct.

47. Match the items of List-I with List-II and indicate the correct code.

List–I	***List–II***
(a) Absolute Cost Advantage Theory	1. The empirical evidence based on US export of labour intensive goods challenging the factor endowment theory.
(b) Comparative Cost Advantage Theory	2. A country having a direct cost advantage in the production of a product on account of greater efficiency.
(c) Factor Endowment Theory	3. A country should produce and export a commodity that primarily involves a factor of production abundantly available within the country.
(d) Leontief Paradox	4. A country should specialize in the production and export of a commodity in which it possesses greatest relative advantage.

Codes:

	(a)	(b)	(c)	(d)
A.	2	4	3	1
B.	2	4	1	3
C.	2	1	3	4
D.	1	4	3	2

48. Match the items of List-I with List-II and indicate the code of correct matching:

List–I	*List–II*
(*a*) Accommodating capital flow	1. Creation of international reserve assets by the IMF and their allocation among member countries in order to improve international liquidity.
(*b*) Autonomous capital flow	2. Estimate of foreign exchange flow on account of either variations in the collection of related figures or unrecorded illegal transactions of foreign exchange.
(*c*) SDR Allocation	3. Inflow of foreign exchange to meet the balance of payments deficit, normally from the IMF.
(*d*) Statistical discrepancy	4. Flow of loans/investments in normal course of business.

Codes:

	(*a*)	(*b*)	(*c*)	(*d*)
A.	1	2	4	3
B.	3	4	1	2
C.	3	4	2	1
D.	3	1	2	4

49. Statement I : TRIMs agreement refers to conditions or restrictions imposed on foreign investors.

Statement II : TRIMs agreement specifically forbids imposing restrictions on operations of an enterprise which result in protecting domestic products and making imports disadvantageous.

Codes:

A. Statement I is correct, but II is incorrect.
B. Statement II is correct, but I is incorrect.
C. Both the statements I and II are correct.
D. Both the statements I and II are incorrect.

50. Assertion (A) : Revenue from indirect taxes was the major source of tax revenue till tax reforms were taken during nineties.

Reason (R) : Traditionally India's tax regime relied heavily on indirect taxes including customs and excise.

Codes:

A. Both (A) and (R) are correct, but (R) is not the correct explanation of (A).
B. (A) is correct, but (R) is not correct.
C. Both (A) and (R) are correct and (R) is the correct explanation of (A).
D. Both (A) and (R) are incorrect.

ANSWERS

1	**2**	**3**	**4**	**5**	**6**	**7**	**8**	**9**	**10**
B	B	C	A	A	C	D	B	A	A
11	**12**	**13**	**14**	**15**	**16**	**17**	**18**	**19**	**20**
C	B	D	D	C	C	B	D	C	A
21	**22**	**23**	**24**	**25**	**26**	**27**	**28**	**29**	**30**
B	B	A	B	D	D	B	A	A	C
31	**32**	**33**	**34**	**35**	**36**	**37**	**38**	**39**	**40**
B	B	C	D	C	B	B	C	B	B
41	**42**	**43**	**44**	**45**	**46**	**47**	**48**	**49**	**50**
C	C	D	A	D	C	A	B	C	C

EXPLANATORY ANSWERS

1. **Corporate culture** is an important factor for determining the internal environment of any company. In a closed and threatening type of corporate culture the business decisions are taken by top level managers while the middle level and lower level managers have no say in business decision-making. This leads to lack of trust and confidence among subordinate officials of the company and secrecy pervades throughout the organisation. This results in a sense of alienation among the lower level managers and workers of the company. In an open and participating culture, business decisions are taken by the lower level managers and top management has a high degree of confidence in the subordinates.

2. Social attitudes towards business and management determine how many people get attracted to private business as an activity and to management as a career. If business gets social sanction as a respectable profession, the occupational structure of a country will reflect a sizable category of professional managers. On the other hand, if more and more of the active labour force joins professional management, the social attitude towards business and its management also changes.

   If the workers cultivate an attitude of confrontation, rather than cooperation, with management, a repressive economic system may be needed to cope with industrial disorder. On the other hand, if the attainment of rapid economic growth is the target, the management must bring about a labour productivity revolution and the wages may be based on productivity of labour rather than profitability of business. To operate on productivity-based wages is cooperate on the system of incentives and positive attitudes of labour. The attainment of a specific economic objectives is, thus, conditioned by a specific social attitude and discipline.

4. There have been changes in the priorities of development and emphasis on objectives through the plans. For example, the development priority shifted from agriculture in the First Plan to basic and heavy industries in the Second Plan. The Third Plan recognized the importance of export promotion and the Fourth Plan emphasized self-reliance as an objective of development. 'Growth with Social Justice' has been receiving added emphasis since the Fifth Plan. The Fifth Plan, which realized that 'a direct attack on poverty' was necessary for rapid eradication of poverty, formulated a specific package of programmes, known as the *minimum needs programmes,* to improve the living conditions of the poor and these programmes have been continued, with modifications, in the subsequent plans.

5. **The Competition Act, 2002**

   The objective of the Competition Act, 2002 include:

   - Prohibition of anti-competitive agreements.
   - Prohibition of abuse of dominant position.
   - Regulation of combination.

6. Consolidated financial statements of a group of companies are prepared on the basis of single economic entity concept.

   Definition : Single Economic Entity Concept suggests that companies associated with each other through the virtue of common control operate as a single economic unit and therefore the consolidated financial statements of a group of companies should reflect the essence of such arrangement.

   Explanation : Consolidated financial statements of a group of companies must be prepared as if the entire group constitutes a single entity in order to avoid the misrepresentation of the scale of group's activities.

   It is therefore necessary to eliminate the effects of any inter-company transactions and balances during the consolidation of group accounts such as the following:

- Inter-company sales and purchases
- Inter-company payables and receivables
- Inter-company payments such as dividends, royalties and head office charges
- Inter-company transactions must be eliminated as if the transactions had not occurred in the first place. Examples of adjustments that may be required to eliminate the effects of inter-company transactions include:
- Elimination of unrealized profit or loss on the sale of assets member companies of a group
- Elimination of excess or deficit depreciation expense in respect of a fixed asset purchased from a member company at a price that was higher or lower than the net book value of the asset in the books of the seller.

9. Standard Cost for Direct Labour : The labour engaged in the manufacture of a product is known as direct labour. The wages paid to such workers can be known as direct wages. If the wages paid to workers cannot be directly assigned to a particular product, these will be known as indirect wages. The time required for producing a product should be ascertained and labour should be properly graded. Different grades of workers will be paid different rates of wages. The setting of standards for direct labour cost will involve: (1) Standard labour time and (2) Labour rate standard.

Standard labour time indicates the time taken by different categories of workers for performing a particular job. The method for determining direct labour cost will be different for different jobs but general principles can be followed for arriving at this cost.

The labour rate standard refers to the expected wage rates to be paid for different categories of workers past wage rates and demand supply principle may not be safe guide for determining standard labour rates. The anticipation of expected changes in labour rates will be an essential factor. In case there is an agreement with workers for payment of wage rates in the coming period then these rates should be used.

If a premium or bonus scheme is in operation then anticipated extra payment should also be included. Where piece rate system is used then standard cost will be fixed per piece. The object of fixing standard labour time and labour rate is to derive maximum efficiency in the use of labour.

10. Value Per Share

$$= \frac{\text{Expected Rate of Return}}{\text{Nominal Rate of Return}} \times \text{Paid up value}$$

$$= \frac{5}{10} \times 50 = 25.$$

12. Relationship between price elasticity and total revenue

Total revenue from the sale of a good is equal to the price times the quantity. Price elasticity is an important concept because if demand is elastic an increase in sales price results in a decrease in total revenue for all producers. If demand is unitary total revenue remains the same if price changes, and total revenue increases if price is increased when demand is inelastic. These relationships are shown in the following table:

Effect of Price Changes on Various Types of Goods

Price Change	*Elastic Demand E > 1*	*Inelastic Demand E < 1*	*Unitary Demand E = 1*
Price increase	Total revenue decreases	Total revenue increases	Total revenue does not change
Price decrease	Total revenue increases	Total revenue decreases	Total revenue does not change

13. $AP_L = \frac{Q}{L} = -\frac{L^3}{L} + \frac{15L^2}{L} + \frac{10L}{L}$

$= -L^2 + 15L + 10 \quad [\because L = 5]$

$= -(5)^2 + 15 \times 5 + 10$

$= -25 + 75 + 10 = 60.$

14. The Kinked demand curve model was developed by Paul Sweezy in 1939. The model attempts at explaining as to why prices are rigid or sticky in spite of moderate changes in demand and cost under conditions of oligopoly. The argument, which is generally given, is that in such market structures where there are only a few firms which are interdependent on each other if a firm reduces its price other firms in the industry will also match the decrease in price. Hence, the firm, which initially reduced the price, will not be in any way better off. If a firm increases its price, other firms in the industry will not increase their price. Hence, the firm which initially increased the price will suffer a loss. Hence, firms are unwilling to change the price of their good.

The assumptions in the model are as follows:

(*i*) The firms recognize their interdependence but do not collude in any way.

(*ii*) The behavioural assumption is that firms in the industry match decreases in the price but not any increases. A price decrease by one firm in the industry leads to a decrease in the price by the others and hence the firm will not benefit in any way. A price increase by one firm is not matched by a price increase by the others and hence the firm would lose its customers. Thus, there is a non-price competition between the firms.

15. A penetration pricing policy involves setting prices of products relatively low compared to those of similar products in the hope that they will secure wide market acceptance, which will allow the company to raise the prices at a later date. Such a policy if often adopted when the firm expects competition from similar products within a short time and when large-scale production and marketing will produce substantial reductions in overall costs. The low price is adopted with the aim of keeping out the competition and it is essential that the company should maintain its low-price position since the market is highly price sensitive. Production and distribution costs are expected to fall as sales volumes increase. A penetration pricing policy is appropriate when demand is elastic. The marketers obtained as many customers as possible through a low price and established a position for their product in the market.

16. Probability Sampling : It is also known as random sampling or chance sampling. Under this design, each item of the universe has equal chance of inclusion in the sample. It is a lottery method in which units are picked up from the whole group by some mechanical process. The results obtained from such a sample can be assured in terms of probability, *i.e.,* we can measure the errors of estimation or the significance of results obtained from a random sample. The is why probability sampling techniques are considered superior to deliberate sampling techniques. Some other sampling techniques under probability sampling are the following:

- Simple random sampling
- Systematic sampling
- Stratified sampling
- Cluster sampling
- Multistage sampling
- Sequential sampling
- Multiphase sampling
- Double sampling

Non-probability Sampling Procedures : Non-probability samples are used when the representativeness is not particularly the primary issue. From these samples, one cannot estimate sampling error. Hence, these are also called 'uncontrolled sampling methods'. This sampling procedure does not afford any basis for estimating the probability that each item in the population has a chance of being included in the example. This type of sampling is also called as deliberate sampling, purposive sampling and judgement sampling. In other words, under non-probability sampling the investigators purposively choose the particular units of the universe for constituting a sample on the basis that the sample will be a typical or representative of the whole. In such a design, personal element has a chance of entering into the selection of the sample.

The investigators may select a sample which shall yield results favourable to their point of view and if this happens, the entire enquiry may get vitiated. There is always the danger of bias entering into this type of sampling technique. But if the investigators are impartial and take sound judgement, the results obtained from the analysis of deliberately selected sample may be reliable. Quota sampling also is a non-probability sampling. Here, the interviewers are simply given quotes to be filled from different strata, with some restriction on how they are to be filled. Actually, the selection of the items for the sample is left to the interviewer's discretion. This type of sampling is very convenient and relatively inexpensive, but they do not possess the characteristic of random samples. Quota samples are judgement samples and inference drawn are not amenable to statistical treatment in a formal way.

Major forms of non-probability sampling procedures are as follows:

- Convenience sampling
- Purposive sampling
- Quota sampling

18. Properties of Correlation Coefficient

Property-1 : Pearsonian correlation coefficient can not exceed 1 numerically. In other words it lies between –1 and +1.

Symbolically, $-1 \leq r \leq 1$

In other words, $r = \pm 1$ implies perfect positive correlation between the variables and $r = -1$ implies perfect negative correlation between the variables.

Property-2 : Correlation coefficient is independent of the change of origin and scale.

Property-3 : Two independent variables are uncorrelated but the converse in not true.

19. Since the coefficient of correlation is the G.M. between the regression coefficients, therefore,

$$r^2 = 0.8 \times 0.2 = 0.16$$

$$\therefore \quad r = \pm 0.4$$

Since r has the same sign as the two regression coefficients so r must be +ve. Hence $r = 0.4$.

21. PERT was originally developed in 1958 and 1959 to meet the needs of the 'age of massive engineering' where the techniques of Taylor and Gantt were inapplicable. The Special Projects Office of the U.S. Navy, concerned with performance trends on large military development programs, introduced PERT on its Polaris Weapon System in 1958, after the technique had been developed with the aid of the management consulting firm of Booz, Allen, and Hamilton. Since that time, PERT has spread rapidly throughout almost all industries. At about the same time, the DuPont Company initiated a similar technique known as the critical path method (CPM), which also has spread widely, and is particularly concentrated in the construction and process industries.

In the early 1960s, the basic requirements of PERT/time as established by the Navy were as follows:

- All of the individual tasks to complete a program must be clear enough to be put down in a network, which comprises events and activities; *i.e.,* follow the work breakdown structure.
- Events and activities must be sequenced on the network under a highly logical set of ground rules that allow the determination of critical and subcritical paths. Networks may have more than one hundred events, but not fewer than ten.

- Time estimates must be made for each activity on a three-way basis. Optimistic, most likely, and pessimistic-elapsed-time figures are estimated by the person(s) most familiar with the activity.

23. **Upward Communication** occurs when lower-level employees communicate with those at higher levels—for example, when a subordinate tells a manager about a problem employees are having meeting a customer's request. Encouraging upward communication can help managers check that subordinates understand their goals and instructions, keep managers informed of employee challenges and complaints, and cultivate acceptance and commitment by giving employees the opportunity to express ideas and suggestions. Despite its potential benefits, getting subordinates to give upward feedback can be challenging. Subordinates often filter bad news, fearing that their boss does not really want to hear it. Being approachable, accessible, and creating a culture of trust and openness can help subordinates feel more comfortable giving upward feedback. Managers should avoid overreacting, becoming defensive, or acting blameful, and should respect confidentiality when a subordinate shares potentially controversial or negative information. Attitude surveys, an open-door policy, and regular face-to-face meetings with subordinates can also foster upward communication. One of the best ways to make subordinates comfortable sharing information may be sympathetically listening to them during your daily informal contacts with them in and outside of the workplace. This can build the trust required for subordinates to share their ideas and honestly communicate negative information.

25. Henry Fayol, a Frenchman, was the first person who issued a complete statement on a theory of general management. Born from relatively well-to-do parents, Fayol was graduated as a mining engineer and started his career as a junior executive of a coal mining and iron foundry company in 1860. In 1888, when the company was near bankruptcy, Fayol took over as Managing Director and rapidly transformed the company into a financially sound organization. After his retirement in 1918, Fayol spent his remaining years lecturing and popularizing his theory of administration. He became especially interested in the application of administrative theory to government.

Although he published earlier papers outlining his general thinking, Fayol's major contribution, *Administration Industrielle et Generale,* was published in 1916. Unfortunately, this work was not translated into English until 1930 and there was only a very limited number of copies. The book was not readily available in English until 1949.

Possibly the most significant of Fayol's work was his discussion of management principles and elements. Fayol stated the following 14 "principles of management", stressing that managers should be flexible in the application of these principles and that allowances should be made for different and changing circumstances. These 14 principles are (1) division of work, (2) authority, (3) discipline, (4) unity of command, (5) unity of direction, (6) subordination of individual interests to the general interests, (7) remuneration, (8) centralization, (9) scalar chain/line of authority, (10) order, (11) equity, (12) stability of tenure personnel, (13) initiative and (14) esprit de corps.

Fayol developed his list of principles from those practices which he had used most often in his work. He used these principles as broad and general guidelines for effective management. The real contribution made by Fayol was not the 14 principles themselves, for many of these were the products of the early factory system, but rather his formal recognition and synthesis of these principles. In presenting his "elements of management", Fayol was probably the first person who outlined what today are called as management functions. Fayol listed planning, organizing, commanding, coordinating and controlling as elements of management. However, he placed the greatest emphasis on planning and organizing because he viewed these elements as primary and essential for the other functions.

27. Synchromarketing : When the demand for the product is irregular due to season, some part of the day or hour-basis, causing ideal capacity or overworked capacities, Synchro-marketing can be used to find ways to alter the same pattern of demand through flexible pricing, promotion and other incentives. For example, in order to attract the customers between 10 am to 6 pm, restaurants offer happy hour pricing.

28. Competition Oriented Marketing Strategies

Marketing has often been termed as a warfare. The battlefield is the customer's mind and the rival forces are competitor firms. It is imperative that the firm also considers principles of this warfare that will give it a competitive edge and hence market leadership. In this section, we shall focus our attention on competition based strategies.

A good starting point is the market and the company's market share in it. A detailed analysis of these two may reveal possible strategic options to a firm in gaining competitive advantage. For example, this analysis may reveal that a certain proportion of the market does not buy the firm's product only because it does not find the product or model satisfying its needs. The firm may even find that not all potential customers are being covered by the company's sales force or distribution outlets. Given Fig. presents these possible sources of competitive differentiation.

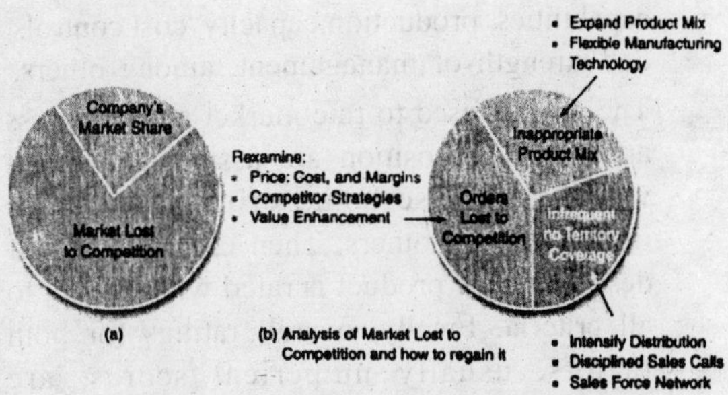

Fig. : *Winning Back Markets*

The point to be noted here is that a firm may lose its market share to competition because of any or all of the following reasons:

(*a*) product/model not offered or not perceived by target customer group as satisfying needs.

(*b*) customers not being covered by the company's sales force and distribution outlets.

(*c*) customers may have been lost to competitors due to poor service by the firm or its sales personnel or product becoming obsolete or more expensive.

To gain a foothold or win back lost customers, the firm has to expand its product mix, distribution coverage, ensure a more disciplined sales call pattern, train marketing and service personnel in customer care, evolve innovative pricing and payment plans to suit customer's needs, and build the brand or corporate image.

29. Management can use the GE business screen to classify SBUs or major products on the basis of two factors: market attractiveness and business position. Each factor is rated according to several criteria. *Market attractiveness* should be judged with respect to market growth rate (similar to the BCG matrix), market size, degree of difficulty in entering the market, number and types of competitors, technological requirements, and profit margins, among other criteria. Business position encompasses market share (as in the BCG matrix), SBU size, strength of differential advantage, research and development capabilities, production capacity, cost controls, and strength of management, among others. The criteria used to rate market attractiveness and business position are assigned different weights because some criteria are more important than others. Then each SBU or, if desired, major product is rated with respect to all criteria. Finally, overall ratings for both factors, usually numerical scores, are calculated for each SBU. On the basis of these ratings, each SBU is labelled as high, medium or low with respect to (1) market attractiveness and (2) business position. For example, an SBU may be judged as having high market attractiveness but medium business position. Following the ratings, an organization's SBUs are plotted on a 3 × 3 grid, as depicted in Figure. The best location for an SBU is the upper left cell because it points to (1) the most attractive market opportunity and (2) the best business position to seize that opportunity. The worst location is the lower right cell, for the opposite reasons. The nine cells have implications with respect to how resources are allocated and, in turn, what marketing strategies are suitable.

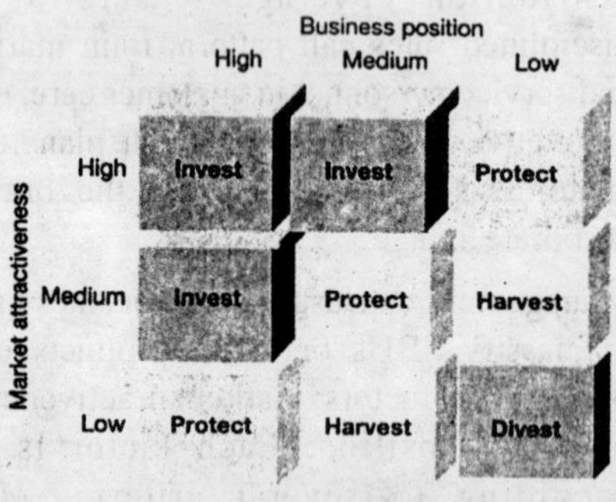

Fig. : *The GE Business Screen*

Every organization has to make decisions aimed at using its limited resources most effectively. That's where planning models can help—determining which SBUs or major products should be stimulated for growth, which ones maintained in their present market positions, and which ones eliminated. An SBU's evaluation, as indicated by its location on the GE business screen, suggests how it should be treated:

Invest strategy : SBUs in the three cells in the upper left of the grid shou'd receive ample resources. To strengthen or at least sustain such SBUs, bold, well-financed marketing efforts are needed. Several years ago, Silicon Graphics, Inc. announced that it would concentrate on producing powerful server computers that can handle challenging technical and Internet applications. The firm's decision seemed to be based on an assessment indicating high market attractiveness and a midrange business position. Xerox Corp is following this strategy with respect to high-end digital copiers, as are several competitors.

Protect strategy : Resources should be allocated selectively to SBUs along the diagonal running from the lower left to the upper right of the grid. This somewhat defensive approach helps an SBU maintain its present market position while it generates cash needed by other SBUs. For example, the firm that makes Precious Moments, small porcelain figurines of children, suffered when demand for collectibles declined. The Enesco Group took several actions, including (a) selling inexpensive Precious Moments trinkets at discount stores in order to promote the brand and (b) distributing the figurines through different channels, including in-home parties.

Harvest strategy : Because they lack an attractive market and a strong business position, SBUs in the two cells just below the three-cell diagonal do not warrant substantial new resources. Instead, expenditures should be curtailed to maximize any remaining profits. An alternative is to sell these SBUs. A case can be made that the Hewlett-Packard Co. is following this strategy with regards to lower-price printers. With growth slowing and profit margins shrinking in this category, H-P is shifting resources from basic printers to higher-growth areas, including digital publishing and multipurpose printer-based machines.

Divest strategy : SBUs in the lower right cell do not have much going for them. Hence, an SBU in this location should not receive any resources. The best approach probably is to eliminate it from the organization's portfolio by selling it or, failing that, shutting it down. When the McDonald's Corp. assessed its portfolio several years ago, the firm decided to divest its Fazoli's and Donatos Pizzeria divisions and keep two "promising concepts," Chipotle Mexican Grill and Boston Markets, in addition to its famous namesake division. Firms typically employ more than one of these four strategies and adjust them over time.

30. Kotler defined these terms as:

(*a*) **Product Idea :** A possible product that the company might offer to the market.

(*b*) **Product Concept :** An elaborated version of the idea expressed in meaningful consumer terms.

(*c*) **Product Image :** The particular picture that consumers acquire of an actual or potential product.

31. Calculation of Working Capital : Difference between current assets and current liabilities is known as 'fund'. In other words, 'fund' means working capital. Before preparing fund flow statement opening and closing working capital is calculated by using the following formula:

Working Capital = Current Assets – Current Liabilities

By comparing opening and closing working capital, increase or decrease in working capital is calculated. If working capital increases, it shows applications on uses of fund. If working capital decreases it shows sources of funds. To study change in working capital, "Statement of working Capital" is prepared.

Statement of Variation or Changes in Working Capital

In fund flow statement difference between total sources and total applications is shown. This change in working capital should be unified working by preparing working capital schedule. Format of statement in change in working capital has been given below:

Rules of Preparing Statement of Changes in Working Capital

1. An increase in current assets increases working capital.
2. A decrease in current assets decreases working capital.
3. An increase in current liabilities decreases working capital.
4. An decrease in current liabilities increases working capital.

32. Financial Leverage and the Shareholders' Return : The primary motive of a company in using financial leverage is to magnify the shareholders' return under favourable economic conditions. The role of financial leverage in magnifying the return of the shareholders is based on the assumptions that the fixed-charges funds (such as the loan from financial institutions and banks or debentures) can be obtained at a cost lower than the firm's rate of return on net assets (RONA or ROI). Thus, when the difference between the earnings generated by assets financed by the fixed-charges funds and costs of these funds is distributed to the shareholders, the earnings per share (EPS) or return on equity (ROE) increases. However, EPS or ROE will fall if the company obtains the fixed-charges funds at a cost higher than the rate of return on the firm's assets. It should, therefore, be clear that EPS, ROE and ROI are the important figures for analyzing the impact of financial leverage.

33. Cost of capital means interest on debts or dividend on shares. Debt is a cheaper source of finance in comparison to equity capital because rate of interest is lower than the return expected by equity shareholders and the tax deductibility of interest further reduces the cost of debt. The preference share capital is also cheaper than equity capital, but not as cheap as debt. Thus, optimum capital structure should include sufficient amount of debt since it is the cheapest source of finance.

35. The cost of capital is the minimum required rate of return which firm must earn on its funds in order to satisfy the expectation of its supplier of funds. If the return from capital budgeting proposals is more than cost of capital then difference will be added to wealth of shareholders.

The concept of cost of capital has a role to play in capital budgeting as well as in finalizing the capital structure for the firm. The cost of capital depends upon the risk free interest rate and risk premium, which depends upon the risk of investment and risk of firm.

The cost of capital may be defined in terms of (1) explicit cost, which the firm pays to supplier, and (2) implicit cost. *i.e.,* opportunity cost of funds to firm. The cost of capital is calculated in after tax terms.

Different sources of funds available to firm may be grouped into Debt, Preference share capital, Equity share capital and retained earning and these sources have their specific cost of capital. However the overall cost of capital of the firm may be ascertained as the weighted average of these specific costs of capital.

36. An organisation is made up of four resources, *i.e.,* men, money, material and machines. Of them the first one is the living resource and the other three are non-living *i.e.,* non-human resource. It is the human resource, formerly termed as 'manpower' that make use of nonhuman resources. Hence, people are the most significant resources for any organisation. Human resource are heterogeneous in the sense that they differ in personality, perception, devotions, values, attitudes, motives , mode of thoughts and social background also. Their behaviour to stimuli is often inconsistent and unpredictable. Therefore, motivational tools also vary accordingly. For example, while increase in salary may satisfy one psychological needs, recognition may satisfy the esteem needs. While other resources depreciate, human resource appreciate with the passage of time. Given the highly competitive and complex business environment, attracting and retaining the qualified and competent employees have become a real challenge of the day for the managers. The 'rule of thmb' has become obsolete and redundant. The need of the new perspective is to have right people for right jobs that offers "competitive advantage" for "core competency" to the organisation to survive and thrive in the competitive business environment.

37. Human resource planning is important to organisation because it benefits the organisation in several ways. The important ones are mentioned below:

1. Human resource planning meets the organisation need for right type of people in right number at right times.
2. By maintaining a balance between demand for and supply of human resources, human resource planning makes optimum use of human resources, on the one hand, and reduces labour cost substantially, on the other.
3. Careful consideration of likely future events, through human resource planning might lead to the discovery of better means for managing human resources. Thus, forceable pitfalls might be avoided.
4. Manpower shortfalls and surpluses may be avoided, to a large extent.
5. Human resource planning helps the organisation create and develop training and succession planning for employees and managers. Thus, it provides enough lead time for internal succession of employees to higher positions through promotions.
6. It also provides multiple gains to the employees by way of promotions, increase in emoluments and other perquisites and fringe benefits.

7. Some of the problems of managing change may be foreseen and their consequences mitigated. Consultation with affected groups and individuals can take place at an early stage in the change process. This may avoid resistance for change.
8. Human resource planning compels management to asses critically the strength and weaknesses of its employees and personnel policies on continuous basis and, in turn, take corrective measures to improve the situation.
9. Through human resource planning, duplication of efforts and conflict among efforts can be avoided, on the one hand, and coordination of worker's efforts can be improved, on the other.
10. Last but not means the least, with increase in skill, knowledge, potentialities, productivity and job satisfaction, organisation becomes the main beneficiary. Organisation is benefitted in terms of increase in prosperity/production, growth, development, profit and thus, an edge over its competitors in the market.

38. Contents of Job Description and Job Specification : The contents of job description and job specification are presented in the following Table:

Table : *Job Contents*

Job Description	*Job Specification*
A statement containing items such as • Job title • Location • Job summary • Duties • Machines, tools, and equipment • Materials and forms used • Supervision given or received • Working conditions • Hazards	A statement of human qualifications necessary to do the job. Usually contains such items as • Education • Experience • Training • Judgement • Initiative • Physical effort • Physical skills • Responsibilities • Communication skills • Emotional characteristics • Unusual sensory demands such as sight, smell, hearing.

40. Organizational Analysis : Entails detailed analysis of organizational structure, objectives, human resources, resource allocation and utilization and future plans. An in-depth analysis of these factors would facilitate an understanding of deficiencies that need to be corrected. Organization analysis consists of the following elements:

- **Analysis of Objectives:** Based on organizational objectives, specific goals and strategies for various departments and sections are stated as detailed operational targets in the light of changing environment.
- **Resource Utilization Analysis :** The allocation of human, physical and financial resources and their efficient utilization in meeting the operational targets are analysed for determining specific work flows as well as the contribution of human resources.
- **Organization Climate Analysis :** Analysis of organizational climate through attitudinal surveys helps to identify strengths and weaknesses of the organization.
- **Environmental Scanning :** As the organization affects and also gets affected by the environmental factors, political, social, economic and technological, therefore understanding of the environment is essential.

43. The Industrial Finance Corporation of India was set up in July 1948 by the Government of India. It was established under the IFCI Act, 1948 with the basic objective of providing finance to the industries in private sector. At present it also providing financial assistance to cooperative, joint, public sector units. It provides loans for expansion, diversification and modernisation of existing units. It also underwrites and directly subscribes to industrial securities, merchant banking services and lease finance. It renders financial assistance both in rupees and foreign currencies to the corporate sector.

The small scale industries, proprietary and partnership concerns were not eligible for financial assistance from the IFCI. It did not grant assistance for the purpose of working capital. It did not provide assistance for the acquisition of capital goods for commercial or trading purposes. It did not grant loans in foreign currencies for purchasing of raw materials, imports or payments of royalties, interest and dividends.

The IFCI (Amendment) Act, 1986 has made it possible for the Corporation to provide assistance inter alia for medical, health or other allied services.

44. SIDBI was set up on April 2, 1990 as a wholly owned subsidiary of IDBI, under an Act of the Parliament, viz., Small Industries Development Bank of India Act, 1989. The objectives of SIDBI are to serve as the principal financial institution for promotion, financing and development of industry in the small scale sector and to coordinate the functions of the institutions engaged in promoting, financing or developing industry in the small scale sector. The paid-up capital of SIDBI is ₹ 450 crore. Earlier this was entirely held by IDBI. In order to provide greater functional autonomy and operational flexibility to SIDBI from IDBI. SIDBI Act was amended in September 2000, which *inter alia,* envisages transfer of IDBI's share holding in SIDBI to the extent of 51% to public sector banks, LIC, GIC and other institutions owned and/or controlled by GOI. SIDBI functions as the principal financial institution for financing, developing and promoting the small-scale industrial sector. A major part of SIDBI's financial assistance, initially, was by way of refinance of term-loans and bills rediscounting. However, it has gradually diversified and expanded its lending operations by way of direct lending as well as support through the existing institutions and banks.

45. Off-Balance Sheet items : Those are items that generate income for the bank but do not appear in the bank's balance sheet. Examples of such items are letters of credit, guarantees, acceptances and various types of derivatives *i.e.,* forward contracts.

46. Theory of Absolute Cost Advantage : Adam Smith was one of the forerunners of the classical school of thought. He propounded a theory of international trade in 1776, which is known as the theory of absolute cost advantage. He was of the opinion that productive efficiency differed among different countries because of diversity in the natural and acquired resources possessed by them. The differences in natural advantage manifests in varying climate, quality of land, availability of minerals, water, and other natural resources; while the difference in acquired resources manifests in different levels of technology and skills available. A particular country should specialise in producing only those goods that it is able to produce with greater efficiency, that is at lower cost; and exchange those goods with other goods of their requirements from a country that produces those other goods with greater efficiency or at lower cost. This will lead to optimal utilisation of resources in both the countries. Both countries will gain from trade insofar as both of them will get the two sets of goods at the least cost.

Adam Smith explains the concept of absolute advantage in a two commodity, two country framework.

48. • Balance of trade = Export of goods – Import of goods

• Balance of current account = Balance of trade + Net earnings on invisibles.

• Balance of capital account = Foreign exchange inflow – Foreign exchange outflow, on account of foreign investment, foreign loans, banking transactions, and other capital flows.

• Overall balance of payments = Balance of current account + Balance of capital account + Statistical discrepancy.

If the overall balance of payments is in surplus, the surplus amount is used for repaying the borrowings from the IMF and then the rest is transferred to the official reserves account. On the contrary, when the overall balance is found in deficit, the monetary authorities arrange for capital flows to cover up the deficit. Such inflows make take the form of drawing down of foreign exchange reserves or official borrowings or purchases (drawings) from the IMF. From this point of view, capital inflows are bifurcated into autonomous and accommodating ones. If the inflow of funds on the capital account is for meeting the overall balance of payments deficit, it is termed as accommodating or compensatory capital flow. In other words, accommodating capital inflows aim at putting the balance of payments in equilibrium. On the other hand, autonomous capital flows take place regardless of such considerations. A foreigner paying back the loan or the inflow of foreign direct investment is an apposite example of autonomous capital inflow. This is why autonomous capital inflow goes "above-the-line", while accommodating capital inflow goes "below-the-line".

Accommodating capital flow is the inflow of foreign exchange to meet the balance of payments deficit, normally from the IMF.

Autonomous capital flow refers to flow of loans/investment in normal course of a business.

Statistical discrepancy refers to estimate of foreign exchange flow on account of either variations in the collection of related figures or unrecorded illegal transaction of foreign exchange.

SDRs allocation is the creation of international reserve assets by the IMF, and their allocation among member countries in order to improve international liquidity.

49. Agreement on Trade-Related Investment Measures (TRIMs)

The agreement on TRIMs is related to the measures (conditions and restrictions) imposed by some countries on foreign investment. Incidentally, restrictive measures on foreign investment were widely imposed by developed countries. The agreement on TRIMs aims to eliminate or modify the conditions and restrictions on foreign investment that are not consistent with the rules and regulations of the WTO. In case of modification of the unreasonable conditions, a transition period is allowed to the parties concerned. The transition period allowed is two years for developed countries, five years for underdeveloped countries, and seven years for less developed countries.

Some important provisions of this agreement are as follows:

• No country can impose any performance clause on foreign investors in respect of foreign-exchange earnings, foreign equity participation, and transfer of technology.

• Foreign investors should be treated on par with national investors.

• There should be no restriction in the area of foreign investment—it should be open.

• There should be no restriction on the import of raw materials and intermediate components related to foreign investment.

PAPER-III

Note: *This paper contains* ***seventy five (75)*** *objective type questions of* ***two (2)*** *marks each. All questions are compulsory.*

1. Put the following steps of strategic Management Process in correct sequence :

(*a*) Scanning and Evaluation of Business Environment

(*b*) Formulating strategies

(*c*) Implementation of Corporate Strategy

(*d*) Deciding about the Mission of the organisation

(*e*) Setting Corporate Level Objective

Codes:

A. (*a*), (*b*), (*c*), (*d*) and (*e*)

B. (*d*), (*a*), (*b*), (*c*) and (*e*)

C. (*d*), (*a*), (*e*), (*c*) and (*b*)

D. (*d*), (*a*), (*e*), (*b*) and (*c*)

2. Match the items of List-I with those of List-II and indicate the code of correct matching.

List-I	***List-II***
(*a*) Indian Railways	1. Government Company
(*b*) Unit Trust of India	2. Department Undertaking
(*c*) Bharat Heavy Electricals Limited	3. Statutory Corporation

Codes:

	(*a*)	(*b*)	(*c*)
A.	1	2	3
B.	2	3	1
C.	2	1	3
D.	3	2	1

3. Identify the correct statement from the following:

A. The liability of the Karta is limited.

B. A joint Hindu family business continues to exist on the death of a co-partner.

C. A joint Hindu family business ceases to exist on the death of the Karta.

D. A joint Hindu family business comes into existence by Hindu law.

4. **Statement I** : "Working in harmony with the community and environment around us and not cheating our customers and workers we might not gain anything in the short run but in the long term it means greater profits and shareholders value".

Statement II : According to Mahatma Gandhi, capitalist class owns wealth or capital as trustees of the society.

Codes:

A. Statement I is correct, but II is incorrect.

B. Statement II is correct, but I is incorrect.

C. Both the statements I and II are incorrect.

D. Both the statements I and II are correct.

5. Match the items of List-I with items of List-II and indicate the code of correct matching.

List-I	***List-II***
(*a*) Principle of Separate Entity	1. Valuing Plant and Machinery at cost less depreciation.
(*b*) Principle of Conservatism	2. Recording punctuality and honesty of employees of an organization.
(*c*) Principle of Money Measurement	3. Capital contributed by proprietor is shown as liability in Balance Sheet.
(*d*) Historical cost concept	4. Valuing inventories at cost or market price whichever is less.

Codes:

	(*a*)	(*b*)	(*c*)	(*d*)
A.	3	2	1	4
B.	3	4	2	1
C.	4	3	1	2
D.	3	1	2	4

6. Which of the following is not true?

A. When all the forfeited shares are not reissued, the forfeited shares account will also show as credit balance equal to gain on forfeiture of shares not yet reissued.

B. Loss on reissue of shares cannot be more than gain on forfeiture of those shares.
C. At the time of forfeiture of shares, securities premium is debited along with share capital when premium has not been received.
D. When forfeited shares are issued at premium, the premium amount is credited to Capital Reserve Account.

7. Preparation of Consolidated Balance Sheet of Holding Company and its subsidiary company is done as per:

A. AS 11 B. AS 21
C. AS 22 D. AS 23

8. Amount due to outgoing partner is shown in the balance sheet as his

A. Liability B. Asset
C. Capital D. Loan

9. Match the items of List-I with items of List-II and indicate the code of their correct matching.

List-I	*List-II*
(*a*) Non-price quantity relationships of demand.	1. Extension and contraction of demand.
(*b*) Income effect of a price rise greater than its substitution effect.	2. Ordinal utility approach.
(*c*) Transitivity and consistency of choices.	3. Increase and decrease in demand.
(*d*) Price-quantity relationships of demand.	4. Giffen goods.

Codes:

	(*a*)	(*b*)	(*c*)	(*d*)
A.	4	2	3	1
B.	2	1	4	3
C.	3	4	2	1
D.	1	2	3	4

10. The short-run cost function of a firm is as follows:

$$TC = 200 + 5Q + 2Q^2$$

Where TC = Total Cost
Q = Physical units of the product of the firm

What would be the level of optimum output?

A. 05 B. 10
C. 12 D. 15

11. Short-run demand and total cost functions for a monopoly firm are as under:

Demand function : $Q = 100 - 0.2\ P$
Price function : $P = 500 - 5\ Q$
Cost function : $TC = 50 + 20\ Q + Q^2$

Where Q = Total quantity of the product in physical units.
P = Price of the product per unit
TC = Total cost

What is the profit maximizing output of the pure monopoly firm?

A. 20 B. 35
C. 40 D. 50

12. In which one of the following market situations, the pricing above the prevailing market price is used as a more common practice?

A. Markets where the selling firms face perfect competitive situations.
B. Markets where the selling firms want to gain popularity of the products having high cross elasticity of their demand.
C. Markets where sellers rely on their customers' high propensity to consume a prestigious commodity.
D. Markets where the selling firms have entered into the stages of maturity and saturation.

13. Which one of the following statements is false regarding normal distribution?

A. Mean, Median and Mode always coincide.
B. Within ± 1.96 σ limits from Mean value, the area under the distribution is 99 per cent of the total area.
C. The area under the normal curve represents probabilities for the normal random variable and the total area for the normal probability distribution is one.
D. For every pair of values of Mean and Standard deviation, the curve of the distribution is bell-shaped and symmetric.

14. If unexplained variation between variables X and Y is 36%, what is the coefficient of correlation between the variables?

A. 0.36 B. 0.64
C. 0.60 D. 0.80

15. Which one of the following is the formula to calculate standard error of mean differences of two sample groups?

A. $\frac{\sigma_p}{\sqrt{n}}$ B. $\sqrt{\frac{\sigma_1^2}{n_1}+\frac{\sigma_2^2}{n_2}}$

C. $\frac{\sigma_1^2}{\sigma_2^2}$, when $\sigma_1^2 < \sigma_2^2$ D. $\sqrt{\frac{p_1q_1}{n_1}+\frac{p_2q_2}{n_2}}$

16. A researcher wants to test the significance of the difference between the average performance of the two small sized samples when the information of the population standard deviation is not available, which one of the following hypothesis-testing is suitably used?

A. Z-test B. Chi-square test
C. F-test D. t-test

17. Which of the following statements are *not* correct? Indicate the correct code.

Statement I : Organizational culture means the general pattern of behaviour, belief and values that organization members have in individuality.

Statement II : As per contingency theory of Leadership, people become leader only because of the demand of group members.

Statement III : The group judgement can only be obtained through the formal committees.

Statement IV : Ombudsperson in communication function is a person assigned to investigate employee concerns and providing valuable upward communication link.

Codes:

A. Statements I, II and IV
B. Statements I, III and IV
C. Statements I, II and III
D. Statements II, III and IV

18. Assertion (A) : The organization is a closed system that operates within and interacts with the external environment.

Reasoning (R) : The system approach to management includes the outputs from the external environment on the basis of interactions between management and employees.

Codes:

A. Both (A) and (R) are correct and (R) is the correct reasoning of (A).
B. Both (A) and (R) are correct, but (R) is not the correct explanation of (A).
C. (A) is incorrect while (R) is a correct statement.
D. Both (A) and (R) are incorrect.

19. Match List-I with List-II relating to corporate ethics and indicate the code of their correct matching.

List-I	***List-II***
(*a*) Utilitarian theory	1. Behaviour guiding statements.
(*b*) Code	2. Making public known about unethical company practices.
(*c*) Whistle blowing	3. Society with varied interest groups.
(*d*) Pluralistic society	4. Evaluation of plans with its consequences

Codes:

	(*a*)	(*b*)	(*c*)	(*d*)
A.	1	3	4	2
B.	2	3	4	1
C.	3	1	2	4
D.	4	1	2	3

20. Find out the correct sequence of planning function of the following elements:

(*a*) Diagnosis of opportunity
(*b*) Establishing objectives
(*c*) Identifying and comparing alternatives
(*d*) Formulating derivative plans
(*e*) Choosing an alternative

Codes:

A. (*a*), (*c*), (*b*), (*e*), (*d*) B. (*b*), (*e*), (*a*), (*c*), (*d*)
C. (*a*), (*b*), (*c*), (*e*), (*d*) D. (*a*), (*b*), (*c*), (*d*), (*e*)

21. Creating the capability of making purchases directly from a firm's website is known as

A. Electronic Networking
B. Electronic Transactions
C. Electronic Data Interchange
D. Electronic Information Transfer

22. For the following two statements of Assertion (A) and Reasoning (R) indicate the correct code:

Assertion (A) : The self image could be an individual's own perceived image and actual image based on how others perceive the individual.

Reasoning (R) : Large number of products like credit cards, automobiles, readymade garments, designer ware, cosmetics and perfumes are bought due to self image and demographic variables like income may not be important in purchase decisions for these products.

Codes:

A. Both (A) and (R) are not correct.
B. (A) is correct, but (R) is not correct.
C. (A) is correct and (R) is correct explanation for (A).
D. (A) is not correct, but (R) is correct.

23. Match the media factors given in List-I with examples given in List-II and indicate the code of current matching.

List-I	***List-II***
(*a*) Media class	1. Prime time at 9:00 PM, full page ad of Honda City
(*b*) Media vehicles	2. Magazine, T.V., Radio
(*c*) Media option	3. Flighting, Pulsing
(*d*) Scheduling & timing	4. Times of India, T.V. serial Bhabhi Ji Ghar Pe Hain

Codes:

	(*a*)	(*b*)	(*c*)	(*d*)
A.	2	4	1	3
B.	3	1	4	2
C.	1	2	4	3
D.	4	2	3	1

24. In integrating specialist functions of product management with the line function of sales as major challenge to top management can be achieved by which type of marketing organization?

A. Functional organization
B. Territorial organization
C. Matrix organization
D. None of the above

25. Assertion (A) : The important aspect of dividend policy is to determine the amount of earnings to be distributed to shareholders and the amount to be retained in the firm.

Reasoning (R) : Dividend policy of the firm has its effect on both the long term financing and the wealth of shareholders.

Codes:

A. Both (A) and (R) are correct and (R) is the correct explanation of (A).
B. Both (A) and (R) are correct, but (R) is not the correct explanation of (A).
C. (A) is correct, but (R) is wrong.
D. (R) is correct, but (A) is wrong.

26. Match the items in List-I with items in List-II and indicate the code of correct matching:

List-I	***List-II***
(*a*) ABC Inventory Control System	1. Developing ancillary units around the manufacturing sites and supplying parts to manufacturing units.
(*b*) Just-in-time (JIT) System	2. Enables a company to easily track large items of inventory.
(*c*) Out sourcing System	3. It eliminates the necessity of carrying large inventories and saves carrying cost.
(*d*) Computerized Inventory Control System	4. Tends to measure the significance of each item of inventories in terms of its value.

Codes:

	(a)	(b)	(c)	(d)
A.	2	3	1	4
B.	4	2	3	1
C.	4	3	1	2
D.	3	1	2	4

27. In certainty-equivalent approach, risk adjusted cash flows are discounted at:

A. Accounting Rate of Return
B. Internal Rate of Return
C. Hurdle Rate
D. Risk-free Rate

28. 'That personal leverage can replace corporate leverage' is assumed by

A. Traditional Approach
B. M M Model
C. Net Income Approach
D. Net Operating Income Approach

29. Match the List-I with List-II relating to Human Resource Planning activities and indicate the code of correct matching.

List-I	*List-II*
(a) Forecasting	1. Optimal employment
(b) Inventorying	2. Development activities
(c) Anticipating manpower problems	3. Mathematical projections of industrial trends
(d) Planning programs	4. Projecting present resources into future

Codes:

	(a)	(b)	(c)	(d)
A.	2	1	4	3
B.	1	4	3	2
C.	4	2	1	3
D.	3	1	4	2

30. Which council was established in India by Government of India in the year 1966 to promote safety consciousness among workers in industries?

A. Factory Advise Council
B. National Safety Council
C. National Industrial Council
D. Safety Regulations Council

31. Assertion (A) : Recruitment is positive while selection is negative in its application.

Reasoning (R) : Recruitment aims at increasing the job seekers while selection rejects a large number of unqualified applicants.

Codes:

A. (A) is correct, but (R) is not correct.
B. Both (A) and (R) are correct, but (R) is not the right explanation of (A).
C. Both (A) and (R) are correct and (R) is the right explanation of (A).
D. Both (A) and (R) are incorrect.

32. Match the List-I with List-II relating to Social Security measures in India and indicate the code of correct matching.

List-I	*List-II*
(a) Social Assistance	1. Payable to workers in accidents & injuries during employment.
(b) Social Insurance	2. Covers individual risks primarily.
(c) Commercial Insurance	3. Maternity benefits.
(d) Workmen's Compensation	4. Provident Funds.

Codes:

	(a)	(b)	(c)	(d)
A.	3	4	2	1
B.	4	3	2	1
C.	4	3	1	2
D.	2	1	3	4

33. Match the following items of List-I with the items of List-II and indicate the code of correct matching.

List-I *(Name of Bank)*	*List-II* *(Year of establishment)*
(a) IFCI	1. 1981
(b) SIDBI	2. 1982
(c) NABARD	3. 1948
(d) EXIM Bank	4. 1990

Codes:

	(a)	(b)	(c)	(d)
A.	3	1	2	4
B.	4	2	3	1
C.	4	3	2	1
D.	3	4	2	1

34. With a view to encourage newer classes of entrepreneurs and bringing about wider dispersal of ownership and control of industrial undertakings, IDBI operates a special scheme for supplementing the equity contribution to projects made by small and new entrepreneurs. This scheme is known as

A. Bridge Loan Scheme
B. Soft Loan Scheme for Modernisation
C. Technical Development Fund Scheme
D. Seed Capital Assistance Scheme

35. Which one of the following is not the objective of UTI?

A. To give everyone a chance to indirectly own shares and securities in a large number of select companies.
B. To maximise mobilisation of people's savings by making insurance linked savings adequately attractive.
C. To channelize the pooled savings into productive outlets.
D. To mobilise savings of the community by offering savers the triple benefits of safety, liquidity and profitability of investments.

36. Under which of the following schemes, the IFCI procures equipment for an actual-user industrial concern by making payment to the machinery/equipment supplier, and then resells/transfers the equipment to the actual-user-industrial concern at the same cost, subject, however, to any liability arising out of taxes and other levies, being put to the account of the actual user industrial concern?

A. Equipment Credit Scheme
B. Equipment Procurement Scheme
C. Equipment Finance Scheme
D. Scheme of Equipment Leasing

37. Match the items of List-I with List-II and denote the code of correct matching.

List-I	*List-II*
(*a*) International Bank for Reconstruction and Development	1. 1945
(*b*) International Finance Corporation	2. 1956
(*c*) Asian Development Bank	3. 1966
(*d*) Export-Import Bank of India	4. 1981

Codes:

	(*a*)	(*b*)	(*c*)	(*d*)
A.	1	2	3	4
B.	4	3	2	1
C.	1	3	2	4
D.	2	1	4	3

38. Assertion (A) : International Finance Corporation (IFC) contributes to increase sustainable agriculture opportunities, improve health and education and increase access to financing for micro finance and business client.

Reasoning (R): The IFC has focused on a set of development goals to ensure that its projects are expected to achieve the target.

Codes:

A. Both (A) and (R) are correct, but (R) is not the correct explanation of (A).
B. Both (A) and (R) are correct and (R) is the correct explanation of (A).
C. (A) is correct but (R) is incorrect.
D. Both (A) and (R) are incorrect.

39. Under TRIPS Agreement, patent is granted subject to which of the following?

(*a*) The product or the process is new one.
(*b*) It contains an inventive step.
(*c*) It is capable of industrial application for 15 years from the grant of the patent.
(*d*) It is capable of industrial application for 20 years from the grant of the patent.

Codes:

A. Only (*a*) and (*b*)
B. Only (*a*), (*b*) and (*c*)
C. Only (*a*), (*b*) and (*d*)
D. Only (*a*) and (*d*)

40. Statement I : During the period of prosperity, prices of goods fall and income of people go down. These changes in incomes of the people and prices of goods affect exports and imports of goods and thereby influence the balance of payments.

Statement II : Secular disequilibrium in balance of payments occur because of short-run changes in an economy.

Codes:

A. Statement I is correct, but II is incorrect.
B. Statement II is correct, but I is incorrect.
C. Both the statements I and II are correct.
D. Both the statements I and II are incorrect.

41. Which of the following correctly depicts differences between a merger and an acquisition of stock?

A. An acquisition of stock results in the total absorption of a firm whereas a merger does not.
B. In case of a merger, the firm can deal directly with the shareholders of the acquired firm but not in the case of acquisition of stock.
C. Shareholders of the acquired or target firm vote by their response to a tender offer in an acquisition of stock but cast a formal vote in a merger situation.
D. A formal vote by the acquired firm's shareholders is required for an acquisition of stock but not for a merger.

42. Match the items of List-I with the items of List-II and indicate the correct code:

List-I	*List-II*
(*a*) Value Added Model	1. It is based on the process audit thereby evaluating the corporate social performance.
(*b*) Bauer-Fenn Model	2. It takes into account the social benefits and costs.
(*c*) ABT Model	3. It reflects the impact of a business enterprise on its employees, the local community and the public at large.
(*d*) ESTs Model	4. It shows the value added by the value of production of socially desirable outputs minus the value of socially undesirable effects.

Codes:

	(*a*)	(*b*)	(*c*)	(*d*)
A.	1	2	3	4
B.	4	1	3	2
C.	4	3	2	1
D.	4	1	2	3

43. You are given the following information:

	X-Security	*Market-Security*
Expected Return (%)	15	12
Standard Deviation of the return (%)	6	4
Coefficient of Correlation between the returns	0.4	

What is the Beta-coefficient of security X to measure its systematic risk?

Codes:

A. 1 B. 1.5
C. 0.6 D. 0.4

44. Lease which includes a third party (a lender) is known as

A. Direct lease
B. Sales and lease-back
C. Leveraged lease
D. Inverse lease

45. Which of the following activities should be shown separately in the cash flow statement prepared as per Accounting Standard-3?

(*a*) Cash flow from borrowing activities.
(*b*) Cash flow from operating activities.
(*c*) Cash flow from financing activities.
(*d*) Cash flow from investing activities.
(*e*) Cash flow from miscellaneous activities.

Codes:

A. (*a*), (*b*), (*c*) B. (*a*), (*c*), (*e*)
C. (*b*), (*c*), (*d*) D. (*a*), (*b*), (*e*)

46. Which of the following statements is correct?

A. The oldest stock exchange of India is OTCEI.
B. Sensex is an index number of 30 scrips.
C. In book-building process, the price of the security is announced by the company.
D. Futures and options in shares are traded at all stock exchanges of India.

47. Match the items of List-I (Developers) with the items of List-II (Methods of measuring human assets) and indicate the correct code:

List-I	*List-II*
(*a*) Hekimian and Zones	1. Stochastic Rewards Valuation Model

(*b*) Hermanson	2. Competence Bidding Method
(*c*) R. Likert	3. Adjusted Discounted Future Wages Model
(*d*) Flamholtz	4. Behavioural Variables Model

Codes:

	(*a*)	(*b*)	(*c*)	(*d*)
A.	1	2	3	4
B.	2	3	4	1
C.	4	3	1	2
D.	3	4	2	1

48. The concept of achieving maximum profits through increased consumer satisfaction for raised market share focuses on

A. Product B. Selling
C. Customer D. Production

49. Which of the following is not a measure for quality of service for consumer?

A. Responsiveness B. Competition
C. Empathy D. Tangibility

50. Which of the following is not a targeting strategy?

A. Standardization B. Differentiation
C. Focus D. All of the above

51. Match the items of List-I with items of List-II and indicate the code of correct matching.

List-I	***List-II***
(*a*) Real Needs	1. Expecting good service from car dealer.
(*b*) Unstated Needs	2. Customer expects to be seen by his friends as value-oriented savvy consumer.
(*c*) Delight Needs	3. Customer wants car at low operational cost and not initial cost.
(*d*) Secret Needs	4. Customer receives free insurance on purchase of car.

Codes:

	(*a*)	(*b*)	(*c*)	(*d*)
A.	3	1	4	2
B.	1	3	2	4
C.	2	4	1	3
D.	4	2	1	3

52. **Statement I** : The firm should "stick to its niching" but not necessarily to its niche.

Statement II : Multiple niching is not preferable to single niching.

Codes:

A. Both the Statements are true.
B. Both the Statements are false.
C. Statement I is true, but Statement II is false.
D. Statement II is true, but Statement I is false.

53. A descriptive thought that a person holds about something is called

A. Belief B. Learning
C. Attitude D. Perception

54. Deferment, Autonomy of object, use of the common place, involvement/detachment and use of metaphor are description of which of the following technique?

A. Brainstorming B. Synectics
C. Forced Relationship D. Attribute listing

55. Which of the following statements are correct? Indicate the correct combination:

(*a*) A well motivated individual tends to experience a low degree of morale.
(*b*) A group characterized by a high state of morale may or may not have a high degree of motivation to perform.
(*c*) Morale can always be built up by a combination of rewards and penalties.
(*d*) Organizations, in general, devote more direct attention towards motivational aspects of people's behaviour than the aspects of morale.

Codes:

A. (*a*), (*b*) and (*d*) B. (*c*) and (*d*) only
C. (*a*), (*c*) and (*d*) D. (*b*) and (*d*) only

56. **Assertion (A)** : Organizations are increasingly getting de-jobbed.

Reasoning (R) : Jobs are becoming more amorphous and more difficult to define.

Codes:

A. Both (A) and (R) are correct, but (R) is not the right explanation of (A).
B. Both (A) and (R) are not correct.
C. (A) is correct, but (R) is incorrect.
D. (A) is correct and (R) is right explanation of (A).

57. Which of the following statements relating to incentive payments is correct?

A. In Halsey incentive plan, bonus paid to a worker is equal to 50 per cent of time saved divided by rate per hour.

B. In Rowan incentive plan, bonus paid to employee is equal to the proportion of the time saved to the standard time.

C. In Taylor's differential piece rate system, a worker whose output exceeds standard output is paid 100 per cent of piece rate and a worker whose output falls short of standard is paid only 50 per cent of piece rate.

D. The Rowan incentive plan is the base of all other incentive, payment plans.

58. Match the most common rating errors made during performance appraisal with their right explanations. Indicate the code of correct matching.

List-I (Common Rating Errors)	*List-II (Description)*
(*a*) Leniency	1. Subjective assessment
(*a*) Halo error	2. One aspect of individual's performance influence his entire performance
(*c*) Spillover effect	3. Past performance appraisal ratings unjustifiably influencing current ratings.
(*d*) Rater effect	4. Favouritism and stereotyping

Codes:

	(*a*)	(*b*)	(*c*)	(*d*)
A.	1	2	3	4
B.	2	3	4	1
C.	3	4	2	1
D.	4	3	2	1

59. Which one of the following industrial relations approach believes in state intervention via legislation and the creation of industrial tribunals as supporting management's interest rather than ensuring a balance between the competing groups?

A. Unitary approach

B. Pluralistic approach

C. Marxist approach

D. Judiciary approach

60. What is the term coined for the system of communication and consultation, either formal or informal, by which workers of an organization are kept informed, as and when required, about the affairs of the undertaking and through which they express their opinion and contribute to decision-making process of management?

A. Collective Bargaining

B. Empowerment

C. Workers' participation in management

D. Welfare state

61. Match the items of List-I with those of List-II with regard to operative functions of HRM and indicate the code of correct matching.

List-I	*List-II*
(*a*) Procurement	1. Performance appraisal
(*b*) Development	2. Discipline
(*c*) Integration	3. Induction
(*d*) Maintenance	4. Personnel research

Codes:

	(*a*)	(*b*)	(*c*)	(*d*)
A.	2	1	4	3
B.	1	4	3	2
C.	3	1	2	4
D.	2	3	1	4

62. What is the popular term used for that type of option in Foreign Exchange Market which provides the holder the right to purchase or sell foreign currency at the most favourable exchange rate realized over the life of the option?

A. Forward reversing option

B. Preference option

C. Look-back option

D. Basket option

63. What is the term used popularly for the situation when a speculator, being dominant in the market, expects a drop in the value of a particular currency and he begins selling it forward?

A. International Fisher Effect

B. Bandwagon Effect
C. Interest Rate Parity Effect
D. Relative Version Effect

64. Identify the correct statement.

A. The Maastricht Treaty signed in February 1992 renamed European Community (EC) as European Economic Community (EEC).
B. The main objective of the formation of ASEAN Free Trade Area in 1993 was to soften the restrictions on the movement of professionals in the region and helping poorer countries.
C. The SAARC is a regional grouping scheme among Six South Asian Countries.
D. The European Union, including European Monetary Union, was the biggest and most important regional integrative scheme.

65. Match List-I with List-II relating to benefits and cost of economic integration and identify the code representing correct matching.

List-I	***List-II***
(*a*) Trade creation	1. Movement of production and resources in opposite directions.
(*b*) Trade diversion	2. Become active when a member country does not augment export but simply shifts its imports from low cost source to high cost source.
(*c*) Trade deflection	3. Shifting the locus of production from high cost to low cost centre within the union.
(*d*) Polarisation forces	4. Goods produced in a third country entering a free trade area through a member country having lower tariff.

Codes:

	(*a*)	(*b*)	(*c*)	(*d*)
A.	2	3	4	1
B.	2	4	1	3
C.	3	1	4	2
D.	3	2	1	4

66. What is the situation referred to as, amongst the following, when intra-region trade is duty free but there is variation in tariff structure for import from a third country?

A. Customs Union B. Common Market
C. Free Trade Area D. Economic Union

67. Which of the following statements is not correct relating to comparison of FDI with trade?

A. Only one market can better be served with differentiated products.
B. FDI overcomes tariff and transport cost involved in trade.
C. It reduces financial risk through greater diversification.
D. It creates harmonious political relations.

68. Match List-I with List-II regarding the grouping of Multi-national Corporations and identify the code representing correct matching.

List-I (Type of MNC)	***List-II (Basic feature)***
(*a*) Ethnocentric firms	1. Maintain a balance in home and host market oriented policy.
(*b*) Polycentric firms	2. Seldom distinguish between domestic & global operation policies.
(*c*) Geo-centric firms	3. Follow a host market policy.

Codes:

	(*a*)	(*b*)	(*c*)
A.	3	1	2
B.	3	2	1
C.	2	3	1
D.	2	1	3

69. An equipment was acquired at a cost of ₹ 10 lacs and was put to use in Scientific Research. After one year of research the equipment was brought into another business of the assessee. For charging depreciation, Block of Assets shall be increased by

A. ₹ 10 lacs.
B. Market value of the equipment on the date it was brought into another business.
C. Cost or market value of the equipment, whichever is less.
D. NIL.

70. If an assessee is engaged in the business of growing and manufacturing tea in India, the portion of agricultural income in that case shall be

A. 100% B. 60%
C. 50% D. 40%

71. Which of the following statements is not correct?

A. X is an individual assessee. He pays a monthly rent of ₹ 10,000 pm. He cannot deduct tax at source.

B. On salaries, tax is deducted at source according to provisions of Sec. 192.

C. No tax is deducted at source in respect of interest on securities issued by a domestic company.

D. Bank will deduct tax at source @ 10% if bank fixed deposit's interest credit is more than ₹ 10,000 in a year.

72. X donated ₹ 20,000 to a charitable institution, which is eligible for deduction u/s 80 G, during the financial year 2015-16. His total income during the period was ₹ 1,50,000. How much deduction he can claims u/s 80 G?

A. ₹ 7,500 B. ₹ 10,000
C. ₹ 15,000 D. ₹ 20,000

73. X is employed in a private company at a salary of ₹ 70,000 per month and ₹ 10,000 per month as dearness pay. He received ₹ 2,000 per month as house rent allowance. He paid ₹ 2,500 per month as house rent. What is the exempted portion of house rent allowance?

A. ₹ 2,500 B. ₹ 2,000
C. ₹ 1,000 D. NIL

74. Surcharge is payable by an individual where the total income exceeds

A. ₹ 10 lacs B. ₹ 25 lacs
C. ₹ 50 lacs D. ₹ 1 crore

75. Which one of the following statements is not correct?

A. A person may not have assessable income but still be an assessee.

B. In some cases, the assessment year and the previous year can be same.

C. An Indian company is always resident assessee.

D. Surcharge is additional tax calculated on total income.

ANSWERS

1	2	3	4	5	6	7	8	9	10
D	B	*	D	B	D	B	D	C	B
11	**12**	**13**	**14**	**15**	**16**	**17**	**18**	**19**	**20**
C	C	B	D	B	D	C	D	D	C
21	**22**	**23**	**24**	**25**	**26**	**27**	**28**	**29**	**30**
B	C	A	C	A	C	D	B	D	B
31	**32**	**33**	**34**	**35**	**36**	**37**	**38**	**39**	**40**
C	A	D	D	B	B	A	B	C	*
41	**42**	**43**	**44**	**45**	**46**	**47**	**48**	**49**	**50**
C	B	C	C	C	B	B	C	B	*
51	**52**	**53**	**54**	**55**	**56**	**57**	**58**	**59**	**60**
A	C	A	B	D	D	B	A	C	C
61	**62**	**63**	**64**	**65**	**66**	**67**	**68**	**69**	**70**
C	C	B	D	C	C	A	C	D	B
71	**72**	**73**	**74**	**75**					
C	A	D	D	D					

EXPLANATORY ANSWERS

1. Strategic management may be understood as the process of formulating, implementing and evaluating business strategies to achieve organisational objectives. A more comprehensive definition of strategic management is: *that set of managerial decisions and actions that determine the long-term performance of a corporation. It includes environmental scanning, strategy formulation, strategy implementation and evaluation and control. The study of strategic management, therefore, emphasises monitoring and evaluating environmental opportunities and threats in the light of a corporation's strengths and weaknesses.*

   Strategic management, therefore, involves four steps as given below:

   1. Analyse the opportunities and threats or constraints that exist in the external environment.
   2. Formulate strategies that will match the organisation's strengths and weaknesses with the environmental threats and opportunities.
   3. Implement the strategies.
   4. Evaluate and control activities to ensure that the organisation's objectives are achieved.

2. **Departmental Undertaking**

   Departmental undertakings are public sector enterprises created, managed and controlled by concerned ministries. They are considered part or an extension of the ministry itself and form an integral part of functioning of government. The important areas of concerned ministry are converted into departments and these departments are assigned the duties of looking after those areas.

   Examples of Departmental Undertakings are: Post and Telegraph, The Indian Railways, Defence Production Department, Chittaranjan Locomotives Works etc.

   Statutory Corporation

   A public corporation is a corporate body created by special act of Parliament or legislative assembly. This special Act defines the powers, duties, privileges and pattern of management of the corporation. The entire equity capital is also provided by the government. **Statutory corporation is a corporate person and has the capacity of acting in its own name.** Hence, it has the power of government along with the operational flexibility of private enterprises. Statutory corporations are suitable for enterprises providing public utility services like transportation, insurance, warehousing, banking etc.

   Examples of Statutory Corporation are: Air India, Damodar Valley Corporation, Life Insurance Corporation of India, Indian Airlines Corporation, Industrial Finance Corporation of India, etc.

   Government Company

   Like any other joint stock company, the government company is registered under the provisions of the Companies Act, 1956. According to Section 617 of the Companies Act, **a government company is a company in which not less than fifty one per cent of the paid-up share capital is held by central or state governments.**

   The shares of these companies are purchased in the name of President of India. These companies function on commercial lines and compete with companies in private sector. Operational and financial autonomy helps this form of government undertaking to function effectively, competitively and efficiently.

   Examples: Hindustan Machine Tools, State Trading Corporation of India, Hindustan Aircraft, BHEL, Sindri Fertilisers Ltd.

4. According to N.R. Narayana Murthy– Corporate foremost social responsibility is to create maximum shareholders value working

under the circumstances where it is fair to all its stakeholders, workers, consumers, the community, government and the environment. He points out that by living in harmony with the community and environment around us and not cheating out customers and workers, we might not gain anything in the short-run, but in the long-term it means greater profits and shareholders value.

6. **Meaning of Reissue of Shares :** Reissue of shares is merely a sale of Forfeited Shares and not an allotment of shares. The forfeited shares can be reissued as per the provisions of the Articles of the Company.

Reissue Price of Forfeited Shares : The forfeited shares can be re-issued at par, premium or discount.

Minimum Reissue Price : The Reissue Price of forfeited shares must be at least equal to the difference between the Paid up Value of Reissued Shares and the Amount Forfeited on Reissued Shares. In other words, Reissue Price must not be less than the amount unpaid on Forfeited Shares.

Maximum Amount of Discount which may be allowed on Reissue

Case	*Maximum Permissible Discount on Reissue*
(*a*) When the Forfeited Shares were originally issued at par or at a premium	The amount credited to Forfeited Share Account.
(*b*) When the Forfeited Shares were originally issued at a discount	The amount credited to 'Forfeited Share Account *plus* the amount of original discount.

7. **Consolidation of Accounts**

Holding companies attach to their own balance sheet a consolidated balance sheet to give a more detailed and clear picture of their subsidiaries. Such a consolidated balance sheet is definitely more useful than the separate balance sheet of each of the subsidiaries. For this purpose, the whole group is regarded as one undertaking and hence the total assets as well as liabilities of all the companies in the group are presented in one balance sheet. The profit and loss account of the whole group is also presented in a similar fashion.

Accounting Standard-21 on 'Consolidated Financial Statements' issued by the Institute of Chartered Accountants of India on consolidation of accounts prescribes the accounting principles to be followed by the holding companies in consolidating the balance sheet and profit and loss account with that of the financial statements of the subsidiaries.

8. When the firm is not in a position to pay off the outgoing partner/the deceased partner the debt due to him or her due to the shortage of fund, the amount payable may be transferred to a loan account. In such circumstances, any one of the following methods may be adopted for settlement of the outgoing partner's claim:

1. Repayment of loan by a number of instalments including interest during subsequent years.
2. Repayment of outgoing partner's claim under Section 37 of the Partnership Act.
3. Repayment of outgoing partner's claim/capital balance (after all adjustments) by way of an annuity.

According to this arrangement, an annuity (a fixed amount) is paid to the retired or deceased partner by an agreement for some years or for the lifetime. The amount due to the outgoing partner is transferred to the Annuity Suspense Account. The interest is given at a certain rate on the outstanding balances and any surplus or deficit arising after final payment of the annuity will be distributed among the remaining partners according to their profit-sharing ratio.

10. $\because$ $$TC = 200 + 5Q + 2Q^2 \quad ...(i)$$

We have noted above that an optimum level of output is one that equalizes AC and MC. In other words, at optimum level of output, AC = MC. Given the cost function in Eq. (*i*),

$$AC = \frac{200 + 5Q + 2Q^2}{Q}$$

$$= \frac{200}{Q} + 5 + 2Q \qquad ...(ii)$$

and $$MC = \frac{\partial TC}{\partial Q} = 5 + 4Q \qquad ...(iii)$$

By equating AC and MC equations, *i.e.*, Eqs. (*ii*) and (*iii*), respectively, and solving them for Q, we get the optimum level of output. Thus,

$$\frac{200}{Q} + 5 + 2Q = 5 + 4Q$$

$$\frac{200}{Q} = 2Q$$

$$2Q^2 = 200 \text{ or } Q = 10$$

Thus, given the cost function (*i*), the optimum output is 10.

11. Here, P = 500 − 5Q ...(*i*)

Since, P = 500 − 5Q, by substitution, we get

$$TR = (500 - 5Q)Q$$

$$TR = 500Q - 5Q^2 \qquad ...(ii)$$

Now MR function can be obtained by differentiating the TR-function given in Eq. (*ii*)

$$MR = \frac{\partial TR}{\partial Q} = 500 - 10Q$$

Likewise, MC function can be obtained by differentiating the TC function

$$TC = 50 + 20Q + Q^2$$

$$MC = \frac{\partial TC}{\partial Q} = 20 + 2Q$$

Now that MR and MC functions are known, profit maximising output can be easily obtained. The profit maximising output can be obtained by equating the MR and MC functions given above and finding the solution as shown below.

$$MR = MC$$

$$500 - 10Q = 20 + 2Q$$

$$480 = 12Q$$

$$Q = 40$$

The output Q = 40 is the profit maximising output.

13. Standard Deviation of the Mean

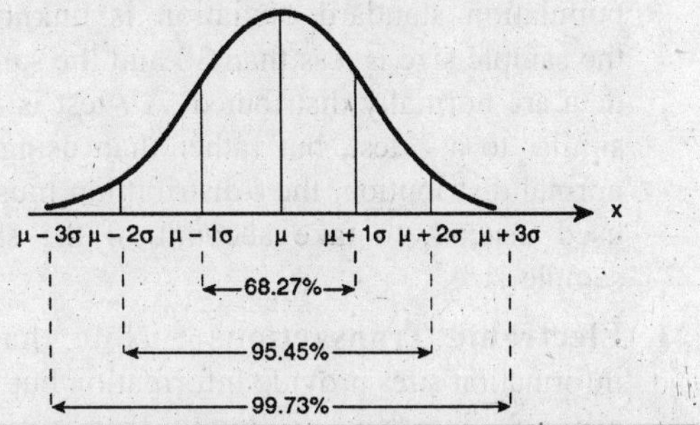

Percent	99.73%	99%	99.45%	95%	90%	80%	68.27%
No. of ± σ's	3.00	2.58	2.00	1.96	1.645	1.28	1.00

Fig. : *Percentage of Area Under the Normal Distribution*

14. ∵ Unexplained Variation = 36%

∴ Explained Variation = 64%

Coefficient of Determination = $r^2 = .64$

∴ $r = \sqrt{.64} = 0.80$.

15. Standard Error of Difference between Two Means

The standard error of difference between two means is the standard deviation of a theoretical distribution of differences between means.

Procedure : Let there be two treatments. Find their means $\bar{x}_1$ and $\bar{x}_2$. Obtain the difference between the means $(\bar{x}_1 - \bar{x}_2)$. If we do this infinite number of times, we would get a distribution of differences between sample means of two groups. These differences would be normally distributed. Their mean would be the true average differences between the populations of two treatments, and the standard deviation of this distribution is called standard error of difference between two means. It is calculated as:

$$\sigma\bar{x} - \bar{y} = \sqrt{(\sigma^2{}_x / n_x + \sigma^2{}_y / n_y)}$$

where, σ^2_x = variance of population x;

σ^2_y = variance of population y,

n_x = sample size of x

and n_y = sample size of y.

16. **The *t*-Test :** A *t*-test is only used when the population standard deviation is unknown, the sample size is less than 30 and the sample data are normally distributed. A *t*-test is very similar to a Z-test, but rather than using the normal distribution, the *t*-distribution must be used instead, to take account of the small sample size.

21. **Electronic Transactions :** Note that e-information sites provide information but they are not designed to make transactions. Creating the capability of making purchases directly from a firm's website is known as electronic transactions (or e-transactions), the next higher level of electronic networking. E-transactions involve more interaction and feedback than e-information. Both consumer product marketers and business-to-business sellers make use of e-transactions.

22. **Self Concept :** Each of us has a self image. This self image is based on the person(s) whom we see as our role models. We then act and behave like these role models, believing that we are them. This affects our dress, hair styles, and almost every other thing including our table manners. This concept of self image has been termed as self concept.

    The self image could be an individual's own perceived image (this may, even be termed as ideal self image) and actual image based on how others perceive the individual. There could, at times, be a conflict between the two. All individuals try to bring about a congruence between these two sets of their images. Recent researches in consumer behaviour, have concluded that a large number of products like credit cards, automobiles, readymade garments, designerware, cosmetics, and perfumes are bought because of this variable. Often a demographic variable like income is not important in purchase decisions for these products.

23. **Media Selection**

    A highly creative advertising copy may not be able to deliver results if there is an improper selection of media or a poor media plan and strategy. In evolving a media plan, decisions have to be taken in respect to the following media factors.

    (*a*) **Media Class :** The refers to the type of medium which is most appropriate to the product and copy. This includes newspapers, magazines, television, radio, billboards, and direct mail.

    (*b*) **Media Vehicles :** They provide the immediate environment for the advertisement. For example, within newspapers, *The Times of India* is a media vehicle, in television Zee TV's Antakshari is the vehicle.

    (*c*) **Media Option :** This refers to the size (full or half page), length (30 or 60 seconds), colour or location (like front page, bottom right, or prime time 9.00 p.m.) of the advertisement in the media vehicle.

    (*d*) **Scheduling and Timing :** This refers to how media options are scheduled over a period of time. The strategic options here are—

    (*i*) *Flighting :* That is, periods of total inactivity.

    (*ii*) *Continuous:* That is, even distribution of advertising during a time period.

    (*iii*) *Pulsing :* That is, a continuous base augmented by intermittent bursts of heavy advertising.

24. **Matrix Form :** Integrating specialist functions of product management with the line function of sales is a major challenge to the top management. Often, this is achieved through a matrix form of organization which appears as shown in Figure.

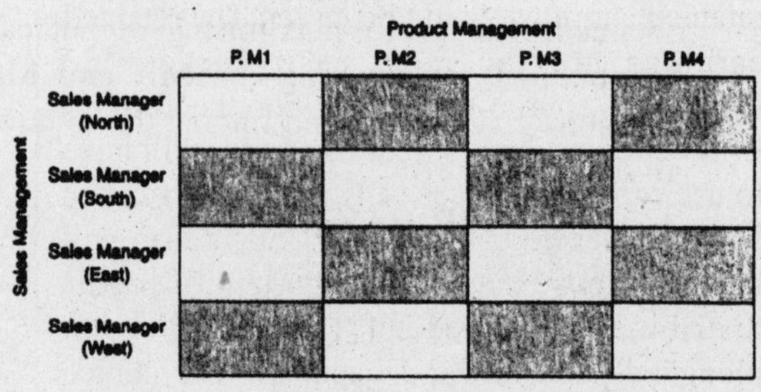

    As may be inferred here, products are profit centres and each product manager relates with each zonal sales manager. This helps in pushing each product across the country and also in evolving product strategies for different geographical areas. In fact, tactical changes are apparent in pushing products across different regions without diluting the core product and communication strategy. This form induces competition among product managers.

The problem often faced here is that of prioritising. Often the sales manager does not know which product he or she should push. This obviously creates room for politicking. Also, as one sales manager remarked on how he settled the issue of prioritisation, 'I listen to the product manager who makes the maximum noise'. It is not uncommon to come across such situations. Another problem of a matrix organisation is that it is difficult to reconcile objectives like profit across products, segments, or regional sales.

25. Dividend policy means the broad approach according to which every year it is determined how much of the net profits are to be distributed as dividend and how much are to be retained in the business. Thus, the dividend policy divide the net profits or earnings after taxes into two parts:

1. Earnings to be distributed as dividend,
2. Earnings retained in the business.

Since dividends are distributed out of the profits, there exists an inverse relationship between dividends distributed and retained earnings in the business. If larger net profits are distributed as dividends, retained earnings would be less and on the contrary, if lesser profits are distributed as dividends, the retained earnings would be larger. The retained earnings are the most easily accessible significant source of finance for the firm. A firm which declares larger dividends will have to use external sources of financing to finance its investment opportunities. Thus, a firm will have to choose between the portion of profits distributed as dividends and the portion ploughed back into the business. The choice is called the dividend policy and it will have its effect on both the long-term financing and the wealth of shareholders.

27. Risk-Adjusted Discount Rate vs Certainty-equivalent : The certainty-equivalent approach recognizes risk in capital budgeting analysis by adjusting estimated cash flows and employs risk-free rate to discount the adjusted cash flows. On the other hand, the risk-adjusted discount rate adjusts for risk by adjusting the discount rate. It has been suggested that the certainty equivalent approach is theoretically a superior technique over the risk-adjusted discount approach because it can measure risk more accurately.

The risk-adjusted discount rate approach will yield the same result as the certainty-equivalent approach if the risk-free rate is constant and the risk-adjusted dicount rate is the same for all future periods.

28. Modigliani-Miller Approach

Modigliani-Miller maintained that under a given set of assumptions, the capital structure and its composition has no effect on the value of the firm. They observed that the financial leverage does not matter and the cost of capital and value of firm are independent of capital structure. There is nothing, which may be called the optimal capital structure. They, in fact, restated the NOI approach and added the behavioural justification for their model. The MM model is based on the following assumptions:

- The capital markets are perfect and complete information is available to all the investors free of cost. The implication of this assumption is that investors can borrow and lend funds at the same rate and can move quickly from one security to another without incurring transaction costs.
- The securities are infinitely divisible.
- Investors are rational and well informed about the risk-return of all the securities.
- All investors have same probability distribution of their expected future earnings.
- There is no corporate income tax. (However, this assumption was relaxed later).
- The personal leverage and the corporate leverage are perfect substitutes.

On the basis of these assumptions, the MM model stated that:

1. The total value of a firm is equal to the capitalized value of operating earnings of the firm. The capitalization is made at a rate appropriate to the risk class of the firm.
2. The total value of a firm is independent of financing mix, *i.e.,* the financial leverage.
3. The cut-off rate for investment decision of a firm depends on the risk class to which the firm belongs, and thus is not affected by the financing pattern of this investment.

29. The components of manpower planning could be briefly stated as follows:

(*a*) **Forecasting** future requirements of manpower, either in terms of mathematical projections of trends in the economy and developments in the industry or of judgemental estimates based upon specific future plans of the company.

(*b*) **Inventorying** present manpower resources and analysing the degree to which these resources are employed optimally.

(*c*) **Anticipating manpower problems** by projecting present resources into the future and comparing them with the forecasting of requirements, to determine their adequacy both quantitatively and qualitatively.

(*d*) **Planning** the necessary programmes of recruitment, selection, training, deployment, utilization, transfer, promotion, development, motivation and compensation so that future requirements will be met.

30. National Safety Council : National Safety Council was set up in 1966 to promote safety consciousness among workers to prevent accidents, minimize dangers and mitigate human suffering. The Council arranges programmes, lectures, seminars and conferences on safety, conducts educational campaigns to arouse consciousness among employers and workers to collect educational and information data. The foundation day of the National Safety Council, *i.e.,* 4th March is celebrated every year as National Safety Day.

31. Table : Distinction between Recruitment and Selection

Recruitment	Selection
1. Recruitment technically precedes selection.	Selection follows recruitment.
2. Recruitment refers to the process of identifying and encouraging potential candidates to apply for jobs in the organisation.	Selection involves choosing the best out of those recruitment.
3. Recruitment is positive as it aims at increasing the number of job seekers (applications) for wider choice or increasing the selection ratio.	Selection, on the other hand, is said to be negative in its application inasmuch as it rejects a large number of unqualified applicants in order to identify those who are suitable for the jobs.
4. In sum, recruitment involves searching.	Selection involves comparing those already searched.

32. Workmen compensation insurance is designed for the benefit of

- Industries/factories
- Commercial establishments
- Contractors in construction, mining, quarrying, repairs, maintenance, etc.

Workmen compensation (WC) insurance policy is a liability insurance policy. It protects the assured (employer) against the legal liabilities to employees arising out of the work done during the course of employment. The workmen compensation insurance covers the employer's liability, if injury is caused to a workman by accident arising out of and in the course of his employment.

Scope: The Workmen Compensation Insurance Policy covers, the employer who is under statutory obligation to take care of and protect the employee in case he/she is injured while on the job or falls ill due to the nature of the job or occupational hazard or could not work due to a job-related injury. Wherever the injury was caused by an accident and if there was permanent disablement which lower the capacity to earn in the type of job the workman was employed at the time of accident, workmen compensation insurance pays the medical bills and provides a portion of the employee's salary/wage until he/she can return to work. The policy also protects the insured from legal liabilities against injury or death of any of his employee who is a "workman" as defined by the Workmen's Compensation Act, 1923.

The Workmen Compensation Insurance Policy provides four main types of benefits to the eligible workers:

- Full payment medical expenses
- Disability income
- Payment for rehabilitation services
- Death benefits.

34. Seed Capital Assistance : Since 1976 IDBI has introduced Seed Capital Assistance Schemes. The objective of these schemes is to help such entrepreneurs who have technically feasible and economically viable projects and possess the enterprise but lack adequate financial resources to put in the promotor's contribution. Thus, Seed Capital Assistance Scheme is intended to make-up or supplement promotor's contribution.

35. The Unit Trust of India (UTI), a public sector investment institution, was established in 1964, under the Unit Trust of India Act, 1963. The share capital of the UTI was subscribed by the IDBI, LIC, SBI and its subsidiaries and other scheduled banks and financial institutions. Sale of units and other savings schemes are the main sources of funds for the Trust.

The main objective of the UTI is to mobilise the savings of the community and channelise them into productive corporate investments so as to provide for growth and diversification of the economy. It is at the same time intended to provide the facility for an equity type of investment to the large and growing number of investors in the small and medium income groups. The UTI mobilises funds from the public through a number of schemes. The savings thus mobilised is channelled into productive activities by the Trust by investing them in the shares and debenture of industrial concerns.

It is one of the main intentions of the UTI to provide opportunity to investors belonging to small and medium income groups to indirectly participate in the ownership of shares and debentures of joint stock companies.

For small investors, the UTI offers the advantages of:

(*i*) considerably reduced risk since funds are invested in a balanced and well distribute portfolio;

(*ii*) the benefit of expert management;

(*iii*) a steady income; and

(*iv*) liquidity.

36. Since 1988-89, IFCI introduced two new schemes of financial assistance, viz., a scheme for equipment leasing and a scheme for equipment procurement. Under the Equipment Leasing Scheme. IFCI provides equipment (imported or indigenous) to the existing industrial concerns by financial lease. Under the Equipment Procurement Scheme, IFCI agrees to procure equipment and then to resell the same, by endorsement of documents, to the eligible existing industrial concerns in the corporate of co-operative sectors.

41. Merger : A merger refers to the absorption of one firm by another. The acquiring firm retains its name and identity, and it acquires all of the assets and liabilities of the acquired firm. After a merger, the acquired firm ceases to exist as a separate business entity.

Here are two important points about mergers:

1. A merger is legally straightforward and does not cost as much as other forms of acquisition. It avoids the necessity of transferring title of each individual asset of the acquired firm to the acquiring firm.

2. The stockholders of each firm must approve a merger. Typically, votes of the owners of two-thirds of the shares are required for approval. In addition, shareholders of the acquired firm have *appraisal rights*. This means that they can demand that the acquiring firm purchase their shares at a fair value. Often the acquiring firm and the dissenting shareholders of the acquired firm cannot agree on a fair value, which results in expensive legal proceedings.

Acquisition of Stock

A second way to acquire another firm is to purchase the firm's voting stock in exchange for cash, shares of stock, or other securities. This process may start as a private offer from the management of one firm to another. At some point the offer is taken directly to the selling firm's stockholders, often by a tender offer. A tender offer is a public offer to buy shares of a target firm. It is made by one firm directly to the shareholders to another firm. The offer is communicated to the target firm's shareholders by public announcements such as newspaper advertisements. Sometimes a general mailing is used in a tender offer. However, a general mailing is difficult because the names and addresses of the stockholders of record are not usually available.

The following factors are involved in choosing between an acquisition of stock and a merger:

1. In an acquisition of stock, shareholder meetings need not be held and a vote is not required. If the shareholders of the target firm do not like the offer, they are not required to accept it and need not tender their shares.
2. In an acquisition of stock, the bidding firm can deal directly with the shareholders of a target firm via a tender offer. The target firm's management and board of directors are bypassed.
3. Target managers often resist acquisition. In such cases, acquisition of stock circumvents the target firm's management. Resistance by the target firm's management often makes the cost of acquisition by stock higher than the cost by merger.
4. Frequently a minority of shareholders will hold out in a tender offer, and thus the target firm cannot be completely absorbed.
5. Complete absorption of one firm by another requires a merger. Many acquisitions of stock end with a formal merger.

43. $\because \quad \beta_x = \dfrac{r_{xm}\sigma_x\sigma_m}{(\sigma_m)^2}$

Here, β_x = Beta coefficient for security X

σ_x = Standard deviation of the possible returns for security X

σ_m = Standard deviation of the possible returns for market security

r_{xm} = correlation coefficient between returns

Here, $r_{xy} = 0.4$, $\sigma_x = 6$, $\sigma_m = 4$

$$\therefore \quad \beta_x = \frac{0.4 \times 6 \times 4}{4 \times 4} = 0.6$$

44. Leverage Lease : Leverage lease is a lease arrangement in which a third party (lender) is involved besides the lessor and the lessee. The lessor borrows a part of the purchase cost (say, 80%) of the asset from the third party (lender). The asset so purchased, is held as a security against the loan. The lender is paid off from the lease rentals directly by the lessee. The surplus after meeting the claim of the lender is received by the lessor (owner). The lessor (owner) is entitled to a depreciation allowance associated with the leased asset.

45. Cash Flow Statement as Prescribed in AS-3

Accounting Standard (Revised)-3 (AS-3) as issued by the ICAI in March 1997, prescribes a specific format for presenting a Cash Flow Statement. Preparation of Cash Flow Statement as per AS-3 is mandatory in respect of accounting periods that are commencing on or after 01 April 2001 (*i.e.*, from the accounting year 2001-02) for the following enterprises:

(*i*) Enterprises that have a turnover of more than ₹ 50 crores during a financial year.

(*ii*) Companies whose shares or debts are listed on a recognized stock exchange in India (Cash Flow Statement of listed companies shall be presented under indirect method only as prescribed in AS-3).

AS-3 prescribes two forms of presentation of Cash Flow Statement, which are as follows:

(*i*) **Direct Method :** Under this method, the Net Cash Flow from Operating Activities is to be calculated directly by deducting the cash outflows from the Operating Activities from Cash Inflows from the Operating Activities.

(*ii*) **Indirect Method :** Under this method, the Net Cash Flow from Operating Activities is to be calculated indirectly by adding back all the non-operating and non-cash items debited and by deducting all the non-operating and non-cash items credited to the Profit & Loss A/c for an accounting year with the Net Profit for that year.

For both the methods, 'Cash' refers to cash in hand, cash at bank (demand deposits alone) and short-term investments or marketable securities. All these combinedly are termed as 'Cash and Cash Equivalents'.

Under both the above methods, Net Cash Flows from the operating, investing and Financing Activities are to be separately shown in the Cash Flow Statement. In other words, *Cash Flow Statement prepared under both the above methods is subdivided into the following three parts:*

(*i*) Net Cash Flows from Operating Activities.
(*ii*) Net Cash Flows from Investing Activities.
(*iii*) Net Cash Flows from Financing Activities.

46. The BSE started publishing an index number of equity prices from 2-1-1986, with the base year 1978-79. It is known as "Sensex". Sensex means sensitive index of 30 scrips selected from the market. The selection is made on the basis of the market activity. The Sensex component of the scrips are always "hot cakes" in the market. They enjoy much status and earn good reputation. Entering into Sensex component means, recording the event in Guinness Book of Records. But it has an outstanding achievement to the corporate sector. Sensex is always depends upon the market situations. The movement is based upon many factors such as government policy, global market movements, bullion market prices, political unrest in the country, sectoral fluctuations, fiscal policy of the government, Central Government budget, railway budget, natural calamities, rainfall, agricultural production and other many factors.

48. Five differences between marketing and selling are given below:

1. **Focus :** The main focus of marketing is on achieving maximum satisfaction of customer's needs and wants. On the other hand, the main focus of selling is on the transfer of ownership and possession of goods from seller to buyer.
2. **Scope :** Selling is a part of marketing which is much wider term.
3. **Mode of profits :** Marketing seeks to increase profits through customer satisfaction. But selling seeks to maximize profits through sales maximisation.
4. **Start and end :** Marketing begins much before the product is produced and continues even after it is sold. On the contrary, selling begins after the product is produced and ends with its sale.
5. **Strategy :** Marketing uses integrated marketing efforts involving strategies for product, price, promotion and distribution. But selling involves efforts like promotion and persuasion.

49. After an extensive research programme, Parasuraman *et al.* (1988) came up with an instrument to measure service quality and termed it SERVQUAL. This is the most frequently used, yet also a highly debated, measurement instrument for service quality. According to this study, the five dimensions of service quality from the customer's perspective are reliability, assurance, tangibility, empathy and responsiveness, and the acronym RATER can be used to denote them:

- **Reliability** refers to the ability of the service provider to deliver its services dependably and consistently.
- **Assurance** refers to the competence of the firm, the courtesy of the employees and the ability to create trust and confidence in customers' minds.

- **Tangibility** considers the service provider's physical facilities, employee appearance and equipment.
- **Empathy** refers to the willingness of the service provider to help customers and provide prompt customer service.
- **Responsiveness** reflects the willingness of employees to help and provide service in a timely fashion.

52. Market-Nicher Strategies : A market-nicher is a company whose products serve market sub-segments not being pursued by firms with larger shares of a given market segment. Many of America's high- and midsize-growth companies follow this strategy. Smart niching companies can attain high margins at low volumes by specializing with respect to a narrowly defined set of end users, vertical levels, geographical areas, product features, quality/price combinations, and so fourth. Kotler says that a company might stick to its niching but not necessarily to its niche. Multiple niching is preferable to pursuing a single niche. An example is Nike who has succeeded by creating new niches continually—cycling, walking, hiking, cheerleading, etc. There is a possible downside however as the firm may be attacked by larger firms once they notice the niches are successful.

53. Beliefs and Attitudes

Through doing and learning, people acquire beliefs and attitudes. These, in turn, influence their buying behaviour. A belief is a descriptive thought that a person has about something. Beliefs may be based on real knowledge, opinion, or faith and may or may not carry an emotional charge. Marketers are interested in the beliefs that people formulate about specific products and services, because these beliefs make up product and brand images that affect buying behaviour. If some of the beliefs are wrong and prevent purchase, the marketer will want to launch a campaign to correct them. People have attitudes regarding religion, politics, clothes, music, food and almost everything else. **Attitude** describes a person's relatively consistent evaluations, feelings and tendencies toward an object or idea. Attitudes put people into a frame of mind of liking or disliking things, of moving toward or away from them. Our camera buyer may hold attitudes such as "Buy the best," "The Japanese make the best electronics products in the world," and "Creativity and self-expression are among the most important things in life." If so, the Nikon camera would fit well into the consumer's existing attitudes.

Attitudes are difficult to change. A person's attitudes fit into a pattern, and to change one attitude may require difficult adjustments in many others. Thus, a company should usually try to fit its products into existing attitudes rather than attempt to change attitudes. For example, McDonald's does not sell beef and pork products in India as it is a religious taboo to eat beef or pork. In some predominantly vegetarian states like Gujarat, it even declares its franchises as "pure vegetarian" and does not offer non-vegetarian products. Moreover, considering the family orientation of Indian consumers, it calls its restaurants "family restaurants," unlike in the United States, where they are called "fast-food outlets." By matching today's attitudes about religion and family orientation, McDonald's has become a great success in the category of fast-food restaurants in India.

54. Synectics : William J.J. Gordon felt that Osborn's brainstorming session produced solutions too quickly, before a sufficient number of perspectives have been developed. Gordon decided to define the problem so broadly that group would have no hint of the specific problem. Gordon described five principles underlying the synectics methods:

Deferment : Look first for viewpoint rather than solutions.

Autonomy of Object : Let the problem take on a life of its own.

Use of Common Place : Take advantage of the familiar as a springboard to the strange.

Involvement/Detachment : Alternate between entering into the pariculars of the problem and standing back from them, in order to see them as instances of a universal.

Use of Metaphor : Let apparently irrelevant, accidental things suggest analogies that are sources of new viewpoints.

56. The relevance of job analysis is becoming vague more now than even before. Firms are becoming increasingly *de-jobbed*—jobs are becoming more amorphous and more difficult to define.

De-jobbing is the result of several changes taking place in business today. Firms need to keep pace with a number of revolutionary forces—accelerating product and technological changes, globalised competition, deregulation, political instability, demographic changes, trend towards a service-oriented society, and the arrival of the information age. Forces like these have changed the playing field on which firms compete. This rapid change has dramatically increased threats for firms. They need to be responsive, flexible, and capable of competing in a global market place.

57. Rowan's Plan

Minimum wages to a worker is also guaranteed under this incentive plan. It differs from Halsey plan only with regard to determination of bonus. In *Rowan's plan,* bonus is calculated on the basis of proportion of time saved.

Let, S = standard time for a job

T = actual time taken by a worker to do the same job

R = hourly wage rate

Working earning as per Rowan's plan

$$= T \times R + \left(\frac{S-T}{S}\right) \times T \times R$$

Merits of Rowan's plan

The following are the merits of Rowan's plan:

1. This incentive plan guarantees minimum wages to all workers.
2. Management shares a percentage of the bonus.

Demerits of Rowan's plan

The demerits of Rowan's plan are as follows:

1. It is relatively difficult to understand and operate this plan.
2. This plan discourages efficient workers as their total earnings reduce if they save more time.
3. Workers do not like management to share their bonus.
4. This is called *regressive plan* because wages increase with output, but at a decreasing rate.

58. Performance appraisals are subject to a wide variety of inaccuracies and biases referred to as 'rating errors'. These errors occur in the rater's observations, judgement, and information processing, and can seriously affect assessment results. The most common rating errors are leniency or severity, central tendency, halo effect, rater effect, primacy and recency effects, perceptual set, performance dimension behaviour, spill over effect, and status effect.

1. **Leniency or Severity Error :** Leniency or severity on the part of the rater makes the assessment subjective. Subjective assessment defeats the very purpose of performance appraisal.
2. **Halo Error :** A halo error takes place when one aspect of an individual's performance influences the evaluation of the entire performance of the individual. In an organisation, an halo error occurs when an employee who works late constantly might be rated high on productivity and quality of output as well as on motivation. Similarly, an attractive or popular employee might be given a high overall rating. Rating employees separately on each of a number of performance measures and encouraging raters to guard against the halo effect are the two ways to reduce the halo effect. It is also referred as 'logic error'.
3. **Rater Effect :** This includes favouritism, stereotyping, and hostility. Excessively high or low scores are given only to certain individuals or groups based on the rater's attitude towards the ratee, not on actual outcomes or behaviours. Sex, age, race state and friendship biases are examples of this type of error.

4. **Spillover Effect :** This refers to allowing past performance appraisal ratings to unjustifiably influence current ratings. Past ratings, good or bad, result in similar rating for the current period although the demonstrated behaviour does not deserve the rating, good or bad.
5. **Status Effect :** It refers to overrating of employees in higher-level job or jobs held in high esteem, and underrating employees in lower-level job or jobs held in low esteem.
6. **Horn Effect :** It is the opposite of Halo Effect. It implies rating a person low in one quality, which in turn influences the rater to give a lower than deserved rating in other qualities. For example, a subordinate is seem coming late to the office (punctuality) may be inferred as poor dependability (does not complete his work in time).

60. Workers' Participation Management

Participation and involvement of workers in the management of industry is practiced in most countries of the world. Workers participation in management has come to stay in both developed and developing countries. Worker's participation is also known as "labour participation" or "employee participation in management". In Germany it is known as co-determination, while in Yugoslavia it is called "self management". The International Labour Organisation has been encouraging member nations to promote the scheme of worker's participation in management. The concept of worker's participation in management is considered as a machanism where workers have a say in the decision-making process of an enterprise.

According to Davis, "It is a mental and emotional involvement of a person in a group situation which encourages him to contribute to goals and share responsibilities in them."

According to Mamoria defines it is a system of communication and consultation either formal or informal by which employees of an organisation are kept informed about the affairs of the undertaking and through which they express their opinion and contribute to management decisions.

62. Look-Back Option: A look-back option gives its holder the right but not an obligation to buy or sell foreign currency at the most favourable exchange rate realized over the life of the option. The strike price of a look-back option is not known till the expiration date. The buyer of a look-back call will buy it at the lowest price and the seller of a look-back put will sell it at the highest price realized during the lifetime of the option. Since this is beneficial to the owner, a higher premium has to be paid.

63. Bandwagon Effect : When a speculator being dominant in the market expects a drop in the value of a particular currency, he begins selling it forward. The other speculators follow the lead. As a result, the currency tends to depreciate despite favourable impact of inflation and interest rate. This factor played a crucial role in the depreciation of rupee during the closing months of 1997.

65. Regional Economic Integration

Trade creation when locus of production shifts from a high cost point to a low cost point.

Trade diversion when locus of production moves from a low-cost point to a high cost point.

Trade deflection when outside goods enter a free trade area through a member country having lowest tariff.

Polarisation of benefits from integration moving away from the weaker partner in favour of the economically stronger partner, leading to intra-region inequality.

66. Free Trade Area : In a free trade area, which involves the least integration, member countries abolish tariff and non-tariff barriers on intra-region trade but they are free to impose tariff on their import from a third country at different rates. Thus tariff abolition is a preferential economic arrangement that aims at encouraging intra-region trade. European Free Trade Association (EFTA) and

North American Free Trade Agreement (NAFTA) are apposite examples of this type of economic integration.

67. FDI is better than trade because:

1. Different markets can better be served with differentiated products.
2. FDI overcomes tariff and transport cost involved in trade.
3. It is a better means to acquire resources from the host county.
4. It reduces financial risk through greater diversification.
5. It creates harmonious political relations.

68. Based on the strategic features, MNCs are grouped as ethnocentric, polycentric, and geocentric. Ethnocentric firms are those that adopt home market oriented policy and seldom distinguish between domestic operation and global operation policies. On the other extreme, polycentric firms operate in foreign countries just to cater to the demand in those countries. This means that they follow a host market oriented policy. Between the two extremes, geocentric firms maintain a balance between the home market and host market oriented policies. They are in fact closer to real situations. It is this behavioural distinction that influences Punnett and Ricks to differentiate between a multi-domestic company and a global company. The former is concerned more with the market of the host country where it operates. The latter is concerned with the global market. It finds the world as a single market and plans to cater it through integrated operations.

69. Assets used in business after it ceases to be used for Scientific Research – Section 43(1) Income Tax Act

In cases where the depreciable asset is used for the business after it ceases to be used for scientific research related to that business and a deduction has been allowed in respect of expenditure on scientific research under Section 35, the actual cost of the asset to the assessee should be taken to be the original cost to the assessee minus the amount of any deduction under Section 35 of the Act, originally allowed.

Note: If capital expenditure for scientific research is incurred after 31-3-1967, the whole of such expenditure is deductible for the relevant previous year. Hence, the cost of such asset for depreciation purposes shall be nil.

70. Under the Income Tax Act, 1961 of rule 8 deals with Income derived from sale of tea grown and manufactured by the seller in India. Here, neither total income will be taken as agricultural income nor as business income. The total Income from sale of tea grown and manufactured divides into 40% of Business Income and 60% of agricultural income.

How to Separate Agricultural and Non-Agricultural Income?

Income from Crop	Agricultural Income	Non-agricultural Income	Rule
Growing and manufacturing Tea in India	60%	40%	8
Manufacture of Latex or latex based crepes or brown crepes or technically specified block rubbers	65%	35%	7A
Coffee grown and cured by seller	75%	25%	7B(1)
Coffee grown, cured, roasted and ground by the seller in India with or without mixing chicory or other flavouring ingredients.	60%	40%	7B(1A)

73. Section 10(13A) & Rule 2A. House Rent Allowance (Partially Exempted Allowance) : House rent allowance (HRA) is given to employee for payment of rent. If no rent is paid exemption is not available. But if rent is paid over 10% of salary then exemption is allowed under section 10(13A).

Previous Paper (Solved)

UGC-NET-Junior Research Fellowship & Assistant Professor Exam

Commerce, July-2016

PAPER-II

Note: *This paper contains **fifty** (**50**) objective type questions of **two** (**2**) marks each. **All** questions are compulsory.*

1. For the following statements of Assertion (A) and Reasoning (R) indicate the correct code from the alternatives given:

Assertion (A) : Liberalization means corporatisation of departmental undertakings and public undertakings.

Reasoning (R) : Freedom to public sector undertakings to access capital market.

Codes :

A. Both (A) and (R) are true and (R) is correct explanation of (A).
B. Both (A) and (R) are true but (R) is not a correct explanation of (A).
C. (A) is true but (R) is false.
D. (A) is false but (R) is true.

2. Match the items of List – I with List – II and indicate the correct code :

List – I	**List – II**
(*a*) Fiscal Policy	(*i*) Mitigation of National hazards
(*b*) Technology Policy	(*ii*) Balance of Payment
(*c*) Macro-Economic Policy	(*iii*) Fiscal Federalism
(*d*) Monetary Policy	(*iv*) Inflation

Codes :

	(*a*)	(*b*)	(*c*)	(*d*)
A.	(*i*)	(*ii*)	(*iii*)	(*iv*)
B.	(*iii*)	(*i*)	(*ii*)	(*iv*)
C.	(*iv*)	(*iii*)	(*i*)	(*ii*)
D.	(*ii*)	(*i*)	(*iv*)	(*iii*)

3. Which of the following factor is not directly responsible for slowing down the growth of infrastructure?

A. High level of perceived political risk.
B. High level of sunk cost.
C. High probability of time and cost over-run.
D. Introduction of competition in all sectors.

4. Out of the following which is not a major component of Gross Domestic Product (GDP)?

A. Personal Consumption Expenditure
B. Gross Private Domestic Investment
C. Net Personal Income
D. Net Exports

5. Which of the following is not a forum of Consumer Dispute Redressal System?

A. Local forum
B. District forum
C. State Forum (State Commission)
D. National Commission

6. X Ltd. purchased 70 per cent of the shares of Y Ltd. at a price of ₹ 1,00,000. Share capital of Y Ltd. was of ₹ 70,000 and its accumulated profits amounted to ₹ 90,000. What would be the amount of Minority Interest in the consolidated Balance Sheet?

A. ₹ 25,000 B. ₹ 70,000
C. ₹ 1,00,000 D. ₹ 40,000

7. Match the items in Column – I with the items in Column – II and indicate the correct code :

Column – I	**Column – II**
(*a*) Debt-Equity ratio	(*i*) $\frac{\text{Net profit before interest and tax}}{\text{Interest on long term loans}}$

(*b*) Proprietary ratio	(*ii*)	$\frac{\text{Equity share capital + Reserves}}{\text{Preference share capital + Interest bearing finance}}$
(*c*) Interest coverage ratio	(*iii*)	$\frac{\text{Long term debts}}{\text{Shareholder's Funds}}$
(*d*) Capital gearing ratio	(*iv*)	$\frac{\text{Shareholder's Funds}}{\text{Total Assets}}$

Codes :

	(*a*)	(*b*)	(*c*)	(*d*)
A.	(*i*)	(*ii*)	(*iii*)	(*iv*)
B.	(*iii*)	(*iv*)	(*i*)	(*ii*)
C.	(*iii*)	(*iv*)	(*ii*)	(*i*)
D.	(*ii*)	(*iii*)	(*iv*)	(*i*)

8. Ram and Shyam are partners in a firm with capital of ₹ 4,80,000 and ₹ 3,10,000, respectively. They admitted Ganesh as a partner with $\frac{1}{4}$th share of profit. Ganesh brings ₹ 3,00,000 as his capital. Ganesh's share of goodwill will be

A. ₹ 1,10,000 B. ₹ 27,500
C. ₹ 17,500 D. ₹ 70,000

9. Which of the following is a deferred revenue expenditure?

A. Legal expenses incurred on the purchase of land.
B. Expenses on a mega advertisement campaign while launching a new product.
C. Expenses incurred on installation of a new machine.
D. Wages paid for construction of an additional room in the building.

10. The amount of depreciation charged to Profit and Loss Account varies every year under :

A. Fixed instalment method
B. Annuity method
C. Diminishing balance method
D. Insurance policy method

11. Ordinal utility analysis of the consumer's behaviour is considered superior to the cardinal utility analysis mainly due to

A. assumption of the rationality of the consumer's behaviour.
B. possibility of the derivation of the consumer's demand.
C. bifurcation of price effects into income and substitution effects.
D. consideration of the available limited resources for satisfying consumer's demand.

12. For the following statements of Assertion (A) and Reasoning (R) indicate the correct code :

Assertion (A) : Price reduction normally leads to an increase in the demand for a commodity.

Reason (R) : Price reduction leads to the entry of new buyers of the commodity in the market.

Codes :

A. (A) is correct but (R) is not correct.
B. (A) is not correct but (R) is correct.
C. Both (A) and (R) are correct and (R) offers full explanation of (A).
D. Both (A) and (R) are correct but (R) does not offer full explanation of (A).

13. The minimum Long Run Average Cost (LAC) can be determined on a

I. LAC curve for a normal production function
II. LAC curve for a linear production function
III. Planning curve
IV. Envelope curve

Codes :

A. I II III B. II III IV
C. I III IV D. I II IV

14. Monopoly is not considered desirable from the point of view of the society mainly because the monopolist endeavours to

A. earn net revenue on sale of all goods including those involving no cost of production.
B. earn net revenue on sale of goods in short run as well as long run.
C. charge different prices for the same product from the different categories of buyers.

D. produce below economic capacity level when he exhibits satisfaction with normal profit only.

15. Product-line pricing strategy includes which combination of the following?

I. Public utility pricing
II. Complementary goods pricing
III. Spare parts pricing
IV. Load factor pricing

Codes :

A. I II III B. II III IV
C. I II IV D. I III IV

16. When the data are classified only on the basis of descriptive characteristics which cannot be quantified is known as

A. Geographical classification
B. Chronological classification
C. Qualitative classification
D. Quantitative classification

17. Which one of the following is a false description?

A. In a moderately asymmetrical distribution, the empirical relationship between Mean, Mode and Median suggested by Karl Pearson is: Mean – Mode = 3 (Mean – Median)
B. Coefficient of variation is an absolute measure of dispersion.
C. Measure of skewness indicates the direction and extent of skewness in the distribution of numerical values in the data set.
D. Kurtosis refers to the degree of flatness or peakedness in the region around the mode of a frequency curve.

18. Match the items of List – I with the items of List – II and indicate the code of correct matching :

List – I	**List – II**
(*a*) Coefficient of determination	(*i*) $\gamma_{xy}\dfrac{\sigma_x}{\sigma_y}$
(*b*) Spearman's Rank correlation coefficient	(*ii*) $1-\dfrac{6\Sigma d^2}{n(n^2-1)}$
(*c*) Regression coefficient of *x* on *y* variable	(*iii*) $\dfrac{\Sigma xy}{n\sigma_x\sigma_y}$
(*d*) Karl Pearson's formula of calculating γ	(*iv*) γ^2

Codes :

	(*a*)	(*b*)	(*c*)	(*d*)
A.	(*i*)	(*ii*)	(*iii*)	(*iv*)
B.	(*i*)	(*iv*)	(*ii*)	(*iii*)
C.	(*iv*)	(*iii*)	(*ii*)	(*i*)
D.	(*iii*)	(*ii*)	(*iv*)	(*i*)

19. **Statement – I :** When the null hypothesis is true but as per the hypothesis-testing, it is rejected, it is known as beta type error in hypothesis testing.

Statement – II : Chi-square test is exclusively a non-parametric test.

Codes :

A. Both the statements are true.
B. Both the statements are false.
C. Statement – I is true while Statement – II is false.
D. Statement – I is false while Statement – II is true.

20. Computers that recognize data as discrete signals are called?

A. Analog computers B. Digital computers
C. Hybrid computers D. Super computers

21. Herbert Simon's concept of administrative man assumes that

(*a*) He has satisfying approach in decision making rather than the maximising approach.
(*b*) He can make decisions without determining all possible alternatives.
(*c*) He is completely rational in decision making.

A. (*a*) only B. (*b*) only
C. Both (*a*) and (*b*) D. (*a*), (*b*) and (*c*)

22. Which of the following statement(s) is/are correct about scalar chain principle as given by Fayol?

(*a*) Each communication, going up or down, must flow through each position in the line authority.

(*b*) Chain of communication cannot be broken under any circumstances.

A. Only (*a*) is correct.
B. Only (*b*) is correct.
C. Neither (*a*) nor (*b*) is correct.
D. Both (*a*) and (*b*) are correct.

23. A mission statement should be

(*a*) Self-explanatory
(*b*) Elaborate
(*c*) Distinctive
(*d*) Feasible

Codes :

A. (*a*) only
B. (*a*) and (*b*)
C. (*a*), (*b*) and (*c*)
D. (*a*), (*c*) and (*d*)

24. Match List – I and List – II and indicate the correct code :

List – I	List – II
(*a*) Equity theory	(*i*) Motivation depends on ratios of inputs and outcomes of self and others.
(*b*) Vroom's theory	(*ii*) People are motivated to achieve a goal to the extent that they expect that certain action will help them to reach the goal.
(*c*) Porter and Lawler model	(*iii*) There exists a complex relationship among motivation, performance and satisfaction.
(*d*) Herzberg's theory	(*iv*) A challenging job that has opportunities for achievement, recognition, responsibility and growth will motivate employees.

Codes :

	(*a*)	(*b*)	(*c*)	(*d*)
A.	(*i*)	(*ii*)	(*iii*)	(*iv*)
B.	(*ii*)	(*i*)	(*iii*)	(*iv*)
C.	(*iii*)	(*ii*)	(*i*)	(*iv*)
D.	(*i*)	(*iii*)	(*ii*)	(*iv*)

25. Assertion (A) : 'Grapevine' tends to be more active during periods of change, excitement, anxiety and sagging economic conditions.

Reason (R) : Employees use this communication to fill in important information gaps and clarify management decisions.

Codes :

A. (A) is right and (R) is wrong.
B. (A) is wrong and (R) is right.
C. Both (A) and (R) are right and (R) explains (A).
D. Both (A) and (R) are right but (R) does not explain (A).

26. Which type of differentiation is used to gain competitive advantage through the way a firm designs its distribution coverage, expertise and performance?

A. Channel differentiation
B. Services differentiation
C. People differentiation
D. Product differentiation

27. Which one of the following is the most likely result of a marketing strategy that attempts to serve all potential customers?

A. All customers will be delighted.
B. Customer-perceived value will be increased.
C. The company will need to follow up with a demarketing campaign.
D. Not all customers will be satisfied.

28. Which of the following is not a primary activity in Michael Porter's value chain?

A. Inbound logistics
B. Operations
C. Outbound logistics
D. Procurement

29. Which of the following represents consistency of results when the test instrument is used repeatedly?

A. Validity
B. Reliability
C. Relativity
D. Sensitivity

30. Assertion (A) : Too many stimuli make a person accommodated to those sensations. Sensory adaptation is a problem that concerns many advertisers, which is why they try to change their advertising campaigns regularly.

Reason (R) : To cut through advertising clutter and to ensure that consumers perceive advertisement, marketers try to increase sensory input.

Codes :

A. (A) is right and (R) is wrong.
B. (A) is wrong and (R) is right.
C. Both (A) and (R) are right but (R) does not explain (A).
D. Both (A) and (R) are right and (R) explains (A).

31. Which of the following is not a feature of payback period method?

A. It is simply a method of cost recovery and not of profitability.
B. It does not consider the time value of money.
C. It does not consider the risk associated with the projects.
D. It is very difficult to calculate.

32. Which of the following is not a source of credit information of prospective customers?

A. Letter of Credit B. Bank Reference
C. Trade Enquiry D. Credit Bureau

33. The portion of earnings which is distributed among shareholders in the form of dividend is called

A. Proprietary Ratio
B. Earnings-yield Ratio
C. Payout Ratio
D. Retention Ratio

34. Select the correct code regarding motives for holding inventories by firms :

(*a*) Transaction motive
(*b*) Environmental motive
(*c*) Precautionary motive
(*d*) Speculative motive
(*e*) Competitive motive

Codes :

A. (*a*), (*b*), (*c*), (*d*) B. (*a*), (*b*), (*d*), (*e*)
C. (*a*), (*d*), (*e*) D. (*a*), (*c*), (*d*)

35. Which of the following formulae is related to operating leverage?

A. $\dfrac{\text{Contribution}}{\text{Operating Profit}}$

B. $\dfrac{\text{Sales} - \text{Variable Cost}}{\text{Earnings before Interest and tax}}$

C. $\dfrac{\text{Percentage change in EBIT}}{\text{Percentage change in sales}}$

D. All of the above

36. Which of the following is ***not*** true in case of HRM?

A. Employees are seen as an investment to be nurtured as well as a cost to be controlled.
B. Conflicts are dealt with by team members within their teams.
C. Preference is for collective bargaining of pay and working conditions.
D. Emphasis is on competitive pay and conditions to stay ahead of competitors.

37. Which one of the following is an advantage of Magazines as a source of recruitment?

A. Less expensive
B. Long lead time for advertisement placement
C. Reach a diverse audience
D. Many unmotivated applicants

38. Examine the following statements and choose the correct code :

Assertion (A) : Human Resource planning must always be seen within the strategy making context.

Reason (R) : Human Resource planning process removed from the realities of the business will be a waste of time.

Codes :

A. Both (A) and (R) are correct.
B. Both (A) and (R) are wrong.
C. (A) is correct, but (R) is wrong.
D. (A) is not correct, but (R) is correct.

39. Match the items of List – I with the items of List – II and select the correct code :

List – I	List – II
(*a*) Golden parachutes	(*i*) The right to purchase a stated number of shares of a company stock at today's price at some time in the future.
(*b*) Gain sharing	(*ii*) An incentive plan that engages employees in a common effort to achieve productivity objectives and share the gains.
(*c*) Stock-option	(*iii*) Payments companies make in connection with a change in ownership or control of a company
(*d*) Annual bonus	(*iv*) Plans designed to motivate short term performance of managers and are tried to company profitability.

Codes :

	(*a*)	(*b*)	(*c*)	(*d*)
A.	(*iii*)	(*i*)	(*ii*)	(*iv*)
B.	(*i*)	(*ii*)	(*iii*)	(*iv*)
C.	(*ii*)	(*iii*)	(*i*)	(*iv*)
D.	(*iii*)	(*ii*)	(*i*)	(*iv*)

40. Which one of the following is not a function of plant council?

A. Recommend and improve safety, health and welfare measures.

B. Determination of productivity schemes taking into consideration the local conditions.

C. Planning, implementation and review of monthly targets and schedules.

D. Review of working of shop level bodies.

41. Assertion (A) : "Banks globally are facing more challenges now, and Macro sustainability is a necessity but not sufficient for sustainable economic growth."

Reason (R) : "Putting regulations in place is only one part and their implementation is equally important for achieving growth and sustainability."

Codes :

A. (A) and (R) both are true and (R) is correct explanation of (A).

B. (A) and (R) both are true but (R) is not the correct explanation of (A).

C. (A) is true and (R) is false.

D. (A) is false and (R) is true.

42. Banking on telephone service includes :

(*i*) Automatic balance voice out

(*ii*) Inquiry all term deposit account

(*iii*) Direct cash withdrawl

(*iv*) Utility bill payment

(*v*) Voice out last five transactions

Codes :

A. (*i*), (*ii*), (*iii*) and (*v*)

B. (*i*), (*ii*), (*iv*) and (*v*)

C. (*ii*), (*iii*), (*iv*) and (*v*)

D. All (*i*), (*ii*), (*iii*), (*iv*) and (*v*)

43. Which one of the following banks currently ranks number one in India in terms of market capitalization?

A. State Bank of India

B. I.C.I.C.I. Bank

C. U.T.I. Bank

D. I.D.B.I. Bank

44. Match the items of Column – I with the items in Column – II and suggest the correct code :

Column – I	Column – II
(*a*) Interbank call market	(*i*) Money market
(*b*) Commercial Bills	(*ii*) Promissory note
(*c*) Commercial paper market	(*iii*) Short-term maturity
(*d*) Treasury bills	(*iv*) Government papers

Codes :

	(*a*)	(*b*)	(*c*)	(*d*)
A.	(*i*)	(*ii*)	(*iv*)	(*iii*)
B.	(*iii*)	(*i*)	(*ii*)	(*iv*)
C.	(*i*)	(*iii*)	(*iv*)	(*ii*)
D.	(*iv*)	(*iii*)	(*ii*)	(*i*)

45. Match the items of List – I with List – II with regard to the BASEL III norms and select the correct code :

List – I	**List – II**
(*a*) Pillar 1	(*i*) Supervisory review process
(*b*) Pillar 2	(*ii*) Market discipline
(*c*) Pillar 3	(*iii*) Minimum regulatory capital requirements based on Risk Weighted Assets (RWAs)

Codes :

	(*a*)	(*b*)	(*c*)
A.	(*i*)	(*ii*)	(*iii*)
B.	(*i*)	(*iii*)	(*ii*)
C.	(*iii*)	(*ii*)	(*i*)
D.	(*iii*)	(*i*)	(*ii*)

46. Assertion (A) : Comparative cost theory is static in character.

Reason (R) : Comparative cost theory is based on fixed supplies of factors of production.

Codes :

A. (A) is correct, but (R) is incorrect.
B. (R) is correct, but (A) is incorrect.
C. (A) and (R) both are correct, but (R) is not the correct explanation of (A).
D. (A) and (R) both are correct and (R) is the correct explanation of (A).

47. Match the items of List – I with List – II with regard to Balance of Payments equilibrium :

List – I	**List – II**
(*a*) Exchange control	(*i*) Exporters surrender foreign exchange to the central bank.
(*b*) Trade Policy Measure	(*ii*) Bank rate raised by the central bank
(*c*) Expenditure reducing policy	(*iii*) Reduction in foreign exchange rate
(*d*) Expenditure switching policy	(*iv*) Enhancing exports by granting subsidies

Codes :

	(*a*)	(*b*)	(*c*)	(*d*)
A.	(*i*)	(*iv*)	(*ii*)	(*iii*)
B.	(*i*)	(*ii*)	(*iii*)	(*iv*)
C.	(*iii*)	(*ii*)	(*iv*)	(*i*)
D.	(*iv*)	(*iii*)	(*ii*)	(*i*)

48. Which among the following is closely associated with intellectual property rights?

A. GATS
B. TRIMS
C. TRIPs
D. MFN

49. What is not correct about International Development Association (IDA)?

(*a*) Following earthquake in 2015, IDA has helped Nepal rebuild and recover.
(*b*) IDA ranks as the highest performing multilateral development bank in 2016.
(*c*) IDA is a subsidiary bank of IBRD.
(*d*) India has procured highest amount of international loan from IDA.

Codes :

A. (*a*) and (*b*)
B. (*c*)
C. (*d*)
D. (*a*) and (*c*)

50. As per the Foreign Trade Policy 2015-2020, a three star export house should have :

A. Export performance (FOB/FOR) of US \$ 100 million during current and previous two years.
B. Export performance (FOB/FOR) of US \$ 500 million during current and previous two years.
C. Export performance (FOB/FOR) of US \$ 1000 million during current and previous two years.
D. Export performance (FOB/FOR) of US \$ 2000 million during current and previous two years.

ANSWERS

1	2	3	4	5	6	7	8	9	10
A	B	D	C	A	*	B	B	B	C
11	**12**	**13**	**14**	**15**	**16**	**17**	**18**	**19**	**20**
C	D	C	D	B	C	B	*	B	B
21	**22**	**23**	**24**	**25**	**26**	**27**	**28**	**29**	**30**
C	A	D	A	C	A	D	D	B	D
31	**32**	**33**	**34**	**35**	**36**	**37**	**38**	**39**	**40**
D	A	C	D	D	C	C	A	D	A
41	**42**	**43**	**44**	**45**	**46**	**47**	**48**	**49**	**50**
A	B	A	B	D	D	A	C	C	A

* Errors might be crept in question

EXPLANATORY ANSWERS

3. Development of proper infrastructure is vital for economic growth of any country. Investors will like to put the capital only in those countries where there is developed infrastructure. Infrastructure consists of many things such as road, railway, port and harbour, airport, electricity, telecommuni-cation, water supply etc. Development of infrastructure is capital intensive and gestation period is high. At the same time return on capital in case of infrastructure projects is small as well as slow. Hence, investors are shy in investing capital in infrastructure projects unless some special incentives and privileges are provided.

Special features of infrastructure projects

(*i*) Large Capital requirement

(*ii*) High sunk cost. A large proportion of the cost has to be irrevocably committed upfront before the project becomes operative

(*iii*) Long gestation periods

(*iv*) Returns are slow to pass in

(*v*) Availability of foreign funds is poor

(*vi*) Sector is sensitive to political environment and policy changes

(*vii*) The services produced are non tradable. The excess services generated can not be stored or exported and deficiency in service can not be met with by imports except for certain exceptions

No single solution applies to different projects as characteristics is different from sector to sector. What applies to road sector does not apply to railways and what applies to railways can not apply to telecommunications sector as the capital requirements are different and so is the method of revenue collection.

4. GDP has four components: personal consumption expenditures, gross private domestic investment, government purchases of goods and services, and net exports of goods and services. The largest component, by a wide margin, is personal consumption expenditures.

5. The National Consumer Disputes Redressal Commission, India is a quasi-judicial commission in India which was set up in 1988 under the Consumer Protection Act of 1986. This Act was enacted to better protect the interests of consumers by creating an alternative disputes resolution mechanism exclusively for consumers. The Act provides for a three-tier approach in resolving consumer disputes. There are three levels of consumer courts called District Consumer Disputes Redressal Forum (District Forum), State Consumer Disputes Redressal Commission (State Commission), and National Consumer

Disputes Redressal Commission (National Commission).

District Forum and State Commission are formed by states with the permission of the Central Government while the National Commission is formed by the Central Government. These courts have not taken away the jurisdiction of the civil courts but have provided an alternative remedy.

The National Commission is the top most layer in the three-level hierarchy of the consumer courts. It was constituted in the year 1988. National Consumer Disputes Redressal Commission's head office is in New Delhi. The commission is headed by a sitting or retired judge of the Supreme Court of India.

7. Different Ratios at Glance

1. Balance Sheet Ratios:

(*a*) Current Ratio $= \dfrac{\text{Current Assets}}{\text{Current Liabilities}}$

(*b*) Liquid/Quick/Acid Test Ratio

$$= \frac{\text{Current Assets} - \text{Stock}}{\text{Current Liabilities} - \text{Bank Overdraft}}$$

(*c*) Proprietary Ratio $= \dfrac{\text{Proprietors's Fund}}{\text{Total Assets}}$

(*d*) Fixed Asset Proprietorship Ratio

$$= \frac{\text{Fixed Assets}}{\text{Proprietor's Fund}}$$

(*e*) Debt-Equity Ratio $= \dfrac{\text{Long-term Loan}}{\text{Proprietor's Fund}}$

(*f*) Capital Gearing Ratio

$$= \frac{\text{Preference Share Capital} + \text{Long-term Loans}}{\text{Equity Shareholders' Fund}}$$

(*g*) Fixed Asset Ratio $= \dfrac{\text{Fixed Assets}}{\text{Proprietors' Fund}}$

(*h*) Share Capital to Reserves and Surplus

$$= \frac{\text{Share Capital}}{\text{Reserves \& Surplus}}$$

2. Revenue Statement Ratios:

(*a*) Gross Profit Ratio $= \dfrac{\text{Gross Profit}}{\text{Sales}} \times 100$

(*b*) Net Profit Ratio

$$= \frac{\text{Net Profit after Tax}}{\text{Sales}} \times 100$$

(*c*) Operating Ratio

$$= \frac{(\text{Cost of Good Sold} + \text{Other Operating Expenses})}{\text{Sales}} \times 100$$

(*d*) Stock Turnover/Velocity Ratio

$$= \frac{\text{Cost of Goods Sold}}{\text{Average Stock}}$$

(*e*) Operating Profit Ratio

$$= \frac{\text{Operating Profit}}{\text{Net Sales}} \times 100$$

(*f*) Contribution Sales Ratio (*i.e.*, P/V Ratio)

$$= \frac{\text{Contribution}}{\text{Sales}} \times 100$$

(*g*) Operating Leverage $= \dfrac{\text{Contribution}}{\text{EBIT}}$

(*h*) Financial Leverage $= \dfrac{\text{EBIT}}{\text{EBT}}$

(*i*) Combined Leverage $= \dfrac{\text{Contribution}}{\text{EBT}}$

(*j*) Interest Coverage Ratio $= \dfrac{\text{EBT}}{\text{Interest}}$

(*k*) Dividend Coverage Ratio

$$= \frac{\text{EBT}}{\text{Total dividend}}$$

3. Mixed/Composite Ratio:

(*a*) Debtors' Velocity/Turnover Ratio

$$= \frac{\text{Credit Sales}}{\text{Receivables}}$$

(*b*) Creditors' Velocity/Turnover Ratio

$$= \frac{\text{Credit Purchases}}{\text{Payables}}$$

(*c*) Fixed Asset Turnover Ratio

$$= \frac{\text{Turnover}}{\text{Fixed Assets}}$$

(*d*) Working Capital Turnover Ratio

$$= \frac{\text{Cost of Goods Sold}}{\text{Working Capital}}$$

(*e*) Total Asset Turnover Ratio

$$= \frac{\text{Turnover}}{\text{Total Assets}}$$

(*f*) Capital Turnover Ratio $= \frac{\text{Turnover}}{\text{Capital Employed}}$

(*g*) Return on Capital Employed/Investment

$$= \frac{\text{Net Profit before Interest \& Tax}}{\text{Capital Employed}} \times 100$$

(*h*) Return on Net Worth

$$= \frac{\text{Net Profit after Interest \& Tax}}{\text{Net Worth}} \times 100$$

(*i*) Return on Equity Shareholders' Fund

$$(\text{ROE}) = \frac{\text{Net Profit after Interest \& Tax} - \text{Preference Dividend}}{\text{Equity Shareholders' Fund}} \times 100$$

(*j*) Earnings per Share (EPS)

$$= \frac{\text{Net Profit after Tax \& Preference Dividend}}{\text{No. of Equity Shares}}$$

(*k*) Dividends per Share (DPS)

$$= \frac{\text{Total Equity Dividend for a Year}}{\text{No. of Equity Shares}}$$

(*l*) Dividend Payout Ratio (D/P Ratio)

$$= \frac{\text{DPS}}{\text{EPS}} \times 100$$

(*m*) Price Earning Ratio (P/E Ratio)

$$= \frac{\text{MPS}}{\text{EPS}} \times 100$$

(*n*) Debt Service Coverage Ratio

$$= \frac{\text{Cash Profit before Interest \& Tax}}{\text{Interest on Loan + Instalment of Loan Due}}$$

8. On the basis of Ganesh's capital, total capital of the firm should be 12,00,000 (300000 × 4).

But the actual capital of the firm is 1090000.

Hence, goodwill = 1200000 − 1090000

= 110000

∴ Ganesh's Share of Goodwill

$$= 110000 \times \frac{1}{4} = 27500.$$

9. Deferred Revenue Expenditure: Deferred Revenue Expenditure is that expenditure which yields benefits which extend beyond a current accounting period, but to relatively a short period as compared to the period for which a capital expenditure is expected to yield benefits. Such expenditure should normally be written-off over a period of 3 to 5 years. The examples of such, expenditure include heavy Advertising Campaign, Research and Development Expenditure.

10. Reducing instalment method: This method is also known as diminishing balance method or written down value method. Under this method, a fixed percentage is written off every year on the book value of the asset at the beginning of the year (original cost less depreciation provided till date). As the book value or written down value will be diminishing each year, the depreciation charged in each instalment will also be diminishing. For example, if the cost of the machinery is ₹ 50,000 and depreciation is @ 10% each year, then the depreciation of the first year will be ₹ 5,000. Next year, the book value is ₹ 45,000, so, the depreciation is only ₹ 4,500 (10% of ₹ 4,500) and so on. Thus, the amount of depreciation goes on decreasing and, therefore, the book value of asset will not become zero after its working life.

Since the depreciation written off each year is on the reduced balance of asset, the amount charged to Profit and Loss Account will be less and less as years go by. And, at the same time, the amount spent on repairs and renewals will be more and more as the asset becomes older and older. This method can be applied to plant and machinery where repairs and heavy additions are made, extensions are quite frequent, and the asset need not to be reduced to zero.

Merits: It tends to give a fairly even charge of depreciation against revenue each year.

1. As and when additions are made to the asset, fresh calculations of depreciation are not necessary.
2. This method is recognised by the Income Tax authorities in India.

Demerits:

1. In subsequent years, the original cost of the asset is altogether lost sight of and the asset can never be reduced to zero.
2. This method does not take into consideration the asset as investment, and the interest.

11. Cardinal utility analysis does not distinguish between the income effect and the substitution effect of the price change. We know that when the price of a good falls, the consumer becomes better off than before, that is, a fall in price of a good brings about an increase in the real income of the consumer. In other words, if with the fall in price the consumer purchases the same quantity of the good as before, then he would be left with some income. With this income he would be in a position to purchase more of this good as well as other goods. This is the income effect of the fall in price on the quantity demanded of a good. Besides, when the price of a good falls, it becomes relatively cheaper than other goods and as a result the consumer is induced to substitute that good for others. This results in the increase in the quantity demanded of that good. This is the substitution effect of the price change on the quantity demanded of the good.

With the fall in price of a normal good, the quantity demanded of it rises because of income effect and substitution effect. But marginal utility analysis does not make clear the distinction between the income and the substitution effects of the price change. In fact, Marshall and other exponents of cardinal utility analysis ignored income effect of the price change by assuming the constancy of marginal utility of money. Thus, marginal utility analysis does not tell us about how much quantity demanded increases due to income effect and how much due to substitution effect as a result of the fall in price of a good. J.R. Hicks rightly remarks, "that distinction between income effect and substitution effect of a price change is accordingly left by the cardinal theory as an empty box which is crying out to be filled."

13. In the long run, all costs are variable. The long-run average cost curve is the envelope of a series of short-run average cost curves. If returns to scale are increasing, long-run average cost (LAC) will be decreasing. If returns to scale are decreasing, LAC will be increasing. The long-run cost functions are used for planning the optimal scale of plant size.

14. Because in Monopoly the demand curve is downward sloping, its point of tangency with the ATC curve will not and cannot be at the lowest level of average cost. It means that even when long-run adjustments are complete, firms art not operating at a level that permits the lowest average cost of production—the efficient scale of the firm. The existing plant, even though optimal for the equilibrium volume of output, is not used to capacity; that is, excess capacity exists at that level of output. Excess capacity occurs when the firm produces below the level where average total cost is minimized.

15. **Product-line pricing:** If sales of one product are linked to sales of another, one product may be priced low in order to stimulate sales, with the linked product being priced high in order to maximise profit. An example is the vehicle spare parts market, while the cars are cheap, the spare parts are expensive.

16. **Qualitative Classification:** In qualitative classification, data are classified on the basis of descriptive characteristics or on the basis of attributes like sex, literacy, region, caste, or education, which cannot be quantified. This is done in two ways:

(*i*) Simple classification: In this type of classification, each class is subdivided into two sub-classes and only one attribute is studied such as: male and female; blind and not blind, educated and uneducated, and so on.

(*ii*) Manifold classification: In this type of classification, a class is subdivided into more than two sub-classes which may be sub-divided further.

19. When we test a hypothesis, we may commit one of two types of errors; α error, or Type I error, the probability of rejecting a true hypothesis; or β error, or Type II error, the probability of accepting a false hypothesis. As the probability of Type I error decreases, the probability of Type II error increases, and vice versa. In most cases, a researcher is trying to show that there is a significant difference (between two means, for instance); that is, the researcher hopes to obtain statistically significant evidence that a null hypothesis is false.

A researcher can increase the probability of rejecting a null hypothesis by testing at a lower level (increasing α), but the cost of this is to make more likely the rejection of a true null hypothesis.

20. A computer is a device which accepts data, performs appropriate operations on this data and then provides the results. Where the input data is in the form of discrete signals which represent numerical values, it is a digital computer. If the data is in the form of continuously varying quantities such as voltage, it is an analogue computer. The digital computer has virtually replaced the analogue computer and will therefore be considered in more detail.

The use of computers for measurement, monitoring and various forms of control is then described by reference to actual systems. Finally simulation, and in particular a diesel plant simulator, is explained in some detail.

21. Simon proposed the model of administrative man as against the model of economic man who takes the maximising decisions. According to him, the administrative man.

(*a*) in choosing between alternatives, tries to satisfy or look for the one which is satisfactory or good enough.

(*b*) recognises that the world he perceives is a drastically simplified model of the real world.

(*c*) can make his choice without first determining all possible alternatives and without ascertaining that these, in fact, are all the alternatives because he satisfies, rather than maximise, and

(*d*) is able to make decisions with relatively simple rule of thumb because he treats the world as rather empty.

Thus, the 'satisficing' administrative man of Simon is different from the 'optimising' economic man, evolved by the classical economic theorists. He ends up with 'satisficing' as he does not have the ability to 'optimise' (maximise).

22. According to Fayol, scalar chain refers to the chain of superiors ranging from the top management to the lowest ranks. All managers are linked together in their positions from highest to the lowest level. Each manager is superior to managers below him but he is also a subordinate to his own superior. The principle of scalar chain suggests that there should be a clear line of authority from top to bottom linking all managers at all levels.

The scalar chain serves as a chain of command as well as a chain of communication. It is considered as a chain of command because orders and instructions issued by higher level managers flow through intermediate managers before reaching lower levels. For example, if the head of the marketing department issues an order to a branch manager, it must pass through managers below the head and above the branch manager.

The scalar chain also works as a chain of communication. All communications, downwards and upwards in the organisation are required to flow through the chain. If reports on results achieved are to be sent by lower to higher levels they must pass through intermediate managers. Similarly, orders and instructions issued by heads of departments to supervisors must flow through intermediate managers.

23. Features of a good Mission Statement

1. Mission should be clear, both in terms of intentions and words used;
2. It should be feasible, neither too high to be unachievable, nor too low to demotivate the people for work.
3. It should be precise but self-explanatory, neither too narrow so as to restrict the organisation's activities, nor too broad to make itself meaningless.
4. It should be distinctive, both in terms of the organisation's contributions to the society and how these contributions can be made.

25. The Grapevine: One type of informal, person-to-person communication network that is not officially sanctioned by the organization is referred to as the grapevine. The grapevine links employees in all directions, ranging from the CEO through middle management, support staff, and line employees. The grapevine will always exist in an organization, but it can become a dominant force when formal channels are closed. In such cases, the grapevine is actually a service because the information it provides helps makes sense of an unclear or uncertain situation. Employees use grapevine rumors to fill in information gaps and clarify management decisions. One estimate is that as much as 70 percent of all communication in a firm is carried out through its grapevine. The grapevine tends to be more active during periods of change, excitement, anxiety, and sagging economic conditions.

26. Channel Differentiation: A company can achieve competitive advantage through the way they design the distribution channel's coverage, expertise and performance.

- **Coverage:** The geographical area of operation.
- **Expertise:** The level of training the channel members are given to handle customers' problem.
- **Performance:** The degree of reliability attached to the channel members' activity.

28. Porter's value chain model described five value generating 'primary activities', namely; 1. Inbound logistics, 2. Operations, 3. Outbound logistics, 4. Marketing and sales, 5. Service.

1. **Inbound logistics:** Activities associated with receiving, storing, and disseminating inputs to the product, such as material handling, warehousing, inventory control, vehicle scheduling, and returns to suppliers.
2. **Operations:** Activities associated with transforming inputs into the final product from, such as machining, packing, assembly, equipment maintenance, testing, printing, and facility operations.
3. **Outbound logistics:** Activities associated with collecting, storing and physically distributing the product to buyers, such as finished goods warehousing, material

handling, delivery vehicle operation, order processing and scheduling.

4. **Marketing and sales:** Activities associated with providing a means by which buyers can purchase the product include advertising, promotion, sales-force, quoting, channel selection, channel relations, and pricing.

5. **Service:** Activities associated with providing service to enhance or maintain the value of the product such as installation, repair, training, parts supply and product adjustment.

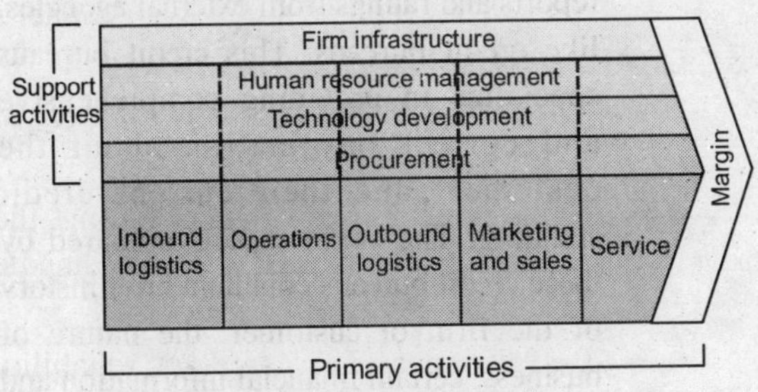

Fig. The value chain

29. Reliability of Research Tool: The quality and adequacy of quantities data can only be assessed by establishing the reliability of an instrument. Reliability is the degree of consistency with which the attributes or variables are measured by an instrument. For example, a blood pressure-measuring instrument gave a reading of 120 mmHg systolic blood pressure; after some time when blood pressure is again measured for the same subject, it gave a reading of 160 mmHg systolic blood pressure. In this situation, this instrument is not considered reliable. However, if a research instrument yields similar or close to similar results on repeated administration of instrument, it is considered as highly reliable research instrument.

Reliability pertains to the consistency of a measure. A test is thought to be reliable if we get the same result in a repeated manner. For example, if a test is designed to scale a trait (e.g. introversion), each time the test is put on a subject, the result should be similar. But, it is unfortunate as it is not possible to calculate the exact reliability; but there are various ways to measure reliability.

Definitions: Reliability is the degree of consistency and accuracy with which an instrument measures the attribute for which it is designed to measure.

'Reliability is defined as the ability of an instrument to create reproducible results.' Therefore, reliability is concerned with consistency of the measurement tools. A tool only can be considered reliable if it measures an attribute with similar results on repeated use.

31. The payback period can be calculated in several ways. The most common one uses the formula:

$$\text{Payback} = \frac{\text{Net investment outlay}}{\text{Net annual cash flow benefits}}$$

When annual cash flow benefits are irregular or investment outlay comes in various time frames, Exhibit 6-1 can be used to determine the payback period. In this case the payback period is four years.

The payback period method is widely used because of its ease of calculation. Because it does not take into consideration the time value of money, however, it has serious. flaws of logic.

Advantages

1. The calculations are easy
2. Choosing the project with shortest payback period has the more favourable short-run effect on earnings per share.
3. The method is easily understood.

Disadvantages

1. The method completely ignores all cash flows beyond the payback period.

2. It does not adjust for risk related to uncertainty.
3. It ignores the time value of money.

Some firms are beginning to use the payback method in combination with one or more of the time value methods described next. When this is done, the payback method is used as a risk measurement while the time value method is used as an indicator of profitability.

32. The following sources can be used to collect the credit information about the individual customers:

(*a*) **Financial Statements:** To assess the financial position and financial performance of a customers, the firm can scrutinize the financial statements of customer's business. The financial statement, e.g., balance sheet, profit and loss account and additional information about seasonal sales, if any, should be sought from the customers. Generally, it is better to insist on the audited financial statements.

(*b*) **Bank Reference:** The necessary information can be collected from the bank in which its customers maintain their accounts. This can be done directly by the firm itself through its direct and confidential enquiry with the bank or the firm can insist on his customer to instruct the bank to provide the necessary information to the firm. Generally, the bankers will not provide any clear cut information to the enquiries made by the firm. However, the information collected from this source may be supplemented with other information collected from other sources.

(*c*) **Trade References:** To obtain credit information, the firm can ask its customers to give the names of a few persons or firms engaged in his line of business. The said persons or firms should be reputed and should have current dealings with the firm's customers. After obtaining trade reference's, the firm can seek information from them directly and personally. While doing so the firm should make his exercise seriously and sincerely, and it should not be treated simply as a formality.

(*d*) **Credit Rating and Reports:** The two sources of credit information—bank reference and trade reference can provide biased information. To overcome this limitation, the firm can obtain credit reports and ratings from external agencies, like credit bureaus. This credit bureaus specialize in providing comprehensive and correct information about the customers and their current credit standing. The credit reports prepared by these credit bureaus contain a brief history of the firm or customer, the nature of business, certain financial information and as to whether payments made by them are prompt or not, etc. No such specialized credit bureaus are available in India at present but the agencies like trade associations and chambers of commerce can provide useful information to their members.

33. Payout Ratio: From the profits of each company, a cash flow termed dividend is distributed among its shareholders. This is the continuous stream of cash flow to the owners of shares, apart from the price differentials (capital gains) in the market. The return to the shareholders, in the form of dividend, out of the company's profit is measured through the payout ratio. The payout ratio is computed as follows:

Payout Ratio = (Dividend per share/Earnings per share) × 100

Percentage of payout ratio can also be used to compute the percentage of retained earnings. Profits available for distribution are either paid as dividends or retained internally for business growth opportunities. Hence, when dividends are not declared, the entire profit is ploughed back into the business for its future investments. The computation of retained earnings ratio (Retention Rate) is as follows:

Retention Rate = 1 – Payout ratio

For example, if a company has an EPS of ₹ 15 and declares a DPS of ₹ 5, the payout ratio is computed as (5/15) × 100 – 33.33 per cent. 'The retention rate is hence (10/15) × 100 or 1 – 33.33 per cent, *i.e.* 66.67 per cent.

34. Inventory Management Motives: Managing inventories involves lack of funds and inventory holding costs. Maintenance of inventory is expensive, then why should firms hold inventories? There are three general motives for holding inventories:

(i) ***The Transaction Motive:*** Transaction motive includes production of goods and sale of goods. Transaction motive facilitates uninterrupted production and delivery of order at a given time (right time).

(ii) ***The Precautionary Motive:*** This motive necessitates the holding of inventories for unexpected changes in demand and supply factors.

(iii) ***The Speculative Motive:*** This compels to hold some inventories to take the advantage of changes in prices and getting quantity discounts.

35. Operating Leverage: It is the tendency of the operating profit to change disproportionately with sales. A company is said to have a high degree of operating leverage if it employs a greater amount of fixed costs and a small amount of variable costs. On the other hand if the company employs a greater amount of variable costs and a smaller amount of fixed costs, it is said to have a low operating leverage. Therefore, the degree of operating leverage will depend on the amount of fixed element in the operating cost structure of the company. In the absence of fixed operating costs there will be no operating leverage.

The operating leverage is calculated for studying the effects on company's income at different levels of sales. It can be determined by the following formula:

$$\text{Operating Leverage} = \frac{\text{Contribution}}{\text{Operating Profit}} \text{ or } \frac{C}{OP}$$

$$\text{or} \quad = \frac{(\text{Total Sales} - \text{Total Variable Costs})}{(\text{Total Sales} + \text{Total Variable Costs}) - \text{Fixed Costs}}$$

Corporate Debt Capacity and Leverage

$$\text{or} \quad = \frac{N(SP - VC)}{N(SP - VC) - FC}$$

where, N is the number of units sold, SP is the selling price per unit, VC is variable cost per unit, FC is the total fixed cost.

Corporate Debt Capacity and Leverage

$$\text{or} \quad = \frac{N(SP - VC)}{N(SP - VC) - FC}$$

where, N is the number of units sold, SP is the selling price per unit, VC is variable cost per unit, FC is the total fixed cost.

The operating leverage may be favourable or unfavourable. Where the contribution exceeds the fixed costs, the operating leverage is termed as favourable, and vice versa.

Degree of operating leverage is the percentage change in profits resulting from a percentage change in sales. It may be put in the form of the following formula:

Degree of Operating Leverage

$$= \frac{\text{Percentage change in Profits}}{\text{Percentage change in Sales}}$$

Operating profit means "Earnings Before Interest and Tax" (EBIT). The operating leverage shows the impact of change in sales on the operating profits. If a company has a high degree or operating leverage, a small change in sales will bring a large change in operating profits. Thus, the operating profits of a company having a high degree of operating leverage increase at a faster rate than the increase in sales. Likewise, the operating profits of such a company also fall at a faster rate than the decrease in its sales.

Most companies do not like operative leverage. It is a very risky situation because a small decrease in sales can excessively damage the company's efforts to increase its profits.

37. Advantages and Disadvantages of Recruitment Media

Medium	Advantages	Disadvantages
Internet	Global reach Fast processing Relatively inexpensive Appeals to youth Technologically savvy More information about job	Many unmotivated applicants EEO/Diversity problems Not effective for low-skilled jobs Spam class (if e-mail)
Newspapers/Magazines	Local audience Tailored to audience Specially outlets Good circulation Good yield ratios for low-skilled jobs	Often ignored/not seen Expensive Long lead time
Direct Mail	Can be well-targeted with good list	Expensive (for better mailing lists) Very long lead time
Television/Radio	Targeted locally More attention to Ad Can attract people not seeking a job	Very expensive Longest lead time Less information regarding jobs

38. Critical Success Factors for Human Resource Planning

- HRP must always be seen within the strategy making context. A planning process removed from the realities of the business will be a waste of time.
- HRP involves the creation of formal and explicit sets of proposals intended to achieve actions that will achieve long term organizational performance.
- HR planners should propose actions that contribute to the long-term corporate success by being prepared for the worst-case scenario and by introducing innovative ways of thinking.
- During the thought processes, flexibility is a must. Opportunities must be available for senior employees to think and play a role in the planning process, thus enhancing employee ownership too.
- It must be process-driven from the very beginning. There should be room for experimentation and scope for improvement too. Various HR scenarios could also be created.

39.

Incentive Program	Description
Piecework Plans	Pay the worker for each unit he or she produces. Be careful to watch the quality of your products, as workers may be focused strictly on numbers rather than quality.
Merit Pay	A salary increase based on the employee's individual

	performance. Usually becomes part of the employee's base salary (not a bonus). Make sure not to throw around these raises carelessly. Established appraisal procedures will help avoid this.
Recognition-Based Awards	Includes "Employee of the Month" programs and less formal recognition such as praise, approval, or expressions of appreciation. Recognition may be given in private or in a public forum (on a website, newsletter, etc.).
Commission Plan	Incentive for salespeople: greatest incentive, as effort clearly produces reward. Watch for neglect of non-selling duties as these often get pushed aside in this program. May lead to quality issues and customer service problems.
Combination Plan	Incentive for salespeople where salary and commission are combined. Good for addressing quality and service issues.
Team Incentives	Tie rewards into the team's overall group performance. These incentives facilitate training, since each member has an interest in getting new members trained as fast as possible. Be aware of slackers, and perceived inequity between group members.
Profit-sharing Plans	All or most employees receive a share of the firm's annual profits which helps develop buy-in to corporate goals.
Employee Stock Ownership Plan (ESOP)	A corporation contributes shares of its own stock to a trust which are later distributed to employees on retirement or separation from service.
Gain-sharing Plans	Engages employees in a common effort to achieve productivity objectives and share the gains.
Annual Bonus	Designed to motivate short-term performance of managers and are usually tied to company profitability.
At-risk Variable Pay Plans	Plans that put some portion of the employee's weekly pay at risk, subject to the firm meeting its financial goals.
Stock Option	The right to purchase a stated number of shares of a company stock at today's price sometime in the future.

Companies also provide various incentives to persuade executives to remain with the firm. This is especially important when there is reason to believe the firm is being stalked by another company that wants to buy it. The target company might then install golden parachute incentives. Golden parachutes (as opposed to golden handcuffs) are extraordinary payments companies make to executives in connection with a change in ownership or control of a company.

40. Plant Council: The plant council was formed in pursuance of the recommendations of the second meeting of the Group of Labour at New Delhi in 1985. The scheme was made applicable to all central public sector undertakings, except those, which are given specific exemption from the operation of the scheme the government.

Features: Following are the features of the plant council:

1. There shall be one plant council for the whole unit.
2. Each plant council should consist of not less than six and not more than eighteen members. There should be parity between the representatives of employees and employers. One-third of the employees' representatives should come from the supervisory staff level.
3. Only such persons as are actually engaged in the unit should be members of the plant council.
4. It's tenure shall be for a period of three years.
5. The chief executive of the unit shall be the chairman of the plant council; the vice-chairman shall be elected from among the employees.
6. The plant council shall appoint one of its members as secretary who will be provided with adequate facilities for the effective discharge of his duties within the premises of the undertaking/establishment.
7. If a person quit the council for whatsoever reason, the member who is nominated to fill the mid-term casual vacancy shall serve on the council for the unexpired period of the term of the council.
8. The council shall meet at least once in quarter.
9. Every decision of the plant council shall be on the basis of consensus and not by voting, and shall be binding on both the employees and the employers.

Functions: The plant council shall normally deal with following matters:

1. Operational Areas

(*a*) Determination of productivity schemes taking into consideration the local conditions;

(*b*) Planning, implementation and attainment and review of monthly targets and schedules;

(*c*) Material supply and preventing its shortfall;

(*d*) Housekeeping activities;

(*e*) Improvement in production in general and in critical areas in particular;

(*f*) Quality and technology improvements;

(*g*) Machine utilization, knowledge and development of products;

(*h*) Operational performance figures;

(*i*) Encouragement to and consideration of the suggestion system; and

(*j*) Matters/problems not sorted out at the shop floor level or those that concern more than one shop.

2. Economic and Financial Areas

(*a*) Profit and loss statement, balance sheet;

(*b*) Review of operating expenses, financial results, and cost of sales; and

(*c*) Enterprise performance in financial terms, labour and managerial cost, and market conditions etc.

3. Personal Matters

(*a*) Matters relating to absenteeism;

(*b*) Special problems of women workers; and

(*c*) Initiation and administration of workers programmes.

4. Welfare Area

(*a*) Implementation of welfare schemes, such as medical benefits, house and transport facilities;

(*b*) Safety measures;

(*c*) Township administration; and

(*d*) Control of the habits of gambling, drinking and indebtedness among the workers.

5. Environmental Area

(*a*) Environmental protections; and

(*b*) Extension activities and community development projects.

45. According to Basel Committee on Banking Supervision "Basel III is a comprehensive set of reform measures, developed by the Basel Committee on Banking Supervision, to strengthen the regulation, supervision and risk management of the banking sector".

Thus, we can say that Basel 3 is only a continuation of effort initiated by the Basel Committee on Banking Supervision to enhance the banking regulatory framework under Basel I and Basel II.

Basel 3 measures aim to:

- improve the banking sector's ability to absorb shocks arising from financial and economic stress, whatever the source
- improve risk management and governance
- strengthen banks' transparency and disclosures.

The basic structure of Basel III remains unchanged with three mutually reinforcing pillars.

Pillar 1: Minimum Regulatory Capital Requirements based on Risk Weighted Assets (RWAs) : Maintaining capital calculated through credit, market and operational risk areas.

Pillar 2: Supervisory Review Process : Regulating tools and frameworks for dealing with peripheral risks that banks face.

Pillar 3: Market Discipline : Increasing the disclosures that banks must provide to increase the transparency of banks.

46. Theory of Comparative Cost Advantage: The theory of Comparative Cost Advantage was propounded by Ricardo (1817) and is also known as comparative advantage or comparative cost theory or the classical theory of international trade. According to this theory, every country will produce the goods as per the availability and suitability of resources, like natural endowments, climate, quality of soil, means of transport, human resources and capital and will exchange the surplus with the imports of goods for the production of which it is not well suited or which it cannot produce at all. In brief, all countries must produce and export the goods and commodities in which they have comparative cost advantages and import all those goods and commodities in which they have comparative cost disadvantages.

The comparative cost theory is based on the assumptions of static theory. It assumes fixed quantity of resources. It does not consider the effect of growth and other dynamic factors.

48. Trade Related Intellectual Property Rights (TRIPs): TRIPs agreements are related to intellectual property rights. These intellectual property rights can be with regard to copyright, trade mark, patents, etc. Under TRIPs, owner of patent gets his patent registered for a particular period of time. Any person who wants to use that patent, can use it by paying royalty to the owner of the patent. TRIPs agreement gives this right on various types of intellectual properties.

50. Star Export Houses:

Sr. No	Status Category	Export Performance FOB/FOR in US$ million during current and previous two years
1.	One Star Export House	3
2.	Two Star Export House	25
3.	Three Star Export House	100
4.	Four Star Export House	500
5.	Five Star Export House	2000

PAPER-III

Note: *This paper contains* ***seventy five (75)*** *objective type questions of* ***two (2)*** *marks each.* ***All*** *questions are* ***compulsory****.*

1. Read the following and select the right code:

Statement-I: A custom to be valid should be proved to be immemorial but may not be ancient.

Statement-II: The principle of judicial decision which is only authoritative is known as 'ratio decidendi'.

A. Both the statements are true.
B. Both the statements are false.
C. Statement-I is true but Statement-II is false.
D. Statement-II is true but Statement-I is false.

2. To become a director in a company the person must obtain

A. Business Licence B. Director's Licence
C. TIN D. DIN

3. Which of following is not a "Maharatna" industry in India?

A. CIL B. SAIL
C. OIL D. GAIL

4. Match the items of Column-I with those of Column-II :

Column-I	**Column-II**
(*a*) Exchange control	(*i*) Adverse BOP
(*b*) Price control	(*ii*) Domestic firms
(*c*) Import control	(*iii*) Mass consumption product
(*d*) Legislative control	(*iv*) Industrial location

Codes :

	(*a*)	(*b*)	(*c*)	(*d*)
A.	(*ii*)	(*i*)	(*iii*)	(*iv*)
B.	(*iv*)	(*ii*)	(*iii*)	(*i*)
C.	(*iii*)	(*ii*)	(*i*)	(*iv*)
D.	(*ii*)	(*iii*)	(*i*)	(*iv*)

5. Match the items of List-I with those of List-II and choose the correct code :

List-I	**List-II**
(*a*) Provision for taxation	(*i*) Current Assets
(*b*) Live-stock	(*ii*) Unsecured loans
(*c*) Sundry Debtors	(*iii*) Fixed Assets
(*d*) Interest accrued on unsecured loans	(*iv*) Provisions

Codes :

	(*a*)	(*b*)	(*c*)	(*d*)
A.	(*iv*)	(*iii*)	(*i*).	(*ii*)
B.	(*iv*)	(*iii*)	(*ii*)	(*i*)
C.	(*iii*)	(*iv*)	(*ii*)	(*i*)
D.	(*ii*)	(*i*)	(*iii*)	(*iv*)

6. A, B and C are partners in a firm sharing profits and losses in the ratio of 4 : 3 : 2. They agreed to take D into partnership and gave him $\frac{1}{8}$ share. What will be their new profit sharing ratio?

A. 4 : 3 : 2 : 1 B. 28 : 21 : 14 : 9
C. 28 : 21 : 14 : 8 D. 4 : 1 : 2 : 1

7. From the following information, find out the number of units that must be sold by the firm to earn profit of ₹ 80,000 per year.

Sales price : ₹ 25 per unit
Variable manufacturing costs – ₹ 12 per unit
Variable selling costs – ₹ 3 per unit
Fixed factory overheads – ₹ 5,00,000
Fixed selling costs – ₹ 3,00,000

A. 60,000 units B. 88,000 units
C. 98,000 units D. 1,00,000 units

8. Which of the following is not a cash inflow?

A. Decrease in creditors
B. Decrease in debtors
C. Issue of shares
D. Sale of a fixed asset

9. Match the items of List-I with those of List-II and indicate the correct code from the following:

List-I	**List-II**
(*a*) Postage stamp pricing	(*i*) Equality of marginal and average cost
(*b*) Loss leader	(*ii*) Constant average and marginal cost

(*c*) Economic capacity (*iii*) Product line pricing

(*d*) Reserve capacity (*iv*) Differential pricing

Codes :

	(*a*)	(*b*)	(*c*)	(*d*)
A.	(*iii*)	(*iv*)	(*ii*)	(*i*)
B.	(*iv*)	(*iii*)	(*i*)	(*ii*)
C.	(*ii*)	(*i*)	(*iii*)	(*iv*)
D.	(*i*)	(*ii*)	(*iv*)	(*iii*)

10. For the following two statements of Assertion (A) and Reasoning (R) indicate the correct code :

Assertion (A) : Low initial pricing for new products is regarded as the principal instrument for entering into mass markets.

Reasoning (R) : Firms generally go for production of new products with excess capacity initially.

Codes :

A. Assertion (A) and Reasoning (R) both are correct but (R) does not offer full explanation for (A).
B. Assertion (A) and Reasoning (R) both are wrong.
C. Assertion (A) is correct but Reasoning (R) is wrong.
D. Assertion (A) and Reasoning (R) both are correct and (R) offers full explanation for (A).

11. For the following two statements of Assertion (A) and Reasoning (R) indicate the correct code :

Assertion (A): Gossen's first law of consumption is invariably applicable in case of individuals' consumption behaviour.

Reasoning (R): It serves as an important determinant of demand for the goods and services in the market.

Codes :

A. Assertion (A) and Reasoning (R) both are correct.
B. Assertion (A) and Reasoning (R) both are incorrect.
C. Assertion (A) is correct but Reasoning (R) is incorrect.
D. Assertion (A) is incorrect but Reasoning (R) is correct.

12. Production function for a product is based on certain assumptions. Indicate the correct code from the following :

(*a*) Complementarity
(*b*) Substitutability
(*c*) Product elasticity
(*d*) Specificity

Codes :

A. (*a*) (*b*) (*c*) B. (*b*) (*c*) (*d*)
C. (*a*) (*c*) (*d*) D. (*a*) (*b*) (*d*)

13. Which one of the following is not the characteristic of normal distribution?

A. Mean, median and mode for the normal distribution are equal.
B. The two tails of the normal curve extend to infinity in both directions but never touch the horizontal axis.
C. For different values of standard deviation, the height of the mean ordinate remains the same.
D. The number of independent constraints of normal distribution are N, $\bar{X}$ and σ.

14. Which one of the following formulae is used to calculate the standard error of coefficient of correlation between 25 paired observations of a sample?

A. $\frac{(1-r^2)}{\sqrt{n}}$ B. $\sqrt{\frac{(1-r^2)}{(n-2)}}$

C. $(0.6745)\left(\frac{1-r^2}{\sqrt{n}}\right)$ D. $\sqrt{\frac{(n-2)}{(1-r^2)}}$

15. Read the following statements and choose the correct code :

Statement-I: Non-parametric tests are based on some assumptions about the parent population from which the sample has been drawn.

Statement-II: The standard deviation of the sampling distribution of mean is called standard error of mean.

Codes :

A. Both statements are true.
B. Both statements are false.
C. Statement-I is true while Statement-II is false.
D. Statement-I is false while Statement-II is true.

16. Match the items of List-I with the items of List-II and indicate the code of correct matching :

List-I	List-II
(*a*) Contingency coefficient for any size of contingency table	(*i*) $\sqrt{\frac{N-n}{N-1}}$
(*b*) Statistical approach to decide size of a sample	(*ii*) $\frac{\sigma_p}{\sqrt{n}}$
(*c*) Finite population multiplier	(*iii*) $\sqrt{\frac{x^2}{x^2+n}}$
(*d*) Standard error of mean	(*iv*) $\frac{z^2.\sigma_p^2}{e^2}$

Codes :

	(*a*)	(*b*)	(*c*)	(*d*)
A.	(*i*)	(*ii*)	(*iii*)	(*iv*)
B.	(*iii*)	(*iv*)	(*i*)	(*ii*)
C.	(*i*)	(*iii*)	(*ii*)	(*iv*)
D.	(*iii*)	(*ii*)	(*iv*)	(*i*)

17. Which of the following is a deterioration of mental efficiency, reality testing and moral judgement that results from in-group pressure?

A. Harassment B. Group think
C. Group burnout D. Group control

18. According to Fiedler's contingency model of leadership, favourableness of situation depends on which combination of the following?

(*a*) Leader-member relationship
(*b*) Member-member relationship
(*c*) Leader's position power
(*d*) Degree of task structure
(*e*) Degree of training

Codes :

A. (*a*), (*b*) and (*c*) B. (*a*), (*c*) and (*d*)
C. (*c*), (*d*) and (*e*) D. (*a*), (*b*) and (*e*)

19. The apex body at the highest level of the unit/division, which oversees the functioning of quality circles (QC), is called

A. Facilitator
B. Coordinator
C. Steering committee
D. Supervisory committee

20. Which of the following is related to the practical means of determining a moral course of action?

A. Meta ethics B. Virtue ethics
C. Normative ethics D. Applied ethics

21. Match List-I and List-II and indicate the correct code :

List-I	List-II
(*a*) Convenience goods	(*i*) Consumer purchases them frequently, immediately and with minimal effort.
(*b*) Shopping goods	(*ii*) Consumer compares them on the basis of suitability, quality, price and style.
(*c*) Speciality goods	(*iii*) These are goods with unique characteristics or brand identification.
(*d*) Unsought goods	(*iv*) Consumers are not aware of them and normally do not think of buying them.

Codes :

	(*a*)	(*b*)	(*c*)	(*d*)
A.	(*i*)	(*iv*)	(*ii*)	(*iii*)
B.	(*i*)	(*ii*)	(*iii*)	(*iv*)
C.	(*iv*)	(*iii*)	(*ii*)	(*i*)
D.	(*ii*)	(*i*)	(*iii*)	(*iv*)

22. Which of the following marketing strategies is/are not used in 'growth stage' of the product life cycle?

A. Improving quality and adding new features.
B. Adding new models of product.
C. Entering new market segments.
D. Using awareness and trial communications.

23. Who among the following take(s) both title to and possession of goods from the preceding member(s) and channelize them to the subsequent members?
(*a*) Agent intermediaries
(*b*) Merchant intermediaries
A. (*a*) only B. (*b*) only
C. Both (*a*) and (*b*) D. Neither (*a*) nor (*b*)

24. Which of the following is not a determinant of service quality?
A. Reliability B. Responsiveness
C. Sensitivity D. Assurance

25. Sales of a firm are ₹ 74 lakh, variable costs ₹ 40 lakh, fixed costs ₹ 8 lakh. Operating leverage of the firm will be
A. 1.48 B. 1.78
C. 1.31 D. 2.42

26. From the following techniques of capital budgeting decision, indicate the correct combination of discounting techniques :
I. Profitability index
II. Net present value
III. Accounting rate of return
IV. Internal rate of return

Codes :
A. I II III B. II III IV
C. I II IV D. I III IV

27. Insufficient working capital may result into which combination of the following?
I. Failures to adapt to changes.
II. Enhancement in credit-worthiness of the firm.
III. Reduced availability of trade and cash discounts.
IV. Reduced volume of sales.

Codes :
A. I II III IV B. I III IV
C. I II IV D. I II III

28. Which combination of the following represents the assumptions of the Walter's dividend model?
I. The company has a very long or perpetual life.
II. All earnings are either reinvested internally or distributed as dividend
III. There is no floatation cost for the company.
IV. Cost of capital of the company is constant.

Codes :
A. I II III B. II III IV
C. I II IV D. I III IV

29. Match the items of List-I with the items of List-II and indicate the correct code :

List-I	**List-II**
(*a*) Job specifications	(*i*) The procedure for determining the duties and skill requirements of a job and the kind of person who should be hired for it.
(*b*) Job description	(*ii*) A list of human requirements
(*c*) Job analysis	(*iii*) A list of job's duties, responsibilities, reporting relationships, working conditions and supervisory responsibilities.

Codes :

	(*a*)	(*b*)	(*c*)
A.	(*i*)	(*ii*)	(*iii*)
B.	(*ii*)	(*iii*)	(*i*)
C.	(*iii*)	(*ii*)	(*i*)
D.	(*ii*)	(*i*)	(*iii*)

30. A training technique in which trainees are first shown good management techniques in a film, are asked to play roles in a simulated situation, and are then given feedback and praise by their supervisor is known as.
A. Behaviour modelling
B. Role playing
C. In-house development center
D. Management game

31. Which combination of the following statements is correct about the code of discipline in industry?

(*a*) It aims at preventing disputes by providing for outside agency or adjudication.

(*b*) It is a government imposed involuntary principle of discipline.

(*c*) It restrains the parties from unilateral action.

Codes :

A. (*a*), (*b*) and (*c*) B. (*b*) and (*c*)

C. (*a*) only D. (*c*) only

32. A conciliation proceeding is deemed to be pending until any combination of the following conditions is fulfilled :

(*a*) a settlement is arrived at a memorandum of settlement is signed by parties to the dispute.

(*b*) no settlement is arrived at, the report of conciliation officer is received by the appropriate government.

(*c*) a reference is made to the court of Inquiry, Labour Court, Tribunal or National Tribunal during the pendency of conciliation proceedings.

Codes :

A. only (*a*) is correct.

B. only (*b*) is correct.

C. (*a*) and (*c*) are correct.

D. (*a*), (*b*) and (*c*) are correct.

33. Identify the correct combination of statements with regard to banking in India:

(*a*) For many years the presidency banks had acted as quasi-central banks.

(*b*) The Bank of Hindustan was liquidated during 1829-32.

(*c*) General Bank of India was an unsuccessful bank and was dissolved in 1791.

(*d*) Bank of Calcutta was renamed as Bank of Bengal in 1921.

Codes :

A. (*a*), (*b*) and (*c*) B. (*b*), (*c*) and (*d*)

C. (*a*), (*b*) and (*d*) D. (*a*), (*b*), (*c*) and (*d*)

34. Which combination of the following methods indicates quantitative methods of control of credit creation practiced by the Reserve Bank of India?

(*a*) Bank Rate

(*b*) Open Market Operations

(*c*) Variable Reserve Ratios

(*d*) Credit Rationing

Codes :

A. (*a*), (*b*) and (*c*) B. (*a*), (*b*) and (*d*)

C. (*b*), (*c*) and (*d*) D. (*a*), (*c*) and (*d*)

35. Which one of the following development financial institutions in India has started the special refinance scheme for the resettlement and rehabilitation of voluntary retired workers of the National Textile Corporation of India?

A. IDBI B. SIDBI

C. ICICI D. None of the above

36. Read the following statements and choose the correct code :

Statement-I: Small Industry Development Bank of India (SIDBI) was set up as a wholly owned subsidiary of RBI.

Statement-II: SIDBI has taken over the responsibility of administering small industry development fund managed by IDBI.

Codes :

A. only (I) is correct.

B. Only (II) is correct.

C. Both (I) and (II) are correct.

D. Both (I) and (II) are wrong.

37. Under the Foreign Trade Policy 2015-2020, following additional ports are allowed for export and import :

(*a*) Calicut Airport, Kerala

(*b*) Rajkot Airport, Gujarat

(*c*) Arakonam ICD, Tamil Nadu

(*d*) Ludhiana Airport, Punjab

Codes :

A. (*a*) and (*c*) B. (*a*) and (*d*)

C. (*b*) and (*d*) D. (*c*) and (*d*)

38. Assertion (A): Under FEMA, the receiver of laundered money is to be made culpable, instead of sender/distributor.

Reasoning (R): FEMA differs from the earlier exchange regulation Act FERA with regard to penalties and punishment in case of violation of the Act.

Codes :

A. (A) is correct but (R) is not correct.
B. (A) and (R) both are correct but (R) is not the right explanation of (A).
C. (A) and (R) both are correct and (R) is the right explanation of (A).
D. (A) and (R) both are incorrect.

39. Match the items of List-I with those of List-II with regard to international monetary fund's various schemes :

List-I	List-II
(*a*) Extended Fund Facility (EFF)	(*i*) Repayment period 4 to 10 years
(*b*) Stan Arrangements	(*ii*) Repayment period 3 to 5 years
(*c*) Supplemented Reserve Fund (SRF)	(*iii*) Repayment period 2 to 5 years
(*d*) Poverty Reduction and Growth Facility (PRGF)	(*iv*) Repayment period 10 years

Codes :

	(*a*)	(*b*)	(*c*)	(*d*)
A.	(*i*)	(*ii*)	(*iii*)	(*iv*)
B.	(*iv*)	(*iii*)	(*ii*)	(*i*)
C.	(*iv*)	(*ii*)	(*iii*)	(*i*)
D.	(*i*)	(*iv*)	(*ii*)	(*iii*)

40. Which combination of the following is correct with regard to World Trade Organization (WTO) :

(*a*) WTO initiates peace process among the member countries to enhance international trade.
(*b*) WTO avoids the task of "Settlement of Disputes" among the member countries.
(*c*) WTO administers the "Trade Review Mechanism".
(*d*) WTO cooperates in an appropriate manner with the IMF and the World Bank.

Codes :

A. (*b*), (*c*) and (*d*) B. (*a*) and (*c*)
C. (*c*) and (*d*) D. (*a*), (*b*) and (*d*)

41. Choose the code representing the correct sequence of steps in a merging transaction :

(I) Screening and investigation of merger proposal.
(II) Approval of Central Government
(III) Approval of respective High Courts
(IV) Negotiation Stage
(V) Approval of proposal by Board of Directors, Shareholders and Creditors

Codes :

A. (I) → (V) → (IV) → (III) → (II)
B. (I) → (IV) → (V) → (III) → (II)
C. (I) → (IV) → (III) → (V) → (II)
D. (I) → (III) → (V) → (II) → (IV)

42. Which of the following are the important features of option contracts?

(I) Buyers of option have limited liability.
(II) Options have high degree of risk to option-writers.
(III) Options are exercisable only by buyers of option.
(IV) Buyers of option have all rights which are available to equity shareholders of the concerned companies.

Codes :

A. (I), (II), (III) B. (I), (II), (III), (IV)
C. (I), (II), (IV) D. (I), (III), (IV)

43. Which of the following approaches is adopted for the valuation of human resource according to economic concept?

A. Replacement cost approach
B. Opportunity cost approach
C. Historical cost approach
D. None of the above

44. Match the items of List-I with those of List-II and select the correct code :

List-I	List-II
(*a*) High levered fund	(*i*) Market risk
(*b*) Increase in bank rate	(*ii*) Purchasing power risk
(*c*) Inflation	(*iii*) Financial risk
(*d*) Political instability	(*iv*) Interest rate risk

Codes :

	(a)	(b)	(c)	(d)
A.	(iii)	(i)	(ii)	(iv)
B.	(i)	(iii)	(iv)	(ii)
C.	(iii)	(iv)	(ii)	(i)
D.	(ii)	(iii)	(i)	(iv)

45. Which of the following are the instruments of money market?

(i) Call money market
(ii) Commercial bill market
(iii) Industrial securities market
(iv) Short-term loans market
(v) Treasury bill market

Codes :

A. (i), (ii), (iv), (v)
B. (i), (ii), (v)
C. (i), (ii), (iii), (iv), (v)
D. (i), (ii), (iii), (iv)

46. Accounting Standard-6 is meant for

A. Accounting for Fixed Assets
B. Accounting treatment for goodwill
C. Depreciation Accounting
D. Disclosure of Accounting policies

47. Which of the following is not a feature of OTCEI?

A. Quick transfer and disposal system
B. Nationalised computerised networking
C. Ringless trading system
D. Fragmentation of regional stock exchanges

48. Which of the following requires consumers to interpret ambiguous stimuli?

A. Focus group method
B. Projective techniques
C. Rejective techniques
D. Semantic differential scales

49. Which of the following passes through the four stages of distinctiveness, emulation, mass fashion and decline?

A. Style B. Fashion
C. Fad D. Style and Fashion

50. Which of the following positioning strategies is adopted by marketers to position their product in two categories simultaneously?

A. Point of Difference
B. Point of Parity
C. Straddle Positioning
D. Emotional Positioning

51. Statement (I): Marketing is the process by which a firm profitably translates customer needs into revenue.

Statement (II): Marketing is the messages and/or actions that causes messages and/or actions.

Codes :

A. (I) is correct but (II) is not correct.
B. (II) is correct but (I) is not correct.
C. (I) and (II) both are correct.
D. (I) and (II) both are incorrect.

52. Assertion (A): Odd pricing aims at maximising profit by making micro-adjustments in pricing structure.

Reasoning (R): Odd pricing refers to a price ending in 1, 3, 5, 7, or 9. When examining a price, the first digits carry more weight than the last ones.

Codes :

A. (A) is right and (R) is wrong.
B. (A) is wrong and (R) is right.
C. Both (A) and (R) are right.
D. Both (A) and (R) are wrong.

53. Name the process in which a buyer posts its interest in buying a certain quantity of item and sellers compete for the business by submitting lower bid until there is only one seller left.

A. Internet B. Reverse auction
C. B2B market place D. B2C market place

54. Advertising method in which an advertisement is broadcasted simultaneously on several radio stations and / or television channels is known as

A. Black-out B. Consolidation
C. Road-block D. Cornering

55. Which of the following is the mental condition or attitude of individuals and groups which determines their willingness to cooperate?

A. Motivation B. Morale
C. Excitement D. Delight

56. Which of the following is not provided under the Factories Act, 1948?

A. The certificate of fitness is granted by a certifying surgeon on the application of any young person or a parent or a guardian.

B. An adolescent who has not been granted a certificate of fitness shall be deemed to be a child for the purpose of the act.

C. The certificate of fitness granted or renewed remains valid for a period of six months from the date of issue.

D. Any fee payable for the certificate of fitness shall be paid by occupier and not by the young person or his parent or guardian.

57. Arrange the following steps of developing Behaviourally Anchored Rating Scales (BARS) in the right sequence :

(*a*) Developing performance dimensions
(*b*) Generate critical incidents
(*c*) Scale the incidents
(*d*) Reallocate the incidents
(*e*) Develop the final instrument

Codes :

A. (*a*), (*b*), (*c*), (*d*), (*e*)
B. (*b*), (*a*), (*d*), (*c*), (*e*)
C. (*a*), (*b*), (*d*), (*c*), (*e*)
D. (*a*), (*c*), (*b*), (*d*), (*e*)

58. Within how much period from the close of accounting year, bonus must be paid, if there is no dispute about the payment of bonus?

A. Two months B. Six months
C. Eight months D. Ten months

59. Which of the following statements is correct about Wage Boards in India?

(*a*) A Wage Board is a tripartite body.
(*b*) Labour and management representatives on a Wage Board can be selected from industries other than the one which is investigated
(*c*) Wage Boards are always statutory in nature.
(*d*) Wage Boards work on the principle of living wage.

Codes :

A. (*a*) only B. (*b*) and (*c*)
C. (*c*) and (*a*) D. (*a*), (*b*), (*c*) and (*d*)

60. Who gave the surplus value theory of wage?

A. David Ricardo B. Karl Marx
C. Adam Smith D. F.A. Walker

61. Who gave the systems approach to industrial relations?

A. Beatrice Webb B. John Dunlop
C. Eric Trist D. Henry Fayol

62. Which among the following are multinational corporations?

(*a*) A multinational, decentralized corporation with strong home country presence.
(*b*) A global, centralized corporation that acquires cost advantage through centralized production when cheaper resources are available.
(*c*) An international company that builds on the parent corporations technology and R & D.
(*d*) A transnational enterprise that combines the (*a*), (*b*) and (*c*).

Codes :

A. (*a*) and (*b*) B. (*b*) and (*c*)
C. (*a*), (*b*) and (*c*) D. (*a*), (*b*), (*c*) and (*d*)

63. Which among the following are full member countries of ASEAN?

(*a*) Brunei Darussalam (*b*) Cambodia
(*c*) Vietnam (*d*) Myanmar
(*e*) Sri Lanka

Codes :

A. (*a*), (*b*) and (*e*) B. (*a*), (*b*), (*c*) and (*e*)
C. (*b*), (*c*), (*d*) and (*e*) D. (*a*), (*b*), (*c*) and (*d*)

64. Assertion (A): Capital Account convertibility is introduced only sometime after the introduction of convertibility on current account when exchange rate of currency of a country is relatively stable.

Reasoning (R): Capital Account convertibility is necessary for faster growth and development of economy and it makes foreign exchange rate more stable.

Codes :

A. (A) is correct but (R) is not correct.
B. (A) and (R) both are correct and (R) is the right explanation of (A).
C. (A) and (R) both are correct but (R) is not the right explanation of (A).
D. Both (A) and (R) are incorrect.

65. Statement (I): WTO is only international organization which deals with the rules of trade between organizations.

Statement (II): The limit of holding by individual foreign institutional investors in a company has been raised from 5 to 10% of company's share while the aggregate limit has been increased from 24 to 34%.

Codes :

A. Statement (I) is correct but Statement (II) is false.
B. Statement (II) is correct but Statement (I) is false.
C. Statements (I) and (II) both are correct.
D. Statements (I) and (II) both are false.

66. In case a farmer in India buys a wheat option on future :

(*a*) The farmer must accept a wheat futures contract and not take physical possession of wheat.
(*b*) The farmer must accept delivery of the wheat at a higher price.
(*c*) The farmer has the right to deliver the wheat and will do so only if the price is favourable.
(*d*) The farmer must deliver the wheat at market price.

Codes :

A. (*a*) and (*d*) B. (*d*) only
C. (*c*) only D. (*b*) and (*c*)

67. Sector specific policy of government of India in case of B2B is when

A. FDI is upto 100%
B. FDI is upto 49%
C. FDI is upto 100% subject to condition that the investment in favour of Indian public to the tune of 20% within 5 years to be done.
D. FDI is upto 100% subject to condition that the investment in favour of Indian public to the tune of 26% within 10 years to be done.

68. Statement I: In India a "copyright" of an unpublished book can be registered under copyright Act of India

Statement II: Once granted by the European Patent Office, the proprietor has a patent which is effective in all contracting states of the patent cooperation treaty and the agreement on the trade related aspects of IPR.

Codes :

A. Statement (I) is correct and (II) is false.
B. Statement (II) is correct and (I) is false.
C. Statements (I) and (II) both are correct.
D. Statements (I) and (II) both are false.

69. As per the Income Tax Act, 1961 for the assessment year 2015-16, a deduction u/s 80 QQB for authors of books of literacy, artistic or scientific nature is allowed upto

A. ₹ 1,00,000 B. ₹ 2,00,000
C. ₹ 2,40,000 D. ₹ 3,00,000

70. Gratuity received by a government employee is

A. exempted upto ₹ 3,50,000
B. exempted upto ₹ 10,00,000
C. fully exempted
D. fully taxable

71. Match the items of the List-I with those of the List-II and indicate the correct code :

List-I	List-II
(*a*) Residential status of an individual	(*i*) Section 10 (13A)
(*b*) Agricultural income	(*ii*) Section 10 (10)
(*c*) House rent allowance	(*iii*) Section 6
(*d*) Gratuity	(*iv*) Section 10 (1)

Codes :

	(a)	(b)	(c)	(d)
A.	(i)	(iii)	(ii)	(iv)
B.	(iii)	(iv)	(i)	(ii)
C.	(ii)	(i)	(iii)	(iv)
D.	(iv)	(ii)	(i)	(iii)

72. Match the items of the List-I with List-II and indicate the correct code :

List-I	List-II
(a) House rent allowance	(i) A deduction from income
(b) Casual income	(ii) A step taken by tax authorities
(c) Collection charges of interest on securities	(iii) Taxable income
(d) Best judgement assessment	(iv) Partly taxable allowance

Codes :

	(a)	(b)	(c)	(d)
A.	(iv)	(iii)	(ii)	(i)
B.	(iv)	(iii)	(i)	(ii)
C.	(iii)	(iv)	(i)	(ii)
D.	(ii)	(iv)	(i)	(iii)

73. The statutory limit for deduction u/s 80 GG of Income Tax Act, 1961, for the assessment year 2015-16 is

A. ₹ 2,000 per month
B. ₹ 3,000 per month
C. ₹ 2,500 per month
D. ₹ 5,000 per month

74. For the purpose of assessment under Income Tax Act, 1961, which combination of the following represent income?

(I) Tax-free salary from the private sector employer.
(II) Pin money received by a family member.
(III) Awards received by the sports persons.
(IV) Loss incurred by the assessee.
(V) Perquisites received by employees.

Codes :

A. (I), (II), (III), (IV) B. (II), (III), (IV), (V)
C. (I), (III), (IV), (V) D. (I), (II), (IV), (V)

75. Indicate the correct code for forms for filing Income Tax return from the following Income Tax Return Forms :

(a) ITR-4S (b) ITR-2
(c) ITR-2B (d) ITR-3

Codes :

A. (a), (b) and (c) B. (b), (c) and (d)
C. (a), (b) and (d) D. (a), (c) and (d)

ANSWERS

1	2	3	4	5	6	7	8	9	10
D	D	C	D	A	B	B	A	B	A
11	**12**	**13**	**14**	**15**	**16**	**17**	**18**	**19**	**20**
D	D	C	B	D	B	B	B	C	C
21	**22**	**23**	**24**	**25**	**26**	**27**	**28**	**29**	**30**
B	D	B	C	C	C	B	C	B	A
31	**32**	**33**	**34**	**35**	**36**	**37**	**38**	**39**	**40**
D	D	A	A	B	B	A	C	A	C
41	**42**	**43**	**44**	**45**	**46**	**47**	**48**	**49**	**50**
B	A	B	C	A	C	D	B	B	C
51	**52**	**53**	**54**	**55**	**56**	**57**	**58**	**59**	**60**
C	C	B	C	B	C	B	C	A	B
61	**62**	**63**	**64**	**65**	**66**	**67**	**68**	**69**	**70**
B	D	D	A	C	C	C	C	D	C
71	**72**	**73**	**74**	**75**					
B	B	A	C	C					

EXPLANATORY ANSWERS

1. For a custom to receive recognition it is necessary that it should be ancient and invariable, it should be established by unambiguous evidence, and it should be continuous, certain and ancient.

A valid custom must satisfy the following requirements:

(*i*) It must be ancient. It need to be of immemorial antiquity, but a long usage is absolutely necessary

(*ii*) It must be certain and uniform

(*iii*) It should be continuous

(*iv*) It should be reasonable *i.e.,* should be in accordance with the rules of equity, justice and good conscience,

(*v*) It should not be immoral

(*vi*) It must not be opposed to public policy

(*vii*) It must not be opposed to law.

2. Director Identification Number (DIN) means an identification number allotted by the central government to any individual, intending to be appointed as director or any existing director of a company, for the purpose of his identification as a director of a company.

The provisions as laid down by Companies Act 2013 with regard to DIN are as follows:

1. Every individual intending to be appointed as director of a company shall make an application for allotment of DIN to the central government in such form and manner and along with such fees as may be prescribed (Section 153).
2. The central government shall, within one month from the receipt of the application under Section 153, allot a DIN to an applicant in such manner as may be prescribed (Section 154).
3. No individual, who has already been allotted a DIN under Section 154, shall apply for, obtain or possess another DIN (Section 155).
4. Every existing director shall, within one month of the receipt of DIN from the central government, intimate his/her DIN to the company or all companies wherein she/he is a director (Section 156).
5. Every company shall, within fifteen days of the receipt of intimation under Section 156, furnish the DIN of all its directors to the Registrar or any other officer or authority as may be specified by the central government with such fees as may be prescribed and in such form and manner as may be prescribed [Section 157(1)].
6. Every person or company, while furnishing any return, information or particulars which relate to a director or contain any reference of any director, as are required to be furnished under this Act, shall mention the DIN (Section 158).
7. If any individual or director of a company contravenes any of the provisions of Section 152, Section 155 and Section 156, such individual or director of the company shall be punishable with imprisonment for a term which may extend to six months or with fine which may extend to ₹ 50,000 and where the contravention is a continuing one, with a further fine which may extend to ₹ 500 for every day after the first during which the contravention continues (Section 159).

5. Secured Loans: Long-term loans, which are taken against some security, are included under this head. Debentures and secured loans and advances from banks, subsidiary companies etc fall under this category and are shown separately under this head.

Unsecured Loans: Loans and advances for which no security is given are shown under this heading. This item includes public deposits, unsecured loans and advances from subsidiary companies, short-term loans and advances and other loans and advances from banks.

Current Liabilities and Provisions: Current liabilities refer to such liabilities, which mature within a period of one year. They include sundry creditors, advance payments, un-expired discounts, unclaimed dividends, interest accrued but not paid, and other short-term liabilities. Provisions refer to the amounts set aside out of revenue profits for some specific liabilities payable within a period of one year. Those include provision for taxation, proposed dividends, provision for contingencies, provision for provident fund, provision for insurance, pension and similar staff benefit schemes, etc.

Fixed Assets: The expenditure incurred on various fixed assets are to be shown separately which include goodwill, land, buildings, leaseholds, plant and machinery, railway sidings, furniture and fittings, patents, livestock, vehicles, etc. These assets are shown at cost less depreciation till the date.

Current Assets: Loans and Advances: Current assets include interest accrued on investments, inventories, sundry debtors, bills receivables, cash and bank balances, and other advances like prepaid expenses etc.

Provision for Taxation: This refers to the provision for income tax (corporation tax) chargeable on profits, and it is made by debiting the Profit and Loss Account and crediting the provision for taxation account which is shown on the liabilities side under the heading "current liabilities and provisions" in the balance sheet.

6. D share of profit $= \frac{1}{8}$

Balance available for A, B, C $= \frac{7}{8}$

A's new share $= \frac{7}{8} \times \frac{4}{9} = \frac{7}{8} = \frac{28}{72}$

B's new share $= \frac{7}{8} \times \frac{3}{9} = \frac{7}{24} = \frac{21}{72}$

C's new share $= \frac{7}{8} \times \frac{2}{9} = \frac{7}{36} = \frac{14}{72}$

$\therefore$ New profit = 28 : 21 : 14 : 9

7. Output to earn a profit of ₹ 80,000

$$= \frac{\text{Fixed Expenses} + \text{Profit}}{\text{Selling price per unit} - \text{Marginal cost per unit}}$$

$$= \frac{(500000 + 300000) + 80000}{25 - 15}$$

$$= \frac{800000 + 80000}{10}$$

$$= \frac{880000}{10} = 88{,}000$$

8. Specimen of Cash Flow Statement

(For the year ended....)

Cash Inflow	Amount	Cash Outflow	Amount
	₹		₹
1. Cash Balance (Opening)	—	1. Repayment of loans	—
2. Cash from Operation	—	2. Payment of dividend	—
3. Sale of Fixed Assets	—	3. Purchase of fixed assets	—
4. Issue of Share for cash	—	4. Redemption of debentures for cash	—
5. Issue of Debenture for cash	—	5. Redemption of Preference share for cash	—
6. Raising of long-term loans	—	6. Loss from operation	—
7. Decrease in Debtors	—	7. Decrease in creditors	—
		8. Cash balance at the end	—
	—		—

11. The law of diminishing marginal utility is an important law of consumer' choice. This law is a simple generalization of consumers' behavioural pattern. It is known as the "Gossen's First Law", because the main idea was put for the first time by H.H. Gossen. But Alfred Marshall takes the entire credit as he has propounded and developed it systematically in his famous book in 1890.

13. • The Normal Distribution is also called the Gaussian Distribution after Karl Friedrich Gauss, a German mathematician (1777-1855)

• Characteristics of any Normal Distribution

- Bell-shaped curve
- Unimodal - peak is at the mean
- Symmetric about the mean
- Mean = Median = Mode
- 'Tails' of the curve extend to infinity in both directions

14. The probable error (PE) of coefficient of correlation indicates extent to which its value depends on the condition or random sampling. If r is the calculated value of correlation coefficient in a sample of n pairs of observations, then the standard error SE_r of the correlation coefficient r is given by

$$SE_r = \frac{1-r^2}{\sqrt{n}}$$

The probable error of the coefficient of correlation is calculated by the expression:

$$PE_r = 0.6745\ SE_r = 0.6745 = \frac{1-r^2}{\sqrt{n}}$$

Thus with the help of PE_r we can determine the range within which population coefficient of correlation is expected to fall using following formula:

$$\rho = r \pm PE_r$$

Where ρ (rho) represents population coefficient of correlation.

Remarks

1. If $r < PE_r$ then the value of r is not significant, that is, there is no relationship between two variables of interest.
2. If $r > 6PE_r$ then value of r is significant, that is, there exists a relationship between two variables.

15. Most of the parametric tests viz. t, z, F etc. are based on the Assumption that the distribution of the population from which the sample has been drawn is Normal. But if the distribution of the parent population of the sample is skewed or non-normal these statistical tests fails. Moreover; in most of these (parametric) tests, it is assumed that the population parameters can be fairly estimated from the corresponding sample statistics. But for the data which are nominal in nature or ranked do not give any meaningful result in such attempt.

The statisticians therefore suggested some distribution free tests which are non-normal, which do not depend upon the shape of the curve or for which sample statistics can not be calculated. These tests do not depend upon population parameter and are called non-parametric tests.

Some of the non-parametric tests are :

(*i*) Chi-square test,

(*ii*) Sign test,

(*iii*) Rank-sum test, and

(*iv*) Run test, etc.

Advantages of Non-Parametric Tests:

Non-parametric tests are

(*i*) Distribution free and hence no assumption about the population is required

(*ii*) When sample size is small it is simple to understand and easy to apply.

(*iii*) It is less time consuming and for significant result no further work is necessary.

(*iv*) Applicable to all types of data.

(*v*) Helpful to researchers collecting pilot study data or the medical researchers working with a rase disease.

(*vi*) Make fewer assumptions than classical procedures.

17. Group think: Systematic analysis of the decision-making processes underlying the war in Vietnam and other US foreign policy fiascoes prompted Yale University's Irving Janis to coin the term group think. Modern managers can all too easily become victims of group think, just like professional politicians, if they passively ignore the danger. Janis defines group think as "a mode of thinking that people engage in when they are deeply involved in a cohesive in-group, when members' strivings for unanimity override their motivation to realistically appraise alternative courses of action." He adds, "Group think refers to a deterioration of mental efficiency, reality testing, and moral judgment that results from in-group pressures". Members of groups victimized by group think tend to be friendly and tightly knit.

According to Janis's model, there are eight classic symptoms of group think. The greater the number of symptoms, the higher the probability of group think:

1. ***Invulnerability:*** An illusion that breeds excessive optimism and risk taking.
2. ***Inherent morality:*** A belief that encourages the group to ignore ethical implications.
3. ***Rationalization:*** Protects pet assumptions.
4. ***Stereotyped views of opposition:*** Cause group to underestimate opponents.
5. ***Self-censorship:*** Stifles critical debate.
6. ***Illusion of unanimity:*** Silence interpreted to mean consent.
7. ***Peer pressure:*** Loyalty of dissenters is questioned.
8. ***Mindguards:*** Self-appointed protectors against adverse information.

18. E.E. Fiedler (born 1922), a leading U.S. organisational scientist, introduced the contingency model of leadership in 1967 popularly known as Fiedler contingency model. The model postulates that the leadership effectiveness is based on 'situational contingency' which is the result of interaction of two factors: Least Preferred Coworker and Situational Favourableness.

Fiedler's Contingency Model

Fiedler's contingency model postulates that the leader's effectiveness is based on 'situational contingency' which is a result of interaction of two factors: leadership style and situational favourableness (later called situational control). The leadership style of the leader, thus, fixed and measured by what he calls the least preferred co-worker (LPC) scale, an instrument for measuring an individual's leadership orientation. According to Fiedler, there is no ideal leader. Both low-LPC (task-oriented) and high-LPC (relationship-oriented) leaders can be effective if their leadership orientation fits the situation. The contingency theory allows for predicting the characteristics of the appropriate situations for effectiveness. Three situational components determine the favourableness of situational control are: (*i*) leader-member relations, referring to the degree of mutual trust, respect and confidence between the leader and the subordinates, (*ii*) task structure, referring to the extent to which group tasks are clear and structured, (*iii*) leader position power, referring to the power inherent in the leader's position itself. When there is a good leader-member relation, a highly structured task, and high leader position power, the situation is considered a 'favourable situation'. Fiedler found that low-LPC leaders are more effective in extremely favourable or unfavourable situations, whereas high-LPC leaders perform best in situations with intermediate favourability.

Since personality is relatively stable, the contingency model suggests that improving effectiveness requires changing the situation to fit the leader. This is called job engineering. The organisation or the leader may increase or decrease task structure and position power, also training and group development may improve leader-member relations. A mismatch occurs if a relationship-oriented leader encounters a very favourable or very unfavourable situation or a task-oriented leader faces a situation of intermediate favourableness. Fiedler argues that because leadership behaviour is a personality trait, the leader cannot adapt to the situation and achieve group effectiveness as the model predicts; Fiedler contends the only alternative is to change the situation through job engineering. This called leader-situation match and mismatch.

19. Essentials for a successful Quality Circle programme are as under:

(*a*) **Management Commitment:** Unless strong supportive signals are sent by the top management and felt by the employees, QC Circles take a back seat. Such a situation can have extremely adverse effect on employees. Motivation and implementation of future programmes become very difficult.

(*b*) **Constitute a Steering Committee:** It is an apex body at the highest level of the unit/division which oversees the functioning of QC circles in the unit/division and serves as an advisory body to ensure smooth and effective functioning of the circles. Its dynamic role reflects the commitment stated above.

(*c*) **Facilitator:** He is usually a manager of the shop/department/section. He is responsible for guiding and directing the activities of the QC circles in his area and enthuse other executives also to get involved in supporting QC circles. He facilitates implementation also. His dynamic role is also a manifestation of managements' commitment.

(*d*) **Focus on employee involvement and development:** QC circles often fail because the management's over-riding focus is on cost reduction through QC circles.

Circle programmes are typically in those organizations which focus on involvement instead of cost reduction. Eventually, improvement does lead to lower costs.

(*e*) **Clear definition of 'supervisors' roles:** The level most threatened by increasing employee involvement is that of the supervisors. If this level becomes dissatisfied, it can be very detrimental to the QC circle program. Thus, it is extremely important that supervisors are involved in QC circles, and made to know their role in an environment of increasing employee involvement be defined and communicated.

(*f*) **Management presentation:** Active participation of top management in the presentation session is yet another example of its commitment to quality circles. The manner of organizing the sessions must not reflect pomp and pageantry but bring out the lively enthusiasm and commitment of employees for circle activities; and the results achieved.

20. Ethics is mainly divided into four major areas of study:

1. **Meta-ethics:** about the theoretical meaning and reference of moral propositions and how their truth values (if any) may be determined;

2. **Normative Ethics:** about the practical means of determining a moral course of action;
3. **Applied Ethics:** about how moral outcomes can be achieved in specific situations;
4. **Descriptive Ethics:** also known as comparative ethics, is the study of people's beliefs about morality.

21. Classification of Consumer Goods

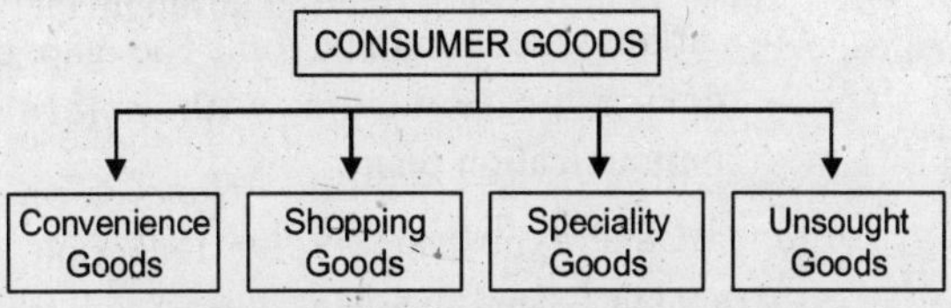

Fig. Classification of Consumer Goods

Consumer goods can be classified into four categories:

1. **Convenience Goods:** These goods are demanded by customers frequently in small quantities, but they must be immediately available at easily accessible retail shops. These are low cost, highly advertised items that are designed for mass markets and are sold to all income classes. All sales promotions devices are liberally used to stimulate consumer demand. These goods have to be distributed through numerous retailers. Examples of convenience goods are daily use items like soaps, detergents, biscuits, cosmetics and so on.

   Because most retail stores sell only a small volume of the total output of a convenience good, it is not economical for the manufacturer to sell directly to all retail outlets. Instead, the manufacturer depends on distributors or retailers to sell the product to the consumers. Intensive distribution is required for convenience goods.

2. **Shopping Goods:** A tangible product for which consumers want to compare quality, price, and perhaps style in several stores before making a purchase is considered a shopping good. These products need search efforts and special visits to central markets, there are not urgent purchases and buyers can postpone buying according to their convenience. They need not have numerous retail outlets. Buyers want to shop around and select goods after comparing quality, terms, style, price, services and so on. Examples of shopping goods are furniture, jewellery, fashion goods, appliances, automobiles.

   As fewer retailers are required, and retail stores typically buy shopping goods in large quantities, it is common for manufacturers to use short channels of distribution. Usually they sell directly to retailers.

3. **Speciality Goods:** A tangible product, for which consumers have a strong brand preference, and are willing to spend substantial time and effort in locating the desired brand is called a speciality good. They are goods with unique features. They demand special shopping efforts. They are sold in speciality shops. Buyers develop brand preferences and make special efforts to buy it. It should be noted that in the modern marketing environment, there is a thin line of difference between shopping and speciality goods.

   Examples of speciality goods can be desired brands of expensive designer clothes (clothes designed by leading designers like J.J. Vallaya or Ritu Beri), expensive sound systems and so on. The most important feature of speciality goods is that consumers insist on a particular brand and are willing to spend considerable effort to find it. Like shopping goods, few retail stores are required to sell speciality goods. Manufacturers may follow exclusive distribution policy for selling speciality goods *i.e.*, opening their own exclusive stores or selling franchisee of exclusive stores.

4. **Unsought Goods:** An unsought good is a new product that the consumer is not yet aware of or he is aware of that product but does not want it at this moment. An example of unsought goods can be a new product to be launched in the market which does not have a ready demand. Another example is personal insurance. Personal selling combined with advertising is the best strategy to sell unsought goods.

23. Merchant Intermediaries: Merchant intermediaries are those channel members who take both title and possession of goods from the preceding member(s) and channelise them to the subsequent member(s) in the channel sequence. Hence, merchant intermediaries are both buyers and sellers of goods.

The merchant middlemen are of four types-wholesalers, semi-wholesalers, retailers and distributors and dealers.

24. One of the service quality models that is well-known and applied in various industries is SERVQUAL introduced by Parasuraman, Zeithaml, and Berry (1985). SERVQUAL is a method used to measure service quality by looking into the gap between users' perception and expectation on a service. With the method, we can know how much the gap is between customer's perception and expectation on a service. The gaps that will be possibly occurred and affect the service quality are:

1. The gap between customer's expectation and management perception. The difference between user's expectation and management's perception about the customer's expectation.
2. The gap between management perception and service quality specification. The gap of management's perception on customer's expectation and service quality specification.
3. The gap between service quality specification and service presentation.
4. The gap between service presentation and marketing communication. The gap of service presentation with external communication team.
5. The gap in the service that is felt.

SERVQUAL scales include five service quality dimensions, which are: Tangibles, Reliability, Responsiveness, Assurance, and Empathy, which are explained as the following (Parasuraman, Zeithaml, and Berry, 1988):

1. Tangibles portray physical facilities, equipment, and appearance of staffs and users attendance.
2. Reliability refers to the ability to provide the promised service accurately reliably.
3. Responsiveness is the willingness to help and give the right attention to users.
4. Assurance is the polite and knowledge-able employees that create trust and conviction.
5. Empathy includes individual's awareness and care to the users.

25. $$\text{Operating Leverage} = \frac{\text{Contribution}}{\text{EBIT}}$$

$$= \frac{\text{Sales} - \text{VC}}{\text{Sales} - \text{VC} - \text{FC}}$$

$$= \frac{74-40}{74-40-8}$$

$$= \frac{34}{26} = 1.3$$

26. There are broadly two methods of capital budgeting: firstly, the non-discounted methods comprising (*a*) Payback Period and (*b*) Average Rate of Return; and secondly, the discounted methods comprising (a) Net Present Value, (*b*) Internal Rate of Return and (*c*) Profitability Index. These are shown in Fig.

Capital Budgeting Techniques

Traditional methods/ Non-discounted cash flow methods	Discounted Cash Flow (DCF) methods
(*a*) Average Rate of Return (ARR) method	(*a*) Net Present Value (NPV) method
(*b*) Payback (PB) method	(*b*) Internal Rate of Return (IRR) method
	(*c*) Profitability Index (PI)

Fig. : Methods of Capital Budgeting

30. Behaviour Modelling

- **Definition:** A training technique in which trainees are first shown good management techniques in a film, are asked to play roles in a simulated situation, and are then given feedback and praise by their supervisors.
- **Behaviour Modelling Involves**
  1. Showing trainees the right (or "model") way of doing something,
  2. Letting each person practice the right way to do it, and
  3. Providing feedback regarding each trainee's performance.
- The basic behaviour modelling procedure can be outlined as follows:
  - **Modelling:** First, trainees watch films or videotapes that show a model person behaving effectively in a problem situation. In other words, trainees are shown the right way to behave in a simulated but realistic situation. The film might thus show a supervisor effectively disciplining a subordinate, if teaching 'how to discipline' is the aim of the training.
  - **Role playing:** Next, the trainees are given roles to play in a simulated situation; here they practice and rehearse the effective behaviours demonstrated by the models.
  - **Social reinforcement:** The trainer provides reinforcement in the form of praise and constructive feedback based on how the trainee performs in the role playing situation.
  - **Transfer of training:** Finally, trainees are encouraged to apply their new skills when they are back on their jobs.
- Measures of learning and skill development were highest for behaviour modelling, followed by the computer-assisted training, and then by conventional instruction.

31. Code of Discipline: Over the years, several legislative measures have been adopted in India to promote discipline and harmony between employees and employers. Sad to relate, the results have not been very encouraging. As a remedy, the Second Five Year Plan has suggested that both employees and employers must formulate and abide by a voluntary Code of Discipline. In pursuance of this suggestion, the Fifteenth Indian Labour Conference suggested a Code of Discipline in 1957. The Central National Labour Organisations (INTUC, AITUC, HMS, UTUC) and Employers' Associations (EFI, AIOIE, AIMO) have agreed to enforce the code with effect from June 1, 1958. The code aims at preventing disputes by providing for voluntary and mutual settlement of disputes through negotiations without the interference of an outside agency. The principles regulating the conduct of the employer and the employee, as provided for in the code, may be listed thus:

Obligations of Both Parties

- It restrains both employers and employees from unilateral action. Both parties must recognise each other's rights and obligations and settle disputes through the existing machinery for the settlement of disputes.
- The parties should not indulge in strikes and lockouts without notice or without exploring possibilities to resolve disputes through negotiations.
- Neither party will resort to coercion, intimidation, victimisation or litigation or adopt unfair labour practices (*e.g.*, go slow, sit down strike, *etc.*).
- Both employers and unions will educate workers regarding their obligations and agree to follow a mutually agreed grievance procedure.

34. The Instruments of Monetary Policy: The monetary authority uses various tools to control the supply of money. These are known as instruments of credit control. These instruments can be divided into two categories-quantitative and qualitative credit controls. There are three main methods of quantitative credit control-bank rate policy, open market operation and changes in statutory reserve requirements. These methods are used to control the quantum of credit on the whole. The qualitative methods of credit control are also known as selective credit control methods. These include credit rationing, direct action, changes in margin requirements, moral suasion, etc.

Methods of Credit Control by RBI

Quantitative Methods	Qualitative Methods
1. Bank Rate Policy	1. Fixation of Margin Requirements
2. Open Market Operations	2. Regulation of Consumer Credit
3. Variation of Cash Reserve Ratios	3. Control through Directives
4. Fixation of Lending Rates of Commercial Banks	4. Rationing of Credit
5. Credit Squeeze	5. Prior Authorisation Schemes
6. 'Repo' Transactions	6. Moral Sausion
	7. Direct Action.

35. Since 1992-93, SIDBI liberalized its terms of assistance and simplified procedures, with a view to widen its scope for larger coverage of schemes. Some of the salient features of SIDBI can be listed as follows:

(*a*) SIDBI has been operating Single Window Scheme (SWS) which is enlarged to cover units in identified areas. The extent of refinance against cash credit sanctioned by banks under SWS was raised from 50 to 70 per cent.

(*b*) SIDBI provides refinance facilities under automatic refinance scheme (ARS). The limit of term loans under ARS was initially fixed at ₹ 10 lakhs but later was raised to ₹ 50 lakhs and the extent of refinance has been raised from 75 to 90 per cent.

(*c*) SIDBI has introduced equipment financing for assistance to existing well-run small scale units for technology upgradation/modernization.

(*d*) SIDBI has introduced a refinance scheme for resettlement of voluntarily retired workers of National Textile Corporation (NTC) and help them to buy upto four looms.

(*e*) SIDBI has set up a venture capital fund to assist entrepreneurs.

Within a short span of time, SIDBI has emerged as a major player in the field of finance for the small-scale sector.

37. The new policy recognizes two new ports for importing and exporting: Calicut Airport in Kerala state and the Arakkonam Inland Container Depot (ICD) in Tamil Nadu state.

40. WTO has the following five functions to perform:

(1) The WTO provides the framework for implementation, administration and operation of multilateral trade agreements reached at Uruguay Round.

(2) The WTO provides the forum for further negotiations among its member states concerning their multilateral trade relations with regard to the matters included in the agreements reached at Uruguay Round.

(3) The WTO undertakes the task of settlement of disputes among the member states, which arise from their different understandings of the rules and procedure agreed upon.

(4) The WTO administers the 'Trade Review Mechanism'.

(5) In order to evolve a coherent global economic policy to promote free and fair trade among the different countries, WTO cooperates in an appropriate manner with the IMF; World Bank and its affiliated agencies.

41. Various countries have their laws, compliances and regulations regarding mergers. While in the Indian context, a particular process is followed by all the companies undergoing a merger. Broadly speaking, on discussion, various experts have opined that the usual procedure is as follows (while a certain level of discretion is required at some steps):

1. Screening and investigation of a merger proposal.
2. Negotiation between the companies takes place.
3. Drafting of scheme takes place.
4. Notice to board of directors of both companies is sent.
5. Preparation of valuation report and determination of swap ratio is initiated and forwarded.
6. Boards of directors from both the companies approve the proposal
7. Obtaining no objection certificate (NOC) from shareholders of both companies (Under exceptional circumstances, this may be exempted from meeting to reduce time and costs.)
8. Obtaining an NOC from creditors, financial institutions and banks of both the companies.
9. Application submitted to respective High Courts in their regions by both the companies for retaining sanctions. (It is feasible to shift registered office to one jurisdiction for the convenience of both companies.)
10. Furnishing notice of Extraordinary General Meeting (EGM) of shareholders containing details of terms of merger, level of interest of directors along with proxy forms within 21 days to authorities.
11. Publication of an advertisement or notice regarding merger in at least two newspapers within 21 days.
12. Submission of the proof of an advertisement or notice in original as compliance to the High Court on an affidavit.

13. Under chairmanship, majority voting by creditors and shareholders in a meeting is mandatory, to arrive at a valid decision.
14. It is mandatory for the chairman to file a report on this meeting within 7 days to the authorities.
15. Furnishing details on resolutions along with descriptive explanatory statements to the registrar of the companies.
16. Response of High Court to the report submitted by chairman is received within 7 days.
17. Publishing a serving notice of hearing of quotation in two newspapers which should be the same in which the advertisement notice was published earlier.
18. Notice to the central government, *i.e.,* to the regional director (The compliances regarding the Income Tax Act, 1961 (Sec. 72A) are considered or verified.)
19. Objections, if any, are sorted or complied with.
20. High Court sanctions or approvals via order are issued.
21. Certified copy of High Court sanction order is submitted to the Registrar of Companies within 30 days of issue of this order.
22. Integration of both the companies at structural and financial levels takes place.

The more coordinated the process is, the less time-consuming will be the merger procedure. It is noteworthy that similar process is followed for Demerger in India, except for the fact that application in a merger is for integration, while for a de-merger, it is for the purpose of disintegration. The overall procedure is more or less the same.

42. The basic features of options are followings:

1. The option is exercisable only by the owner namely the buyer of the option.
2. Option yield only capital gains.
3. The owner has limited liability
4. Owners of options have no voting rights and dividend right
5. Options have high degree of risk to the option writers
6. Options involving buying counter positions by the option sellers
7. Flexibility in investors needs
8. No certificates are issued by the company
9. Options are popular because they allow the buyer profits from favourable movement in exchange rate

43. The Opportunity Cost Approach: This approach values human resources on the basis of the economic concept of opportunity cost. *Hekimian and Jones* proposed this method to overcome the limitations of the replacement cost method. The human resource values are measured through a competitive bidding process within the firm, based on the concept of opportunity cost. Under this method, "the investment centre managers will bid for the scarce employees they need to recruit. These 'scarce' employees come from within the firm and include only those who are the subject of recruitment request made by an investment centre manager. In other words, employees not considered 'scarce' are not included in the human asset base of the organization.

Under this approach, the divisional or investment centre manager may bid for the services of the various personnel he requires. This bid price is then included in the investment base. The maximum bid price may go to the extent of the capitalized value of the extra profits likely to be generated by the ability and competence of the executive.

For example, assume that a company has a capital base of ₹ 20,00,000 and it earned profits of the amount of ₹ 2,00,000. The return on investment (ROI) of the particular industry to which the company belongs is 12%. If the services of a particular executive are acquired, it is expected that the profits will increase by ₹ 60,000 over and above the target profit.

If we capitalize ₹ 60,000 at 12% rate of return, it works to ₹ 5,00,000. The company may bid upto ₹ 5,00,000 for the executive. However, the maximum bid can go upto the capitalized value of ₹ 1,00,000, the actual excess profit expected to be generated by the executive, *i.e.*, ₹ 8,33,333.

Hekimian and Jones believe that this approach provides for more optimal allocation of personnel and sets the quantitative base for planning, evaluating and developing the human assets of the firm.

44. **The Risks of Investing:** The basic types of investment risk are business risk, financial risk, market risk, purchasing power risk, interest rate risk, liquidity risk, and event risk. Other things being equal, you'd like to reduce your exposure to these risks as much as possible.

Business Risk: When investing in a company, you may have to accept the possibility that the firm will fail to maintain sales and profits, or even to stay in business. Such failure is due either to economic or industry factors or, as is more often the case, to poor management decisions. Business risk is the degree of uncertainty surrounding the firm's cash flows and subsequent ability to meet operating expenses on time. Companies that are subject to high degrees of business risk may experience wide fluctuations in sales, may have widely erratic earnings, and can experience substantial operating losses every now and then.

Financial Risk: Financial risk concerns the amount of debt used to finance a firm, as well as the possibility that the firm will not have sufficient cash flows to meet these obligations on time. Look to the company's balance sheet in order to get a handle on a firm's financial risk. As a rule, companies that have little or no long-term debt are fairly low in financial risk. This is the case particularly if the company also has a healthy earnings picture. The problem with debt financing is that it creates principal and interest obligations that must be met regardless of how much profit the company is generating.

Market Risk: Market risk results from the behaviour of investors in the securities markets that can lead to swings in security prices. These price changes can be due to underlying intrinsic factors, as well as to changes in political, economic, and social conditions or in investor tastes and preferences. Essentially, market risk is reflected in the price volatility of a security: the more volatile the price of a security, the greater its market risk.

Purchasing Power Risk: Changes in the general level of prices within the economy also produce purchasing power risk. In periods of rising prices (inflation), the purchasing power of the dollar declines. This means that a smaller quantity of goods and services can be purchased with a given number of dollars. In general, investments (such as stocks and real estate) whose values tend to move with general price levels are most profitable during periods of rising prices, whereas investments (such as bonds) that provide fixed returns are preferred during periods of low or declining price levels.

Interest Rate Risk: Fixed-income securities-which include notes, bonds, and preferred stocks—offer investors a fixed periodic return and, as such, are most affected by interest rate risk. As interest rates change, the prices of these securities fluctuate, decreasing with rising interest rates and increasing with falling rates. For example, the prices of fixed-income securities drop when interest rates increase, giving investors rates of return that are competitive with securities offering higher levels of interest income. Changes in interest rates are due to fluctuations in the supply of or demand for money.

45. The important money market instruments are commercial papers, certificate of deposits, treasury bills, commercial bills call money repurchase agreements (Repos), Inter-bank participation certificates etc. The assets which are used as credit instruments are known as near money assets. The markets where these financial assets are traded are called the sub-markets of money market. Call money market, treasury bill market, commercial bill market, commercial paper market, certificate of deposit market, acceptance market, etc. are various components of money markets.

46. The ICAI issued the Accounting Standard (AS-6) "Depreciation Accounting" in November 1982 which was superseded by revised standard of the same number, that came into effect in respect of accounting periods commencing on or after 1st April 1995. The revised standard defines depreciation and depreciable assets, sets out the significance of depreciation, specifies the fixed assets excluded from its scope and coverage, and prescribes the principles and norms of standard accounting treatment for various aspects of depreciation accounting. These include determinants of depreciation, methods of depreciation, statutory requirements and compliances, consistency principle and depreciation charge in special cases, and disclosure requirements in financial statements prepared on historical cost basis, including revaluation.

48. Projective Techniques: Projective tests require the respondent to decide what the other person would do in a certain situation. These techniques explore the underlying motives of individuals who consciously or unconsciously get involved in rationalisations and concealment because they may be reluctant in admit certain weaknesses or desires. Projective techniques involve a variety of disguised tests containing ambiguous stimuli such as untitled pictures, incomplete sentences, inkblots, word-associations and other-person characterisations. The respondent taking the test is required to describe, complete or explain the meaning of different ambiguous stimuli. It is believed that respondents' inner feelings influence their perceptions of ambiguous stimuli. By taking the tests, they project their inner thoughts revealing their underlying needs, wants, aspirations, fears and motives, whether or not the respondents are fully aware of them. Some examples of projective techniques are:

- **Thematic Apperception Techniques (TAT):** Respondents are shown pictures or cartoons concerning the product or the topic under study and asked to describe what is happening in the picture. It is believed that respondents will actually reveal their own motivations, attitudes, personalities and feelings about the situation.
- **Word Association Test:** This is a relatively old and simple technique. Respondents are read a series of words or phrases, one at a time and asked to answer quickly with the first word that comes to mind after hearing each one. By responding in rapid succession, it is assumed that they indicate what they associate most closely with the word or phrase spoken and reveal their true feelings.

- **Sentence Completion Test:** The interviewer reads the beginning of a sentence and the respondent is required to finish it. This technique is believed to be useful in uncovering the images consumers have about products and stores. The information collected can be used to develop promotional campaigns.
- **The Third-Person Technique:** The inter-viewer asks the respondent to describe a third person. For this, respondents are presented with some information about the person. It is believed that when they describe a neighbour or a third person, they usually respond without hesitation and in doing so, they express their own attitudes or motives as they infer the attitudes or motives of someone else.
- **Laddering (Means-End Chain Model):** This is a relatively new research method for data collection. The assumption here is that very specific product attributes are linked at levels of increasing abstraction to terminal values. The consumer concerned has highly valued end states and chooses among alternative means to attain these goals, and therefore products are valued as the means to an end. Laddering uses in-depth probing directed toward uncovering higher-level meanings at attribute (benefit) level and the value level.

49. Style, Fashion, and Fad Life Cycles: Three special categories of product life cycles should be distinguished-styles, fashions, and fads (Figure). A style is a basic and distinctive mode of expression appearing in a field of human endeavour. Styles appear in homes (colonial, ranch, Cape Cod); clothing (formal, casual, funky); and art (realistic, surrealistic, abstract). A style can last for generations, and go in and out of vogue. A fashion is a currently accepted or popular style in a given field. Fashions pass through four stages: distinctiveness, emulation, mass-fashion, and decline.

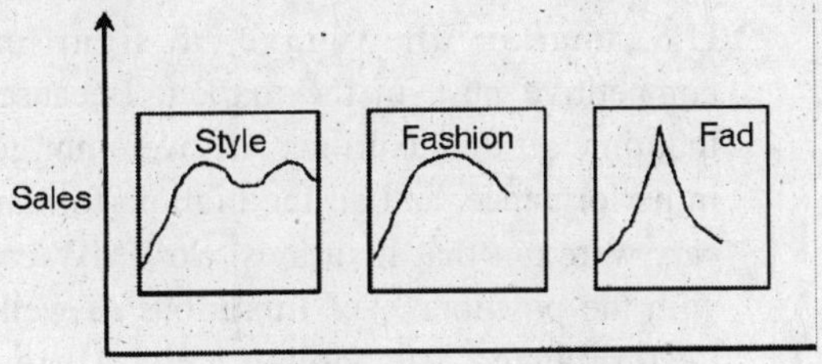

Fig.: Product Life Cycles in Terms of Style, Fashion and Fad

The length of a fashion cycle is hard to predict. Chester Wasson believes that fashions end because they represent a purchase compromise, and consumers start looking for missing attributes. For example, as automobiles become smaller, they become less comfortable, and then a growing number of buyers start wanting larger cars.

Furthermore, too many consumers adopt the fashion, thus turning others away. William Reynolds suggests that the length of a particular fashion cycle depends on the extent to which the fashion meets a genuine need, is consistent with other trends in the society, satisfies societal norms and values, and does not exceed technological limits as it develops.

Fads are fashions that come quickly into public view, are adopted with great zeal, peak early, and decline very fast. Their acceptance cycle is short, and they tend to attract only a limited following of those who are searching for excitement or want to distinguish themselves from others. They often have a novel or capricious aspect, such as body piercing and tattooing. Fads do not survive because they do not normally satisfy a strong need. The marketing winners are those who recognize fads early and leverage them into products with staying power.

50. Straddle positioning is the kind of positioning where the brands are looking for position itself in two categories simultaneously.

For example in 1980s when BMW entered the U.S. market they gave a significant competitive push in the market. Because at that time all the luxurious cars were not good in performance, and all the high performance cars were not that luxurious. So BMW came with the positioning of Luxurious as well as Performance. The slogan (The Ultimate Driving Machine) also very well supports the cause. Also the Mahindra Scorpio had positioned itself as Luxury and Adventure.

In the case of Scorpio the brand can have -1 POP (points of parity) in Luxury and POD (point of differentiation) in Adventure, when comparing to Luxurious category and 2 POP (points of parity) in Adventurous and POD (point of differentiation) in Luxury, when comparing to Adventurous category. So the brand can enjoy double benefit in terms of customer as well as competitor. Similarly we can relate this to BMW also.

Again Domino's pizza has the similar kind of positioning *i.e.*, by Product attribute and Desirable benefit. Product attribute by promoting fresh pizza and Desirable benefit by home delivery service. Again it works for this particular brand.

53. A reverse auction is the process in which a buyer posts its interest in buying a certain quantity of items with notations concerning quality, specification, and delivery timing, and sellers compete for the business by submitting successively lower bids until there is only one seller left. Reverse auctions create tremendous "power" for the buyer because multiple sellers are competing for the same business.

54. The practice of airing television or radio ads on several stations simultaneously is called a road-block. The advantages of this strategy are that you get multiple exposures, reach people who frequently switch stations, and are more likely to benefit from word-of-mouth or viewers talking you up after the ads have run.

55. Professor Flippo in his book, Principles of Personnel Management describes morale as a "mental condition or attitude of individuals and group which determines their willingness to cooperate".

According to Flippo, "Good morale is evidenced by employee enthusiasm, voluntary conformance with regulations and orders, and a willingness to cooperate with others in the accomplishment of the organization's objectives". Conversely, "poor morale is evidenced by surliness, cases of insubordination, discouragement, and dislike of job, company, and associates".

57. Behaviourally Anchored Rating Scales (BARS): 'BARS' is a performance appraisal method combining rating and critical incidents. It is a more objective and accurate method than the two methods separately. Rather than having excellent, good, average, and so forth, the form has several statements that describe the employee's performance, from which the manager selects the one that best describes the employee's performance for that task. Standards are clear when good BARS are developed.

Developing BARS typically requires five steps:

1. ***Generate critical incidents:*** Ask persons who know the job (job holders and/or supervisors) to describe specific illustrations (critical incidents) of effective and ineffective performance.
2. ***Develop performance dimensions:*** Have these people cluster the incidents into a smaller set of (5 or 10) performance dimensions, and define each dimension, such as "conscientiousness".

3. ***Reallocate incidents:*** Another group of people who also know the job then reallocate the original critical incidents. They get the cluster definitions and the critical incidents, and must reassign each incident to the cluster they think it fits best. Retain a critical incident if some percentage (usually 50% to 80%) of this second group assigns it to the same cluster, as did the first group.
4. ***Scale the incidents:*** This second group then rates the behaviour described by the incident as to how effectively or ineffectively it represents performance on the dimension (7- to 9-point scales are typical).
5. ***Develop a final instrument:*** Choose about six or seven of the incidents as the dimension's behavioural anchors.

59. The Constitution of India committed the government to evolve a wage policy. Successive five-year plans have also devoted necessary attention to the need for a wage policy. Following the recommendations of the First and Second Plans, the Government of India constituted wage boards for important industries in the country. A wage board is a tripartite body comprising representations from the government, owners, and employees. Technically speaking, a wage board can only make recommendations, and wage policies are normally implemented through persuasion.

60. The Surplus Value Theory of Wages (Marxian): This theory owes its development to Karl Marx (1818-1883). According to this theory, the labour was an article of commerce, which could be purchased on payment of 'subsistence price'. The price of any product was determined by the labour time needed for producing it. The labourer was not paid in proportion to the time spent on work, but much less, and the surplus went over, to be utilised for paying other expenses.

61. 'Systems' approach was developed by John Dunlop. He views industrial relations system as a sub-system of society. According to Dunlop, the core elements of the systems model of industrial relations are actors, *certain contexts, an ideology which binds* the industrial relations system together and body of rules created to govern the actors at the workplace.

63. On August 8, 1967, ASEAN (Association of South-East Asian Nations) came into existence with five member countries named: Indonesia, Philippines, Malaysia, Singapore and Thailand. Brunei joined ASEAN after her Independence in 1984. Vietnam also became the member of ASEAN in 1995. Laos and Myanmar got its membership in 1997 and in April 1999. Cambodia also became the member of ASEAN, with the object of securing mutual understanding and cooperation. At present the total membership of ASEAN stands at ten.

69. Deduction in respect of royalty income, etc., of authors of certain books other than text books [Section 80QQB]

(*i*) Under section 80QQB, deduction of up to a maximum ₹ 3,00,000 is allowed to an individual resident in India in respect of income derived as author *i.e.*, the deduction shall be the income derived as author or ₹ 3,00,000, whichever is less.

(*ii*) This income may be received either by way of a lumpsum consideration for the assignment or grant of any of his interests in the copyright of any book.

(*iii*) Such book should be a work of literary, artistic or scientific nature, or of royalties or copyright fees (whether receivable in lumpsum or otherwise) in respect of such book.

(*iv*) However, this deduction shall not be available in respect of royalty income from textbook for schools, guides, commentaries, newspapers, journals, pamphlets and other publications of similar nature.

70. Death-cum-retirement Gratuity under Section 10(10): Gratuity is the amount paid by the employer to the employee for the meritorious service rendered by him. The employee may receive Gratuity at the time of:

(*a*) leaving the job

(*b*) his death

For government employees: Any death-cum-retirement gratuity received by the Government employees are fully exempted from Tax. The entire amount is fully exempt from tax.

For non-government employees: Gratuity received by the non-government employees can be classified into two categories, namely:

- Covered by the Payment of Gratuity Act
- Not covered by the Payment of Gratuity Act

The provisions relating to gratuity for non-government employees are given below.

From the actual gratuity received, the least of the following will be deducted and the balance will be taxable.

Covered by the Payment of Gratuity Act	Not covered by the Payment of Gratuity Act
(*a*) Notified limit ₹ 10,00,000 (*b*) Actual gratuity received (*c*) 15 days average salary for every completed year of service. Fraction for 6 months or more is to be rounded off to one year. **Note:** Salary = Basic Pay + DA + Commission on turnover achieved. Average salary shall be calculated by taking 26 days as the maximum number of working days in a month.	(*a*) Notified limit ₹ 10,00,000 (*b*) Actual gratuity received (*c*) 1/2 month's average salary for every completed year of service. Fraction of service to be ignored. **Note:** Salary = Basic Pay + DA + Commission on turnover achieved. Average salary means average of the salary drawn during 10 months before the calendar month of retirement.

73. Section 80GG allows the Individuals to a deduction in respect of house rent paid by him for his own residence. Such deduction is permissible subject to the following conditions:

(*a*) The Individual has not been in receipt of any House Rent Allowance from his employer specifically granted to him which qualifies for exemption under section 10(13A) of the Act.

(*b*) The Individual files the declaration in Form No. 10BA.

(*c*) The employee does not own:

(*i*) Any residential accommodation himself or by his spouse or minor child or where such Individual is a member of a Hindu Undivided family, by such family, at the place where he ordinarily resides or performs duties of his office or carries on his business or profession; or

(*ii*) At any other place, any residential accommodation being accommodation in the occupation of the Individual, the value of which is to be determined under Section 23(2)(a) or Section 23(4)(a) as the case may be.

(*d*) He will be entitled to a deduction in respect of house rent paid by him in excess of 10% of his total income, subject to a ceiling of 25% thereof or ₹ 2,000/- per month (₹ 5000/- Proposed *w.e.f.* F.Y.

2016-17), whichever is less. The total income for working out these percentages will be computed before making any deduction under section 80GG. In other word eligibility will be least amount of the following:

1. Rent paid minus 10 per cent the adjusted total income.
2. ₹ 2,000 per month (₹ 5000/- Proposed *w.e.f.* F.Y. 2016-17).
3. 25 per cent of the adjusted total income.

The deduction will also not be available to an assessee if any residential accommodation is owned by the assessee at any other place, which he is occupying, and the concessions in respect of self-occupied house are claimed by him for that property. In such a case, no deduction will be allowed in respect of the rent paid, even if the person does not own any residential accommodation at the place where he ordinarily resides.

YOUR SPACE

Previous Paper (Solved)

UGC (NET) JRF & Assistant Professor Exam
Commerce, December-2015

PAPER-II

Note : *This paper contains* ***fifty (50)*** *objective type questions of* ***two (2)*** *marks each.* ***All questions are*** *compulsory.*

1. Environmental degeneration does **not** consist of:

A. Land degeneration and soil erosion

B. Problem of over grazing and ecological degeneration

C. Floods

D. None of the above

2. Which of the following is **not** the main objective of "Fiscal Policy of India"?

A. To increase liquidity in economy

B. To promote price stability

C. To minimize the in-equality in income and wealth

D. To promote employment opportunities

3. Liberalization means:

A. Reducing number of reserved industries from 17 to 8

B. Liberating the industry, trade and economy from unwanted restriction

C. Opening up economy to the world by attaining international competitiveness

D. Free determination of interest rate

4. Assertion (A): Industrialization of an economy is considered synonymous with growth.

Reasoning (R): The transfer of resources from agrarian to industrial may be capital or labour or both.

Codes:

A. Both (A) and (R) are true and (R) is correct explanation of (A)

B. Both (A) and (R) are true but (R) is not the correct explanation of (A)

C. (A) is true but (R) is false

D. (A) is false but (R) is true

5. Globalization is the term used to describe process of removal of restriction on which one of the following?

A. Foreign trade B. Investment

C. Both A and B D. None of the above

6. Interest on loan taken for the purchase of fixed assets is a:

A. Revenue Expenditure

B. Capital Expenditure

C. Deferred Revenue Expenditure

D. Capital Loss

7. Dual Aspect Concept results in the following accounting equation:

A. Revenue = Expenses

B. Capital + Profits = Assets + Expenses

C. Capital + Liabilities = Assets

D. Capital + Drawings = Owner's Equity

8. Match the items in **Column-1** with the items in **Column-2.**

Column-1	**Column-2**
(*a*) Materiality Concept	(*i*) The same accounting method used by a firm from one period to another
(*b*) Going Concern Concept	(*ii*) An inappropriate assumption of a firm being bankrupt
(*c*) Historical Cost Concept	(*iii*) A normal basis used for accounting assets
(*d*) Consistency Concept	(*iv*) Relates to the importance of an item or event

Codes:

	(*a*)	(*b*)	(*c*)	(*d*)
A.	(*iv*)	(*ii*)	(*iii*)	(*i*)
B.	(*i*)	(*ii*)	(*iii*)	(*iv*)
C.	(*ii*)	(*iii*)	(*iv*)	(*i*)
D.	(*iv*)	(*ii*)	(*i*)	(*iii*)

9. 'X' Ltd. has a liquid ratio of 2 : 1. If its stock is ₹ 40,000 and its current liabilities are of ₹ 1 Lac, its current ratio will be:

A. 1.4 times B. 2.4 times
C. 1.2 times D. 3.4 times

10. 'Comparison of the financial statements of the current year with the performance of previous years of the same firm', is known as:

A. Trend Analysis
B. Horizontal Analysis
C. Intra-firm comparison
D. All of the above

11. The Marshallian utility analysis is based on a less valid assumption of:

A. cardinal measurability of the utility
B. given marginal utility of money
C. diminishing marginal utility of the goods
D. additivity of the utility

12. Match the items of the **List-I** with those of the **List-II** and indicate the **correct** code.

List-I	List-II
(*a*) Convexity of the indifferences curve to origin	(*i*) Indifference curve analysis
(*b*) Quantity of certain goods sacrificed for a large quantity of other goods	(*ii*) Consumer's equilibrium
(*c*) Equality of the ratio of the marginal utilities with that of the prices of the two goods	(*iii*) Substitutability/ complementarity of the two goods
(*d*) Separation of substitution and income effects from the total price effect	(*iv*) Marginal rate substitution

Codes:

	(*a*)	(*b*)	(*c*)	(*d*)
A.	(*iv*)	(*ii*)	(*i*)	(*iii*)
B.	(*iii*)	(*iv*)	(*ii*)	(*i*)
C.	(*iii*)	(*i*)	(*iv*)	(*ii*)
D.	(*i*)	(*iii*)	(*ii*)	(*iv*)

13. Firms producing and selling a large variety of goods will generally follow:

A. Cost plus pricing B. Marginal pricing
C. Skimming pricing D. Product line pricing

14. For the following two statements of **Assertion (A)** and **Reasoning (R)** indicate the **correct** code:

Assertion (A): All firms under perfect competition in long run earn only normal profit.

Reasoning (R): All firms under perfect competition in long run operate at the minimum average cost level.

Codes:

A. (A) and (R) both are correct
B. (A) is correct but (R) is not correct
C. (A) is not correct but (R) is correct
D. (A) and (R) both are incorrect

15. Match the items of **List-I** with those of **List-II** and indicate the **correct** code.

List-I	List-II
(*a*) Substitute Goods	(*i*) Negative Cross Elasticity
(*b*) Complementary Goods	(*ii*) Low Price Elasticity
(*c*) Giffen Goods	(*iii*) Positive Cross Elasticity
(*d*) High Income Group Consumption Goods	(*iv*) Positive Price Elasticity

Codes:

	(*a*)	(*b*)	(*c*)	(*d*)
A.	(*iii*)	(*iv*)	(*ii*)	(*i*)
B.	(*iii*)	(*i*)	(*iv*)	(*ii*)
C.	(*ii*)	(*iii*)	(*i*)	(*iv*)
D.	(*i*)	(*ii*)	(*iii*)	(*iv*)

16. Which one of the following is **not** a method of studying association of attributes?

A. Concurrent Deviation Method
B. Proportion Method
C. Yule's Method
D. Coefficient of Contingency

17. Identify which of the following steps would be included in hypothesis testing:
(*a*) State the null and alternative hypothesis.
(*b*) Set the significance level before the research study.
(*c*) Eliminate all outliers.
(*d*) Obtain the probability value using a computer program such as SPSS.
(*e*) Compare the probability value to the significance level and make the statistical decision.

Codes:
A. (*a*), (*c*) and (*d*) B. (*c*), (*d*), and (*e*)
C. (*a*), (*b*), (*d*) and (*e*) D. (*b*), (*c*), (*d*) and (*e*)

18. Select the methods of finding out correlation from the following:
(*a*) Karl Pearson's Method
(*b*) Spearman's Rank Method
(*c*) Yule's Method
(*d*) Coefficient of Contingency
(*e*) Concurrent Deviation Method

Codes:
A. (*a*), (*b*), (*c*) B. (*a*), (*b*), (*c*), (*d*)
C. (*a*), (*b*), (*e*) D. (*c*), (*d*), (*e*)

19. A set of data can be distinguished from other set of data by means of:
A. Central value and dispersion
B. Central value, dispersion and skewness
C. Central value, dispersion, skewness and Kurtosis
D. None of the above

20. The advent of computers in research has led to:
A. Limitations of options in analysis
B. Tremendous amount of flexibility with marginal increase in cost
C. Myopic exposure of statistics to the researcher
D. None of the above

21. Who among the following is **not** related to the planning function given by Taylor?
A. Route clerk B. Time and cost clerk
C. Inspector D. Disciplinarian

22. Match the following:

(Book)	**(Author)**
(*a*) Functions of the Executive	(*i*) Charles Babbage
(*b*) On the Economy of Machinery and Manufactures	(*ii*) Henri Fayol
(*c*) The Effective Executive	(*iii*) Chester Barnard
(*d*) General and Industrial Administration	(*iv*) Peter Drucker

Codes:

	(*a*)	(*b*)	(*c*)	(*d*)
A.	(*i*)	(*ii*)	(*iii*)	(*iv*)
B.	(*iii*)	(*i*)	(*iv*)	(*ii*)
C.	(*iv*)	(*iii*)	(*i*)	(*ii*)
D.	(*iii*)	(*iv*)	(*i*)	(*ii*)

23. The classical organisation theory treats organisation as a/an:
A. Open system B. Closed system
C. Technical system D. Macro system

24. Which of the following is a systematic interactive forecasting method that relies on a panel of experts?
A. Pay-off matrix B. Game theory
C. Queing theory D. Delphi technique

25. According to Hersey and Blanchard's situational approach to leadership, the 'participating style' of leadership has:
A. High task and low relationship orientation
B. High task and high relationship orientation
C. Low task and high relationship orientation
D. Low task and low relationship orientation

26. Which of the following is **not** a reason for the failure of new products?
A. Good idea but overestimated market size
B. Correctly positioned new product, not promoted effectively or overpriced
C. Development costs are lower than or equal to estimated or expected
D. Competitors fight back harder than expected

27. Which one of the following is **true** for the calculation of overall market share ?

A. (Customer penetration) × (Customer loyalty) × (Price selectivity)

B. (Customer loyalty) × (Customer selectivity) × (Price selectivity)

C. (Customer selectivity) × (Price selectivity) × (Customer penetration)

D. (Customer penetration) × (Customer loyalty) × (Customer selectivity) × (Price selectivity)

28. .... is wielded by a manufacturer that threatens to withdraw a resource or terminate a relationship if intermediaries fail to cooperate.

A. Coercive Power B. Legitimate Power
C. Expert Power D. Reference Power

29. When the consumers favour those products which offer the most quality, performance or innovative features, then it is called as:

A. Production concept
B. Product concept
C. Sales concept
D. Marketing concept

30. Match the items of **List-I** with **List-II** where the PLC curve patterns are given for different categories.

List-I	**List-II**
(*a*) Product category	(*i*) One of several variant shapes
(*b*) Product forms	(*ii*) Longest PLC
(*c*) Products	(*iii*) Standard PLC
(*d*) Branded Products	(*iv*) Short or long PLC

Codes:

	(*a*)	(*b*)	(*c*)	(*d*)
A.	(*iii*)	(*iv*)	(*ii*)	(*i*)
B.	(*i*)	(*ii*)	(*iv*)	(*iii*)
C.	(*iv*)	(*ii*)	(*i*)	(*iii*)
D.	(*ii*)	(*iii*)	(*i*)	(*iv*)

31. The term 'capital structure' implies:

A. Share Capital + Reserves + Long-Term Debts
B. Share Capital + Long and Short-Term Debts
C. Share Capital + Long-Term Debts
D. Equity and Preference Share Capital

32. A company has issued 10 per cent perpetual debt of ₹ 1 lac at 5 per cent premium. If tax rate is 30 per cent, then the cost of debt will be:

A. 10 per cent B. 15 per cent
C. 6.66 per cent D. 8.21 per cent

33. "Dividend is not relevant in determining the value of the company". Who among the following held this opinion?

A. J.E. Walter B. Ezra Soloman
C. Modigliani-Miller D. M.J. Gordon

34. The formula $\frac{Q}{2}$ is used to compute the:

A. Total ordering cost
B. Total carrying cost
C. Opportunity cost
D. Re-order point

35. Financial Leverage is measured by:

A. $\frac{EBIT}{EAT}$ B. $\frac{EBIT}{EBT}$

C. $\frac{EAIT}{EBT}$ D. $\frac{C}{EBIT}$

36. Which of the following is a key role of HR Manager as defined by Ulrich et al (2009)?

A. Personnel Administrator
B. Business Ally
C. Payroll Advisor
D. Organizational Geographer

37. Which of the following is the most serious problem that might arise due to excessive reliance on internal recruitment?

A. reduced job performance
B. high labour turnover
C. lack of motivation
D. internal resistance

38. Match the methods of performance appraisal given in **List-I** with the explanations given in the **List-II.**

List-I	**List-II**
(*a*) Behaviourally Anchored Rating Scale (BARS)	(*i*) Evaluator keeps a log of critical incidents to evaluate performance

(*b*) Management By Objectives (MBO)	(*ii*)	Evaluator indicates on a scale how often the appraise was actually observed engaging in the specific behaviours already identified
(*c*) Critical incident method	(*iii*)	Evaluator rates on the scale described in the form of critical incidents
(*d*) Behaviour observation scale	(*iv*)	Systematic and organized approach that allows management to focus on achievable goals

Codes:

	(*a*)	(*b*)	(*c*)	(*d*)
A.	(*ii*)	(*iv*)	(*i*)	(*iii*)
B.	(*i*)	(*iv*)	(*ii*)	(*iii*)
C.	(*iii*)	(*iv*)	(*i*)	(*ii*)
D.	(*ii*)	(*i*)	(*iv*)	(*iii*)

39. The internal factors affecting the wage mix include:

(*a*) Relative worth of the job
(*b*) Area wage rates
(*c*) Employer's ability to pay
(*d*) Manpower market conditions

Codes:

A. (*a*), (*b*) and (*c*) B. (*a*) and (*c*)
C. (*b*), (*c*) and (*d*) D. All of the above

40. Match the items of **List-I** with the items of **List-II.**

List-I		**List-II**
(*a*) Giri Approach	(*i*)	The utility of non-violence as the means of conflict resolution.
(*b*) Industrial Sociology Approach	(*ii*)	Organizations are made up of people and the success of management lies in its dealing with these people.
(*c*) Gandhian Approach	(*iii*)	Voluntary negotiations between employers and employees are a means of settling disputes.
(*d*) Human Relations Approach	(*iv*)	Investigating the underlying trends and patterns in the cause and effect of industrial disputes.

Codes:

	(*a*)	(*b*)	(*c*)	(*d*)
A.	(*ii*)	(*iii*)	(*i*)	(*iv*)
B.	(*iii*)	(*iv*)	(*i*)	(*ii*)
C.	(*i*)	(*iii*)	(*ii*)	(*iv*)
D.	(*i*)	(*ii*)	(*iv*)	(*iii*)

41. Assertion (A) : Taking of deposits and granting of loans single out banks.

Reasoning (R) : Banks act as intermediaries when they mobilize savings from surplus units to shortage units in order to finance productive activities.

Codes:

A. Assertion (A) is correct and Reasoning (R) is the correct explanation of (A).
B. Both Assertion (A) and Reasoning (R) are correct but (R) is not the correct explanation of (A).
C. Assertion (A) is correct but Reasoning (R) is incorrect.
D. Reasoning (R) is correct but Assertion (A) is incorrect.

42. "Skimming" in e-banking refers to:

A. Identifying fraudsters copying vital information from credit cards
B. Multiple transactions by one credit card
C. Conversion of a debit card into credit card
D. None of the above

43. Match the items of **List-I** with **List-II** in terms of functions of a bank.

List-I (Activities)		**List-II (Functions)**
(*a*) Underwriting	(*i*)	Primary Functions
(*b*) Transfer of funds	(*ii*)	Granting Advances
(*c*) Overdraft	(*iii*)	Utility Functions
(*d*) Recurring Deposits	(*iv*)	Agency Functions

Codes:

	(*a*)	(*b*)	(*c*)	(*d*)
A.	(*i*)	(*ii*)	(*iv*)	(*iii*)
B.	(*iv*)	(*iii*)	(*ii*)	(*i*)
C.	(*iii*)	(*iv*)	(*ii*)	(*i*)
D.	(*ii*)	(*iv*)	(*iii*)	(*i*)

44. Which among the following is **not** a subsidiary of Reserve Bank of India?

(*a*) Deposit Insurance and Credit Gaurantee Corporation of India.

(*b*) Bharatiya Reserve Bank Note Mudran Private Limited.

Codes:

A. Only (*a*) B. Only (*b*)
C. Both (*a*) and (*b*) D. Neither (*a*) nor (*b*)

45. Which among the following is **not** associated with NABARD ?

(*a*) NIEAF (*b*) BIRD
(*c*) RIDF (*d*) SHPI

Codes:

A. (*a*) only B. (*b*) only
C. (*b*) and (*c*) only D. None of the above

46. Examine the following statements and choose the **correct** code:

Statement - (I): Companies with Low cash reserves normally prefer Licensing mode rather than Foreign Direct Investment.

Statement - (II): Cash rich firms normally prefer Foreign Direct Investment.

Codes:

A. Both (I) and (II) are correct
B. Both (I) and (II) are wrong
C. (I) is correct but (II) is wrong
D. (I) is not correct but (II) is correct

47. Which one of the following is **not** a feature of Business Process Outsourcing (BPO)?

A. It enables executives to concentrate on strategy
B. It improves process and saves money
C. It decreases organizational capabilities
D. None of the above

48. The major outcome of the Bretton Woods Conference was:

A. Establishment of IMF and IFC
B. Establishment of IBRD and IFC
C. Establishment of IBRD and ADB
D. Establishment of IMF and IBRD

49. Which one of the following is an important activity of the World Bank borrowings?

A. It borrows in the international capital market
B. It borrows on currency on swap agreements
C. It borrows under the discount net programme
D. All of the above

50. Which one of the following statements is **false**?

A. IFC was established in July 1956
B. IFC encourages the growth and development of Public Sector Enterprises in member countries
C. IFC is an affiliate of the World Bank
D. IFC encourages the growth of productive private enterprises in member countries

ANSWERS

1	2	3	4	5	6	7	8	9	10
D	A	C	B	C	B	C	A	B	D
11	**12**	**13**	**14**	**15**	**16**	**17**	**18**	**19**	**20**
B	B	D	A	B	A	C	C	C	B
21	**22**	**23**	**24**	**25**	**26**	**27**	**28**	**29**	**30**
C	B	B	D	C	C	D	A	B	D
31	**32**	**33**	**34**	**35**	**36**	**37**	**38**	**39**	**40**
A	C	C	B	B	B	D	C	B	B
41	**42**	**43**	**44**	**45**	**46**	**47**	**48**	**49**	**50**
A	A	C	D	D	A	C	D	D	B

EXPLANATORY ANSWERS

2. **Objectives of Fiscal Policy:** Fiscal policy has a multi-dimensional role. It particularly aims at improving economic growth and ensuring social justice to people. Objectives of fiscal policy differ from country to country depending upon the socio-economic policy of the country. The objectives of fiscal policy will be different for a developed country and for a developing country. Even among developing countries, objectives will differ depending upon the type of economic system (*i.e.*, socialism, capitalism, mixed economy) prevailing in that country.

   The objectives of fiscal policy in any developing countries are:
   (*a*) Mobilisation of resources for investment.
   (*b*) Accelerating the pace of economic development.
   (*c*) Minimising inequalities of income and wealth through transfer of income.
   (*d*) To prevent the evil effects of slump and boom conditions.
   (*e*) To increase employment opportunities.
   (*f*) To contain inflationary and deflationary tendencies in the country.

3. Liberalization is defined as laws or rules being liberalized, or relaxed, by a government. Economic liberalization is generally described as the relaxing of government regulations in a country to allow for private sector companies to operate business transactions with fewer restrictions. With reference to developing countries, this term denotes to opening of their economic borders to multinationals and foreign investment. Many economist explained that economic liberalization is "opening up" to the rest of the world with regards to trade, regulations, taxation and other areas that generally affect business in the country.

5. **Globalisation** is the term used to describe the process of removal of restrictions on foreign trade, investment, innovations in communications and transport systems. These changes have encouraged nations to reduce the high levels of protection between countries and to adopt policies to liberalise their economies in order to increase their volume of trade. People are linked together economically and socially by trade, investments and governance. These links are spurred by information, communication and transportation technologies.

   Globalisation of the economy means integrating the economy with the rest of the world. This involves dismantling of high tariff walls, i.e., reduction of import duties thereby facilitating the transition from a protected economy to an open economy, removal of non-tariff restrictions on trade such as exchange control and import licensing, quotas allowing Foreign Direct Investment (FDI) and Foreign Portfolio Investment (FPI), allowing companies to raise capital abroad and encouraging domestic companies to grow beyond national boundaries. In the process of globalisation, national economies are integrated in several fundamental ways—through trade, finance, production and a growing web of global treaties and institutions. Both foreign investment and international trade volume have grown rapidly over the last few years. Firms go global as part of their business strategy mainly because of three reasons:
   (*i*) They get access to more markets and customers.
   (*ii*) They can create better 'brand' by way of expansion so that the acceptance at home market also increases.
   (*iii*) There could be a saturation point in the domestic business.

6. Any expenditure which is incurred for purchase of any fixed asset is called capital expenditure. Capital expenditure yields benefit over a long period, hence they are shown in the asset side of balance sheet.

7. Dual Aspect or Double Entry principle or concept provides that each transaction has dual or two aspects i.e. it results in debit and credit of the same amount. This is the reason that Debit and Credit Side of Trial Balance and Assets & Liabilities sides of Balance Sheet tally with each other. For example, if Gaurav purchases goods for ₹ 500 on credit from Gunjan, the Goods Account shall be debited with ₹ 500 and Gunjan's Account shall be credited with the same amount. Further, if Gaurav purchases goods for ₹ 500 by cash payment, this shall also have two aspects i.e. Goods Account shall be debited with ₹ 500 and Cash Account shall be credited with ₹ 500. Hence in both the examples ₹ 500 have been debited and credited. In the first example, liability in the form of creditor in the name of Gunjan will be created and in the second example, the assets in the form of cash have decreased by ₹ 500. This follows that by each transaction either liability or asset shall increase or decrease.

   We know, Total of Assets equal to Total Liabilities. The liabilities consist of Capital and other liabilities. This can be shown in equation form as follows:

   Assets = Capital + Liabilities

   Or

   Capital = Assets – Liabilities

   From the above equation, it is clear that the owner's share of the assets of the firm is always what is left out of assets after paying off outsiders. Above is called the Accounting Equation.

8. **Consistency:** Conformity from period to period with unchanging policies and procedures.

   Going Concern Concept: Accounting is based on the assumption that the business firm has an indefinite period of existence.

   Materiality: Materiality refers to the importance of an item or event to be recorded. Only material item *i.e.* the knowledge of which would influence the decision of an informed investor should be recorded.

   Historical Cost: It is an accounting concept under which an asset (resource or service) is recorded at cost (price actually paid for it). It is the acquisition cost. It is not the market price. Realisable values are ignored.

9. $$\text{Current Ratio} = \frac{\text{Current Assets}}{\text{Current Liabilities}}$$

   $\Rightarrow$ Liquid Assets = Current Assets – Stock Here Stock = 40000

   Given that

   $$\text{Liquid Ratio} = \frac{\text{Liquid Assets}}{\text{Current Liabilities}}$$

   $$\Rightarrow \frac{2}{1} = \frac{\text{Liquid Assets}}{100000}$$

   $\Rightarrow$ Liquid Assets = 200000

   Since

   Liquid Assets = Current Assets – 40000

   $\Rightarrow$ Current Assets = 240000

   $$\therefore \quad \text{Current Ratio} = \frac{240000}{100000} = 2.4 \text{ times.}$$

10. Financial statements provide us information regarding the financial position of the business and the values of different assets, liabilities and capital. The values of these items are changing. In this way, comparison of financial statements is a tool, which expresses the changes in the different items of financial statement. It points at future prospects of the business in addition of exposing the current achievements.

    In the words of FAULKE "*Comparative analysis is the study of trend of the same items and computed from two or more financial statements of the same business enterprise on different dates.*"

    Financial statements can be compared both inter-firm and intra-firm. In case of inter-firm comparison financial statements of two or more firms are compared, whereas in case of intra-firm comparison financial statements of the same enterprise for two or more years are compared. *Intra-firm comparison is also termed as trend analyses. It indicates the trend of the profitability, operational efficiency and financial soundness of the business enterprise.* Trend analysis may also be named as horizontal analysis, because each accounting variable is placed and analysed horizontally.

11. Marshall assumes that the marginal utility of money remains constant. It is unrealistic. The constancy of marginal utility of money implies that there is no income effect of a change in price. But when the price of a commodity changes, the real income of the consumer also changes. With the change in real income, marginal utility of money will change and this would have an effect on the demand for the good though the total money income available with the consumer remains the same. But utility analysis ignores all these and does not take cognizance of the change in real income and its effect on demand for goods.

13. Product-line pricing means establishing and adjusting the prices of multiple products within a product line. When marketers use product-line pricing, their goal is to maximize profits for an entire product line rather than to focus on the profitability of an individual product item. Product-line pricing can provide marketers with pricing flexibility. Thus, marketers can set prices so that one product is profitable, whereas another is less profitable but increases market share by virtue of having a low price and, therefore, selling more units.

Before setting prices for a product line, marketers evaluate the relationship among the products in the line. When products in a line are complementary, sales increases in one item raise demand for other items. For instance, desktop printers and toner cartridges are complementary products. However, when products in a line function as substitutes for one another, buyers of one product in the line are unlikely to purchase one of the other products in the same line. In this case, marketers must be sensitive to how a price change for one of the brands may affect the demand not only for that brand but also for the substitute brands. For instance, if decision makers at Procter & Gamble were considering a price change for Tide detergent, they would likely also be concerned about how the price change might influence sales of other detergents, such as Cheer, Bold, and Gain.

When marketers employ product-line pricing, they have several strategies from which to choose. These include captive pricing, premium pricing, bait pricing, and price lining.

15. The responsiveness of demand for one product to changes in the price of another product is called cross-elasticity of demand. It is defined as:

$$\eta_{xy} = \frac{\text{Percentage change in quantity demanded of product } x}{\text{Percentage change in price of product } y}$$

Cross-elasticity can vary from minus infinity to plus infinity. Complementary goods have negative cross-elasticities and substitute goods have positive cross-elasticities.

The price elasticity of demand is always a negative number due to the inverse relationship between quantity demanded and price. Economists often omit the minus sign for simplicity, but the negative relationship still holds, since a positive sign would imply that the demand curve slopes upwards. This is a very rare phenomenon. Sir Robert Giffen once described the case of a positive relationship between price and quantity, and consequently a good with a positive price elasticity is referred to as a *Giffen good.*

When the demand elasticity is high, the quantity demanded is very sensitive to a change in price; and likewise, when the elasticity is low, the quantity demanded is relatively insensitive to a change in price. Thus a demand elasticity of zero implies that the product is entirely insensitive to any change in price, or perfectly inelastic. A demand elasticity between zero and one (if we ignore the negative sign) indicates relative inelasticity, whereas demand elasticities between one and infinity imply relative elasticity.

16. In statistics, two attributes are said to be associated when both the attribute are more commonly found together than is ordinarily expected. In the words of *Yule and Kendel, "In statistics A and B are associated only if they together in a greater number of cases then is to be expected if they are independent"*. Evidently A and B are disassociated if this number is less than expected for independence.

Methods of Determining Association

Following are the main methods for determining the association between the two attributes:

1. Frequency Method
2. Proportion Method
3. Yule's Coefficient of Association
4. Coefficient of Colligating
5. Coefficient of Contingency.

17. Hypothesis Testing: A sampling investigation produces a result which has to be compared with the one expected, on the basis of population parameter. Due to the laws of chance, it is possible that any particular sample may produce a result which is out of accord with the one expected. Before acting hastily we must try to determine whether the difference is significant and cannot arise merely because of sampling. We must therefore subject our judgement to an appropriate test for significance in order to see that the disparity between the observed and expected result arose solely due to sampling.

Steps in Hypothesis Testing

1. State the null and alternative hypotheses.
2. Set the *significance level* before analyzing the data. (Most educational researchers use .05 as the significance level. Note that the significance level is also called the *alpha level* or, more simply, *alpha*).
3. Obtain the *probability value* based on the analysis of your empirical data using a computer program such as SPSS. (Note that probability value is also called the *p* value).
4. Compare the probability value to the significance level and make the statistical decision.

18. Methods of Studying Correlation:

Correlation can be determined by the following methods:

1. **Graphic Methods:**
   (*i*) Scatter Diagram
   (*ii*) Correlation Graph
2. **Algebraic Methods:**
   (*i*) Karl Pearson's Coefficient of Correlation
   (*ii*) Spearman's Rank Correlation Method
   (*iii*) Concurrent Deviation Method

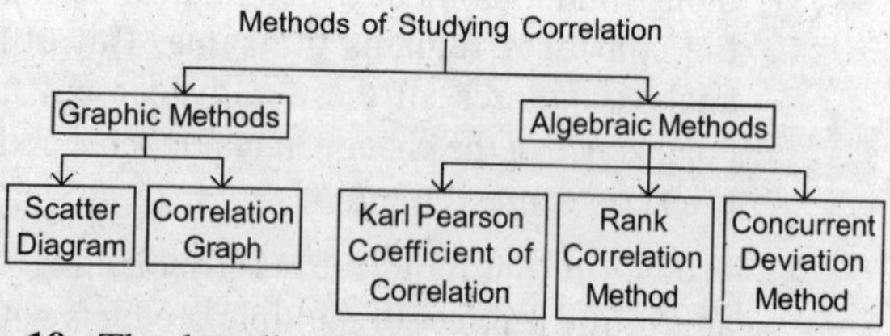

19. The data distribution can be described with four characteristics:

- Measures of location
- Measures of dispersion
- Skewness
- Kurtosis

21. Taylor suggested work organisation based on functional foremanship. This system requires total eight persons i.e., four for planning aspect and four for doing aspect. Those involved in planning aspect are (i) route clerk, (ii) instruction card clerk, (iii) time and cost clerk, and (iv) disciplinarian. The persons involved in doing aspect of work are (i) speed boss, (ii) inspector, (iii) repair boss, and (iv) gang boss. Each one of them gives instruction to workers on different aspects concerning them as follows:

(*i*) *Route Clerk:* He plans the sequence of operations and instructs the workers concerned about it.

(*ii*) *Instruction Card Clerk:* He prepares detailed instructions to the workers regarding different aspects of work such as special tools etc. to be used, techniques of operations, the number of operations and the proper speed to be maintained.

(*iii*) *Time and Cost Clerk:* He maintains all records relating to workers such as time devoted to different jobs, their pay and allowance, leave etc. He also maintains cost records.

(*iv*) *Disciplinarian:* He maintains, discipline in the shop and deals with cases of breach of discipline and absenteeism.

(*v*) *Speed Boss:* He ensures that machines are run at their proper speed and proper tools are being used.

(*vi*) *Inspector:* He inspects the work done by workers, demonstrates to the workers to ensure that quality of the product is being maintained.

(*vii*) *Repair Boss:* He is responsible for the repair of the machine and he ensures that the worker keeps his machine in good order.

(*viii*) *Gang Boss:* He is to assemble and set up tools and machines and to instruct the workers to make all their personal motions in the quickest and best way.

22. • Babbage, Charles: *On the Economy of Machinery and Manufactures.* Philadelphia: Carey & Lea, 1832.

• Barnard, Chester I: *The Functions of the Executive.* Cambridge, Mass.: Harvard University Press, 1938.

• Fayol, Henri: *General and Industrial Management.* London: Pitman, 1967.

Peter Drucker was known as the "father of modern management'. His book "The Effective Executive" is one of the most helpful books on the subject of effectiveness in the workplace.

23. The classical theory is described as a "static model" of organisation, that is, it treats an organisation as a "closed system", uninfluenced by the external environment. The systems approach to organisational analysis highlighted this drawback of classical theory.

24. The Delphi technique was developed by the RAND Corporation in the late 1960's, as a forecasting methodology. Later, the U.S. government enhanced it as a group decision-making tool.

The tool works formally or informally, in large or small contexts, and reaps the benefits of group decision making while insulating the process from the limitations of group decision-making. The process involves a lot of ranking and re-ranking based on criteria and constraints.

The Delphi method is a structured communication technique, originally developed as a systematic, interactive forecasting method which relies on a panel of experts. Delphi is based on the principle that forecasts (or decisions) from a structured group of individuals are more accurate than those from unstructured groups. This has been indicated with the term "collective intelligence".

The Delphi Technique is used when some degree of confidentiality should exist or participants are not comfortable formally giving feedback on a topic. Delphi is also a more formalized approach to gaining consensus.

The procedure is to:

- Pick a facilitation leader.
- Select a panel of experts.
- Identify a straw man criteria list.
- The panel ranks the criteria.
- Re-rank the criteria.
- Identify project constraints and preferences.
- Rank projects by constraint and preference.
- Analyze the results and feedback to panel.
- Re-rank the projects until it stabilizes.

25. **Situational Theory:** Hersey and Blanchard's situational leadership theory (2000) addresses follower readiness as a factor in determining leadership style and considers *task behaviour* and *relationship behaviour.*

High task behaviour and low relationship behaviour is called a *telling leadership* style. A high task, high relationship style is called a *selling leadership* style. A low task and high relationship style is called a *participating leadership* style. A low task and low relationship style is called a *delegating leadership* style.

26. There are several reasons for the failure of new products. Although an idea may be good, the market size may have been overestimated. Perhaps the actual product was not designed as well as it should have been. Or maybe it was incorrectly positioned in the market, priced too high, or advertised poorly. A high-level executive might push a favourite idea despite poor marketing research findings. Sometimes the costs of product development are higher than expected, and sometimes competitors fight back harder than expected.

27. According to professor Kotler, a useful way of analyzing market share movements is in terms of the following four components.

Overall market share = Customer penetration × customer loyalty × customer selectivity × price selectivity

where

Customer penetration is the percentage of all customers who buy from this company.

Customer loyalty consists of purchases from this company by its customers expressed as a percentage of their total purchases from all suppliers of the same products.

Customer selectivity is the size of the average customer purchase from the company expressed as a percentage of the size of the average customer purchase from an average company.

Price selectivity is the average price charged by this company expressed as a percentage of the average price charged by all companies.

28. Producers vary greatly in how they manage their distributors. They can draw on the following types of power to elicit cooperation.

Coercive power is wielded by a manufacturer that threatens to withdraw a resource or terminate a relationship if intermediaries fail to cooperate. This power is quite effective if the intermediaries are highly dependent upon the manufacturer. But the exercise of coercive power produces resentment and can lead the intermediaries to organize countervailing power.

Reward power occurs when the manufacturer offers intermediaries an extra benefit for performing specific acts or functions. Reward power typically produces better results than coercive power but can be overrated. The intermediaries are conforming to the manufacturer's wishes not out of conviction but because of an external benefit. They may come to expect a reward every time the manufacturer wants a certain behaviour to occur. If the reward is later withdrawn, the intermediaries feel resentment.

Legitimate power is wielded when the manufacturer requests a behaviour that is warranted by the contract. Thus, General Motors may insist that its dealers carry certain inventory levels as part of the franchise agreement. The manufacturer feels it has this right and the intermediaries have this obligation. As long as the intermediaries view the manufacturer as a legitimate leader, legitimate power works.

Expert power can be applied when the manufacturer has special knowledge that the intermediaries value. For example, a manufacturer may have a sophisticated system for sales-lead generation or for distribution sales training. This is an effective form of power, if intermediaries would perform poorly without this help. Once the expertise is passed on to the intermediaries, however, this basis of power weakens. The manufacturer must continue to develop new expertise so that the intermediaries will want to continue cooperating.

Referent power occurs when the manufacturer is so highly respected that intermediaries are proud to be identified with it. Companies such as IBM, Caterpillar, McDonald's and Hewlett Packard have high referent power. To the extent possible, manufacturers will gain cooperation best if they would resort to referent power, expert power, legitimate power and reward power in that order and generally avoid using coercive power.

29. The Product Concept: It assumes that consumers will prefer those products that offer quality, performance or innovative features. So, a company that favours this philosophy should devote its full energy to offer quality products or services. For example, the Saravana Bhavan Hotel chain in Chennai city is well known for its high quality vegetarian dishes. Customers come again and again to enjoy the high quality delicious food items which include a range of fast food items along with traditional local Chettinada items to the satisfaction of customers. Saravana Bhavan consider that its strength lies in high quality vegetarian dishes and it is able to attract repeat customers.

Companies that adopt the product concept must continuously strive for improving product or service quality.

31. Capital Structure: Firm's long term financing is termed as capital structure and this is represented generally by long-term debt, preference shares and equity share capital.

Capital structure = Long-term funds

or

Capital structure calculated as follows—

	Rs.
Equity share capital	—
Add : Preference share capital	—
Add : Reserve	—
Add : Surplus	—
Add : Long-term loans	—
Capital structure	—

Optimum capital structure is the point where the market value of the shares is the maximum and at this point the average weighted cost of capital is minimum.

32. At premium $K_i = \dfrac{10000}{105000} = 9.52\%$

After tax cost $K_d = K_i\,(1 - t)$

$= 9.52\,(1 - 0.30)$

$= 9.52 \times 0.7 = 6.66\%$

33. Miller and Modigliani (1961) showed that dividend policy is not relevant in determining the value of a firm if some well-defined conditions are met. The conditions include:

1. Perfect capital markets (including rational investors, perfect information available to all and certainty).
2. No transaction costs.
3. Investors are not taxed.
4. The investment policy of the firm is set and the amount invested is not affected by the dividend policy.

Assume a firm intends to invest \$100 and it has generated \$100 of income. It could retain the \$100 and the investors have an increased \$100 investment in the firm. But assume the firm pays a \$100 dividend. To invest \$100 it must obtain \$100 from its stockholders. After the stockholders invest \$100 in the firm the net change in the stockholders cash is zero, and the stockholders with the dividend are in the identical financial situation as the stockholders when zero dividends were paid. Our conclusion will change when investor taxes are introduced.

However, if some of the assumptions stated are relaxed, the conclusion that the amount of dividends paid (or more exactly, the dividend policy) is irrelevant in determining the present value of the common stock is not true.

34. The total carrying costs will be the product of the average inventory units and the carrying cost per unit. If Q is the order size and usage is assumed to be steady, the average inventory will be:

$$\text{Average inventory} = \frac{\text{Order size}}{2} = \frac{Q}{2}$$

and total carrying costs will be:

Total carrying cost = Average inventory × Per unit carrying cost

$$\text{TCC} = \frac{Q}{2} \times \text{Per unit carrying cost}$$

35. Financial leverage results from the presence of fixed financial cost namely interest & preference dividend. These fixed charges do not vary with the EBIT. They are to be paid regardless of the EBIT available to pay them.

Capital Employed consist of two types of funds:

1. Funds with fixed interest or dividend (Long Term Debt & Preference Capital).
2. Funds without fixed interest or dividend (Equity Share Capital & Retained Earnings)

On debts company has to pay fixed rate of interest irrespective of its earnings. Similarly on preference capital, company has to pay fixed rate of dividend. The equity shareholders are entitled to the remainder of the profits of the firm after all prior obligations are met.

Financial leverage involves the use of funds obtained at a fixed cost in the hope of increasing the returns to the shareholders.

$$\text{Financial Leverage} = \frac{\text{EBIT}}{\text{EBT}}$$

36. University of Michigan Professor David Ulrich proposes six competencies that Human Resources professionals must master if they are going to provide a value-added service within their organization. They are:

- Credible Activist
- Cultural Steward
- Talent Manager/Organizational Designer
- Operational Executor
- Business Ally
- Strategic Architect.

37. Internal recruitment is a process where the existing capable employee will be recruited to the higher post by analyzing the promotion and transfer options with in the organization. The methods and sources usually adopted for internal recruitment are job posting system, promotions and transfers, current employee referral, recruiting former employee and organizational databases. External recruitment is limited to entry level jobs. Often the higher posts are filled through internal recruitment process. The following table provides the pros and cons of internal and external recruitment.

38. Methods or Techniques of Performance Appraisal: The number of different performance appraisal methods or techniques is available for evaluating the performance of the employees. These methods try to explain how management can establish standards of performance and devise ways and means to measure and evaluate the performance of employees. There is no full-proof method of evaluating the performance of employees. Every method suffers from certain drawbacks in spite of some merits. These methods can broadly be divided into traditional and modern methods.

A. Traditional Methods	B. Modern Methods
1. Unstructured method	1. BARS–Behavioural Anchored Rating Scale method.
2. Straight ranking method	2. Result Oriented Appraisal or MBO method.
3. Paired comparison method	3. Assessment centre method
4. Man to man comparison method	4. Human Resource Accounting method
5. Grading method	5. Psychological Appraisal method
6. Graphic rating method	6. 360 degree appraisal
7. Forced choice method	
8. Check list method	
9. Weight check list method	
10. Free essay method	
11. Critical incidents method	
12. Field review method	
13. Confidential reports.	

OR

METHODS

A. Traditional Methods	B. Modern Methods
1. Essay Appraisal Method	1. Management By Objectives (MBO) Method
2. Straight Ranking Method	2. 360 Degree Appraisal Method
3. Paired Comparison Method	3. Assessment Centers Method
4. Critical Incidents Methods	4. Behaviorally Anchored Rating Scales Method (BARS)
5. Field Review Method	5. Human Resource Accounting Method
6. Checklist Method	6. Grading Method
7. Graphic Ratings Scale Method	7. Potential Appraisal Method
8. Forced Distribution Method	8. Self Appraisal Method
9. Forced Choice Method	
10. Confidential Report Method	

39. External and Internal Factors Affecting the Wage Mix

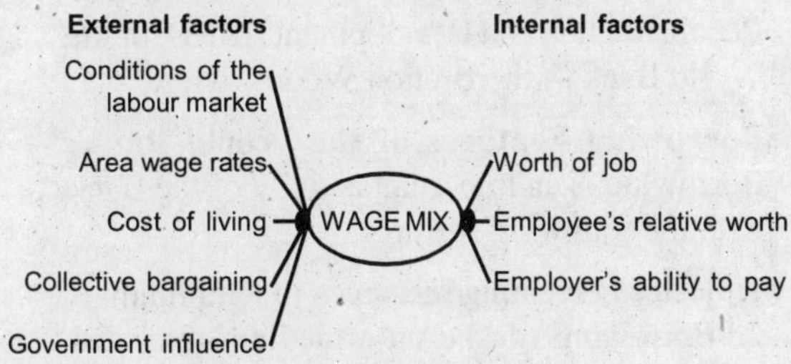

40. Several approaches have been developed for the study of industrial relations. These approaches are: (i) the unitary approach, (ii) the pluralist approach, (iii) the system approach, (iv) the social action approach, (v) the Marxist approach, (vi) the Gandhian approach, (vii) the human relations approach, (viii) the Giri approach, (ix) the industrial sociology approach, and (x) the Oxford school approach.

Fig.: *Approaches Industrial Relations*

42. Credit card fraud: This type of fraud involves individuals and shady companies that pretend to (or actually do) sell a service or product via credit card, for the purpose of collecting the victim's credit card information and using it to make fraudulent purchases. Transferring the information from the card to another counterfeit card is a practice called *skimming*.

44. The Reserve Bank has fully owned four subsidiaries: National Housing Bank (NHB), the National Bank for Agriculture and Rural Development (NABARD), the Deposit Insurance and Credit Guarantee Corporation of India (DICGC) and Bharatiya Reserve Bank Note Mudran Private Limited (BRBNMPL).

The Reserve Bank has a majority stake in the State Bank of India and a minority stake in the Infrastructure Development Finance Company (IDFC).

46. Companies – with low cash reserves – normally prefer the licensing mode over foreign direct investment (FDI). Merck entered Israel by issuing to Teva Pharmaceutical, an Israel company, in order to save the expenses of establishing in Israel. In contrast, cash rich firms may prefer FDI. Firms enter through FDI in order to take advantage of economies of scale and synergies between their domestic and international operations.

47. Business Process Outsourcing (BPO): Business process outsourcing is the long-term contracting out – of non-core business processes – to an outside provider to help achieve increased shareholder value.

Features of Business Process Outsourcing (BPO):

To enable executives to concentrate on strategy: An important aspect – of business process outsourcing – is its ability to free corporate executives from some of their day-to-day process management responsibilities and enable them to concentrate on strategic issues. Traditionally, executives spend 80 per cent of their time managing details and only 20 per cent on strategy. Once a process is successfully outsourced, the ratio can be reversed. Executives get more control over the most valuable resource *i.e.*, time. Time to explore new revenue streams; to accelerate other projects; and to focus on their customers.

To improve processes and save money: Companies – that outsource business processes

– are often able to re-engineer those processes and capture new efficiencies. Then they can re-allocate resources to other important projects and leverage their investment in technology. For example, processes – that are handled in a shared production environment for multiple companies – save everyone money. In most cases, high-calibre subject-matter exports are brought in to design and manage these processes, bringing with them best practices; innovation; and years of experience.

Increase organisational capacities: With this expertise, often comes increased capability. In addition to doing things more efficiently, organisations can expand to deliver new products and services to customers. Then there are the factors of scalability and scope. Companies – that want to grow internationally – must continuously invest in infrastructure and find talent around the world. Many outsourcing providers are already established globally and can help make the growth process run smoothly.

48. The International Monetary and Financial Conference of the United and Associated Nations was convened in Bretton Woods, New Hampshire, on July 1, 1944. By the time the conference ended on July 22, 1944, based on substantial preparatory work, it had defined the outlines of the postwar international economic system. The conference also resulted in the creation of the International Monetary Fund (IMF) and the International Bank for Reconstruction and Development (IBRD, or the World Bank)—the Bretton Woods twins.

49. Borrowing Features of the World Bank: Borrowing is an important activity of the Bank with the following features:

1. Helps in creating resources to lend funds.
2. Borrowing can be on a medium-term and long-term basis from the international capital market.
3. Borrowing can be done under currency Swap Agreements and Discount net programme.
4. The main borrowing instruments are Central Bank facility and US dollar dominated facility of the member countries.
5. World Bank borrows from commercial banks and other financial institutions with the help of Floating Rate Notes.

50. The International Finance Corporation (IFC) was established on 20 July, 1956 as an affiliate of the World Bank Group. IFC gives loans to promote private sector. It finances projects in infrastructure, mining, chemicals, cement, construction materials, manufacturing and timber. It focuses on promoting private sector investment in developing countries in order to reduce poverty and improve people's standard of living.

PAPER-III

Note : *This paper contains **seventy five (75)** objective type questions of **two (2)** marks each. **All** questions are **compulsory**.*

1. The method being used for Transferring Complex Technology is known as:
A. Licensing Agreement
B. Transfer of Technology
C. Turnkey Contract
D. None of the above

2. Which of the following is **not** a 'force' in the "Porter Five Forces Model" ?
A. Buyers
B. Suppliers
C. Complementary produce
D. Industry rivalry

3. LIBOR term is used for:
A. Deposit rate in European market
B. Interest rate in Euro currency market
C. Deposit rate applicable to interbank loans in London
D. Interest rate in Euro bond market

4. Which of the following characterises the early stage financial crises?

A. Falling the price of residential properties
B. Excessive euphoria about the future price of certain assets
C. Excessive pessimism about future assets price
D. Stragnating share price

5. Assertion (A): In 1991 Government decided to allow all foreign investments to any industry without any restrictions.

Reason (R): Government has enhanced the investment limit of small scale industrial units.

Codes:

A. Both (A) and (R) are true and (R) is the correct explanation of (A)
B. Both (A) and (R) are true but (R) is not the correct explanation of (A)
C. (A) is true but (R) is false
D. (A) is false but (R) is true

6. When a business is purchased, any amount paid in excess of the total of assets, minus the liabilities taken, is called:

A. Share Premium B. Goodwill
C. Capital Employed D. Working Capital

7. Indicate the **correct** code as regards the sources of funds for a Funds Flow Statement from the following:

(*a*) Increase in working capital
(*b*) Decrease in working capital
(*c*) Writing off the intangible/fictitious assets
(*d*) Issuing equity shares for acquisition of a building for office
(*e*) Charging depreciation on fixed assets

Codes:

A. (*a*), (*c*), (*d*) B. (*b*), (*c*), (*e*)
C. (*a*), (*d*), (*e*) D. (*b*), (*c*), (*d*)

8. Which of the following statements are **correct**?

(*a*) Analysis and interpretation of financial statements, is a function of accounting.
(*b*) Profit and Loss account is prepared for ascertaining financial position of a firm.
(*c*) Goodwill is a wasting asset.
(*d*) Balance Sheet is prepared for ascertaining financial position of a firm.

Select the **correct** answer using the codes given below:

Codes:

A. (*a*) and (*b*) B. (*a*) and (*c*)
C. (*a*) and (*d*) D. (*b*) and (*c*)

9. Match the items of **List-I** with those of the **List-II** and indicate the **correct** code for the following.

List-I	List-II
(*a*) Debtors Turnover Ratio	(*i*) Solvency Ratio
(*b*) Proprietary Ratio	(*ii*) Liquidity Ratio
(*c*) Operating Ratio	(*iii*) Activity Ratio
(*d*) Acid Test Ratio	(*iv*) Profitability Ratio

Codes:

	(*a*)	(*b*)	(*c*)	(*d*)
A.	(*ii*)	(*iv*)	(*iii*)	(*i*)
B.	(*iii*)	(*ii*)	(*i*)	(*iv*)
C.	(*iii*)	(*i*)	(*iv*)	(*ii*)
D.	(*iv*)	(*iii*)	(*ii*)	(*i*)

10. For the following two statements of **Assertion (A)** and **Reasoning (R)**, indicate the **correct** code.

Assertion (A) : Cash Flow Statement as per the financial statements as well is incapable in revealing the overall financial position of a firm.

Reasoning (R) : Cash is an important constituent of the working capital based on the recorded facts only.

Codes:

A. (A) and (R) both are correct and (R) is an explanation of (A)
B. (A) is correct but (R) is not correct
C. (A) is not correct but (R) is correct
D. (A) and (R) both are incorrect

11. For the following two statements of **Assertion (A)** and **Reasoning (R),** indicate the **correct** code:

Assertion (A): The quantity of a commodity demanded invariably changes inversely to changes in its price.

Reasoning (R): The price effect is the net result of the positive substitution effect and negative income effect.

Codes:

A. (A) and (R) both are correct
B. (A) is correct but (R) is incorrect
C. (A) is incorrect but (R) is correct
D. (A) and (R) both are incorrect

12. Economic capacity of a plant represents its:
A. maximum physical output level
B. average output level over a period
C. break-even output and sales level
D. output level that equates the average and the marginal costs

13. Match the items of **List-I** with those of the **List-II** and indicate the **correct** code.

List-I	List-II
(*a*) Excess capacity of the plant	(*i*) Cost reduction with output expansion
(*b*) Resorting to New Technology	(*ii*) Constant cost with output expansion
(*c*) Setting up of the Training Institutions	(*iii*) Internal economies
(*d*) Reserve capacity of the plant	(*iv*) External economies

Codes:

	(*a*)	(*b*)	(*c*)	(*d*)
A.	(*i*)	(*iii*)	(*iv*)	(*ii*)
B.	(*iii*)	(*i*)	(*iv*)	(*ii*)
C.	(*ii*)	(*iii*)	(*i*)	(*iv*)
D.	(*iv*)	(*ii*)	(*iii*)	(*i*)

14. In case the elasticity of demand on an average revenue curve is equal to unity, the marginal revenue will be:
A. more than unity
B. equal to unity
C. equal to a fraction of unity
D. equal to zero

15. Match the items of the **List-I** with those of the **List-II** and indicate the **correct** code.

List-I	List-II
(*a*) Trade Channel Discount	(*i*) Oligopoly Pricing
(*b*) Loss Leadership	(*ii*) Locational Price Differentials
(*c*) Pricing being non - responsive to changes in the demand and the cost	(*iii*) Differential Pricing
(*d*) Basing Point Pricing	(*iv*) Product - Line Pricing

Codes:

	(*a*)	(*b*)	(*c*)	(*d*)
A.	(*iv*)	(*iii*)	(*ii*)	(*i*)
B.	(*iii*)	(*iv*)	(*i*)	(*ii*)
C.	(*ii*)	(*iii*)	(*iv*)	(*i*)
D.	(*i*)	(*ii*)	(*iii*)	(*iv*)

16. Statement-I: When a null hypothesis gets rejected in statistical hypothesis testing, it is known as II type - error in hypothesis testing.

Statement-II: When a sample is small sized and parametric value of the standard deviation is not known, z - test is the most appropriate test for hypothesis testing.

Codes:

A. Both statements are correct
B. Both statements are incorrect
C. Statement-I is correct while statement-II is incorrect
D. Statement-I is incorrect while statement-II is correct

17. The following are the estimated regression equations for x and y variables:
$x = 0.85y$
$y = 0.89x$

With this information, the value of the coefficient of correlation would be:
A. 0.87 B. 0.86
C. 0.89 D. 0.75

18. The power of the statistical hypothesis testing is denoted by:
A. α (alpha) B. β (beta)
C. $1 - \alpha$ D. $1 - \beta$

19. Match the items of **List-I** and **List-II** and indicate the code of **correct** matching of the items.

List-I	List-II
(a) $\dfrac{z^2.\sigma_p^2}{e^2}$	(i) Measurement for Kurtosis
(b) $\dfrac{\lvert \bar{X}_1-\bar{X}_2\rvert}{\sqrt{\sigma_p^2\left(\dfrac{1}{n_1}+\dfrac{1}{n_2}\right)}}$	(ii) Calculated value of F ratio
(c) $\dfrac{\mu_4}{\mu_2^2}$	(iii) Statistical approach to find out the size of sample
(d) $\dfrac{\sigma_{s_1}^2}{\sigma_{s_2}^2}$	(iv) Calculated z value of mean differences

Codes:

	(a)	(b)	(c)	(d)
A.	(i)	(ii)	(iii)	(iv)
B.	(ii)	(iv)	(iii)	(i)
C.	(iii)	(iv)	(ii)	(i)
D.	(iii)	(iv)	(i)	(ii)

20. Assertion (A): A reasonably large sized sample drawn randomly from a given population contains almost all the characteristics of the population.

Reason (R): As per the sampling theory, the assertion is based only on the 'Law of Inertia of Large Numbers'.

Codes:

A. Assertion (A) is correct and Reason (R) as per the sampling theory is also fully correct
B. Assertion (A) is correct but the Reason (R) as per the sampling theory is not fully correct
C. Both Assertion (A) and Reason (R) are incorrect
D. Assertion (A) is incorrect but the Reason (R) is sufficient as per the sampling theory

21. Which of the following approaches of team building is based on the belief that each person possesses positive and negative characteristics that must be owned up to a permitted expression?

A. Process approach
B. Gestalt approach
C. Role analysis approach
D. Parallel learning structure approach

22. Which of the following factors lead to group cohesiveness?

(a) Agreement on group goals
(b) High intra-group competition
(c) Frequent interaction of members
(d) Personal attractiveness

Codes:

A. (a) and (b) B. (a), (b) and (c)
C. (a), (c) and (d) D. (a), (b) and (d)

23. Assertion (A): 'Uncertainty Avoidance' is one of the dimensions of cultural differences, as identified by Geert Hofstede.

Reasoning (R): 'Uncertainty Avoidance' is the extent to which people feel threatened by ambiguous situations. To avoid such situations, organisations provide greater career stability, make more formal rules and reject deviant behaviours.

Codes:

A. (A) is wrong (R) is right
B. Both (A) and (R) are wrong
C. Both (A) and (R) are right and (R) is the correct explanation of (A)
D. Both (A) and (R) are right but (R) is not the correct explanation of (A)

24. Which of the following is the internal conflict or anxiety that occurs when people receive information incompatible with their value systems, prior decisions and knowledge?

(a) Polarisation
(b) Cognitive dissonance
(c) Premature evaluation
(d) Projection

Codes:

A. (a) and (b) B. Only (b)
C. Only (d) D. (a), (b), (c) and (d)

25. Matrix organisation structure is essentially a violation of the principle of:

A. Unity of Command
B. Scalar Chain
C. Unity of Direction
D. Division of Labour

26. Which of the following statements is **not true**?
A. One sided messages work best with audiences those are initially predisposed to communicator's position.
B. Two sided arguments work best with audiences who are similar and not opposed.
C. Two sided messages tend to be more effective with better educated audiences.
D. Two sided messages tend to be more effective with audiences those are likely to be exposed to counter propaganda.

27. In the course of converting to a marketing-oriented company, a company may face which of the following hurdles?
A. Organised resistance
B. Slow learning
C. Fast forgetting
D. All of the above

28. A person's distinguishing psychological characteristics that lead to relatively consistent and enduring responses to his or her environment is called:
A. Life style B. Self-concept
C. Personality D. Attitude

29. When electronic markets permit prices to change faster even daily as a function of demand and supply then this practice is called:
A. competitive pricing
B. e-marketing pricing
C. yield management pricing
D. none of the above

30. Match the strategies given in **List-I** with the examples given in **List-II**.

List-I (Strategies)	**List-II (Examples)**
(*a*) Differential Pricing	(*i*) Customer lounges to sit in while waiting for a table at service centres, etc.
(*b*) Complimentary Service	(*ii*) Breakfast service by McDonald's and mini vacation and weekends by hotels
(*c*) Reservation System	(*iii*) Low prices for early and evening movies, weekend discounts for car parking rentals
(*d*) Non-peak Demand Cultivation	(*iv*) Airlines, Hotels and Physicians employ extensively

Codes:

	(*a*)	(*b*)	(*c*)	(*d*)
A.	(*i*)	(*iii*)	(*ii*)	(*iv*)
B.	(*iv*)	(*ii*)	(*i*)	(*iii*)
C.	(*ii*)	(*i*)	(*iv*)	(*iii*)
D.	(*iii*)	(*i*)	(*iv*)	(*ii*)

31. From investor's point of view, the cost of capital is:
A. Interest Rate
B. Market Value
C. Yield of Capital Sacrifice
D. Stock Exchange Value

32. Formula for net cash inflow of a project is:
A. Sales – Operating Expenses – Interest – Tax
B. Sales – Operating Expenses
C. Net Profit after tax + Depreciation
D. Gross Profit + Depreciation

33. Concentration Banking is a method of:
A. Decentralised collection
B. Centralised collection
C. Direct collection
D. Payment only through cheques

34. In case, cost of capital is 10%, EPS ₹ 10, IRR 8% and Retention Ratio is 60%, then the value of equity share as per Gordon's Model will be:
A. ₹ 100 B. ₹ 87
C. ₹ 90 D. ₹ 77

35. A firm with high operating leverage has:
A. Low fixed cost in its production process
B. High variable cost in its production process
C. High fixed cost in its production process
D. Low variable cost in its production process

36. Match the items of **List-I** with **List-II** according to 'The Harvard Framework' developed for HRM.

List-I	List-II
(a) Stakeholder's interest	(i) Work systems
(b) Situational factor	(ii) Cost-effectiveness
(c) HRM policy choice	(iii) Individual well-being
(d) HR outcome	(iv) Government
(e) Long-term consequence	(v) Business strategy

Codes:

	(a)	(b)	(c)	(d)	(e)
A.	(iv)	(i)	(ii)	(iii)	(v)
B.	(v)	(iv)	(ii)	(i)	(iii)
C.	(iv)	(v)	(i)	(ii)	(iii)
D.	(i)	(v)	(ii)	(iii)	(iv)

37. The committees which promote worker's participation in management are usually established only at the:

A. Corporate level B. Plant level
C. Shop-floor level D. All of the above

38. Choose the **correct** code for the statements given below.

Statement (I): T-group and sensitivity training are not the same.

Statement (II): T-group participants belong to a diverse groups and may not be familiar with each other.

Statement (III): T-group training sessions are well structured.

Codes:

A. Statements (I) and (II) are correct
B. Only (II) and (III) statements are correct
C. All the three statements are correct
D. Only statement (II) is correct

39. A review is heavily influenced only by any one characteristic of the employee whose performance is being reviewed is known as:

A. Recency of Events Error
B. Central Tendency
C. Logical Error
D. Halo Effect

40. Which one of the following tests is **not** recommended for the top level positions?

A. Presentations
B. Role plays
C. Interviews
D. Leaderless group discussions

41. Select the major principles which banks strive to incorporate in their working from the following:

(a) Profitability (b) Labour welfare
(c) Social welfare (d) Safety
(e) HRD (f) Liquidity

Codes:

A. (a), (b), (d), (e) B. (a), (c), (d), (f)
C. (c), (d), (e), (f) D. (a), (b), (c), (d)

42. Identify the years in which different phases of Bank Nationalisation took place in India:

(a) 1950 (b) 1955
(c) 1969 (d) 1949
(e) 1980

Codes:

A. (a), (b), (c), (d) B. (b), (c), (e)
C. (b), (d), (e) D. (c), (d), (e)

43. 'SWIFT' stands for:

A. Society for Worldwide Inter-bank Fund Transfer
B. Society for Worldwide Inter-bank Fast Transmission
C. Society for Worldwide Inter-bank Financial Telecommunications
D. None of the above

44. Select the techniques of monetary control adopted by RBI from the following:

(a) Cash Reserve Ratio
(b) Statutory Liquidity Ratio
(c) Bank Rate
(d) Currency Rate

Codes:

A. (a), (b), (c), (d) B. (b), (c), (d)
C. (a), (c), (d) D. (a), (b), (c)

45. Which of the following is **not** a development banking institution?

A. IDBI B. IFCI
C. EXIM Bank D. ICICI

46. Which of the following is **not** a characteristic of bartering internationally?

A. Bartering can be time - consuming
B. Bartering can be expensive
C. Bartering is a type of service export and import
D. Bartering can be risky

47. **Assertion (A):** International business has grown in more recent years at a faster pace than global production.

Reason (R): Growth through trade has increased, but growth through foreign direct investment has not.

Codes:
A. Both (A) and (R) are correct
B. (A) is correct but (R) is incorrect
C. (A) is incorrect but (R) is correct
D. Both (A) and (R) are incorrect

48. Identify the multinational corporations (MNCs) from the following:

(*a*) IOCL	(*b*) GAIL
(*c*) SBI	(*d*) SAIL
(*e*) Tata Steel	(*f*) Bharat Petroleum

Codes:
A. (*a*), (*b*), (*c*), (*d*) B. (*b*), (*c*), (*d*), (*e*)
C. (*c*), (*d*), (*e*), (*f*) D. (*a*), (*c*), (*e*), (*f*)

49. **Statement-I:** Legal agreements between two countries govern how both the countries tax earnings.

Statement-II: International Law may determine how and whether companies can operate in a certain locale.

Codes:
A. Both the statements are true
B. Both the statements are false
C. Statement-I is true but Statement-II is false
D. Statement-I is false but Statement-II is true

50. Which of the following is an example of an issue for which an agreement has **not** been made between two or more countries?
A. Restricting harmful emissions
B. Deep-sea mining in non-coastal areas of the oceans
C. Preserving endangered species
D. Banning the use of certain pesticides

51. Match the items of **List-I** with **List-II**.

List-I	**List-II**
(*a*) Intangible Assets	(*i*) Ind AS 31
(*b*) Impairment of Assets	(*ii*) Ind AS 34
(*c*) Interim Financial Reporting	(*iii*) Ind AS 36
(*d*) Interests in Joint Ventures	(*iv*) Ind AS 38

Codes:

	(*a*)	(*b*)	(*c*)	(*d*)
A.	(*i*)	(*ii*)	(*iii*)	(*iv*)
B.	(*iv*)	(*iii*)	(*ii*)	(*i*)
C.	(*iv*)	(*i*)	(*ii*)	(*iii*)
D.	(*iv*)	(*ii*)	(*i*)	(*iii*)

52. **Assertion (A):** Human Resource Accounting is the measurement of the cost and value of people to the organization.

Reasoning (R): Human Resource Accounting involves measuring costs incurred by the organizations to recruit, select, hire, train and develop employees and judge their economic value to the organization.

Codes:
A. Assertion (A) and Reasoning (R) are correct and (R) is the right explanation of (A)
B. Assertion (A) and Reasoning (R) are correct and (R) is not the right explanation of (A)
C. Assertion (A) is correct but Reasoning (R) is incorrect
D. Both Assertion (A) and Reasoning (R) are incorrect

53. For the discharge of its functions efficiently, SEBI has been vested with the following powers:
(*a*) to approve by-laws of stock exchanges
(*b*) to direct the stock exchanges to amend their by-laws
(*c*) inspect the books of accounts and call for periodical returns from recognized stock exchanges
(*d*) inspect the books of accounts of financial intermediaries
(*e*) compel certain companies to list their shares in one or more stock exchanges
(*f*) registration of brokers

Codes:
A. (*a*), (*b*), (*c*) and (*f*)
B. (*a*), (*c*), (*d*) and (*f*)
C. (*b*), (*c*), (*d*), (*e*) and (*f*)
D. (*a*), (*b*), (*c*), (*d*), (*e*) and (*f*)

54. Consider the following characteristics:
(*a*) High risk high return opportunity
(*b*) Small and medium size enterprise
(*c*) Private equity stakes in start-ups
(*d*) Investment fund
The above attributes are found in:
A. Mutual Funds
B. Venture Capital Funds
C. Qualified Institutional Buyers
D. Domestic Institutional Investors

55. Identify the **incorrect** statement(s), regarding money market, among the following:
(*a*) The call money market deals in short-term finance repayable on demand, with a maturity period varying from one day to 14 days.
(*b*) Treasury bills are instruments of short-term borrowing by the Government of India, issued as promissory notes under discount.
(*c*) A reduction in the repo rate helps banks to get money at a cheaper rate.
(*d*) Money market mutual funds invest money in specifically, high-quality and very short maturity-based money market instruments.

Codes:
A. (*a*) and (*c*) B. (*b*)
C. (*d*) D. None of the above

56. "Buyers are less price sensitive when they **cannot** easily compare the quality substitutes". Which of the following factors of price sensitivity is reflected from this statement?
A. Substitute - awareness effect
B. Unique value effect
C. Price quality effect
D. None of the above

57. The model of decision support where there is recommendation of the type of advertisement with humourous and 'slice of life' kinds of appeals to use for given marketing goals and characteristics of products, target markets and competitive situations is known as:
A. MEDIAC B. PROMOTOR
C. ADCAD D. COVERSTORY

58. Which of the following statements is **not** true?
A. Marketing profitability analysis measures the profitability of different marketing activities.
B. Marketing efficiency studies try to determine how various marketing activities could be carried out more efficiently.
C. Each company needs to reassess periodically its marketing effectiveness through a control instrument called marketing audit.
D. All the above are true

59. Industry boundaries are blurring at an incredible rate as companies are recognizing that the new opportunities lie at the intersection of two or more industries, it is called:
A. Globalization
B. Customization
C. Industry convergence
D. Acquisition

60. A picture of two characters is presented, with one making a statement. Respondents are asked to identify with the other and fill in the empty balloon.
This description belongs to which one of the following projective techniques?
A. Thematic Apperception Test
B. Picture Completion Test
C. Sentence Completion Test
D. Story Completion Test

61. Match the items of **List-I** with the items of **List-II**.

List-I (Job Analysis)	**List-II (Examples)**
(*a*) Task	(*i*) Payroll processing
(*b*) Element	(*ii*) Compensation policy administrator
(*c*) Duty	(*iii*) Compensation design manager
(*d*) Position	(*iv*) Compensation specialist
(*e*) Job	(*v*) Preparing forms
(*f*) Occupation	(*vi*) Signing pay-cheques

Codes:

	(a)	(b)	(c)	(d)	(e)	(f)
A.	(i)	(ii)	(iii)	(iv)	(v)	(vi)
B.	(v)	(vi)	(i)	(ii)	(iii)	(iv)
C.	(vi)	(v)	(iv)	(ii)	(iii)	(i)
D.	(vi)	(i)	(ii)	(iii)	(iv)	(v)

62. In which of the following types of collective bargaining, one party gains at the expense of the other?

A. Distributive bargaining
B. Integrative bargaining
C. Centralized bargaining
D. None of the above

63. Which one of the following dispute settlers **cannot** make a binding decision?

A. Arbitrator
B. Adjudicator
C. Conciliator
D. Industrial tribunal member

64. Ensuring the safety, health and welfare of the employee is the primary purpose of which one of the following Acts?

A. The Factories Act, 1948
B. The Payment of Wages Act, 1936
C. The Equal Remuneration Act, 1976
D. The Industrial Disputes Act, 1947

65. Match the items of **List-I** with the items of **List-II** and select the **correct** code:

List-I	List-II
(a) Pension scheme	(i) Health Care for family
(b) Personal security	(ii) Severance Pay
(c) Financial assistance	(iii) Provident Fund
(d) Allowance	(iv) Transport Allowance

Codes:

	(a)	(b)	(c)	(d)
A.	(i)	(ii)	(iii)	(iv)
B.	(iii)	(i)	(ii)	(iv)
C.	(iii)	(ii)	(i)	(iv)
D.	(i)	(iv)	(ii)	(iii)

66. Examine the following statements and choose the **correct** answer.

Statement-I: FIIs do not invest in unlisted securities. They participate only through Stock Exchanges.

Statement - II: FIIs cannot invest at the time of initial allotment.

Codes:

A. Both the statements are wrong
B. Both the statements are correct
C. Statement-I is correct but the statement-II is wrong
D. Statement-I is wrong but the statement-II is correct

67. Which one of the following is **not** a member country in the Association of South-East Asian Nations (ASEAN)?

A. Singapore
B. Malaysia
C. Thailand
D. Vietnam

68. Match the items of **List-I** with the items of **List-II** and select the **correct** answer with the codes given below.

List-I	List-II
(a) SAARC	(i) Philippines
(b) ASEAN	(ii) Canada
(c) EU	(iii) Afghanistan
(d) NAFTA	(iv) Hungary

Codes:

	(a)	(b)	(c)	(d)
A.	(ii)	(iv)	(i)	(iii)
B.	(iv)	(ii)	(i)	(iii)
C.	(iii)	(i)	(iv)	(ii)
D.	(iii)	(iv)	(ii)	(i)

69. Which among the following are criticisms given against World Trade Organization (WTO)?

(a) It is not a democratic and transparent institution.

(b) It has domination of international trade by rich countries for the benefit of their individual interests.

(c) It encourages a 'race to the bottom' in wages by pitting workers against each other rather than promoting internationally recognized labour standards.

(*d*) It is seeking to privatize essential public services.

Codes:

A. (*b*), (*c*) and (*d*)
B. (*a*), (*b*) and (*c*)
C. (*a*), (*b*) and (*d*)
D. (*a*), (*b*), (*c*) and (*d*)

70. Domestic Currency tends to depreciate owing to:

A. Constant inflation rate
B. Lowering of inflation rate
C. High inflation rate
D. All of the above

71. Consider the following conditions:

(*a*) An individual is in India for a period of 182 days in the financial year in which he is getting his salary income.

(*b*) An individual is in India for a period of 60 days or more during financial year in which he gets his salary and 365 days or more during 4 years immediately preceding to that financial year.

If one of the above conditions is satisfied, as per the provisions of Income Tax Act, 1961, he is:

A. Resident but not ordinarily resident of India
B. Non-resident citizen of India
C. Resident and categorised citizen of India U/S 29
D. Ordinary resident of India

72. Agriculture income is exempted from income tax under the following section of Income Tax Act, 1961:

A. 2 (1A) B. 10 (1)
C. 10 (2) D. 10 (4)

73. Match the items of **List-I** with **List-II**.

List-I	**List-II**
(*a*) When the assessee is in default or is deemed to be in default in making payment of tax, including the tax deducted at source	(*i*) Section 271 (1) (*c*)
(*b*) Failure to pay the advance tax as directed by the Assessing Officer	(*ii*) Section 273 (1)
(*c*) Concealment of particulars of income or furnishing of inaccurate particulars of income	(*iii*) Section 201 (1)

Codes:

	(*a*)	(*b*)	(*c*)
A.	(*i*)	(*ii*)	(*iii*)
B.	(*iii*)	(*ii*)	(*i*)
C.	(*iii*)	(*i*)	(*ii*)
D.	(*ii*)	(*i*)	(*iii*)

74. Assertion (A): Tax evasion is undertaken by employing unfair means.

Reasoning (R): Payment of tax is avoided through illegal means or fraud for tax evasion.

Codes:

A. Assertion (A) is correct and Reasoning (R) is the right explanation of (A)
B. Assertion (A) is correct but Reasoning (R) is not the right explanation of (A)
C. Both Assertion (A) and Reasoning (R) are correct independently and (R) may be considered as an explanation of (A)
D. Both Assertion (A) and Reasoning (R) are incorrect

75. Which among the following are necessary documents to file Income Tax Return for an employed person in India?

(*a*) Adhar Card
(*b*) PAN Card
(*c*) Form No. 16 issued by employer

Codes:

A. (*a*) only
B. (*a*) and (*b*)
C. (*a*), (*b*) and (*c*)
D. (*b*) and (*c*)

ANSWERS

1	2	3	4	5	6	7	8	9	10
C	C	C	B	D	B	B	C	C	A
11	**12**	**13**	**14**	**15**	**16**	**17**	**18**	**19**	**20**
C	D	A	D	B	B	B	D	D	B
21	**22**	**23**	**24**	**25**	**26**	**27**	**28**	**29**	**30**
B	C	C	B	A	B	D	C	C	D
31	**32**	**33**	**34**	**35**	**36**	**37**	**38**	**39**	**40**
C	C	A	D	C	C	D	A	D	B
41	**42**	**43**	**44**	**45**	**46**	**47**	**48**	**49**	**50**
B	B	C	D	C	C	B	D	A	B
51	**52**	**53**	**54**	**55**	**56**	**57**	**58**	**59**	**60**
B	A	D	B	D	D	C	D	C	B
61	**62**	**63**	**64**	**65**	**66**	**67**	**68**	**69**	**70**
B	A	C	A	B	A	*	C	D	C
71	**72**	**73**	**74**	**75**					
D	B	B	A	D					

EXPLANATORY ANSWERS

1. **Methods of Technology Transfer**

1. Contract for Sale of Plant and Machinery: Under such contract, one country sells plant machinery, equipment to the other country. Such contract provides for transfer of operational technology. The foreign supplier provides the information regarding method of operating plant, machinery, equipment.

2. Licensing Agreement: In this transfer, the transferee units enters into licensing agreement with transferor units. Under this agreement, technical support, expertise is provided by transferor unit (licensor) to transferee unit (licensee). These agreements are also called technological collaborations. The transferee unit pays royalty to transferor unit for use of technology of licensor.

3. Training to Employees: In this case, transferor nation imparts training of unpatented manufacturing techniques, production process, handling equipments, etc. to the employees of transferee nation. The employees of transferee nation attend training programmes in transferor nation. Sometimes, foreign technical experts are also employed in the transferee nation for operating technology and training employees of transferee nation.

4. Complete Transfer: When technology is complex in nature, then transfer of technology is done through *turnkey* contracts. Here, the transferor provides details of drawings, designs, method of installation, operating, maintaining, supervising, etc. to the transferee. The transferor company completes the project from scratch to end stage. When the project is complete, it is handed over to transferee company. For example, technology for setting up power project is transferred through *turnkey contracts.*

2. Michael Porter developed a framework for classifying and analyzing the characteristics of an industry's environment. His five forces model of competition examines competitive forces

that influence the profitability potential in an industry or of a segment within an industry. Each force can reduce the probability that a firm can earn profits while competing in an industry. Potential entrants, substitute products, suppliers, buyers, and rivalry among existing firms are the five forces that affect the profitability potential of an industry. Firms competing in an industry want to understand these forces so they can position themselves in the industry to maximize their ability to earn profits. Firms thinking of entering and industry need to understand these forces to decide whether the industry's profitability potential is sufficient to support entry into that industry.

3. **London Interbank Offered Rate (LIBOR):** The deposit rate applicable to interbank loans in London. LIBOR is used as the reference rate for many international interest rate transactions.

4. In the early stages of a financial crisis prices of assets such as shares or houses or commodities start to rise. An expectation takes root that prices will continue to rise and buyers rush into the market. An excessive euphoria develops based on the assumption that asset prices will continue to increase.

6. To an accountant, goodwill is the "excess of cost over the market value" of net assets purchased by a company. In other words, "net assets" are the difference between the value of a company's total assets and its total liabilities. When one business purchases another, it may be willing to pay more for that business than the market value of the individual assets minus any liabilities. This is referred to in accounting as *goodwill.*

   Why might a company be willing to pay more than market value for the net assets of another company? Because the purchaser is also acquiring intangibles—the reputation of the products or service of the purchased company, the quality of its personnel, brand-name recognition, and so on. Conceptually, goodwill represents an amount paid for the above-average earnings of a company caused by these factors. Accounting principles allow only purchased goodwill to be recorded in the accounts; internal development of a business reputation is not assigned a value and recorded. Goodwill has an indefinite economic life and is not amortized; however, like other intangibles with an indefinite life, goodwill is subject to an impairment test.

7. Funds flow statement is a statement of sources and uses of funds. It analyses and explains changes in net working capital between two balance sheet dates.

   According to S.C. Kuchhal. "The statement of showing sources and uses of funds is popularly known as funds flow statement. It is a condensed report of how the activities of the business have been financed and how the financial resources have been used during the period covered by the statement."

   The major sources of funds are:

   (*a*) Depreciation of fixed assets.
   (*b*) Amortization of fictitious or intangible assets.
   (*c*) Loss on sale of fixed assets or investments.
   (*d*) Gifts given, damages paid, etc.
   (*e*) Appropriation of profits such as transfer to general reserve, or any specific reserve.
   (*f*) Proposed dividend.
   (*g*) Provision for taxation.

8. Balance Sheet is a financial statement that summarizes a company's assets, liabilities and shareholders' equity at a specific point in time. These three balance sheet segments give investors an idea as to what the company owns and owes, as well as the amount invested by the shareholders.

   The balance sheet show:

   Assets = Liabilities + Shareholders' Equity

   A balance sheet thus, provides detailed information about a company's assets, liabilities and shareholders' equity.

   Assets are things that a company owns that have value. This typically means they can either be sold or used by the company to make products or provide services that can be sold. Assets include physical property, such as plants, trucks, equipment and inventory. It also includes things that can't be touched but nevertheless exist and have value, such as trademarks and patents. And cash itself is an asset. So are investments a company makes.

9. The accounting ratios can be classified according to their functions, such as, liquidity, solvency, activity and profitability.

(*i*) **Liquidity ratios:** Liquidity is the short-term solvency of an enterprise, *i.e.*, the ability of the business enterprise to meet its short-term obligation as and when they are due. The liquidity ratios, therefore, are also called the short-term solvency ratios. The most common ratios which measure the extent of liquidity are current ratio, liquid ratio and acid test ratio.

(*ii*) **Solvency ratios:** These ratios are used to judge the long-term financial soundness of any business. Solvency means the ability of the enterprise to meet its long-term obligations on the due date. Usually, debt—equity ratio, total assets to debt ratio, proprietary ratio and interest coverage ratio are calculated to judge the solvency of the concern.

(*iii*) **Activity/turnover ratios:** These ratios indicate the efficiency with which capital employed is rotated in the business. Some of the important activity ratios are stock turnover, debtors (receivable) turnover, creditors (payable) turnover, fixed assets turnover and working capital turnover.

(*iv*) **Profitability ratios:** These ratios give an indication of the efficiency with which the operations of business are carried on. There are two major types of profitability ratios: (1) profitability in relation to sales and (2) profitability in relation to investment.

12. Up to the economic capacity of the plant, average costs are always higher than marginal costs; beyond that point, marginal costs exceed average costs. At economic capacity, where average cost is at a minimum, average cost equals marginal cost.

14. Elasticity of demand can be written as:

$$Ed = \frac{\text{Average Revenue}}{\text{Average Revenue} - \text{Marginal Revenue}}$$

$$Ed = \frac{AR}{AR - MR}$$

where, MR = Marginal revenue, AR = Average revenue, and Ed = Value of elasticity of demand.

Now, on the basis of above formula, can we find out the relationship between MR and AR at various point elasticities of demand.

If $Ed = 1$, then $MR = 0$

If $Ed = 2$, then MR equals half the AR

If $Ed > 1$, then $MR > 0$

If $Ed < 1$, then MR is negative

These situations can also be illustrated with the help of a diagram as in below.

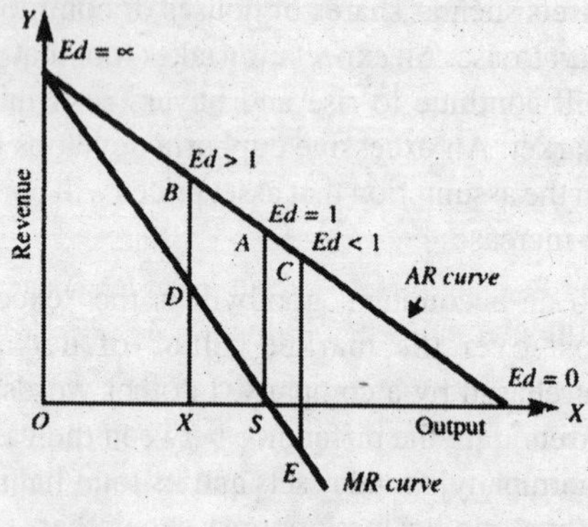

17. Coefficient of Correlation = $\sqrt{0.85 \times 0.89}$

$= 0.86.$

18. Power of a hypothesis test

$$\begin{aligned}\text{Power} &= P(\text{reject } H_0 \mid H_1 \text{ is true})\\ &= 1 - P(\text{type II error})\\ &= 1 - \beta\end{aligned}$$

That is, the power of a hypothesis test is the probability that it will reject when it's supposed to.

21. Gestalt Approach: This approach focuses more on the individual rather than the group. The major advocate of this orientation is Stanley M. Herman. Gestalt theory is based on the belief that persons function as whole or total; each person possesses positive and negative characteristics; and people get into trouble when they get fragmented. The goal of this theory is awareness, integration, maturation, authenticity, self-regulation, and behaviour change. The primary thrust is to make the individual stronger, more authentic, and more in touch with own feelings. The Gestalt practitioner fosters the expression of positive and negative feelings, encourages people to stay with transactions, structures and exercises that cause individuals to become more aware of what they want from others, and pushes towards greater authenticity for everyone. The practitioner usually works within a group, but the focus is usually on individuals.

22. Group Cohesiveness: The perception of group attractiveness that brings individuals together is called "cohesion". When cohesiveness is strong, there is a willingness on the part of all members to trust one another and to sacrifice personal gain to further the team's goals. Team norms and cohesiveness, then, combine to shape the performance expectations that influence member productivity.

If a team consists simply of a collection of individuals, each pursuing his or her individual interests, the group will lack cohesion and will not function effectively.

When norms are strong and when they favour high productivity, cohesiveness then provides the social pressure needed to encourage members to excel. A group requires a personal commitment from all members if it is to develop a strong culture and attain its most difficult goals.

Factors increasing Cohesiveness: The following factors can facilitate to incease the cohesiveness of the work group.

(*i*) Agreement on Group Goals
(*ii*) Frequency of Interaction
(*iii*) Personal Attractiveness
(*iv*) Inter-group Competition
(*v*) Favourable Evaluation
(*vi*) Group Size
(*vii*) Pleasant experiences with the group
(*viii*) Lack of Domination
(*ix*) Gender of Members
(*x*) Previous Success

24. Cognitive dissonance is the psychological barriers that can interfere with effective communication. Davis and Newstrom describe cognitive dissonance as:

The internal conflict and anxiety that occurs when people receive information incompatible with their value system, prior decision, or other information they may have. Since people do not feel comfortable with dissonance, they try to obtain new communication inputs, change their interpretation of the inputs, reverse their decision, or change their values. They may even refuse to believe the dissonant input, or they rationalize it out of the way.

25. The matrix structure can be best described as one that assigns specialists from different functional departments to work on one or more projects led by a project manager. One of the most characteristic features of matrix organization is that it requires dual reporting authority for the organizational members, which is in sharp contrast to the principle of unity of command. It thus tries to curtail the duplicating costs by using the same pool of functional people to assist in various divisions or projects. This is also superior to any particular type of departments as it employs specialists in each area. One of the most common examples of matrix organization is perhaps a university or a degree college with a number of different departments with the respective Head of the Departments along with an overall head of the entire organization in the form of Vice Chancellor or the Principal. The faculty members are answerable to both their respective department heads as well as the overall Head of the Organization (Vice Chancellor or the Principal).

One of the major advantages of matrix structure is that it minimizes the problem of coordination. It also ensures the availability of experts to all projects, along with effective communication and feedback system. It also proves to be economical as only the required number of people is allotted to the specific project.

However, it is not without its weak spots. Matrix organizations require people to work under dual authority, which violates the principle of unity of command and often proves to be confusing. It also fosters conflict because of heterogeneity of team members.

26. A message's effectiveness depends on its structure as well as its content. Extensive research has been carried out one the relative effectiveness of three types of structure:

1. **Conclusion drawing:** This structure raises the question whether the manager should draw a definite conclusion for the customer, or let the customer draw the conclusion for themselves. It is generally thought that it is best to allow customers to reach their own decision, as conclusion-drawing causes negative reactions particularly in the following situations:
   - It the communicator is untrustworthy, the customer might resent the attempt to influence them.
   - It the issue is simple or the audience is intelligent (example physicians), they might be annoyed at the attempt to explain the obvious.
   - If the issue is highly personal, the audience might resent the communicator's attempt to draw a conclusion for them.
2. **One- or two-sided argument:** This structure raises the question of whether the communicator should only praise the product or also mention some of its shortcomings. It may seem obvious that only one-sided presentations would be the most effective, but this structure does have its limitations:
   - One-sided messages work best with audiences that are initially predisposed to the product's position — two-sided arguments work better with audiences who are opposed.
   - Two-sided arguments work better with more intelligent audiences (note-physicians).
   - Two-sided arguments are more effective with audiences who are likely to be exposed to counter-propaganda.
3. **Order of presentation:** This structure raises the question whether the communicator should raise the strongest argument first or last. In the case of the one-sided argument presenting the strongest message first has the advantage of establishing attention and interest. In the two-sided argument it is better to present the strongest argument last if the audience is opposed to the product, *i.e.*, start with the other side's argument to disarm the customer and then conclude with your own strong argument.

27. In the course of converting to a marketing orientation, a company faces three hurdles: organized resistance, slow learning, and fast forgetting.

28. Philip Kotler defines personality in the following manner:

By personality we mean "the person's distinguishing psychological characteristics that lead to relatively consistent and enduring responses to his or her own environment".

31. Cost of capital may be viewed in different ways: (i) From investors' view point – the measurement of the sacrifice made by him with regard to capital formation, (ii) Firms view point – it is the minimum required rate of returns needed to justify the use of capital, and (iii) Capital expenditure point – it is the minimum required rate of return used to value cash flows.

32. A firm's cash flow generally differs from its profit after tax because some of the revenues/ expenses shown on its profit and loss account may not have been received/paid in cash during the year. The relationship between net cash flow and profit after tax is as follows:

Net cash flow = Profit after tax – Non-cash revenues + Non-cash expenses

An example of non-cash revenue is accrued interest income that has not yet been received. It increases the bottom line but is not matched by a cash inflow during the accounting period—the cash inflow would occur in a subsequent period. An example of a non-cash expense is depreciation.

In practice, analysts define the net cash flow as:

Net cash flow = Profit after tax + Depreciation + Amortisation

33. Concentration Banking: In this system of decentralised collection of accounts receivable, large firms which have a large number of branches at different places, select some of the strategically located branches as collection centres for receiving payment from customers. Instead of all the payments being collected at the head office of the firm, the cheques for a certain geographical area are collected at a specified local collection centre. Under this arrangement, the customers are required to send their payments (cheques) to the collection centre covering the area is which they live and these are deposited in the local account of the concerned collection centre, after meeting local expenses, if any. Funds beyond a predetermined minimum are transferred daily to a *central* or *disbursing* or *concentration* bank or account. A concentration bank is one with which the firm has a major account-usually a disbursement account. Hence, this arrangement is referred to as concentration banking.

Concentration banking, as a system of decentralised billing and multiple collection points, is a useful technique to expedite the collection of accounts receivable. It reduces the time needed in the collection process by reducing the *mailing* time. Since the collection centres are near the customers, the time involved in sending the bill to the customer is reduced. Moreover, the time-lag between the despatch of the cheque by the customer and its receipt by the firm is also reduced. Mailing time is saved both in respect of sending the bill to the customers as well as in the receipt of payment.

34. Gordon's Formula

$$P_0 = \frac{\text{Earning Per Share } (1 - RR)}{\text{Cost of Capital} - (RR \cdot IRR)}$$

$$= \frac{10(1-0.60)}{0.10-(0.60 \times 0.08)} = \frac{10 \times (0.40)}{0.052}$$

$$= 77.$$

35. An organization's cost structure plays an important role in determining its cost-volume-profit relationships. A firm with proportionately high fixed costs has relatively high operating leverage. The result of high operating leverage is that the firm can generate a large percentage increase in net income from a relatively small percentage increase in sales revenue. On the other hand, a firm with high operating leverage has a relatively high break-even point.

37. Under the Janata Government regime a 21-member Committee on Workers' participation in industry was set up in September 1977, under the chairmanship of Ravindra Varma the then Union Labour Minister. The committee submitted its report in 1979. It has recommended a three-tier system of participation at shop floor, plant and corporate or Board levels. Flexibility is advocated to suit the ethos and special features of individual undertakings. The recommendations of the Committee were considered at the 31st session of the Labour Ministers' Conference in July 1980. Most of the recommendations were generally endorsed.

39. Halo effect: The halo effect occurs when a manager's positive or negative rating of a subordinate on one characteristic or criterion affects the way he rates the other characteristics, including the overall evaluation. For example, if the employee has successfully added value to the organisation through the development of higher skills, he may be rated satisfactorily overall, even if he has not added value in other areas that were agreed upon. Likewise, failure in one area may negatively influence an overall rating. This is known as a negative halo, or the devil's horns effect. Being aware of this problem is major step towards avoiding it.

41. Profitability, liquidity, safety and social welfare (justice) are the major principles which banks strive to incorporate in their working.

42. **Nationalisation of Banks:**

- 14 top commercial banks were nationalised on July 1969.
- In 1980, another six commercial banks were nationalised.
- On July 1, 1955, the State Bank of India and its associate banks commonly known as the State Bank of India Group, were nationalised.
- Presently, 27 commercial banks are working in the public sector.
- Out of these 27 commercial banks, 19 banks are nationalised.

43. SWIFT stands for: Society for Worldwide Interbank Financial Telecommunications. SWIFT is a Cooperative Society registered in May 1973 in Brussels, Belgium. In an era of information technology SWIFT offers unique message processing services and provides a very fast, accurate and authenticated transfer of financial messages on global basis. It is a cooperative society of international banks and operates a computerized telecommunication system, which allows rapid, economical, secure and accurate transmission system for essential financial data. SWIFT services enable the retail as well as corporate customers to transfer funds around the world.

44. The RBI, as the central bank of the country, formulates and conducts the monetary policy. Monetary policy refers to the use of the techniques of monetary control to achieve the broad objectives of (a) maintaining price stability and (b) ensuring adequate flow of credit to productive sectors so as to assist growth. A country's monetary policy creates conditions for growth by influencing the cost and availability of money and credit. It uses instruments directed towards regulating the money supply and the cost and availability of credit in the economy. The important techniques/tools/instruments of monetary control that are adopted by the RBI include: Open Market Operations (OMOs); Bank Rate; Refinance; Cash Reserve Ratio (CRR); Statutory Liquidity Ratio (SLR); Liquidity Adjustment Facility (LAF); and Repo Rates.

45. The structure of financial institutions (FIs) in India is widely diversified and includes National and State level development financial institutions, insurance corporations and investment institutions. For purposes of classification, the financial institutions can be classified into three broad heads; (i) All-India Financial Institutions, (ii) State-level Institutions (SFCs and SIDCs), and (iii) Other Institutions (ECGC and DICGC). All-India Financial Institutions can be further reclassified under four broad heads—All-India Development Banks (IDBI, ICICI, SIDBI, IIBI and IFCI); Specialized-Financial Institutions (EXIM Bank, RCTC, ICICI Venture, TFCI and IDFC); Investment Institutions (UTI, LIC, and GIC and its subsidiaries); and Refinance Institutions (NABARD and NHB).

46. Barter trading is less common and not much popular due to its cumbersome, time-consuming, risky, and expensive nature.

47. International business has grown in most recent years at a faster pace than global production. Reason for this is:

1. Rapid increase in and expansion of technology.
2. Liberalization of government policies on cross-border movement of trade and resources.
3. Development of institutions that support and facilitate international trade.
4. Increased global competition.

51. Ind AS 29: Financial Reporting in Hyper-inflationary Economies.

Ind AS 31: Interests in Joint Ventures.

Ind AS 34: Interim Financial Reporting.

Ind AS 36: Impairment of Assets.

Ind AS 38: Intangible Assets.

52. Human Resource Accounting (HRA) is similar in principle to the preparation of an accounting statement. Just as financial accounting reflects the cost of assets such as buildings, land, machinery, HRA tries to place a value on organisational human resources by formulating a human resource balance sheet. Here human resources are presented as assets, not as expenses. HRA, thus, shows the investment the organisation makes in its people and how the value of these people changes over time. (See Walker) According to the American Association of Accountants (AAA), HRA is "a process of identifying and measuring data about human resources and communicating this information to interested parties". Flamhoitz defined HRA as "accounting for people as an organisational resource. It involves measuring the costs incurred by organisations to recruit, select, hire, train and develop human assets. It also involves measuring the economic value of people to the organisation".

Thus, precisely stated, human resource accounting is the art of valuing, recording and presenting systematically the worth of human resources in the books of account of an organization. This definition reveals the following important characteristics of human resource accounting:

- Valuing the human resources of a company in a systematic way.
- Recording the valuation in the books of account.
- Presenting the information in the financial statements of the business.

53. **Powers of SEBI:** Securities and Exchange Board of India has been vested with powers for effective discharge of its functions. These powers can be outlined as follows:

- To give license to any individual for dealing in a given areas.
- To delegate its power (which SEBI exercises).
- The power for awarding monetary penalties.
- Judging and prosecuting in cases of violation of the rules/provisions of the Companies Act, 1956.
- To impose fines/fees/other charges on intermediaries related to performance of their functions.
- Passing mandatory orders on firms for listing their shares on one or more stock exchanges.
- Asking stock exchanges to amend their bye-laws.
- According approval on the bye-laws of stock exchanges/SEBI.
- To carry out inspection of books of accounts and demand periodical returns from the recognized stock exchanges.
- Inspection of books of accounts of financial intermediaries.

54. Venture capital funds are pooled investments that manage money from investment banks or wealthy investors to invest in start-up, small, and medium-size enterprises that are characterized as high-risk/high-return opportunities. A vulture capitalist fund is a type of fund that focuses on buying distressed firms at very low prices. This usually happens when the firm files for bankruptcy.

Venture capital is basically the second or third stage of a traditional start-up financing sequence. In the first stage, the entrepreneur invests his or her own funds called seed capital. Then an angel investor brings in additional funds for first stage existence and expansion. Venture capital funds are then utilized to establish the firm. These venture capital firms obtain their investment funds from wealthy individuals, investment banks, endowments, pension funds, insurance companies, and other financial institutions. The fund raising involves circulating a prospectus to potential investors. The first round and second round of venture capital funding involves substantial cash investments and managerial assistance. Venture capital fund managers receive annual management fees (usually 2% of invested capital) and a part of the fund's net profit. Venture capitalist funds select companies to invest in after an extensive due-diligence process. Firms are selected based on criteria in which opportunities exist for venture capital funds to grow their investments rapidly and to exit within a designated time frame. The exit process, known as the harvest strategy, takes place within 3-10 years, usually through an initial public offering (IPO) or merger or sale of the company.

56. FACTORS AFFECTING CUSTOMERS' SENSITIVITY TO PRICE

Buyer's perceptions and preferences

Unique-value effect: Customers are less price-sensitive when they perceive the product or service provides unique benefits; there are no acceptable substitutes.

Price-quality effect: Customers are less price-sensitive when they perceive the product or service offers high quality, prestige, or exclusiveness.

Buyer's awareness of and attitude toward alternatives

Substitute-awareness affect: Customers are less price-sensitive when they are relatively unaware of competing brands or substitute products or services.

Difficult-comparison effect: Customers are less price-sensitive when it is difficult to objectively compare the quality or performance of alternative brands or substitutes.

Sunk-investment effect: Customers are less price-sensitive when the purchase is necessary to gain full benefit from assets previously bought.

Buyer's ability to pay

Total-expenditure effect: Customers are less price-sensitive when their expenditure for the product or service is a relatively low proportion of their total income.

End benefit effect: Customers—particularly organizational buyers purchasing raw materials or component parts—are less price-sensitive when the expenditure is a relatively small proportion of the total cost of the end product.

Shared cost effect: Customers are less price-sensitive when part of the cost of the product or service is borne by another party (*e.g.*, when part of the cost of medical services is covered by health insurance, or when a salesperson's travel costs are covered by an expense account).

Inventory effect: Customers are less price-sensitive in the short run when they cannot store large quantities of the product as a hedge against future price increases.

57. Here are examples of decision models that have been used by marketing managers.

BRAND AID: A flexible marketing mix model focused on consumer packaged goods whose elements are a manufacturer, competitors, retailers, consumers and the general environment. The model is contains sub models for advertising pricing and competition. The model celebrated with creative branding of judgement, historical analysis, tracking field experimentation and adaptive control.

CALL PLAN: A model to help sales people determine the number of calls to make per period to each prospect and current client. The model takes into account travel time as well as selling time. The model was tested in the United States airlines with an experimental group that managed to increase its sales ever a matched control group by 8 percentage points.

DETAILER: A model to help sales people determine which customer to call on and which products to represent on each call. This model was largely developed for pharmaceutical detail people calling on physicians, where they could represent no more than three products on a call. In two applications, the model yield strong profit improvements.

GEOLINE: A model for designing sales and services territories that satisfies three principles. The territories equalize sales workloads, each territories consists of adjacent areas and the territories are compact several successful application were reported.

MEDICAL: A model to help an advertising buy media for a year. The media planning model includes market-segment delineation sales potentials estimation, diminishing marginal returns, forgetting, timing issues and competitors media schedules.

Some models now claim to duplicate the way expert marketers normally make their decision, some recent expert system models includes:

PROMOTER: Evaluations sales promotions by determining baseline sales (what sales would have been without promotion) and measuring the increase over baseline associated with the promotion.

ADCAD: Recommends the types of advertising (humorous, slice of life and so on) to use given them marketing goals, product characteristics, target marketing and competitive situation.

COVER STORY: Examines a mass of syndicated sales data and writes English Language memo reporting the highlights.

59. Kotler and Keller (2005) have observed that 'the marketplace isn't what it used to be'. It is radically different as a result of major, sometimes interlinking societal forces that have created new behaviours, new opportunities and new challenges. Some of the forces described by them are:

- **Changing technology**
- **Globalization**
- **Deregulation**
- **Privatization**
- **Customer empowerment**
- **Heightened competition**
- **Industry convergence**

60. Open-ended questions

Name	Description
Completely unstructured	A question that respondents can answer in an almost unlimited number of ways.
Word association	Words are presented, one at a time, and respondents mention the first word that comes to mind.
Sentence completion	Incomplete sentences are presented, and respondents are asked to complete them.
Picture completion	A picture of two characters is presented, with one making a statement. Respondents are asked to identify with the other and fill in the empty balloon.
Thematic Apperception Tests (TATs)	A picture is presented, and respondents are asked to make up a story about what is happening or may happen in the picture.

61.

Job family	A category in which similar occupations are grouped together. Training managers, compensation managers and recruitment managers can be combined with other occupations in the field of human resources and placed in the job family of human resource professional.
Occupation	Jobs that are combined across organisations based upon the skills, efforts and responsibilities required by the job, e.g. compensation specialist.
Job	A group of positions that are similar enough in their job elements, tasks and duties to be covered by the same job analysis, e.g. payroll manager.
Position	The combination of all the duties required of the person performing a job. Each person in an organisation holds a position, e.g. compensation policy administrator.
Duty	Several distinct tasks that are performed by an individual to complete a work activity for which they are responsible, e.g. payroll processing.
Task	An identifiable unit of work activity that is produced through the application of methods, procedures and techniques, e.g. preparing payroll forms.
Element	The smallest practical unit into which any work activity can be subdivided, e.g. signing pay cheques.

62. Distributive Bargaining: A bargaining process is described as distributive bargaining when the parties to the bargaining process have conflicting needs, interests and goals. In such a situation, the employers and employees normally adopt opposing positions. Normally, this type of bargaining is adversarial in character and a hostile environment prevails in the discussion. In this kind of bargaining, one party's gain is another party's loss as their needs are mutually exclusive. Economic issues like wages revisions, benefits, bonuses, leaves, and workloads become the major agenda of distributive bargaining. Similarly, controversial issues like employee dismissal, discharge and other disciplinary actions can also be the subject-matter of distributive bargaining. This kind of bargaining is normally a distressing experience for both the parties since they have to bring in enormous pressure on the other party. For instance, the employees' unions may hold the threat of a strike during the bargaining, while the employers may counter it with the threat of a lock-out and even disputing the union status as the real representative of the employees. Depending upon the power equation, one party finally gains at the expense of another in distributive bargaining.

64. The Factories Act of 1948 has several sections which deal with employee safety and health. The primary purpose of this act is to regulate safety, health and welfare of the employees working in factories located anywhere in India. It is a central act enforced by the state governments. According to this act, "factory" means any premises where ten or more workers are working on any day of the preceding twelve months, and in any part of which a manufacturing process is being carried out with the aid of power (twenty or more workers must work in places where operations are carried out without the aid of power).

66. Foreign Institutional Investor (FII) means an institution established or incorporated outside India which proposes to make investment in securities in India. They are registered as FIIs in accordance with Section 2(*f*) of the SEBI (FII) Regulations 1995.

There are certain beliefs about FIIs:

1. FIIs do not invest in unlisted entities. They participate only through stock exchanges
2. FIIs cannot invest at the time of initial allotment.

67. The Association of Southeast Asian Nations (ASEAN) was formed in 1967 by the five founding members, namely, Indonesia, Malaysia, the Philippines, Singapore and Thailand (also known as ASEAN-5). Brunei joined in 1984 and Vietnam, in 1995. Laos and Myanmar were admitted in 1997 and Combodia, in 1999.

69. Main Reasons to Oppose the World Trade Organization:

1. The WTO is Fundamentally Undemocratic.
2. The WTO Tramples Labour and Human Rights.
3. The WTO would Privatize Essential Services.
4. The WTO is Destroying the Environment.
5. The WTO is Increasing Inequality.
6. The WTO Hurts Poor, Small Countries in Favour of Rich Powerful Nations.
7. The WTO Undermines Local Level Decision Making and National Sovereignty.

70. A depreciation is a fall in the external value of one currency against another, for example the Australian dollar might depreciate against the US dollar so that one Australian dollar buys less of the US currency.

72. Agricultural Income [Section 10(1)]

As per section 10(1), agricultural income earned by the taxpayer in India is exempt from tax.

Agricultural income is defined under section 2(1A) of the Income-tax Act. As per section 2(1A), agricultural income generally means:

(*a*) Any rent or revenue derived from land which is situated in India and is used for agricultural purposes.

(*b*) Any income derived from such land by agriculture operations including processing of agricultural produce so as to render it fit for the market or sale of such produce.

(*c*) Any income attributable to a farm house subject to satisfaction of certain conditions specified in this regard in section 2(1A).

Previous Paper (Solved)

UGC (NET) JRF & Assistant Professor Exam Commerce, June-2015

PAPER-II

Note : *This paper contains* ***fifty (50)*** *objective type questions of* ***two (2)*** *marks each.* ***All*** *questions are compulsory.*

1. The world's first electronic stock market is:
A. KOSPI B. Nikkie
C. NASDAQ D. Dow Jones

2. The Human Development Index (HDI) is introduced by :
A. UNDP B. UNICEF
C. IMF D. World Bank

3. Examine the following statements and choose the **correct** code:

Assertion (A) : American style option, compared to European style, provides more freedom to option holders in exercising the option.

Reason (R) : American style option can be exercised only at a specified date which is generally the expiration date.

Codes :
A. Both (A) and (R) are correct.
B. Both (A) and (R) are wrong.
C. (A) is correct, but (R) is wrong.
D. (A) is not correct, but (R) is correct.

4. From the statements given below, identify the **correct** code:

Statement (I): The key strategy behind acquiring a company is to create shareholder's value.

Statement (II) : Conglomeration is a merger between two companies that have common business areas.

Statement (III) : MRTP Act got replaced by the Competition Act, 2002 in India.

Codes :
A. All the three statements are correct.
B. Statements (I) and (II) only are correct.
C. Statements (I) and (III) only are correct.
D. Statement (II) only is correct.

5. From the following, identify the tools of fiscal policy:
(*i*) Public expenditure
(*ii*) Open market operations
(*iii*) Deficit financing
(*iv*) Taxation
(*v*) Reserve requirements

Codes:
A. (*i*), (*iii*), (*iv*) and (*v*)
B. (*i*), (*ii*), (*iv*) and (*v*)
C. (*ii*) and (*v*)
D. (*i*), (*iii*) and (*iv*)

6. The basic difference between a static budget and flexible budget is that:
A. A flexible budget considers only variable costs but a static budget considers all costs.
B. Flexible budgets allow management latitude in meeting goals, whereas static budget is based on fixed standards.
C. A flexible budget is applicable for a single department only but a static budget for entire production facility.
D. A flexible budget can be prepared for any production level within a relevant range but a static budget is based on one specific level of production.

7. A retiring partner continues to be liable for obligations incurred after his retirement:
A. If unpaid amount is transferred to his loan account.
B. If he does not give public notice.
C. If he starts a similar business elsewhere.
D. In all the situations till he survives.

8. In what order, the following assets are shown in the balance sheet of a company?

(*i*) Trade receivables
(*ii*) Cash
(*iii*) Furniture and fittings
(*iv*) Investment in shares and debentures

Codes :

A. (*ii*), (*i*), (*iv*), (*iii*) B. (*i*), (*ii*), (*iii*), (*iv*)
C. (*iii*), (*iv*), (*i*), (*ii*) D. (*iv*), (*iii*), (*ii*), (*i*)

9. When opening stock is ₹ 50,000, closing stock is ₹ 60,000 and the cost of goods sold is ₹ 2,20,000, the stock turnover ratio is:

A. 2 times B. 3 times
C. 4 times D. 5 times

10. If : Stock turnover ratio is = 6 times

Average stock = ₹ 8,000

Selling price = 25% above cost

What is the amount of gross profit?

A. ₹ 2,000 B. ₹ 4,000
C. ₹ 10,000 D. ₹ 12,000

11. A rectangular hyperbola shaped demand curve on all its points has:

A. Equal slopes of the price demand curve
B. Price elasticity equal to unity
C. Varying price elasticity
D. Both slope and price elasticity equal

12. In case of short-run equilibrium, a perfectly competitive firm while earning abnormal profits operates at an output level where:

A. Marginal cost is the minimum
B. Average cost is the minimum
C. Both marginal cost and average cost are equal
D. Marginal cost is higher than average cost

13. Which one of the following statements is **false**?

A. Normally, a price demand curve slopes downward from left to right
B. Economies of scale and economies of scope are the same
C. For optimization, equality between marginal cost and marginal revenue is a necessary condition but it is not a sufficient one
D. Law of variable proportions denotes input-output relationship during short-run

14. Match the items of List-I with the items of List-II.

List-I	List-II
(*a*) Law of diminishing marginal utility	(*i*) Cross demand
(*b*) Relationship between price of one commodity and demand for other commodity	(*ii*) Oligopoly
(*c*) Skimming the cream policy	(*iii*) Cardinal approach
(*d*) Price rigidity	(*iv*) Pioneer pricing

Codes :

	(*a*)	(*b*)	(*c*)	(*d*)
A.	(*i*)	(*ii*)	(*iii*)	(*iv*)
B.	(*iii*)	(*i*)	(*ii*)	(*iv*)
C.	(*ii*)	(*iv*)	(*i*)	(*iii*)
D.	(*iv*)	(*iii*)	(*ii*)	(*i*)

15. The following are the demand and supply equations in a perfectly competitive market:

$$P = 12 + 0.3\, Q_s$$
$$P = 40 - 0.4\, Q_d$$

The equilibrium market price would be:

A. 24 B. 10
C. 40 D. 20

16. Which of the following is **not** an accounting software package?

A. Quick Books B. Sage one
C. Sage M D. Sage 50

17. Which one of the following formula is used to calculate probable error of correlation-coefficient between two variables of '*n*' pairs of observations?

A. $0.6745\left[\frac{1-r^2}{\sqrt{n}}\right]$ B. $0.5758\left[\frac{1-r^2}{\sqrt{n}}\right]$

C. $0.675\left[\frac{1-r^2}{n}\right]$ D. $0.5758\left[\frac{1-r^2}{n}\right]$

18. If the population is heterogeneous, which one of the following probability sampling methods is more appropriate?

A. Sequential sampling
B. Quota sampling
C. Double sampling
D. Stratified sampling

19. Which of the following relating to normal distribution is **not** correct?

(*i*) Co-efficient of skewness is three
(*ii*) It is mesokurtic
(*iii*) Mean deviation for it is $\frac{2}{3}\sigma$
(*iv*) $\mu \pm 2\sigma$ covers 95.45% area
(*v*) Mean, median and mode are equal
(*vi*) The standard normal variate z has mean one and SD zero

Codes:

A. (*i*), (*iii*) and (*vi*) B. (*iii*), (*iv*) and (*v*)
C. (*i*), (*iii*) and (*v*) D. (*i*), (*iii*) and (*iv*)

20. Which one of the following statements is **false**?

A. Both correlation and regression co-efficients have same sign
B. Arithmetic mean of the regression co-efficients is always more than the correlation co-efficient
C. Regression co-efficients are independent of both the origin and scale
D. Correlation co-efficient is the square root of two regression co-efficients

21. Match the items of List-I with the items of List-II.

	List-I		List-II
(*a*)	"He who can manage, can manage anything".	(*i*)	Henry Fayol
(*b*)	"Due to these experiments, a factory does not remain a factory, it is converted into a laboratory".	(*ii*)	William B. Cornell
(*c*)	"Management succeeds or fails as human relations in business are intelligently or unintelligently handled".	(*iii*)	F.W. Taylor
(*d*)	"A place for everything, and everything in its place".	(*iv*)	Lawrance A. Appley

Codes :

	(*a*)	(*b*)	(*c*)	(*d*)
A.	(*i*)	(*ii*)	(*iii*)	(*iv*)
B.	(*i*)	(*ii*)	(*iv*)	(*iii*)
C.	(*iv*)	(*iii*)	(*ii*)	(*i*)
D.	(*iii*)	(*ii*)	(*i*)	(*iv*)

22. Assertion (A): Management is mainly associated with economic affairs.

Reason (R) : Big business houses are the result of effective financial management.

Codes :

A. (A) is correct, and (R) is the right explanation of (A).
B. Both (A) and (R) are correct but (R) is not the right explanation of (A).
C. (A) is incorrect but (R) is correct in isolation.
D. Both (A) and (R) are incorrect.

23. Areas of establishing objectives under MBO are:

(*i*) Market Standing
(*ii*) Innovation
(*iii*) Industrial Relations
(*iv*) Public Accountability
(*v*) Productivity
(*vi*) Industrial Policy

Codes :

A. (*iii*), (*iv*), (*v*) and (*vi*)
B. (*i*), (*ii*), (*iv*) and (*v*)
C. (*i*), (*ii*), (*v*) and (*vi*)
D. (*ii*), (*iii*), (*iv*) and (*v*)

24. Match the items of List-I with List-II.

	List-I		List-II
(*a*)	Management of Tomorrow	(*i*)	Chris Argyris
(*b*)	Motivation and Personality	(*ii*)	Fredrick Hergberg
(*c*)	The Motivation of Work	(*iii*)	L.F. Urwick
(*d*)	Personality and Organisation	(*iv*)	A.H. Maslow

Codes :

	(*a*)	(*b*)	(*c*)	(*d*)
A.	(*i*)	(*iv*)	(*ii*)	(*iii*)
B.	(*iii*)	(*iv*)	(*i*)	(*ii*)
C.	(*iv*)	(*iii*)	(*ii*)	(*i*)
D.	(*iii*)	(*iv*)	(*ii*)	(*i*)

25. Narayan Murthy Committee revised its recommendations on Corporate Governance as on 29th October 2004 which diluted the following areas:

(*i*) Independence of Directors
(*ii*) Whistle Blower Policy
(*iii*) Performance evaluation of Non-Executive Directors
(*iv*) Mandatory training of Non-Executive Directors

Codes :

A. (*i*), (*ii*) and (*iii*) only
B. (*i*) and (*iii*) only
C. (*i*), (*ii*) and (*iv*) only
D. All (*i*), (*ii*), (*iii*) and (*iv*)

26. The service marketing mix is an extended marketing mix and includes:

(*i*) People
(*ii*) Process
(*iii*) Service
(*iv*) Physical evidence

Codes :

A. (*ii*), (*iii*) and (*iv*)
B. (*i*), (*ii*) and (*iii*)
C. (*i*), (*ii*) and (*iv*)
D. (*i*), (*iii*) and (*iv*)

27. Black box model in marketing relates to:

A. Marketing planning
B. Marketing mix
C. Marketing control
D. Consumer behaviour

28. Items, considered part of the augmented product, do **not** include:

A. Guarantee
B. Warranty
C. Complementary products
D. Channels of distribution

29. Which of the following is **not** a type of direct marketing?

A. Direct mail marketing
B. Retail marketing
C. Telemarketing
D. Email direct marketing

30. 'Press release' is a part of:

A. Public relations B. Advertising
C. Sales promotion D. None of the above

31. In capital budgeting, the term capital rationing implies:

A. that no retained earnings are available
B. that limited funds are available for investment
C. that no external funds can be raised
D. that no fresh investment is required in current year

32. In certainty equivalent approach, adjusted cash flows are discounted at:

A. Accounting Rate of Return
B. Internal Rate of Return
C. Hurdle Rate
D. Risk Free Rate

33. Combined leverage is calculated as:

A. Operating Leverage + Financial Leverage
B. Operating Leverage – Financial Leverage
C. Operating Leverage × Financial Leverage
D. Operating Leverage ÷ Financial Leverage

34. Which of the following is **not** true with reference to capital budgeting?

A. Capital budgeting is related to asset replacement decisions
B. Cost of capital is equal to minimum required return
C. Existing investment in a project is not treated as sunk cost
D. Timing of cash flows is relevant

35. What is Economic Order Quantity?

A. Cost of an order
B. Cost of stock
C. Reorder level
D. Optimum order size

36. Which of the following is **not** a basic objective of HRM?

A. To attract HR into the organisation
B. To develop and motivate HR for better performance
C. To have the reward and punishment system for HR
D. To integrate and maintain HR in the organisation

37. What is 'gate hiring'?
A. To select people who approach on their own for employment in the organisation
B. To select people who are recommended by the employees
C. To select people from public employment exchanges
D. To select people supplied by labour contractors

38. Matching essential managers and essential positions is a step in the process of:
A. Career Cycle
B. Succession Planning
C. Career Planning
D. Career Stages

39. The barriers to effective performance appraisal are:
(*i*) Psychological blocks of managers
(*ii*) Faulty assumptions of the parties concerned
(*iii*) Technical pitfalls
(*iv*) Faulty written communications

Codes :
A. All are correct
B. Only (*ii*) and (*iii*) are correct
C. Only (*i*) and (*ii*) are correct
D. Only (*i*), (*ii*) and (*iii*) are correct

40. Who has developed the 'Systems Approach' of industrial relations?
A. John Dunlop B. Garry S. Becker
C. Michael J. Jucius D. Edwin B. Flippo

41. In 1992, the banking sector reforms were introduced as per:
A. C. Rangarajan Committee Report
B. M. Narasimham Committee Report
C. Suresh Tendulkar Committee Report
D. Sukhamoy Chakrabarty Committee Report

42. For the purpose of extending rural banking and agro finance, the NABARD:
A. Directly lends and monitors the rural borrowers
B. Refinances the banks extending rural finance
C. Refinances the rural borrowers obtaining credit from banks
D. Directly finances the rural borrowers and gets refinance from government

43. When RBI grants loan to commercial banks and charges interest on it, it is called:
A. Rapo rate
B. Reverse Rapo rate
C. Sweep stack rate, basic rate
D. Bank rate

44. E-banking business is essentially regulated by the Information Technology Act, 2000, under which personal signature is replaced by:
A. Encrypted signature
B. Image signature
C. Digital signature
D. Online signature

45. In order to control inflation and ensure stability in money market:
A. The RBI works under the direction of ministry of finance, government of India
B. The RBI acts independently and can refuse the government directive
C. The RBI acts under the board of directors
D. The RBI's board of governors shall abide by the government directive

46. In respect of international business, a project is called a turnkey project because:
A. The licensee agrees to construct an entire plant in his home county and hands over the key
B. The lincensor starts the operation and hands over the key of the operating plant to the licensee
C. The licensor starts the operation and then invites the licensee and hands over the key to complete the remaining work
D. The licensor and the licensee jointly carry out the project and agree to share profit equally

47. Match the items of List-I with List-II.

List-I	List-II
(*a*) Bretton woods conference	(*i*) WTO
(*b*) Soft loan window	(*ii*) World Bank
(*c*) Geneva	(*iii*) IFC
(*d*) Loan to private sector	(*iv*) IDA

Codes :

	(a)	(b)	(c)	(d)
A.	(i)	(iii)	(ii)	(iv)
B.	(iv)	(iii)	(ii)	(i)
C.	(ii)	(iv)	(i)	(iii)
D.	(iv)	(ii)	(iii)	(i)

48. Assertion (A): The member nations, consistently finding balance of payments crisis, may approach the Wold Bank seeking financial accommodation to mitigate the crisis.

Reason (R) : The member nations facing balance of payments crisis can approach the IMF seeking redressal of the BOP crisis.

Codes :

A. (A) is correct, and (R) is correct explanation of (A).
B. (A) is correct, but (R) is wrong.
C. (R) is correct and (A) is wrong.
D. Both (A) and (R) are wrong.

49. In computation of balance of payments, overall balance of payments =

A. Balance of current account + Balance of capital account + Statistical discrepancy
B. Export of goods and invisibles – Import of goods
C. Foreign exchange inflow – Foreign exchange outflow
D. Export of goods and invisibles + Import of goods and invisibles

50. The instrument chosen for enhancement of international liquidity is:

A. Society for Worldwide Inter bank Financial Telecommunications (SWIFT)
B. Special Drawing Rights (SDRs)
C. Multilateral Netting
D. Netting of Payments

ANSWERS

1	2	3	4	5	6	7	8	9	10
C	A	C	C	D	D	B	C	C	D
11	**12**	**13**	**14**	**15**	**16**	**17**	**18**	**19**	**20**
B	D	B	C	A	C	A	D	A	C
21	**22**	**23**	**24**	**25**	**26**	**27**	**28**	**29**	**30**
C	C	B	D	D	C	D	D	B	A
31	**32**	**33**	**34**	**35**	**36**	**37**	**38**	**39**	**40**
B	D	C	C	D	C	A	B	D	A
41	**42**	**43**	**44**	**45**	**46**	**47**	**48**	**49**	**50**
B	B	D	C	B	B	C	C	A	B

SOME SELECTED EXPLANATORY ANSWERS

1. NASDAQ: Opened to trading in 1971, the National Association of Securities Dealers Automatic Quotations (NASDAQ) was the world's first electronic stock market. Initially a computer bulletin board system, with no contact between buyers and sellers, it gradually expanded to include trade and volume reporting, automated trading systems and was the first U.S. stock market to allow online trading. It merged with the London Stock Exchange in 1992, forming the first intercontinental partnership of securities markets. In 1998 it merged with AMEX, forming the second-largest U.S. stock exchange, although that partnership lasted only six years. NASDAQ Stock Market, Inc. was formed as a public company in 2000. NASDAQ is known for specializing in technology based stocks, although virtually every industry is listed.

2. The Human Development Index (HDI) was introduced in 1990 by the United Nations Development Programme (UNDP). Unlike the narrow GNP measure (which is based solely on income), the HDI includes three key components, longevity, knowledge, and income which are combined into a composite human development index to arrive at an 'average deprivation index.'

5. Fiscal Policy is a part of economic policy of the government which is related to government income and expenditure. It includes public expenditure policy, taxation policy, public debt policy and deficit financing. It is aimed at achieving certain objectives like—rapid economic development, reduction in economic inequalities, promoting capital formation etc.

Techniques/Tools/Areas/Components/Instruments/Scope of Fiscal Policy

Fiscal policy has four techniques as under:
A. Public Expenditure Policy
B. Taxation Policy
C. Public Debt Policy
D. Deficit Financing

6. **Static budget:** A quantified plan that projects revenues and costs for only one level of activity.
Flexible budget: A quantified plan that projects revenues and costs for varying levels of activity.

7. **Incoming partner:** A person who is admitted as a partner into an already existing firm with the consent of all the existing partners is called as "incoming partner". Such a partner is not liable for any act of the firm done before his admission as a partner.
Outgoing partner: A partner who leaves a firm in which the rest of the partners continue to carry one business is called a retiring or outgoing partner. Such a partner remains liable to third parties for all acts of the firm until public notice is given of his retirement.

9. Stock Turnover Ratio = $\dfrac{\text{Cost of Goods Sold}}{\text{Average Stock}}$

$$\because \text{Average Stock} = \frac{\text{Opening Stock + Closing Shock}}{2}$$

$$= \frac{50000 + 60000}{2} = \frac{110000}{2} = 55000$$

$$\therefore \text{Stock Turnover Ratio} = \frac{220000}{55000} = \frac{220}{55}$$

$$= 4 \text{ times.}$$

10. Stock Turnover Ratio = $\dfrac{\text{Cost of Goods Sold}}{\text{Average Stock}}$

$$6 = \frac{\text{Cost of Goods Sold}}{8,000}$$

$$\text{Cost of Goods Sold} = 8,000 \times 6 = 48,000$$

$$\text{G.P.} = \frac{25}{100} \times 48,000$$

$$= ₹\ 12,000.$$

11. **Demand with unit elasticity:**

$$h = \frac{\Delta x/x}{\Delta p/p} = 1 \Rightarrow \frac{\Delta x}{x} = \frac{\Delta p}{p}$$

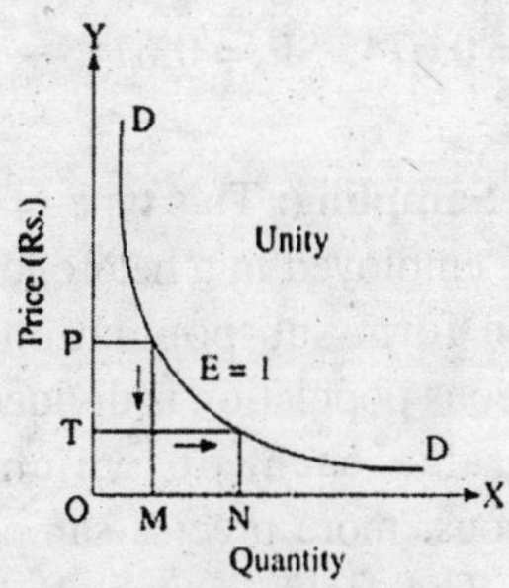

⇒ when the elasticity of demand is unity, any proportionate change in the price causes an equal proportionate change in the quantity demanded. Here, the shape of the demand curve is a rectangular hyperbola.

15. In equilibrium

$$Q_d = Q_s$$

$$\Rightarrow \frac{40 - P}{0.4} = \frac{P - 12}{0.3}$$

$$\Rightarrow 12 - 0.3P = 0.4P - 4.8$$

$$\Rightarrow 0.7P = 12 + 4.8 \Rightarrow 0.7P = 16.8$$

$$\Rightarrow P = \frac{168}{7} = 24.$$

16. Online bookkeeping relies on a Web-based computer application rather than desktop bookkeeping software. Popular online account services that charge a monthly fee include *FreshBooks, Harvest, QuickBooks Online, Sage One, Zoho Books, Outright, Xero, Hashoo, FreeAgent, LessAccounting, WorkingPoint, Cheqbook, Intaaact, Clear Books* and *Kashflow.*

17. The probable error (PE) of coefficient of correlation indicates extent to which its value depends on the condition of random sampling. If r is the calculated value of correlation coefficient in a sample of n pairs of observations, then the standard error SE_r of correlation coefficient r is given by

$$SE_r = \frac{1-r^2}{\sqrt{n}}$$

The probable error of the coefficient of correlation is calculated by the expression:

$$PE_r = 0.6745\ SE_r = 0.6745\frac{1-r^2}{\sqrt{n}}.$$

18. Stratified Sampling: This type of sampling is commonly employed in a heterogeneous field. If we can form sub-populations so that a heterogeneous population is divided into parts, called strata, each of which is fairly homogeneous, more precise sampling can be achieved. The field is thus divided into a number of strata, and a sample or samples are drawn independently in each stratum.

19. Seven features of normal distributions are listed below.

1. Normal distributions are symmetric around their mean.
2. The mean, median and mode of a normal distribution are equal.
3. The area under the normal curve is equal to 1.0.
4. Normal distributions are denser in the center and less dense in the tails.
5. Normal distributions are defined by two parameters, the mean (μ) and the standard deviation (σ).
6. 68% of the area of a normal distribution is within one standard deviation of the mean.
7. Approximately 95% of the area of a normal distribution is within two standard deviations of the mean.

20. Properties of Regression Coefficients

1. Correlation coefficient is the geometric mean between the regression coefficients. Symbolically, $r = \sqrt{b_{xy} \cdot b_{yx}}$.
2. If one of the regression coefficients is greater than unity, the other must be less than unity. (Both of them may be less than unity).
3. Regression coefficients are independent of the change of origin but not scale.
4. Both the regression coefficients will have the same sign and correlation coefficient also has the same sign as that of regression coefficients.

23. One of the major emphases of the MBO process is on "Key Result Areas" (KRAs). KRAs indicate the present state of organization's health and the top management perspective for the future. Examples of KRAs applicable to most of the business organizations are—profitability, market standing, innovation, productivity, worker performance, financial and physical resources, manager performance and public responsibility. The list of KRAs gets considerably changed over the period in response to new needs and opportunities. The achievement in a particular KRA also provides the impetus for a new KRA in future.

25. SEBI instituted a committee under the chairmanship of Mr. N.R. Narayana Murthy which recommended enhancements in corporate governance. SEBI has incorporated the recommendations made by the Narayana Murthy Committee on Corporate Governance in Clause 49 of the listing agreement. The revised Clause 49 has been made effective from January 1, 2006.

The revised Clause 49 on corporate governance made major changes in the definition of independent directors, strengthening the responsibilities of audit committees, improving quality of financial disclosures, including those relating to related party transactions and proceeds from public/rights/preferential issues, requiring Boards to adopt formal code of conduct, requiring CEO/CFO certification of financial statements and for improving disclosures to shareholders.

26. In determining the best way to present a good or service for consumers' consideration, marketeers have many decisions to make, so they need many tools. The marketeer's strategic toolbox is called the marketing mix, which consists of the tools that are used to create a desired response among a set of predefined consumers. These tools include the *product* itself, the *price* of the product, the *promotional* activities that introduce it to consumers and the *place* where it is available.

27. Black box model: Consumer behaviour can be defined as a study of human behaviour within the consumer role and includes all the steps in the decision-making process. The study must go beyond the explicit act of purchase to include an examination of less observable processes as well as a discussion of why, where and how a particular purchase occurs.

Consumer behaviour is an area of study that draws on the work of scholars and practitioners from many diverse disciplines. Most studies of consumer behaviour attempt to explain the so called black box model, as shown in Figure. This is essentially a model of stimulus and response. The mind of a consumer is analogous to a black box, in that the box, like the mind, does not permit the observation of processes within it. Mental activities between a stimulus and the resulting response cannot be observed, causing difficulty in comprehending why a person decides to take a particular action. Scholars have been attempting for many years to draw some conclusion, based on their observation of the input and output activity about what takes place inside that black box.

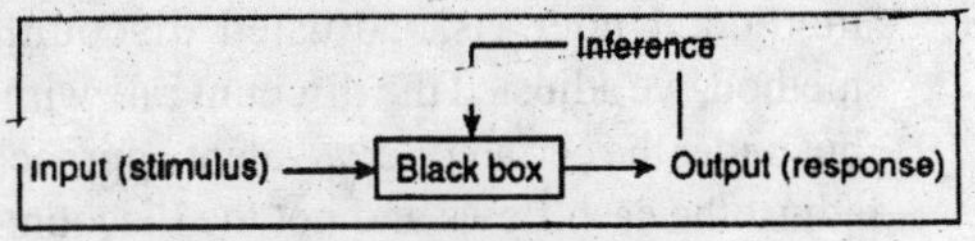

Fig. *Black box model*

There are four major perspectives employed to explain the internal operation of the black box. These four perspectives are:

(1) Economics, (2) Social biology, (3) Behavioural sciences, and (4) Marketing.

28. Augmented Product: Marketeers often surround their actual products with goods and services that provide additional value to the customer's purchase. While these factors may not be the key reasons leading customers to purchase; for some, their inclusion strengthens the purchase decision; their omission may cause others not to buy. Among these are guarantees, service networks, delivery, after-sales service, and credit facilities. They provide ways to enhance the offering, can be used to counter objections or resolve doubts in the customer's mind, and can be an important source of differentiation from the competition.

Items considered part of the augmented product include the following:

(1) Guarantee, (2) Warranty, (3) Customer Service, (4) complementary Products and (5) Accessibility.

31. When firms have to take investment decisions under the constraint of fund availability it is termed as capital rationing. Capital budgeting decisions taken when the amount of funds available with the firm is limited are termed as capital rationing decisions. Thus, lesser the funds available with the firm, lesser will be the number of profitable investment projects accepted by the firm. Under capital rationing, the usual capital budgeting decisions have to be restructured in order to maintain the profitability and value addition of the firm.

32. The certainty-equivalent approach avoids demerits of the risk-adjusted discount rate method. Under risk-adjusted discount rate method, we adjusted the discount rate with risk; but under the certainty-equivalent approach, we adjust the cash flows and not the discount rate. This way the demerits of risk-adjusted discount rate method are done away with.

Certainty-equivalent approach involves two steps:

(*a*) The first step is the determination of the certainty-equivalent coefficient.

(*b*) The second step is the determination of the present value of the future expected cash flows.

33. Combined leverage is the product of operating leverage and financial leverage. The operating leverage has its effects on operating risk and is measured by the percentage change in EBIT due to percentage change in sales. The financial leverage has its effects on financial risk and is measured by the percentage change is EPS due to percentage change in EBIT. Since both these leverages are closely concerned with ascertaining the ability to cover fixed charges (fixed-operating costs in the case of operating leverage and fixed-financial costs in the case of financial leverage), if they are combined, the result is total leverage and the risk associated with combined leverage is known as total risk. Symbolically, Degree of combined leverage (DCL).

$$DCL = DOL \times DFL$$

Substituting the value of DOL and DFL, we have

$$DCL = \frac{\%\text{ change in EBIT}}{\%\text{ change in sales}} \times \frac{\%\text{ change in EPS}}{\%\text{ change in EBIT}}$$

$$= \frac{\%\text{ change in EPS}}{\%\text{ change in sales}}$$

$$\text{or } DCL = \frac{\text{Contribution}}{\text{EBIT}} \times \frac{\text{EBIT}}{\text{EBIT} - \text{I}}$$

$$= \frac{\text{Contribution}}{\text{EBIT} - \text{I}}$$

Thus, the DCL measures the percentage change in EPS due to percentage change in sales.

35. **Economic Order Quantity (EOQ) model:** An inventory management technique for determining an item's optimal order quantity, which is the one that minimises the total of its order costs and carrying costs. The EOQ model takes into account various operating and financial costs and determines the order quantity that minimises total inventory costs.

37. **Gate Hiring and Contractors:** The concept of gate hiring is to select people who approach on their own for employment in the organisation. This happens mostly in the case of unskilled and semiskilled workers. Gate hiring is quite useful and convenient method at the initial stage of the organisation when large number of such people may be required by the organisation.

38. A succession plan to fill key positions over a period of time is essential for the survival and success of an organisation. The purpose of succession planning is to identify and develop people to replace current incumbents in key positions in cases of resignation, retirement, promotion, growth, etc. Succession can be from within or from outside the organisation. Succession by people from within provides opportunities to employees for advancement in their careers. In some professionally managed companies, every key executive is usually asked to identify two or three best juniors who could replace him in his job should the need arise. Complete dependence on internal sources may however cause conflicts and stagnation in the organisation. Similarly, complete dependence on outside talent may cause stagnation in the careers of present employees which may in turn lead to a sense of frustration and job dissatisfaction.

39. There are certain barriers, which work against the effective appraisal system. Identification of these barriers is essential, so that suitable measure may be adopted to reduce their impact to a possible minimum level. These barriers can be grouped in three categories, they are:

1. Faulty Assumptions
2. Psychological Blocks
3. Technical Pitfall.

40. Environmental or External Theories or System Model: This approach is developed by economists. This is 'systems' approach developed by John Dunlop. He views industrial relations system as a sub-system of society. According to Dunlop, the core elements of the systems model of industrial relations are actors, *certain contexts, an ideology which binds* the industrial relations system together and body of rules created to govern the actors at the workplace.

41. In India, financial sector reforms were undertaken in the early stages of economic reform, pursuant to the recommendations, of the Committee on Financial Sector Reforms (Narasimham Committee), which submitted its report in 1992. This was followed by another Committee on Banking Sector Reforms (Narasimham Committee II), which submitted its report in 1998. As a result of measures taken pursuant to the recommendations of these Committees, the adoption of prudential norms relating to capital adequacy, income recognition, asset classification, provisioning standards and valuation of investment portfolio in India are now close to international best practices.

43. Reserve Bank of India (Central Bank) is Controller of credit and this is its important function. It controls the volume of loans granted by the commercial banks. It supervises that the banks should not grant too much or too low loans to industry and general public. As grant of too much loans will create inflation and prices will tend to rise. Therefore, the volume of credit should be just adequate to meet the needs of the industry and commerce. Both inflation and deflation are bad for economy. The Central Bank can control the volume of credit by various methods *e.g.*, regulation of bank rate, open market operation, change in reserve ratio and selective credit control policies. The principal methods used by RBI can be classified into two categories as follows:

I. Quantitative or General Methods, and

II. Qualitative or Selective Methods

46. In a turnkey project agreement, a firm agrees to construct an entire plant in a foreign country and make it fully operational. It is known as turnkey because the licensor starts the operation and hands over the key of the operating plant to the licensee. Agreements for turnkey projects normally take place where the initial construction part of the plant is more complex than the operational part. Such projects are either self-engineered or made to specifications. In case of the former, it is the licensor who decides the design of the project. In the latter, it is the lincensee who takes such decision. In both cases, the contract involves either a fixed price or a cost-plus price. In a fixed-price contract, the risk of cost over-runs lies with the licensor.

49. Balance of Payments

- Balance of trade = Export of goods – Import of goods
- Balance of current account = Balance of trade + Net earnings on invisibles
- Balance of capital account = Foreign exchange inflow – Foreign exchange outflow, on account of foreign investment, foreign loans, banking transactions, and other capital flows
- Overall balance of payments = Balance of current account + Balance of capital account + Statistical discrepancy

50. Special Drawing Rights (SDRs) is also known as the paper gold. It is a form of international reserve created by IMF in 1969. It was created to solve the problem of international liquidity. They are not paper notes or currency. It was created by the group of ten agreed countries. They are international units of account in which the official accounts of the IMF are kept.

PAPER-III

Note : *This paper contains* ***seventy five*** *(75) objective type questions of* ***two*** *(2) marks each.* ***All*** *questions are compulsory.*

1. GNP at market prices – Indirect taxes + subsidies is referred to as:
A. GNP at factor cost
B. GDP at factor cost
C. NNP at factor cost
D. NDP at factor cost

2. EDI system got legal recognition under which one of the following Acts?
A. Electronics Act, 1996
B. Right to Data Act, 1998
C. DGFT Act, 1999
D. Information Technology Act, 2000

3. Following statements are related to futures contracts. Choose the statements that are **not** true:
(*a*) Purchase of a futures contract is called short position.
(*b*) Currency futures are traded on an exchange in standardised form and in fixed quantity.
(*c*) Default risk in futures contract is high compared to forward contract.

Codes:
A. only (*a*) and (*b*)
B. only (*a*) and (*c*)
C. (*a*), (*b*) and (*c*)
D. only (*b*)

4. From the following, identify the trading blocks in the world and choose the **correct** code:
(*a*) European Union
(*b*) North American Free Trade Agreements
(*c*) South Asian Association of Regional Co-operation
(*d*) Central American Common Market
(*e*) Central African Customs Union

Codes:
A. (*a*), (*b*) and (*c*)
B. (*a*), (*b*), (*c*) and (*d*)
C. (*a*), (*b*), (*c*), (*d*) and (*e*)
D. (*a*), (*b*) and (*e*)

5. Match the items of List-I with items of List-II and choose the **correct** code:

List-I	**List-II**
(*a*) Carroll Model	(*i*) International trade
(*b*) Corlett-Hague Rule	(*ii*) Interest rate
(*c*) Hecksher Ohlin Theorem	(*iii*) Principles of taxation
(*d*) Knut Wick sell's Theory	(*iv*) Social responsibility of business

Codes :

	(*a*)	(*b*)	(*c*)	(*d*)
A.	(*iv*)	(*iii*)	(*i*)	(*ii*)
B.	(*iii*)	(*ii*)	(*i*)	(*iv*)
C.	(*iii*)	(*i*)	(*ii*)	(*iv*)
D.	(*ii*)	(*iii*)	(*i*)	(*iv*)

6. Labour Rate of Pay Variance can be calculated by which one of the following equations?
A. Budgeted Labour Costs – Actual Labour Costs
B. (Standard Hours – Actual Hours) × Actual Wage Rate
C. (Standard Wage Rate – Actual Wage Rate) × Actual Hours Worked
D. (Standard Wage Rate – Actual Wage Rate) × Standard Hours Worked

7. Given :

Margin of Safety	₹ 80,000
Profit	₹ 20,000
Sales	₹ 3,00,000

What is the amount of Fixed Cost?
A. ₹ 1,00,000 B. ₹ 75,000
C. ₹ 55,000 D. ₹ 20,000

8. Preparation of consolidated statement of accounts as per AS - 21 is:
A. Optional
B. Mandatory for Private Ltd. Companies
C. Mandatory for Listed Companies
D. Mandatory for all Companies

9. Which one of the following is **not** true of cash Budget?

A. The shortage or excess of cash would appear in a particular period
B. All inflows would arise before outflows for those periods
C. Only revenue nature cash flows are shown
D. Proceeds from issue of share capital is shown as an inflow

10. Study the following transactions:
(*a*) Raising of short-term loans
(*b*) Goods purchased for cash
(*c*) Payment of bonus in the form of shares
(*d*) Issue of shares in lieu of raw materials
Flow of funds is:
A. (*a*), (*b*), (*c*) and (*d*)
B. (*b*), (*c*) and (*d*)
C. (*c*) and (*d*)
D. Only (*d*)

11. When a consumer increases units of X-commodity by giving up some units of Y-commodity and even to attain the same level of satisfaction, the marginal rate of substitution, will be calculated by:
A. Change in X-Commodity divided by change in Y-Commodity
B. Change in X-Commodity divided by marginal utility of Y-Commodity
C. Change in Y-Commodity divided by change in X-Commodity
D. Change in Y-Commodity divided by marginal utility of X-Commodity

12. The following is the demand function in the small market:
$Q = 50 - 5P$
Where 'Q' denotes quantity in physical units and 'P' denotes price of the commodity. At price ₹ 5, the point price elasticity of demand would be:
A. Zero
B. Equal to unity
C. Highly elastic
D. Highly inelastic

13. Match the items of List-I with the items of List-II and find out the correct matching.

List-I Production functions	List-II Name of the shapes of returns to scale
(*a*) $Q = 10.2\ K^{0.19}\ L^{0.88}$	(*i*) Constant Returns to scale
(*b*) $Q = 1.01\ L^{0.75}\ K^{0.25}$	(*ii*) Diminishing Returns to scale
(*c*) $Q = 0.84\ L^{0.63}\ K^{0.3}$	(*iii*) Increasing Returns to scale

Codes:

	(*a*)	(*b*)	(*c*)
A.	(*i*)	(*ii*)	(*iii*)
B.	(*ii*)	(*i*)	(*iii*)
C.	(*ii*)	(*iii*)	(*i*)
D.	(*i*)	(*iii*)	(*ii*)

14. In the short-run, when a simple monopoly firm attains equilibrium and earns only normal profit, its level of output will correspond to:
A. Lowest average cost
B. Average cost above optimum level of output
C. Average cost equals marginal cost
D. Marginal cost much below average cost

15. Which one of the following is a **false** statement?
A. Ramsey pricing rates to the methodology of pricing to situations where firms are regulated and the maximization of allocative efficiency is the objective of pricing together with the objective of profit-maximization.
B. Peak-load pricing is a pricing practice where price varies with time of the day.
C. Value-pricing is the practice of pricing where the price is set based on its value to the customer.
D. Two-part tariff refers to a price structure which has two parts—a lump sum charge and a variable charge.

16. All the properties of order, interval and zero origin are simultaneously possessed by :
A. Nominal Data B. Interval Data
C. Ratio Data D. Ordinal Data

17. Under which of the following situations, chi-square test is applicable?

(*a*) testing homogeneity
(*b*) testing goodness of fit
(*c*) testing equality of two sample means
(*d*) testing equality of two sample proportions
(*e*) testing independence of attributes

Codes:

A. Only (*a*), (*b*) and (*c*)
B. Only (*a*), (*b*) and (*e*)
C. Only (*c*), (*d*) and (*e*)
D. Only (*a*), (*c*) and (*e*)

18. Which one of the following is **not** the **correct** statement regarding sampling distribution of mean?

A. Sampling distribution of mean is normally distributed for large sized samples.
B. Sampling distribution of mean is normally distributed for small sized samples drawn from not normally distributed population.
C. '*t*' distribution is not normally distributed.
D. Mean of the sampling distribution of mean is equal to the parametric value of mean.

19. Consider the following statements and identify the **wrong** statements:

Statement-I: Accepting null hypothesis, when it is false, is called a level of significance.

Statement-II: 1–α is called power of a test.

Statement - III : Critical value of Z-static for two-tailed test at 5% level of significance is 1.96.

Codes:

A. Statements I, II and III
B. Statements I and III
C. Statements II and III
D. Statements I and II

20. The process of thoroughly checking the collected data to ensure optimal quality level is referred to as :

A. Validation B. Editing
C. Classification D. Entry

21. Statement-I: Management is the art of knowing what you want to do and then seeing that it is done in the best and the cheapest way.

Statement-II: Management is the process of planning and regulating the activities of an enterprise.

A. **Statement** (I) is correct, but (II) is incorrect
B. **Statement** (II) is correct, but (I) is incorrect
C. Both the **statements** (I) and (II) are incorrect
D. Both the **statements** (I) and (II) are correct

22. Assertion (A) : No business runs itself, even on momentum ..... every business needs repeated stimulus.

Reasoning (R): The management is the dynamic, life giving element in every business, without its leadership, the resources of production remain as resources and never become production.

A. Assertion (A) and Reasoning (R), both are correct, and (R) is the correct explanation of (A).
B. Assertion (A) and Reasoning (R), both are correct, but (R) is not the correct explanation of (A).
C. Assertion (A) is correct, but Reasoning (R) is incorrect.
D. Reasoning (R) is correct, but Assertion (A) is incorrect.

23. Match the items of **List-I** with **List-II** :

List-I	**List-II**
(*a*) Credit Mobilier	(*i*) Charles Babbage
(*b*) Charleton Twist Company	(*ii*) Henry Fayol
(*c*) Difference Engine	(*iii*) Claud Henri Saint Simon
(*d*) Commentry Four Chambault	(*iv*) Robert Owen

Codes:

	(*a*)	(*b*)	(*c*)	(*d*)
A.	(*iii*)	(*iv*)	(*i*)	(*ii*)
B.	(*iii*)	(*i*)	(*iv*)	(*ii*)
C.	(*i*)	(*iii*)	(*iv*)	(*ii*)
D.	(*ii*)	(*i*)	(*iv*)	(*iii*)

24. Find out the **correct** combination of statements with regards to business ethics :

(*a*) Business ethics is the behaviour that a business adheres to in its daily dealings.
(*b*) The ethics of a particular business can be diverse.
(*c*) Business ethics has normative and descriptive dimensions.

A. Only (*a*) and (*b*) B. Only (*a*) and (*c*)
C. Only (*b*) and (*c*) D. All (*a*), (*b*) and (*c*)

25. Which one of the following is **not** correct about business ethics?

A. Business ethics reflects the philosophy of business.
B. Business ethics is a form of applied ethics.
C. Business ethics is governed by the Government Policies.
D. Ethics are the standards which govern decisions on daily basis.

26. A marketing network consists of :

A. The tasks to devise marketing activities.
B. The tasks of hiring, training and motivating employees.
C. The activities that help in designing and implementing the marketing programmes.
D. The company and its supporting stakeholders with whom it has built mutually profitable business relationships.

27. Target marketing involves which of the following activities?

(*a*) Market positioning
(*b*) Market targeting
(*c*) Market behaviour
(*d*) Market segmentation

Codes:

A. (*a*) and (*b*)
B. (*b*) and (*d*)
C. (*a*), (*b*) and (*d*)
D. (*b*), (*c*) and (*d*)

28. The pricing strategy which adjusts the basic price to accommodate differences in customers, products and locations is called :

A. Differentiated pricing
B. Promotional pricing
C. Geographical pricing
D. Price discounts and allowances

29. Horizontal marketing system comprises:

A. the producer, wholesaler and retailer acting in a unified system.
B. multichannel marketing.
C. two or more marketing channels to reach one or more customer segments.
D. two or more unrelated companies put together resources to exploit an emerging market.

30. Match the items of List-I with the items of List-II:

List-I	List-II
(*a*) Face-to-face interaction with one or more prospective purchasers	(*i*) Sales promotion
(*b*) Any paid form of nonpersonal promotion	(*ii*) Public relations
(*c*) Short-term incentives to encourage purchase	(*iii*) Personal selling
(*d*) Programmes to promote company's image	(*iv*) Advertising

Codes:

	(*a*)	(*b*)	(*c*)	(*d*)
A.	(*iii*)	(*iv*)	(*ii*)	(*i*)
B.	(*iii*)	(*iv*)	(*i*)	(*ii*)
C.	(*ii*)	(*i*)	(*iii*)	(*iv*)
D.	(*ii*)	(*iii*)	(*i*)	(*iv*)

31. Which of the following techniques for appraisal of investment proposals are based on time value of money?

(*a*) Accounting Rate of Return
(*b*) Internal Rate of Return
(*c*) Profitability Index Method
(*d*) Earnings Per Share

Codes :

A. (*a*) and (*b*) B. (*b*) and (*c*)
C. (*a*) and (*d*) D. (*a*), (*b*) and (*d*)

32. On the basis of the following information, what will be the EBIT corresponding to financial indifference point?

Total capital outlay ₹ 60,00,000

Financing Plans

(*a*) 100% Equity @ ₹ 10/- per share
(*b*) Debt-equity ratio 2 : 1

Rate of interest 18% p.a., corporate tax rate 40%

A. ₹ 10,00,000 B. ₹ 12,00,000
C. ₹ 10,80,000 D. ₹ 12,80,000

33. Which one of the following assumptions is **not** included in the James E. Walter Valuation model?

A. All financing by retained earnings only
B. No change in the key variables such as EPS and DPS
C. The firm has finite life
D. All earnings are either distributed as dividends or invested internally immediately

34. Match the items of List-I with the items of List-II and find out the correct matching.

List-I (Formulae)	**List-II (Type of leverages)**
(a) $\frac{\text{Contribution}}{\text{EBIT}}$	(i) Financial leverage
(b) $\frac{\text{EBIT}}{\text{Earnings before Tax (EBT)}}$	(ii) Super-leverage
(c) $\frac{\text{Contribution}}{\text{EBT}}$	(iii) Operating leverage

Codes:

	(a)	(b)	(c)
A.	(ii)	(iii)	(i)
B.	(i)	(ii)	(iii)
C.	(iii)	(ii)	(i)
D.	(ii)	(i)	(iii)

35. Statement-I: Working capital leverage measures the responsiveness of Return on Equity for changes in current Assets.

Statement-II : When the annual demand for an item is 3200 units, unit cost ₹ 6, inventory carrying charges 25% p.a. and cost of one procurement ₹ 150, the economic ordering quantity would be 700 units.

Codes:

A. Both statements are correct
B. Both statements are incorrect
C. Statement-I is correct and Statement-II is incorrect
D. Statement-I is incorrect and Statement-II is correct

36. Match the items of List-I with the items of List-II:

List-I Conventional HRM	**List-II Strategic HRM**
(a) Staff specialists	(i) Fast and proactive
(b) Slow and reactive	(ii) People and knowledge
(c) Capital and products	(iii) Line managers
(d) Cost centre	(iv) Investment centre

Codes:

	(a)	(b)	(c)	(d)
A.	(ii)	(i)	(iii)	(iv)
B.	(ii)	(iii)	(i)	(iv)
C.	(iii)	(ii)	(i)	(iv)
D.	(i)	(ii)	(iii)	(iv)

37. Which one of the following is a traditional method for selection of personnel?

A. Interview B. Selection Test
C. Phrenology D. Aptitude Test

38. The method of training in crafts, trades and technical areas is known as :

A. Vestibule training
B. Coaching
C. Mentoring
D. Apprenticeship

39. Behaviourally Anchored Rating Scale is a technique used for :

A. Selection
B. Succession Planning
C. Performance appraisal
D. Recruitment

40. Which one of the following is **not** a mechanism of managing stress?

A. Rust out B. Cognitive therapy
C. Job enrichment D. Networking

41. Interest earned by a depositor against a deposit with a commercial bank for custodial service :

A. is a fund based income
B. is a fee based income
C. is a combination of fund and fee based gain
D. is a commitment based gain

42. Match the items in List-I with the items in List-II:

List-I	List-II
(*a*) ATM card	(*i*) NPA
(*b*) Debts due for more than 30 days	(*ii*) John Shephard Barron
(*c*) Micro finance	(*iii*) State Finance Corporations Act
(*d*) State level finance corporations	(*iv*) NABARD

Codes:

	(*a*)	(*b*)	(*c*)	(*d*)
A.	(*i*)	(*iii*)	(*ii*)	(*iv*)
B.	(*ii*)	(*i*)	(*iv*)	(*iii*)
C.	(*iv*)	(*iii*)	(*ii*)	(*i*)
D.	(*ii*)	(*i*)	(*iii*)	(*iv*)

43. Assertion (A): A well-developed money market is the basis for an effective monetary policy. It is in the money market that the Central Bank comes into contact with the financial sectors of the economy as a whole and it is through the liquidity in the market that influences the cost and availability of credit.

Reasoning (R): A well-organised money market is an essential condition for the successful operation of the Central Banking policies, and for holding the conditions of liquidity within the bounds of what the monetary authorities consider desirable.

A. (A) is true but (R) is false
B. (R) is true but (A) is false
C. (A) is true and (R) offers correct explanation to (A)
D. Both (A) and (R) are false

44. The operations of banks and financial institutions are regulated by:

A. The RBI Act, 1934 only
B. The Banking Regulation Act, 1949 only
C. Information Technology Act, 2000 only
D. All of the above

45. To operationalise online, internet, mobile banking, debit card and credit card tools, some of the essential ingredients are :

A. Compliance with the Information Technology Act, 2000
B. Satellite connection
C. Selection of a portal and server
D. All of the above

46. Any country consistently facing balance of payment deficiency can approach:

A. The World Bank
B. The Smithsonian Institute
C. IMF
D. The IMF and the IBRD

47. Counter-trade means:

A. A sort of bilateral trade where one set of goods is exchanged for another set of goods and a seller provides a buyer with deliveries.
B. A company takes full responsibility for making its goods available in the target market by selling directly to the end-users.
C. The companies in two separate sovereigns agree to exchange one set of goods for another set of goods.
D. A set of multilateral trade where one of goods and services may be exchanged for another set of goods and services among the trading partners.

48. The floating rate system is characterised by :

A. the market forces that determine the exchange rate between two currencies.
B. the central banking authorities of the two countries mutually agree upon the rate.
C. help realigning the par value of major currencies.
D. the rate of exchange mutually agreed upon between IMF and its member nations.

49. A practice of selling a commodity in a foreign market at a price lower than the domestic price; and even at equal to the cost of production to capture foreign market is known as :

A. Gouging B. Forging
C. Dumping D. Forfeiting

50. The highest percentage of export from India went to which of the following regions in 2013-14?

A. OECD countries B. USA
C. SAARC D. Latin America

51. Match the items of List-I with the items of List-II and select a **correct** code:

List-I	List-II
(*a*) SEBI	(*i*) Exchange for small companies
(*b*) RBI	(*ii*) Secondary market in treasury bills
(*c*) STCI	(*iii*) Regulation of secondary market
(*d*) OTCEI	(*iv*) Ad-hoc treasury bills

Codes :

	(*a*)	(*b*)	(*c*)	(*d*)
A.	(*iv*)	(*ii*)	(*iii*)	(*i*)
B.	(*iii*)	(*iv*)	(*ii*)	(*i*)
C.	(*iii*)	(*i*)	(*ii*)	(*iv*)
D.	(*ii*)	(*iii*)	(*i*)	(*iv*)

52. X Ltd. goes into liquidation and a new company Z Ltd. purchases the business of X Ltd. It is a case of :

A. Amalgamation
B. Absorption
C. Internal reconstruction
D. External reconstruction

53. When the cost incurred on recruiting, training and developing the employees is considered for determining the value of employees, it is called:

A. The replacement cost approach
B. The historical cost approach
C. The opportunity cost approach
D. None of the above

54. In India, NIFTY and SENSEX are calculated on the basis of :

A. Market capitalisation
B. Paid up capital
C. Free-float market capitalisation
D. Authorized share capital

55. Financial Instruments which are issued with detachable warrants and are redeemable after certain period is known as:

A. Deep Discount Bonds
B. Secured Premium Notes
C. Bunny Bonds
D. Junk Bonds

56. Which of the following can be used by a company as communication mix to reach the target customers?

(*a*) Advertising
(*b*) Sales promotion
(*c*) Events and experiences
(*d*) Public relations
(*e*) Direct marketing
(*f*) Personal selling

Codes:

A. (*a*), (*b*), (*d*) and (*f*)
B. (*a*), (*b*), (*e*) and (*f*)
C. (*a*), (*b*), (*d*), (*e*) and (*f*)
D. (*a*), (*b*), (*c*), (*d*), (*e*) and (*f*)

57. In addition to motivation, learning and memory, which one of the following is included in the main psychological processes affecting consumer behaviour?

A. Perception B. Life cycle
C. Life style D. Social class

58. Match the items of List-I with the items of List-II:

List-I	List-II
(*a*) Geographic Segmentation	(*i*) Gender, income, religion
(*b*) Demographic Segmentation	(*ii*) Knowledge, attitude, response
(*c*) Psychographic Segmentation	(*iii*) Regions, cities, neighbourhoods
(*d*) Behavioural Segmentation	(*iv*) Lifestyle, personality traits, values

Codes:

	(*a*)	(*b*)	(*c*)	(*d*)
A.	(*ii*)	(*iv*)	(*iii*)	(*i*)
B.	(*ii*)	(*iv*)	(*i*)	(*iii*)
C.	(*iv*)	(*ii*)	(*i*)	(*iii*)
D.	(*iv*)	(*i*)	(*ii*)	(*iii*)

59. Which one of the following is **not** a stage in the product life cycle?

A. Introduction B. Growth
C. Equilibrium D. Decline

60. Which one of the following is **correct** statement in respect of co-branding?

A. Co-branding is an umbrella branding of goods of a company.
B. In co-branding, two or more well-known existing brands are combined into a joint product.
C. Co-branding is the process of combining two brands for promoting brand equity.
D. All of the above

61. Which one of the following is **not** a punishment?
A. Withholding of increments
B. Demotion
C. Transfer
D. Suspension

62. Assertion (A) : Job evaluation is essentially a job rating process, not unlike the rating of employees.

Reasoning (R): Job evaluation is a practice which seeks to provide a degree of objectivity in measuring the comparative value of jobs within an organisation and among similar organisations.
A. Both **Assertion (A)** and **Reasoning (R)** are correct
B. Both **Assertion (A)** and **Reasoning (R)** are incorrect
C. **Assertion (A)** is correct, but **Reasoning (R)** is incorrect
D. **Reasoning (R)** is correct, but **Assertion (A)** is incorrect

63. Identify the **correct** combinations from the following:

Skills	Training and Development Methods	Target Trainees
(a) Knowledge	Deliberation/Lecture	Managerial
(b) Multi-skills	Vestibule training	Operative
(c) Decision-making skills	Management game	Managerial
(d) Behavioural skills	Sensitivity training	Supervisory

Codes:
A. (*a*), (*b*) and (*c*) B. (*a*), (*c*) and (*d*)
C. (*b*), (*c*) and (*d*) D. (*a*), (*b*) and (*d*)

64. Which among the following are **not** part of staffing process?
(*a*) Human Resource Planning
(*b*) Recruitment
(*c*) Selection
(*d*) Induction and Orientation
(*e*) Training and Development
(*f*) Performance Appraisal
(*g*) Transfers
(*h*) Separations

Codes:
A. (*e*), (*f*), (*g*) and (*h*)
B. (*g*) and (*h*)
C. (*f*) and (*h*)
D. None of the above

65. Match the items of List-I with List-II:

List-I	List-II
(*a*) INTUC	(*i*) 1920
(*b*) AITUC	(*ii*) 1947
(*c*) CITU	(*iii*) 1955
(*d*) BMS	(*iv*) 1970

Codes:

	(*a*)	(*b*)	(*c*)	(*d*)
A.	(*i*)	(*ii*)	(*iii*)	(*iv*)
B.	(*ii*)	(*i*)	(*iv*)	(*iii*)
C.	(*ii*)	(*i*)	(*iii*)	(*iv*)
D.	(*iii*)	(*i*)	(*iv*)	(*ii*)

66. Assertion (A): Amended Patent Act, in compliance with WTO, provides for grant of product patent as well as a process patent for a period of 20 years from the date of application.

Reasoning (R): Under the Act, patent may be granted to an invention which means a new product or process involving an inventive step and capable of industrial application, a technical advance over existing knowledge.

Codes:
A. Both (A) and (R) are true but, (R) is not correct explanation to (A).
B. (A) is false, but (R) is correct.
C. Both (A) and (R) are true and (R) is correct explanation to (A).
D. (A) is correct, but (R) is false.

67. Which of the following have been recognised under the intellectual property eligible for creation of rights as per WTO mandate?

(*a*) Computer software, music disc, performing art

(*b*) Geographical indicator

(*c*) Global positioning system

(*d*) Journals, books, seeds, design, brand

Codes:

A. (*a*), (*b*) and (*c*)

B. (*d*), (*c*) and (*a*)

C. (*a*), (*b*) and (*d*)

D. (*c*), (*a*) and (*b*)

68. NAFTA came into force from January, 1994 embracing:

A. The USA, Canada, Cuba, Trinidad and Tobago

B. The USA, Canada, Mexico

C. Cuba, Mexico, USA, Havana

D. Trinidad, The USA, Mexico

69. A common market is one where :

A. all the trading nations agree commonly to levy a common and uniform tariff rate for all goods.

B. all the trading nations agree commonly to rationalise tariff and non-tariff barriers mutually to promote intra-region trade.

C. there is a customs union along with free intra-union movement of factors of production.

D. there is an economic union along with free intra-union movement of residents.

70. The Maastricht Treaty of February, 1992 renamed the European Community (EC) as:

A. the European Union (EU)

B. the European Economic Union (EEU)

C. the European Monetary Union (EMU)

D. the European Economic Community (EEC)

71. In which of the following cases, Assessing Officer has the discretion to assess the income of the previous year in the previous year or in the subsequent assessment year?

A. Shipping business of non-residents

B. Association of Persons (AOP) or Body of Individuals (BOI) formed for a particular event or purpose

C. Assessment of persons likely to transfer property to avoid tax

D. Discontinued business

72. Rental income received by a foreign individual, from another foreign individual, in respect of the property situated in Delhi is taxable in the hands of :

A. Resident and Ordinarily Resident (OR) only

B. Ordinarily Resident (OR) and Not Ordinarily Resident (NOR) only

C. Non Resident (NR) only

D. Ordinarily Resident (OR), Not Ordinarily Resident (NOR) and Non Resident (NR)

73. Which of the following income is **not** chargeable under the head 'income from business and profession'?

A. Profits and Gains carried on by an assessee during the previous year.

B. Income derived by a trade professional or similar association from specific services performed for its members.

C. Income from the activity of owning or owning and maintaining race horses.

D. Salary received by a partner of a firm from the same firm.

74. Mr. A earned a capital gain of ₹ 100 lakhs on 31-2-2014 from the sale of a long term capital asset (land) within the limits of Jaipur corporation. If he invests ₹ 60 lakhs, out of ₹ 100 lakhs, in Rural Electricity Corporation Bonds approved under Sec. 54 EC in 20-2-2014, what is the amount of exemption he can claim under Sec. 54 EC of Income Tax Act for the AY 2014-15?

A. ₹ 60 lakhs B. ₹ 50 lakhs

C. ₹ 100 lakhs D. ₹ 30 lakhs

75. Under which of the following situations, the Appellate Tribunal can rectify the mistake in the order passed by it under Sec 254 (2) of Income Tax Act?

(*a*) If subsequent decision of the Supreme Court/High Court is available on the subject after the Appellate Tribunal's order

(*b*) If an assessee applies for rectification of the Tribunal's order by raising fresh grounds before the Tribunal

(*c*) If the omission or mistake is on the part of Appellate Tribunal

(*d*) If the order is passed by the Appellate Tribunal under an erroneous impression of fact or law

Codes:

A. (*a*), (*b*) and (*c*)
B. (*b*), (*c*) and (*d*)
C. (*a*), (*c*) and (*d*)
D. only (*c*) and (*d*)

ANSWERS

1	2	3	4	5	6	7	8	9	10
A	D	B	C	A	C	C	C	C	D
11	**12**	**13**	**14**	**15**	**16**	**17**	**18**	**19**	**20**
C	B	C	D	A	C	B	B	D	A
21	**22**	**23**	**24**	**25**	**26**	**27**	**28**	**29**	**30**
D	A	A	D	C	D	C	A	D	B
31	**32**	**33**	**34**	**35**	**36**	**37**	**38**	**39**	**40**
B	C	C	A	B	B	C	D	C	A
41	**42**	**43**	**44**	**45**	**46**	**47**	**48**	**49**	**50**
A	B	C	D	D	C	A	A	C	A
51	**52**	**53**	**54**	**55**	**56**	**57**	**58**	**59**	**60**
B	D	B	C	B	D	A	*	C	B
61	**62**	**63**	**64**	**65**	**66**	**67**	**68**	**69**	**70**
C	A	B	D	B	C	C	B	B	A
71	**72**	**73**	**74**	**75**					
D	D	C	*	C					

SOME SELECTED EXPLANATORY ANSWERS

1. Market price refers to the actual transacted price and it includes indirect taxes—custom duty, excise duty, sales tax, service tax etc.

Factor cost refers to the actual cost of the various factors of production includes government grants and subsidies but it excludes indirect taxes.

Relationship between market price and factor cost.

GNP at factor cost = GNP at market price – indirect taxes + subsides

GDP at factor cost = GDP at market pirce – indirect taxes + subsides

2. The IT Act, 2000 is an act to provide legal recognition for transactions carried out by means of electronic data interchange and other means of electronic communication, which is commonly referred to as "electronic commerce". It involves the use of alternatives to paper-based methods of communication and storage of information, to facilitate electronic filing of documents with the Government agencies and further to amend the Indian Penal Code, the Indian Evidence Act, 1872, the Banker's Book's Evidence Act, 1891 and the Reserve Bank of India Act, 1934 and for matters connected therewith or incidental thereto.

3. Futures Contract means a legally binding agreement to buy or sell the underlying security on a future date. Future contracts are the organized/standardized contracts in terms of quantity, quality (in case of commodities), delivery time and place for settlement on any date in future. The contract expires on a pre-specified date which is called the expiry date of the contract. On expiry, futures can be settled by delivery of the underlying asset or cash. Cash settlement enables the settlement of obligations arising out of the future/option contract in cash.

6. **Labour Rate of Pay Variance:** It is that portion of labour cost variance which is due to the difference between the standard rate specified and actual rate paid. It is calculated as follows:

Labour Rate Variance = AT (SR – AR)

= Actual Time (Standard Rate – Actual Rate)

When actual rate is less than the standard rate, it will be favourable and vice-versa. It arises due to the following reasons:

(*i*) Change in the wage rate
(*ii*) Less wages paid to new workers
(*iii*) Overtime work done
(*iv*) Persons of different grades are employed than specified

7. $\because$ Margin of Safety $= \dfrac{\text{Profit}}{\text{P/V Ratio}}$

$$\Rightarrow \quad \frac{P}{V}\text{ Ratio} = \frac{20000}{80000} = 25\%$$

$$\text{and} \quad \frac{P}{V}\text{ Ratio} = \frac{\text{Contribution}}{\text{Sales}} \times 100$$

$$25 = \frac{\text{Contribution}}{300000} \times 100$$

$$\Rightarrow \quad \text{Contribution} = 25 \times 3000 = 75000$$

$$\therefore \quad \text{Profit} = \text{Contribution} - \text{Fixed cost}$$

$$\text{Fixed cost} = \text{Contribution} - \text{Profit} = 75000 - 20000 = 55000.$$

8. The objective of AS-21 is to provide guidelines, principles and procedure to prepare consolidated financial statements for a group of enterprises under the control of a holding company. These consolidated Financial Statements are prepared to provide financial information about the economic activities of the "group". (Holding and its subsidiaries).

While preparing consolidated financial statements, a holding company should include all its subsidiaries (domestic and foreign) except where:

(*i*) Control subsidiary is temporary due to its subsequent disposal in near future or
(*ii*) the subsidiary operates under severe long term restrictions and cannot transfer funds to its holding (parent) Company.

Consolidation Procedure as per AS-21

Consolidation is mandatory only for listed companies as per the listing agreement. Consolidation is done as per general rules of preparation of financial statements of individual companies. Significant accounting policies and notes which are necessary for presenting a true and fair view of consolidated financial statements should also be disclosed.

9. **Cash Management Planning through Budgeting:** Cash budget can be called as summary statements of cash flows over a projected time period. To synchronize cash receipts and cash payments a cash budget should be prepared. A cash budget will consider only cash receipts and cash payments and ignore the non-cash items. The objective of cash budet is to identify periods of shortage of funds and excess of requirements of cash. It helps to plan the production schedule and to find out the requirements of seasonal variations of funds. It avoids excess cash balances and arranges funds at favourable terms. Since funds can be analyzed in time, the opportunities of cash discounts and other advantages can be taken.

The significance of cash budgeting can be summarized in the following:

- It identifies periods of shortage of cash and periods of surplus cash

- It helps the firm take advantage of cash discounts
- It prevents the firm from having excess accumulation of funds
- It procures funds on the most favoured terms
- It plans the schedules of firm for an even and smooth flow of funds throughout the year so that it does not face a shortage.

11. **Marginal Rate of Substitution (MRS):** It is the rate at which a consumer is willing to substitute good Y for good X.

$$\text{MRS} = \frac{\text{Loss of Good Y}}{\text{Gain of Good X}} \text{ or } -\frac{\Delta Y}{\Delta X}$$

Indifference Curve: is a curve showing different combination of two goods, each combination offering the same level of satisfaction to the consumer.

Characteristics of IC.

12. $E_d = -\frac{dQ}{dP}\cdot\frac{P}{Q}$

$\therefore \quad \frac{dQ}{dP} = -5$

$\therefore \quad E_d = (-)(-5)\cdot\frac{5}{25} = 1.$

13. **Cobb-Dogulas Production Function**

The Cobb-Dogulas may be expressed as

$$Q = AK^{\alpha}L^{\beta}$$

where Q = output, K = Capital input,
L = Labout input

A, α and β are positive parameters and also $\alpha > 0, \beta > 0, L > 0$ and $K > 0$.

Returns to Scale: The sum of the exponents $(\alpha + \beta)$ gives information about returns to scale. If $(\alpha + \beta) > 1$, it exhibits increasing returns to scale and if $(\alpha + \beta) < 1$, it exhibits diminishing returns to scale. If $(\alpha + \beta) = 1$, it exhibits constant returns to scale.

14. **Monopoly Firm Earning Normal Profit:** In this diagram, at point T, marginal revenue and marginal costs are equal and the firm produces OQ output.

The price is OP or QR which touch average cost and average revenue curves at point R

As the rice is equal to average cost at R the monopoly firm earns only normal profits.

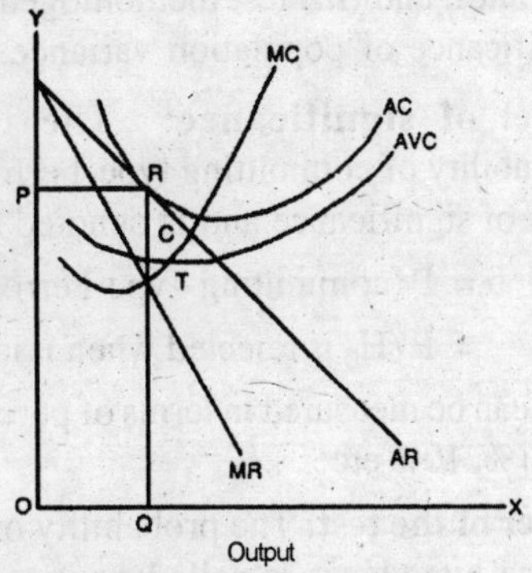

16. There are four levels of data measurement. Ranked from top to bottom in order of complexity and information content these are:

1. Ratio data
2. Interval data
3. Ordinal data
4. Nominal data

Each level of measurement is characterized by its properties. Nominal measurement has just one property: CLASSIFICATION. Ordinal measurement has two properties: CLASSIFICATION and ORDER. Interval measurement has three properties: CLASSIFICATION, ORDER and EQUAL INTERVALS. Ratio data has four properties: CLASSIFICATION, ORDER, EQUAL INTERVALS and TRUE ZERO.

17. The chi-square test is an important test amongst the several tests of significance developed by statisticians. Chi-square, symbolically written as χ^2 (Pronounced as Ki-square), is a statistical measure used in the context of sampling analysis for comparing a variance to a theoretical variance. As a non-parametric test, it can be used to determine if categorical data shows dependency or the two classifications are independent. It can also be used to make comparisons between theoretical populations and actual data when categories are used. Thus, the chi-square test is applicable in large number

of problems. The test is, in fact, a technique through the use of which it is possible for all researchers to (*i*) test the goodness of fit; (*ii*) test the significance of association between two attributes, and (*iii*) test the homogeneity or the significance of population variance.

19. Level of significance: The maximum probability of committing type-I error is called level of significance and is denoted by α.

$$\alpha = \text{P (committing Type-I error)}$$
$$= \text{P (}H_0\text{ is rejected when it is true)}$$

This can be measured in terms of percentage *i.e.* 5%, 1%, 10% etc ... .

Power of the test: The probability of rejecting a false hypothesis is called power of the test and is denoted by $1 - \beta$.

Power of the test

$$= \text{P (}H_0\text{ is rejected when it is false)}$$
$$= 1 - \text{P (}H_0\text{ is accepted when it is false)}$$
$$= 1 - \text{P (Committing Type-II error)}$$
$$= 1 - \beta$$

- A test for which both α and β are small and kept at minimum level is considered desirable.
- The only way to reduce both α and β simultaneously is by increasing sample size.
- The type-II error is more dangerous than type-I error.

21. According to **E.W. Taylor,** "Management is the art of knowing what you want to do and then seeing that it is done in the best and cheapest way".

"Management is a social process entailing responsibility for effective (or efficient) planning and regulation of the operations of an enterprise." **—E.F.L. Brech**

24. Business ethics is the behaviour that a business adheres to in its daily dealings with the world (Borgerson and Schroeder, 2008). The ethics of a particular business can be diverse (Solomon, 1983). They apply not only to how the business interacts with the world at large, but also to their one-on-one dealings with a single customer (Solomon, 1991).

Business ethics can be both normative and a descriptive discipline (Abrams, 1954). As a corporate practice and a career specialization, the field is primarily normative. In academic research descriptive approaches are also taken.

25. Business ethics (also known as corporate ethics) is a form of applied ethics or professional ethics that examines ethical principles and moral or ehtical problems that arise in a business environment. It applies to all aspects of business conduct and is relevant to the conduct of individuals and business organizations as a whole. Applied ethics is a field of ethics that deals with ethical questions in many fields such as medical, technical, legal and business ethics.

Business ethics reflects the philosophy of business, of which one aim is to determine the fundamental purposes of a company. If a company's purpose is to maximize shareholder returns, then sacrificing profits to other concerns is a violation of its fiduciary responsiblity. Corporate entities are legally considered as persons in USA and in most nations. The 'corporate persons' are legally entitled to the rights and liabilities due to citizens as persons.

26. According to **Kotler** (2006) "A marketing network consists of the company and its supporting stakeholders.... with whom it has built mutually profitable business relationships."

27. Target Marketing recognizes that different groups of customers have different needs and might also desire different core benefits from the same service. It sought the different needs and preferences of the consumers and instead of trying to satisfy them with the same type of services, the firm designed complete marketing programmes for each of these sub-groups.

Benefits of Target Marketing

- The market size is large and the service firm may not have sufficient resources to address it, neither would it perhaps want to do so.

- Customers are scattered all over the geographical spread, making it practically impossible to reach every potential buyer. Targeting was far more cost-effective.
- Competitors are entrenched, making entry and survival difficult. Therefore, smaller firms can seek niche or specialized markets.
- Customer requirements from the service vary widely. Targeting a segment or two — to the exclusion of the rest — increases the chances of meeting most of customers' demands.
- It generated customer loyalty.

There are three stages to Target Marketing:

- Market segmentation
- Market Targeting
- Market Positioning

28. **Differentiated Pricing:** Companies often adjust their basic price to accommodate differences in customers, products, and locations. *Price discrimination* occurs when a company sells a product or service at two or more prices that do not reflect a proportional difference in costs. In *first-degree price discrimination,* the seller charges a separate price to each customer depending on the intensity of his or her demand. In *second-degree price discrimination,* the seller charges less to buyers who buy a larger volume. In *third-degree price discrimination,* the seller charges different amounts to different classes of buyers.

29. Horizontal marketing system or horizontal channel is a channel arrangement in which two or more unrelated companies put together resources or programmes to exploit a new marketing opportunity. Adler calls this symbiotic marketing. By working together, companies can combine their capital, production capabilities, or marketing resources to accomplish more than any one company could alone. Companies might join forces with competitors or non-competitors. They might work with each other on a temporary or permanent basis, or they may create a separate company.

The number of horizontal marketing system has increased dramatically in recent years. The examples of this kind are Sugar Syndicate of India, Associated Cement Company, Maruti, Hero Honda etc. The reasons for horizontal channels are—the ever-changing markets, cut-throat competition, changing pace of technology, excess capacity and so on.

31.
- Payback and Accounting rate of return methods do not consider the time value of money. Hence, these are identified as traditional methods.
- The modern methods are Internal rate of return and net present value methods. These consider the time value of money.
- Internal rate of return is that rate which equates the present value of future cash inflows to the original investment.
- Profitability index is the ratio between 'present value of future cash inflows' to 'capital outlay'. The higher the index is, the higher is the profitability and vice versa.

32. Alternatives in Financing and its Financial Charges

(*a*) By issue of 6,00,000 equity shares of ₹ 10 each amounting to ₹ 60 lakhs. No financial charges are involved.

(*b*) By raising the funds in the following way:

Debt = ₹ 40 lakhs

Equity = ₹ 20 lakhs (2,00,000 equity shares of ₹ 10 each)

Interest payable on debt = $40,00,000 \times \frac{18}{100}$

= ₹ 7,20,000

The difference point between the two alternatives is calculated by:

$$\frac{(\text{EBIT} - I_1)}{E_1} = \frac{(\text{EBIT} - I_2)(1-T)}{E_2}$$

Where, EBIT = Earnings before interest and taxes

I_1 = Interest charges in Alternative (a)

I_2 = Interest charges in Alternative (b)

T = Tax rate

E_1 = Equity shares in Alternative (a)

E_2 = Equity share in Alternative (b)

Putting the values, the break-even point would be as follows:

$$\frac{(EBIT-0)(1-0.40)}{6,00,000} = \frac{(EBIT-7,20,000)(1-0.40)}{2,00,000}$$

$$\frac{(EBIT)(0.60)}{6,00,000} = \frac{(EBIT-7,20,000)(0.60)}{2,00,000}$$

$$\frac{EBIT(0.60)}{3} = \frac{0.60(EBIT-7,20,000)}{1}$$

$$EBIT = 3EBIT - 21,60,000$$

$$-2\,EBIT = -21,60,000$$

$$EBIT = \frac{21,60,000}{2}$$

$$EBIT = 10,80,000.$$

33. James E. Walter has presented a model in 1963, which explains the relevance of dividend for valuation of shares or maximization of wealth. The investment policy of a firm cannot be separated from its dividend policy and both are, according to Water, interlinked. The choice of an appropriate dividend policy affects the value of an enterprise. The key argument in support of the relevance proposition of Water's model is the relationship between the return on firm's investment or its internal risk of return (r) and its cost of capital or required rate (k). The firm would have an optimum dividend polity, which will be determined by the relationship of r and k.

Walter's model is based on the following assumptions.

1. The firm finances all investment through retained earnings; that is debt or new equity is not issued.
2. The firm's rate of return (r) and cost of capital (k) are constant.
3. All earnings are either distributed as dividend or retained internally immediately.
4. There is no change in the earnings per share EPS and dividend per share DPS. They may be changed in the models to determine the results.
5. The firm has a very long or infinite life.

37. Selection as a process is not new to organizations. It has been practised in one form or the other in practically all organizations. The history of selection suggests that formerly stereotyped impressions of personality and characteristics were used as a basis for selection. The nineteenth century particularly, saw the growth of several "pseudo-scientific" methods like phrenology, physiognomy, and graphology. They were utilized to make decisions concerning the individuals' conduct and predisposition. It is difficult to evaluate these methods because casual observation and introspection by their very nature are incapable of providing scientific proof of their effectiveness.

Phrenology: One of the most popular doctrines of the early nineteenth century was the phrenology of Gall, Spurzheim, and Coombe. It assumed that the strength of each faculty was indicated by prominent bumps on certain parts of the skull. Thirty-seven faculties and propensities like combativeness, sentiment, and perception were identified, and judgements on the conduct and character were made on the basis of these bumps. Gall did not provide any evidence that these faculties were independent of each other and that they were fundamental to all behaviour. It is now known that traits and abilities are not all located in the brain and it is also very difficult to locate one trait that does not have an effect on the others. Indeed, it has been said that "the bumps on a man's skull tell more about his wife's character than his own."

39. There are three commonly used performance appraisal methods: (1) Checklists; (2) Graphic

Rating Scales; and (3) Behaviourally Anchored Rating Scales.

Evaluation on Behaviourally Anchored Rating Scales: This technique is based on the concept that one can assess an employee's performance by evaluating his behaviour or action over a particular situation. It is applied on Behaviourally Anchored Rating Scales and is commonly known as BARS. While practising this technique, the employee is asked to describe a specific incident of his effective or non-effective performance behaviour. In some cases, the employees are asked to identify the broad sets of job activities for which the supervisors have generated sets of critical incidents representing behavioural pattern in the form of action, and describing them as 'very good', 'good', or 'poor' performance. The choice made by the employee in a given situation is assessed on the behavioural observation scale. The comparison is made with the expected performance level. The parameters used in the system, which can be identified in the critical incidents, are human relations, consciousness, organisational ability, observational power, knowledge and judgement.

41. There are two categories of sources of income for a financial services company, namely: (*i*) Fund based and (*ii*) Fee based.

Fund based income comes mainly from interest spread (the difference between the interest earned and interest paid), lease rentals, income from investments in capital market and real estate. On the other hand, fee based income has its sources in merchant banking, advisory services, custodial services, loan syndication, etc. In fact, a major part of the income is earned through fund-based activities. At the same time, it involves a large share of expenditure also in the form of interest and brokerage. In recent times, a number of private financial companies have started accepting deposits by offering a very high rate of interest. When the cost of deposit resources goes up, the lending rate should also go up. It means that such companies have to compromise the quality of its investments.

Fee based income, on the other hand, does not involve much risk. But, it requires a lot of expertise on the part of a financial company to offer such fee-based services.

43. A well-developed money market is the basis for an effective monetary policy. If is in the money market that the Central Bank comes into contact with the financial sectors of the economy as a whole and it is through varying the liquidity in the market and thereby influencing the cost and availability of credit that the Bank achieves its economics objectives.

The important functions of a well developed money market may be listed down in more precise terms as follows:

1. By providing various kinds of credit instruments suitable and attractive for different sections, a money market augments the supply of funds.
2. Efficient working of a money market helps to minimise the gluts and stringencies in the money market due to the seasonal variations in the flow of and demand for funds.
3. A money market helps to avoid wide seasonal fluctuations in the interest rates.
4. A money market, by augmenting the supply of funds and making them readily available to the legitimate borrowers, helps in making funds available at cheaper rates.
5. A well-organised money market, through quick transfer of funds from one place to another, helps to avoid the regional gluts and stringencies of funds.
6. It enhances the amount of liquidity available to the entire country.
7. A money market, by providing profitable investment opportunities for short-term surplus funds, helps to enhance the profit of financial institutions and individuals.

46. IMF performs the following functions:

(*i*) Providing short-terms credit to member countries for meeting temporary difficulties due to adverse balance of payments.

(*ii*) Reconciling conflicting claims of member-countries.

(*iii*) Providing a reservoir of currencies of member-countries and enabling members to borrow on another's currency.

(*iv*) Promoting orderly adjustment of exchange rates.

(*v*) Advising member-countries on economic, monetary and technical matters.

47. Counter-trade is a sort of bilateral trade where one set of goods is exchanged for another set of goods. In this type of external trade, a seller provides a buyer with deliveries and contractually agrees to purchase goods from the buyer equal to the agreed percentage of the original sale contract value (US Department of Commerce, 1978). Counter-trade is classified broadly as:

1. Commercial counter-trade such as classical barter, counter-purchase and pre-compensation.
2. Industrial counter-trade such as buy-back agreements, develop for import arrangements, and framework agreements.

48. Floating Rate System: In a floating-rate system, the market forces that determine the exchange rate between two currencies. The advocates of the floating-rate system put forth two major arguments. One is that the exchange rate varies automatically according to the changes in the macro-economic variables. As a result, there is no gap between the real exchange rate and the nominal exchange rate. The country does not need any adjustment, which is often required in a fixed rate regime and so it does not have to bear the cost of adjustment (Friedman, 1953). The other argument is that this system possesses insulation properties, meaning that the currency remains isolated from the shocks emanating from other countries. It also means that the government can adopt an independent economic policy without impinging upon the external sector performance (Friedman, 1953).

49. Dumping is recognized as a form of international price discrimination where exports are priced lower than domestic sales. Dumping is a special case of price discrimination, when the practice of price discrimination is extended to two or more countries.

"*The art of selling a commodity at a lower price in a foreign market and at a higher price in home market is called dumping*". Home market is controlled or protected and the foreign market is free or open. It is a lesser-known but widely practiced phenomenon-both openly and subtly, in diverse forms and with varying motives. Its effects can be long lasting and deeply damaging, particularly for the developing countries.

Selling in foreign markets at a price below the cost of production is also considered dumping. Dumping of a commodity may also be defined to exist so long as it export price is lower than its domestic price.

52. Amalgamation: When two or more companies that exist as on date combine together to form a new company, then it is called "amalgamation".

In this case, all the combining companies will get liquidated. A new company will be formed to take over their business.

To illustrate, X Ltd and Y Ltd, the two existing companies, combine together to form Z Ltd, a new company X Ltd and Y Ltd will get liquidated A new company Z Ltd is formed to run the business.

Absorption: When one existing company takes over the business of two or more older existing companies, it is called "absorption". The other two or more existing companies (i.e., companies whose business are taken over) will get liquidated. At the same time, no new company will be floated.

To illustrate, X Ltd, one existing company, takes over other two existing companies Y Ltd and Z Ltd. Y Ltd and Z Ltd will get liquidated. X Ltd continues to do its business and no new company will be formed. In other words, X Ltd absorbs the other two companies Y Ltd and

Z Ltd. X Ltd continues to do its business whereas Y Ltd and Z Ltd will be liquidated.

External reconstruction: When an existing company is liquidated and in its place a new company is floated but with the same shareholders, it is known as "external reconstruction". Shareholders will remain unaltered but company's name and structure will be new.

To illustrate, X Ltd is liquidated but the existing shareholders continue their status as shareholders and a new company Y Ltd is formed.

53. Human resource accounting is the process of estimating the cost benefit of investments on human resources with a view to assessing its value to the organization.

There are two approaches to the study of human resource accounting cost-based approach and value-based approach.

The cost-based approach includes (*i*) historical cost, (*ii*) replacement cost, (*iii*) opportunity cost, and (*iv*) standard cost.

As per the historical cost approach, the value of HR is the cumulative cost incurred on recruiting, training and developing the employees.

As per the replacement cost approach, the value of HR means the aggregate cost of recruiting, training and developing persons as suitable replacements.

As per the opportunity cost approach, the value of HR calculates the sacrifices made for choosing a decision pertaining to human resources.

According to the standard costing approach, the value of HR is the standard cost fixed for various HR functions like hiring and training.

As per the opportunity cost approach, the value of HR calculates the sacrifices made for choosing a decision pertaining to human resources.

According to the standard costing approach, the value of HR is the standard cost fixed for various HR functions like hiring and training.

The value-based approach includes (*i*) the present value of future earnings model, (*ii*) the certainty equivalent model, (*iii*) the reward valuation model, (*iv*) the human asset multiplier model, (*v*) the unpurchased goodwill model, (*vi*) the causal, intervening, and end-result model, (*vii*) the five-dimensional model, and (*viii*) the aggregate payment model.

54. The Bombay Stock Exchange Index S&P BSE Sensex: S&P BSE SENSEX is scientifically designed and based on globally accepted construction and review methodology index, is for large companies on the Bombay Stock Exchange. First compiled in 1986, S&P BSE SENSEX is a basket of 30 constituent stocks representing a sample of large, liquid and representative companies. The base year of SENSEX is 1978-79 and the base value is 100. The index is widely reported in both domestic and international markets through print as well as electronic media. The index was initially calculated based on the 'Full Market Capitalization' methodology but was shifted to the free-float methodology with effect from September 1, 2003. The 'Free-float Market Capitalization' methodology of index construction is regarded as an industry best practice globally.

The National Stock Exchange Index – S&P CNX Nifty: The Standard and Poor's CRISIL NSE Index 50 or S&P CNX Nifty nicknamed Nifty 50 or simply Nifty, is the leading index for large companies on the National Stock Exchange (NSE). The NSE is the largest stock exchange in India. NSE is located in Bombay. It is the third largest in the world in terms of trading volume as well as the second fastest growing in the world today. NSE started its operations in 1994. The Nifty, leading index for large companies on the NSE, is a diversified 50 stock index accounting for 23 sectors of the Indian economy and offers investment managers exposure to the Indian market in one portfolio. The Nifty stocks represent about 60 percent of the total market capitalization of the NSE. From inception, the index used full market capitalization as weight assigned to different constituents.

55. Secured premium notes (SPNs): SPN is issued along with a detachable warrant, and is redeemable after a notified period with features of medium to long-term notes. Each SPN has a warrant attached to it which gives the holder the right to apply for, or seek allotment of one equity share, provided the SPN is fully paid. The conversion of detachable warrant into equity shares is done within the time limit notified by the company. There is a lock-in-period for SPN during which no interest is paid for the invested amount.

57.

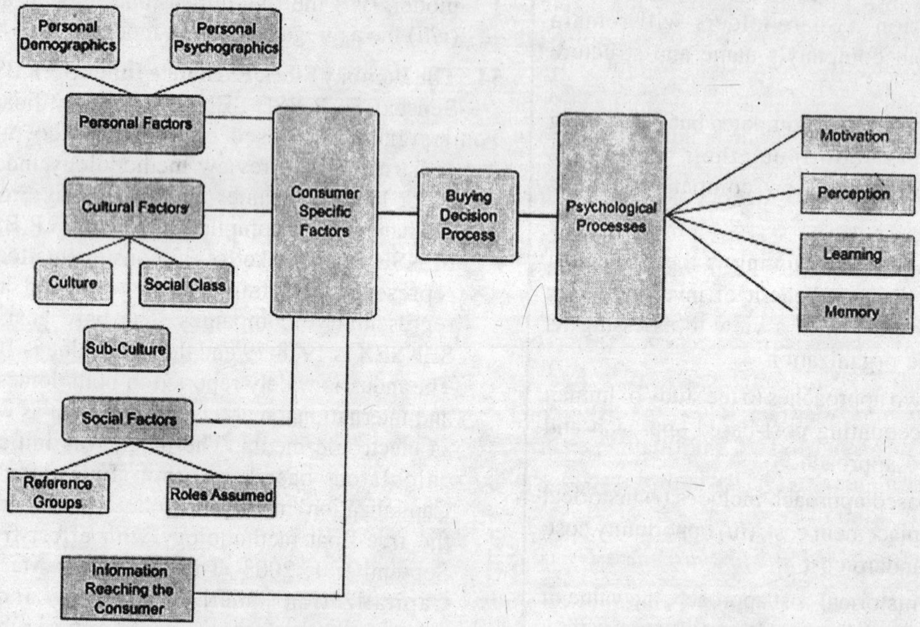

Fig. *Consumer-specific Factors Affecting Buying Behaviour*

59. The product life cycle has four stages as shown in the diagram namely: Introduction stage – Growth stage – Maturity stage and Decline stage. As the product moves through different stages of its life cycle, sales volume and profitability changes from stage to stage. A detailed study of each stage is necessary in terms of its basic features, so that a marketeer make necessary changes in his marketing mix. Product life cycle is simply a graphic presentation of the sales history of a product in distinct stages as illustrated in the given diagram.

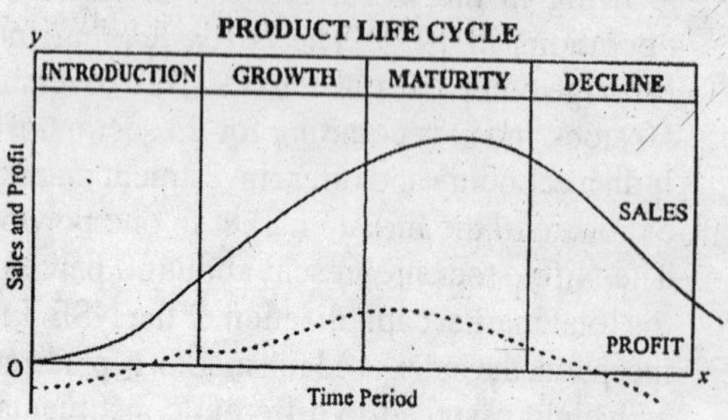

60. Co-Branding: Sometimes products feature more than one brand. A good example is the emergence of co-branding—also called dual branding or brand bundling—in which two or more well-known existing brands are combined into a joint product and/or marketed together in some fashion.

Co-branding's main advantage is that a product may be convincingly positioned by virtue of the multiple brands involved, generating greater sales from the existing target market and opening more opportunities with new consumers and channels. Co-branding also can reduce the cost of product introduction because two well-known images are combined, accelerating potential adoption. Finally, co-branding may help marketers learn more about consumers and how other companies approach them.

Co-branding must be carefully managed to minimize the risks and lack of control from aligning with another brand. First, unsatisfactory performance could hurt both of the brands. Second, if one brand participates in a number of co-branding arrangements, over-exposure might dilute the transfer of any association. Third, a company with several co-branding arrangements may focus less on its existing brands.

61. Types of Penalties: For various types of misconduct, there are various types of punishments/penalties. These punishments/ penalties can be divided into major penalties and minor penalties. The table given below shows the kind of penalties.

Table: ***Types of Punishment/Penalties***

Minor Penalties	*Major Penalties*
1. Oral Warning	1. Withholding increments
2. Written reprimand	2. Demotion/stopping promotion
3. Loss of privileges	3. Discharge
4. Suspension	4. Dismissal

64. Human resources are the most important resources of an organization. Related to human resources is the staffing process which is a continuing step-by-step procedure to keep the organization supplied with the right people in the right positions at the right time. There are eight steps in the staffing process: (1) human resource planning; (2) recruitment; (3) selection; (4) induction and orientation; (5) training and development; (6) performance appraisal; (7) transfers; and (8) separations.

67. Intellectual Property (IP): It is basically intangible property that is created at the mind of the humans before being converted to material forms. Property here is the human thought process and the protection accorded to such thought process. For example, idea, business method, invention etc.

Intellectual Property Rights (IPR): As the name indicates Intellectual Property Rights are exclusive rights over the creations of the mind. A creator can have exclusive rights over his creation for a certain period of time depending upon the type of Intellectual Property.

These items of intellectual properties can be classified into two main categories:

(*a*) Industrial Property rights

(*b*) Copyright and related rights

The industrial properties rights include rights in form of patents, trade marks, industrial designs, and geographic indication of source. The copyrights and related rights items include all literary works which range from articles, newspaper items, novels, story books, poetry books, drawings, photographs, paintings, architectural design, music, dance, films and artistic performances.

68. North American Free Trade Agreement (NAFTA): The NAFTA, embracing three member countries, namely, the United States of America, Canada, and Mexico, came into force from January 1994.

69. Common Market: The common market involves common external tariff that is found in a customs union. Over and above, it also involves free movement of factors of production such as labour, capital, enterprise, and technology among the member states. As a result, there are chances for best allocation of resources in a common market leading to maximisation of benefits from resource utilisation among the member states.

70. The Maastricht Treaty, which was signed in February 1992 and came into force from November 1993, renaming the EC as the European Union (EU), called for a close link between the European economic union and the European monetary union. It set up monetary and fiscal targets for the countries participating in the monetary union.

71. **Discontinued business (Sec. 176):** When any business or profession has been discontinued in any assessment year, the income for the period from the expiry of the previous year for that assessment year up to date of such discontinuance may at the discretion of the Assessing Officer, be charged to tax in that assessment year at the rates specified for the payment of advance tax in Part III of the Annual Finance Act in that year [Sec. 176(2) r.w. Sec 2(9) of the Annual Finance Act]. Separate assessments are to be made for each complete previous year and the last broken year. The Assessing Officer has also the discretion to tax the income of the discontinued business in the normal assessment year.

Previous Paper (Solved)

UGC (NET) JRF & Assistant Professor Exam Commerce, December-2014

PAPER-II

Note: *This paper contains* ***fifty*** *(50) objective type questions of* ***two*** *(2) marks each.* ***All*** *questions are compulsory.*

1. The responsibility of the organization to the workers includes:

(*i*) The payment of fair wages

(*ii*) Arrangement of proper training and education of the workers

(*iii*) The installation of an efficient grievance handling system

(*iv*) Welfare of family members

(*v*) The provision of the best possible working conditions

Identify the correct combination:

A. (*i*), (*ii*), (*iii*) and (*v*)

B. (*ii*), (*iii*), (*iv*) and (*v*)

C. (*i*), (*ii*), (*iii*) and (*iv*)

D. (*i*), (*iii*), (*iv*) and (*v*)

2. Match the items of List–I with List–II:

List–I	**List–II**
(*a*) Industries Development Regulation Act	(*i*) 1947
(*b*) Import and Export Control Act	(*ii*) 1948
(*c*) Foreign Exchange Management Act	(*iii*) 1951
(*d*) Factories Act	(*iv*) 1999

Identify the correct combination:

Codes:

	(*a*)	(*b*)	(*c*)	(*d*)
A.	(*i*)	(*iii*)	(*iv*)	(*ii*)
B.	(*iii*)	(*i*)	(*ii*)	(*iv*)
C.	(*iii*)	(*i*)	(*iv*)	(*ii*)
D.	(*iii*)	(*iv*)	(*ii*)	(*i*)

3. Which among the following is not a correct sequential combination?

A. Macro Environment → Economic Environment → National Income → Pattern of Income Distribution

B. Business Environment → Internal Environment → Business Ethics → Payment of Fair Wages

C. Business Environment → External Environment → Micro Environment → Suppliers

D. Macro Environment → External Environment → Customers → Prospects of Business Development

4. Which among the following is not a correct combination?

A. Industrial Policy – 1948

B. Industrial Policy Statement – 1977

C. Industrial Policy Statement – 1980

D. Industrial Policy Statement – 1991

5. Statement–I: The industrial policy of the Government of India is aimed at increasing the tempo of industrial development.

Statement–II: After the New Industrial Policy–1991, the Balance of Trade for India has always been positive.

Codes:

A. Statement I is correct, but II is incorrect.

B. Statement II is correct, but I is incorrect.

C. Both Statements I and II are correct.

D. Both Statements I and II are incorrect.

6. Current Ratio 2.5, Liquid Ratio 1.5 and Working Capital ₹ 60,000. What is Current Assets?

A. ₹ 60,000

B. ₹ 80,000

C. ₹ 1,00,000

D. ₹ 1,20,000

7. X, Y, Z are sharing profits in the ratio of 6 : 5 : 3. A is admitted into partnership for 1/8th share. The sacrificing ratio of X, Y and Z is
A. Equal
B. 6 : 5 : 3
C. 5/14, 4/14, 5/14
D. 4 : 5 : 5

8. Accounting information given by a company:

Total assets turnover	3 times
Net profit margin	10%
Total assets	₹ 1,00,000

The net profit is
A. ₹ 10,000   B. ₹ 15,000
C. ₹ 25,000   D. ₹ 30,000

9. "Make sufficient provisions for future losses, but do not anticipate future profits." This statement is in accordance to the concept of:
A. Matching
B. Objectivity
C. Conservatism
D. Materiality

10. When a firm is dissolved, profit or loss on realisation is shared by the partners
A. Equal
B. In the ratio of their capital balances
C. In the profit sharing ratio
D. In the ratio laid down in Garner *vs.* Murray

11. The inverse relationship between variations in the price and quantity demanded is not due to
A. Income Effects
B. Substitution Effects
C. Future Expectations
D. Law of Diminishing Marginal Utility

12. Consumer is said to be in equilibrium, maximizing his total utility, when
A. the marginal utilities of the two goods consumed are equal.
B. the proportions of the marginal utilities and respective prices are equal.
C. the consumer gets full satisfaction from the consumption.
D. the consumer feels satisfied with his expenditure on the various goods.

13. Match the items of the following two lists and suggest the correct code:

List–I	List–II
(*a*) Zero Income Elasticity	(*i*) Substitute goods
(*b*) Unit Cross Elasticity	(*ii*) Complementary goods
(*c*) Positive Cross Elasticity	(*iii*) Indifferent goods
(*d*) Negative Cross Elasticity	(*iv*) Independent goods

Choose the correct option:

Codes:

	(*a*)	(*b*)	(*c*)	(*d*)
A.	(*iii*)	(*ii*)	(*i*)	(*iv*)
B.	(*ii*)	(*iii*)	(*iv*)	(*i*)
C.	(*iii*)	(*iv*)	(*i*)	(*ii*)
D.	(*iv*)	(*i*)	(*ii*)	(*iii*)

14. Statement (A): The isoquant curves are drawn convex to the origin due to diminishing technical rate of substitution.

Statement (B): The lesser the convexity of the isoquant curve the greater the possibility of the complementarity of the two inputs.

Codes:
A. Statements (A) and (B) both are correct.
B. Statement (A) is correct but (B) is incorrect.
C. Statement (A) is incorrect but (B) is correct.
D. Statements (A) and (B) both are incorrect.

15. Match the items of the List–I with those of List–II and suggest the correct code:

List–I	List–II
(*a*) Constant average cost over a range of output	(*i*) Economic capacity
(*b*) Average cost becomes constant momentarily	(*ii*) Reserve capacity
(*c*) Normal average cost is a U-shaped curve	(*iii*) Production and Managerials costs effects
(*d*) Modern Long-run average cost is L-shaped	(*iv*) Economies and Dis-economies

Codes:

	(*a*)	(*b*)	(*c*)	(*d*)
A.	(*i*)	(*ii*)	(*iii*)	(*iv*)

B. (*ii*) (*iii*) (*iv*) (*i*)
C. (*iii*) (*iv*) (*ii*) (*i*)
D. (*ii*) (*i*) (*iv*) (*iii*)

16. Which one of the following is not probability sampling method?
A. Simple Random Sampling
B. Cluster Sampling
C. Judgemental Sampling
D. Systematic Sampling

17. The research carried out to expand the knowledge of a particular field is known as
A. Applied research
B. Qualitative research
C. Quantitative research
D. Basic research

18. In univariate data analysis t-test is used when the data are in the form of
A. Metric data with one sample
B. Non-metric data
C. Non-metric data with independent variable
D. Metric data with independent two sample

19. To show the trend for a variable, which one of the presentation method is used?
A. Histogram B. Frequency polygon
C. Line graph D. Scatter graph

20. Which one of the following objectives is not the objective of secondary data collection?
A. Identify the problem
B. Test the hypotheses of the relevant present problem
C. Better define the problem
D. Interpret primary data more insightfully

21. The structure of an organisation in which there is separation of ownership and management is called
A. Sole proprietorship
B. Partnership
C. Company
D. Cooperative society

22. When a person transacts with a company on matters which is beyond the power of the company, the person will be governed by the Doctrine of
A. Management by Exception
B. Constructive Notice
C. Indoor Management
D. Self Management

23. Assertion (A): MBO is effective way of planning and organizing the work.
Reason (R): Employees participate in setting the objectives.
Codes:
A. Both (A) and (R) are true.
B. Both (A) and (R) are false.
C. (A) is true, but (R) is false.
D. (A) is false, but (R) is correct.

24. The appropriate sequence of the formation of a company are in the following order:
A. Promotion, commencement of business and incorporation
B. Promotion, incorporation, capital subscription and commencement of business
C. Capital subscription, promotion, incorporation and commencement of business
D. Incorporation, capital subscription, commencement of business and promotion

25. Delegation of authority makes the size of the organization:
A. Smaller organization
B. Larger organization
C. Very big organization
D. It does not affect the size of the organization

26. Managerial Grid suggests the following as the best leader behaviour:
A. High structure and high consideration
B. Low structure and low consideration
C. High concern both for production and people
D. Low concern both for production and people

27. Marketing strategy development is also known as
A. Marketing Control
B. Marketing Exercise
C. Marketing Planning
D. Situation Analysis

28. For most people, the purchase of cheese for daily use can be described as a

A. Completely novel buy
B. Modified re-buy
C. Routine re-buy
D. High involvement product

29. The promotion mix of a company consists of these–

A. Marketing communication, promotion decisions
B. Personal selling, product objectives
C. Advertising, personal selling, sales promotion, publicity and public relations
D. Consumer psychology, buyers motives, brand equity

30. Rational buying motives that determine purchase decisions are mostly based on

A. Price factor
B. Psychological factors
C. Quality of product
D. Advertisement

31. Statement–I: Capital structure refers to composition of long-term funds.

Statement–II: These include equity share capital, preference share capital, debentures, all debts and all reserves.

A. Both Statements I and II are correct.
B. Statement I is correct but Statement II is incorrect.
C. Statement I is incorrect but Statement II is correct.
D. Both statements are incorrect.

32. Match the items of the following two lists and suggest the correct code:

List–I	List–II
(*a*) Pay-back Rate of Return	(*i*) Discounted Cash Flow Technique
(*b*) Internal Rate of Return	(*ii*) Compounded values of investments and returns
(*c*) Benefit Cost Ratio	(*iii*) Crude method for project evaluation
(*d*) Net Terminal Value Method	(*iv*) Varying sized projects evaluation

Codes:

	(*a*)	(*b*)	(*c*)	(*d*)
A.	(*ii*)	(*iii*)	(*i*)	(*iv*)
B.	(*iii*)	(*i*)	(*iv*)	(*ii*)
C.	(*i*)	(*iv*)	(*ii*)	(*iii*)
D.	(*iv*)	(*ii*)	(*iii*)	(*i*)

33. Match the items of the following two lists and suggest the correct code:

List–I	List–II
(*a*) Realised yield method	(*i*) Cost of equity share capital
(*b*) Taxation	(*ii*) Cost of equity capital
(*c*) Cost of total capital employed	(*iii*) Cost of debt capital
(*d*) Dividend growth is a consideration	(*iv*) Weighted cost of capital

Codes:

	(*a*)	(*b*)	(*c*)	(*d*)
A.	(*iv*)	(*iii*)	(*ii*)	(*i*)
B.	(*ii*)	(*iv*)	(*i*)	(*iii*)
C.	(*ii*)	(*iii*)	(*iv*)	(*i*)
D.	(*i*)	(*ii*)	(*iii*)	(*iv*)

34. Cash Flow Management involves:

I. Lock-box system
II. Marketable securities
III. Playing the float
IV. Concentration Bank Account

Codes:

A. I, II and III only
B. II, III and IV only
C. I, III and IV only
D. I, II and IV only

35. Dividend capitalisation model was developed by

A. Ezra Solomon
B. Myron J. Gordon
C. James E. Walter
D. Merton H. Miller and Franco Modigliani

36. The process of narrowing a large number of candidates to a smaller field is called

A. Rushing
B. Recruitment
C. Selection
D. Enrollment

37. According to which theory, people are motivated to the extent to which they expect that their actions will help in achievement of goals?
A. Vroom's Vector Valence Theory
B. Need Theory
C. Z Theory
D. X Theory

38. Match the items of List–I with List–II and select the correct code:

List–I	List–II
(*a*) Getting Effective Leadership in the Industrial Organization	(*i*) Dale Yoder
(*b*) The Nature of Leadership Organization and Management	(*ii*) Alford and Beatty
(*c*) Industrial Management	(*iii*) Douglas McGregor
(*d*) Personnel Management	(iv) Chester I. Bernard

Codes:

	(*a*)	(*b*)	(*c*)	(*d*)
A.	(*i*)	(*ii*)	(*iii*)	(*iv*)
B.	(*iii*)	(*iv*)	(*ii*)	(*i*)
C.	(*iii*)	(*iv*)	(*i*)	(*ii*)
D.	(*iv*)	(*iii*)	(*ii*)	(*i*)

39. Match the items of List–I with List–II:

List–I	List–II
(*a*) AITUC	(*i*) Indian National Congress
(*b*) BMS	(*ii*) Socialists
(*c*) INTUC	(*iii*) Rashtriya Swayamsevak Sangh
(*d*) CITU	(*iv*) Communist Party of India

Identify the correct combination:
Codes:

	(*a*)	(*b*)	(*c*)	(*d*)
A.	(*iv*)	(*iii*)	(*ii*)	(*i*)
B.	(*iv*)	(*i*)	(*ii*)	(*iii*)
C.	(*iv*)	(*iii*)	(*i*)	(*ii*)
D.	(*iv*)	(*i*)	(*iii*)	(*ii*)

40. The main characteristics of Weber's bureaucracy are:
A. Specialization
B. Hierarchy of authority
C. System of rules
D. All of the above

41. Match the items of List–I with List–II:

List–I	List–II
(*a*) RBI Nationalization	(*i*) 1964
(*b*) Imperial Bank Nationalization	(*ii*) 1949
(*c*) Nationalization of 14 Commercial Banks	(*iii*) 1955
(*d*) Establishment of IDBI	(*iv*) 1969

Identify the correct combination:
Codes:

	(*a*)	(*b*)	(*c*)	(*d*)
A.	(*i*)	(*ii*)	(*iii*)	(*iv*)
B.	(*ii*)	(*iii*)	(*i*)	(*iv*)
C.	(*iii*)	(*ii*)	(*iv*)	(*i*)
D.	(*ii*)	(*iii*)	(*iv*)	(*i*)

42. As per the RBI Act, 1934, the following functions are described as the functions of a Central Bank:
(*i*) Banking functions
(*ii*) Advisory functions
(*iii*) Supervisory functions
(*iv*) Promotional functions
Identify the correct combination:
A. (*i*), (*iii*) and (*iv*)
B. (*i*), (*ii*) and (*iv*)
C. (*ii*), (*iii*) and (*iv*)
D. Only (*i*) and (*iii*)

43. Phishing is an attempt to acquire:
A. Loan from unauthorized firms
B. Sensitive information such as username, password, etc.
C. Personal information from banks
D. None of the above

44. What is Call Money?
A. Money borrowed or lent for a day or overnight.
B. Money borrowed for more than one day but upto 3 days.

C. Money borrowed for more than one day but upto 7 days.
D. Money borrowed for more than one day but upto 14 days.

45. The Regulatory Authority of Regional Rural Banks is
A. NABARD
B. Central Government
C. State Government
D. Sponsor Bank

46. Which of the following is not ensured to the consumer in the globalization?
A. Lower prices
B. Better selection
C. Clear origin of goods and services
D. Improved services

47. In international trade which of the following is a non-tariff trade barrier?
A. Quotas B. Import bans
C. Export controls D. Anti dumping laws

48. Match the items of List–I with items in List–II and select a correct code:

List–I	List–II
(*a*) Current Account	(*i*) Official Capital
(*b*) Capital Account	(*ii*) Reserves from foreign countries
(*c*) Unilateral Payments	(*iii*) Reparations
(*d*) Official Statement Account	(*iv*) Visible Exports and Imports

Codes:

	(*a*)	(*b*)	(*c*)	(*d*)
A.	(*i*)	(*iii*)	(*ii*)	(*iv*)
B.	(*iv*)	(*i*)	(*ii*)	(*iii*)
C.	(*iv*)	(*i*)	(*iii*)	(*ii*)
D.	(*iii*)	(*ii*)	(*i*)	(*iv*)

49. Match the items of List–I with the items in List–II and select a correct code:

List–I	List–II
(*a*) Vishesh Krishi Upaj Yojana	(*i*) Scheme intended to reduce difficulties of exporters
(*b*) EPCG	(*ii*) Duty Entitlement Pass Book
(*c*) DFRC	(*iii*) To boost exports of fruits, vegetables, flowers, minor forest produce etc.
(*d*) DEPB	(*iv*) Relating to import of duty free fuel

Codes:

	(*a*)	(*b*)	(*c*)	(*d*)
A.	(*iv*)	(*i*)	(*ii*)	(*iii*)
B.	(*iv*)	(*iii*)	(*i*)	(*ii*)
C.	(*iii*)	(*iv*)	(*ii*)	(*i*)
D.	(*iii*)	(*i*)	(*iv*)	(*ii*)

50. Which of the following is not the agency of World Bank?
A. MIGA B. ICSID
C. ADB D. IDA

ANSWERS

1	2	3	4	5	6	7	8	9	10
A	C	D	D	A	C	B	D	C	C
11	**12**	**13**	**14**	**15**	**16**	**17**	**18**	**19**	**20**
C	B	C	B	D	C	D	D	C	B
21	**22**	**23**	**24**	**25**	**26**	**27**	**28**	**29**	**30**
C	B	A	B	B	C	C	C	C	B
31	**32**	**33**	**34**	**35**	**36**	**37**	**38**	**39**	**40**
B	B	C	C	B	C	A	B	C	D
41	**42**	**43**	**44**	**45**	**46**	**47**	**48**	**49**	**50**
D	A	B	A	A	C	B	C	D	C

SOME SELECTED EXPLANATORY ANSWERS

1. Responsibility toward employees

- The successful organization depends to a very large extent on the morale of the employees.
- The payment of fair wages.
- The provision of best possible working conditions.
- The establishment of fair work standards and norms.
- The provision of labour welfare facility.
- Arrangement for proper training and education of the worker.
- Reasonable and proper chance for promotion.
- Proper recognition, appreciation and encouragement of skills.
- The installation of efficient grievance handling system.
- An opportunity for participation in a management decision.

4. The year 1991 saw the beginning of a new era in the history of industrial policy in India. It was on July 24, 1991 that the Government of India announced a new industrial policy as an important chapter of its New Economic Policy focusing on liberalisation, privatisation and globalisation of the economy. It was a significant departure from the existing regime of controls, regulations and licences. The economy was opened up to new horizons of international competition and industrialisation was expected to cope with the emerging challenges of competitive growth based on cost-saving technology and devoid of state protection.

6. Working Capital = ₹ 60,000

i.e., Current Assets – Current Liabilities

Therefore, Current Assets – Current Liabilities = ₹ 60,000

or 2.5 – 1 = ₹ 60,000

(Current Ratio is 2.5 which means Current Assets are 2.5 times of Current Liabilities).

or 1.5 = ₹ 60,000

1 = ₹ 40,000

Therefore, Current Liabilities = ₹ 40,000

Current Assets are

2.5 × ₹ 40,000 = ₹ 1,00,000.

9. The preamble of accounting prudence insists on **convention of conservatism** that implies that one should anticipate future losses and provide for such losses in the books of accounts but future profits should never be provided in the books of accounts. According to this convention, inventory items are to be shown in the books of accounts (specifically final accounts) at the cost or market value, whichever is lower.

10. Section 48 of the Partnership Act provides the following rules for the settlement of accounts between the partners:

(*a*) **Payment of losses:** Losses shall be paid first out of profits, next out of capital and lastly, if necessary, by the partners individually in their profit sharing ratio.

(*b*) **Distribution of assets:** Assets of the firm are first to be applied in paying the debts of the firm to the third parties; next in paying to each partner retably what is due to him from the firm for advances as distinguished from capital; and the residue to be divided among the partners in the proportion in which they were entitled to share profits.

12. According to **Samuelson,** *"A consumer gets maximum satisfaction when the ratio of marginal utilities of all commodities and their price is equal."*

$$\frac{MU_1}{P_1} = \frac{MU_2}{P_2} = \frac{MU_3}{P_3}$$

If prices of the commodities are equal, then maximum satisfaction to the consumer can be indicated in the following equation:

$$MU_1 = MU_2 = MU_3$$

In the above equations MU_1, MU_2, MU_3, refers to the marginal utility of first, second and third commodity P_1, P_2 and P_3 refer to the price of first, second and third commodity.

13. **Zero Income Elasticity of Demand:** Income elasticity of demand is zero, when change in the income of consumer evokes no change in his demand. Demand for necessaries like, salt, has zero income elasticity of demand.

Cross Elasticity of Demand		
1. Substitutes	Positive	Price increase of a substitute leads to an increase in quantity demanded of this good.
2. Comple-mentary	Negative	Price increase of a complement leads to a decrease in quantity demanded of this good.

14. The Law of Diminishing Marginal Rate of Technical Substitution (MRTS) could be explained only if it is convex to the origin. The rate at which one factor is substituted for another factor is known as Technical Substitution.

16. The probability sampling includes the simple random sampling, stratified sampling, systematic sampling, cluster sampling, and multi-stage sampling which permits randomisation whereas the non-probability sampling that lags randomisation includes convenience sampling, judgement sampling, quota sampling, double sampling and snowball sampling.

17. Business research is conducted either to expand knowledge about a particular aspect or to find a solution to a particular problem. Business research studies can be classified into two categories–basic research and applied research. **Basic research** refers to a focused, systematic study or investigation undertaken to discover new knowledge or interpretations and establish facts or principles in a particular field. In other words, it is a research aimed primarily at gaining knowledge rather than solving a pragmatic problem. The underlying motive is to increase knowledge about particular phenomena by testing, refining and elaborating theory without concern for practical application.

18.

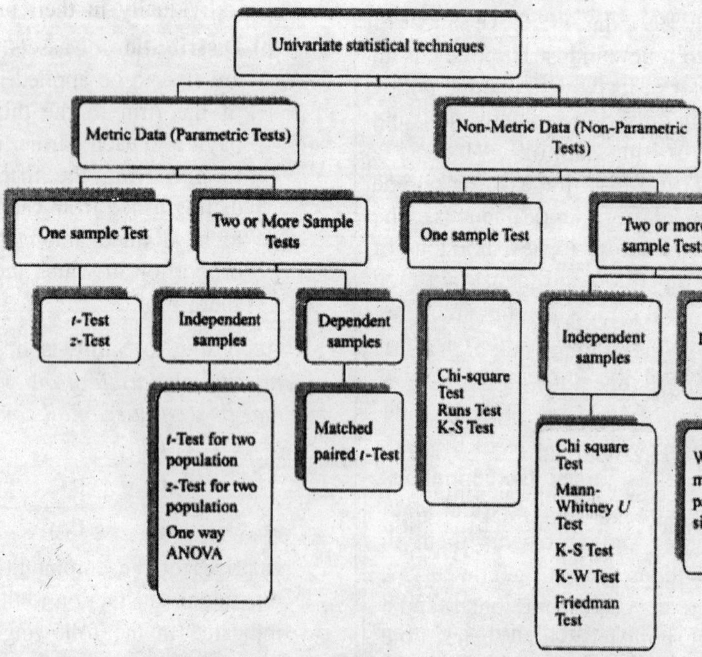

Fig. : *Classification of univariate statistical techniques*

A broad classification of univariate statistical techniques is shown in the figure. Univariate statistical techniques are categorized on the basis of metric or non-metric data. Type of data whether it is metric or non-metric presents a base for selecting appropriate test statistics. Parametric tests are applied for metric data and non-parametric tests are applied for non-metric data. Selection of appropriate test statistics is based on one, two, or more than two samples from the population. When one sample is taken from one population, *z*- or *t*-test is applied for data analysis. When the sample size is more than 30 (a large sample), *z*-test statistic is used, and when sample size is less than or equal to 30 *t*-test statistic is used. In the category of parametric tests, two or more samples tests can be further classified on the basis of independent samples or related (dependent) samples category. When two independent samples are taken from two populations and the intention of the researcher is to find the mean difference of the population through sample means, then *z*- and *t*-tests are applied for large and small samples, respectively. When two samples are dependent on each other, matched-paired *t*-test is used. When a researcher wants to compare more than two samples taken from more than two populations. ANOVA technique is used.

19. Charts can be of the following types:

- Line Graphs
- Pie Charts
- Bar Charts.

Line Graphs : A type of graph that highlights trends by drawing connecting lines between data points is known as a line graph. A line graph is a bar graph with the tops of the bars represented by points joined by continuous lines. A line graph takes statistical data presented in tables and represents them in rising and falling lines, steep or gentle curves. Line graphs have an X-axis (horizontal) and a Y-axis (vertical), both labelled. When a time lines, steep or gentle curves. Line graphs have an X-axis (horizontal) and a Y-axis (vertical), both labelled. When a time variable is used, the X-axis is numbered for the time period, which is the independent variable, and the Y-axis is numbered for what is being measured, which is the dependent variable. Line graphs represent data that change with time, such as cycles, fluctuations, trends, distributions, increases and decreases in profits, employment, energy levels and temperatures. A line graph shows trends in data clearly, and hence, it is possible to predict the future trends for which data have not been collected.

21. A company is collectively owned by the shareholders who entrust the task of management to their elected representatives called the directors. The salient features of a company are as follows:

- The company is a distinct legal "person", separate from its owners, the shareholders. It can own assets, incur liabilities, enter into contracts, sue and be sued in its name.
- The liability of the shareholders of a company is limited to the share capital subscribed to by them. Once this amount is fully paid up, they have no further obligation.
- A company must pay taxes on its profits. Moreover, shareholders of the company are liable to pay taxes on the dividend received by them. So, in effect, there is double taxation.
- Setting up and managing a company is more complicated than setting up and managing other forms of organisation because companies are governed by the Indian Companies Act, a very elaborate and comprehensive piece of legislation.

In proprietorships, partnerships, and cooperative societies, owners are actively involved in management. But in companies, particularly large public limited companies, owners typically are not active managers. Instead, they entrust this responsibility to professional managers who may have little or no equity stake in the firm. There are several reasons for the separation of ownership and management in such companies:

- Most enterprises require large sums of capital to achieve economies of scale. Hence it becomes necessary to pool capital from thousands or even hundreds of thousands of owners. It is impractical for many owners to participate actively in management.
- Professional managers may be more qualified to run the business because of their technical expertise, experience, and personality traits.
- Separation of ownership and management permits unrestricted change in owners through share transfers without affecting the operations of the firm. It ensures that the 'knowhow' of the firm is not impaired, despite changes in ownership.
- Given economic uncertainties, investors would like to hold a diversified portfolio of securities. Such diversification is achievable only when ownership and management are separated.

22. The term **'constructive notice'** means the presumption of notice in certain circumstances. We know that the 'memorandum' and 'articles' of association of a company are registered with the Registrar of Companies. The office of the Registrar is a public office. Therefore, on registration, these documents become the 'public documents'. They are open for public inspection in Registrar's office. It is, therefore, the duty of every person dealing with the company to inspect these documents, and make sure that his contract with the company is in accordance with the provisions of these documents. He will be presumed to have read the documents and to know their contents. This kind of presumed knowledge of these documents is called the 'constructive notice' of memorandum and articles of association. If any person enters into a contract with the company which is contrary to the provisions of memorandum and articles of association, he will not get any right under such contract.

23. Management by objectives refers to the set of goals that are measurable, verifiable and tangible. Management by objectives (MBO) is used for planning, organising, actuating and controlling organisational activities. Objectives are determined after thorough analysis of the internal and external environment relating to the organisation. The SWOT, i.e., strength, weakness, opportunities and threats, analysis is used to formulate objectives. MBO was coined by Peter Drucker 45 years ago, who suggested that the setting of objectives and appraising the results based thereon, leads to improvement of performance. It is used to motivate people by providing satisfaction of achievement and rewards. The organisational objectives are translated into specific objectives of succeeding offices, viz. division, branches and so on. Individual objectives are decided on the basis of the departmental objectives. Each employee's performance is compared with their respective objectives. If employees achieve the goals they are satisfied. Moreover, they are rewarded for the achievement of the objective if the achievements are outstanding.

The objective relation to the organisation's total performance is determined through identification of various sub-objectives of marketing, production, quality, service, employees' development and other activities. Objectives are developed in quantitative terms so that they can be easily achieved and used for measurement. Employees are made aware of MBO. They are prepared and motivated to achieve the objectives. They are developed accordingly to implement the objective plans. MBO is not fixed, but is flexible as per the requirements. Individual objects are used for motivation. The superior-subordinate relationship is strengthened. Responsibilities, power and duties are defined accordingly to achieve objectives. The goal setting theory is fully applicable in MBO.

24. 'A company is an artificial person created by law'—the saying implies that a company is created by the provisions of law. Being an 'artificial person', the birth of a company is not a free and natural process. It is a process that involves a long exercise. The promoters of a company have to fulfil many legal requirements before the formation of a company. Formation here means giving the company an 'entity' and making it functional in the field of business and commerce.

The formation of company is a step-by-step process involving various stages. These stages involve a change from one step to the next–from the conception of the company, to the possibility of its doing business and the kind of business it will do, and finally, to the commencement of the company when it becomes operative. Basically, there are four stages in the formation of a company. These are:

1. Promotion of a company
2. Incorporation or registration of the company.
3. Its capital subscription, and
4. Commencement of business.

All these stages are a part of the process of formation of a company. And all are essential in the formation of a public company, whereas for a private company, only the first two stages are necessary because a private company can commence its business as soon as it receives the certificate of incorporation. A public company, on the other hand, has to collect its capital from the public, and needs to have a certificate of commencement of business before it can do so.

25. The process by which authority passes from one managerial level to another is known as delegation. As organization grows in size and complexity, no one person can perform all the tasks or exercise all the authority that is needed to accomplish goals.

Delegation of authority is not the same as division of work. As Fayol says, 'division of work permits reduction in the number of objects to which attention and effort must be directed and has been recognized as the best means of making use of individuals and of groups of people'.

Authority is required in order to perform some task. It implies responsibility. Once an individual gets the authority to do a job, it becomes obligatory on his part to discharge his duty. This is responsibility.

According to the principle of organization, every manager has to delegate a part of their authority to their subordinates and by doing that 'the manager multiples himself'. While moving downwards, delegated authority and responsibility so created becomes less and less. This is otherwise known as 'the concept of tapering authority'.

26. Managerial Grid

(*i*) It is the most important approaches of leadership styles formulated by **Blake** and **Mountain.**

(*ii*) They refer that the leadership styles has both the factors of task-oriented and relation-oriented in different degrees.

(*iii*) According to them the managers are more concerned with people and production rather than the quantity of production giving out by the group.

(*iv*) Concern for production means that the attitudes of managers towards:

(*a*) Policy decisions, procedures and processes.

(*b*) Develop research; staff service and their efficiency of work and production output.

(*c*) Personal commitment towards goal achievement and responsibility and

(*d*) To satisfy inter-personal relations.

The managerial grid is based on two underlying dimensions:

(*i*) Concern for production

(*ii*) Concern for people

The authors have prepared a 9 by 9 grid for the above dimensions as shown in figure:

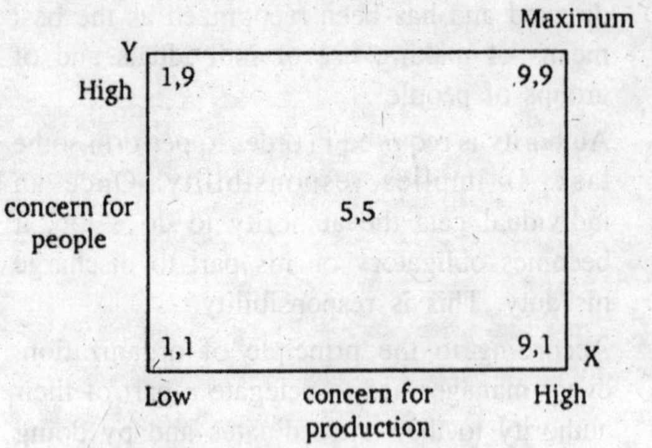

Fig.: *The Managerial grid*

The following is the brief description of the five leadership style:

1. The point 1,1

(*i*) Poor management and low concern for people and production.

(*ii*) Less leadership care with no intention for increasing production.

(*iii*) Same as Laissez-faire style.

2. The point 1,9

(*i*) High concern for people but low concern for production.

(*ii*) Leader pay more attention to the welfare of people and make them friendly.

3. The point 9,9

(*i*) High concern for people and production. It is the best style of the management.

(*ii*) Employees are taken into full confidence and motivate them to produce at their highest capacity.

4. The point 9,1

(*i*) Low concern for people but high concern for production.

(*ii*) Shows rigid attitude towards employees to get high level of production.

(*iii*) Same as autocratic style.

5. The point 5,5

(*i*) Equal level of concern for both people and production.

(*ii*) Adopted middle path.

❖ **Conclusion :** The best style is 9,9 which implies the maximum concern for people and production.

27. A strategy process model provides a framework that gives a logical sequence or 'roadmap' to follow to ensure inclusion of all key activities of strategy development and implementation. In a marketing context, these strategy development and implementation activities are coordinated through a marketing plan, and the process of creating this is known as 'marketing planning'. McDonald (2003) defines marketing planning simply as:

The planned application of marketing resources to achieve marketing objectives...... Marketing planning is simply a logical sequence and a series of activities leading to the setting of marketing objectives and the formulation of plans for achieving them.

29. Main elements of promotion mix are as follows:

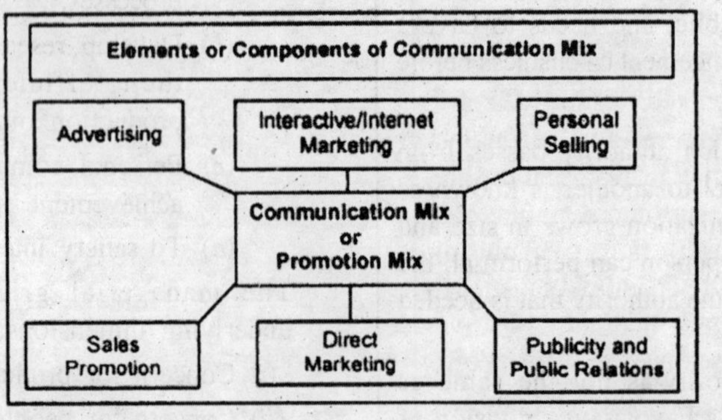

Promotion mix consists of all the activities aimed at persuading customers to buy the product. It includes communication activities undertaken to inform and convince customers. The various elements of promotion mix are as under:

(*a*) **Advertising :** It includes activities concerned with providing product information to customers through newspapers, radio, television and other media. It is paid for by the seller and is non-personal communication.

(*b*) **Personal selling :** It refers to face-to-face communication between a seller or his representative and the buyer. Sales persons of an enterprise assist and persuade the prospective buyers to buy the product.

(*c*) **Sales promotion :** It means increasing immediate sales through short-term incentives such as samples, special discount offers, prize contests, coupons, etc. These are aimed at supporting advertising and personal selling and are of non-recurring nature.

(*d*) **Publicity :** It means the mention of a company or its product in newspapers, journals, radio, etc. A favourable report, by the news media, on a company or event has a significant impact on customers. Publicity is not paid by the seller and it is non-personal communication. It is relatively a minor form of promotion because the seller has no control over what the media will mention.

(*e*) **Public Relations:** Public relations refer to various practices used to build good relations with various sections of public. Public relation is the firm's relationship with the public, *i.e.,* customers, employees, suppliers, stockholders, government officials, society and general public, etc. It aims to establish and maintain positive image of the firm among various sections of society. Firm uses publicity and various other tools like participation in social activities, fund raising for social events, sponsorship of special events, donations to charitable institutes; get-together of employees, suppliers, customers, shareholders, etc., to maintain good public relations. It enhances the image of the product and firm. It also helps to overcome negative image.

30. Emotional buying motives are based on personal feelings such as hunger, thirst, security, prestige, pride etc. Numerous advertisements are based on emotional motives. For example, film star Karina propagates, *"Lux soap is the only mystery of my beauty."*

Rational motives are based on man's reasoning, logic and ability. In this case, buyer decides his buying motive prior to actual purchase. For example, a buyer respond favourable towards an advertising of pressure cooker that it saves time and fuel both.

Another stage in which purchase done under emotional and rational motives may also arise. For example, buying a colour television may be influenced by emotional motive, but decision to which brand is to be purchased is influenced by rational motive.

34. An important aspect of efficient cash management is to expedite the collection of cheques. Two important methods for expediting the collection process are: (*i*) concentration banking, and (*ii*) lock-box system.

Concentration Banking: The key elements of concentration banking are as follows:

- The major bank account of the company is set up with a concentration bank, generally situated in the same place where the company is headquartered.
- Customers are advised to mail their remittances to collection centres closest to them.
- Payments received in different collection centres are deposited in local banks which in turn transfer them to the concentration bank.

Lock Box System : The salient features of the lock box system are as follows:

- A number of post-office boxes are rented by the company in different locations.
- Customers are advised to mail their remittances to the lock boxes.
- Banks are instructed and authorised to pick up the cheques from the lock boxes and deposit them in the company's account.

Playing the Float : Playing the float is another way of maximizing cash availability. *The float is the difference between the total amount of cheques drawn and the actual amount shown in the bank account.*

Thus, the float means that the firm's actual bank balance is greater than the bank balance shown in the firm's book. This float is caused by transit and processing delays. If the size of the float can be estimated accurately, the funds available in the form of excess bank balance can be invested to even earn a return. However, it is a risky practice and has to be followed quite consciously.

35. Gordon's Model : Myron J. Gordon in his work, *The Investment, Financing and Valuation of the Corporation,* developed dividend growth capitalization model. In this model, Gordon made a basic assumption that future dividend receipts on a stock determine the value of the equity. The basic rationale behind Gordon's model is that the worth of the share of a given company is no more than the current and future dividend receipts of its shareholders. Dividends are the cash flows that are returned to the shareholder.

37. Vector Vroom's expectancy theory advocates that people will be driven to choose a particular task and carry it out in a particular mode because they expect such actions will lead them to attain something which they value. Therefore, the intensity of efforts people put in is generally equivalent to the sum of value they attach to the outcome of such efforts. This theory consists of three vital elements. These are:

Valence: It is the 'value of an outcome' of an effort. Degree of value to an outcome varies from person to person. For example, hike in annual compensation may not be valued equally by all people though the increase is same. Therefore, people who value hike in compensation are most likely to put in more efforts than those who value it less.

Expectancy: This is 'expectation' on the part of people that a particular action or a set of actions would lead to produce the outcome they desire to achieve, which in turn gets them what they value. For example, some employees may expect that performing beyond targets will help them climb the career ladder fast.

Instrumentality: It is concerned with 'mechanisms' people use to attain goals. For example, people who are interested to grow fast in their career may employ two mechanisms. Firstly, they choose to perform exceedingly well in their jobs with an expectation that this ensures them a quick promotion. Secondly, this promotion is perceived as a mechanism to reach higher level in the career. Here, performing exceedingly well is the first level outcome and promotion is the second level outcome.

39. 1. **AITUC** (All India Trade Union Congress) was established in 1920 as an outcome of the resolution passed by the organized workers of Bombay and its first President was Lala Lajpat Rai.

2. **INTUC** (Indian National Trade Union Congress) was established in 1947 as an outcome of the resolution by Central Board of the Hindustan Mazdoor Sevak Sangh, a labour organization working under the direction of the National-Congress-minded labour leaders on the Gandhian philosophy of Sarvodaya. S.C. Banerjee was the first President of INTUC.

3. **UTUC** (United Trade Congress) was formed in 1949 with the aim of establishing a 'pure' trade union, free from the control of political parties. The leadership was dominated by various left-wing political groups.
4. **BMS** (Bharatiya Mazdoor Sabha) was the outcome of a decision taken by the Jana Sangh in its convention in 1954 and is viewed as a productivity-oriented, non-political trade union based on a triple ideology–
   (*i*) nationalize labour,
   (*ii*) labourize the industry and
   (*iii*) industrialize the nation.
5. **CITU** was established in 1971 as a result of the split in the AITUC, which was a sequel to the split in the CPI, a new centre, owing to its allegiance to the CPI (M).

40. The main characteristics of Waber's Bureaucracy are:

- A division of labour based on functional specialization.
- A well-defined hierarchy of authority.
- A system of rules covering the rights and duties of positional incumbents.
- A system of procedures for dealing with work situations.
- Impersonality of interpersonal relations.
- Promotion and selection based on technical competence.

43. Phishing (pronounced 'fishing') is a type of social engineering in which an attacker attempts to obtain sensitive information from a user by masquerading as a trusted entity in an e-mail or instant message sent to a large group of often random users. The attacker attempts to obtain information such as usernames, passwords, credit card numbers, and details about the user's bank accounts.

44. Call money market is that part of the national money market where the day-to-day surplus funds, mostly of banks, are traded. Call/notice money is the money borrowed or lent on demand for a very short period, usually for a day, it is known as call (overnight) money. Interbank market for deposits of maturity beyond 14 days is referred to also as the *term money market.* Banks, Primary Dealers (PDs), development finance institutions, insurance companies and select mutual funds are currently the participants in call/notice money market.

45. NABARD's role and functions can be enumerated below:

(*a*) NABARD initiates measures toward institution building for improving absorptive capacity of the credit delivery system, including monitoring, formulation of rehabilitation schemes, restructuring of credit institutions, training of personnel, etc.

(*b*) It coordinates the rural financing activities of all the institutions engaged in developmental work at the field level and maintains liaison with the Government of India, State Governments, the Reserve Bank of India and other national level institutions concerned with policy formulation.

(*c*) It prepares, on annual basis, rural credit plans for all the districts in the country. These plans form the base for annual credit plans of all rural financial institutions.

(*d*) It undertakes monitoring and evaluation of projects refinanced by it.

(*e*) It promotes research in the field of rural banking, agriculture and rural development.

(*f*) It functions as a regulatory authority, supervising, monitoring and guiding cooperative banks and regional rural banks.

47. Tariff-barrier means imposing import-duty; and non-tariff barriers refer to restricting imports through import-licensing, import-quota (quantitative restriction) or banning the imports.

50. The **World Bank Group** is part of the UN family, but operates autonomously. The Group is made up of five legally and financially independent agencies:

- International Bank for Reconstruction and Development (IBRD).
- International Development Agency (IDA).
- International Finance Corporation (IFC).
- Multilateral Investment Guarantee Agency (MIGA), and
- International Centre for Settlement of Investment Disputes (ICSID).

IBRD and IDA are jointly referred to as the World Bank, IBRD grants loans at market rates to middle income and poorer countries with good credit records, while IDA is responsible for low income countries (LICs). IDA funds are allocated in the form of either grants or loans with favourable terms.

The World Bank Group

The International Bank for Reconstruction and Development IBRD	**The International Development Association IDA**	**The International Finance Corporation IFC**	**The Multilateral Investment Guarantee Agency MIGA**	**The International Center for Settlement of Investment Disputes ICSID**
Established : 1945 Aims to reduce poverty in Middle income and craditworthy poor countries by promoting sustainable development through loans, guarantees, and nonlending services.	Established : 1960 Provides interest-free credits to poorest countries	Established : 1956 invests in sustainable private enterprises in developing countries provides long-term loans and guarantees	Established : 1988 Encourages foreign investment in developing countries by providing loan guarantees.	Established : 1966 Provides international facilities for conclution and artitration of investment disputes.

PAPER-III

Note: *This paper contains **seventy five** (75) objective type questions of **two** (2) marks each. **All** questions are compulsory.*

1. Match the items of List–I with List–II:

List–I (International Economic Groups)	**List–II (Year of Establish-ment)**
(*a*) European Union (EU)	(*i*) 1973
(*b*) European Free Trade Association (EFTA)	(*ii*) 1992
(*c*) Caribbean Community (CARICOM)	(*iii*) 1985
(*d*) South Asian Association for Regional Cooperation (SAARC)	(*iv*) 1960

Codes:

	(*a*)	(*b*)	(*c*)	(*d*)
A.	(*ii*)	(*iv*)	(*iii*)	(*i*)
B.	(*ii*)	(*iv*)	(*i*)	(*iii*)
C.	(*iv*)	(*ii*)	(*i*)	(*iii*)
D.	(*iii*)	(*i*)	(*ii*)	(*iv*)

2. The important objectives of WTO are:

(*i*) To improve the quality of technology in the member countries.
(*ii*) To improve the standard of living of people in the member countries.
(*iii*) To ensure full employment and broad increase in effective demand.
(*iv*) To enlarge production and trade of goods.
(*v*) To increase trade of services.

Codes:

A. (*i*), (*ii*), (*iii*) and (*iv*)
B. (*ii*), (*iii*), (*iv*) and (*v*)
C. (*i*), (*ii*), (*iii*) and (*v*)
D. (*i*), (*iii*), (*iv*) and (*v*)

3. Assertion (A): The industrial growth in India has been hampered by the burden of many controls and regulations.

Reason (R): The New Industrial Policy seeks to liberate the industry from the shackles of Licensing System.

Codes:

A. Assertion (A) is correct, but Reason (R) is not correct.
B. Assertion (A) is correct and Reason (R) is right explanation of (A).
C. Both Assertion (A) and Reason (R) are correct.
D. Both Assertion (A) and Reason (R) are incorrect.

4. Internal environment of a business includes:

(*i*) Business ethics and moral standards
(*ii*) Business and managerial policies
(*iii*) Prospects of business development
(*iv*) Government rules and regulations
(*v*) Industrial relations

Codes:

A. (*i*), (*ii*), (*iv*) and (*v*)
B. (*ii*), (*iii*), (*iv*) and (*v*)
C. (*i*), (*ii*), (*iii*) and (*iv*)
D. (*i*), (*ii*), (*iii*) and (*v*)

5. Identify the incorrect combination from the following:

	Finance Commi-ssion	**Constituted (Year)**	**Report Submitted (Year)**	**Chairman**
A.	1st	1951	1953	K.C. Neogi
B.	7th	1977	1978	J.M. Shelat
C.	11th	1998	2000	N.K.P. Salve
D.	13th	2007	2009	V.L. Kelkar

6. A flexible budget requires careful study and classification of expenses into

A. Product expenses and period expenses
B. Past and current expenses
C. Administrative, selling and factory expenses
D. Fixed, semi-variable and variable expenses

7. Responsibility accounting aims at collecting and reporting costing information

A. Department-wise
B. Cost centre-wise
C. Function-wise
D. Product-wise

8. Return on Investment (RoI) is computed as
A. Net Profit Ratio × Capital Turnover Ratio
B. Operating Net Profit Ratio × Shareholders Fund
C. Net Profit / Sales
D. Cost of Sales / Capital Employed

9. Margin of Safety is calculated by using

A. $\frac{\text{Profit}}{\text{P/V Ratio}}$ B. $\frac{\text{Fixed Cost}}{\text{Contribution}}$

C. $\frac{\text{Break Even Sales}}{\text{Sales}}$ D. $\frac{\text{Profit}}{\text{Sales}}$

10. Pre-acquisition profit in subsidiary company is considered as
A. Revenue profit B. Capital profit
C. Goodwill D. Minority interest

11. **Assertion (A):** The financial statements prepared on historical cost basis result into an erosion of capital in the long run.
Reason (R): Maintaining the books of accounts as per Current Purchasing Power Technique only may contain the inflationary pressure.
In the context of above two statements, which one of the following is correct one?
A. Both (A) and (R) are true and (R) is the correct explanation of (A).
B. Both (A) and (R) are true, but (R) is not the correct explanation of (A).
C. (A) is true, but (R) is false.
D. (A) is false, but (R) is true.

12. Secondary market intermediaries for corporate securities in India are
I. Investors
II. Jobbers
III. Brokers and sub-brokers
IV. Portfolio consultants
Codes:
A. I, II and III only B. II, III and IV only
C. II and III only D. III and IV only

13. The type of lease requiring an agreement between the financier and lessor is known as
A. Financial lease B. Sale and lease back
C. Leveraged lease D. Operating lease

14. Match the various stock exchanges in List–I with the years of their establishment in List–II as follows and suggest the correct code:

List–I	List–II
(*a*) National Stock Exchange (NSE)	(*i*) 1875
(*b*) MCX Stock Exchange (MCX-SX)	(*ii*) 1992
(*c*) Bombay Stock Exchange (BSE)	(*iii*) 2000
(*d*) Interconnected Stock Exchange of India (ISEI)	(*iv*) 2008

Codes:

	(*a*)	(*b*)	(*c*)	(*d*)
A.	(*ii*)	(*iv*)	(*i*)	(*iii*)
B.	(*ii*)	(*iii*)	(*iv*)	(*i*)
C.	(*i*)	(*iii*)	(*ii*)	(*iv*)
D.	(*iii*)	(*ii*)	(*iv*)	(*i*)

15. Monopolists prefer to sell the products in the markets with
A. Elastic demand
B. Unitary elastic demand
C. Inelastic demand
D. Absence of elasticity of demand

16. **Assertion (A):** In long run under Perfect Competition all firms invariably get only normal profit.
Reason (R): All firms incur minimum average cost and incur no selling cost due to absence of product differentiation.
Codes:
A. Assertion (A) and Reason (R) both are correct.
B. Assertion (A) is correct, but Reason (R) is incorrect.
C. Assertion (A) is incorrect, but Reason (R) is correct.
D. Assertion (A) and Reason (R) both are incorrect.

17. **Assertion (A):** Differential pricing structure is designed to accommodate the various categories of buyers.
Reason (R): It aims at increasing sales and revenues and driving the competitors out from the market.

Codes:

A. Assertion (A) and Reason (R) both are correct.

B. Assertion (A) is correct, but Reason (R) is incorrect.

C. Assertion (A) is incorrect, but Reason (R) is correct.

D. Assertion (A) and Reason (R) both are incorrect.

18. Cost-plus pricing is considered appropriate for:

I. Product Tailoring

II. Public Utility Pricing

III. Refusal Pricing

IV. Monopoly Pricing

Codes:

A. I and II only B. I, II and III only

C. II, III and IV only D. III and IV only

19. For promoting sales advertising endeavours may be made as per

I. Competitive parity

II. Objective and task

III. Tied sales

IV. All-one-can-Afford

Codes:

A. I and II only

B. II, III and IV only

C. I, II and IV only

D. III and IV only

20. In the hypothesis testing procedure a researcher may commit type II error in which of the following conditions?

A. When the true null hypothesis is rejected.

B. When the alternative hypothesis is accepted.

C. When the false null hypothesis is accepted.

D. When the true null hypothesis is accepted.

21. Which one of the following tenets is not correct in the context of Central Limit Theorem?

A. If a population from which a sample is drawn is normally distributed the sampling distribution of mean (SDM) will be normal for all sample sizes.

B. The mean of the SDM is the population mean.

C. If the population is not normal from which the sample is drawn, the SDM is not normal for any sample size.

D. If the population is not normal from which a sample is drawn, the SDM approaches normality as the sample size increases.

22. Which one of the following is not an example of tax evasion?

A. Submitting misleading documents.

B. Not maintaining proper accounts of income earned.

C. Suppression of facts.

D. Interpreting the tax law in ones own way to minimise tax liability.

23. Which one of the following is not the purpose of performance-monitoring research?

A. To provide feedback for evaluation and control.

B. To indicate things that are not going as planned.

C. To help the organisation to plan various activities.

D. It is required to explain why something went wrong.

24. The transformation of raw data into a form that will make them easy to understand and interpret, rearranging and manipulating data to generate information is called

A. Descriptive research

B. Descriptive analysis

C. Causal research

D. Exploratory research

25. Assertion (A): The span of management at the upper level is generally narrow while at the lower level span is wide.

Reason (R): The task allocated to subordinates at the lower level of management are more specific and precise and thus making supervision easy and simple.

Suggest correct code:

A. (A) is correct, but (R) is wrong.

B. (A) is wrong, but (R) is correct.

C. Both (A) and (R) are correct.

D. Both (A) and (R) are wrong.

26. Match the following:

List–I	List–II
(*a*) To check the quality of work	(*i*) Speed loss
(*b*) To see that work is completed in time	(*ii*) Inspector
(*c*) To check absenteeism of workers	(*iii*) Instruction and check
(*d*) To issue instructions regarding methods of work	(*iv*) Shop discipline

Select the code:

Codes:

	(*a*)	(*b*)	(*c*)	(*d*)
A.	(*iii*)	(*ii*)	(*i*)	(*iv*)
B.	(*ii*)	(*i*)	(*iv*)	(*iii*)
C.	(*ii*)	(*i*)	(*iii*)	(*iv*)
D.	(*iv*)	(*iii*)	(*i*)	(*ii*)

27. F.W. Taylor called "The Military type of Foreman" to

A. Unity of Command
B. Span of Control
C. Delegated Legislature
D. Department

28. Match the items of List–I with List–II:

List–I	List–II
(*a*) Commentary Four Chambault	(*i*) F.W. Taylor
(*b*) Midvale Steel Works	(*ii*) Claud Henry Saint Simon
(*c*) Charleton Twist Company	(*iii*) Henry Fayol
(*d*) Credit Mobilier	(*iv*) Robert Owen

Codes:

	(*a*)	(*b*)	(*c*)	(*d*)
A.	(*iii*)	(*ii*)	(*iv*)	(*i*)
B.	(*i*)	(*ii*)	(*iii*)	(*iv*)
C.	(*iii*)	(*i*)	(*ii*)	(*iv*)
D.	(*iii*)	(*i*)	(*iv*)	(*ii*)

29. Assertion (A): The risk condition exists when decision makers have absolutely no idea of what the results of an implemented alternative would be.

Reason (R): When operating under complete uncertainty condition, decision makers usually find that sound decisions are a matter of chance.

In the context of the two statements, which one of the following is correct?

Codes:

A. Both (A) and (R) are correct.
B. Both (A) and (R) are wrong.
C. (A) is correct, but (R) is wrong.
D. (A) is wrong, but (R) is correct.

30. Assertion (A): In product concept, focus is on innovating and improving products.

Reason (R): In selling concept, consumers are persuaded to buy products.

Codes:

A. Both (A) and (R) are true.
B. (A) is true, but (R) is false.
C. (A) is false, but (R) is true.
D. Both (A) and (R) are false.

31. Which of the following is not a method of segmenting a market?

A. Behavioural segmentation
B. Psychographic segmentation
C. Benefits segmentation
D. Customer segmentation

32. Consumer attitudes and beliefs about diet, health and nutrition are influenced by

A. Economic environment
B. Cultural environment
C. Social environment
D. Natural environment

33. Select the phases of Product Life Cycle:

1. Initiation
2. Decline
3. Boom
4. Introduction
5. Maturity
6. Growth

Codes:

A. 1, 3, 5, 6 B. 1, 2, 3, 4
C. 4, 6, 5, 2 D. 2, 3, 5, 6

34. Which of the following is not a product-mix strategy?

A. Trading up B. Alteration
C. Simplification D. Value addition

35. "Relationship" in marketing means

A. Relation between buyer and seller
B. Relation between sales person

C. Relation between company and consumers
D. All of the above

36. Match the items of List–I with the items of the List–II:

List–I (Company Name)	List–II (Brand)
(*a*) HUL	(*i*) Cerelac
(*b*) ITC	(*ii*) Eclares
(*c*) Nestle	(*iii*) Vivel
(*d*) Cadbury	(*iv*) Sunsilk

Codes:

	(*a*)	(*b*)	(*c*)	(*d*)
A.	(*iv*)	(*iii*)	(*i*)	(*ii*)
B.	(*i*)	(*ii*)	(*iii*)	(*iv*)
C.	(*iv*)	(*ii*)	(*iii*)	(*i*)
D.	(*iv*)	(*iii*)	(*ii*)	(*i*)

37. The following are the steps in designing the market driven distribution:
1. Know what customers want
2. Determine the costs
3. Review assumptions
4. Decide on the outlet
5. Compare alternatives
6. Implement changes

Select the right sequence of the steps from the codes given below:
A. 1, 4, 2, 5, 3, 6 B. 1, 2, 3, 5, 4, 6
C. 1, 3, 4, 5, 2, 6 D. 2, 3, 4, 5, 6, 1

38. Which of the following are consumption values that customers look for in any product or service in a society?
1. Functional value
2. Social value
3. Money value
4. Emotional value
5. Maximum value

Codes:
A. 1, 2, 3, 5 B. 1, 3, 4, 5
C. 5, 4, 3, 2, 1 D. 1, 2 and 4

39. Franchising is a practice of:
A. Leasing for a prescribed period of time, the right to use firm's successful business model and brand.
B. Selling out a successful business model and brand.
C. Hiring a firm's successful business model and brand.
D. None of the above.

40. Underwriters of the security issues are required to
A. Purchase the securities underwritten
B. Work as agent of the company for marketing the securities
C. Manage the issues of the securities
D. Take up securities not subscribed by investors

41. The optimum capital structure of a company is planned as per considerations of
I. Profitability
II. Solvency
III. Marketability of shares
IV. Control

Codes:
A. I, II and IV only B. II, III and IV only
C. I and II only D. III and IV only

42. Assertion (A): Investors in capital market seem to be inclined for fixed income securities.
Reason (R): Debt instruments now have active secondary market.

Codes:
A. Assertion (A) and Reason (R) both are correct and (R) is correct explanation of (A).
B. Assertion (A) and Reason (R) both are correct, but (R) is not correct explanation of (A).
C. Assertion (A) is correct, but Reason (R) is incorrect.
D. Assertion (A) is not correct, but Reason (R) is correct.

43. Insufficient working capital in any enterprise may also result into
I. Failure to adapt to changes
II. Overcapitalisation
III. Reduced availability of trade and cash discounts
IV. Reduced volume of production and sales

Codes:
A. I, II and III only B. I, III and IV only
C. II and III only D. I and IV only

44. Assertion (A): Arbitrage keeps the cost of capital constant despite change in the capital structure.

Reason (R): It ensures compensating inverse change in cost of equity capital with a change in the cost of debt capital.

Codes:

A. Assertion (A) and Reason (R) both are correct and (R) is correct explanation of (A).
B. Assertion (A) and Reason (R) are correct, but (R) is not correct explanation of (A).
C. Assertion (A) is correct, but Reason (R) is incorrect.
D. Assertion (A) is not correct, but Reason (R) is correct.

45. Assertion (A): High morale and high productivity go hand-in-hand.

Reason (R): Workers do not have their own ways for relief from fatigue and monotony.

Codes:

A. Both (A) and (R) are true.
B. (A) is true, but (R) is false.
C. (A) is false, but (R) is true.
D. Both (A) and (R) are false.

46. Relationship at work is the source of

A. Status anxiety B. Managerial stress
C. Legitimate power D. Expert power

47. Match the group of words in List–I with the group of words in List–II:

List–I	List–II
(*a*) Grievances	(*i*) Profit sharing
(*b*) Impact of technology	(*ii*) Effective planning
(*c*) Adjustment to technology	(*iii*) Index of low morale
(*d*) Morale improvement	(*iv*) Changes in occupation

Codes:

	(*a*)	(*b*)	(*c*)	(*d*)
A.	(*i*)	(*ii*)	(*iii*)	(*iv*)
B.	(*iv*)	(*iii*)	(*ii*)	(*i*)
C.	(*iii*)	(*ii*)	(*iv*)	(*i*)
D.	(*iii*)	(*iv*)	(*ii*)	(*i*)

48. Assertion (A): Functional conflict is a type of institutionalised conflict.

Reason (R): Politics is a kind of emergent conflict.

Codes:

A. Both (A) and (R) are true.
B. (A) is true, but (R) is false.
C. (A) is false, but (R) is true.
D. Both (A) and (R) are false.

49. Formal conflict is a kind of

A. Goal Conflict
B. Organisational Conflict
C. Role Conflict
D. Emergent Conflict

50. One of the objectives of organisational change is

A. Increased motivation
B. Greater innovation
C. Solving inter-group problems
D. Changes in an organisation's level of adaptation to its environment

51. Assertion (A): Job design relates to the manner in which tasks are put together to form complete job.

Reason (R): The matrix organisation is a project organisation plus a functional organisation.

Codes:

A. Both (A) and (R) are true.
B. (A) is true, but (R) is false.
C. (A) is false, but (R) is true.
D. Both (A) and (R) are false.

52. HRD as a total system includes the following major sub-systems:

1. Performance Appraisal
2. Career Planning
3. Role Analysis
4. ABC Analysis
5. Rewards

Select the correct answer from the codes.

Codes:

A. 1, 2, 3, 4
B. 1, 2, 3, 5
C. 2, 3, 4, 5
D. 1, 3, 4, 5

53. Which of the following is not true about employee grievances?

A. Grievance is a sign of employee's discontent with job or its nature.

B. Grievance provides a downward channel of communication.

C. Grievance arises only when an employee feels that injustice has been done to him.

D. Grievance can be real or imaginary.

54. Which of the following is not a component of Job Analysis?

A. Job Description B. Role Analysis

C. Job Summary D. Job Specification

55. As per the Master Circular on "Prudential Norms on Capital Adequacy – Basel I Framework", elements of Tier I capital include:

(*i*) Authorised Capital (Ordinary shares), statutory reserves, all other free reserves (disclosed), if any.

(*ii*) Paid-up capital (Preference shares).

(*iii*) Perpetual Non-Cumulative Preference Shares (PNCPS).

(*iv*) Innovative Perpetual Debt Instruments (IPDI).

Codes:

A. (*i*) and (*ii*) only B. (*ii*) and (*iii*) only

C. (*i*) and (*iii*) only D. (*iii*) and (*iv*) only

56. What is true about the Basel Committee on Banking Supervision (BCBS)?

(*i*) BCBS is an Indian National Committee of banking supervisory authority.

(*ii*) BCBS was established by a group of 19 nationalized commercial banks.

(*iii*) BCBS was established in 1996.

(*iv*) It provides a forum for regular cooperation on banking supervisory matters.

Codes:

A. (*i*) and (*ii*) only B. (*ii*) and (*iii*) only

C. (*iii*) and (*iv*) only D. (*iv*) only

57. Under the Cooperative Bank structure, the apex institution is

A. National Cooperative Bank

B. State Cooperative Bank

C. District Cooperative Bank

D. IDBI Bank

58. What is SLR ratio of a bank?

A. Ratio of total deposits against total investments.

B. Amount deposited by the bank with the Central Bank in the form of cash, gold and securities.

C. Amount that commercial banks are required to maintain before providing credit to customers.

D. Amount that commercial banks deposit with the foreign banks.

59. Assertion (A): The USA remains the world's largest FDI recipient country.

Reason (R): The global economic crisis of 2009, causes a reduction of global FDI flows took place to USA.

Select the correct code:

Codes:

A. Both (A) and (R) are correct and (R) is the correct explanation of (A).

B. (A) is correct, but (R) is not correct.

C. Both (A) and (R) are incorrect.

D. Both (A) and (R) are correct, but (R) is not correct explanation of (A).

60. As per the South Asia Free Trade Agreement, 1993 of SAARC, the member countries have to bring their duties down to

A. 25 per cent by 2006

B. 15 per cent by 2006

C. 10 per cent by 2007

D. 20 per cent by 2007

61. Which of the following is the correct combination?

(*i*) A GSA allows an MNE to enter into activities that might too costly and risky to pursue on its own.

(*ii*) A GSA does not allow a firm to enhance economics of scale.

(*iii*) A GSA does not allow a firm to bypass entry barriers into a target foreign country.

(*iv*) A GSA allows a firm to acquire partner knowledge.

Codes:

A. (*i*), (*iv*) are correct.

B. (*i*), (*ii*) are correct.

C. (*i*), (*ii*), (*iii*) and (*iv*) are correct.
D. (*ii*) and (*iii*) are correct.

62. Which of the following are the outcomes of the Sixth Ministerial Conference of WTO which was held at Hong Kong in December 2005?
Select the correct combination:
(*i*) Resolve to complete the Doha Work Programme fully and to conclude negotiations in 2006.
(*ii*) Amendments to TRIPS agreement reaffirmed to address public health concerns of developing countries.
(*iii*) To continue export subsidies in agriculture upto 2018.
(*iv*) Duty free, quota free market access for all LDC's products to all developed countries.

Codes:
A. (*i*), (*ii*) and (*iv*) B. (*i*), (*ii*), (*iii*) and (*iv*)
C. (*i*) and (*iii*) only D. (*ii*) and (*iv*) only

63. Which of the following is not a function of Foreign Exchange Market?
A. Stabilization function
B. Hedging function
C. Credit function
D. Transfer function

64. **Assertion (A):** The impact of depreciating Indian Rupee leads to less competition for Indian firms from imports.
Reason (R): The depreciating Indian Rupee results in downward pressure on inflation.
Select the correct code:
Codes:
A. Both (A) and (R) are correct.
B. (A) is false, but (R) is correct.
C. Both (A) and (R) are false.
D. (A) is true, but (R) is false.

65. In which of the following Stock Exchanges the GDR's are listed?
(*i*) London Stock Exchange
(*ii*) New-York Stock Exchange
(*iii*) Luxembourg Stock Exchange
(*iv*) Bombay Stock Exchange
(*v*) Singapore Stock Exchange
(*vi*) Hong Kong Exchange
Identify the correct combination:
A. (*i*), (*ii*) and (*iii*)
B. (*i*), (*iv*), (*v*) and (*vi*)
C. (*iii*), (*iv*), (*v*) and (*vi*)
D. (*i*), (*iii*), (*v*) and (*vi*)

66. **Statement I:** FIIs do not invest in unlisted entities. They participate only through stock exchanges.
Statement II: FIIs cannot invest at the time of initial allotment.
Select the correct code:
Codes:
A. Statements I and II are correct.
B. Statement I is true and II is false.
C. Statement I is false and II is correct.
D. Statements I and II are false.

67. ADRs' and GDRs' are an excellent means of investment to invest in India for
A. NRIs' B. Foreign nationals
C. Both A and B D. None of the above

68. Which of the following is not provided by EXIM Bank, for financing overseas investments?
A. Term loans to Indian Companies upto 80% of their equity investment in overseas JV/WOS.
B. Term loans to Indian Companies towards upto 100% of loan extended by them to the overseas JV/WOS.
C. Term loan to overseas JV/WOS towards part financing.
D. Guarantee facility to the overseas JV/WOS for raising term loan/working capital

69. Under Section 271C of the Income Tax Act, 1961 the amount of penalty for failure to deduct tax at source is
A. 10% of tax which is otherwise deductible under Section 194C.
B. 100% of tax which is otherwise deductible under Section 194C.
C. 200% of tax which is otherwise deductible under Section 194C.
D. 300% of tax which is otherwise deductible under Section 194C.

70. Match the following items of List–I and List–II and select the correct answer from the codes given below:

List–I (Sections)	**List–II (Maximum Deduction)**
(*a*) Section 80C of I.T. Act	(*i*) ₹ 10,000
(*b*) Section 80D of I.T. Act	(*ii*) ₹ 40,000
(*c*) Section 80 DDB of I.T. Act	(*iii*) ₹ 1,00,000
(*d*) Section 80 TTA of I.T. Act	(*iv*) ₹ 15,000

Codes:

	(*a*)	(*b*)	(*c*)	(*d*)
A.	(*iii*)	(*i*)	(*iv*)	(*ii*)
B.	(*iii*)	(*iv*)	(*ii*)	(*i*)
C.	(*iv*)	(*iii*)	(*ii*)	(*i*)
D.	(*ii*)	(*iii*)	(*i*)	(*iv*)

71. In which of the following cases, income of previous year is assessable in the previous year itself?

A. A person in employment.

B. A person engaged in illegal business.

C. A person who is running charitable business.

D. A person leaving India permanently.

72. Long term capital loss can be set off from which of the following?

A. Short term capital gain only

B. Long term capital gain only

C. Income from business and profession

D. Capital gain head of income

73. In which of the following long term assets, cost indexation benefit is allowed?

A. Debentures issued by a company

B. Self generated goodwill of a business

C. Bonus shares allotted on 1-4-2000

D. Jewellery

74. Calculate the Gross Annual Value from the following details:

Municipal Value	–	₹ 45,000
Fair Rental Value	–	₹ 50,000
Standard Rent	–	₹ 48,000
Actual Rent	–	₹ 42,000

A. ₹ 50,000 B. ₹ 48,000

C. ₹ 45,000 D. ₹ 42,000

75. Minimum Alternate Tax (MAT) is imposed on

A. All companies

B. Public Limited Companies only

C. Private Limited Companies only

D. Partnership Firms and Companies

ANSWERS

1	2	3	4	5	6	7	8	9	10
B	B	A	D	C	D	B	A	A	B
11	**12**	**13**	**14**	**15**	**16**	**17**	**18**	**19**	**20**
B	B	C	A	A	C	B	B	C	C
21	**22**	**23**	**24**	**25**	**26**	**27**	**28**	**29**	**30**
C	D	C	B	C	B	A	D	D	A
31	**32**	**33**	**34**	**35**	**36**	**37**	**38**	**39**	**40**
D	B	C	D	C	A	A	D	A	D
41	**42**	**43**	**44**	**45**	**46**	**47**	**48**	**49**	**50**
A	C	B	A	D	B	D	A	B	D
51	**52**	**53**	**54**	**55**	**56**	**57**	**58**	**59**	**60**
A	B	B	C	D	D	B	C	A	D
61	**62**	**63**	**64**	**65**	**66**	**67**	**68**	**69**	**70**
A	A	A	D	D	D	C	B	B	B
71	**72**	**73**	**74**	**75**					
D	B	D	B	A					

SOME SELECTED EXPLANATORY ANSWERS

1. The European Union (EU) is a supranational and intergovernmental union of 25 independent, democratic member states. The European Union is the world's largest confe-deration of independent states, established under that name in 1992 by the Treaty on European Union (the Maastricht Treaty).

The European Free Trade Association (EFTA) was established on May 3, 1960 as an alternative for European states that were not allowed or did not wish to join the European Community.

The Caribbean Community and Common Market or CARICOM was established by the Treaty of Chaguaramas which came into effect on August 1, 1973. The first four signatories were Barbados, Jamaica, Guyana and Trinidad and Tobago.

The South Asian Association for Regional Cooperation (SAARC) was established on 8th December, 1985 by the heads of states or Governments of Bangladesh, Bhutan, India, Maldives, Nepal, Pakistan and Sri Lanka.

4. Internal Environment includes internal factors of the business which can be controlled by business. It refers to environment within the organisation. It includes objectives of business, managerial policies, different departments of the organisation, management and employees of the organisation, labour management relationship; barnd image and corporate images, physical resources including infrastructure available with the business, vision and thinking of top management, research and development activities of organisation, working conditions in the organisation, morale and commitment of human resources etc. Internal environment includes 5 Ms, *i.e., man, material, money, machinery, management* available with business. The components of internal environment are usually within the control of business.

External Environment refers to external aspects of the surroundings of business enterprise which have influence on the functioning of business. The external aspects of the surroundings are by and large, beyond the control of business. External environment includes factors outside the firm which can provide opportunities or pose threats to the firm. The success of a business enterprise depends to a great extent on its awareness about its surroundings, environment and adaptability to changes in the environment.

Internal Environment of Business: The following components are more important for a business:

- Business and managerial policies
- The object of business
- Business ethics and standards
- Availability of resources
- Capability of business and prospects for development
- Production methods used and plant machinery
- Labour management relations
- Work environment
- Structure of organisation
- Business policies and strategies
- Management Information Systems (MIS)
- Opinion towards social responsibility

External Environment of Business: External factors largely affect the business. They are not controllable by the business. They include the following:

- Physical environment (e.g., Climate and geography)
- Demographic environment (e.g., Migration of population, settlement, etc.)
- Economic environment
- Technological environment
- Historical environment
- Social environment
- Political environment
- Legal environment
- Ethical environment
- Cultural environment
- International environment

5. Finance Commissions

Sl. No.	Name	Appointed in	Submitted Report in	Name of the Chairman
1.	First Finance Commission	1951	1952	K.C. Neogy
2.	Second Finance Commission	1956	1957	K. Santhanam
3.	Third Finance Commission	1960	1961	A.K. Chanda
4.	Fourth Finance Commission	1964	1965	Dr. P.V. Rajamannar
5.	Fifth Finance Commission	1968	1969	Mahavir Tyagi
6.	Sixth Finance Commission	1972	1973	Brahmananda Reddy
7.	Seventh Finance Commission	1977	1978	J.M. Shelat
8.	Eighth Finance Commission	1982	1984	Y.B. Chavan
9.	Ninth Finance Commission	1987	1989	N.K.P. Salve
10.	Tenth Finance Commission	1992	1994	K.C. Pant
11.	Eleventh Finance Commission	1998	2000	A.M. Khusro
12.	Twelfth Finance Commission	2002	2004	Dr. C. Rangarajan
13.	Thirteenth Finance Commission	2007	2009	Dr. Vijay Kelkar

6. On the basis of flexibility of production capacity, Budget is classified into three parts: (*i*) Fixed Budget; (*ii*) Flexible Budget; and (*iii*) Current Budget.

(*i*) **Fixed Budget:** Fixed Budget is prepared for a particular level of production. This type of Budget is suitable for a static production level condition. According to ICWA, London, *'Fixed Budget is a Budget which is designed to remain unchanged irrespective of the level of activity actually attained."*

(*ii*) **Flexible Budget:** A Flexible Budget consists of a series of Budgets prepared in respect of different levels of activity during a Budget period. A Flexible Budget is a series of Fixed Budgets prepared for different levels of production. It is useful in case of those concerns whose level of activity rapidly changes due to unforeseen changes in the business condition. According to ICWA, London, *'Flexible Budget is a Budget which, by recognizing the difference between Fixed, Semi-Fixed and Variable Costs, is designed to change in relation to the level of activity attained."*

(*iii*) **Current Budget :** This budget relates to the current business activities of a concern and is prepared under current conditions for a very short period. Accoding to ICWA, London, *'Current Budget is a Budget which is established for use over a short period of time and is related to Current Conditions.'*

7. Responsibility Accounting: Collection, summarization and reporting of financial information about various decision centers *(responsibility centers)* throughout an organization; also called *activity accounting* or *profitability accounting.* It traces costs, revenues, or profits to the individual managers who are primarily responsible for making decisions about the costs, revenues, or profits in question and taking action about them. Responsibility accounting is appropriate where top management has delegated authority to make decisions. The idea behind responsibility accounting is that each manager's performance should be judged by how well he or she manages those items under his or her control. **Responsibility Center:** Unit in the organization that has control over costs, revenues, or investment funds. For accounting purposes, responsibility centers are classified as Cost Centers, Revenue Centers, Profit Centers, and Investment Centers. A well-designed responsibility accounting system should clearly define *responsibility centers* in order to collect and report revenue and cost information by areas of responsibility.

8. **Du Pond Control Chart:** Du Pond employed a variation of ROI for control purposes. Capital employed turnover ratio multiplied by the net profitability ratio would also give the return on investment (ROI). Capital employed turnover ratio is turnover divided by capital employed. The net profitability ratio reveals the relationship between net profit and sales and is calculated by dividing net profit by sales turnover.

DU Pond Control Chart

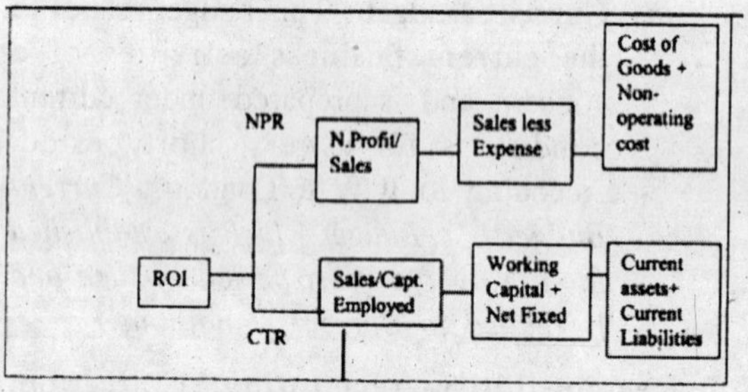

ROI = Return on investment
NPR = Net profit ratio
CTR = Capital employed turnover ratio

9. Margin of Safety is calculated by deducting Break-Even Sales from actual amount of sales.

Thus, Margin of Safety = Actual Sales – Break Even Sales. As contribution is expressed as a percentage of sales (*i.e.,* P/V ratio), Margin of Safety may also be expressed as percentage of actual sales. Accordingly, percentage will be presented as below:

Margin of safety (Sales)/Actual sales × 100

Margin of safety also be calculated with the help of the following formula (*i.e.,* with the use of P/V ratio):

Margin of Safety = Profit/(P/V Ratio)

The above formula has been developed from the original formula *i.e.,* Actual sales BEP sales. This is explained below:

Margin of Safety = Actual sales – BEP sales

Now, P/V Ratio = Contribution/Sales

i.e., Sales = Contribution/(P/V ratio)

= Fixed cost + Profit/(P/V Ratio)

Where as Break Even Sales

= Fixed cost/(P/V Ratio)

Margin of safety = Profit/(P/V Ratio)

10. The profits earned by the subsidiary company before the holding company acquires its control, is known as *pre-acquisition profit* or *capital profit.* Undrawn pre-acquisition profit is taken into consolidation for calculation of goodwill or capital reserve. It is split between cost of control (goodwill/capital reserve calculation) and minority interest.

The profits earned by the subsidiary company after the holding company acquires its control, is known as *post-acquisition profit* or *revenue profit,* which can be distributed as dividend. It should be noted that post-acquisition profit of a subsidiary company do not form part of the goodwill or capital reserve calculation.

Minority shareholders are not concerned whether the profits are pre-acquisition or post-acquisition. Post-acquisition profit is apportioned between holding company and minority shareholders. The share of holding company is added with its profit, while the share of the minority shareholders form a part of the calculation of minority interest.

12. **Secondary Market:** Players are—Issuers of securities, namely, companies, intermediaries like brokers, sub-brokers, etc., and the investors who bring in their savings and funds into the market.

Stock brokers of various categories, viz., client brokers, floor brokers, Jobbers, Arbitraguers, Badla financiers, and dealers.

The secondary market is a market where scrips are traded. Secondary market is a place provides liquidity to which, the scrips issued in the primary market. The growth of secondary market, thus, is dependent upon primary market. More the number of companies entering in the primary market, the greater is the volume of trade at the secondary market. Trading activities in the secondary market take place through recognised stock exchanges. It involves buying and selling of securities on the floor of the exchanges through its members.

13. **Leveraged lease:** A leveraged lease is arranged when the equipment is very costly. Leveraged leases are of course, financial leases in which the lessor borrows part of the purchase price of the leased asset using lease contracts as the security of the loan. In a leveraged lease, the debt finances the cost of the leased asset without recourse to the lessor. The financier enjoys recourse over the lessee. The leveraged lease has a longer maturity period owing to its high value. Generally, there are three parties in the leveraged lease, which include the lessor, the lessee and the lender of funds. The lessor provides equity funds which may be about 20 to 30 per cent of the cost of the asset and is generally termed as equity participant. The lender is called the debt participant who lends about 70 to 80 per cent of the cost of the asset. The lender obtains an assignment on the lease rentals payable by the lessee. The lease rentals are routed through a trustee who administers the transaction.

15. The elasticity of demand is one at the quantity where marginal revenue equals zero, demand is elastic (greater than one in absolute value) at quantities where marginal revenue is positive, and demand is inelastic (less than one in absolute value) at quantities where marginal revenue is negative. Like a competitive firm, the monopoly maximizes profits by producing the quantity that equates marginal cost and marginal revenue. Since marginal cost is positive, it must equal marginal revenue where marginal revenue is positive, meaning that demand is elastic. Thus, when maximizing profits, a monopoly always operates on the elastic portion of its demand curve.

18. **Role of Cost-plus Pricing**

(*a*) **For Product Tailoring :** Many times there already exists a great deal of competition in the field where a firm wishes to enter. As such a common level of prices has already been established in the market. Under such circumstances, the producers can first determine the price and work back by calculating the retailers marginal distribution costs, own profit and what remains is the cost of production. A product that is first in such a cost by its design, composition, etc., is then selected for production. This is known as product-tailoring.

(*b*) **For Refusal Pricing:** When products are supplied according to specifications given by the customer; minimum price can be decided by full cost method. For example, while supplying school uniforms, minimum price below which the offer cannot be accepted, can be fixed on the basis of this method.

(*c*) **For Monopsony Pricing:** When there is only one or very few buyers for a product, it is desirable to charge full cost price only. This is so because the bulk buyers are mostly business concerns who may otherwise decide to produce the commodity themselves. For example, let us suppose, the university wants to get some books printed. The printing press should charge at 'full cost' rates otherwise the University may decide to print the books in its own press if rates quoted are high.

(*d*) **For Public Utility Pricing:** When the Government (or a private company) supplies public utilities like electricity, water, telephone, etc., to the people, cost of service, is considered as the proper basis. Even when an element of profit is included in price, the method is cost plus pricing.

19. The promotional budgets consisting of advertising, sales promotion, direct marketing and publicity, of companies marketing industrial products or services are not large enough in comparison with those of the consumer products. There are four common methods used to set a promotion budget. These are: (*i*) Affordable method, (*ii*) Percentage-of-sales method, (*iii*) Competitive-parity method and (*iv*) Objective task mehtod.

20. In the testing of hypotheses we may commit two types of errors: (1) reject the null hypothesis when it is true (Type I error) or (2) accept the null hypothesis when it is false (Type II error).

21. The **Central Limit Theorem** is arguably the most important theorem in statistics. The branch of statistics known as inferential statistics relies heavily on this theorem. When you make inferences about a population mean based on information from a sample, you must know the relationship between the population from which your sample is taken and the sampling distribution of sample means. The Central Limit Theorem describe that relationship.

Properties of the Central Limit Theorem

1. If repeated samples of size n, where $n \geq 30$, are selected from ANY population with mean μ and standard deviation σ, then the sampling distribution of sample means will approximate a normal distribution. As the sample size increases, the approximation improves.
2. If the population from which the samples are drawn is normally distributed, then the sampling distribution of sample means will be normally distributed for any sample size.
3. The mean of a sampling distribution of sample means is equal to the population mean: $\mu_3 = \mu$.
4. The sampling distribution of sample means has a variance that is inversely proportional to the sample size: $\sigma_3^2 = \dfrac{\sigma^2}{n}$.
5. The sampling distribution of sample m has a standard deviation that is equ the standard deviation of the popul divided by the square root of the sa size: $\sigma_i = \dfrac{\sigma}{\sqrt{n}}$.

22. Meaning of Tax Evasion : Any illegal me which leads to reduction of tax liabili known as Tax Evasion. The tax evasic resorted to by applying following dish means:

1. Concealing the income.
2. Claiming excessive expenditure.
3. Falsification of accounts.
4. Wilful violation of rules.

E.g. claiming depreciation where no asset in the business or claiming depreciatio the assets which is used for reside purposes. It is basically a fraudulent me of reduction in tax liability.

What Are the Evil Consequences of Avoidance or Tax Evasion?

(*a*) There is a substantial loss of much ne public revenue.

(*b*) It encourages generation of black mo thereby directly increasing the inflat

(*c*) Hidden loss to the society, where by s of the best brains indulge in legal disp

(*d*) Then there arises a sense of injustic honest taxpaying citizens who pays t regularly by tax planning habits.

(*e*) Ethics are in the back business for a tax dodgers.

23. Performance-monitoring research specific type of evaluation research regularly provides feedback for evaluation control. It also indicates whether things a are not going as planned. Performa monitoring research may be required to ex why something 'went wrong.'

24. Descriptive analysis: The elemen transformation of raw data in a way describes the basic characteristics suc central tendency, distribution and variabi

Descriptive research: Describes characteristics of objects, people, groups, organizations or environments; tries to "paint a picture" of a given situation.

27. **Functional Foremanship:** F.W. Taylor replaced the existing "linear" system with new kind of system, known as the "functional foremanship". In the linear system or the military type of organisation, each worker is subordinate to only one boss. In the system of functional foremanship, each worker is subordinate to more than one boss or many supervisors. Taylor thus divided work not only among workers, but also at the supervisory level. In his system of functional foremanship, the workers received orders from eight narrowly specialised supervisors. Four of them (route clerk, instruction card man, time clerk and disciplinarian) were responsible for planning and the remaining four (gang boss, speed boss, inspection foreman and repair boss) for execution. He believed that in this functional type of organisation, the foreman can be trained scientifically and quickly and specialisation becomes easy. This technique was developed to improve the quality of work as single supervisor may not be an expert in all the aspect of the work. The scheme of functional foremanship is an extension of principle of specilisation at the supervisory level.

31. The phrase market segmentation means, division of the market of a certain product or service. To quote Philip Kotler, 'Market segmentation' is the act of dividing a market into distinct groups of buyers who might require separate products and/or marketing mixes. The company identifies different ways to segment the market and develops profiles of the resulting market segments.

Willion J. Stanton defines market segmentation as follows: "Market segmentation consists of taking the total heterogenous market for a product and dividing it into several sub-markets or segments each of which tends to be homogenous in all significant aspects."

Thus, market segmentation is a technique of dividing the customers of a product or service who may differ in their wants, resources, geographical locations, buying attitudes and buying practices, into several homogenous groups. Any of the mentioned variables might be used as bases for market segmentation.

The common bases of marketing segmentation are mentioned in the following diagram:

- Geographic Segmentation.
- Demographic Segmentation
- Economic Segmentation
- Psychographic Segmentation
- Behavioural Segmentation
- Volume Segmentation
- Benfit Segmentation.

33. A product follows the normal PLM (product lifecycle management) graph. It follows five stages: development, introduction, growth, maturity, and decline. The ideal maturity period should end with another phase of boom and beginning of a slowdown.

37. **Market or Customer-driven Distribution System:** Stern and Sturdivant (1991) have suggested an eight-step process to create a market-driven distribution system. This is based on their detailed marketing research. They suggest that consumer research throws up ideal distribution alternatives. According to Stern and Sturdivant, the eight steps in the market-driven distribution system are:

- Step 1 : Know what customers want
- Step 2 : Decide on the outlets
- Step 3 : Determine the cost
- Step 4 : Bound up 'ideal'
- Step 5 : Compare the alternatives
- Step 6 : Ascertain the gap between the 'ideal' and actual distribution system
- Step 7 : Review the assumptions
- Step 8 : Implement changes in the system as required.

38. Consumption Values: Sheth proposed five consumption values to explain collectively the buyers' multiple-facet decision process of purchasing what they wanted. The first is functional value, which emphasized on the consumption utility of a particular product/ service. Everyone's preference may differ and usually depend on his/her own budget, and purpose. Secondly, the linking to the buyer will influence his/her purchasing decision. The third is that reflects the purchasing feeling and enthusiasm surrounding a specific intention, atmosphere or situation. The buyer may be eager to purchase the on sale product or service that gives the buyer new knowledge or special consumption experience. Besides, some technological products are usually used under considering the condition of compatibility or network externality.

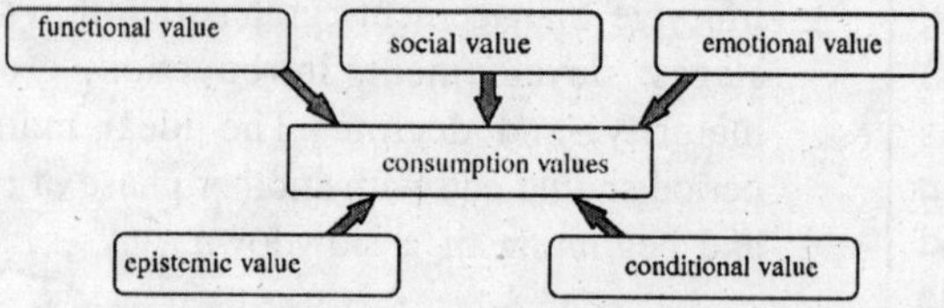

Fig. *Five consumption values.*

39. Franchising: Franchising is the practice of leasing for a prescribed period of time, the right to use a firm's successful business model and brand. The word 'franchise' is of Anglo-French derivation-from franc, meaning free-and is used both as a noun and as a (transitive) verb. For the franchisor, the franchise is an alternative to building 'chain stores' to distribute goods that avoids the investments and liability of a chain.

41. Optimum Capital Structure: The capital structure is said to be the optimum when the firm has selected such a combination of equity and debt so that the wealth of the firm is maximum. Where capital structure is optimum, the cost of capital is minimum and market price per share is maximum.

Features of an Optimum Capital Structure

1. **Profitability:** The capital structure is said to be optimum if it tends to minimise cost of financing and maximise earning per equity share.
2. **Flexibility:** The capital structure should be flexible so that the company can raise necessary funds as and when needed.
3. **Conservation:** The capital structure should be flexible so that the debt portion does not exceed the limit which the company can afford.
4. **Solvency:** The capital structure should be such that the firm does not run the risk of becoming insolvent either due to non-availabiltiy of funds or fresh loans, etc.
5. **Control :** The capital structure should be designed in such a way that it involves minimum risk of loss of control of the company.

46. The workplace is an important source of both demands and pressures causing stress, and structural and social resources to counteract stress.

The workplace factors that have been found to be associated with stress and health risks can be categorised as those to do with the content of work and those to do with the social and organisational context of work. Those that are intrinsic to the job include long hours, work overload, time pressure, difficult or complex tasks, lack of breaks, lack of variety, and poor physical work conditions (for example, space, temperature, light).

Unclear work or conflicting roles and boundaries can cause stress, as can having responsibility for people. The possibilities for job development are important buffers against current stress, with under promotion, lack of training, and job insecurity being stressful. There are two other sources of stress, or buffers against stress: relationships at work, and the organisational culture. Managers who are critical, demanding, unsupportive or bullying create stress, whereas a positive social dimension of work and good team working reduces it.

49. Organisational conflicts include intra-individual, interpersonal, intergroup conflict and structural conflict. The causes of organisational conflicts are incompatible goals, incompatible means, incompatible resource allocation, problem of status incongruities and difference in perceptions.

Types of Organisational Conflicts: Organisational conflicts are hierarchical, functional, line-staff conflicts and formal-informal conflicts. Hierarchical conflicts refer to the conflicts between various levels of the organisation; conflicts between top management and middle management is an example of this. Conflicts between management and employees are also related to hierarchical conflicts. Functional conflicts are related to conflicts between functional departments, as for example conflicts relating to production and marketing management, conflicts relating to finance and personnel management and so on... Line and staff conflicts are concerned with line personnel and staff members. Conflects related to formal and informal organisations are discussed under formal-informal conflict. Organisational conflicts include several causes of conflicts such as the level, merit and experience of different employees in the same cadres. Project and material organisations create conflicts because of inherent problems.

50. Organisational change has a number of goals, explicit and implied. Greiner and Barnes categorise the most obvious common goals as; higher performance, acceptance of new techniques, increased motivation, greater, innovation, enhanced cooperation, decreased turnover, etc.

Underlying these goals are two basic objectives:

- Changes in an organisation's level of adaptation to its environment.
- Changes in the internal behavioural patterns of employees.

51. **Job design** is the way the tasks are combined to form a complete job. It specifies the tasks that make up the job. Job design involves determining:

(*a*) What is to be done (*i.e.*, responses)?

(*b*) How it is to be done (*i.e.*, tools, etc.)?

(*c*) Why it is to be done (*i.e.*, purpose)?

According to Fred Luthans: The matrix organization is a project organization plus a functional organization.

52. **Mechanism of Human Resource Development:** Some mostly used methods or techniques or sub-systems of HRD for developing the competencies and motivation of individuals in an organisation and building the organisation's climate are explained in Figure.

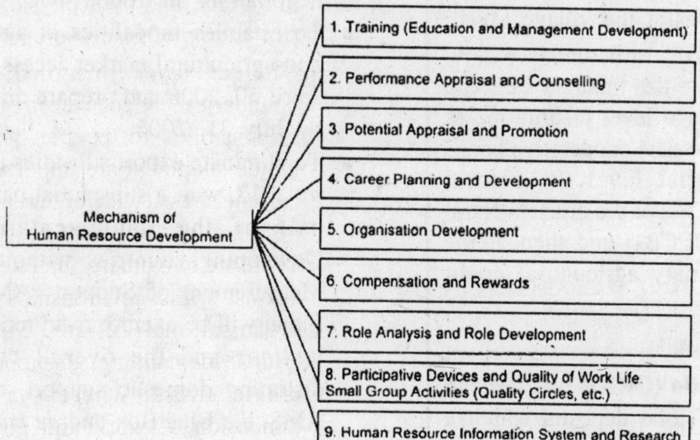

54. Job analysis is important form the view point of manpower planning, recruitment, selection and placement, induction of new trainees, promotion and transfer, training and development, job evaluation, performance appraisal, etc. It shows that the study of job analysis occupies an important place in the study of Huyman Resource Management. In Job analysis, as a process, by collecting necessary information, study is done relating to operations and responsibilities of a specific job. Dale Yoder describes job analysis as "the procedure by which the facts with respect to each job are systematically discovered and noted:. Job descriptions, job specification, job evaluation, etc. are the important job analysis components.

56. **Basel Committee on Banking Supervision (BCBS):** A committee of banking supervisory authorities that provides a forum for regular cooperation on banking supervisory matters. Its objective is to enhance understanding of key supervisory issues and improve the quality of banking supervision worldwide. The BCBS also develops guidelines and supervisory standards in various areas, including the international standards on capital adequacy, the Core Principles for Effective Banking Supervision, and the Concordat on cross-border banking supervision.

57. Cooperative banks have a three-tier set-up with the state cooperative bank at the apex, the district cooperative bank at the district level and the primary credit societies at the village level. The cooperative banking structure is federal in character, with three-tier linkages between state, district and village level institution. At the state level, we have state cooperative banks (SCBs), at the district level the central cooperative banks (CCBs) or the district central cooperative banks (DCCBs) and then at the village level the primary agricultural credit societies (PACSs).

58. **Variable Reserve Ratio:**

(*i*) **Cash Reserve Ratio (CRR):** It is defined as that portion of total deposits which a commercial bank is required to keep with the RBI in the form of cash reserves. In a situation of excess demand, RBI raises the CRR. This will reduce the cash deposits left with commercial banks to be loaned out. In case of deflation, RBI lowers the CRR.

(*ii*) **Statutory Liquidity Ration (SLR):** It is defined as the portion of total deposits which a commercial bank has to keep with itself in the form of liquid assets. In a situation of excess demand, RBI raises the SLR. The result is reduction in surplus cash reserves of the commercial banks which can be offered for credit. This will discourage credit in an economy. In a deflationary situation, RBI lowers the SLR.

60. In 1993, SAARC countries signed an agreement to gradually lower tariffs within the region, in Dhaka. Eleven years later, at the 12th SAARC Summit at Islamabad, SAARC countries devise the South Asia Free Trade Agreement which created a framework for the establishment of a free trade area covering 1.4 billion people. This agreement went into force on January 1, 2006. Under this agreement, SAARC members will bring their duties down to 20 per cent by 2007.

62. **Key Outcomes and Timelines of Hong Kong Ministerial Declaration:**

- Resolve to complete the Doha Work Programme fully, and to conclude negotiations in 2006.
- To establish modalities in agriculture and non-agricultural market access (NAMA) by April 30, 2006 and prepare draft Schedules by July 31, 2006.
- To eliminate export subsidies in agriculture by 2013, with a substantial part in the first half of the implementation period. Developing countries without Aggregate Measurement of Support (AMS), such as India, will be exempt from reductions in *de minimis* and the overall cut in trade-distorting domestic support, consisting of AMS, the Blue Box and *de minimis,* that is

entitlement to provide Amber Box subsidies up to 10 per cent of value.

- To submit a second round of revised services' offers by July 31, 2006 and submit final draft schedules by October 31, 2006.
- Amendment to TRIPS Agreement reaffirmed to address public health concerns of developing countries.
- In cotton, export subsidies to be eliminated by developed countries in 2006 and trade-distorting domestic subsidies to be reduced more ambitiously and over a shorter period of time.

Functions:

(*i*) Foreign exchange market facilitates transfer of purchasing power across different countries of the world. This is called Transfer function.

(*ii*) Foreign exchange market facilitates credit for international trade. This is called Credit function of the market.

(*iii*) Foreign exchange market facilitates protection against risks of foreign exchange. This is called Hedging function of the market.

Global Depository Receipts: A global depository receipt (GDR) is issued outside of the company's home country and outside of the United States. The depository bank that issues GDRs is generally located (or has branches) in the countries on whose exchanges the shares are traded. A key advantage of GDRs is that they are not subject to the foreign ownership and capital flow restrictions that may be imposed by the issuing company's home country because they are sold outside of that country. The issuing company selects the exchange where the GDR is to be traded based on such factors as investors' familiarity with the company or the existence of a large international investor base. The London and Luxembourg exchanges were the first ones to trade GDRs. Other stock exchanges trading GDRs are the Dubai International Financial Exchange, the Singapore Stock Exchange, and the Hong Kong Stock Exchange.

68. Exim Bank encourages Indian companies to invest abroad for, inter alia, setting up manufacturing units and for acquiring overseas companies to get access to the foreign market, technology, raw materal, brand, IPR etc. For financing such overseas investments, Exim Bank provides:

(*a*) Term loans to Indian companies up to 80% of their equity investment in overseas JV/ WOS.

(*b*) Term loans to Indian companies towards up to 80% of loan extended by them to the overseas JV/ WOS.

(*c*) Term loans to overseas JV/WOS towards part financing.

(*d*) Guarantee facility to the overseas JV/ WOS for (i) raising term loan/working capital.

69. Section - 271C, Income-tax Act, 1961

Penalty for failure to deduct tax at source:

271C. 27 (1) If any person fails to—

(*a*) deduct the whole or any part of the tax as required by or under the provisions of Chapter XVII-B; or

(*b*) pay the whole or any part of the tax as required by or under—

(*i*) sub-section (2) of section 115-O; or

(*ii*) the second proviso to section 194B, then, such person shall be liable to pay, by way of penalty, a sum equal to the amount of tax which such person failed to deduct or pay as aforesaid.

(2) Any penalty imposable under sub-section (1) shall be imposed by the 29[Joint] Commissioner.

71. Assessment Year – S. 2(9): Section 2(9) defines an "Assessment year" as, ***"the period of twelve months starting from the first day of April every year"*** An assessment year begins on 1st April every year and ends, on 31st March of the next year. For example, Assessment year 2012-13, means, the period of one year beginning on 1st April, 2011 and ending on 31st March, 2012.

In an assessment year, income of the assessee during the previous year is taxed at the rates prescribed by the relevant Finance Act. It is therefore, also called as the "Tax Year"

Previous Year - S 2(34) & S. 3

Defintion: Section 3 defines "Previous year" as ***"the financial year immediately preceding the assessment year".***

Income earned in one financial year is taxed in the next financial year. The year in which income is earned is called the "previous year" and the year in which it is taxed is called the "assessment year".

Exception: There are some exceptions to the rule that income of the previous year is taxable in the next assessment year. In such cases, the income of is taxed in the previous year itself. As a result, in such case, a financial year becomes the previous year as well as the assessment year.

These exceptions are provided to ensure safeguards to smooth collection of income tax from a class of taxpayers who may not be traceable till the commencement of the normal assessment year.

The Exceptions referred to above are:

(*a*) Income of non-residents from shipping business–S.172;

(*b*) Income of persons leaving India either permanently or for a long period of time and not likely to return back–S. 173-174;

(*c*) Income of bodies formed for short duration for a particular event or purpose–S 174A;

(*d*) Income of a person trying to alienate his assets with a view to avoiding payment of tax–S. 175

(*e*) Income of a discontinued business–S. 176

(*f*) Realisation of written off bad debts–S 41(1)

(*g*) Dividend income–S 56

72. Capital Loss (Sec. 74): From the assessment year 2003-2004 and subsequent years, following provisions govern the carry forward and set-off of capital losses:

(*i*) **Carry forward [Sec. 74(1)]:** Unabsorbed capital losses, short-term or long-term, can be carried forward for 8 assessment years, immediately succeeding the assessment years, in which the loss was first computed.

(*ii*) **Conditions for carry forward:**

(*a*) Return of loss should be furnished within the time-limit under Sec. 139(1).

(*b*) Carry forward and set-off is allowed to the same assessee who incurred the loss.

(*iii*) **Set-off of short-term capital losses:** A short-term capital loss may be set-off against short-term capital gain as well against long-term capital gains, assessable for that year.

However, a short-term capital loss cannot be set-off against the income of any other head [Sec. 71(3)].

(*iv*) **Set-off of long-term capital loss:** A long-term capital loss can be set-off only against long-term capital gains, assessable for that assessment year.

It cannot be set-off against the income of any other head [Sec. 71(3)].

74. (*a*) Municipal Value – ₹ 45,000

(*b*) Fair Rental Value – ₹ 50,000

(*c*) Higher of (*a*) or (*b*) – ₹ 50,000

(*d*) Standard Rent – ₹ 48,000

(*e*) Expected Rent

(Lower of (*c*) or (*d*) – ₹ 48,000

GAV = Expected Rent

= 48,000.

75. In 1996-97, the Government of India imposed the Minimum Alternate Tax (MAT) on companies, which escaped corporate tax net by using the provisions of exemptions, deduction, incentives, differential rate of depreciation, etc.

Previous Paper (Solved)

UGC (NET) JRF & Assistant Professor Exam Commerce, June-2014

PAPER-II

Note : *This paper contains* **fifty (50)** *objective type questions of* **two (2)** *marks each.* **All** *questions are compulsory.*

1. There is acute shortage of electricity in some of the states in India. This reflects a problem in which type of business environment?

A. Economic B. Demographic
C. Politico-legal D. Socio-cultural

2. Match the items given in List-I and List-II.

List-I	List-II
(*a*) Economic liberalisation	(*i*) IT-enabled services
(*b*) Out sourcing	(*ii*) SFIO
(*c*) Corporate frauds	(*iii*) Macro economic stability
(*d*) Second generation reforms	(*iv*) Increased competition

Indicate the correct combination :

Codes :

	(*a*)	(*b*)	(*c*)	(*d*)
A.	(*i*)	(*ii*)	(*iii*)	(*iv*)
B.	(*i*)	(*iii*)	(*ii*)	(*iv*)
C.	(*ii*)	(*iii*)	(*iv*)	(*i*)
D.	(*iv*)	(*i*)	(*ii*)	(*iii*)

3. Which of the following is true?

A. A consumer court setup under the Consumer Protection Act, does not have the power to punish for its contempt.
B. Professional services are outside the purview of the CPA.
C. A consumer court cannot force a person indulging in misleading advertising to confess his quit.
D. None of the above.

4. Match the items/terms given in List-I with those given in and List-II.

List-I	List-II
(*a*) BIS	(*i*) Print Media
(*b*) CERC	(*ii*) Minimum support price for agricultural products
(*c*) CACP	(*iii*) Quality of manufactured products
(*d*) PCI	(*iv*) Comparative product testing

Indicate the correct answer :

Codes :

	(*a*)	(*b*)	(*c*)	(*d*)
A.	(*iv*)	(*iii*)	(*ii*)	(*i*)
B.	(*i*)	(*ii*)	(*iii*)	(*iv*)
C.	(*iii*)	(*iv*)	(*ii*)	(*i*)
D.	(*ii*)	(*iii*)	(*iv*)	(*i*)

5. Which one among the following is ***not*** the salient feature of industrial policy since 1991?

A. Enormous expansion of the private sector.
B. Redefining the role of public sector.
C. Limited exposure of Indian industry to foreign competition.
D. Pruning of the list of items reserved for SSI units.

6. A, a partner in a firm, is drawing ₹ 500 regularly on the 16th of every month. He will have to pay interest at the given rate in a year on ₹ 6000 for the total period of

A. 5 months B. 6 months
C. 7 months D. 12 months

7. Subsequent expenditures that extend the useful life, improve the quality of output, or reduce operating costs of an existing asset beyond their originally estimated levels are

A. Capital expenditures
B. Revenue expenditures
C. Deferred Revenue expenditures
D. None of the above

8. Marginal-costing technique is useful for
A. Make or Buy decisions
B. Profit planning
C. Shut-down decisions
D. All of the above

9. Which one is not a feature of budgetary control?
A. A tool for management control.
B. An instrument of delegation and authority.
C. An instrument for evaluating the overall performance.
D. A statement of budget and forecasts.

). The Debt-Equity Ratio of a company is 2 : 1. In this relation, match the following :

List-I	List-II
(*a*) Issue of equity shares	1. No change on the ratio
(*b*) Cash received from debtors	2. Reduce the ratio
(*c*) Redemption of debentures	3. No change on the ratio
(*d*) Purchased goods on credit	4. Reduce the ratio

Codes :

	(*a*)	(*b*)	(*c*)	(*d*)
A.	1	2	3	4
B.	2	3	4	1
C.	1	3	4	2
D.	2	4	1	3

. Which one of the following does not explain the basic nature of Business economics?
A. Behaviour of firms in theory and practice.
B. Distribution theories like rent, wages and interest along with the theory of profit.
C. Use of the tools of economic analysis in clarifying problems in organising and evaluating information and in comparing alternative courses of action.
D. Integration of economic theory with business practices for the purpose of facilitating decision-making.

12. At a point of satiety for a commodity the marginal utility is
A. Negative
B. Positive
C. Zero
D. Highly positive

13. A rectangular hyperbola shaped demand curve on all its points has
A. Equal slopes and equal point elasticities.
B. Unequal slopes and unequal point elasticities.
C. Unequal slopes and equal point elasticities.
D. Equal slopes and unequal point elasticities.

14. **Assertion (A) :** A perfectly competitive firm is not a price-maker but is a price-taker.
Reason (R) : The firm is interested in deciding the level of output only.
Codes :
A. Both (A) and (R) are true.
B. Both (A) and (R) are false.
C. (A) is false, while (R) is true.
D. (A) is true, but (R) is not a correct explanation of (A).

15. Match the items of List-I with the items of List-II.

List-I	List-II
(*a*) A market having high price elasticity.	I. Skimming pricing
(*b*) A market having high price inelasticity	II. Differential pricing
(*c*) A market having several segments differing prominently with regard to price elasticities of their demand.	III. Penetrating pricing

Codes :

	I	II	III
A.	(*b*)	(*c*)	(*a*)
B.	(*a*)	(*b*)	(*c*)
C.	(*b*)	(*a*)	(*c*)
D.	(*a*)	(*c*)	(*b*)

16. Which one of the following options deals with the process of making estimates, predictions and decisions?
A. Descriptive statistics

B. Inferential statistics
C. Probability theory
D. None of the above

17. A hypothesis test is being performed for a process in which a Type-I error will be very costly, but a Type-II error will be relatively inexpensive and unimportant. Which of the following would be the best choice for alpha (α) in this test ?

A. 0.10 B. 0.05
C. 0.01 D. 0.50

18. If the dependent variable increases as the independent variable increases in an estimating equation, the coefficient of correlation will be in the range

A. 0 to (–) 1 B. 0 to (–) 0
C. 0 to (–) 0.05 D. 0 to 1

19. **Assertion (A) :** When there is an evidence of a linear relationship between two variables, it may not always mean an independent-dependent relationship between the two variables.

Reason (R) : The causal relationship between the two variables may not imply a reasonable theoretical relationship between the two.

Choose the right answer from the following statements :

Codes :

A. Both (A) and (R) are true and (R) is the correct explanation.
B. Both (A) and (R) are true, but (R) is not the correct explanation.
C. (A) is true, but (R) is false.
D. (A) is false, but (R) is true.

20. **Assertion (A) :** User interface is most critical task in DSS design

Reason (R) : DSS is used by outside Customers frequently.

A. (A) is correct, but (R) is wrong.
B. Both (A) and (R) are wrong.
C. (A) is wrong, but (R) is correct.
D. Both (A) and (R) are correct.

21. Which of the following is not true about Matrix Organisation?

A. It is relatively permanent.
B. Its project managers authority is distributed reasonably.
C. There is slow information processing.
D. Its project heads have to share resources with functional heads.

22. Consider the following leadership styles :

1. Telling 2. Autocratic
3. Selling 4. Motivating
5. Participating 6. Delegating
7. Charismatic

Select the four styles of leadership explained by Hersey and Blauchard.

A. 1, 2, 6 and 7 B. 2, 3, 4 and 5
C. 1, 3, 5 and 6 D. 4, 5, 6 and 7

23. Given below are two statements, one labelled as Assertion (A), and the other labelled as Reason (R).

Assertion (A) : Classical organisations believed in the use of authority to achieve coordination.

Reason (R) : Classical thinkers consider organisation is an open system.

Codes :

A. (A) is correct, but (R) is incorrect.
B. Both (A) and (R) are correct.
C. (A) is incorrect, but (R) is correct.
D. Both (A) and (R) are incorrect.

24. Who has modified Maslow's Hierarchical levels of needs and developed ERG model?

A. Frederick Herzberg
B. David C. McClelland
C. Douglas McGregor
D. Clayton Alderfer

25. Taylor's differential piece work plan provides that

A. All labourers should be assigned different amount of work.
B. All labourers should be put in different time-period.
C. Those who produce above standard should receive higher wages than those producing below standard.
D. Payment should be the same on a fixed standard.

26. Which one of the following stages of the marketing research process is most expensive?
A. Data analysis
B. Data collection
C. Developing the research plan
D. Report writing

27. The people to adopt a new product first are called
A. Early adopters B. First users
C. Initial adopters D. Innovators

28. A concept in retailing that helps explain the emergence of new retailers is called the _______ hypothesis.
A. Product life cycle
B. Service assortment
C. Retail life cycle
D. 'Wheel-of-retailing'

29. Manufacturers of cars and motor cycles typically seek _______ distribution.
A. selective B. intensive
C. exclusive D. None of these

30. Which method of setting advertising budget is most scientific and logical?
A. All-you-can afford method
B. Competitive parity method
C. Objective-and-task method
D. Percentage-of-sales method

31. Assertion (A) : Weighted average cost of capital should be used as a hurdle rate for accepting or rejecting a capital budgeting proposal.
Reason (R) : It is because by financing in the proportions specified and accepting the project, yielding more than the weighted average required return, the firm is able to increase the market price of its stock.
Codes :
A. Both (A) and (R) are false.
B. Both (A) and (R) are true.
C. (A) is true, while (R) is false.
D. (A) is false, while (R) is true.

32. A firm wants to know the Degree of Operating Leverage (DOL) with the following information:
Current level of sales : 6000 units
Break-even point sales : 4000 units
What would be the DOL?
A. 1.50 B. 0.67
C. 3.00 D. None of the above

33. Assertion (A) : When two or more investment proposals are mutually exclusive, ranking the proposals on the basis of IRR, NPV and PI methods may give contradictory results.
Reason (R) : The contradictory results in the ranking are due to differing dimensions relating to the scale of investments, cash flow patterns and project lives.
Indicate the correct answer :
Codes :
A. Both (A) and (R) are true.
B. (A) is true, but (R) is a necessary condition, but not a sufficient condition.
C. Both (A) and (R) are false.
D. Both (A) and (R) are true and (R) explains the reason sufficiently.

34. Which one of the following assumptions is not covered in the Walter's Model of the dividend policy?
A. All financing is done through retained earnings.
B. Firm's business risk does not change due to additional investments.
C. The firm has an infinite life.
D. The key variables like EPS and DPS keep on changing.

35. Which one of the following emphasizes the qualitative aspects of working capital management?
A. Gross working capital
B. Quick working capital
C. Net working capital
D. None of the above

36. Which of the following training methods exposes the newly recruited employee to the various business functions, divisions and departments ?
A. Orientation
B. Vestibule Training

C. Transition Analysis
D. Role playing

37. Match the names of the Authors given below with the motivational theories they are associated with

List-I	**List-II**
1. Herzberg	(*a*) ERG Theory
2. McGregor	(*b*) Three-need theory
3. Alderfer	(*c*) Theory X and Theory Y
4. David McClelland	(*d*) Two-factor theory

Codes :

	1	2	3	4
A.	(*a*)	(*b*)	(*c*)	(*d*)
B.	(*d*)	(*c*)	(*b*)	(*a*)
C.	(*b*)	(*a*)	(*d*)	(*c*)
D.	(*d*)	(*c*)	(*a*)	(*b*)

38. Who was closely associated with industrial relations in India?
A. B. Kurien
B. Gadgil
C. V.V. Giri
D. Vinoba Bhave

39. Under the Trade Union Act 1926, how many minimum number of members are required for a trade union to be registered?
A. 5 B. 7
C. 9 D. 11

40. The idea that a manager tends to be promoted to a level of his incompetence is referred to as
A. the advancement principle
B. the Paul principle
C. the Peter principle
D. the job design principle

41. Which of the following committees is intended to review the working of the monetary system in India?
A. Narasimham Committee
B. Tandon Committee
C. Sukhamoy Chakravarty Committee
D. Deheja Committee

42. Match the items of List-I with those in List-II and select the correct answer.

List-I	**List-II**
(*a*) Bank Rate Policy	1. Involving the shortening of the currency of bills eligible for rediscount
(*b*) Credit Rationing	2. Involving the Purchase and sale of securities in the open market
(*c*) Variable Reserve System	3. Involving the alteration of discount rate
(*d*) Open Market Operations	4. Involving the variation of the minimum reserves

Codes :

	(*a*)	(*b*)	(*c*)	(*d*)
A.	1	4	2	3
B.	2	1	3	4
C.	4	2	1	3
D.	3	1	4	2

43. Match the items of List-I with the items of List-II and select the correct answer using the codes given below the lists.

List-I	**List-II**
(*a*) Rural Industries Programme	(*i*) Meant for various target groups like Rural youth, Ex-serviceman, women and Scheduled Castes/ Tribes
(*b*) Mahila Vikas Nidhi Scheme	(*ii*) Aim at ensuring flow of credit to the dis-advantaged sections of the society
(*c*) Entrepreneur-ship Development Programme	(*iii*) Commercial exploitation of local resources
(*d*) Micro Credit Scheme	(*iv*) Provides assistance to voluntary organizations for the benefit of women

Codes :

	(*a*)	(*b*)	(*c*)	(*d*)
A.	(*i*)	(*iii*)	(*ii*)	(*iv*)
B.	(*ii*)	(*iv*)	(*i*)	(*iii*)
C.	(*iv*)	(*ii*)	(*iii*)	(*i*)
D.	(*iii*)	(*iv*)	(*i*)	(*ii*)

44. According to the FDI Policy of the Government of India (2012), the FDI in banks is limited to
A. 20% in Nationalised Banks and 74% in Private Sector Banks.
B. 20% in Nationalised Banks and 49% in Private Sector Banks.
C. 16% in Nationalised Banks and 74% in Private Sector Banks.
D. 49% in Nationalised Banks and 51% in Private Sector Banks.

45. According to the recent guidelines (2013) of the Reserve Bank of India the Private Sector Banks are required to have a minimum paid up equity capital of
A. ₹ 300 crores
B. ₹ 200 crores
C. ₹ 400 crores
D. ₹ 500 crores

46. International trade theory which provides that capital intensive country should export labour-intensive goods and import capital goods is referred to as
A. Leontief Paradox
B. Heckscher-Ohlin Theory
C. Mercantilism Theory
D. Theory of Comparative Advantage

47. Which of the following is not a form of economic integration in the context of intra-regional trade?
A. Customs Union
B. European Union
C. Economic Union
D. African Union

48. 'Crawling Peg System' means
A. Fixed Exchange Rate System
B. Floating Exchange Rate System
C. Hybrid of Fixed and Floating Excha[illegible] System
D. None of the above

49. From the following modes of internatio[illegible] business, identify the mode which invol[illegible] strategic alliance
A. Franchising
B. Leasing
C. Turnkey Project
D. Joint venture

50. Which of the following expressions amoun[illegible] the import restriction measures?
(*i*) Currency control
(*ii*) Establishment of EPZs
(*iii*) Tariff cuts
(*iv*) Imposition of tariffs
(*v*) Imposition of non-tariff barriers

Codes :
A. (*i*), (*ii*) and (*iii*)
B. (*i*), (*iv*) and (*v*)
C. (*iii*), (*iv*) and (*v*)
D. (*ii*), (*iii*) and (*v*)

ANSWERS

1	2	3	4	5	6	7	8	9	10
A	D	A	C	C	B	A	D	D	B
11	**12**	**13**	**14**	**15**	**16**	**17**	**18**	**19**	**20**
B	C	C	D	A	B	C	D	A	A
21	**22**	**23**	**24**	**25**	**26**	**27**	**28**	**29**	**30**
C	C	A	D	A	B	D	D	C	C
31	**32**	**33**	**34**	**35**	**36**	**37**	**38**	**39**	**40**
B	C	B	D	C	A	D	C	B	C
41	**42**	**43**	**44**	**45**	**46**	**47**	**48**	**49**	**50**
C	D	D	A	D	A	D	C	D	B

SOME SELECTED EXPLANATORY ANSWERS

3. Consumer Protection Act, 1986: India is a vast country having a majority of poor consumers who are disorganised. Therefore, the Government enacted an Act in 1986 to protect the rights and interest of consumers in the market. This Act normally recognises consumer rights and has also established a redressal system unique in the world. This Act was amended in 1993, 1999 and 2002.

6. Interest on drawings can be calculated by applying the following two methods:

(1) Product Method, (2) Average Period Method

Product Method: Under this method, the amount of drawings for each period is multiplied by the period for which the amount is going to be used. Then, the product is summed up and the following formula is used to find the interest on drawings.

Interest on Drawings

$$= \text{Product} \times \frac{\text{Rate of interest}}{100} \times \frac{1}{12}$$

If the amount is withdrawn at irregular period of months:

It is easier to calculate under Product Method.

Average Period Method: Interest on drawings is to be calculated with reference to the average of the periods for which the money is withdrawn.

Interest on Drawings:

$$= \text{Total drawings} \times \frac{\text{Rate of interest}}{100} \times \frac{\text{Average period}}{12}$$

Calculation of Average Period: The average period is calculated to take the period for the average of the periods applicable to the first instalment and the last instalment.

$$\text{Average Period} = \frac{\text{Beginning period of use + Ending period of use}}{2}$$

(*a*) *If the fixed amount is withdrawn in t beginning of every month:*

Take the period at the average of the perio applicable to the first and last instalment.

The period of first instalment is 12 months.

The period of last instalment is 1 month.

$$\text{Average period} = \frac{12 + 1}{2} = 6\tfrac{1}{2} \text{ months}$$

(*b*) *If the fixed amount is withdrawn in t middle of every month:*

Take the period at the average of the perio applicable to the first and last instalment.

The period of first instalment is $11\frac{1}{2}$ months

The period of last instalment is ½ month.

$$\text{Average period} = \frac{11\frac{1}{2} + \frac{1}{2}}{2} = \frac{12}{2} = 6 \text{ months}$$

From Question, Fixed Amount is drawing in t middle of every month.

∴ Average Period is 6 months.

7. Capital expenditures are expenditures for t acquisition of assets. Subsequent expenditur that extend the useful life, improve the qual of output, or reduce operating costs of existing asset beyond their originally estimat levels are capital expenditures.

By making use of marginal-costing techniqu one can achieve the main objectives of busine organization, such as—(1) Better decisio making and (2) A proper device to control nee

The task of arriving at a proper decision-maki is facilitated by the application of margin costing technique making decisions relating fixation of selling prices, selection of profitab product mix, diversification of products, ma or buy decisions, alternative methods manufacture, shut-down decisions, cost cont and profit planning.

12. Law of Diminishing Marginal Utility

This law lies at the centre of cardinal approach. This law is based on the satiabil characteristic of human wants, that a single want taken separately at a time can be fully satisfied. According to the law, "other things being equal, as the quantity of commodity consumed or acquired by the consumer increases, the marginal utility of the commodity tends to diminish."

This law is also known is as 'First Law of Gossen'. Marginal utility curve slops downward from left to right which indicates that as consumption units increases, the marginal utility diminishes. Point of satiety (in given figure) reaches where the marginal utility is zero. After point B, utility becomes negative which denotes disutility.

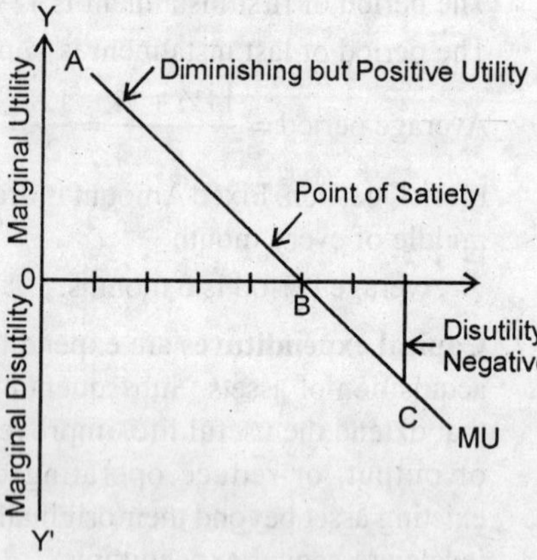

15. A pricing strategy is an approach or a course of action designed to achieve pricing and marketing objectives. The major categories of pricing strategies are differential pricing, new-product pricing, product-line pricing, psychological pricing, professional pricing and promotional pricing. When marketers employ differential pricing, they charge different buyers different prices for the same quality and quantity of products. Negotiated pricing, secondary-market discounting, periodic discounting and random discounting are forms of differential pricing. Two strategies used in new-product pricing are price skimming and penetration pricing. With price skimming, the organisation charges the highest price that buyers who most desire the product will pay. A penetration price is a low price designed to penetrate a market and gain a significant market share quickly. Product-line pricing establishes and adjusts the prices of multiple products within a product line. This category of strategies includes captive pricing, premium pricing, bait pricing and price lining. Psychological pricing attempts to influence customer's perceptions of price to make a product's price more attractive. Psychological pricing strategies include reference pricing, bundle pricing, multiple-unit pricing, everyday low prices, odd-even pricing, customary pricing and prestige pricing. Professional pricing is used by people who have great skill or experience in a particular field, therefore allowing them to set the price.

16. Statistical inference is the process of making an estimate, prediction, or decision about a population based on sample data. Because populations are almost always very large, investigating each member of the population would be impractical and expensive. It is far easier and cheaper to take a sample from the population of interest and draw conclusions or make estimates about the population of the basis of information provided by the sample. However, such conclusions and estimates are not always going to be correct. For this reason, we build into the statistical inference a measure of reliability. There are two such measures: the confidence level and the significance level.

18. The simple correlation coefficient provides this information when only two variables are involved. It measures the degree of association between the dependent variable and the independent variable. The coefficient of simple correlation may range from –1 to +1. A negative coefficient means that one variable tends to decrease in value as the other increases. A positive coefficient means that one variable tends to increase in value as the other variable increase. If the coefficient is zero, there is no association between the variables.

21. Project Organisation vs. Matrix Organisation

Projects organisation	Matrix organisation
1. Purely temporary	1. Relatively permanent
2. Project manager's authority could range from very low to very high.	2. Project managers' authority distributed reasonably.
3. Low information processing	3. High information processing
4. Power struggles avoidable in case of projects having limited life span.	4. Power struggles a distinct possibility-between functional managers and project managers.
5. In the aggregate project form, project manager takes charge of information, resources and people.	5. Project heads have to share resources with functional heads.

22. Hersey and Blanchard's situational theory (1988) suggests four styles of leadership that can be used in different situations. The four styles are telling, selling, participating and delegating.

1. Telling is a very directive style. It involves giving explicit direction about how the tasks should be accomplished.
2. Selling involves providing direction, but also includes seeking inputs from others before making decisions.
3. Under delegating style the employees assume responsibility for their work and for the success of their organization.
4. Participative style is already described above.

24. Clayton Alderfer reformulated Maslow's Needs Hierarchy Theory. He modified and reduced Maslow's five levels of needs to three levels and labeled them as needs for:

Herzberg's Two Factors	Maslow's Hierarchy of Needs	Alderfer's ERG Needs
Motivators	Self-actualisation	Growth
	Esteem	
Hygiene Factors	Social	Relatedness
	Safety	Existence
	Physiological	

27. The adoption of new technology products can be described in a diffusion process. The first group of prople that tries the product is called innovators, the second, early adopters, the third, early majority, the forth, late majority and the fifth, laggards.

28. Wheel-of-retailing concept: A concept of retailing, states that new types of retailers usually begin as low-margin, low-price, low-status operations but later evolve into higher-priced, higher-service operations, eventually becoming like the conventional retailers they replaced.

29. There are three alternative distribution strategies:

(*i*) **Intensive Distribution:** This involves maximum exposure by placing the product in as many outlets as possible. This policy provides access to all possible buyers. Greater stability in sales volume can be achieved. A large sales volume is possible and distribution overheads are widely spread. Intensive distribution is appropriate for frequently purchased low priced products which involve little buying effort e.g., toilet soap, detergent, bread, nuts, bolts, lubricants, cold drink, cigarette etc.

(*ii*) **Selective Distribution:** Selective distribution involves exposure to certain target customers through more than one but less than all outlets. The producer sells his product through selected outlets. It provides the advantages of better dealer relationships. Selective distribution is suitable for products that buyers seek out and are prepared to spend some buying efforts e.g., designer shirts, cosmetics, television sets, electronic equipment. Such as washing machines, air conditions, music systems etc.

(*iii*) **Exclusive Distribution:** Exclusive distribution implies selling the product through one outlet in each market. Every dealer sells the product in a restricted market and does not deal in competitive brands. This strategy provides greater participation and motivation of the dealer, greater willingness on his part to maintain inventory and after sale service, and a more co-ordinated physical distribution system. Specialisation in selling promotes efficiency. In India, this arrangement may, however, face legal problems under the Consumer Protection Act, MRTP Act, Exclusive distribution is useful when greater participation of seller is required. Technical complex products requiring installation and after sales services, products requiring cultivation of brand loyality or exclusive image e.g. refrigerators, automobiles, cosmetics, music systems, washing machines, computers, mobile phones, digital camera's etc., are examples of such products.

32. $\text{DOL} = \dfrac{Q}{Q - Q_{BE}}$

$$\text{DOL} = \frac{6000}{6000-4000} = \frac{6000}{2000} = 3.00.$$

34. Walter's Valuation Model : Prof. James E. Walter suggests that dividend policy and investment policy of a firm are interlinked and hence the dividend decision always affects the value of a firm. His proposition clearly states the relationship between the firm's internal rate of return (i.e., Ra) and its cost of capital (i.e., Rc). In short, in case the firm's return on investment is more than the cost of capital, it must retain its earnings and otherwise it should distribute its earnings to the shareholders.

Assumptions: The critical assumptions of Walter's Model are as follow:

1. All financing is done through retained earnings: external sources of funds like debt or new equity capital are not used.
2. With additional investments undertaken, the firm's business risk does not change. It implies that *r* and *k* are constant.
3. There is no change is the key variables, namely, beginning earnings per share, E, and dividends per share, D. The value of D and E may be changed in the model to determine results, but, any given value of E and D are assumed to remain constant in determining a given value.
4. The firm has perpetual (or very long) life.

35. Difference between Net Working Capital and Gross Working Capital

S.No.	Net Working Capital	Gross Working Capital
1.	Net working capital is qualitative in nature.	Gross working capital is quantitative in nature.
2.	It is indicating the firm's ability to meet its operating expenses and current liability	It is pointing out the total amount available for financing the current assets.
3.	It is expressed as current assets minus current liabilities.	It indicates the total sum of current assets.
4.	It is a concept that is very popular in accounting system.	It is a concept that is very popular in financial management circles.
5.	Net concept is suitable for sole traders and partnership firms.	Gross concept is suitable for companies.
6.	It is useful to find out the true financial position of a company.	It does not reveal the true financial position of a company.
7.	Increase in bank loans cannot increase working capital. Retained profits, sale of fixed assets will increase net working capital.	Every increase in borrowing will increase the gross working capital.

38. Former President of India V.V. Giri's deep concern for the well-being of the working class made him write two popular books on labour issues entitled *Industrial Relations* and *Labour Problems in the Indian Industry.* According to him, in the tree of socialism, the root comprises human beings. Giri observed that "it is an essential condition to maintain mutual trust and confidence between the employer and employee to obtain the goal of rapid economic development and social justice." The Giri approach in industrial relations focuses on the relevance and importance of voluntary negotiations between the employers and the employees as a means of settling disputes.

39. Registration of a trade union is not compulsory but is desirable since a registered trade union enjoys certain rights and privileges under the Trade Union Act 1926. A minimum of seven workers of an establishment (or seven employers) can form a trade union and apply to the Registrar of Trade Unions for its registration. Seven or more members of a trade union may, by subscribing their names to the rules of the trade union and by complying with the provisions of the Act with respect to registration, apply for registration of the trade union under the Act. The minimum age limit for membership of a trade union is 15 years unless the rules of a particular trade union provide for higher age limit. However, to be an office-bearer the person has to be above 18 years of age.

40. The Peter principle, named after Dr. Laurence Peter, is the Management theory that people tend to be promoted to one level beyond their competency. As stated in Peter's book *The Peter Principle—Why Things Always Go Wrong* (coauthored with Raymund Hull), "In a hierarchy every employee tends to rise to his own level of incompetence."

41. For the first time since its establishment, the Reserve Bank of India set up in December, 1982, a committee under the Chairmanship of Prof. Sukhamoy Chakravarty to undertake a comprehensive review of the working of the monetary system in our country. The Committee submitted its report in April, 1985.

46. Leontief's Paradox: With the help of import-export statistics of America eminent economist and Nobel Laureate Leontief has proved wrong the conclusion of Heckscher-Ohlin Theory that a capital intensive country exports capital intensive goods and a labour intensive country exports labour intensive goods. Leontief's conclusion was competely contrary to this concept. That is why his conclusion is referred to a Leontief Paradox. Taking 1947 as the base year, Leontief prepared an intput-output schedule of 192 industries of America. On the basis of this schedule, he calculated the consumption of labour and capital involved in exports and import substitutes worth one million dollars each. In this respect he concluded that America being a capital intensive country was exporting labour intensive goods and importing capital intensive goods. It is what is called Leontief's Paradox.

48. A Crawling peg system is a hybrid of the fixed and flexible exchange rate systems. Under this system, while the value of the currency is fixed in terms of a reference currency, the peg itself keeps changing in line with economic fundamentals, thus letting the market forces play a role in the determination of the exchange rate. The advantages of a crawling peg is that, though it gives a relatively stable exchange rate (changes in which are fairly predictable), the rate is never too much out of line with the underlying fundamentals of the economy.

PAPER-III

Note : *This paper contains **seventy five** (75) objective type questions of **two** (2) marks each. **All** questions are compulsory.*

1. The Competition Act, 2002, seeks to regulate
- A. Anti-competitive agreements
- B. Mergers and amalgamation
- C. Unfair trade practices
- D. A and B above

2. Indicate the true statement :
- A. Large industrial houses are outside the purview of the Competition Act, 2002
- B. There is no provision for curbing frivolous complaints under the CPA.

C. The Trade Marks Act, 1999 does not apply to services.
D. All of the above are true.

3. The time limit for filing a complaints before the District forum under the Consumer Protection Act, 1986 is
A. one year
B. two years
C. three years
D. There is no such time limit.

4. The Foreign Investment Promotion Board (FIPB) revamps the rules and regulations pertaining to
A. Accounting of Foreign Investment
B. Investment by NRIs
C. Foreign investments
D. All of the above

5. Which of the legislation(s) do (does) not form part of the legal environment of business in India?
A. The Drugs and Cosmetics Act, 1940
B. The Prevention of Food Adulteration Act, 1954
C. The Monopolies and Restrictive Trade Practices Act, 1969
D. Both B and C above

6. What is the underlying concept that support the immediate recognition of an estimated loss?
A. Substance over form
B. Consistency
C. Matching
D. Prudence

7. Which is ***not*** the limitation of budgetary control?
A. Budgets are based on forecasts which may not be true
B. Installation and operation of a system of budgetary control is costly.
C. Budget is a tool of management and not a substitute of management.
D. Budgets do not pinpoint the lack of efficiency or the presence of it.

8. Profit volume ratio of an enterprise is 40%. To offset 10% decrease in selling price, how much sales must be increased?
A. 10% B. 20%
C. 25% D. 40%

9. If debt is ₹ 220, cash balance is ₹ 20 and equity is ₹ 300, then the gearing ratio is
A. 20% B. 40%
C. 50% D. 30%

10. Responsibility accounting aims to
A. ensure that a manager is punished if things go wrong.
B. ensure that costs become the responsibility of a specific manager.
C. allocate costs to all areas of a business.
D. reduce the costs that a department incurs.

11. Find the correct matching of the items of List-I with the items of List-II given below :

List-I	**List-II**
(*a*) Normal Profit	I. Excess of total revenue over total explicit cost
(*b*) Economic profit	II. Total revenue equals total economic cost
(*c*) Accounting profit	III. Excess of total revenue over total of explicit and implicit costs and a normal rate of return

Codes :

	I	II	III
A.	(*c*)	(*a*)	(*b*)
B.	(*b*)	(*a*)	(*c*)
C.	(*a*)	(*b*)	(*c*)
D.	(*a*)	(*c*)	(*b*)

12. Assertion (A) : A monopoly firm's revenue curve is downward sloping from left to right.
Reason (R) : The monopoly firm does not simultaneously enjoy the freedom to determine both price and quantity to be sold according to its whims and fancy.
Codes :
A. Both (A) and (R) are true.
B. Both (A) and (R) are false.
C. (A) is true, but (R) is false.
D. (A) is false, but (R) is true.

13. The equilibrium level of output for a perfect competitive firm is given by the point where :
A. MR = MC

B. MR < MC
C. MR > MC
D. MR = MC and MC starts rising

14. Match the following :

List-I	List-II
(*i*) Dumping	(*a*) Monopolistic competitive firm
(*ii*) Kinked Revenue Curve	(*b*) Oligopoly firm
(*iii*) Horizontal straight line revenue curve	(*c*) Perfectively competitive firm
(*iv*) Large number of buyers and sellers with differentiated products	(*d*) Discriminatory monopoly

Codes :

	(*i*)	(*ii*)	(*iii*)	(*iv*)
A.	(*a*)	(*d*)	(*c*)	(*b*)
B.	(*b*)	(*d*)	(*a*)	(*c*)
C.	(*d*)	(*b*)	(*c*)	(*a*)
D.	(*a*)	(*b*)	(*c*)	(*d*)

15. Penetrating pricing strategy is appropriate when
A. price elasticity of demand in the market is highly inelastic.
B. price elasticity of demand in the market is uncertain.
C. price elasticity of demand in the market is highly elastic.
D. income elasticity of demand in the market is negatively elastic.

16. Assertion (A) : The expected values should be atleast 5 to apply the chi-square test.

Reason (R) : The chi-square distribution provides an adequate approximation of the sampling distribution.

Indicate the correct answer from the following :

Codes :
A. Both (A) and (R) are true, and (R) is the right explanation.
B. Both (A) and (R) are true, but (R) is not the correct explanation.
C. (A) is true, but (R) is false.
D. (A) is false, but (R) is true.

17. In a decision problem having four possible alternative decisions and six possible states of nature, the pay-off table will include
A. Four payoffs
B. Six payoffs
C. Twenty four payoff
D. Ten payoff

18. The mathematical formula for joint probabilities P(AB) = P(A/B) × P(B), holds when
A. The events are statistically independent.
B. The events are statistically dependent.
C. The event is either independent or dependent.
D. None of the above

19. Which one of the following statements is the correct interpretation of P-value of less than 0.01 in hypothesis testing?
A. There is *overwhelming* evidence to infer that the alternative hypothesis is true.
B. There is *strong* evidence to infer that the alternative hypothesis is true.
C. There is *weak* evidence to indicate that the alternative hypothesis is true.
D. There is *no* evidence to infer that the alternative hypothesis is true.

20. Two lists of items are given below :

List-I	List-II
(*i*) Charles Babbage	(*a*) Mossai
(*ii*) Herbert A. Simon	(*b*) HTML
(*iii*) Tim Berners Lee	(*c*) Computer Design
(*iv*) Maarc Andreessen	(*d*) Decision model

Which one of the following is the correct match?

Codes :

	(*i*)	(*ii*)	(*iii*)	(*iv*)
A.	(*c*)	(*b*)	(*a*)	(*d*)
B.	(*a*)	(*c*)	(*d*)	(*b*)
C.	(*b*)	(*a*)	(*c*)	(*d*)
D.	(*c*)	(*d*)	(*b*)	(*a*)

21. Which of the following statements are true about informal organization?
1. It arises spontaneously.
2. It reflects individual and group goals.
3. It tends to be permanent and stable.
4. It tends to be small and manageable.
5. Its basic purpose is to improve human relations.

6. Its basic purpose is to achieve organisation's goals.

Codes :

A. 1, 2, 3 and 5 B. 1, 2, 4 and 6
C. 1, 2, 4 and 5 D. 2, 3, 5 and 6

22. Which of the following is ***not*** true about an employee-centered leader as identified by Michigan researchers?

A. Treats subordinates as human beings.
B. Shows concern for their well being.
C. Focuses on work standards and close supervision.
D. Encourages and involves them in goal setting.

23. According to Talcott Parson, organizations can be classified primarily into four categories, based on functions. Which of the following is not an organization in Parson's scheme?

A. Political organisations
B. Integrative organisations
C. Pattern maintenance organisations
D. Commercial organisations

24. An MBO programme usually involves the following steps :

1. Establishing unit's objectives
2. Establishing organisational goals
3. Negotiating or agreeing
4. Reviewing the performance
5. Creating action plans

Indicate the correct sequence of the above steps from the following codes :

A. 1, 2, 3, 4, 5 B. 2, 1, 3, 5, 4
C. 2, 3, 1, 4, 5 D. 5, 4, 3, 2, 1

25. Match the following :

List-I	List-II
(*a*) Fayol	(1) Economy and Society
(*b*) Taylor	(2) General and Industrial Administration
(*c*) Weber	(3) Principles of Organization
(*d*) Mooney and Reilly	(4) Shop Management

Codes :

	(*a*)	(*b*)	(*c*)	(*d*)
A.	(3)	(4)	(1)	(2)
B.	(2)	(4)	(1)	(3)
C.	(1)	(3)	(2)	(4)
D.	(4)	(3)	(2)	(1)

26. A primary group influencing the buyer behaviour is a

A. Family
B. Professional association
C. Religious group
D. Trade Union

27. After conducting the business analysis for developing a new product, a company must do

A. Idea generation
B. Product positioning
C. Product development and testing
D. Test marketing

28. Match the items in List-I with those in List-II :

List-I	List-II
(*a*) Post purchase behaviour	(*i*) AIDA
(*b*) Personal selling	(*ii*) ACMEE
(*c*) Everitt M. Rogers	(*iii*) Diffusion of Innovation
(*d*) Salesperson training	(*iv*) Cognitive dissonance

Indicate the correct matching :

Codes :

	(*a*)	(*b*)	(*c*)	(*d*)
A.	(*i*)	(*ii*)	(*iii*)	(*iv*)
B.	(*iv*)	(*ii*)	(*iii*)	(*i*)
C.	(*iii*)	(*ii*)	(*i*)	(*iv*)
D.	(*iv*)	(*i*)	(*iii*)	(*ii*)

29. Which type of retail stores generally has the highest operating costs?

A. Department store
B. Supermarket
C. Chain store
D. Co-operative Store

30. Indicate the correct statement :

A. India has been a pioneer in social marketing.
B. Advertising Standards Council of India is a statutory body set up by the government of India.
C. Both A and B are incorrect.
D. Both A and B are correct.

31. Match the items of List-I with the items of List-II :

List-I	List-II
(a) Trade credit and other payables that arise in the firm's day-to-day operations	(i) Maturity Financing
(b) Financing and asset needs over time	(ii) Factoring
(c) A tool for accelerating the collection from the customers	(iii) Spontaneous financing
(d) Seeking financial service to finance on its debtors' balances	(iv) Lockbox system

Codes:

	(a)	(b)	(c)	(d)
A.	(iv)	(iii)	(ii)	(i)
B.	(iii)	(ii)	(iv)	(i)
C.	(ii)	(iv)	(i)	(iii)
D.	(i)	(ii)	(iii)	(iv)

32. Indicate the cost of equity capital, based on capital asset pricing model, with the following information :

Beta coefficient – 1.40

Risk-free rate of interest – 9%

Expected Rate of Return on equity in the market – 16%

A. 9.8% B. 18%

C. 18.8% D. 16%

33. The degree of super-leverage would be calculated by :

A. Adding DOL (Degree of Operating Leverage) and DFL (Degree of Financial Leverage)
B. Dividing DOL with DFL
C. Multiplying DOL and DFL
D. Subtracting DOL from DFL

34. Interim cash inflows are reinvested at a rate of return equal to the internal rate of return is the built-inmechanism for

A. Net Present Value Method
B. Internal Rate of Return Method
C. Profitability Index Method
D. None of the above

35. Who formulated the following model for estimating the market price of equity share?

$$P = \frac{D + \frac{R_a}{R_c}(E - D)}{R_c}$$

Where, P = Market price of equity share

D = DPS

E = EPS

E – D = Retained earning per share

R_a = Internal rate of return on investment

R_c = Cost of capital

A. Modigliani-Miller
B. Myron-Gordon
C. James E. Walter
D. Clarkson and Elliot

36. Indicate the quantitative methods of job evaluation

A. Ranking methods and Job comparison method
B. Point rating method and Factor comparison method
C. Grading method and Job classification method
D. Factor comparison method and Ranking method

37. Match the items of List-I with those List-II :

List-I	List-II
(1) Career goals	(a) The process where in an executive serves as a guide
(2) Career path	(b) The future positions one strives to reach as part of career
(3) Career counselling	(c) The sequential pattern of jobs that form a career
(4) Mentoring	(d) Guiding people on their possible career path

Codes:

	(1)	(2)	(3)	(4)
A.	(b)	(c)	(d)	(a)
B.	(a)	(b)	(c)	(d)
C.	(d)	(c)	(b)	(a)
D.	(c)	(b)	(a)	(d)

38. The process of receiving and welcoming an employee when he first joins a company and giving him the basic information he needs to settle down quickly and happily and starts working, is referred to as

A. Placement B. Orientation
C. Job Rotation D. Counselling

39. Which is ***not*** relevant of succession planning?

A. Analysis of the demand for managers
B. Review of existing executives
C. Planning individuals career paths
D. Recruitment to meet immediate needs

40. Where does recognition of an Employee fall in Maslow's hierarchy of needs theory?

A. Self-actualisation B. Security needs
C. Social needs D. Esteem needs

41. The profitability of public-sector banks is low due to

(*i*) Over-cautions approach to lending
(*ii*) Reserve Bank Policies
(*iii*) High Overhead Costs
(*iv*) Social-sector lending

Identify the correct code :

Codes :

A. (*i*) and (*ii*) B. (*i*) and (*iv*)
C. (*i*), (*iii*) and (*iv*) D. (*ii*) and (*iii*)

42. Match the items of List-I with those List-II and select correct answer :

List-I	List-II
(1) Narasimham Committee	(*a*) Lending under consortium arrangement
(2) Shetty Committee	(*b*) Frauds and Malpractices in banks
(3) Ghosh Committee	(*c*) Securities operations of banks and financial institutions
(4) Janakiraman Committee	(*d*) Financial system in India

Codes :

	(*a*)	(*b*)	(*c*)	(*d*)
A.	(3)	(4)	(2)	(1)
B.	(2)	(3)	(4)	(1)
C.	(4)	(2)	(3)	(1)
D.	(3)	(4)	(1)	(2)

43. Which of the following financial institutions is ***not*** with in the supervisory Purview of Reserve Bank of India ?

A. Foreign Commercial Banks Operating in India
B. Regional Rural Banks
C. Mutual Funds
D. State Co-operative Banks

44. The Repo and Reserve Repo rates are resorted to by the RBI as a tool of

A. Credit Control
B. Settlement Systems
C. Currency Management
D. Liquidity Control

45. Which one of the following institutions is promoted by the IFCI :

A. Credit Analysis and Research Ltd. (CARE)
B. Rashtriya Gramin Vikas Nidhi (RGVN)
C. Clearing Corporation of India Ltd. (CCIL)
D. Small Industries Development Bank of India (SIDBI)

46. Indicate the right sequence of the stages of internationalization :

(*i*) Multinational Company
(*ii*) Global Company
(*iii*) Transnational Company
(*iv*) International Company

Codes :

A. (*i*) (*iv*) (*ii*) (*iii*)
B. (*iv*) (*i*) (*iii*) (*ii*)
C. (*i*) (*iv*) (*iii*) (*ii*)
D. (*iv*) (*i*) (*ii*) (*iii*)

47. Which of the following is ***not*** one of the components of 'International Reserve'?

A. Special Drawing Rights
B. Reserve Position in IMF
C. Monetary Gold
D. Money Market Instruments

48. Match the items given in List-I with the most appropriate items in List-II :

List-I	List-II
(*a*) UNCTAD	(*i*) Foreign investment
(*b*) WTO	(*ii*) Developing Countries
(*c*) TRIMS	(*iii*) UNDP
(*d*) ITC	(*iv*) General Council

Codes :

	(*a*)	(*b*)	(*c*)	(*d*)
A.	(*ii*)	(*iv*)	(*i*)	(*iii*)
B.	(*iii*)	(*iv*)	(*i*)	(*ii*)
C.	(*iv*)	(*ii*)	(*i*)	(*iii*)
D.	(*iii*)	(*ii*)	(*i*)	(*iv*)

49. Duty levied on the value of goods imported is referred to as

A. Ad valorem Duty B. Compound Duty

C. Specific Duty D. Import Duty

50. Which of the following can be included in the current account of the balance of payments?

(*i*) Purchase of goods from abroad

(*ii*) Sale of services abroad

(*iii*) Workers' remittances from abroad

(*iv*) Sale of copyright to foreigners

(*v*) Direct investment in equity capital

Codes :

A. (*i*), (*ii*) and (*iii*)

B. (*i*), (*ii*) and (*iv*)

C. (*i*), (*ii*), (*iii*) and (*v*)

D. (*i*), (*ii*), (*iii*) and (*iv*)

51. Which of the following items would be specifically included in the statement of cash flows constructed in compliance with AS-3?

A. Conversion of debt to equity

B. Acquiring an asset through lease

C. Operating and non-operating cash flow information

D. Purchasing a building by giving a mortgage to the seller

52. Fixing the value of an employee depending upon his productivity, promotability, transferability and retainability is the core of the

A. Certainty equivalent model

B. Stochastic Reward Valuation model

C. Human asset multiplier model

D. Present value of future earnings model

53. Which of the following refers to a situation in which the merger of companies results in over 25% of the market in the hands of the merged companies?

A. 'Gateway' condition

B. Restrictive practice

C. 'Share of supply' test

D. 'Asset' test

54. Which of the following is true?

A. Systematic risk is diversifiable but unsystematic risk is non-diversifiable.

B. Systematic risk is non-diversifiable but unsystematic risk is diversifiable.

C. Both systematic and unsystematic risks are diversifiable.

D. Both systematic and unsystematic risks are non-diversifiable.

55. Match the following :

List-I (Explanation)	**List-II (Term)**
(*a*) It involves using the version of master file and the update transactions used to create the current file to recreate the current master file if it becomes damaged.	(1) Audit Trail Controls
(*b*) It involves copying the whole or a portion of the data-base to some back up medium, typically magnetics tape.	(2) Dumping
(*c*) It stores current and historical data extracted from various operations systems and consolidates for management reporting and analysis.	(3) Grandfather, Father, Son
(*d*) It maintains the chronology of events that occur either to the database definition or the database itself.	(4) Data warehouse for Accounting

Codes :

	(a)	(b)	(c)	(d)
A.	(3)	(2)	(4)	(1)
B.	(3)	(1)	(2)	(4)
C.	(1)	(3)	(2)	(4)
D.	(4)	(3)	(2)	(1)

56. Which one is ***not*** a major component of holistic marketing?
A. Relationship marketing
B. Integrated marketing
C. Internal marketing
D. Socially responsible marketing

57. The final step in target marketing is
A. Market Analysis
B. Market Positioning
C. Market Segmentation
D. Market Targeting

58. The most recent consideration in product packaging is
A. Cost effectiveness
B. Product protection
C. Product promotion
D. Economy

59. Distribution logistics (also termed as 'market logistics') does not include
A. Distribution channel
B. Inventory
C. Transportation
D. Warehouses

60. Most of the money spent in measuring the effectiveness of advertising is spent on
A. Communication-response research
B. Pre-testing the advertisements
C. Post-testing the advertisements
D. Sales-response research

61. Which of the following is ***not*** included in the model of the systems approach to human resource management?
A. Departmentation
B. Recruitment
C. Performance Appraisal
D. Promotion

62. Which one of the following is ***not*** an example of Herzberg's hygiene factors?
A. Advancement
B. Interpersonal relations
C. Job security
D. Work conditions

63. Which of the following two forms of collective bargaining were identified by Chamberlain and Kuhn?
A. Integrative Bargaining and Distributive Bargaining
B. Conjunctive Bargaining and Cooperative Bargaining
C. Integrative Bargaining and Cooperative Bargaining
D. Distributive Bargaining and Conjunctive Bargaining

64. Who observed that a worker's behaviour and sentiments are closely related?
A. Peter Drucker B. Elton Mayo
C. F.W. Taylor D. Dale Yoder

65. What is ***not*** an operative function of HRM?
A. Procurement B. Development
C. Organising D. Integration

66. The total number of Special Economic Zones notified by the Government of India till March 2011 under the SEZ Act, 2005 is
A. 154 B. 184
C. 286 D. 386

67. The different forms of IMF assistance are given below. Identify the one which is mainly meant for Less Developed Countries (LDCs)
A. Credit Tranche Drawing
B. Extended Fund Facility
C. Compensatory Financing Facility
D. Structural Adjustment Facility

68. In the context of globalization, 'Levitt Thesis' means
A. Standardisation strategy to respond to the worldwide homogenised market and expand the market through aggressive low pricing
B. Customise products to regional markets

C. Customise products to meet the national market

D. None of the above

69. Which one of the following is an internal hedging technique?

A. Leading

B. Netting

C. Both A and B above

D. Swap

70. Business conglomerates have different names in different countries. Which country's conglomerates are called 'Chaebols'?

A. Japan B. South Korea

C. Germany D. China

71. Mr. X, a non-resident, earned ₹ 36,000 as interest on German Development Bonds. Of this, he received one-sixth in India. The amount to be included as interest for the computation of his Gross Total Income is

A. ₹ 36,000 B. ₹ 30,000

C. ₹ 6,000 D. Nil

72. Consider the following problem relating to a let-out house property :

Municipal value – ₹ 60,000

Fair rent – ₹ 68,000

Standard rent under the Rent Control Act – ₹ 62,000

Annual Rent received – ₹ 65,000

The Gross Annual Value of the property will be

A. ₹ 68,000 B. ₹ 62,000

C. ₹ 65,000 D. ₹ 60,000

73. From the following, identify by the web-based financial software :

A. Private Equity Software

B. Share Accounting Software

C. Wealth Management Software

D. WINGS 2013

74. Which of the following are true in tax planning?

(*i*) It is futuristic in its approach.

(*ii*) It has limited scope compared to tax management.

(*iii*) The benefits arising from it are limited particularly in the short run.

(*iv*) Its main objective is to reduce the tax liability.

Codes :

A. (*i*), (*ii*) and (*iii*) B. (*i*) and (*ii*)

C. (*i*) and (*iv*) D. (*ii*), (*iii*) and (*iv*)

75. The benefits of debt financing over equity financing are likely to be highest in which of the following situations?

A. High marginal tax rates and low non-interest tax benefits

B. Low marginal tax rates and low non-interest tax benefits

C. High marginal tax rates and high non-interest tax benefits

D. Low marginal tax rates and high non-interest tax benefits.

ANSWERS

1	2	3	4	5	6	7	8	9	10
D	C	B	C	D	D	D	B	B	B
11	**12**	**13**	**14**	**15**	**16**	**17**	**18**	**19**	**20**
A	A	D	C	C	A	C	B	A	D
21	**22**	**23**	**24**	**25**	**26**	**27**	**28**	**29**	**30**
C	C	D	B	B	A	C	D	A	A
31	**32**	**33**	**34**	**35**	**36**	**37**	**38**	**39**	**40**
C	C	C	B	C	B	A	B	D	D
41	**42**	**43**	**44**	**45**	**46**	**47**	**48**	**49**	**50**
C	B	C	D	B	D	D	A	A	A

51	52	53	54	55	56	57	58	59	60
C	B	C	B	A	C	B	C	A	B
61	**62**	**63**	**64**	**65**	**66**	**67**	**68**	**69**	**70**
A	A	B	B	C	D	C	A	C	B
71	**72**	**73**	**74**	**75**					
C	C	D	C	A					

SOME SELECTED EXPLANATORY ANSWERS

1. The new competition law formulated by Competition Commission of India (CCI) called the *Competition Act* was enacted in the year 2002 to replace the Monopolies and Restrictive Trade Practices (MRTP) Act of 1969. The Competition Act 2002 seeks to prohibit anti-competitive agreements, abuse of dominant positions, and regulate mergers and acquisitions. The Act defines a *combination* as any merger or acquisition in which the firms' combined assets or turnover exceeds ₹ 1,000 crore (approximately $250 million) and ₹ 3,000 crore (approximately $750 million), respectively, in India or $500 million and $1,500 million, respectively, worldwide. M&As that fall below these thresholds are not considered combinations and are outside the ambit of the Act.

3. Section 24A provides period within which the complaint must be filed before the Consumer Fora. This Section 24A, a new provision has been inserted by the Consumer Protection (Amendment) Act, 1993, w.e.f. 18-6-93.

S. 24A provides:

The District Forum, the State Commission or the National Commission shall not admit a complaint unless it is filed within two years from the date on which the cause of action has arisen.

6. Prudence concept: This deals with "exercising caution in an uncertainty situation" on the values of assets and liabilities.

- It states that profit should be recognised when it is reasonably certain that it can be earned e.g. when sale activities are completed and losses should be recognised as soon as it anticipated.
- It's also implies that, where there are two possible values available, great caution should be taken not to understate or overstate the assets and liabilities.

8. Suppose selling price per unit is Re. 1 and units sold are 100.

	Present Position	**After reduction of 10% in selling price**
	₹	₹
Sales	100	90
Less: Variable cost	60	60
Contribution	40	30
Total sales in order to offset decrease in selling price		—
$\frac{\text{Sales} \times \text{Present Contribution}}{\text{New Contribution}}$ % Increase in Sales		$\frac{90}{30} \times 40$ = ₹ 120 = 20%

9. Gearing is the relationship between an entity's debt capital and equity capital. It is calculated as follows:

Net debt divided by enterprise value, that is,

$$\frac{D}{D+E}$$

Net debt is calculated as total debt less the amount of cash and cash equivalents in the balance sheet. For example, if debt is ₹ 220, cash balance is ₹ 20 and equity is ₹ 300, gearing is

$$\frac{220-20}{200+300} \text{ or } 40\%.$$

10. Responsibility accounting is one of the systems of control. It is related with fixing responsibilities on executives of the undertaking on the basis of objectives of the organisation. Under this system, costs are assigned to responsibility centres rather than to product. It is a method of measuring the performance of various divisions of an organisation. Responsibility accounting requires that each executive should be held responsible for the activities which are under his/her control. Such a policy is highly useful in making planning and control more effective.

13. Marginal Revenue–Marginal Cost Approach: According to this approach, producer strikes his equilibrium when two conditions are satisfied:

(*i*) MR = MC, and

(*ii*) MC is rising (or MC curve cuts MR curve from below).

17. Payoff: A numerical value resulting from each possible combination of alternatives and states of nature is called payoff. The payoff values are always conditional values because of unknown states of nature.

A tabular arrangement of these conditional outcome (payoff) values is known as *payoff matrix*, as shown in given Table.

General Form of Payoff Matrix

States of Nature	*Courses of Action (Alternatives)*			
	S_1	S_2	...	S_n
N_1	p_{11}	p_{12}	...	p_{1n}
N_2	p_{21}	p_{22}	...	p_{2n}
⋮	⋮	⋮		⋮
N_n	p_{n1}	p_{n2}	...	p_{nn}

18. If events A and B are not statistically independent but are statistically *dependent* events, the joint probability of both A and B occurring is

$$P(AB) = P(A) \times P(B|A)$$

or $P(B) \times P(A|B)$

joint probability both A and B occur = simple probability one event occurs × conditional probability the other will occur given occurrence of the first event

23. According to Talcott Parsons, organizations can be classified primarily into four categories based on functions:

(*a*) *Economic organizations:* Economic organizations are primarily concerned with producing something of value to the society. They are wedded to a philosophy of generating surplus/profit. Industrial, commercial and trading concerns are included in this category.

(*b*) *Political organizations:* Political organizations survive on the basis of service to society. They help in achieving the basic values cherished by the society. They collect resources from the society, employ them judiciously and help in maintaining peace and stability in the society. All governmental agencies are included in this category.

(*c*) *Integrative organizations:* Integrative organizations are concerned with social control and maintenance. Police departments and other protective organizations (courts, etc.), are included in this category.

(*d*) *Pattern maintenance organizations:* Pattern maintenance organizations like educational institutions, research institutions, religious organizations, clubs, etc., are primarily concerned with long-term interests of society (culture, knowledge, values etc).

27. Steps in Developing New Products: The process of developing a new product consists of seven phases:

1. Idea generation
2. Screening
3. Concept testing
4. Business analysis
5. Product development
6. Test marketing
7. Commercialization

32. Cost of Equity Capital = Risk free rate of Interest + Beta Coefficient (Expected Rate of Return – Risk free rate of Interest)

= 9 + 1.40 (16 – 9)

= 9 + 1.40 (7) = 18.8%.

36.

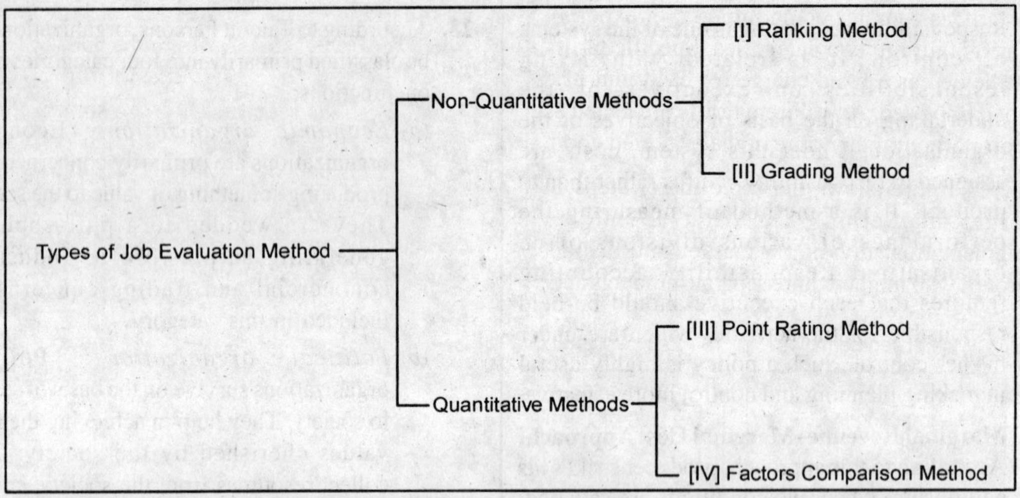

39. A typical succession planning involves the following activities:

1. Analysis of the demand for managers and professionals by company level, function, and skill.
2. Audit of existing executives and projection of likely future supply from internal and external sources.
3. Planning of individual career paths based on objective estimates of future needs, and drawing on reliable performance appraisals and assessments of potential.
4. Career counselling undertaken in the context of a realistic understanding of the future needs of the firm, as well as those of the individual.
5. Accelerated promotions, with development targeted against the future needs of the business.
6. Performance-related training and development, to prepare individuals for future roles as well as current responsibilities.
7. Planned strategic recruitment, not only to fill short-term needs but also to provide people for development to meet future needs.
8. The actual activities by which openings are filled.

44. Repo/ready forward/repurchase (buy-back) transaction/deal is an agreement between a seller and a buyer stipulating the sale and later repurchase of securities at a particular price and date. It is essentially a short-term loan to the seller with securities issued as collateral. Similarly, the buyer purchases the securities with an agreement to sell the same back to the seller on an agreed date in future, at a prefixed price. For the buyer of the securities, it becomes a reserve repo deal or a buy-back arrangement. In a standard ready forward transaction (repo) when a bank, for instance, sells securities to, say, a mutual fund, it simultaneously enters into a contract with the latter to repurchase them at a predetermined date and price in the future. Both sale and repurchase prices are determined prior to entering into the deal. In return for the securities, the bank receives cash from the mutual fund, which can be used to meet temporary cash requirements. After the expiry of the repo period, the bank would buy back the securities from the mutual fund and return the cash.

46. Many labels have been attached to international business ventures over the years. They have been called international companies, multinational companies, global companies, and transnational companies.

49. A tariff is a tax levied on imports (or exports). Tariffs fall into two categories. Specific tariffs are levied as a fixed charge for each unit of a good imported. Ad valorem tariffs are levied as a proportion of the value of the imported good.

57. Given figure shows the three major steps in target marketing. The first is market segmentation, dividing a market into distinct groups who might require separate products and/or marketing mixes. The company identifies different ways to segment the market and develops profiles of the resulting market segments. The second step is market targeting, evaluating each segment's attractiveness and selecting one or more of the market segments. The third step is market positioning, developing competitive positioning for the product and an appropriate marketing mix.

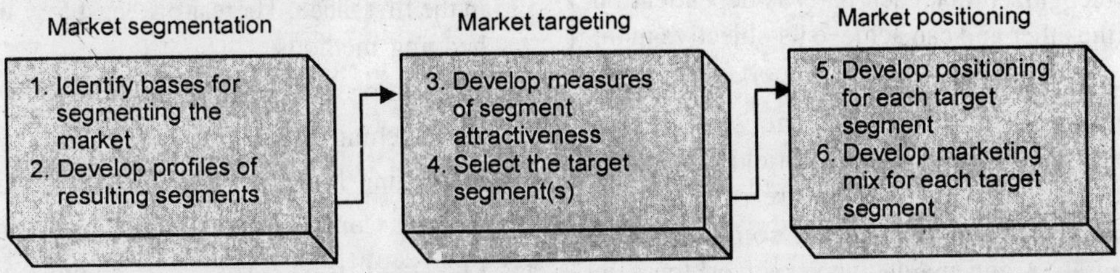

59. *Distribution logistics* primarily concerns sales processes that generally begin with a customer ordering materials and indicating a desired delivery date. Using this information, a sales order is generated. Depending on the delivery date, shipping activities are initiated such that the materials reach the customer in a timely manner. *Warehouse logistics* takes over the task of commissioning and material provision. As soon as the materials have left the warehouse, a goods issue is booked to update stock and inventory management values.

A carrier can be commissioned to deliver the materials. *Transport logistics,* in a cross-sectional function, takes on the task of booking the transport planning and the transport itself. At the end of the sales procedure, an invoice is produced for the customer. As soon as the customer has paid for the materials, payment receipt is recorded in Accounting.

62.

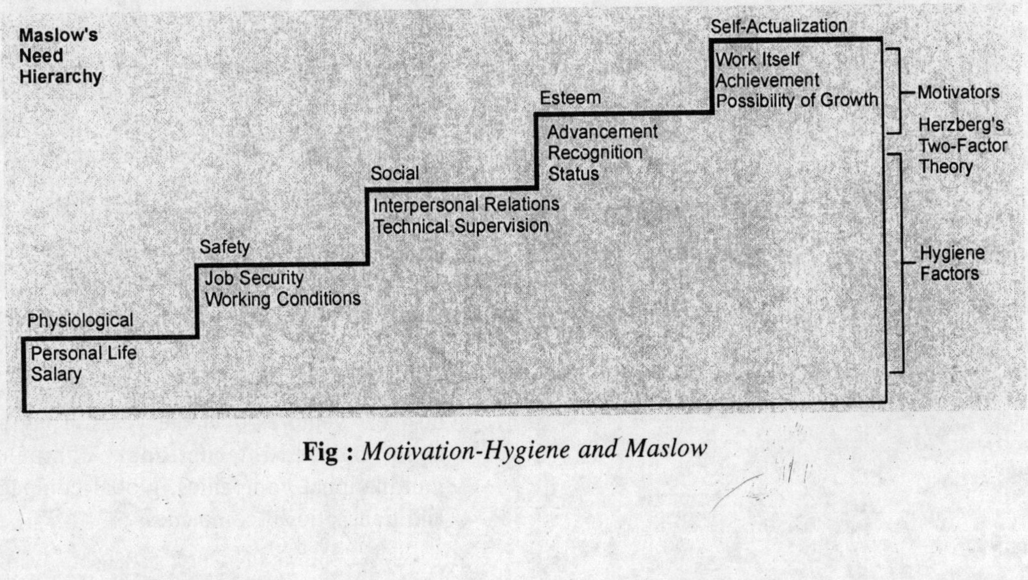

Fig : *Motivation-Hygiene and Maslow*

63. Forms of Collective Bargaining: It has two basic forms as identified by Chamberlain and Kuhn (1965):

- *Conjunctive bargaining,* which arises from the absolute requirement that some agreement be reached so that the operations on which these are dependent, may continue and result in a working relationship.
- *Cooperative bargaining* in which it is recognized that each party is dependent on the other and can achieve its objective more effectively if it wins the support of the other.

65. Operative functions are the specialised functions related to a specific field. In case of HRM, operative functions are related with procurement, development, compensation, integration and maintenance of workforce in the organisations. These functions are also known as "service functions" or "staff functions".

68. Levitt feels that standardisation can help expand the market. "When the global producer offers his lower costs internationally, his patronage expands exponentially. He not only reaches into distant markets, but also attracts customers who previously held to local preferences and now capitulate to the attractions of lesser prices. The strategy of standardisation not only responds to worldwide homogenised markets but also expands those markets with aggressive low pricing.

69. The internal hedging methods are the techniques which arises from the company. It is an integral part of company's regulatory treasury to prevent an exposed position arising in the first place. There are at least four internal hedging methods.

1. Leading and Lagging Method,
2. Matching Method,
3. Netting Method,
4. Inter-Company Foreign Exchange Contracts.

72. Municipal Value (MRV) — ₹ 60,000
Fair Rent (FRV) — ₹ 68,000
whichever is higher

FRV — ₹ 68,000
Standard Rent — ₹ 62,000
whichever is lower

Expected Rent Value — ₹ 62,000
Rent Received — ₹ 65,000
whichever is high

Therefore, the gross annual value = 65,000

Previous Paper (Solved)

UGC-JRF/NET & Lectureship Exam Commerce, December, 2013

PAPER-II

Note : *This paper contains* ***fifty (50)*** *objective type questions, each question carrying* ***two (2)*** *marks each. Attempt* ***all*** *the questions.*

1. Who is the fiscal agent and advisor to Government in monetary and financial matters?

A. NABARD B. SBI
C. RBI D. None of the above

2. Match the items of List–I with the items of List–II :

List–I	*List–II*
(*a*) National Manufacturing Competitiveness Council (NMCC)	1. Industrial Licensing Policy
(*b*) National Investment Fund (NIP)	2. Eleventh Five Year Plan
(*c*) The Industries (Development and Regulation) Act (IDRA), 1951	3. The Competition Act, 2002
(*d*) Increase in Employment	4. Public Sector Undertakings

Codes :

	(*a*)	(*b*)	(*c*)	(*d*)
A.	4	1	2	3
B.	3	4	1	2
C.	1	2	3	4
D.	4	3	2	1

3. Kyoto Protocol pertains to

A. Capital formulation
B. Globalisation
C. Environmental protection
D. Unemployment reduction

4. Uruguay Round pertains to

A. WTO B. IMF
C. GATT D. World Bank

5. Which of the following are outside the scope of the Consumer Protection Act, 1986?

A. Newspaper industry
B. Services provided under contract of personal service
C. Banking industry
D. Both **(A)** and (B)

6. Which of the following is 'true' regarding the Prudence Principle of Accounting?

A. Taking care of the future losses
B. Taking care of the future profits
C. Taking care of bad debts
D. Taking care of inventory and depreciation

7. Which of the following is a non-operating expense?

A. Salary of Managing Director
B. Depreciation
C. Advertisement expenditure
D. Interest on loan

8. A and B are partners sharing profits in the ratio of 3 : 2. Their books showed goodwill at ₹ 3,000. C is admitted with 1/4th share of profits and brings ₹ 10,000 as his capital. But he is not able to bring in cash for his share of goodwill ₹ 3,000. How will you treat this?

A. Goodwill is raised by ₹ 12,000
B. C will remain as debtor for ₹ 3,000
C. C's A/c is debited for ₹ 3,000
D. Goodwill is raised by ₹ 9,000

9. If there is mutual indebtedness between the transferor company and the transferee company in business combination, which of the following is correct?

A. No adjustment is required in the books of the transferor company.

B. Adjustment is required in the books of the transferor company.
C. No adjustment is required in the books of the transferee company.
D. None of the above

10. Improvement of profit-volume ratio can be done by
A. Increasing selling price
B. Altering sales mixture
C. Reducing variable cost
D. All of the above

11. Business Economics is a subject which
A. studies economic relationships
B. studies economic activities at the aggregate level
C. deals with the tools of economics used for decision-making in business
D. studies optimum allocation of limited resources

12. Match List–I with List–II and select the correct code for the answer :

List–I	***List–II***
(*a*) Cross elasticity is zero	1. Price = AVC
(*b*) Shut-down point	2. Two commodities are independent
(*c*) Slutsky theorem	3. Transformation line
(*d*) Production Possibility Curve	4. Substitution effect

Codes :

	(*a*)	(*b*)	(*c*)	(*d*)
A.	2	4	1	3
B.	3	2	4	1
C.	1	3	2	4
D.	2	1	4	3

13. Assertion (A) : The demand curve has negative slope showing inverse relationship between price and the quantity demanded.
Reason (R) : This applies only to Giffen goods.
Codes :
A. Both (A) and (R) are true.
B. (A) is true, but (R) is false.
C. (A) is false, but (R) is true.
D. Both (A) and (R) are false.

14. The consumer is said to be in equilibrium when he plans his expenditure on *x*, *y* and *z* commodities in such a way that he ultimately attains :
A. $MU_x = MU_y = M_z$
B. $\frac{MU_x}{P_x} = \frac{MU_y}{P_y} = \frac{MU_z}{P_z}$
C. $\frac{MU_x}{P_x} = \frac{MU_y}{P_y} = \frac{MU_z}{P_z} = MU_m$
D. $\frac{MU_x}{P_x} < \frac{MU_y}{P_y} < \frac{MU_z}{P_z} < MU_m$

15. Match the items in List–I with those in List–II and select the correct code for the answer :

List–I	***List–II***
(*a*) Monopoly	1. Price Taker
(*b*) Monopolistic competition	2. Homogeneous product's price maker
(*c*) Perfect competition	3. Heterogeneous product
(*d*) Oligopoly	4. Price Rigidity

Codes :

	(*a*)	(*b*)	(*c*)	(*d*)
A.	2	3	1	4
B.	1	2	4	3
C.	3	4	2	1
D.	4	1	3	2

16. Match the following items in List–I with most suitable options in List–II :

List–I	***List–II***
(*a*) Fisher	1. Inverse probability
(*b*) Karl Pearson	2. Normal Distribution
(*c*) Thomas Baye's	3. Correlation Coefficient
(*d*) Karl Gauss	4. Index Numbers

Codes :

	(*a*)	(*b*)	(*c*)	(*d*)
A.	4	3	2	1
B.	4	3	1	2
C.	4	2	3	1
D.	4	2	1	3

17. The law of statistics, which says 'Moderately large number of items chosen at random from a large group possess the characteristics of the large group', is referred to as :

A. The Central Limit Theorem
B. The Law of Statistical Regularity
C. The Law of Inertia of Large Numbers
D. None of the above

18. A distribution, where the value of arithmetic mean is maximum as compared to median and mode, is

A. Normal distribution
B. Positively-skewed distribution
C. Negatively-skewed distribution
D. None of these

19. The most appropriate average to be used to compute the average rate of growth in population is

A. Arithmetic mean B. Median
C. Geometric mean D. Harmonic mean

20. "The life expectancy of people in Kerala is more than that of Tamil Nadu." This statement is an example of

A. Descriptive Hypothesis
B. Causal Hypothesis
C. Correlational Hypothesis
D. None of the above

21. Match the items of List–I with the items of List–II and choose the correct answer :

List–I	***List–II***
(*a*) Intrapersonal communication	1. Information sharing
(*b*) Element of a communication event	2. Development of 'will' to work
(*c*) Objective of organisational communication	3. Thinking
(*d*) Goals of organisational communication	4. Purpose

Codes :

	(*a*)	(*b*)	(*c*)	(*d*)
A.	1	2	3	4
B.	3	4	2	1
C.	2	3	1	4
D.	4	3	2	1

22. According to the Boston Consulting Group, a business which has a high growth rate but a weak market share is referred to as a

A. Cash Cow B. Dog
C. Question Mark D. Star

23. 'No ideas are ever criticized' and 'the more radical the ideas are the better' – are the rules of which decision-making process?

A. Programmed decision-making
B. Non-programmed decision-making
C. Brainstorming
D. Group discussion

24. According to McClelland's Needs Theory, which of the following is not a motivating need?

A. Need for Power
B. Need for Security
C. Need for Achievement
D. Need for Affiliation

25. In the managerial grid, developed by Blake and Mouton, a manager who has high consideration for production but little concern for people is known as

A. 1.1 Management B. 1.9 Management
C. 9.1 Management D. 5.5 Management

26. Which of the following is *not* the major component of holistic marketing?

A. Relationship marketing
B. Integrated marketing
C. Customer satisfaction
D. Socially-responsible marketing

27. Which of the legislations listed below do not form part of the marketing environment of India?

A. The Drugs and Cosmetics Act, 1940
B. The Prevention of Food and Adulteration Act, 1954
C. The Monopolies and Restrictive Trade Practices Act, 1969
D. Both (B) and (C)

28. The set of all actual and potential buyers of a product is known as

A. Customer group B. Industry
C. Market D. None of the above

29. In the model of consumer behaviour given by Philip Kotler, what constitutes the marketing stimuli?

A. Marketing environment
B. Four P's of marketing
C. Consumer needs and wants
D. None of the above

30. The factor that exerts the broadest and deepest influence on consumer behaviour is

A. Culture
B. Sub-culture
C. Social class
D. Income

31. Which one of the following is not among the assumptions of the Modigliani-Miller model?

A. Perfect capital market
B. Equivalent risk classes
C. Unity for dividend payout ratio
D. Absence of taxes

32. The most suitable coverage ratio for deciding the debt capacity of a firm is

A. Interest Coverage Ratio
B. Cash Flow Coverage Ratio
C. Debt Service Coverage Ratio
D. Fixed Assets Coverage Ratio

33. Which one of the following is the most popular method for estimating the cost of equity?

A. Capital asset pricing model
B. Dividend yield method
C. Gordon's dividend discount model
D. Earnings yield method

34. Which one of the following is not the internal factor affecting the weighted average cost of capital of a firm?

A. Investment policy of the firm
B. Capital structure of the firm
C. Dividend policy followed
D. Market risk premium for the firm

35. Most common approach for analysing the capital structure of a firm is

A. Ratio Analysis
B. Cash Flow Analysis
C. Comparative Analysis
D. Leverage Analysis

36. Who propounded "Theory Z"?

A. William Ouchi
B. Peter F. Drucker
C. Joseph H. Jurau
D. Douglas McGregor

37. Another name for MATRIX organisation is

A. Flexible organisation
B. Geographic organisation
C. Project organisation
D. None of the above

38. Which of the following are methods of on-the-job training?

(*i*) Coaching
(*ii*) Vestibule training
(*iii*) Demonstration
(*iv*) Role-playing
(*v*) Apprenticeship training

Select the right answer from the following codes:

A. (*i*), (*ii*), (*iii*), (*iv*)
B. (*i*), (*iii*), (v)
C. (*ii*), (*iii*), (*iv*)
D. (*i*), (*ii*), (*iii*), (*iv*), (v)

39. The idea that a manager tends to be promoted to the level of his incompetence is referred to as

A. The advancement principle
B. The Parkinson's law
C. The Peter principle
D. The job design principle

40. **Assertion (A) :** The emphasis in industrial psychology has shifted from the studies of the isolated individual and the physical environment to the consideration of motivation and morale.

Reason (R) : A motivated employee with a high morale will always give high productivity.

Codes :

A. Both (A) and (R) are correct, and (R) is the right explanation of (A).
B. Both (A) is correct, but (R) is not correct.
C. Both (A) and (R) are incorrect.
D. Both (A) and (R) are correct, but (R) is not the right explanation of (A).

41. Match the following items of List–I and List–II in terms of functions of commercial banks:

List–I	*List–II*
(*a*) Letter of reference	1. Advancing loans
(*b*) Sale of gold coins	2. Receiving deposits
(*c*) Recurring Account	3. Non-banking function
(*d*) Overdrafts	4. Agency function

Codes :

	(*a*)	(*b*)	(*c*)	(*d*)
A.	1	2	3	4
B.	4	3	2	1
C.	4	2	3	1
D.	1	3	2	4

42. Which of the following are included under representation functions of a bank?

(*i*) Payment of cheques and bills
(*ii*) Providing remittance facilities
(*iii*) Underwriting of securities
(*iv*) Advancing clean credit
(*v*) Allowing overdrafts on current account
(*vi*) Purchase and sale of securities

Codes :

A. (*i*), (*ii*), (*iii*) and (*iv*)
B. (*iii*), (*iv*), (*v*) and (*vi*)
C. (*i*), (*ii*), (*iii*) and (*vi*)
D. (*ii*), (*iii*), (*v*) and (*vi*)

43. Call money rate is applicable for a very short period to

A. Inter bank advances
B. Bank to Reserve Bank advances
C. Reserve Bank to Bank advances
D. Commercial Banks to Industrial Banks advances

44. Match the following List–I with List–II :

List–I (Name of Securities)	*List–II (Type of Securities)*
(*a*) Bonds of Land Development Banks	1. Semi-Government Securities
(*b*) Treasury Bills	2. First Order Securities
(*c*) Shares of a Public Ltd. Co.	3. Personal Securities

Codes :

	(*a*)	(*b*)	(*c*)
A.	1	2	3
B.	2	1	3
C.	3	2	1
D.	1	3	2

45. Reserve Bank of India controls the activities of some of the following banks in India:

(*i*) Commercial Banks
(*ii*) Cooperative Banks
(*iii*) Foreign Banks
(*iv*) Rural Banks

Codes :

A. (*i*), (*ii*) and (*iii*)
B. (*i*), (*iii*) and (*iv*)
C. (*ii*), (*iii*) and (*iv*)
D. (*i*), (*ii*), (*iii*) and (*iv*)

46. Match the following List–I with List–II and select the correct answer:

List–I	*List–II*
(*a*) Comparative Cost Theory of International Trade	1. Gottfried Haberler
(*b*) International Trade Theory of Opportunity Cost	2. J.S. Mill
(*c*) Factor Endowment Theory of International Trade	3. David Ricardo
(*d*) Doctrine of Reciprocal Demand	4. Hecksher-Ohlin

Codes :

	(*a*)	(*b*)	(*c*)	(*d*)
A.	3	2	4	1
B.	1	3	2	4
C.	3	1	4	2
D.	2	1	4	3

47. Identify the one, from the following, which is not a type of disequilibrium in the balance of payments of a country:

A. Cyclical disequilibrium
B. Secular disequilibrium
C. Structural disequilibrium
D. Sectoral disequilibrium

48. The participants who take advantage of different exchange rates in different markets are

A. Speculators B. Arbitrageurs
C. Hedgers D. Investors

49. Assertion (A) : The liability of the option buyer is limited in the currency options market.
Reason (R) : Option buyer need not exercise the option if the exchange rate is not favourable for him.

Codes :
A. (R) is correct and (A) is wrong.
B. (A) is correct and (R) is wrong.
C. Both (A) and (R) are correct.
D. Both (A) and (R) are wrong.

50. An MNC that maintains a balance between the home market and host market oriented policies is

A. Ethnocentric firm B. Polycentric firm
C. Geocentric firm D. None of the above

ANSWERS

1	2	3	4	5	6	7	8	9	10
C	B	C	C	B	A	D	D	A	D
11	**12**	**13**	**14**	**15**	**16**	**17**	**18**	**19**	**20**
C	D	B	C	A	B	B	B	C	C
21	**22**	**23**	**24**	**25**	**26**	**27**	**28**	**29**	**30**
B	C	C	B	C	C	D	C	B	A
31	**32**	**33**	**34**	**35**	**36**	**37**	**38**	**39**	**40**
C	B	A	D	C	A	C	B	C	B
41	**42**	**43**	**44**	**45**	**46**	**47**	**48**	**49**	**50**
B	C	A	A	D	C	D	B	C	C

SOME SELECTED EXPLANATORY ANSWERS

1. As government banker, the central bank conducts the banking accounts of government departments and enterprises. It gives short-term loans to government in anticipaion of collection of taxes or the raising of loans from the public. The central bank also makes extraordinary advances to government during depression, war or other national emergencies. It conducts transactions on behalf of the government involving the purchases or sales of foreign currencies. Besides these services, the central bank also performs various other services such as to act as the financial agent of the government. It acts generally as financial adviser to the government. It manages the national debt and gives the much-sought-after advice to the government on important matters of economic policy, such as the extent to which deficit financing may be resorted to by the government for accelerating economy's planned economic development without inflation, devaluation of the currency, foreign trade policy, etc. In India, the Reserve Bank of India has advised the Government of India on various important economic policy matters including the stability of prices, funding of the national debt, amount of deficit financing which the economy can absorb etc. during the past five decades.

3. The Kyoto Protocol is an historical agreement in that it was the first international agreement in which many of the the world's industrial nations concluded a verifiable agreement to reduce their emissions of six greenhouse gases in order to prevent global warming. The major feature of the Kyoto Protocol is that it sets binding targets for 37 industrialized countries and the European community for reducing emissions. These amount to an average of five per cent against 1990 levels over the five-year period 2008-2012. The Kyoto Protocol was adopted in Kyoto, Japan, on 11 December 1997 and entered into force on 16 February 2005. 184 Parties of the Convention have ratified its Protocol to date. It is an international agreement linked to the United Nations Framework Convention on Climate Change.

4. The Uruguay Round is the name given to the eighth round of international talks and agreements on economic issues undertaken by the General Agreement on Tariffs and Trade (GATT). The Uruguay Round of multilateral trade negotiations was initiated by the United States in 1985 and was formally launched in September 1986 at Punta del Este, Uruguay. The Round was launched at a time when significant structural shifts had occurred in most of the industrialised countries. The service industry had grown and was continuing to expand while at the same time communication technologies were revolutionised. It also came at a time when there was a certain degree of crisis in international agricultural markets (eg. declining agricultural export earnings and growing protectionism) and when major reconfiguration of global economic and political balance of forces was emerging.

5. As per section 2(1)(c), of the Consumer Protection Act, 1986, following may form the subject-matter of complaint:
- an unfair trade practice or a restrictive trade practice adopted by any trader;
- defect in the goods purchased;
- deficiency in service;
- over-charging of price;

In the context of the subject-matter of the present article, it is important to note two important definitions provided in the Act. "Service" [Section 2(1)(o)] has been defined in the Act to mean service of any description and includes the provision of facilities in connection with banking, financing, insurance, transport, processing, supply of electrical or other energy etc. but does not include the rendering of any service free of charge or under a contract of personal service.

As per section 2(1)(g), "deficiency" means any fault, imperfection, shortcoming or inadequacy in the quality, nature and manner of performance required to be maintained under any law or in pursuance of a contract or otherwise.

6. Prudence Principle: This principle is generally used in case of uncertainities in respect of some business incidents, economic events that may happen in future. According to this principle, all possible losses must be recognized but all possible incomes must not be taken into consideration until and unless they are realized. It has a drawback as it may be used to create secret reserve and thus financial statements may not state the true and fair view of state of affairs of business. Thus it should be applied caustiously.

For example : closing stock is valued at lower of cost or net realisable value or making the provision for doubtful debts and discount on debtors in anticipation of actual bad debts and discount.

7. Non-operating Expenses are incurred on activities which are not the main revenue producing activities. But these may be required for more effective, smooth functioning of the business, but still these are not necessary considering the nature of business activities.

Examples:
1. Loss by fire
2. Loss on sale of fixed assets (selling of fixed assets is not the main business activity)
3. Interest on loan taken, debentures (these are only for financing the business, but these are not main business activities themselves)
4. Bank charges
5. Dividends paid
6. Loss by theft, etc.

10. Profit volume ratio is the ratio of contribution denoting the difference between sales and variable cost. Since in the short term fixed cost does not change, Profit/volume ratio also measures the rate of change of profit due to change in the volume of sales. Thus Profit/ Volume ratio is expressed as Profit/Volume $= \frac{C}{S} = \frac{S-V}{S}$. It is influenced by sales and variable or marginal cost. If the sales price increases without corresponding increase in marginal cost the contribution increases and the Profit volume ratio improves. Similarly if the marginal cost is reduced with sale price remaining same Profit/Volume ratio improves. One fundamental property of Profit/Volume ratio is that it remains same at various levels of operation and thus break even points, required selling prices to maintain profits at various levels etc. can be easily calculated by suitable application of this ratio.

11. Managerial Economics (also called *Business Economics*), a subject first introduced by Joel Dean in 1951, is essentially concerned with the economic decisions of business managers. It is a branch of Economics that applies microeconomic analysis to specific business dicisions (i.e., Economics applied in business decision-making). Managerial Economics help managers to learn the economic principles which are relevant to decision-making in such areas as production, personnel, marketing and finance. A clear understanding of economic principles will help the manager in his activities. For example, XYZ Ltd. has limited financial, human, and physical resources. XYZ Ltd. managers seek to maximize the financial return from these limited resources. They should apply Managerial Economics to develop pricing and advertising strategies, design their organizations, and manage purchasing.

13. A good for which demand increases as the price increases, and falls when the price decreases. A Giffen good has an upward-sloping demand curve, which is contrary to the fundamental law of demand which states that quantity demanded for a product falls as the price increases, resulting in a downward slope for the demand curve. A Giffen good is typically an inferior product that does not have easily available substitutes, as a result of which the income effect dominates the substitution effect. Giffen goods are quite rare, to the extent that there is some debate about their actual existence. The term is named after the economist Robert Giffen.

14. When a consumer spends his fixed income on more than one commodity, he compares the marginal utilities of different commodities with a view to getting maximum satisfaction. He spends a unit of money on that commodity which gives him more marginal utility. He will compare the marginal utility of different commodities that he gets in return for each unit (one rupee) of money. He will spend his money on the commodity which yields him maximum marginal utility. But according to law of diminishing marginal utility, as a consumer buys more and more units of a commodity, its marginal utility goes on diminishing. The consumer stops the purchase of a commodity when its marginal utility becomes less than the marginal utility of another commodity. He will then shift his purchase to the other commodity. In this way, the consumer goes on substituting goods giving more marginal utility for the goods giving less marginal utility. Finally, he arrives at a situation where the last unit of money spent on different commodities yields him equal marginal utility. This will be the position of his equilibrium. Since marginal utility of money is assumed to be constant, it can also be stated that in equilibrium marginal utility of each commodity will be equal to marginal utility of money. That is,

$MU_x = MU_y =$ MU of money

$$\frac{MU_x}{P_x} = \frac{MU_y}{P_y} = \frac{MU_z}{P_z} = MU_m$$

In short, consumer's equilibrium requires that,

a consumer's money income should be spent so that the last rupee spent on each good purchased yields the same amount of marginal utility.

17. **Theoretical basis of Sampling:** There are two important laws which determine the possibility of reaching valid conclusions about a population on the basis of sample study. These two laws are :

1. Law of Statistical Regularity
2. Law of 'Inertia of Large Numbers'.

Law of Statistical Regularity: The law of statistical regulatory is based on the mathematical theory of probability. According to King, 'The law of statistical regularity lays down that a moderately large number of items chosen at random from a large group are almost sure on the average to possess the characteristics of the large group'.

Law of 'Inertia of Large Numbers' : 'Law of Inertia of large numbers' is a corollary of the law the **law of statistical regularity** and plays a vital role in theory of sampling. The law states that samples of larger size show higher degree of stability. Thus, greater is the size of the sample, more accurate and stable the results are likely to be.

18. **Comparison among Mean, Median and Mode :**

1. A distribution in which the values of mean, median and mode coincide, i.e., mean = median = mode, is known as symmetrical distribution.
2. For a moderately asymmetrical distribution, the location of mean, median and mode do not coincide. In case of positively skewed curve the mean will have the highest value, the mode the lowest and the median will be about one-third the distance from the mean towards the mode. On the other hand, for a negatively skewed curve, mean will be the lowest, mode would be the largest and median would be approximately at the one-third distance from mean towards mode.

The empirical relationship for moderately skewed distribution may be put in the form of formula given below–

Mode = 3 median – 2 mean.

19. **Applications of Geometric Mean**

1. **Useful in Index Numbers :** Geometric mean is extensively used in index numbers, since it measures relative change.
2. **Useful in a Series of Geometric Progression :** Geometric mean provides a satisfactory measure of the economic phenomena which grew at geometric progression, like population, compound interest rate, etc.
3. **Average Rate of Growth :** Geometric mean is used to find the average rate of growth. The average rate of growth can be determined by using the following formula, which is called as *compound interest formula*, i.e.,

$$P_n = P_0(1+r)^n \quad \text{or} \quad r = n\sqrt{\frac{P_n}{P_0}} - 1$$

(where P_n = value in period 'n' value in period zero or in the beginning. r = rate of growth; n = number of years.) This formula is used to find any one of the four values P_n, P_0, r and n, if other three are given.

20. Correlational relationships state merely that the variables occur together in some specified manner without implying that one causes the other.

22. The Boston consulting Group matrix (at right) consists of four cells in a 2 × 2 configuration, which allows plotting of the stages of a business's products. The four cells are:

- The top right-hand cell relates to queries or question marks. These are relatively weak in a fast growing market, that is, they have high growth, but low market share. Frequently they are promising new products that have yet to establish themselves fully in the market. At this point in the cycle the products are vulnerable to competition and are carrying a high initialisation cost overhead.
- The top left-hand cell relates to stars. These are the top performers, product leaders in a fast growing market, with high market

share and high growth, that contribute significantly to the profitiability of the business.

- The bottom left-hand cell relates to the cash cows. These are leading products with high but static market share, that generate a high cash flow. Their initialisation costs have all been amortised, and the products are established and reliable. They are a source of internal funds for developing new products and supporting them into the market.
- The bottom right-hand cell contains the dogs. These are low volume, no growth, low market share products, with little or no contribution to profitability.

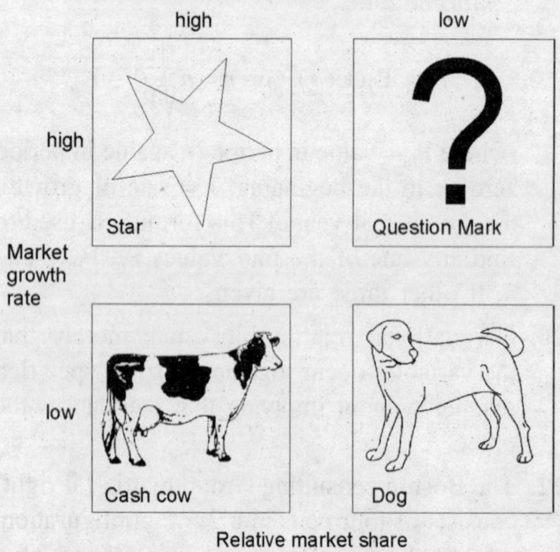

23. Brainstorming: This technique was developed by Alex F. Osborn who is fondly known as the father of brainstorming. The purpose of this approach is to improve solving by finding new and unusual solutions. In the Brainstorming session, a multiplication of ideas is sought. The rules are as follows:

1. No ideas are ever criticized.
2. The more radical the ideas are the better.
3. The quantity of idea production is stressed.
4. The improvement of ideas by others is encouraged.

Brainstorming, which emphasizes group thinking, was widely accepted in business circles.

24. McClelland's Achievement Theory of Motivation

- Harward Psychologist David C. McClelland proposed achievement theory of motivation. This theory is also known as acquired-needs theory.
- McClelland's achievement theory states that our needs are acquired or learned on the basis of our life experiences.
- He proposed three major needs or motives that motivate human behaviour.
- He measures these needs using the Thematic Appreciation Test (TAT), in which participant write stories about pictures that are purposely ambiguous. The stories are then scored according to the achievement, affiliation and power themes that they contain. The assumption is that individuals write about themes that the important to them.

According to him these three needs are:

(*i*) Need for achievement (nAch)
(*ii*) Need for affiliation (nAff) and
(*iii*) Need for power (nPow)

McClelland feels that every individual wants all the above three needs in work place but the individuals differ in behaviour and motivation.

25. The managerial grid theory suggests that managers combine two styles simultaneously, but in differing proportions. One style is job- or task-centred. The other style is employee-centred. The managerial grid developed by Blake and Mouton (1981) plots the two dimensions on a chart on scales 1 to 9. The vertical axis represents increasing concern for people, and the horizontal axis, an increasing concern for production. A manager rated at 1.1 is wholly ineffective. A manager at 1.9 has great concern for people, but is ineffective in achieving the task. A manager at 9.1 is task-driven with little concern for people. Managers at the midpoints (5.5) show balance. The ideal is 9.9, high regard for people, combined with optimum focus on results.

26. A holistic marketing concept is based on the development, design, and implementation of marketing programs, processes, and activities that recognize their breadth and interdependencies. Holistic marketing recognizes that 'everything matters' with marketing and that a broad, integrated perspective is necessary to attain the best solution. Four main components of holistic marketing are: relationship marketing, integrated marketing, internal marketing, and socially responsible marketing.

28. The concepts of exchange and relationships lead to the concept of a market. A market is the set of actual and potential buyers of a product. These buyers share a particular need or want that can be satisfied through exchange relationships.

29. Marketing stimuli consist of the Four Ps: products, price, place and promotion. Other stimuli include major forces and events in the buyer's environment: economic, technological, political, and cultural. All these inputs enter the buyer's black box, where they are turned into a set of observable buyer responses: product choice, brand choice, dealer choice, purchase timing, and purchase amount. The marketer wants to understand how the stimuli are changed into responses inside the consumer's black box, which has two parts.

Marketing and other stimuli	
Marketing	**Other**
Product	Economic
Price	Technological
Place	Political
Promotion	Cultural

↓

Buyer's black box
- Buyer characteristics
- Buyer decision process

↓

Buyer responses
- Product choice
- Brand choice
- Dealer choice
- Purchase timing
- Purchase amount

First, the buyer's characteristics influence how he or she perceives and reacts to the stimuli. Second, the buyer's decision process itself affects the buyer's behaviour. We look first at buyer characteristics as they affect buyer behaviour and then discuss the buyer decision process.

30. Consumer purchasers are influenced strongly by cultural, social, personal and psychological characteristics as shown in Fig. For the most part, marketers cannot control their factors but they should take them into account while formulating marketing strategies.

Cultural
- Cultural
- Sub-cultural
- Social Class

↓

Social
- Reference
- Group
- Family
- Role and Status

↓

Personal
- Age and Life Cycle stage
- Occupation
- Economic Situation
- Life Style
- Personality and self-concept

↓

Psychological
- Motivation
- Perception
- Learning
- Beliefs and Attitudes

↓

Buyer

Fig.: *Factors Influencing Consumer Behaviour*

Cultural Factors : Cultural factors exert the broadest and deepest influence on consumer behaviour. The marketer needs to understand the role played by the buyer's culture, subculture and social class.

31. Modigliani and Miller (MM) Hypothesis: Modigliani and Miller Hypothesis is in support of the irrelevance of dividends. Modigiliani and Miller argue that firm's dividend policy has no effect on its value of assets and is, therefore of no consequence, *i.e.*, dividends are irrelevant to shareholders wealth. According to them, 'Under conditions of perfect capital markets, rational investors, absence of tax discrimination between dividend income and capital appreciation, given the firm's investment policy, its dividend policy may have no influence on the market price of shares'.

The hypothesis is based on the following assumptions:

1. Capital Markets are perfect–All investors have perfect cost-free information.
2. Expected future earnings constant.
3. Initial assumption of no taxes.
4. Firms can be classified into 'equivalent risk' classes.

32. Debt capacity : The technique of cash flow analysis is helpful in determining a firm's debt capacity. Debt capacity is the amount, which a firm can service easily even under adverse conditions; it is the amount that the firm should employ. There may be lenders who are prepared to lend to the firm at higher interest rates. But the firm should borrow only if it can service debt without any problem. A firm can avoid the risk of financial distress if it can maintain its ability to meet contractual obligation of interest and principal payments. Debt capacity, therefore, should be thought in terms of the operating cash flows servicing debt rather than debt ratios. A high debt ratio is not necessarily bad. If a firm can service high amount of debt without much financial risk, it will increase shareholders' wealth. On the other hand, a low debt ratio can prove to be burdensome for a firm, which has liquidity problem. A firm faces financial distress (or even insolvency) when it has cash flow problem. It is dangerous to finance a capital-intensive project out of borrowings, which has built in uncertainty about the earnings and cash flows.

33. Estimating the Cost of Equity : To estimate the cost of equity, we must determine the expected rate of return of the company's stock. Since expected rates of return are unobservable, we rely on asset-pricing models that translate risk into expected return. The most common asset-pricing model is the capital asset pricing model (CAPM). Other models include the Fama-French three-factor model and the arbitrage pricing theory (APT). The three models differ primarily in how they define risk. The CAPM defines a stock's risk as its sensitivity to be stock market, whereas the Fama-French three-factor model defines risk as a stock's sensitivity to three portfolios: the stock market, a portfolio based on firm size, and a portfolio based on book-to-market ratios. The CAPM is the most common method for estimating expected returns, so we begin our analysis with that model.

34. Factors Affecting WACC : Weighted average cost of capital is affected by a number of factors. They are divided into two categories such as:

(*a*) Controllable Factors (Internal Factors)

(*b*) Uncontrollable Factors (External Factors)

(*a*) Controllable Factors : Controllable factors are those factors that affect WACC, but the firm can control them. They are:

(*i*) Capital Structure Policy: As we have assured, a firm has a given target capital structure where it assigns weights based on that target capital structure to calculate WACC. However, a firm can change its capital structure or proportions of components of capital that affect its WACC. For example, when a firm decides to use more debt and less equity, which will lead to reduction of WACC. At the same time increasing proportion of debt in capital structure increases the risk of both debt and equity holder, because it increases fixed financial commitment.

(*ii*) Dividend Policy : The required capital may be raised by equity or debt or both. Equity capital can be raised by issue of new equity shares or through retained earnings.

Sometimes companies may prefer to raise equity capital by retention of earnings, due to issue of new equity shares, which are expensive (they involve flotation costs). Firms may feel that retained earnings is less costly when compared to issue of new equity. But if it is different it is more costly, since the retained earnings is income that is not paid as dividends hence, investors expect more return and so it affects the cost of capital.

(iii) **Investment Policy :** While estimating the initial cost of capital, generally we use the starting point as the required rate of return on the firm's existing stock and bonds. Therefore, we implicitly assume that new capital will be invested in assets of the same type and with the same degree of risk. But it is not correct as no firm invest in assets similar to the ones that currently operate, when a firm changes its investment policy. For example, investment in diversified business.

(b) **Uncontrollable Factors:** The factors that are not possible to be controlled by the firm and mostly affects the cost of capital. These factors are known as External factors.

(i) **Tax Rates:** Tax rates are beyond the control of a firm. They have an important effect on the overall cost of the capital. Computation of debt involves consideration of tax. In addition, lowering capital gains tax rate relative to the rate on ordinary income makes stocks more attractive and reduces cost of equity and lower the overall cost of capital.

(ii) **Level of Interest Rates:** Cost of debt is interest rate. If interest rates increases, automatically cost of debt also increases. On the other hand, if interest rates are low then the cost of debt is less. The reduced cost of debt decreases WACC and this will encourage an additional investment.

(iii) **Market Risk Premium:** Market risk premium is determined by the risk in investing proposed stock and the investor's aversion to risk. Market risk is out of control risk, i.e., firms have no control on this factor.

35. Comparative Analysis : A common approach to analysing the capital structure of a firm is to compare its debt ratio with that of other firms. Perhaps the simplest way to do is to compare a firm's debt ratio to the average debt ratio of the industy to which the firm belongs. Such analysis assumes that firms belonging to the same industry are comparable and, on average, they are more or less operating at their optimal capital structure. However, both the assumptions are questionable. Firms within the same industry may not be comparable because of differences in size, capital intensity, product mix, operating risks, tax status, and so on. Further, because firms try to follow the industry average, the average debt ratio of the industry may not represent what is optimal for it.

36. Other Theories of Motivation

1. Achievement Motive Theory—*David McClelland* (1953).
2. Positive Reinforcement Theory (Behaviour Modification Theory or Operant Conditioning Theory)—*B.F. Skinner* (1953).
3. Management by Objectives (MBO) Theory—*Peter Drucker* (1955).
4. Maturity-Immaturity Theory—*Chris Argyris* (1957)
5. Theory X and Theory Y—*Douglas McGregor* (1960)
6. Expectancy Theory or VIE Theory (Valence, Instrumentality and Expectancy)—*Victor Vroom* (1964)
7. Equity Theory—*J. Stacy Adams* (1965)
8. Performance-Satisfaction Theory—*Porter and Lawler* (1968)
9. Goal Setting Theory—*Edwin Locke* (1968)
10. ERG (Existence, Relatedness and Growth Needs) Theory—*Clayton Alderfer* (1972)
11. Attribution Theory—*Harold Kelley* (1973)
12. Theory Z—*William Ouchi and Alfred Jaeger* (1978)

Theory Z : It would be relevant at this stage to make a passing mention about Theory Z propounded by William Ouchi in his 1981 book, *'Theory Z : How American Management can meet the Japanese Challenge'*. Theory Z was often referred to as Japanese style management. It advocated a mix of all that was best about Theory Y and modern Japanese management, which placed a large amount of trust and freedom with workers and assumed that workers would have a strong loyalty and interest in team work and the organization. It placed greater reliance on the attitude and responsibility of workers unlike McGregor's Theory Y which focused on the management. Since it lacked the elegance of McGregor's model, Theory Z did not become very popular in management circles.

38. **Training Methodologies :** The commonly used training methodologies in an organization are explained below. These training methodologies can be divided into : (*a*) on-the-job and (*b*) off-the-job.

On-the-job training methodologies:

- apprenticeship training
- job instruction training
- coaching, understudy
- demonstration

Off-the-job training methodologies:

- class room lectures, seminars, conferences, symposiums
- simulation exercises
- experiential learning
- computer modelling
- vestibule training
- programmed learning

39. **Peter's Principle :** Peter Principle is regarded as the most penetrating social and psychological discovery of the century. Laurence J. Peter, Professor at University of Southern California, was originator of this model and made it popular worldwide through his book titled, *The Peter Principle* published in 1969. The important Peter's laws include the following:

1. Managers tend to be promoted to their level of incompetence. The idea is that people are often promoted for their past performance and not for their competence to handle the promoted level which is usually more complex and demand more skills. Every position tends to be filled by an employee incompetent to execute the duties. The net result is that most of the higher levels of bureaucracy will be filled by incompetent people, who got there because they were quite good at doing a different task than the one they are expected to do.
2. Work is accomplished by those who have not yet reached to their level of incompetence: This is obvious because only competent people can deliver the goods.
3. Competence always contains the seed of incompetence. In other words, an employee who is competent in a particular skill/ discipline not necessarily makes him as competent in other skills. In contrast, his/ her total occupation with acquiring mastery in a given skill makes them ignorant of other things.
4. Employees in hierarchy do not really object to incompetence in their colleagues.
5. Internal consistency is more valued than efficiency.
6. Impostors tend to congregate in the mid to upper levels of large organizations because one impostor cannot spot another impostor.

43. **The Call Money Market :** Call money market is that part of the national money market where the day-to-day surplus funds of banks are traded. The maturity of the loans made in this market varies between one day to a fortnight. The main purpose of the operation of this market is to adjust the reserves of banks and supply of funds to the market which arises out of the reserves of banks with the central banking system.

47. **Types of Disequilibrium:** Disequilibrium in balance of payments may be of the following kinds:

1. Cyclical Disequlibrium: Disequilibrium caused by trade cycles is called cyclical disequilibrium. Terms of trade and growth of trade undergo a change as a result of trade cycles. Consequently, balance of payments in influenced. Cyclical disequilibrium can be corrected by import-export adjustment.

2. **Secular Disequilibrium:** When an economy undergoes intensive changes, it causes secular or long-term disequilibrium in the balance of payments.
3. **Structural Disequilibrium:** When structural changes take place in some sectors of the economy, then they effect import-export trade of the country resulting into structural disequilibrium.
4. **Fundamental Disequilibrium:** When a country suffers chronic disequilibrium in its balance of payments, then according to International Monetary Fund, it will be called fundamental disequilibrium.
5. **Temporary Disequilibrium:** Short-term factors account for temporary disquilibrium in balance of payments. For instance, when crops are washed away by floods in certain regions of India and to make good the loss the country is forced to import foodgrains on a large-scale while her exports remain constant, then the balance of payments will turn unfavourable. This sort of disequilibrium is called temporary or short-term disequilibrium.

48. **Traders in Derivatives Market:** There are three types of traders in the derivatives market:
• Hedger, • Speculator, • Arbitrageur.

Hedger : A hedge is a position taken in order to offset the risk associated with some other position. A hedger is someone who faces risk associated with price movement of an asset and who uses derivatives as a means of reducing that risk. A hedger is a trader who enters the futures market to reduce a pre-existing risk.

Speculator : While hedgers are interested in reducing or eliminating risk, speculators buy and sell derivatives to make profit and not to reduce risk. Speculators willingly take increased risks. Speculators wish to take a position in the market by betting on the future price movements of an asset. Futures and options contracts can increase both the potential gains and losses in a speculative venture. Speculators are important to derivatives markets as they facilitate hedging, provide liquidity, ensure accurate pricing, and help to maintain price stability. It is the speculators who keep the market going because they bear risks which no one else is willing to bear.

Arbitrageur : An arbitrageur is a person who simultaneously enters into transactions in two or more markets to take advantage of the discrepancy between prices in these markets. For example, if the futures price of an asset is very high relative to the cash price, an arbitrageur will make profit by buying the asset and simultaneously selling futures. Hence, arbitrage involves making profits from relative mispricing. Arbitrageurs also help to make markets liquid, ensure accurate and uniform pricing, and enhance price stability.

50. According to Vernon and Wells Jr. (1986), MNCs represent a cluster of affiliated firms located in different countries that:
1. are linked through common ownership
2. draw upon a common pool of resources
3. respond to a common strategy.

All this shows a high degree of integration among different units of the firm. Based on the strategic features, MNCs are grouped as ethnocentric, polycentric and geocentric (Perlmutter, 1969; Perlmutter and Heenan, 1974). Ethnocentric firms are those that adopt home market oriented policy and seldom distinguish between domestic operation and global operation policies. On the other extreme, polycentric firms operate in foreign countries just to cater to the demand in those countries. This means that they follow a host market oriented policy. Between the two extremes, geocentric firms maintain a balance between the home market and host market oriented policies.

PAPER-III

Note : *This paper contains* ***Seventy Five (75)*** *objective type questions, each question carrying* ***two (2)*** *marks each. Attempt* ***all*** *the questions.*

1. The present regime of subsidies can be improved by focussing on

(*i*) Reducing the overall scale of subsidies.

(*ii*) Making subsidies as transparent as possible.

(*iii*) Giving a specific amount to the Member of Parliament for subsidies.

(*iv*) Setting clear limits on duration of any new subsidy scheme.

(*v*) Eliminating system of periodic review of subsidies

(*vi*) Using subsidies for well-defined economic objectives.

Codes :

A. (*i*), (*ii*), (*iii*) and (*iv*)

B. (*ii*), (*iii*), (*iv*) and (*v*)

C. (*i*), (*iii*), (*iv*) and (*vi*)

D. (*i*), (*ii*), (*iv*) and (*vi*)

2. Which of the following is not regulated by The Competition Act, 2002?

A. Abuse of dominant position

B. Anti-competitive agreements

C. Medical negligence

D. Predatory pricing

3. The freedom of private enterprise is the greatest in the free market economy. This is characterized by which of the following assumptions?

(*i*) The factors of production (labour, land, capital) are privately owned and production occurs at the initiative of the private enterprise.

(*ii*) Income is received in monetary form by the sale of services of the factors of production and from the profits of the private enterprise.

(*iii*) Members of the free market economy have freedom of choice in so far as consumption, occupation, savings and investments are concerned.

(*iv*) The free market economy is not planned, controlled or regulated by the government.

(*v*) The free market economy is prone to corrupt practices.

Codes :

A. (*i*), (*ii*) and (*iii*)

B. (*i*), (*ii*), (*iii*) and (*iv*)

C. (*i*), (*ii*), (*iii*), (*iv*) and (*v*)

D. (*ii*), (*iii*), (*iv*) and (*v*)

4. The important responsibilities of a business to the customers are

(*i*) To ensure family welfare of the customers.

(*ii*) To understand customer needs and to take the necessary measures to satisfy these needs.

(*iii*) To ensure health condition of the customers.

(*iv*) To ensure that the product supplied has no adverse effect on the customer.

(*v*) To provide an opportunity for being heard and to redress genuine grievances.

Codes :

A. (*i*), (*ii*), (*iii*), (*iv*) and (*v*)

B. (*i*), (*ii*), (*iii*) and (*iv*)

C. (*ii*), (*iv*) and (*v*)

D. (*ii*), (*iii*), (*iv*) and (*v*)

5. The rationale of expanding role of the public sector stems mainly from which of the following factors?

(*i*) The failure of the private sector in certain crucial areas

(*ii*) The exploitation of the society by the private sector

(*iii*) The revenue need of the Central Government

(*iv*) The demand of economic justice

(*v*) The need for accelerating the pace of economic growth

Codes :

A. (*i*), (*ii*), (*iii*) and (*iv*)

B. (*ii*), (*iii*), (*iv*) and (*v*)

C. (*i*), (*iii*), (*iv*) and (*v*)

D. (*i*), (*ii*), (*iv*) and (*v*)

6. Which of the following factors may lead to a sick industrial unit?

(*i*) Shortage of funds and faulty financial management
(*ii*) Investment by the FIIs in Indian industries
(*iii*) Unauthorized FDI in Indian industries
(*iv*) Lack of experience on the part of promoters
(*v*) Technological factors including obsolete or improper technology

Codes :

A. (*i*), (*ii*), (*iii*) and (*iv*)
B. (*ii*), (*iii*), (*iv*) and (*v*)
C. (*i*), (*iv*) and (*v*)
D. (*i*), (*ii*) and (*iii*)

7. Indicate what is *not* correct in respect of the Consumer Protection Act, 1986.

A. No complaint can be entertained in respect of a product purchased more than 2 years back.
B. A complaint against medical negligence can be filed by legal heir or representative of the deceased.
C. A complaint involving a claim of ₹ 15 lakhs is to be filed before the State Commission.
D. Both (A) and (C)

8. If bonus shares are issued out of pre-acquisition profit, it will have

A. Direct effect on the Consolidated Balance Sheet
B. No effect on the Consolidated Balance Sheet
C. No effect on Net Profit
D. None of the above

9. The present value of the future contributions of employees is one of the methods of

A. HR Accounting
B. Inflation Accounting
C. Social Accounting
D. Responsibility Accounting

10. A standard which can be attained under the most favourable working conditions is called

A. Attainable Standard
B. Basic Standard
C. Current Standard
D. Ideal Standard

11. Which of the following ratios are taken into consideration by a banker before sanctioning the loan?

A. Proprietory Ratio
B. Stock-Turnover Ratio
C. Debt-Equity Ratio
D. All of the above

12. Match the items of the following two lists:

List–I	***List–II***
(*a*) Zero-base Budgeting	1. Internal Reconstruction
(*b*) Goodwill or Capital Reserve	2. Earnings Per Share
(*c*) Reduction of Capital	3. Control of Expenditure
(*d*) Basic & Diluted	4. Business Combination

Codes :

	(*a*)	(*b*)	(*c*)	(*d*)
A.	3	4	2	1
B.	4	3	1	2
C.	4	1	3	2
D.	3	4	1	2

13. Assertion (A): Dividend paid out of pre-acquisition profit by the subsidiary company to the holding company is deducted from the cost of investment.

Reason (R): Dividend paid out of pre-acquisition profit by the subsidiary company should be treated as a return of capital to the holding company. Which one of the following is correct?

A. Both (A) and (R) are correct.
B. (A) is correct, but (R) is wrong.
C. (A) is wrong, but (R) is correct.
D. Both (A) and (R) are wrong.

14. Given below are two statements, one labelled as Assertion (A) and the other labelled as Reason (R):

Assertion (A): Increasing the value of closing inventory increases profit.

Reason (R): Increasing the value of closing inventory reduces cost of goods sold.

In the context of the above two statements, which of the following is correct?

Codes:

A. Both (A) and (R) are correct.
B. Only (A) is correct.
C. Only (R) is correct.
D. Both (A) and (R) are wrong.

15. Match the items of List–I with the items of List–II and select the correct code for the answer :

List–I	***List–II***
(*a*) Multiple plants	1. $MRP_T = MC = MRP_X = MRP_{PY}$
(*b*) Cost-plus pricing	2. $MRT = MC = MR_1 = MR_2$
(*c*) Multiple markets	3. $MR = MC_T = MC_A = MC_B$
(*d*) Multiple products	4. P = (1 + m) ATC

Codes :

	(*a*)	(*b*)	(*c*)	(*d*)
A.	4	2	1	3
B.	1	3	4	2
C.	2	1	3	4
D.	3	4	2	1

16. A measure of the responsiveness of quantity demanded to changes in the price of a related good is known as

A. Cross Elasticity of Demand
B. Substitution Elasticity of Demand
C. Complementary Elasticity of Demand
D. Price Elasticity of Demand

17. If the total cost is ₹ 260 and the total variable cost is ₹ 60, what will be total fixed cost if output is (*a*) 100 units and (*b*) 200 units?

A. ₹ 200 and ₹ 200
B. ₹ 100 and ₹ 200
C. ₹ 260 and ₹ 100
D. ₹ 160 and ₹ 100

18. Optimal input combination to minimize the cost for a given output will be at the point where :

A. Isocost is tangent to Isoquant
B. MRTS between inputs is equal
C. Any movement from optimum point will lead to low level of output
D. All the above conditions are fulfilled.

19. What kinds of actions can be taken to put the rivals at a disadvantageous position under oligopoly market?

A. Commitments B. Threats
C. Promises D. All the above

20. There is no exceptions to the law of demand in the case of

A. Giffen goods
B. Normal goods
C. Articles of conspicuous consumption
D. Ignorance of the buyer

21. What is the degree of elasticity of demand in case the demand is represented by a straight line parallel to the *x*-axis?

A. $e > 1$ B. $e = 0$
C. $e = \propto$ D. $e < 1$

22. If a chi-square test is to be performed on a contingency table with 3 rows and 4 columns, how many degrees of freedom should be used?

A. 6 B. 12
C. 8 D. 9

23. Assertion (A) : If regression coefficient of X on Y is greater than one, regression coefficient of Y on X must be less than one.

Reason (R) : The geometric mean between two regression coefficients is the co-efficient of correlation. On the basis of the above, choose the appropriate answer:

A. (A) and (R) are correct.
B. (A) is correct, but (R) is not correct.
C. (A) is not correct, but (R) is correct.
D. Both (A) and (R) are not correct.

24. If the sum of squares of deviations within samples is 140 with 12 degrees of freedom and the sum of squares of deviations between samples is 190 with 2 degrees of freedom, the test statistic will be

A. 81.4 B. 12.28
C. 8.14 D. 1.22

25. The regression equation of profits (X) on sales (Y) of a firm is given as : 3Y – 5X + 110 = 0. If the sales of the firm is ₹ 44,000, the profit will be

A. ₹ 23,370 B. ₹ 26,422
C. ₹ 24,422 D. ₹ 21,370

26. Cricketer 'A' scores on an average 40 runs with a standard deviation of 5. Scores of players 'B' and 'C', on an average, are 75 and 90 with standard deviations 10 and 18 respectively. Arrange the players in the descending order of consistency:

A. A, B and C
B. C, B and A
C. B, A and C
D. C, A and B

27. Among the following, choose the most suitable 'test' that can be applied to examine the influence of one factor on different groups:

A. 't' test
B. 'F' test
C. 'Chi-square' test
D. None of the above

28. A machine produced 20 defective articles in a batch of 400. After overhauling, it produced 10% defectives in a batch of 300. Which test of hypothesis can be applied to the above situation to examine whether the machine has improved?

A. Test of significance of a sample proportion (two-tail test)
B. Test of significance of a sample proportion (one-tail test)
C. Test of significance of difference between two sample proportion (two-tail test)
D. Test of significance of difference between two sample proportion (one-tail test)

29. Strategies and policies

A. are not closely related
B. give direction
C. are the framework for performance appraisal
D. Both (A) and (B)

30. According to Vroom's Expectancy Theory of Motivation,

A. Force = valence divided by expectancy
B. Force = valence × expectancy
C. Force = strength of an individual preference for an outcome
D. Valence = probability that a particular action shall lead to a desired outcome

31. In the managerial grid, the managers who have little or no concern for production but are concerned only for people are known as what type of managers?

A. 1.1 Management B. 5.5 Management
C. 9.1 Management D. 1.9 Management

32. According to the Boston Consulting group, a business, which has a strong market share in a low growth industry is referred to as a

A. Dog B. Cash Cow
C. Star D. Question mark

33. Which of the following are major principles of leading?

(*i*) Principle of motivation
(*ii*) Principle of continuous development
(*iii*) Principle of harmony of objectives
(*iv*) Principle of open competition
(*v*) Principle of communication clarity

Select the correct answer from the codes given below:

Codes :

A. (*i*), (*ii*), (*iii*), (*v*)
B. (*i*), (*ii*), (*iii*), (*iv*), (*v*)
C. (*i*), (*iii*), (*iv*), (*v*)
D. (*i*), (*iii*), (*v*)

34. The following are the steps of management control process :

(*i*) Taking corrective action from standards
(*ii*) Establishing standards
(*iii*) Measuring actual performance
(*iv*) Comparing performance against standard

Select the correct sequence of these steps from the codes given below :

Codes :

A. (*i*), (*ii*), (*iii*), (*iv*) B. (*ii*), (*iii*), (*iv*), (*i*)
C. (*iii*), (*iv*), (*i*), (*ii*) D. (*ii*), (*iv*), (*i*), (*iii*)

35. Consider the following:

(*i*) Planning is today's action for tomorrow's decision.
(*ii*) Planning is forward looking while controlling is looking back.
(*iii*) Motivation is about getting voluntary willingness of subordinates for action.
(*iv*) Line and staff organisation is the oldest form of organisation.

Select the correct statements from the codes given below:

Codes:

A. (*ii*) and (*iii*) are correct.
B. (*i*), (*ii*) and (*iv*) are correct.
C. (*i*), (*iii*) and (*iv*) are correct
D. All are correct.

36. Which is *not* one of the stages in the consumer buying-decision process?
A. Purchase decision
B. Post-purchase behaviour
C. Problem recognition
D. Cultural factors

37. At which stage of product-life-cycle are the pricing decisions most complex?
A. Decline B. Growth
C. Introduction D. Maturity

38. Which one is not an element of market logistics?
A. Inventory
B. Order-processing
C. Warehousing
D. Supply chain management

39. Under which legislation, the manufacturers and distributors are required to declare Maximum Retail Price (MRP) on packaged commodities?
A. The Bureau of Indian Standards Act, 1986
B. The Consumer Protection Act, 1986
C. The Standards of Weights and Measures Act, 1976
D. The Essential Commodities Act, 1955

40. In modern marketing, which of the following functions of a distribution middleman is gaining maximum importance?
A. Making persuasive communication
B. Price negotiation
C. Keeping adequate inventory
D. Gathering market information

41. Which method of setting the advertising budget of a company is considered to be the most scientific?
A. All-you-can-afford method
B. Percentage of sales method
C. Competitive-parity method
D. Objectives and tasks method

42. Match the items of List–I with those of List–II and indicate the correct combination from the codes given below :

List–I	***List–II***
(*a*) AIDA Model	1. Consumer behaviour
(*b*) Hierarchy of effects model	2. Marketing communication
(*c*) Howard and Sheth model	3. Consumer buying-decision process
(*d*) Information search	4. Advertising effectiveness

Codes :

	(*a*)	(*b*)	(*c*)	(*d*)
A.	1	2	3	4
B.	2	3	4	1
C.	2	4	1	3
D.	4	1	3	2

43. Inability of the firm to meet its obligations results in financial distress which may lead to bankruptcy resulting into the following:
1. Distress sale of assets at lower price.
2. Legal and administrative costs for bankruptcy.
3. Dilution of stakeholders' commitment to the firm.
4. Stretching of payments to suppliers and creditors.

The direct costs of such financial distress may be
A. 1 and 4 B. 2 and 3
C. 1 and 2 D. 3 and 4

44. Mutually exclusive projects can be more accurately ranked as per
A. Internal rate of return method
B. Net Present Value Method
C. Modified Internal Rate of Returns Method
D. Accounting or Average Rate of Return Method

45. Which one of the following does not constitute a Standalone Risk Analysis?
A. Simulation Analysis
B. Break-even Analysis
C. Corporate Risk Analysis
D. Scenario Analysis

46. Financial leverage in a firm is positively affected by

A. Intensity of tangible assets
B. Operating leverage
C. Profitability
D. Tax Rate

47. Which combination of the following two statements (A) and (R) is correct?

Assertion (A) : The IRR of a project is the discount rate which reduces its NPV to zero.

Reason (R) : A project is worth accepting if the IRR exceeds the cost of capital.

Codes :

A. (A) is right, but (R) is wrong.
B. Both (A) and (R) are correct.
C. (A) is wrong, but (R) is correct.
D. Both (A) and (R) are wrong.

48. Assertion (A) : A company should pay minimum dividend to its shareholders.

Reason (R) : Dividends are heavily taxed than capital gains.

Codes :

A. Both (A) and (R) are correct.
B. Both (A) and (R) are incorrect.
C. (A) is not correct, but (R) is correct.
D. (A) is correct, but (R) is wrong.

49. Dividend irrelevance hypothesis is implied in the

A. Traditional Model
B. Walter Model
C. Gordon Model
D. M.M. Model

50. Which one of the following does not serve the main objective of performance appraisal?

A. Developmental uses
B. Administrative uses
C. Ethical and moral values
D. Organisational objectives

51. Statement (I) : Job evaluation is a technique of assessing the worth of each job in comparison with others throughout an organization.

Statement (II) : Job evaluation and job rating are one and the same for employees' appraisal purposes.

Codes :

A. Statement (I) is correct, but Statement (II) is incorrect.
B. Statement (II) is correct, but Statement (I) is incorrect.
C. Both the Statements (I) and (II) are correct.
D. Both the Statements (I) and (II) are incorrect.

52. Match the items of List–I with the items of List–II and select the correct answer:

List–I	*List–II*
(*a*) Job Rotation	1. Involves conscious efforts, to organise tasks, duties and responsibilities into a unit of work to achieve certain objectives.
(*b*) Job Design	2. Involves movement of employees from job to job
(*c*) Job Evaluation	3. Seeks to improve both task efficiency and human satisfaction and more opportunity for individual growth
(*d*) Job Enrichment	4. The formal process by which the relative worth of various jobs in the organisation is determined for pay purpose.

Codes :

	(*a*)	(*b*)	(*c*)	(*d*)
A.	1	2	3	4
B.	4	3	2	1
C.	3	4	2	1
D.	2	1	4	3

53. Assertion (A) : Merit rating of an employee is the process of evaluating the employees performance on the job in terms of the requirements of the job.

Reason (R) : Employees' merit rating is a technique for fair and systematic evaluation of an employee's capacities and abilities and performance on the specific job.

Codes :

A. Both (A) and (R) are correct, and (R) is the right explanation of (A).

B. Both (A) and (R) are correct, but (R) is not the right explanation of (A).
C. Both (A) and (R) are incorrect.
D. (R) is correct, but (A) is incorrect.

54. The major provisions for employees' health and safety are contained in
A. The Industrial Disputes Act, 1947
B. The Factories Act, 1948
C. The Industrial Employment (Standing Orders) Act, 1946
D. The Employees' Compensation Act, 1923

55. Indicate your choice through the codes given below:
1. A club is an industry under the Industrial Disputes Act, 1947
2. Factory as defined under the Factories Act, 1948 includes a mine.
3. For purpose of the payment of bonus to employees, the gross profits earned by a bank is to be calculated in the manner specified in Schedule – I of the Payment of the Bonus Act, 1965.
4. Various labour laws do not apply to public sector undertakings.

Codes :
A. While 1 and 2 are correct, others are not.
B. All the statements are correct.
C. Only 1 is correct, others are incorrect.
D. Only 1 is incorrect, all others are correct.

56. Match the items of List–I with the items of List–II and select the correct answer:

List–I	***List–II***
(*a*) Abraham Maslow	1. Achievement Motivation Theory
(*b*) Herzberg	2. ERG Theory
(*c*) Alderfer	3. Two Factor Theory
(*d*) McClelland	4. Need Hierarchy Theory

Codes :

	(*a*)	(*b*)	(*c*)	(*d*)
A.	1	2	3	4
B.	4	3	2	1
C.	3	2	1	4
D.	4	3	1	2

57. Assertion (A) : The Central Bank of the country is responsible to maintain stability of the monetary standard which involves currency circulation.
Reason (R) : The Central Bank is the only authorized entity to do so.

Codes :
A. (A) and (R) both are correct.
B. (A) and (R) both are incorrect.
C. (A) is correct, but (R) is incorrect.
D. (R) is correct, but (A) is incorrect.

58. Identify the quantitative credit control methods among the following :
(*i*) Bank Rate
(*ii*) Credit Rationing
(*iii*) Open Market Operations
(*iv*) Variable Reserve Ratio
(*v*) Selective Credit Control
(*vi*) Liquidity Ratio

Codes :
A. (*i*), (*ii*), (*iii*) and (*iv*)
B. (*ii*), (*iii*), (*iv*) and (*v*)
C. (*i*), (*ii*), (*v*) and (*vi*)
D. (*i*), (*iii*), (*iv*) and (*vi*)

59. The following activities are mainly related to which organization?
(*i*) Micro Finance
(*ii*) Rural Finance
(*iii*) Self Help Groups
(*iv*) Cooperative Banks Finance
A. Industrial Finance Corporation of India
B. Ministry of Finance
C. Reserve Bank of India
D. National Bank for Agriculture and Rural Development

60. PIN in banking transaction is known as
A. Postal Index Number
B. Permanent Identification Number
C. Personal Identification Number
D. Public Interlocking Numeric

61. Reserve Bank of India was nationalized on
A. January 26, 1948
B. January 01, 1949
C. January 26, 1950
D. January 01, 1956

62. When a banking company is placed under moratorium under Section 45 of the Banking (Regulation) Act, 1949, the RBI must prepare a scheme of

A. VRS for staff
B. Capital Buy-Back
C. Reconstruction of the company or amalgamation with any other bank
D. IPO of the bank

63. Match the following items of List–I with List–II :

List–I	*List–II*
(*a*) SWIFT	1. 1996
(*b*) NEFT	2. 1988
(*c*) BASEL I Accord	3. 1973
(*d*) BASEL II Accord	4. 2004

Codes :

	(*a*)	(*b*)	(*c*)	(*d*)
A.	1	2	3	4
B.	2	3	1	4
C.	4	3	2	1
D.	3	1	4	2

64. The main features of TRIMS are :

(*i*) All restrictions on foreign capital are imposed.
(*ii*) No restriction is imposed on any area of investment.
(*iii*) Restrictions on repatriation of dividend is eliminated.
(*iv*) Imports of raw material is allowed freely.
(*v*) No limit on the extent of foreign investment.

Indicate the correct combination

A. (*i*), (*ii*), (*iii*) and (*v*)
B. (*ii*), (*iii*), (*iv*) and (*v*)
C. (*iii*), (*iv*) and (*v*)
D. (*iv*) and (*v*)

65. Assertion (A): TRIPS requires an understanding about the scope of the new patent regime.

Reason (R): Patent protection will be extended to micro-organisms, non-biological and micro-biological processes and plant varieties.

Codes:

A. (A) and (R) are not related with each other.
B. (R) is related with (A).
C. (A) is independent of (R).
D. While (R) is related with TRIMS, (A) is related with TRIPS.

66. Possible impact of WTO on various aspects of the Indian economy :

(*i*) Quantitative restriction will be allowed.
(*ii*) Second hand cars will be imported.
(*iii*) There will be dumping of Chinese goods.
(*iv*) Increase in population.
(*v*) Child labour exploitation
(*vi*) Unemployment will increase

Which combination is appropriate?

A. (*i*), (*ii*), (*iii*)   B. (*iii*), (*iv*), (*v*)
C. (*ii*), (*iii*) & (*vi*)   D. (*iv*), (*v*) & (*vi*)

67. Assertion (A): Economic integration abolishes cross-national economic discrimination.

Reason (R): Geographical proximity is an important reason for economic integration.

Codes :

A. (R) does explain (A).
B. Both (A) and (R) are correct.
C. Both (A) and (R) are not correct.
D. (A) is correct, but (R) is not correct.

68. Match the items of List–I and items of List–II and select the correct answer:

List–I	*List–II*
(*a*) Free Trade Area	1. MERCOSUR
(*b*) Customs Union	2. European Union
(*c*) OEEC	3. EFTA
(*d*) Common Market	4. Marshall Plan

Codes :

	(*a*)	(*b*)	(*c*)	(*d*)
A.	1	2	3	4
B.	2	4	1	3
C.	3	1	4	2
D.	4	3	2	1

69. Assertion (A) : A futures contract specifies in advance the exchange rate to be used, but it is not as flexible as a forward contract.

Reason (R) : A futures contract is for specific currency amount and a specific maturity date.

Codes :

A. (R) is a correct explanation of (A).
B. (R) is not a correct explanation of (A).

C. (A) and (R) are not related with each other.
D. (R) is irrelevant for (A).

70. Out of the following, which are the important objectives of IMF?

(*i*) To promote exchange rate stability
(*ii*) To create standby reserves
(*iii*) To print International currency notes
(*iv*) To establish a multilateral system of payments.
(*v*) To maintain orderly exchange rate stability
(*vi*) To create employment

Codes :

A. (*ii*), (*iv*), (*v*), (*vi*) B. (*iii*), (*v*), (*vi*)
C. (*i*), (*ii*), (*iv*), (*v*) D. (*i*), (*ii*), (*v*), (*vi*)

71. Given that :

Fair rent of a let out house property is ₹ 75,000. Its Municipal value is ₹ 60,000, standard rent is ₹ 72,000 and actual rent received is ₹ 63,000. What is the Gross Annual Value of this house property?

A. ₹ 60,000 B. ₹ 63,000
C. ₹ 72,000 D. ₹ 75,000

72. Match the items of List–I with the items of List–II.

List–I	***List–II***
(*a*) Amount deposited in PPF	1. 80-IA
(*b*) Profits and gains from undertakings engaged in infrastructure development	2. 80-G
(*c*) Contribution to National Defence Fund	3. 80-IAB
(*d*) Profits and gains by an undertaking engaged in the development of Special Economic Zone	4. 80-C

Codes :

	(*a*)	(*b*)	(*c*)	(*d*)
A.	4	3	2	1
B.	4	1	2	3
C.	4	1	3	2
D.	2	1	3	4

73. Which of the following deductions will not come under Sec. 80 of the Income Tax Act?

A. Deduction in the case of a person with disability
B. Deduction for interest paid on loan taken for pursuing higher education
C. Deduction for interest on loan taken for the construction/purchase of house property
D. Deduction for repayment of any instalment of principal amount borrowed for the purchase/construction of house property

74. X purchased a land in the P.Y. 1997-98 for ₹ 50,000. This land was sold by him during the P.Y. 2009-10 for ₹ 8,00,000. The fair market value of this land on 1-4-81 was ₹ 1,20,000. If the Cost Inflation Index for the A.Y. 2010-11 is 632, his capital gain for the A.Y. 2010-11 will be

A. ₹ 4,84,000
B. ₹ 7,50,000
C. ₹ 6,80,000
D. ₹ 41,600

75. Any amount of money received in excess of ₹ 50,000 without consideration is fully taxable in the hands of

A. Individuals
B. Individuals and HUF
C. Individuals, HUF and Company
D. All assessees

ANSWERS

1	2	3	4	5	6	7	8	9	10
D	C	B	C	D	C	C	B	A	D
11	**12**	**13**	**14**	**15**	**16**	**17**	**18**	**19**	**20**
C	D	A	A	D	A	A	D	D	B
21	**22**	**23**	**24**	**25**	**26**	**27**	**28**	**29**	**30**
C	A	A	C	B	A	B	D	B	B

31	32	33	34	35	36	37	38	39	40
D	B	D	B	A	D	D	D	C	D
41	42	43	44	45	46	47	48	49	50
D	C	C	B	C	A	B	A	D	C
51	52	53	54	55	56	57	58	59	60
A	D	B	B	A	B	C	D	D	C
61	62	63	64	65	66	67	68	69	70
B	C	B	B	A	C	B	C	A	C
71	72	73	74	75					
C	B	C	D	B					

SOME SELECTED EXPLANATORY ANSWERS

2. The Government of India appointed a committee in October. 1999 to examine the existing MRTP Act for shifting the focus of the law from curbing monopolies to promoting competition and to suggest a modern competition law. Pursuant to the recommendations of this committee, the Competition Act, 2002, was enacted on 13 January 2003. The Competition Act, 2002, covers those anti-competitive practices that have an appreciable adverse effect (AAE) in India. The Act covers anti-competitive agreements, e.g., Cartel and Abuse of Dominent Position. The Act provides that the issues of anti-competitive agreements and abuse of dominant position should be determined in 'relevant market' in which core issues may cause or likely to cause AAE on competition. Further, the Act requires regulator to determine dominance not solely on basis of market share but to look into number of factors including market share. For this purpose, the regulator is vested with substantial powers including power to declare agreements void, levy stringent fines and penalties, and to block mergers which are a threat to healthy competition. The salient features of the Competition Act are (*i*) anti-competitive agreements, (*ii*) prohibition of abuse of dominant positions by an enterprise, and (*iii*) regulation of combinations such as acquisitions, mergers, joint ventures, takeovers, and amalgmations. Of these, the first two features govern pricing practices such as price-fixing and predatory pricing.

7. Time frame within which a complaint can be filed : Section 24A of the Act provides that a consumer dispute can be filed within two years from the date on which the cause of action arises. A number of amendments were made to the Consumer Protection Act of 1986 (and amended in 1991 and 1993). The President gave his assent on 17-12-2002 after the Rajya Sabha passed it on 17-11-2002 (Act No. 62 of 2002). These are effective from 15-3-2003.

Definitions : A Complainant is 2 (b) IV–one or more consumers, where there are numerous consumers having the same interest may make a complaint. **2(b)V–**in case of death of a consumer, his legal heir or representative may also make a complaint.

8. Issue of Bonus Shares by the Subsidiary Company : Treatment of issue of bonus shares by the subsidiary company will depend upon the source from which the bonus shares are issued. Bonus Shares may be issued out of pre-acquisition profits or reserves or post acquisition profits or reserves of the subsidiary company.

(*i*) **Treatment of issue of Bonus Shares out of Pre-acquisition Profits :** Issue of bonus shares out of pre-acquisition profits or reserves will have no effect on the consolidated Balance Sheet. It is so because holding company's share in pre-acquisition profits is reduced on account of issue of bonus shares and on the other hand paid-up value of shares held by holding company increases.

(*ii*) **If the Bonus Shares are issued out of Post acquistion profits :** Issue of bonus shares out of post acquisition profits will have effect on the consolidated Balance Sheet. The share of holding company shall reduce in revenue profits and the paid up value of shares held by the holding company.

9. 'Human resource accounting' refers to accounting for human beings, the most important organisational resource. The accounting of human resource deals with the measurement of costs which are associated with recruiting, selecting, hiring, training, placing and developing the employees of an organisation. It also involves measuring the present economic value of human resources to an organisation.

The primary objective of accounting for human resources is not merely to account but also to help the management in planning and controlling the contribution of people to organisations and to society at large. Human resource accounting is also expected to improve financial decisions made both internally as well as externally regarding the functioning of an organisation. Information regarding human resources and changes thereof may provide the management with valuable aids for monitoring efficiency of employees, regulating organisation behaviour, reducing absentecism and improving human relations.

10. Different Types of Standards and Their Fixation : For arriving at the standard cost for each element, we need two standards, namely, basic standards and current standards. Standards may also be classified as ideal standards and expected or attainable standards.

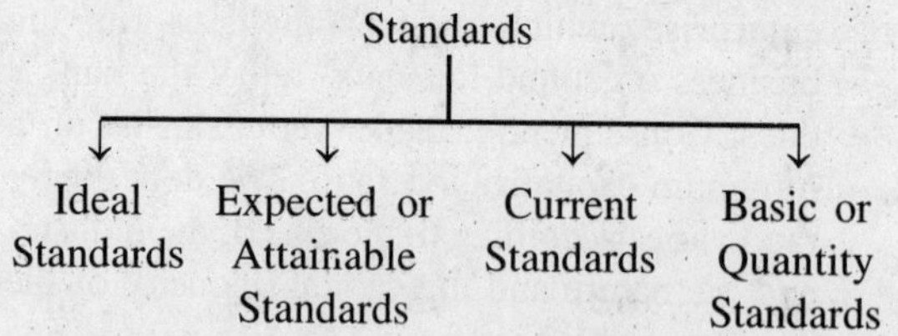

Ideal Standards : Ideal standards are the standards that can be attained under the most favourable conditions. It takes into consideration, performance under very efficient conditions which are rarely achieved in practice. In other words, they are highly theoretical in nature.

Basic or Quantity Standards: Quantity standards are known as basic standards and are permanent in nature. For example, the quantity of materials required to produce a product and labour hours required to produce a product are examples of basic standards. So long as the product design remains constant, the basic standards will not change.

Current Standards : Current standard is a standard that is fixed for a shorter period of, say, 3–6 months. Rate standards such as material price, labour rate etc. are examples of current standards.

Expected Standards : Expected standards are the standards, which are anticipated during the budgeted period. Hence, we should take into consideration, the likely conditions and circumstances that are expected to prevail in that future period. While setting up these standards, provision should be made for unavoidable and normal wastages. Therefore, these standards are realistic in nature.

11. The capitalization ratio or the debt equity ratio is used as a yardstick to make credit decisions and determine the size of the exposure that can be granted to the borrowers. In general, commercial banks define debt equity ratio as the ratio of total outside liabilities to equity, and term lending institutions define it as the ratio between funded debt and equity. The prescription of a benchmark debt equity ratio ensures that the borrowers have a reasonable stake in the enterprise, which induces them to run the business on sound lines and repay the bank's dues. Consequently, banks should insist on a minimum capitalization ratio. The debt equity ratio varies according to the size of the industry and the nature and the capital intensity of the projects, and ranges from 2.5 : 1 to 4.0 : 1. The ratios for industrial projects are different from those applicable to other types of business, but most often, the difference is only marginal.

17. Relation between Total Cost, Total Fixed Cost and Total Variable Cost : Total cost is the sum of each input (fixed and variable) used in the production. Therefore to obtain the firm's total cost (TC) at a given output, we have to add fixed cost (TFC) and its total variable cost (TVC). Thus,

$$TC = TFC + TVC$$

TFC is constant with respect to output changes. Therefore, in short run, the change in total cost resulting from a change in the level of output is equal to the change in total variable cost.

At zero level of output, TVC is zero.

$$TC = TFC + TVC$$
$$TC = TFC + \text{zero}$$
$$\therefore \quad TC = TFC$$

Hence TC and TFC are equal at zero level of output. Therefore, TC curve starts from starting point of TFC.

Also, TC – TVC = TFC,

that is, total cost and total variable cost differ by the amount of total fixed costs, which remains constant at every output. Thus, TC and TVC curves are parallel to each other. In other words, TC curve have the same shape as TVC curve but will lie above the TVC curve.

Here, TC = 260

and TVC = 60

Since TFC is constant with respect output changes.

∴ In both cases TFC will be Rs. 200.

19. Managers can make strategic moves to achieve better outcomes for themselves, usually to the detriment of their rivals. Only credible strategic moves matter; rivals ignore any commitments, threats, or promises that will not be carried out should the opportunity to do so arise. There are three types of strategic moves: *commitments, threats and promises*.

(*a*) Managers make commitments by announcing, or demonstrating to rivals in some other way, that they will bind themselves to take a particular action or make a specific decision *no matter what action or decision is taken by its rivals.*

(*b*) Threats, whether they are made explicitly or tacitly, take the form of a conditional statement, "If you take action A, I will take action B, which is undesirable or costly to you."

(*c*) Promises, like threats, are also conditional statements that must be credible to affect strategic decisions. Promises take the conditional form, "If you take action A, then I will take action B which is desirable or rewarding to you."

21. Perfectly Elastic Demand : When the demand for product changes–increase or decrease even when there is no change in price, it is known as perfectly elastic demand. The demand curve here is a straight line parallel to X-axis, which indicates that demand changes even though the price remains unchanges. This is shown in Figure where DD is the demand curve which is parallel to X-axis.

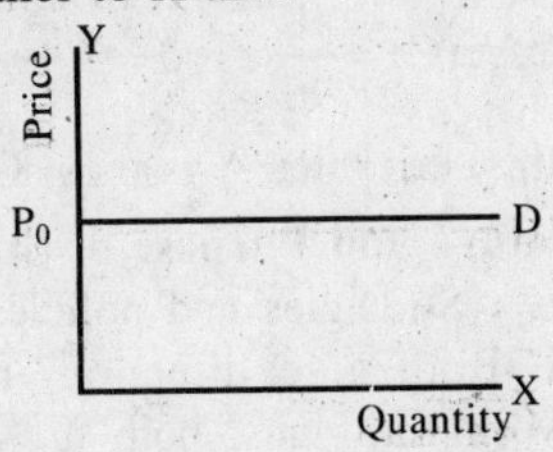

Fig. *Perfectly Elastic Demand*

22. The critical value of χ^2 depends on the degrees of freedom. The degrees of freedom = (the number of rows-1) multiplied by (the number of colums-1). In our case, there are 3 rows and 4 columns. So the degrees of freedom = (3 – 1). (4 – 1) = 6.

24. ANOVA Table : The technique of analysis of variance is referred to as ANOVA. A table showing the source of variation, the sum of squares, degrees of freedom, mean square (variance) and the formula for the F-ratio is known as ANOVA table.

Computation of Test Statistic : The actual analysis of variance is carried out on the basis of ratio between the variances. This ratio forms the test statistic known as *F-statistic, given by*

$$\text{F-statistic} = \frac{\text{Variance between the samples}}{\text{Variance within the samples}}$$

Following Table is based on information given in question.

Source of Variation	*Sum of squares*	*Degree of freedom*	*Mean sum squares*	*Variance ratio (F)*
Between varieties	190	2	95	F = 95/11.67
Within varieties	140	12	11.67	= 8.14
Total	330	14		

26. Since Coeff. of variation (C.V.) = $\frac{\text{S.D.}}{\text{A.M.}} \times 100$

$$\therefore \quad \text{C.V.(A)} = \frac{5}{40} \times 100 = 12.5\%$$

$$\text{C.V.(B)} = \frac{10}{75} \times 100 = 13.33\%$$

$$\text{C.V.(C)} = \frac{18}{90} \times 100 = 20\%$$

From this, cricketer A is most Consistent.

29. The Nature and Purpose of Strategies and Policies : Strategies and policies are closely related. Both give direction, both are the framework for plans, both are the basis of operational plans, and both affect all areas of managing. The term *strategy* (which is derived from the Greek word *strategos,* meaning "general") has been used in different ways. Authors differ in at least one major aspect. Some writers focus on both the end points (mission/purpose and goals/objectives) and the means of achieving them (policies and plans). Others emphasize the means to the ends in the strategic process rather than the ends per se. Strategy refers to the determination of the mission (or the fundamental purpose) and the basic long-term objectives of an enterprise, followed by the adoption of courses of action and allocation of resources necessary to achieve these aims. Therefore, objectives are part of strategy formulation.

Policies are general statements or understandings that guide manager's thinking in decision-making. The ensure that decisions fall within certain boundaries. They usually do not require action but are intended to guide managers in their commitment to the decision they ultimately make.

The essence of policy is discretion. Strategy, on the other hand, concerns the direction in which human and material resources will be applied in order to increase the chance of achieving selected objectives.

30. The Expectancy Theory of Motivation: Victor H. Vroom holds that people will be explaining to do things to reach a goal if they believe in the worth of that goal and if they can see that what they do will help them in achieving it. In a sense, this is a modern expression of what the German priest Martin Luther observed centuries ago when he said, "Everything that is done in the world is done by hope." In greater detail, Vroom's theory is that people's motivation toward doing anything will be determined by the value they place on the outcome of their effort (whether positive or negative) multiplied by the confidence they have that their effort will materially aid in achieving a goal. In his own terms, Vroom's theory may be stated as

Force = Valence × Expectancy

where *force* is the strength of a person's motivation, *valence* is the strength of an individual's preference for an outcome, and *expectancy* is the probability that a particular action will lead to a desired outcome. When a person is indifferent about achieving a certain goal, a valence of zero occurs; there is a negative valence when the person would rather not achieve the goal. The result of either would be, of course, no motivation. Likewise, a person would have no motivation to achieve a goal if the expectancy were zero or negative. The Force exerted to do something will depend on both valence and expectancy.

31. **The Four Extreme Styles:** Blake and Mouton recognize four extremes of style. Under the 1.1 style (referred to as impoverished management), managers concern themselves very little with either people or production and have minimum involvement in their jobs; to all intents and purposes, they have abandoned their jobs and only mark time or act as messengers communicating information from superiors to subordinates. At the other extreme are the 9.9 managers, who display in their actions the highest possible dedication both to people and to production. They are the real "team managers", who are able to mesh the production needs of the enterprise with the needs of individuals.

    Another style is 1.9 management (called country club management by some), in which managers have little or no concern for production but are concerned only for people. They promote an environment in which everyone is relaxed, friendly, and happy and no one is concerned about putting forth coordinated effort to accomplish enterprise goals. At another extreme are the 9.1 managers (sometimes referred to as autocratic task managers), who are concerned only with developing an efficient operation, who have little or no concern for people, and who are quite autocratic in their style of leadership.

    By using these four extremes as points of reference, every managerial technique, approach, or style can be placed somewhere on the grid. Clearly, 5.5 managers have medium concern for production and for people. They obtain adequate, but not outstanding, morale and production. They do not set goals too high and are likely to have a rather benevolently autocratic attitude toward people. The managerial grid is a useful device for identifying and classifying managerial styles, but it does not tell us why a manager falls into one part or another of the grid. To determine the reason, one has to look at underlying causes, such as the personality characteristics of the leader or the followers, the ability and training of managers, the enterprise environment and other situational factors that influence how leaders and followers act.

32. See Dec. 2013, Paper II explanation.

33. **Major Principles or Guides of Leading :** For the managerial function of leading, several principles or guides, have been suggested by Koontz and Weihrich:

    1. **Principle of harmony of objectives :** The more managers can harmonize the personal goals of individuals with the goals of the enterprise, the more effective and efficient the enterprise will be.
    2. **Principle of motivation :** Since motivation is not a simple cause and effect matter, the more managers carefully assess a reward structure, look upon it from a situation and contingency point of view, and integrate it into the entire system of managing, the more effective a motivational program will be.
    3. **Principle of leadership :** Since people tend to follow those who, in their view, offer them a means of satisfying their personal goals, the more managers understand what motivates their subordinates and how these motivators operate, and the more they reflect their understanding in carrying out their management actions, the more effective they are likely to be as leaders.
    4. **Principle of communication clarity:** Communication tends to be clear when it is expressed in a language and transmitted in a way that can be understood by the receiver. The responsibility of the sender is to formulate the message so that it is understandable to the receiver. This responsibility pertains primarily to written and oral communication and points to the necessity for planning the message, stating the underlying assumptions, and applying

the generally accepted rules for effective writing and speaking.

5. **Principle of communication integrity :** The greater the integrity and consistency of written, oral and non-verbal messages, as well as of the moral behaviour of the sender, the greater the acceptance of the message by the receiver.
6. **Principle of supplemental use of informal organization :** Communication tends to be more effective when managers utilize the informal organization to supplement the communication channels of the formal organization.

Informal organizational is a phenomenon managers must accept. Information, true or not, flows quickly through the informal organization. Consequently, managers should take advantage of this device to correct misinformation and to provide information that cannot be effectively sent or appropriately received through the formal communication systems.

36. Buying Decision Process : Sales people must understand that household and individual consumers as well as business (or industrial) buyers pass through certain stages or steps in buying a product. In consumer markets, individual and household consumers make buying decisions based on five mental stages of buying process, as shown in Fig. These are : (*a*) problem (or need) recognition, (*b*) information search (or collection), (*c*) evaluation of alternatives, (*d*) purchase decision and (*e*) post purchase behaviour.

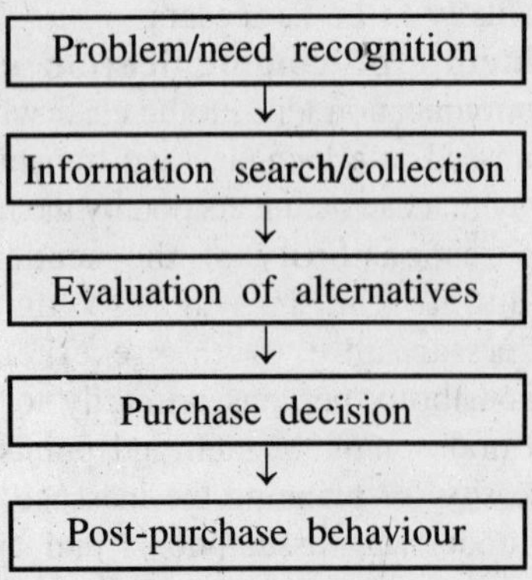

38. According to Philip Kotler, "physical distribution involves planning, implementing and controlling the physical flow of materials and final goods from points of origin to points of use to meet customer needs at a profit". Physical distribution is also known as 'marketing logistics'. The main elements of physical distribution are as follows:

(*a*) Storage or warehousing
(*b*) Inventory control
(*c*) Order processing
(*d*) Transportation.

These elements are interrelated as decision on one element may influence decisions on other elements.

39. The MRP on all packages is a requirement under the Legal Metrology Act, 2009. Under the Act, the Legal Metrology (Packaged Commodities) Rules, 2011, have been framed. [The Act and Rules were earlier called the Standards of Weights and Measures Act, 1976 and the Standards of Weights and Measures (Packaged Commodities) Rules, 1977]. The Rules require the manufacturer/packer to make certain declarations on every pre-packed commodity. The declarations include the name of the product, the quantity and the 'Maximum Retail Sale Price'. The manufacturer is free to fix the MRP. However, once the price is declared on the package, no person can alter or obliterate the declared price or make a sale at a price higher than the MRP. The MRP is inclusive of all taxes.

41. Determining the Advertising Budget: The advertising budget, or the total amount of money a firm allocates to advertising activities for a specific time period, is difficult to determine because the effects of advertising are difficult to measure. There are many factors that can determine a firm's decision about the appropriate level to fund advertising activities, including the geographic size of the market, the distribution or density of customers, the types of products advertised, sales volume relative to the competition, and the firm's own historical advertising budget. There are several different ways to determine an appropriate advertising budget:

- **Percentage of Sales Approach:** This approach is the most widely used method for determining the advertising budget. The approach is simple, straightforward, and based on what the firm traditionally spends on advertising. The obvious flaw of this approach is its implied assumption that sales create advertising. Also, during periods of declining sales, setting the budget as a percentage of sales may be a mistake because reduced advertising is often not the best strategy.
- **Objectives and Task Approach:** This approach requires that the firm lay out its goals for the advertising campaign and then list the tasks required to accomplish specific advertising objectives. The firm calculates and sums the costs of each task to determine the total budget. The major drawback of this approach is that the level of effort needed to accomplish advertising objectives is difficult to know with certainty.
- **Competitive Matching Approach:** This approach involves firms attempting to match major competitor's advertising expenditures in absolute dollars. Many firms review competitive advertising and compare competitor's expenditures across various media in relation to their own spending levels. This competitive tracking can occur at the national and regional levels and at least can provide a benchmark for comparing advertising resources to market share movements.
- **Arbitrary Approach :** Intution and personal experience set the advertising budget under this approach. The arbitrary approach can lead to mistakes in budgetting because it is not necessarily scientific, objective, or logical. On the other hand, deciding how much to spend on advertising is not an exact science.

The most popular and scientific methods is called objective and task method. In this method, the marketing budgets are decided on the basis of converting objectives into tasks. For each task the marketing manager can come up with a cost structure and spending details. This will help in determining the budget by summing up of all the expenses for achieving all the tasks. The following table explains the steps involves in arriving at a budget through the objective and task method.

44. The NPV and IRR methods make the same accept-reject decisions for independent projects, but if projects are mutually exclusive then ranking conflicts can arise. In such cases, the NPV method should generally be relied upon.

47. IRR is the discount rate that equals the present value of cash flows inflows to the present value of the capital invested (cash outflows), i.e., NPV is zero. IRR decision rules are:

- When the IRR exceeds the cost of capital–accept.
- When the IRR equals the cost of capital, the project meets the cost of capital but yields no surplus–indifference.
- When the IRR is less than the cost of capital–reject.
- As with NPV, sources of cash flows and the accounting treatment of income and expenditure flows are irrelevant to IRR calculations. IRR has a high sensitivity to errors in forecasted cash flows.

49. According to MM hypothesis, in perfect market situation the dividend policy of a firm is irrelevant as it does not affect the value of the firm. The value of the firm depends on the firm's earning which results from its investment policy. Thus, split of earning decision between dividend and retained earnings is not significant in determining the value of the firm. The hypothesis is based on following assumptions.

(*a*) Capital market are perfect and investors are rational. Information is freely available.

(*b*) Floation costs are nil.

(*c*) There are no taxes.

(*d*) Investment and dividend decisions are independent.

(*e*) Investment opportunities and future profits of firms are known with certainty (assumption dropped later).

50. Broadly, performance appraisal serves four objectives–

(*i*) developmental uses,

(*ii*) administrative uses/decisions,

(*iii*) organisational maintenance/objectives, and

(*iv*) documentation purposes. Following Table outlines these and specific uses more clearly.

Multiple Purposes of Performance Assessment

General Applications	*Specific purpose*
Developmental Uses	Identification of individual needs Performance feedback Determining transfers and job assignments Identification of individual strengths and developmental needs
Administrative Uses/Decisions	Salary Promotion Retention or termination Recognition of individual performance Lay-offs Identification of Poor performers
Organisational Maintenance/Objectives	HR planning Determining organisation training needs Evaluation of organisational goal achievement Information for goal identification Evaluation of HR systems Reinforcement of organisational development needs
Documentation	Criteria for validation research Documentation for HR decisions Helping to meet legal requirements

51. Job Evaluation : Job evaluation is concerned with rating the job and not the employees. It should help in deciding how much a particular job is worth.

Job evaluation is a technique used to establish the relative worth of jobs in a job hierarchy. It is a comparative process which defines the relative position of one job to another. It enables the organisation to fix the fair and equitable wage or salary level. It is basically an attempt to find a measure by which the relative payments made to different jobs are internally consistent. Methods of job evaluation includes ranking method, job classfication method and point rating method.

53. Merit Rating : Merit rating or employee rating or performance rating is the comparative appraisal of merits of individual employee, *vis-a-vis* other employees. It is a systematic evaluation of an employee performance on the job in terms of requirements of the job. It is the process of ranking or grading employees on the basis of their actual on the job performance in comparison with standards of performance already laid down and the performance of other employees. Employee rating is done by the supervisor or some other officer competent to do this work. Merit rating is also called as efficiency rating. It should be noted that there is difference between merit rating and performance appraisal. In merit rating, evaluation of the performance of employees performing their jobs is done. Merit rating evaluates merits of an employee on the basis of their qualities and traits. It may indicate their abilities, capacities, potentials, but it does not measure their work or performance. While performance appraisal is a process of evaluation of an employee's performance on his job in terms of the requirements of his job and is action oriented. In merit rating, an employee is rated or judged on the basis of what he is and not on the basis of what he does as is done in performance appraisal.

54. **Safety in Factories:** The legislation for regulating various aspects relating to safety, health and welfare of workers employed in factories is contained in the Factories Act, 1948. The Act is a Central enactment aiming at the protection of workers employed in factories from occupational hazards. The respective State Governments and UT Administrations frame rules under the Act and enforce provisions of the Act through their factory inspectorate. The Directorate General Factory Advice Service and Labour Institute (DGFASLI) Mumbai, renders technical advice to States/UTs in the implementation of the provisions of the Factories Act. The DGFASLI also undertakes support research facilities through five regional labour institutes at Mumbai, Kolkata, Chennai, Kanpur and Faridabad. It carries out promotional activities through education and training in issues concerning occupational safety and health.

The Factories Act prescribes a 48 hours week for adult workers and forbids employment of children below the age of 14 in any factory. The Act also lays down the minimum standards of lighting, ventilation, safety, welfare services which employers must provide in their factories. The factories employing women workers over 30 are required to provide a creche for their children, rest rooms and shelters. Lunch rooms are required to be provided by factories employing more than 150 workers. Factories with 250 workers or more have to compulsorily appoint welfare officers.

The Factories Act was amended in 1987 to impose a general duty on employers to ensure health and safety of workers. A general duty has been imposed on designers, manufacturers, importers and suppliers to ensure that the articles designed, manufactured, imported are without risk to health and safety of workers.

56.

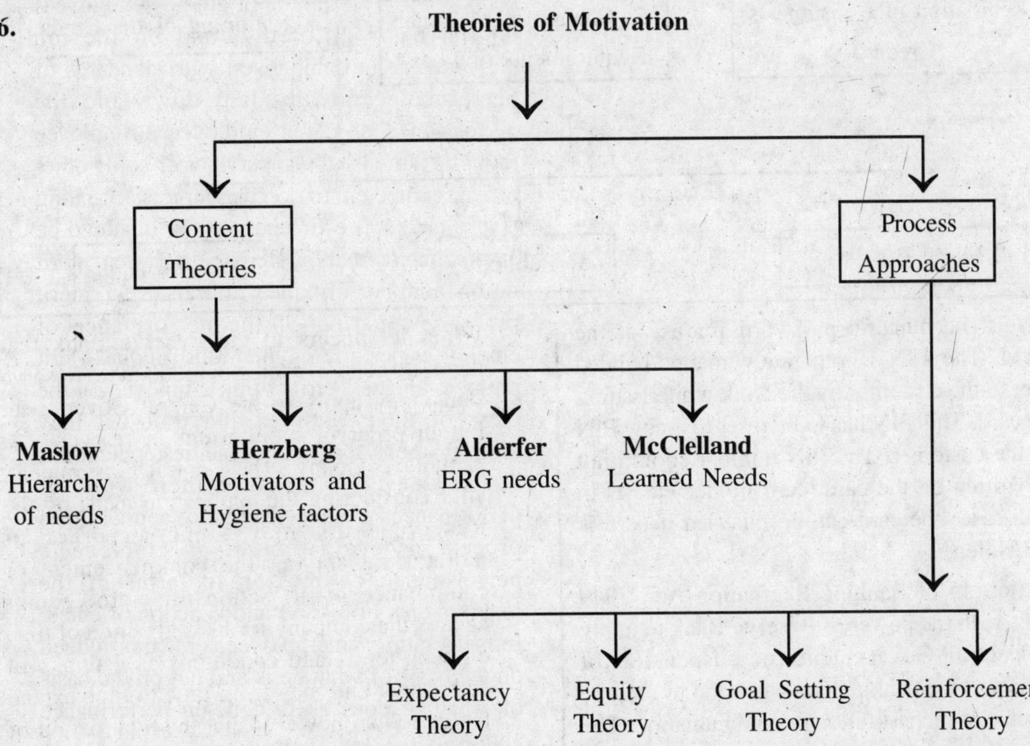

Fig. *Classification of Major Motivation Theories*

58.

Methods of Credit Control

Central Bank usually controls credit by two methods–Quantitative Credit Control and Qualitative Credit Control.

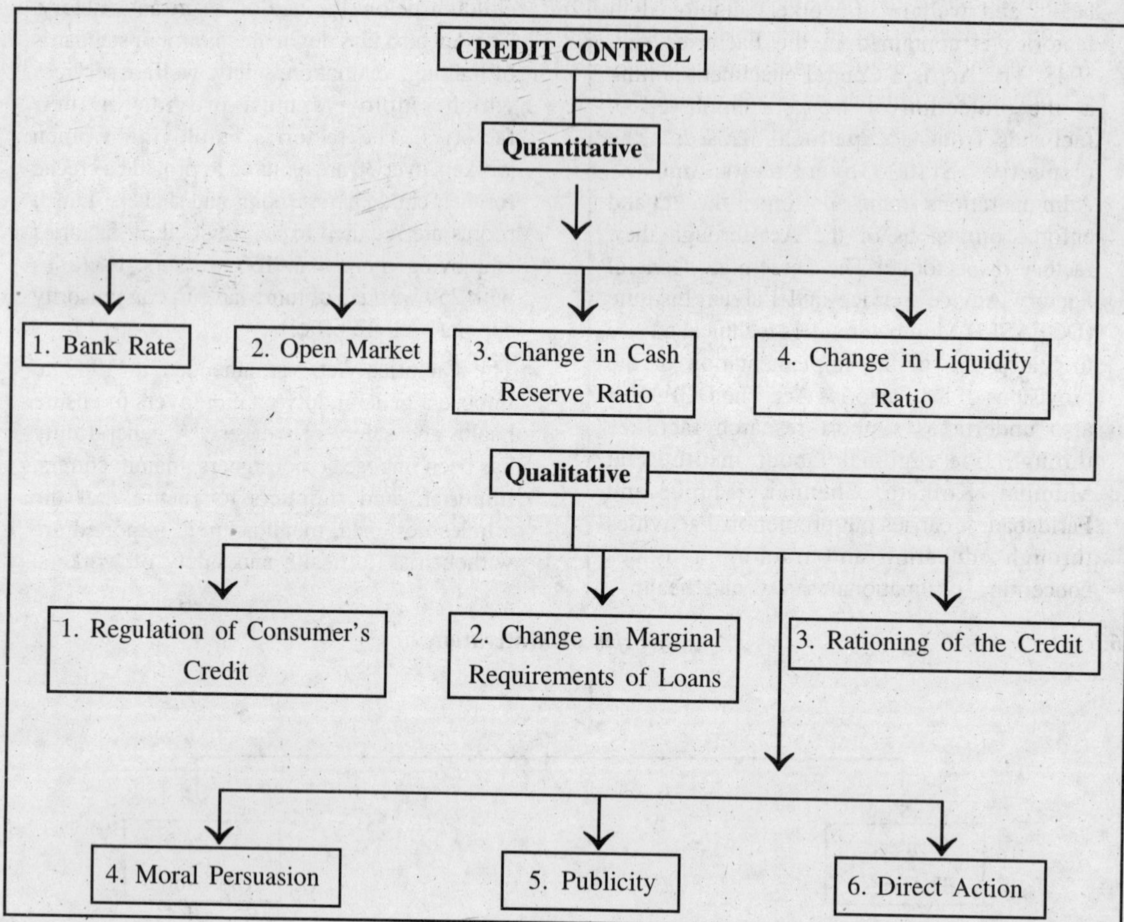

60. PIN is the numeric password for use at the ATM. The PIN is separately mailed/handed over to the customer by the bank while issuing the card. This PIN has to be reset to a new PIN by the customer. The PIN number should not be written on the card, card holder etc. as in such cases the card can be misused if card is lost/stolen.

62. Section 45 of Banking Regulation Act, 1949 deals with the power of Reserve Bank to apply to Central Government for suspension of business by a banking company and to prepare scheme of reconstitution or amalgamation. The provisions of this section are stated below.

When it appears to the Reserve Bank that there is good reason so to do, the Reserve Bank may apply to the Central Government for an order of moratorium in respect of a banking company. The Central Government, after considering the application made by the Reserve Bank may make an order of moratorium staying the commencement or continuance of all actions and proceedings against the company for a fixed period of time on such terms and conditions as it thinks fit and proper and may from time to time extend the period so however that the total period of moratorium shall not exceed six months.

Except for directions given by the Central Government, the banking company shall not during the period of moratorium make any payment to any depositors or discharge any liabilities or obligations to any other creditors.

71. Gross Annual Value (GAV) = Higher of Actual Rent Received or Expected Rent

Expected Rent = Higher of Fair Rent or Municipal Valuation but subject to Standard Rent

= 72000

∴ GAV = Higher of Actual Rent (63000) or expected Rent (72000)

= 72000.

74. Indexed Cost of Acquisition

$$= \frac{\text{Fair Market Value as on 01/04/81} \times \text{Cost Inflation Index for the Year in which asset is transferred}}{\text{Cost Inflation Index for 1981-82}}$$

$$= \frac{120000 \times 632}{100} = 758400$$

Capital Gain = 800000 − 758400 = 41600.

Previous Paper (Solved)

UGC-NET COMMERCE, JUNE–2013

PAPER–II

Note : *This paper contains **fifty (50)** objective type questions, each question carrying **two (2)** marks. **All** questions are compulsory.*

1. Direct supervision over depositories and mutual funds is undertaken by

A. NBFCs

B. RBI

C. SEBI

D. All of the above

2. In the call/notice money market, which of the following participants is allowed to trade?

A. All Banks, Primary Dealers and Mutual Funds

B. All Corporates

C. Only Commercial Banks

D. All of the above

3. Match the items of List-I with the items of List-II and select the correct answer:

	List-I		*List-II*
(*i*)	Private ownership and Free Enterprise.	(*a*)	Secondary Market
(*ii*)	Government ownership and Central Authority.	(*b*)	Capitalism
(*iii*)	The market for the sale and purchase of previously issued securities.	(*c*)	Primary Market
(*iv*)	The market for new long term capital.	(*d*)	Socialism

Codes :

	(*i*)	(*ii*)	(*iii*)	(*iv*)
A.	(*b*)	(*d*)	(*a*)	(*c*)
B.	(*a*)	(*b*)	(*c*)	(*d*)
C.	(*b*)	(*d*)	(*c*)	(*a*)
D.	(*a*)	(*c*)	(*b*)	(*d*)

4. The apex consumer court in India is referred to as

A. The Consumer Education and Research Centre.

B. The Consumer Unity and Trust Society.

C. National Consumer Disputes Redressal Commission.

D. None of the above

5. Who is Chairman of 13th Finance Commission?

A. Dr. C. Rangarajan

B. Mr. Vimal Jalan

C. Dr. Vijay C. Kelkar

D. None of the above

6. Insurance expenses paid to bring an equipment from the place of purchase to the place of installation is a type of

A. Revenue expenditure

B. Capital expenditure

C. Deferred revenue expenditure

D. Operating expense

7. ABC Ltd was incorporated with an authorised Share Capital of ₹ 1,00,000 equity shares of ₹ 10 each. The Board of Directors of the company decided to allot 10,000 shares credited as fully paid to the promoters of the company for their services. Which account should be debited in the books of ABC Ltd.?

A. Promoters' Account

B. Services Account

C. Goodwill Account

D. Share Capital Account

8. In a reconstruction scheme, the reduction of capital may take the form of

A. Reducing the liability of the shareholders in respect of any unpaid amount on the shares held by them.

B. Paying-off any paid-up share capital which is in excess of its requirement.
C. Cancelling any paid-up share capital which is lost or unrepresented by available assets.
D. All of the above.

9. While determining the normal rate of return for the valuation of shares in Market Value Method, which of the following should be taken into consideration?
A. The degree of risk involved.
B. The current rate of interest on gilt-edged securities.
C. Weighted average cost of capital.
D. All of the above.

10. Master budget is a
A. Functional Budget
B. Operating Budget
C. Summary Budget
D. Financial Budget

11. **Assertion (A):** Want-satisfying power of a commodity is called its utility.

Reason (R): Utility may not have the characteristic of morality.

Codes:
A. Both (A) and (R) are correct.
B. (A) is correct, but (R) is not correct.
C. Both (A) and (R) are not correct.
D. (R) is correct, but (A) is not correct.

12. Match the items of List-I with those in List-II and select the correct code for the answer:

List-I	***List-II***
(*a*) Contraction of Demand	(*i*) Non-Price change effect
(*b*) Decrease in Demand	(*ii*) Demand curve remains the same
(*c*) Increase in Demand	(*iii*) Price change effect
(*d*) Expansion of Demand	(*iv*) Shifts the Demand curve

Codes:

	(*a*)	(*b*)	(*c*)	(*d*)
A.	(*iii*)	(*i*)	(*iv*)	(*ii*)
B.	(*iv*)	(*iii*)	(*ii*)	(*i*)
C.	(*i*)	(*ii*)	(*iii*)	(*iv*)
D.	(*ii*)	(*iv*)	(*i*)	(*iii*)

13. **Assertion (A):** As the proportion of one variable factor in a combination with fixed factor is increased, after a point the marginal product of the factor will diminish.

Reason (R) : Beyond the level of optimum combination of inputs leads to this.

Codes:
A. (R) is appropriate reason of (A).
B. (R) is not appropriate reason of (A).
C. (A) and (R) are not related with each other.
D. (A) is independent of (R).

14. Match the items of List-I with the items of List-II and select the correct answer.

List-I	***List-II***
(*a*) Indifference Curve	(*i*) Slopes downward to the right
(*b*) Demand Curve	(*ii*) P = AR = MR = d
(*c*) Perfect Competition	(*iii*) Oligopoly
(*d*) Price Leadership	(*iv*) Convex to the origin

Codes:

	(*a*)	(*b*)	(*c*)	(*d*)
A.	(*ii*)	(*iii*)	(*iv*)	(*i*)
B.	(*iii*)	(*iv*)	(*i*)	(*ii*)
C.	(*iv*)	(*i*)	(*ii*)	(*iii*)
D.	(*i*)	(*ii*)	(*iii*)	(*iv*)

15. Price, Marginal Revenue and Elasticity are related to each other. When $e = 1$, then:
A. MR > 0 B. MR < 0
C. MR = 0 D. MR = 1

16. Consider the following statistical tests:
(*i*) 'F' test.
(*ii*) 't' test
(*iii*) 'z' test
(*iv*) 'Chi-square' test

Which of these are parametric tests?
A. (*i*), (*ii*) and (*iv*) B. (*i*), (*iii*) and (*iv*)
C. (*i*), (*ii*) and (*iii*) D. (*ii*), (*iii*) and (*iv*)

17. The difference between sample statistic and its corresponding population parameter is
A. Sampling error
B. Measurement error
C. Coverage error
D. Non-response error

18. Match the items in List-I with items in List-II.

List-I	*List-II*
(*i*) Level of significance	(*a*) Sample mean is equal to population mean
(*ii*) Standard deviation of sampling distribution	(*b*) Parameters
(*iii*) Numerical value that describes the characteristics of the population	(*c*) Type-I error
(*iv*) Normally-distributed population	(*d*) Standard error

Codes:

	(*i*)	(*ii*)	(*iii*)	(*iv*)
A.	(*d*)	(*c*)	(*a*)	(*b*)
B.	(*c*)	(*d*)	(*b*)	(*a*)
C.	(*c*)	(*b*)	(*d*)	(*a*)
D.	(*d*)	(*b*)	(*c*)	(*a*)

19. Kendall's co-efficient of concordance is used to

A. Test the difference among two or more sets of data.

B. Test the relationship between variables.

C. Test the variations in the given data.

D. Test the randomness of samples.

20. Which of the following softwares are used for data processing?

(*i*) EXCEL

(*ii*) ACCESS

(*iii*) SPSS

(*iv*) STAR

(*v*) PASW

Codes:

A. (*i*), (*ii*), (*iii*) and (*v*)

B. (*ii*), (*iii*), (*iv*) and (*v*)

C. (*iii*) and (*iv*)

D. (*i*), (*iii*) and (*iv*)

21. Match the items of List-I with the items of List-II and select the correct answer.

List-I	*List-II*
(*i*) Grapevine	(*a*) Task group
(*ii*) Formal group	(*b*) Field force theory
(*iii*) Informal group	(*c*) Gossip
(*iv*) Kurt Lewin	(*d*) National group

Codes:

	(*i*)	(*ii*)	(*iii*)	(*iv*)
A.	(*c*)	(*a*)	(*d*)	(*b*)
B.	(*d*)	(*c*)	(*b*)	(*a*)
C.	(*a*)	(*b*)	(*c*)	(*d*)
D.	(*b*)	(*a*)	(*d*)	(*c*)

22. Who has suggested that achievement motivation among individuals and nations can be developed through training courses?

A. MeClelland B. Alderfer

C. Maslow D. Herzberg

23. Assertion (A): When span of control is wide co-ordination and control becomes difficult.

Reason (R): In a narrow span, levels of authority reduces.

Codes:

A. Both (A) and (R) are true and (R) is the correct explanation of (A).

B. Both (A) and (R) are true, but (R) is not a correct explanation of (A).

C. (A) is true, but (R) is false.

D. (A) is false, but (R) is true.

24. The general pattern of behaviour, shared belief and values that members have in common is known as

A. Organisation climate

B. Organisation culture

C. Organisation effectiveness

D. Organisation matrix

25. Which of the following is not a principle of management according to Henry Fayol?

A. Subordination of individual interest over the organisational interest

B. Esprit de crops

C. Unity of Managers

D. Unity of Direction

26. Which of the following concepts is based on development, design and implementation of marketing programmes, processes and activities that recognise their breadth and interdependence?

A. Product concept
B. Sales concept
C. Societal marketing concept
D. Holistic marketing concept

27. The concept of marketing-mix, consisting of the 4 P's of marketing, was developed by
A. E. Jerome McCarthy
B. Peter F. Drucker
C. Philip Kotler
D. William J. Stonton

28. The selling concept is most likely to be used by firms which sell
A. Convenience goods
B. Shopping goods
C. Speciality goods
D. Unsought goods

29. Match the items of List-I with those of List-II and select the correct answer from the codes given below:

List-I	*List-II*
(*a*) Everitt M. Rogers	(*i*) Service Quality Model
(*b*) J.D. Power	(*ii*) Three types of marketing for services
(*c*) Parasuraman, Zeithamal and Berry	(*iii*) Quality rating of automobiles
(*d*) Gronroos	(*iv*) Diffusion of innovation

Codes:

	(*a*)	(*b*)	(*c*)	(*d*)
A.	(*iii*)	(*ii*)	(*i*)	(*iv*)
B.	(*i*)	(*ii*)	(*iii*)	(*iv*)
C.	(*ii*)	(*i*)	(*iv*)	(*iii*)
D.	(*iv*)	(*iii*)	(*i*)	(*ii*)

30. Consumer attitudes and beliefs about diet, health and nutrition are influenced by
A. Economic environment
B. Cultural environment
C. Social environment
D. Natural environment

31. Positive NPV in project appraised by a firm may not occur an account of
A. Economics of scale
B. Market reach
C. Product differentiation
D. Intangible benefits

32. In case the projects are divisible under capital rationing an appropriate project appraisal method is
A. Net Present Value Method
B. Profitability Index Method
C. Internal Rate of Return Method
D. Payback Period Method

33. Permanent working capital is generally financed through
A. Long term Capital Funds
B. Government Assistance
C. Internal Financing
D. Short term loans from Banks

34. The appropriate ratio for indicating liquidity crisis is
A. Operating ratio
B. Sales turnover ratio
C. Current ratio
D. Acid test ratio

35. Who proposed a model to apply economic order quantity concept of inventory management to determine the optimum cash holding in a firm?
A. Keith V. Smith
B. Miller and Orr
C. William J. Baumol
D. J.M. Keynes

36. Which of the following is *not* included in the model of the systems approach to Human Resource Management?
A. Human Resource Planning
B. Recruitment and Selection
C. Performance appraisal
D. Departmentation

37. It is generally easy to measure the performance of the
A. Industrial Relations Manager
B. Research and Development Manager
C. Sales person
D. All of the above

38. Which one of the following is *not* a monetory incentive to sales people?
A. Bonus
B. Staff meeting
C. Travelling allowance
D. Both (B) and (C)

39. Statement (*i*): Sound industrial relations are essential to achieve individual, team goals and organizational goals.

Statement (*ii*): Congenial labour management relations create an atmosphere of harmony and low rate of absenteeism.
A. Statement (*i*) is true, but (*ii*) is false.
B. Statement (*ii*) is true, but (*i*) is false.
C. Both statements are true.
D. Both statements are false.

40. Out of the following, which are the schemes of Social Security?
(*i*) Provident Fund Scheme
(*ii*) Health Insurance Scheme
(*iii*) Job Guarantee Scheme
(*iv*) Maternity Benefit Scheme
(*v*) Merit Promotion Scheme
(*vi*) Compulsory and Voluntary Social Insurance Scheme
(*vii*) Child Insurance Scheme

Codes:
A. (*i*), (*ii*), (*iv*) and (*vi*)
B. (*ii*), (*i*), (*v*) and (*vii*)
C. (*iii*), (*v*), (*iv*) and (*vi*)
D. (*iv*), (*vii*), (*iii*) and (*ii*)

41. RBI ensures that banks operate within the set norms by conducting ______ inspections and ______ monitoring.
A. on site, off site B. off site, on site
C. on site, field D. field, on site

42. Under Section 37 of the Banking (Regulation) Act, a moratorium order can be issued by the High Court for a maximum total period of
A. One month
B. Six months
C. One year
D. One and a half year

43. Bonds or debentures issued by Securitization company should bear interest not less than
A. Bank Rate
B. Prime Lending Rate
C. 1.5% over the Bank Rate
D. 1.5% over the Saving Rate

44. Section 131 of the Negotiable Instruments Act extends protection to the ______
A. Collecting Banker
B. Paying Banker
C. Advising Banker
D. Confirming Banker

45. When a customer, by a letter has advised the bank not to honour/pay a particular cheque, such letter is called ______
A. Cancellation letter B. Garnishee letter
C. Mandate D. None of the above

46. Flow of foreign loans and investments affect
A. Trade balance
B. Current Account balance
C. Capital Account balance
D. None of the above

47. Concessions mainly multinational in character come under the principle of
A. Non-discrimination
B. Reciprocity
C. Market Access
D. Fair Competition

48. From the following identify the one which is not a commercial counter trade?
A. Classical barter
B. Counter purchase
C. Pre-compensation
D. Buy-back agreement

49. If the spot price is higher than the strike price in a call option, it is referred to as
A. At-the-money B. In-the-money
C. Out-of-the-money D. Premium

50. Identity the item which does not include under Current Account transaction.
A. Services
B. Non-monetary movement of gold
C. Unilateral transfer
D. Investment income

ANSWERS

1	2	3	4	5	6	7	8	9	10
C	C	A	C	C	B	C	D	D	C
11	12	13	14	15	16	17	18	19	20
A	A	A	C	C	C	A	B	B	A
21	22	23	24	25	26	27	28	29	30
A	*	C	B	C	D	A	D	D	B
31	32	33	34	35	36	37	38	39	40
D	B	A	D	C	D	C	D	C	A
41	42	43	44	45	46	47	48	49	50
A	B	C	A	D	C	B	D	B	B

SOME SELECTED EXPLANATORY ANSWERS

2. The money market is a market for short-term financial assets that are close substitutes of money. The most important feature of a money market instrument is that it is liquid and can be turned over quickly at low cost and provides an avenue for equilibrating the short-term surplus funds of lenders and the requirements of borrowers. The call/notice money market forms an important segment of the Indian money market. Under call money market, funds are transacted on overnight basis and under notice money market, funds are transacted for the period between 2 days and 14 days.

Participants

Participants in call/notice money market currently include Scheduled Commercial Banks, Co-operative Banks, Primary Dealers (PDs), development finance institutions, insurance companies and select mutual funds. Of these, banks and PDs can operate both as borrowers and lenders in the market. Non-bank institutions, which have been given specific permission to operate in call/notice money market can, however, operate as lenders only.

Eligibility for Transactions in Call/Notice Money Market

Borrowing
1. Scheduled Commercial Banks
2. Co-operative Banks
3. Primary Dealers (PDs)

Lending
1. Scheduled Commercial Banks
2. Co-operative Banks
3. Primary Dealers (PDs)
4. Select all-India Financial Institutions
5. Select Insurance Companies
6. Select Mutual Funds

4. **National Consumer Disputes Redressal Commission (National Commission)**

The National Commission is the Apex body of the Consumer Forums of the three tier system excerpted in the The Consumer Protection Act, 1986 (CPA). The "National Commission" has been set up under the provision of Section 9 of the Act. The place of National Commission is at New Delhi. The original jurisdiction with regard of pecuniary jurisdiction is above ₹ 1 crore and all complaints wherein the value of claim is above One crore are filed before the National Commission. The National Commission also acts as an Appellate Court over the matter decided by the any of state commission in India. Apart the appellate powers the National Commission also has revisional and review powers. The president National Commission is a retired judge of Supreme Court of India. The National Commission has apart from the president at least four other members to assist the president and out of these four members one member is required to be a woman.

5. **Finance Commission:** According to Article 280 of Indian Constitution, the President appoints a Finance Commission after every five years. This provision is also a fundamental feature of Indian Constitution which is not found in any other Constitution. The Finance Commission was appointed two years after the implementation of Indian Constitution and every five years thereafter. The President has the power to appoint a new Finance Commission even before the expiry of five years, if he deems it necessary. In other words, the appointment of the Finance Commission is a continuous process according to our Constitution. Finance Commission, generally, presents its recommendations regarding the allocation of revenue between the centre and the state so that there is no discord between the centre and the states. Main objective of the Finance Commission is to assess the financial requirements of the states to determine amount of grants in aid to be given to various states and to strengthen the Federal financial system.

Finance Commission	Chairman
1st (1951)	Mr. K.C. Nyogi
2nd (1956)	Mr. K.A. Santhanam
3rd (1961)	Mr. A.K. Chanda
4th (1966)	Mr. R.V. Rajamannar
5th (1968)	Mr. Mahavir Tyagi
6th (1972)	Mr. Brahmananda Reddy
7th (1977)	Mr. J.M. Shelat
8th (1982)	Mr. Y.B. Chavan
9th (1987)	Mr. N.K.P. Salve
10th (1992)	Shri K.C. Pant
11th (1998)	Prof. A.M. Khusro
12th (2004)	Dr. C. Rangarajan
13th (2008)	Dr. Vijay L. Kelkar

7. **Issue of shares to promoters:** Issue of shares to promoters as reward for their service. Here goodwill a/c is debited and share capital is credited.

   Goodwill a/c .....Dr

   Share Capital a/c

8. **Meaning:** Capital Reduction is the repayment or writing down of a company's different classes of capital, as a result of large accumulated losses or an excess of funds without profitable use.

   Though Capital Reduction may be effected when a company accumulates huge surplus funds far in excess of its requirements, but it is more usually followed, when a company passes through a period of financial difficulties, accumulates losses or has its assets over-valued.

   Objective of Capital Reduction: When new capital has to be introduced to revive a company, the success of a new issue would however, almost certainly be jeopardised by the existence of accumulated losses. Therefore, it is prudent and usual to write-off these losses by putting a reconstruction scheme into effect.

   The objective of Capital Reduction is the resumption of the payment of normal dividends out of the expected future profits without the necessity of using those profits to write-off the debit balance of the Profit and Loss Account.

   Procedure: In order to effect Share Capital Reduction, the following formalities must be completed in accordance with the Companies Act, 1956 (Sec. 100 to 104).

   (*i*) The company must be authorised by its articles of association to reduce the share capital. If there is no provision in the article in this respect, it must pass a Special Resolution to alter its articles of association. It should be noted that an authority to do so contained in the memorandum is of no avail. (Re: Dexine Patent Packing and Rubber Co.)

(ii) The company must pass a Special Resolution to reduce the share capital.

(iii) The company must apply, by petitions, to the Court for an order confirming the reduction. If the court is satisfied that the creditor's interests have been secured, it may confirm the reduction. However, it may impose terms and conditions including a direction that the word "and reduced" should be added after the name of the company for a certain period of time, and that the company should publish the reasons for such reduction. (For failure to add the words "and reduced" a penalty of ₹ 500 is payable.)

(iv) The company has to deliver to the Registrar a certified copy of the Court's order and a minute approved by the Court showing the details of the shares for registration.

(v) The Registrar will then register the order and the minute.

(vi) After registration of these, the Resolution to reduce the share capital shall take effect.

(vii) Notice of the registration shall be published in such a manner as the Court may direct.

Form of Reduction: The reduction of capital may take any of the following forms:

(i) The company may reduce the liability of the shareholders in respect of any unpaid amount on the shares held by them.

(ii) The company may pay-off any paid-up share capital which is in excess of its requirements.

(iii) The company may cancel any paid-up share capital which is lost or unrepresented by available assets.

9. **Yield Valuation Method:** This method is also known as Market Value Method. The word 'yield' means a rate of return relating cash invested to cash received (or expected to be received). Yield may be 'Earning yield' or 'Dividend yield'. They are as under:

Earning Yield: A company cannot grow and can never be in a position to increase its dividends, if it distributes all of its profits as dividends. There are also legal restrictions by the Companies Act for distribution of profits as dividends. Therefore, a shareholder will have interest both in the retained profits as well as distributed profits. Under this method, shares are valued on the basis of the earnings expected by using an average of recent years as the best indicator of what future earnings of the company will be. Under this method, value of each share is calculated by applying the following formula:

$$\text{Value Per Share} = \frac{\text{Expected Rate of Earnings (ERE)}^{*}}{\text{Normal Rate of Return (NRR)}} \times \text{Face Value of Share}$$

*Expected Rate of Earnings (ERE)

$$= \frac{\text{Profit after Tax}}{\text{Paid-up Value of Shares}} \times 100$$

While fixing the normal rate of return, the degree of risk involved and the current rate of interest on gilt-edged securities should also be taken into consideration.

10. **Master Budget:** It is the overall budget for the entire enterprise. It covers summarized figures for different activities of a firm. The other names for master budget are 'summary budget' or "finalized profit plan". Master budget includes both the budgeted position of the profit and loss and balance sheet. Master budget is prepared by the budget committee of the enterprise. This master budget acts as a target for the whole firm.

Definition: A master budget is defined as a budget which is prepared from, or summarizes, the functional budgets. It is defined as "a summary of the budget schedules in capsule form made for the purpose of presenting, in one report, the highlights of the budget forecast". Master budget is also called **summary budget**. According to ICMA of England, it is defined as "The summary budget incorporating its component functional budgets and which is finally approved, adopted and employed". It is prepared by the budget committee.

Advantages of a master budget are:

1. A summary of all functional budgets in capsule form is available for reference.
2. This indicates total position of business during the budget period.
3. It tells about the budgeted profit or loss.
4. This highlights on assets and liabilities of business during the budget period.

11. In economics, the term 'utility' is used for that specific quality of a good or service which leads to satisfaction of our wants. **Want satisfying capacity of a good is called utility.** According to **Jevons,** "*Utility refers to abstract quality whereby an object serves our purpose.*" Utility has the following main features:

(i) **Utility is Subjective:** Utility is subjective because it deals with the mental satisfaction of a man. A thing may have different utility for different persons. Liquor has utility for a drunkard but for a person who is **teetotaller,** liquor has no utility. Peasants of Haryana get very little utility from coffee whereas peasants of Kerala derive lot of utility from its consumption. Utility, therefore, is subjective.

(ii) **Utility is Relative:** Utility of a commodity never remains the same. It varies with time and place. Cooler has utility in the summer but not during the winter season.

(iii) **Utility is not Essentially Useful:** A commodity having utility need not be useful. Liquor and cigarette are not useful, but if these things satisfy the want of an addict then they have utility for him.

(iv) **Utility is Independent of Morality:** Utility has nothing to do with morality. Use of opium or liquor may not be proper from the moral point of view, but as these intoxicants satisfy wants of the opium-eaters and drunkards, they have utility.

12. Extension in demand means rise in demand in response to fall in the price of a commodity, other things being equal. It is expressed by the movement from a higher point to a lower point along the same demand curve. On the other hand, **increase in demand** refers to rise in demand in response to change in the determinants of demand (like tastes, income of the consumer, price of substitutes) other than the price. It is expressed by the upward shift of the entire demand curve.

Contraction in demand means fall in demand in response to a rise in the price of a commodity, other things being equal. It is expressed by the movement from a lower point to a higher point on the same demand curve. On the other hand, **decrease in demand** means fall in demand in response to change in determinants of demand, other than the price. It is expressed by a downward shift of the entire demand curve.

15. The relation between marginal revenue, price and price elasticity, *for linear or curvilinear demands,* is

$$MR = P\left(1+\frac{1}{E}\right)$$

where E is the price elasticity of demand and P is product price. When demand is elastic ($|E| > 1$), $|1/E|$ is less than 1, $1 + (1/E)$ is positive, and marginal revenue is positive. When demand is inelastic ($|E| < 1$), $|1/E|$ is greater than 1, $1 + (1/E)$ is negative, and marginal revenue is negative. In the case of unitary price elasticity ($E = -1$), $1 + (1/E)$ is 0, and marginal revenue is 0.

16. Types of Tests:

1. Parametric test.
2. Non-parametric test.

Parametric Test:

1. Parametric tests are more powerful. The data in this test is derived from interval and ratio measurement.
2. In parametric tests, it is assumed that the data follows normal distributions.

Examples of parametric tests are (*a*) Z-Test, (*b*) T-Test and (*c*) F-Test.

3. Observations must be independent i.e., selection of any one item should not affect the chances of selecting any others be included in the sample.

Non-parametric Test:

Non-parametric tests are used to test the hypothesis with nominal and ordinal data.

1. We do not make assumptions about the shape of population distribution.
2. These are distribution-free tests.
3. The hypothesis of non-parametric test is concerned with something other than the value of a population parameter.
4. Easy to compute. There are certain situations particularly in marketing research, where the assumptions of parametric tests are not valued. *Example:* In a parametric test, we assume that data collected follows a normal distribution. In such cases, non-parametric tests are used. Example of non-parametric tests are (*a*) Binomial test (*b*) Chi-Square test (*c*) Mann-Whitney U test (*d*) Sign test. A binomial test is used when the population has only two classes such as male, female; buyers, non-buyers, success, failure etc. All observations made about the population must fall into one of the two tests. The binomial test is used when the sample size is small.

17. Sampling error is simply the difference between the sample statistic and the unknown population parameter it is intended to estimate. The sampling error is expressed as the difference between the sample mean and the unknown population mean $(\bar{X} - \mu)$.

19. Kendall's Coefficient of Concordance: A measure to find out the degree of association among the ranking of '*n*' objects by '*n*' respondents or judges. It ranges between '0' and '+1' and its value is denoted as '*w*'.

21. Force Field Analysis: A tool, developed by social psychologist Kurt Lewin, which is used to analyze the opposing forces involved in causing/resisting any change. It is shown in balance-sheet format with forces that will help (driving forces) listed on the left and forces that hinder (restraining forces) listed on the right.

Grapevine is the most uncontrolled form of communication which spreads in all directions informally and unofficially by means of gossip and rumor and at a very fast pace just like a grape fruit vine and that is how it got its name.

- ***Formal groups*** are created by an organization and are designed to direct members toward some important organizational goal
  - ***Command groups*** are determined by the connections between individuals who are a formal part of the organization
  - ***Task groups*** are formed around some specific task
- ***Informal groups*** develop naturally among an organization's personnel without any direction from the management of the organization within which they operate
  - ***Interest group***
  - ***Friendship group***

23. Span of Control: The number of people under a manager is an important feature of an organization's structure. The number of subordinates who report directly to an executive or supervisor is called the **span of control**. The implications of differences in the span of control for the shape of an organization are straightforward. Holding size constant, narrow spans build a *tall* organization that has many reporting levels. Wide spans create a *flat* organization with fewer reporting levels. The span of control can be too narrow or too wide. The optimal span of control maximizes effectiveness because it is (1) narrow enough to permit managers to maintain control over subordinates but (2) not so narrow that it leads to overcontrol and an excessive number of managers who oversee a small number of subordinates.

Actually, the optimal span of control depends on a number of factors. The span should be wider when (1) the work is clearly defined and unambiguous, (2) subordinates are highly trained and have access to information, (3) the manager is highly capable and supportive, (4) jobs are similar and performance measures are comparable, and (5) subordinates prefer autonomy to close supervisory control. If the opposite conditions exist, a narrow span of control my be more appropriate.

24. **Meaning and Definition of Culture**

Culture can be inferred from what people say, do and think within an organizational setting. It sets the tone for the company and establishes implied rules for the way people should behave. Weihrich, Cannice and Koontz have defined it as the general pattern of behaviour, shared beliefs and values that members have in common.

Organizational culture has been called the corporate soul—the spirit and the ethos that percolates all aspects of organizational behaviour. In fact, McShane has defined organizational culture as the values and assumptions shared within an organization. Organization culture directs everyone in the organization towards the "right way" of doing things.

Stephen Robbins defines it as a system of shared meaning which distinguishes the organization from other organizations. Newstrom has defined organizational culture as a set of assumptions, beliefs, values and norms that are shared by an organization's members.

The organizational culture is important for a firm's success because of the following reasons:

1. It gives an organizational identity to employees and defines what the oganization represents.
2. It is an important source of stability and continuity to the organization and provides a sense of security to its members.
3. It helps the employees to know what is going on in the oganization and provides a ready context for events which could be confusing.
4. The culture of the organization helps to stimulate employee enthusiasm for their tasks.

25. **Fundamental Principles of Management:** Principles advocated by Henry Fayol: (*i*) Division of work, (*ii*) Authority and responsibility, (*iii*) Discipline, (*iv*) Unity of command, (*v*) Unity of direction, (*vi*) Subordination of Individual to General Interest, (*vii*) Remuneration to employees, (*viii*) Centralisation and Decentralisation, (*ix*) Scalar Chain, (*x*) Order, (*xi*) Equity, (*xii*) Stability of personnel, (*xiii*) Initiative, and (*xiv*) Esprit de corps.

26. **Holistic Marketing:** This concept is based on the development, design and implementation of marketing programs, processes and activities that recognize their breadth and interdependence. Holistic marketing recognize that everything matters with marketing. It integrates all the aspect of the business like internal marketing, relationship marketing, integrated marketing and social responsibility.

27. 'Marketing mix is the mixture of controllable marketing variables that the firm uses to pursue the sought level of sales to target markets.' (Kotler, 1984).

There are dozens of marketing mix elements, but in his book *Basic Marketing: A Managerial Approach* (1981) McCarthy popularised the four Ps approach – product, price, place and promotion.

28. **The Selling Concept:** The selling concept holds that consumers, if left alone, will ordinarily not buy enough of the organization's products. The organization must therefore undertake an aggressive selling and promotion effort.

The concept assumes that customers typically show buying resistance and have to be coaxed into buying and the company has to use a whole battery of effective selling and promotion tools to stimulate more buying. The selling concept is practiced most aggressively with unsought goods, the goods that buyers normally do not think of buying. The perfect example is selling of insurance. The seller here is not selling a tangible produce, but a promise, and that too more often after a person's death. Hard selling techniques are a requirement for this industry. The industries like these have perfected various sales techniques to locate prospects and hard sell them on the product benefits.

31. **Intangible benefits:** Benefits that cannot be measured in financial terms, such as improved morale or employee safety.

    Net present value: The sum of discounted benefits minus the development costs.

    Limitations of Net Present Value: Although NPV measurement is widely used for making investment decisions, a disadvantage of NPV is that it does not account for uncertainty after the project decision has been made.

    NPV is unable to deal with intangible benefits, which decreases its value for strategic issues and projects.

32. **Capital Rationing:** Capital rationing refers to situation in which, the company attempts to select the combination of projects that will provide the greatest increment to firm value, subject to some budget constraints. Managers should accept all attractive investment opportunities, but some objective or subjective reasons cause the choice of only the best projects. It is important to understand that this approach is inconsistent with the goal of value maximization. Regardless of how high the opportunity cost of capital may be, the firm should accept all the projects if their NPVs are positive. That it makes no sense to say that capital rationing exists because financing becomes to much expensive. In selecting investment projects under capital rationing, it is necessary to understand that some projects are divisible and others are indivisible. Projects that should be accepted or rejected in their entirety are indivisible. The company should choose the combination of indivisible projects that maximizes the sum of their NPVs without exceeding the budget constraints. On the other hand, projects may be divisible. When projects are divisible, the profitability index criterion is appropriate to make the right decision. Projects may be ranked using PI values from highest to lowest, and then the highest-ranked projects that do not exceed the imposed capital budget may be selected.

33. Working capital can be (*i*) permanent and (*ii*) temporary. While the permanent component reflects the need for a certain irreducible level of current assets on a continuous and uninterrupted basis, the temporary portion is needed to meet seasonal and other temporary requirements. While permanent working capital requirements should be financed from long-term sources, short-term funds should be used to finance temporary working capital needs of a firm.

34. **Quick Ratio (Acid Test Ratio):** This is the measure of liquidity of a company. This relates quick assets to current liabilities to test the critical liquidity position of a company. The computation of quick ratio is as follows:

    Quick ratio = Quick assets/Current liabilities

    Quick assets are the assets that can be easily converted into cash or cash equivalents. The current asset that is a major problem to a business enterprise is its inventory holding. Inventory has to be converted into sales to make it into a cash equivalent. Till then the value of the inventory cannot be considered as a cash equivalent. Hence current assets excluding inventory is termed quick assets. These quick assets may be equal to the current liabilities of a company. A very low ratio indicates the short-term debt trap of a company and a very high ratio compared to industry standards indicates too much of asset holding that do not yield high returns to the company.

35. William J. Baumol Model (Inventory Model): William J. Baumol's mathematical model is based on the combination of inventory theory with monetary theory. In determination of optimum level of cash of a company, economic order quantity model is used in the standard inventory situation. According to this model, the optimum cash level is that level of cash where the carrying cost and transaction cost are the minimum. In other words, the optimum level of cash is one at which that point where carrying costs and transmission costs are equal. It indicates optimum level of cash required by the company. The carrying cost of holding cash refers to the interest foregone on marketable securities, whereas transaction cost represents the cost of liquidating marketable securities into cash. The formula for determining optimum cash balance is:

$$C = \sqrt{\frac{2UP}{S}}$$

where,

C = Optimum cash balances (i.e., optimum amount of cash to be withdrawn each time)

U = Annual (monthly) cash disbursement (total amount of transaction demand)

P = Fixed cost per transaction

S = Opportunity cost of one rupee per annum (Cost of carrying cash inventory interest rate on marketable securities for the period involved)

36. Human Resource Management (HRMN) is the specialized field in management devoted to strategies and techniques for the effective utilization of people. The field of HRMN deals with human resource planning, the recruitment and selection of employees, training and development, performance appraisal, compensation and benefits and employee/labour relations.

38. In many cases, sales motivation depends on the quality of management provided by the first-line sales supervisor. Through day-to-day contact, the manager sets the style and tone for the salesperson's relationship with the company. However, personal supervision is limited by the time available to the manager, and sales incentives (including compensation) must also be used to motivate salespeople. A sales incentive can be defined as anything that is used to reward sales personnel for their accomplishments.

TYPES OF INCENTIVES

Nonfinancial Incentives:

- Recognition
- Sales contests and incentive programs
- Sales meetings
- Sales training

Financial Incentives (Direct)

- Salary
- Commission
- Bonus

Indirect Financial Rewards

- Fringe benefits

40. Social Security protects not just the subscriber but also his/her entire family by giving benefit packages in financial security and health care. Social Security schemes are designed to guarantee at least long-term sustenance to families when the earning member retires, dies or suffers a disability. Thus the main strength of the Social Security system is that it acts as a facilitator – it helps people to plan their own future through insurance and assistance. The success of Social Security schemes however, requires the active support and involvement of employees and employers.

The principal social security laws enacted in India are the following:

1. The Employees' State Insurance Act, 1948 (ESI Act) which covers factories and establishments with 10 or more employees and provides for comprehensive medical care to the employees and their families as

well as cash benefits during sickness and maternity, and monthly payments in case of death or disablement.

2. The Employees' Provident Funds & Miscellaneous Provisions Act, 1952 (EPF & MP Act) which applies to specific scheduled factories and establishments employing 20 or more employees and ensures terminal benefits to provident fund, superannuation pension, and family pension in case of death during service. Separate laws exist for similar benefits for the workers in the coal mines and tea plantations.
3. The Employees' Compensation Act, 1923 (WC Act), which requires payment of compensation to the workman or his family in cases of employment related injuries resulting in death or disability.
4. The Maternity Benefit Act, 1961 (M.B. Act), which provides for 12 weeks wages during maternity as well as paid leave in certain other related contingencies.
5. The Payment of Gratuity Act, 1972 (P.G. Act), which provides 15 days wages for each year of service to employees who have worked for five years or more in establishments having a minimum of 10 workers.

41. The Banking Regulation Act, 1949 empowers the Reserve Bank of India to inspect and supervise commercial banks. These powers are exercised through on-site inspection and off site surveillance.

42. Under Section 37 of Banking Regulation Act, a moratorium order can be issued by High Court for a maximum total period of 6 months.

43. Guidelines to banks/ FIs on sale of Financial Assets to Securitisation Company (SC)/ Reconstruction Company (RC)

The securities (bonds and debentures) offered by SC/RC should satisfy the following conditions:

(*i*) The securities must not have a term in excess of six years.

(*ii*) The securities must carry a rate of interest which is not lower than 1.5% above the Bank Rate in force at the time of issue.

(*iii*) The securities must be secured by an appropriate charge on the assets transferred.

(*iv*) The securities must provide for part or full prepayment in the event the SC/RC sells the asset securing the security before the maturity date of the security.

(*v*) The commitment of the SC/RC to redeem the securities must be unconditional and not linked to the realization of the assets.

(*vi*) Whenever the security is transferred to any other party, notice of transfer should be issued to the SC/RC.

44. Section 131 of the Negotiable Instruments Act 1881 extends protection to the Collecting Banker.

According to section 131 of the NI Act:

"A banker who has in good faith and without negligence received payment for a customer of a cheque crossed generally or specially to himself shall not, in case the title to cheque proves defective, incur any liability to the true owner of the cheque by reason only of having received such payment."

The collecting banker is given statutory protection subject to fulfilment of following conditions:

1. The cheque must be a crossed cheque.
2. The payment must be received for a customer.
3. Payment must be received in good faith and without negligence.

46. Under current account of the BoP, transactions are classified into merchandise (exports and imports) and invisibles. Invisible transactions are further classified into three categories. The first component is Services comprising travel, transportation, insurance, government not included elsewhere (GNIE), and miscellaneous. Miscellaneous services include communication, construction, financial, software, news agency, royalties, management, and business services.

The second component of invisibles is income. Transfers (grants, gifts, remittances, etc.) which do not have any quid pro quo form the third category of invisibles.

Under capital account, capital inflows can be classified by instrument (debt or equity) and maturity (short- or long-term). The main components of capital account include foreign investment, loans, and banking capital.

47. Reciprocity means that affiliates of foreign firms are given the same treatment in the host country as the host country's firms are given in the nation they call headquarters.

48. Counter-trade: Counter-trade is a sort of bilateral trade where one set of goods is exchanged for another set of goods. In this type of external trade, a seller provides a buyer with deliveries and contractually agrees to purchase goods from the buyer equal to the agreed percentage of the original sale contract value (US Department of Commerce, 1978). Counter-trade is classified broadly as:

1. Commercial counter-trade such as classical barter, counter-purchase and pre-compensation.
2. Industrial counter-trade such as buy-back agreements, develop for import arrangements, and framework agreements.

49. In-the-Money Option: An in-the-money (ITM) option is an option that would lead to a positive cashflow to the holder if it were exercised immediately. A call option on the index is said to be in-the-money when the current index stands at a level higher than the strike price (that is, spot price > strike price). If the index is much higher than the strike price, the call is said to be deep ITM. In the case of a put, the put is ITM if the index is below the strike price.

At-the-Money Option: An at-the-money (ATM) option is an option that would lead to zero cashflow if it were exercised immediately. An option on the index is at-the-money when the current index equals the strike price (that is, spot price = strike price).

Out-of-the-Money Option: An out-of-the-money (OTM) option is an option that would lead to a negative cashflow if it were exercised immediately. A call option on the index is out-of-the-money when the current index stands at a level that is less than the strike price (that is, spot price < strike price). If the index is much lower than the strike price, the call is said to be deep OTM. In the case of a put, the put is OTM if the index is above the strike price.

PAPER–III

Note: *This paper contains* ***seventy five (75)*** *objective type questions of* ***two (2)*** *marks each.* ***All*** *questions are compulsory.*

1. Under the provisions of the Industries (Development and Regulation) Act, 1951, a licence is necessary for

A. changing the location of an existing industrial undertaking.
B. producing or manufacturing a 'new article' in an existing industrial undertaking.
C. establishing a new undertaking.
D. All of the above.

2. Match the items of List-I with the items of List-II and select the correct answer.

List-I	*List-II*
(*i*) Political and Legal Environment	(*a*) Important for industries directly depending on imports or exports.
(*ii*) Demographic Environment	(*b*) Close relationship with the economic system and economic policy.
(*iii*) Economic Environment	(*c*) Related to natural resources.

(*iv*) Geographical and Ecological Environment	(*d*) Occupational and spatial mobilities of population having implications for business.

Codes :

	(*i*)	(*ii*)	(*iii*)	(*iv*)
A.	(*b*)	(*d*)	(*c*)	(*a*)
B.	(*b*)	(*d*)	(*a*)	(*c*)
C.	(*a*)	(*b*)	(*c*)	(*d*)
D.	(*a*)	(*b*)	(*d*)	(*c*)

3. Match the items of List-I with the items of List-II and select the correct answer:

List-I	***List-II***
(*i*) SLR	(*a*) Working in the field of consumer protection.
(*ii*) SIDBI	(*b*) Credit control.
(*iii*) CUTS	(*c*) Industrial policy.
(*iv*) ILPIC	(*d*) Facilitating Small Scale Industries.

Codes:

	(*i*)	(*ii*)	(*iii*)	(*iv*)
A.	(*a*)	(*c*)	(*d*)	(*b*)
B.	(*b*)	(*d*)	(*a*)	(*c*)
C.	(*a*)	(*b*)	(*c*)	(*d*)
D.	(*a*)	(*c*)	(*b*)	(*d*)

4. Match the following:

List-I	***List-II***
(*i*) National Stock Exchange	(*a*) Marks the beginning of the process of dematerialisation of shares of the participating companies.
(*ii*) National Securities Depository Limited	(*b*) Facilitation of equal access to investors across the country.
(*iii*) Securities and Exchange Board of India	(*c*) To foster the development of an active secondary market for Government Securities.
(*iv*) Securities Trading Corporation of India	(*d*) Abolition of Capital issues control and retaining the sale authority for new capital issues.

Codes:

	(*i*)	(*ii*)	(*iii*)	(*iv*)
A.	(*b*)	(*a*)	(*d*)	(*c*)
B.	(*a*)	(*b*)	(*c*)	(*d*)
C.	(*a*)	(*b*)	(*d*)	(*c*)
D.	(*d*)	(*c*)	(*b*)	(*a*)

5. The United Nations Conference on Trade and Development (UNCTAD) was set up in -

A. 1944 B. 1954
C. 1960 D. 1964

6. Indicate the ground on which a complaint under the Consumer Protection Act, 1986, shall be invalid.

A. A product having short weight.
B. A service provided free of cost.
C. A misleading advertisement given in newspaper.
D. None of the above.

7. Out of the following, which are the four components of food security?

(*i*) Food availability
(*ii*) Food market
(*iii*) Food accessibility
(*iv*) Food utilization
(*v*) Food credit

Codes:

A. (*iii*), (*iv*) and (*v*)
B. (*i*), (*iii*) and (*iv*)
C. (*i*), (*ii*) and (*iii*)
D. (*i*), (*ii*) and (*iv*)

8. Performance evaluation of a responsibility centre can be done by

A. ROI B. Return on sales
C. EVA D. All of the above

9. Social Balance Sheet shows

A. Social costs
B. Social revenues
C. Value of employees of the organization
D. All of the above

10. Which of the following comes under efficiency ratios?

A. Average collection period
B. Inventory turnover ratio
C. Fixed assets turnover ratio
D. All of the above

11. Match the items of the following two lists:

List-I	List-II
(*i*) Statement of changes in Working Capital	(*a*) Cash Flow Statement
(*ii*) Deferred Tax	(*b*) Fixed Assets
(*iii*) Three activities	(*c*) Funds Flow Statement
(*iv*) Impairment Loss	(*d*) Balance Sheet

Codes:

	(*i*)	(*ii*)	(*iii*)	(*iv*)
A.	(*a*)	(*b*)	(*c*)	(*d*)
B.	(*c*)	(*d*)	(*b*)	(*a*)
C.	(*c*)	(*d*)	(*a*)	(*b*)
D.	(*d*)	(*c*)	(*a*)	(*b*)

12. Match the items of the following two lists and indicate the correct answer:

List-I	List-II
(*i*) Earning ability of firm	(*a*) Basis of Accounting
(*ii*) Conservatism	(*b*) P/V ratio
(*iii*) Cash profit	(*c*) Cash flow statement
(*iv*) Cash and Accrual	(*d*) Prudence

Codes:

	(*i*)	(*ii*)	(*iii*)	(*iv*)
A.	(*b*)	(*d*)	(*c*)	(*a*)
B.	(*b*)	(*a*)	(*d*)	(*c*)
C.	(*c*)	(*d*)	(*a*)	(*b*)
D.	(*c*)	(*d*)	(*b*)	(*a*)

13. Given below are two statements, one labelled as Assertion (A) and the other labelled as Reason (R).

Assertion (A): Only the relevant costs should be taken into consideration for decision-making.

Reason (R): All variable costs are relevant costs and all fixed costs are irrelevant costs.

In the above two statements, which one alternative of the following is correct?

Codes:

A. Both (A) and (R) are correct.
B. Only (A) is correct, but (R) is wrong.
C. Only (R) is correct, but (A) is wrong.
D. Both (A) and (R) are wrong.

14. Given below are two statements, one labelled as Assertion (A) and the other labelled as Reason (R):

Assertion (A): Variance analysis is undertaken for planning and control of costs.

Reason (R) : Future costs are taken into consideration in budgeting and standard costing.

In the above two statements, which one alternative of the following is correct?

Codes:

A. Both (A) and (R) are correct and (R) is the Reason for (A).
B. Both (A) and (R) are correct and (R) is not the Reason for (A).
C. (A) is correct, but (R) is wrong.
D. (A) is wrong, but (R) is correct.

15. **Assertion (A):** Mark-up pricing is a method of determining price.

Reason (R): P = ATC + (m × ATC) is the expression for that.

Codes:

A. (A) is correct but (R) is not correct.
B. Both (A) and (R) are correct.
C. Both (A) and (R) are not correct.
D. (R) is correct, but (A) is not correct.

16. Match the items of List-I with the items of List-II and select the correct answer.

List-I	List-II
(*a*) Economic profit	(*i*) Total Revenue Explicit cost
(*b*) Accounting profit	(*ii*) Buyers and Sellers exchanging
(*c*) Collusion/Cartel	(*iii*) Total Revenue – Total cost
(*d*) Market	(*iv*) Oligopoly

Codes:

	(a)	(b)	(c)	(d)
A.	(iii)	(i)	(iv)	(ii)
B.	(i)	(ii)	(iii)	(iv)
C.	(iv)	(iii)	(ii)	(i)
D.	(ii)	(iv)	(i)	(iii)

17. Which one is not the item of economic cost to the business?

A. Owner supplied resources.
B. Market supplied resources.
C. Implicit costs.
D. Non-monetary opportunity costs of using owner supplied resources.

18. Demand must have the elements

A. Desire
B. Want
C. Quantity, Price and Time
D. All of the above

19. Match the items of List-I and items of List-II and select the correct code for the answer.

List-I	*List-II*
(a) Utilitarian Approach	(i) Marginal Rate of Substitution
(b) Ordinal Approach	(ii) Budget line & Indifference Curve
(c) Price-Consumption Curve	(iii) $U = f(x, y)$
(d) Consumer Equilibrium	(iv) $MRS_{xy} = MRS_{yx}$

Codes :

	(a)	(b)	(c)	(d)
A.	(i)	(iv)	(iii)	(ii)
B.	(ii)	(iii)	(iv)	(i)
C.	(iii)	(i)	(ii)	(iv)
D.	(iv)	(ii)	(i)	(iii)

20. The Learner Index measures

A. Market power
B. Price
C. Price-Marginal cost
D. None of the above

21. Match the items of List-I and items of List-II and select the correct answer.

List-I	*List-II*
(a) Perfect competition	(i) Different prices for the same product
(b) Monopolistic competition	(ii) Dominant strategy
(c) Oligopoly	(iii) Product differentiation
(d) Discriminating Monopoly	(iv) Identical product

Codes:

	(a)	(b)	(c)	(d)
A.	(iv)	(iii)	(ii)	(i)
B.	(i)	(ii)	(iii)	(iv)
C.	(ii)	(iv)	(i)	(iii)
D.	(iii)	(i)	(iv)	(ii)

22. If there are 8 possible classes under consideration for a goodness of-fit, the number of degrees of freedom will be

A. 8
B. 7
C. 6
D. Cannot be determined from the given information.

23. Identify from the following, the test statistic for which the value of numerator should always be greater than that of denominator.

A. 'Chi-square' B. 'F' value
C. 'Z' value D. 't' value

24. Which of the following tests can be applied to ordinal scale data?

(i) Chi-square test
(ii) 'Z' test
(iii) Kruskal-Wallis test
(iv) Wilcoxon Mann-Whitney test

Codes:

A. (i), (ii) and (iii) B. (ii), (iv) and (iii)
C. (i), (iii) and (iv) D. (i), (ii) and (iv)

25. Which of the following tests can be based on the normal distribution?

A. Difference between independent means
B. Difference between dependant means
C. Difference between proportions
D. All of the above

26. From the following, identify one situation where 'F' test *cannot* be used?

A. To compare more than two population means.
B. To test the hypothesis about a single population variance.
C. To test the hypothesis about two-population variance.
D. To study about randomized block design.

27. Which statistical test should be applied to test the effectiveness of 'special coaching' on the marks scored by the students?
A. Paired 't' test B. 'Chi-square' test
C. 'Z' test D. 'F' test

28. In a linear equation, $y = a + bx$, 'a' refers to
A. Slope
B. Y-intercept
C. Dependant variable
D. Independent variable

29. Which among the following is the most popular approach for accomplishing the results?
A. Management by exception
B. Reward system
C. Management by objectives
D. Mentor system

30. The managerial function of organizing involves
A. Reviewing and adjusting plan in the light of changing conditions.
B. Establishing programme for the accomplishment of objectives.
C. Creating structure of functions and duties to be performed.
D. Getting things done through others.

31. A leader who identifies what subordinates need to do to achieve objectives, clarify organizational roles and tasks, set up an organization structure, reward performance and provide for the social needs of their followers, is
A. a transformational leader
B. a participative leader
C. a transactional leader
D. an autocratic leader

32. Which of the following is *not* an assumption of theory X?
A. An average human being has an inherent dislike of work and will avoid it if he can.
B. An average human being prefers to be directed, seeks to avoid responsibility, has relatively little ambition, and want security above all.
C. An average human being learns under proper conditions, not only to accept responsibility but also to seek it.
D. Most people must be coerced, controlled, directed and threatened with punishment to get them put forth adequate effort.

33. If a network of interpersonal relationship that arise when people associate with each other is an informal organization, then find out which of the following is *not* an informal organization?
A. The "machine shop" group
B. Customers' group
C. The "sixth floor" group
D. The "Friday evening bowling" gang

34. Which of the following are sources of ethics?
(*i*) Religion
(*ii*) Legal system
(*iii*) Economic system
(*iv*) Culture
(*v*) Family system

Select the correct answer from the codes given below:
A. (*i*), (*ii*), (*iii*), (*v*)
B. (*i*), (*ii*), (*iv*)
C. (*i*), (*iv*), (*v*)
D. (*i*), (*ii*), (*iii*), (*iv*), (*v*)

35. Which of the following has refined Maslow's theory of motivation by proposing a hierarchy of three needs?
A. MeClelland B. Aldorfer
C. Herzburg D. Vroom

36. Which segmentation approach is the most compatible with the spirit of the marketing concept?
A. Benefit sought B. Income
C. Social class D. Family size

37. The description of a product's quality, features, style, brand name and packaging identifiers the

A. Actual product

B. Augmented product

C. Core product

D. Tangible product

38. Consider the following statements and find out the correct alternative from the codes given below:

(*i*) A firm's marketing information system is a component of its marketing research system.

(*ii*) The most common forms of marketing researches conducted in most of the firms are the measurement of market potential and the analysis of market share.

(*iii*) Survey research is seldom used for studying consumer perception and attitudes.

(*iv*) The concept of cognitive dissonance is relevant to study consumer's post-purchase behaviour.

Codes:

A. All the statements are true.

B. All the statements are false.

C. (*i*) is false and the rest are true.

D. (*ii*) and (*iv*) are true and the rest are false.

39. In India, which pricing practice is *not* permissible?

A. Penetrating pricing

B. Skimming pricing

C. Predatory pricing

D. None of the above

40. Consider the following statements and find out the correct alternative from the codes given below:

(*i*) A good salesman is one who can sell refrigerator to an Eskimo.

(*ii*) Salesmen are born, not made.

(*iii*) Physical distribution is an area where high cost-savings is possible.

Codes:

A. (*i*) and (*iii*) are correct.

B. (*i*) and (*ii*) are correct.

C. (*ii*) and (*iii*) are correct.

D. All are correct.

41. Which form of retail outlet has the highest operating costs?

A. Super market

B. Consumer co-operative store

C. Department store

D. Retail chain store

42. Consider the following statements and indicate the correct alternative from the codes given below:

(*i*) The product management system often turns out to be costly.

(*ii*) When customers belong to different user groups with distinct buying preferences and practices, a market management organization is not suitable.

(*iii*) Advertising department has the closest interface with the finance department of the company.

Codes:

A. (*i*) and (*ii*) are correct.

B. (*ii*) and (*iii*) are correct.

C. Only (*i*) is correct.

D. All are correct.

43. Match the statements in List-I with dividend models in List-II as follows:

List-I	*List-II*
(*a*) Dividend Capitalisation Approach.	(*i*) Traditional Model
(*b*) Dividend Policy has a bearing on the share valuation.	(*ii*) Gardon Model
(*c*) Stock Market places more weight on dividends than on retain earnings.	(*iii*) Walter Model
(*d*) Dividend payout is irrelevant to the value of the firm.	(*iv*) Modigliani and Miller Model

Codes:

	(*a*)	(*b*)	(*c*)	(*d*)
A.	(*ii*)	(*iii*)	(*i*)	(*iv*)
B.	(*i*)	(*ii*)	(*iv*)	(*iii*)
C.	(*iv*)	(*i*)	(*iii*)	(*ii*)
D.	(*iii*)	(*iv*)	(*ii*)	(*i*)

44. Venture capital financing at starting stage is generally not done through

A. Debt instruments

B. Deep discount bonds

C. Equity shares

D. Conditional loans

45. Match the statements in List-I with the types of lease in the List-II as follows:

List-I	*List-II*
(*a*) Lessor transfers all risks and rewards of an asset to the lessee.	(*i*) Indirect lease
(*b*) Lessor transfers the assets to the lessee but bears the cost of maintenance	(*ii*) Operating lease
(*c*) The owner of the asset sells it to the lessor who in turn leases it back to the owner (now lessee)	(*iii*) Finance lease
(*d*) Lessor owns/acquires the assets that are leased to a given lessee.	(*iv*) Direct lease

Codes:

	(*a*)	(*b*)	(*c*)	(*d*)
A.	(*ii*)	(*iii*)	(*iv*)	(*i*)
B.	(*i*)	(*iv*)	(*ii*)	(*iii*)
C.	(*iii*)	(*ii*)	(*i*)	(*iv*)
D.	(*iv*)	(*i*)	(*iii*)	(*ii*)

46. Full details for the issue of ADRs by a company must be furnished within 30 days from the date of its closure to

A. Securities and Exchange Commission (SEC)

B. Reserve Bank of India (RBI)

C. Securities and Exchange Board of India (SEBI)

D. Company Law Board (CLB)

47. The degree to which the returns of the two securities change together, is reflected by

A. Correlation B. Leverage

C. Covariance D. Beta

48. The transfer by a company of one or more of its business divisions to another newly set up company is called

A. Demerger

B. Merger

C. Equity Carve-out

D. Disinvestment

49. What combination of the following factors influences the working capital requirement?

(*i*) Market Conditions

(*ii*) Production Policy

(*iii*) Firm's goodwill

(*iv*) Supply conditions

Codes:

A. (*i*), (*ii*) and (*iii*)

B. (*ii*), (*iii*) and (*iv*)

C. (*i*), (*iii*) and (*iv*)

D. (*i*), (*ii*) and (*iv*)

50. Which of the followings are the modern method of performance appraisal?

(*i*) 360 degree performance appraisal.

(*ii*) Graphic rating scale.

(*iii*) Management By Objectives (MBO).

(*iv*) Forced distribution method.

(*v*) Behaviourally Anchored Rating Scales (BARS).

Select the correct answer from the codes given below:

A. (*i*), (*ii*), (*iii*) B. (*ii*), (*iv*), (*v*)

C. (*i*), (*iii*), (*v*) D. (*iv*), (*ii*), (*i*)

51. Which of the following principle serves as a warning to organizations not to take the selection and promotion process lightly?

A. Promotion Principle

B. Drucker Principle

C. Validity Principle

D. Peter Principle

52. According to D. Katz morale has four dimensions:

(*i*) Jobs satisfaction
(*ii*) Satisfaction with wages and promotional opportunities.
(*iii*) Identification with company.
(*iv*) Pride in the work group.
(*v*) Top Management Support.

Select the correct combination.

A. (*i*), (*ii*), (*iii*) and (*iv*)
B. (*i*), (*ii*), (*iii*) and (*v*)
C. (*i*), (*ii*), (*iv*), and (*v*)
D. (*i*), (*iii*), (*iv*) and (*v*)

53. HRM is viewed as a management process, consisting of four functional activities:

(*i*) Acquisition
(*ii*) Motivation
(*iii*) Development
(*iv*) Resolution of industrial disputes
(*v*) Maintenance

Select the correct combination.

A. (*i*), (*ii*), (*iii*) and (*iv*)
B. (*i*), (*ii*), (*iii*) and (*v*)
C. (*i*), (*ii*), (*iv*) and (*v*)
D. (*i*), (*iii*), (*iv*) and (*v*)

54. O C TA PA C stands for

A. Order, Co-ordination, Trust, Authority, Personality and Cooperation.
B. Openness, Confrontation, Trust, Authenticity, Pro-action and Collaboration.
C. Organization, Conflict, Team, Authority, People and Collaboration.
D. Oneness, Compromise, Tress pass, Authority, Protection and Combination.

55. Technique of 'Transaction Analysis' was developed by

A. Elton Mayo
B. Peter Drucker
C. Eric Berne
D. Adam Smith

56. Which one of the following methods is *not* a demand forecasting method of Human Resource Planning?

A. Managerial judgement
B. Managerial grid
C. Work study techniques
D. Statistical techniques

57. Transaction of Internet Banking excludes

A. Withdrawal of cash anywhere in India.
B. Statement of account for a specific period.
C. Transfer of funds from one account to another account.
D. Balance enquiry.

58. Which among the following is *not* a category of Non-Performing Assets?

A. Substandard Assets
B. Doubtful Debts
C. Loss Assets
D. Devaluated Assets

59. When a loan will be NPA?

A. Interest and/or loan instalments overdue for more than 90 days.
B. Account is out of order for more than 90 days in case of overdraft/cash credit.
C. Bill remains overdue for more than 90 days.
D. All of the above.

60. **Assertion (A):** "The problem of rural credit is not primarily one of rural credit, it may be said to be one of rural minded credit."

Reason (R) : The Indian economy has yet to come out of rural mentality.

Codes:

A. Both (A) and (R) are correct.
B. Both (A) and (R) are incorrect.
C. (A) is correct, but (R) is incorrect.
D. (R) is correct, but (A) is incorrect.

61. Match the items of List-I with the items of List-II and select the correct answer:

List-I	*List-II*
(*i*) Debit card	(*a*) Several storage
(*ii*) Credit card	(*b*) Online recovery of amount
(*iii*) Electronic purse	(*c*) Image processing use
(*iv*) Cheque function	(*d*) Revolving credit

Codes:

	(i)	(ii)	(iii)	(iv)
A.	(c)	(a)	(d)	(b)
B.	(a)	(b)	(d)	(c)
C.	(d)	(c)	(a)	(b)
D.	(d)	(c)	(b)	(a)

62. Assertion (A): The Indian economy could survive in the recent global recession due to its strong banking system.

Reason (R) : The Indian economy contains a large amount of black money.

Codes:

A. Both (A) and (R) are correct and (R) is the explanation of (A).
B. Both (A) and (R) are correct, but (R) is not the correct explanation of (A).
C. (R) is correct, but (A) is not the appropriate assertion of (R).
D. Both (A) and (R) are incorrect.

63. Assertion (A): Most of the development bank in India have setup private commercial banks after the introduction of capital adequacy norms.

Reason (R) : Development banks in India have not adhered to their basic objectives.

Codes:

A. (A) and (R) both are correct, and (R) is correct explanation of (A).
B. (A) and (R) both are correct, but (R) is not a correct explanation of (A).
C. (A) is correct, but (R) is incorrect.
D. (R) is correct, but (A) is incorrect.

64. Match the following items of List-I with List-II:

List-I	*List-II*
(a) Brettonwoods conference	(i) 1947
(b) General Agreement on Trade and Tariffs	(ii) 1964
(c) ACCRA conference	(iii) 1944
(d) United Nations Conference on Trade and Development	(iv) 2008

Codes:

	(i)	(ii)	(iii)	(iv)
A.	(b)	(d)	(a)	(c)
B.	(b)	(d)	(c)	(a)
C.	(b)	(c)	(d)	(a)
D.	(c)	(a)	(b)	(d)

65. The forces that lend momentum to the process of globalization have been identified by Michael Porter include the following:

(i) Fluid global capital market.
(ii) Technological restructuring.
(iii) Decreasing religious command.
(iv) Ethnic decontrol.
(v) New-global competitors.
(vi) End of the 'cold war' in 1990s.

Codes:

A. (vi), (v), (iv) and (iii)
B. (vi), (iii), (ii) and (i)
C. (vi), (v), (ii) and (i)
D. (iv), (iii), (ii) and (i)

66. Statement (I): Green Box subsidies include amount spent on Government services such as research, disease control, infrastructure and food security.

Statement (II) : Blue Box subsidies are certain direct payments made to farmers, to limit production, and are certain government assistance programmes to encourage agriculture and rural development.

Codes:

A. Statement (I) is correct, but (II) is not correct.
B. Statement (II) is correct, but (I) is not correct.
C. Both statement (I) and (II) are correct.
D. Both statement (I) and (II) are incorrect.

67. Assertion (A): The major economic powers have succeeded in creating a new international regime where the profits and the dominance of their transnational corporations will be the decisive consideration.

Reason (R) : This regime will legitimise the process of progressive erosion of the sovereign economic space of the third-world countries.

A. Both (A) and (R) are correct, and (R) is the right explanation of (A).

B. Both (A) and (R) are correct, but (R) is not the right explanation of (A).
C. Both (A) and (R) are incorrect.
D. (R) is correct, but (A) is not correct.

68. Assertion (A): The 'Balance of Payments' presents a classified record of all receipts on account of goods exported, services rendered and capital received by 'residents' and payments made by them on account of goods imported and services received from capital transferred to 'non-residents' or 'foreigners".

Reason (R): The 'Balance of Payments' of a country is a systematic record of all economic transactions between the 'residents' of a country and the rest of the world.

A. Both (A) and (R) are correct and (R) is the right explanation of (A).
B. Both (A) and (R) are correct, but (R) is not the right explanation of (A).
C. (R) is correct, but (A) is not correct.
D. Both (A) and (R) are incorrect.

69. Which among the following is not rightly explained?

(*i*) M_1 = Currency with the public + demand deposits of the public.
(*ii*) $M_2 = M_1$ + Post Office Savings Deposits.
(*iii*) $M_3 = M_1$ + Time Deposits of the public with Banks.
(*iv*) $M_4 = M_3$ + Total Post Office Deposits.
(*v*) M_1 = Narrow money
(*vi*) M_3 = Broad money

A. Only (*v*) and (*vi*)
B. Only (*i*) and (*iii*)
C. Only (*vi*)
D. None of the above

70. Which of the followings are not effect of dumping on importing country?

(*i*) Domestic industry might be affected adversely by a decline in sales and profits.
(*ii*) If dumping is continued for a longer period, survival of the domestic industry may be threatened.
(*iii*) Dumping may create BOP problems for the country.
(*iv*) It finds market for its surplus production.

Codes:

A. (*i*), (*ii*), (*iii*) and (*iv*)
B. (*ii*), (*iii*) and (*iv*)
C. (*iii*) and (*iv*)
D. Only (*iv*)

71. Donation to National Children's Fund will come in which of the following deduction under Sec. 80G of Income Tax Act, 1961.

A. 100 per cent deduction without any qualifying limit.
B. 50 per cent deduction without any qualifying limit.
C. 100 per cent deduction subject to qualifying limit.
D. 50 per cent deduction subject to qualifying limit.

72. If the taxable income of a domestic company for the Assessment Year 2011-12 is ₹ 9,00,000, its tax liability will be

A. ₹ 2,76,800 B. ₹ 2,78,100
C. ₹ 3,70,800 D. ₹ 3,70,880

73. Unabsorbed depreciation which could not be setoff in the same assessment year, can be carried forward upto

A. 4 years B. 8 years
C. 10 years D. Indefinite period

74. If the book profits of a partnership firm is ₹ 1,10,000, the remuneration admissible to working partners under Sec. 40(*b*) of the Income Tax Act, 1961 is

A. ₹ 1,10,000 B. ₹ 1,50,000
C. ₹ 99,000 D. None of the above

75. Which of the following expenses is inadmissible while computing income from other sources?

A. Interest paid on amounts borrowed to meet tax liabilities.
B. Collection charges paid to the banker or any other person to collect interest/ dividend.
C. Interest on loan taken to invest in securities.
D. Depreciation on let-out machinery and plant.

ANSWERS

1	2	3	4	5	6	7	8	9	10
D	B	B	A	D	B	B	D	C	D
11	**12**	**13**	**14**	**15**	**16**	**17**	**18**	**19**	**20**
C	A	B	B	B	A	B	D	C	A
21	**22**	**23**	**24**	**25**	**26**	**27**	**28**	**29**	**30**
A	D	B	C	D	B	A	B	C	C
31	**32**	**33**	**34**	**35**	**36**	**37**	**38**	**39**	**40**
C	C	B	C	B	A	A	D	C	A
41	**42**	**43**	**44**	**45**	**46**	**47**	**48**	**49**	**50**
C	C	A	B	C	B	C	A	D	C
51	**52**	**53**	**54**	**55**	**56**	**57**	**58**	**59**	**60**
D	A	B	B	C	B	A	D	D	C
61	**62**	**63**	**64**	**65**	**66**	**67**	**68**	**69**	**70**
B	B	C	A	C	C	B	A	D	D
71	**72**	**73**	**74**	**75**					
B	B	D	B	A					

SOME SELECTED EXPLANATORY ANSWERS

1. Industries (Development and Regulation) Act 1951

This act came into force on May 8, 1952, and was supplemented by "Registration and Licensing of Industries Undertaking Rules 1952". It empowers the Government of India to issue industrial licenses and regulate growth of the industry in the country in such a way as to subserve the common good. Its provisions apply to all industrial undertakings manufacturing any of the items included in the First Schedule to this Act.

An industrial licence is a written permission from the government to an industrial undertaking to manufacture specific articles included in the schedule. Under the provisions of the Act, a licence in necessary for:

(*a*) Setting up a new industrial undertaking;

(*b*) Manufacturing a "new article" or diversification;

(*c*) Substantial expansion, that is, more than 25 per cent of the licensed capacity;

(*d*) Carry on business (CoB) for the undertakings, which were earlier in the delicensed list for one reason or another but now are in the ambit of the licensing provisions; and

(*e*) Change of location.

3. CUTS and Consumer Protection

Consumer Unity & Trust Society (CUTS) is a registered Indian NGO established in 1984, pursuing social justice and economic equity within and across borders. CUTS serves on several policy, making bodies of the Government of India. CUTS was responsible for the enactment and strengthening of the dynamic Consumer Protection Act, 1986 (COPRA), the likes of which has not been seen anywhere in the world. It developed a draft National Consumer Policy at the request of Ministry of Consumer Affairs (MoCA), Government of India (GoI).

Industrial Licensing Policy Inquiry Committee (ILPIC) (1969)

In July 1969, an Industrial Licensing Inquiry Committee (ILPIC) was appointed to examine the shortcomings in licensing policy. The Committee felt that the licensing policy had not succeeded in preventing the practice of pre-empting capacity by large houses; it had not ensured development of industries according to announced licensing policies; it did not prevent investment in non-priority industries etc. In 1969, the MRTP Act was passed by the Government and following the report of Industrial Licensing Policy Inquiry Committee, a number of new restrictions were put on the large industrial houses in the industrial licensing policy announced in 1970.

5. Established by the UN General Assembly in December 1964, United Nations Conference on Trade and Development (UNCTAD) serves as the focal point within the United Nations for deliberation and negotiations in the field of international trade and related issues of international economic cooperation. The main conference held once in four years, reviews the work carried out by the organization in the preceding four years and decides the work programme for the next four years.

6. The Indian Parliament enacted Consumer Protection Act in December, 1986. It came into force on April 15, 1987. By July 1987, all the provisions came into operation. Rights of consumers have been given a statutory recognitions. Three-tier grievance redressal machinery at the District, State and National level has been constituted.

7. Food security refers to the availability of food and one's access to it. A household is considered food-secure when its occupants do not live in hunger or fear of starvation. According to the World Resources Institute, global per capita food production has been increasing substantially for the past several decades.

   Food availability, food utilization, and food access are the principle variables that define household food security.

8. Performance measures for investment centres usually attempt to assess how well managers are utilizing the invested capital of the division to produce income. The three most common measures of investment centre performance are return on investment (ROI), residual income (RI), and economic value added (EVA®). Traditionally, the most common investment centre performance measure is ROI. ROI is calculated as the ratio of investment centre income to invested capital. An investment centre's ROI can be improved by increasing either the sales margin or capital turnover. Residual Income (RI) is an alternative to ROI and is the net operating income that an investment centre is able to earn above the imputed interest charge on its invested capital. Economic value added or EVA® is an adaptation of residual income and is an investment centre's after-tax operating profit minus the total annual cost of capital.

Performance measures used to evaluate investment centres are:
• Return on investment, which is defined as $\text{ROI} = \dfrac{\text{Operating Income}}{\text{Investment Centre Assets}}$ • Residual income, which is defined as Divisional operating income – (Divisional investment base × Minimum capital charge) • Economic Value Added, which is defined as net operating profit after taxes (NOPAT) – (Capital investment × Cost of capital)

9. "Human Resource Accounting may be defined as the measurement and reporting of the cost and value of people as organisational resources. It involves accounting for investment in people and their replacement costs, as well as accounting for the economic values of people to an organisation."

   In companies, the value of their human resources will be reflected in their annual reports - not forming part of the audited financial statements. It reflects the value of its human resources in the social balance sheet appended as supplemental information to the annual report.

   An employee to the firm is described as the value of 'the present value of the difference between wage and marginal revenue product'. An employee's value derives from the ability of the firm to pay less than the marginal revenue product.

10. Turnover Ratios (Efficiency Ratios)

Turnover ratios may be also termed as *efficiency ratios* (or) *performance ratios* (or) *activity ratios.* Turnover ratios highlight the different aspects of financial statement to satisfy the requirements of different parties interested in the business. It also indicates the effectiveness with which different assets are utilised in a business. Turnover means the number of times the assets are converted or turned over into sales. This ratio indicates the rate at which different assets are turned over.

Depending upon the purpose, the following activities or turnover ratios are commonly used:

1. Inventory Ratio (or) Stock Turnover Ratio (Stock Velocity)
2. Debtors Turnover Ratio (or) Receivable Turnover Ratio (Debtor's Velocity) (*a*) Debtors Collection Period
3. Creditors Turnover Ratio (or) Payable Turnover Ratio (Creditor's Velocity) (*a*) Debt Payment Period
4. Working Capital Turnover Ratio
5. Fixed Assets Turnover Ratio
6. Capital Turnover Ratio

13. Relevant Cost: Relevant costs are those which are pertinent to a decision another words. These are the cost which are influenced by a decision. Expected future costs which differ for alternative course. It is not essential that all variable costs are relevant and all fixed costs are irrelevant. Fixed or variable costs that differ for various alternatives are relevant costs. Examples of relevant costs one:

1. All variable costs
2. Fixed costs with vary with the decision are relevant costs.
3. Incremental costs.

15. Mark-up Pricing (Cost-plus Pricing): A method of determining price by setting price equal to average total cost plus a portion (*m*) ATC as a marku-up. One popular alternative technique for pricing is called *cost-plus pricing*. Firms using cost-plus pricing determine their price by setting price equal to the projected average total cost (ATC) plus a percentage of this average total cost as a markup:

$$P = ATC + (m \times ATC)$$
$$= (1 + m)ATC$$

Where m is the markup on unit cost.

18. Meaning of Demand: For a common man, the terms like desire, want and demand have same meaning or connotation but in economics they are used in different senses. A desire for a commodity means a mere idea or wish for that commodity. A desire become want when two more elements joint it, namely, ability to pay (money or means) and willingness to pay (or spend). In other words, a want is an effective desire *i.e.* desire for satisfaction of which we have not only means (money) but are also ready to sacrifice (spend) the same. Like want demand has also three components, namely, quantity demanded, price and time. Demand for a commodity refers to the quantity of the commodity that will be purchased at a specific price in given period of time & other things being constant.

20. The Lerner index, named after the economist Abba Lerner, describes a firm's *market power*. It is defined by:

$$L = \frac{P - MC}{P}$$

where P is the market price set by the firm and MC is the firm's *marginal cost*. The index ranges from a high of 1 to a low of 0, with higher numbers implying greater market power. For a perfectly competitive firm (where P = MC), L = 0; such a firm has no market power.

23. The F-distribution is named after the famous statistician R. A. Fisher. It is also sometimes known as the Fisher F distribution or the Snecedor-Fisher F distribution. F is the ratio of two variances.

The F-distribution is most commonly used in Analysis of Variance (ANOVA) and the F test (to determine if two variances are equal). The F-distribution is the ratio of two chi-square distributions, and hence is right skewed. It has a minimum of 0, but no maximum value (all values are positive).

24. There are two basic families of statistical techniques and methods—parametric methods, which are based on data measured on an interval or ratio scale, and non-parametric methods, where the variables are measured on a nominal or ordinal scale. Thus, depending on the nature of data measurement, a whole range of parametric and non-parametric methods can be used to compare differences across groups on some variable.

Parametric Test and Non-parametric Test

Goal	*Parametric Test* *Gaussian Population*	*Non-parametric Test* *Rank, Score or Measurement*	*Non-parametric Test* *Binomial (Two Possible Outcomes)*
Compare one group to a hypothetical value	One-sample *t* test	Wilcoxon test	Chi-square or binomial test
Compare two unpaired groups	Unpaired *t* test	Mann-Whitney test	Fisher's test
Compare two paired groups	Paired t test	Wilcoxon test	McNemar's test
Compare three or more unmatched groups	One-way ANOVA	Kruskal-Wallis test	Chi-square test
Compare three or more matched groups	Repeated-measures ANOVA	Friedman test	Cochran Q

27. A paired sample t-test is used to determine whether there is a significant difference between the average values of the same measurement made under two different conditions. Both measurements are made on each unit in a sample, and the test is based on the paired differences between these two values.

28. In a linear equation $y = a + bx$ the, first constant, *a*, is the intercept, and the second, *b*, is the slope. The intercept, *a*, is defined as the value of Y when the value of X is 0 (the starting point of the straight line that intersects the *y*-axis). The slope, *b*, is the rate of change of Y for a unit change in the value of X, which provides the angle of the straight line. Given the starting point and the angle of the straight line, the linear function can be used to predict the values of the dependent variable (Y) for a given value of the independent variable (X).

29. The concept of 'Management by Objectives' was introduced in 1954 by the great management thinker 'Peter Drucker'. Management by objectives is an important practicing style of management to accomplish the objectives of an organization in an effective way. Many management thinkers prior to 1954 have also emphasized the importance of objectives in the success of management but Peter Drucker has made it a philosophy and today it is recognized as the most dynamic and exciting practice in the area of management.

Peter Drucker explains MBO as a process whereby performance, goals and objectives are set in order to achieve the expected results through the participation of organizational members. It is an important tool to motivate the managers to work as a team for achieving the organizational goals. According to George S. Ordiorne, the system of Management by objectives can be described as a process whereby the superior and subordinate managers of an organization jointly identify its common goals, define such individual's major areas of responsibility in terms of results expected of him, and use these measures as guides for operating the unit and assessing the contribution of each of its members.

Management by Objectives is also known as management by results and goals setting approach. Dale D. McConkey has preferred the term management by results and has defined it, as an approach to management planning and evaluation in which specific targets for a year, or some length of time, are established for each manager, on the basis of the results which each must achieve if the overall objectives of the company are to be realized. At the end of this period the actual results achieved are measured against the originals goals *i.e.* against the expected results, which each manager knows he is responsible for achieving.

31. Transactional and Transformational Leadership

Managing involves carrying out the managerial functions effectively and efficiently. One of these functions relates to leading in general and to leadership in particular. A distinction can be made between transactional and transformational leaders. **Transactional leaders** identify what subordinates need to do to achieve objectives, clarify organizational roles and tasks, set up an organization structure, reward performance, and are considerate for the social needs of its followers. Such leaders work hard and try to run the organization effectively and efficiently.

Transformational leaders articulate a vision and inspire followers. They also have the capacity to motivate, shape the organizational culture, and create a climate favourable for the organizational change. Companies such as IBM and AT&T have programs to promote transformational leadership designed to transform their organizations quickly in order to be more responsive to the rapid changes in the environment. There are many similarities between transformational leaders and charismatic leaders with the former being noted for initiating innovation and change. When one thinks of charismatic leaders, one thinks of people such as Winston Churchill, Martin Luther King, and also, Mother Teresa, who inspired people through her selfless service to the poor.

33. Informal Organization: Chester Barnard, author of the management classic *The Functions of the Executive,* described an informal organization as any joint personal activity without conscious joint purpose, although contributing to joint results. It is much easier to ask for help on an organizational problem from someone you know personally, even if he or she may be in a different department, than from someone you know only as a name on an organization chart. The informal organization is a network of interpersonal relationships that arise when people associate with each other. Thus, informal organizations—relationships not appearing on an organization chart—might include the machine shop group, the sixth floor crowd, the Friday evening bowling gang, and the morning coffee "regulars."

35. Alderfer's ERG Theory

Alderfer had given a refined version of Maslow's hierarchy of needs. He proposed a hierarchy of three needs, viz., existence needs, relatedness and growth needs.

'Existence needs' refers to provision of the basic needs, inclusive of, what Maslow described as the physiological and safety needs. The 'relatedness' implies the need for maintaining the significant interpersonal needs or the social and status needs. This is what Maslow termed as the social and the external needs. Then, the growth needs, which cover the intrinsic need for personal growth and development is what Maslow called the 'self-actualization needs'.

37. Each product or service offered to customers can be viewed on three levels. The *core product* consists of the core problem-solving benefits that consumers seek when they buy a product. The *actual product* exists around the core and includes the quality level, features, design, brand name, and packaging. The *augmented product* is the actual product plus the various services and benefits offered with it, such as warranty, free delivery, installation, and maintenance.

39. Predatory pricing occurs, where a dominant enterprise charges low prices over a long enough period of time so as to derive a competitor from the market or deter others from entering the market and then raises prices to recoup its losses. The greater the diversification of the activities of the enterprise in terms of products and markets and the greater its financial resources, the greater is its ability to engage in predatory behaviour.

41. Department Stores: Department stores are large-scale retailing enterprises which carry a number of product lines. Most department stores carry three major types of merchandise—readymade garments, home appliances and furnishings, housewares, and other soft goods.

In a department store, each department handles one type of merchandise, and is headed by a department buyer. The buyer enjoys considerable autonomy and functions as a decentralized unit with centralized control. The departmental head is called the buyer because his main job is to buy the merchandise. Majority of shoppers in department stores are women, although different departments appeal to different sections of the population. For example, the sports department may have special appeal to sportsmen, and music department to teen-agers. Some department stores pursue the policy of dealing in low priced goods and high sales volume whereas others carry only prestigious brand names and cater only to the affluent sections of society.

Department stores have certain merits and limitations. They provide a wider variety of merchandise than any other kinds of retail store. They also provide a high level of services to their customers, and there are a number of sales people on the floor to help customers. They provide tremendous scope for one-stop shopping. On the other hand, operating costs of department stores are higher than other retailing institutions.

44. Deep Discount Bonds (DDBs) are in the form of zero interest bonds. These bonds are sold at a discounted value and on maturity face value is paid to the investors. In such bonds, there is no interest payout during lock-in period.

These are issued at a large discount to their maturity value. As a long-term instrument, these are not suited to venture capital investment.

47. Covariance reflects the degree to which the returns of the two securities vary or change together. A positive covariance means that the returns of the two securities move in the same direction whereas a negative covariance implies that the returns of the two securities move in opposite direction.

48. **Demerger:** A demerger involves the transfer by a company of one or more of its business divisions to another company which is newly set up. For example, the Great Eastern Shipping Company transferred its offshore division to a new company called The Great Offshore Limited. The company whose business division is transferred is called the demerged company and the company to which the business division is transferred is called the resultant company.

Equity Carveout: In an equity carveout, a parent company sells a portion of its equity in a wholly owned subsidiary. The sale may be to the general investing public or a strategic investor.

51. **The Peter Principle:** Errors in selection are possible, perhaps even common. According to Laurence J. Peter and Raymond Hall, authors of *The Peter Principle*, managers tend to be promoted to the level of their incompetence. Specifically, if a manager succeeds in a position, this very success may lead to promotion to a higher position, often one requiring skills that the person does not possess. Such a promotion may involve work that is over the manager's head. While the possibility of individual growth muse not be overlooked, the Peter Principle can serve as a warning not to take the selection and promotion process lightly.

54. OCTAPACE is an instrument that can help us to find out about the organizational culture. The eight dimensions of OCTAPACE culture are Openness, Confrontation, Trust, Authenticity, Pro-action, Autonomy, Collaboration, and Experimentation.

55. The term "Transactional Analysis" was first used by Dr. Eric Berne in 1957. This technique gained further momentum after the publication of his two books, i.e. Transactional Analysis in Psychotherapy (l961) and Games People Play (1964). Thomas A. Harris developed the concept further in 1967 through his book 'I am OK. You are OK'.

Originally, TA was basically a technique used in Psychotherapy. Later on, it was used in improving inter-personal relationships and Communication. TA concentrates on the rational and analytical side of human behaviour, which is observable. TA is concerned with transactions between people- both verbal and non-verbal, physical and emotional, implicit or explicit.

This technique presupposes the existence of three ego states-Parent ego state; Adult ego state; and Child ego state; acquired by an individual since childhood. Each ego state is a distinct source of particular behaviour. However, one does not stay in only one ego state; instead, a person switches occasionally from one to another, as can be noted through observing behaviour and listening to what is said and how it is said.

56. Demand Forecasting: One of the important aspects of demand forecasting is forecasting of the quality of human resource (skill, knowledge, values, capabilities etc.), in addition to quantity of human resources. Important forecasting methods are:

(*a*) Managerial judgement
(*b*) Statistical techniques
(*c*) Econometric models
(*d*) Work study techniques
(*e*) Delphi Technique
(*f*) Flow models

58-59. NPA is a classification used by *financial institutions* that refer to loans that are in jeopardy of *default*. Once the borrower has failed to make interest or principal payments for 90 days the loan is considered to be a non-performing asset. Non-performing assets are problematic for financial institutions since they depend on interest payments for income. Troublesome pressure from the economy can lead to a sharp increase in *non-performing loans* and often results in massive write-downs.

With a view to moving towards international best practices and to ensure greater transparency, it has been decided to adopt the '90 days overdue' norm for identification of NPA, from the year ending March 31, 2004. Accordingly, with effect from March 31, 2004, a non-performing asset (NPA) shall be a loan or an advance where;

- Interest and/or installment of principal remain overdue for a period of more than 90 days in respect of a term loan,
- The account remains 'out of order' for a period of more than 90 days, in respect of an Overdraft/Cash Credit (OD/CC),
- The bill remains overdue for a period of more than 90 days in the case of bills purchased and discounted,
- Interest and/or installment of principal remains overdue for two harvest seasons but for a period not exceeding two half years in the case of an advance granted for agricultural purposes, and
- Any amount to be received remains overdue for a period of more than 90 days in respect of other accounts.

Classification

Banks are required to classify non-performing assets further into the following three categories based on the period for which the asset has remained non-performing and the realisability of the dues:

1. *Sub-standard assets:* a sub-standard asset is one which has been classified as NPA for a period not exceeding 12 months.
2. *Doubtful Assets:* a doubtful asset is one which has remained NPA for a period exceeding 12 months.
3. *Loss assets:* where loss has been identified by the bank, internal or external auditor or central bank inspectors but the amount has not been written off, wholly or partly.

Sub-standard asset is the asset in which bank have to maintain 15% of its reserves. All those assets which are considered as non-performing for period of more than 12 months are called as Doubtful Assets. All those assets which cannot be recovered are called as Loss Assets.

66. Amber Box : All subsidies which are supposed to distort production and trade fall into the amber box i.e. all agricultural subsidies except those which fall into the blue and green boxes. These include government policies of *minimum support prices* (as MSP in India) for agricultural products or any help directly related to production quantities (as power, fertilisers, pesticides, irrigation, etc).

Green Box: The agricultural subsidies which cause minimal or no distortions to trade are put under the green box. They must not involve price support.

This box basically includes all forms of government expenses which are not targeted at a particular product and all direct income support programmes to farmers which are not related to current levels of production or prices. This is a *very wide box* and includes all government subsidies like—public storage for food security, pest and disease control, research and extension, and some direct payments to farmers that do not stimulate production like restructuring of agriculture, environmental protection, regional development, crop and income insurance, etc.

Blue Box: This is the amber box with conditions. The conditions are designed to reduce distortions. Any subsidy that would normally be in the amber box, is placed in the blue box if it requires farmers to go for a certain production level. These subsidies are nothing but certain direct payments (i.e. direct set-aside payments) made to farmers by the government in the form of assistance programmes to encourage agriculture, rural development, etc.

70. In economics, "*dumping*" is a kind of predatory pricing, especially in the context of international trade. It occurs when manufacturers export a product to another country at a price either below the price charged in its home market or below its cost of production.

72.

Taxable Income	Rate	Tax Amount
900000	30%	270000
Income Tax Amount		270000
Add: Education Cess (EC) @ 2% on Income Tax Amount		5400
Add: Secondary & High Education Cess @ 1% on Income Tax Amount		2700
Total Tax Payable		278100

73. The tax authorities allow current period tax losses to be carried forward to future periods and deducted from future taxable profits, subject to conditions. Tax loss carry forwards would represent future economic benefits, provided an enterprise can make profits in the future find claim the deduction from future taxable profits. In India, tax loss can be carried forward for eight years, after which it lapses. The tax depreciation component of tax loss (commonly known as *unabsorbed depreciation* in India) can be carried forward for an indefinite number of years.

74. *Remuneration and interest* paid by a firm to its partners is allowed as a deduction to the firm if all the following conditions are satisfied:

A. Remuneration can be paid only to a *Working partner.* Interest can be paid to working as well as non-working partner.

"*Working partner*" means an *individual* who is actively engaged in conducting the affairs of the business or profession of the firm of which he is a partner.

From the definition of working partner it is clear that remuneration can be paid to a working partner who is an *individual.* Interest can be paid to any partner (e.g. interest can be paid to a partner which is an HUF).

B. Payment of remuneration and interest should be authorized by the partnership deed and should be in accordance with the terms of the partnership deed. In other words, either *amount of remuneration* payable to partners or *manner of quantification* of remuneration should be mentioned in the partnership deed. Similarly, rate of interest on capital should be specified in the partnership deed.

C. The payment of *remuneration* and *interest* should relate to a period falling after the date of partnership deed.

That means, the partnership deed should not provide for payment of remuneration and interest from retrospective effect (i.e. any earlier period prior to the date of partnership deed).

D. The payment of *interest* to a partner should not exceed the amount calculated at the rate of 12% per annum simple interest (any amount in excess shall be disallowed).

E. The payment of remuneration should not exceed the following amounts:

Book Profit	Allowable remuneration
If Book Profit is negative.	1,50,000
If Book Profit is positive: On first 3 Lakhs of Book Profit	1,50,000 or 90% of Book Profit, whichever is more.
On the balance of Book Profit	60% of Book Profit

Previous Paper (Solved)

UGC-NET COMMERCE, DECEMBER–2012

PAPER–II

*Note: This paper contains **fifty** (50) objective type questions, each question carrying **two** (2) marks. Attempt **all** the questions.*

1. GDP at factor cost is

A. P(Q) + P (S) B. GDP – IT – S

C. GDP + DT + S D. GDP – DT + S

2. Which one is not the main objective of fiscal policy in India?

A. To increase liquidity in the economy

B. To promote price stability

C. To minimize the inequalities of income and wealth

D. To promote employment opportunities

3. Which one is not an element of internal environment?

A. Marketing capability

B. Operational capability

C. Money and Capital market

D. Personnel capability

4. Out of the following, which four benefits are available to host countries from MNCs?

i. Transfer of technology

ii. Learning of business mannerism

iii. Strategic information sharing

iv. Creation of jobs

v. Entertainment

vi. Better utilisation of resources

vii. Enhancing social contacts

viii. Improved competition in local economy

A. i, iii, v, vii B. ii, iv, vi, viii

C. i, iv, vi, viii D. iii, vi, vii, viii

5. Environmental degradation does not consist of

A. Land degradation and soil erosion

B. Problem of overgrazing and ecological degradation

C. Floods

D. None of the above

6. Which one of the following concepts is used as fund in the preparation of Funds Flow Statement?

A. Current Assets

B. Working Capital

C. Cash

D. All Financial Resources

7. Window dressing is prohibited due to

A. Conservative Convention

B. Convention of Disclosure

C. Convention of Materiality

D. Arrear of book accounts

8. **Assertion (A) :** Ratio analysis is one of the tools employed to know the financial health of a concern.

Reason (R) : Ratio analysis is not the only technique available to take investment decision.

Codes :

A. Both (A) and (R) are true and (R) is the correct explanation of (A)

B. Both (A) and (R) are true, but (R) is incorrect explanation of (A)

C. (A) is true, but (R) is false

D. (A) is false, but (R) is true

9. Which of the following relate to measures of non-financial performance of a concern?

i. Customer satisfaction

ii. Business process improvement

iii. Economic value added

iv. Learning organisation

Choose the right combination.

A. i, iii, ii, iv B. ii, iv, iii

C. iv, i, iii D. i, ii, iv

10. Consider the following parties :

i. Secured creditors
ii. Unsecured creditors
iii. Partners who have granted loans
iv. Partners who have contributed over and above profit sharing ratio

Arrange them in correct sequence in the event of dissolution of a firm.

A. ii, i, iii, iv B. i, ii, iii, iv
C. i, ii, iv, iii D. ii, i, iv, iii

11. Which kind of economics explains the phenomenon of cause and effect relationship?

A. Normative B. Positive
C. Micro D. Macro

12. **Assertion (A):** Marginal cost and differential cost do not convey the same meaning in all the circumstances.

Reason (R): Differential cost increases or decreases due to change in fixed cost.

Codes :

A. (A) is true, but (R) is false
B. (A) is false, but (R) is true
C. (A) and (R) are correct and (R) is correct explanation of (A)
D. Both (A) and (R) are correct, but (R) is not the correct explanation of (A)

13. Consider the following :

i. Pricing objectives
ii. Pricing methods
iii. Pricing strategies
iv. Pricing decisions

Arrange them in correct sequence :

A. i, iii, ii, iv B. i, iv, iii, ii
C. ii, i, iv, iii D. iv, ii, iii, i

14. A commodity is used for multiple purposes, then the demand for it is known as

A. Joint Demand
B. Composite Demand
C. Direct Demand
D. Autonomous Demand

15. Match List-I with List-II and select the correct answer.

List-I	***List-II***
(*a*) Administered price	1. Landed cost of imports
(*b*) Parity pricing	2. Liberalized economy
(*c*) Competitive price	3. Public enterprise
(*d*) Discriminating price	4. Fixed by Government

Codes :

	(a)	*(b)*	*(c)*	*(d)*
A.	1	2	3	4
B.	2	3	4	1
C.	3	4	2	1
D.	4	2	1	3

16. Sample design involves the following :

i. Sampling unit
ii. Size of samples
iii. Type of universe
iv. Source list
v. Sampling procedure

Which one of the following sequence is correct?

A. i, ii, iii, iv, v B. iii, iv, i, ii, v
C. iii, i, iv, ii, v D. iii, v, i, iv, ii

17. Which one of the following is not a measure of dispersion?

A. Quartile
B. Range
C. Mean Deviation
D. Standard Deviation

18. If $bxy = 0.25$ and $byx = 0.64$, correlation coefficient is

A. 0.16 B. 0.40
C. 0.89 D. 0.30

19. Sturge's rule is used to find out directly

A. Number of classes in a continuous distribution
B. Size of class limits
C. Direction of the classification
D. None of the above

20. Which of the following software has applications in both Mathematics and Statistics?

A. SPSS B. SAS
C. R D. None of the above

21. Match the following :

(*a*) The Practice of Management		1. Henry Fayol
(*b*) Philosophy of Management		2. F.W. Taylor
(*c*) Scientific Management		3. Oliver Sheldon
(*d*) General and Industrial Administration		4. Peter F. Drucker

Codes :

	(*a*)	(*b*)	(*c*)	(*d*)
A.	1	2	3	4
B.	4	3	2	1
C.	4	3	1	2
D.	3	4	2	1

22. **Assertion (A) :** All decisions taken through mental process are rational.

Reason (R): Decision making is a mental process.

Codes :

A. (R) is correct, but (A) is not correct.
B. (A) is correct, but (R) is not correct.
C. Both (A) and (R) are correct.
D. Both (A) and (R) are not correct.

23. The Narasimham Committee made separate recommendations for the reforms of:

A. Manufacturing sector
B. Banking sector
C. Agriculture sector
D. Insurance Sector

24. Which among the following are parts of job description?

i. Duties performed
ii. Job summary
iii. Job identification
iv. Supervision given
v. Delegation of authority

A. i, ii, iii and iv B. ii, iii, iv and v
C. i, iii, iv and v D. i, ii, iii and v

25. Appointment of independent directors is the part of Corporate Governance as per the

A. SEBI
B. Indian Companies Act
C. Government of India
D. RBI

26. A method for achieving maximum market response from limited marketing resources by reorganising differences in the response characteristics of various parts of the market is known as

A. Market targeting
B. Market positioning
C. Market segmentation
D. Market strategy

27. Who plays their significant role in distribution of goods when they do not sell to ultimate users or consumers?

A. Retailer B. Wholeseller
C. Mediator D. Commission agent

28. In Marketing Mix, which four P's are covered?

A. Product, Price, Place, Promotion
B. Product, Price, Power, Promotion
C. Product, Price, Penetration, Promotion
D. Product, Price, Positioning, Promotion

29. Which research includes all types of researches into human motives when it refers to qualitative research designed to uncover the consumer's subconsciousness or hidden motivations?

A. Motivational Research
B. Marketing Research
C. Managerial Research
D. Price Research

30. False and misleading claims and vulgarity in advertisements do not match with

A. Aggressive advertising
B. Ethics in advertising
C. Mass level of advertising
D. Sales promotion

31. Arrange the following steps involved in capital budgeting in order of their occurrence:

i. Project selection
ii. Project appraisal
iii. Project generation
iv. Follow up
v. Project execution

A. ii, iii, i, v, iv B. iii, ii, i, v, iv
C. i, iii, ii, v, iv D. i, ii, iii, v, iv

32. Which method does not consider the time value of money?

A. Net Present Value
B. Internal Rate of Return
C. Average Rate of Return
D. Profitability Index

33. Which formula is used to measure the degree of Operating leverage?

A. $\frac{\text{EBIT}}{\text{Sales}}$ B. $\frac{\text{C}}{\text{EBIT}}$

C. $\frac{\text{EBIT}}{\text{EBT}}$ D. $\frac{\text{EBIT}}{\text{C}}$

34. Which one is more appropriate for cost of retained earnings?

A. Weighted Average Cost of Capital
B. Opportunity cost to the firm
C. Expected rate of return by the investor
D. None of the above

35. Match the following with the most suitable option.

List-I	*List-II*
(*a*) Modigliani-Miller approach	1. Commercial paper
(*b*) Net Operating income approach	2. Working capital
(*c*) Short-term money market instrument	3. Capital structure
(*d*) Factoring	4. Arbitrage

Codes :

	(*a*)	(*b*)	(*c*)	(*d*)
A.	4	3	1	2
B.	3	4	1	2
C.	3	2	1	4
D.	4	2	3	1

36. During which plan was the National Apprenticeship Training Scheme introduced?

A. 1st Five Year Plan
B. 2nd Five Year Plan
C. 4th Five Year Plan
D. Annual Plans

37. Match the following :

List-I	*List-II*
(*a*) An ordinary person does not want to work on his own	1. Hierarchy Theory
(*b*) An individual is willing to work on his own	2. Hygiene Theory
(*c*) Motivational Factors	3. X-Theory
(*d*) Esteem Needs	4. Y-Theory

Codes :

	(*a*)	(*b*)	(*c*)	(*d*)
A.	1	2	3	4
B.	3	4	1	2
C.	1	4	2	3
D.	3	4	2	1

38. Arrange the following staffing procedures in the correct sequence :

i. Determining sources of Personnel supply.
ii. Preparing personnel specifications.
iii. Selection of personnel.
iv. Determining personnel characteristics.

A. ii, i, iv, iii   B. i, ii, iii, iv
C. ii i, iii, iv   D. ii, iii, i, iv

39. Which among the following is not a voluntary method for prevention and settlement of disputes?

A. Collective Bargaining
B. Standing Orders
C. Joint Consultation
D. Works Committee

40. **Statement–I :** It is no better to pay employees for little than to pay too much.

Statement–II : Competent employees will remain competent forever.

A. Statement I is true, but II is false
B. Statement II is true, but I is false
C. Both Statements I and II are true
D. Both Statements I and II are false

41. Match the following:

(*a*) Credit Control	1. MCA
(*b*) Corporate Control	2. SEBI
(*c*) IPO Control	3. IRDA
(*d*) ULIP Control	4. RBI

Codes :

	(*a*)	(*b*)	(*c*)	(*d*)
A.	4	2	3	1
B.	4	1	2	3
C.	2	3	4	1
D.	4	1	3	2

42. Which one among the following has not started Commercial Banking?

A. SIDBI B. IDBI
C. ICICI D. UTI

43. What is OTP in credit card transactions?

A. Odd Transaction Password
B. Owner's Trading Passcode
C. One Time Password
D. One Time Pincode

44. The powers of Controller of Capital Issues of India is now shifted to

A. Ministry of Finance
B. SEBI
C. AMFI
D. Ministry of Corporate Affairs

45. The success of E-banking depends upon:

i. Multi-layer Security System
ii. Risk and Surveillance Management
iii. Updated Flawless Softwares
iv. Stringent Legal Frame-work

A. i and ii B. i, ii and iii
C. ii, iii and iv D. i, ii, iii and iv

46. International liquidity comprises which four of the following?

i. Gold held by Central Banks
ii. Gold held by families
iii. Forex Reserve held by Commercial Banks
iv. Mineral wealth
v. SDRs
vi. Borrowing facilities
vii. NRIs FDRs
viii. Credit facilities available under SWAP

A. i, ii, iii, iv B. ii, iii, iv, viii
C. i, iii, v, viii D. iii, iv, vii, viii

47. Which among the following are important bodies of WTO?

i. Dispute Settlement Body
ii. NAFTA
iii. Trade Policy Review Body
iv. ASEAN
v. Council for Trade in Goods
vi. IBRD
vii. Council for Trade related aspects of Intellectual Property Rights
viii. GATT

An appropriate combination is

A. i, ii, iii, iv B. ii, iii, iv, v
C. i, iii, v, vii D. iv, v, vi, viii

48. Which one is not the source of External Finance?

A. WTO Funds
B. World Bank Group
C. Export Credit
D. Foreign Direct Investment

49. Which one is called Bretton-Wood Twins?

A. IBRD and IDA B. IMF and IFC
C. IMF and IBRD D. IDA and IFC

50. UNCTAD stands for

A. United Nations Committee on Tariff and Development
B. United Nations Conference on Trade and Deficit
C. United Nations Conference on Trade and Development
D. Union of Nations Cause for Trade and Development

ANSWERS

1	2	3	4	5	6	7	8	9	10
B	A	C	C	D	B	B	A	D	B
11	**12**	**13**	**14**	**15**	**16**	**17**	**18**	**19**	**20**
B	C	A	B	B	C	A	B	A	D
21	**22**	**23**	**24**	**25**	**26**	**27**	**28**	**29**	**30**
B	A	B	A	A	C	B	A	A	B
31	**32**	**33**	**34**	**35**	**36**	**37**	**38**	**39**	**40**
B	C	B	B	A	B	D	A	D	A
41	**42**	**43**	**44**	**45**	**46**	**47**	**48**	**49**	**50**
B	A	C	B	B	C	C	A	C	C

SOME SELECTED EXPLANATORY ANSWERS

2. Fiscal Policy is a part of economic policy of the government which is related to government income and expenditure. It includes public expenditure policy, taxation policy, public debt policy and deficit financing. It is aimed at achieving certain objectives like — rapid economic development, reduction in economic inequalities, promoting capital formation, etc. Fiscal Policy is related to income and expenditure of government. It refers to budgetary policy of government. It is also known as Tax and Expenditure Policy of government. The Fiscal Policy is of great importance for both developed and developing countries. It is an instrument for promoting economic growth, employment, social welfare, etc. Fiscal Policy may be defined as the part of government economic policy which deals with taxation, government expenditure, borrowings, deficit financing and management of public debts in an economy. Government's public expenditure and public revenue policy have a great bearing on the economic equality and economic development of the country.

Objectives of Fiscal Policy of India:

1. To mobilise resources for rapid economic development of the country
2. To increase the rate of saving in the country so that sufficient financial resources can be obtained from within the economy
3. To increase the rate of investment in the economy, so as to promote capital formation
4. To remove poverty and unemployment
5. To reduce economic inequality
6. To reduce regional disparities
7. To achieve economic stability
8. To ensure optimum utilisation of resources
9. To support private sector
10. To achieve favourdble balance of payments

3. The dynamics of the internal environment are understood in terms of the complex interplay of organisational resources and behaviour, strengths and weaknesses, synergistic effects, and the competencies of the organisation.

Organisational capability is the inherent capacity or potential of an organisation to use its strengths and overcome its weaknesses in order to exploit opportunities and face threats in its external environment. These are the outcomes of the knowledge possessed by an organisation which is regarded as a learning system.

Organisational capability is described in terms of the six areas of finance, marketing, operations, personnel, information management, and general management. Financial capability factors relate to the availability, usage and management of funds. Marketing capability factors relate to the pricing, promotion and distribution of products or services. Operations capability factors relate to the production of products or services and the use of material resources. Personnel capability factors relate to the existence and use of human resources and skills. Information management capability factors relate to the design and management of the flow of information from outside into and within, an organisation for the purpose of decision-making. General management capability relates to the integration, coordination, and direction of the functional capabilities towards common goals.

6. A funds flow statement may be prepared on the basis of any of the alternative concepts of funds (*e.g.* cash, working capital, total financial resources among others), though the working capital concept is more popular and widely used. A cash flow statement can be prepared on 'cash' concept only. Thus, the latter statement uses the narrower concept of fund while analysing the financial position of a firm during a period.

7. Window-dressing, *i.e.*, showing a position better than what it is, is not permitted. Conservatism results in understatement of income, assets and capital and overstatement of liabilities and provisions. This results in the creation of what is called 'secret reserve'. This, however, conflicts with the convention of adequate disclosure.

11. In positive economics we derive propositions, theories and laws following central rules of logic. These theories, laws and propositions explain the cause and effect relationship between economic variables. In normative economics value is meant the conceptions of the people about the feeling–good feeling or bad feeling.

12. Although Differential Cost Analysis is often confused with Marginal Costing, they are not synonymous. Differential Cost Analysis has some similarities and some dissimilarities as well with Marginal Costing. A comparative analysis between Differential Cost Analysis and Marginal Costing is done as follows:

Similarities:

(i) Both Differential Costing as well as Marginal Costing are techniques of cost analysis.

(ii) Both the techniques are used by the management in its process of Decision Making.

(iii) Both the techniques arc based on the classification of costs into Fixed Cost and Variable Cost. When there is no change in the Fixed Cost due to a change in the volume of production or sales, Differential Cost becomes equal to the Marginal Cost.

Dissimilarities:

(i) In Marginal Costing, Profit–Volume Ratio (P/V Ratio), contribution margin, contribution per unit of limiting factor and so on are the main parameters for evaluation of performance and Decision Making. On the other hand, in the Differential Cost Analysis, Differential Costs are compared with differential revenues to select the best alternative in the process of Decision Making.

(ii) Marginal Costing excludes all Fixed Costs from its analysis, whereas Differential Cost Analysis includes all identifiable Fixed Costs.

(iii) Marginal Cost may be incorporated into the system of accounting, whereas Differential Costs are separately calculated as an aid to the management for a Decision Making purpose.

14. Composite demand refers to the demand for one commodity in order to satisfy two or more wants. For example, demand for milk is a composite demand. Some people demand milk to prepare cheese, others to prepare curd and still others to prepare sweet meats etc. Total demand for milk is called composite demand.

17. Measures of dispersion describe how spread out or scattered a set or distribution of numeric data is. There are different bases on which the spread of data can be measured.

(a) ***Spread about the mean.*** This is concerned with measuring the distance between the items and their common mean. There arc two measures of this type used:
  (i) the mean deviation
  (ii) the standard deviation

(b) ***Central percentage spread of items.*** These measures have links with the median.
  (i) the 10 to 90 percentile range
  (ii) the quartile deviation

(c) ***Overall spread of items.*** This measure is called the range.

18. If bxy = 0.25 and byx = 0.64, correlation coefficient is = $\sqrt{0.25 \times 0.64} = \sqrt{.16} = 0.4$

19. Regarding the number of classes and size of the class interval, Sturges rule may be noted. His formula for number of classes is :
$K = 1 + 3.222 \log N$
where K = Number of classes,
N = Number of observations
As an illustration, if $N = 10$, $K = 1 + 3.322 \log 10 = 4.322 \simeq 4$
and if $N = 100$, $K = 1 + 3.322 \log 100 = 7.644 \simeq 8$

$$\text{Size of the class interval} = \frac{\text{Range}}{1 + 3.322 \log N}$$

where Range = The difference between the maximum and minimum value of the collected data.

24. A job description usually contains the following Information:

(a) **Job Identification :** This includes the job title, alternative title, department and division, plant and code number of the job. The job title helps to identify the job and department and division indicate the name of the department, its place, whether maintenance, mechanical or any other department.

(b) **Job Summary :** It is a brief write-up what the job is all about. In fact, it is a quick capsule explanation of the job in one or two sentences.

(c) **Job Duties and Responsibilities :** This portion of the job description gives a comprehensive list of duties to be performed. It is regarded as the heart of the job description. Job duties also make clear the job activities. Responsibilities related to the custody of cash, supervision, training to subordinates are also described In this part.

(d) **Relation to other jobs :** This section makes clear the vertical relationship of work flow and procedures and also the location of the job in the organisation by indicating the job immediately below or above it in the job hierarchy.

(e) **Supervision :** This section is obviously related to the supervision making clear the number of employees to be supervised alongwith their job titles, the extent and degree of supervision involved *i.e.,* general intermediate or close supervision.

(f) **Information about machines, tools and equipments, materials :** In this part, information relating to major type or trade name of the machines, tools, equipments and raw materials used is given.

(g) **Working Conditions :** It specifies the conditions under which the employees have to work *i.e.,* heat, cold, dust, moisture, fumes, etc. Because of this, job holders get an idea about the environment in which they have work.

(h) **Hazards :** Many jobs are hazardous involving the risks of accidents. Hazardous conditions are particularly noted making clear the nature of risks of life, limbs as well as the possibilities of their occurrence.

28. The marketing mix is that range of tools, or levers, used by marketers to influence demand and gain competitive advantage. There are four levers: product, place, promotion and price, traditionally known as the 'four P's' and shown in figure.

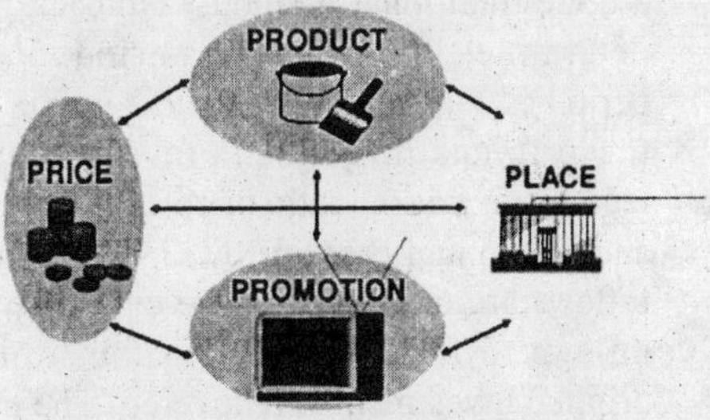

29. Quantitative research is based on the measurement of quantity or amount. It is applicable to phenomena that can be expressed in terms of quantity. Qualitative research, on the other hand, is concerned with qualitative phenomenon, *i.e.*, phenomena relating to or involving quality or kind. For instance, when we are interested in investigating the reasons for human behaviour, we quite often talk of "Motivation Research", an important type of qualitative research. This type of research aims at discovering the underlying motives and desires, using in depth interviews for the purpose. Other techniques of such research are word association tests, sentence, completion tests, story completion test and similar other projective techniques. Attitude or opinion researches *i.e.*, research, designed to find out how people feel or what they think about a particular subject or institution is also qualitative research. Qualitative research is specially important in the behavioural sciences where the aim is to discover the underlying motives of human behaviour. Though such research we can analyses the various factors which motivate people to behave in a particular manner or which make a people like or dislike a particular thing. It may be stated, however, that to apply qualitative research in practice is relatively a difficult job and therefore, while doing such research, one should seek guidance from experimental psychologists.

32. There are different methods used to appraise the long-term investment proposals. They are (a) Payback method (b) Accounting rate of return (c) Internal Rate of Return and (d) Net present value method (e) Profitability index. Payback method and accounting rate of return are the traditional methods. Payback method determines the payback period. Payback period is the minimum period within which the original investment in the project is recovered. It is the ratio of cost of the proposal and the annual cash inflows. Where the cash inflows are uneven, take the cumulative cash inflows to find the period within which the original investment is recovered. The projects with minimum payback are preferred.

Payback and Accounting rate of return methods do not consider the time value of money. Hence these are identified as traditional methods. The modem methods are Internal rate of return and net present value methods. These consider the time value of money. Internal rate of return is that rate which equates the present value of future cash inflows to the original investment. Net present value is the difference between the present value of future cash inflows and the original investment. The higher the NPV, the higher is the profitability of the proposal. Profitability index is the ratio between 'personal value of future cash inflows' to 'capital outlay'. The higher the index is, the higher is the profitability and *vice versa.*

34. The cost of retained earnings represents an opportunity cost in terms of the return on their investment in another enterprise by the firm whose cost of retained earnings is being considered.

36. The National Apprenticeship Scheme was launched in 1959, initially on voluntary basis. The Apprentices Act 1961 came into force on March 1, 1962. In the beginning, the Act envisaged training of trade apprentices. The training of Graduates and Diploma Holders in Engineering and Technology as Graduate and Technician Apprentices was brought within the purview of the Act through an amendment in 1973. The Apprentices Act was, further, amended in 1986 to bring within its purview the training of students passing out of the (10+2) vocational stream as Technician (Vocational) Apprentices. The training of this category of apprentices commenced in terms of the requisite Rules notified by the Government in October, 1987.

42. **Small Industries Development Bank of India (SIDBI):** For the benefit of small-scale industrial units, Small Industries Development Bank of India (SIDBI) was established in the year 1989. SIDBI is a subsidiary unit of IDBI. The main objectives of SIDBI are as follows:

(i) To provide adequate financial aid to small-scale industries.

(ii) To promote modernisation and technical upgradation of small-scale units.

(iii) To facilitate the marketing of products of small scale industries in India and abroad.

(iv) To promote employment by giving special assistance to labour intensive small scale industries.

43. **One-time passward (OTP):** A temporary passward that is only valid for a single login session or transaction.

49. IBRD and its associate institutions as a group are known as the World Bank. The Second World War damaged economies of most of the countries particularly of those who were directly involved in the war. In 1945, it was realised to concentrate on reconstructing these war affected economics. Besides, it was also given a thought to develop underdeveloped economies in a planned way. IBRD was established in December 1945 with the IMF on the basis of the recommendation of the Bretton Wood Conference. That is the reason why IMF and IBRD are called 'Bretton Wood Twins'.

50. UNCTAD is the acronym of United Nations Conference on Trade and Development established in 1964. To discuss the trade and development problems of member countries, three yearly conferences were held by United Nations Organisation (UNO). The permanent secretariat of UNCTAD was in Geneva. Now WTO–the World Trade Organisation–replaced UNCTAD. WTO was set up in 1995. WTO now formulates the policies and frameworks within which the member countries adjust and adjudicate their trade policies, mediates in trade disputes and conferences of WTO are had at regular interval.

PAPER–III

*Note: This paper contains **seventy five (75)** objective-type questions, each question carrying **two (2)** marks. **All** questions are compulsory.*

1. In accounting, profit prior to incorporation is treated as

A. Revenue Reserve
B. Secret Reserve
C. Capital Reserve
D. General Reserve

2. Receipts and Payments Account is prepared by

A. Manufacturing concerns
B. Non-Trading concerns
C. Trading concerns
D. Companies registered under Companies Act, 1956

3. Owners equity stands for

A. Fixed Assets minus Fixed Libilities
B. Fixed Assets minus Current Liabilities
C. Current Assets minus Fixed Liabilities
D. Total Assets minus Total outside Liabilities

4. When the Debt Turnover Ratio is 4, what is the average collection period?

A. 5 months   B. 4 months
C. 3 months   D. 2 months

5. Which of the following will result into sources of funds?

(*i*) Increase in current assets
(*ii*) Decrease in current assets
(*iii*) Increase in current liabilities
(*iv*) Decrease in current liabilities

Codes:

A. (*i*) and (*iv*)   B. (*ii*) and (*iii*)
C. (*i*) and (*iii*)   D. (*ii*) and (*iv*)

6. In marginal costing, contribution is equal to

A. Sales – Fixed cost
B. Sales – Variable cost
C. Sales – Profit
D. Sales – Variable cost + Fixed cost

7. The funds available with a company after paying all claims including tax and dividend is called

A. New Profit
B. Net Operating Profit
C. Capital Profit
D. Retained Earnings

8. **Assertion (A):** Accounting information refers to only events which are concerned with business firm

Reason (R): Accounting information is presented in financial statements

Codes:

A. (A) is correct, but (R) is wrong
B. Both (A) and (R) are correct
C. (A) is wrong, but (R) is correct
D. Both (A) and (R) are wrong

9. When average cost is declining

A. Marginal cost must be declining
B. Marginal cost must be above average cost
C. Marginal cost must be below average cost
D. Marginal cost must be rising

10. ABC Ltd. has declared 40% dividend. Which one of the following does it mean?

A. The company has declared 40% of net profit as dividend
B. The company has declared 40% of profits after tax as dividend
C. The company will provide dividend 40% on issued capital
D. The company will provide dividend 40% on paid-up capital

11. The main objective of Accounting Standards is
A. To prepare the accounting reports which is easily understood by common man
B. To comply with the legal formalities
C. To harmonise the diversified accounting practices
D. To comply with the requirements of the International Accounting Standards (IAS)

12. Given below are two statements :
I. Activity ratios show where the company is going.
II. Balance Sheet ratios show how the company stand.

Codes :
A. I is correct, but II is wrong
B. Both I and II are correct
C. I is wrong, but II is correct
D. Both I and II are wrong

13. Income and Expenditure Account of non-profit organisation is a
A. Real Account
B. Nominal Account
C. Personal Account
D. Representative Personal Account

14. Which of the following statements are correct?
I. Inventory includes raw materials, finished goods and work-in-progress
II. Inventory is a part of the working capital
III. Inventory includes goods likely to be purchased

Codes :
A. I, II and III B. II and III
C. I and III D. I and II

15. If the current ratio is 2 : 1 and working capital is ₹60,000, what is the value of the Current Assets?
A. ₹60,000 B. ₹1,00,000
C. ₹1,20,000 D. ₹1,80,000

16. Which of the following steps of purchase decision process is in sequence?
1. Problem recognition
2. Search for alternatives
3. Evaluation of alternatives
4. Purchase action
5. Post purchase action

Codes :
A. 1, 3, 2, 4, 5 B. 1, 2, 4, 3, 5
C. 2, 1, 3, 5, 4 D. 1, 2, 3, 4, 5

17. What is customer value?
A. Ratio between the customer's perceived benefits and the resources used to obtain these benefits
B. Excess of satisfaction over expectation
C. Post purchase dissonance
D. None of the above

18. Match the items of List-I with items of List-II.

	List-I	*List-II*
(*a*)	The silent mental repetition of information	1. Encoding
(*b*)	The process by which we select a word or visual image to represent a perceived object	2. Rehearsal
(*c*)	Where information is kept temporarily before further processing	3. Working Memory
(*d*)	The stage of real memory in which information is processed and held for just a brief period	4. Store house

Codes :

	(a)	*(b)*	*(c)*	*(d)*
A.	2	1	4	3
B.	1	2	3	4
C.	3	2	1	4
D.	4	3	2	1

19. Fill in the blanks :

	Statements	**Alternatives**
(*a*)	Loyal customers ____ products.	1. Less attention
(*b*)	Loyal customers are ____ sensitive.	2. Cheaper

(*c*) Loyal customers pay ____ to competitor's advertising.	3.	Less price
(*d*) Serving existing customer is ____.	4.	Buy more

Codes :

	(*a*)	(*b*)	(*c*)	(*d*)
A.	3	1	2	4
B.	4	3	1	2
C.	2	1	3	4
D.	4	3	2	1

20. **Assertion (A) :** High customer expectations lead to dissatisfaction as product performance never matches them.

Reason (R) : Product performance is always customer specific.

Codes :

A. Both (A) and (R) are correct.
B. Both (A) and (R) are incorrect.
C. (A) is correct, but (R) is incorrect.
D. (R) is correct, but (A) is incorrect.

21. VAT is imposed
A. Directly on Consumers
B. On final stage of production
C. On all stages from production to final sales
D. None of the above

22. Which is used for short-term sales achievement?
A. Personal selling
B. Advertising
C. Sales Promotion
D. Public Relations

23. Public distribution system relates to
A. Marketing system
B. Retailing system
C. Industrial system
D. Selling system

24. Who do buy more, complain less, spread positive word of mouth, ensure a large customer base and repeat business?
A. Satisfied customers
B. Delighted customers
C. Industrial customers
D. None of the above

25. There are impulses which persuade a customer to buy certain products without evaluating the positive and negative value of the same.
A. Emotional motives
B. Blind motives
C. Egoistic motives
D. All of the above

26. Which subject is relevant to the study of consumer behaviour?
A. Economics B. Psychology
C. Sociology D. All of the above

27. Find an incorrect statement.
A. Consumer attitude can be summarized as evaluation of an object.
B. Attitudes are learned.
C. Attitudes are synonymous with behaviour.
D. Attitudes have motivational qualities.

28. Who is considered Father of Scientific Management?
A. Peter Drucker B. F.W. Taylor
C. Victor Vroom D. Henry Fayol

29. Who did give the concept of hierarchy of needs ?
A. Fredrick Herzberg
B. Victor Vroom
C. Douglas Mcgregor
D. A.H. Maslow

30. **Assertion (A) :** Management is a continuous process.
Reason (R) : Managers first plan, then organise and finally perform the function of controlling.

Codes :

A. Both (A) and (R) are correct and (R) is correct explanation of (A).
B. Both (A) and (R) are correct, but (R) is not a correct explanation of (A).
C. (A) is correct, but (R) is incorrect.
D. (A) is incorrect, but (R) is correct.

31. Induction of employees relates to
A. Organisational awareness
B. Training programme
C. Introduction
D. Assignment of duties

32. 'Kinked' demand curve is related with
A. Monopoly
B. Discriminating monopoly

C. Oligopoly
D. Perfect competition

33. Who is not associated with HRM?
A. Michael J. Jucius
B. Dale Yodar
C. Edvoin B. Flippo
D. K.K. Devit

34. Merit rating is not known as
A. Efficiency Rating
B. Service Rating
C. Job Rating
D. Experience Rating

35. Match the items of List-I with the items of List-II.

	List-I	*List-II*
(*a*)	FEMA	1. 1986
(*b*)	Indian Factories Act	2. 1999
(*c*)	Industrial Dispute Act	3. 1948
(*d*)	Consumer Protection Act	4. 1947

Codes :

	(*a*)	(*b*)	(*c*)	(*d*)
A.	4	2	3	1
B.	3	1	2	4
C.	2	3	4	1
D.	1	4	3	2

36. If price of any commodity decreases by 20% and the demand for that commodity increases by 40%, then elasticity of demand would be
A. perfectly elastic
B. perfectly inelastic
C. unit elastic
D. highly elastic

37. Which of the following statements is true?
A. In case of inferior goods, the income effect is negative, although the substitution effect is positive.
B. In inferior goods, the income and substitution effects are positive.
C. In inferior goods, the income and substitution effects are negative.
D. In case of inferior goods, the income effect is positive although the substitution effect is negative.

38. In perfect competition, the demand curve of a firm is
A. Vertical
B. Horizontal
C. Positively sloped
D. Negatively sloped

39. Which one is not non-financial incentive?
A. Additional bonus on minimum wasteful expenditure.
B. Permanent job.
C. Participatory decision making.
D. Recognition of individuality.

40. HRM does not include
A. job evaluation
B. performance appraisal
C. sales promotion
D. job enrichment

41. The term (1-B) is called
A. Level of the test
B. Power of the test
C. Size of the test
D. None of the above

42. The area under normal distribution covered within μ ± 36 limits is
A. 0.6827 B. 0.9545
C. 0.9973 D. 1.0000

43. Sampling distribution of mean is very close to the standard normal distribution when
A. Population is normally distributed.
B. Population is not normally distributed, but sample size is large.
C. Both A and B.
D. Neither A nor B.

44. If the value of co-efficient of determination is 0.64, what is the value of co-efficient of correlation?
A. 0.40 B. 0.80
C. 0.08 D. 0.04

45. Which one of the following is not a source of conflict in project ranking in capital budgeting decision as per NPV and IRR?
A. Independent Investment Project
B. No Capital Budget Constraints
C. No time disparity
D. None of the above

46. Match the following :

	List-I	*List-II*
(*a*)	Trade policy	1. Economic conditions

(*b*) Trade flows	2. Economic policies
(*c*) Price trends	3. Global linkages
(*d*) Internal sectoral linkages	4. Structure and Nature of Economy

Codes :

	(*a*)	(*b*)	(*c*)	(*d*)
A.	3	1	2	4
B.	2	3	1	4
C.	1	2	3	4
D.	1	2	4	3

47. Which one of the following is not a benefit of privatisation?
A. Encourage entrepreneurship
B. Concentration of economic power
C. Better management of enterprise
D. Freedom from bureaucracy

48. 'BOLT' system in the Indian Securities market is related to
A. National Stock Exchange
B. Bombay Stock Exchange
C. Over the Counter Exchange of India
D. Multi Commodity Stock Exchange

49. Which one of the following is not a money market instrument?
A. Commercial paper
B. Participatory certificates
C. Warrants
D. Treasury Bills

50. Which one is related with microfinancing?
A. SHG
B. Anganwadi workers
C. Women Entrepreneurs
D. None of the above

51. Which one of the following is not an element of internal environment?
A. Mission/Objectives
B. Human Resources
C. Customers
D. Shareholders' values

52. The presence of fixed costs in the total cost structure of a firm results into
A. Financial leverage
B. Operating leverage
C. Super leverage
D. None of the above

53. "The cost of capital declines when the degree of financial leverage increases." Who advocated it?
A. Net operating income approach
B. Net income approach
C. Modigliani-Miller approach
D. Traditional approach

54. A view that the dividend policy of a firm has a bearing on share valuation advocated by James E. Walter is based on which one of the following assumptions?
A. Retained earnings is only source of financing
B. Cost of capital does not remain constant
C. Return on investment fluctuates
D. All of the above

55. Match the following :

List-I	*List-II*
(*a*) Matching approach	1. Dividend Policy
(*b*) Structural ratios	2. Inventory Management
(*c*) Ordering quantity	3. Financing Working Capital
(*d*) Bonus shares	4. Capital Structure

Codes :

	(*a*)	(*b*)	(*c*)	(*d*)
A.	1	2	3	4
B.	3	4	1	2
C.	3	4	2	1
D.	2	1	3	4

56. Assertion (A) : Operating style of the international business can be spread to the entire globe.

Reason (R) : The style is limited to the internal economy only.

Codes :
A. Both (A) and (R) are true.
B. (A) is true, but (R) is false.
C. (A) is false, but (R) is true.
D. Both (A) and (R) are false.

57. The Comparative Cost Advantage Theory was given by
A. David Ricardo
B. Adam Smith

C. Raymond Vernon
D. Michael E. Porter

58. The companies globalise their operations through different means
A. Exporting directly
B. Licensing/Franchising
C. Joint ventures
D. All of the above

59. The components of W.T.O. are
A. Ministerial Conference
B. Disputes Settlement Body
C. Director General
D. All of the above

60. India is not associated with
A. SAARC B. NAFTA
C. BRICS D. None of the above

61. Which one of the following is true statement?
A. A balance of trade deals with export and import of invisible items only.
B. A balance of payment deals with both visible and invisible items.
C. The current account is not a component of balance of payment.
D. All of the above

62. SDRs are popularly known as
A. Currency Notes B. Paper Gold
C. Silver Coin D. Gold Coin

63. Which one is not international institution?
A. IMF B. IDA
C. IBRD D. TRAI

64. **Assertion (A) :** Indent may be open or closed. Open indent does not specify the price and other details of the goods. The closed indent specifies the brand, price, number, packing, shipping mode, insurance, etc.

Reason (R) : This is required as a part of export procedures.

Codes :
A. Both (A) and (R) are correct.
B. Both (A) and (R) are not correct.
C. (A) is true, but (R) is false.
D. (R) is true, but (A) is false.

65. When a population is heterogeneous, it is divided into groups, so that there is homogeneity within the group and heterogeneity between the groups, and some items are selected at random from each group. It is a case of:
A. Cluster Random Sampling
B. Systematic Random Sampling
C. Quota Sampling
D. Stratified Random Sampling

66. Match the items of List-I with items of List-II.

List-I	*List-II*
(*a*) Selective credit control	1. Consumer Credit Regulation
(*b*) Encourage credit for desirable use	2. Cash Reserve Ratio
(*c*) Quantitative credit control	3. Variation in Margin
(*d*) Bank Rate	4. Re-discounting Rate

Codes :

	(a)	*(b)*	*(c)*	*(d)*
A.	4	2	3	1
B.	3	1	2	4
C.	1	3	2	4
D.	2	1	3	4

67. **Assertion (A) :** Use of paper money is replaced by plastic money. The future will see the electronic money clearance through satellite networking.

Reason (R) : RBI is encouraging e-banking.

Codes :
A. (A) is false, but (R) is true.
B. (A) is true, but (R) is false.
C. Both (A) and (R) are false.
D. Both (A) and (R) are true.

68. Which one is not Finance Company?
A. Hire-Purchase Finance Company
B. IRDA
C. Mutual Benefit Finance Companies
D. Loan Companies

69. The Securities and Exchange Board of India was not entrusted with the function of
A. Investor Protection.
B. Ensuring Fair practices by companies.
C. Promotion of efficient services by brokers.
D. Improving the earnings of equity holders.

70. Which one is not Non-Marketable securities?
A. Corporate Securities
B. Bank Deposits
C. Deposits with Companies
D. Post Office Certificates and Deposits

71. Minimum Alternative Tax (MAT) under Sec.115 JB of the Income Tax Act is applicable on
A. Partnership firm
B. Association of persons
C. Certain companies
D. All types of companies

72. For the Assessment Year 2011-12, deduction under Sec. 80G is available without any limit but at the rate of 50% on
A. Prime Minister's National Relief Fund
B. National Foundation for Communal Harmony
C. Jawahar Lal Nehru Memorial Fund
D. Chief Minister Relief Fund

73. Interest on capital paid by a firm to its partners, under the Income Tax Act, 1961, is allowed
A. 6% B. 12%
C. 15% D. 18%

74. Under capital gains head of the Income Tax Act, the income from sale of Household Furniture is
A. Taxable Income B. Capital Gain
C. Revenue Gain D. Exempted Income

75. Under Section 80E of the Income Tax Act, 1961 deduction in respect of payment of interest on loan taken for higher education shall be allowed up to
A. ₹10,000 B. ₹15,000
C. ₹20,000 D. Without any limit

ANSWERS

1	2	3	4	5	6	7	8	9	10
C	B	D	C	B	B	D	B	C	D
11	**12**	**13**	**14**	**15**	**16**	**17**	**18**	**19**	**20**
C	B	B	D	C	D	A	A	B	B
21	**22**	**23**	**24**	**25**	**26**	**27**	**28**	**29**	**30**
C	C	B	B	D	D	C	B	D	A
31	**32**	**33**	**34**	**35**	**36**	**37**	**38**	**39**	**40**
C	C	D	C	C	D	A	B	A	C
41	**42**	**43**	**44**	**45**	**46**	**47**	**48**	**49**	**50**
B	C	C	B	D	B	B	B	C	A
51	**52**	**53**	**54**	**55**	**56**	**57**	**58**	**59**	**60**
C	B	B	A	C	B	A	D	D	B
61	**62**	**63**	**64**	**65**	**66**	**67**	**68**	**69**	**70**
B	B	D	C	D	B	D	B	D	A
71	**72**	**73**	**74**	**75**					
C	C	B	D	D					

SOME SELECTED EXPLANATORY ANSWERS

1. (i) Profit prior to incorporation is a capital profit and hence it should be transferred to Capital Reserve Account. Capital Reserve may be used to write off Goodwill, Share Issue Expenses, Discount on Issue of Debentures, etc.

(ii) Loss prior to incorporation should be debited to Goodwill Account.

(iii) Post-incorporation profit/loss should be transferred to Profit and Loss Appropriation Account.

2. The technique of preparing the final accounts of a non-trading concern is similar to that used for preparing the final accounts of a trading concern. These are prepared on the basis of Cash Book and Ledger. The final accounts of non-trading concerns consist of the following
   1. Receipts and Payments Account
   2. Income and Expenditure Account
   3. Balance Sheet

4. **Debtors Turnover Ratio and Average Collection Period:** Debtors or receivables are current assets of business. The debtors turnover ratio measures how quickly the debtors or receivables of business are realised. It also indicates how efficiently the debtors of business are being realised. It is an indicator of the liquidity of debtors. This ratio establishes relationship between credit sales and average debtors.

   Accounts receivable include debtors and bills receivable. Average receivables are calculated by dividing the sum of opening and closing balances of receivables by two.

   Debtors Turnover Ratio

   $$= \frac{\text{Credit Sales}}{\text{Average Accounts Receivable}}$$

   In case information about credit sales and average debtors is missing, this ratio is calculated on the basis of total sales and closing balance of receivables.

   Debtors Turnover Ratio

   $$= \frac{\text{Total Sales}}{\text{Accounts Receivable (Closing)}}$$

   The second ratio related to debtors turnover is the average collection period. This ratio is calculated by dividing the days in a year by debtors turnover ratio. This ratio indicates to what extent the debtors have been collected in time.

   Average Collection Period

   $$= \frac{\text{Months or Days in a year}}{\text{Debators Turnover Ratio}}$$

   From question

   Average Collection Period

   $$= \frac{\text{12 months}}{\text{Debtors Turnover Ratio}} = \frac{12}{4} = 3 \text{ months}$$

6. The marginal costing technique advocates that fixed costs are not relevant for the purpose of planning. It considers only marginal costs for efficient planning of expenses and profit. The logic is simple; fixed costs would remain fixed over a short period of time, hence should be ignored. Difference between sales and variable costs is called profit in marginal costing. This term "profit" has a different connotation also, namely Contribution. A firm which can maximize profit (contribution) can automatically maximize net profit, fixed costs remaining constant.

9. The relationship between average cost and marginal cost can be expressed thus:

   If Average Cost is falling Marginal Cost will be less than Average Cost.

   If Average Cost is rising Marginal Cost will be higher than Average Cost.

   If Average Cost is constant Marginal Cost will be equal to Average Cost.

11. Accounting Standards are the guidelines, principles, methods, customs, usage and business environment for accounting. In India, the Accounting Standard are authorised by the Accounting Standard Board (ASB) constituted by Institute of Chartered Accountants of India (ICAI) in the year 1977. The main objective of the accounting standards is to harmonise the diversified accounting practices and policies. The international body to monitor the accounting standards is International Accounting Standards Committee (IASC).

13. An Income and Expenditure Account may be defined as a summary of incomes and expenditures of the accounting year. Income and Expenditure Account is similar to the Profit and Loss Account of business or profit organisations. It is prepared on accrual basis. It is prepared at the end of the year and includes only revenue items. The terms "Profit" or "Loss" are substituted by the words "Surplus" (excess of income over expenditure)

or "Deficit" (excess of expenditure over income).

Following are the features of Income and Expenditure Account :

(i) It is a nominal account.

(ii) Debit side of this account records expenditures while credit side records incomes.

(iii) It is prepared on accrual basis.

(iv) It records incomes and expenditures of only revenue items relating to the current accounting year.

15. $\because$ Current Ratio = $\dfrac{\text{Current Assets}}{\text{Current Liabilities}} = \dfrac{2}{1}$

and Current Assets – Current liabilities = working capital $\Rightarrow 2 - 1 = 1$

If working capital is Rs. 1, then current assets is 2.

If working capital is 60,000, then

Current assets is $\dfrac{2}{1} \times 60{,}000$

$\therefore$ Current assets = 120,000

17. Customer value is defined as "the ratio between the customer's perceived benefits (economic, functional and psychological) and the resources (monetary, time, effort, psychological) used to obtain those benefits."

Customer's perceived value is the difference between the prospective customer's evaluation of all the benefits and cost of an offering and perceived alternatives. Hence, customer perceived value is thus based on the difference between what customer gets and what he gives for different possible choices. The marketer can increase the value of the customer by providing/adding functional or emotional benefits to the products or by reducing the cost.

22. Sales promotion is a dynamic and flexible sales tool. Two related definitions are:

1. The short-term achievement of marketing objectives by schematic means.
2. Immediate or delayed incentives to purchase, expressed in cash or in kind.

28. Scientific Management. F.W. Taylor is regarded as the father of scientific management movement. According to him, scientific management is 'the art of knowing exactly what you want men to do and then seeing that they do it in the best and cheapest way'. In the words of F.W. Taylor, "Scientific Management is the substitution of exact scientific investigations and knowledge for the old individual judgement or opinion in all matters relating to the work done in the shop".

According to Peter Druker, "Scientific Management is the operational study of work, the analysis of work into its simplest element and the systematic improvement of the workers performance of each element."

29. Among the most widely referred to motivation theories, Maslow's Hierarchy of Needs Theory is quite prominent. He sees human needs in the form of a hierarchy, starting in an ascending order from the lowest to the highest needs and concludes that when one set of needs is satisfied then the need for the other set arises.

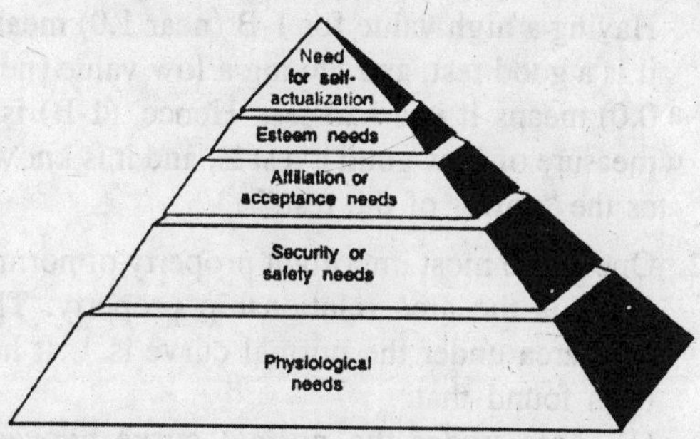

Fig. Maslow's hierarchy of needs.

31. Induction is the process of introducing new employees to the company, to their supervisors and co-workers (if there are any), and to their jobs.

32. The theory of the kinked demand curve was developed by Paul Sweezy (1939) in order to explain why oligopolistic prices tend to be more stable than prices in other market structures.

34. The task of evaluating employee performance is known by various terms, namely: (a) performance rating, (b) efficiency rating, (c) merit rating, (d) employee evaluation, (e) service rating, (f) personnel rating, (g) performance review, and (h) performance appraisal.

38. In perfect competition a firm is a price-taker. This follows from the fact that the product is homogeneous and the firm is too small to affect market price.

The graphical expression of the demand curve for a firm which is a price-taker, is a horizontal straight line drawn at the going market price.

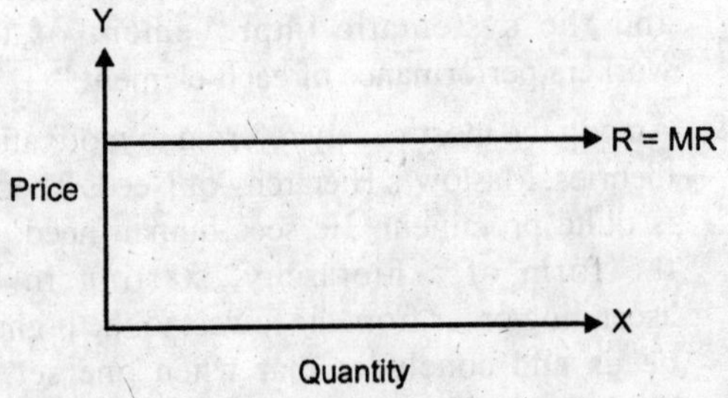

41. Rejecting a null hypothesis when it is false is what every good hypothesis test should do. Having a high value for 1-B (near 1.0) means it is a good test, and having a low value (near 0.0) means it is a bad test. Hence, (1-B) is a measure of how good a test is, and it is known as the "power of the test."

42. One of the most important property of normal curve is the area relationship property. The total area under the normal curve is 1. It has been found that:

(1) Area under the normal curve between $\mu - 1\sigma$ and $\mu + 1\sigma$ is 0.6826, *i.e.,* Mean $\pm 1\sigma$ covers 68.26% area under the normal curve.

(2) Area under the normal curve between $\mu - 2\sigma$ and $\mu + 2\sigma$ is 0.9545, *i.e.,* Mean $\pm$ 2σ covers 95.45% area under the normal curve.

(3) Area under the normal curve between $\mu - 3\sigma$ and $\mu + 3\sigma$ is 0.9973, *i.e.,* Mean $\pm$ 3σ covers 99.73% area under the normal curve.

44. Coefficient of determination = $r^2 = 0.64$

$\therefore$ Coefficient correlation

$$= \sqrt{r^2} = \sqrt{0.64} = 0.8$$

49. The Money Market is that segment of the financial markets wherein financial instruments having maturities of less than one year are traded. These different instruments are listed as follows:

1. Call money and notice money
2. Repos
3. Inter-bank term money
4. Bill of Exchange
5. Treasury bill
6. Inter-bank Participation Certificate
7. Certificate of deposit
8. Commercial Paper
9. Intercorporate deposit

50. Microfinance means providing very poor families with very small loans (micro credit) to help them engage in productive activities or grow their tiny businesses. Traditionally microfinance was focused on providing a much standardised credit product. The poor, just like anyone else, need a diverse range of financial instruments to be able to build assets, stabilise consumption and protect themselves against risks. Over time, microfinance has come to include a broader range of services (credit, savings, money transfers, payment services, insurance, etc.) as it is realised that the poor who lack access to traditional formal financial institutions require a variety of financial products. This helps them generate income which allows them to care for themselves and their families. Micro finance is thus regarded as the dignified way of crossing the poverty line.

53. According to this approach, the cost of debt and the cost of equity do not change with a change in the leverage ratio. As a result, the average cost of capital declines as the leverage ratio increases. This is because when the leverage ratio increases, the cost of debt, which is lower than the cost of equity, gets a higher weightage in the calculation of the cost of capital.

This approach has been suggested by David Durand. According to this approach, capital structure decision is relevant to the valuation of the firm.

57. The principle of Comparative Advantage was developed by David Ricardo in his book entitled "Principles of Political Economy and Taxation" published in 1817. He stated that the gains from trade accrue to both sides even when a country has no absolute advantage whatsoever. As long as price ratios differ between countries every country will have a comparative advantage, an ability to find some goods it can produce at a lower relative cost disadvantage than other goods. It should export these goods in exchange for those goods which have a relatively higher cost disadvantage. It can be summed up that trade between two countries can benefit both countries if each country exports the goods in which it has comparative advantage.

60. The North American Free Trade Agreement (NAFTA) is an agreement signed by Canada, Mexico, and the United States, creating a trilateral trade bloc in North America. The agreement came into force on January 1, 1994. It superseded the Canada–United States Free Trade Agreement between the U.S. and Canada.

61. Balance of payment of a country is a systematic record of all economic transactions completed between its residents and the residents of remaining world during a year. In other words, the balance of payments shows the relationship between one country's total payment to all other countries and its total receipts from them. Balance of payment is a comprehensive term which includes both visible and Invisible items. Balance of payment not only include visible export & import but also invisible trade like shipping, banking, insurance, tourism, royalty payments, payments of interest on foreign debts. In accounting sense, balance of payments is always in equilibrium in accounting sense due to double entry accounts. Disequilibrium in balance of payment may appear. When the total revenue from international trade and investment exceeds total expenditure a situation of surplus balance of payment arises and when expenditure *i.e.* payment side becomes greater, it takes the shape of deficit balance of payment

62. For increasing international liquidity, IMF created a scheme called Special Drawing Rights (SORs). It is also known as paper gold. This scheme was started by IMF to overcome acute shortage of international liquidity. International liquidity means ability to pay for its imports. If any country is not in a position to make payment of its imports *i.e.* its balance of payments is unfavourable, then that country can use SDRs for meeting such deficits in balance of payments. This scheme was started in the year 1969. In this scheme, member countries are allotted quotas of SDRs. SDRs are like coupons which can be exchanged for currencies required by holder of SDRs for making international payment.

63. The Telecom Regulatory Authority of India (TRAI) is the independent regulator of the telecommunications business in India.

68. Insurance Regulatory and Development Authority (IRDA) is an autonomous apex statutory body which regulates and develops the insurance industry in India. It was constituted by a Parliament of India act called Insurance Regulatory and Development Authority Act, 1999 and duly passed by the Government of India. The agency operates its headquarters at Hyderabad, Andhra Pradesh where it shifted from Delhi in 2001.

70. Non-Marketable Securities—Securities which do not constitute an important part of the capital market, e.g., bank deposits, deposit with companies, loans and advances of banks and financial institutions, post office certificates and deposits, etc.

Previous Paper (Solved)

UGC-NET COMMERCE, JUNE–2012

PAPER–II

*Note: This paper contains **fifty** (50) objective-type questions, each question carrying **two** (2) marks. Attempt **all** of them.*

1. Which of the following denote the structural changes in Indian economy?

A. Primary sector contribution has gone down.
B. Service sector contribution has gone up.
C. Secondary sector has not changed much.
D. All of the above

2. Broad Money has to be sensitized through:

A. CRR
B. SLR
C. Repo Rate
D. All of the above

3. Which one is not an element of legal environment?

A. Act of Parliamentarians in Lok Sabha
B. Indian Contract Act, 1872
C. Indian Partnership Act, 1932
D. Negotiable instruments Act, 1881

4. Out of the following, which are four dimensions of Human Development Index?

(*i*) Life Expectancy
(*ii*) Literacy Level
(*iii*) Success Rate of Marriages
(*iv*) Standard of Living
(*v*) Crime Rate
(*vi*) Corruption Level
(*vii*) Economic Entitlement
(*viii*) Foreign Visits

Codes :

A. (*i*), (*ii*), (*vi*) and (*viii*)
B. (*i*), (*ii*), (*iv*) and (*vii*)
C. (*ii*), (*iii*), (*vi*) and (*vii*)
D. (*iii*), (*v*), (*vii*) and (*viii*)

5. Public Enterprise is defined as:

A. An organisation run by joint efforts of Centre and State Governments.
B. An organisation which caters to the needs relating to public utilities.
C. An organisation in which capital is invested by public.
D. An organisation owned and managed by public authorities for definite set of public purposes.

6. Match List-I with List-II and select the correct answer :

List-I

(*a*) Measurement of income
(*b*) Recognition of expense
(*c*) Basis of realization
(*d*) Identification of revenue

List-II

(*i*) Accrues to the equity of owners
(*ii*) Recognition of revenue
(*iii*) Matching revenue with expenses
(*iv*) Accounting period

Codes :

	(*a*)	(*b*)	(*c*)	(*d*)
A.	(*i*)	(*ii*)	(*iii*)	(*iv*)
B.	(*ii*)	(*i*)	(*iii*)	(*iv*)
C.	(*iii*)	(*iv*)	(*i*)	(*ii*)
D.	(*iii*)	(*iv*)	(*ii*)	(*i*)

7. Consider the following items:

(*i*) Debentures (*ii*) Prepaid rent
(*iii*) Interest accrued (*iv*) Bank overdraft

Which of them are current liabilities?

A. (*i*), (*ii*), (*iii*) and (*iv*)
B. (*iv*)
C. (*ii*), (*iii*) and (*iv*)
D. (*i*), (*ii*) and (*iii*)

8. Conversion cost is the sum of:
A. Indirect wages and factory overhead
B. Direct wages, direct expenses and factory overhead
C. Direct material cost and indirect wages
D. Prime cost and selling & distribution overhead

9. Assertion (A): Premium received on issue of shares is credited to share premium account but not to Profit and Loss account.

Reasoning (R): Since share premium is not a trading profit, it is not distributed to shareholders.
A. Both (A) and (R) are true but (R) is not correct explanation to (A).
B. (A) is false but (R) is correct.
C. Both (A) and (R) are true and (R) is correct explanation of (A).
D. (A) is correct but (R) is false.

10. Consider the following:
(*i*) Basic defensive and interval ratio
(*ii*) Current ratio
(*iii*) Superquick ratio
(*iv*) Quick ratio

Arrange these ratios in sequence to reflect the liquidity in descending order.
A. (*ii*), (*iv*), (*iii*) and (*i*)
B. (*i*), (*ii*), (*iv*) and (*iii*)
C. (*iv*), (*ii*), (*iii*) and (*i*)
D. (*iii*), (*iv*), (*i*) and (*ii*)

11. Normally Demand curve slopes:
A. Upward B. Downward
C. Horizontal D. Vertical

12. Which of the following refers to Perfect Competition?
(*i*) There are restrictions on buyers and sellers
(*ii*) There are no restrictions on movement of goods
(*iii*) There are no restrictions on factors of production
Correct one is
A. only (*i*) and (*ii*) B. only (*ii*) and (*iii*)
C. only (*i*) and (*iii*) D. only (*i*)

13. Assertion (A): Total utility will be maximum when marginal utility to price of respective products are equal.

Reason (R): Deviation from this situation leads to reduction in maximum utility.
A. (A) and (R) are not correct.
B. (A) is correct but (R) is not correct.
C. (A) and (R) are correct.
D. (A) is incorrect, (R) is correct.

14. Match List-I with List-II and select the correct answer.

List-I	*List-II*
(*a*) Survival	(*i*) Economic Objective
(*b*) R.O.I	(*ii*) Natural Urge
(*c*) Growth	(*iii*) Business Purpose
(*d*) Innovation	(*iv*) Primary Objective

Codes :

	(*a*)	(*b*)	(*c*)	(*d*)
A.	(*ii*)	(*iii*)	(*iv*)	(*i*)
B.	(*ii*)	(*i*)	(*iii*)	(*iv*)
C.	(*i*)	(*ii*)	(*iii*)	(*iv*)
D.	(*iv*)	(*iii*)	(*ii*)	(*i*)

15. Consider the oligopoly models :
(*i*) Sweezy's kinked demand curve model
(*ii*) Newman and Morgenstern Game Theory model
(*iii*) Cournal's duopoly model
(*iv*) Baumal's sales maximisation model

Arrange them in correct sequence as per order of evolution.
A. (*iv*), (*iii*), (*ii*), (*i*)
B. (*ii*), (*i*), (*iii*), (*iv*)
C. (*iii*), (*i*), (*ii*), (*iv*)
D. (*i*), (*iii*), (*ii*), (*iv*)

16. Which of the following is not a restricted random sampling technique?
A. Stratified sampling
B. Simple random sampling
C. Systematic sampling
D. Multistage sampling

17. Classification of respondents only on the basis of gender is an application of:
A. Ordinal scale B. Nominal scale
C. Interval scale D. Ratio scale

18. Karl Pearson's co-efficient of correlation between two variables is:

A. the product of their standard deviations

B. the square root of the product of their regression co-efficients

C. the co-variance between the variables

D. None of the above

19. Statistical software packages for research in social sciences include:

A. SPSS B. STATA

C. MiniTab D. All of the above

20. F-test is used to test the significance of the differences between/among

A. Two sample mean

B. More than two samples mean

C. Variance of two samples

D. B and C

21. Match the following:

List-I	*List-II*
(*a*) The Practice of Management	(*i*) Henry Fayol
(*b*) Philosophy of Management	(*ii*) F.W. Taylor
(*c*) Scientific Management	(*iii*) Oliver Sheldon
(*d*) General and Industrial Administration	(*iv*) Peter F Drucker

Codes :

	(a)	*(b)*	*(c)*	*(d)*
A.	(*i*)	(*ii*)	(*iii*)	(*iv*)
B.	(*iv*)	(*iii*)	(*ii*)	(*i*)
C.	(*iv*)	(*iii*)	(*i*)	(*ii*)
D.	(*iii*)	(*iv*)	(*ii*)	(*i*)

22. Identify the correct sequence of steps involved in planning:

(*i*) Selecting the best course of action

(*ii*) Establishing the sequence of activities

(*iii*) Establishment of objectives

(*iv*) Evaluating alternative courses

(*v*) Determining alternative courses

A. (*i*), (*ii*); (*iii*), (*iv*) and (*v*)

B. (*iii*), (*v*), (*iv*), (*ii*) and (*i*)

C. (*v*), (*iv*), (*iii*), (*ii*) and (*i*)

D. (*iii*), (*v*), (*iv*), (*i*) and (*ii*)

23. Assertion (A): One can be sure about future course of actions by making good plans.

Reasoning (R): Planning brings certainty in future course of actions of an organisation.

A. (R) is correct but (A) is not correct.

B. (A) is correct but (R) is not correct.

C. Both (A) and (R) are correct.

D. Both (A) and (R) are not correct.

24. According to Kieth Devis, which one is not a barrier of communication?

A. Physical Barriers

B. Technological Barriers

C. Personal Barriers

D. Linguistic Barriers

25. While establishing relation between Maslow's and Herzberg's theories, which Needs of Hierachy Theory will fall under the Hygiene Factors?

A. Self actualisation, esteem and social needs

B. Esteem, social and safety needs

C. Social, safety and physiological needs

D. Only social needs

26. Howard-Sueth model of consumer behaviour is popularly known as:

A. Machine Model

B. Human Model

C. Marketing Model

D. Purchase Model

27. To generate and facilitate any exchange intended to satisfy human needs or wants such that the satisfaction of these wants occur with minimal detrimental impact on the natural environment is known as:

A. Aggressive marketing

B. Operating marketing

C. Green marketing

D. All of the above

28. All the activities involved in selling goods or services directly to final consumers for personal non-business uses are done by:

A. Wholesalers

B. Retailers

C. Mediators

D. Commission Agents

29. To manage a business well is to manage its future and to manage the future is to manage information is termed as:

A. Management information system
B. Marketing information system
C. Future information system
D. General information system

30. DAGMAR approach in marketing is used to measure:

A. Public relations
B. Advertising results
C. Selling volume
D. Consumer satisfaction

31. Which one is not an important objective of Financial Management?

A. Profit Maximisation
B. Wealth Maximisation
C. Value Maximisation
D. Maximisation of social benefits

32. Which one refers to cash inflow under payback period method?

A. Cash flow before depreciation and taxes
B. Cash flow after depreciation and taxes
C. Cash flow after depreciation but before taxes
D. Cash flow before depreciation and after taxes

33. The concept of present value is based on the:

A. Principle of compounding
B. Principle of discounting
C. A and B
D. None of the above

34. Cost of capital from all the sources of funds is called:

A. Specific cost
B. Composite cost
C. Implicit cost
D. Simple Average cost

35. Match the following with most suitable option:

(*a*) Modigiliani-Miller Approach	(*i*) Commercial papers
(*b*) Net Operating Income Approach	(*ii*) Working Capital Management
(*c*) Short term Money Market Instrument	(*iii*) Capital Structure
(*d*) Factoring	(*iv*) Arbitrage

Codes :

	(*a*)	(*b*)	(*c*)	(*d*)
A.	(*iv*)	(*iii*)	(*i*)	(*ii*)
B.	(*iii*)	(*iv*)	(*i*)	(*ii*)
C.	(*iii*)	(*ii*)	(*i*)	(*iv*)
D.	(*iii*)	(*ii*)	(*iv*)	(*i*)

36. Which four are the factors influencing the Human Resource Management of an organisation?

(*i*) Size of workforce
(*ii*) Employee Expectations
(*iii*) Composition of workforce
(*iv*) Political influence
(*v*) Changes in technology

A. (*i*), (*ii*), (*iii*) and (*iv*)
B. (*i*),(*ii*), (*iii*) and (*v*)
C. (*i*), (*ii*), (*iv*) and (*v*)
D. (*i*), (*iii*), (*iv*) and (*v*)

37. **Assertion (A):** One can not be sure about the quality of appraisal on the basis of length of service.

Reasoning (R): Initial appraisal and promotional appraisal are done separately and differently since the length of service is different.

A. (R) is correct but (A) is not correct.
B. (A) is correct but (R) is not correct.
C. (A) and (R) both are correct.
D. (A) and (R) both are not correct.

38. Which of the following are covered under the scope of Human Resource Management?

(*i*) Forecasting Human Resource Needs
(*ii*) Replacement Planning
(*iii*) Human Resource Dynamics
(*iv*) Human Resource Development Planning
(*v*) Human Resource Audit

A. (*i*), (*iii*), (*v*)
B. (*i*), (*ii*), (*iii*), (*iv*)
C. (*iii*), (*v*)
D. (*i*), (*ii*), (*iii*), (*iv*), (*v*)

39. On which of the following, at the initial stage, the Indian IT companies relying more for getting good IT professionals?
A. Job Portals
B. Placement Agencies
C. Campus Placement
D. All of the above

40. **Statement (*i*):** Labour always get a major share of productivity gains.

Statement (*ii*): Partial stoppage of work by workers amounts to strike.
A. Statement (*i*) is true but (*ii*) is false.
B. Statement (*ii*) is true but (*i*) is false.
C. Both statements are true.
D. Both statements are false.

41. Imperial Bank was established on January 27, 1921 on the advise of:
A. J. M. Keynes
B. Lord Illingworth
C. King George V
D. Winston Churchill

42. Read the following events:
(*i*) Allowing convertibility of rupee at the market rate in the current account
(*ii*) Nationalisation of general insurance business
(*iii*) Establishment of IDBI
(*iv*) Nationalisation of life insurance business
(*v*) Capital adequacy norms for commercial banks

Arrange the events in the ascending order of their occurrence:
A. (*iv*), (*iii*), (*ii*), (*i*), (*v*)
B. (*v*), (*iv*), (*iii*), (*ii*), (*i*)
C. (*i*), (*ii*), (*iii*), (*v*), (*iv*)
D. (*i*), (*v*), (*ii*), (*iv*), (*iii*)

43. In India, the Commercial Banks are given license of operation by:
A. The Government of India
B. The Ministry of Finance
C. Reserve Bank of India
D. Banking Companies Regulation Act, 1949

44. The provisions of General Reserve in Banking Companies are made keeping in view the provisions of:
A. Indian Companies Act, 1956
B. Banking Companies Act, 1949
C. SEBI Act, 1992
D. Statutory Auditor

45. Which among the following is not true with regard to merchant banker?
(*i*) It can accept deposits.
(*ii*) It can advance loans.
(*iii*) It can do other banking activities.
(*iv*) It can be manager to a public issue.
A. (*i*), (*ii*) and (*iii*) B. (*ii*), (*iii*) and (*iv*)
C. (*i*), (*iii*) and (*iv*) D. (*ii*) and (*iv*)

46. Balance of Payments can be made favourable if:
A. Exports are increased
B. Imports are increased
C. Devaluation of money
D. A and C

47. Which one is not an objective of IMF?
A. To promote international monetary co-operation
B. To ensure balanced international trade
C. To finance productive efforts according to peace-time requirement
D. To ensure exchange rate stability

48. EPCG denotes:
A. Export Potential and Credit Guarantee
B. Earning Promotion and Credit Guarantee
C. Export Promotion and Credit Guarantee
D. Export Potential and Credit Goods

49. Which one of the following matches correspond to the Member and Observer countries of the SAARC?
(*i*) India, Pakistan, Bangladesh, Bhutan, Nepal, Sri Lanka, Afghanistan, Maldive
(*ii*) Iran, China, Japan, USA, South Korea, European Union
(*iii*) Pakistan, Nepal, India, Bangladesh, Iran
(*iv*) UK, USA, North Korea, South Africa
A. (*iii*) and (*iv*) B. (*ii*) and (*iv*)
C. (*i*) and (*ii*) D. (*ii*) and (*iii*)

50. Which one is not an international organisation?
A. SAARC B. ASEM
C. ASEAN D. CBDT

ANSWERS

1	2	3	4	5	6	7	8	9	10
D	D	A	B	D	D	B	B	C	A
11	**12**	**13**	**14**	**15**	**16**	**17**	**18**	**19**	**20**
B	B	C	A	C	B	B	B	D	D
21	**22**	**23**	**24**	**25**	**26**	**27**	**28**	**29**	**30**
B	D	A	B	C	A	C	B	A	D
31	**32**	**33**	**34**	**35**	**36**	**37**	**38**	**39**	**40**
D	D	B	B	A	C	D	D	C	B
41	**42**	**43**	**44**	**45**	**46**	**47**	**48**	**49**	**50**
A	A	C	B	A	D	C	C	C	D

PAPER–III

***Note:** This paper contains seventy five (75) objective-type questions, each question carrying two (2) marks each. All questions are compulsory.*

1. If Opening Stock is ₹ 10,000, Net Purchases ₹ 70,000, Wages ₹ 2,500, Carriage inward ₹ 500 and Closing Stock ₹ 15,000, what is the Manufacturing Cost?

A. ₹ 65,000 B. ₹ 83,000
C. ₹ 68,000 D. ₹ 73,000

2. What does a high payout ratio indicate?

A. A High Earning Per Share (EPS)
B. The management is not ploughing back enough profit.
C. The management is ploughing back profit.
D. The company is earning high profit.

3. Which one of the following statements is true?

A. Capital expenditure does not affect the profitability of a concern but revenue expenditure does.
B. Capital expenditure affects the profitability of a concern directly but revenue expenditure does not.
C. Capital expenditure affects the profitability of a concern indirectly but revenue expenditure affects directly.
D. Both capital expenditure and revenue expenditure affect the profitability of a concern directly.

4. Identify the true statement of the following :

(*i*) Balance Sheet is always prepared from the point of view of the business but not from that of the owners.
(*ii*) The financial relationship of the business to its owners is shown in the Balance Sheet.
(*iii*) Balance Sheet is always related to a period of time.

Codes :

A. (*i*) and (*ii*) B. (*ii*) and (*iii*)
C. (*i*) and (*iii*) D. (*i*), (*ii*) and (*iii*)

5. X and Y are partners in a firm sharing profits in the ratios of 2 : 1. Z is admitted with a 1/3 profit sharing. What will be the new profit sharing ratio of X, Y and Z?

A. 3 : 3 : 3 B. 4 : 3 : 2
C. 4 : 2 : 3 D. 2 : 3 : 4

6. Which one of the following will not affect the working capital?

A. Realisation of cash from debtors.
B. Sale of plant and machinery in cash.
C. Issue of equity shares.
D. Redemption of debentures.

7. Given below are two statements, one labelled as Assertion (A) and the other labelled as Reason (R) :

Assertion (A): When a company earns profit prior to its incorporation, it is called capital profit.

Reason (R): Capital profit cannot be used for distribution as dividend to the shareholders.

In the context of the above two statements, which one of the following is correct?

Codes:

A. (A) is correct, but (R) is wrong.
B. Both (A) and (R) are correct.
C. (A) is wrong, but (R) is correct.
D. Both (A) and (R) are wrong.

8. Reconstruction of a company takes place when:

(*i*) the company is undercapitalised
(*ii*) company has incurred heavy losses which must be written off
(*iii*) the company is overcapitalised

Which one of the following is correct?

A. (*i*) and (*ii*) only
B. (*i*) and (*iii*) only
C. (*ii*) and (*iii*) only
D. All the above

9. Match the items of List-I with the items of List-II and select the correct answer using the codes given below the lists:

List-I	***List-II***
(*a*) Leverage Ratio	(*i*) Short-term solvency
(*b*) Liquidity Ratio	(*ii*) Earning capacity
(*c*) Turnover Ratio	(*iii*) Relationship between debt and equity
(*d*) Profitability Ratio	(*iv*) Efficiency of Asset Management

Codes :

	(*a*)	(*b*)	(*c*)	(*d*)
A.	(*ii*)	(*i*)	(*iv*)	(*iii*)
B.	(*iii*)	(*ii*)	(*i*)	(*iv*)
C.	(*iv*)	(*iii*)	(*i*)	(*ii*)
D.	(*iii*)	(*i*)	(*iv*)	(*ii*)

10. Given below are two statements, one labelled as Assertion (A) and the other labelled as Reason (R):

Assertion (A): Sinking fund is a charge against Profit and Loss Account.

Reason (R): Sinking fund is created for repayment of a long term liability.

In the context of the above two statements, which one of the following is correct?

Codes :

A. (A) is correct, but (R) is wrong.
B. Both (A) and (R) are correct.
C. (A) is wrong, but (R) is correct.
D. Both (A) and (R) are wrong.

11. Match List-I with List-II and select the correct answer using the codes given below the lists:

List-I	***List-II***
(*a*) Goodwill of a company	(*i*) Current liability
(*b*) Overdraft	(*ii*) Fixed Assets
(*c*) Preliminary Expenses	(*iii*) Reserves and Surplus
(*d*) Premium on Issue of Shares	(*iv*) Fictitious Assets

Codes :

	(*a*)	(*b*)	(*c*)	(*d*)
A.	(*ii*)	(*i*)	(*iv*)	(*iii*)
B.	(*i*)	(*ii*)	(*iv*)	(*iii*)
C.	(*i*)	(*ii*)	(*iii*)	(*iv*)
D.	(*ii*)	(*i*)	(*iii*)	(*iv*)

12. In India, which of the following is prepared on the guidelines of AS-3 (Accounting Standard -3)?

A. Balance Sheet of a Company
B. Funds Flow Statement
C. Cash Flow Statement
D. Consolidated Financial Statement

13. What is the correct sequence of the following actions required for the preparation of financial accounts?

(*i*) Trading accounts
(*ii*) Making adjusting entries

(*iii*) Balance Sheet
(*iv*) Profit and Loss Account

Select the correct answer from the codes given below:

Codes :

A. (*iv*), (*ii*), (*i*), (*iii*)
B. (*ii*), (*iv*), (*iii*), (*i*)
C. (*ii*), (*i*), (*iv*), (*iii*)
D. (*iv*), (*ii*), (*iii*), (*i*)

14. The main effect of inflation on the financial statement is:

A. Profits are understated
B. Overstatement of Assets
C. Adequacy of funds for replacement of assets
D. Erosion of capital

15. Present value of future earnings is a model of Human Resources Accounting suggested by:

A. Brauch Lev & ABA Schwartz
B. Jaggi & Lau
C. S.K. Chakraborty
D. Eric Flamhaltz

16. Which element of the promotion mix do wholesalers generally apply to obtain their promotional objective?

A. Advertising
B. Personal Selling
C. Trade Promotion
D. Direct Marketing

17. Who has given 'fourteen Principles of Management'?

A. Barnard   B. Henry Fayol
C. F.W. Taylor   D. Flemming

18. What is M.B.O?

A. Management by Objective
B. Multiple Business Organisation
C. Management by Organisation
D. Multiplicity of Business Operations

19. Match items in List-II with items in List-I :

List-I	*List-II*
(*a*) Mega Marketing	(*i*) Advertising
(*b*) Penetration Price	(*ii*) Kotler
(*c*) Promotion Mix	(*iii*) Low price
(*d*) Customer Satisfaction	(*iv*) Post Purchase Behaviour

Codes :

	(*a*)	(*b*)	(*c*)	(*d*)
A.	(*i*)	(*ii*)	(*iii*)	(*iv*)
B.	(*iii*)	(*i*)	(*ii*)	(*iv*)
C.	(*iv*)	(*iii*)	(*ii*)	(*i*)
D.	(*iii*)	(*iv*)	(*i*)	(*ii*)

20. Statement (A): Sales promotion has a strong impact on consumer behaviour in rural India.

Reason (R): Rural people in India give utmost significance to sales promotion schemes.

Codes :

A. Statement (A) is correct but Reason (R) is incorrect.
B. Statement (A) is incorrect, but Reason (R) is correct.
C. Both Statement (A) and Reason (R) are correct.
D. Both Statement (A) and Reason (R) are incorrect.

21. Market sub-divided on the basis of behavioural characteristics is called:

A. Segmentation   B. Aggregation
C. Precision   D. None of the above

22. What is mass marketing?

A. Offering the same products and marketing mix to all consumers.
B. Offering variety of products to the entire market.
C. Offering differentiated products to all customers.
D. Following concentrated marketing strategy.

23. Which concept of marketing is based on the assumption that superior products sell themselves?

A. Production   B. Marketing
C. Societal   D. Product

24. In broader sense, marketing communication includes:
A. Product B. Price
C. Place D. All

25. Physical distribution provides:
A. Place utility
B. Time utility
C. Place and Time utility
D. Form utility

26. What is relevant to place variable of marketing mix?
A. Branding
B. Price penetration
C. Sales personnel motivation
D. None

27. Find incorrect statement:
A. Marketers arouse emotional motives
B. Marketers satisfy rational motives
C. Marketers formulate different sales promotions for different motives
D. None of the above

28. Non-store marketing includes:
A. Home selling
B. V.P.P.
C. Vending Machines
D. All of the above

29. What is customer delight?
A. Performance equal to expectation
B. Performance less than expectation
C. Performance more than expectation
D. Expectation more than performance

30. Which terms are often used interchangeably in marketing literature?
A. Concept, method, philosophy
B. Concept, approach, technique
C. Orientation, concept, philosophy
D. Philosophy, system, concept

31. Which one of the following is not the operative function of HRM?
A. Development B. Controlling
C. Compensation D. Integration

32. Which one of the following is not in sequence of personnel training procedure?
(*i*) Instructor Preparation
(*ii*) Present the task
(*iii*) Try out performance
(*iv*) Training preparation
(*v*) Follow up
A. (*i*), (*ii*), (*iii*), (*iv*), (*v*)
B. (*ii*), (*i*), (*iv*), (*iii*), (*v*)
C. (*i*), (*iv*), (*ii*), (*iii*), (*iv*)
D. (*iii*), (*i*), (*ii*), (*v*), (*iv*)

33. Under which method of performance appraisal one person is compared with all others for the purpose of placing them in a simple order of work?
A. Grading
B. Person to Person comparison
C. Ranking
D. None of the above

34. Which one of the following is not the fundamental procedure that should be considered for the collective bargaining?
A. Prenegotiation phase
B. Selection of Negotiators
C. Tactic and Strategy of Bargaining
D. None of the above

35. Assertion (A): Inevitably the firm must go to the external sources for lower entry jobs.
Reason (R): For positions where required qualification/experience are not met.

Codes :
A. Both (A) and (R) are not correct.
B. (A) is true, but (R) is false.
C. (R) is true, but (A) is false.
D. Both (A) and (R) are correct.

36. Match the following items of List-I and List-II:

List-I	***List-II***
(*a*) Asbestos	(*i*) Lung Cancer
(*b*) Benzene	(*ii*) Cancer
(*c*) Ethylene Disbromide	(*iii*) Leukemia
(*d*) Kerosene	(*iv*) Acute Nervous System Depression

Codes :

	(a)	***(b)***	***(c)***	***(d)***
A.	(*iv*)	(*ii*)	(*iii*)	(*i*)
B.	(*iv*)	(*iii*)	(*ii*)	(*i*)
C.	(*i*)	(*iii*)	(*ii*)	(*iv*)
D.	(*iii*)	(*iv*)	(*ii*)	(*i*)

37. **Assertion (A):** Business Economics is tool centrics facilitating decision making in business.

Reason (R): It provides an analytical understanding of economic activities.

Codes :
A. Both (A) and (R) are not correct.
B. Both (A) and (R) are correct.
C. (A) is true, but (R) is false.
D. (R) is true, but (A) is false.

38. Demand has the following elements:
A. Quantity B. Price
C. Time D. All the above

39. A perfectly competitive firm attains equilibrium when:
A. AC = AR B. MR = MC
C. MC = AC D. TC = TR

40. The purpose of job evaluation is:
A. Fixation of Responsibility
B. Promotion
C. Wage Determination
D. Transfer to a better job

41. For testing of hypothesis $H_0 : M_1 = M_2$ and $H_1 : M_1 < M_2$, the critical value of Z at 5% level of significance when size of sample is more than 30 is:
A. 1.96 B. 2.32
C. 1.645 D. 2.5758

42. Which of the following is the non-random method of selecting samples from a population?
A. Stratified Sampling
B. Quota Sampling
C. Systematic Sampling
D. Cluster Sampling

43. If the two regression coefficients are 0.8 and 0.2, then the value of coefficient of correlation is:
A. + 0.16 B. – 0.40
C. – 0.16 D. + 0.40

44. Which one of the following is a relative measure of dispersion?
A. Standard deviation
B. Variance
C. Coefficient of variation
D. None of the above

45. **Assertion (A):** Internal factors of business environment are controllable factors.

Reason (R): The company can alter or modify such factors to suit the environment.

Codes :
A. Both (A) and (R) are correct.
B. (A) is correct, but (R) is incorrect.
C. Both (A) and (R) are incorrect.
D. (A) is incorrect.

46. The concept of 'Rolling Plan' in India was introduced by the:
A. BJP Government
B. Janta Government
C. Congress Government
D. All of the above

47. Which one of the following is an obstacle to globalisation?
A. Wide base B. Niche markets
C. Obsolescence D. Competition

48. 'VSAT' technology is first followed for online trading by:
A. BSE B. OTCEI
C. NSE D. ISE

49. Match the following:

List-I (*Years*)	*List-II* (*Act*)
(*a*) 1956	(*i*) Consumer Protection Act
(*b*) 1986	(*ii*) Indian Companies Act
(*c*) 1992	(*iii*) Securities and Exchange Board of India
(*d*) 2002	(*iv*) Securitisation Act

Codes :

	(*a*)	(*b*)	(*c*)	(*d*)
A.	(*ii*)	(*i*)	(*iii*)	(*iv*)
B.	(*i*)	(*ii*)	(*iii*)	(*iv*)
C.	(*ii*)	(*iii*)	(*i*)	(*iv*)
D.	(*i*)	(*iv*)	(*iii*)	(*ii*)

50. The flagship project of Government of India launched for generating guaranteed employment in rural areas is known as:
A. PMRY B. MNREGA
C. JRY D. NREP

51. The conflicts in project ranking in capital budgeting as per NPV and IRR may arise because of:

A. Size disparity B. Time disparity
C. Life disparity D. All the above

52. The degree of financial leverage reflects the responsiveness of:
A. Operating income to changes in total revenue
B. EPS to changes in EBIT
C. EPS to changes in total revenue
D. None of the above

53. The overall capitalisation rate and the cost of debt remain constant for all degrees of financial leverage is advocated by:
A. Traditional Approach
B. Net Income Approach
C. Net Operating Income Approach
D. M-M-Approach

54. Which of the following is not included in the assumptions on which Myron Gordon proposed a model on stock valuation?
A. Retained earnings, the only source of financing
B. Finite life of the firm
C. Taxes do not exist
D. Constant rate of return on firm's investment

55. Match the following:

	List-I		*List-II*
(*a*)	Factoring services	(*i*)	Cash Management
(*b*)	Economic Order Quantity	(*ii*)	Receivable Management
(*c*)	Commercial paper	(*iii*)	Inventory Management
		(*iv*)	Working Capital Financing

Codes :

	(*a*)	(*b*)	(*c*)
A.	(*i*)	(*iii*)	(*ii*)
B.	(*iii*)	(*ii*)	(*i*)
C.	(*ii*)	(*iii*)	(*iv*)
D.	(*ii*)	(*i*)	(*iii*)

56. **Assertion (A):** International business focuses on global resources, opportunities to buy/sell worldwide.

Reason (R): The efforts of IMF, World Bank and WTO to liberalise their economies led to globalisation.

Codes :
A. Both (A) and (R) are true.
B. Both (A) and (R) are false.
C. (A) is true, but (R) is false.
D. (A) is false, but (R) is true.

57. Match the items of List-I with items of List-II:

	List-I		*List-II*
(*a*)	Wider Market	(*i*)	Modes of Entry
(*b*)	Turn key Projects	(*ii*)	Goal of International Business
(*c*)	Expanding the production capacities	(*iii*)	Advantages of International Business
(*d*)	Geocentric approach	(*iv*)	Stage of Globalisation

Codes :

	(*a*)	(*b*)	(*c*)	(*d*)
A.	(*iv*)	(*ii*)	(*iii*)	(*i*)
B.	(*iii*)	(*i*)	(*ii*)	(*iv*)
C.	(*i*)	(*ii*)	(*iii*)	(*iv*)
D.	(*iv*)	(*iii*)	(*ii*)	(*i*)

58. BRICS includes:
A. Bhutan, Romania, Indonesia, Chile and South Korea
B. Brazil, Russia, Indonesia, Chile and Sudan
C. Brazil, Russia, India, China and South Africa
D. Britain, Russia, India, Czechoslovakia, Sri Lanka

59. Out of the following, one is not related with WTO:
A. TRIPS B. Ministerial Conference
C. TRIMS D. TRAI

60. Balance of Payment includes components:
A. Current Account, Capital Account, Unilateral Payments Accounts, Official Settlement Account
B. Revenue Account, P & L Account, Capital Account, Official Account
C. Trade Account, Activity Account, Revenue Account, Currency Account

D. Forex Account, Trade Account, Funds Account

61. **Assertion (A) :** International Monetary Fund was set up in 1944.

Reason (R) : To promote international monetary cooperation through a permanent institution which provides machinery for consultation and collaboration on international monetary problems.

Codes :

A. Both (A) and (R) are false.
B. Both (A) and (R) are true.
C. (A) is true, but (R) is false.
D. (R) is true, but (A) is false.

62. The commercial banks do not perform one function out of the following:

A. Mobilisation of savings
B. Giving Loans and Advances
C. Issuing Currency Notes
D. Financing Priority Sectors

63. There are two lists of items, match the items of List-I with items of List-II:

List-I	*List-II*
(*a*) Reserve Bank of India	(*i*) NPA
(*b*) EXIM Bank	(*ii*) Facilitating Small Scale Industries
(*c*) SIDBI	(*iii*) Credit Control
(*d*) Capital Adequacy	(*iv*) Export/Import Financing

Codes :

	(*a*)	(*b*)	(*c*)	(*d*)
A.	(*i*)	(*ii*)	(*iii*)	(*iv*)
B.	(*iv*)	(*iii*)	(*ii*)	(*i*)
C.	(*ii*)	(*iii*)	(*iv*)	(*i*)
D.	(*iii*)	(*iv*)	(*ii*)	(*i*)

64. One of the items is not related with e-banking :

A. Demand Draft B. SPNS
C. ECS D. ATM

65. **Assertion (A):** The Treasury Manager uses the derivatives in the Bond market as well as in Forex market.

Reason (R): It helps risk coverage.

Codes :

A. Both (A) and (R) are false.
B. Both (A) and (R) are true.
C. (A) is true, but (R) is false.
D. (R) is true, but (A) is false.

66. Factoring and forfeiting have not taken off in the Indian economy due to lack of expertise and experience. One is not included in the factoring services rendered:

A. Purchase of book debts and receivables.
B. Prepayment of debts partially or fully
C. Giving advice
D. Covering the credit risk of the suppliers

67. Which one is not the form of FDI?

A. Purchase of existing assets in foreign currency
B. New Investment in property, plant, equipment
C. Making investment in the mutual funds
D. Transfer of many types of assets

68. Match the items of List-I with items of List-II:

List-I	*List-II*
(*a*) Measures towards globalization	(*i*) Globalisation
(*b*) Off-shoring	(*ii*) FEMA
(*c*) FERA	(*iii*) Liberalise the inflow of FDI
(*d*) Mr. Aruthur Dunkel	(*iv*) Uruguay Round

Codes :

	(*a*)	(*b*)	(*c*)	(*d*)
A.	(*iii*)	(*i*)	(*ii*)	(*iv*)
B.	(*ii*)	(*i*)	(*iii*)	(*iv*)
C	(*iv*)	(*ii*)	(*i*)	(*iii*)
D.	(*i*)	(*ii*)	(*iv*)	(*iii*)

69. Which one of the following is not the advantage of MNCs to the host country?

A. Increase in social activity
B. Increase in economic activity
C. Utilisation of natural resources
D. R & D efforts enhanced

70. India suffered from deficit balance both in trade balance and net invisibles, hence, took up a number of steps to manage this problem.

Which one is not appropriate for this?

A. Export control

B. Current Account Convertibility
C. Liberalised Export Policy
D. Unified Exchange Rate

71. Mr. James, a citizen of U.S., arrived in India for the first time on 1st July, 2010 and left for Nepal on 15th December, 2010. He arrived to India again on 1st January 2011 and stayed till the end of the financial year 2010-11. His residential status for the assessment year 2011-12 is:
A. Resident (ordinarily resident)
B. Not ordinarily resident
C. Non-resident
D. None of the above

72. The value of free accommodation in Delhi provided by employer in the private sector is:
A. 10% of salary B. 15% of salary
C. 20% of salary D. 25% of salary

73. Which of the following is not a capital asset under capital gains head of income?
A. Stock in tradc
B. Goodwill of business
C. Agricultural Land in Delhi
D. Jewellery

74. Match the items of List-I with List-II:

List-I		List-II
(*a*) Tax Planning	(*i*)	Making suitable arrangement of TDS
(*b*) Tax Avoidance	(*ii*)	Understatement of Income
(*c*) Tax Evasion	(*iii*)	Availing deduction under Section 10A of IT Act.
(*d*) Tax Administration	(*iv*)	Misinterpreting the provisions of the IT Act

Codes :

	(*a*)	(*b*)	(*c*)	(*d*)
A.	(*ii*)	(*i*)	(*iv*)	(*iii*)
B.	(*i*)	(*iv*)	(*iii*)	(*ii*)
C.	(*iii*)	(*iv*)	(*ii*)	(*i*)
D.	(*iv*)	(*i*)	(*iii*)	(*ii*)

75. Under the Income Tax Act, 1961 unabsorbed depreciation can be carried forward for set-off purpose:
A. For 4 years
B. For 5 years
C. For 8 years
D. For unspecified period

ANSWERS

1	2	3	4	5	6	7	8	9	10
C	B	C	A	C	A	B	C	D	C
11	**12**	**13**	**14**	**15**	**16**	**17**	**18**	**19**	**20**
A	C	C	D	A	C	B	A	B	A
21	**22**	**23**	**24**	**25**	**26**	**27**	**28**	**29**	**30**
A	A	D	D	C	C	D	D	C	C
31	**32**	**33**	**34**	**35**	**36**	**37**	**38**	**39**	**40**
B	C	C	D	D	C	B	D	B	C
41	**42**	**43**	**44**	**45**	**46**	**47**	**48**	**49**	**50**
C	B	D	C	A	B	C	C	A	B
51	**52**	**53**	**54**	**55**	**56**	**57**	**58**	**59**	**60**
D	B	C	B	C	A	B	C	D	A
61	**62**	**63**	**64**	**65**	**66**	**67**	**68**	**69**	**70**
B	C	D	A	B	C	C	A	A	A
71	**72**	**73**	**74**	**75**					
B	B	A	C	D					